Communications
in Computer and Information Science   134

Ran Chen (Ed.)

Intelligent Computing and Information Science

International Conference, ICICIS 2011
Chongqing, China, January 8-9, 2011
Proceedings, Part I

 Springer

Volume Editor

Ran Chen
The Key Laboratory of Manufacture and Test
Chongqing University of Technology
Chongqing, 400054, P. R. China
E-mail: sanshyuan@hotmail.com

Library of Congress Control Number: Applied for

CR Subject Classification (1998): I.2, H.4, H.3, C.2, H.5, D.2

ISSN   1865-0929
ISBN-10   3-642-18128-7 Springer Berlin Heidelberg New York
ISBN-13   978-3-642-18128-3 Springer Berlin Heidelberg New York

springer.com

© Springer-Verlag Berlin Heidelberg 2011

Typesetting: Camera-ready by author, data conversion by Scientific Publishing Services, Chennai, India
Printed on acid-free paper   06/3180

Preface

The 2011 International Conference on Intelligent Computing and Information Science (ICICIS 2011) was held in Chongqing, China, during January 8–9, 2011. The aim of the conference series is to provide a platform for researchers, engineers, academicians as well as industrial professionals from all over the world to present their research results and development activities in intelligent computing and information science. This two-volume set of CCIS 134 and CCIS 135 communicates the latest progress and research results in the theory, methods, and technology in the field of intelligent computing and information science if it also presents an update on the international trends, which will drive the global communication and cooperation in production, education and research in this field.

We received more than 600 submissions which were reviewed by international experts, and 230 papers were selected for presentation. We believe the proceedings provide the reader with a broad overview of the latest advances in the field of intelligent computing and information science.

On behalf of the guest editors for this special issue, I would like to thank the National 863 Program of China and the National Science Fund of China. I also thank the conference organization staff and the members of the International Technical Committees for their hard work.

We look forward to seeing all of you next year at ICICIS 2012.

October 2010

Ran Chen

ICICIS 2011 Committee

Conference Chairman

Ran Chen   Chongqing University of Technology, China

Publication Chair

Wenli Yao   Control Engineering and Information Science
Research Association, Hong Kong
International Frontiers of Science and
Technology Research Association

International Technical Committees

Peifu Chen	Chongqing Aerospace Polytechnic College, China
Lin Mi	Chongqing University of Technology, China
Viranjay M. Srivastava	Jaypee University of Information Technology, Solan, India
Liu Yunan	University of Michigan, USA
Mir Mahdi Zalloi	Iran
Wang Liying	Institute of Water Conservancy and Hydroelectric Power, China
Zhou Liang	Donghua University, China
Chenggui Zhao	Yunnan University of Finance and Economics, China
Rahim Jamian	Universiti Kuala Lumpur Malaysian Spanish Institute, Malaysia
Li-Xin GUO	Northeastern University, China
Wen-Sheng Ou	National Chin-Yi University of Technology, Taiwan R.O.C.
Hsiang-Chuan Liu	Asia University, Japan
Mostafa Shokshok	National University of Malaysia, Malaysia
Ramezan ali Mahdavinejad	University of Tehran, Iran
Wei Fu	Chongqing University, China
Anita Kova Kralj	University of Maribor, Slovenia
Tjamme Wiegers	Delft University of Technology, The Netherlands
Gang Shi	Inha University, South Korea
Zengtao Chen	University of New Brunswick, Canada
Bhagavathi Tarigoppula	Bradley University, USA

Co-Sponsored by

Control Engineering and Information Science Research Association
International Frontiers of science and technology Research Association
Chongqing Xueya Conferences Catering Co., Ltd
Chongqing University of Technology

Table of Contents – Part I

Table of Contents – Part II

Some Analysis and Research of the AdaBoost Algorithm

Peng Wu and Hui Zhao

Computing Center, Henan University,
Kaifeng, China
hehe9840@126.com, 33237509@qq.com

Abstract. The AdaBoost algorithm enables weak classifiers to enhance their performance by establishing the set of multiple classifiers, and since it automatically adapts to the error rate of the basic algorithm in training through dynamic regulation of the weight of each sample, a wide range of concern has been aroused. This paper primarily makes some relevant introduction of Adaboost, and conducts an analysis and research of several aspects of the algorithm itself.

Keywords: adaboost algorithm, boosting algorithm, analysis and research.

1 Introduction

AdaBoost is a kind of self-adaptive Boosting algorithm which enhances the performance of weak classifiers by establishing the set of multiple classifiers. Since it automatically adapts to the error rate of the basic algorithm in training through dynamic regulation of the weight of each sample, a wide range of concern has been aroused. The Boosting method stems from the theoretical analysis of the learning model PAC (Probably Approximately Correct). Kearns and Valiant proposed the concepts of strong learning and weak learning. In the learning model of PAC, if there exists a polynomial learning algorithm to identify a group of concepts, and the recognition accuracy is very high, this group of concepts are strong learning; but if this learning algorithm's rate of correct identification is just slightly better than that of random guessing, then this group belongs to the weak learning; Kearns and Valiant proposed the issue of equivalence between the weak learning algorithm and the strong learning algorithm, namely whether the weak learning algorithm can be promoted into the strong learning algorithm. If the two are equivalent, then when learning the concepts, we can elevate an algorithm which is slightly better than random guessing to a strong learning algorithm only if we find it. In 1990, Schapire published the first Boosting method. Freund then made improvement to it and put forward a much better method BBM (boost-by-majority). Boosting will produce a series of classifiers before and after the training. The training set used in each classifier is a subset provided from the general training set, and whether each sample will appear in that subset or not depends on the performance of the previously produced classifiers. As for the samples which are judged to be incorrect by the already existing classifiers, they will appear with a larger probability in the new training subset, making the subsequent classifiers more focus on dealing with the issue of differentiating samples, which seems quite difficult for the existing classifiers. The Boosting method can enhance the generalization ability of a given algorithm, but that algorithm needs to know the lower limit of a weak classifier's learning accuracy, which in practical problems is very difficult to achieve. The AdaBoost algorithm brought forth by Freund and Schapire's in 1995 is a great improvement to the Boosting algorithm.

2   Analysis and Research of Several Aspects of AdaBoost

AdaBoost is the most representative algorithm in the Boosting family. It maintains the distribution of one set of probabilities for training samples, and adjusts this probability distribution for each sample during each iteration. Specific learning algorithm is used to generate the member-classifier and calculate its error rate on training samples. AdaBoost will use this error rate to adjust the probability distribution of training samples. The role of changing weights is to set a greater weight for the incorrectly classified sample and reduce its weight if the sample is classified correctly. Finally, by way of the weighted voting of single classifiers, a strong classifier will be established.

Pseudocode of AdaBoost under two kinds of classification are as follows:

Input: the set of given samples $L = \{(x_1, y_1), (x_2, y_2) \cdots (x_N, y_N)\}, y_i \in \{+1, 0\}$, +1 represents the positive sample, 0 represents the negative sample, the total number of all the samples is N. Distribution of the initialized sample's weight: $w_i^1 = \dfrac{1}{N}$.

Conduct the loop of $t = 1, \cdots, T$, as follows:

the normalized weight:
$$w_i^t = \frac{w_i^t}{\sum\limits_{j=1}^{N} w_j^t} ;$$

The weak classifier which selects and classifies with the smallest error rate under the set of samples and the distribution of current weights h_t;

To record the error rate of that weak classifier's classification
$$\varepsilon_t = \sum_{i=1}^{N} w_i^t |h_t(x_i) - y_i| ;$$

Update of the sample's weight : $w_i^{t+1} = w_i^t \beta_t^{1-e_i}$. Among them, $e_i = 0$ represents that x_i is correctly classified, and $e_i = 1$ indicates that x_i is incorrectly classified;

Output:
$$H(x) = \begin{cases} 1, & \sum\limits_{t=1}^{T} \alpha_t h_t(x) \geq \dfrac{1}{2} \sum\limits_{t=1}^{T} \alpha_t \\ 0, & otherwise \end{cases}$$
. Among them,

$\alpha_t = \log \dfrac{1}{\beta_t}$.

AdaBoost has the advantage of being fast, simple and easy to program. It does not require a prior knowledge of the weak classifier, and it can look for the weak assumptions by nimbly combining with any methods. When given adequate training samples and a weak classifier with medium accuracy, Adaboost can provide the theoretical assurance for learning. The birth of AdaBoost subverts the ideas of the traditional learning system's design, people no longer attempting to design a learning algorithm that is accurate in the entire sample space, but focusing on finding out the algorithm of weak learning that is only slightly better than random guessing, which is very easy to achieve.

When a sample is correctly classified, namely when $y_i = h_t(x_i)$,

$$e_i = 0 \text{ , } w_i^{t+1} = w_i^t \beta_t^{1-e_i} = w_i^t \beta_t = w_i^t \frac{\varepsilon_t}{1-\varepsilon_t} \text{ ;}$$

When a sample is incorrectly classified, namely when $y_i \neq h_t(x_i)$,

$$e_i = 1 \text{ , } w_i^{t+1} = w_i^t \beta_t^{1-e_i} = w_i^t \text{ ,}$$

$\because$ The error rate of a weak classifier's classification $\varepsilon_t < 0.5$,

$$\therefore \quad \frac{\varepsilon_t}{1-\varepsilon_t} < 1 \text{ ;}$$

Therefore, when a sample is correctly classified, $w_i^{t+1} = w_i^t \frac{\varepsilon_t}{1-\varepsilon_t} < w_i^t$, that is to

say, its weight is reduced;

When a sample is incorrectly classified, $w_i^{t+1} = w_i^t$, that is to say, its remains

unchanged;

After the normalization of weights, it is obvious that the incorrectly classified samples' weights increase, while the correctly classified samples' weights decrease. In the next round of iteration, the algorithm will give more attention to samples that are incorrectly classified during the last round of iteration, meeting the idea of upgrading.

AdaBoost is an iterative algorithm, whose core idea is to train different classifiers (weak classifiers) for the same training set, then bring these weak classifiers together and form a stronger final classifier (the strong classifier). The algorithm itself is achieved by changing the distribution of data, and it determines the weight of each sample according to whether the classification of each sample in every training set is correct or not as well as the general classification's accuracy during last time. Give the new data set whose weights have been modified to the lower classifiers for training. Finally fuse the classifiers obtained in each training and take it as the final decision classifier. The use of the adaBoost classifiers can eliminate unnecessary characteristics of the training data, and place the key on the crucial training data.

In AdaBoost algorithm, different training sets are achieved by adjusting the corresponding weight of each sample. In the beginning, the corresponding weights of all the samples are the same, and among them, n is the number of samples. Train a weak classifier under this distribution of samples. For the sample which is incorrectly classified, increase its corresponding weight; for the correctly classified sample, reduce its weight. In this way, incorrectly classified samples will be protruded, thus obtaining a new distribution of samples. Under the new distribution of samples, train the weak classifiers once again and get weak classifiers. Then according to this, after the loops of T times, T weak classifiers can be obtained. Boost these T weak classifiers by a certain weight and then get the final desired strong classifier.

Do some explanation for the output decision-making expression of the finally generated strong classifier:

$$\frac{1}{2}\sum_{t=1}^{T}\alpha_t = \sum_{t=1}^{T}\frac{1}{2}\log\frac{1-\varepsilon_t}{\varepsilon_t} = \sum_{t=1}^{T}\log\left(\frac{1-\varepsilon_t}{\varepsilon_t}\right)^{\frac{1}{2}} = \log\left[\prod_{t=1}^{T}\left(\frac{1-\varepsilon_t}{\varepsilon_t}\right)^{\frac{1}{2}}\right]$$

$$\sum_{t=1}^{T}\alpha_t h_t(x_i) - \frac{1}{2}\sum_{t=1}^{T}\alpha_t = \log\frac{\prod_{t=1}^{T}\left(\frac{1-\varepsilon_t}{\varepsilon_t}\right)^{h_t(x_i)}}{\prod_{t=1}^{T}\left(\frac{1-\varepsilon_t}{\varepsilon_t}\right)^{\frac{1}{2}}} = \log\left[\prod_{t=1}^{T}\left(\frac{1-\varepsilon_t}{\varepsilon_t}\right)^{h_t(x_i)-\frac{1}{2}}\right]$$

Among them, $\log\dfrac{1-\varepsilon_t}{\varepsilon_t} > 0$, namely, the output of the final strong classifier depends on whether the decision outcome of all the weak classifiers' integrated votes is greater that the average outcome of their votes.

If we understand it on the surface by the strong classifier's expression: suppose that among all the weak classifiers, the probability of voting "yes" equals that of voting "no", then we can calculate an average probability, namely the average result of

voting is $\dfrac{1}{2}\left(\sum_{t=1}^{T}\alpha_t \times 1 + \sum_{t=1}^{T}\alpha_t \times 0\right) = \dfrac{1}{2}\sum_{t=1}^{T}\alpha_t$. Therefore, the result of the

strong classifier's output is the final result obtained after making a comparison of the weighted sum of all the weak classifiers' votes to the average result of voting.

Suppose in the AdaBoost algorithm, the error rate of classification of the weak classifiers selected during the T cycles are $\varepsilon_1, \varepsilon_2, \ldots, \varepsilon_T$,

Make a classification using the finally generated strong classifier. Its upper bound of the classification's errors is $\varepsilon \leq 2^T \prod_{t=1}^{T}\sqrt{\varepsilon_t(1-\varepsilon_t)}$.

In this upper bound, we make $\gamma_t = \dfrac{1}{2} - \varepsilon_t$, thus the upper bound of the classification's errors can be written as:

$$\varepsilon \leq 2^T \prod_{t=1}^{T}\sqrt{\frac{1}{4} - \gamma_t^2} = \prod_{t=1}^{T}\sqrt{1 - 4\gamma_t^2}$$

$$= e^{\ln\sqrt{1-4\gamma_1^2}} \times \cdots \times e^{\ln\sqrt{1-4\gamma_T^2}} = e^{\frac{1}{2}\sum_{t=1}^{T}\ln(1-4\gamma_t^2)} \leq e^{-2\sum_{t=1}^{T}\gamma_t^2}$$

From the above we can see that the smaller the weak classifiers' error rates on classification are, the lower the final strong classifier's error rate on classification is. However, the error rates of weak classifiers generally are only slightly lower than 0.5, so the decrease of the strong classifier's error rate of classification is mainly completed relying on increasing the number of weak classifiers.

3 Summary

This article first gives a sketch of the Adaboost algorithm's background theories and development, then elaborates on the classification algorithm AdaBoost, and studies and deduces the mechanism of that algorithm. It mainly conducts an analysis and research of the AdaBoost algorithm from several aspects, the update of samples' weights, the determination of strong classifiers' output, and the error rate of the strong classifier for classification. The main ideas of Adaboost are highly accurate rules obtained after the weighted combination of a series of rough rules. Among them, the advantage of the algorithm lies in that it's easy to implement; and the accuracy of classification is very high. Its drawbacks are that the Adaboost is susceptible to the interference of noise, which is also the shortcoming of most algorithms; and that the effect of implementing the algorithm depends on the choice of weak classifiers. Currently, the research and application of the AdaBoost algorithm largely focus on the issue of classification, while in recent years, some problems about the application to the regression also begin to arouse people's attention. In terms of application, the AdaBoost series have solved: problem of the two-type-result, the single label with multiple results, the multi-label with multiple results, the large single-label, and regression. The algorithm actually is a simple upgrading process of the weak classification algorithm, which can improve the ability of data classification through constant training.

References

1. Xiao-long, Z., Fang, R.: Study on combinability of SVM and AdaBoost algorithm. Application Research of Computers (2009)
2. Hui-Xing, J., Yu-Jin, Z.: Fast Adaboost Training Algorithm by Dynamic Weight Trimming. Chinese Journal of Computers (2009)
3. Kearns, M., Valiant, L.G.: Learning Boolean formulae or finite automata is as hardas factoring. Harvard University Aiken Computation Laboratory (1998)
4. Schapire, R.E.: The Strength of weak learnability. Machine Learning (1990)
5. Freund, Y.: Boosting a weak learning algorithm by majority. Information and Computation (1995)
6. Freund, Y., Schapire, R.E.: A decision-theoretic generalization of online learning and an application to boosting. In: Vitányi, P.M.B. (ed.) EuroCOLT 1995. LNCS, vol. 904, Springer, Heidelberg (1995)

Simulation the Heat Flow Field in Cooler of Rotary Calcining Kiln

Yonggang Liu[1,2], Jishun Li[1,2], Xianzhao Jia[1,2], Weimin Pan[1], and Zhiming Liao[1]

[1] Henan University of Science and Technology, Luoyang, 471003, China
[2] Henan Key Lab for Machinery Design and Transmission System, Luoyang, 471003, China

Abstract. Cooler is the key device of rotary calcining kiln to produced limestone. Through design processes, better heat exchange can be obtained. According to the structural features and working principles of rotary calcining kiln, the finite element model of cooler is built. Then the convection heat transfer coefficient is calculated on the theory of heat transfer. On the simulation analysis of the heat transfer of the cooler based on the Flotran of ANSYS, the distribution of temperature in cooler is given. The results show that the surface temperature drops to 450°C, after which it gradually rise until maturity. In additional, the convection heat transfer coefficients increase with the velocity of gas at the entrance of cooler. So the low-temperature region increases and more limestone down to a lower surface temperature.

Keywords: Heat Flow Field, Temperature, ANSYS/Flotran, Cooler.

1 Introduction

Rotary calcining kiln is the main equipment which produces active lime in steel mill. The rotary calcining kiln with cooler could produces high quality active lime with larger particle size range limestone and it improves the use ratio of rough material a lot [1, 2]. According to research of the cooler, the theoretical basis to transform the devices could be got to improve the thermal efficiency and save energy [3-5]. The material and the air flow reversely, lots of parameters and large range of temperature change in the cooler. So it is hard to calculate by number method. At present, there is only a little research to heat flow field in cooler. As a general finite element software, ANSYS has been used in many research fields such as mechanics, electricity, temperature field, flow field and so on [5-9]. In this paper, the finite element model of the cooler was built. And the method that calculates the heat flow field of the gas-solid two-phase flow was researched on the basis of heat transfer theory and the coupling of the temperature field and the flow field. With the analysis of the calculating result, it could provide some useful theoretical direction on the optimal design of the cooler [8-10].

2 Convection Heat Transfer Coefficient

Heat exchange occurs by convection between gas and limestone in cooler. The convection heat transfer coefficient (CHTC) is expressed as

R. Chen (Ed.): ICICIS 2011, Part I, CCIS 134, pp. 6–11, 2011.

$$h = \frac{\lambda C \operatorname{Re}^m}{l} \tag{1}$$

Where, h is CHTC; l is the diameter of limestone; λ is the thermal conductivity of the gas; Re is the Reynolds number of the gas; C and m is constants.

The cooling gas is air in cooler. The constants of gas at different temperatures are shown in Table 1. The average velocity of gas in cooler is 5m/s. So the CHTC is listed in Table 2 by equation (2), where the diameter of limestone is 0.25m. The CHTC decreases with the temperature of limestone.

Table 1. Constants of gas

Temperature $^{\circ}C$	Thermal conductivity W/(m K)	Kinematic Viscosity m^2/s	Specific heat J/(kg K)	Density kg/m^3
300	0.0460	0.00004833	1047	0.615
500	0.0574	0.00007938	1093	0.456
700	0.0671	0.0001154	1135	0.362
900	0.0763	0.0001551	1172	0.301

Table 2. Parameters table of CHTC

Temperature $(^{\circ}C)$	300	500	700	900
CHTC $(W/(m^2K))$	26.312	24.338	22.850	21.820

3 FEM

Cooler is composed of four parts: kiln hood, main grate bars and aniseed- cleaning device, cooling chamber and feeding device, support device. The framework of cooler is shown in Fig. 1.

The temperature of limestone in cooler depends on cooler part of the internal space for cooling limestone. To improve the cooling efficiency of the heat flow field analysis, a two-dimensional section of cooler was adopted to substitute the three-dimensional model of cooler. The finite element model of cooler is shown in Fig. 2. The circular parts are the limestone to be cooled. Others are the low-temperature gas. Through the several vents and air duct in the lower part of cooler, gas enters into the cooler. In this model, the boundary shall be that the lower entrance of cooling gas.

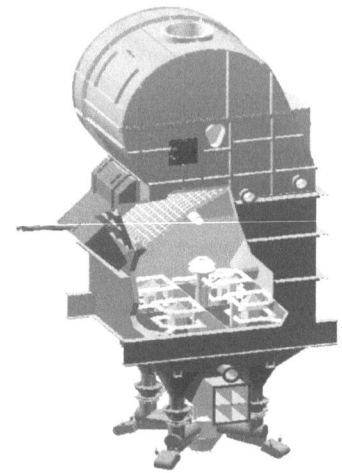

Fig. 1. Framework of Cooler

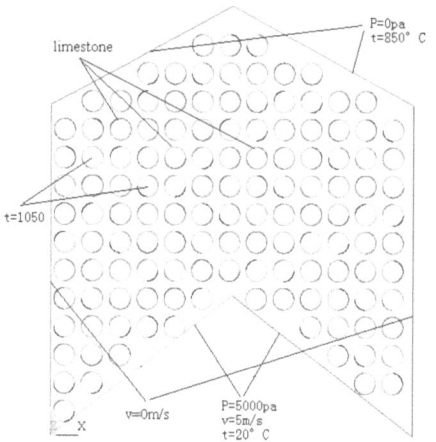

Fig. 2. Two-dimensional model of Cooler

The main chemical change in the rotary calcining kiln is decomposition of limestone. Chemical equation is expressed as $CaCO_3 \longrightarrow CaO + CO_2$. The calcium oxide enters into the cooler after the calcination of limestone. In addition, the carbon dioxide gas enters into the preheater. Thermal conductivity of limestone is 0.12W/(mK). Specific heat is 0.834KJ/(kgK). Density is 3.32×10^3kg/m^3. The cooling gas is mainly dry air.

The pressure of gas is 5000Pa, the temperature is $20\,^{\circ}$C and the velocity is 5m/s at the entrance. The pressure of gas is 0Pa and the temperature is $850\,^{\circ}$C at the exit. The initial temperature of limestone is $1050\,^{\circ}$C. And the velocity of x and y direction is 0 both the fixed wall. The boundary conditions are shown in Fig. 2.

The 2-dimention element FLUID141 is adopted. FLUID141 could be divided into quadrilateral with 4 nodes or triangle with 3 nodes which has several DOFs such as speed, pressure, temperature, turbulence kinetic energy. In order to ensure the convergence and the precision of the results, quadrilateral element was chosen. In additional, the element edge length was defined as 0.008.

4   Results and Discussion

Arrangement and particle size of limestone had little effect on the temperature field by the analysis of cooler. So limestone with the Ordered Arrangement and particle size 0.28m ware researched. The temperature field of cooler is shown in Fig. 3.

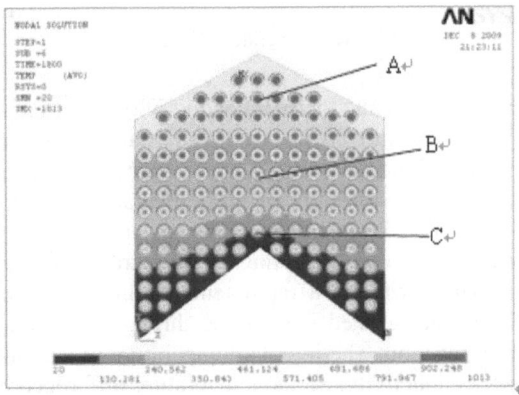

Fig. 3. Temperature field of cooler

If the entrances of cooler are doubled, the pressure and velocity of gas in the model should be increased with the increase of the cooling gas. Assuming constant pressure, the velocity of gas in the model is doubled. Then the CHTCs between the gas and limestone are shown in Table 3 by equation 1.

Table 3. CHTC in cooler

Temperature (^{o}C)	300	500	700	900
CHTC (W/(m^{2}K))	39.52	36.74	34.43	32.87

Fig. 4 shows the temperature field of cooler at different velocity of gas. The low-temperature region increases clearly with the increase of the pressure and velocity of gas from Fig.4. The surface temperature of limestone in lower part of cooler also decreased compared with Fig.3. But there is a little change in the internal temperature of limestone. Mainly due to the increase of velocity of gas, the CHTC increases. So the surface temperature of limestone would drop fast. Internal heat transfer of

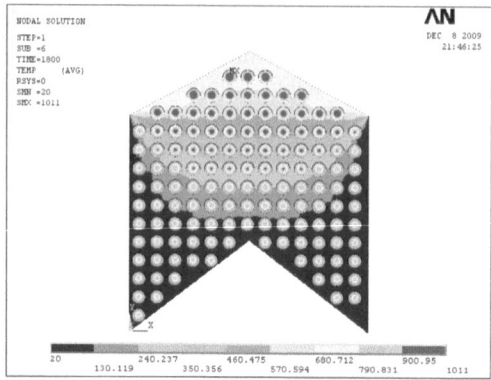

Fig. 4. Temperature field of cool

limestone is accomplished by the thermal conductivity. Thermal conductivity has not changed here leading to the little change of the internal temperature of limestone.

Temperature curves of the limestone surface with different CHTC are shown in Fig. 5. There is only a little different of the temperature curve in the CHTCs. The temperature drops to about $450^{\circ}C$, then picks up and stabilizes finally. When the limestone just touched the cold gas, the temperature difference between gas and limestone is large. There will be a rapid temperature drop process. However, the internal heat of limestone reached the surface through conduction, and then passed through the air by convection. The internal temperature of limestone slows down due to the lower thermal conductivity. So the temperature difference between internal and surface of limestone is big within a certain period. Heat conduction occupied a leading role in this time. So limestone surface temperature has gradually increased and eventually stabilized.

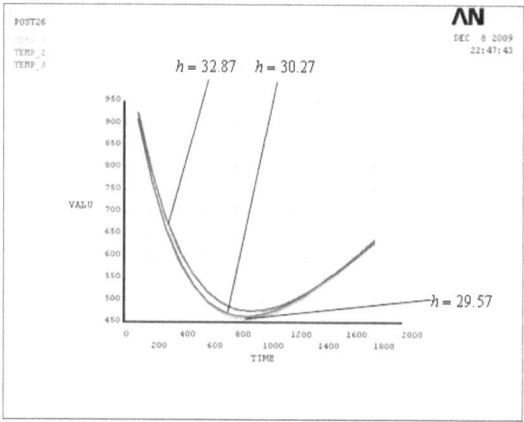

Fig. 5. Temperature of the limestone with different CHTC

5 Conclusion

The CHTCs were calculated due to structural features of cooler and the experimental correlation of the air cross-flow tube bundles. A series of finite models are established. The heat flow field of limestone in cooler was analyzed by FEM in detail. The distribution of temperature in cooler is given. Results showed the surface temperature drops to a certain temperature, after which it gradually rise until maturity. In additional, the CHTCs increase with the velocity of gas at the entrance. So the low-temperature region increases and more limestone down to a lower surface temperature.

Acknowledgments

This work was financially supported by the National Key Technology R&D Program of China (No.2007BAF26B03), Innovation Scientists and Technicians Troop Construction Projects of Henan Province, Doctor Subject Foundation of Henan University of Science and Technology.

References

1. Qi, T.M., Lu, J., Zhang, Y.F.: The Development of the Active Lime Rotary Kiln in Steel Mill. Cement Engeneering 6, 34 (1995)
2. Duan, Y.Z.H.: Discussion on the Key Parameter Calculation Method of Active Lime Rotary Kiln. Minting and Processing Equipment 19, 103 (2008)
3. Zhang, K.B.: Discussion to Energy Saving and Consumption Reduction of Active Lime Rotary Kiln and Resource Synthetic Utilization. Minting and Processing Equipment 10, 152 (2007)
4. Wang, W., Li, Y.C.H.: Progress of the Simulation of Particle Fluid Two Phase Flow. Progress in Chemistry 12, 208 (2000)
5. Liu, Y.G., Li, J.S.H., Li, L.: Modeling of Mechanical and Electrical Behavior of Piezoelectric Fiber Composites. In: Proceedings of the ASME International Mechanical Engineering Congress and Exposition, IMECE 2009, vol. 4, pp. 343–349 (2009)
6. Carvel, R.O., Beard, A.N., Jowitt, P.W.: The influence of tunnel geometry and ventilation on the heat release rate of fire. Fire Technology 40(5) (2004)
7. Liu, Y.G., Li, J.S.H., Xue, Y.J.: The Effect of Polymer on Piezoelectric Fiber Composites Actuators. In: Proceedings of the 2009 18th IEEE International Symposium on Applications of Ferroelectrics, Xi'an, China, August 23-27 (2009)
8. Li, X.T., Wang, M.T., Du, F.S.H.: FEA on Hot Strip Continuous Rolling Process with Multi-field Coupling. China Mechanical Engeneering 17,1955 (2006)
9. Zhou, J.Z.H., Guo, H.F., Xu, D.P.: Finite Element Simulation for the Temperature Field in Multi-layer Thin-wall Metal Part Formed by DMLS. China Mechanical Engeneering 18, 2618 (2007)
10. Yang, S.H.M., Tao, W.S.H.: Heat Transfer. Higher Education Press (1998)

Teaching Platform Scheme of *Engineering Testing* Curriculums Based on LabVIEW

Tingrui Liu[*], Xiuhua Sui[*], and Huibin Liang[*]

Mechanical & Electronical Institute
Shandong University of Science & Technology, Qingdao 266510, China
Liutingrui9999@163.com, suixh@126.com, binhui0166@163.com

Abstract. *Engineering testing* courses are the core curriculums for the electromechanical majors. They are imperative or elective courses for the majors of *Mechanical Design Manufacture and Automation, Testing Control Instrument and Meter, Material Moulding and Control, and Process Equipmemt and Control.* There is one problem which commonly exists in the textbooks and the problem, lacking of numeralization, visualization, and engineering description, has impact on students' understanding and absorbing of the professonal knowledge. Grounded on the problem, the paper researches on teaching platform scheme of *Engineering Testing* courses based on LabVIEW, expatiates on engineering examples approaches, and demonstrates numeralizing procession of typical principles and typical signals.

Keywords: Engineering testing; teaching platform; LabVIEW.

1 Introduction

The core curriculums of *Engineering testing* courses include *Engineering testing and signal processing, Mechanical Engineering measuring and testing techniques, Sensor techniques.* The essential contents of the courses include two parts, which are sensor testing hardware parts, and signal analysis parts on the basis of Fourier Transform (FT). Taking *Engineering testing and signal processing* as the example, the main contents can be divided as signal acquirement and testing, and another part signal analysis approaches.

The concrete contents of *Engineering testing and signal processing* are listed as follows,

- Fourier series and FT, signal frequency spectrum analysis
- The static characteristics and dynamic characteristics of testing equipments
- Parts of sensors including electromotive species, photoelectric series, and digital transducer
- Signal transform including amplifying, filtering, moddemod, etc.

---

[*] Sponsor: Qunxing Project of Shandong University of Science and Technology (qx101002).

R. Chen (Ed.): ICICIS 2011, Part I, CCIS 134, pp. 12–17, 2011.

- Digital signal processing, its main contents are Fast Fourier Transform(FFT) and signal correlation
- Measuring of temperature, vibration and displacements
- Application of virtual instruments

Grounded on long-term theoretical and practical teaching, the members of the teaching group found one important problem which commonly exists in the textbooks and has impact on students' understanding and absorbing of the specialty knowledge. The problem is clarified and decomposed as follows.

2   Lacking of Numeralization, Visualization, and Engineering Description

Firstly, Lacking of engineering description. The theoretical parts, including the theoretical parts of the hardwares, are independent from one another and there are no the practical cases to link the differnt parts, especially the cases to link virtual instruments and the other parts. It mainly concludes as,

The singnal analysis parts are independent from one another and there are no the systematic applicable cases. The different part clarify the different kind of singnal processing methods which are tedious, complicate and abstract. There is no the vivid way to illustrate the process of singnal changing. The immediate consquences of the problems is that it seems for the students to learn the absolute mathematics matter, which negativly influences students' interests on the subjects and, in turn, their understanding and absorbing of the speciality knowledge. In all the chpaters of the books, there is no a systematic case to illustrate that after a signal is acquired, firstly make Fourier series unfolding or FT, then make frequency spectrum analysis or other equivalent transformation, up to signal simulation time domain display, to show the fact that the tested singnal can reflect the real signal in theory. Further more, as the modern measuring means, the virtual instruments parts are only introduced in a general way, there are no related teaching examples linking practical testing processing cases to make the teaching.

Secondly, Lacking of numeralization and visualization. There are no the software operation and vivid visual display of the dynamic process, especially about dynamic descriptions of basic principles, such as FFT, frequency shift, filtering, and aliasing processes. The students may look upon the signal transformation as a pure mathematics process.

3   Teaching Platform Scheme Based on LabVIEW

To solve the problem mentioned above, this teaching project scheme will realize numerical teaching platform baesd on LabVIEW, including utilizing two practical examples to link all parts of the textbooks, and visualizing the basic principles and typical signals dynamic processes. The flow diagram of the scheme is illustrated in Fig.1.

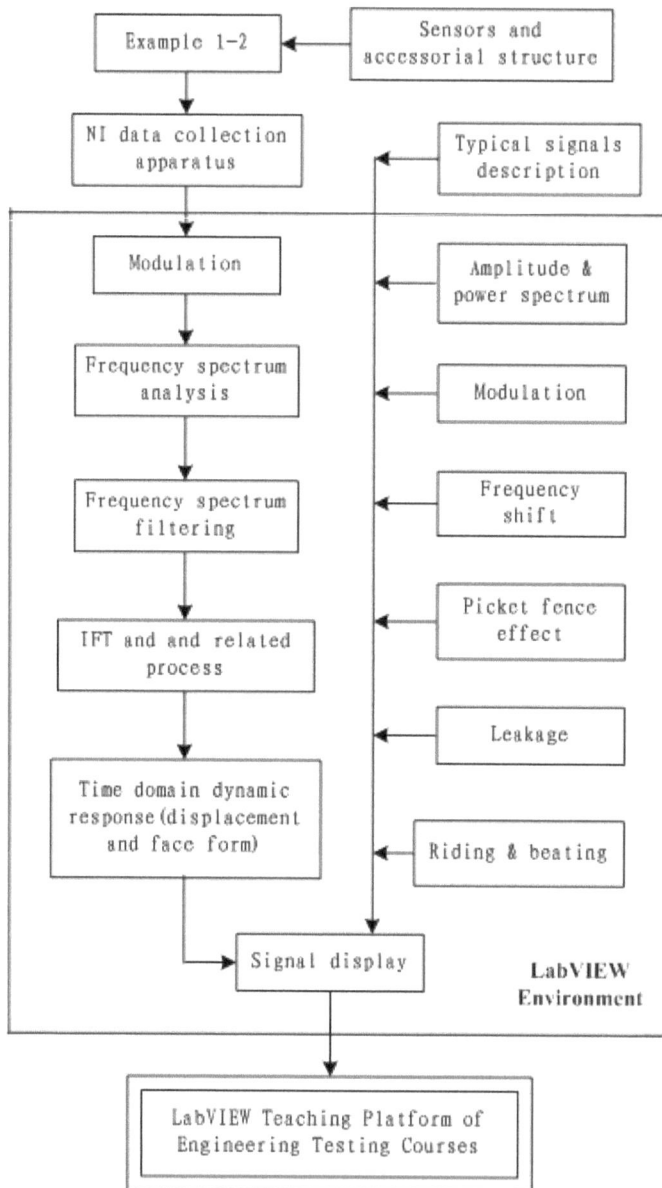

Fig. 1. The flow diagram of the scheme

3.1 Scheme Target One

Utilizing interface technology to induct large-scale engineering simulation examples in Matlab, so as to realize dynamic demojnstration of complicated engineering examples in LabVIEW. In view of apparent advantages of Matlab in complex engineering computing, to complicated testing and analysis, the edition of *m* files of

Matlab can be finished in advance, then make compatibility of m files and MathScript. MathScript of LabVIEW, and can add text programme oriented maths into LabVIEW. The main core of the MathScript is an advanced programing language that includes complex grammar and functions can be used in signal processing, signal analysis, and related mathematical process [1]. MathScript provides more than 600 species built-in functions, and allows the user to build new customed functions. The related example and its processes are clarified as follows,

Firstly, to build complicated example, the measuring of microcosmic surface of precise components, to compute surface roughness and demonstrate wavefront. The testing hardware platform uses CCD sensor, Piezo ceramics sensor,and Michelson interferometer to show the surface quality testing based on FFT spectrum analysis. It mainly demonstrates frequency spectrum transformation and testing consequence. The example combines signal analysis and sensor testing parts, the whole course can be fulfilled in Matlab, the flow diagram of which can be illustrated in Fig. 2.

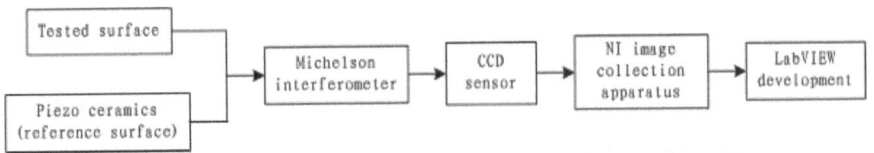

Fig. 2. The flow diagram of the processes of the complicated example

Secondly, to utilize the interface between LabVIEW and Matlab to induct codes above mentioned, so as to realize in LabVIEW. Based on Activex automation, the devise can control running state of Matlab server. Another based on COM and DLL technologies, the devise can greatly break away from Matlab environment with high efficiency and occupying few resources, which can bring conditions for fault diagnosis and real-time processing. Integrating application above technologies can acquire perfect programming consequences [2]. Mixing programming principles scheme is illustrated in Fig. 3.

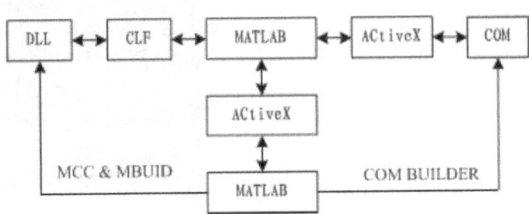

Fig. 3. Mixing programming principles scheme

3.2 Scheme Target Two

To conceive natural frequency testing research of cantilever beam based on LabVIEW [3]. The scheme grounded on PC hardware, combining necessary sensor, NI signal regulating apparatus, and NI data collection module, builds natural frequency testing hardware system with programming in LabVIEW. The devise uses force hammer to stimulate signals to testing the uniform strength beam (see Fig. 4).

The hammer strikes the cantilever surface, with data collecting by data collecting card. After signals regulating, curves of amplitude frequency spectrum and real frequency spectrum can be displayed in front board. Every time collecting frequency can be acqured after analyzing functional curves of frequency responses. The natural frequencise of the uniform strength beam can be got after processing of data with error theories and by taking the average of data post processing [3], simultaneous the time responses can be got afater IFFT.

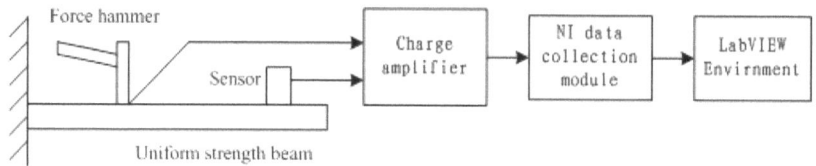

Fig. 4. The hardware structure of beam testing

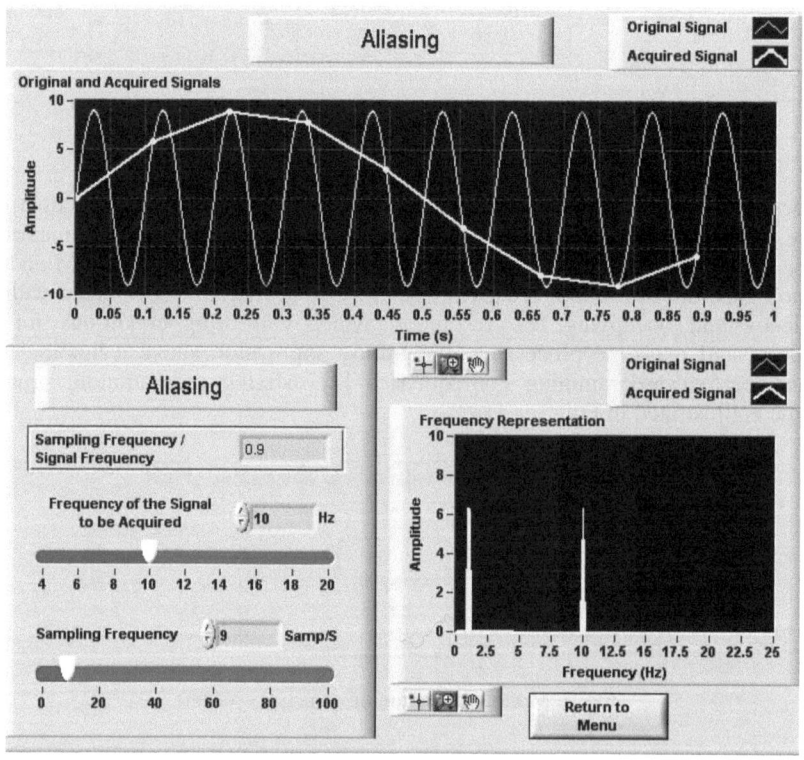

Fig. 5. Aliasing

3.3 Scheme Target Three

To devise dynamic display of basic principles and typical signals based on LabVIEW [4]. NI provides a complete platform to setup interaction teaching tools, to show signal and image conception, and can make signalsimulation by built-in functions of LabVIEW. The LabVIEW digital filter tools devise digital filter interactively, The LabVIEW DSP module makes program for digital signal processor and fulfils prototype devise.

The scheme will adopt LabVIEW DSP module and digital filter tools to demonstrate all sorts of concepts, such as discrete time signal and system, impulse response, convolution, frequency aliasing, picket fence effect, amplitude modulation and frequency modulation, riding and beating, different filters and their responses, stroboscope, sampling principles, windows for frequency analysis, all kinds of FFT transformation (from FFT time scaling and FFT time shifting to frequency domain averaging and frequency shift), and spectrogram etc. The students can allocate self-devised filters in NI Speedy-33DSP sheet card, and testify its validity with real-time signals. They can also can allocate filters in DSP and makle real-time debug and redesign. Fig.5 illustrates aliasing, which developed by NI.com/China [4].

4 Conclusion

In the scheme of LabVIEW teaching platform development, the principles covering FT and Fourier series, and their related contents are fully reflected. The teaching cases can reflect all the core theories of different chapters. All the core theories are integrated and can be visually displayed in the cases. Especially in LabVIEW, the whole process, from basic processing to filtering, frequency domain, modulation, sampling, time damain, and windowing, even advanced signal processing can be found in NI websites[5] as some examples, so the schme is advisable and feasible in practical way.

References

1. NI.com /China: Go Deep into LabVIEW MathScript (in Chinese)
2. Shen, L., Sen, L., et al.: Study on Program Method of LabVIEW Mixs with Matlab and Engineering Applications. Instrument Technique and Sensor 1(1), 22–25 (2007) (in Chinese)
3. Quan, L., Yingfu, G., et al.: Research on Natural Frequency of Cantilever Beam Based on LabVIEW. Electronic Measurement Technology 9, 85–88 (2009) (in Chinese)
4. NI.com /China: LabVIEW Processing Lab-E,
   ftp://ftp.ni.com/pub/branches/china/Signal%20Processing%20Lab-E.zip

Software Development Cost and Time Forecasting Using a High Performance Artificial Neural Network Model

Iman Attarzadeh and Siew Hock Ow

Department of Software Engineering
Faculty of Computer Science & Information Technology
University of Malaya, 50603 Kuala Lumpur, Malaysia
attarzadeh@siswa.um.edu.my, show@um.edu.my

Abstract. Nowadays, mature software companies are more interested to have a precise estimation of software metrics such as project time, cost, quality, and risk at the early stages of software development process. The ability to precisely estimate project time and costs by project managers is one of the essential tasks in software development activities, and it named software effort estimation. The estimated effort at the early stage of project development process is uncertain, vague, and often the least accurate. It is because that very little information is available at the beginning stage of project. Therefore, a reliable and precise effort estimation model is an ongoing challenge for project managers and software engineers. This research work proposes a novel soft computing model incorporating Constructive Cost Model (COCOMO) to improve the precision of software time and cost estimation. The proposed artificial neural network model has good generalisation, adaption capability, and it can be interpreted and validated by software engineers. The experimental results show that applying the desirable features of artificial neural networks on the algorithmic estimation model improves the accuracy of time and cost estimation and estimated effort can be very close to the actual effort.

Keywords: Software Engineering, Software Project Management, Software Cost Estimation Models, COCOMO Model, Soft Computing Techniques, Artificial Neural Networks.

1 Introduction

Accurate and consistent software development effort prediction in the early stage of development process is one of the critical tasks in software project management. Project managers use effort estimation to make on-time and better managerial decisions during project development life cycle and especially for determination of project details, allocation of project resources, project tasks, schedule controlling, and process monitoring. In software development process, the effort directly related to software schedule, cost and manpower factors that are critical and important for any project. The software development effort estimation is counted as a very complex process because of essential project factors such as development environments, platform factors, human factors, product factors, customers' needs, and finally the

R. Chen (Ed.): ICICIS 2011, Part I, CCIS 134, pp. 18–26, 2011.
© Springer-Verlag Berlin Heidelberg 2011

difficulty of managing such large projects. During last decades, the governments and many mature organisations invest on software development to achieve their purpose.

Therefore, the accurate estimation of project time, cost, and staffing are needed to effectively plan, monitor, control and assess software development companies and project managers. The effort estimation in software engineering is based on two large methods: algorithmic methods and non-algorithmic methods. Algorithmic methods carry a mathematical formula that is inferred from regression model of historical data and project attributes. Constructive Cost Model (COCOMO) [1, 2] and Function Points [3] (FP) are two well-known methods of this category. Non-algorithmic methods [4, 5, 6], usually, are based on heretical projects information and comparing new project activities to past projects, then make estimation on the new project tasks. Expert judgment and analogy-based estimation [5] are two samples of non-algorithmic methods. This research work intends to use the soft computing approach, artificial neural networks, to propose a novel software effort estimation model incorporating constructive cost model to improve the precision of software effort estimation.

2 Related Work

Wittig and his colleagues proposed a simple neural network for software cost estimation. The purpose of that research was to examine the performance of back-propagation training algorithm. First, they used a metric model, $(SPQR/20^2)$, to generate adequate data for the experiment. Second, they used a set of actual experiments from developed past software. In both methods, Function Points (FPs) method used as the measurement method of the input parameter, Size, and the development hours used as the unit of system output, Effort [7]. The experiments results in their research work show the ability of neural networks to make better estimation. Samson et al. used another mathematical model, Cerebellar Model Arithmetic Computer (CMAC). Then applied proposed neural networks architecture on the CMAC to make effort estimation based on software code size. The CMAC model proposed by Albus [8] and it is an approximation perceptron function. The established model based on neural networks was trained on COCOMO dataset in order to estimate software development effort from size of software. Also, they used linear regression techniques in same manner to compare the acquired data. The results of the proposed prediction model performed better than linear regression on the same data set. In other research, Boetticher used more than 33,000 different experiments data, collected from separate software companies, to examine the proposed neural network [9].

He used different software metrics such as size, complexity, objects, and vocabulary to estimate software effort using neural networks. Boetticher in another research used bottom-up approach to apply the past experiments on the two separate neural networks. The bottom-up approach uses data collected from software products rather than software projects. In that model, the Source Lines of Code (SLOC) metric used as the input of neural network model to estimate the project effort. Karunanitthi et al., also, proposed a cost estimation model based on artificial neural networks [10]. The established neural network was able to generalise from trained datasets. The model results show better effort estimation results than other compared models. Srinivasan et al. applying machine leaning approaches based on neural networks and regression trees to algorithmic cost estimation models [11].

They reported that the main advantages of learning systems such as adaptable and nonparametric. However, they did not discuss on the used dataset and how divided it for training and validation process. In another research, Khoshgoftaar et al. considering a case study on the real time estimation software. They used a primary neural network model to establish a real time cost estimation model [12, 13]. But the presented validation process of their model is not adequate. Shepperd and Schofield presented a software estimation model based on analogy. This research was one the basic work on that time [14]. They used the information of past projects to make estimation for new projects. The proposed method was a heuristic method, so they could not make a good evaluation of the performance of their proposed model. Jorgenson examined many parameters in cost estimation based on expert judgment. His research established some essential parameters that affects on software development process [15].

3   The Proposed Artificial Neural Network Based on COCOMO Model

The constructive cost model, COCOMO, is a mathematical and regression-based effort estimation model that was proposed and establishes by Barry Boehm in 1981 [1, 2]. The calculation of effort based on the COCOMO post architecture model is given as:

$$Effort = A \times [Size]^B \times \prod_{i=1}^{17} Effort\ Multiplier_i \qquad (1)$$

$$where\ B = 1.01 + 0.01 \times \sum_{j=1}^{5} Scale\ Factor_j$$

In the equation "1":

A: Multiplicative Constant
Size: Size of the software project measured in terms of KSLOC or FP.

The proposed artificial neural network architecture is customised to adopt the widely used algorithmic model, COCOMO model. The input and output parameters of COCOMO model are categorised as follow [1, 2]:

- Size parameter – Input parameter: software size based on thousands source lines of code.
- Five Scale Factors (SF) – Input parameter: scale factors are based software productivity variation and project's activities.
- Seventeen Effort Multipliers (EM) - Input parameter: effort multipliers are based on project attributes, product attributes, personnel attributes, and hardware attributes.
- Effort – Output parameter: the calculated effort is based on person-month (PM) unit.

In the new proposed model, twenty five input parameters are defined that corresponds to number of SFs and EMs as well as two bias values. Therefore, the input layer in the new artificial neural network includes 25 nodes. However, in order to customise the COCOMO model in the new ANN model, a specific ANN layer as a hidden layer and a widely used activation function, Sigmoid, with some data pre-processing for input and hidden layer are considered. The ANN architecture and configuration shows in Figure 1.

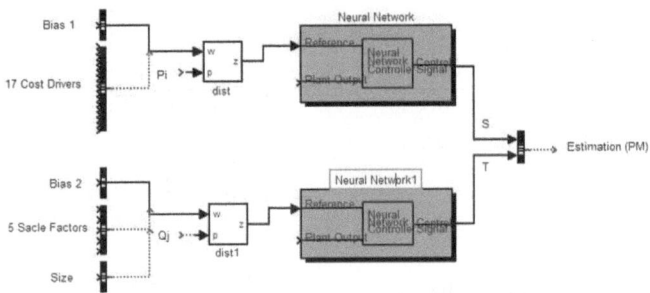

Fig. 1. The proposed COCOMO II model based on artificial neural networks

In the proposed ANN, the scale factors and effort multipliers values are pre-processed to log (SF_i) and log (EM_i), also the input size of the product in KSLOC is considered as one of the initial weights for scale factors. The Sigmoid function is considered as the activation function of hidden layer. It defined by $f(x) = \frac{1}{1+e^{-x}}$. The assigned weights of nodes in the input layer to hidden layer are defined by P_i for Bias1 and each input log (EM_i) for $1 \leq i \leq 17$. On the other hand, the assigned weights of each SF_j in the input layer to hidden layer are defined as $q_j + \log(size)$ for $1 \leq j \leq 5$ by Bias2. 'S' and 'T' are the final weights of nodes from the hidden layer to the output layer as shown in Figure 1. 'S' and 'T' are the values of the relevant nodes in the hidden layer and in the output layer the identity function uses them to generate the final effort value.

One of the additional contributions in the new ANN architecture is using pre-processed Log(Size) to the weight q_j of SF's input for adjusting the weights q_j. Another major contribution of the new ANN architecture compared to previous models is the training approach of the new artificial neural network. In order to customise the COCOMO model in the new ANN architecture, the initial values of weights 'S' and 'T' are adjusted to the offset of the nodes values in the hidden layer. The network inputs initialise to a random data from the data set at the beginning of training. The network output, effort estimation, would be inferred from the equation of COCOMO model, in "1", by using the initial values of Bias1 as Log (A) and Bias2 as 1.01. The network weights are initialised as $p_i = 1$ for $1 \leq i \leq 17$ and $q_j = 1$ for $1 \leq j \leq 5$. The nodes values in the hidden layer generated by propagating the values of input nodes into the network as follow:

$$f\left(p_o \cdot Bias1 - \sum_i^{17} p_i \times log(EM_i)\right) = sigmoid\left(Bias1 - \sum_i^{17} p_i \times log(EM_i)\right) =$$
$$\frac{A \cdot \prod_{i=1}^{17} EM_i}{1 + A \cdot \prod_{i=1}^{17} EM_i} = \alpha \tag{2}$$

$$f\left((q_o - log(size)) \times Bias2 - \sum_{=1}^{5}(q_i - log(size))(SF_i)\right) = sigmoid\left(log(size) \times \right.$$
$$\left(Bias2 - \sum_{=1}^{5} SF_i\right) = \frac{Size^{1.01 - \sum_{=1}^{5} SF}}{1 - Size^{1.01 - \sum_{=1}^{5} SF}} = \beta \tag{3}$$

Then initialisation of weights 'S' and 'T' as follow:

$$S = \frac{\beta}{2(1-\alpha)(1-\beta)} \quad \text{and} \quad T = \frac{\alpha}{2(1-\alpha)(1-\beta)} \tag{4}$$

The network output calculated as:

$$PM = S*\alpha + T*\beta = \frac{\alpha\beta}{(1-\alpha)(1-\beta)} = A. Size^{1.01+\sum_{j=1}^{5} SF_j} * \prod_{i=1}^{17} EM_i \tag{5}$$

4   Results and Discussion

Experiments were done by taking three different datasets as follow:

- First dataset, Dataset #1, the projects information from COCOMO dataset - COCOMO dataset involves 63 different projects.
- Second dataset, Dataset #2, the projects information from NASA projects - NASA dataset involves 93 different projects.
- Third dataset, Dataset #3, the artificial dataset that created based on the ANN – The artificial dataset involves 100 different projects information from the COCOMO and NASA datasets.

Therefore, in this research work has used 256 projects information from three different datasets, to evaluate the proposed artificial neural network estimation model. Finally, by aggregation of the obtained results from the ANN model, the accuracy of the proposed model compares to other estimation models.

4.1   Evaluation Method

The two most widely accepted evaluation methods are used for model evaluation, which are as follows:

- Mean Magnitude of Relative Error (MMRE)
- Pred(L): probability of a project having a relative error of less than or equal to L that called Pred(L) or prediction at level L. The common value of L is 25%.

The first evaluation method, Magnitude of Relative Error (MRE) is defined as follows:

$$MRE_i = \frac{|Actual\ Effort_i - Predicted\ Effort_i|}{Actual\ Effort_i} \tag{6}$$

The MRE is calculated for all predicted effort in the datasets, for all observations i. Another related evaluation method is the Mean MRE (MMRE) that can be achieved through the aggregation of MRE over multiple observations (N) as follows:

$$MMRE = \frac{1}{N} \sum_{i}^{N} MRE_i \qquad (7)$$

Therefore, usually, the aggregation of the measures used to overcome the problem. In fact, the aggregate measure less sensitive to large values. In the second evaluation method, a complementary criterion is the prediction or estimation at level L, Pred(L) = K/N, where k carries the number of observations of MRE (or MER) that less than or equal to L, and N equals total number of observations. Thus, Pred(25%), for example, means the percentage of projects which were estimated with a MRE (or MER) less or equal than 0.25. The proposed artificial neural network estimation model was trained and evaluated based on the three described datasets in the previous sections. At the first attempt, the COCOMO dataset, 63 projects, applied to the new ANN model. The system results, effort estimation, recorded step by step in a table for future comparisons.

The MRE is calculated based on the estimated effort and corresponding actual effort form the dataset. Finally, the aggregation of the results, MMRE, computes to avoid any sensitivity to large values. Then the Pred(25%) also calculated as the second evaluation method. Same approach applied for NASA dataset, Dataset #2, and Artificial dataset, Dataset #3. All the 256 projects used to the evaluation of the proposed ANN estimation model. The comparison of the obtained results from Dataset #1, #2, and #3 that applied on the new artificial neural network cost estimation model and COCOMO model shows more accuracy in case of effort estimation by the new ANN estimation model. Table 1 shows, the used datasets on one side and the other side, the MMRE and Pred(25%) corresponding values to the models. In fact, all datasets first applied to the proposed ANN model then applied to the COOCMO model, widely used cost estimation model. The final results shown in Table 1 as follows.

Table 1. Comparison between performance of the new model and COCOMO II

Dataset	Model	Evaluation	
		MMRE	Pred (25%)
Dataset #1	COCOMO II	0.581863191	30%
	Proposed Model	0.413568265	40%
Dataset #2	COCOMO II	0.481729632	40%
	Proposed Model	0.468142057	50%
Dataset #3	COCOMO II	0.526316925	40%
	Proposed Model	0.453826571	40%
Mean	COCOMO II	0.529969916	36.6%
	Proposed Model	0.445178964	43.3%

In this research work three different datasets has applied to the proposed artificial neural network cost estimation model and the COCOMO model. For each set of data, dataset, the MMRE and Pred(25%) measures were calculated for models evaluation. The MMRE and Pred(25%) values for each dataset to consider the performance of each dataset separately as in shown in Table 1. The final results of 256 applied projects shows that the MMRE for the proposed ANN estimation model is 0.445178964 and the Pred(25%) values equals 43.3% when compared to COCOMO model with MMRE = 0.529969916 and Pred(25%) = 36.6%.

Obviously, the results show that the MMRE of proposed ANN model is less than the MMRE of COCOMO model. As it state above, if the value of MMRE is closed to 0, it means the amount of occurred error, the difference of actual effort and estimated effort, is very low. In the other words, it means the accuracy of estimated effort in the ANN estimation model is better than the COCOMO model. When the value of Pred(25%) in the ANN estimation model, 43.3%, compared to the corresponding value in the COCOMO model, 36.6%, it shows that the proposed model provides accurate results than the COCOMO model. If the value of Pred(25%) measure is closed to 100%, it means most of estimated results are closed to the actual results. Therefore, the accuracy of the ANN estimation model is obviously better than the COCOMO model. According to the stated analysis based on the two evaluation methods, MMRE and Pred, the artificial neural network cost estimation model shows better results in case of accuracy of the estimated results. That is one of the good achievements of this research work. Table 2 shows the comparison between the proposed ANN model and the COCOMO model in case of percentage of accuracy in the two examined model.

Table 2. Accuracy of the proposed model

Model	Evaluation	MMRE
Proposed Model vs. COCOMO II	COCOMO II	0.529969916
	Proposed Model	0.445178964
	Improvement %	9.28%

When the percentage of improvement in the ANN estimation model and the COCOMO model is calculated, the result shows 9.28% improvement in case of the accuracy of the estimation with the propose model. In summary, the experimental results from the two effort estimation models confirm the capabilities and better performance of the proposed ANN model in case of accuracy of the estimation when compared to the COCOMO model. Most of the selected data with the proposed ANN effort estimation model resulted in a more precise estimations when compared to the COCOMO model.

5   Conclusion

In software engineering and especially in software project management providing the accurate and reliable software attributes estimation in the early stages of the software development process is one the essential, critical, and crucial issues. It always has been the center of attention for software engineers and project managers as well as mature software companies and organisations. Software development attributes usually have properties of vagueness and uncertainty when the human judgment used to measure them. Using the ability of artificial neural networks to provide accurate estimations can overcome the characteristics of vagueness and uncertainty that exists in software development attributes. However, utilising adaptive neural network architecture plays a key role in coming up with reliable and accurate effort estimation model. Appling soft computing techniques, e.g. artificial neural networks, can be a considerable attempt in the area of software project management and estimation. One of the main objectives of this research work is to use artificial neural network, as an applicable technique, for software effort estimates that performs better and accurate estimation than other techniques, e.g. COCOMO model, on a given datasets. In this research work a novel artificial neural network presented to handle the uncertainty and imprecision of software effort estimation. The proposed model has shown applying artificial neural network as an applicable technique on the algorithmic cost estimation models accurate estimation is achievable. The ANN effort estimation model has shown better and accurate software effort estimates in view of two evaluation methods, the MMRE and Pred (0.25), as compared to the COCOMO model. The percentage of improvement in the proposed model, 9.28%, demonstrate that utilising artificial neural networks in software effort estimation can be an applicable and feasible approach to address the problem of vagueness and uncertainty exists in software development attributes. Furthermore, the proposed ANN effort estimation model presents better estimation accuracy as compared to the algorithmic COCOMO model. The applying other soft computing techniques for other software engineering weakness can also is considered in the future.

References

[1] Boehm, B.: Software Engineering Economics. Prentice-Hall, Englewood Cliffs (1981)
[2] Boehm, B., Abts, C., Chulani, S.: Software Development Cost Estimation Approaches – A Survey, University of Southern California Center for Software Engineering, Technical Reports, USC-CSE-2000-505 (2000)
[3] Putnam, L.H.: A General Empirical Solution to the Macro Software Sizing and Estimating Problem. IEEE Transactions on Software Engineering 4(4), 345–361 (1978)
[4] Srinivasan, K., Fisher, D.: Machine Learning Approaches to Estimating Software Development Effort. IEEE Transactions on Software Engineering 21(2), 123–134 (1995)
[5] Molokken, K., Jorgensen, M.: A review of software surveys on software effort estimation. In: IEEE International Symposium on Empirical Software Engineering, ISESE, pp. 223–230 (2003)
[6] Huang, S., Chiu, N.: Applying fuzzy neural network to estimate software development effort. Applied Intelligence Journal 30(2), 73–83 (2009)
[7] Witting, G., Finnie, G.: Using Artificial Neural Networks and Function Points to Estimate 4GL Software Development Effort. Journal of Information Systems 1(2), 87–94 (1994)
[8] Samson, B.: Software cost estimation using an Albus perceptron. Journal of Information and Software 4(2), 55–60 (1997)
[9] Boetticher, G.D.: An assessment of metric contribution in the construction of a neural network-based effort estimator. In: Proceedings of Second International Workshop on Soft Computing Applied to Software Engineering, pp. 234–245 (2001)
[10] Karunanitthi, N., Whitely, D., Malaiya, Y.K.: Using Neural Networks in Reliability Prediction. IEEE Software Engineering 9(4), 53–59 (1992)

[11] Srinivasan, K., Fisher, D.: Machine learning approaches to estimating software development effort. IEEE Transaction on Software Engineering 21(2), 126–137 (1995)

[12] Khoshgoftar, T.M., Allen, E.B., Xu, Z.: Predicting testability of program modules using a neural network. In: Proceeding of 3rd IEEE Symposium on Application-Specific Systems and Software Engineering Technology, pp. 57–62 (2000)

[13] Khoshgoftar, T.M., Seliya, N.: Fault prediction modeling for software quality estimation: comparing commonly used techniques. Journal of Empirical Software Engineering 8(3), 255–283 (2003)

[14] Shepperd, M., Schofield, C.: Estimating Software Project Effort Using Analogies. IEEE Transactions on Software Engineering 23(11), 736–743 (1997)

[15] Jorgenson, M.: A review of studies on expert estimation of software development effort. Journal of Systems and Software 70(4), 37–60 (2004)

A Weighted Combination Method of Target Identity Identification

Jin Hongbin, Lan Jiangqiao, and Li Hongfei

Air Force Radar Academy, Wuhan, China
Jhb760817@sina.com

Abstract. Evidence theory is widely used in the target identity identification. Dempster-Shafer theory (DST)'s result is unreliable when the conflict becomes high, and Dezert-Smarandanche theory (DSmT) reduces the basic belief assignment in the lowly conflicting condition, so this paper presents a weighted target identity identification method that interacts DST and DSmT to overcome their weakness. The method calculates the similarity as a weighted factor to adaptive combine evidence. The examples are tested and veritied the effectiveness and applicability of the method.

Keywords: Target identity identification; DSmT; DST; Interactive combination.

1 Introduction

Target identity identification is an important content in information fusion which is full of vitality. Target identity identification is not only the foundation of situation and threat assessment but also providing supports for battlefield decisions. The category and behavior of targets become more and more complex especially in the environment of information confronting, which makes the traditional method based on single sensor difficult to obtain satisfying result. DST provides a useful evidence combination rule to fuse and update new evidence for multi-sensor targets' identity. But D-S evidence theory will obtain a result which is against instinct when the conflict becomes high [1].

Dezert and Smarandache present a new evidence reasoning theory—DSmT [2] to solve the limitation of DST. The DSmT changes the frame of DST and proposes a series effective combination rules. DSmT obtains a satisfying result in high conflicting condition, but the calculation is considerable and the basic belief assignment reduced in the lowly conflicting condition. So considering the figure of two theories, this paper presents a weighted combination method of target identity identification. The method interacts DST and DSmT based on the similarity to adaptive combine evidence. The method can combine highly conflicting evidence and lowly conflicting evidence effectively.

2 PCR Rule

Proportional conflict redistribution rules (PCR rules) [3-6] is present by Dezert and Smarandache based on the DSmT. PCR rules distribute conflicting belief in a certain

R. Chen (Ed.): ICICIS 2011, Part I, CCIS 134, pp. 27–32, 2011.

proportion to the combination belief, which make better use of the evidence. PCR rules are composed of PCR1 to PCR6 rule according to distributing proportion. PCR6 rule computes the distributing proportion following the logic of the sum of evidence's bba to consider as the most reasonable PCR rule. PCR6 rule between two evidence is defined as follows:

Let's $\Theta = \{\theta_1, \theta_2, \ldots, \theta_n\}$ be the frame of the fusion problem under consideration and two belief assignments m_1, m_2 : $G^\Theta \to [0,1]$ such that $\sum_{Y \in G^\Theta} m_i(Y) = 1$, $i = 1,2$. The PCR6 rule for two evidences is defined $\forall (X \neq \phi) \in G^\Theta$ by:

$$m_{\mathrm{PCR6}}(X) = \sum_{\substack{X_i \cap X_j = X, X_i, X_j \in G^\Theta}} m_1(X_i)m_2(X_j) + \sum_{\substack{X_i \in G^\Theta \setminus \{X\} \\ c(X_i \cap X) = \phi}} [\frac{m_1(X)^2 m_2(X_i)}{m_1(X) + m_2(X_i)} + \frac{m_2(X)^2 m_1(X_i)}{m_2(X) + m_1(X_i)}] \quad (1)$$

PCR6 rule does well in dealing with low conflicting evidence, but the bba of result reduces compared with Dempster rule of combination as a result of the increase of elements involved. So PCR6 rule is less than Dempster rule of combination in lowly conflicting condition.

3   Similarity Measurement of Evidence

The association of Similarity between evidence can estimate the support grade between evidence. The common methods for estimation of similarity between evidence are distance and angle similarity. Common distance method includes Euclidean distance, Manhattan distance, Minkowski distance etc. These three distance methods don't take into account the intersection of sets , result is unreliable in some condition. So a important consideration of similarity measure is the management of intersection. Jousselme distance solved this problem [8], but Jousselme distance brought new problem that the cardinal of focal elements used incorrectly in the method. Considering the character of angle similarity and Jousselme distance, we present the angle similarity method based on cardinal as the quantitative analysis of similarity measurement of evidence. Angle similarity between evidence can measure by their cosine. The method is defined as:

Let's $\Theta = \{\theta_1, \theta_2, \ldots, \theta_n\}$ be the frame of the fusion problem under consideration and two belief assignments $m_1, m_2 : 2^\Theta \to [0,1]$ such that $\sum_{Y \in 2^\Theta} m_i(Y) = 1$, $i = 1,2$. The angle similarity between m_1 and m_2 is defined $\forall (X \neq \phi) \in 2^\Theta$ by

$$\cos(m_1, m_2) = \frac{\langle m_1, m_2 \rangle}{\sqrt{\|m_1\|^2 \cdot \|m_2\|^2}} \quad (2)$$

where $\|m\|^2 = \langle m, m \rangle$, and $\langle m_1, m_2 \rangle$ defined as

$$\langle m_1, m_2 \rangle = \sum_{i=1}^{2^\Theta} \sum_{j=1}^{2^\Theta} m_1(X_i)m_2(X_j)d(i,j) \quad X_i, X_j \in 2^\Theta \quad (3)$$

(3) into (2)

$$\cos(m_1,m_2) = \frac{\sum_{i=1}^{2^\Theta}\sum_{j=1}^{2^\Theta} m_1(X_i)m_2(X_j)\frac{|X_i \cap X_j|}{|X_i \cup X_j|}}{\sqrt{\left(\sum_{i=1}^{2^\Theta}\sum_{j=1}^{2^\Theta} m_1(X_i)m_1(X_j)\frac{|X_i \cap X_j|}{|X_i \cup X_j|}\right)\cdot\left(\sum_{i=1}^{2^\Theta}\sum_{j=1}^{2^\Theta} m_2(X_i)m_2(X_j)\frac{|X_i \cap X_j|}{|X_i \cup X_j|}\right)}} \tag{4}$$

Let's $d(i, j)$ the ratio between intersection's cardinal and union's cardinal

$$d(i, j) = d(j,i) = \frac{|X_i \cap X_j|}{|X_i \cup X_j|} \quad X_i, X_j \in 2^\Theta \tag{5}$$

Angle similarity is more reasonable than distance , distance method used the cardinal of focal elements incorrectly so the result of distance is imprecise. Angle similarity solves this problem, so angle similarity is a better method in similarity measure between evidence. Example Let's $\Theta = \{\theta_1, \theta_2, \theta_3\}$ be the frame, there're three evidence.

E_1: $m_1(\theta_2) = 0.2$, $m_1(\theta_3) = 0.8$; E_2: $m_2(\theta_1 \cup \theta_2) = 0.8$, $m_2(\theta_3) = 0.2$;

E_3 : $m_3(\theta_1) = 1$, $m_3(\theta_3) = 0$. **Jousselme distance**: $d(m_1, m_2) = 0.9381$; $d(m_2, m_3) = 0.9381$; $d(m_1, m_3) = 1.296$ **angle similarity**: $\cos(m_1, m_2) = 0.3529$; $\cos(m_2, m_3) = 0.4851$; $\cos(m_1, m_3) = 0$.

The two method both give the result that the similarity between m_1, m_3 is least. Jousselme distance educes that the similarity between m_1, m_2 is as same as that between m_2, m_3 . The result is obviously incorrect when angle similarity educes a reasonable result. Angle similarity is more useful in similarity measurement of evidence.

4 Method of Target Identity Identification

Experts already recognize the validity of DST when the conflict is low, but the result's bba of DSmT reduces for the increase of involved elements. In the highly conflicting condition, DSmT solve DST's problem that DST is not able to combine conflicting focal elements. So single identification theory can't deal with the evidence in real application. The weighted combination method of target identity identification combines evidence with different combination rules, and the result of different combination rules is weighted in a proper probability to identify different kinds of targets. DST chooses the Dempster rule of combination, DSmT chooses the PCR6 rule.

The process of weighted combination method of target identity identification is defined as follows:

Let's $\Theta = \{\theta_1, \theta_2, \dots, \theta_n\}$ be the frame of the fusion problem under consideration and k belief assignments $m_1, m_2 \cdots m_k$: $2^\Theta \to [0,1]$ such that $\sum_{Y \in 2^\Theta} m_i(Y) = 1$, $i = 1, 2 \cdots k$.

Step 1 calculate the angle similarity by formula (4) ,to obtain $\cos(.)$;

Step 2 combine the evidence with Dempster rule to obtain $m_{\text{DS}}(.)$;

Step 3 combine the evidence with PCR6 rule by formula (1) ,to obtain $m_{\text{PCR6}}(.)$;

Step 4 ensure the weighted factor by angle similarity, and weight sum $m_{\text{DS}}(.)$ and $m_{\text{PCR6}}(.)$ to obtain combination belief :

$$m_{\text{weighted}}(X) = \cos(.) \cdot m_{\text{DS}}(.) + \left[1 - \cos(.)\right] \cdot m_{\text{PCR6}}(.) \tag{6}$$

Combine the new evidence with the result of weighted combination to form dynamic fusion.

5 Analysis on Number Examples

To validate the method presented in this paper, we compare and analyze the methods by two classical number examples. One is highly conflicting example, the other is a lowly conflicting example. The methods compared are: Dempster rule of combination, Yager rule of combination, PCR6 rule and weighted combination method. The background of example: Let consider there are five sensors in the identification system, the frame of discernment is Shafer model, the attributes of air target are Friend (F), Hostile (H), Neutral (N), $\Theta = \{F, H, N\}$.

The bba of a time is shown in Table 1 and Table 3, The identification result by different method is shown in Table 2 and Table 4.

The identification result in table 2 shows that the result of Dempster rule is against instinct, determines the attribute Hostile. Yager rule assigns all conflict to unknown Θ which is't useful for the decision. PCR6 rule eliminates the "wrong" evidence and obtains a reasonable result which shows its validity in dealing with highly conflicting evidence. And the weighted combination method obtains a result that the bba support Friend increases to 0.73168 better than PCR6 rule. The result in table 4 shows that Dempster rule has a perfect result when the conflict is low. The bba supports Friend is 0.98406. PCR6 rule reduces bba of Friend to 0.78146 for the increase of elements involved. The bba of Friend obtained by weighted combination method is 0.95422 only 0.03 less than that of Dempster rule which is also a satisfying result. Form the two examples we can conclude that Dempster rule and PCR6 rule has obvious limitation when the weighted combination method can deal with conflicting evidence of different degree.

Table 1. bba obtained by five sensors （highly conflicting example）

evidence / attribute	m_1	m_2	m_3	m_4	m_5
F	0.5	0	0.55	0.55	0.5
H	0.2	0.9	0.1	0.1	0.2
N	0.3	0.1	0.35	0.35	0.3

Table 2. The identification result of highly conflicting example

Method	Results	$m_1 - m_2$	$m_1 - m_3$	$m_1 - m_4$	$m_1 - m_5$
Dempster Rule of combination	$m(F)$	0	0	0	0
	$m(H)$	0.85714	0.63158	0.32877	0.24615
	$m(N)$	0.14286	0.36842	0.67123	0.75385
Yager rule of combination	$m(F)$	0	0	0	0
	$m(H)$	0.18	0.018	0.0018	0.00036
	$m(N)$	0.03	0.0105	0.00368	0.00110
	$m(\Theta)$	0.79	0.9715	0.99452	0.99854
PCR6 rule	$m(F)$	0.20238	0.36997	0.51013	0.58902
	$m(H)$	0.68512	0.44823	0.25794	0.18146
	$m(N)$	0.11250	0.18180	0.23193	0.22952
weighted combination method	$m(F)$	0.12624	0.33732	0.58411	0.73168
	$m(H)$	0.74983	0.46463	0.18305	0.09239
	$m(N)$	0.12392	0.19805	0.23284	0.17593

Table 3. bba obtained by five sensors （lowly conflicting example）

evidence / attribute	m_1	m_2	m_3	m_4	m_5
F	0.5	0.9	0.55	0.55	0.5
H	0.2	0	0.1	0.1	0.2
N	0.3	0.1	0.35	0.35	0.3

Table 4. The identification result of lowly conflicting example

Method	Results	$m_1 - m_2$	$m_1 - m_3$	$m_1 - m_4$	$m_1 - m_5$
Dempster rule of combination	$m(F)$	0.93750	0.95930	0.97371	0.98406
	$m(H)$	0	0	0	0
	$m(N)$	0.06250	0.04070	0.02629	0.01594
Yager rule of combination	$m(F)$	0.45	0.24750	0.13613	0.06807
	$m(H)$	0	0	0	0
	$m(N)$	0.03	0.0105	0.00367	0.00110
	$m(\Theta)$	0.52	0.7420	0.8602	0.93083
PCR6 rule	$m(F)$	0.84144	0.82073	0.80496	0.78146
	$m(H)$	0.04606	0.02267	0.01826	0.05510
	$m(N)$	0.11250	0.15660	0.17678	0.16344
weighted combination method	$m(F)$	0.92404	0.94174	0.95105	0.95422
	$m(H)$	0.00645	0.00282	0.00221	0.00754
	$m(N)$	0.06951	0.05544	0.04674	0.03824

6 Conclusion

This paper presents a weighted combination method of target identity identification based on DST and DSmT. The method chooses angle similarity as the basis of weighted factor interacts DST and DSmT to combine evidence. The method can obtain a satisfying result in lowly conflicting condition and solve the problem in highly conflicting condition. But this method needs to calculate the similarity between evidence which increases the calculation; Dempster rule of combination can't be applicable in free DSm model and hybrid model which limits its applied area.

References

1. Zadeh, L.A.: Review of Shafers A mathematical theory of evidence. AI Magazine 5(3), 81–83 (1984)
2. Dezert, J.: Foundations for a new theory of Plausible and Paradoxical reasoning. Information and Security Journal 12(1), 26–30 (2002)
3. Smarandache, F., Dezert, J.: An introduction to DSm Theory of Plausible, Paradoxist, Uncertain, and Imprecise Reasoning for Information Fusion. Octogon Mathematical Magazine 15(2), 681–722 (2007)
4. Smarandache, F., Dezert, J.: Proportional conflict redistribution for information fusion. In: Smarandache, F., Dezert, J. (eds.) Advances and Applications of DSmT for Information Fusion(Collected Works), vol. II, pp. 3–66. American Research Press, Rehoboth (2006)
5. Smarandache, F., Dezert, J.: Information fusion based on new proportional conflict redistribution rules. In: 8th International Conference on Information Fusion, Philadelphia, PA, USA, vol. 2, pp. 25–28 (2005)
6. Scholte, K.A., van Norden, W.L.: Applying the PCR6 Rule of Combination in Real Time Classification Systems. In: 12th International Conference on Information Fusion, Seattle, USA, pp. 1665–1672 (2009)
7. Jousselme, A.L., Dominic, G., Bosse, E.: A new distance between two bodies of evidence. Information Fusion 2(2), 91–101 (2001)

Fault Diagnosis of Power Transformer Based on BP Combined with Genetic Algorithm

Weiguo Zhao[1], Yanning Kang[2], Gangzhu Pan[3], and Xinfeng Huang[4]

[1] Hebei University of Engineering, Handan, 056038, China
[2] Dept. of Economics & Management, Shijiazhuang University, Hebei, 050035, China
[3] School of Software, Hebei Normal University, Shijiazhuang 050016, China
[4] Zhang-fuhe Irrigation Water Supply Management Office of Handan City,
Handan 056001, China

Abstract. In this paper, we synthetically applied genetic algorithm (GA) and artificial neural network (ANN) technology to automatically diagnose the fault of power transformer. The optimization based on the genetic algorithm is executed on the neural network thresholds and weights values. The test results show that the optimized BP network by genetic algorithm has an excellent performance on training speed and diagnosis reliability, and its prediction accuracy outperforms traditional BP in fault diagnosis of power transformer.

Keywords: fault diagnosis; power transformer; BP; genetic algorithm.

1 Introduction

Power transformers are important equipments in power systems. Diagnosis of potential faults concealed inside power transformers is the key of ensuring stable electrical power supply to consumers. Some combustible and noncombustible gases can be produced when a power transformer operates in a hostile environment, such as corona discharge, overheating of the insulation system and low-energy sparking [1]. Dissolved gas analysis (DGA) is a well-known technique to detect incipient faults of a power transformer [2]. The fault-related gases mainly include hydrogen (H2), methane (CH4), acetylene (C2H2), ethylene (C2H4) and ethane (C2H6). In recent years, various fault diagnostic techniques of power transformer have been proposed, including the conventional ratio methods and artificial intelligence methods. The conventional ratio methods are coding systems that assign a certain combination of codes to a specific fault type based on experience.

In this paper, we use BP to design a near optimal network architecture firstly, then the genetic algorithm is used to train the interconnection weights and thresholds of artificial neural network. The experiment results obtained by GA-BP model are feasible, valid and accurate in fault diagnosis of power transformer.

2 The GA-BP Algorithm

ANN is mathematical models with a highly connected structure inspired by the structure of the brain and nervous systems. ANN processes operate in parallel, which

R. Chen (Ed.): ICICIS 2011, Part I, CCIS 134, pp. 33–38, 2011.
© Springer-Verlag Berlin Heidelberg 2011

differentiates them from conventional computational methods [3]. ANN consist of multiple layers - an input layer, an output layer and one or more hidden layers as shown in Fig. 1. Each layer consists of a number of nodes or neurons which are interconnected by sets of correlation weights. The input nodes receive input information that is processed through a non-linear transfer function to produce outputs to nodes in the next layer. These processes are carried out in a forward manner hence the term multi-layer feed-forward model is used. A learning or training process uses a supervised learning algorithm that compares the model output to the target output and then adjusts the weight of the connections in a backward manner.

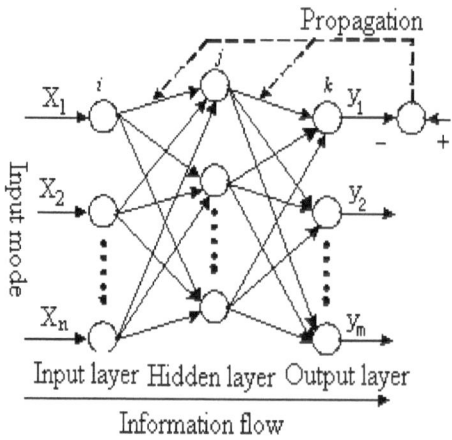

Fig. 1. Structure of BP neural network

2.1 Genetic Algorithm

(GA). GA is a kind of search and optimized algorithm that have been produced from simulating biologic heredities and long evolutionary processes of creatures. It stimulates the mechanism of "survival competitions; the superior survive while the inferior are eliminated, the fittest survive." The mechanism searches after the optimal subject by means of a successive iterative algorithm. Ever since the late 80s, GA, as a new cross discipline which has drawn people's attention, has already shown its increasing vitality in many fields [4].

GA stimulates reproduction, mating, and dissociation in natural selection and natural heredity procedures. Each possible solution to problems is taken as an individual among population, and each individual is coded as character string; each individual is evaluated in response to predefined objective functions and a flexibility value given. Three of its elemental operators are selection, crossing, and mutagenesis [5].Its main features are as follows:

(1) GA is to acquire the optimal solution or quasi-optimal ones through a generational search rather than a one-point search; (2) GA is capable of global optimum searching; (3) GA is a parallel process to population change, and provides intrinsic parallelism; (4) The processed object of GA is the individuals whose parameter set is coded rather than the parameters themselves, and this very feature enables GA to be used extensively [3].

2.2 The GA-BP Model

There have been some successful applications of BP networks in bankruptcy prediction, but BP has drawbacks due to its use of gradient descent. It often converges to an inferior solution and gets trapped in a long training time [4]. One way to overcome gradient-descent-based training algorithms' shortcomings is genetic algorithm-back propagation model, GA can then be used effectively in the evolution to find a near-optimal set of connection weights globally without computing gradient information. GA can treat large, complex, and multimodal spaces. Considerable research and applications have been conducted on the evolution of connection weights.

The major steps of our GA-BP model can be explained further as follow in Fig. 2:

1) Design a near optimal network architecture by the given input and output specimens. In this step, it is very important to find the optimal number of hidden layer nodes. Initiate several network architectures, train each network on the training set for a certain number of epochs using BP algorithm. The number of epochs is specified by user. After that we can get a near optimal network architecture.

2) Encode the network. In this step, we use the real-number representation, in which each variable being optimized is represented by a conventional floating-point number, which can get a higher accuracy than binary representation. And the connection weights and network threshold are encoded by an ordered string of certain length. Each one is represented by one bit in this string.

3) Generate an initial population of network at random.

4) Define the fitness function. We always use the squared-error loss function in BP networks, so the fitness function follows as:

$$F(\omega,\theta)=1/\sum\sum(y_i\text{-}f(y_i))^2 \tag{4}$$

5) Run an evolvement process. After sorting the population members of the previous generation in an ascending order based on the fitness value, the process of creating a new generation consists of three main steps:

① selection: We use the methods of elitist selection. The process of assigning the few best members from the old generation to the new generation ensures a gradual improvement of the solution.

② crossover: The crossover operator provides a thorough search of the sample space to produce good individuals. The crossover operator is given by:

$$S_a' = cS_a+(\ 1\text{-}c\ )S_b \quad c\in[0.1] \tag{5}$$

$$S_b' = cS_b+(\ 1\text{-}c\ )S_a \quad c\in[0.1] \tag{6}$$

③ mutation: The mutation operator performs mutation to randomly selected individuals to avoid the local optimum. The mutation operator is defined by:

$$S_a'=\text{-}S_a \tag{7}$$

6) Calculate the value of fitness function for each individual. An individual with a higher fitness function value has a higher probability to be selected to propagate a new generation. With the use of crossover and mutation operations, the parents with

the best solutions from among the previous generation are selected to breed the next generation.

7) If the best network found is acceptable or the maximum number of generations has been reached, stop the evolutionary process. Otherwise, go to step 5).

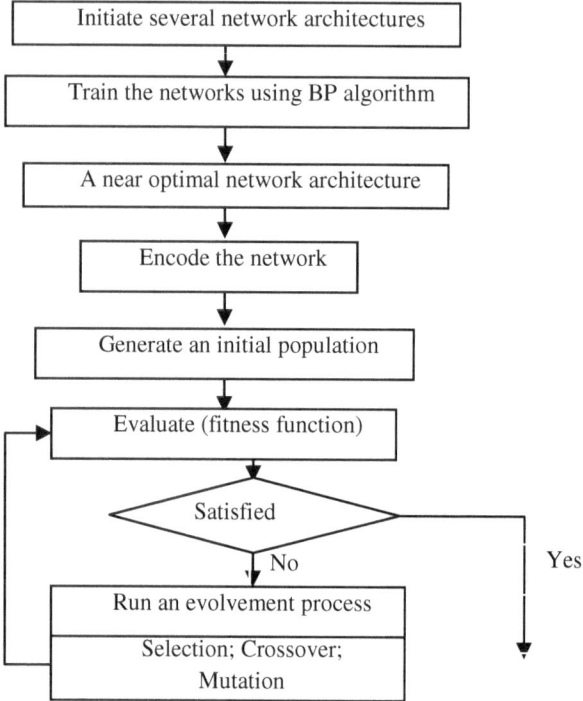

Fig. 2. The overall procedure of GA-BP

3   Experimental Analysis

The analytical base of diagnosis is some diagnostic gas content obtained by DGA. The content information reflects the states of transformer. These diagnostic gases include H_2, CH_4, $_2H_6$, $_2H_4$ and C_2H_2. The four types of transformer state are to be identified, including normal state, thermal heating, low-energy discharge and high-energy discharge. Table 1 shows fault datasets training and test sets for the experiments [6, 7].

From Fig. 3, we can see the average square error for 1000 epochs in the network training process by GA-BP and BP, respectively, where y-axis id the value of squared error for each learning epoch, and the x-axis is the number of the machine learning epochs in the training process. The minimum of the sum-error in the training process by GA-BP is 2.79×10^{-3}, and that of BP is 9.59×10^{-3}. So the precision of GA-BP is mostly increased compared to the traditional BP.

Table 1. Fault datasets training and test sets for the experiments

Fault type	Fault number	Training samples	Test set samples
Normal state	5	1	4
Thermal heating	25	2	13
High-energy discharge	15	3	2
Low-energy discharge	5	4	6

A comparison with a BP neural network is made in order to evaluate the method properly. The ANN is one hidden-layer ANN, the ANN is trained using fast back-propagation method. Training parameters are set as follows: learning rate is 0.02, and Momentum constant is 0.9. The weights and biases are initialized randomly. The BP network is trained with the same training samples, and the same testing samples are used too in testing. The target error is set as 0.01, 0.005, and 0.001. The results of the comparison between the two methods are shown in Table 2.

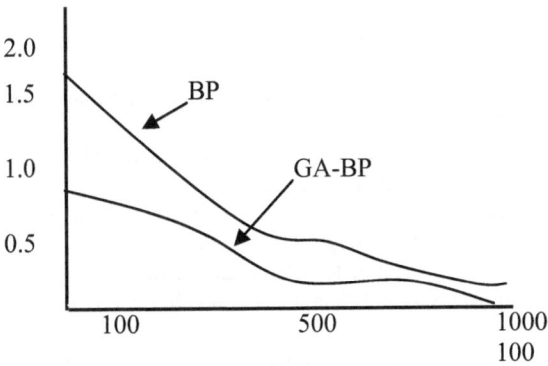

Fig. 3. Training error in 1000 epochs of BP and GA-BP

Table 2. Comparison between BP neural network and DDAG-SVM

Method	Target error(MSE)	Training accuracy	Test accuracy
GA-BP	0.01	99.73%	99.52%
BP1	0.01	99.04%	97.81%
BP2	0.005	99.42%	98.26%
BP3	0.001	99.62%	96.31%

Compared with BP network, the result in Table 2 shows that fault diagnosis of power transformer based on GA-BP classifier is more robust, and needs much less training time. One can also find that BP network can improve the result by reducing error. When target error is drop down from 0.01 to 0.005, error is down too. But when target error is small enough, due to the over-fitting, one cannot improve the result by reducing the target error anymore.

4 Conclusion

By using the GA for optimizing the weights of the artificial neural networks can be shorten the time of the convergence. At the same time, this method can simultaneously searches in many directions, thus greatly increasing the probability of finding a global optimum. According to the experiment results, the model we propose has higher prediction accuracy in fault diagnosis of power transformer. The proposed method has a large potential in practice.

Aknowledgement

Project supported by the Science Research Foundation of Hebei Education Department of China(No. 2009422) and Natural Science Foundation of Hebei Province of China (No. E2010001026).

References

1. Altman, E., Hotchkiss, E.: Corporate Financial Distress and Bankruptcy, 3rd edn. J. Wiley & Sons, England (2005)
2. Beaver, W.: In Empirical Research in Accounting. Selected studies supplement to the Journal of Accounting Research 4(1), 71–127 (1996)
3. Altman, E.I.: Financial Ratio Discriminant Analysis and the Prediction of Corporate Bankruptcy. Journal of Finance 23(3), 589–609 (1999)
4. Altman, E.I., Macro, G., Varetto, R.: Corporate Distress Diagnosis Comparisons Using Linear Discriminant Analysis and Neural Networks. Journal of Banking and Finance 18(3), 505–529 (1994)
5. Cristinanini, N., Shawe-Taylor, J.: Support Vector. Machines and other kernel-based learning methods. Cambridge. University Press, Cambridge (2000)
6. Lv, G., Cheng, H., Zhai, H., Dong, L.: Fault Diagnosis of Power Transformer Based on Multi-layer SVM Classifier. Electric power systems research 75(1), 9–15 (2005)
7. Song, X., Chen, W., Jiang, B.: Sample reducing method in SVM based on K-closed Sub-clusters. International Journal of Innovative Computing Information and Control 4(7), 1751–1760 (2008)

The Complexities of Implementing Cluster Supply Chain – Case Study of JCH

Xiao Xue[1], Jibiao Zhang[2], and Yang Wang[1]

[1] Lab of Service Science, Henan Polytechnic University,
Jiaozuo, Henan, P.R. China
jzxuexiao@126.com
[2] Digital Easy Company, China Classification Society,
Beijing, P.R. China
jbzhang@ccs.org.cn

Abstract. As a new type of management pattern, "cluster supply chain" (CSC) can help SMEs to face the global challenges through all kinds of collaboration. However, a major challenge in implementing CSC is the gap between theory and practice in the field. In an effort to provide a better understanding of this emerging phenomenon, this paper presents the implementation process of CSC in the context of JingCheng Mechanical & Electrical Holding co., ltd.(JCH) as a case study. The cast study of JCH suggests that the key problems in the practice of cluster supply chain: How do small firms use cluster supply chain? Only after we clarify the problem, the actual construction and operation of cluster supply chain does show successful results as it should be.

Keywords: Supply Chain, Cluster Supply Chain, Virtual Alliance, Service System.

1 Introduction

Porter proposed that today's economic map of the world is dominated by clusters: geographic concentrations of linked businesses that enjoy unusual competitive success in their field (Porter, 1998). Currently, the globalization of economy and the ease of transportation & communication have led many companies to move some or all of their operations to locations with low wages, taxes, and utility costs. For stable, labor-intensive activities such as manufacturing assembly and software localization, low factor costs are often decisive in driving location choices. In the context, China becomes the dominant makers of steel, coke, aluminum, cement, chemicals, leather and other goods, which drives the rapid growth of its economy in recent years. Some well-known industrial clusters have earned a certain reputation in the world, such as textile and clothing cluster in Huzhou, Zhejiang Province, electronic products manufacturing cluster in Dongguan, Guangdong Province.

However, China's industrial cluster is still in its initial stage, and faces some critical problems now. Many cluster members are only geographically concentrated, while their managers can't demonstrate the advantages of virtual organizational alliance fully (interrelated, interdependent and specialized division of labor). Their

R. Chen (Ed.): ICICIS 2011, Part I, CCIS 134, pp. 39–44, 2011.

competitive advantage mainly relies on cheap labor and high consumption of natural resources. For many export-oriented clusters in China, they only occupy the low end of global value chain, such as those links for processing and manufacturing, thus there is a real possibility of losing the competitive edge to cost competitors in developing countries like Viet Nam, Philippines and Malaysia. With the advent of financial crisis and the intensification of environmental damage, it is becoming more and more difficult to remain the existing development pattern.

Based on the background, the concept of "cluster supply chain (CSC)" is put forward as a new business pattern which integrates the advantages of industrial cluster and supply chain management to help SMEs to move beyond this stage (jizi Li, 2006). As a result, SMEs can achieve a breakthrough in some critical links of the value chain (e.g. strategy development, core technology and workflow optimization) and even compete with industry giants in international market. This paper focuses on giving some theoretical suggestions and practical approaches to help to bridge the barrier mentioned above. JingCheng mechanical & electrical holding co., ltd.(JCH) is a state-owned enterprise group in Beijing, which consist of more than 30 manufacturing companies and 30 related institutes presently. The reform of JCH will serve as a case study to explain the advantages and challenges of implementing cluster supply chain. The rest of this paper is organized as follows. Section 2 gives the research questions and methodology in the field. Section 3 presents the completed process of implementing cluster supply chain through the case study of JCH. The concluding remarks will be given in section 4.

2   Research Question and Methodology

Research on managing cluster supply chain has blossomed, and has been accompanied by research across a range of academic disciplines, with each discipline making use of its own theoretical lens, such as Economic Science [1], Management Science [2], Social Science [3], and Information Science [4], to analyze and explain this kind of business pattern. CSC has brought new demands to a company's capability and the whole cluster's operation pattern. Despite much effort from government, research institutes and SMEs, there still exist substantial gaps between theories developed and what is actually occurring in practice. The existence of clear definition and conceptual frameworks on how to implement the new business pattern has been lacking, leaving a fragmented field open to the danger of a lack of generality.

JingCheng mechanical & electrical Holding co., ltd.(JCH) is a state-owned enterprise group in Beijing, which is committed to provide professional, high quality mechanical & electrical equipments and services to worldwide customers. The formation of JCH can be viewed as being the result of state-owned enterprise reform, whose assets were authorized by Beijing government in 1995 and 2000 respectively. Currently, JCH owns more than 30 manufacturing companies with great variety in the products, wide range in the services and 30 related institutes presently. Those firms are geographically concentrated in an area within radius of less than 50 km. Furthermore, they all belong to machinery industry, which are mainly in the following five areas: printing machines(such as Beiren Printing Machinery Co., Ltd), CNC machine tools(such as Beijing No1 Machine plant、Beijing No2 Machine plant), construction machinery(such as Beijing BEIZHONG Steam Turbine Generator Co., Ltd, JingCheng Heavy Industry Co., Ltd), environmental protection (such as Jingcheng Environment Protection Co., Ltd), power generation equipment (such as Beijing Mechanical and Electrical Co., Ltd, Beijing BEIKAI Electronic Co., Ltd, Beijing Electric Wire & Cable General Factory, Beijing Electric Motor Co., Ltd etc.).

With the increasingly fierce competition of market, it is important to improve the core competitiveness of JCH through reorganization and resources integration of sub-firms, which is also local government's original intention for the reformation. Although JCH has achieved a dramatic increase in scale, most of its subsidiaries are still weak in strength, lack of innovation, slow in market reaction. Because of the isolation and self-dependency of those sub-firms, each firm has its own supply chain and management mode, namely often responsible for purchasing, inventory, transportation and sales independently. As a result, it is difficult to conduct the synergy between those sub-firms to enhance the overall competitiveness of JCH. Therefore, it has become a critical problem for JCH how to make full use of the advantages of grouping, such as resource sharing and risk sharing, to create the "1 +1> 2" effect in competitiveness, creativity and anti-risk ability.

This paper will conduct an in-depth study on the implementation of CSC, which takes JCH as an example, and focus on giving some theoretical suggestions and practical approaches to the following question: How do small firms use cluster supply chain? The methodology adopted for this research was a case study. According to [5], the case study approach is useful in theory building and enables a rigorous and holistic investigation. The subject of the research – strengthen the competiveness of cluster by CSC – is emergent in nature as there are not many typical examples. Therefore, this study, through the consideration of a single case study, would lead to the development of new ideas and theories. The process is divided into two steps:

Step 1: Data collection. Data collection was carried out using the following techniques: **(i)** Documentation. Documented information relating to the collaboration process was analyzed. The documented information includes data on the analysis of spend across the cluster community, the breakdown of cost, and the details of members in the collaboration. **(ii)** Interviews. Ten semi-structured interviews are held with key personnel in the case study organization. Interviews were held continuously over a six month period. Many of the interviews enabled the research team keep track of the evolution of the collaboration process. The key people interviewed include product manager, process and technology manager and general manager. **(iii)** Participant observation. At the end of the collaboration process, the research team participated in a brainstorming and discussion session. The session was focused on identifying and analyzing potential business models for the case study organization.

Step 2: Data analysis. The availability of both qualitative and quantitative data from multiple sources of evidence (documentation, multiple interviews and participant-observation) facilitated the method of triangulation. For example, data from service customers about their spending across product categories combined with data from the interviews with the service providers led to identification of complexities relating to product choice for collaboration. Similarly, data from the documentation combined with information from the brainstorming and discussion session identified alternative business models and their advantages and disadvantages.

3 Case Study

The development history and current situation of JCH can be viewed as critical determinants in making CSC possible. Firstly, the relevance of those sub-firms decides that the amount of common materials and parts is huge, which facilitates implementing the collaboration across different supply chains. In 2008, the demand of MRO (Maintenance, Repair and Operations) for JCH's subsidiaries is about 162 million RMB, or 24 million dollars. According to the survey of domestic research agencies, the existing procurement costs can be reduced about 10 percent to 20 percent (i.e. at least 16 million RMB, or 2.3 million dollars can be saved) by means of the integration and optimization along supply chain. Secondly, geographical concentration has been proved to create a unique environment in which a large pool of skilled workers has been developed and refined, deep relationships have been formed, and a closely-knit social network is in place to support group norms of behavior. Lastly, as the headquarters of those sub-firms, it is natural for JCH to act as the role of coordination institution, which provides all kinds of service infrastructure to identify the cooperation flow, streamline the working relationship and support the collaboration between its subsidiaries.

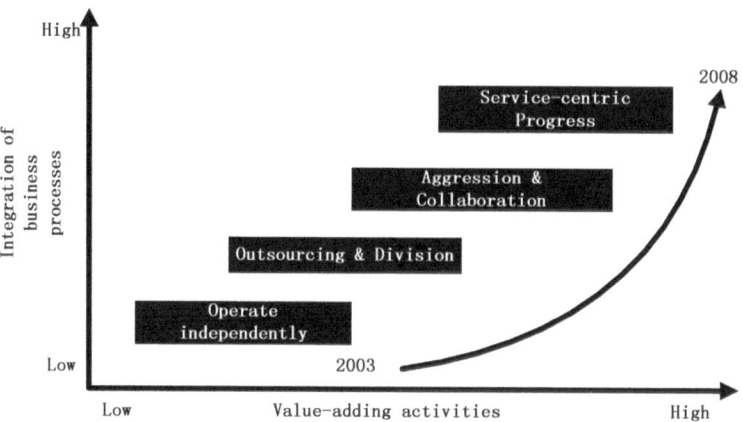

Source: Based on Annual Reports of JCH (from 2003 to 2008)

Fig. 1. The development phases of implementing CSC strategy in JCH

The implementation of cluster supply chain needs to follow the "step-by-step" policy, which extends from the selection and procurement of material, to the delivery of the finished machinery product to the final customers. As shown in figure 1, in terms of JCH, the process of applying CSC pattern can be divided into four gradual phases, which are introduced and discussed in further details.

(1) Operate independently
At the beginning, each sub-firm in JCH is responsible for all links of its value chain. As a result, it is difficult for them to reduce high interactive costs among partners, improve product quality, speed up the response to market, and maximize the whole

JCH performance. While the pride and desire to look good in JCH prompt sub-firms to compete with each other, the motivation for doing so is typically based on a desire to maintain its position within the community, rather than an overt attempt to beat its partners. Therefore, it is feasible for JCH to synthesize relevant enterprise resources to provide a package of industrial services. Furthermore, a set of performance expectations need to be identified, with a general knowledge of regulating the acceptance or dismissal of prospective business partners.

(2) Outsourcing & Division

Because of resources and capability constraints, it is no profit for a single company to burden all links of supply chain. Therefore, those links which can not or do not be implemented personally can be outsourced to other enterprises in the cluster. As a result, the close and flexible specialized division of labor between enterprises begins to form and professional industrial service providers begin to emerge. In this phase, core enterprise plays a leading role, which attracts a lot of supporting firms together.

In 2003, several companies of JCH jointly sponsored and founded Global Industrial Supply Co., Ltd. (GIS), which furnishes them with an efficient means of obtaining inputs from a deep and specialized supplier base. By sourcing the procurement of raw material and components to GIS partially, manufacturers are able to reduce the need to inventory, minimize labor requirements, reduce costs of market entry, and lower the risk that suppliers will overprice or renege on commitments. Based on the principle of voluntary and mutually beneficial, sub-firms of JCH begin to outsource more and more non-core business to GIS, such as warehousing & distribution, cutting, and steel rod cutting. Against the background, Jingcheng Taichang Machinery Co., Ltd was separated from GIS in 2004, which offers professional machining services, such as cutting, welding, and pre-processing in order to meet the specific requirements of some high-growth companies.

(3) Aggression & Collaboration

In the previous phase, the core-enterprise centric aggression is still a quasi-network organization, which has not yet evolved into a complete cluster supply chain. With more and more companies join the organization, core enterprise begin to be relegated to a secondary position, while the related services supporting firms begin to occupy the dominant position. The supporting service system can improve the communication between buyer and seller and make it easier for suppliers to provide goods and services. Thus, a large number of small and medium enterprises can be linked together by those related services firms, which supports the collaboration along the whole supply chain to make a relatively complete supply chain network possible.

These new organizational practices demand a new way of thinking about JCH – a community that accommodates firms which are linked by supporting service system. In this phase, GIS is not just a industrial logistics company, which acts as an "industrial collaborative service platform" which offers all kinds of specialized services for customers, such as warehousing, packing and transportation, pooling procurement, order management, stock management and product sales, etc. As the milestone of cluster supply chain formation, GIS strives for coordinating activities and resources across firm boundaries to optimize the collective productivity of JCH.

(4) Service-centric progress

Because of limited margin of profit, cluster supply chain needs to scatter from this original region to other regions, which leads to the continuously and dynamically changes in the organization structure. The key motivation for small companies to join CSC is to realize long-term benefits and potential business opportunities. During the process, the development of service system is increasingly key factors for their successes, which can provide SMEs with a cost-effective gateway to global markets.

For policy makers, the implementation of cluster supply chain can facilitate the internationalization of small- and medium-sized enterprises (SMEs). This is particularly true for JCH because sub-firms need to expand or relocate their production facilities in order to achieve more market access and lower production costs. Currently, GIS begins to offer services to enterprises outside JCH, which has become the biggest supplier of silicon steel in provinces of North China. By means of the service system provided by GIS, SMEs will not need to go through a lengthy, incremental process to participate in global markets.

4 Conclusions

To further maximize effectiveness and efficiency (internal and external), and enhance competitive advantage of industrial cluster in China, cluster supply chain is viewed as a crucial activity. The implementation of cluster supply chain, however, is not straightforward or easy. In order to face the above challenge, this paper focuses on giving some theoretical suggestions and practical approaches to help to bridge the barrier mentioned above by means of the case study of JCH. The development process of JCH serves as clues to explain the advantages and challenges of implementing cluster supply chain. In the next step, we will consider how to encapsulate enterprise resources into services better, which will build a solid foundation for the collaboration between partners in cluster supply chain.

Acknowledgments. This work is supported by National Nature Science Foundation under Grant 60905041, Fundamental Science Research Foundation of Henan Province under Grant 092300410216, and Young Scientist Foundation of HPU under Grant 649100.

References

1. Patti, A.L.: Economic clusters and the supply chain: a case study. Supply Chain Management: An International Journal. Vol 11(3), 266–270 (2006)
2. Towers, N., Burnes, B.: A Composite Model of Supply Chain Management and Enterprise Planning for Small and Medium Sized Manufacturing Enterprises. Supply Chain Management: An International Journal 13(5), 349–355 (2008)
3. Villa, A., Dario, A., Marchis, V.: Analysing Collaborative Demand and Supply Networks in a Global Economy. In: Road Map, A. (ed.) A Road Map to the Development of European SME Networks, pp. 1–21. Springer, London (2009)
4. Siau, K., Tian, Y.: Supply chains integration: architecture and enabling technologies. Journal of Computer Information Systems 44(3), 67–72 (2004)
5. Meredith, J.: Building operations management theory through case and field research. Journal of Operations Management 11(3), 239–256 (1998)

Fault Diagnosis of Rolling Bearing Based on Lyapunov Exponents

Liying Wang[1], Huang Meng[2], and Yanning Kang[3]

[1] Institute of Water Conservancy and Hydropower, Hebei University of Engineering,
Handan, 056038, China
[2] Shandong Vocational College of Water Conservancy, Rizhao, 276826, China
[3] Dept. of Economics & Management, Shijiazhuang University, Hebei, 050035, China

Abstract. The nonlinear behavior of rolling bearing is studied. The Lyapvnov exponent is estimated from an experimental time series based on its different state. The experimental results show that the Lyapvnov exponent is different for the different state and can be used as characteristics for recognizing the rolling bearing's fault. The rule for fault diagnosis of rolling bearing is extracted by using Lyapvnov exponent.

Keywords: phase space reconstruction, maximum Laypunov exponent, fault diagnoses, rolling bearing.

1 Introduction

Rolling bearing is the vulnerable components of the machine, according to statistics, 30% of failures are caused by the bearing of rotating machinery, so fault diagnosis and monitoring of the rolling bearing is the focus [1]. In the diagnosis technology of fault diagnosis and condition monitoring, vibration monitoring is one of the main methods. Characteristics of vibration signals in time and frequency domain are extracted to identify the fault parameter in Traditional diagnostic techniques against. In fact, due to the impact of different bearing fault state, nonlinear, friction, clearance and external load, if we can accurately describe the system in state space, the failure behavior can be correctly distinguished.

Nonlinear vibration system under different input conditions shows complex motive characteristics[2], Poincare section, power spectrum, phase diagram, time-domain waveform diagram and maximum Laypunov exponent can be used to judge whether the system enter the chaotic state[3].

In the fault diagnosis to complex machinery, we usually use the quantitative indicators; maximum Laypunov exponent can quantitatively describe the nonlinear systems [4]. In this paper, maximum Laypunov exponent based on time series was researched and was used to diagnoses the railway truck bearing. The numerical results show that the maximum Laypunov exponent can be used as indicators of bearing condition and is a great potential fault diagnosis method.

2 Lyapunov Exponent Spectrums and Its Calculation

The basic characteristic of chaotic motion is extremely sensitive to initial conditions [5]. The track generated by two very close initial value separates with the exponent

R. Chen (Ed.): ICICIS 2011, Part I, CCIS 134, pp. 45–50, 2011.
© Springer-Verlag Berlin Heidelberg 2011

over time, Lyapunov exponent is a quantitative description of the volume of this phenomenon and is the average which relates with the characteristics of contraction and expansion in different directions of the phase space orbit, each Lyapunov exponent can be seen as the average of the local deformation in the relative movement and at the same time is determined by the evolution of the system for a long time. Therefore, Lyapunov exponent is not local variable, but the overall characteristic of the system. In the spectrum, the smallest Lyapunov exponent decides the speed of convergence and the largest Lyapunov exponent decides the speed of divergent. Lyapunov exponent is a very important parameter that is used to characterize chaotic attractor "singular" of the nonlinear systems, which are widely used to characterize the behavior of nonlinear systems.

The theory of chaotic phase-space reconstruction is used to analyze the measured signal, because it can more accurately reflect the essential characteristics of the system. Thus, when calculating the Lyapunov exponent, two respects must be paid attention: One is the proper phase-space reconstruction, that is the right choice of reconstruction parameters (embedding dimension m and delay time interval τ), these parameters have great impact on the calculated result of Lyapunov exponent, in this paper, embedding dimension and delay time interval are choose based on the average displacement - Simultaneous false neighbor ; The second is to choose a suitable algorithm to calculate Lyapunov exponent, the literature given the method of calculating the index by Matrix[6].

It should be noted that noise has a greater impact on the calculating of Lyapunov exponent, in order to obtain a true description of the state, the collected time-domain signal must be filter to reduce the noise. The iterative calculation process shown in Fig. 1.

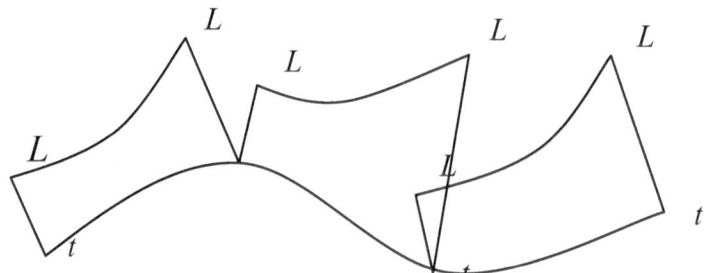

Fig. 1. Iterative calculation process of Laypunov exponent

3   Calculated Results and Its Analyses of Maximum Laypunov Exponent

In this paper, based on three different states of style 197726, both drive, the vibration signals were measured, the time-domain waveforms are shown in Fig. 2, Fig. 3 and Fig. 4, the abscissa is the signal sampling points, and the vertical axis is the amplitude of acceleration. Among them, the bearing show in Fig. 2 is in good condition; the bearing shows in Fig. 3 that the outer ring t is failure; the bearing show in Fig. 4 is roller failure.

The method of wavelet denoising was used to reduce the noise, after denoising [7], the time-domain waveforms are shown in Fig. 5, Fig. 6 and Fig. 7. With comparison, in order to actually calculate the maximum Lyapunov exponent, noise must be reduced. Selecting the same computing conditions, the maximum Lyapunov exponent is calculated from the de-noised signal, the relationship between points and the maximum Lyapunov exponent is shown in Fig. 8, in figure, a, b, c respectively represents the maximum Lyapunov exponent of the normal bearing, outer ring fault bearings and roller bearing fault[8].

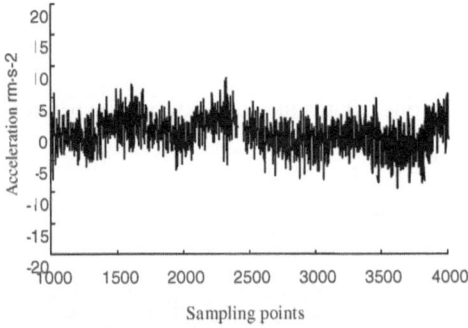

Fig. 2. The normal time-domain waveform before lowering noise

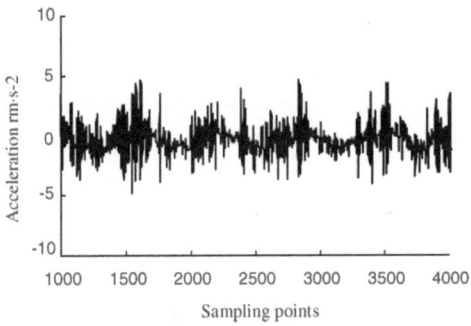

Fig. 3. The normal time-domain waveform after lowering noise

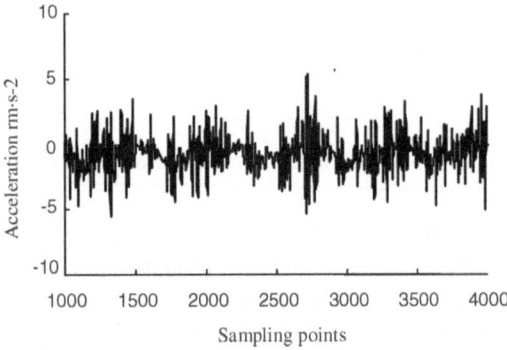

Fig. 4. The outer ring failure time-domain waveform before lowering noise

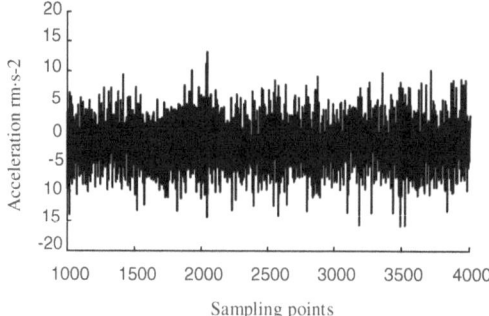

Fig. 5. The outer ring failure time-domain waveform before lowering noise

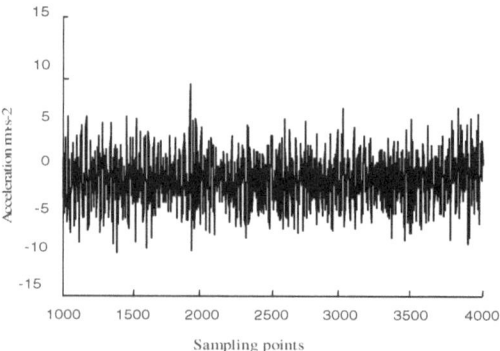

Fig. 6. The roller failure time-domain waveform before lowering noise

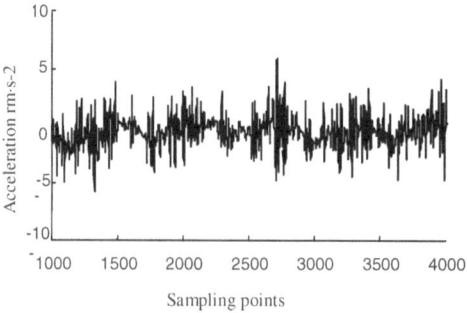

Fig. 7. The roller failure time-domain waveform before lowering noise

As can be seen from the figures, the maximum Lyapunov exponent is different in different state of bearing, so the maximum Lyapunov exponent can be used to reflect the motion characteristics of vibration system, the maximum Lyapunov exponent is the largest in normal bearing.

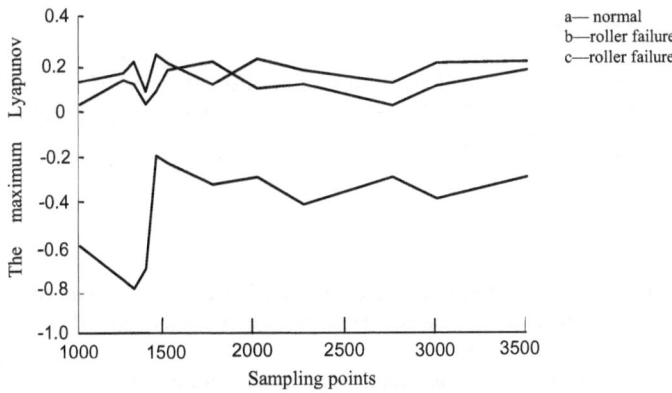

Fig. 8. The relationship between the maximum Lyapunov exponent and sampling points

Using the same method, the maximum Lyapunov exponent can be calculated in different driving modes calculated results are shown in Table 1:

Table 1. The maximum Lyapunov exponent in different driving modes

driving modes	fault styles		
	normal bearing	outer ring	roller bearing
Both sides	-0.477 5	0.036 4	0.124 6
Left	-0.355 9	0.571 5	0.929 7
right	-1.371 9	0.749 5	0.191 5

From the table 1, we can see that the maximum Lyapunov exponent in normal bearing is less than zero whether in any driving mode, while the maximum Lyapunov exponent in the outer and roller failure is greater than zero, thus the maximum Lyapunov exponent can be used as the characteristics of fault diagnosis and condition monitoring.

4 Conclusions

In this paper, based on three different states of railway truck bearing, the maximum Lyapunov exponent of vibration signals was calculated, the results shows that the maximum Lyapunon exponent is different in different states; the maximum exponent can be as the characteristic to diagnose the failure. The study is a new method to judge the states of the bearing; it has a great significance to improve the accuracy of the fault diagnosis and state identification.

Aknowledgement

Project supported by the Science Research Foundation of Hebei Education Department of China (No. 2009422) and Natural Science Foundation of Hebei Province of China (No. E2010001026).

References

1. Liao, B.: Machinery fault diagnosis based, pp. 62–57. Metallurgical Industry Press (2005)
2. Holger, K., Thomas, S.: Nonlinear Time Series Analysis, pp. 159–176. Cambridge University, Cambridge (2000)
3. Cai, J.: Application on Extracting Feature in State Monitoring and Fault Diagnosis. Journal of Chongqing University 1, 12–16 (2003)
4. Li, H., Zhang, H.-Q., Yang, S.-P.: Bearing fault diagnodis based on EMD and teager kaiser energy operator. Journal of Vibration and Shock 27, 16–22 (2008)
5. Zhang, X.: Modern signal processing, pp. 64–132. Tsinghua University Press, Beijing (2002)
6. Xue, N.: The application of MATLAB on the digital signal processing, pp. 21–50. Tsinghua University Press, Beijing (2003)
7. Brie, D.: Modeling of the Spalled Rolling Element Bearing Vibration Signal: An Overview and Some New Re2sult. Mechanical Systems and Signal Processing 14, 353–369 (2000)
8. Yang, Z., Zhang, R.: Analysis of Panel Thermal Flutter Using Maximum Lyapunov Exponent. Journal of Northwestern Polytechnical University 26, 24–29 (2009)

New Encryption Scheme of One-Time Pad Based on KDC

Xin Xie[1], Honglei Chen[2], Ying Wu[3], Heng Zhang[3], and Peng Wu[3]

[1] School of Information Engineering East China Jiaotong University
Nanchang, China
xienew@gmail.com
[2,3] School of Information Engineering East China Jiaotong University
Nanchang, China
chenhonglei.521@163.com

Abstract. As more and more leakage incidents come up, traditional encryption system has not adapted to the complex and volatile network environment, so, there should be a new encryption system that can protect information security very well, this is the starting point of this paper. Based on DES and RSA encryption system, this paper proposes a new scheme of one time pad，which really achieves "One--time pad" and provides information security a new and more reliable encryption method.

Keywords: OTP; KDC; Security.

1 Introduction

As the security issues of the Internet become more and more serious, how to effectively protect information security is the reality every information system must face, preventing information disclosure has been the focus of research in the field of information security. The traditional encryption technology such as DES, RSA provide safeguard for information security over the past and present time, but with the development of technology, the traditional encryption technology encounter severe challenges, these encryption technology can no longer well resist various attacks. Based on characteristics of traditional encryption system, this paper introduce KDC technology, and puts forward a new scheme of one time pad, which makes better use of advantages of RSA and DES.

2 Existing Encryption Scheme

Now DES (Data Encryption Stardard) is the most extensive application of symmetric encryption, which is adopted as federal information processing standards by America's national bureau in 1997.

DES adopts 64-bit packet length and 64-bit key length, it inputs 64-bit plain text and gets 64-bit ciphertext output after 16 iteration transform. The advantage of DES is fast speed, which is still used in many fields. Weakness is the difficult key distribution and bad resistance to brute-force attack. Public-key cryptosystem is based

R. Chen (Ed.): ICICIS 2011, Part I, CCIS 134, pp. 51–55, 2011.
© Springer-Verlag Berlin Heidelberg 2011

on the difficulty of factorization of large numbers, which is based on function instead of the substitution and replacement. public key is asymmetrical, it uses two different keys, one is public, the other is secret, each can be used in encryption or decryption. The advantages of RSA algorithms are quite simplicity and high security, the algorithm encryption is separated from encryption algorithm, and it makes the key distribution more convenient. Weakness is very troublesome to produce keys, so it is difficult to realize one-time pad, encryption speed is very slow, the time it costs is more 100-1000 times than DES.

3 One-Time Pad Scheme Based on KDC

The online version of the volume will be available in LNCS Online. Members of institutes subscribing to the Lecture Notes in Computer Science series have access to all the pdfs of all the online publications. Non-subscribers can only read as far as the abstracts. If they try to go beyond this point, they are automatically asked, whether they would like to order the pdf, and are given instructions as to how to do so.

3.1 Overview of KDC

KDC (Key Distribution Center) is an important part of Kerberos Protocal and it can manage and distribute the public keys. Due to its recognized safety and credibility KDC is currently the most effective method of Key Distribution.

KDC in kerberos usually provides two services: authentication service and ticket-granting service. The main idea of the article is that, according to KDC having storing the information between communicating parties such as user name, public keys and so on, when users in the process of communication to verify the identity of the other, he directly sends the user's public-key, name to KDC, after receiving validation request, KDC query database, if it can find the corresponding user information then KDC sends validation information, the authentication is end. Otherwise, authentication fails because the information user submit is invalid or user information does not exist.

3.2 The Process of Producting Temporary Session Key

Suppose the communication parties have get their digital certificates and store their public keys in KDC so that some user can timely query them as shown in figure 1. The communication parties can get the other party's public key through KDC. Assume one party is Alice and the other party is Bob. The word "request" is the symbol that Alice sets up the temporary session. The word "random" is the symbol that stand for a random number in every session. This random number can resist replay attack. The word is the confirmation symbol. The word "refuse" is the symbol that refuses the process of consulting the session key. The word "success" is the symbol that the process of consulting the session key is successful. The word "failded" is the symbol that consulting the session key is not successful.

1)   Alice sends Bob the session request Msg (request, random, PKa, userID_a), which is encrypted by Bob's public key—PKb. Alice and Bob both store the random. Through KDC Bob checks whether PKa belongs to the user whose ID is userID_a.If the check is successful, Bob sends Alice Msg (ACK, random, Pkb, userID_b) which is encrypted by Alice's public key—Pka and go to the next step. Otherwise, Bob sends Msg (refuse, random) and session is over.

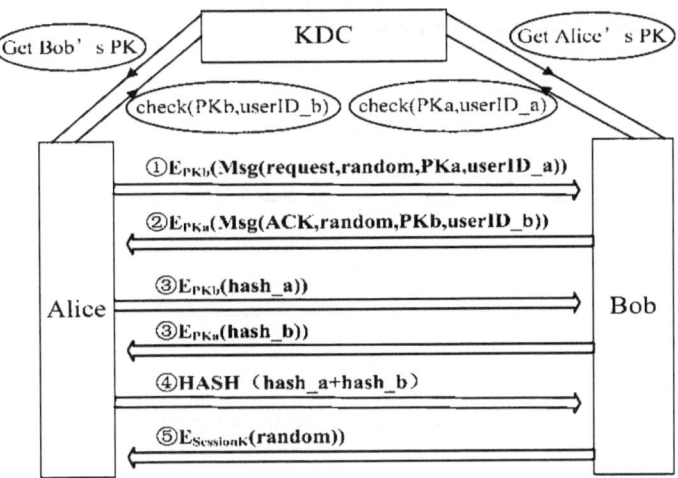

Fig. 1. OTP based on KDC

In a similar way, after receiving Msg (ACK, random, PKb, userID_b), Alice checks whether PKb belongs to the user whose ID is userID_b. Alice verifies this random received and the stored random. If both checks are sucessful, go to next step, otherwise, Alice sends Msg (refuse, random) to Bob and session is over.

2) The communication parties respectively product their hash values hash_a and hash_b on the basis of their system time, configuration, OS version and so on. Then send their hash values to the other party after they are encrypted by the other party's PK.

3) The communication parties decrypt the information received from the other party with their own secret key—SK. They both get hash_a and hash_b and combine hash_a with hash_b. Through a hash computing they get another hash value— hash_ab.Select specific 64 bits from the hash_ab as the temporary session key— SessionK.

4) The communication parties need verify the consistency of SessionK. They encrypt random with

5) SessionK and send it to the other party. After receiving it they decrypt it with SessionK and get the random. If the random is equal to the one they have stored, they send Msg (success, random) to the other party. The temporary session is sucessful. Otherwise, one party send Msg (failed, random) and go to step 1 to resume a temporary session.

6) In the following communication, the communication parties encrypt the information with SessionK. During temporary session, encryption algorithm is DES.

3.3 The Process of Data Transmission

1) Alice adopts EDS algorithm and encrypts plain text with temporary session key— SessionK to get ciphertext.

2) The ciphertext is transmited to Bob through Internet. Bob decrypts the ciphertext with SessionK to get plain text.

3) Once the temporary session is over, temporary key must be deleted and will be newly created again in next temporary session.

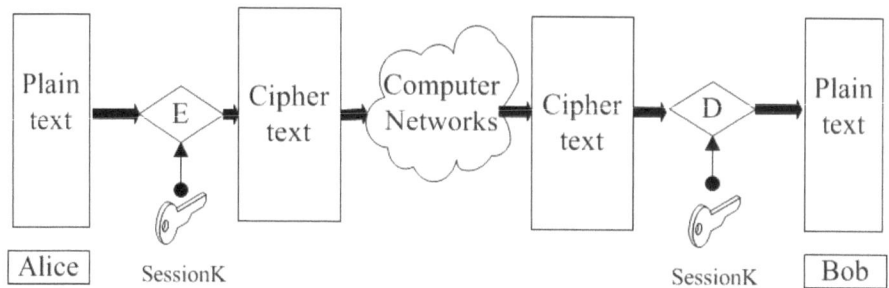

Fig. 2. The process of data transmission

4 Security Analysis

1) Identity authentication of the communication parties. The traditional schemes of OTP lack effective identity authentication of communication parties so there is hidden danger in information exchange process. But when this scheme sets up temporary, Alice and Bob can check the other party's identity and PK through KDC. This way can guarantee the valid identity and reliability of communication parties and avoid network deception.

2) The creation of temporary session key needs the participation of communication parties. The communication parties are equal and there is no problem of low confidence level when key is created by one party. The creation of temporary session key also needs the participation of RSA encryption technology. The hash values are encrypted by RSA so the temporary session key is security.

3) When one party sets up a session, it must create a random number which is used to identify every session. In the process of creating temporary session, two partis can check the consistency of random number so it can tesist replay attack.

4) After temporary session key is created, two partis can communicate with each other. But in the whole process the session key is not transmitted through network. So this protects the security of session key. Moreover, session key is deleted after every session. So brute-force attack is invalid and it's hard to get useful information during the short session.

5) Because every computer has different status at each moment, the hash value is different. This can ensure that temporary session key is different every time, truely realising "one time, one pad". This way simplifies the management and distribution of key and make users convenience to use this scheme.

5 Conclusion

It is difficult to manage the DES keys. DES cann't well resist brute-force attack. But its key is short and its encryption process has fast speed and high efficiency. So DES is suit to the field where there is large data to be encrypted. RSA has better security and the management of its key is easy. But its encryption process has low speed and it is used to encrypt small amounts of data. For the advantages and disadvantages of DES and RSA, this paper draws lesson from both schemes, combines KDC, introduces identity authentication, key distribution and management and so on, reduces the length of key, simplifies key distribution and management, which can enhance the security of information transmission. Once session key is created successfully, communication partis can transmit information security. When session is over, temporary session key is deleted and it truly realises "one time, one pad".

References

[1] Zhang, B., Sun, S.: One-time Pad Encryption Technology Based on RSA. Computer security 3, 53–55 (2009)

[2] Wang, W., Guo, X.: Design on DES algorithm of one-time pad. Computer security 5, 17–78 (2006)

[3] Wang, Y., Zhu, F.: Security Analysis of One-time System and Its Betterment. Journal of Sichuan University 5(39), 222–225 (2007)

[4] Zhang, Y., Feng, D.: A Practical One-Time-Pad-Like Block Cipher Scheme. Journal of Beijing University of Posts and Telecommunications 4(28), 101–104 (2005)

[5] Wang, Y.: Analysis of Secure Limitation of One-Time System and Its Origin. Electronic Technology 1, 71–75 (2008)

[6] Patil, S., Devare, M., Kumar, A.: International. Modified One Time Pad Data Security Scheme: Random Key Generation Approach. Journal of Computer Science and Security (IJCSS) 3(2), 138–145

[7] Shannon, C.: Communication Theory of Secrecy Systems. Bell System Technical Journal 28, 656–715 (1949)

[8] Nagaraj, N., Vaidya, V., Vaidya, P.G.: Revisiting the One-Time Pad. (2008), http://arxiv.org/abs/cs/0508079

Three Dimensional Canonical Correlation Analysis and Its Application to Facial Expression Recognition

Lei Gang, Zhang Yong, Liu Yan-Lei, and Deng Jing

Chengdu Aeronautic Vocational and Technical College, Chengdu 610021, China
cdleigang@gmail.com

Abstract. Based on the traditional canonical correlation analysis (CCA) and two-dimensional canonical correlation analysis (2DCCA), a generalized three dimensional canonical correlation analysis (3DCCA) is proposed. If a three dimensional pattern has a pair of observations (For any pattern space, there has two observation spaces), 3DCCA can find a relevant subspaces of the two observation spaces, in which the projections of the two observations are irrelevant. It can reduce the curse of dimensionality by avoiding the vectorization process and can effectively solve the singular sample covariance matrix problem as well. Finally, our algorithm is validated by the experiments on JAFFE face database. Comparison of other methods, in our method not only the computing complexity is lower, but also the recognition performance is better.

Keywords: Canonical correlation analysis; Three dimensional data; Feature fusion; Face recognition; Facial expression recognition.

1 Introduction

Subspace learning is an important direction in pattern analysis research area, most traditional vector based algorithms, such as principal component analysis(PCA) [1], independent component analysis(ICA)[2], linear discriminate analysis (LDA) [3], canonical correlation analysis (CCA)[4] have gained wide applications. The first step of the above algorithms is to input object as 1D vector, which can be called as vectorization process. However, the vectorization process may be faced with three problems: 1) curse of dimensionality dilemma and high computation cost; 2) small sample number always leads to singular sample covariance matrix; 3) vectorization process may destroy the object's underlying spatial structures. In order to solve the above problems, some recent works have started to consider an image as a 2D matrix for subspace learning and generate some traditional vector based algorithms to 2D matrix based algorithms, such as 2DPCA[5], 2DLDA [6], 2DCCA[7]. However, many color images, videos and some other dates are naturally 3D objects. For example, gray-scale video sequences can be viewed as 3D objects with column, row and time axes. In the active area of face recognition research, three-dimensional face detection and recognition using 3D information with column, row and depth axes has emerged as an important research direction. So, it is essential to study the 3D version pattern analysis algorithms, which can be used on 3D objects directly. In this paper, we propose a method named as three dimensional canonical correlation analysis (3DCCA) which can conduct canonical correlation analysis on 3D source data.

R. Chen (Ed.): ICICIS 2011, Part I, CCIS 134, pp. 56–61, 2011.

2 Overview of Canonical Correlation Analysis (CCA)

Among the traditional 1D subspace learning algorithms, recently CCA and kernel CCA (KCCA) were successfully applied to content-based retrieval, face recognition and facial expression recognition. CCA is a powerful multivariate analysis method, the goal of which is to identify and quantify the association between two sets of variables. If a pattern space has two observation spaces, CCA can find a more accurate relevant subspace of the two observation spaces, which has more semantic description information. CCA firstly seeks a pair of projections on the relevant subspace of the variables in the two sets, which has the largest correlation. Next, it seeks a second pair of projections of the variables which has the largest correlation among all pairs uncorrelated with the initially selected pair, and so on. That is, CCA represents a high-dimensional relationship between two sets of variables with a few pair of canonical variables.

Considering two set of multivariate random vector data $\{\ \mathbf{x}_t \in \mathbf{R}^m,\ t=1,..,N\}$ and $\{\ \mathbf{y}_t \in \mathbf{R}^m,\ t=1,..,N\}$, their mean vector are denoted by $\overline{\mathbf{x}}$ and $\overline{\mathbf{y}}$. Centering the original data $\tilde{\mathbf{x}}_t = \mathbf{x}_t - \overline{\mathbf{x}}$ and $\tilde{\mathbf{y}}_t = \mathbf{y}_t - \overline{\mathbf{y}}$ respectively, we get the centered zero mean random vector set $\{\ \tilde{\mathbf{x}}_t \in \mathbf{R}^m,\ t=1,..,\ N\}$, $\{\ \tilde{\mathbf{y}}_t \in \mathbf{R}^m,\ t=1,..,N\}$. In computer vision, $\tilde{\mathbf{x}}_t$ and $\tilde{\mathbf{y}}_t$ can be regarded as a pair of different observations of the same original data, for example, images captured from different sensors (infrared ray or visible light) of the same original object; images captured under different visible light conditions (clear or dark); different image features described by different methods (spatial domain or frequency domain). CCA finds a pair of projections $\mathbf{u}_1$ and $\mathbf{v}_1$ that maximize the correlation $\rho_1 = \mathrm{cov}(\mathbf{u}_1^T\tilde{\mathbf{x}}, \mathbf{v}_1^T\tilde{\mathbf{y}}) / \sqrt{\mathrm{var}\left(\mathbf{u}_1^T\tilde{\mathbf{x}}\right)\mathrm{var}\left(\mathbf{v}_1^T\tilde{\mathbf{y}}\right)}$ between the projections of $\tilde{\mathbf{x}}_1^* = \mathbf{u}_1^T\tilde{\mathbf{x}}$ and $\tilde{\mathbf{y}}_1^* = \mathbf{v}_1^T\tilde{\mathbf{y}}$. The projections $\tilde{\mathbf{x}}_1^*$ and $\tilde{\mathbf{y}}_1^*$ are called the first pair of canonical variates. Then finding the second pair of canonical variates $\tilde{\mathbf{x}}_2^*$ and $\tilde{\mathbf{y}}_2^*$ which is uncorrelated with their first canonical variates $\tilde{\mathbf{x}}_1^*$ and $\tilde{\mathbf{y}}_1^*$, and so on. In order to study the correlation of $\tilde{\mathbf{x}}$ and $\tilde{\mathbf{y}}$, we only need analyze the correlation of a few pairs of canonical variants.

3 Deduction of Three Dimensional Canonical Correlation Analysis

In traditional 1D CCA case, it is essential to reshape the two observations to 1D vectors. Such reshaping might break the spatial structure of data and also increase the computational complexity known as dimensionality disaster. Literature [7] proposed 2DCCA, which directly conduct canonical correlation analysis on 2D image data. Because some source dates are naturally 3D structures as described in section 1, we generate CCA and 2D-CCA to a 3D version as follows:

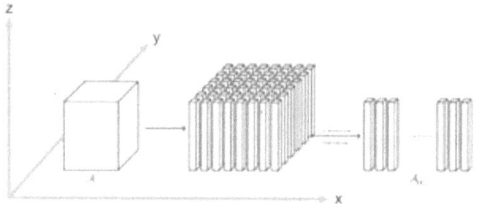

Fig. 1. Illustration of mode- flattening of a 3D pattern

3.1 Notations

A 3D pattern which has three axes of dimensions $I_\mathbf{x}, I_\mathbf{y}, I_\mathbf{z}$ is denoted by calligraphic letter $\mathcal{A} \in \mathbf{R}^{I_x \times I_y \times I_z}$. $I_\mathbf{x}, I_\mathbf{y}, I_\mathbf{z}$ are the dimensions of x, y, z directions. An element of $\mathcal{A}$ is denoted as $\mathcal{A}_{i,j,k}$, $1 \le i \le I_\mathbf{x}$, $1 \le j \le I_\mathbf{y}$, $1 \le k \le I_\mathbf{z}$. The inner product of any two 3D patterns $\mathcal{A}$ and $\mathcal{B}$ is defined as $\langle \mathcal{A}, \mathcal{B} \rangle = \sum_{i,j,j} \mathcal{A}_{i,j,k} \mathcal{B}_{i,j,k}$. The norm of $\mathcal{A}$ is defined by $\| \mathcal{A} \| = \sqrt{\langle \mathcal{A}, \mathcal{A} \rangle}$. By flattening a 3-D pattern according the x direction, we can get a matrix named as mode- x flattened matrix, which is denoted by $\mathcal{A}_{(x)} \in \mathbf{R}^{I_x \times (I_y \times I_z)}$. The illustration of mode- x flattening is shown in Fig. 1. The rows and columns of $\mathcal{A}_{(x)}$ are $I_\mathbf{x}$ and $\left(I_\mathbf{y} \times I_\mathbf{z} \right)$ respectively. The product of $\mathcal{A}_{(x)}$ by matrix $\mathbf{U}$ is denoted by $\mathbf{U}^T \mathcal{A}_{(x)}$ or $\mathcal{A}_{\times x} \mathbf{U}$, these two notations are equal.

3.2 Three Dimensional Canonical Correlation Analysis

Now we consider two sets of 3D dates $\{ \mathcal{A}_t \in \mathbf{R}^{I_{x_1} \times I_{y_1} \times I_{y_1}} \}_{t=1}^N$ and $\{ \mathcal{B}_t \in \mathbf{R}^{I_{x_2} \times I_{y_2} \times I_{y_3}} \}_{t=1}^N$ which are realizations of 3D random variable $\mathcal{A}$ and $\mathcal{B}$, respectively. We define mean of $\mathcal{A}_t$ and $\mathcal{B}_t$ as $M_\mathcal{A} = \frac{1}{N} \sum_{t=1}^N \mathcal{A}_t$ and $M_\mathcal{B} = \frac{1}{N} \sum_{t=1}^N \mathcal{B}_t$. Then the centered 3D data are denoted by $\tilde{\mathcal{A}}_t = \mathcal{A}_t - M_\mathcal{A}$, $\tilde{\mathcal{B}}_t = \mathcal{B}_t - M_\mathcal{B}$. 3DCCA is to seek transforms $\mathbf{u}_x$, $\mathbf{u}_y$, $\mathbf{u}_z$, and $\mathbf{v}_x$, $\mathbf{v}_y$, $\mathbf{v}_z$ such that correlation between $\mathcal{A}_{\times x} \mathbf{u}_x \times y \mathbf{u}_y \times z \mathbf{u}_z$ and $\mathcal{B}_{\times x} \mathbf{v}_x \times y \mathbf{v}_y \times z \mathbf{v}_z$ is maximized. Similar to CCA optimization, the optimization function of 3DCCA is formulated as:

$$J_1 = \underset{u_x, u_y, u_z, v_x, v_y, v_z}{\arg\max} \text{cov}\left(\mathcal{A}_{xx}\mathbf{u}_{xxy}\mathbf{u}_{yxz}\mathbf{u}_z, \mathcal{B}_{xx}\mathbf{v}_{xxy}\mathbf{v}_{yxz}\mathbf{v}_z\right)$$

$$\text{s.t. } \text{var}\left(\mathcal{A}_{xx}\mathbf{u}_{xxy}\mathbf{u}_{yxz}\mathbf{u}_z\right) = 1 \tag{1}$$

$$\text{var}\left(\mathcal{B}_{xx}\mathbf{v}_{xxy}\mathbf{v}_{yxz}\mathbf{v}_z\right) = 1$$

Because equation (1) is equivalent to a higher order nonlinear optimization problem with a higher order nonlinear constraint; it is difficult to find a closed form solution. Alternatively, we search for an iterative optimization approach to solve the objective function. For concise, we only detailly describe the solution of transforms $\mathbf{u}_x$ and $\mathbf{v}_x$ according to x direction. And the y and z directions' transforms are the same. Given $\mathbf{u}_y, \mathbf{v}_y$, $\mathbf{u}_z, \mathbf{v}_z$ are fixed, we define the following matrices:

$$\Sigma_{AB}^x = \frac{1}{N}\sum_{t=1}^{N}\left(\tilde{A}_{txy}\mathbf{u}_{yxz}\mathbf{u}_z\right)_{(x)}\left(\tilde{B}_{txy}\mathbf{v}_{yxz}\mathbf{v}_z\right)_{(x)}^T, \Sigma_{AA}^x = \frac{1}{N}\sum_{t=1}^{N}\left(\tilde{A}_{txy}\mathbf{u}_{yxz}\mathbf{u}_z\right)_{(x)}\left(\tilde{A}_{txy}\mathbf{v}_{yxz}\mathbf{v}_z\right)_{(x)}^T, \Sigma_{BB}^x = \frac{1}{N}\sum_{t=1}^{N}\left(\tilde{B}_{txy}\mathbf{u}_{yxz}\mathbf{u}_z\right)_{(x)}\left(\tilde{B}_{txy}\mathbf{v}_{yxz}\mathbf{v}_z\right)_{(x)}^T$$

Also because of $\text{cov}\left(\mathcal{A}_{xx}\mathbf{u}_{xxy}\mathbf{u}_{yxz}\mathbf{u}_z, \mathcal{B}_{xx}\mathbf{v}_{xxy}\mathbf{v}_{yxz}\mathbf{v}_z\right) = \mathbf{u}_x^T\Sigma_{AB}^x\mathbf{v}_x$, function (1) can be rewritten as equation (3):

$$\underset{\mathbf{u}_x, \mathbf{v}_x}{\arg\max} \ \mathbf{u}_x^T\Sigma_{AB}^x\mathbf{v}_x$$

$$s.t. \ \mathbf{u}_x^T\Sigma_{AA}^x\mathbf{u}_x = 1 \tag{2}$$

$$\mathbf{v}_x^T\Sigma_{BB}^x\mathbf{v}_x = 1$$

And the Lagrangian functions of equation (3) can be rewritten as :

$$J = \mathbf{u}_x^T\Sigma_{AB}^x\mathbf{v}_x + \lambda_{u_x}(1 - \mathbf{u}_x^T\Sigma_{AA}^x\mathbf{u}_x) + \lambda_{v_x}(1 - \mathbf{v}_x^T\Sigma_{BB}^x\mathbf{v}_{xx}) \tag{3}$$

Solve $\dfrac{\partial J}{\partial \mathbf{u}_x} = 0$ and $\dfrac{\partial J}{\partial \mathbf{v}_x} = 0$, leads to:

$$\Sigma_{AB}^x\mathbf{v}_x - 2\lambda_{u_x}\Sigma_{AA}^x\mathbf{u}_x = 0 \tag{4}$$

$$\Sigma_{BA}^x\mathbf{u}_x - 2\lambda_{v_x}\Sigma_{BB}^x\mathbf{v}_x = 0 \tag{5}$$

Here $\Sigma_{BA}^x = \Sigma_{AB}^{x}{}^T$, by multiplying $\mathbf{u}_x^T$ and $\mathbf{v}_x^T$ to the both sides of equation (4) and (5), according to the two constrains $\mathbf{u}_x^T\Sigma_{AA}^x\mathbf{u}_x = 1$ and $\mathbf{v}_x^T\Sigma_{BB}^x\mathbf{v}_x = 1$, we have $\mathbf{u}_x^T\Sigma_{AB}^x\mathbf{v}_x = 2\lambda_{u_x}$ and $\mathbf{v}_x^T\Sigma_{BA}^x\mathbf{u}_x = 2\lambda_{v_x}$. Saliently, $2\lambda_x = 2\lambda_y = \lambda$. So the solution of $\mathbf{u}_x$ and $\mathbf{v}_x$ is changed to the following generalized eigenvalue problem:

$$\begin{bmatrix} 0 & \Sigma_{AB}^x \\ \Sigma_{BA}^x & 0 \end{bmatrix}\begin{bmatrix} \mathbf{u}_x \\ \mathbf{v}_x \end{bmatrix} = \lambda\begin{bmatrix} \Sigma_{AA}^x & 0 \\ 0 & \Sigma_{BB}^x \end{bmatrix}\begin{bmatrix} \mathbf{u}_x \\ \mathbf{v}_x \end{bmatrix} \tag{6}$$

In a similar way, given $\mathbf{u}_x, \mathbf{v}_x, \mathbf{u}_z, \mathbf{v}_z$ are fixed, the transforms $\mathbf{u}_y$ and $\mathbf{v}_y$ can be solved. The same as the solution of $\mathbf{u}_z$ and $\mathbf{v}_z$. An iterative calculating process is used to get the final solutions until convergence. In our numerical experiments, it takes only a few iterations for convergence. The d largest generalized eigenvectors in (6) determines $\mathbf{U}_x = \left(\mathbf{u}_{x_1}, \mathbf{u}_{x_2}, ..., \mathbf{u}_{x_d} \right)$ and $\mathbf{V}_x = \left(\mathbf{v}_{x_1}, \mathbf{v}_{x_2}, ..., \mathbf{v}_{x_d} \right)$. In a similar manner, we can get the projection matrices $\mathbf{U}_y, \mathbf{V}_y$ and $\mathbf{U}_z, \mathbf{V}_z$. In our proposed 3DCCA, the generalized eigenvalue problem for much smaller size matrices, compared to the traditional CCA, which can reduce the computation cost dramatically. Finally the dimension decreased 3D dates $\mathcal{A}_{\times x} \mathbf{U}_{\times\times y} \mathbf{U}_{y\times z} \mathbf{U}_z$ and $\mathcal{B}_{\times x} \mathbf{V}_{\times\times y} \mathbf{V}_{y\times z} \mathbf{V}_z$ are for the next classification. In this paper, the nearest-neighbor classifier is used for recognition.

4   Experiments and Analysis

The JAFFE database used in this study contains 213 images of female facial expressions. Each image has a resolution of 200*180 pixels. The number of images corresponding to each of seven categories of expressions (neutral, happiness, sadness, surprise, anger, disgust and fear) is almost the same. The images in the database are grayscale images in tiff file format. The expression expressed in each image along with a semantic rating is provided in the database that makes the database suitable for facial expression research. Some images are shown in Fig. 2.

Fig. 2. Sample expressions of two persons from the JAFFE database

Gabor wavelets can derive desirable local facial features characterized by spatial frequency, spatial locality, and orientation selectively to cope with the image variations. This paper we encode the original face image to a pair of two correlative 3D representations which correspond to 5 scales 8 orientations and 8 scales 5 orientations Gabor features respectively. The task here is to investigate how well CCA, 2DCCA and 3DCCA can accurately recognize the facial expressions. In this paper, we choose 3 face images of the same expression each person and sum to 210 face images for experiments. Each expression has 30 face images. The image set was randomly partitioned into the gallery and probe set with different numbers. For ease of representation, the experiment is named as Gm/Pn which means that the random m images per expression are selected for training data and the remaining n images for testing of the same expression. We extract the 5*8=40 Gabor features in the down-sample positions with 5 different scales 8 different orientations and the exchanged parameters to construct pair feature representations. And each image is encoded as a pair of 3D dates of dimensions 25*23*40. The nearest-neighbor classifier is used for recognition. For CCA, image Gabor representations are reshaped to 25*23*40=23000 dimension vectors, and always result in out of memory error in our experiments because of the eigenvalue decomposition of a 23000*23000 matrix. For 2DCCA, image Gabor representations are reshaped to 200*115 and 125*184 2D matrices according to x and y direction flattening. And for 3DCCA, image Gabor representations are 25*23*40 3D patterns. We randomly choose 5, 10, 15 facial images per expression for testing and the remaining samples for training. And repeat the experiments three times. The average best facial expression recognition rate is shown in table 1. In terms of classification accuracy, 3DCCA is better than 2DCCA. Also, because of the smaller eigenvalue decomposition matrix, 3DCCA can decrease the feature extraction time cost.

Table 1. Recognition accuracies comparison of 3DCCA and 2DCCA

Recognition rate	G10/P20	G15/P15	G20/P10	G25/P5
2DCCA	0.5143	0.6381	0.7524	0.8571
3DCCA	0.5881	0.6667	0.8190	0.9143

5 Conclusions

In this paper, we generate the traditional CCA algorithm to 3D data, which can effectively preserve the spatial structure of the source data and effectively decrease the possibility of singular problem of high dimensional matrix's eigenvalue decomposition. Be compared with other methods, experiments show that our proposed 3DCCA has better recognition rate as well as decreases the computation cost.

References

1. Wang, H., Leng, Y., et al.: Application of image correction and bit-plane fusion in generalized PCA based face recognition. Pattern Recognition Letters 28(16), 2352–2358 (2007)
2. Hu, H.: ICA-based neighborhood preserving analysis for face recognition. Computer Vision and Image Understanding 112(3), 286–295 (2008)
3. Zheng, W.-S., Lai, J.H., et al.: Perturbation LDA: Learning the difference between the class empirical mean and its expectation. Pattern Recognition 42(5), 764–779 (2009)
4. Sun, T., Chen, S.: Class label versus sample label-based CCA. Applied Mathematics and Computation 185(1), 272–283 (2007)
5. Yongwon, J., Hyung Soon, K.: New Speaker Adaptation Method Using 2-D PCA. IEEE Signal Processing Letters 17(2), 193–196
6. Wen-Hui, Y., Dao-Qing, D.: Two-Dimensional Maximum Margin Feature Extraction for Face Recognition. IEEE Transactions on Systems, Man, and Cybernetics, Part B: Cybernetics 39(4), 1002–1012 (2009)
7. Lee, S., Choi, S.: Two-dimensional canonical correlation analysis. IEEE Signal Processing Letters 14(10), 735–738 (2007)

Technology Barriers Analysis on Bearing Industry Based on Relational Matrix Method

Xianzhao Jia[1,2], Feng Lv[1], Yonggang Liu[1,2], and Juan Wang[1]

[1] School of Mechatronics Engineering, Henan University of Science and Technology, Luoyang, 471003, China
[2] Henan Key Lab for Machinery Design and Transmission System, Luoyang, 471003, China

Abstract. Statuses of bearings industry are analyzed. The main elements of industrial targets are identified and calculated in light of the weighted average by the scientific statistics and analysis methods. Technical barriers are got in the term of expert judgments based on the weights of industrial targets. Then the matrix is built. The industry targets which need to overcome key technical barriers are selected. By means of the breakthrough in these technical barriers, the technological upgrading of the industry will be promoted.

Keywords: Technical Barriers; Analysis Matrix; Weight; Industry Targets.

1 Introduction

Relational matrix method is commonly used to the comprehensive evaluation, which is mainly expressed in matrix form the relation between the related evaluation index of every substitute scheme with the importance and value evaluation amount of specific targets. Usually the system is multi- target, therefore, the system evaluation index is not the only, and not always measure the scale of every index are monetary units, in many cases is not the same, the system evaluation of the difficulty lies. Accordingly, H. Chestnut proposed comprehensive method is based on specific evaluation system to determine the system of evaluation index system and its corresponding weight, and calculate the comprehensive evaluation value of every substitute scheme about system evaluation, that is, calculated weighted sum of every substitute scheme evaluation values. The key of the relational matrix method is to determine the relative importance of every substitute scheme (that is the weight W_j), and based on the evaluation scale of the given evaluation index about evaluation subject ,determine the value evaluation amount of evaluation index(V_{ij}). [1]

Bearings are indispensable supports of modern machine parts, which are widely used to aviation, aerospace, navigation, military industry and other fields, known as the machine's "joint." Bearing quality directly affects the performance and level of a variety of matching host and equipment, thereby the level of the whole machinery industry. Bearing industry is one of the basic industries in national economy. The Chinese bearing industry has developed rapidly since Eleventh Five-Year, and it

R. Chen (Ed.): ICICIS 2011, Part I, CCIS 134, pp. 62–68, 2011.

becomes the third largest bearings producer next to Japan and Sweden. There is still a great disparity with world powers, therefore, it is essential to analysis the technical barriers of the bearing industry in determined industry objective when Twelfth Five-Year comes. [2]

2 Importances

The bearing industry in the clear status, and based on future market demand for industrial products and services, through the scientific statistics and analysis methods, concise expert on the industry with the future direction's decision, determine the objectives of the bearing industry [3], see the table 1.

Fill the eight goals in the first line and in the first row of the judgment matrix, multiple comparison their importance, forming the matrix. $C = \left| c_{ij} \right|_{m \times n}$ Express the importance judgment matrix formed in industrial target which need priority development. C_{ij} Indicate that the importance of industry target i compared with industry target j.

$$c = \begin{bmatrix} 1 & 3 & 1/2 & 2 & 3 & 2 & 3 & 2 \\ 1/3 & 1 & 1/3 & 1/3 & 1/3 & 1/2 & 2 & 2 \\ 2 & 3 & 1 & 2 & 2 & 3 & 3 & 3 \\ 1/2 & 3 & 1/2 & 1 & 1/3 & 3 & 1 & 1/2 \\ 1/3 & 3 & 1/2 & 3 & 1 & 3 & 2 & 1 \\ 1/2 & 2 & 1/3 & 1/3 & 1/3 & 1 & 3 & 3 \\ 1/3 & 1/2 & 1/3 & 1 & 1/2 & 1/3 & 1 & 2 \\ 1/2 & 1/2 & 1/3 & 2 & 1 & 1/3 & 1/2 & 1 \end{bmatrix}$$

Judgment matrix   elements C_{ij} with assignment score criterion   are as follows: 1——target i and target j of the considerable importance; 3——target i is important than the target j; 5——target i compared to target j, target i is extreme important; 2, 4——advisable middle value. Compared with the every two target, through expert evaluation, estimating judgment matrix of the target importance [4], and then calculate eigenvectors $W = [W_1, W_2, \ldots W_i]^T$. Among

$W_i = \overline{W_i} \sum_{i=1}^{m} \overline{W_i}$, W_i is the importance for the target i, by the ahp and weighted score criterion, derived important values in table 2. [5]

Table 1. Industry Target Elements

Number	Industry Target Elements
I	improve product design manufacture capabilities and level
II	increased industrial concentration, promote clustering development
III	improve product performance and expand product standard and type
IV	reduce costs
V	improve the quality of industrial workers
VI	expand the industrial scale, increase market share
VII	improve the social service system of industry
VIII	optimization system, mechanism

Table 2. The importance obtained by the ahp and weighted score criterion

Index	$\overline{W_i}$	W_i	Weighted Score V_i
I	1.23	0.092	7.7
II	0.53	0.039	3.3
III	1.60	0.121	10
IV	1.01	0.076	6.3
V	1.17	0.088	7.3
VI	0.83	0.062	5.2
VII	0.24	0.018	1.5
VIII	0.29	0.022	1.8

3 Barriers

Technical barriers are the technical difficulties that need to overcome in the process of achieving industry targets. Technical barriers analysis is based on future market demand and industrial development targets, analysis to achieve the industry targets which affect the technology (including process) barriers. The key is screened out the more difficult to solve the key technical problems from the existing technology barriers. Through the breakthrough of these technical barriers, promote the technology upgrade of the whole industry, achieving industry targets. [6]

To drive the technology upgrade from the whole bearing industry, achieve the bearing industry targets, according the market demand ,the requirements of target industries, combined with the literature and the bearing business of customer interviews information and experts advice, put forward technical difficulties in bearing industry, concise technical barriers elements of bearing industry.

The process of refining technical barriers elements are listed below.

(1) Classify: Based on the these elements in common, such as attributes, divided into 6 categories ① product design ② materials and heat treatment ③ processing ④ test and device ⑤ detection ⑥ others.

(2) Generalize: Complicated with the concept of the same or similar related content and standard words.

(3) Analyze: Delete not constitute a relevant items on bearing technical barriers.

(4) Held expert forum convened: Bearing Technical Barriers held a special meeting on whether to become a technical barrier elements, elements of technical barriers to the formulation of norms, terms and other issues were fully discussed and reached consensus.

(5) Solicit the views of thematic leader: Put through the classification, inductive, concise and sorting out, "technology barriers elements of bearing industrial questionnaire" sent to focus group leader, to seek the views of head.

(6) Solicit expert opinion: After the head of the modification "technology barriers elements of bearing industrial questionnaire "and then sent to experts, to seek expert's advice.

Through classify, generalize, analysis, comprehensive, influx experts opinions, the final condensed into the following 12 key technical difficulties of bearing industry technology areas: A: bearing raceway and the flange surface quenching technology B: parts ferrule material of smelting and casting technology C: large bearing reliability test methods; D: materials nondestructive testing technology; E: quenching technology inside and outside the ring gear; F: large load bearing rings to turning instead of grinding technology; G: technology of parts forging process; H: large-size rings, roller precision machining technology; I: precision grinding, ultra-precision NC machine J: test equipment design and manufacturing technology; K: cage processing technology; L: bearing test parameters design technology.

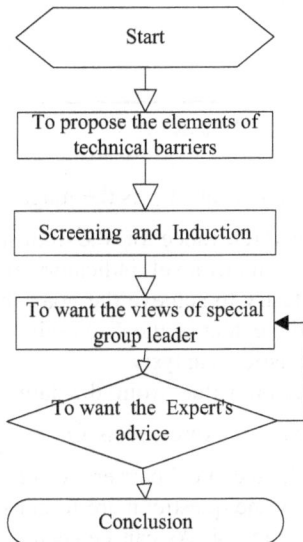

Fig. 1. The process of refining technical barriers elements

4 Correlations

The purpose of industry targets correlation analysis with technical barriers is to use matrix analysis to establish correlation analysis matrix with industry targets and technical barriers, ultimately obtained the order of technical barriers elements with the correlation of industry targets.

Basis on the main industry targets elements, according to the technical barriers elements obtained from experts in the judge of technical barriers, build analysis matrix, selected to achieve the industry targets of priority development technology. See the Table 3 [7]. Matrix elements of the horizontal as industry targets sequences, by the numbers 1, 2, 3 ... represent; Matrix elements of the vertical as technical barriers sequence, by the A, B and C ... represent.

Table 3. Industry target elements associated analysis with elements of technical barriers (1)

The Judgment Value Of Technical Barriers V_{ji}	The Importance Of Industry Targets V_i							
	V_1 7.7	V_2 3.3	V_3 10	V_4 6.3	V_5 7.3	V_6 5.2	V_7 1.5	V_8 1.8
V_{Ai}	3	2	1	1	-3	-2	-1	2
V_{Bi}	3	0	-2	0	2	1	3	-3
V_{Ci}	2	3	1	1	-2	2	2	-2
V_{Di}	0	-1	-1	0	2	-1	1	2
V_{Ei}	-1	-2	0	1	3	1	-2	-2
V_{Fi}	-1	0	-2	3	2	0	3	0
V_{Gi}	1	0	-2	3	2	0	3	0
V_{Hi}	0	-1	-1	1	2	1	1	2
V_{Ii}	3	2	1	0	-3	-2	-1	2
V_{Ji}	3	3	1	2	-3	0	-3	-3
V_{Ki}	-1	-2	-2	1	-3	1	-2	-2
V_{Li}	1	-2	0	2	1	-2	1	3

Note: i=1,2,3,4,5,6,7,8; j=A,B,C,D,E,F,G,H,I,J,K,L.

The judgment value of technical barriers V_{ij} is the judge value of the experts given about technical barriers elements relevance of the industry targets, divided into positive and negative categories, multi-level indicators that can be used. Expert judgments on the basis of an industry to achieve the goal, the obstacles to their level of technical barriers and hinder the extent of the size divided +3, +2, +1, 0, -1, -2, -3, obtained by questionnaire and statistical analysis.

Calculated association evaluation value from the table 3 obtained the data in table 4. Association evaluation value is expressed as $G_j = \sum \left(v_i \times v_{ji} \right)$.

Regard the ranking results of the technical barriers which realized with the difficult degree and then sent to experts by the questionnaire to consult expert's opinion, and reached identical results. See the table 4. As can be seen from table 4, the technical barriers as the boundary of position 6, ranking the best six shows the key technical problems with the bigger hinder in these 8 industry targets, post-ranking 6 shows the key technical problems to these eight industry targets affected not significant. Obtained the evaluation value is based on the key technical difficulties association with each corresponding industry target, the merit obtained by the comprehensive consideration, the final value obtained by re-arrangement, from the ranking results can be seen: Because it has the most relevant with every industry targets, the large bearing reliability test methods is the most difficult to solve technical difficulties in these key technical problems. The others like that.

5   Results and Discussion

The associated analysis results in industry target elements and technical barriers, with the bearing industry in China at this stage of the basic agreement.

(1) Large bearing reliability test methods: At present, China only Luoyang LYC bearing limited company has a similar large turntable bearing comprehensive performance test-bed. The next few years should focus on establishing the appropriate test bed for bearing life test done to improve reliability.

(2) Bearing test parameters design technology: As the large gap between domestic and foreign, by selecting test methods, of similarity to the experimental study and determine ways to improve design load.

Table 4. Industry target elements associated analysis with elements of technical barriers (2)

Elements Of Technical Barriers	Evaluation Value G_j	Order From Hard to Easy
bearing raceway and the flange surface quenching technology	15.8	6
parts ferrule material of smelting and casting technology	22	4
large bearing reliability test methods	38.6	1
materials nondestructive testing technology	1.2	12
quenching technology inside and outside the ring gear	14.3	7
large load bearing rings to turning instead of grinding technology	10.3	9
technology of parts forging process	18	5
large-size rings, roller precision machining technology	12.7	8
precision grinding, ultra-precision nc machine	9.5	10
test equipment design and manufacturing technology	24.1	3
cage processing technology	4.3	11
bearing test parameters design technology	30.8	2

(3) Test equipment design and manufacturing technology: In order to narrow the gap with advanced countries, the key from the conditions simulation, the state's testing and test data acquisition and processing are three aspects to improve.

(4) Parts ferrule material of smelting and casting technology: Low level of automation, the lack of large-scale NC machine tools and machining center is China's current situation, through smelting and casting technology research, and based on the mechanical properties, process ability, and the performance of the hardening heat treatment and harden ability of research, improve smelting and forging techniques.

(5) Technology of parts forging process: The current high precision, high reliability bearing materials also need to import from abroad, so to simulate and analyze the forging process to determine the temperature, pressure, forging speed key parameters is necessary.

(6) Bearing raceway and the flange surface quenching technology: As the heat treatment of instability in China, the future focus on designing reasonable quench apparatus, determining the optimal quenching process, selecting the proper heat treatment process parameters and improving the bearing raceway and the flange surface hardening techniques.

6 Conclusion

In short, the bearings industry should be proper sequence from the emphasis needs to start in order to overcome technical barriers. And other non-key technical barriers have a choice to break, through such a series of breakthroughs that can bring the whole bearing industry to upgrade technology and achieve bearing industry targets.

Acknowledgments

This work was financially supported by the National High-tech R&D Program of China (No.2009AA044902), Soft Science Project of Henan Province (No. 102400410011), Innovation Scientists and Technicians Troop Construction Projects of Henan Province.

References

1. Yu, X.C., Sh, X.: Engineering Tutorials. Qinghua University Press (2007)
2. Ji, Z.J., Jia, X.Z., Wang, Y.J.: Luoyang Bearing Industry Cluster Study. Bearing 11, 43–46 (2008)
3. China Bearing Industry Association. 2007 Development Report of China's bearing industry, pp. 1–8. China Bearing Industry Association, Beijing (2008)
4. Wang, Q.: Analysis based on fuzzy weights of customer demand. Hubei Institute of Technology 2, 54–57 (2004)
5. Lv, F., Guo, Z.W.: Quality Function Deployment using logistics service quality improvement. Industrial Engineering 5, 91–94 (2009)
6. Wang, J., Jia, X.Z., Zhang, J.: Analysis on Technical Barriers of Bearing Industry Based on Incidence Matrix Method. Bearing 9, 61–63 (2010)

Optimizational Study on Computing Method of Channel Earthwork Based on MATLAB

Yuqiang Wang[1], Jianqiang Zhang[2], and Yinghua Wang[1]

[1] Zhejiang Water Conservancy and Hydropower College, Hangzhou, 310018, China
wangyq@zjwchc.com
[2] Zhejiang Hangzhou Economic and Technological Development Zone River Regulation
Center Consideration
52882689@qq.com

Abstract. The calculation of channel transition earthwork volume is the basic work of channel design and construction. Traditional calculation is complicated and low precision. The study is based on the strong calculation function and user-friendly interface of MATLAB. Analyzing the traditional calculation and the principle, I recommend a calculation by using the interpolation of quadratic B-spline function and integral, which makes the calculation simpler, more accurate and for reference.

Keywords: channel, earthwork volume, MATLAB, B-spline function integral, optimizational study.

Introduction

The calculation of channel transition earthwork volume is the basic work of channel design and construction. Traditional calculation always adopts grid method, slice method and analytical method to calculate the Cut and fill area of Cross Section. Then it calculates the earthwork volume by using the average cross- section method or average distance method[1,2]. But it is cockamamie and low accuracy and it can't adapt to the acquirement of modern technology. As the development of science technology, it is essential to study the new method of earthwork volume which can meet the real demand of projects. This essay puts forward the calculation of earthwork volume which is based on the theory basis of PT PoinT location coordinate method[3] and quadratic B-spline function. PT PoinT location coordinate method calculates the the Cut and fill area of every construction stake. Then, we can consider it as a math problem[4]. It means that we know a series of stake number and the cut and fill area. We adopt quadratic B-spline function to interpolate it and use integral method to get the integral value of two stake numbers, which is the earthwork volume. This method is of simple calculation model, which adapts to the calculation of earthwork volume for channels and roads' linear engineering. It is adaptable to complex landform. And it also has good effect for calculating some particular forms, such as variable cross-section and twist surface.

R. Chen (Ed.): ICICIS 2011, Part I, CCIS 134, pp. 69–76, 2011.

1 The Theory Basis of PT PoinT Location Coordinate Method [5]

The theory basis of PT PoinT location coordinate method for studying the land-leveling and terrace design nowadays is a rigorous method which makes use of Polyhedron vertex coordinates to calculate Polyhedron geometry character. It defines each side of Polyhedron as oriented. Someone calls it as directed Polyhedron[6]. Because the basic calculation formula is derived from vector(directed line) --- oriented polygon --- oriented Polyhedron. And it is also called vector method. But for universal meaning, it is more reasonable to be called PT PoinT location coordinate method and it's also the reason for changing the name.

Although PT PoinT location coordinate method is not applied to the calculation of channel earthwork volume, it is undoubted to solve the basic theoretical questions of channel earth area calculation. It means that PT PoinT location coordinate method is the theory basis of channel earth area calculation.

2 Area Calculation of Directed Areas of Polygons

2.1 The Concept of Directed Areas of Polygons

Directed areas of polygons which are in the same space plane belong to directed area. Its property "directed area" has three descriptions: definite normal direction (normal direction only points to one side of the plane); definite steering (in the right handed coordinate system, the steering of polygons is made by right-hand rule based on its normal direction); directed boundary (the direction of directed boundary is the same to steering).

The third description is easily to use the vertices sequence to show the polygon. As shown in 1a. it is a pentagon $M_1M_2M_3M_4M_5$ (M_i is shown as I in the figure). Two sides of directed areas of polygons can be intersected. Apparently, when it happens, the polygon falls into doubled-sided area which has different normal direction and steerings.

The normal direction which is the basic direction of area vector of directed areas of polygons is the vector based on its real area. To double-sided directed areas of polygons, area vector is the sum of areas of two sides. $\vec{S}$ stands for area vector, easy to understand $\vec{S}_{12345} = \vec{S}_{54321}$.

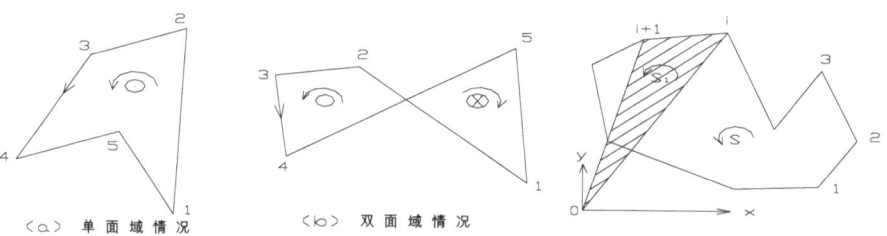

(a) 单面域情况   (b) 双面域情况

Fig. 1. Directed planar polygon   **Fig. 2.** Area calculation of Directed polygon

2.2   Area Formulas of Directed Areas of Polygons in xy Coordinate Plane

According to vector algebra, the directed area vector $\triangle M_0M_iM_{i+1}$ is (Figure 2)

$$\vec{S}_i = \frac{1}{2}\vec{R}_i \times \vec{R}_{i+1}$$

Radius vector of $\vec{R}_i$ ——Mi is $\overrightarrow{OM}_i$.

As $\vec{S}_i$ is parallel to axis z, we consider the area of $\triangle M_0M_iM_{i+1}$ S_i as algebraic quantity. When $\vec{S}_i$ is the same direction to axis z, S_i is the positive value, or it is negative value; when $\vec{S}_i = 0$, $S_i = 0, |S_i| = |\vec{S}_i|$.

According to superposition principle and two vector product determinants, we can get that xy plane has an expression formula which is applied to the area S of directed n areas polygon.

$$S = \frac{1}{2}\sum_{i=1}^{n}\begin{vmatrix} x_i & x_{i+1} \\ y_i & y_{i+1} \end{vmatrix} \tag{1}$$

It can easily get that when polygon has anticlockwise boundary, the area is positive value or the area is negative value. When polygon has double sides, the area is the sum of two sides.

2.3   Polygon Topology Changes into Planar Network

To the N areas polyhedron fixed by the directed area S_i ($i=1\sim n$), we use S_i to stand for the name and $\vec{S}_i$ of i side, use $\vec{S}_i$ to stand for the area vector and fix every side $\vec{S}_i$ which is intersected in the same apex as outer normal, or inner normal.

Polyhedron also can be double-sided polyhedron. Figure 3a, 3b show the hexahedral of one side and double sides. Pay attention, the extreme point of two sides intersection line in double-sided polyhedron, as Figure 3b shows, A, B can't be the apex of the polyhedron. According to the concept of directed area, the normal which consist of the same side can be outer normal or inner normal.

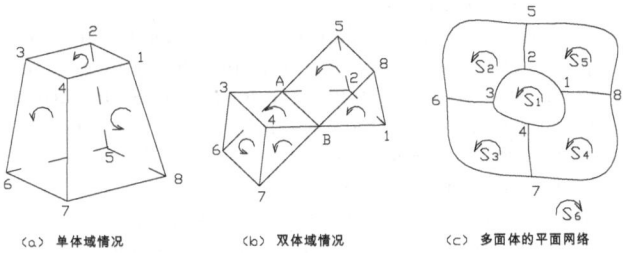

(a) 单体域情况   (b) 双体域情况   (c) 多面体的平面网络

Fig. 3. The polyhedron confirmed by directed planar polygon

To overcome the difficulties of clearly showing the steering and area number in stereogram, we need to change polyhedron topology into planar network[7]. Make network correspond to the apex of polyhedron, so the work of steering and area number can be done at network. There is big difference between figure 3a and 3b, but they all can change into the network in figure 3c. compared 3a with 3c, it's easy to find that the inner arc area of S_1, S_2 are anticlockwise steering. Because the outer normal of corresponding area is vertical after the transformation. The bottom surface $M_8M_7M_6M_5$ has changed into outer arc area which is overlapped with other arc areas. It's difficult to label S_6 and we transfer it to the outside of the area. Apparently, the steering of S_6 is clockwise. The label of figure 3c is also applied to 3b.

3   The Calculating Program Implementation of Channel Cut and Fill Cross Section Area Based on MATLAB [8]

With the previous concept and area calculations of directed areas of polygons,we can easily program subprogram to calculate cut and fill cross section area rigorously. As the area calculation of left and right sides of the channel is the same, to be simplified, we choose the right side of the channel as the calculation unit. As Figure 4 shows.

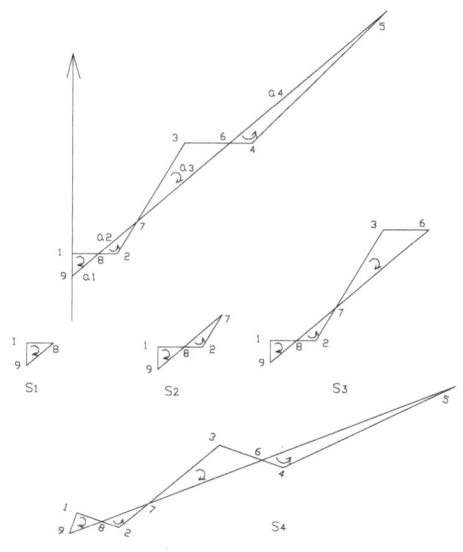

From the view of point coordinate method, we consider the right side as a directed areas of polygon which consist of transversal ground level (broken line), channel design section and y axe. And number every apex. And the apex coordinate of directed areas of polygon has formed and been stored in correlative database table for user's convenience. Table 5 shows the most complex situation in cross section, which has most intersection points. Broken line 12345 is the cross hatching line of right-sided channel, straight line 56789 shows the transversal ground level of the testing construction stake. The intersection points are changeable because of the variety of ground. Si and iai are directed areas, which set clockwise is plus sign to be applied to earth fill area; while anticlockwise is minus sign to be applied to excavated volume area.

We will study the implementation method of earthwork volume of earth fill and excavated volume cross sections as follows[9].

The calculation of the program of the half side of channel Cut and fill cross section area is named *area(xy( ), at, aw)*, several groups of parameters *xy( )* are defined as a planar array of 9 rows and 2 arrays, which conveys 9 node coordinates; *at, aw* are the unknown earth fill and excavated volume areas. It contains a function *ds(xy( ))*, several groups of parameters. *xy( )*is defined as a the Variable Data Array which conveys the unknown apex coordinates. This function can calculate directed areas of 4 directed areas of polygons $S_1=S_{189}$, $S_2=S_{1279}$, $S_3=S_{12369}$, $S_4=S_{123459}$.

After that, we reorder it, remove the directed areas of zero and record the number of non-zero directed areas.

Then

$$
\begin{cases}
S_1 = a_1 \\
S_2 = a_1 + a_2 \\
S_3 = a_1 + a_2 + a_3 \\
S_4 = a_1 + a_2 + a_3 + a_4
\end{cases}
\Rightarrow
\begin{cases}
a_1 = S_1 \\
a_2 = S_2 - S_1 \\
a_3 = S_3 - S_2 \\
a_4 = S_4 - S_3
\end{cases}
$$

Accumulate the positive value and negative value of a_1, a_2, a_3, a_4, and the results are channel areas of earth fill and excavated volume.

4   The Interpolation Calculation of Quadratic B-Spline Function

After the measurement of the channel, it gets the Cut and fill cross section area summation of construction stake which is a group of discreet coordinates. The key point is to choose the proper interpolation method to make the discrete point as curve equation and then calculate the earthwork volume. Cubic Spline Function can make it but because of the smoothness of cubic spline[10], it easily makes inflection points in some undulant terrain, which is unmatched to real situation. And non isometric node quadratic B-spline function easily adapts to the interpolation of channel Cut and fill area of Cross Section function and the actual topography change, which is consistent with the man-made treatment of ground level.

4.1   The Interpolation Algorithm of Quadratic B-Spline Function[11,12,13,14,15]

The concept of spline function is introduced by American mathematician I.Schoenberg in 1946. Because spline function has the property of subsection and low degree and it doesn't have instability of high degree interpolation. B-spline function(Basic Spline function) is spline function which has limited support and can be the spatial fundus of spline function and haas many good properties. The method of B-spline has united, universal, effective standard algorithm and accessory technology. It is of powerful function of showing and designing free-form curved surface. It is one of the most popular description of shape math. The mathematics model and calculation of quadratic B-spline function is perfect.

4.2   Construct and Solve Quadratic B-Spline Function as $a=l_0<l_1<\cdots<l_m=b$, Every Position

Table 4 correspond to a group of channel earth fill or excavated cross section A_0, $A_1 \cdots A_m$. Let $N=m-1$, choose the node

$$x_0 = l_0 = a$$
$$x_i = \frac{l_i + l_{i+1}}{2}, \qquad i = 1, 2, \cdots, N-1$$
$$x_N = l_m = b$$

Then add new node and expand it as

$$x_{-2} < x_{-1} < a = x_0 < x_1 < \cdots < x_N = b < x_{N+1} < x_{N+2}$$

Choose $x_{-2} = x_0 - 2(x_1 - x_0)$, $\qquad\qquad x_{-1} = x_0 - (x_1 - x_0)$

$\qquad\quad x_{N+1} = x_N + (x_N - x_{N-1})$, $\qquad x_{N+2} = x_N + 2(x_N - x_{N-1})$

Get it from recurrence relation

$$B_{i,0}(x) = \begin{cases} 1, & x_i < x \le x_{i+1} \\ 0, & 其它 \end{cases} \qquad i = -2, -1, \cdots, N+1$$

$$B_{i,1}(x) = \frac{x - x_i}{x_{i+1} - x_i} B_{i,0}(x) + \frac{x_{i+2} - x}{x_{i+2} - x_{i+1}} B_{i+1,0}(x) \quad i = -2, -1, \cdots, N$$

$$B_{i,2}(x) = \frac{x - x_i}{x_{i+2} - x_i} B_{i,1}(x) + \frac{x_{i+3} - x}{x_{i+3} - x_{i+1}} B_{i+1,1}(x) \quad i = -2, -1, \cdots, N-1$$

Cut and fill area of Cross Section function $A(x) \approx S(x) = \sum_{i=-2}^{N-1} \alpha_i B_{i,2}(x)$ and calculate the

coefficient α_i.

Construction stake,

$$S(l_0) = \sum_{i=-2}^{N-1} \alpha_i B_{i,2}(l_0) = A_0$$

$$S(l_1) = \sum_{i=-2}^{N-1} \alpha_i B_{i,2}(l_1) = A_1$$

$$\cdots \cdots$$

$$S(l_m) = \sum_{i=-2}^{N-1} \alpha_i B_{i,2}(l_m) = A_m$$

The matrix versions is $B \partial = \beta$

$$\begin{bmatrix} B_{-2,2}(l_0) & B_{-1,2}(l_0) & \cdots & B_{N-1,2}(l_0) \\ B_{-2,2}(l_1) & B_{-1,2}(l_1) & \cdots & B_{N-1,2}(l_1) \\ \vdots & \vdots & \ddots & \vdots \\ \vdots & \vdots & & \vdots \\ B_{-2,2}(l_m) & B_{-1,2}(l_m) & \cdots & B_{N-1,2}(l_m) \end{bmatrix} \begin{bmatrix} \alpha_{-2} \\ \alpha_{-1} \\ \vdots \\ \vdots \\ \alpha_{N-1} \end{bmatrix} = \begin{bmatrix} A_0 \\ A_1 \\ \vdots \\ \vdots \\ A_m \end{bmatrix}$$

Coefficient matrix B is tridiagonal positively definite matrix, and it can calculates linear equations to get coefficient α_i.

5   Rigorous Method of Cut and Fill Area Earthwork Volume in Any Two Cross Sections

After calculating the coefficient α_i of Cut and fill area of Cross Section function $A(x) \approx S(x) = \sum_{i=-2}^{N-1} \alpha_i B_{i,2}(x)$, we can get it by using integral method. Because the integral process is very complex, this essay adopts MATLAB to calculate it, only using simple source program(because of the thesis length, it will not go into particulars). Program steps: ①produce area moment of cross section; ②use polyfit $(x, s, 2)$ to simulate faultage area function; ③write functional matrix of quadratic B-spline function to get the coefficient; ④write quadrature program to calculate earthwork volume.

6   Practical Examples

The design of a agrouted masonry Torsion area shows l =3m, H1=3m, H2=2.5m, b1=b2=B1=0.42m, B2=1.42. After calculation, Canal Transition Earthwork is just as table 1 shows. It also states the utility and low calculation error of the formulas in this essay and the result of literature[3], which gets the calculation of actual earthwork volume based on numerical method [16,17,18].

Table 1. The result of earthwork volume

design parameter (m)		design elevation (m)		initiating terminal area (m3)	intermediate terminal area (m³)	termination area (m³)	the length of changeover form (l)	Earthwork volume(m³)			
								Actual earthwork volume	average section method	Calculation of literature[19]	This algorithm
b_1 0.42		h_1	3								
b_2 0.42				1.26	2.074	2.3	3	5.4	5.34	5.358	5.401
B_1 0.42		h_2	2.5								
B_2 1.42											
		relative error (%)							1.11%	0.78%	0.02%

From the result (table 1), average section method is of high calculation error. Althouth the calculation error of literature[19] is fewer than average section method, only 0.78%, the formula is more complex, especially the calculation of end-face coordinate. This essay only calls simple programs and the largest calculation error is only 0.02% which shows the simpleness and high precision.

References

[1] Henan Agricultural University Chief Editor. surveying. China Agriculture Press, Beijing (1979)

[2] Xinan Agricultural University Chief Editor. surveying. China Agriculture Press, Beijing (1981)

[3] Cai, J., Xin, Q.: Soil and water conservation project—vector method. Soil and Water Conservation Academic Journal 9(1), 77–81, 85 (1995)

[4] Luo, Y.: Study on Software Development of Channel Earthwork Volume Calculation. Northwest A & F University (2004)

[5] Wang, Y., Lai, L.: The Explration in Calculation Model about the Area of Filling-in and Excavation of Canal Cross Section. Zhejiang Water Conservancy And Hydropower College (3), 40–43 (2007)

[6] Cai, J.: The Regular Method of Calculating the Geometrical and Mechanical Characteristic Values of Prismatic Section. Northwest Agriculture University Journal of Northwest Sci-tech University of Agriculture And Forestry 23(3), 69–73 (1995)

[7] Tan, Y.: The Introduction of Topology. Sichuan Education Press, Sichuan (1987)

[8] Liu, B., et al.: Visual Basic How to Program. Tsinghua University Press, Beijing (2000)

[9] Yang, L.: Visual Basic How to Program. China Water Power Press, Beijing (2002)

[10] Luo, Y., Zhang, K., et al.: The Application of MATLAB in the Calculation of Channel Earthwork Volume. Journal of Irrigation and Drainage (Junior College) 22, 94–96 (2003)

[11] Deng, J., et al.: Computational Method. Xi'an Jiaotong University Press, Xi'an (1985)

[12] Schumaker, L.L.: Spline functions: basic theory. John Wiley & Sons, New York (1981)

[13] Bojanov, B.D., Hakopian, H.A., Sahakian, A.A.: Spline functions and multivariate interpolations. Kluwer Academic Publishers, London (1993)

[14] Cox, M.G.: The numerical evaluation of B-splines. J. Inst. Maths. Applications 10 (1972)

[15] Gordon, W.J., Riesenfeld, R.F.: B-spline curves and surfaces. Quart.Appl.Math. (1946)

[16] Wang, M.: MATLAB and Scientific Calculation, 2nd edn. China Power Press, Beijing (2003)

[17] Yang, X.: The Application of Numerical Methods to earthwork volume calculation in River embankment. Shuili Tiandi (8), 42 (2002)

[18] Liu, B., Xu, M.: Visual Basic How to Program. Tsinghua University Press, Beijing (2000)

[19] Wang, M., Song, T., Luo, Y.: Essential deficiency and improvement of the average cross-section method calculating the cannel earthwork volume. Journal of Northwest A&F University (Natural Science Edition) 32(9), 118–122 (2004)

A New Co-training Approach Based on SVM for Image Retrieval

Hui Liu[1,*], Hua Han[1], and Zhenhua Li[2]

[1] School of Computer Science and Technology, Shandong Economic University,
Jinan 250014, Shandong, China
[2] School of Control Science and Engineering, Shandong University,
Jinan 250061, Shandong, China
liuh_lh@sdie.edu.cn

Abstract. It's difficult to collect vast amounts of labeled data and easy for unlabeled data in collecting image characters. Therefore, it is necessary to define conditions to utilize the unlabeled examples enough. In this paper we present a new co-training approach based on SVM to define two learners, both learners are re-trained after every relevance feedback, and then each of them gives every image in a rank. Experiments show that using co-training idea in CBIR is beneficial, and achieves better performance than some existing methods.

Keywords: Content-based Image Retrieval, SVM, Unlabeled Data, Co-training.

1 Introduction

In recent years, some researches have introduced semi-supervised learning in Content Based Image Retrieval (CBIR). Different from traditional supervised learning which only makes use of labeled data, semi-supervised learning makes use of both labeled and unlabeled data. Generally, it's difficult to collect vast amounts of labeled data and easy for unlabeled data, moreover, the unlabeled data can be used to better describe the intrinsic geometrical structure of the data space, and hence improve the image retrieval performance.

So, learning from unlabeled examples has become a hot topic during the past few years, there are two main machine learning paradigms for this purpose: semi-supervised learning and active learning [1]. In semi-supervised learning there is a kind of co-training algorithm, which impliedly utilizes the clustering hypothesis or manifold hypothesis, and two or more learners. During the course of training, these learners select some unlabeled samples with high confidence to label each other, for updating the model continually.

---

* This work was supported by the Defence Industrial Technology Development Program (Grant No. B1420080209-08), the National Nature Science Foundation of China (Grant Nos. 61003104) and the Technical Plan Project of Shandong Province (Grant No. J07YJ11).

R. Chen (Ed.): ICICIS 2011, Part I, CCIS 134, pp. 77–81, 2011.

2   Co-training Method

The earliest co-training algorithm (the normal co-training algorithm) [2] was presented by A.Blum and T.Mitchell in 1998. It assumes that features can be split into two sets, each sub-feature set is sufficient to train a good classifier. After this, K.Nigam and R.Ghani[3] carried out experiment research about the problem that co-training algorithm hasn't abundant redundancy view, which indicates that when the attribute set is big enough, we can randomly partition the set into two views and can obtain better effect based on this. In 2000, S.Goldman and Y.Zhou[4] presented a new co-training algorithm that using two different classifiers instead of abundant redundancy view. Similarly Zhou and Li [5] propose 'tri-training' which uses three learners. If two of them agree on the classification of an unlabeled point, the classification is used to teach the third classifier.

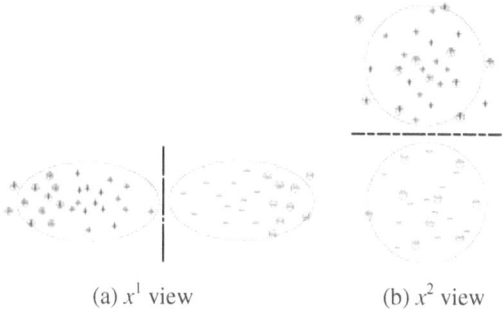

(a) x^1 view   (b) x^2 view

Fig. 1. Conditional independent assumption on feature split. With this assumption the high confident data points in x^1 view, represented by circled labels, will be randomly scattered in x^2 view.

One way to look at the co-training problem is to view the distribution D as a weighted bipartite graph, which we write as $G_D(X_1, X_2)$. The left-hand side of G_D has one node for each point in X_1 and the right-hand side has one node for each point in X_2. There is an edge (x_1, x_2) if and only if the example (x_1, x_2) has non-zero probability under D. We give this edge a weight equal to its probability.

3   Proposed Co-training Approach for Image Retrieval

From the view of machine learning, a normal user query is a labeled positive example, while the image database is a collection of unlabeled data, which is assumed that the database contains no annotation. Here let U denote the unlabeled data set while L denotes the labeled data set, $L = P \cup N$ where P and N respectively denote the sets of labeled positive examples and negative examples. Originally, U is the whole database DB, P is {query}, and N is empty. Let $|D|$ denote the size of a set D. Then the sizes of the original U, P and N are $|DB|$, 1, and 0, respectively.

In relevance feedback, the user may label several images according to whether they are relevant or not to a *query*, which could be viewed as providing additional positive or negative examples. Let $P*$ and $N*$ denote the new positive and negative examples, respectively. Since the feedback is usually performed on images in the database, both $P*$ and $N*$ are subsets of DB. Therefore, the relevance feedback process changes L and U. As for L, its positive subset P is enlarged to be $P \cup P*$, and its negative subset N is enlarged to be $N \cup N*$; but as for U, since some of its elements have been moved to L, it is shrunk to $U - (P* \cup N*)$.

Inspired by the co-training, our method attempts to exploit U to improve the performance of retrieval. Concretely, this method employs two learners. After obtaining the enlarged P and N, both learners are re-trained and then each of them gives every image in U a rank. Here the rank is a value between -1 and +1, where positive/negative means the learner judges the concerned image to be relevant/irrelevant, and the bigger the absolute value of the rank, the stronger the confidence of the learner on its judgement. Then, each learner will choose some unlabeled images to label for the other learner according to the rank information. After that, both the learners are re-trained with the enlarged labeled training sets and each of them will produce a new rank for images in U. The new ranks generated by the learners can be easily combined via summation, which results in the final rank for every image in U. Then, images with the top *resultsize* ranks are returned. Here *resultsize* specifies how many relevant images are anticipated to be retrieved. This parameter could be omitted so that all the images in the database are returned according to descending order of the real value of their ranks.

In our mehtod, in order to avoid a complicated learning process so that the real time requirement may be met, a very simple model is used, as shown in Eq.1, where $i \in \{1, 2\}$ is the index of the learner, x is the image or feature vector to be classified, P_i and N_i are respectively the set of labeled positive and negative examples in the current training set of L_i, Z_{norm} is used to normalize the result to (-1,1), ε is a small constant used to avoid a zero denominator, and Sim_i is the similarity measure adopted by L_i.

$$L_i(x, P_i, N_i) = (\sum_{y \in P_i} \frac{Sim_i(x, y)}{|P_i| + \varepsilon} - \sum_{z \in N_i} \frac{Sim_i(x, z)}{|N_i| + \varepsilon}) / Z_{norm} \qquad (1)$$

Here the similarity between the two d-dimensional feature vectors x' and y' is measured by the reciprocal of the Minkowski distance, as shown in Eq.2 where ζ is a small constant used to avoid a zero denominator.

$$Sim_i(x, y) = 1/((\sum_{j=1}^{d} |x_j' - y_j'|^{P_i} + \zeta) \qquad (2)$$

Indeed, the learners defined in Eq.2 are quite trivial, whose performance is determined by the contents of P_i and N_i.

4   Experiments

We used an image database with name COREL and size 3865. The COREL images can be considered as scenery and non-scenery. Scenery part has 2639 images consisting images containing the defined semantic categories, while non-scenery part has 1226 images including different kinds of textures, indoor, animals, molecules, etc.

Because the statistical average top-k precision is used as the performance measurement.

Table 1. Experimental results on top-20 images

method category	MRF		FGM		Our method	
	precision	recall	precision	recall	precision	recall
SKY	0.9568	0.9320	0.9538	0.9323	0.9605	0.9135
WATER	0.8336	0.8099	0.885	0.8669	0.88	0.9619
TREE_GRASS	0.88	0.8893	0.905	0.8702	0.9412	0.9160
FALLS_RIVER	0.8538	0.8631	0.9471	0.8859	0.9829	0.8745
FLOWER	0.9244	0.8736	0.912	0.9192	0.9385	0.9953
EARTH_ROCK_MO UNTAIN	0.9306	0.7893	0.9402	0.8429	0.9077	0.9042
ICE_SNOW_MOUN TAIN	0.913	0.7969	0.9496	0.8659	0.9302	0.9195
SUNSET	0.8504	0.8915	0.9012	0.8649	0.9633	0.9112
NIGHT	0.7703	0.7703	0.8313	0.7860	0.7829	0.8560
SHADING	0.697	0.5331	0.7234	0.6615	0.8119	0.6381

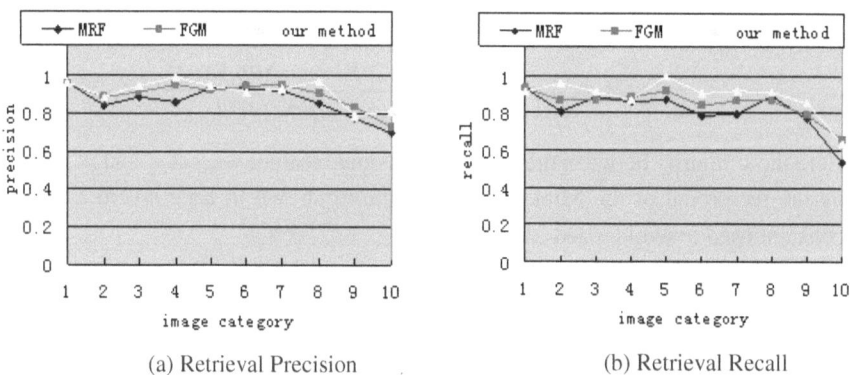

(a) Retrieval Precision   (b) Retrieval Recall

Fig. 2. Experimental results on top-20 images

Table 1 and Fig. 2 show our results along with those of previous works. Our method presents a new fuzzy set framework combining Markov random field (MRF) and morphological idea, uses the Fuzzy Attributed Relational Graphs (FARGs) to model the vagueness associated with the attributes of image objects and their relationships. It solves the problem of "all-or-nothing" definition that leads to unsatisfactory results in several situations, and does better work on image retrieval precision and recall than traditional methods.

5 Conclusion

In this paper, we present a new co-training approach applying in image retrieval, which combines the Support Vector Machines (SVM) and relevance feedback method. The new algorithm employs two learners, both learners are re-trained and then each of them gives every image in a rank, that means the learner judges the concerned image to be relevant/irrelevant, and each learner will choose some unlabeled images to label for the other learner according to the rank information. Experimental results show that in this new method the unlabeled can be used to enhance the retrieval performance, and in our image retrieval system, the proposed method achieves better performance than some existing methods, such as MRF and FGM.

There are still several questions that remain unclear. We have found that only if some unlabeled data satisfying the model assumption and the distribution of labeled data can be identified, using them in co-training method might be better than simply trying to use all the unlabeled data or randomly picking some to use, which is another issue to be explored in the future. We are currently working on these problems.

References

1. Zhou, Z.-H., Chen, K.-J.: Enhancing Relevance Feedback in Image Retrieval Using Unlabeled Data. ACM Journal Name (TBD), 1–25 (2006)
2. Blum, A., Mitchell, T.: Combining labeled and unlabeled data with co-training. In: Proceedings of the 11th Annual Conference on Computational Learning Theory (COLT 1998), Wisconsin, MI, pp. 92–100 (1998)
3. Nigam, K., Ghani, R.: Analyzing the effectiveness and applicability of co-training. In: Proceedings of the 9th ACM International Conference on Information and Knowledge Management (CIKM 2000), McLean, VA, pp. 86–93 (2000)
4. Goldman, S., Zhou, Y.: Enhancing supervised learning with unlabeled data. In: Proceedings of the 17th International Conference on Machine Learning (ICML 2000), San Francisco, CA, pp. 327–334 (2000)
5. Zhou, Z.-H., Li, M.: Tri-training: exploiting unlabeled data using three classifiers. IEEE Transactions on Knowledge and Data Engineering 17, 1529–1541

Recognizing Human Activities Using Non-linear SVM Decision Tree

Haiyong Zhao, Zhijing Liu, and Hao Zhang

School of Computer Science and Technology, Xidian University, Xi'an, P.R. China
zhaohaiyongym@163.com, liuzhijing@vip.163.com,
zhanghao@mail.xidian.edu.cn

Abstract. This paper presents a new method of human activity recognition, which is based on $\Re$ transform and non-linear SVM Decision Tree (NSVMDT). For a key binary human silhouette, $\Re$ transform is employed to represent low-level features. The advantage of the $\Re$ transform lies in its low computational complexity and geometric invariance. We utilize NSVMDT to train and classify video sequences, and demonstrate the usability with many sequences. Compared with other methods, ours is superior because the descriptor is robust to frame loss in superior because the descriptor is robust to frame loss in activities recognition, simple representation, computational complexity and template generalization. Sufficient experiments have proved the efficiency.

Keywords: feature extraction, activity recognition, $\Re$ transform, NSVMDT.

1 Introduction

Even great efforts have been made for decades, the recognition of human activities is still an immature technology that attracted plenty of people in computer vision[1]. Reliable and effective solutions to this problem would be highly useful in many areas, such as behavioral biometrics [2], contend-based video analysis [3], security and surveillance [4], [5]. A large amount of work has been done on the active topic over the past decades, as the reviews [6], [7], [8], [9] have summarized.

Building a general and effective activity recognition and classification system is a challenging task, due to the various parameters from the environment, objects and activities. Variations in the environment can be caused by cluttered or moving background, camera motion, occlusion, weather and illumination. Variations in the objects are caused by differences in appearance, size or posture of the objects or due to self-motion which is not itself part of the activity. Variations in the activity can make it difficult to recognize semantically equivalent activities.

As in many vision-related problems, feature extraction is an element operation for the recognition of human activities. This paper describes a simple and unique representation of activities with $\Re$ transform as the template, since they are detected and extracted based on the whole image from the video sequence, rather than some parts of the image. This is contrary to the work of Gorelick et al [10], where a whole image sequence is represented as a space-time shape.

R. Chen (Ed.): ICICIS 2011, Part I, CCIS 134, pp. 82–92, 2011.

In machine learning, there are two main approaches to perform classification: generative learning or discriminative learning. It has been shown that discriminative classifiers often achieve better performance than generative classifiers in supervised learning. For example, support vector machines (SVMs) directly maximize the margin of a linear separator between two sets of points in the vector space. Since the model is linear and simple, the maximum margin criterion is more appropriate than maximum likelihood or other generative model criteria. In computer vision, person detection and recognition have been dominated by SVM [11] frameworks which surpass maximum likelihood generative models. Thus, in activity classification with labeled training samples in this paper, support vector machines would be superior to the generative classifiers.

In this paper, a smart surveillance system is proposed, whose framework is described as follows:

(I) Detecting and locating people by background subtraction approach.

(II) Extracting shape feature and representing a posture by $\Re$ transform.

(III) Recognizing activities of people by SVM multi-class classifier. The Support Vector Machine technology and the decision tree have combined into one multi-class classifier, which called Non-linear SVM Decision Tree (NSVMDT).

The rest of the paper is organized as follows. Section 2 describes the extraction of the human blobs by background subtraction and the information of the features. Section 3 introduces the structure design of the multi-class support vector machine classifier (NSVMDT). In Section 4, experiments are performed to demonstrate the effectiveness of the method. The conclusion is given in Section 5.

2 Feature Extraction of Activities

2.1 Background Modeling and Subtraction

The first step in our proposed system is to segment motion targets in a surveillance video shot by a camera mounted on the wall. Extracting moving blobs provides a focus of attention for later processes like activity recognition, where only those changing pixels are subject to consideration. However, changes of illumination, shadow and repetitive motion from clutter make the segmentation unreliable. Several motion detection approaches such as background subtraction, temporal difference, and optical flow are generally used, where the background subtraction is particularly popular especially under the situations with a relatively static camera. It attempts to detect moving targets in an image by subtracting a reference background image from the current image pixel-wisely. In our case, a non-parameter background model [12] is adopted, where the probability density function at each pixel is worked out from multiple samples by kernel density estimation technique.

Suppose that $x_1, x_2, \ldots, x_N$ are N temporally sampled features in a pixel position, the observation at time t is x_t, and its probability density function can be estimated using kernel density as:

$$p(x_t) = \sum_{i=1}^{N} \alpha_i K_h(x_t - x_i) \qquad (1)$$

where K_h is a kernel function with window length h, a_i is the normalized coefficient, and usually $a_i=1/N$.

In (12), kernel function K_h is chosen as normal distribution $N(0,\Sigma)$ where Σ is kernel bandwidth. Supposing the kernel bandwidth of three color components is independent one another and the bandwidth of the jth component is σ_j^2, then $\Sigma = diag(\sigma_1^2, \sigma_2^2, \sigma_3^2)$, where diag (.) denotes a diagonal matrix. The probability density function of x_t can be written as:

$$p(x_t) = \frac{1}{N} \sum_{i=1}^{N} \prod_{j=1}^{d} \frac{1}{\sqrt{2\pi\sigma_j^2}} e^{-\frac{(x_{t_j} - x_{i_j})^2}{2\sigma_j^2}} \tag{2}$$

Where d is the number of color components. The kernel bandwidth σ can be estimated by calculating the median absolute deviation over samples. A pixel is considered as the foreground pixel if p (x_t) < th, where the threshold th is a global threshold. In the model-updating phase, a long-term model and blind update are used. In order to eliminate illumination influence and noise, shadow detection and removal, morphologic processing and connectivity component analysis are employed. Experiments show that this method can also shape an integrated object contour, ensure the connectivity of moving object, and the detection result is quite good, as shown in Fig. 1.

(a)Background image   (b)Current frame image   (c)Extracted contour

Fig. 1. The results of human contour extraction

2.2 Feature Extraction

Feature Extraction is a key bridge between low level image features and high level activity understanding [13], [14]. We extract and represent activity features by $\mathfrak{R}$ transform, which is defined by which is an extended Radon transform [15].

Two dimensional Radon transform is the integral of a function over the set of lines in all directions, which is roughly equivalent to finding the projection of a shape on any given line. For a discrete binary image f(x, y), its Radon transform is defined by [16]:

$$\begin{aligned} T_{R^f}(\rho,\theta) &= \int_{-\infty}^{\infty} \int_{-\infty}^{\infty} f(x,y)\delta(x\cos\theta + y\sin\theta - \rho)dxdy \\ &= R\{f(x,y)\} \end{aligned} \tag{3}$$

Where $\theta \in [0,\pi]$, $\rho \in [-\infty, \infty]$ and $\delta(.)$ is the Dirac delta-function,

$$\delta(x) = \begin{cases} 1 & if \ x = 0 \\ 0 & otherwise \end{cases} \tag{4}$$

However, Radon transform is sensitive to the operation of scaling, translation and rotation, and hence an improved representation, called $\Re$ Transform, is introduced [16], [21]:

$$\Re_f(\theta) = \int_{-\infty}^{\infty} T_{R^f}^2(\rho,\theta)d\rho \tag{5}$$

$\Re$ transform has several useful properties in shape representation for activity recognition [16],[21]:

(1) Translate the image by a vector $\bar{\mu} = (x_0, y_0)$,

$$\int_{-\infty}^{\infty} T_{R^f}^2((\rho - x_0 \cos\theta - y_0 \sin\theta),\theta)d\rho$$
$$= \int_{-\infty}^{\infty} T_{R^f}^2(v,\theta)d\rho = \Re_f(\theta) \tag{6}$$

(2) Scale the image by a factor α,

$$\frac{1}{\alpha^2} \int_{-\infty}^{\infty} T_{R^f}^2(\alpha\rho,\theta)d\rho$$
$$= \frac{1}{\alpha^3} \int_{-\infty}^{\infty} T_{R^f}^2(v,\theta)d\theta = \frac{1}{\alpha^3} \Re_f(\theta) \tag{7}$$

(3) Rotate the image by an angle θ_0,

$$\int_{-\infty}^{\infty} T_{R^f}^2(\rho,\theta+\theta_0)d\rho = \Re_f(\theta + \theta_0) \tag{8}$$

According to the symmetric property of Radon transform, and let $v=-\rho$,

$$\int_{-\infty}^{\infty} T_{R^f}^2(-\rho,\theta\pm\pi)d\rho = -\int_{\infty}^{-\infty} T_{R^f}^2(v,\theta\pm\pi)dv$$
$$= \int_{-\infty}^{\infty} T_{R^f}^2(v,\theta\pm\pi)dv = \Re_f(\theta\pm\pi) \tag{9}$$

From equations (6)-(9), one can see that:

(1) Translation in the plane does not change the result of $\Re$ transform.

(2) A scaling of the original image only induces the change of amplitude. Here in order to remove the influence of body size, the result of $\Re$ transform is normalized to the range of [0, 1].

(3) A rotation of θ_0 in the original image leads to the phase shift of θ_0 in $\Re$ transform. In this paper, recognized activities rarely have such rotation.

(4) Considering Equation (9), the period of $\Re$ transform is π. Thus a shape vector with 180 dimensions is sufficient to represent the spatial information of silhouette.

Therefore, $\Re$ transform is robust to geometry transformation, which is appropriate for activity representation. According to [17], $\Re$ transform outperforms other moment based descriptors, such as Wavelet moment, Zernike moment and Invariant moment, on similar but actually different shape sequences, and even in the case of noisy data.

We represent activity features with $\Re$ transform and modeling by the average of $\Re$ transform. The red curve in the third column is shown in Fig. 2. The activities in dataset, i.e. walk, run, bend, jump, crouch and faint, are defined by 1 to 6 respectively.

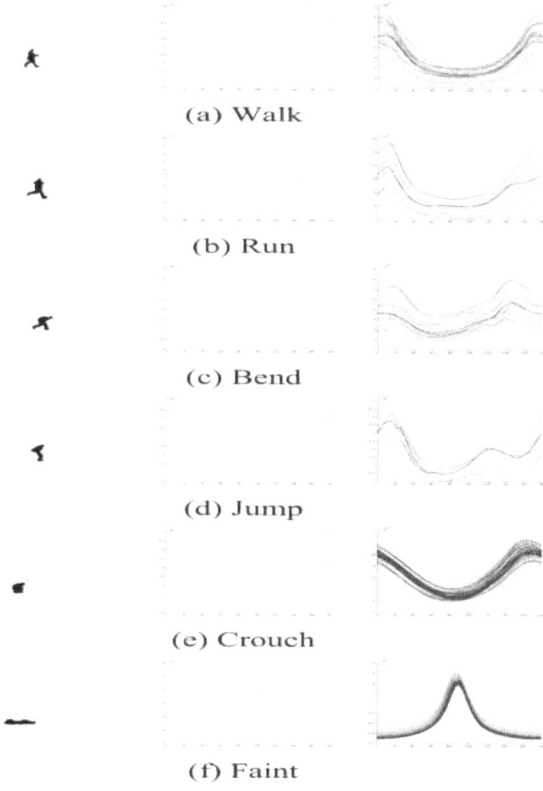

(a) Walk

(b) Run

(c) Bend

(d) Jump

(e) Crouch

(f) Faint

Fig. 2. The $\Re$ transform of single and multiple frames for different activities

3 Action Learning and Classification

SVM is designed for two-class problems both positive and negative objects exist, but practical classification applications are multi-class problems. In this paper, SVM is extended to non-linear by using kernel functions. Then non-linear SVM combines with decision tree to solve multi-class classification problems. We call this method is NSVM Decision Tree.

In the case of non-linear, we can calculate the relativity separability measure between class i and class j after non-linear mapping.

For input sample z_1 and z_2, non-linear mapping map them into the feature space H, then the Euclidean distance between z_1 and z_2 in H is:

$$d^H(z_1, z_2) = \sqrt{K(z_1, z_1) - 2K(z_1, z_2) + K(z_2, z_2)} \tag{10}$$

Where K(.,.)is the kernel function. In the space H, m_Φ is the class center and $m_\Phi = \dfrac{1}{n}\sum_{i=1}^{1}\Phi(x_i)$, here n is the number of samples within class.

For the training samples $\{x_1, x_2,..., x_n\}$ of a given class, the mapping Φ map them into feature space H, the distance between training sample x and class center m_Φ is:

$$d^H(x, m_\Phi) = \sqrt{K(x, x_i) - \frac{2}{n}\sum_{i=1}^{n}K(x, x_i) + \frac{1}{n^2}\sum_{i=1}^{n}\sum_{j=1}^{n}K(x_i, x_j)} \tag{11}$$

then in feature space the class variance can be get:

$$\sigma^H = \frac{1}{n-1}\sum_{i=1}^{n}d^H(x_i, m_\Phi) \tag{12}$$

Therefore, the relativity separability measure between class i and class j in feature space H is:

$$rsm_{ij}^{H} = \frac{d^H(m^i_\Phi, m^j_\Phi)}{(\sigma_i^H + \sigma_j^H)} \tag{13}$$

If $rsm_{ij}^{H} \geq 1$, then there is no overlap between class i and class j, and if $rsm_{ij}^{H} < 1$, there is overlap between them. The bigger the rsm_{ij}^{H}, the more easily separated between class i and class j.

We then define rsm_{ij}^{H} as the relativity separability measure of class i from the others, and we have the formula:

$$rsm_i^{H} = \min_{\substack{j=1,...,k \\ j \neq i}} rsm_{ij}^{H} \tag{14}$$

From the formula we can know that the relativity separability measure of class i is the minimum one between class i and the others.

4   Experiment Analysis and Discussion

4.1   Experiment Data

The videos used are taken from activity database shot by Institute of Automation, Chinese Academy of Sciences (CASIA). In this database, there are two sets of activities, including single person and two interactive persons. Each of them is screened in 3 visual angles, i.e. horizontal, vertical and angle. The dataset of single person contains 8 classes per angle, including 11 or 16 flips (320×240, 25fps) respectively. All flips are shot outdoors by stationary camera, including 16 persons in 8 types of activities. In our system, the video flips of single person in horizontal view, i.e. walk, run, bend, jump, crouch and faint, are used for experiment, as shown in Fig. 3.

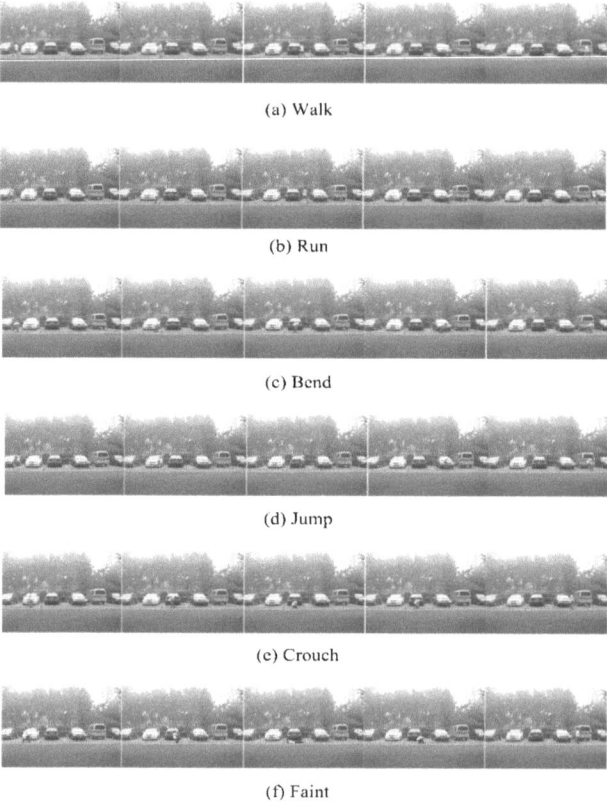

(a) Walk

(b) Run

(c) Bend

(d) Jump

(e) Crouch

(f) Faint

Fig. 3. The sequences of activities

The features of each action type are extracted using the method proposed in this paper. The resultant silhouettes contain holes and intrusions due to imperfect subtraction, shadows and color similarities with the background. To train the activity models, holes, shadows and other noise are removed manually. The synthetic data are taken as ground truth data.

The raw data include such cases as disjoint silhouettes, silhouettes with holes and silhouettes with missing parts. Compared with the ground truth data, they are incomplete data. Shadow and other noises may add an extra part to the human silhouette, and thus induce redundant data. The incomplete data and redundant data are of low quality, and thus they are used for testing the performance of the $\Re$ transform. Fig. 4 shows some such examples.

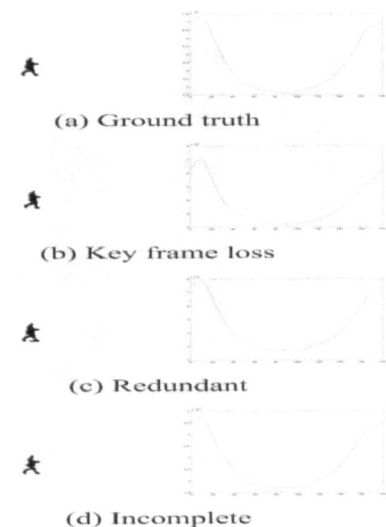

(a) Ground truth

(b) Key frame loss

(c) Redundant

(d) Incomplete

Fig. 4. The $\Re$ transform for data of different qualities

In order to test the robustness of $\Re$ transform, we select the frame with less feature information rather than the frames shown in Fig.2. In other words, we use the frames near the key one to substitute. These artificially generated data are defined as key frame loss data.

Fig. 4 shows the $\Re$ transform of the walking shape in different data case. For the cases of incomplete data and ground truth data, the $\Re$ transform is similar, but the transform of redundant data varies significantly in the peak of the curve. In fact, $\Re$ transform is sensitive to the redundant data, which will have negative effect on activity recognition.

4.2 Result Analysis

Fig. 5 illustrates the recognition results with $\Re$ transform and NSVMDT in different data. Note that there are more activity sequences in each probe class, which are different with gallery data. Fig. 6 concludes that, in spite of the high similarities between running and walking, misclassifications never occur in the case of key frame loss data and incomplete data. The $\Re$ transform descriptor captures both boundary and internal content of the shape, so they are more robust to noise, such as internal holes and separated shape. While in the case of silhouette with shadow, the performance of $\Re$ transform is slightly worse than other cases. This shows that $\Re$ transform is suitable for the background segmentation methods with low false positive rate but keeping some false negative rate. Generally speaking, low level features based on $\Re$ transform are effective for recognizing similar activity even in the case of noisy data.

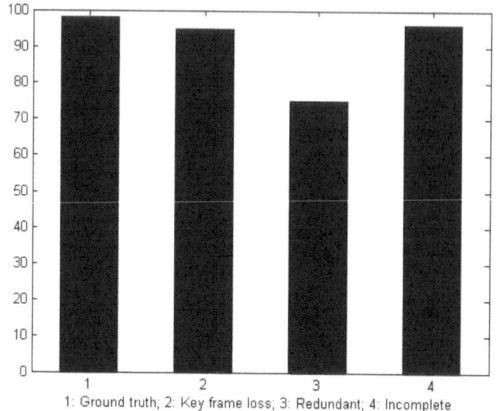

100
90
80
70
60
50
40
30
20
10
0
1
2
3
4
1: Ground truth; 2: Key frame loss; 3: Redundant; 4: Incomplete

Fig. 5. The recognition rates of $\Re$ transform with different data

	Walk	Run	Bend	Jump	Crouch	Faint
Walk	97.25	3.85		3.13		
Run	2.75	96.15		3.13		
Bend			100			
Jump				93.75		
Crouch					100	
Faint						100

Fig. 6. The confusion matrix of six activities (%)

4.3 Result Analysis

As shown in Table 1, our method not only outperforms other three methods, but also has three advantages as follow. Firstly, it has lower computational complexity. The key frames extracted from video sequences are utilized in feature matching, so that it costs less time compared with Chen's work [18], which matches features in two sequences. Secondly, its representation is simple. Though Oikonomopoulos' work [19] represents activities with a codebook in details, it is more complex and ambiguous than our method using $\Re$ transform descriptor. Finally, our method is general for different activities. We only use one descriptor, $\Re$ transform, to represent six different activities and extract their features, while Ikizler's work [20] uses HOR and velocity to implement it. In general, our method has made significant improvement in many aspects.

Table 1. Comparison of our method to other methods that have reported results

Method	Average accuracy (%)
Chen et al [18]	85.9
Oikonomopoulos et al [19]	93.0
Ikizler and Duygulu [20]	94.7
Our method	95.3

5 Conclusion

In this paper, we have approached the problem of human activity recognition and used a new pose descriptor based on $\Re$ transform. Our pose descriptor is simple and effective, since we extract activity features from a human silhouette in the whole image. We show that, by effective classification using NSVMDT, reliable human activity recognition is possible. We demonstrate the effectiveness of our method over the state-of-the-art datasets in activity recognition literature, which is CASIA dataset. Our results are intuitively comparable and even superior to the results presented by the pioneers.

References

1. Turaga, P., Chellappa, R., Subrahmanian, V.S.: Octavian Udrea: Machine Recognition of Human Activities: A Survey. J. IEEE Trans. Circuits Syst. Video Technol. 18, 1473–1488 (2008)
2. Sarkar, S., Phillips, P.J., Liu, Z., Vega, I.R., Grother, P., Bowyer, K.W.: The Human ID gait challenge problem: Data sets, performance, and analysis. J. IEEE Trans. Pattern Anal. Mach. Intell. 27, 162–177 (2005)
3. Rui, Y., Huang, T.S., Chang, S.F.: Image retrieval: Current techniques, promising directions and open issues. J. Visual Commun. Image Represent. 10, 39–62 (1999)
4. Vaswani, N., Roy-Chowdhury, A.K., Chellappa, R.: Shape activity: A continuous-state HMM for moving/deforming shapes with application to abnormal activity detection. J. IEEE Trans. Image Process. 14, 1603–1616 (2005)
5. Zhong, H., Shi, J., Visontai, M.: Detecting unusual activity in video. In: 2004 IEEE Conference on Computer Vision and Pattern Recognition, pp. 819–826. IEEE Press, Los Alamitos (2004)
6. Aggarwal, J.K., Cai, Q.: Human motion analysis: A review. J. Computer vision and Image Understanding 73, 428–440 (1999)
7. Gavrila, D.M.: The visual analysis of human movement: A survey. J. Computer vision and Image Understanding 73, 82–98 (1999)
8. Pavan, T., Rama, C., Subrahmanian, V.S., Octavian, U.: Machine Recognition of Human Activities: A Survey. J. IEEE Trans. Circuits Syst. Video Technol. 18, 1473–1488 (2008)
9. Poppe, R.: Vision-based human motion analysis: An overview. J. Computer Vision and Image Understanding 108, 4–18 (2007)
10. Gorelick, L., Blank, M., Shechtman, E., Irani, M., Basri, R.: Actions as space-time shapes. J. IEEE Trans. Pattern Anal. Mach. Intell. 29, 2247–2253 (2007)

11. Nakajim, A.C., Itoh, N., Pontil, M.: Object recognition and detection by a combination of support vector machine and rotation invariant phase only correlation. In: 15th International Conference on Pattern Recognition, pp. 4787–4790. IEEE Comput. Soc., Los Alamitos (2000)
12. Elgammal, A., Harwood, D., Davis, L.: Non-parametric model for background subtraction. In: Vernon, D. (ed.) ECCV 2000. LNCS, vol. 1843, pp. 751–767. Springer, Heidelberg (2000)
13. Pla, F., Ribeiro, P., Santos-victor, J., Bernardino, R.: Extracting Motion Features for Visual Human Activity Representation. In: Marques, J.S., Pérez de la Blanca, N., Pina, P. (eds.) IbPRIA 2005. LNCS, vol. 3522, pp. 537–544. Springer, Heidelberg (2005)
14. Hongeng, S., Nevatia, R., Bremond, F.: Video-based event recognition: activity representation and probabilistic recognition methods. J. Comput. Vision Image Understandi. 96, 129–162 (2004)
15. Tabbone, S., Wendling, L., Salmon, J.-P.: A new shape descriptor defined on the Radon transform. J. Comput. Vision Image Understanding 102, 42–51 (2006)
16. Deans, S.R.: Applications of the Radon Transform. Wiley Interscience Publications, Chichester (1983)
17. Ying, W., Kaiqi, H., Tieniu, T.: Human Activity Recognition Based on $\Re$ Transform. In: The 2007 IEEE Comput. Soc. Conf. Comput. Vision Pattern Recognition, pp. 3722–3729. IEEE Society, Minneapolis (2007)
18. Yan, C., Qiang, W., Xiangjian, H.: Using Dynamic Programming to Match Human Behavior Sequences. In: The 10th International Conference on Control, Automation, Robotics and Vision, pp. 1498–1503. IEEE, NJ (2008)
19. Oikonomopoulos, A., Pantic, M., Patras, I.: B-spline Polynomial Descriptors for Human Activity Recognition. In: The 2008 IEEE Computer Society Conference on Computer Vision and Pattern Recognition Workshops, pp. 1–6. IEEE Press, NJ (2008)
20. Ikizler, N., Duygulu, P.: Histogram of oriented rectangles: A new pose descriptor for human action recognition. J. Image and Vision Computing 27, 1515–1526 (2009)

Research on Logistics Service Providers Selection Based on AHP and VIKOR

Lu Shan

Management-Business School of Hunan University of Commerce, 410205 Changsha, China
lushan20031020@163.com

Abstract. The logistics service providers supply a kind of service which is a service product, thus there is a plenty of uncertainty and fuzzy in selecting logistics service providers. AHP is first used to calculate the weights of logistics services providers evaluations and then VIKOR method developed for multi-criteria optimization determining a compromise solution is applied to select the logistics services providers. The latter method provides a maximum "group utility" for the "majority" and minimum of an individual regret for the "opponent". This decision making process of logistics services providers selection is verified to be scientific and feasible through the empirical research.

Keywords: logistics services providers; providers selection; VIKOR method; AHP.

1 Introduction

It is a haunted problem for many enterprises to select the best partner from a lot of logistics services providers when the logistics business outsourcing is conducted. Rational selection of logistics services providers takes advantage of the enterprises' profession and cost to achieve such goals as logistics routing optimization, the logistics links efficiency increase with every link joined together well. With the advantage of the node firms' core business, they benefit from it and consolidate their core competence. Therefore, it is significantly important for the enterprises to select logistics services providers so as to strengthen the supply chain competence as well as improve the ability to respond to the demands of end customers.

The traditional supply chain providers selection issues focus on the providers that offer the products but the third-party logistics providers offer the logistics demanders a kind of service rather than a real product, namely service products. Thus, there is a plenty of uncertainty and fuzzy in the selection of logistics service providers. At present, many methods are applied for logistics services providers selection at home and abroad, for examples, the fuzzy comprehensive evaluation method[1], the Analytic Hierarchy Process(AHP)[2], the Principal Component Analysis(PCA), TOPSIS[3], and the Data Envelopment Analysis(DEA)[4]. Whereas, some of these methods consider only the overall satisfaction (i.e. maximum "group utility") and some consider

R. Chen (Ed.): ICICIS 2011, Part I, CCIS 134, pp. 93–98, 2011.

only the regret of the selection of wrong alternative(i.e.. minimum of the individual regret of the "opponent"). In VIKOR linear normalization considering the decision makers' preference, the VIKOR determines a compromise solution, providing a maximum "group utility" for the "majority" and minimum of an individual regret for the "opponent". Although VIKOR is similar to TOPSIS, it is improved in data normalization. AHP is first used to calculate the weights of logistics services providers evaluations and then VIKOR method applied to select the logistics services providers in this paper. At the end of this paper, this method is verified by an example of logistics services providers selection.

2 Determination of Evaluation Indices of Logistics Services Providers Selection

From the research on the third-party logistics by Steven E. et. al, "benefit of customers" and "reliability" are the most important elements in selection of the third-party logistics[5]. As a result, such evaluation indices representing the third-party logistics service characteristics as service level, service quality are listed in the index system. The strategic allied win-win relationship should be established between the logistics services providers and logistics demanders, thus, the strategic allied relationship consolidation is also an important factor from the view of enterprise alliance and history[6]. In view of this, this paper classifies the criteria of logistics services providers selection into service price, service quality, service ability and alliance. The service price is represented by service quoted price, the strain capacity of price, etc. The service quality is represented by the delivery accuracy rate and perfectness ratio of goods, etc. The service ability is represented by on-time delivery, information exchange ability, etc. The alliance is represented by the compatible strategic ideas and sharing of benefits and risks.

3 Method of Logistics Services Providers Selection Based on AHP and VIKOR

3.1 VIKOR Method

The VIKOR method was presented as a multi-criteria decision making method by Opricovic. It determines a compromise solution, based on the reference points[7]. The positive-ideal solution and negative-ideal solution should first be defined in the basic principle of VIKOR method. The positive-ideal solution is the best alternative according to the criteria, while the negative-ideal solution, the worst. The compromise ranking-list is determined according to the "closeness" between the evaluation value and the ideal alternative[8].

Determine the positive-ideal solution and negative-ideal solution.

$$f_i^* = [(\max_j f_{ij} \mid i \in I_1), (\min_j f_{ij} \mid i \in I_2)] \forall i \tag{1}$$

$$f_i^- = [(\min_j f_{ij} \mid i \in I_2), (\max_j f_{ij} \mid i \in I_2)] \forall i \tag{2}$$

where j is the alternative and i is the criterion; f_{ij} is the value of i th criterion function for the alternative j, obtained by the questionnaire; I_1 is the set of efficiency evaluation criteria, I_2 is the set of cost evaluation criteria; f_i^* the positive-ideal solution, f_i^- negative-ideal solution.

Compute the values S_j and R_j

$$S_j = \sum_{j=1}^{n} [\omega_i (f_i^* - f_{ij}) / (f_i^* - f_i^-)] \forall j \tag{3}$$

$$R_j = \max_i [\omega_i (f_i^* - f_{ij}) / (f_i^* - f_i^-)] \forall j \tag{4}$$

where ω_i are the weights of i th criteria, obtained by AHP; S_j is the group utility of the alternatives, and the less S_j, the greater the group utility; R_j is the individual regret of the "opponent", and the less R_j, the smaller the individual regret.

Compute the value Q_j expressing the benefit ration generated by alternatives

$$Q_j = \lambda \frac{S_j - S^*}{S^- - S^*} + (1 - \lambda) \frac{R_j - R^*}{R^- - R^*}$$

where

$$S^* = \min\{S_j, j = 1, \cdots, n\} \quad , \quad S^- = \max\{S_j, j = 1, \cdots, n\} \quad ,$$

$$R^* = \min\{S_j, j = 1, \cdots, n\}, \quad R^- = \max\{S_j, j = 1, \cdots, n\}$$

λ is introduced as weight of the strategy of "the majority of criteria" . When $\lambda > 0.5$, "voting by majority rule" is needed, or "by consensus" $\lambda \approx 0.5$, or "with veto" $\lambda < 0.5$. Here $\lambda = 0.5$ expresses a maximum group utility and minimum individual regret[8].

Rank the alternatives in ascending order and obtain three ranking lists with the best alternative listed with the first position.

Propose as a compromise solution the alternative which is ranked the best by the measure Q_j (minimum) if the following two conditions (C1 & C2) are satisfied:

C1. "Acceptable advantage": $Q(b^F) - Q(b^S) \geq 1/(n-1)$ where b^F is the alternative with second position in the ranking list by Q while b^S is the alternative with first position in the ranking list by Q. n is the number of alternatives.

C2. "Acceptable stability in decision making": Alternative b^F must also be the best ranked by S or/and Q. This compromise solution is stable within a decision making process. Ranked by Q, S of the alternative with first position is better than the alternative with second position or R of the alternative with first position is better than the alternative with second position. When there are several alternatives, the condition C2 should be determined to be satisfied or not between the first, second and third alternative.

Criteria: if the relation between the first position alternative and the second position alternative satisfies both C1 and C2, the first position alternative is the best one. If the relation between the first position alternative and the second position alternative satisfies C2, both the alternatives are the best ones. If the relation between the first position alternative and the other alternatives doesn't satisfy C1 but only C2, the alternatives not satisfying C1 are the best[9].

3.2 Determine the Weights by AHP

The basic principle of AHP is decomposing the complex decision into its decision elements building a hierarchy and then making comparisons between each possible pair in each cluster to determine their relative importance (as a fuzzy judgment matrix). The weighs of present level's elements related to the upper criterion are obtained by the characteristic root and eigenvector calculated[10]. The judgment matrix expresses the comparison of relative importance between present level's related elements and upper level's one element.

4 Empirical Analysis

Four logistics services providers are selected to be evaluated through the previous index system and models.

Determine the weights by AHP: the index weights are obtained by the experts according to the fuzzy matrix constructed by index system. The each index weight are obtained by AHP as $W = (0.26, 0.37, 0.16, 0.21)$.

Evaluate the four logistics services providers by VIKOR: the index elements evaluation values are obtained after the initial data from the four logistics services providers are dimensionless processed and normalized, illustrated as Table 1.

Table 1. Data dimensionless and normalized from four logistics services providers

Alternatives(firms)	Service price	Service quality	Service ability	alliance
b_1	1	1	0.865	0.728
b_2	0.893	0.926	0.913	0.962
b_3	0.746	0.912	1	1
b_4	0.949	0.989	0.957	1

Determine the positive-ideal solution and negative-ideal solution of alternatives with the criteria.

The positive-ideal solution f_i^* =(1,1,1,1), The negative-ideal solution f_i^- = (0.746,0.912, 0.865,0.728).

According to the VIKOR, S,R,Q of the four logistics services providers are presented in Table 2.

Table 2. Four logistics services providers order by S,R,Q

	b_1	b_2	b_3	b_4
S	0.370 (2)	0.553 (3)	0.630 (4)	0.149 (1)
R	0.210 (2)	0.311 (3)	0.370 (4)	0.052 (1)
Q	0.4786 (2)	0.8281 (3)	1 (4)	0 (1)

According to C1 of VIKOR, acceptable advantage $Q(b^F) - Q(b^S) \geq 1/(n-1) =$ 0.333, b_1 and b_2, b_1 and b_3, b_1 and b_4, b_2 and b_4, b_3 and b_4 all satisfy C1 except for b_2 and b_3, and four logistics services providers satisfy C2. So the conclusion can be drawn that b_4 is the best alternative and b_1 is the better alternative, the preference order is $b_4 > b_1 > b_2 > b_3$. This result is acceptable in the logistics services providers selection so that it is verified to be valid.

5 Conclusion

The traditional supply chain providers selection issues focus on the providers that offer the products but the third-party logistics providers offer the logistics demanders a kind of service rather than a real product, namely service products. Thus there is a plenty of uncertainty and fuzzy in selection of logistics service providers. AHP is first used to calculate the weights of logistics services providers evaluations and then VIKOR method is applied to select the logistics services providers make the decision making process more scientific. However, with the development of science and technology, many elements need to be considered to improve the method and index system of logistics services providers selection in the practical selection of logistics services providers.

Acknowledgement

The work in the paper is supported by Hunan Nature Sciences Fund item (10JJ6112), Research Project of China Society of Logistics (2010CSLKT162) and Outstanding

Youth of Scientific Research Project of Hunan Provincial Education Department (09B056).

References

1. Sanjay, J., Shankar, R.: Selection of Logistics Service Provider: An Analytic. Network Process (ANP) Approach, Omega 3, 274–289 (2007)
2. Isklar, G., Alptekin, E., Buyuksozk, G.: Application of a hybrid intelligent decision support model in logistics outsourcing. Computers & Operations Research 12, 3701–3714 (2007)
3. Wang, J., Cheng, C., Huang, K.: Fuzzy Hierarchical TOPSIS for Supplier Selection. Applied Soft Computing 9, 377–386 (2009)
4. Saen, R.F.: A Mathematical Model for Selecting Third-party Reverse Logistics Providers. International Journal of Procurement Management 2, 180–190 (2009)
5. Saen, R.F.: A Mathematical Model for Selecting Third-party Reverse Logistics Providers. International Journal of Procurement Management 2, 180–190 (2009)
6. Qiao, H., Zhao, Q.: Research on Third Party Logistics Service Capability Maturity Model. In: International Conference 2008 Service Operations, Logistics and Informatics, pp. 2858–2861. IEEE Press, Los Alamitos (2008)
7. Opricovic, S., Gwo-Hshiung, T.: Compromise solution by MCDM methods: a comparative analysis of VIKOR and TOPSIS. European Journal of Operational Research 2, 445–455 (2004)
8. Xiao, Z.X.: A note on the subjective and objective integrated approach to determine attributes weights. European Journal of Operational Research 2, 530–532 (2004)
9. Tong, L.I., Chen, C.C., Wang, C.H.: Optimization of multi-response processes using the VIKOR method. International Journal of Advanced Manufacturing Technology 11, 1049–1057 (2007)
10. Lee, A.H.I., Kang, H.Y., Wang, W.P.: Analysis of priority mix planning for semiconductor fabrication under uncertainty. International Journal of Advanced Manufacturing Technology 3, 143–157 (2006)

Research on Digitized Scenario for Tactical Internet Simulative Training

Jian-jun Shen, Hua Tian, and Zhi-chun Gan

Dept. of Information Warfare, Commanding Communications Academy,
No. 45, Jiefang Park Road, Wuhan, China
shjj06@126.com

Abstract. The scenario of Tactical Internet simulative training can't be realized directly through the scenario systems and methods in existence. For solving this problem, firstly this paper introduced the new concept called digitized scenario, which can describe the meaning of scenario more exactly than the old simulation scenario. Secondly, this paper constructed the framework of digitized scenario, and it settled such issues as composition of digitized scenario system, scenario generating flow and data architecture. Thirdly, this paper built up the general data model for script situation, and it settled the problem of situation setting. Finally, this paper proposed the method of describing scenario files based on eXtensible Markup Language (XML), and it settled such problems as generation, verification and distribution of scenario files. The paper's work has been applied in the Tactical Internet simulative training system, and it also has good directive value to the developing of other communication network simulative training system.

Keywords: Tactical Internet, Simulative Training, Digitized Scenario, Situation Setting, XML.

1 Introduction

Along with the continuous development of computer simulation technology in the military domain, military simulation systems become more and more complicated. It requires the initial data and actions to be prearranged before the simulation running begins. So, traditional scenarios, such as text, diagrams and oral orders that were used to organize and induce military trainings and maneuvers, are being replaced by the simulation scenario, which provides the simulation systems with supporting data and running environment. At first, the simulation scenarios were mainly used to create simulation data, and functioned as scenario modules in simulation systems such as JWARS [1], JSIMS [2], JMASS [3] and etc. Subsequently, for solving some problems including software reuse, it has evolved into a kind of independent system, such as STAGE [4] produced by VPI.

Tactical Internet (TI) is a maneuvering communication system oriented to digital battle fields, and represents the advancing direction of the maneuvering communication systems all over the world. TI has unique characteristics, its network

R. Chen (Ed.): ICICIS 2011, Part I, CCIS 134, pp. 99–105, 2011.
© Springer-Verlag Berlin Heidelberg 2011

organization and application is complex, and it is relevant to such factors as battle field environment, battle forces and communication networks, so the scenario of TI simulative training system (TISTS) could not be generated by the scenario systems in existence directly, but to develop special ones.

Due to traditional scenarios in text couldn't be directly recognized and applied by computers, the simulation scenario was academically put forward. But, in this paper, it is deemed that the simulation scenario could not yet reflect the characteristics of the information age, and is easy to be confused conceptually. Therefore, the concept called digitized scenario is creatively brought forward here. This concept can uniformly describe all scenarios that can be directly recognized and applied by computers. Digital scenario is defined as digitized imagination and assumption for the attempts, situations and combat developments of both sides according to the combat simulation task. It is the fundamental data to organize and induce modern combat simulation, and can be directly recognized and applied by computers. The representation form of digitized scenario is the structural and formalized data.

2 Framework of Digitized Scenario

2.1 Composition of Digitized Scenario System

The digitized scenario system of TISTS is composed of fundamental data management, scenario management, network organization, parameter planning, situation setting and scenario generation, shown as Fig. 1.

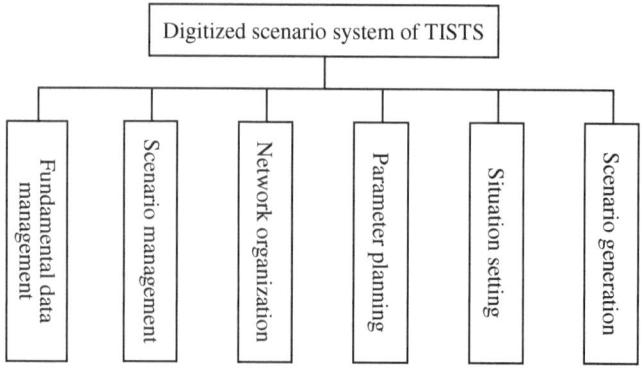

Fig. 1. Composition of digitized scenario system

In Fig. 1:

• Fundamental data management is used to managing the fundamental data, which is necessary when writing the digitized scenario.

• Scenario management is used to implement such jobs as resource management, scenario editing, scenario input and scenario distribution, etc.

• Network organization is used to confirm the grouping circumstance, and decide network types, network quantity, network members, network topologies and etc.

• Parameter planning is used to plan initial running parameters of all equipments in the network.

• Situation setting is used to arrange the roles of trainees and preset training situations, including role arrangement, script situation setting and writ situation setting.

• Scenario generation is used to transform the final scenario data to XML file, and verify and validate the scenario.

2.2 Generating Flow of Digitized Scenario

According to the characteristics and requirements of TI operating in combat and the system composition shown as Fig. 1, the generating flow of scenario system can be concluded to 14 steps, shown as Fig. 2.

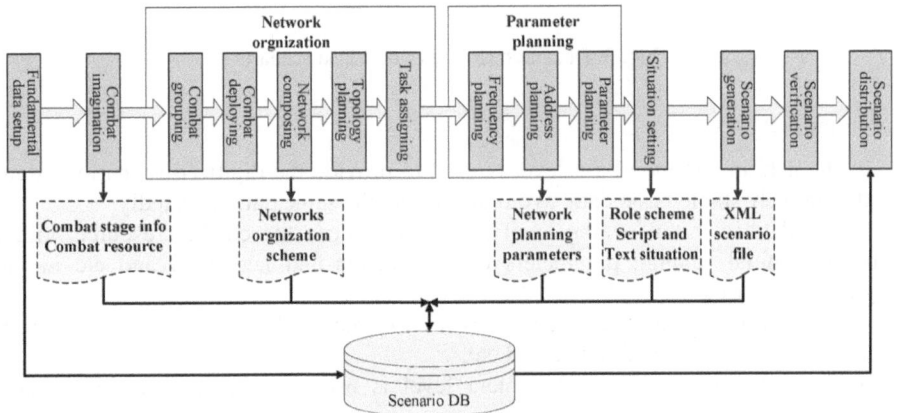

Fig. 2. Generating flow of digitized scenario

In Fig. 2, based on the comparatively close relationship about functions, the following five processes, combat grouping, combat deploying, network composing, topology planning and task assigning, are combined as network organizing; the following three processes, frequency planning, address planning and all networks' parameter planning, are combined as parameter planning.

2.3 Data Architecture of Digitized Scenario

In the digitized scenario of TISTS, the types of data are various, and the quantity of data is huge. Thus, constructing the data architecture reasonably can not only simplify the developing process of the scenario system, but also promote the data storing efficiency. The data architecture of TISTS is shown as Fig. 3.

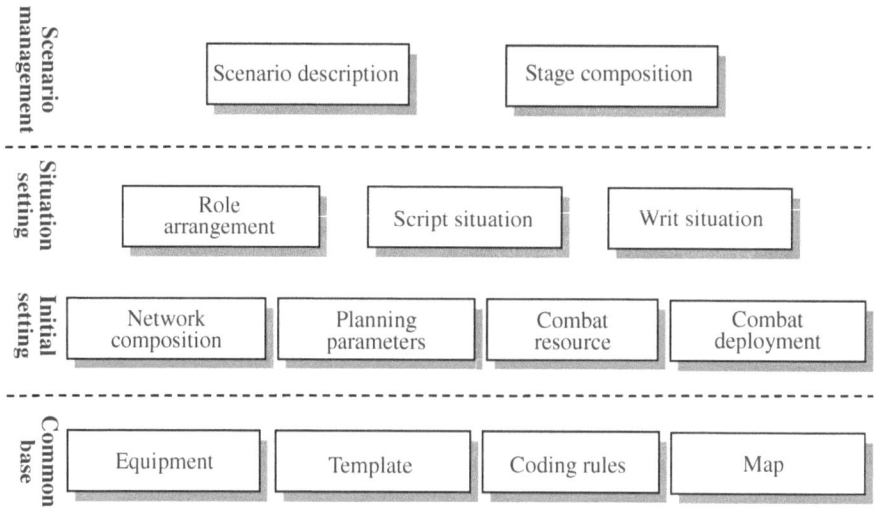

Fig. 3. Data architecture of digitized scenario

In Fig. 3:

• The data in common base level is used to provide the digitized scenario system with relatively stable basic data, avoid generating the same data repeatedly.

• The data in initial setting level is used to record the combat resource, initial situation, initial running parameters of equipments and networks, and etc in the digitized scenario.

• The data in situation setting level is used to record the role arrangement, script situation data, writ situation data and etc.

• The data in scenario management level is used to manage scenario's basic information and stages' composition and etc.

Each type of data in Fig. 3 also is composed of several kinds of detailed data.

3   Situation Setting

In TISTS, situation setting is mainly used to simulate setting various battlefield situations, such as communication equipments' malfunction, electronic interference, firepower damage, opening and withdrawing of equipments, etc. It creates a battlefield environment nearly as real ones, so that the trainees' abilities to handle various situations can be trained. The function of situation setting is similar to the supplementary scenarios in traditional scenario, but the later are mainly implemented by the ways of text in paper and oral order, and they can't be recognized and applied by computer simulation system directly, so new situation setting type should be adopted in TISTS.

The situation setting of TISTS is divided to three types: script situation, writ situation and role arrangement situation. As the script situation setting is the most difficult, only the script situation setting is researched in the following. The script situation is the battlefield situation which can be parsed automatically by computers and denoted by a formatted parameter collection. Each parameter indicates certain composition element of relative battlefield situation.

Battlefield situation can mostly be described by script situation in TISTS. Due to the uncertainty and complexity of battlefield situation, every kind of object, such as combat units, communication network systems, single equipment and even modules of equipment, may has various kinds of combat situation. Thus, the key point of script situation setting is to conclude battlefield situation relative to TI, and then abstract these situation and construct corresponding models for the convenience of implementation.

According to the analysis of TI and its combat actions, the script situation in digitized scenario of TISTS can be concluded and classified into 11 types as the following, shown as Table 1.

Table 1. Types of script situation

No.	Types
1	maneuvering/transferring
2	opening/withdrawing
3	enable/disable
4	parameter adjusting
5	communication repairing
6	firepower damage
7	electronic interference
8	network attacking
9	equipment malfunction
10	traffic changing
11	environment influence

Based on the classification of script situation above mentioned, it's necessary to analyze the elements of each situation type, and abstract the most essential data characteristics from script situation. Thereby a general data model can be built up and then be parsed and executed by computers. The general data model of script situation is shown as Table 2.

4   Scenario Files' Generation, Verification and Distribution Based on XML

In the editing process of digitized scenario, various kinds of scenario data are stored in databases, but ultimately these data should be used by each federate of TISTS. Therefore, it's necessary to adopt a kind of standardized describing means to transform and output the whole scenario as a file with normative format, so that each federate can load and use scenario data. As a result, the scenario is independent of specific simulation applications, and the generality and reusability are promoted.

Table 2. General data model of script situation

Basic information	Executing entity	Setting target	Start/end time	Chosen model	Setting parameter	Assistant information
situation name situation type type code	entity name entity no. military mark index team code entity position	target name target no. military mark index team code target position	start time end time	model name model no.	parameter quantity parameter name parameter no. parameter value	scenario no. stage no.

Considering such characteristics of XML language as self-description, hierarchy, independency to platforms, etc., it's an advisable choice to utilize XML specifications to generate scenario data. This issue mainly needs resolving the transformation between the database and XML files, including three parts: choice of mapping manner, establishment of mapping rules and definition of modes.

Due to the great scale and complicated structure of the XML scenario files in TISTS, the efficiency would be low and the error rate would be high if adopting manual checking and verifying way, so the automatically way should be applied. Considering the characteristics of XML language, the XML schema [5] mechanism is chosen. XML Schema can automatically check and verify the structure, attribute and data types, including format checking and validity verifying. This mechanism can avoid several deficiencies that manual checking would bring out.

After the XML scenario files pass the verification, it can be distributed to every federate to drive them into running. The distribution of XML scenario file is shown as Fig. 4.

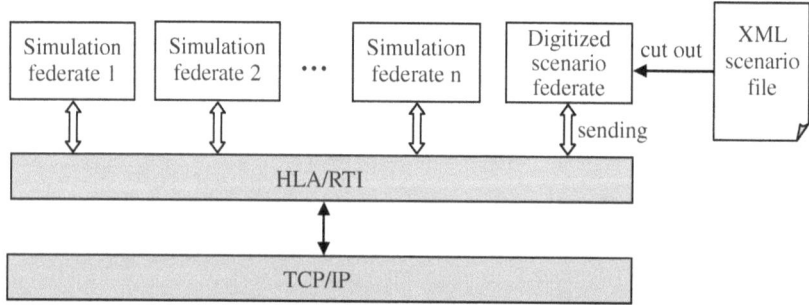

Fig. 4. The distribution of XML scenario file

The digitized scenario system of TISTS utilizes High Level Architecture (HLA) [6] to distribute scenario file. In Fig. 4, after logging in the simulative training system, each federate send request to the digitized scenario system, then the digitized scenario system cut out the initial XML scenario file suitable for the corresponding federate and send it back to federates.

5 Conclusions

In order to settle the scenario problem of Tactical Internet simulative training, this paper brought out the concept of digitized scenario, and then gave the corresponding schemes of digitized scenario's framework, situation setting and scenario file description respectively. The digitized scenario is a new concept, it can describe the meaning of scenario used in simulative training more exactly and clearly. All research work about digitized scenario in this paper has been put into practice in TISTS and proved good. It is worthy to be put into more applications.

References

1. Maxwell, D.T.: An Overview of the Joint Warfare System (JWARS) (2006),
   http://www.dtic.mil/jwars
2. Joint Simulation System (JSIMS) – FY01 Activity (2005),
   http://www.globalsecurity.org
3. McCauley, B., Hill, J., Gravitz, P.: JMASS 98 – Engagement Level Simulation Framework. In: Proceeding of the 2000 Spring SIW Conference, 00S-SIW-148 (2000)
4. STAGE Scenario 5.0 Simulation Reference Guide. eNGENUITY Technologies Inc. (2004)
5. Walmsle, P.: Definitive XML Schema. Prentice Hall PTR, Englewood Cliffs (2001)
6. The Institute of Electrical and Electronics Engineers: IEEE Std 1516-2000 for Modeling and Simulation (M&S) High Level Architecture (HLA) – Framework and Rules (2000)

Numerical Simulation for the Timoshenko Beam Equations with Boundary Feedback

Dian-kun Wang and Fu-le Li[*]

College of Science and Information, Qingdao Agricultural University,
266109 Qingdao, China
nianwo@163.com, lfl2004666@126.com

Abstract. In this paper, a vibrating Timoshenko beam with boundary feedback is considered. A linearized three-level difference scheme for the Timoshenko beam equations is derived by the method of reduction of order on uniform meshes. The unique solvability, unconditional stability and convergence of the difference scheme are proved. The convergence order in maximum norm is of order two in both space and time. The validity of this theoretical analysis is verified experimentally.

Keywords: Timoshenko beam; Finite difference method; Solvability; Convergence; Stability.

1 Introduction

The boundary control problem, as already pointed out by Xu and Feng[12], plays a very important role with the rapid development of high technology such as space science and flexible robots. A number of authors (see[1-7,12]) have considered control problems associated with the Timoshenko beam and obtained many interesting results. In this article, we consider the following vibrating Timoshenko beam problem (system (I)) with one end fixed:

$$w_{tt} + \delta w_t - \frac{1}{d^2}(w_{xx} - \phi_x) = f_1(x,t),\ 0 \le x \le l, 0 < t \le T,$$

$$\phi_{tt} + \delta \phi_t - \phi_{xx} - \frac{1}{d^2}(w_x - \phi) = f_2(x,t),\ 0 \le x \le l, 0 < t \le T,$$

with boundary conditions

$$w(0,t) = 0,\quad \phi(0,t) = 0,\quad 0 \le t \le T,$$
$$w_x(l,t) - \phi(l,t) = \alpha w_t(l,t) + g_1(t),\quad 0 \le t \le T,$$
$$\phi_x(l,t) = -\beta \phi_t(l,t) + g_2(t),\quad 0 \le t \le T,$$

and initial condition

$$w(x,0) = g_3(x),\ w_t(x,0) = g_4(x),\ 0 \le x \le l,$$
$$\phi(x,0) = g_5(x),\ \phi_t(x,0) = g_6(x),\ 0 \le x \le l,$$

---

[*] Corresponding author.

R. Chen (Ed.): ICICIS 2011, Part I, CCIS 134, pp. 106–111, 2011.
© Springer-Verlag Berlin Heidelberg 2011

where δ and d represent a damping constant and the thickness of the beam respectively. α, β are given positive gain feedback constants, $w(x,t)$ is the transversal displacement and $\phi(x,t)$ is the rotational angle of the beam. Feng et al. [2] and Semper[10] discussed some semi-discrete and fully discrete scheme using the Galerlin method and the partial projection finite element method respectively. They obtained optimal convergence rates with constants independent of the beam thickness when assuming that a smooth solution exists. Cheng and Xue[1], Franca and Loula[3], Jou[6] studied Timoshenko beam problems using different finite element methods and obtained many interesting results. Li and Sun[8], Li et al.[9] studied the numerical solution of Timoshenko beam using the finite difference method. In this article, we consider finite difference simulation for the vibrating Timoshenko beam equations (I).

We use the notations in [8,9] and construct the following difference scheme (system (II)) for system (I):

$$\frac{\overline{m}}{2}(\delta_t^2 y_{i-\frac{1}{2}}^k + \delta_t^2 y_{i+\frac{1}{2}}^k) - A_s G[\delta_x^2 y_i^{\overline{k}} - \frac{1}{2}(\delta_x \theta_{i-\frac{1}{2}}^{\overline{k}} + \delta_x \theta_{i+\frac{1}{2}}^{\overline{k}})] = \frac{1}{2}[(f_1)_{i-\frac{1}{2}}^k + (f_1)_{i+\frac{1}{2}}^k],$$

$$\frac{1}{2}\overline{m}r^2(\delta_t^2 \theta_{i-\frac{1}{2}}^k + \delta_t^2 \theta_{i+\frac{1}{2}}^k) - EI\delta_x^2 \theta_i^{\overline{k}} - \frac{1}{2}A_s G[(\delta_x y_{i-\frac{1}{2}}^{\overline{k}} + \delta_x y_{i+\frac{1}{2}}^{\overline{k}}) - (\theta_{i-\frac{1}{2}}^{\overline{k}} + \theta_{i+\frac{1}{2}}^{\overline{k}})] - \frac{1}{2}P(\delta_x y_{i-\frac{1}{2}}^{\overline{k}}$$

$$+ \delta_x y_{i+\frac{1}{2}}^{\overline{k}}) = \frac{1}{2}[(f_2)_{i-\frac{1}{2}}^k + (f_2)_{i+\frac{1}{2}}^k],$$

$$w_0^k = 0, \phi_0^k = 0,$$

$$\delta_x w_{M-\frac{1}{2}}^{\overline{k}} - \phi_M^k = -\alpha D_t w_M^k - \frac{h}{2}[\delta_x \phi_{M-\frac{1}{2}}^{\overline{k}} + d^2(\delta_t^2 w_{M-\frac{1}{2}}^k + \delta D_t w_{M-\frac{1}{2}}^k) - d^2(f_1)_{M-\frac{1}{2}}^k] + (g_1)^k,$$

$$\delta_x \phi_{M-\frac{1}{2}}^{\overline{k}} = -\beta D_t \phi_M^k - \frac{h}{2}[-\frac{1}{d^2}(\delta_x w_{M-\frac{1}{2}}^{\overline{k}} - \phi_{M-\frac{1}{2}}^{\overline{k}}) + \delta_t^2 \phi_{M-\frac{1}{2}}^k + \delta D_t \phi_{M-\frac{1}{2}}^k - (f_2)\phi_{M-\frac{1}{2}}^k] + (g_2)^k,$$

$$w_i^0 = (g_3)_i, \quad w_i^1 = (g_3)_i + \tau(g_4)_i + \frac{\tau^2}{2}[\frac{1}{d^2}((g_3)_i'' - (g_5)_i') - \delta(g_4)_i + (f_1)_i^0],$$

$$\phi_i^0 = (g_5)_i, \quad \phi_i^1 = (g_5)_i + \tau(g_6)_i + \frac{\tau^2}{2}[(g_5)_i'' + \frac{1}{d^2}((g_3)_i' - (g_5)_i) - \delta(g_6)_i + (f_2)_i^0].$$

The outline of this paper is as follows. In section 2, the difference scheme is derived by the method of reduction of order (see[11]). In section 3, the solvability, convergence and stability of the difference scheme are proved. In section 4, some numerical results are presented to test and verify the theoretical results. Finally, we summarize the result of this paper in section 5.

2 The Derivation of the Difference Scheme

We followe the idea in [8,9] and define the grid functions:

$$W_i^k = w(x_i, t_k), V_i^k = v(x_i, t_k), \Phi_i^k = \phi(x_i, t_k), \Psi_i^k = \psi(x_i, t_k).$$

Let $v = w_x$ and $\psi = \phi_x$, using the Taylor expansion and neglecting the small terms which are two order with respect to τ and h, we construct the difference scheme (system (III)) as follows:

$$\delta_t^2 w_{i-\frac{1}{2}}^k + \delta D_{\bar{t}} w_{i-\frac{1}{2}}^k - \frac{1}{d^2}(\delta_x v_{i-\frac{1}{2}}^{\bar{k}} - \psi_{i-\frac{1}{2}}^{\bar{k}}) = (f_1)_{i-\frac{1}{2}}^k,$$

$$v_{i-\frac{1}{2}}^k - \delta_x w_{i-\frac{1}{2}}^k = 0,$$

$$\delta_t^2 \phi_{i-\frac{1}{2}}^k + \delta D_{\bar{t}} \phi_{i-\frac{1}{2}}^k - \delta_x \psi_{i-\frac{1}{2}}^{\bar{k}} - \frac{1}{d^2}(v_{i-\frac{1}{2}}^{\bar{k}} - \phi_{i-\frac{1}{2}}^{\bar{k}}) = (f_2)_{i-\frac{1}{2}}^k,$$

$$\psi_{i-\frac{1}{2}}^k - \delta_x \phi_{i-\frac{1}{2}}^k = 0,$$

$$w_0^k = 0, \quad \phi_0^k = 0, \quad v_M^{\bar{k}} - \phi_M^{\bar{k}} = -\alpha D_{\bar{t}} w_M^{\bar{k}} + (g_1)^k, \quad \psi_M^{\bar{k}} + \beta D_{\bar{t}} \phi_M^k = (g_2)^k,$$

$$w_i^0 = (g_3)_i, \quad w_i^1 = (g_3)_i + \tau(g_4)_i + \frac{\tau^2}{2}\frac{1}{d^2}[((g_3)_i'' - (g_5)_i') - \delta(g_4)_i + (f_1)_i^0],$$

$$\phi_i^0 = (g_5)_i, \quad \phi_i^1 = (g_5)_i + \tau(g_6)_i + \frac{\tau^2}{2}[(g_5)_i'' + \frac{1}{d^2}((g_3)_i' - (g_5)_i) - \delta(g_6)_i + (f_2)_i^0].$$

At the $(k+1)$-th time level, we regard system (III) as a system of linear algebraic equations with respect to unknowns $\{w_i^{k+1}, \phi_i^{k+1}, v_i^{k+1}, \psi_i^{k+1}\}$.

We have the following theorem.

Theorem 1. The difference scheme (system(III)) is equivalent to system (II) and following equations:

$$v_{i-\frac{1}{2}}^0 = \delta_x w_{i-\frac{1}{2}}^0, \quad v_{i-\frac{1}{2}}^1 = \delta_x w_{i-\frac{1}{2}}^1, \quad 1 \leq i \leq M,$$

$$\psi_{i-\frac{1}{2}}^0 = \delta_x \phi_{i-\frac{1}{2}}^0, \quad \psi_{i-\frac{1}{2}}^1 = \delta_x \phi_{i-\frac{1}{2}}^1, \quad 1 \leq i \leq M,$$

$$v_i^{\bar{k}} = \delta_x w_{i+\frac{1}{2}}^{\bar{k}} - \frac{h}{2}[\delta_x \phi_{i+\frac{1}{2}}^{\bar{k}} + d^2(\delta_t^2 w_{i+\frac{1}{2}}^k + \delta D_{\bar{t}} w_{i+\frac{1}{2}}^k) - d^2(f_1)_{i+\frac{1}{2}}^k], \quad 0 \leq i \leq M-1,$$

$$v_M^{\bar{k}} = \delta_x w_{M-\frac{1}{2}}^{\bar{k}} + \frac{h}{2}[\delta_x \phi_{M-\frac{1}{2}}^{\bar{k}} + d^2(\delta_t^2 w_{M-\frac{1}{2}}^k + \delta D_{\bar{t}} w_{M-\frac{1}{2}}^k) - d^2(f_1)_{M-\frac{1}{2}}^k],$$

$$\psi_i^{\bar{k}} = \delta_x \phi_{i+\frac{1}{2}}^{\bar{k}} - \frac{h}{2}[-\frac{1}{d^2}(\delta_x w_{i+\frac{1}{2}}^{\bar{k}} - \phi_{i+\frac{1}{2}}^{\bar{k}}) + \delta_t^2 \phi_{i+\frac{1}{2}}^k + \delta D_{\bar{t}} \phi_{i+\frac{1}{2}}^k - (f_2)_{i+\frac{1}{2}}^k], \quad 0 \leq i \leq M-1,$$

$$\psi_M^{\bar{k}} = \delta_x \phi_{M-\frac{1}{2}}^{\bar{k}} + \frac{h}{2}[-\frac{1}{d^2}(\delta_x w_{M-\frac{1}{2}}^{\bar{k}} - \phi_{M-\frac{1}{2}}^{\bar{k}}) + \delta_t^2 \phi_{M-\frac{1}{2}}^k + \delta D_{\bar{t}} \phi_{M-\frac{1}{2}}^k - (f_2)_{M-\frac{1}{2}}^k].$$

3 Analysis of the Difference Scheme

In this section we will discuss the solvability, convergence and stability of the difference scheme (system (II)).

Lemma 1. Suppose $\{w_i^k, \phi_i^k, v_i^k, \psi_i^k\}$ be the solution of

$$\delta_t^2 w_{i-\frac{1}{2}}^k + \delta D_i w_{i-\frac{1}{2}}^k - K(\delta_x v_{i-\frac{1}{2}}^{\bar{k}} - \psi_{i-\frac{1}{2}}^{\bar{k}}) = (P_1)_{i-\frac{1}{2}}^k,$$

$$v_{i-\frac{1}{2}}^k - \delta_x w_{i-\frac{1}{2}}^k = (P_2)_{i-\frac{1}{2}}^k,$$

$$\delta_t^2 \phi_{i-\frac{1}{2}}^k + \delta D_i \phi_{i-\frac{1}{2}}^k - \delta_x \psi_{i-\frac{1}{2}}^{\bar{k}} - K(v_{i-\frac{1}{2}}^{\bar{k}} - \phi_{i-\frac{1}{2}}^{\bar{k}}) = (P_3)_{i-\frac{1}{2}}^k,$$

$$\psi_{i-\frac{1}{2}}^k - \delta_x \phi_{i-\frac{1}{2}}^k = (P_4)_{i-\frac{1}{2}}^k,$$

$$w_0^k = 0, \quad \phi_0^k = 0, \quad v_M^{\bar{k}} - \phi_M^{\bar{k}} = -\alpha D_i w_M^{\bar{k}} + (P_5)^k, \quad \psi_M^{\bar{k}} + \beta D_i \phi_M^k = (P_6)^k,$$

$$w_i^0 = 0, \quad \phi_i^0 = 0, \quad w_i^1 = (P_7)_i, \quad \phi_i^1 = (P_8)_i.$$

Let

$$F(k) = \left\| \delta_t w^{k+\frac{1}{2}} \right\|^2 + \left\| \delta_t \phi^{k+\frac{1}{2}} \right\|^2 + \frac{1}{2}(\left\| \psi^{k+1} \right\|^2 + \left\| \psi^k \right\|^2) + \frac{K}{2}(\left\| v^{k+1} - \phi^{k+1} \right\|^2 + \left\| v^k - \phi^k \right\|^2).$$

Then, we have

$$F(k) \le (1 + \frac{3}{2}\tau)^k [F(0) + \frac{3}{2}\tau \sum_{n=1}^{k} G(n)], \quad 1 \le k \le N-1,$$

Where

$$G(n) = \frac{2}{4\delta+1} \left\| (P_1)^n \right\|^2 + \frac{1}{2\delta+1} \left\| (P_3)^n \right\|^2 + 2K^2 \left\| (P_4)^n \right\|^2 + \frac{K}{2\alpha} \left| (P_4)^n \right|^2 + \frac{1}{2\beta} \left| (P_6)^n \right|^2$$

$$+ 2K \left\| D_i (P_2)^n \right\|^2 + 2 \left\| D_i (P_4)^n \right\|^2.$$

Theorem 2. The difference scheme (system (II)) is uniquely solvable. The proof is similar to the proof of Theorem 1 in [8], we omit it. Using Lemma 1, we can easily obtain the following Theorem:

Theorem 3. The solution $\{w_i^k, \phi_i^k\}$ of the difference scheme (system (II)) is convergent to the solution $\{W_i^k, \Phi_i^k\}$ of the problem (system (I)) with the convergence order of $O(\tau^2 + h^2)$ in the L_∞ norm.

Theorem 4. The difference scheme (system (II)) is stable to the initial values and the in homogeneous terms.

4 Numerical Example

To test the difference scheme, we consider a simple initial and boundary value problem. The coefficients are choosed to be $l = T = \pi, \delta = d = 1, \alpha = 3.5, \beta = 4.1$. The right hand functions $f_1(x,t), f_2(x,t)$ and the functions in the initial and boundary conditions are determined by the exact solution (see[10])

$$w(x,t) = [\frac{\pi}{2}\sin(x) + (1.0 - d^2)(\frac{x^2}{2} - \frac{\pi}{2}x)]\cos(t)$$

and

$$\phi(x,t) = [\frac{\pi}{2}\cos(x) + (x - \frac{\pi}{2})]\cos(t).$$

The numerical results are presented in tables 1-3. In table 3, the maximal errors are defined as follows:

$$\|w - w_{h\tau}\|_{\infty} = \max_{0 \le k \le N}\{\max_{0 \le i \le M}|w(x_i, t_k) - w_i^k|\}, \quad \|\phi - \phi_{h\tau}\|_{\infty} = \max_{0 \le k \le N}\{\max_{0 \le i \le M}|\phi(x_i, t_k) - \phi_i^k|\}.$$

Suppose $\tau = h$ and $\|w - w_{h\tau}\| \approx c_1 h^{p_1}$, $\|\phi - \phi_{h\tau}\| \approx c_2 h^{p_2}$. Using the data in table 3, we obtain the linear fiting functions of w and ϕ:

$$-\log\|w - w_{h\tau}\|_{\infty} \approx -1.1237 + 2.0025(-\log h),$$
$$-\log\|\phi - \phi_{h\tau}\|_{\infty} \approx 0.3269 + 1.9918(-\log h).$$

That is to say, $p_1 = 2.0025$ and $p_2 = 1.9918$ respectively, which is in accordance with our theoretical analysis results.

Table 1. The errors of the numerical solutions of w at $t = 1$

$M \setminus x$	1/5	2/5	3/5	4/5	1
40	1.2323e-3	1.8092e-3	1.8651e-3	1.2742e-3	1.2339e-4
80	3.0557e-4	4.5077e-4	4.6410e-4	3.1732e-4	3.1327e-5
160	7.6524e-5	1.1250e-4	1.1572e-4	7.9155e-5	7.8949e-6
320	1.9105e-5	2.8101e-5	2.8899e-5	1.9766e-5	1.9818e-6
640	4.7765e-6	7.0213e-6	7.2215e-6	4.9388e-6	4.9649e-7

Table 2. The errors of the numerical solutions of ϕ at $t = 1$

$M \setminus x$	1/5	2/5	3/5	4/5	1
40	2.3945e-4	1.5459e-4	9.6784e-5	2.0893e-4	1.6398e-4
80	5.9170e-5	3.8541e-5	2.3893e-5	5.2429e-5	4.1256e-5
160	1.4920e-5	9.6222e-6	5.9254e-6	1.3106e-5	1.0349e-5
320	3.7224e-6	2.4037e-6	1.4784e-6	3.2743e-6	2.5917e-6
640	9.3142e-7	6.0073e-7	3.6943e-7	8.1816e-7	6.4844e-7

Table 3. The maximum errors of the numerical solutions of w and ϕ

M	40	80	160	320	640
$\| w - w_{h\tau} \|_{\infty}$	1.9080e-3	4.7505e-4	1.1855e-4	2.9613e-5	7.3997e-6
$\| \phi - \phi_{h\tau} \|_{\infty}$	4.6268e-4	1.1710e-4	2.9463e-5	7.3893e-6	1.8503e-6

5 Conclusion

In this study, we construct a finite difference scheme for a vibrating Timoshenko beam, and have proved that the scheme is uniquely solvable, unconditionally stable and second order convergent in L_∞ norm. The numerical experiment shows that the results are in accordance with our theoretical analysis. Next, we will consider the system of nonhomogeneous undamped Timoshenko beam with both ends free and give a high-order difference scheme as much as possible.

Acknowledgments. This research is supported by Shandong Provincial Natural Science Foundation (ZR2009AL012) and Shandong Provincial Education Bureaus Science and Technology Plan (J09LA12).

References

1. Cheng, X.L., Xue, W.M.: Linear finite element approximations for the Timoshenko beam and the shallow arch problems. J. Comput. Math. 20(1), 15–22 (2002)
2. Feng, M.F., Xie, X.P., Xiong, H.X.: Semi-discrete and fully discrete partial projection finite element methods for the vibrating Timoshenko beam. J. Comput. Math. 17(4), 353–368 (1999)
3. Franca, L.P., Loula, A.F.D.: A new mixed finite element method for the Timoshenko beam problem. RAIRO Modél. Math. Anal. Numér. 25(5), 561–578 (1991)
4. Ghayesh, M.H., Balar, S.: Non-linear parametric vibration and stability analysis for two dynamic models of axially moving Timoshenko beams. Appl. Math. Model. 34, 2850–2859 (2010)
5. Hou, S.H., Yan, Q.X., Feng, D.X.: Stabilization of coupled nonuniform Timoshenko beam system. Nonlinear Anal. Theory Methods Appl. 63(5-7), e2329–e2333 (2005)
6. Jou, J., Yang, S.Y.: Least-squares finite element approximations to the Timoshenko beam problem. Appl. Math. Comput. 115(1), 63–75 (2000)
7. Khaji, N., Shafiei, M., Jalalpour, M.: Closed-form solutions for crack detection problem of Timoshenko beams with various boundary conditions. Internat. J. Mech. Sci. 51, 667–681 (2009)
8. Li, F.L., Sun, Z.Z.: A finite difference scheme for solving the Timoshenko beam equations with boundary feedback. J. Comput. Appl. Math. 200, 606–627 (2007)
9. Li, F.L., Wu, Z.K., Huang, K.M.: A difference scheme for solving the Timoshenko beam equations with tip body. Acta Math. Appl. Sinica (English Series) 24, 337–352 (2008)
10. Semper, B.: Semi-discrete and fully discrete Galerkin methods for the vibrating Timoshenko beam. Comput. Methods Appl. Mech. Engrg 117, 353–360 (1994)
11. Sun, Z.Z.: A new class of difference schemes for linear parabolic equations in 1-D. Math. Numer. Sinica. 16(2), 115–130 (1994)
12. Xu, G.Q., Feng, D.X.: The Riesz basis property of a Timoshenko beam with boundary feedback and application. IMA Journal of Appl. Math. 67, 357–370 (2002)

A Study on Technology Architecture and Serving Approaches of Electronic Government System

ChunNian Liu[1], YiYun Huang[1], and Qin Pan[2]

[1] School of Information Engineering, Nanchang University,
330031, Nanchang, China
[2] School of Economics Management, HuaZhong Agricultural University,
430070 Wuhan, China
pan81706@163.com

Abstract. As E-government becomes a very active research area, a lot of solutions to solve citizens' needs are being deployed. This paper provides technology architecture of E-government system and approaches of service in Public Administrations. The proposed electronic system addresses the basic E-government requirements of user friendliness, security, interoperability, transparency and effectiveness in the communication between small and medium sized public organizations and their citizens, businesses and other public organizations. The paper has provided several serving approaches of E-government, which includes SOA, web service, mobile E-government, public library and every has its own characteristics and application scenes. Still, there are a number of E-government issues for further research on organization structure change, including research methodology, data collection analysis, etc.

Keywords: E-government; technology architecture; serving approaches.

1 Introduction

During the past decades, study on E-government has witnessed significant progress. Torres, Pinal, & Acierate argued that since the late 1990s, governments at all levels have launched electronic government projects to provide electronic information and services for citizens and businesses[1]. Yao G and Lin P claimed that E-government projects for local governments should be designed and developed by local government informatization offices. At present, E-government systems in Chinese central government or local governments have lower capabilities of service delivery compared with developed countries[2]. In the world, different countries are usually divided into different areas, and different areas have their own web portals and IT systems[3]. Torres suggested E-government can be broadly defined as a government's use of ICT, particularly Web-based Internet applications, to enhance the access rates and delivery quality of government information and service to citizens, business partners and other agencies and entities[4]. The construction and management of E-government systems are becoming an essential element of modern public administration. The paper will try to analyze the development of E-government and technology architecture and serving approaches of electronic government system.

R. Chen (Ed.): ICICIS 2011, Part I, CCIS 134, pp. 112–117, 2011.
© Springer-Verlag Berlin Heidelberg 2011

2 The Essence and Development Routes of E-Government System

E-government is the use of information and communications technologies (ICT) to transform government by making it more accessible, effective and accountable, and allows the public sectors to provide citizens, business partners and administrative staff with information that is based on life-events and business situations. Based on functionality, complexity and maturity, E-government development should usually follow such routes: In the primary stage, it mainly constructs the management of government automation office and public web sites, which is becoming an essential element of modern public administration. In the middle stage, E-government provides Social multiplication services that present online interfaces to deal with transactions on the user side, which is the important service of E-government. In the high stage, the construction and management of digital cities, where the cataloged information is usually presented on static web sites and usually organized with different levels of layers, plays a significant role in public management.

3 The Technology Architecture of E-Government System

The design of E-government system is to not only rely on computers to fulfill its function, which is not simply the traditional digital data, but also to use the power of modern science and technology to make up for the lack of manual operations. So, we can create the innovation means of the management mechanism so that it can play a key role in its democratic management and improve the transparency of information services, and to ensure that all information open, just and fair for the citizens. [5] E-government is concerned with the intense usage (application) of electronic media such as the Internet and other telecommunication facilities to support a modern public administration.

In the construction of E-government, the key is to build a stable and mature framework for the implementing of E-government system. We should designate some appropriate criterions which can avoid working in parallel and take advantage of the operating of information communication. The normal framework of E-government describes the distribution and mutual relation of the various subsystems, modules and the components in the system. The whole is divided into three levels: application layer, component layer and data layer.

(1) Interface

It decrypts about professional applications of user interaction in information processing, including some related communications standard of end-users, such as Web browser access, mobile phone / PDA, etc, which is, multi-access transmission channels of the client and e-government system.

(2) Application layer

1) Business application systems: including the Government internal Office applications, external applied service system and office business management systems, include: government websites, office automation systems, electronic

document exchange system, decision support system, various government on-line service systems, etc.

2) Component-based system: It uses a programming tool to package business logic rules, disposes of a large-scale distributed system with unified planning. And it realizes the reuse of software, reduces the development cycle of software, achieves the cross-platform. The system is built based on the current distributed component technology and multi-layer structure.

The main basic components of E-government are: the electronic payment platform, data security systems, information portal systems, e-forms systems, workflow systems, content management system (CMS).

3) Middleware: It is a basic complex software which is between system software and application software. Distributed applications software shares resources in different technologies with using the software. The middleware is located on the system software of client-server, and manages computer resources and network communications. The constitute of E-government software systems includes various middleware, the function of which are: integrating the data resources, providing heterogeneous distribution data resources, supporting solution for application integration, realizing the share and exchange interface of government information and related data. There are some common middleware: the middleware of data access, the middleware of transaction processing, the middleware of distributed object, the middleware of and application services, and so on.

(3) Basic network platform

1) Computer and network hardware: including a variety of PC, servers, network routers, optical fiber, switches, and other types of hardware.

2) System software: including the operating system, database, and other serve system software. Manage the software. In the E-government network construction program, we should consider the network saturation, the network transmission and the internet protocol, routing protocol, address management, and so forth.

(4) E-government security system

E-government security system: from the physical layer, network layer, system layer the application layer, even the management of all aspects, It ensures the security and reliance of government management and business information resources in E-government system and business.

(5) E-government standard system

E-government standard system is the essential guarantee of E-government construction, and penetrates from the beginning to the end. The final goal of E-government is to establish a unified E-government, so it should build a unified standard to facilitate various business systems, promote various government departments to work interoperability and share resources. The standard system includes: information technology standards, information security standards and management standards.

Therefore, it is esteemed that through this paper, E-government practitioners will be able to obtain a macro perspective of the various activities involved in the implementation of E-government and thus be able to take appropriate actions in the strategic planning and managing of their respective E-government implementation initiative towards the achievement of the desired outcomes.

4 The Serving Approaches of E-Government

4.1 The Serving Approach Based on SOA

Service Oriented Architecture (SOA) provides a design framework for realizing rapid and low-cost system development and improving total system quality. SOA uses the Web services standards and technologies and is rapidly becoming a standard approach for enterprise information systems. SOA is an architectural style for building software applications that use services available in a network such as the web. It promotes loose coupling between software components so that they can be reused. Applications in SOA are built based on services. A service is an implementation of a well-defined business functionality, and such services can then be consumed by clients in different applications or business processes.

SOA allows for the reuse of existing assets where new services can be created from an existing IT infrastructure of systems. In other words, it enables businesses to leverage existing investments by allowing them to reuse existing applications, and promises interoperability between heterogeneous applications and technologies. In the meantime, SOA depends on data and services that are described using some implementation of metadata which meets the following two criteria: (1) the metadata must be in a form which software systems can use to configure themselves dynamically by discovery and incorporation of defined services, and also to maintain coherence and integrity(2). the metadata must also be in a form which system designers can understand and manage at a reasonable cost and effort.

According to the traditional way of integration, we always use the peer-to-peer module. To build an SOA a highly distributable communications and integration backbone is required. Web services are software systems designed to support interoperable machine-to-machine interaction over a network. This interoperability is gained through a set of XML-based open standards, such as WSDL, SOAP, and UDDI. These standards provide a common approach for defining, publishing, and using web services. Sun's Java Web Services can be used to develop state-of-the-art web services to implement SOA, which enables you to build and deploy web services in your IT infrastructure on the application server platform. It provides the tools you need to quickly build, test, and deploy web services and clients that interoperate with other web services and clients.

4.2 The Serving Approach Based on Web Service

The model will allow the public sector to provide citizens, business partners and administrative staff with information that is based on life-events and business situations, hence increasing the effectiveness, efficiency and quality of public services. This model was citizen-focused and pledged to ensure consistency and integration with central government initiatives. There is evidence of this trend as many government information and services are available exclusively online[6].

The technical objectives of the E-government project include the specification and development of: (1) The next generation of an E-government portal and the supporting network architecture. The portal will feature a number of advanced characteristics, for example access from different devices. (2) The service repository. It will be the source containing the interpretations of online services in terms of data and information (structured around the life-events and according to the respective governmental processes). (3) A Mark-up Language which should be the portal and of all public repositories. It will be implemented as an XML derivative that should become an open standard for data exchange and information sharing among horizontally.

4.3   The Serving Approach Based on Mobile E-Government

Mobile E-government is the combining product of e-traditional E-government and mobile communication platform, which is the main part of E-government. And it is based on the mobile wireless Internet platform, promote the Chief activate through mobile data services and information technology, including management and service. It can help transmit information to public without network constraints in order to improve efficiently government management.

4.4   The Serving Approach Based on Public Library

In this model, libraries might serve as gateways and/or providers to communities who seek information in a complex of intermingled paper and digital information environments. Research by Loretta and Groin, has demonstrated that many titles once only available in a depository library are now freely available on the Internet [7]. And despite librarians concerns to the contrary, research by Asher, Yi, and Knapp suggests that users prefer electronic access to the library's print copy, even when they must bear the printing costs [8]. Librarians have sought to help users locate government information by including records for both physical format and electronic government documents into their online catalogs and by merging government documents reference services into their centralized reference services [9]. Clearly, providing access to government information sources via the library's online catalog has significantly increased and improved citation patterns.

5   Conclusions

The main objective of this paper is to present a secure, interoperable framework of E-government system and several serving approaches of E-government. The proposed electronic system addresses the basic E-government requirements of user friendliness, security, interoperability, transparency and effectiveness in the communication between small and medium sized public organizations and their citizens, businesses and other public organizations. The emergence of the web service technology permitted to extend it to a distributed source of functionality. Public service information is placed online through the Web sites of agencies and departments. Mobile E-government is a new application model. The model of E-government is focus on its mobility. The approach based on public library is significantly altered in this new web-based redistribution model. Today, public libraries still struggle with these same issues, as well as more recent issues, continually working to obtain adequate resources and political support for the provision of information services through the Internet. Libraries have a long, well-established social role of providing information; people trust libraries because of it. Libraries have a vested interest in ensuring that the information they provide is authentic and that they are trusted to do so. Still, there are a number of E-government issues for further research on organization structure change, including research methodology, data collection analysis, etc.

References

1. Jaeger, P.T.: The endless wire: e-government as a global phenomenon. Government Information Quarterly 20(4), 323–331 (2003)
2. Yao, G., Lin, P.: International E-government case studies. Peking University Press, Beijing (2005)
3. China.Org.cn The local administrative system in China's political system (2007), http://www.china.org.cn/english/Political/28842.htm (access on 4-6- 2007)
4. Layne, K., Lee, J.: Developing fully functional e-government four stage model. Government Information Quarterly 18(2), 122–136 (2001)
5. Barber, B.: Three scenarios for the future of technology and strong democracy. Political Science Quarterly 113(4), 573–589 (1998)
6. Thomas, J.C., Strait, G.: The new face of government: Citizen-initiated contacts in the era of e-government. Journal of Public Administration Research and Theory 13(1), 83–102 (2003)
7. Aldrich, D., Bertot, J.C., McClure, C.R.: E-government initiatives, developments, and issues. Government Information Quarterly 19, 349–356 (2002); Jaeger, P. T.: The endless wire: E-government as global phenomenon. Government Information Quarterly, 20(4), 323–331 (2003).
8. Asher, C., Yi, H., Knapp, S.: Effective Instruction Needed to Improve Students' Use of Government Information. Journal of Government Information 29, 293–301 (2002)
9. Libraries who are not depository libraries have long-since begun to understand this—see, C. Dianna Weatherly: A U.S. Government Publications Collection in a Non-Depository Research Library: A Case Study. Journal of Government Information 23(4), 471–489 (1996)

Construction and Development of CRM Technology and Industry Chain in China

ChunNian Liu[1], YongLong Wang[1], and Qin Pan[2]

[1] School of Information Engineering, Nanchang University,
330031, Nanchang, China
[2] School of Economics Management, HuaZhong Agricultural University,
430070 Wuhan, China
pan81706@163.com

Abstract. CRM is any application or initiative designed to help an organization optimize interactions with customers, suppliers, or prospects via one or more touch points. CRM has been interpreted and used in different ways by researchers in the various disciplines and researchers have identified a variety of technologies related to CRM. This paper highlights the implementation from the technology level and contributes to some successful factors in CRM application. The development of CRM is not fully developed in China. There are many critical factors that determine the CRM market development. Construction and development of CRM industry chain in China is a valuable research field and the paper provided some suggestions and analyses on it. In future, it requires our joint efforts of many aspects from every walk of life to make sure that CRM industry chain can improve and maturate gradually.

Keywords: CRM; Construction; technology; industry chain.

1 Introduction

Customer relationship management (CRM), firstly proposed by Gartner Group, is the means to manage such relationships with customers, aiming at enhancing their competitive positions. It comprises a set of processes and enabling systems supporting a business strategy to build long term, profitable relationships with specific customers.[1] The rapid growth of the Internet and its associated technologies has greatly increased the opportunities for marketing and has transformed the way relationships between companies and their customers are managed.[2]Over the years, CRM has built up a great deal of academic, technological, and industrial knowledge around its core concept, that is looking after customers better. [3] CRM is changing many industries and influencing many customers and business. Yet, many business failed in the CRM implementation. The paper will try to analyze some complex questions on CRM and give some predictors about future CRM development trend.

R. Chen (Ed.): ICICIS 2011, Part I, CCIS 134, pp. 118–123, 2011.

2 Definition, Types and Core Technologies for CRM

2.1 Definition

Since CRM has been interpreted and used in different ways by researchers in the various disciplines, it makes sense for us to bring together these diverse views [4][5]: CRM is any application or initiative designed to help an organization optimize interactions with customers, suppliers, or prospects via one or more touch points-such as a call center, salesperson, distributor, store, branch office, web, or email-for the purpose of acquiring, retaining, or cross-selling customers. (Goodhue, Wixom, and Watson, 2002); CRM is combination of software and management practices to serve the customer from order through delivery and after-sales service. (Wright, Stone, and Abbott, 2002) [4]; CRM is a core business strategy that integrates internal processes and functions and external business networks to create and deliver value to targeted customers at a profit. It is grounded on high quality customer data and enabled by information technology. (Ang and Buttle, 2002); CRM is the infrastructure that enables the delineation of and increase in customer value, and the correct means by which to motivate valuable customers to remain loyal-indeed, to buy again. (Dyche, 2002); CRM is a business strategy aimed at gaining long-term competitive advantage by optimally delivering customer value and extracting business value simultaneously.(Kellen, 2002); CRM is managerial efforts to manage business interactions with customers by combining business processes and technologies that seek to understand a company's customers. (Kim, Suh, and Hwang , 2003); CRM is a blueprint for turning for an enterprise's customers into an asset by building up their value.(Kirkby, 2002); CRM is a good CRM program enables customers to easily access the information they need at any time and includes a 24-by-27 web site, fast email tools and the ability to discuss problems with a human being rather than an electronic answering system. (Rembrandt, 2002); CRM is a business strategy combined with technology to effectively manage the complete customer life cycle. (Smith, 2002).

Customer is the core resource of business, so the core of CRM is customer value management. It classifies customer value into underlying value, model value and product value. Therefore, customer can be classified into underlying customer, model customer and product customer. It improves customer satisfaction and loyalty by meeting the individual needs of customer and keeping direct relationship with customer. On the basis of that, it helps business to find more valuable customer by a quantitative evaluation of the customer value, so as to shorten the sales cycle, reduce the sale cost, reduce inventories and increase market share, improving the viability and competitiveness fully. It provides the entire business management from marketing to customer service. At the same time, it conduct a deep data analysis and synthesis from customer buying behavior and orientation in order to tap more potential corporate customers and provide scientific quantified guidance for the future direction of product development, making enterprises maintain a permanent development ability in the rapidly changing market .

2.2 Types

CRM programs when carefully planned and successfully implemented promise a great deal of benefits for both customers and businesses. This represents a rationale for the adoption and implementation of CRM. That is to say, the promise of a CRM strategy is customer loyalty, retention, repeat business and profits.[6]

CRM programs are classified into different types (1)in the context of customer types and life cycles, there are four types of CRM programs: win back or save, prospecting, loyalty, and cross-sell/up-sell(Tan al 2002); (2)in the context of technology, CRM is of three types (Crosby and Johnson 2001; The Hindu Business Line 2002). M-Trilogix labels theses types as "the CRM technology ecosystem" which include operational, analytical and collaborative CRM applications: [2] a. Operational CRM: Focuses on the automation of business processes such as order management, customer service, marketing automation, sales automation, and field service. b. Analytical CRM: Focuses on the analysis of customer characteristics and behaviors so as to support the organization's customer management strategies. c. Collaborative CRM: This type consists of technologies that assure enterprise-customer interaction across all contact channels.

Of the above two classifications, I prefer the latter one, because technology plays an important role in the implementation of CRM. Also, Customer Relationship Management (CRM) put "marketing management" at the core of the system. It is reasonable to classify CRM into three types—operational, analytical and collaborative CRM. Besides, the customer types are not so definite and may cause troubles.

2.3 The Core Technology of CRM

CRM consists of four dimensions: (1) Customer Identification; (2) Customer Attraction; (3) Customer Retention; (4) Customer Development. CRM begins with customer identification, which is referred to as customer acquisition in some articles. [7]. Customer segmentation involves the subdivision of an entire customer base into smaller customer groups or segments, consisting of customers who are relatively similar within each specific segment [8]. Customer Attraction is the phase following customer identification. After identifying the segments of potential customers, organizations can direct effort and resources into attracting the target customer segments. Customer Retention is the activity that a selling organization undertakes in order to reduce customer defections. Customer development is a parallel process to product development, which means that you don't have to give up on your dream. Researchers have identified a variety of technologies related to CRM, including:

- Product development through customer DB analysis
- Product development through customer involvement
- Development of customized products
- Customer mileage reward programs
- Real-time customer services
- Managing customer loyalty
- Managing customer complaints
- Developing member-only access to website
- Customer database development
- Customer categorization based on spending
- Customize service depending on customer categories
- CRM application system implementation
- Ability to provide fashion information via email and catalogs

- Managing customers' anniversaries
- Developing sales promotion strategies
- Providing products and services in one place
- Providing price discount depending on customer categories
- Localization of strategies through customer analysis

3   Construction of CRM Industry Chain

3.1   CRM Consulting Firm

In order to make readers more acquainted with those manufacturers, some manufacturers are listed in the following.

Akup: Found at Taiwan in 1995.--Orienting the whole GreatChina region, with lots of successful customers.--Entering China in 1999, 30% of its marketing income from taiwan, 40% from mainland, 30% from singapore and southeast Asia.--CTE, IVR, multi-channel integration, data mining, integration Enterprise Ⅰ, multi-channel customer calling center integration, SFA, calling service, customer behavior analysis tool, E-mail management field service and industrial application eBroderage.

Oracle CRM: Found in Germany SAP company in 1972, entering China in 1991. SAP system installation for 44 500 times. Product-user more than10 000 000. BI, product configuration, system integration, all-electronic. Besides tipical CRM business field, including product and price configuration, data mining and so on.

SalesLogix: Foreign advanced middle-small business CRM product. Found by Pat Sullivan. Close integration with Outlook, ROI analysis on sales promotion, mobile synchronization. SalesLogix 5.2 business function includes sales, marketing e-business and customer support module. Feature-rich in analytical and operational application. Citrix provides the ability of convenient data synchronize.

Siebel: Found by Pat Tom Siebel in 1993.The founder of CRM concept and CRM software development. A comprehensive business coverage for CRM, one-time development tools, multiple integrated way, the automation business of allocation process, and a neat product line. Siebel 7.0 has more 200 functional module, 20 industrial application, fat clients, thin clients, wireless customers, products e-Series, CTI integrated calling centre, provides customer intelligence analysis for data market, such as customer, service and marketing.

3.2   CRM Consulting Firm

The CRM implementation won't be successful without the participation of professional consulting firm. The consulting fee accounts for 7% of the total fee in the CRM implementation. The implementation of the CRM professional consultants can play a role as follows:

(1) The enterprise needs to carry out research to help the users define needs, and mine their potential needs.

(2) Reengineering the original business management process to help optimize the management process.

(3) With the combination of CRM management software, giving solutions to the problems related.

(4) Organizing the implementation of the CRM software.

(5) Supporting the second development.

3.3 CRM Training Seminars and Agencies

CRM project implementation training is throughout the entire process of CRM project implementation, including: (1) project team training; (2) end-user software training; (3) technical staff training; (4) the new process and data analysis of training. The content of such training is determined by the CRM vendor according to specific project characteristics and the function modules of products so as to ensure successful implementation of CRM projects.

The most famous CRM Training agencies are Siebel CRM, and SAP ERP, but there are some other companies provide CRM training courses. For example, Zisco company launched the "Marketing of the six competitive management" course. It changed the CRM training routine, and is not a simple or pure theory or the description about the product functions. It based on advanced marketing and management philosophy, combined with the actual operation and management of enterprises in the status quo, at the same time, used CRM product as a complementary tool to deeply explicit the customer relationship management system in the enterprise application.

4 Conclusions

CRM is any application or initiative designed to help an organization optimize interactions with customers, suppliers, or prospects via one or more touch points. Customer is the core resource of business, so the core of CRM is customer value management. CRM has been interpreted and used in different ways by researchers in the various disciplines and researchers have identified a variety of technologies related to CRM. The development of CRM is not fully developed in China. There are many critical factors that determine the CRM market development. The implementation of the CRM professional consultants can play a role. CRM project implementation training is throughout the entire process of CRM project implementation. It based on advanced marketing and management philosophy, combined with the actual operation and management of enterprises.

In future, it requires our joint efforts of many aspects from every walk of life to make sure that CRM industry chain can improve and maturate gradually. I think there are some features of the future development trend of CRM in China.

(1) CRM will continue to keep its high speed of increase and business will apply the whole set of information management solution schema which combines the application of CRM and other information systems (eg. ERP). Besides, the number and sum for CRM manufactures resigning will increase in some degree.

(2) A few years later, CRM manufacturers will undergo a heavy storm, those who don't have any competition in any industry will close or be merged by others. The completion between CRM manufacturers will become clear and the brand position of CRM will become stable gradually.

(3) Some middle-low business will take the operation pattern of CRM software service outsourcing into consideration in the coming future.

(4) CRM industrials will pay more attention to the Web service ability, real-time, industry-specific and system integration.

(5) Traditional way can't be abandoned, while modern ways can't be refused. In the aspect of customer relationship establishment and maintenances, Chinese business in future need not only traditional personal relationship, emotion investment to keep it, but also CRM computer systems to deepen the overall understanding of customers.

References

1. Ling, R., Yen, D.C.: Customer relationship management: An analysis framework and implementation strategies. Journal of Computer Information Systems 41, 82–97 (2001)
2. Ngai, E.W.T.: Customer relationship management research (1992–2002): An academic literature review and classification. Marketing Intelligence, Planning 23, 582–605 (2005)
3. Birchfield, D.: CRM Sites Galore. New Zealand Management 49(3), 14 (2002)
4. Wright, L.T., Stone, M., Abbott, J.: The CRM imperative Practice theory in the telecommunications industry. Journal of Database Marketing 9(4), 339–349 (2002)
5. Winer, R.S.: A Framework for Customer Relationship Management. California Management Review 43(4), 89–105 (2001)
6. Wift, R.S.: Accelerating customer relationships: Using CRM and relationship technologies. Prentice Hall PTR, Upper Saddle River (2001)
7. Kracklauer, A.H., Mills, D.Q., Seifert, D.: Customer management as the origin of collaborative customer relationship management. Collaborative Customer Relationship Management - taking CRM to the next level, 3–6 (2004)
8. Woo, J.Y., Bae, S.M., Park, S.C.: Visualization method for customer targeting using customer map. Expert Systems with Applications 28, 763–772 (2005)

Multi Scale Adaptive Median Filter for Impulsive Noise Removal

Xiangzhi Bai, Fugen Zhou, Zhaoying Liu, Ting Jin, and Bindang Xue

Image Processing Center, Beijing University of Aeronautics and Astronautics,
Beijing 100191, China
jackybxz163@163.com

Abstract. Adaptive median filter has been an efficient algorithm for impulsive noise removal. However, if the noises are very heavy, adaptive median filter may still remain noise regions in result image. Actually, noise pixels usually exist in different scales of image. So, a multi scale adaptive median filter is proposed in this paper. The multi scale adaptive median filter is a sequence of adaptive median filter using maximum windows with increasing sizes. Because the noises exist at multi scales could be identified, multi scale adaptive median filter could efficiently filter very heavy noises in image. Experimental results show that multi scale adaptive median filter could be very efficient even though the impulsive noises are very heavy.

Keywords: Adaptive median filter, multi scale, impulsive noise removal.

1 Introduction

Noises heavily destroy image contents, which affects the applications of images. Especially, impulsive noises, which appear as very large or very small gray values in image, usually completely ruin image contents. So, efficiently removing impulsive noises is very important and meaningful. Many algorithms have been proposed [1-7] to remove impulsive noises. Among them, the median type filters perform well. Classical median filter [1] is widely used for impulsive noise removal. However, if the noise is heavy, median filter could not correctly recovery the real image contents [1, 2]. Center weighted median filters [3] could achieve a satisfaction result if the percentage of impulsive noises is not very high. But, heavy impulsive noises will decrease the performance of center weighted median filters. Although pixel-wise MAD [4] does not need optimizing parameters or pre-training, and has good filtering performance, it could not well process images with high percentage of impulsive noises. Switching median filter [5] and adaptive soft-switching median filter [6] are switching-based median filters. Although the high corrupted image could be recovered, the decision for switching conditions should be correctly determined. Adaptive median filter [7] could filter images with high percentages of impulsive noises. The maximum window size S_{max} used in adaptive median filter determines the performance of adaptive median filter. To well filter the high percentage of noises, a very large window size S_{max} should be used. However, the performance of adaptive median filter is also suppressed if the noises are very heavy.

R. Chen (Ed.): ICICIS 2011, Part I, CCIS 134, pp. 124–129, 2011.

Heavy noises are usually not easy to be filtered using only one adaptive median filter with a very large S_{max}. Actually, heavy noises usually exist at different scales of image. So, consecutively removing impulsive noises using S_{max} with increasing sizes in adaptive median filters may achieve a good performance. In light of this, a multi scale adaptive median filter is proposed in this paper. A class of adaptive median filters using S_{max} with increasing sizes is serialized to form the multi scale adaptive median filter. Because the noises at different scales could be efficiently filtered, the proposed filter could remove high percentage of impulsive noises. Simulation results indicate that the proposed filter could well recovery noise images even with very high impulsive noises (up to 90%).

2 Multi Scale Adaptive Median Filter

2.1 Algorithm

Let $AMF_w(f)$ represent the adaptive median filter on image f. w is the maximum window size used in adaptive median filter. In the result of adaptive median filter, the gray value of each pixel is a selective output. If the pixel is determined as noise pixel, the gray value of the pixel is replaced by the median value of one window whose size is not larger than the size of w. Otherwise, the gray value of the pixel keeps unchanged. The determination of the noise pixel is based on the gray value of the pixels in window with size not larger than the size of w. And, the window is determined by one iterative procedure.

It has been proved that the size of window w will affect the performance of adaptive median filter [2]. And, the effective window sizes for different percentages of impulsive noises have also been researched [2, 7]. Actually, because the noises may exist at different scales of image, even the window size is efficient for one percentage of impulsive noises, adaptive median filter may not efficiently remove all the noises existed at different scales. Especially, if the impulsive noise is very heavy, the performance of adaptive median filter with only one w is not very efficient. To efficiently filter heavy noises at different scales, the multi scales of adaptive median filter with increasing sizes of w should be used.

Suppose t scales should be used to filter the impulsive noises existed at image f. The size of w at the firstly used scale is m. Then, the impulsive noises existed at the scale i could be filtered by adaptive median filter as follows $(m \leq i \leq n, n=2 \times t+1)$. i usually is odd number and should be larger than m.

$$f_R^i = AMF_w^i(f).$$

Heavy noises could not be completely filtered by adaptive median filter using w with a small size. The noises existed at large scale should be filtered by w with a large value. So, heavy noises could be filtered through a sequence of adaptive median filter using w with increasing sizes as follows.

$$f_R = AMF_w^n(...(AMF_w^{m+2}(AMF_w^m(f)))...). \tag{1}$$

Based on expression (1) and the procedure of adaptive median filter, the implementation of multi scale adaptive median filter is demonstrated below.

Multi Scale Adaptive Median Filter (MSAMF)

Let $s_{i,j}^{\min,w_{cur}}$, $s_{i,j}^{med,w_{cur}}$ and $s_{i,j}^{\max,w_{cur}}$ represent the minimum, median and maximum gray values in the current window with size w_{cur}, respectively.

Let $f_R = f$;

For each w from m to n with increasing step 2

    For each w_{cur} from 3 to w with increasing step 2

        Calculate $s_{i,j}^{\min,w_{cur}}$, $s_{i,j}^{med,w_{cur}}$ and $s_{i,j}^{\max,w_{cur}}$;

        If $s_{i,j}^{\min,w_{cur}} < s_{i,j}^{med,w_{cur}} < s_{i,j}^{\max,w_{cur}}$

                If $s_{i,j}^{\min,w_{cur}} < f_R(i,j) < s_{i,j}^{\max,w_{cur}}$

        $f_R(i,j) = s_{i,j}^{med,w_{cur}}$;

      End;

          Else

                If $w_{cur} < w$

        $w_{cur} = w_{cur} + 2$;

      Else

              $f_R(i,j) = s_{i,j}^{med,w}$;

      End;

          End;

  End;

  End;

The procedure of MSAMF indicates that, impulsive noises existed at small scale could be removed by using w with small size. And, the remained noises at large scales could be subsequently removed by using w with large size. Therefore, the noises existed at different scales could be efficiently removed.

2.2 Parameter Selection

The parameters used in MSAMF are m and n. m is a small size of the used window in MSAMF. The procedure of MSAMF indicates that the smallest size of window, which is 3, has been used. And, m should be larger than 3. So, m is set as 5. n is the largest size of the used window in MSAMF. n could be selected following the percentage of the impulsive noises of image. The heavier the impulsive noise is, the larger the n is. Usually, n could be selected following Table 1.

Table 1. *n* for different percentages of impulsive noises

Percentage of impulsive noises	n
0<noise level≤30%	5
30%<noise level≤50%	7
50%<noise level≤60%	9
60%<noise level≤70%	11
70%<noise level≤80%	13
80%<noise level≤90%	15

3 Experimental Results

To demonstrate the efficiency of MSAMF, the Lena images with very high percentage of impulsive noises are used. Also, adaptive median filter are used to do the comparison. Because it has been proved that, adaptive median filter could achieve a better performance than many other median type filters [2], so we do not choose other algorithms to do the comparison. Fig. 1 is the comparison of Lena image with 80% impulsive noises. Fig. 1(a) is the original image. Fig. 1(b) is the noise image with 80% impulsive noises. Fig. 1(c) is the result of adaptive median filter. Fig. 1(d) is the result of MSAMF. Fig. 1 indicates that MSAMF could filter more noises than AMF and the visual effect of Fig. 1(d) is better than Fig. 1(c).

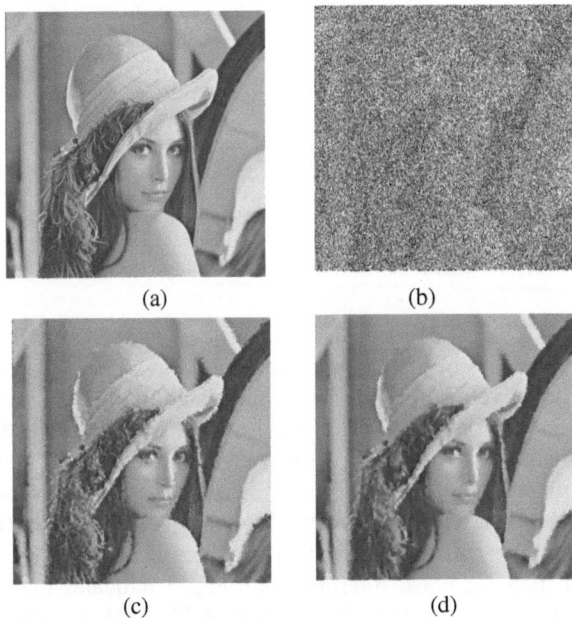

(a)   (b)

(c)   (d)

Fig. 1. Comparison results (80% impulsive noises). (a) Original Lena image; (b) Noise image with 80% impulsive noise; (c) Result of adaptive median filter; (d) Result of MSAMF.

Fig. 2 is the comparison of Lena image with 90% impulsive noises. Because the noise is very heavy, there are still many noises in the result of adaptive median filter (Fig. 2(b)). However, MSAMF filters more noises and recovery more image details than adaptive median filter (Fig. 2(c)).

(a)   (b)   (c)

Fig. 2. Comparison results (90% impulsive noises). (a) Noise image with 90% impulsive noises; (b) Result of adaptive median filter; (c) Result of MSAMF.

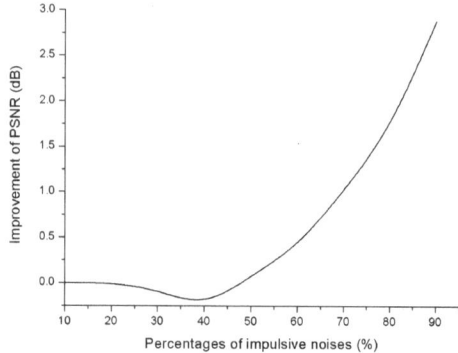

Fig. 3. Improvement of PSNR versus percentage of impulsive noises

To do a quantity comparison and show the efficiency of MSAMF on more images with different percentages of impulsive noises, the improvement of PSNR of MSAMF comparing with adaptive median filter is demonstrated in Fig. 3. The improvement of PSNR is the difference of the PSNR of the result of MSAMF and the PSNR of the result of adaptive median filter. Fig. 3 shows that if the noise is not very heavy (<50%), the improvement of MSAMF is not very efficient. That is because adaptive median filter could filter small percentage of impulsive noises very efficiently. But, if the noise is very high (≥50), MSAMF could apparently improve the performance of adaptive median filter for noise filtering. And, Fig. 3 indicates that, the heavier the impulsive noise is, the better the performance of MSAMF is. Therefore, MSAMF could be efficiently used to filter very heavy noises in image.

4 Conclusions

Heavy noises dramatically destroy the visual effect of images. It is very important to efficiently remove noises in image. Adaptive median filter is one efficient median type filter for impulsive noise removal. However, it is not very efficient for heavy noise removal. Heavy noises usually exist at different scales of image. In light of this, a multi scale adaptive median filter, which is a sequence of adaptive median filter using maximum windows with increasing sizes, is proposed in this paper. Multi scale adaptive median filter could efficiently remove impulsive noises at different scales. So, the very heavy impulsive noises could be removed. Experimental results show that multi scale adaptive median filter performs better than adaptive median filter and could be efficiently used in images with very heavy impulsive noises (up to 90%).

Acknowledgments. This work is partly supported by the National Natural Science Foundation of China (60902056), the Aeronautical Science Foundation of China (20090151007), and the Natural Science Foundation of Beijing (3102020). The authors are grateful to Dr. Yan Li at Peking University, Beijing, China, for many helpful discussions and comments.

References

1. Bovik, A.: Handbook of Image and Video Processing. New York, Academic (2000)
2. Chan, H.R., Ho, C.-W., Nikolova, M.: Salt-and-Pepper Noise Removal by Median-Type Noise Detectors and Detail-Preserving Regularization. IEEE Transactions on Image Processing 14, 1479–1485 (2005)
3. Chen, T., Wu, H.R.: Adaptive Impulse Detection Using Center-Weighted Median Filters. IEEE Signal Processing Letters 8, 1–3 (2001)
4. Crnojevic, V., Senk, V., Trpovski, Ž.: Advanced Impulse Detection Based on Pixel-Wise MAD. IEEE Signal Processing Letters 11, 589–592 (2004)
5. Zhang, S., Karim, M.A.: A New Impulse Detector for Switching Median Filters. IEEE Signal Processing Letters 9, 360–363 (2002)
6. Eng, H.-L., Ma, K.-K.: Noise Adaptive Soft-Switching Median Filter. IEEE Transactions on Image Processing 10, 242–251 (2001)
7. Hwang, H., Haddad, R.A.: Adaptive Median Filters: New Algorithms and Results. IEEE Transactions on Image Processing 4, 499–502 (1995)

GA-Based Optimization Approach of Fractional Linear Neural Network and Its Application

Guowei Yang[1] and Lei Guo[2]

[1] College of Information Engineering, Nanchang Hangkong University
330063 Nanchang, China
Ygw_ustb@163.com
[2] School of Instrumentation Science and Opto-electronics Engineering, BeiHang University
100191 Beijing, China

Abstract. A GA-based optimization method of fractional linear neural network (FNN) is proposed. Firstly, the GA is used to optimize the weight of fractional linear neural network. A solution near the global optimum will be found. Then the global optimum in the local area can be obtained with back propagation algorithm for the FNN to train the network based on the solution. The simulation results show that the GA-based new approach to optimize the fractional neural network is feasible and effective.

Keywords: GA, fractional linear neural network, BP algorithm for fractional neural network, prediction of rainfall.

1 Introduction

The most widely used neural network is the multilayer feed-forward perception in which the connection weight training is normally completed by a back-propagation (BP) learning algorithm. However, despite its popularity as an optimization tool for neural network training, the BP algorithm also has several drawbacks. For instance, the disadvantages of falling into a local minimum and inconsistent and unpredictable performance could not be avoided. Thus, improving a BP network's convergence during training is very necessary as well as important. Genetic algorithm (GA), based on Darwin's theory, is considered to be a heuristic, stochastic, combinatorial, optimization technique based on the biological process of natural evolution developed by Holland (1975). The genetic algorithm has been used extensively in artificial neural network (ANN) optimization and is known to achieve optimal solutions fairly successfully. Recently some investigations into neural network training using genetic algorithms have been successfully employed to overcome the inherent limitations of the BP. Especially there are some articles concerning BP network in meteorologic forecasting that has been published in the literature. For instance, Zhang et al. (2005) investigated the effectiveness of the GA evolved BP network for rainfall-runoff forecasting and its application to annual rainfall-runoff in the upper reach of the Yellow River[1]. Their results showed that the GA-based BP network model gives superior predictions. In 2006, Wu et al. used GA to find the weight values of a changed BP network architecture[2]. In their study, they investigated the effectiveness

R. Chen (Ed.): ICICIS 2011, Part I, CCIS 134, pp. 130–135, 2011.
© Springer-Verlag Berlin Heidelberg 2011

of the GA evolved BP network for rainfall forecasting and its application to monthly rainfall in the Guangxi Zhuang Autonomous Region. Also, their results showed that the established model gives satisfying predictions.

According to some mathematical definitions, linear function is reciprocal to fractional linear function. In 2007, Yang et al. submitted a new promising feed-forward network architecture, which using fractional linear function as each hidden neuron's input of BP network. Their study concerned demonstrated that the fractional linear neural network has more extensive approaching ability compared with traditional BP network[3]. However, just like the BP algorithm we mentioned above, some similar disadvantages may still exist in the process of training fractional neural network. Consequently, it is sure to be instructive to investigate into combining GA with training algorithm of fractional neural network so as to avoid existed drawbacks. At present, there is quite few article concerning fractional neural network in meteorologic forecasting that has been published in the literature. Considered above, this paper investigates the effectiveness of genetic algorithm evolved fractional linear neural network for rainfall forecasting and its application to predict the rainfall in Daqing, Heilongjiang province, China. To evaluate the performance of the genetic algorithm-based fractional neural network, conventional BP neural network is also involved for a comparison purpose. The simulation results showed that the model of GA-based fractional NN is feasible as a tool for rainfall forecasting.

2 The Proposed Model

In this paper, the best fractional neural network architecture is: 12–25–12 (12 input units, 25 hidden neurons, 12 output neurons).

The input data contains information for a period of 15 years (1990-2004). Experimental data of 15 years are used to design the GA-based fractional neural network model used for the prediction rainfall of overall 2004. Furthermore, data from 1991 to 2003 constitute the training set and remaining data from 2004 is used in testing phase. This means that hundred and sixty eight individual samples (precipitation per month between 1990 and 2003) were used for training and 12 individual samples (precipitation per month in 2004) were used for testing. The output data were normalized at a boundary of [0.125, 0.590] by division of every output power into 273.4.

To improve the learning performance of FNN, the GA proposed is used to find the initial value of parameters of fractional neural network, and is implemented as follows:

Step 1: Randomly generate initial population of real coded strings for the parameters of initial weight of network.

Step 2: Evaluate fitness function of each chromosome in the population. The better chromosomes will return higher values in this process.

Step 3: Stop and output the optimum solutions after the specified number of generation (maxgenterm T); otherwise proceed.

Step 4: Generate some new chromosomes (offspring) from the parents through genetic operations, which are as follows:

    a. Use roulette wheel selection to select the better chromosomes to be parent generation in the mating pool. The chromosomes with a higher fitness value have a higher probability of contributing one or more offspring in the next generation.

    b. Produce new offspring by crossing from their parent generation. The offspring are expected to be more fit than the parents.

    c. Randomly choose some chromosomes from new offspring for mutation operation. This operator can create new genetic material in the population to maintain the population's diversity.

Step 5: Proceed to step 2.

A crucial issue in the design of a genetic algorithm is the choice of the fitness function. As the basic process of GA includes evaluating each chromosomes according to a defined fitness function, the fitness of every chromosome in the population is evaluated by measuring the value of the total mean square error. The better chromosomes will obtain smaller mean square error and return higher fitness function values in this process accordingly. So the fitness function in the study is given by

$$
f = \frac{1}{\frac{1}{M}\sum_{p=1}^{M}\left(y_{p}-\hat{y}_{p}\right)^{2}} = 1 \Bigg/ \frac{1}{M}\sum_{p=1}^{M}\left(Y_{p}-W_{p}^{2}\frac{1}{1+e^{\left(-\sum_{i=1}^{R}W_{p}^{1}\frac{x_{p,i}-a_{i}}{\left(x_{p,1}-a_{1}\right)^{2}+...+\left(x_{p,R}-a_{R}\right)^{2}}+B_{p}^{1}\right)}}+B_{p}^{2}\right)^{2}
$$

where W_{p}^{1} and W_{p}^{2} are the connection weights between the input and hidden neuron, and between the hidden neuron and output neuron referring to pth sample respectively, B_{p}^{1} and B_{p}^{2} are hidden neuron thresholds and output neuron thresholds referring to pth sample respectively.

The deployment of the optimal solution search requires the tuning of some features related with the GA, for example population size, selection and crossover functions, mutation rate, migration, etc. which we mentioned above. Although some general guidelines about such selections exist in the relevant literature [4, 5], optimal setting is strongly related to the design problem under consideration and can be obtained through the combination of the designer's experience and experimentation. By many efforts and experiments, parameters are set in this study as follows:

- Number of generation: 300 generations.
- Population size: 60;
- Selection function: roulette
- Reproduction: Elite count: 0.
- Mutation: Mutation probability: 0.01; Mutation function: non-Uniform.

Crossover function: arithXover, Crossover rate: 0.9.

3 Implementation of Optimization Algorithm

The GA-based fractional neural network learning process consists of two stages: Firstly employing GA to search for optimal or approximate optimal connection weights and thresholds for the fractional neural network, then using the fractional neural networks BP algorithm to adjust the final weights. The steps involved in training a GA-based fractional neural network by the use of back propagation algorithm are as follows:

Step 1: Initializing the populations randomly. The GA consists of population of 60 individuals evolving during 300 generations.

Step 2: Presenting all inputs X_p as well as desired outputs Y_p to the network.

Step 3: Computing the corresponding network outputs $\hat{Y}_p$ and errors according to X_p, Y_p, updating connection weights and thresholds.

Step 4: Evaluating the fitness of every chromosome by measuring the value of the total mean square error, see Eqs. (3). Rank the chromosome according to the relative fitness.

Step 5: Forming the population of the next generation by applying the roulette wheel selection, crossover and mutation operator to the chromosomes of the intermediate population.

Step 6: Turning to the next step on condition that the stopping criterion is satisfied, Otherwise, go back to the step 3.

Step 7: Applying BP algorithm for fractional NN on GA established initial connection weights and thresholds which got from step 5.

Step 8: Updating the connection weights and thresholds by BP algorithm. If the value of the total mean square error (MSE) is smaller than a predefined value e, save and provide for future prediction rainfall.

4 Results and Discussion

Rainfall is illustrative of a nonlinear process and its forecasting with relatively limited data makes it very complex phenomenon. In order to evaluate the performance of the genetic algorithm -based fractional neural network model, conventional BP neural network was also applied with the same data sets used in the GA–FNN model.

The simulation results are given below.

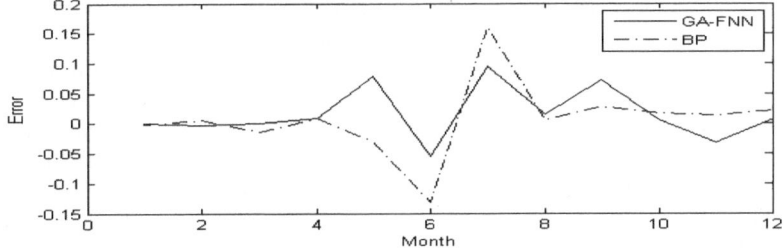

Fig. 1. The error performance comparison of GA–FNN and BP neural network

Table 1. The prediction results comparison of GA–fractional linear network and BP network

	Month	Jan.	Feb.	Mar.	Apr.	May.	Jun.
	Actual rainfall	1.2	1.9	0.2	8.2	43.3	14.1
GA-BP	Predicted rainfall	0.9	2.5	0.05	5.9	22.0	29.2
	Relative error	25.0%	31.6%	75.0%	28.0%	49.2%	107.1%
BP	Predicted rainfall	1.3	0.2	4.1	6.0	51.5	49.9
	Relative error	8.33%	89.5%	1950%	26.8%	18.9%	253%
	Month	Jul.	Aug.	Sep.	Oct.	Nov.	Dec.
	Actual rainfall	74.0	115.6	30.9	11.1	11.3	6.0
GA-BP	Predicted rainfall	47.9	111.5	11.3	9.7	20.1	4.1
	Relative error	35.3%	3.5%	63.4%	12.6%	77.9%	31.7%
BP	Predicted rainfall	30.3	113.9	23.3	6.5	7.7	0
	Relative error	59.1%	1.47%	24.6%	41.4%	31.9%	100%

Fig. 1 shows the error performance comparison of GA–FNN and BP network, which gives the performance of GA–FNN is better than that of the pure BP models in general.

Table 1 gives the results for the two different models of the training phase. This table shows that the convergence speed of GA–FNN model is faster than that of the BP network models, as the GA-FNN decreases chance of being trapped in a local minimum and increases chance of finding stable results.

5 Conclusions

In this article, the advantages and the key issues of the genetic algorithm evolved fractional linear neural network has been presented to model the rainfall in Daqing area. Our methodology adopts a real coded GA strategy and hybrid with back-propagation algorithm for fractional linear neural network. The genetic operators are carefully designed to optimize the neural network, avoiding problems premature convergence and permutation. The study reported in this article has led to the conclusion that the predictive performance of the proposed model is slightly better than that of the traditional BP neural network in general. The experiment with real rainfall data has showed that the genetic algorithm-based fractional linear neural network model is a feasible forecasting method for rainfall problems.

One problem when considering the combination of neural network and genetic algorithm for rainfall forecasting is the determination of the optimal neural network topology. Our neural network topology described in this experiment is determined by trial and error method. A substitute method is to apply the genetic algorithm for fractional neural network structure optimization, which will be a part of our future work.

Acknowledgments. This work is supported by the National Natural Science Foundation of China (No.60973048, No. 60673101), the National 863 Project (No.2006AA01Z123, No.2006AA04Z110), the National Natural Science Foundation of Shandong Province (No.Y2007G30), the Science and Technology Project of Shandong Province (No.2007GG3WZ04016).

References

1. Zhang, S., Zhang, X., Wang, L., Ding, J., Liu, G.: Study on annual precipitation and runoff forecast based on artificial neural network in the upper reach of yellow river. China Rural Water and Hydropower 1, 41–44 (2005)
2. Wu, Q., Zhang, Q., Wa, J.: Application of ANN in weather forecast. Computer Engineering 31, 176–179 (2005)
3. Yang, G., Wang, S., Yan, Q.: Research of fractional linear neural network and its ability for nonlinear approach. Chinese Journal of computers 30(2), 189–199 (2007)
4. Goldberg, D.E.: Genetic algorithm in search optimization and machine learning. Addison-Wesley, Reading (1989)
5. Goldberg, D.E.: The design of innovation. Kluwer Academic Publishers, Massachusetts (2002)

Study of Unicyclic Graph with Maximal General Randić Index R_α for $\alpha < 0$

Deqiang Chen[*]

Department of Information Science and Technology
East China University of Political Science and Law, Shanghai 201620, China
dqchen2009@gmail.com

Abstract. A unicyclic graph is a simple connected graph that contains exactly one cycle. The general Randić index $R_\alpha(G)$ for a graph G is defined as $\sum_{uv}(d_u d_v)^\alpha$, where uv is an edge of G, d_u and d_v are degrees of u and v, respectively, $\alpha \in R$ and $\alpha \neq 0$. In this paper, it is proved that the cycle C_n is the unique extremal unicyclic graph with maximal general Randić index R_α for $\alpha \in (-0.58, 0)$, which implies the result obtained by Gao and Lu. Moreover, we characterize the extremal unicyclic graph with maximal general Randić index R_α for $\alpha \to -\infty$.

Keywords: unicyclic graph; the general Randić index; extremal problem.

1 Introduction

It is well known that in 1975 M. Randic [1] introduced the *Randić index* or the *connectivity index* as one of the many graph-theoretical parameters derived from the graph underlying some molecule. For a simple connected graph G, its Randić index $R(G)$ is defined as the sum of the weights $(d_u d_v)^{-\frac{1}{2}}$ over all edges uv of G. That is,

$$R(G) = \sum_{uv}(d_u d_v)^{-\frac{1}{2}}, \tag{1}$$

where d_u and d_v stand for the degrees of the vertices u and v, respectively, and the summation goes over all edges uv of G.

In 1998, Bollobás and Erdös [2] generalized it to the following *general Randić index* and denoted by $R_\alpha(G)$. That is,

$$R_\alpha(G) = \sum_{uv}(d_u d_v)^\alpha, \tag{2}$$

where d_u and d_v are the degrees of the vertices u and v, respectively, the summation goes over all edges uv of G and α is a real number not equal to 0.

[*] Supported by Special Research Fund in Shanghai Colleges and Universities to Select and Train Outstanding Young Teachers (No. hzf09009).

R. Chen (Ed.): ICICIS 2011, Part I, CCIS 134, pp. 136–141, 2011.
© Springer-Verlag Berlin Heidelberg 2011

Firstly, we give some terminology and notations. For others not defined here, please refer to [1] and [3]. The degree of vertex u in a graph is denoted by d_u. A path $P = u_0 - u_1 - \cdots - u_{t-1} - u_t$ in a graph is called a *pendent path of length* t if it satisfies $d_{u_0} > 2$, $d_{u_1} = \cdots = d_{u_{t-1}} = 2$ and $d_{u_t} = 1$. Especially, we call the vertex u_t a *leaf*. A simple connected graph is called *unicyclic* if it contains exactly one cycle. Obviously, a unicyclic graph with n vertices has n edges. For $n \geq 3$, let C_n and S_n denote the cycle and the star with n vertices. Let S_n^+ denote the unicyclic graph obtained from the star S_n by joining its two vertices of degree 1.

There are many results concerning the Randić index and the general Randić index of unicyclic graphs. In [4], the authors gave sharp lower and upper bounds on the Randić index of unicyclic graphs. For $\alpha < -1$, Li, Wang and Zhang [5] characterized the extremal unicyclic graph with the minimal general Randić index. In [6], the authors discussed the unicyclic graphs with maximal general Randić index and they also gave the structure description for the graphs with maximal general Randić index for $\alpha > 0$. At the end of [6], they said that the extremal problem of finding the unicyclic graphs with maximal R_α for $\alpha < 0$ is much more complicated.

In this paper, we will prove that the cycle C_n is the unique unicyclic graph with the maximal general Randić index R_α for $-0.58 < \alpha < 0$. This result implies Theorem 1 in [4] obtained by Gao and Lu. Moreover, we character the unicyclic graphs with maximal $R_\alpha(G)$ for $\alpha \to -\infty$.

2 Some Lemmas

Lemma 1. Suppose G_1 is a unicyclic graph with a cycle S and a vertex $u \notin S$ is adjacent to $j(j \geq 0)$ pendent paths and $d_u - 1 - j$ leaves. Transform G_1 into a new unicyclic graph G_2 by changing the pendent paths and the leaves into a new path with the vertices. See Figure 1. Then $R_\alpha(G_1) \leq R_\alpha(G_2)$ for $\alpha \in (-0.58, 0)$.

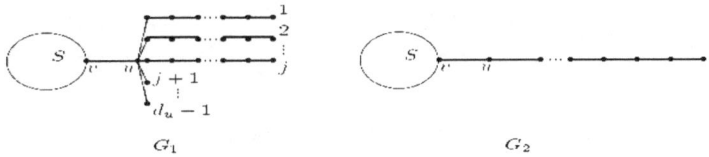

Fig. 1. The change for the case in Lemma 1

Proof. $d_u = 1$ and $d_u = 2$ are trivial cases. Suppose $d_u \geq 3$ and v is the adjacent vertex of u. The vertex v is not a leaf nor in the pendent paths. By comparing, we have $R_\alpha(G_1) - R_\alpha(G_2) = j(d_u^\alpha 2^\alpha - d_u^\alpha + 2^\alpha - 4^\alpha) + (d_u - 1)(d_u^\alpha - 4^\alpha) + (d_v^\alpha d_u^\alpha - d_v^\alpha 2^\alpha)$ $+ (4^\alpha - 2^\alpha)$. Note that $d_u^\alpha 2^\alpha - d_u^\alpha + 2^\alpha - 4^\alpha$ is positive for $d_u \geq 3$ and $j \leq d_u - 1$.

Case 1: $d_u \geq 4$. Then $R_\alpha(G_1) - R_\alpha(G_2) \leq 3(4^\alpha 2^\alpha + 2^\alpha - 2 \cdot 4^\alpha) + (d_v^\alpha 4^\alpha - d_v^\alpha 2^\alpha)$ $+(4^\alpha - 2^\alpha) < 3(4^\alpha 2^\alpha + 2^\alpha - 2 \cdot 4^\alpha) + 4^\alpha - 2^\alpha < 0$ for $\alpha \in (-0.58, 0)$. Therefore, $R_\alpha(G_1)$ $-R_\alpha(G_2) \leq (d_u - 1)(d_u^\alpha 2^\alpha + 2^\alpha - 2 \cdot 4^\alpha) + (d_v^\alpha d_u^\alpha - d_v^\alpha 2^\alpha) + (4^\alpha - 2^\alpha) < 0$ for $d_u \geq 4$ and $\alpha \in (-0.58, 0)$.

Case 2: $d_u = 3$. If $2 \leq d_v \leq 5$, then $R_\alpha(G_1) - R_\alpha(G_2) \leq 2(6^\alpha + 2^\alpha - 2 \cdot 4^\alpha)$ $+(d_v^\alpha 3^\alpha - d_v^\alpha 2^\alpha) + (4^\alpha - 2^\alpha) < 0$ for $\alpha \in (-0.58, 0)$. If $d_v \geq 6$, then without loss of generality, suppose $v \in S$ and v has neighbors $u_1, \cdots, u_j, u_{j+1}, \cdots, u_{d_v-2} \notin S$, $d_{u_1}, \ldots, d_{u_j} \geq 4$ and $d_{u_{j+1}} = \ldots = d_{u_{d_v-2}} = 3$ $(u \in u_{j+1}, \cdots, u_{d_v-2})$. Shown as G_3 in Figure 2. We can transform G_3 to G_4 as follows. By similar method as above, it is easy to prove that $R_\alpha(G_3) < R_\alpha(G_4)$ for $\alpha \in (-0.58, 0)$.

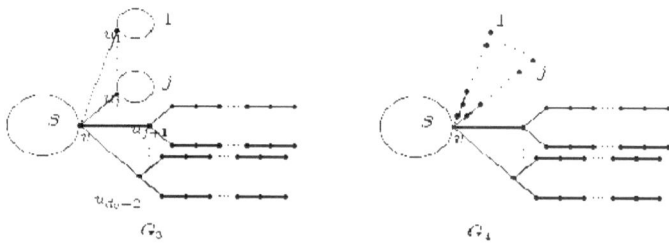

Fig. 2. The first change for Case 2 in Lemma 1

Transform G_4 into a new unicyclic graph G_5 as follows: delete a pendent path adjacent to v , and attach it to a leaf M of G_4 . See Figure 3. By comparing, we have

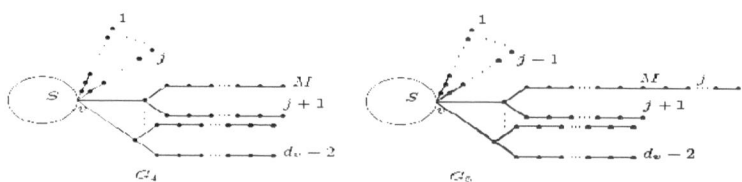

Fig. 3. The second change for Case 2 in Lemma 1

$R_\alpha(G_4) - R_\alpha(G_5) \leq j2^\alpha d_v^\alpha - (j-1)2^\alpha (d_v - 1)^\alpha + (d_v^\alpha - (d_v - 1)^\alpha)(j2^\alpha + j3^\alpha + 3^\alpha(d_v - 2))$ $-2 \cdot 4^\alpha \leq j(2^\alpha + 3^\alpha)(d_v^\alpha - (d_v - 1)^\alpha) + 3^\alpha(d_v - 2)(d_v^\alpha - (d_v - 1)^\alpha) + 2^\alpha((d_v - 1)^\alpha - 2^\alpha) + 2^\alpha$ $-4^\alpha \leq 2^\alpha((d_v - 1)^\alpha - 2^\alpha) + 2^\alpha - 4^\alpha + 3^\alpha(d_v - 2)(d_v^\alpha - (d_v - 1)^\alpha) < 0$ for $\alpha \in (-0.58, 0)$.

If G_6 is a unicyclic graph with the following structure, then transform G_6 into a new unicyclic graph G_7 as follows: delete the edge vu_2 and connect u_2 to a leaf M. See Figure 4.

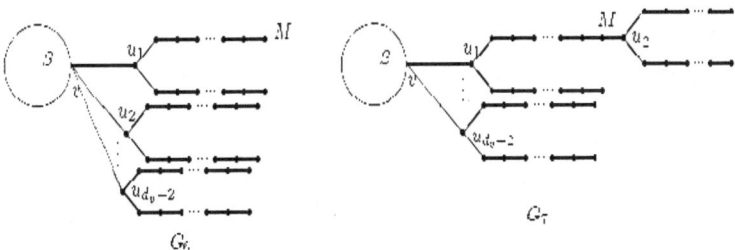

Fig. 4. The third change for Case 2 in Lemma 1

By comparing, we have $R_\alpha(G_6) - R_\alpha(G_7) \le (j \cdot 2^\alpha + 3^\alpha (d_v - 2 - j))(d_v^\alpha - (d_v - 1)^\alpha)$
$+ 3^\alpha (d_v - 1)^\alpha + 2^\alpha - 6^\alpha - 4^\alpha \le 3^\alpha (d_v - 2)(d_v^\alpha - (d_v - 1)^\alpha) + 3^\alpha (d_v - 1)^\alpha + 2^\alpha - 6^\alpha - 4^\alpha < 0$
for $\alpha \in (-0.58, 0)$.

Similar discussion can be done for the case $v \notin S$ and the results still hold.

By above discussion, we conclude that $R_\alpha(G_1) \le R_\alpha(G_2)$ for $\alpha \in (-0.58, 0)$.

Lemma 2. Suppose G_8 is a unicyclic graph with a cycle S. A vertex $v \in S$ is adjacent to j pendent paths and $d_v - 2 - j$ leaves. Transform G_8 into a new unicyclic graph G_9 as follows: delete the pendent paths and the leaves and form a new path adjacent to v. See Figure 5. Then $R_\alpha(G_8) \le R_\alpha(G_9)$ for $\alpha \in (-1, 0)$.

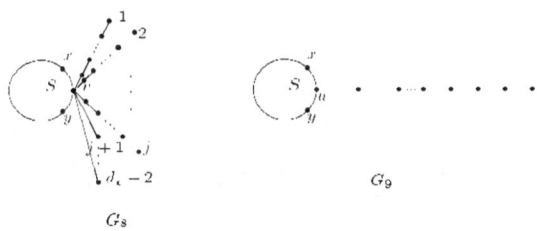

Fig. 5. The change for the case in Lemma 2

Proof. Assume v has neighbors x and y on the cycle S and $d_v = a$, $d_x = b$ and $d_y = c$. Obviously $b \ge 2, c \ge 2$. $a = 3$ is a trivial case and the result is direct. Suppose $a \ge 4$, then $R_\alpha(G_8) - R_\alpha(G_9) = (a^\alpha - 3^\alpha)(b^\alpha + c^\alpha) + j((2a)^\alpha + 2^\alpha - 4^\alpha - a^\alpha) + 4^{\alpha+1} - a4^\alpha - 6^\alpha - 2^\alpha + (a-2)a^\alpha$. Since $j \le a - 2$, then $R_\alpha(G_8) - R_\alpha(G_9) \le (a^\alpha - 3^\alpha)(b^\alpha + c^\alpha) + (a-2)((2a)^\alpha + 2^\alpha - 4^\alpha - a^\alpha) + 4^{\alpha+1} - a4^\alpha - 6^\alpha - 2^\alpha + (a-2)a^\alpha < 0$ for $\alpha \in (-1, 0)$. The proof is completed.

Lemma 3. Let G_{10} (not a cycle) be a unicyclic graph with a cycle S satisfying the following two conditions: (1) All vertices in G_{10} are of degree 1 , 2 or 3 . (2) A vertex v is of degree 3 if and only if $v \in S$. Suppose $d_v = 3$, $x, y \in S$ are adjacent to v and v is an end of a pendent path. Transform G_{10} into a new unicyclic graph G_{11} as follows: delete the edge xv and connect x to the leaf M of the pendent path. See Figure 6. Then $R_\alpha(G_{10}) < R_\alpha(G_{11})$ for $\alpha \in (-0.58, 0)$.

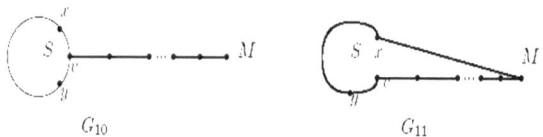

G_{10} G_{11}

Fig. 6. The change for the case in Lemma 3

Proof. Suppose $d_x = a$ and $d_y = b$, then $R_\alpha(G_{10}) - R_\alpha(G_{11}) \le (3a)^\alpha + (3b)^\alpha + 6^\alpha - (2a)^\alpha - 4^\alpha - 4^\alpha = (a^\alpha + b^\alpha + 2^\alpha)(3^\alpha - 2^\alpha) + 2^\alpha - 4^\alpha$. There are altogether four cases (1) $a = 2, b = 2$; (2) $a = 2, b = 3$; (3) $a = 3, b = 2$ and (4) $a = 3, b = 3$. For each case, $R(G_{10}) - R(G_{11}) \le (2 \cdot 3^\alpha + 2^\alpha)(3^\alpha - 2^\alpha) + 2^\alpha - 4^\alpha \le 2 \cdot 9^\alpha - 2 \cdot 6^\alpha + 6^\alpha - 4^\alpha + 2^\alpha - 4^\alpha \le 2 \cdot 9^\alpha - 6^\alpha - 2 \cdot 4^\alpha + 2^\alpha < 0$, for $\alpha \in (-0.58, 0)$. Then the proof is completed.

3 Main Results

Theorem 1. Among the unicyclic graphs with n vertices, the cycle C_n has the maximal general Randic index R_α for $\alpha \in (-0.58, 0)$ and S_n^+ has the minimal general Randic index R_α for $\alpha \in (-0.58, 0)$.

Proof. For each unicyclic graph G with n vertices, we can always use Lemma 1, Lemma 2 and Lemma 3 to change G into the cycle C_n step by step. In the process, the general Randić indices keep increasing for $\alpha \in (-0.58, 0)$. Similarly, we can always use Lemma 1, Lemma 2 and Lemma 3 to change G into the unicyclic graph S_n^+ step by step. In the process, the general Randić indices keep decreasing for $\alpha \in (-0.58, 0)$. So C_n and S_n^+ has the maximal and minimal general Randic index for $\alpha \in (-0.58, 0)$, respectively.

Theorem 2. Among the unicyclic graphs with n vertices, when $\alpha \to -\infty$, the unicyclic graph with a triangle u, v, w and $\frac{n-3}{2}$ pendent paths of length 2 adjacent to u has the maximal general Randic index R_α for odd n ; the unicyclic graph with a quadrilateral u, v, w, x and $\frac{n-4}{2}$ pendent paths of length 2 adjacent to u has maximal general Randic index R_α for even n .

Proof. Because the general Randić index $R_\alpha(G)$ for a graph G is the sum of $(d_u d_v)^\alpha$, where (u, v) is an edge of G and d_u, d_v are the degrees of the vertices u, v, respectively. For a unicyclic graph, $d_u d_v \geq 2$ and for $\alpha \to -\infty$, $\frac{3^\alpha}{2^\alpha} \to 0$, $\frac{4^\alpha}{2^\alpha} \to 0$, $\frac{5^\alpha}{2^\alpha} \to 0$, $\cdots$. So 2^α s are the main part of $R_\alpha(G)$. The unicyclic graph with maximal general Randic index R_α for $\alpha \to -\infty$ must have as many edges (x, y) as possible, where $d_x = 1, d_y = 2$. If n is odd, then a unicyclic graph has at most $\frac{n-3}{2}$ such edges. If n is even, then a unicyclic graph has at most $\frac{n-4}{2}$ such edges. With this condition, by comparing each case that is possible, we have the result of the theorem.

References

1. Randić, M.: On the Characterization of Molecular Branching. J. Amer. Chem. Soc., 6609–6615 (1975)
2. Bollobás, B., Erdös, P.: Graphs with Extremal Weights. Ars. Combin., 225–233 (1998)
3. Li, X., Gutman, I.: Mathematical Aspects of Randic-Type Molecular Structure Descriptors. Univ. Kragujevac, Kragujevac (2006)
4. Gao, J., Lu, M.: On the Randić Index of Unicyclic Graphs. MATCH Commun. Math. Comput. Chem. 2, 377–384 (2005)
5. Li, X., Wang, L., Zhang, Y.: Complete Solution for Unicyclic Graphs with Minimum General Randić Index. MATCH Commun. Math. Comput. Chem., 391–408 (2006)
6. Li, X., Shi, Y., Xu, T.: Unicyclic Graphs with Maximum General Randić Index for a > 0. MATCH Commun. Math. Comput. Chem., 557–570 (2006)

Study on Molecular Dynamics Simulation of Calcium Silicate Hydrate (C-S-H) Gels

Peng Hu[1] and Wei Dai[2,*]

[1] School of Mathematics and Physics, Huangshi Institution of Technology, China
qingwahp@yahoo.com.cn
[2] School of Economics and Management, Huangshi Institution of Technology, China
dweisky@163.com

Abstract. C-S-H gels-the main cement hydration product, have an important impact on the properties of cement and caused a wide range of study on it. Simulation technology of molecular dynamics is summarized, the basic principles of molecular dynamics and simulation of molecular dynamics of C-S-H gels are introduced, and development trend about simulation of molecular dynamics of C-S-H gel is finally predicted in this paper. It is designed to provide information and ideas to academics engage in computer simulation of cement-based materials.

Keywords: C-S-H gels; molecular dynamics; quantum chemistry; computer simulation.

1 Introduction

C-S-H gel, as the most important hydration product of cement-based material, accounting for 60-70% of hydration products, has an important impact on the performance of cement. Reasons for calcium silicate hydrate in cement paste being called C-S-H gels are as follows: (1) its smaller particles, in the size range of colloidal particles, in general, it can not be observed under the microscope; (2) it is mostly amorphous state, only a dispersive diffraction peaks occurs between 0.28-0.32nm when using the method of X-Ray diffraction, and complete structural information can not be found; (3) C-S-H gel is nonstoichiometric compound with volatile compounds, and it changes with the cement composition, the environment and hydration time [1].

In recent years, with the development and renewal of research tools, knowledge and understanding of C-S-H gel is deepening. Commonly, C-S-H gel is divided into C-S-H(I) and C-S-H(II) according to calcium silicon ratio, they are both layered structures, only differ in length of chain and spacing of different layers. With the development of computer technology, the effective integration of relationship between microstructure and macroscopic properties of cement-based composite material and computer technology makes remarkable achievements in the area of design and performance evaluation of materials. Macroscopic properties of material are dependent

---

* Corresponding author.

R. Chen (Ed.): ICICIS 2011, Part I, CCIS 134, pp. 142–147, 2011.

on their microstructure under the premise of specific chemical composition [2]. So, we can establish some models relying on the experimental and theoretical studies on microstructure of cement-based material, and display them effectively using computer so as to provide new ideas for people to study the mechanism of hydration of cement and modification.

2 Simulation of Molecular Dynamics

Simulation of molecular dynamics has been widely used since the mid-fifties. It has become an important method together with Monte Carlo method and its application has been involved in chemical reactions, heavy ion collision, microstructure and other branches of learning [3]. The so-called simulation of molecular dynamics means simulation of the movement of the nucleus using computer in the many-body systems consist of the nuclear and electronic, and calculating the structure and nature of computing systems. Each nucleus's motion is regarded following Newton's law of motion in the experiential potential field provided by all the other nuclei and electrons. This method can provide microstructure, particle motion and clear images of the relationship between particles and the macroscopic nature, which can contribute to extraction of new concepts and theories.

Simulation of molecular dynamics is under the assumption that particle motion can be dealt with classical mechanics. For a system formed by the many isolate particles, the particle motion can be determined by the Newtonian equations of motion. In the process of simulation of molecular dynamics, by solving the Newtonian motion equations can obtain a series of configuration of atoms in the system. Current common algorithms for solving equations of motion are: (1) Verlet algorithm; (2) Velocity-Verlet algorithm; (3) Leap-frog algorithm; (4) Gear algorithm [4]. In addition, a reasonable initial configuration and speed enable computing systems relax rapidly to balance. Initial configuration and velocity can be determined through the experimental data, theoretical model, or a combination of both. After determining the initial model, the choice of potential function is critical. At present, potential function is mainly two-body potential and many-body potential. In fact, many-body potential can more accurately represent the potential function of polyatomic systems. Equilibrium simulation of molecular dynamics is carried out under certain ensemble; there are four types of balanced ensemble: NPT, NVT, NHP, NVE, the former two categories is frequently used, and NHP and NVE method can also be combined with the actual model in order to achieve better simulation results.

3 Simulation of Molecular Dynamics of C-S-H Gels

Early study of C-S-H gels only involved XRD, DTA and chemical analysis, and obtained the average composition of C-S-H gels. In the 50's of last century, Grudemo[5] firstly observed calcium silicate hydrate using electron microscopy, and determined its structure using electron diffraction, finally he found that it was colloidal size particle, but had crystal structure. This conclusion coordinated the controversy on whether the strength of cement came from colloidal or crystal at the time. Then

Taylor[6] proposed that it was more accurate that C-S-H gel was expressed as hydration products in Portland cement on the basis of the research, since it is not compounds with fixed composition. His opinion has been recognized in cement sector and has being used till now. In the mid-70s, as the emergence of scanning electron microscopy (SEM), sample preparation could be achieved only using cement bulk directly instead of cement powder prepared with plenty of water prepared by Grudemo. So the observation was closer to the practicality. Diamond [7], found C-S-H has follow four kinds of morphology with the extension of hydration time when he observe cement paste with the SEM- fibrous, honeycomb, irregular and other large particles and the porous internal hydration products. This result, although not comprehensive, but it is a leap forward in understanding morphology of C-S-H gels. On the basis of previous studies, scholars from various countries conducted further researches, and proposed a series of structural models, such as class Tobermorite and Jennite model [8], solid solution model [9], hypothesis of nano-structure and intermediate structure [10]. However, these models are based on their respective theories backed by research; inevitably there are limitations of their own, which brought a big problem for further study on cement. At present, Taylor theory is gradually accepted by the majority for it fits experimental facts better. Taylor thinks the cement hydration products mainly made by solution of the Tobermorite and Jennite, and the proportion of Tobermorite and Jennite in calcium silicate hydrate is different under different Ca/Si ratio, there is a certain transformation between the two. People often can only imagine on the structure of calcium silicate hydrate, before the simulation of molecular dynamics applied to the study of cement-based materials and simulation of molecular dynamics allowed the researchers to construct a fine three-dimensional structure model of calcium silicate hydrate according to crystallographic data tested by different means. The model is clear and intuitive, and staff can revise and comprise the model easily in order to make the model more realistic, make the results obtained from various simulations more accurate.

As the complexity and uncertainty of cement hydration system structure of C-S-H gel is still unknown. People have done much work using simulation technology molecular dynamics. The mid-90s of last century, Faucon [12] simulated the structure of hydrated calcium silicate with the Ca/Si between 0.66 and 0.83, he inputted Tobermorite structure of 0.9 nm found by Hamid, and simulated the cause of instability of structure of the calcium silicate hydrate, fracture mechanism silicate chain and the effect on structure after replacing silicon with cation (Al^{3+}) using isovolumic method molecular dynamics. The results show that: with the Ca/Si increases, the bridge silicon-oxygen tetrahedron becomes unstable, but the chain will not break; if water molecules exist in the structure, the chain break between bridge silicon-oxygen tetrahedron and non-bridge silicon-oxygen tetrahedron and form two Q1, meanwhile water molecules are decomposed and are connected to the two new Q1 to ensure the four-coordination of silicon. If Al^{3+} replaces Si^{4+} in bridge silicon-oxygen tetrahedron, the chain does not break up and replace, if Al^{3+} replaces Si^{4+} in non-bridge silicon-oxygen tetrahedron in the participation of water molecules, the chain break between bridge silicon-oxygen tetrahedron and non-bridge silicon-oxygen tetrahedron. In 2007, J.S.Dolado[13], came from University of Bonn in Germany, conducted

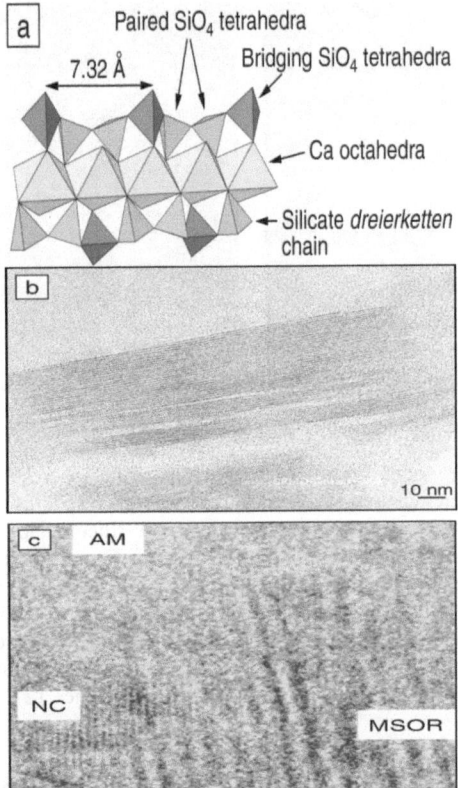

Fig. 1. a) Model of calcium silicate hydrate (C-S-H) at Ca/Si = 0.66, with a central double layer of calcium ions connected on each side to chains of silica tetrahedral. b) Transmission electron microscopy (TEM) image of C-S-H prepared by reaction of lime with amorphous silica at Ca/Si =1. c) High-resolution TEM micrograph of the hydrated region in a "real," dense, C-S-H paste. AM, NC, and MSOR indicate amorphous, nanocrystalline, and mesoscopically ordered regions, respectively. The distance between layers is 1.5 nm. [a), b), c) adapted from Reference 11].

follow-up simulation of calcium silicate hydrate system with different Ca/Si ratio using TREMOLO software, and the obtained physical parameters such as the density were in good agreement with the measured values. It verified the accuracy of the structure model used and the potential function, it also visually illustrated that with the increase of the ratio of calcium silicon, calcium silicate hydrate structure has gradually changed from the long chain to short chain structures, and the structural changed from the Tobermorite to Jennite. It validated the correctness of the theory of Taylor solution from a certain extent. In 2009, Roland J.-M.Pellenq [15] in the United States simulated the adsorption of water molecules in the C-S-H gels through Material Studio software, using simulation of molecular dynamics and Monte Carlo algorithm, and obtained the structural model which was in good agreement with actual results.

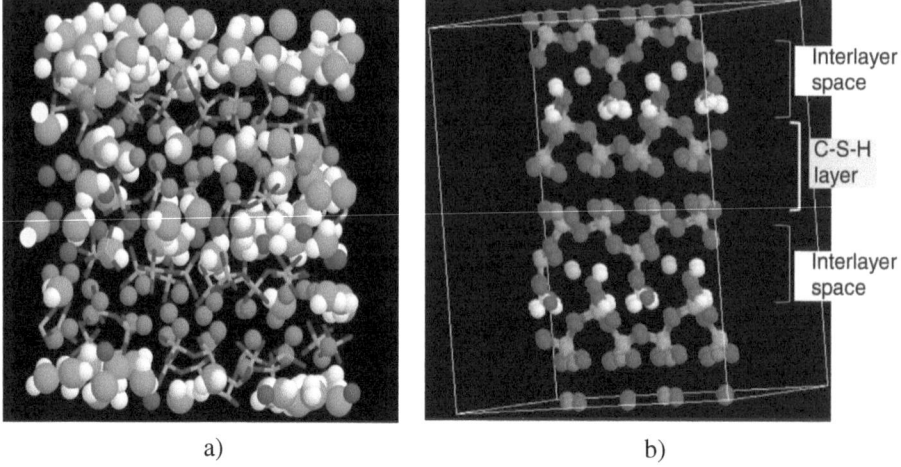

a)   b)

Fig. 2. a) the molecular model of C-S-H: the blue and white spheres are oxygen and hydrogen atoms of water molecules, respectively; the green and gray spheres are inter and intra-layer calcium ions, respectively; yellow and red sticks are silicon and oxygen atoms in silica tetrahedral (adapted from Reference 14) b) A relaxed configuration of tobermorite-like C-S-H (Hamid's structure), after potential-energy minimization, at Ca/Si = 0.83 with four H_2O molecules per unit cell in the interlamellar space. Hydrogen atoms are white, oxygen atoms are red, layer calcium ions are dark grey, interlayer calcium ions are light grey, and silicon atoms are yellow-brown. Note the short distance between the interlayer calcium ions and the closest oxygen atom from the neighboring layer. (Adapted from reference 12).

4   Development Trends of Simulations of Molecular Dynamics of C-S-H Gels

While the simulation of molecular dynamics of C-S-H gel is increasingly widespread and a series of achievements was made, researches on C-S-H gels faced new difficulties and opportunities mainly in the following areas with the complexity of cement system and increased uncertainty of structure of hydration products.

(1) Molecular modeling is a new interdisciplinary field its application to real study needs the combination of knowledge about mathematics, physics, theoretical chemistry, computer science and chemical engineering, etc. It sets up very large threshold for the general research workers, and thus molecular modeling studies can not truly be a means of study accepted by the general.

(2) At present, as research methods and means are different for various research teams, so the choice of potential function has changed dramatically, they can be to some extent in line with the actual situation, but not very comprehensive, there are certain deviation. With the theory of molecular dynamics simulation continues to mature, a form of simple, accurate potential function is bound to occur in order to bring greater convenience to researchers, making the field of simulation of molecular dynamics more complete.

(3) In order to improve certain properties of cement, a certain degree of admixture are needed to mix in, but the mechanism of admixture are not yet mastered. If the

method of molecular dynamics were implied, may be can help us understand the mechanism at the atomic level, and can predict many unknowns about the performance. It supplied great help for the related studies.

(4) With the progress of research tools, understanding of the nature of the C-S-H gel is in constant development and more comprehensive, it is also our understanding of the laws of objective things. In addition, researches of C-S-H gel is not only the theoretical study of the problem, its characteristics are closely related with performance of cement and concrete. Therefore, the understanding of structure and properties of C-S-H gels, especially grasp chemical structure chemical structure for C-S-H model can improve the performance, durability and quality of concrete materials.

References

1. Young, N.: New Progress on Structure Model of C-S-H gel. Nanjing University of Chemical Technology 20(2), 78–85 (1998)
2. Shi, C., Feng, N., Liu, Z.: Introduction of Materials Science. Chemical Industry Press, Beijing (2002)
3. Chen, Z., Xu, W., Tang, L.: Theory and Practice of Molecular Modeling. Chemical Industry Press, Beijing (2007)
4. Wen, Y., Zhu, R., et al.: Technology on Simulation of Molecular Dynamics. Progress on Mechanics (2003)
5. Grudemo, A.: Discussion of the structure of cement hydration compounds-Bernal J D. In: Proceedings of the third International Symposium on the Chemistry of Cement, London, p. 247 (1952)
6. Taylor, H.F.W.: Cement Chemistry, pp. 142–152. Academic press, London (1990)
7. Diamond, S.: Hydraulic cement pastes: Their structure and properties. Cement and Concrete Association, Slough, UK, K, p. 2 (1976)
8. Taylor, H.F.W.: Cement Chemistry, 2nd edn., pp. 128–134. Thomas Telford, London (1997)
9. Grutzec, M.W., Laros, T.J., Kwan, S.: Characteristics of C-S-H gels. In: Proceeding of the 10th ICCC, p. 2067. Gothenburg, Sweden (1997)
10. Viehlan, D., Li, J.F., Yuan, L.J., et al.: Mesostructure of calcium silicate hydrate (C-S-H) gels in Portland cement paste: Short-range ordering, nanocrystallinity, and local compositional order. J. Am. Ceram. Soc. 9(7), 1731–1744 (1996)
11. Pellenq, R.J.-M., Van Damme, H.: Why Does Concrete Set? The Nature of Cohesion Forces in Hardened Cement-Based Materials. Mrs Bulletin 136, 319–323 (2004)
12. Hamid, S.A.: The crystal structure of the 11 Å natural tobermorite Ca2.25 [Si3O7.5 (OH) 1.5].1H2O. Zeitschrift fur Kristallographie 154, 189–198 (1981)
13. Dolado, J.S., Griebel, M., Hamaekers, J.: A Molecular Dynamics Study of Cementitious Calcium Silicate Hydrate (C-S-H) Gels. INS Preprint No.0701 (2007)
14. Pellenq, R.J.-M., Kushima, A., Shahsavari, R., Van Vliet, K.J., Buehler, M.J., Yip, S., Ulm, F.-J.: A realistic molecular model of cement hydrates. PANS 106(38), 16102–16107 (2009)

Apply Ensemble of Lazy Learners to Biomedical Data Mining

Liu Pengfei[1] and Tang Wulei[2]

[1] College of Science, South China Agricultural University, Guangzhou, 510642, China
[2] Guangdong Soft-Park, Guangzhou, 510663, China
pfliu@scau.edu.cn, tangwl@gdsoftpark.com

Abstract. Disease stat can be predicted from biomedical data studies by machine learning. However, many available biomedical data feature high dimensional or imbalanced, and these always led to high false positive or false negative rate in prediction. How to construct suitable machine learning model is the key to the performance.

This article describes a novel approach that applies PSO boosted ensembles of lazy learners to mining biomedical data. The learned model is evaluated on three published data sets during 10-fold cross-validation; Experiment result reveals that the proposed model can tackle data interference and performs better than other available rule learning methods.

Keywords: Lazy learning, Ensemble, Biomedical, PSO.

1 Introduction

Data mining are being increasingly applied on the analysis of biomedical data sets. It was demonstrated that rule models can be applied to biomarker profiling studies that produce understandable models [1, 2]. Furthermore, Gopalakrishnan *et al.* [3] described an approach that uses a Bayesian score to evaluate rule models during biomarkers mining. Chanho and Sung-Bae proposed evolutionary computation for optimal ensemble classifier in lymphoma cancer classification [4] and showed classifiers ensemble method would be a good way for biological data mining. However, we believe above mentioned mining model can be further improved, both from classifiers ensemble aspect and evolutionary algorithm aspect while considering data features. Susmita *et al.* proposed an adaptive optimal ensemble classifier via bagging and rank aggregation with applications to high dimensional data [5].

How to promote the accuracy of biomedical data mining still remains a great challenge. In this article, we apply Particle swarm optimization Boosted Ensemble of Lazy Learning (PBELL) to solving the issue, while the ensemble model is optimized with boosted weight scores vector.

The remainder of the article is organized as follows. Section 2 presents PBELL algorithm and implementation. Section 3 describes experimental setup and results of applying PBELL to three published data sets. Section 4 presents conclusions.

R. Chen (Ed.): ICICIS 2011, Part I, CCIS 134, pp. 148–154, 2011.

2 Methods and Implementation

It is well known that more complex classification functions yield lower training errors yet run the risk of poor generalization in machine learning studies [6]. Take this fact into consideration and refer to the practice, we employ the simple but very powerful classification algorithm called case-based reasoning, or known as lazy learning. Lazy learning belongs to the local methods but goes to the extreme of locality idea. The use of the lazy learning approach allows the generalization delayed until it is given a test sample [7]. Lazy learning with information-theoretic similarity matching was demonstrated to be superior over other machine-learning approaches in various comparative studies [8]. Contrary to global approximations, lazy learning does not suffer from data interference [9] and this feature is very helpful.

There are many lazy learning implementations such as IB1, IBk, lazy Bayesian rules. IB1 determines the type of test samples through one of its neighbors, while IBk by its k neighbors around. Lbr is a lazy semi-naive Bayesian classifier that designed to alleviate the attribute interdependence problem of naive Bayesian classification. To classify a test example, Lbr creates a conjunctive rule that selects a most appropriate subset of training examples and induces a local naive Bayesian classifier using this subset. Lbr can significantly improve the performance of the naive Bayesian classifier [10]. Here we choose LBR as the lazy learning implementation in mining model.

Ensemble is a learning paradigm where many basic learners are jointly used to solve a predicting problem and make prediction more robust and accuracy. Ensemble learning's leverage comes from the diversity of multiple classifiers [11]. Ensemble researches had shown that the aggregated output of a lazy learning ensemble can be more accurate than any single predictor [12].

The computing time would increase exponentially with the classifiers growth while using traditional optimized method to calculate ensemble's all possible weight vectors. Therefore it has great need to use evolution method for finding optimal weight vector efficiently. In this situation, many PSO or GA based ensemble optimization methods were proposed and worked well [13, 14].

PSO performs optimization without explicit gradient knowledge of the problem by maintaining a population of candidate solutions called particles and driving them around in the search-space according to fitness function. The movements of the particles are guided by the best found positions in the search-space, which are continually updated as better positions are found by the particles [15]. Compared to genetic algorithms, PSO can converge to the optimal solution more quickly in most cases, so we choose PSO as the optimizing method.

We propose a novel PSO boosted ensemble of lazy learners to solve biomedical data mining issue. PSO based boosting optimization model revokes some basic classifiers repeatedly in a series of rounds to update a distribution of weights that indicates the importance of each classifier. On each round, the weight of each classifier is updated according to the position of the corresponding particle; this strategy enables ensemble generate more robust and accuracy prediction.

Kazemi *et al.* proposed a multi-objective PSO optimization that used different groups of particles to proceed with differing goals [16]. This article also uses multi-objective similar real-value coded PSO in ensemble optimization problem.

Supposing the ensemble has k classifiers that each particle in the swarm would have k dimensions while each dimension's position representing one classifiers' weight.

All classifiers' weights compose of an instance of weight vector. In the updating period, the weight vector should satisfy the normalization condition in expression (1).

$$ST: \quad \Omega = \sum_{i=1}^{K} w_i = 1 \quad 0 \le w_i \le 1 \tag{1}$$

Where k is the number of classifiers, and w_i is the weight factor of classifier i. As we know, precision is the proportion of the true positives against all positive results. To improve the performance of the minor class, here we assume the minor class as positive samples. In first swarm the model tries to optimize the precision goal which refers to expression (2), thus promotes minor class's performance.

$$Precision = \frac{tp}{tp + fp} \tag{2}$$

At second swarm, the model tries to optimize the MCC goal which refers to expression (3).

$$MCC = \frac{(tp \times tn) - (fp \times fn)}{\sqrt{(tp + fp) \times (fp + tn) \times (tn + fn) \times (fn + tp)}} \tag{3}$$

Here tp means the proportion of true negatives; fp means the proportion of false positives; fn means the proportion of false negatives; tn means the proportion of true negatives.

Two fitness functions that globally evaluate the particles are defined as expression (4) and (5). Each fitness function works in its corresponding swarm. The fitness functions can effectively distinguish the excellent particles in ensemble's weight vector optimizing course. Each swarm exchanges some best particles with the other during evolution course.

$$fitness(first\ swarm) = \frac{1}{2} \log \sqrt{\frac{precision_i}{1 - precision_i}} \tag{4}$$

The $precision_i$ in expression (4) is the training prediction on the N examples of the corresponding ensemble under weight matrix i.

$$fitness(second\ swarm) = \frac{1}{2} \log \sqrt{MCC} \tag{5}$$

Both metrics are used to assess the performance of validation in training procedure, and they are less dependent on the scaling and magnitude of the training sets than other performance metrics. The bigger are the precision and MCC, the better is the performance.

To increase diversity of ensemble and tackle high dimension data effectively, Ref. [17] used feature selection method; this article applies Partial Least Squares regression (PLS-regression) approach to estimating importance of features and selecting suitable features while encountering high dimensional data. PLS-regression is a statistical method that finds a linear regression model by projecting the predicted variables and the observable variables to a new space [18].

Sampling from both classes is repeated until training sets are enough for the classifiers in ensemble. This article uses simple random sampling with replacement strategy [19] from both original classes. To estimate the real performance, the model performs double cross-validation where inner cross-validation is used to construct weight vector based on PSO evolution algorithm followed by outer 10-fold cross-validation to test the performance of the ensemble.

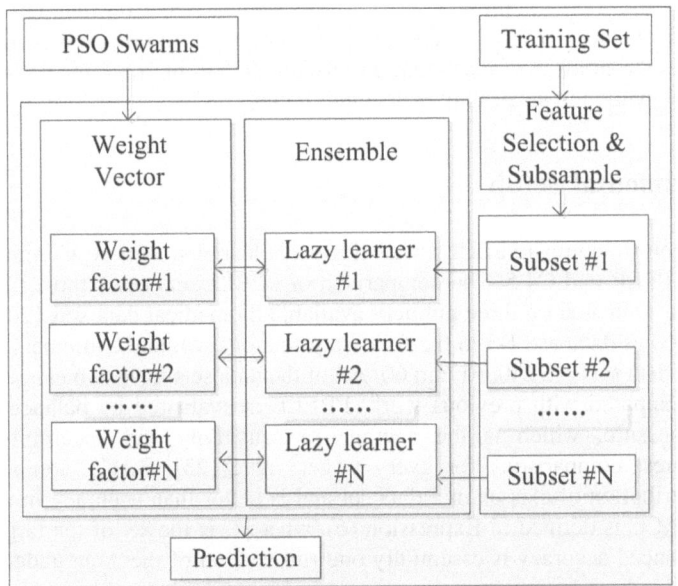

Fig. 1. Framework of PSO boosted lazy learner ensemble

Figure 1 illustrates the framework of PSO boosted lazy learners ensemble.

The working cycle of PBELL lists as following.

Input: {Sequence of N examples $(x_1, y_1),...,(x_N, y_N)$ with labels $y_i \in Y = \{1,...,k\}$

Distribution D over the examples by sampling N;

Basic learning models C of Lazy Learner;

Integer T specifying number of iterations;

Weight vector $w_i^1 = W(i)$ *for* $i = 1,...,N$. }

1. Initialize positions and speeds of particles represent C on D;

2. Set ensemble's weight vector W according to all particles' positions;

3. Calculate fitness of each particle according to expression (4) and (5) by ensemble's prediction;

4. Compare individual current fitness and its experienced best one; assign the better one as its current best one;

5. Determine current best fitness value in entire swarm;

6. Update particles' velocity parameters according to current best fitness values;

7. Exchange best particles with the other while preset criterions are satisfied;

8. Repeat step 2 ~ 7 until stopping criteria T is satisfied;

9. Obtain best weights vector W and test the predicting performance.

In actual optimization, number of iterations T can be set a big enough value. For example, 1500 can be a suitable one in our experiments. In other cases, T can be set according to the number of classifiers in ensemble. Too big of T may waste a lot of running time while too small may course not mature.

3   Experimental Setup

In this section we compare PBELL with three rule learners, namely, Conjunctive Rule Learner, RIPPER and C4.5. The comparison of PEBLL and other three rule learning methods are evaluated on three publicly available biomedical data sets [20-22] which are numbered as database 1-3 in the following sections, while the numbers of samples in the three data sets are 240, 61 and 60. All of the data sets have two classes.

To be compared with previous work, PBELL is evaluated by balanced accuracy (BACC) measure, which is the average of sensitivity and specificity over all one-versus-rest comparisons for every target value [23]. BACC compensates for skewed distribution of classes in a data set and is better than accuracy in imbalanced data set. BACC is defined in Expression (6), where C is the set of the target variable values. Balanced accuracy is essentially one run version of the Area under the Curve (AUC).

$$\text{BACC} = \frac{\sum_c Sensitivity(c) + Specificity(c)}{|C|} \tag{6}$$

The definitions of sensitivity and specificity are defined in expression (7) and (8), where meanings of tp, tn, fp and fn can refer to above section.

$$Sensitivity = \frac{tp}{tp + fn} \tag{7}$$

$$Specificity = \frac{tn}{tn + fp} \tag{8}$$

Table 1 shows the BACC values from 10-fold cross-validation on the three datasets depicted above. Except PBELL's values, other values come from Ref. [3]. Where BRL1 stands for BRL with beam search size (memory of particular size) 1 and BRL1000 represents BRL with beam search size 1000. Ripper and C4.5 are classical classifiers methods and wildly used in data mining and report many successful cases [24, 25].

Table 1. Comparison of the Predicting Performance

#	Ripper	C4.5	BRL1	BRL1000	PBELL
1	44.81	42.93	43.31	49.63	51.14
2	98.65	100	100	100	100
3	25.54	38.56	45.00	63.75	65

From the experiments, PBELL exceeds other three rule learning models overall. There are several advantages of PBELL that compared with other traditional machine learning models and the most important is that it can tackle different types of biomedical data sets and produce more robust and accuracy results by basic classifiers ensemble method. This feature enables biomedical scientists just use one kind of ensemble model in different occasions instead of attempting different mining models to get best performance one.

4 Conclusions

The application of machine learning method to analyzing biomedical datasets has become more and more important. In this article, we present and evaluate a novel approach that complements existing methods for certain biomedical data mining and is helpful for biomedical research. It is reasonable to forecast that the classifiers ensemble would be applied to more and more fields.

We have shown that using PSO boosted lazy learning ensemble approach to generate biomedical data mining model allows a more accurate result in the biomedical data mining. The basic PBELL algorithm presented here can be extended in many ways, including implementation with different boosted methods or different basic classifiers ensemble.

References

1. Gopalakrishnan, V., Ganchev, P., Ranganathan, S., et al.: Rule learning for disease-specific biomarker discovery from clinical proteomic mass spectra. In: Li, J., Yang, Q., Tan, A.-H. (eds.) BioDM 2006. LNCS (LNBI), vol. 3916, pp. 93–105. Springer, Heidelberg (2006)
2. Gopalakrishnan, V., Williams, E., Ranganathan, S., et al.: Proteomic data mining challenges in identification of disease-specific biomarkers from variable resolution mass spectra. In: SIAM Bioinformatics Workshop. Society of Industrial and Applied Mathematics International Conference on Data Mining, Lake Buena Vista, FL (2004)
3. Gopalakrishnan, V., Lustgarten, J.L., Visweswaran, S., Cooper, G.F.: Bayesian rule learning for biomedical data mining. Bioinformatics 26(5), 668–675 (2010)
4. Park, C., Cho, S.-B.: Evolutionary Computation for Optimal Ensemble Classifier in Lymphoma Cancer Classification. In: Carbonell, J.G., Siekmann, J. (eds.) ISMIS 2003. LNCS (LNAI), vol. 2871, pp. 521–530. Springer, Heidelberg (2003)
5. Datta, S., Pihur, V., Datta, S.: An adaptive optimal ensemble classifier via bagging and rank aggregation with applications to high dimensional data. BMC Bioinformatics 11, 427 (2010)

6. Viola, P., Jones, M.: Fast and Robust Classification using Asymmetric AdaBoost and a Detector Cascade. Advances in Neural Information Processing System 14, 1311–1318 (2001)
7. Aha, D.W.: Lazy learning. Lazy learning, 7–10 (1997)
8. van den Bosch, A., Weijters, T., van den Herik, H.J.: When small disjuncts abound, try lazy learning: A case study. In: Proceedings Seventh Benelearn Conference, pp. 109–118 (1997)
9. Atkeson, C.G., Moore, A.W., Schaal, S.: Locally weighted learning. Artificial Intelligence Review 11(1-5), 11–73 (1997)
10. Zheng, Z., Webb, G.I., Ting, K.M.: Lazy Bayesian Rules: A Lazy Semi-Naive Bayesian Learning Technique Competitive to Boosting Decision Trees. In: Proc. 16th International Conf. on Machine Learning, pp. 493–502 (1999)
11. Schapirere, R.E.: The strength of weak learnability. Machine Learning 5(2), 197–227 (1990)
12. Zenobi, G., Cunningham, P.: An Approach to Aggregating Ensembles of Lazy Learners that Supports Explanation. In: Craw, S., Preece, A.D. (eds.) ECCBR 2002. LNCS (LNAI), vol. 2416, pp. 121–160. Springer, Heidelberg (2002)
13. Chen, Y., Zhao, Y.: A novel ensemble of classifiers for microarray data classification. Applied Soft Computing 8(4), 1664–1669 (2008)
14. Wang, X., Wang, H.: Classification by evolutionary ensembles. Pattern Recognition 39, 595–607 (2006)
15. Kennedy, J., Eberhart, R.: Particle Swarm Optimization. In: Proceedings of IEEE International Conference on Neural Networks, vol. IV, pp. 1942–1948 (1995)
16. Parsopoulos, K.E., Vrahatis, M.N.: Particle swarm optimization method in multiobjective problems. In: Proceedings of ACM Symp. on Applied Computing, Madrid The Association for Computing Machinery, pp. 603–607. ACM Press, New York (2002)
17. Kim, K.-J., Cho, S.-B.: An evolutionary algorithm approach to optimal ensemble classifiers for DNA microarray data analysis. IEEE Transactions On Evolutionary Computation 12(3), 377–388 (2008)
18. Wold, S., SjÄolstrÄom, M., Erikson, L.: PLS-regression: A Basic Tool of Chemometrics. Chemometrics and Intelligent Laboratory Systems 130, 58–109 (2001)
19. Rocke, D.M., Dai, J.: Sampling and Subsampling for Cluster Analysis in Data Mining: With Applications to Sky Survey Data. Data Mining and Knowledge Discovery 7(2), 215–232 (2003)
20. Rosenwald, A., Wright, G., Chan, W.C., et al.: The use of molecular profiling to predict survival after chemotherapy for diffuse large-B-cell lymphoma. N. Engl. J. Med. 346, 1937–1947 (2002)
21. Alon, U., Barkai, N., Notterman, D.A., et al.: Broad patterns of gene expression revealed by clustering analysis of tumor and normal colon tissues probed by oligonucleotide arrays. Proc. Natl. Acad. Sci. USA 96, 6745–6750 (1999)
22. Iizuka, N., Oka, M., Yamada-Okabe, H., et al.: Oligonucleotide microarray for prediction of early intrahepatic recurrence of hepatocellular carcinoma after curative resection. The Lancet 361(9361), 923–929 (2003)
23. Sokolova, M., Japkowicz, N., Szpakowicz, S.: Beyond Accuracy, F-score and ROC: a Family of Discriminant Measures for Performance Evaluation. In: Sattar, A., Kang, B.-h. (eds.) AI 2006. LNCS (LNAI), vol. 4304, pp. 1015–1021. Springer, Heidelberg (2006)
24. Witten, I.H., Frank, E.: Data Mining: Practical Machine Learning Tools and Techniques. Morgan Kaufmann, San Francisco (2005)
25. Quinlan, J.R.: Bagging, Boosting, and C4.5. In: Proceedings of the Thirteenth National Conference on Artificial Intelligence, pp. 725–730 (1996)

Molecular Dynamics Simulation on Calcium Silicate Hydrate Doped Organic Molecules

Wei Dai[1,2,*], Zhonghe Shui[1], and Ping Duan[1]

[1] School of Materials Science and Engineering, Wuhan University of Technology, Wuhan, China
[2] School of Economics and Management, Huangshi Institution of Technology, Huangshi, China
dweisky@163.com, mre.shui@yahoo.com.cn, dp19851128@sina.com

Abstract. The interactions between organic molecules and calcium silicate hydrate were studied using molecular simulation techniques. Representative model of calcium silicate hydrate-Hamid model was selected as the initial structure of this simulation. Method of molecular mechanics (MM) and molecular dynamics (MD) were employed for simulation and calculation of C-S-H doped with styrene-acrylate, and the most stable conformation with lowest energy was obtained. Solubility parameters were calculated by analyzing the data of molecular trajectory combined with cohesive energy density (CED) of the structure. The results show that: doped calcium silicate hydrate have significant growth in the bulk modulus, compressibility and other mechanical performance parameters, compatibility of styrene-acrylate and calcium silicate hydrate is better, that is unanimous with test results.

Keywords: molecular dynamics simulation; calcium silicate hydrate; styrene-acrylate.

1 Introduction

With the rapid development of society, high strength and high-performance cement-based materials have become the main development direction of construction materials. To improve the performance of traditional cement-based materials, a variety of polymers were added into cement mortar and concrete, so that physical and chemical properties such as compressive and flexural strength, hydration rate and the curing time, water resistance have been considerably improved. Therefore, people have also study the micro-mechanism of polymers on cement hydration. Yousuf, Prince, Tritt-Goc and Gu Ping [1-4] have used XRD, FTIR, TG-DTA, MRI, MP, and SPI and other modern technology to study the effects of naphthalene and melamine super plasticizer on the cement hydration, and to monitor the changes of microstructure and pore structure in the hydration process of cement. In many polymer modifiers, especially styrene-acrylate, epoxy and other organic polymer materials are the most prominent; Xu Yajun studied the modification mechanism of the styrene-acrylate

---

* Corresponding author.

R. Chen (Ed.): ICICIS 2011, Part I, CCIS 134, pp. 155–160, 2011.
© Springer-Verlag Berlin Heidelberg 2011

copolymer on cement mortar and the microscopic structure of the blends system [5-7]. But overall, researches on modification of polymer on cement hydrate productions are still at the practical application level results from restrictions of testing means, the mechanism researches are not enough.

With the rapid development of quantum mechanics and computer technology, molecular simulation technology has become an indispensable means for scientific research, it can not only provides a qualitative description and can simulate the quantitative relationship between structure and properties of molecular systems, simulate the molecular structure and behavior using model at atomic level molecular, and then simulate various physical and chemical properties of molecular systems [8]. In this paper, molecular modeling software Materials Studio was used to construct the initial three-dimensional structure of calcium silicate hydrate, the most stable three-dimensional molecular structure of silicon calcium hydrate mixed with organic molecules was obtained using molecular mechanics (MM) and molecular dynamics (MD), compatibility between styrene-acrylate and silicon calcium hydrate and the modification effect was studied. The results show that the results of simulation are in good agreement with the test results.

2   Molecular Simulation

2.1   Model

Because of the complex and uncertainty of cement hydration process, the true structure of hydration products was still unknown. Representative model of calcium silicate hydrate-Hamid model [9] was selected as infrastructure, two basic structural unit of calcium silicate hydrate model and styrene-acrylate organic molecules were constructed and were shown in Fig.1 to Fig.3.

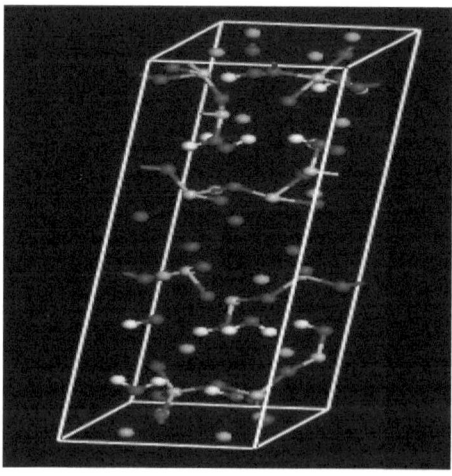

Fig. 1. Three-dimensional molecular structure of calcium silicate hydrate

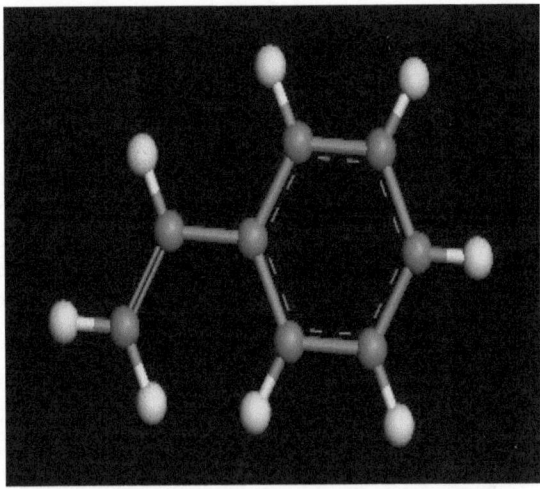

Fig. 2. Molecular structure of styrene monomer

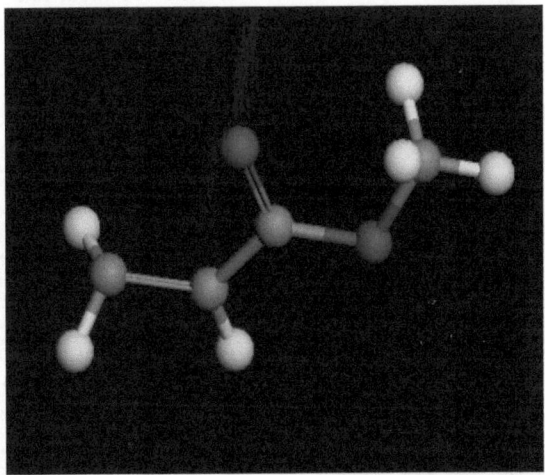

Fig. 3. Molecular structure of methyl acrylate

2.2   Simulation Process and Method

These researches were completed using the Materials Studio molecular modeling software from Accelrys company in U.S.A. First the model was constructed using 3D modeling unit in Amorphous Cell, the structure of calcium silicate hydrate-Hamid model was input in the basic unit, the model temperature was 300K and density was 2.18g/cm^3. In styrene-crylate modified simulation, a certain amount of styrene and methyl acrylate monomer structure was input according to doping proportion. After the 3D model was built, the most stable three-dimensional molecular structure was obtained using molecular mechanics (MM) method provided by the most optimal

(Minimizer), methods of conjugate gradient, the steepest descent and Newton. In the process of MD molecular dynamics calculations, the temperature consistent with modeling temperature and NVT ensemble was employed in dynamics simulations, the dynamics simulation time was 80ps, step length was 1fs, force field was Compass force field, using Verlet velocity for integration sum. In calculating the system's non-bond interaction, cutoff values of 0.9nm was used in the van der Waals interaction and Coulomb interaction, the van der Waals interaction was dealed with by atomic sum, the electrostatic interaction was dealed with by Ewald sum. After dynamics calculation, solubility parameters, mechanical properties and other parameters were obtained according to the molecular trajectories, and simulation results were in good agreement with the experimental data.

3 Results and Discussion

3.1 Structure Analysis

After simulation calculation, the most stable three-dimensional structure of calcium silicate hydrate doped with organic molecules was obtained, and it can be visually observed from the graph the status of calcium silicate hydrate and styrene-acrylate within the cell.

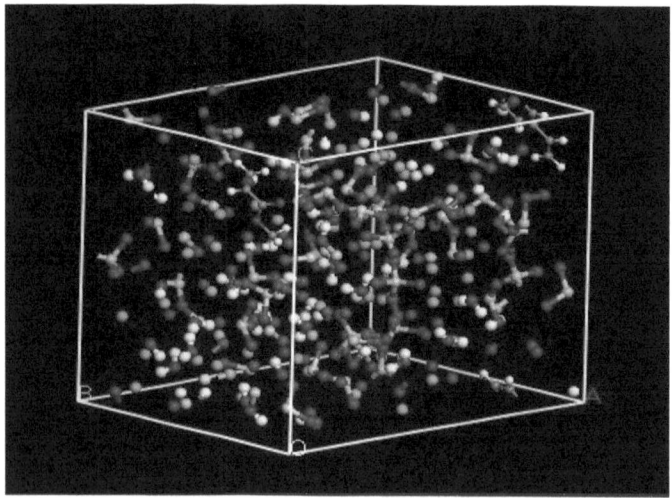

Fig. 4. The most stable organic molecular structure of doped calcium silicate hydrate

As can be seen from Fig. 4, because styrene and methyl acrylate are in the calcium silicate hydrate cell, so the cell structure become more dense, the original organic molecules monomer dissociated, the original obvious the layered structure of calcium silicate hydrate was disrupted, the system disorder degree increases, system reached minimum energy state.

3.2 Solubility Parameter

Solubility parameter (SP) is physical constant which measures the compatibility of liquid material. Its physical meaning of material per unit volume of the square root of cohesive energy density (CED) .The more similar the solubility parameters of the two materials are, the better the blend effective is. If the difference between them is more than 0.5, it is generally difficult to blend evenly. Solubility parameters of doped and pure calcium silicate hydrate can be obtained according to analysis of molecular trajectories, which are shown in Table 1.

Table 1. Solubility parameters of C-S-H in different status

Status of C-S-H	CED (J/m^3)	SP $(J/cm^3)^{1/2}$
Pure C-S-H	2.551e+008	15.971
Doped C-S-H	2.642e+008	15.601

From Table 1, the different value of solubility parameters of C-S-H in different status is 0.37, which is in the acceptable scale. It means the compatibility of styrene-acrylate and calcium silicate hydrate is fine, the polymers blended well into calcium silicate hydrate, it is unanimous with the most stable molecules structure in Fig.4. The simulation results supplied sustain for modification mechanism, and they're in good agreement with the test results.

3.3 Mechanical Properties

We can get the bulk modulus, cut modulus, condensability of the most stable system, and compare them with those of pure C-S-H.

Table 2. Mechanical properties parameters of C-S-H in different status

Status of C-S-H	Bulk modulus(GPa)	Shear modulus(GPa)	Compressibility (1/TPa)
Pure C-S-H	7.7932	5.9639	129.7492
Doped C-S-H	2.2117	0.1171	485.7125

From Table 2, bulk modulus and cut modulus of C-S-H doped with polymers decrease significantly, however, the condensability increases. Actually, transmutation resistance of doped C-S-H increases, this maybe because the polymers blended well into calcium silicate hydrate, it results in the changes of the initial cell, so as to the system can resist outside changes; this means the modification is successful.

4 Conclusions

The interactions between organic molecules and calcium silicate hydrate were studied using molecular simulation techniques in this paper, and the following conclusions are obtained.

(1) The compatibility of styrene-acrylate and calcium silicate hydrate is fine, the polymers blended well into calcium silicate hydrate, transmutation resistance of doped C-S-H increases, so as to the system can resist outside changes, this means the modification is successful.

(2) As newly research method, Molecules simulation has advantages over traditional means in material study, such as high efficiency, veracity, and low resource consuming. It will be spread in future.

Acknowledgement. This research has been supported by the National Fundamental Scientific Research Project (P.R.China), relevant to "Basic research in Environmentally Friendly Concrete (2009CB623201)" and the Fundamental Research Funds for the Central Universities (2010-IV-079), gratitude for Materials Studio software provided by School of Materials Science and Engineering, Wuhan University of Technology.

References

1. Yousuf, M., Mollah, A., et al.: Chemical and physical effects of sodium lignosulfonate superplasticizer on the hydration of Portland cement and solidification/stabilization consequences. Cement and Concrete Research (25), 671–682 (1995)
2. Prince, W., Edwards-Lajnef, M., Aitcin, P.C.: Interaction between ettringite and a polynaphthalene sulfonate superplasticizer in a cementitious paste. Cement and Concrete Research (32), 79–85 (2002)
3. Tritt-Goc, J., Pilewski, N., Kocielski, S., Milia, F.: The influence of the superplasticizer on the hydration and freezing processes in white cement studied by 1H spin-lattice relaxation time and single point imaging. Cement and Concrete Research 30, 931–936 (2000)
4. Gu, P., Xie, P., Beaudoin, J.J., et al.: Investigation of the retarding effect of superplasticizers on cement hydration by impedance spectroscopy and other methods. Cement and Concrete Research 24, 433–442 (1994)
5. Xu, Y.J., Li, X.C., Weng, T.Y., et al.: Study on blending system of Benzene-third polymer latex-mortar (I) Modification mechanism and microstructure status of blending system. Journal of Beijing University of Chemistry Industry 25(4), 28–32 (1998)
6. Xu, Y.J.: Study on blending system of Benzene-third polymer latex-mortar (II) Effect of SAE on mortar properties. Journal of Beijing University of Chemistry Industry 26(1), 21–23 (1999)
7. Xu, Y.J.: Study on blending system of Benzene-third polymer latex-mortar (III) Effect of modifier on mortar strength. Journal of Beijing University of Chemistry Industry 26(4), 44–45 (1999)
8. Cong, Y.F., Liao, K.J., Zhai, Y.C.: Application of molecule simulation in SBS modified bitumen. Journal of Chemistry Industry 56(5), 769–773 (2005)
9. Hamid, S.A.: The crystal structure of the 11Å natural Tobermorite Ca2.25 [Si3O7.5 (OH) 1.5].1H2O. Zeitschrift für Kristallographie 154, 189–198 (1981)

Construction of Energy Management and Control Information System in Iron and Steel Enterprise

Wen Qiang Sun, Jiu Ju Cai, and Yong Liu

State Environmental Protection Key Laboratory of Eco-industry,
Northeastern University, 110819 Shenyang, China
neu20031542@163.com

Abstract. The contribution of energy management and control information system (EMS) to energy conservation and emission reduction of iron and steel industry was expounded in this paper. According to the different management modes and system coverage of iron and steel enterprises, three basic application categories of EMS were summarized. Then, the application functions and their descriptions were studied in detail, followed by the introduction of the relationship between EMS and other information systems. Finally, the comprehensive evaluation indices and recommended standards of EMS were given. It provides a guideline for iron and steel enterprises to construct EMS, beneficial to the energy conservation and environmental protection.

Keywords: Energy Management and Control Information System, Iron and Steel Enterprise, Application Function, Evaluation Index.

1 Introduction

Energy management and control information system (EMS) is one of the system energy conservation technologies. EMS is an integrated management and control computer system with complete functions of energy monitoring, management, analysis and optimization. It plays a key role in enterprises' automation and information and is still in its early stage in iron and steel industry [1-3].

Energy consumption accounts for 20 to 40% of the cost of steel. The energy consumption depends on equipment level, process flow, product mix and energy management level. It is constructing an integrated EMS that can support digital energy management technologies and improve enterprise performance in energy conservation. Considering many iron and steel enterprises have been starting constructing EMS [4,5], the objective of this paper is to introduce advanced experience and methods of EMS construction, to introduce the application scope, basic functions, implementation approach, environmental requirements and general principle, to guide enterprises towards constructing EMS, and to contribute for the energy conservation and emission reduction of iron and steel enterprises.

R. Chen (Ed.): ICICIS 2011, Part I, CCIS 134, pp. 161–166, 2011.

2 Basic Application Categories of EMS

The construction method, management mode, system coverage, technology category and management benefit of EMS will vary at different development stages of EMS in iron and steel enterprises.

(1) EMS Supported by Complete Flat Management. EMS supported by complete flat management blends energy management and production according to the flat-type production-directing pattern and centralized-through management system. It is harmonious in the integrated energy management and control, energy balance, and production. It is of remarkable to recycle and reuse secondary energies, with leading energy efficiency and operating rate in iron and steel industry. It has excellent technologies and its operation management and human resource meet the requirements of industrialization and modernization. It has an integrated function of data acquisition, processing and analysis, control and schedule, balance and prediction, and comprehensive energy management.

(2) EMS Supported by Incomplete Flat Management. Hierarchical management is still used in production-directing pattern and whole management mode of EMS supported by incompetent flat management; while centralized management is used in energy management and data acquisition. Some essential energy balance points have the function of centralized management, forming an effective coordination with dynamic energy balance. However, further improvements are expected with respect to online control technology and management guarantee system. EMS of this category can integrate and control the functions of data acquisition, processing and analysis, control and schedule, balance and prediction, and comprehensive energy management. It has higher recovery and reuse rate of secondary energies, with relatively advanced energy efficiency and operating rate in iron and steel enterprises. It basically fulfils the goal of "zero emission".

(3) EMS Based on Data Acquisition. Enterprise class energy data acquisition network covers managements among processes and has relatively excellent functions of data acquisition, processing and analysis. It has infrastructures for energy management, basically meeting the requirement of integrated information and industrialization in early stage. The category of EMS develops energy management and control centre (EMCC) and integrated guarantee system by combining energy management and environmental protection. It has no phenomenon of energy waste and is above average in energy utilization and energy consumption indices.

3 Construction of EMS

The application functions of EMS in iron and steel enterprises are shown in Fig. 1, and the description of these functions is given in Table 1.

EMS plays an important role in information system of iron and steel enterprises. The relationship between EMS and ERP (enterprise resource planning), MES (manufacturing execution system) and PCS (process control system) is presented in Fig. 2.

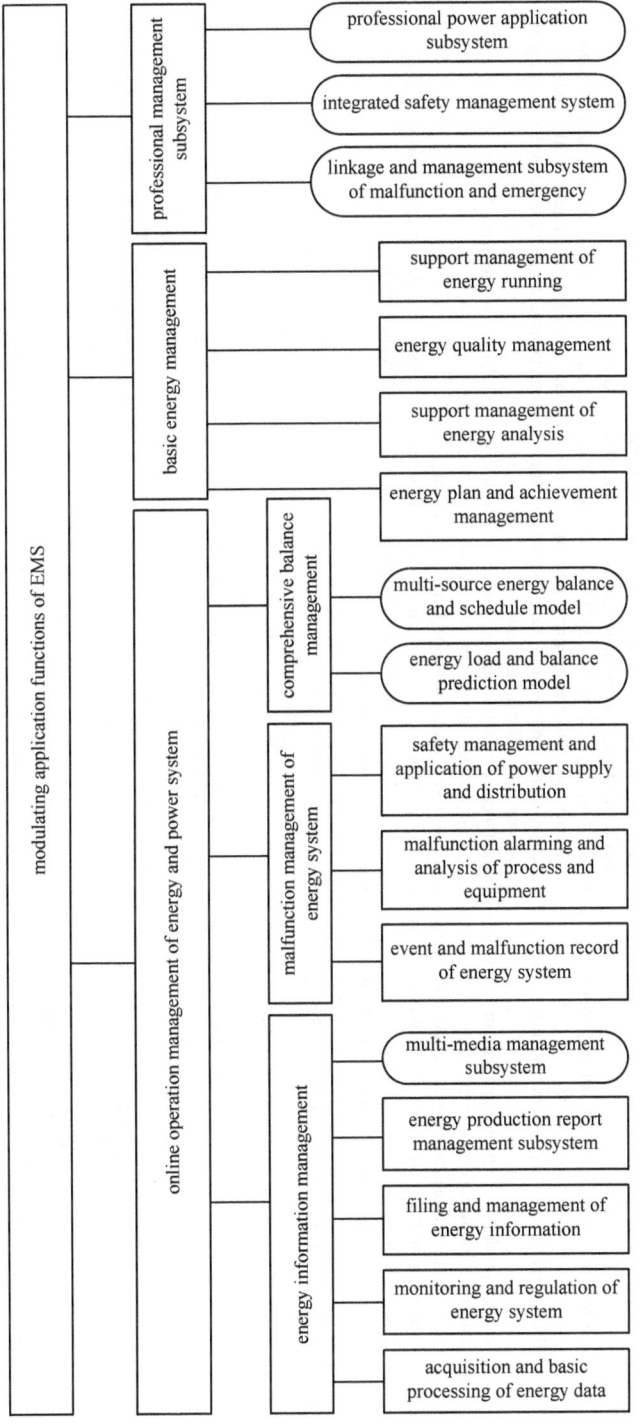

Fig. 1. Configuration of application functions of EMS. Those in rounded rectangular represent selectable functions.

Table 1. Description of application functions

application function	brief description
acquisition and basic processing of energy data	completeness, accuracy, timeliness, individuality and security of data; necessary temperature and pressure compensation, data filing and backdating; meet the requirements of monitoring, control and management; reasonable quantity of information points
monitoring and regulation of energy system	remote and regulation key spots (energy balance and schedule related); safety measurements; effective preplan management; human-computer interface complying with industrial standards
filing and management of energy information	short-term and long-term filing; personalized query and management interface; record and filing of information and malfunction
energy production report management subsystem	instantaneous report (in energy sources), schedule log and daily management report
multi-media management subsystem	video monitoring and analysis of certain spots
event and malfunction record of energy system	record of event order, malfunction and operation
malfunction alarming and analysis of process and equipment	classed malfunction alarming; malfunction time-series analysis; accident preplan analysis; linkage with control system; analysis and implementation of emergency off-load
safety management and application of power supply and distribution	operational and overhaul safety management
energy load and balance prediction model	systematic load prediction, including power load prediction, daily power consumption, gas system prediction, oxygen-nitrogen-argon prediction, etc.; load quantity management
multi-source energy balance and schedule model	optimization and schedule of energy system according to load prediction and balance prediction; whole balance and economic schedule of enterprises' energy system
energy plan and achievement management	energy supply-and-demand plan; acquisition of actual generation, consumption and release of energy sources; management and analysis of energy consumption indices
support system of energy analysis	historical energy data analysis, comparison of energy supply & demand and energy consumption achievement & plan; calculation of technical and economic energy indices
energy quality management	monitoring and management of the energy quality indices of energy sources (water, gas, etc.); energy quality report; trend analysis of energy quality indices
support system of energy running	stability and safety of energy supply
linkage and management subsystem of malfunction and emergency	preplan treatment and emergency linkage caused by malfunction, error and others; preplan formation and management based on configuration technology
integrated safety management system	professional safety management modules, including authority and access management
professional power application subsystem	flow calculation; short-circuit calculation

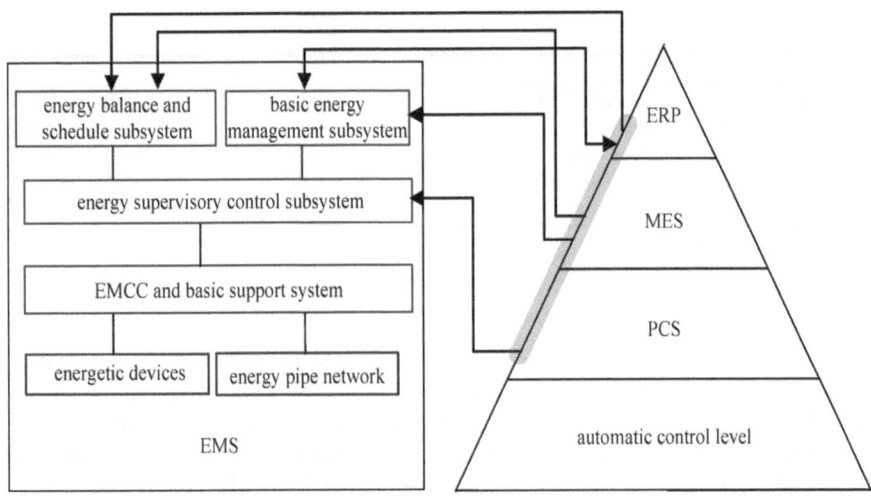

Fig. 2. The relationship between EMS and ERP/MES/PCS

3.1   Relationship between EMS and Enterprise Information Systems

According to the infrastructure and function division, EMS requests energy statistical information, energy quality information, production plan of main processes and over-haul plan of key lines from relative modules of information systems (ERP and MES). These are used to prepare complete energy management report, energy consumption analysis and reliable information for the prediction of energy system. Simultaneously, EMS supplies information system detailed energy analysis data to prepare cost analysis report and management report.

3.2   Relationship between EMS and Supervisory Control System of Main Processes

EMS should obtain the online production information of main processes with the re-quirements of application functions, especially those related to energy balance and schedule, such as production rhythm, operation status, energy consumption status and tendency, abnormality and malfunction status of system. If these are gotten, the operation management, balance scheduling and abnormality analysis will be established scientifi-cally, exactly and timely, resulting in a steady and economic production process.

4   Comprehensive Evaluation Indices

The economic and managerial evaluation indices of EMS are: enhancement rate of labor productivity, reduction rate of BFG (blast furnace gas) release, growth rate of LDG (Linz-Donatiwz process gas) recovery, increase rate of comprehensive energy data accuracy, and perfection efficiency of management flow. Recommended evalua-tion standards are given in Table 2.

Table 2. Evaluation indices

score	10	30	50	80
enhancement rate of labor productivity (%)	>30	>50	>70	100
reduction rate of BFG release (%)	<30	<50	<70	<100
growth rate of LDG recovery (%)	>20	>30	>40	>50
increase rate of comprehensive energy data accuracy (%)	>30	>50	>70	100
perfection efficiency of management flow		unfinished		finished

5   Conclusions

Based on the development stages, EMS is reducible to three categories: EMS supported by complete flat management, EMS supported by incomplete flat management, and EMS based on data acquisition. EMS can be divided into five types of modules and subdivided into seventeen application functions. Corresponding modules of EMS are correlated with other information systems such as ERP, MES and PCS, to obtain a steady and economic process. The economic and managerial indices of EMS are proposed at the end of this paper.

Acknowledgments. This work is sponsored by the Fundamental Research Funds for the Central Universities (No. N090602007), China. The authors greatly acknowledge CISA for her references.

References

1. Cai, Y.P., Huang, G.H., Yang, Z.F., Tan, Q.: Identification of Optimal Strategies for Energy Management Systems Planning under Multiple Uncertainties. Appl. Energy 86, 480–495 (2009)
2. Avouris, N.M.: Abstractions for operator support in energy management systems. Int. J. Elec. Power 23, 333–341 (2001)
3. Wu, M., Shen, D.Y., Rao, L.C., Gui, W.H.: A Distributed Computer Energy Management and Control System. Control Eng. Pract. 1, 469–478 (1993)
4. Fang, Y.J., Wang, Y.T., Li, S.H.: Realization of the Energy Information Metering and Management System of Metallurgical Industry. Control. Autom. 20, 99–100 (2004) (in Chinese)
5. Qian, W.P., Zhu, X.R.: SCADA for Energy Source Data in Shasteel. Metall. Ind. Autom. 6, 54–56 (2007) (in Chinese)

Review of Dynamic Modeling and Simulation of Large Scale Belt Conveyor System

Qing He and Hong Li

National Engineering Laboratory for Biomass Power Generation Equipment,
School of Energy Power and Mechanical Engineering, North China Electric Power University,
Beijing 102206, China
hqng@163.conm

Abstract. Belt conveyor is one of the most important devices to transport bulk-solid material for long distance. Dynamic analysis is the key to decide whether the design is rational in technique, safe and reliable in running, feasible in economy. It is very important to study dynamic properties, improve efficiency and productivity, guarantee conveyor safe, reliable and stable running. The dynamic researches and applications of large scale belt conveyor are discussed. The main research topics, the state-of-the-art of dynamic researches on belt conveyor are analyzed. The main future works focus on dynamic analysis, modeling and simulation of main components and whole system, nonlinear modeling, simulation and vibration analysis of large scale conveyor system.

Keywords: Modeling and Simulation; Dynamic, Vibration; Belt Conveyor.

1 Introduction

Belt conveyor is widely used in all kinds of industry fields, such as electric power, coal, mine, metallurgy, chemical, port, architecture and food supplies. It is one of the most important devices to transport bulk material of long distance. Nowadays, the transporting system is becoming larger and more using curve line. Long distance, high speed, large-capacity, high power and multi-drive is the main trend [1, 2]. It is very significant to study on conveyor system, which is helpful to improve the efficiency and productivity of conveyor, guarantee safe, reliable and stable running.

Many research institutions, engineers and technicians did a lot of deep researches on design theory, calculation methods, system control methods, design standards and design analysis system. The traditional design of belt conveyor was thought more about static properties than dynamic properties. Otherwise, if only thinking static properties when designing, choosing type and using, some serious problems will happen, such as unstable starting-up or failure starting, sharp rising belt tension, belt skidding, running deviation, irrational system design, too high safe factor and so on. The recent researches on dynamic properties of conveyor are introduced. The main research of conveyor dynamics is analysis. The further research is prospected.

R. Chen (Ed.): ICICIS 2011, Part I, CCIS 134, pp. 167–172, 2011.
© Springer-Verlag Berlin Heidelberg 2011

2 State-of-the-Art of Belt Conveyor

2.1 Dynamic Model of Large Scale Belt Conveyor

Large scale belt conveyor is a mechanical system composed of several subsystems. The more complicated of mechanical system is and the more functions the system have, the better running properties and the higher reliable system will be. So, traditional assembly design using static methods is not enough for the reliable system. Dynamic properties are the most important factors of a function completed and performance excellent system. Belt is one of the most important parts of conveyor system. The belt properties will greatly affect the functions of the system. So it is necessary to model and simulate belt and system, and analyze dynamic properties.

Dynamic Model of Belt. Many researches on dynamic model of belt conveyor are done by research institutes and individuals. Obvious viscoelasticity properties of belt were found in researches. So, modeling of adhesive tape means viscoelasticity modeling. There are several main viscoelasticity model including Maxwell model, Kevin model, three-element model which Kevin model and elastic element are in series [4] and five-element composite rheological model, and so on. Because of different properties and suitable conditions, the models are used by different researchers. For example, in the new conveyor design and analysis software, Helix Delta-T6, which developed by Helix Technologies Pty Ltd, Australia, a finite element model of the conveyor to perform the dynamic analysis is used. During modeling, the conveyor is broken up into segments, and for each segment, Kelvin solid model is used. The dynamic calculation process uses sophisticated variable step Runge Kutta method integrators for solving the complex differential equations [5]. Conveyor Dynamics, Inc. started to research belt conveyor system from 1967 and five-element composite rheological model is used in the simulation software BELTSTATV [6]. The model is also applied by L.K. Nordell and J.K. David. Some Chinese researchers use Kelvin model for dynamic analysis [7]. All the models have some advantages and disadvantages. Using composite element can calculate the final distortion at the condition of short time or infinite long loads. The more composite elements are the better accuracy of simulation will be. But, at the same time, increasing the number of composite elements will make the mechanics equation of the model become more complicated, which will bring some trouble for actual calculation. So, it is the main concern of researchers to choose high efficient conveyor model.

Dynamic Model of Conveyor System. Applying mathematic model derived by using centralized method and two functions related to time and the speed of drive roller to express the hydraulic coupling system driving force of motor, Kim [8,9] built the system analysis model and the motion equation of main parts including belt, drive, head roller, tail roller and take-up device and so on. Using multi-body dynamics analysis method, Han [8, 10] built dynamic analysis model of whole conveyor system. W.G. Song [11] built the mechanics and mathematics models of belt unit, drive unit and take-up unit. Combining the above unit models, the dynamic equation of whole conveyor system was built. In order to recognize the transport routes of belt conveyor with turning curve automatically, D.Z. Tang [12] set up the routes morphological function, modeled the system based on it, and developed auto-modeling software.

2.2 Nonlinear of Belt and Whole System

There are some properties of belt conveyor, such as nonlinear and with time-variant parameters. It is very important to set up exact nonlinear mathematics model to simulate and forecast the dynamic properties according to the above properties. W.R.B. Morrison [13] applied nonlinear model of belt material in 1988. G. Suweken [14] studied the weakly nonlinear of belt. Under the condition of running tensions defined, numerical integration method using non-linear stiffness gradients is used to generate transient forces during starting and stopping by A. Harrison [15].

Analyzing the actual running, J.G. Shi [16] built a nonlinear, time-variant, dynamic coupled finite element model of belt conveyor, studied the motivitiy transfer principle of bulk-solid material, constructed a shape function of belt conveyor route, and realized the computer automatic modeling. According to analyze the belt sag and the change of tension, G.B. Li pointed out the coefficients of stiffness metric and damping metric in motion differential equation are time-variable and nonlinear. With a discrete element model, he set up a nonlinear motion equation of belt conveyor based on belt sag and discussed the affect to motion differential equation caused by nonlinear [17]. He also built the mathematic model of a drive system with three motors and hydraulic couplings, discussed increment equation successive linearized and Newmark β step by step integration method [18].

2.3 Effect of Vibration on Dynamic Performance

Vibration is one of the important content of dynamic research of belt conveyor. The researches related on vibration are concentrated on analysis of factors affected vibration, longitudinal vibration, transverse vibration, lateral vibration, solving main vibration mode, vibration analysis, studying the methods reducing and eliminating vibration of key parts.

G. Suweken [19] discussed an initial-boundary value problem for a linear wave (string) equation, which was used to build a simple model to describe the vertical vibrations of a conveyor belt. G. Suweken and W.T. Horssen [14] studied the transversal vibration and weakly nonlinear, set up a single equation of motion according a coupled system of partial differential equations describing the longitudinal and transversal vibrations of the belt, and put forward the approximate solution method and two time-scales perturbation method. I.V. Andrianova [20] analyzed transversal vibration of conveyor belts and described the vibration with finite or infinite mode-representations.

Y.F. Hou and X.J. Liu and et al [21-22] analyzed the running vibration of high speed and long distance belt conveyor, pointed out the two factors affected vibration, one is the dynamic properties of belt, the other is the external factors which produce stimulation. They built discrete viscoelasticity model, simulated the dynamic performance of belt, measured dynamic parameters, and analyzed the influencing mode of boundary conditions with different tension and excitation frequency. Y.J. Li [23] studied viscoelasticity vibration equation and the calculation methods of displacement solution and dynamic tension, provide a design method limiting and eliminating viscoelasticity vibration of belt conveyor. According to dynamic equation, G.B. Li [24, 25] analyzed natural characteristics of belt conveyor in theory, derived its intrinsic frequency equation, and built the main vibration model on the four-order intrinsic frequency and two-order intrinsic frequency of a conveyor with and without load. X.H. Lu [26] pointed out that there were three kinds of vibration of belt, which are longitudinal, transverse and lateral vibration, built the mathematics model and longitude vibration equation. Through experiments designed to establish the dynamic properties of belt material, Y.F. Hou studied some properties which have not been tested previously under conditions appropriate for the ISO/DP9856 standard. These properties included the natural vibration frequency of longitudinal vibration and transverse vibration, and the response to an impulse excitation. It was observed that the stress wave propagation speed increased with tension load and that tension load was the main factor influencing longitudinal vibration [27]. T.L. Qin analyzed the main factors of automatic take-up device, including the structure and the elastic wave produced in starting, stopping and loading. According to these, he built the model of automatic take-up and simulated it. He pointed out the main measures of reducing vibration of automatic take-up. The measures include reducing tension, limiting inertia force, increasing braking torque and add automatic tension buffer [28].

2.4 Dynamic Analysis and Simulation of Operating Conditions

L.K. Nordell [7] discussed the main problem of building stress and strain viscoelasticity model, put forward the method analyzing dynamic instant force during starting and stopping, forecasted the instant properties with simulation tools.

W.G. Song [23, 29-31] studied the dynamic tension curve of belt when starting with constant, trapezoid, sinusoid, triangle, parabola and rectangle acceleration, analyzed better starting mode and starting time, provided design basis of parts. According to examples, J.G. Shi [16,17,32] analyzed the dynamic properties during starting, freely stopping, abnormal loads, belt broken, emergent stopping and lose power in starting, simulated dynamic curves, developed dynamic analysis algorithm that control starting and stopping process and optimal methods. Regarding conveyor as an elastic continuum, J. Wang [33] built mechanical model of belt with inertia, elastic, damping distribution, simulated dynamic properties of changing load starting.

3 Future Works

Conveyor is composed by parts and assemblies, such as belt, idler, driver, brake, transmission, take-up, and so on. It is a complex mechanical system. Because of geography, there are lines and curves in whole route. Dynamic analysis include modeling for parts, assemblies and whole system, designing dynamic, solving dynamic equation and calculating dynamic loads. It is the basis for whole system to analyze all key parts and build exact mechanical models for them.

The requirement of long distance and high speed, the dynamic property become more remarkable [2], are extraordinary complicated, and have nonlinear. Strain is related to not only stress and load history, but also time, frequency, temperature, material, and so on. The nonlinear relationship between strain and stress, lag property, creep property, relaxation property, dynamic elastic modulus and other factors should be considered. So, it is the core to study nonlinear dynamic theory of belt and whole system, build nonlinear dynamic model, analyze and simulate dynamic properties and nonlinear dynamic response using viscoelasticity theory, system dynamics, vibration mechanics and finite discrete element method, which is important for optimal design of long conveyor.

There are many kinds of vibration, such as longitudinal, transverse and lateral vibrations of belt, vibration of idler and frame [2,4], which impact dynamic properties of long distance and high speed conveyor seriously. So it is very necessary to study the mutual effects and coupling relationship of all kinds of vibration, build multi-freedom spatial mechanics model of belt, put all the parts in a system to model and simulate, which is useful to optimize dynamic properties of system.

4 Summary

The main research, situation and shortage of dynamics of large scale belt conveyor are analyzed specially. The future works focus on dynamic analysis, modeling and simulation of main components and whole system, nonlinear modeling, simulation and vibration analysis of large scale conveyor system.

Acknowledgments. This work is supported by the Program for Changjiang Scholars and Innovative Research Team in University (PCSIRT0720).

References

1. Pu, X.L., Wang, G.Q., Yue, Y.J.: Summarization on Foreign Dynamic Analysis Software for Belt Conveyor. Mining & Processing Equipment 11 (2007)
2. Dong, D.Q.: Research on Dynamics Behavior of Large Scale Belt Conveyor and its Application. North China Electric Power University (2008)
3. Chen, J., Dai, J.L.: The Current Developing Situation of Dynamic Analyzed Technology of Long Distance Belt Conveyor. Colliery Mechanical & Electrical Technology 1 (2003)
4. Li, G.B.: Dynamics and Design of Belt Conveyor. China Machine Press, Beijing (1998)
5. Information on, http://www.helixtech.com.au/
6. Information on, http://conveyor-dynamics.com/beltstat/
7. Nordell, L.K., Ciozda, Z.P.: Transient Belt Stresses during Starting and Stopping: Elastic Response Simulated by Finite Element Methods. Bulk Solids Handling 4(1), 93–98 (1984)
8. Wang, F.S., Hou, Y.F.: Research in Modeling Belt Conveyor Dynamics. China Mining Magazine 11 (2008)
9. Kim, W.J.: Transient Dynamic Analysis of Belt Conveyor System using the Lumped Parameter Method. Bulk Solids Handling 15(3), 573–577 (1995)
10. Han, H.S., Park, T.W.: Analysis of a Long Belt Convey or System Using the Multibody Dynamics Program. Bulk Solids Handling 16(4), 543–549 (1996)
11. Song, W.G., Liu, H.Y., Wang, Y.: Research on Dynamic and Computer Simulation of the Belt Conveyor. Chinese J. of Mechanical Engineering 9 (2003)

12. Tang, D.Z.: Automatic Modeling and Simulation of the Dynamic Design of Belt Conveyer. J. of Heilongjiang Institute of Science 5 (2004)
13. Morrison, W.R.B.: Computer Graphics Techniques for Visualizing Belt Stress Waves. Bulk Solids Handling 8(4), 221–227 (1988)
14. Suweken, G., Horssen, W.T.: On the Weakly Nonlinear, Transversal Vibrations of a Conveyor Belt with a Low and Time-varying Velocity. J. of Sound and Vibration 264(1), 117–133 (2003)
15. Harrison, A.: Non-linear Belt Transient Analysis-A Hybrid Model for Numerical Belt Conveyor Simulation. Bulk Solids Handling 28(4), 242–247 (2008)
16. Shi, J.G., Mao, J., Liu, K.M.: Research on Dynamic Modeling and Simulation of Belt Conveyor. Coal Mine Machinery 5 (2009)
17. Li, G.B., Li, R.Q., Wei, J.Z.: Simulation of Belt Conveyor Dynamics Based on Geometry Nonlinearity. China Mechanical Engineering 1 (2007)
18. Li, G.B., Cao, L.Y., Li Ru, R.Q.: Modeling and Simulation of Nonlinear Dynamics for an Overland Belt Conveyor. Machine Design & Research 8 (2008)
19. Suweken, G., Horssen, W.T.: On the Transversal Vibrations of a Conveyor Belt Using a String-Like Equation. In: Proc. of ASME Design Eng. Tech. Conf., vol. 6B, pp. 1109–1116 (2001)
20. Andrianov, I.V., Horssen, W.T.: On the Transversal Vibrations of a Conveyor Belt: Applicability of Simplified Models. J. of Sound and Vibration 333(3-5), 822–829 (2008)
21. Hou, Y.F.: Study on the Dynamic Performance and Controlling Methods of Belt Conveyor. China University of Mining & Technology (2006)
22. Liu, X.J., Hou, Y.F., Lu, C.D.: Computer Aided Dynamic Design of High Speed Belt Conveyor. Hoisting and Conveying Machinery 3 (2004)
23. Li, Y.J.: Dynamic Analysis and Soft Starting Design of Belt Conveyor. J. of China Coal Society 3 (2002)
24. Li, G.B.: Study on the Intrinsic Behavior of Belt Conveyer System. Hoisting and Conveying Machinery 12 (2005)
25. Li, G.B.: Predicting and Controlling of Belt Conveyor Dynamic Characteristics by Computer Simulation. Hoisting and Conveying Machinery 2 (2005)
26. Lu, X.H.: Longitudinal Vibration Equation of Conveyor Belt. Coal Mine Machinery 1 (2009)
27. Hou, Y.F., Meng, Q.R.: Dynamic Characteristics of Conveyor Belts. J. of China University of Mining & Technology 7 (2008)
28. Qin, T.L., Wei, J.: Vibration Analysis on Automatic Take-up Device of Belt Conveyor. In: Proc. of SPIE, vol. 7129, 71291U1-7
29. Song, W.G., Wang, D.: The Dynamic Computer Simulation of Long Distance Belt Conveyor with 7.6 km. J. of China Coal Society 4 (2004)
30. Zhang, Y., Zhou, M.S., Yu, Y.: Analysis of Dynamic Properties of Long Distance Belt Conveyor. Mining & Processing Equipment 5 (2008)
31. Zhao, X.C., Zhang, Y.D., Meng, G.Y.: Dynamic Simulation to the Belt during the Soft Start of Belt Conveyor Based on Matlab. Mining & Processing Equipment 5 (2007)
32. Li, Y.X., Hao, S.S., Zhou, G.L.: Dynamic Analysis of Belt Conveyer Break Stage. J. of Heilongjiang Institute of Science and Technology 3 (2008)
33. Wang, J., Meng, G.Y., Shi, L.: Dynamics Simulation of Variable Load Starting in Belt Conveyors. Hoisting and Conveying Machinery 12 (2008)

Identification of Network Traffic Based on Radial Basis Function Neural Network*

Yabin Xu and Jingang Zheng

School of Computer
Beijing Information Science and Technology University
Beijing, China
xyb@bistu.edu.cn, tianhuo1191@sina.com

Abstract. A method of network traffic identification based on RBF (Radial Basis Function) neural network is proposed by analysis of the current status of the network environment. By using the public data set and the real-time traffic for a combination of supervised learning, this method constructs a reasonable training set and testing set to experiment and implement the network traffic identification based on RBF neural. The experiments prove the identification method in the application of network traffic has the characteristics of high accuracy, low complexity and high recognition efficiency, and the practical feasibility in real-time traffic identification.

Keywords: RBF neural network, traffic identification, traffic classification, real-time identification.

1 Introduction

With the development of network technology, network traffic has been changed from the traditional flow which is represented to the services such as FTP, TELNET and HTTP to the new flow represented to the services such as P2P and IM service. The traditional traffic identification methods have been unable to meet the network requirements. Accurate traffic identification method has become an important issue of the network technology research and development. Good traffic identification technology can help network administrators control the users' network application when necessary. And traffic classification also plays an important role in finding traffic intrusion, malicious attacks and new network applications.

RBF neural network is a neural network which issues to solve high-dimensional space curve surface fitting (approximation) problem. It can find a curved surface which fits the training data best from a multi-dimensional space and interpolates the elements to the test data by the multi-dimensional space [1]. When receiving the external

* Enhancing Project for Science and Research Level of Beijing Information Science & Technology University (5028123400).
Funding Project for Academic Human Resources Development in Institutions of Higher Learning under the Jurisdiction of Beijing Municipality (PHR201007131).

stimulus, the neurons in the local area where accept the stimulus in the neural network has the strongest response and the neighbor neurons are reduced as the increase of radial distance between with the ones in the local area. The hidden layer of neural network provides a set of functions which construct an arbitrary "basis" to the hidden layer when they extended to the hidden space in the input mode. The functions in this set are called radial basis function.

RBF neural networks are generally divided into three layers: input layer, hidden layer and output layer. The input layer is built up by several sources(perception units), which connect the network with the external environment .The hidden layer takes the vectors obtained from the input space to the hidden space by nonlinear transformation. The output layer is linear, which responds to the activation pattern (signal) on the role of the input layer. In general, the hidden space has a high dimensions on the purpose of that map the input vector in the input layer to a high-dimensional space. So under the Cover theorem, the input vector is more likely to achieve linear reparability [2].

RBF network is a computing model which Express the mapping just like (1)

$$H: U_{input} \rightarrow U_{output} \qquad (1)$$

"$U_{input} \subseteq R^n$" is the n-dimensional input space and "$U_{output} \subseteq R^m$" is the m-dimensional output space. Both above represent the characteristics of the input data set values and the type of the value of the output data set. The point in "U_{input}" denoted by "$x = (x_1, x_2, ..., x_n)^-$". The point in "$U_{output}$" denoted by "$t = (t_1, t_2, ..., t_m)^-$". The number of hidden layer units has a direct bearing on the requirement of the problem and the number of input/output units. The huge number of hidden layer units will result in learning time too long and the error is not necessarily the best. And it can lead to a poor fault tolerance without the ability of identifying the new samples that not previously seen. So there must be an optimum number of hidden layer units. The (2) can be used to select the best number of hidden layer unit as a reference [3]:

$$h = \sqrt{n + m} + a \qquad (2)$$

The "n" is the number of input neuron. The "m" is the number of output layer neuron. The "a" is the constant for the 1 to 10. RBF network has the "sense-association-reaction" structure which constructs by sensory neurons(S), association neurons (A) and reaction neurons (R) is as Fig.1.

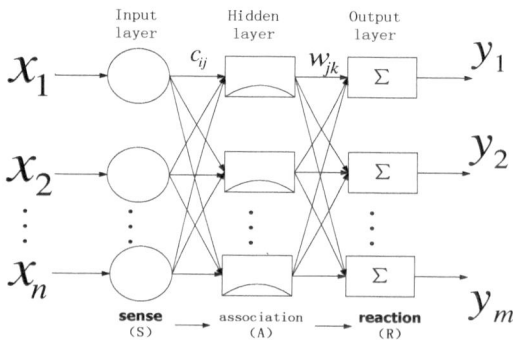

Fig. 1. System Structure of RBF neural network

General, RBF network consists of n sensory neurons and h association neurons and m reaction neuron by (3):

$$\text{NN}_{\text{RBF}}^{n>,h>,m} = < V_G, A_G, IF, OF, WA, OA > \qquad (3)$$

The "V_G" shows the set of neuron which includes "S", "A" and "R". The "A_G" represents the connection that include the connection of "S" to "A" (denoted as "C"), recording the connection intensity between them; include the connection of "A" to "R" (denoted as "W"), recording the connection intensity between them. "IF" represents input vector. "OF" represents output vector. "WA" represents the work algorithm just like gradient descent algorithm and least squares. It is used to solve the value in "W". "OA" represents organization algorithm just like center self-organization selection method, which is an unsupervised learning method. It is used to solve the value of "C". RBF network is a feed-forward type network. After pushing into the RBF network from sensory neurons layer, the information is passed to the association neurons layer. After transformed by "A", the information is passed to the reaction neurons layer."R" makes the information a linear combination and passed to the end to finish the work as (4) shows:

$$IF = S \mid A \rightarrow R = OF \qquad (4)$$

2   Identification Process

The network traffic identification process based on RBF neural is divided into four parts: (1) Data acquisition process. (2) Data preprocessing. (3) Data training process. (4) Test data classification process. The focus will be on building a good model of RBF neural network for testing network traffic samples and classifying the network application by the feature of RBF neural network classification. As below:

(1) Data Acquisition Module created by data acquisition process extracts the network connection records and analyzes the features to select the appropriate network feature attributes to be the original input value by "features extract", which means to select the best subset of features from the network feature set as the original input value and select the appropriate network attributes as neural network input values. Denoted "x_i" ($0<i<n$).

(2) The input value that has been extracted is mapped to range [-1, 1] and eliminated the dependence of port in the classification process. The data after preprocessed is called classification process.

(3) The preprocessed input set submitted to the neural network to be trained and generate the training model, As (5):

$$\begin{cases} C: & S \rightarrow A \\ W: & A \rightarrow R \end{cases} \qquad (5)$$

(4) The generated RBF model is used to predict the type of test data, which is the output, denoted "y_j" ($0<j<m$). The algorithm here is Least Squares RBF network training. The mapping is achieved by a regression model like (6):

$$t = \phi\omega + \epsilon \qquad (6)$$

"ϵ" is error vector between the desired output and the actual output like (7):

$$\epsilon = \frac{1}{2} \sum_{k=1}^{m} \left(t^k - y^k \right)^2 \tag{7}$$

"t^k" is target output and "y^k" is actual output.

The other important parameter in the least square method is admissible parameter "ρ". The "ρ" is a real number whose absolute value is in range (0, 1).It is important to the balance between accuracy and complexity of the network. If it is set too close to one, the network will be high-precision mapping approach, but it would lead a large number of centers and over fitting. If too small, it will lead to relatively poor performance of the network model, but significantly reduced network size.

The main standard of network traffic identification processes are recognition accuracy and recognition efficiency. With the high accuracy of pattern classification algorithm characteristics and advantage of the least square method, it can meet an increasingly complex network environment. The following experiment shows that.

3   Experiment

This experiment adopts the equivalent random, average value of several training methods that combines the existing data set and real-time data set. The existing data set comes from Genome Campus research institution in Cambridge University which is built up by the sample of 24-hour traffic.

Table 1. Genome Campus sample statistics data set

Category	Flow Number	Percentage %	Application
ATTACK	94	0.494	Internet virus attacks
DATABASE	183	0.962	postgres, sqlnet oracle, ingres
FTP-CONTROL	22	0.116	ftp-control
FTP-DATA	72	0.378	ftp-data
FTP-PASV	177	0.930	ftp-pasv
INTERACTIVE	8	0.042	ssh, klogin, rlogin, telnet
MAIL	1278	6.716	imap, pop2/3, smtp
P2P	116	0.610	KaZaA, BitTorrent, GnuTella
SERVICES	77	0.405	X11, dns, ident, ldap, ntp
WWW	16612	87.303	www
OTHER	389	0.204	KaZaA, BitTorrent,Half-Life
Total	19028	100	

The real-time data set comes from one hour real-time monitoring for the traffic of a university laboratory. Table 1 and Table 2 respectively shows the composition of the contents of two sets of data.

The Experimental procedure is as follows:

(1) The experiments perform 10 times randomized training and testing on the data set and uses the TCP data as the test data. Complete two-way TCP stream is constituted by 249 properties [4]. The experiment removed the port

information to eliminate the dependence on the port. So in the experiments there are 248 neurons in the input layer. Two sets (set 1 and set 2) contains the type of traffic are 11 species and 8 species. The numbers of neurons in output layer in the two experiments are 11 and 8. Set number of hidden layer neurons is 260 and 262 referencing (2). For the output error parameter ε and ρ, we choose ε = 1.0E-8, ρ = 0.1 after numerous tests.

(2) The data from the preprocessed data set concentration of random data as the experimental data to extract. The set extracted is divided into two sets: training set about 66%, and testing set about 34%. In order to simulate the real network environment, the training and testing set are selected randomly by category in extraction process. Table 3 shows the result.

As Table 3 shows, the RBF neural network in classification has the advantage to be applied to network traffic identification and the average recognition rate has been more than 96%. With the training set size increases, the recognition accuracy will be a corresponding increase. The combination of sample concentration ratio of each category and number shows that the more

Table 2. Laboratory sample statistics data set

category	Flow Number	percentage %	Application
DATABASE	329	1.382	postgres, sqlnet oracle, mysql
FTP	1701	7.147	ftp
INTERACTIVE	2	0.084	ssh, klogin,rlogin, telnet
MAIL	2726	11.453	imap, pop3, smtp
P2P	94	0.395	Thunder,BitTorrent
SERVICES	220	0.924	X11, dns, ident, ldap, ntp
WWW	18559	77.976	www
OTHER	170	0.714	QQGame, Real Media
Total	23801	100	

Table 3. The experimental results

Category	recognition rate %	
	Set 1	*Set 2*
ATTACK	86.3	
DATABASE	98.8	99.6
FTP-CONTROL	96.2	
FTP-DATA	99.7	99.6
FTP-PASV	91	
INTERACTIVE	65.5	66
MAIL	98.1	98.7
P2P	93.4	89.6
SERVICES	99.7	99.2
WWW	98	97.8
OTHER	98.1	98.1
Total	97.0448	97.4454

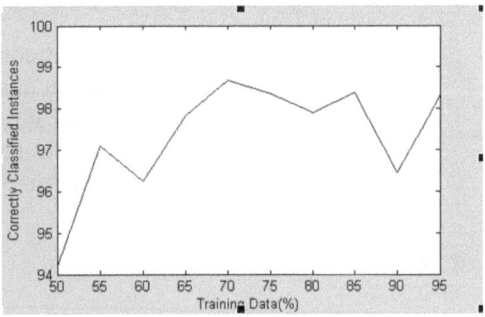

Fig. 2. The relationship between training model and test accuracy

the support samples are , the more detailed of the description that can represent the categories much possible, the better of the study ability of the neural network constructed by the samples and stronger the convergence and the generalization ability of the model.

(3) During the experiment, the building of training model is associated with the size of test data. The size of data model should coordinate the average network traffic. Mixture of the two samples were generated from a new random sample of 50% to 95% of the data as the training set and the remaining data as the test set for testing. The results shown in Fig. 2:

As the figure shows below, the smaller the size of the training set is, the higher the speed of the model building and the data testing, and the accuracy is low. Small training set is suitable of the complex network environment.

With the growth of the training model, the training complex is improved continuously and the test accuracy reaches to peak precision gradually. That is, when the model is built in reason, the neural network built by the training model can identify the network traffic with the best performance.

When the training model is too large, the method will appear over-fitting phenomenon. Model complexity is too high and the interaction between the vector properties is too large. The training time began to increase and the recognition rate goes down. So analysis of the network size and traffic flow content plays an important role to create an excellent training model to meet the requirement of network traffic identification.

(4) In order to prove that the method is feasible in real-time flow identification, the experiment below extracts the data for 1 minute in the data set represented by Table 2, the number of which is about 400 containing about 280 P2P flows. We extract all the P2P flows to be the data set on behalf of the network services. To improve the testing accuracy and simulate the real-time identification, the experiment extracts the first 70% flows of each kind of P2P applications as the training set and the last 30% as the testing set. Test results show in Table 4:

As Table 4 shows that, when confronting the small size sample and high frequency real-time identification of network traffic, the method of RBF neural network has the characteristics that fast, efficient and less resource. It is proved the method based on RBF neural network traffic identification competent to identify the requirements of real-time traffic.

4   Conclusion

This paper presents a machine learning method of RBF neural network traffic identification. Through tested both in open data set and real-time data set, the method is proved to have the characteristics of high identification rate, fast and low resources consumption and the relationship between the scale of the model and the identification efficiency. It further evidence the practical feasibility in real-time traffic identification based on RBF neural network.

References

1. Zhongzhi, S.: Neural Network. Higher Education Press, Beijing (2009)
2. Cover, T.M.: Geometrical and statistical properties of system of linear inequalities with applications in pattern recognition. IEEE Transactions on Electronic Computer 14, 326–334 (1965)
3. Fei Sike Technology R&D center: Matlab Application. Electronic Industry Press, Beijing (2005)
4. Moore, A.W., Zuev, D.: Discriminators for use in flow-based classification. Intel Research, Cambridge (2005)

Thermal Hotspots in CPU Die and It's Future Architecture

Jian Wang[1,2] and Fu-yuan Hu[1]

[1] University of Science and Technology of Suzhou, Suzhou, Jiangsu, China, 215011
[2] School of Electronics, University of Glamorgan, Pontypridd CF37 1DL, UK
wangjiansuzhou@sina.com

Abstract. Owing to the increasing core frequency and chip integration and the limited die dimension, the power densities in CPU chip have been increasing fastly. The high temperature on chip resulted by power densities threats the processor's performance and chip's reliability. This paper analyzed the thermal hotspots in die and their properties. A new architecture of function units in die ---- hot units distributed architecture is suggested to cope with the problems of high power densities for future processor chip.

Keywords: temperature; hotspot; CPU chip; die; reliability; architecture.

1 Introduction

Large power dissipation or high temperature produces thermal hotspots in CPU die. With increasing core frequency and chip integration, the power densities in die have increased very fast. This problem has already threated processor performance and chip's reliability [1-5].

We described the distribution of hotspots in die in Section 2, analyzed the heat conducting in Section 3, pointed out the bottleneck for processor performance in Section 4. In Section 5, a hot units distributed architecture for future processor die is suggested. Section 6 is the conclusions.

2 Distribution of Hotspots in Die

2.1 Numbers and Positions of Hotspots

At any time, a CPU chip consumes power depending on its workloads. That is, each function unit in a chip consumes different amount of power from time to time. So the numbers and positions of the hotspots in a die are variant.

In a die, function units such as processor cores, I-Caches and D-Caches are often hotspots. Other units may be a hotspot at some time, too. For example, when matrixes multiplication is run, the floating unit will be a hotspot. Fig. 1 shows temperatures and hotspots of a die under different workloads [6].

R. Chen (Ed.): ICICIS 2011, Part I, CCIS 134, pp. 180–185, 2011.

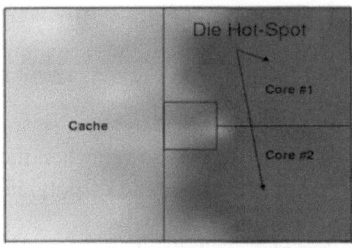 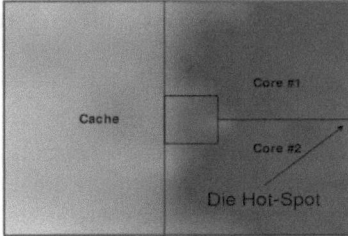

Fig. 1. Thermal behavior and hot spots at different applications

2.2 Real Distribution of Hotspots

Actually, in addition to the hotspots with the highest temperatures, there are some other spots with higher temperatures. In Fig. 1 we can see some potential hotspots which appear to have very high temperatures.

Qwing to the inefficiency of heat transferring, the spot with the highest temperature may not be the spot generating the largest amount of heat. Fig. 2 has two temperature curves along the diagonal of a die, one is a real line and the other is a dashed line. The dashed is the measured data and the real is the anticipated [7]. In the middle of the measured curve, there are two peaks and a valley between them. From the bottom of the valley to the top of the peaks, the temperature changes 10°C in the distance of only 1mm. On the right slope of the dashed line, the temperature descends 8°C in the distance of 0.5mm and then ascends 5°C again in the distance of 1mm.

Therefore, while the temperature of one spot is below the critical value, its adjacent area may exceed the maximum sufferance value. Furthermore, even the complete thermal maps of one die are obtained, there would be differences from die to die, owing to the thickness of substrate and the material nomogeneity [8].

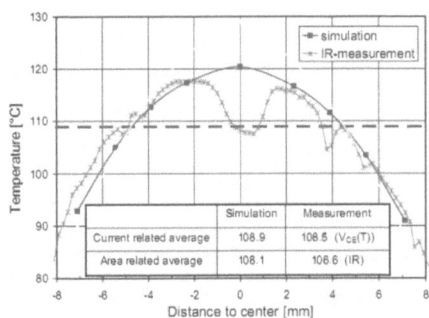 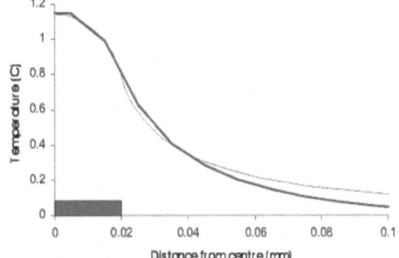

Fig. 2. Comparison of the IR camera simulation

Fig. 3. Real distribution curve of reading and temperature around hotspot

3 Dissipated Power Gradient around Hotspots

3.1 Heat Conducting Model

With heat conducting around a hotspot, the temperature gets lower when the distance becomes larger. We say that there are temperature grads around hotspots. Fig. 3 is an example of real temperature curve around a hotspot [9].

For simplification, we assume the die is a thin plate and the chip runs time-invarient workloads. A hotspot can be considered a time-dependent point source of heat. At any time, any spot's temperature submits to the following formula:

$$T(x,t) = \frac{Q}{2\pi\lambda x}\left[1 - \mathrm{erf}\left(\frac{x}{\sqrt{4\alpha t}}\right)\right] = \frac{Q}{2\pi\lambda x}\left[1 - \frac{2}{\sqrt{\pi}}\sum_{n=0}^{\infty}(-1)^n \frac{r^{2n+1}}{\prod\limits_{n=1}^{n} n(2n+1)}\right]. \tag{1}$$

where $r = \dfrac{x}{\sqrt{4\alpha t}}$, T is temperature, x is the distance between the measuring point and source point, Q is the heat emitted from the source at any time, α is the thermal distribution ratio of material, λ is a parameter related to die material. In steady state when $t\to\infty$, point x has temperature value as follows:

$$T(x) = \frac{Q}{2\pi\lambda x}. \tag{2}$$

3.2 Temperature Pole at Hotspot

Because of heat conduction, the temperature distributing around the hotspot presents a shape like a pole. Paci [9] showed us several steady states of temperature distribution in Fig. 4 and Fig. 5.

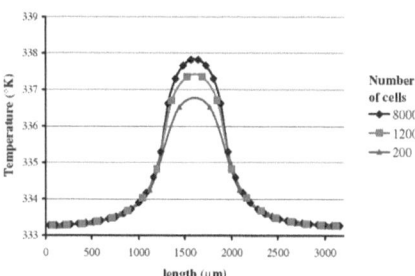
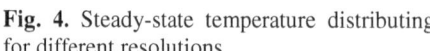
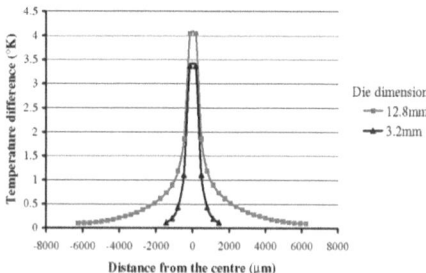

Fig. 4. Steady-state temperature distributing for different resolutions

Fig. 5. Steady-state temperature distributing for two different die dimensions

4 Bottle-Neck in Future

Fig. 6 is the temperature map of a 4-processor die under a task. The hottest parts are the processor cores and their instruction caches. In Fig. 7, not only the temperatures of cores and I-caches, do that of other units rise, too! We notice that though the core frequency and die dimension are not changed, the cores and caches get closer.

For the example in Fig. 8, when the frequency is augmented by 10 times, the temperature differences increases with 10.77 times, which is a little more than the ideal number 10. Furthermore, when the die dimensions are minished by 2 times, the temperature differences increases from 1.5°C to 2.8°C. Since the temperature poles get closer, the powers in processors and Caches overlapp with each other. This arises the temperature of processors and Caches more than expected. Also, it arises the temperature of memories rising more than intended, too [9].

From Figs. 2 through 8, the width of the hotspot poles is about 2mm or less. This implies us that if two hotspots is nearer than 2mm, their temperature poles may overlap. Then the temperature would rise higher than we expected at one hotspot or

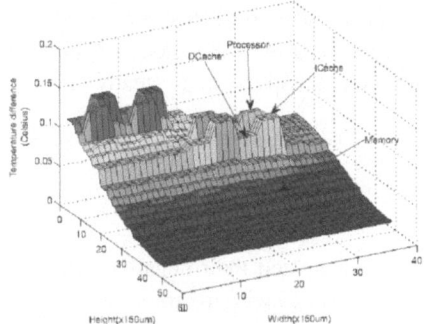

Fig. 6. Temperature differences of a 4-processor chip at 100 MHz

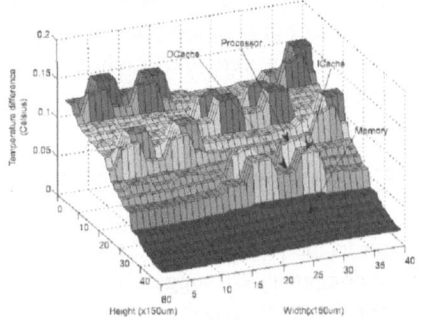

Fig. 7. Temperature differences of a 10-processorchip 100 MHz

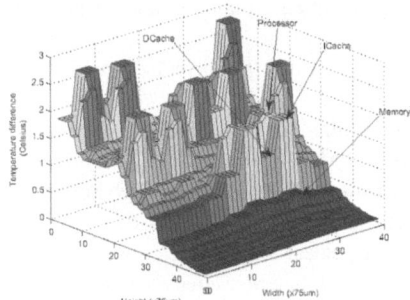

Fig. 8. Temperature differences of the die in Fig. 7 at 1 GHz on a scaled die size

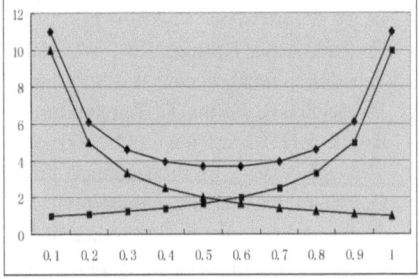

Fig. 9. Temperature curves of two Hotspots when they are too close

both or somewhere between them. From formulae 1 and 2, we simulate to obtain the effect if two hotspots are too close. The heat generated from two hotspots splice to make the temperature between them higher (seeing Fig. 9).

5 Hot Units Distributed Architecture for Future

To solve the above problems and bottleneck in microprocessor dies, we propose the idea of distributed function unit architecture. That is, hot function units in one die are scattered so that the distances between them are long enough. In this structure, cores are far from each another, caches are far from each other, even a core is far from its cache(s). With this new distributed function unit architecture, the energy now dissipated in one smaller region can be balanced in larger region. Then the crowded hotspots would be scattered and the heat generated from hotspots can be conducted to the surrounding easily.

Actually, our idea has existed in several software approaches for chip's dynamical thermal management (DTM). The goal of various operating system scheduling strategies for DTM is minimizing the numbers of hot spots. By means of apportioning workloads among different function units in processor, the scheduling strategies balance the temperature distribution on the die for a set of tasks [1-5]. Those approaches lowered the highest temperature on hotspots and steady average temperature in die.

6 Conclusions

Facing to the problem of hotspots in CPU die, we analyzed their negative effects to future computer. We suggest a new die architecture to cope with the trend of more and closer hotspots in a die.

References

1. Balakrishnan, S., Ramanan, J.: Power-Aware Operating System Using ACPI (2007), http://www.cs.wisc.edu
2. Coskun, A.K., Rosing, T.S., Whisnant, K.A., Gross, K.C.: Temperature-Aware MPSoC Scheduling for Reducing Hot Spots and Gradients
3. Jayaseelan, R., Mitra, T.: Temperature Aware Scheduling for Embedded Processors
4. Brooks, D., Martonosi, M.: Dynamic Thermal Management for High-Performance Microprocessors. In: Proceedings of the 7th International Symposium on High Performance Computer Architecture, Monterrey, Mexico (January 2001)
5. Cheng, A.M.K., Feng, C.: Predictive Thermal Management for Hard Real-time Tasks
6. Rotem, E., Hermerding, J., Aviad, C., Harel, C.: Temperature Measurement in the Intel Core Duo Processor. Intel Document Published August 2008, 45nm Desktop Dual Core Processors Intel Core 2 Duo processor E8000 and E7000 series

7. Scheuermann, U.: Chip Temperature Measurement without Additional Sensors
8. Gunther, S.H., Binns, F., Carmean, D.M., Hall, J.C.: Managing the Impact of Increasing Microprocessor Power Consumption. Intel Technology Journal Q1 (2001)
9. Paci, G., Poletti, F., Benini, L., Marchal, P.: Exploring temperature-aware design in low-power MPSoCs

A Modified Nearest Neighbor Classification Approach Based on Class-Wise Local Information

Deqiang Han[*], Chongzhao Han, and Yi Yang

Institute of Integrated Automation, Xi'an Jiaotong University, Xi'an,
Shaanxi, 710049, China
deqhan@gmail.com, czhan@mail.xjtu.edu.cn, yyjiafei@gmail.com

Abstract. Nearest Neighbor (NN) is a nonparametric classification approach, which is simple yet effective. In NN, the classification decision only uses the information of distance, thus its classification performance is always undermined by the outliers. To solve such a problem, a modified nearest neighbor classification method is proposed by using class-wise local information. For a given test sample, its corresponding nearest neighbor in each class can found and the corresponding distance information can be derived. At the same time, the class distributions in the neighborhood of the test sample's nearest neighbors in each class can be obtained, which is considered as the class-wise local information and can represent the possibility for the nearest neighbor in each class to be the outlier. The classification decision criterion is designed by jointly utilizing the distance information and the class-wise local information. Experimental results show that the proposed method is rational and effective.

Keywords: Nearest Neighbor, Neighborhood-based Classification, Pattern Classification.

1 Introduction

Pattern classification [1] is one of the essential problems in the fields of machine learning and artificial intelligence. Due to the simplicity and effectiveness, the neighborhood-based pattern classification approaches are widely used in many applications such as audio classification [2], face recognition [3], text categorization [4], etc. Among the neighborhood-based pattern classification approaches, nearest neighbor (NN) is the simplest yet effective one, which is nonparametric. It has been proved that has asymptotic error rate that is at most twice the Bayes error rate [5].

But it should be noted that the performance of NN might be affected by the quantity of samples, the representative capacity of samples and the existence of outliers (i.e. the noisy sample or the isolated sample) etc. To resolve such problems, several generalized or modified nearest neighbor classifier were proposed, such as the k-nearest neighbor (k-NN), the error rate of which is asymptotically approximate to the Bayes error rate. But in practical use of k-NN, the choice of the parameter k might be a trouble issue. There still exist other types of generalized or modified

---

[*] Corresponding author.

R. Chen (Ed.): ICICIS 2011, Part I, CCIS 134, pp. 186–192, 2011.
© Springer-Verlag Berlin Heidelberg 2011

neighborhood-based classifiers such as the nearest feature line (NFL) [2], graphic neighbor (GN) and surround neighbor (SN) [6], etc. NFL can improve the representative capacity of the samples. This is helpful for the resolving of the small sample size problem, but it will arouse the problem of trespass inaccuracies and tremendous increase of computational complexity. GN and SN also have the drawbacks of high computational complexity. What is more crucial is that almost all the neighborhood-based classifiers' performances will be influenced by the outliers or noisy samples.

To counteract the effects of the outliers or noisy samples thus improve the classification performance, we modify the traditional NN by using class-wise local information. For a given query sample, its corresponding nearest neighbors in each class are found and the corresponding distances can be calculated. We further calculate the class distribution surrounding the query sample's NN in each class, which can be used as the class-wise local information. Such a type of information can represent the possibility of each class's NN to be the outlier. By jointly using the distance information obtained and the class-wise local information derived, the decision criterion is designed. The experimental results provided can verify that the proposed classification approach is rational and effective.

2 Nearest Neighbor Classifier and the Outlier

The traditional NN is implemented as follows.

Suppose that $X^i = \{x_1^i, x_2^i, ..., x_{N(i)}^i\}$ are the training samples belonging to class i, $i = 1,...,M$. $N(i)$ is the quantity of the samples belonging to class i. Given a query (test) sample x_q, find its corresponding nearest training sample point x_j^i from all training samples, then x_q is labeled as class i. The NN is simple yet effective and its implementation is nonparametric. It has been proved that NN has asymptotic error rate that is at most twice the Bayes error rate. That is to say if infinite number of training samples are available, half of the information in classification is provided by the nearest neighbor. But NN still has some drawbacks which confine its performance.

For example, the small sample size (SSS) problem, which means that when the feature dimension is far larger than the sample size, NN is always not competent for classification. This is not hard to understand because NN in fact can be considered as an effective approximation of the real probability distribution of class. The corresponding efficiency is guaranteed by some certainty quantity of training samples. When the sample quantity is too limited, the performance will be restricted. Like other nonparametric approach, without the probability distribution, there will be no meaningful conclusions [1].

The computational complexity is also a defect of NN, because all the training samples will be traversed in the procedure of the classification based on NN.

For NN, there still exists another important factor, i.e. the influence of the outlier, which confines its performance. How to counteract the negative effect of the outliers in NN is the aim of this paper. The outlier is illustrated in Figure 1.

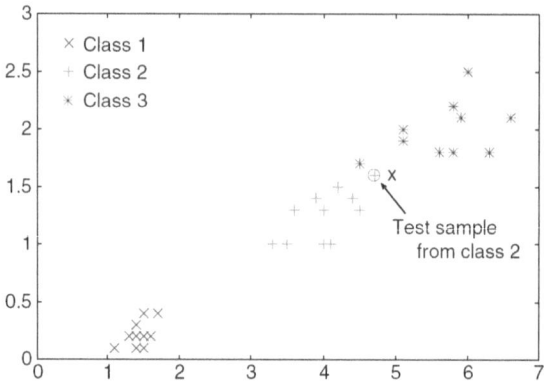

Fig. 1. Illustration of the Outlier Point

In Fig. 1, the sample point pointed by the arrow is belonging to class 2 while its nearest neighbor is belonging to class 3. According to the rule of NN, such a query sample is labeled as class 3. That is to say the query sample is misclassified, which is due to the existence of an outlier belonging to class 3.

The outlier can not be deleted arbitrarily. This is due to that some outliers can be considered as the noisy points but some other outliers can provide important information. To resolve the problem of outliers, there have emerged several methods. Many researchers aim to detect the outliers. For the rule of NN, Mitani, etc [7] design an approach to detect the outliers based on their class-wise local information defined. In their work, for each query sample and in each class, k nearest neighbors are found. Then in each class, the centroid of the k nearest neighbors is derived. Based on the distances between the query sample and the centroids in each class, the classification decision can be made. In [8], based on the work of Mitani et al., the information provided by the centroids of all the samples in each class are also considered to make the decision. The reason for the negative effect of the outliers for the classification is that only the distance is used to make the decision. If other types of auxiliary information could be added in, it will be helpful for the NN classification. In this paper, we propose a modified NN classifier by jointly using a new type of class-wise local information and the distance, which is introduced in the next section.

3   Modified NN Classifier Based on Class-Wise Local Information

The implementation procedure of the proposed classification is as follows.

1) For a query sample x_q , find the its nearest sample x_{NN_i} in $X^i = \{x_1^i, x_2^i, ..., x_{N(i)}^i\}$ belonging to each class i , where $i = 1, ..., M$ represents the class label. Calculate the corresponding distance d_{min}^i :

$$x_{NN\_i} \triangleq x_{j*}^i, j* = \arg\min_j \left\| x_q - x_j^i \right\|, j = 1, ..., N(i) \tag{1}$$

$$d^i_{\min} = \left\| x_{NN\_i} - x_q \right\|$$ (2)

where $N(i)$ represents the number of training samples belonging to class i and $\| \ \|$ represents a kind of distance, e.g. the Euclidean distance.

2) In each class i, for the x_{NN_i} (i.e. the NN of x_q in class i), find its corresponding k nearest neighbors in all the training samples belonging to class i;

3) In each class i, calculate the number of samples belonging to class i in k nearest neighbors of x_{NN_i}, which is denoted by $k^i_{NN\_i}$. Then calculate the class-wise local class distribution information (i.e. the ratio of the samples belonging to class i) as follows:

$$\rho^i_{NN\_i} = \frac{k^i_{NN\_i}}{k}$$ (3)

4) Make the classification decision according to (4) and (5)

$$d'_i = \frac{d^i_{\min}}{\rho^i_{NN\_i}}$$ (4)

$$\text{class of } x_q \equiv \min_i d'_i$$ (5)

In (3), the $\rho^i_{NN\_i} \in [0,1]$ can be regarded as the possibility of x_{NN_i} (the NN of x_q in class i) to be an outlier. If $\rho^i_{NN\_i}$ is relatively large, then x_{NN_i} has relatively low possibility to be an outlier. If $\rho^i_{NN\_i}$ is relatively small, then x_{NN_i} has relatively high possibility to be an outlier. In (4), the distance information are modified by using the class-wise local classification distribution information described in (3). That is to say the decision is not only made based on the distance but also based on the possibility of NN in each class to be the outlier. The shortest distance can not assure the correctness of the classification if the NN is just the outlier. Thus both the distance and the class-wise local information are used in the decision-making, better classification performance can be expected.

4 Experiments

1) Classification problem of two classes with Gaussian distribution
We generate the artificial two-class dataset with known probability density. Any sample in our dataset has two dimensions (x, y). x is a Gaussian distributed variable and y is a uniform distributed variable. Their joint – probability density function is as follows [9]:

$$p_{class1}(x,y) = \begin{cases} \dfrac{1}{\sqrt{2\pi}\sigma(b-a)} \exp[-\dfrac{1}{2}(\dfrac{x}{\sigma})^2], & a \le y \le b, \\ 0, & otherwise; \end{cases}$$

$$p_{class2}(x,y) = \begin{cases} \dfrac{1}{\sqrt{2\pi}\sigma(b-a)} \exp[-\dfrac{1}{2}(\dfrac{x-\mu}{\sigma})^2], & a \le y \le b, \\ 0, & otherwise; \end{cases}$$

(6)

where μ denotes the distance between the two Gaussian centers. Totally 500 samples are generated. Here $b-a=3$ and $\mu=3.5$. Class 1 and class 2 each have 250 samples. Randomly select 125 training samples from each class, the remainder are reserved as test samples. The k parameter used for our proposed approach is $k=5$. The experimental results are listed in Table 1.

Table 1. The classification performance on Gaussian distribution dataset

Classifier	Mean classification accuracy
NN	94.87%
This paper	95.79%

2) UCI dataset –iris [10]

There are totally 3 classes of plants in iris dataset including Setosa, Versicolor and Virginicia. The feature dimension of the sample is 4. The first two feature dimensions represent the length and width of the sepal, respectively. And the last two feature dimensions represent the length and width of the petal, respectively.

All feature values are normalized to lie between 0 and 1 based on (7):

$$a_i = \frac{v_i - \min v_i}{\max v_i - \min v_i}$$

(7)

where v_i denotes the actual value of attribute i. Maximum and minimum operations are over all samples.

Each dataset is randomly divided into 5 disjoint subsets of approximately equal size. For each time, we select three subsets to constitute the training set and treat the remainder as the testing set. Thus, there are totally $C_5^3 = 10$ different trials over each dataset. The average classification performances across the 10 trials are computed. The k parameter used for our proposed approach is $k=5$. The experimental results are listed in Table 2.

Table 2. The classification performance on iris dataset

Classifier	Mean classification accuracy
NN	94.93%
This paper	95.96%

3) Ripley dataset [11]

The well-known Ripley dataset problem consists of two classes where the data for each class have been generated by a mixture of two Gaussian distributions. The training set consists of 250 patterns (125 patterns belong to each class) and the testing set consists of 1000 patterns (500 patterns belong to each class). The k parameter used for our proposed approach is $k = 5$. The experimental results are listed in Table 3.

Table 3. The classification performance on Ripley dataset

Classifier	Mean classification accuracy
NN	85.00%
This paper	87.20%

4) Remote sensing dataset

The Landsat TM images of some district in Beijing are used. Each sample has 6 bands of TM images. The classes used here are semi-bare land, rice field and corn field. Each class has 800 samples. Randomly select 400 training samples from each class, the remainder are reserved as test samples. The k parameter used for our proposed approach is $k = 5$. The experimental results are listed in Table 4.

Table 4. The classification performance on TM data

Classifier	Mean classification accuracy
NN	96.00%
This paper	97.20%

Based on all the experimental results listed above, it can be concluded that our proposed approach can effectively improve the classification accuracy.

5 Conclusions

In this paper, the class-wise local information are used to modify the NN classifier to counteract the negative effect of the outliers and to improve the classification accuracy. Both the class distributions around nearest neighbor in each class and the distance are used to make the classification decision. The experimental results listed in section 4 show that our proposed approach is rational and effective.

It should be noted that there still exist drawbacks in our proposed approach. The first one is the computational complexity. In the proposed approach, several traverse procedures are needed which will arouse large computation burden thus our approach is not appropriate to the large sample size applications. The second one is that in our proposed approach, there exists the problem of the choice of parameter k. Inappropriate choice of k will do harm to the classification performance. The choice of parameter k in our paper depends on the experience. How to reduce the computational complexity and how to select an appropriate parameter are both our important works in the future.

Acknowledgments

This work is supported by Grant for State Key Program for Basic Research of China (973) No. 2007CB311006.

References

1. Duda, R.O., Hart, P.E., Stork, D.G.: Pattern Classification, 2nd edn. John Wiley & Sons, New York (2001)
2. Li, S.Z.: Content-based audio classification and retrieval using the nearest feature line method. IEEE Transactions on Speech and Audio Processing 8(5), 619–625 (2000)
3. Jiang, W.H., Zhou, X.F., Yang, J.Y.: Face recognition using wavelet transform and nearest neighbor convex hull classifier. Control & Automation 24, 212–214 (2008) (in Chinese)
4. Chen, C.Y., Chang, C.C., Lee, R.C.T.: A near pattern-matching scheme based upon principal component analysis. Pattern Recognition Letters 16, 339–345 (1995)
5. Bian, Z.Q., Zhang, X.G.: Pattern Recognition, 2nd edn. Tsinghua University Press, Beijing (2000) (in Chinese)
6. Chaudhuri, B.B.: A new definition of neighborhood of a point in multi-dimensional space. Pattern Recognition Letters 17, 11–17 (1996)
7. Mitani, Y., Hamamoto, Y.: A local mean-based nonparametric classifier. Pattern Recognition Letters 27, 1151–1159 (2006)
8. Zeng, Y., Yang, Y.P., Zhao, L.: Nearest neighbour classification based on local mean and class mean. Control & Decision 24, 547–550, 556 (2009)
9. Du, H., Chen, Y.Q.: Rectified nearest feature line segment for pattern classification. Pattern Recognition 40, 1486–1497 (2007)
10. Blake, C.L., Merz, C.L.: UCI repository of machine learning databases[DB/OL] (1998), (Online), http://www.ics.uci.edu/~mlearn/MLRepository.html
11. Ripley, B.D.: Pattern Recognition and Neural Networks. Cambridge University Press, Cambridge (1996)

The Kinematics and Dynamics Simulation of the Collision between the Rigid Rod and the Ground

Lulu Gao[1] and Wenli Yao[2,*]

[1] College of Mechanical and Electronic Engineering, Shandong University of Science and
Technology, Qingdao 266510, P.R. China
gaolulu1979@163.com
[2] Department of Engineering Mechanics, Qingdao Technological University,
Qingdao 266520, China
ywenli1969@sina.com

Abstract. For the single rigid rod has the non-fixed point smoothing contact impact to the ground in the motion process, analyzing the motion situation of the before and after collision between the rigid rod and the ground. Base on the geometric characteristics of this construction, giving the method to judge which endpoint of the rod impacts the ground firstly. Using the MATLAB to simulate the motion situation of the before and after collision of the rigid rod.

Keywords: contact impact model, plane motion, simulation.

1   Introduction

The problem of the single rigid rod non-fixed point smoothing contact impact to the ground had been introduced in some textbooks[1], but lots of the textbooks only analysis the content which about the collision process. The non-fixed point impact is when the systems impact in the motion process, the position of collision point which at the object changed with the initial condition, the system parameters and the time and so on[2]. The single rigid rod contacts and impacts to the ground in the motion process is the non-fixed collision. So in the motion process of the rigid rod, we must analysis the problem about when and which point will be contact impact to the ground. We will analysis the contact impact model, the motion condition after collision and if there has many times collision. This paper will analysis when and which point will be contact impact to the ground by solving the minimum distance between the potential pair of contact points. When we analysis the collision process of this model, we will use the method of Newton coefficient of restitution.

Supposing the model as following: a uniform rigid rod, the length is l, the mass is m, the centroid is C, at the initial position ,the rigid rod has no initial velocity, then it will do plane motion, analyzing the motion situation of the before and after collision between the rigid rod and the ground. The model as shown in Fig.1.

---

* Corresponding author.

R. Chen (Ed.): ICICIS 2011, Part I, CCIS 134, pp. 193–198, 2011.

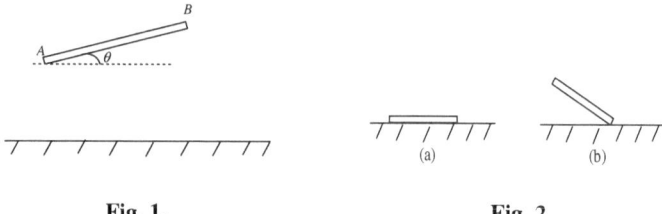

Fig. 1.   Fig. 2.

2 The Kinematics Equation and the Kinetic Equation of the Rigid Rod Plane Motion

From the model which we show in Fig.1, we can know there may be have two kinds contact impact model when the rigid rod impacts to the ground, as shown in Fig.2. (a) the condition of the contact and impact between the whole rigid rod and the ground; (b) the condition of the contact and impact between the one endpoint of the rigid rod and the ground.

When the two endpoints contact and impact to the ground at the same time, then the contact impact model is (a);when there is only one endpoint contacts and impacts to the ground, then the contact impact model is(b).

For this model, we must analysis which endpoint of the rigid rod impacts the ground firstly, the most important of this problem is solving the distance between the ground and the two endpoints in the motion process. Now we establish the coordinate system, it as shown in Fig.3:

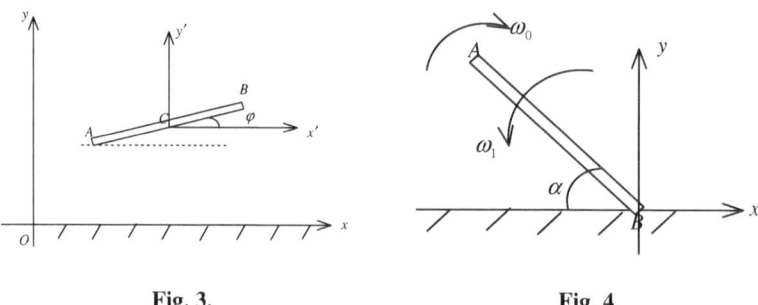

Fig. 3.   Fig. 4.

The coordinate system which takes the centroid C as grid origin is the moving co-ordinate system, the coordinate system which takes the ground as grid origin is the fixed coordinate system. Then at any time, we can get the position of any point of the rod by the kinematics equation and the kinetic equation of the plane motion.

The kinematics equation of the rigid body plane motion is:

$$x_C = f_1(t), \qquad y_C = f_2(t), \qquad \varphi = f_3(t).$$

Then when the rigid rod do the plane motion, the coordinate of the A, B in the fixed coordinate system can be obtain, expressing them as following:

$$x_{OA} = x_C \mp \frac{l}{2}\cos\varphi, \quad y_{OA} = y_C \mp \frac{l}{2}\sin\varphi.$$

$$x_{OB} = x_C \pm \frac{l}{2}\cos\varphi, \quad y_{OB} = x_C \pm \frac{l}{2}\sin\varphi.$$

The kinetic equation of the rigid body plane motion is:

$$m\frac{d^2 x_C}{dt^2} = \sum F_x^{(e)}, \quad m\frac{d^2 y_C}{dt^2} = \sum F_y^{(e)}, \quad J_C \frac{d^2\varphi}{dt^2} = \sum M_C(\mathbf{F}^{(e)}).$$

where J_C is the moment of inertia of the rigid rod rotation around centroid.

At any time, we can get the position of A, B by the kinematics equation and the kinetic equation of the rigid body plane motion. We can judge which endpoints of the rigid rod impacts the ground firstly by test the value of y_{OA}, y_{OB} at any time. The method as follows:

If at one time, there are (1) $y_{OA} = 0$; (2) the direction of v_A^n is vertically downwards, and $v_A^n > 0$, then the A point contacts and impacts to the ground;

Otherwise at one time, there are (1) $y_{OB} = 0$; (2) the direction of v_B^n is vertically downwards, and $v_B^n > 0$, then the B point contacts and impacts to the ground. where v_A^n, v_B^n is the vertically velocity of the two points A, B respectively.

3 Analyzing the Collision Process between the Rigid Rod and the Ground

Analyzing the collision process between the rigid rod and the ground. Here we suppose the point B of the rod impacts to the ground, then the coordinate of the point A can be obtain, we write it as y'_{OA}. The momentary before collision, we write angular velocity of the rod is ω_0, the velocity of the point B is v_B, the velocity of the centroid C is v_C, the angle between the rod and the ground is α, these element can be obtained by the kinetic equation of the rigid body plane motion. The momentary after collision, we write angular velocity of the rod is ω_1, the velocity of the point B is v'_B, the velocity of the centroid C is v'_C. Showing in Fig.4.

The impulsive equation of the rigid body plane motion is:

$$mv'_{Cx} - mv_{Cx} = \sum I_x. \tag{1}$$

$$mv'_{Cy} - mv_{Cy} = \sum I_y. \tag{2}$$

$$J_C\omega_1 - J_C\omega_0 = \sum M_C(\mathbf{I}^{(e)}).$$ (3)

Because here is a smoothing contact and impact, so the collision impulse only exists in y direction, $I_x = 0$. For the rod do the plane motion, the following results are achieved:

$$\mathbf{v}_B = \mathbf{v}_C + \mathbf{v}_{BC}, \quad \mathbf{v}'_B = \mathbf{v}'_C + \mathbf{v}'_{BC}.$$

Projecting these two equations to y direction, yields:

$$v_{By} = v_{Cy} + \frac{l}{2}\omega_0\cos\alpha, \quad v'_{By} = v'_{Cy} + \frac{l}{2}\omega_1\cos\alpha.$$ (4)

The coefficient of restitution is:

$$k = \frac{v'_{By}}{v_{By}} = 1.$$ (5)

Because

$$v_{Cy} = v_C, \quad \alpha = \arcsin\frac{y'_{OA}}{l}.$$ (6)

From Eq.(1) to Eq.(6), we can obtain:

$$\omega_1 = \frac{12v_C\cos\alpha + (3\cos^2\alpha - 1)l\omega_0}{(3\cos^2\alpha + 1)l}, \quad v_{Cy} = \frac{v_C + l\omega_0\cos\alpha - 3v_C\cos^2\alpha}{1 + 3\cos^2\alpha}.$$

Because this model is the rigid rod contacts and impacts to the ground, so after the collision, under the effect of the angular velocity and the velocity of the centroid, the rigid rod will continue to motion and impact to the ground again. In this collision, the problem of which endpoint will be impact to the ground can be solved by the first part of this paper.

4 Numerical Example

In order to prove the correctness of the method, we have the following numerical example.

A uniform rigid rod, the length is $l = 1$ m, the mass is $m = 2$ kg, the coordinate of the centroid is $x_C = 0.6$, $y_C = 3$. At the initial time, the rigid rod at the horizontal position, has no initial velocity, then it will do plane motion under the effect of the moment of the couple $M = 0.5$, the direction of the M is clockwise. As shown in Fig.5. The beginning time is $t = 0$, we get the following results by MATLAB

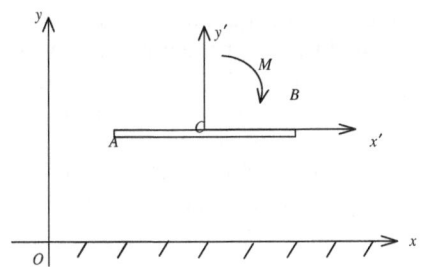

Fig. 5.

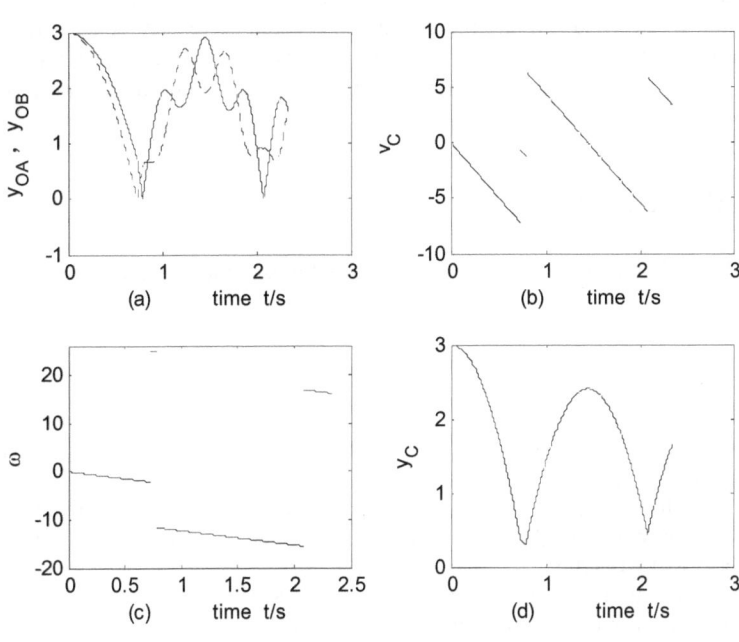

Fig. 6.

numerical simulation: (here, we only give the rod motion situation figure of the former three times before and after contact impact).

In Fig.6 (a), in the fixed coordinate system, the change curve of the ordinate of A is the black real line; the change curve of the ordinate of B is the black dashed line. If the value of ordinate is 0, then the rigid rod impacts to the ground; the time which the two curve intersection is the time of rod at the horizontal position in the plane motion process. For this numerical example, we can obtain information from the Fig.6(a), the endpoint B impacts the ground firstly, after a time endpoint A impacts the ground, then the endpoint A impacts the ground again. The Fig.6(a) gives the curve about the ordinate of the two endpoints change with the time, this curve is only shows the change of the former three times before and after contact impact, hence we know, after the third collision ,the rod will impacts ground again and again in the plane motion process. In Fig.6 (b), the negative value of the velocity denotes the direction of the velocity is vertically downwards, the positive value denotes the direction of the velocity is vertically upwards. In Fig.6(c), the negative value denotes the direction of the angular velocity is clockwise, the positive value denotes the direction of the angular velocity is anticlockwise. The time of the velocity and the angular velocity value jumping is the time of the rod impacts to the ground.

5 Conclusion

This paper analysis the situation of the non-fixed point smoothing contact impact between the single rigid rod and the ground, we obtain there may be have many times collision between the rod and the ground. Giving the method to judge which endpoint of the rod impacts to the ground firstly, and numerical simulation the process by the MATLAB.

Acknowledgements

The authors thank for the support of the Chinese State Natural Science Fund 10872118.

References

1. Theoretical Mechanics Department of Harbin Institute of Technology: Theoretical Mechanics. Higher Education Press (2005)
2. Li, J., Qinchao, L., Qi, W.: Dynamic Analysis of Two_Degree_of_Freedom Oblique Impact System With Non_Fixed Impact Positions. J. Applied Mathematics and Mechanics 26(7), 810–818 (2005)
3. Lixiao, W., Caishan, L.: Dynamic Simulation and Kinetic Description of Revolute Joint with Spatial Clearanc, vol. 41(5), pp. 679–687. Peking University Press, Beijing (2005)

Research on Innovative Practice Teaching System Based on the High-End Practice Teaching Environment for Software Engineering Speciality*

Jianli Dong, Cunhua Li, Zhaohui Ji, and Junming Wu

School of Computer Engineering, Huaihai Institute of Technology,
Lianyungang, 222005, China
dongjl1019@sina.com

Abstract. Through the analysis of current culture status of undergraduate engineering applied talents, the paper points out that the main reason causing the lack of student integrated application and practice innovation abilities is the poor construction of high-end practice environment. And then, how to enhance the practice environment construction and practical teaching innovation as well as building an appropriate innovation practice teaching system for engineering applied talents are systematically discussed. It is very obvious that the application and promotion of this kind of innovative practice teaching system could enhance the practice innovation abilities and entrepreneurial and employment awareness of the graduates.

Keywords: high-end practice environment, practice teaching system, software engineering speciality, exam-oriented education, practice base.

1 Introduction

Undergraduate engineering practical teaching is considered as a group of the experiment, training, practice, engineering case studies and other general practice teaching. Although, experiment, training, and practice all have practical features, their teaching goals, means and methods are different from each other. Experimental teaching is mainly a practice teaching form for students' basic skills training associated with professional based courses or professional courses theory teaching processes. By the ways of demonstration, validation and design the technical verification and implementation is finished as well as the basic operating skills; Professional practice focuses on understanding and recognizing the social needs to professional technologies and its application and development, its goal is to train the observation and adaptation abilities of students; Professional training, which between the professional experiment and training, is a kind of practical teaching processes for culturing the comprehensive application and practical innovation abilities. Systematic specialized core course experiments and basic

---

* This project is supported by Fund of Jiangsu Education Reform Research Project (Grant No. JG09004) and Chinese Association of Higher Education's Special Project (Grant No. 2010YHE009).

R. Chen (Ed.): ICICIS 2011, Part I, CCIS 134, pp. 199–204, 2011.

operation skills could be a foundation of professional training, but, systematic and advanced professional technologies and applied abilities also provide a solid foundation for later professional practice, which even is helpful for students to understand and adapt to society faster. The three links of practical teaching form three levels of teaching. They oppose each other and also complement each other. Experiment, training and practice constitute complete practice teaching system for culturing undergraduate innovative applied talents.

Take the development of high-end practice environment of undergraduate software engineering in Huaihai Institute of Technology for example, this paper focus on the problems of innovative practice teaching system research and building based on high-end practice environment.

2   The Building System of the High-End Practice Environment

In current Higher Education in China, the based experimental environment of undergraduate engineering applied specialties already has a considerable scale after several years of construction, especially after the Ministry of Education's activities of "Evaluation of undergraduate education", the construction of basis professional laboratory have achieve a new level. However, it is the lack of university's internal and external high-end practice environment construction which restrain the development of higher education and the formation of school characteristics. What is high-end practice environment? Here we give the specific definition: high-end practice environment (also known as high-end training and practice base) is experiment, practice, training and other facilities and sites for professional talents which is in social development more cutting-edge technology and could able to meet the needs of culturing current undergraduate students in late high school comprehensive applied abilities and innovative abilities. It's mainly forms including: Firstly, universities and governments (including central and local government) to build together; Secondly, cooperation in the Establishment of Universities and Enterprises; Thirdly, opening undergraduate professional integrated laboratories or training centers that university self-built; Fourthly, created by cooperation of the government and business; Fifthly, opening undergraduate training center that enterprise self-built (currently widespread in the community); Sixthly, the inner production and research environment of modern enterprises could be seen as the undergraduate professional talents training and practice base or research and development center.

Objectively speaking, the training of software engineering applied innovative talents must require the support of high-end practice teaching and learning environment. That is, the first-class practice environment, first-class technology and equipment, first-class faculty and excellent management system is the basic conditions to ensure the first-class software engineering talents, especially for the cultivation of high-quality software professionals. So, in the process of practice environment building, we particularly emphasized large-scale integrated high-end practice environment construction. Two main directions should be take attention on, one is inner school construction including central and local governments build together, national and provincial Demonstration Laboratory and so on; another is outside school high-end practice bases construction which are built together with enterprises as well as professional build. The basic principles of internal and external laboratory and practice base

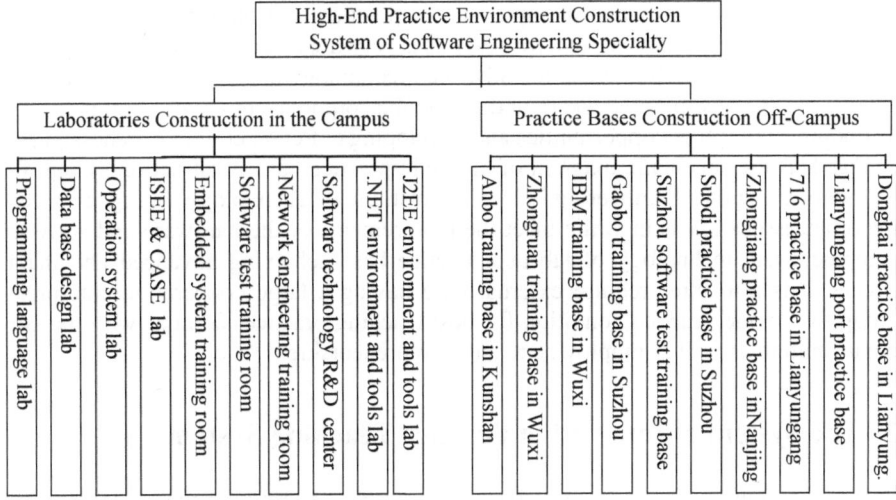

Fig. 1. Construction system of high-end practice bases and laboratories

construction are high-end configuration, the development of practice running and the property of binding the industry, learning and research as one. These three character- istics are the basic principles of the common property of internal and external school high-end practice environment construction. On the other hand, to the construction of external school practice environment, the enterprise feature of practice-based must be emphasized.

The principle of high-end, stress the advanced of hardware and software environ- ment configuration and equipment of practice environment construction (including laboratory or practice base, et.al.), which could represent the current mainstream technological level existing in social and economic development and professional field. This is very important, especially for the construction of Key Laboratory of the inner school central and local governments building together, the repetitive low-quality basis laboratory must be resolutely stopped. Otherwise, it would raise the widening gap with social development. Opening principle, emphasis on laboratory and practical bases must be able to open to teachers and students, which not only meet the needs of ex- periment, design, training and practice and other general practice but also meet the requirement of innovation, research and development, competitions and other practical activities; opening to teachers is to become the high-end research and project devel- opment platform for teachers; open to the public is to become the practice base pro- vided social technology services and training talents for enterprises. The combining principle stressed that the high-end practice environment must focus on the combina- tion of practical and theoretical teaching, the combination of experimentation, training and research, the combination of practice environment and social technology service, the combination of the construction of practice teaching base and the corporation with enterprises and other construction and operation mechanism. Emphasize on the com- bining principle is focus on the comprehensive benefits and social potential of high-end practice environment construction and application, and play their due role in many aspects such as practice creative abilities, research, social service and so on. What must be take more attention is that the inner school practice environment must considered co-operation with the modern enterprises, this is very important and urgent not only for the university to absorb and use the advanced technology and equipment resource of enterprises, but also for students to understand the corporate culture or training as well as finding employment opportunities and developing entrepreneurial awareness [4,5].

Fig. 1. is the schematic diagram of high-end practice base construction system for School of Computer Engineering in Huaihai Institute of Technology. In Fig. 1., a very important issues exists in while meet the requirements of the hardware and software equipment and technology of lab and practice base achieving advanced and mainstream, it is also must require external base having a large cooperation enterprises group to provide practice condition for post teaching practice, familiar with the corporate culture as well as employment and entrepreneurship.

3   The System of Innovation Practice Teaching System

Practice teaching is the most effective and direct way to training the comprehensive application and practice innovation abilities. The objectives, plans, content, environment and requirements of practical teaching should be clearly developed and implemented according to professional education and the school regulations.

To the traditional practice teaching in universities, practical teaching system establishment should focus on practice teaching programs, practice environment and management systems. Practice teaching program have systematically and clearly plan and description in general professional training programs, including course experiment, curriculum design, professional training, social practice and graduation design and so on. For each practice teaching course, its name, general outline, content, assessment methods, achievements evaluation should have a clear planning, they should be archived and issued executive in the form of documents, becoming the fundamental basis of implementing practical teaching and its management. Practice environment mainly include training plan adapting to the experiment, training, internships and other places and facilities, consisting of two types of internal and external school. Generally speaking, internal school practice environment construction give first place to professional basic laboratory, external take training and practice base construction as the principal thing. Practice teaching management system is the standards of implementing practice teaching tasks, including teaching resources management, teaching staff, teaching process, teaching effectiveness, teaching quality, assessment and evaluation, cooperation agreements and other rules and regulations [6,7].

To implement the innovation of software engineering teaching system, the first thing is to adjust and plan the professional knowledge and course systems according to professional training and social needs. And the original computer knowledge and curriculum systems which have no obvious professional characteristics should be break. So, we adjusted the original professional training program combining the requirements of software engineering professional basic theory and practice ability training in and aboard, increasing the theoretical and practical courses such as software testing, software project management, software quality assurance and management, integrated software engineering environment, large-scale software construction techniques, net environment and new technologies, J2EE environment and new technologies and so on. It can be seen that the adjustment of these courses, which not only highlights the characteristics of specialized knowledge and curriculum systems but also broaden the content and scope of professional theory and practice teaching, established a solid foundation for students to learn frontier knowledge of software engineering, master advanced professional technology and improve the comprehensive application and innovative ability.

With the update of professional knowledge and curriculum system, the corresponding practice teaching environment must be ensured. The practice teaching environment shown in fig 1. adapts to this innovation practice teaching system very well.

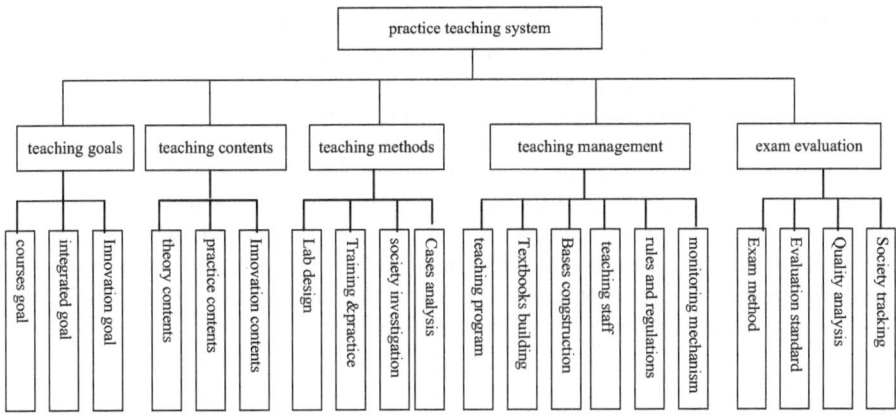

Fig. 2. Practice Teaching System

It does not mean the high-end software engineering professional talents could be trained naturally with internal and external high-end practice environment. It also needs to develop scientific and standardized practice teaching management system. The process and quality control of external practice teaching, which is the bottlenecks of current external practice and training in universities, must be give adequate attention. From overall situation of undergraduate professional talents training, our school researched and developed the management system which consisted with the practice teaching characteristics. In this respect, we firstly guaranteed the quality of external practice base. So, by critical review from nature and development potential of enterprise, infrastructure and technical equipment of base, instructor qualifications, teaching management standard, the base environment safety, quality of student life, size and number of enterprise alliance and other aspects, we choose a number of enterprises which have advanced resource and favorable conditions for running school as the software engineering high-end practice teaching base of our school, and signed long-term cooperation agreement with each practice base to clear responsibilities, rights and interests of each party. The teaching process and quality control of external practice base is an important and complex problem. So, we explore a set of new mechanism adapting to external base management in the corporation with outside base. We study and develop a series of specific management regulations and standards in all respect such as internal and external professional knowledge extension, complementary teaching resources, alternative course credit, practice process monitoring, teaching quality assessment, management system standards, quantitative employment indicators, curriculum and professional build together and so on, which make the cooperation of universities and base have rule-based, legal basis, clearly responsibility, rights and benefits, and finally achieving win-win cooperation. Fig 2. is the schematic diagram of practice teaching system [8].

4   Conclusion

Through the high-end practice base construction and practice teaching innovation of our school in recent years, the software engineering professional talents training quality and practice creative abilities have been significantly improved, gradually showing the professional education characteristics of "the grassland, enough stamina". We deeply feel in teaching practice that the training of undergraduate applied innovation talents is must strengthen the high-end practice environment construction and pay attention to the training of comprehensive application and practical creative ability while keeping the advantage of systematic and integrity of traditional theory education, this is our success experience. It has been proved that it is correct and effective to emphasize enhancing the training quality of software engineering professional talents in the high-end practice environment, and the rising of the employment rate and the rate of passing postgraduate entrance exams is the best proof.

References

1. Dong, J., Wang, J.: Research on Innovative Education Thoughts and Teaching Methods for China Universities. In: 2009 International Conference on Information Management, Innovation Management and Industrial Engineering, Xi'an, vol. 3, pp. 379–382. IEEE Computer Society, Los Alamitos (2009)
2. Dong, J., Wang, Q.: Research and Practice on the Innovative Teaching Mode of Software Engineering Synthesis Design. In: The 1st International Conference on Information Science and Engineering, Track 10. IEEE Computer Society, Nanjing (2009)
3. Yang, H., Wang, Z.: Research in the Construction of Off-Campus Practice Base in the New Period. J. Journal of Yangzhou University (Higher Education Study Edition) 11(3), 87–89 (2007) (in Chinese)
4. Wang, W., Yao, A., Sun, W.: Research and Practice of the Construction of Off- campus Practical Teaching Base. J. Journal of Anhui Agri. Sci. 35(29), 9383–9385 (2007) (in Chinese)
5. Zhang, Z., Zhao, Z., Zheng, Y., Wu, J.: Construction and Practice of Practice Base Outside School. J. Experiment Science & Technology 7(1), 139–141 (2009) (in Chinese)
6. Huang, S., Yang, L., Zhang, Z.: Constructing Practice Bases for Engineering Specialties and Study on New Practice Modes. J. Journal of Guangdong University of Technology (Social Sciences Edition) 4(4), 52–55 (2004) (in Chinese)
7. Meng, F.: Student-oriented Teaching Quality Evaluation System of Universities and Its Construction. J. Higher Education Research and Evaluation 2, 84–89 (2009) (in Chinese)
8. Zhang, S.: The Construction and Evaluation of Modern Engineering Professinal Practice and Teaching Basees. J. Journal of ShanDong Institute of Business and Technology 22(5), 104–109 (2008) (in Chinese)

Chaotic Artificial Bee Colony Used for Cluster Analysis

Yudong Zhang, Lenan Wu[*], Shuihua Wang, and Yuankai Huo

School of Information Science and Engineering, Southeast University, Nanjing China
zhangyudongnuaa@gmail.com, wuln@seu.edu.cn

Abstract. A new approach based on artificial bee colony (ABC) with chaotic theory was proposed to solve the partitional clustering problem. We first investigate the optimization model including both the encoding strategy and the variance ratio criterion (VRC). Second, a chaotic ABC algorithm was developed based on the Rossler attractor. Experiments on three types of artificial data of different degrees of overlapping all demonstrate the CABC is superior to both genetic algorithm (GA) and combinatorial particle swarm optimization (CPSO) in terms of robustness and computation time.

Keywords: partitional clustering; variance ratio criterion; artificial bee colony; Rossler attractor.

1 Introduction

Cluster analysis or clustering is the assignment of a set of observations into subsets without any priori knowledge so that observations in the same cluster are similar in some sense [1]. Clustering is a method of unsupervised learning, and a common technique for statistical data analysis used in many fields, including machine learning, data mining, pattern recognition, image analysis and bioinformatics.

In this study, we focus our attention on partitional clustering. K-means clustering [2] and the fuzzy c-means clustering (FCM) [3] are two typical algorithms of this type. They are iterative algorithms and the solution obtained depends on the selection of the initial partition and may converge to a local minimum of criterion function value if the initial partition is not properly chosen [4]. In these decades, evolutionary algorithms were proposed to clustering problem since they are not sensitive to initial values and able to jump from local minimal point. For example, Lin applied genetic algorithm (GA) for clustering for k-anonymization [5]. Jarboui [6] proposed a combinatorial particle swarm optimization (CPSO) method for partitional clustering problem. However, those algorithms still suffers from being trapped into local extrema.

Artificial Bee Colony (ABC) algorithm was originally presented by Dervis Karaboga [7] under the inspiration of collective behavior on honey bees with better performance in function optimization problem compared with GA, differential evolution (DE), and PSO [8]. In order to improve the performance of ABC, we propose a chaotic ABC (CABC) method based on the Rossler attractor of chaotic theory.

---

[*] Corresponding author.

R. Chen (Ed.): ICICIS 2011, Part I, CCIS 134, pp. 205–211, 2011.

2 Partitional Clustering Problem

The problem of partitional clustering can be depicted as follows. Suppose there are n samples $\boldsymbol{O}=\{o_1, o_2, \ldots, o_n\}$, in a d-dimensional metric space to be clustered into k groups/clusters so that the objects in a cluster are more similar to each other than to objects in different groups. Each $o_i \in R^d$ represents a feature vector consisting of d real valued measures describing the feature of the objects. Suppose the clusters are denoted as $\boldsymbol{C}=\{c_1, c_2, \ldots, c_k\}$, then they should obey three following statements

$$c_i \neq \phi \ \text{ for } \ i = 1, 2, \ldots, k$$
$$c_i \cap c_j = \phi \ \text{ for } \ i \neq j \tag{1}$$
$$\bigcup c_i = \{1, 2, \ldots, n\}$$

Our task is to find the optimal partition $\boldsymbol{C}^*$ that has the best adequacy in terms to all other feasible solution. Two important issues should be solved for translating the clustering problem into an optimization problem. One is the encoding strategy, and the other is the criterion function.

2.1 Encoding Strategy

The search space was determined of n-dimension due to n-objects. Each dimension represents an object and the ith bee $X_i = \{x_{i1}, x_{i2}, \ldots, x_{in}\}$ corresponds to the affection of n objects, such that $x_{ij} \in \{1, 2, \ldots, k\}$, where k denotes the number of classes. Suppose $n=9$, $k=3$, the first cluster contains the 1st, 4th, and 7th object, the second cluster contains the 2nd, 5th, and 8th object, and the third cluster contains the 3rd, 6th, and 9th object. The encoding of this cluster solution is illustrated in Fig. 1.

Cluster	Object
I	1,4,7
II	2,5,8
III	3,6,9

	x_{i1}	x_{i2}	x_{i3}	x_{i4}	x_{i5}	x_{i6}	x_{i7}	x_{i8}	x_{i9}
X_i	1	2	3	1	2	3	1	2	3

Fig. 1. An example of encoding representation

2.2 Criterion Function

There are several criteria that have been proposed to measure the adequacy or similarity in which a given data set can be clustered. The most common used partitional clustering strategy is the variance ratio criterion (VRC). Its definition is depicted as

$$VRC = \frac{B}{W} \times \frac{n-k}{k-1} \tag{2}$$

Here W and B denote the within-cluster and between-cluster variations. As a consequence, compact and separated clusters are expected to have small values of W and large values of B. Hence, the better the data partition, the greater the value of VRC. The normalization term $(n-k)/(k-1)$ prevents the ratio to increase monotonically with the number of clusters, thus making VRC an optimization (maximization) criterion.

3 Artificial Bee Colony

ABC is introduced by mimicking the behavior of natural bees to construct a relative good solution of realistic optimization problems. The colony of artificial bees contains three groups of bees: employed bees, onlookers and scouts. First half of the colony consists of the employed artificial bees and the second half includes the onlookers. For every food source, there is only one employed bee, viz., the number of employed bees is equal to the number of food sources. The employed bee of an abandoned food source becomes a scout. The detailed main steps of the algorithm are given below [9].

Step 1. Initialize the population of solutions x_{ij} and evaluate the population;
Step 2. Repeat;
Step 3. Produce new solutions (food source positions) v_{ij} in the neighborhood of x_{ij} for the employed bees using the formula

$$v_{ij} = x_{ij} + \Phi_{ij}\left(x_{ij} - x_{kj}\right) \tag{3}$$

Here k is a solution in the neighborhood of i, Φ is a random number in the range [-1, 1]. Evaluate the new solutions;
Step 4. Apply the greedy selection process between x_i and v_i;
Step 5. Calculate the probability values P_i for the solutions x_i by means of their fitness values using the equation

$$P_i = \frac{f_i}{\sum\limits_{i=1}^{SN} f_i} \tag{4}$$

Here SN denotes the number of solutions, and f denotes the fitness value;
Step 6. Normalize P_i values into [0, 1];
Step 7. Produce the new solutions (new positions) v_i for the onlookers from the solutions x_i, selected depending on P_i, and evaluate them;
Step 8. Apply the greedy selection process for the onlookers between x_i and v_i;
Step 9. Determine the abandoned solution (source), if exists, and replace it with a new randomly produced solution x_i for the scout using the equation

$$x_{ij} = \min_j + \varphi_{ij} * \left(\max_j - \min_j\right) \tag{5}$$

Here φ_{ij} is a random number in [0, 1];
Step 10. Memorize the best food source position (solution) achieved so far;
Step 11. Go to Step 2 until termination criteria is met.

4 Chaotic ABC

Chaos theory is epitomized by the so-called butterfly effect established by Lorenz [10]. Attempting to simulate numerically a global weather system, Lorenz discovered that minute changes in initial conditions steered subsequent simulations towards radically different final results, rendering long-term prediction impossible in general. Sensitive dependence on initial conditions is not only observed in complex systems, but even in the simplest logistic equation.

4.1 Rossler Attractor

In this study we chose the Rossler equation as the chaos number generator. The Rossler equations are a system of three non-linear ordinary differential equations, which define a continuous-time dynamical system that exhibits chaotic dynamics associated with the fractal properties of the attractor [11]. Some properties of the Rossler system can be deduced via linear methods such as eigenvectors, but the main features of the system require non-linear methods such as Poincare maps and bifurcation diagrams. Compared to the Lorenz attractor, the Rossler has 3 advantages [12]: I) Simpler; II) Having only one manifold; III) Easier to analyze qualitatively. The well-known 3D Rossler equation is shown below

$$\begin{cases} x' = -(y+z) \\ y' = x+ay \\ z' = b+z(x-c) \end{cases} \tag{6}$$

Here a, b, and c are parameters. When they are selected as specific values (such as $a = 0.1$, $b = 0.1$, and $c = 14$ [13]), the point series $[x(t), y(t), z(t)]$ in 3D space will exhibit chaotic property as called "spiral chaos" shown in Fig. 2(a). It indicates that an orbit within the attractor follows an outward spiral close to the $[x, y]$ plane around an unstable fixed point. Once the graph spirals out enough, a second fixed point influences the graph, causing a rise and twist in the z-dimension.

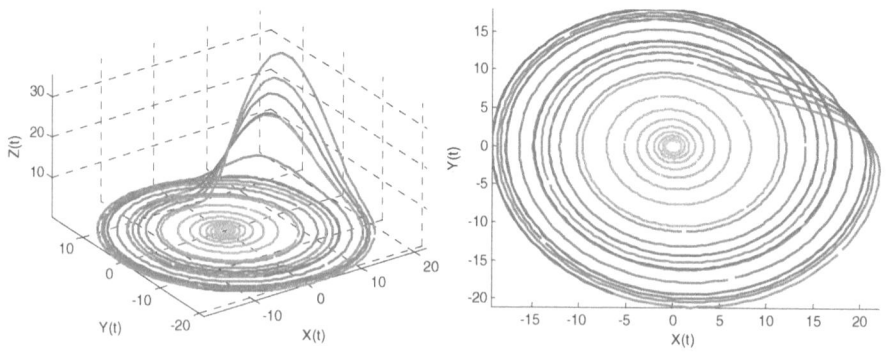

Fig. 2. A Rossler chaotic number generator with $a=0.1$; $b=0.1$; $c=14$. (a) 3D vision; (b) x-y plane vision (From Blue to Purple).

4.2 Procedures of CABC

The parameters (Φ_{ij}, φ_{ij}) in traditional ABC were generated by pseudo-number generator (RNG). The RNG can not ensure the ergodicity in solution space due to the pseudo random property. Therefore, using the chaotic-number generator (CNG) instead of RNG can guarantee the ergodicity of (Φ_{ij}, φ_{ij}). We employ Equ. (8) to generate random numbers series [$x(t)$, $y(t)$, $z(t)$], then set $z(t)=0$, and let $\Phi_{ij}=2*x(t)-1$ since its range lies in [-1, 1], and $\varphi_{ij.}=y(t)$.

5 Experiments

Let $n=200$, $k=4$, and $d=2$. Non-overlapping, partially overlapping, and severely overlapping artificial data were generated randomly from a multivariate Gaussian distribution. The distributions of the data were shown in Fig. 3.

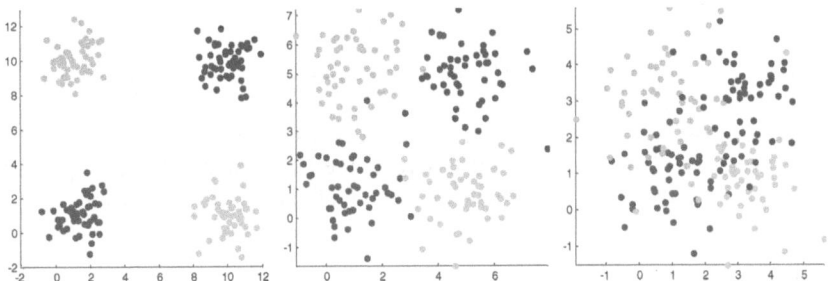

Fig. 3. Artificial Data: (a) Non-overlapping; (b) Partially Overlapping; (c) Severely Overlapping

The proposed CABC was tested in comparison with the GA [5] and CPSO [6] algorithm. Each algorithm was run 100 times to reduce the randomness. The results are listed in Table 1, indicating that for non-overlapping instances, the CPSO and CABC can found global maxima of 1524.6 with 100% success rate. Conversely, the GA is trapped at local maxima of 195.04 at worst runs, so the mean VRC of GA is 1102.0. For partially overlapping instances, the GA, CPSO, and CABC can find the maximal VRC of 303.7, the mean VRCs of those algorithms are 280.1, 284.0, and 295.4, respectively, and the worst VRCs are 254.3, 248.9, and 276.3, respectively. For severely overlapping instances, the GA, CPSO, and CABC can find the maximal VRC of 179.5, the mean VRCs are 133.9, 151.4, and 166.8, respectively, and the worst VRCs are 80.4, 106.1, and 149.3, respectively. Tab. 1 indicates that the mean VRC and worst VRC of the proposed CABC algorithm is higher than the corresponding VRC of either GA or CPSO, therefore, the CABC is more robust than both GA and CPSO.

Moreover, the average time of each algorithm was listed in Table 2. For non-overlapping instances, the average computation time of GA, CPSO, and CABC are 2.97, 2.89, and 2.45 in seconds, respectively. For partially overlapping instances, the average computation time of GA, CPSO, and CABC are 3.55, 3.65, 2.88 in seconds, respectively. For severely overlapping instances, the average computation time of GA,

Table 1. Experimental results for artificial data sets for 100 different runs

Instances	VRC	GA	CPSO	CABC
	Best	**1524.6**	**1524.6**	**1524.6**
Non-overlapping	Mean	1102.0	**1524.6**	**1524.6**
	Worst	195.04	**1524.6**	**1524.6**
	Best	**303.7**	**303.7**	303.7
Partially overlapping	Mean	280.1	284.0	**295.4**
	Worst	254.3	248.9	**276.3**
	Best	**179.5**	**179.5**	179.5
Severely overlapping	Mean	133.9	151.4	**166.8**
	Worst	80.4	106.1	**149.3**

Table 2. Average Computation Time (s)

Instances	GA	CPSO	CABC
Non-overlapping	2.97	2.89	**2.45**
Partially overlapping	3.55	3.65	**2.88**
Severely overlapping	4.48	4.33	**3.57**

CPSO, and CABC are 4.48, 4.33, and 3.57 in seconds, respectively. Table 2 indicates that the average computation time of CABC is the least among all three approaches, besides, this time increases as along as the degree of overlapping increases.

6   Conclusions

In this paper, we first investigate the optimization model including both the encoding strategy and the criterion function of VRC. Afterwards, a CABC algorithm was developed for partitional clustering. Experiments on three types of artificial data of different degrees of overlapping all demonstrate the CABC is more robust and costs less time than either GA or CPSO.

References

1. Coomans, D., Smyth, C., Lee, I., Hancock, T., Yang, J.: Unsupervised Data Mining: Introduction. In: Stephen, D.B., Tauler, R., Beata, W. (eds.) Comprehensive Chemometrics, pp. 559–576. Elsevier, Oxford (2009)
2. Bellec, P., Rosa-Neto, P., Lyttelton, O.C., Benali, H., Evans, A.C.: Multi-level bootstrap analysis of stable clusters in resting-state fMRI. Neuro. Image 51, 1126–1139 (2010)
3. Ayvaz, M.T., Karahan, H., Aral, M.M.: Aquifer parameter and zone structure estimation using kernel-based fuzzy c-means clustering and genetic algorithm. Journal of Hydrology 343, 240–253 (2007)
4. Chang, D.-X., Zhang, X.-D., Zheng, C.-W., Zhang, D.-M.: A robust dynamic niching genetic algorithm with niche migration for automatic clustering problem. Pattern Recognition 43, 1346–1360 (2010)

5. Lin, J.-L., Wei, M.-C.: Genetic algorithm-based clustering approach for k-anonymization. Expert Systems with Applications 36, 9784–9792 (2009)
6. Jarboui, B., Cheikh, M., Siarry, P., Rebai, A.: Combinatorial particle swarm optimization (CPSO) for partitional clustering problem. Applied Mathematics and Computation 192, 337–345 (2007)
7. Karaboga, N., Kalinli, A., Karaboga, D.: Designing digital IIR filters using ant colony optimisation algorithm. Engineering Applications of Artificial Intelligence 17, 301–309 (2004)
8. Karaboga, D., Basturk, B.: On the performance of artificial bee colony (ABC) algorithm. Applied Soft Computing 8, 687–697 (2008)
9. Singh, A.: An artificial bee colony algorithm for the leaf-constrained minimum spanning tree problem. Applied Soft Computing 9, 625–631 (2009)
10. Peng, B., Liu, B., Zhang, F.-Y., Wang, L.: Differential evolution algorithm-based parameter estimation for chaotic systems. Chaos, Solitons & Fractals 39, 2110–2118 (2009)
11. Hammami, S., Benrejeb, M., Feki, M., Borne, P.: Feedback control design for Rössler and Chen chaotic systems anti-synchronization. Physics Letters A 374, 2835–2840 (2010)
12. Ahmed, E., El-Sayed, A.M.A., El-Saka, H.A.A.: On some Routh-Hurwitz conditions for fractional order differential equations and their applications in Lorenz, Rössler, Chua and Chen systems. Physics Letters A 358, 1–4 (2006)
13. Ghosh, D., Saha, P., Roy Chowdhury, A.: Linear observer based projective synchronization in delay Rössler system. Communications in Nonlinear Science and Numerical Simulation 15, 1640–1647 (2010)

A DVE Time Management Simulation and Verification Platform Based on Causality Consistency Middleware

Hangjun Zhou[1,2], Wei Zhang[1], Yuxing Peng[1], and Sikun Li[1]

[1] Key Laboratory of Science and Technology for National Defence of Parallel and
Distributed Processing,
School of Computer Science, National University of Defense Technology,
Chang Sha, Hu Nan, 410073, P.R. of China
{zhouhangjun,weizhang,yxpeng,skli}@nudt.edu.cn
[2] Department of Information Management, Hunan University of Finance and Economics,
Chang Sha, Hu Nan, 410205, P.R. of China

Abstract. During the course of designing a time management algorithm for
DVEs, the researchers always become inefficiency for the distraction from the
realization of the trivial and fundamental details of simulation and verification.
Therefore, a platform having realized theses details is desirable. However, this
has not been achieved in any published work to our knowledge. In this paper,
we are the first to design and realize a DVE time management simulation and
verification platform providing exactly the same interfaces as those defined by
the HLA Interface Specification. Moreover, our platform is based on a new designed causality consistency middleware and might offer the comparison of
three kinds of time management services: CO, RO and TSO. The experimental
results show that the implementation of the platform only costs small overhead,
and that the efficient performance of it is highly effective for the researchers to
merely focus on the improvement of designing algorithms.

Keywords: DVE, HLA, time management, distributed simulation and verification platform, causality consistency middleware.

1 Introduction

Generally, a DVE [1] is established according to HLA standards [2] which regulates
that the whole simulation environment is regarded as a federation consisting of federates and RTI (Run Time Infrastructure).

In HLA/RTI, Time Management is developed to ensure the consistency of the delivery order of messages and events at each federate in a DVE. In an early version of
Time Management Design Document, the following five message ordering mechanisms were suggested [2]: Receive Order (RO), Priority Order, Causal Order (CO),
Causal and Totally Ordered, and Time Stamp Order (TSO).

However, in the versions of the currently available RTI, merely two kinds of time
management mechanisms are realized: RO and TSO. With RO mechanism, messages
are delivered by federates in their receiving turn, which costs little control overhead
and suitable for real-time simulations. Nevertheless, the temporal anomalies could

R. Chen (Ed.): ICICIS 2011, Part I, CCIS 134, pp. 212–218, 2011.

happen with RO if the receiving order of messages is not identical to their generated order due to the network latency. TSO is able to eliminate these kinds of anomalies, but the computation overhead is too significant to satisfy the real-time property.

In the above five mechanisms, CO is developed from the "happened before" relation and uses logical time [3] to preserve the consistent delivery order of messages. Therefore, it is thought to be more feasible to use real-time CO instead of TSO to carry out time management in many DVEs. However, if the CO is realized with embedded mode in RTI, there would be compatibility problems when RTI is updated. In order to improve the code reusability, we design and implement a common CO distributed middleware running between each federate and RTI. By using the standard HLA programming interfaces, the middleware could fulfill the consistent time management at all federates. Moreover, based on the CO middleware, we are first to propose and establish a time management simulation and verification platform which aims at simplifying the design and realization of consistency preservation algorithms for DVEs. The experiments demonstrate that the platform incurs small control overhead and has a sound performance and scalability. More importantly, it could effectively offer the fundamental simulation functions so as to free the researchers to pay more attention to improve the efficiency of the algorithm design.

In the rest of the paper, a CO discussion is given in section 2. The working modes of the platform are proposed in section 3. Section 4 illustrates the design principle and distributed algorithms. Section 5 describes the architecture of the verification platform. Experiments are implemented in section 6. Conclusions are summarized in section 7.

2   Causality Consistency Delivery

One of the most important issues in DVEs is causality. In related works, Lamport's "happened before" relation, which is denoted as " $\rightarrow$ " is used to capture the causality relation between the events of a distributed execution.

Definition 1 ("happened before" relation). Given that e_1, e_2 is any two event in a distributed system, the "happened before" relation between e_1, e_2 could be described as follows:

1) $e_1 \rightarrow e_2$, if e_1 and e_2 are events in the same process of the distributed systems and e_1 comes before e_2;
2) $e_1 \rightarrow e_2$, if e_1 is the sending of a message by one process and e_2 is the receipt of the same message by another process;
3) $e_1 \rightarrow e_2$, if there exists an event e_3 satisfying $e_1 \rightarrow e_3$ and $e_3 \rightarrow e_2$.

If e_1 and e_2 meets any one of three above items, it is said e_1 happens before e_2. As can be seen, "happened before" relation is a partial and non-reflexive order. Based on the "happened before" relation, the causal order is defined as follows:

Definition 2 (Causal Order). Given that e_1, e_2 is any two event in a distributed system, if $e_1 \rightarrow e_2$ and both e_1 and e_2 have been received by a process, then the causal order delivery must ensure that e_1 is delivered before e_2.

3 Working Modes of the Platform

In a serverless DVE, each federate utilizes the local RTI to communicate with others and preserve the consistent delivery order of events. However, the time management service offered by the current versions of RTI merely concerns about RO and TSO that may not effectively applicable in large-scale DVEs. Therefore, we propose a causality consistency control middleware which is designed to distributedly function between each federate and it local RTI. In the middleware, two causal order algorithms have been encapsulated: the IDR [4] and the Prakash method [5]. Among them the former is majorly applied to maintain CO in the broadcast communication pattern and the latter in the multicast pattern.

On the other side, considering the possible damages due to the direct application of the newly proposed consistency algorithms in DVEs running on WAN, it is necessary to firstly verify new algorithms in the simulation LAN environment. Thereby, a LAN network latency simulator is proposed to generate the message transmission delay of WAN. Both the middleware and the latency simulator are deployed into the platform. The framework of the simulation and verification platform is described in Fig. 1.

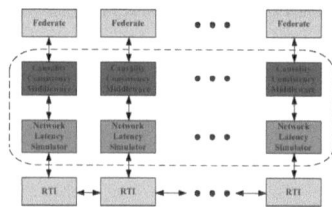

Fig. 1. The framework of the simulation and verification platform

In order to satisfy the different verification requirements of designed algorithms, we propose four kinds of working modes of the platform based on its framework:

Plain-Mode: if designers want to testify and compare the performances of RO and TSO in a DVE running on LAN or other networks having small transmission delay, this mode could be set in the platform without the functions of causality consistency middleware and network latency simulator.

CO-Mode: if a new CO algorithm is completed, this mode could be used to evaluate its effectiveness with the encapsulated methods of the middleware in DVEs on LAN or similar networks. In this mode, only the middleware works while the simulator doesn't.

Delay-Mode: if designers would like to verify how the RO and TSO would effect in DVEs on WAN through a LAN, this mode with the solitary function of the latency simulator could be utilized.

CO-Delay-Mode: if there needs to verify the performance of CO algorithms on the time management of a DVE on WAN through a LAN, this mode could be suitable with the functions of both the causality middleware and the network latency simulator.

4   Design Principle and Distributed Algorithms

In this section, we firstly introduce the major design principle of the platform based on the CO-Delay-Mode, and then the relevant distributed algorithms are proposed.

As can be seen in Fig. 2, *midRtiAmb* and *midFedAmb* respectively inherit *RTIambassador* and *FederateAmbassador*. When sends a message containing an event, a federate calls *midRtiAmb* to use *coModule* to add causal control information into the message. Then, *midRtiAmb* calls *dlyRtiAmb* to transfer the message to RTI. When receives a message, RTI calls *dlyFedAmb* to calculate if the message should buffer into *dlyMsgQueue* or transfer to *midFedAmb*. Through the control information, *midFedAmb* calls *coModule* to check if the message meet the delivery condition. If not, buffer it into *midMsgQueue*. Otherwise, transfer the message to the federate.

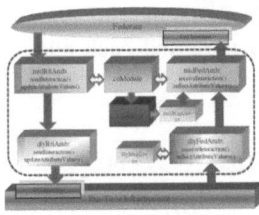

Fig. 2. The design principle of the platform with the CO-Delay-Mode

It is known to us that the message transfer mechanism is the pivot of time management service. The following part describes two distributed algorithms individually about the procedure of sending a message and the one of receiving it.

Algorithm 1. Distributed CO Algorithm of Sending A Message	**Algorithm 2.** Distributed CO Algorithm of Receiving A Message
Input: messge *M* containing event *e* generated at a federate	**Input:** messge *M* received by the local *RTI* through the network
Output: *M* containing event *e* and causal control information and network delay value	**Output:** *M* containing event *e* but without *CI* and ΔT

1 *federate → midRtiAmb* ;   // federate transfers *M*
                                        // to *midRtiAmb*
	1 *RTI → dlyFedAmb* ; // *RTI* transfers *M*
	                                        // to *dlyFedAmb*

2 *midRtiAmb → coModule* ; // *midRtiAmb* calls // *coModule*	2 *if*(*CheckDelay*( )) // check if ΔT is over
3 *coModule*.calculate(*CI*) ; // *CI*--causal control // information	3 *dlyRtiAmb → midFedAmb* ; 4 *else*
4 *M ← CI* ; // add *CI* into *M*	5 {*BufferdlyMsgQueue*(*M*) ; return ; } // if *M* // still needs to delay, buffer it
5 *midRtiAmb → dlyRtiAmb* ;	6 *midFedAmb → coModule* ;

6 *dlyRtiAmb*.simulate(ΔT) ; // ΔT--network delay
                                        // value
	7 *if*(*CheckCO*( )) // check if the delivery
	                                        // condition of *M* is satisfied

7 *M ← ΔT* ;	8 *midFedAmb → federate* ;

8 *dlyRtiAmb → RTI*;   // transfer *M* to the
                                        // local *RTI*
	9 *else*

	10 {*BuffermidMsgQueue*(*M*) ; return ; }
9 End	11 End

As for the messages being buffered in the *dlyMsgQueue* and *midMsgQueue*, the platform has the particular thread to scan them periodically. Once a message in either of the two queues meets the requirement to be not buffered, it would be transferred to the correspondent module immediately.

5   Architecture of the Simulation and Verification Platform

For better understanding of the functions of the DVE simulation and verification platform, the architecture of it is described from two aspects: software and hardware.

Fig. 3(a) illustrates the software architecture of the distributed platform. The entire structure could be divided into two parts: Data Acquisition and Data Generation. Simulation Control Server creates the federation when a DVE initiates and acquires the real-time data from Simulation Clients through socket communications; Federates transmit the generated simulation data to Simulation Clients through IPC and commutes each other through RTI; the Network Latency Simulator between Federates and RTI generates the simulation delay values of WAN; the Causality Consistency Middleware is set between the Federates and Network Latency Simulator. The consistency control algorithms could be effectively verified in this platform which has realized the fundamental functions for the designers.

Fig. 3(b) demonstrates the hardware architecture of the platform in our lab. The platform is distributedly executed on 30 nodes pertaining to 3 Domains. The Hardware Network Simulator connects each Domain and generates impairments of WAN. In a Domain, PCs nodes and other kinds of computing nodes connect each other through wired and wireless devices, and each node has the software network delay simulator.

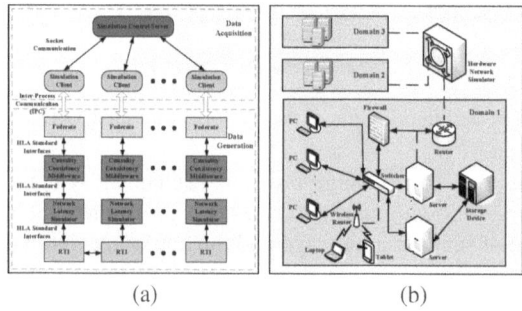

(a)   (b)

Fig. 3. The software and hardware architectures of the platform

6   Experimental Results and Analysis

In order to evaluate the effectiveness of the DVE simulation and verification platform, a distributed real-time air battle simulation is developed to implement several experiments in our laboratory. The GUI of the platform is shown in Fig. 4(a). In this platform, the designer doesn't have to consider about how to realize the fundamental details of a consistent control algorithm, such as generating WAN latency, the connection manner between RTI and application, etc. Thus, they could pay more attention on how to enhance the performance and correctness of an algorithm. After the experiments, the platform explicitly displays the statistical data and analysis results, of which the GUI example is depicted in Fig. 4(b).

Furthermore, to estimate the performance of the CO middleware, we compare CO, RO and TSO in multiple experiments with different federate scales. As shown in Fig. 5(a), the average messages delivery time of RO is relatively the least at each scale; on the contrary, the overhead of TSO is the largest for using the conservative

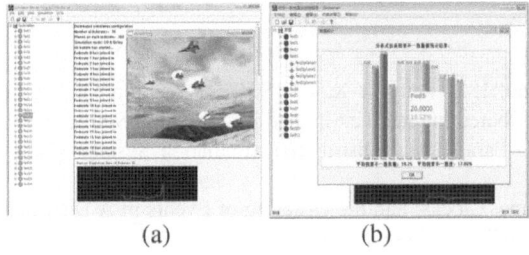

(a)   (b)

Fig. 4. The verification GUI of several functions realized in the platform

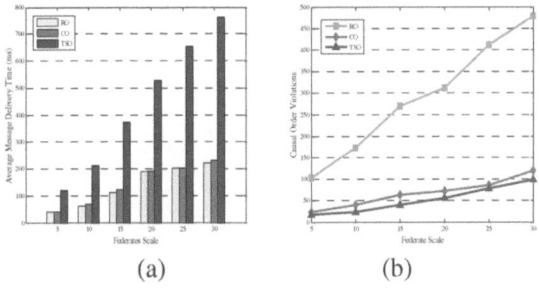

(a)   (b)

Fig. 5. The performance evaluation of CO middleware

time mechanism; because the CO middleware merely incurs a little more overhead than RO at each scale, it could meet the real-time requirement of DVEs. Fig. 5(b) displays the results about the correctness of time management in DVEs. It can be seen the CO middleware could almost achieve the identical effects with TSO in the experiments.

7 Conclusion

In this paper, based on the pivot causality consistency middleware, a DVE simulation and verification platform is firstly proposed and realized to free the designer from the fundamental details of a consistent control algorithm to focus more on how to improve the design efficiency. The experimental results and the analysis demonstrate the effectiveness of the work.

Acknowledgement

This research work is supported by the National High-tech R&D Program of China under Grant No.2009AA01Z142 and the National Basic Research Program of China under Grant No. 2011CB302601. We also thank the anonymous reviewers for their valuable comments and insightful suggestions.

References

1. Zhang, W., Zhou, H.J., Peng, Y.X., Li, S.K.: Asynchronous Time Consistency Control Methods in Distributed Interactive Simulation. Journal of Software 6, 1208–1219 (2010)
2. Fujimoto, R.M.: Parallel and Distributed Simulation Systems. Wiley Interscience, New York (2000)
3. Lamport, L.: Time, Clocks, and the Ordering of Events in A Distributed System. Communications of the ACM 7, 558–565 (1978)
4. Hernandez, S.P., Fanchon, J., Drira, K.: The Immediate Dependency Relation: An Optimal Way to Ensure Causal Group Communication. Annual Review of Scalable Computing 3, 61–79 (2004)
5. Prakash, R., Raynal, M., Singhal, M.: An Adaptive Causal Ordering Algorithm Suited to Mobile Computing Environments. Journal of Parallel and Distributed Computing 2, 190–204 (1997)

Ways of and Gains from Foreign Communication through Computer in China's College Bilingual Teaching[*]

Ailing Gong[1], Tingrui Liu[2], and Yan Liu[1]

[1] Economics & Business School, Qingdao Technological University
Qingdao, China, 266033
gongai9999@163.com
[2] Mechanical & Electronical Institute, Shandong University of Science & Technology
Qingdao, China, 266510
Liutingrui9999@163.com

Abstract. Foreign communication is very important in china's college bilingual education since the original textbook written in English is adapted for teaching. Foreign communication through computer is affordable to many instructors. Based on teaching practices, the paper introduces ways of foreign communication through computer in bilingual teaching and summarizes gains from the communication.

Keywords: Bilingual teaching; foreign communication through computer; original textbook; teaching concept; gains.

1 Introduction

Bilingual teaching (BT) is commonly deemed as teaching by two different languages. The definition and connotations differ from one country to another. In many countries including China, it is defined as teaching with English as one teaching language and Chinese as the other. In China's college education, the foreign original textbook written in English is required to use in the bilingual teaching courses.

College bilingual teaching has been favored by some people and opposed to by other since it come to being in china, and the disputes still exists until nowadays. However, under the background of economic globalization, adapting the internationally authoritative, original textbook for teaching and using English as one of the teaching languages has positive effects for the students, which is undeniable.

The original textbooks that are used in bilingual teaching are written under the background of foreign culture and foreign education environment. The textbook embodies the foreign teaching approaches and teaching concept with which Chinese instructors are not familiar. For many Chinese college bilingual instructors, both to master the textbook thoroughly and to instruct the student effectively are not easy job.

---

[*] Qingdao Technological University: Project to establish the low-cost foreign communication via internet in bilingual teaching; Project to establish the model bilingual teaching class; Qunxing Project of Shandong University of Science & Technology (qx101002).

R. Chen (Ed.): ICICIS 2011, Part I, CCIS 134, pp. 219–224, 2011.
© Springer-Verlag Berlin Heidelberg 2011

It is almost impossible for the Chinese instructor to fulfill bilingual teaching independently. So, to communicate with foreign experts or counterparts is indispensable in the bilingual teaching. Since to communicate physically cross national border is too expensive for many instructors to afford, communication through computer is sensible and advisable.

2 The Necessity and Feasibility of Foreign Communication in Bilingual Teaching

The aim of bilingual teaching is to instruct students the most authoritative, advanced knowledge by adapting the foreign original textbook. Since there is obvious gap between domestic textbook and foreign one, it takes pains for the instructor to master the textbook thoroughly. Furthermore, the original textbook is under the background of foreign culture and some parts are very hard to understand for the Chinese instructors who have no the experiences of living abroad. To understand the culture, the communication is necessary. For example, in the textbook of *international marketing* which is by *Philip R. Cateora,* there is a paragraph which reads *U.S president sent an unintentional message to some Australian protesters when he held up his first two fingers with the back of his hand to the protesters. Meaning to give the victory sign, he was unaware that in Australia the same hand gesture is equivalent to holding up the middle finger in the United States.* But what is the meaning of holding up the middle finger in the United States? If you have no the relevant cultural background, it is hard to understand. In addition, the textbook embodies the foreign teaching approaches and concept with which Chinese instructors are not familiar. If instructors can communicate with foreign counterpart and ask for help, all puzzles might be solved.

The face-to-face communicate is ideal since it is direct and effective. So the communication in person is more recommended if it is possible. However, the cost of physically cross-border communication is so high that is prohibitive for most instructors in China. Thanks to the development of internet technology, the communication through computer makes the otherwise expensive international communication at so low cost that it is affordable to many instructors in china. Email-links, on-line talk and sharing electric teaching resources are efficient way to communicate internationally.

3 Ways of Foreign Communication through Computer

3.1 To Connect with the Author and Share the Electronic Teaching Resources

Usually the foreign textbook is accompanied by lots of electronic teaching resources which include the PowerPoint, instructor's manual, test bank, video clip and so on. If you connect with author by email, asking for the resources, usually he or she will give you what you need. Let's take the *international marketing* by *Cateora* for example, which we adapt for bilingual teaching. The textbook is accompanied by very rich electronic teaching resources which are shown in an website. We found the email address of the author by visiting the website of the university where the author works.

By sending email we tell him what we need. The author forwarded our request to the Mc Graw Hill education and through its agent in china we got the password of the website and shared the rich teaching resources.

3.2 To Invite a Foreign Experts or Counterpart to Be the *Online* Teaching Consultant

We have invited Doctor *Cynthia Moody* who is the professor in South California University as our teaching consultant. By sending email or online chat, we asked her many questions concerning the teaching contents, teaching approaches and teaching concept. Thanks to her kindness and the wonderful internet technology, the problems are solved immediately. It is advisable for the Chinese instructors to communicate with the consultant through computer asking for help to solve the puzzle and problems frequently arising in the process of bilingual teaching.

3.3 To Guide the Students to Communicate with Foreign Students

Since teaching and learning are indivisible, it is very necessary for the instructor to guide the students to communicate with the foreign students. The immediate aim of communication is for the students to exchange their experience, gains and lessons from the bilingual learning. Furthermore, frequent foreign communications can widen the students' horizon and cultivate their global awareness and the students will be more knowledgeable, understanding and wiser. Thanks to the teaching consultant, we have exchanged the MSN account with the students of South California University and guide the student to communicate online.

The followed is from a student's online survey on foreign consumer's attitude on china's product:

How do you think of made-in china products?
Michael Padik: I like them but I'd rather buy products form America since they are more trustworthy.

Gerona: I think the Chinese should test more closely on the products due to past experience with recoil.

Coach: their quality is okay, can be better, and should be re-constructed to a safer manner.

…

Do you have lots of made-in-china products at your home?
Michael : yes , I do
Gerona: no
Coach: more than I probably know….

4 Gains from Foreign Communication

4.1 The Horizon of Both the Instructor and Student Get Widened

Before communication, when confronted with a set of questions on bilingual teaching and learning, both the instructor and student react spontaneously on the basis of knowledge -knowledge that is a product of our culture. Although it is the original textbook that is adopted for teaching, we seldom stop to think about the result of the reaction; we simply react. Thus when faced with a problem in another culture, our tendency is to react instinctively and refer to our SRC for a solution. Our reaction, however, is based on meanings, values, symbols and behavior relevant to our own culture and usually different from those of the foreign culture. Such decisions are often not good ones.

After frequent foreign communication, global awareness is obtained gradually for us. We realized that the similarity is an illusion. Teaching concept and approach are quite different between China and western countries. The textbook is under the quiet different background and the differences are embodied in the textbook in turn. Only after we realize the gap, can we improve ours to bridge the gap.

4.2 The Bilingual Teaching is Reoriented

To lecture in both English and Chinese was deemed as the orientation of bilingual teaching before foreign communication, so the instructor focused mainly on how to express in English. The higher percentage of English expression was regarded as the most important factor when the instruction quality is evaluated.

After frequent communication, we realize that the bilingual teaching connotes much more than what we have been aware of. To lecture partly in English is certain in bilingual teaching since the original textbook written in English is adapted in teaching. However, it is also realized that the teaching concept and teaching approach are advanced in western countries that we must adjust and improve ours as so to bridge the gap.

So we reorient the bilingual teaching; that is, by adopting the original textbook which is far and away internationally authoritative one, the advanced international teaching concepts and approaches should be embodied in the bilingual teaching. To lecture partly in English is certain in bilingual teaching, but English expression is just means of teaching, rather than destination.

4.3 The Instructor Gets Answers to Questions on the Teaching Contents Which Puzzle the Instructor

For many Chinese college bilingual instructors, to master the textbook thoroughly is not an easy job. They have many puzzles and questions on the teaching contents. As mentioned-above, in the textbook of *international market* which is by *Philip R. Cateora,* the author gives an example to illustrate the cultural conflict which puzzles the instructor. By sending email to the foreign consultant asking for the answer, the puzzle is easily solved. The reply reads *"about your question, in the U.S. this is an obscene gesture. . . very offensive. . . it's usually used when someone is angry. Literally it means "screw you" - a nicer word for an allusion to fornication. In Brazil, this is symbolized by the U.S. hand gesture for "ok" (holding the thumb and index finger together in a circle. Cross-cultural communication (especially non-verbal) is tricky!!!"*

4.4 The Instructor Adapts More Advanced Teaching Concept Which Stresses Cultivating the Student' Initiative and Creativity

In China's class teaching, the instructor usually plays the role of actor while as the student plays the role of audience. Before the class, the instructor takes pains in making preparation; mastering the textbook and searching for the relevant teaching material to enrich the content while as the students almost do nothing. In the class, the instructor usually lectures like acting while as the student listens like audience.

After foreign communication we realize that western teaching concept attaches great importance to cultivating students' initiative and creativity. Instructors play the role of director rather than actor; students play the role of actor instead of audience. The teaching concept is instructing students in fishing, rather than giving students fish.

Let's take the part on social responsibility in *international marketing* as an example to illustrate the point. Before the communication and under the traditional teaching approach, the instructor at first explains the relevant definitions and then introduces cases to illustrate the points in detail. After communication, the approach is changed. After explaining the definition, the instructor assigns students a debate topic:

Nestle had introduced infant formula to developing countries. Advertising, promotions of infant formula using testimonials from nurses and midwives and abundant free samples were used to encourage a change in behavior. It was very successful marketing program, but the consequences were unintentionally dysfunctional. In Nicaragua (and numerous other developing countries), as a result of the introduction of the formula, a significant number of babies annually were changed from breast feeding to bottle feeding before the age of six months, in the united states, with appropriate refrigeration and sanitation standards, a similar pattern exists with no apparent negative consequences, in Nicaragua, however, where sanitation methods are inadequate, a substantial increase in dysentery and diarrhea and a much higher infant mortality rate resulted. Who is mainly responsible for the tragedy? Nestle or Nicaragua itself?

So the student have to discuss the problem, search for the relevant material to support their opinion and write paper for presentation--- all the task which were finished by the instructor are to be finished by the student. Students participate more and they no longer passively sit and listen.

5   Comparison of Students' Feedback on Instruction

5.1 It's about Students' Attitude towards Bilingual Teaching

A. I like bilingual teaching.
B. I can accept bilingual teaching.
C. I don't like bilingual teaching, but I negatively accept it.
D. I oppose to bilingual teaching.

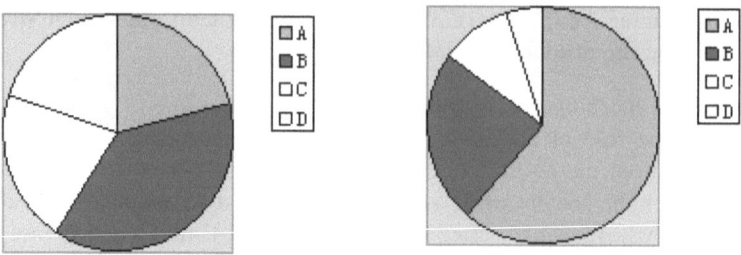

Fig. 1. Attitude towards bilingual teaching before (left) and after (right) communication

5.2 It Is about Students' Gain from Bilingual Teaching

A. I have learnt the advanced professional concept and my English is also improved.
B. My horizon is widened and I learned the advanced professional concepts.
C. Although I have some improvement in English, the subject study is hindered.
D. No gains at all.

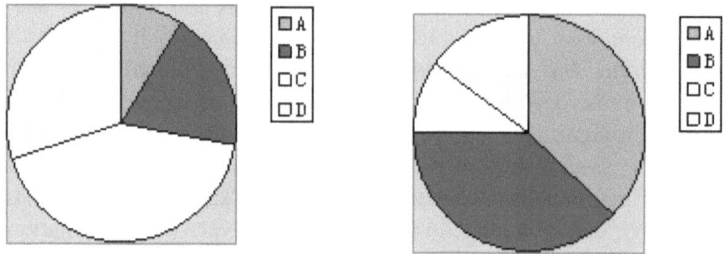

Fig. 2. Feedback on gains from bilingual teaching before (left) and after (right) communication

Reference

1. Ailing, G., Tingrui, L.: Practical Ways of College Bilingual Teaching. In: The First International Workshop on Educational Technology and Computer Science (ETCS 2009), vol. 1, pp. 40–42 (2009)

Correction Method for Photoelectric Theodolite Measure Error Based on BP Neural Network

Hai-yan Li and Yun-an Hu

Department of Control Engineering, Naval Aeronautical and Astronautical University,
Yantai 264001, China

Abstract. The least square method is used widely to correct the system error in photoelectric theodolite, but it depends on the model tightly and neglects the residuals during modeling. A system error correction method based on BP neural network is put forward firstly, and then a class of stylebooks are chosen and fully enlarged. Finally, some stylebooks are chosen to train the BP neural networks and the remainders are used to validate the approach ability of BP neural network. The simulation results prove BP neural networks can attain ideal effect for error correction.

Keywords: photoelectric theodolite; measure error; least square method; BP neural network.

1 Introduction

Photoelectric theodolite is a kind of photoelectric measure equipment which can track and measure in real-time[1]. During measuring objects by photoelectric theodolite, the measure errors (errors between measure value and real value of object position) influence directly the orientation precision of objects[2] and must be measured and corrected.So it is important to study appropriate ways to measure and correct the system error to improve the precision of photoelectric theodolite.

Synthesized stars calibration method is usually used in error measure of photoelectric theodolite outdoors, and least square method is adopted in data processing to correct the errors[3]. But the least square method depends on the model tightly and can only calculate the second order of multinomial, so we should study another method to improve the precision.

This paper studied the error correction methods based on synthesized stars calibration method deeply. To overcome the shortcoming of least square method, an error correction method based on BP neural network was put forward. The error estimation model based on BP neural network was built up and the finite stylebooks were enlarged fully. Finally, partial stylebooks were chosen to train the BP neural networks and the remainder stylebooks validated the approach ability of BP neural networks. The simulative results proved the validity of BP neural networks applied in error correction of photoelectric theodolite.

R. Chen (Ed.): ICICIS 2011, Part I, CCIS 134, pp. 225–230, 2011.

2 Principle of Synthesized Stars Calibration Method

Synthesized stars calibration method takes the stars as objects. The theoretical position is looked as real value when the stars are taken photos or real-time measurement and compared with the measure value[4]. The error between them will be gained and processed. After measuring several objects and erecting error equation group, the single system error of photoelectric theodolite will be calculated and the measure results will be corrected according to the error correction formula[5].

2.1 Calculation of Star Theoretical Position

In chronometer coordinate, the position of star in celestial sphere is denoted by equator longitude and declination. But the position of star in earth is denoted by azimuth and elevation. The longitude and latitude and time of observing position must be clear. The theoretical position of star can be calculated according to (1), (2) after correcting atmosphere refraction[6]:

$$A_1 = \tan^{-1}(\cos\delta\sin t / (\cos\delta\sin\phi\cos t - \sin\delta\cos\phi)) \tag{1}$$

$$E_1 = \sin^{-1}(\sin\phi\sin\delta + \cos\phi\cos\delta\cos t) - \Delta\rho \tag{2}$$

Where A_1, E_1 is the azimuth and elevation of star theoretical position; φ is the latitude of observing station; δ is the declination of star; t is the region-time angle; $\Delta\rho$ is the atmosphere refraction, if the temperature(T) and atmosphere pressure(p) is clear, $\Delta\rho$ can be calculated by formula (3) [6]:

$$\Delta\rho = (60.2'' \times 273 / (273 + T) \times p / 760 \times \cot E) \tag{3}$$

2.2 Calculation of Star Measure Value

The single error which influences the precision of angle measure greatly includes orientation error(g), collimation error(C), zero position error(L), horizontal axis error(i), vertical axis error(V) and atmosphere refraction($\Delta\rho$), the star measure value can be calculated by formula (4), (5) [7,8]:

$$A_2 = A - C \bullet \sec E - i \bullet \tan E + V \bullet \sin(A_V - A)\tan E - g + \Delta a \tag{4}$$

$$E_2 = E - V \bullet \cos(A - A) - L + \Delta e \tag{5}$$

Where, A_2, E_2 is the measure value of azimuth and elevation; A, E is the reading of azimuth coder and elevation coder; $\Delta\alpha$, Δe is the miss distance of azimuth and elevation; g, $C \cdot \sec E$, $i \cdot \tan E$, $V\sin(A_V - A)\tan E$ is the correction value for azimuth measure of orientation error, collimation error, horizontal axis error, vertical axis error separately; $L, V \cdot \cos(A_V - A)$ is the correction value for elevation measure of zero position error, vertical axis error. Here A, E, $\Delta\alpha$ and Δe gain by photoelectric theodolite and each single error has a known original value.

3 Neural Network Model Based on Synthesized Stars Calibration

3.1 Neural Network Structure Design and Neural Network Analysis

The neural network doesn't rely on the model and has stronger generalization ability, so we can adopt BP neural networks to correct the error of photoelectric theodolite and approach the function of measure error[9].

Because the error value of photoelectric theodolite is about arcsecond order and the azimuth and elevation is degree order[10], we choose the measure values vectors of azimuth and elevation (A_1, E_1) as input and the error vectors of azimuth and elevation (ΔA, ΔE) as output. The BP neural network's structure design for photoelectric theodolite error correction is shown as Fig.1.

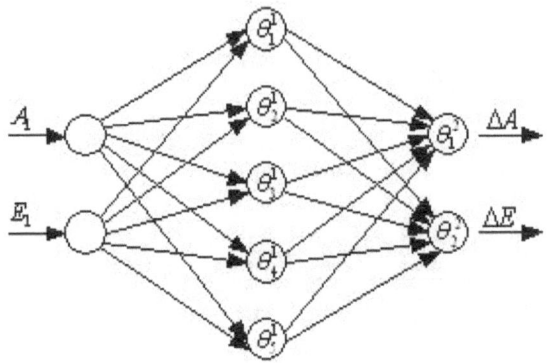

Fig. 1. BP NN structure for error correction

There are three layers in the neural network design: the first layer is input layer and there are two input nodes, and the input stylebooks are measure values of azimuth and elevation; The second layer is latent node layer and we design five latent nodes adopting S transforming function; The third layer is output layer and there are two output nodes and the outputs are error functions of azimuth and elevation adopting linear transforming function.

There are n_q neural units in the $q(q=1,2,3)$ layer. The weight coefficient which connects the j neural unit in the q-1 layer with the i neural unit in the q layer is

$$w_{ij}^{(q)}(i=1,2,\cdots,n_q;j=1,2,\cdots n_{q-1}).$$

The number of neural units in the second layer is five, so the output of each neural units are:

$$s_i^{(2)} = \sum_{j=0}^{n_1} w_{ij}^{(2)} x_j^{(1)} \quad (x_0^{(1)} = \theta_i^{(1)}, w_{i0}^{(2)} = -1) \tag{6}$$

$$x_i^{(2)} = f(s_i^{(2)}) = \frac{1}{1+e^{-\mu s_i^{(2)}}} \tag{7}$$

Where, $i = 1, 2, \cdots, 5$, $n_1 = 2$.

The number of neural units in the third layer is two, the output of each neural units are:

$$s_k^{(3)} = \sum_{j=0}^{n_2} w_{kj}^{(3)} x_j^{(2)} \quad (x_0^{(2)} = \theta_k^{(2)}, w_{k0}^{(3)} = -1) \tag{8}$$

$$x_k^{(3)} = f(s_k^{(3)}) = \frac{1}{1+e^{-\mu s_k^{(3)}}} \tag{9}$$

Where, $k = 1, 2$, $n_2 = 5$.

Designing the cost function of fitting errors as:

$$E = \frac{1}{2} \sum_{p=1}^{P} \sum_{i=1}^{2} (d_{pi} - x_{pi}^{(3)})^2 = \sum_{p=1}^{P} E_p \tag{10}$$

One order grads ways can adjust the connecting weight coefficient to make the cost function E least and the key is calculating [11].

To the third layer:

$$\frac{\partial E_p}{\partial w_{kj}^{(3)}} = \frac{\partial E_p}{\partial x_{pk}^{(3)}} \cdot \frac{\partial x_{pk}^{(3)}}{\partial s_{pk}^{(3)}} \cdot \frac{\partial s_{pk}^{(3)}}{\partial w_{kj}^{(3)}} = -\delta_{pk}^{(3)} x_{pj}^{(2)} \tag{11}$$

where

$$\delta_{pk}^{(3)} = -\frac{\partial E_p}{\partial s_{pk}^{(3)}} = (d_{pk} - x_{pk}^{(3)}) f'(s_{pk}^{(3)})$$

To the second layer

$$\frac{\partial E_p}{\partial w_{ij}^{(2)}} = \frac{\partial E_p}{\partial x_{pi}^{(2)}} \cdot \frac{\partial x_{pi}^{(2)}}{\partial w_{ij}^{(2)}} = -\delta_{pi}^{(2)} x_{pj}^{(1)} \tag{12}$$

where

$$\delta_{pi}^{(2)} = -\frac{\partial E_p}{\partial s_{pi}^{(2)}} = \sum_{n=1}^{2} (\delta_{pk}^{(3)} w_{ki}^{(3)}) f'(s_{pi}^{(2)})$$

We should calculate $\delta_{pk}^{(Q)}$ firstly, and then calculate $\delta_{pi}^{(Q-1)}$ according to formula (12) successively. To the neural network with several layers, we can continue calculating the $\delta_{pi}^{(q)}$ and $\partial E_p / \partial w_{ij}^{(q)}$, $(q = Q - 2, \cdots, 1)$.

3.2 Simulation Analysis

The stylebooks are enlarged fully adopting linear interpolation to train the BP neural network well. We use 610 groups data to train the neural network and 210 groups data to validate the approach effect. The simulative results is shown in Fig.2~Fig.5.

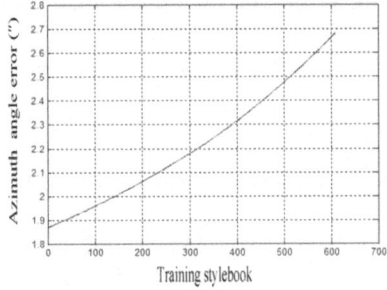

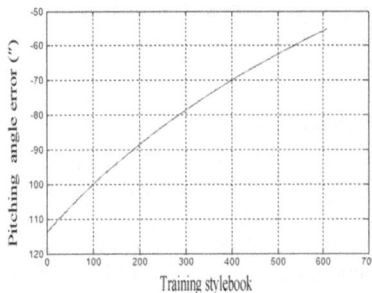

Fig. 2. Azimuth error track curve of training stylebooks

Fig. 3. Elevation error track curve of training stylebooks

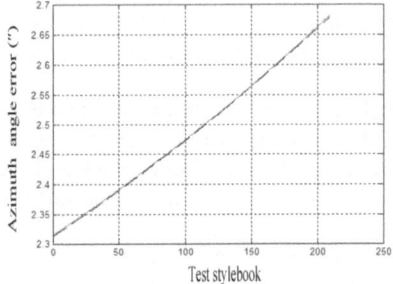

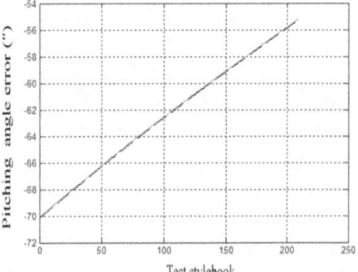

Fig. 4. Azimuth error track curve of test stylebooks

Fig. 5. Elevation error track curve of test stylebooks

Fig.2 and Fig.3 is the track curve of azimuth and elevation error function coming from 610 groups training stylebooks. In the figures, the real line is theoretical error function curve of neural network and the broken line is the error function curve after the neural network has been trained. We can see apparently that the outputs of neural network nearly match the curve of ideal value and realize tracking error function. Fig.4 and Fig.5 is the error value of azimuth and elevation coming from 210 groups test stylebooks. In the figures, the real line is theoretical error value and the broken line is the outputs of neural network. We can see apparently that the trained neural network can simulate the error function exactly, and correct the measure error aroused by system error.

4 Conclusion

The photoelectric theodolite develops forward far instance, high precision and rapid response and its real-time and intelligent performance improve quickly at the same time[12]. This paper adopt BP neural network to correct the system error of photo-electric theodolite and gain better effect than least square method. The simulative results prove the neural network can approach the error with high precision and correct the measure error accurately.

References

1. Zaho-cai, H., Bao-an, H.: Optical measure system. National defence Industry Press, Beijing (2002)
2. Ce, G., Yan-feng, Q.: Real-time error-correction method for photoelectrical theodolite. Optics and Precision Engineering 15(6), 847–851 (2007)
3. Lee, G.: Integrated modeling tools for large ground based optical telescopes. In: SPIE, vol. 5178, pp. 49–62 (2004)
4. Chun-yan, L., Huai-feng, L., Cai-hong, S.: Astronomical calibration method and observation analysis for high-accuracy star sensor. Optics and Precision Engineering 14(4), 558–563 (2006)
5. Guang, J., Jia-qi, W.: Calibration of Pointing Accuracy with Electro optic Phototheodolites by the Star Arc length. Optics and Precision Engineering 7(4), 91–95 (1999)
6. Li-hong, G.: Detecting of Theodolite Outfield Static Precision by Catching Stars. Optics and Precision Engineering 5(1), 119–123 (1997)
7. Hong-lu, H., De-yun, Z., Wei, W., et al.: Angle accuracy assessment of photo-electric tracking system based on star calibration. Opto-Electronic Engineering 33(3), 5–10 (2006)
8. Ke-xin, Z., Hong-lu, H., Chun-lian, S.: Application of Star Calibrating Technology to Metrological Confirmation of Photoelectric Tracking System. Theory and Application 23(5), 8–11 (2003)
9. Hui, L., Xiang-heng, S.: The method of building the digital model of the photoelectric theodolite and its application. Optoelectronic Technology 27(2), 97–100 (2006)
10. Sahan, S., Patrick, R.P.: Hybrid system modeling, simulation and visualization: A crane system. In: SPIE, vol. 5097, pp. 1–10 (2003)
11. Keitzer, S., Verbaneta, W., Greenwald, D., Kimbrell, J.: Deterministic errors in Pointing and Tracking Systems I:Identification and Correction of Static Error. In: SPIE (1991)
12. Wei-guo, Z., Li-you, W., Yu-kun, W., et al.: The Study of Film Theodolite Precision Measurement in Outside by Measuring Star Based on GPS Time System. Journal of Changchun University of Science and Technology 29(4), 27–29 (2006)

The Application of LOGO! in Control System of a Transmission and Sorting Mechanism

Jian Liu and Yuan-jun Lv

Zhejiang Industry Polytechnic College, Shaoxing 312000, China
caicainiao222@163.com, lvyuanjun222@163.com

Abstract. Logic programming of general logic control module LOGO! has been recommended the application in transmission and sorting mechanism. First, the structure and operating principle of the mechanism had been introduced. Then the pneumatic loop of the mechanism had been plotted in the software of FluidSIM-P. At last, pneumatic loop and motors had been control by LOGO!, which makes the control process simple and clear instead of the complicated control of ordinary relay. LOGO! can achieve the complicated interlock control composed of inter relays and time relays. In the control process, the logic control function of LOGO! is fully used to logic programming so that the system realizes the control of air cylinder and motor. It is reliable and adjustable mechanism after application.

Keywords: LOGO ! , control, transmission and sorting mechanism, pneumatic loop.

1 Introduction

Transmission and sorting mechanism has put into wide use in industrial production. Formerly, the control system is adopted by relay-contactor, which defection is obvious, such as high failure rate and hard maintenance. High reliability and high efficiency of device has been demanding. The control system by PLC has been given priority to traditional method. However, many functions of PLC are unwanted and its price is high. LOGO! holds high cost performance and maneuverability. It also holds 8 fundamental functions and 26 specific functions to take the place of relay, contactor, counter etc.

A transmission and sorting mechanism used to deliver and sort work piece has been adopted the control system by LOGO!. Air cylinder, kind of sensors and motor are used as action element or sensitive element. The results show that it is reliable and adjustable mechanism [1-2].

2 The Structure and Working Principle of Device

The total structure of the transmission and sorting mechanism has been showed in Fig.1. It is made up of feed tray, robot manipulator and conveyor. Feed tray is used to

R. Chen (Ed.): ICICIS 2011, Part I, CCIS 134, pp. 231–236, 2011.

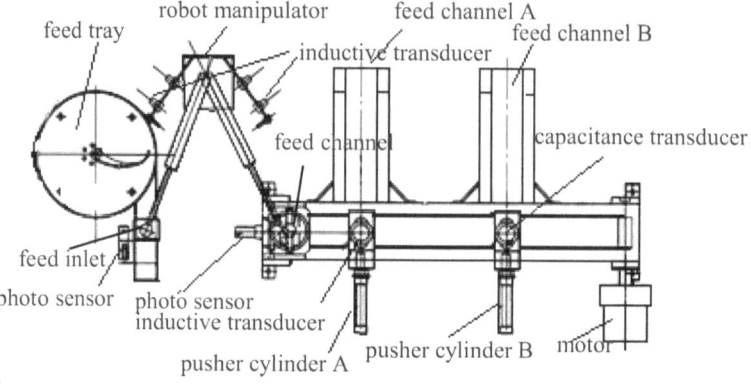

Fig. 1. The model of transmission and sorting mechanism

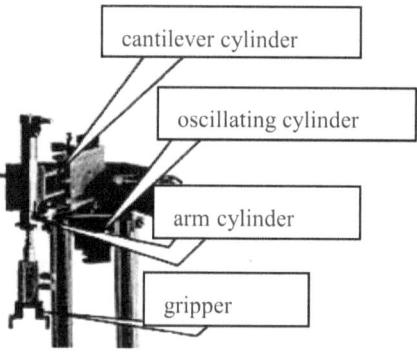

Fig. 2. The structure of robot manipulator

deposit work pieces. It can rotate and send work piece to rollway. Robot manipulator is used to grab work piece to feed inlet, which is located at the left end of conveyor. The structure of robot manipulator is made up of cantilever cylinder, arm cylinder, oscillating cylinder and gripper, which showed in Fig.2. Conveyor is made up of feed channel, pusher cylinder, conveyor belt and motor. It is used to sort plastic and metal material. Then it put them in different feed channel. Many sensors have been installed in the device. For example, the combination of capacitance transducer and inductive transducer are used to detect different material.

The operating principle of this device is represented. Initial position of robot manipulator should be met: Piston rod of cantilever cylinder and arm cylinder is retractile; Blade of oscillating cylinder is in leftmost position; Finger of gripper is in patulous state. When a work piece reaches feed inlet, robot manipulator works as follows: Piston rod of cantilever cylinder puts out. Then piston rod of arm cylinder puts out. Finger of gripper grabs the work piece within 2 seconds. Piston rod of arm cylinder retracts to initial point. Blade of oscillating cylinder reaches to right position. Piston rod of arm cylinder puts out again. Finger of gripper releases the work piece to feed channel. Once the work piece entries in the feed channel, conveyor works as follows: conveyor belt takes the work piece to move towards right. If the work piece is a metal material, pusher cylinder A pushes the work piece to feed channel A. If the work piece is a plastic material, pusher cylinder B pushes the work piece to feed channel B.

3   Analysis of Pneumatic System

Recently, pneumatic components had been applied widely in many industrial fields with their lower cost and higher efficiency. Sketches of control system were built by adding symbols or icons to a drawing area. The pneumatic system in FluidSIM-P was depicted in Fig.3. A model of pneumatic system which went with position feedback had been described. Note this had a mass included and it was one of the standard pneumatic components. Such air pump, air filter, pressure gauge, magnet valve, throttle, air cylinder and so on. Particularly, position switch should be paid attention to control air cylinder, which maximum stroke was defined as "A1", etc.[3-4].

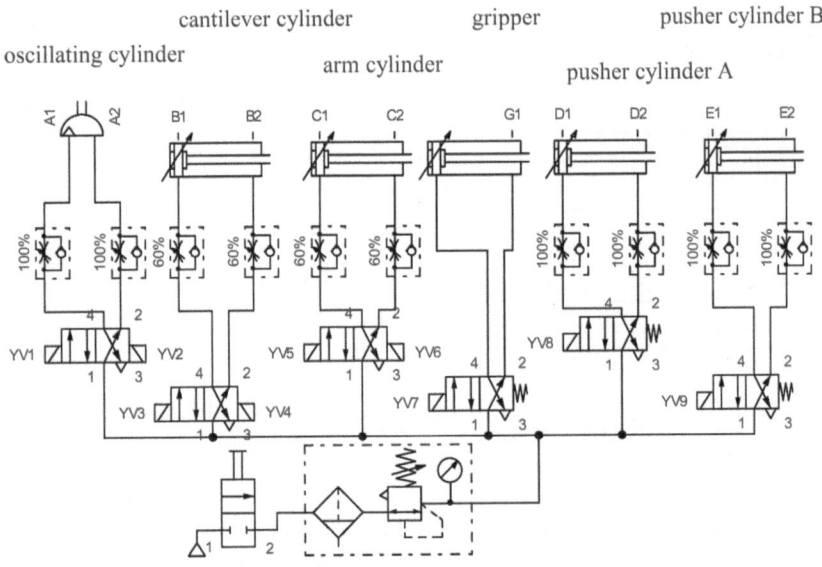

Fig. 3. Pneumatic system of transmission and sorting mechanism

4   Control of LOGO !

When program is designed, a perfection function is finished by many program units. Every unit connected together by input or output signals in different unit. So

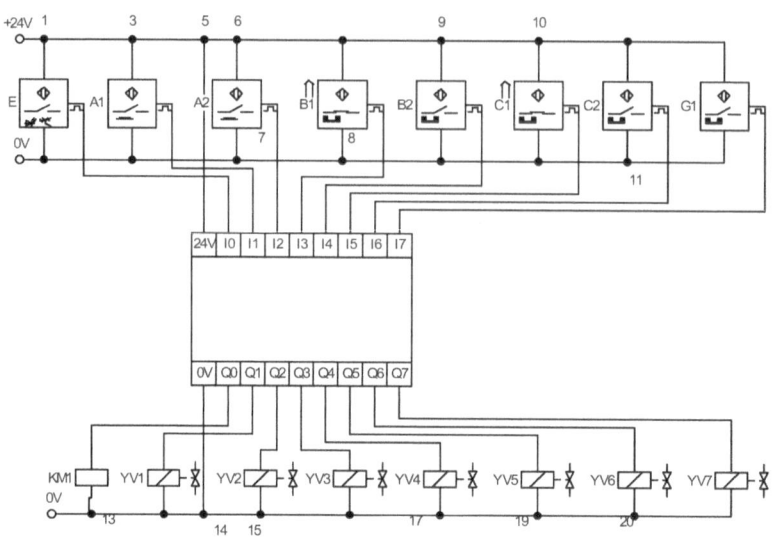

Fig. 4. Wiring connection of control loop on robot manipulator

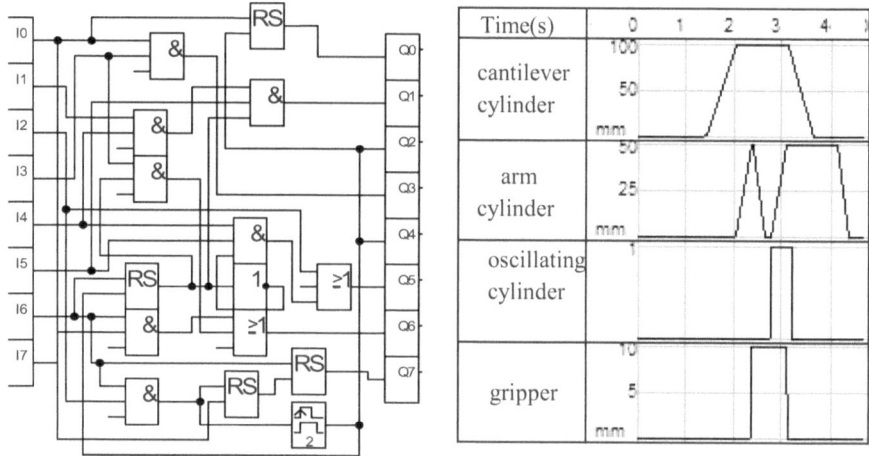

Fig. 5. Numerical control system of robot manipulator

Fig. 6. Pneumatic control simulation result of robot manipulator

transmission mechanism and sorting mechanism could be individual controlled. At last, networking function can be done to accordance each part. A photo sensor was installed around feed inlet. Once a work piece reach feed inlet, the photo sensor had a signal. Then, the robot manipulator worked at the moment. A photo sensor was installed around feed channel. Once a work piece reach feed inlet, the photo sensor had a signal. Then, the conveyor worked at the moment. Electric control loop was needed to finish the working of air cylinder. The general connection diagram of LOGO! was showed in Fig.4, where input channel was made up of position switch and feedback signal knob, output channel was made up of magnet valve and motor.

Pneumatic component had been come in contact with electric element by way of setting same counter mark. For example, the position switch was used to convert signal, which was subjected to a gain and transferred to the solenoid valve, position switch "B1" in Fig.3 was accord with position switch 'B1" in Fig.4. Magnet valve in "YV1" in Fig. 3 was accord with Magnet valve in "YV1" in Fig.4. Output port, input channel and pneumatic loop had been come in contact. Program could be compiled by way of function diagram and imported in LOGO!. One control mode of robot manipulator was showed in Fig.5, but it should meet to other coherent devices and also consider reliability and working efficiency.

The displacement of piston at various times was showed in Fig.6. Among it, horizontal abscissa showed the time (unit: second), longitudinal coordinate showed the displacement (unit: millimeter). The curves indicated the working process of four air cylinders, which chimed with design requirement. So the control loop was reasonable. The control mode of conveyor could be gotten in the same methods. Among, output point Q1 is connected to pusher cylinder A; output point Q2 is connected to pusher cylinder B; output point Q0 is connected to motor. Input point I1 is connected to photo sensor; Input point I2 is connected to capacitance transducer; Input point I3 is connected to inductive transducer.

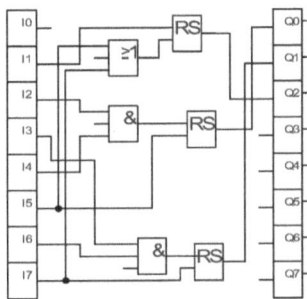

Fig. 7. Numerical control system of conveyor

Fig. 8. The application of the device

AS-interface, called communication modular, has been used to connect two LOGO!. Transmission mechanism and sorting mechanism acted as slave station which holds the function of distributed controller. The parameters should be set up in control panel of LOGO!, such as trigger point and timer.

5 Conclusion

At present, the device had been put into practice and obtained good effect. The main work can be summarized as follows:1. To combine pneumatic system and control system, a sketch is built of engineering systems by adding symbols or icons to a drawing by using FluidSIM-P.2. It's clear that LOGO! control module has superiority and better price and application prospect in similar engineering. The device had been produced and gotten a good performance.

References

[1] LOGO! user manual, the company of SIEMENS, 2 (2005)
[2] Zhi-qi, Z., Ren, Z.: The Application of LOGO in Water Level Control System. Non-Ferrous Metallurgical Equipment (5), 17–20 (2006)
[3] Jian, L., Yuanjun, L.: Pneumatic control of test equipment based on FluidSIM-Pneumatics. Manufacturing Automation (5), 18–30 (2008)
[4] Wen-chen, S., Xue-hui, H., Da-li, C.: The Teaching Application of FluidSIM. Chinese Hydraulics & Pneumatics (6), 73–76 (2007)

Design of Firmware Update Strategy in Tower Mounted Amplifier

Yi Lv[1] and Shuqin Han[2]

[1] Computer Department, University of Electronic Science and Technology of China
ZhongShan Institute
ZhongShan City, China
lvyi9131@gmail.com
[2] Electronic Department, Zhongshan Polytechnic
ZhongShan City, China
shuzi_1225@163.com

Abstract. With rapid development of radio communication, Tower mounted amplifier (TMA) that conform to AISG protocol will be increasingly applied. Remote firmware update function is essential for TMA. In this paper, a method about remote firmware update that conforms to AISG2.0 is proposed. In this paper, defect of traditional firmware storage is given, and the implementation procedure of firmware storing that based on internal flash of STR755 was introduced. According to corresponding specification in aisg2.0, the process of firmware download and activation are provided in detail. The key point of bootloader was given. Application result shows that the strategy is reliable and highly secure.

Keywords: Tower mounted amplifier; firmware update; AISG; bootloader.

1 Introduction

With rapid development of cellular telephone networks, operators keep finding cost effective ways to improve network performance through increased capacity and better coverage. Achieving maximum coverage is often as easy as boosting the uplink signal from the network users cell phone. TMA is one kind of Low Noise Amplifier(LNA) in the BTS(basestation) unlink which will be installed as close as possible to the receive antenna. Appropriately installed Tower Mounted Amplifier(TMA) will significantly improve the quality of uplink signals to improve receiver system sensitivity and voice quality, while expanding the coverage area.

AISG2.0 protocol is the 3rd Generation Partnership Project(3GPP) global standard for the communication of BTS and Antenna line Device (ALD) such as RCU, TMA, RAS. TMA which is conforming to AISG protocol have been broadly supported by system integrators.

Firmware update function of AISG 2.0 protocol makes application update and software defects amending is possible. TMA is installed at the bottom of antenna. The quantity is so large and installation and removal of TMA is so hard. If the TMA does not support remote firmware update feature, when software application repairation is

R. Chen (Ed.): ICICIS 2011, Part I, CCIS 134, pp. 237–242, 2011.

needed in the future, it's not only wasted a mass of human and material resources, but also affect the normal operation of network. As a result, firmware update function is essential for TMA.

2 Selection of Firmware Storing Media

Follow with the AISG2.0 protocol, remote firmware update feature including two processes: download process and firmware activation. AISG2.0 protocol stipulate three elementary procedure(EP) for firmware download process: Download Start, Download App and Download End. Basestation starts download process with sending Download Start EP to TMA. If TMA receives this EP, it will clear the corresponding memory area and initialize download state machine and CRC check value. Download App EP is used to transfer content of new firmware. Download End is used to informing TMA that the download process is finished and TMA will check the integrity of received data and activate it. In AISG2.0 protocol firmware download EP and work flow is given in detail, but there is no clear explanation about the firmware storage strategy and method of activation of new firmware. Different manufacturers can choose different ways.

Method of using external memory is conventional, such as EEPROM memory or serial Data Flash memory. During the process of downloading, received data is loaded into external memory firstly. After the firmware was downloaded and checked successfully, the system shall be rebooted, and then in the boot loader, data storing in external memory will be programmed into flash memory of MCU. There are two defects of this method: Firstly, higher cost, the price of large capacity EEPROM or Data Flash memory is high. Secondly, the safety is terrible. As the result of that the external memory could not be locked, the data in the external memory will be easily cracked. In this paper, a new firmware update method which conforms to AISG2.0 protocol and features high safety was introduced. The major benefit is that the products using this method has higher safety comparing to the method introduced above. Following this method, the receive firmware data was loaded in internal flash of MCU, and the firmware will be activated correctly in bootloader. Progress of updating new firmware will be greatly simplified. The external memory is not needed, and the reliability and safety is greatly improved.

3 Strategy of Firmware Storing and Updating

3.1 Design of Storing Strategy

STR755 was selected as the micro-controller. It has an embedded ARM core and on-chip high-speed single voltage FLASH memory. Up to 128 Kbytes of embedded Flash is available in Bank 0 for storing programs and data. Fig. 1 shows the memory map of bank0.

In logic view, the on-chip flash of Bank 0 was divided into three parts:

[1] Bootloader area, it is used to store bootloader function code. The size of bootloader area is 8 Kbytes, and the start address is 0x20000000.

[2] Firmware running-area, it is used to store the firmware code which was valid for TMA. The size of this area is 56 Kbytes which include Sector 1 to sector 4 of Bank 0. The start address is 0x20002000. The address of firmware was fixed in the progress of link.

[3] Firmware storing-area, it is used to store the received firmware data. The size is 64 Kbytes, and the start address is 0x20010000. Actually, this area is used as data flash to store the received data from base station.

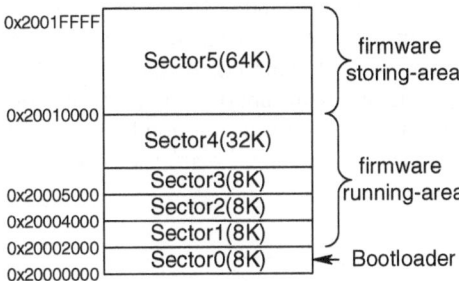

Fig. 1. The memory map of STR755 bank0

Although the Bank 0 was divided into three parts in logic, they are in the same bank. Taking account of the feature that flash memory can not be written while reading, function code about flash memory programming could not be fetched from flash region. The instructions shall be read from SRAM while programming the firmware data into the on-chip flash memory. Load region of functions related to flash memory programming is in flash memory, but execution region is in SRAM. This is configured in the scatter loader file.

3.2 Activation of New Firmware

After new firmware was downloaded into Firmware storing-area successfully, it should be used to replace previous firmware and be validated. This task is implemented in bootloader. In the end of firmware download process, if new firmware is checked successfully by CRC32, the system will reset. Bootloader code at 0x20000000 will be executed first after reset. In bootloader, the integrity of new firmware will be checked again. It will be programmed into firmware running-area only when it is correctly.

Storage area of bootloader code and firmware running-area which will be programmed are in the same bank of flash memory. As we all know, in the same bank, read-while-write feature is not supported. Therefore, the functions that are related to flash programming should be copied into ram region. This coping task is accomplished by configuring these function's execution address starting at 0x40000000 in RAM while its load region starting at 0x20000000 in flash memory.

4 Design of Firmware Download

In Aisg2.0 protocol, there are three Elementary Procedures(EP) for firmware download. The first EP is Download Start which is used to inform TMA that download process will take place at once. On receipt of this EP TMA will transform to the Download Mode state, and then erase the firmware storing-area and initialize the CRC32 value. The second EP is Download App which should be executed several times to transfer firmware data from the BTS to TMA. Before accepting update file, TMA will verify a check field to ensure that the update file is appropriate to itself. This check field is commence with the Vendor Code, hardware version and other vendor-specific designators. In the event of a mismatch, it shall be rejected and an Unknown Command response will be returned. At the end of the update file is CRC32 check sum of the check field and firmware data. TMA could conform that whether the update file is corrupted in the stage of transmission by using CRC32 check sum. This CRC32 polynomial is: $c(x) = x^{32} + x^{26} + x^{23} + x^{22} + x^{16} + x^{11} + x^{10} + x^8 + x^7 + x^5 + x^4 + x^2 + x^1 + x^0$.

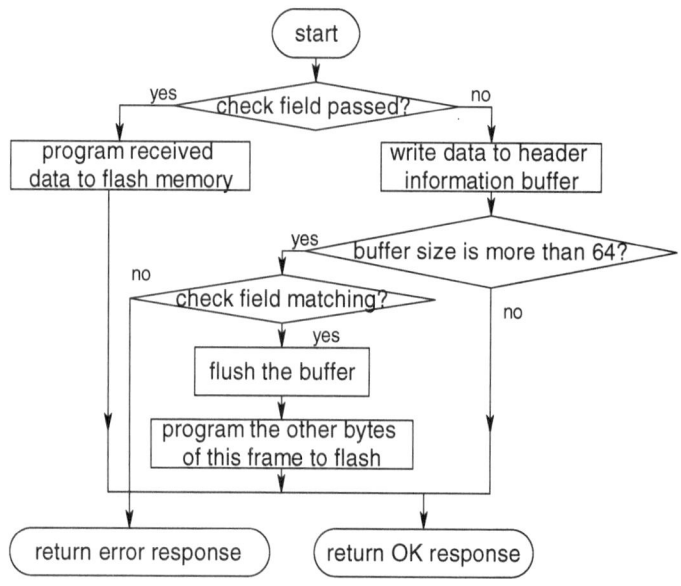

Fig. 2. Flowchart of Download APP EP

TMA will fulfill the check, download and program of firmware with Download App EP. The flowchart is shown as Fig. 2 Firstly, TMA will check the header information of downloaded data. Header information is a check field consist of vender code, hardware version and firmware serial number. If header information is not matched, download data will be rejected and download process will be finished. After checking header information, download data will be program into corresponding flash memory, and then it will be read out to check again to avoid programming error.

The third EP is Download End using which BTS signals the end of firmware transfer to TMA. TMA responds after verifying the CRC32 checksum of the data transferred to memory. Flag in EEPROM will be set to indicate new valid firmware is existing. Then TMA shall reset autonomously after completion of the layer 2 response and activate the new application firmware in bootloader. The sequence of previous EP must be strictly observed.

5   Firmware Activation

This function is realized in bootloader which is in the region starting at 0x20000000. The flowchart is shown as Fig. 3 First of all, reading the flag bits in EEPROM to distinguish whether new firmware is existing. If there is no new firmware, the program will jump to 0x20002000 directly to execute previous application. If the flag bits are set, TMA shall read the size of firmware data, and then check CRC32 checksum. When CRC32 is correct previous data in running-area will be erased. New data in storing-area will be programmed to the running-area. Finally, flag bits in EEPROM shall be erased, and then new application will be executed.

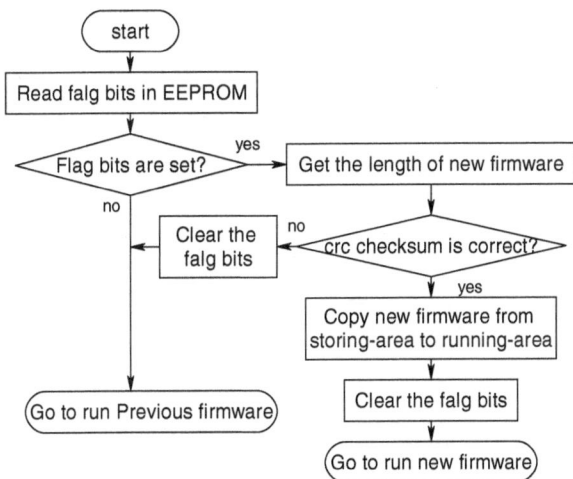

Fig. 3. Flowchart of firmware activation

6   Conclusion

Based on the background of TMA, this paper expounds a firmware update realization method conform to AISG2.0 protocol. The internal Flash memory is made good use for firmware storage. Comparing to using external memory, highly secure and competitive price is the main feature of this method. Application result shows that the strategy is reliable and highly secure.

Acknowledgement

This paper is funded by Youth Foundation, University of Electronic Science and Technology of China, ZhongShan Institute (408YJ03), and supported by Science and Technology Planning Project of ZhongShan City, China.

References

[1] 3rd Generation Partnership Project (3GPP):UTRAN Iuant Interface: Application Part. 3GPP Technical Specification:TS 25.466 V7.1.0 (June 2007)
[2] 3rd Generation Partnership Project (3GPP):UTRAN Iuant Interface: Layer 1. 3GPP Technical Specification:TS 25.461 V6.5.0 (December 2005)
[3] 3rd Generation Partnership Project (3GPP):UTRAN Iuant interface: General aspects and principles. 3GPP Technical Specification:TS 25.460 V6.2.0 (March 2005)
[4] 3rd Generation Partnership Project (3GPP):UTRAN Iuant Interface: Signalling transport. 3GPP Technical Specification:TS 25.462 V6.3.0 (September 2005)
[5] Antenna Interface Standards Group Standard NO.AISG V2.0:Control Interface for Antenna Line Devices (June 2006)

Extraction of Urban Built-Up Land in Remote Sensing Images Based on Multi-sensor Data Fusion Algorithms

Chengfan Li[1], Jingyuan Yin[1,2,*], Junjuan Zhao[1], and Lan Liu[3]

[1] School of Computer Engineering and Science, Shanghai University, 200072 Shanghai, China
david-0904@163.com, jyyin@staff.shu.edu.cn,
junjuanzhao@shu.edu.cn
[2] Earthquake Administration of Shanghai, 200062 Shanghai, China
[3] School of Foreign Languages, Shandong Foreign Languages Vocational College,
262872 Rizhao, China
lanny718@sina.com

Abstract. With the development of the high-resolution remote sensing technology, dynamic monitoring of urban built-up land use high-resolution remote sensing technology already become an important content of urban remote sensing. In this paper we select SPOT5 in 2003 and QuickBird in 2007 as data sources which covers research area, the urban built-up land information has been extracted through SAVI, PRWI and textural features, and analysis the extraction results. The results of this research show that the extraction method based on SAVI, PRWI, textural features could automatic (semi-automatic) extract urban built-up land effectively, and has the characteristics of simplicity, convenience and efficiency.

Keywords: remote sensing, urban built-up land, SAVI, PRWI, multi-sensor data fusion.

1 Introduction

Urban built-up land is where mankind production, living and acts, consists of constructions, roads, and plaza and so on. The urban built-up land automatic (semi-automatic) extraction is a focal study of the city remote sensing. High-resolution remote sensing images can post more detail information of ground targets, and it is easy to classify the land feature more accurately [1]. The construction land and roads have account for 80 percentage of the total area in the urban high-resolution remote sensing images. The urban built-up land as a major part of the some land covers, it is very easy to discriminate the Greenland, roads, forests, water land and barren land. It will be very important for monitoring the urban land use; remote sense mapping and updating the GIS database to automatic (semi-automatic) extract the urban built-up land.

Many researchers have discussed the automatic (semi-automatic) extraction of urban built-up land accurately and quickly in recent years. At present, the methods of extraction included the classification method based on statistics, threshold method of

---

* Corresponding author.

R. Chen (Ed.): ICICIS 2011, Part I, CCIS 134, pp. 243–248, 2011.

optical spectrum structure, normalization index method, textures analysis method and the classification method of geological experts. Xue hui studied the classified method of optical spectral structure has more accuracy in the urban built-up land extraction than any other methods through more experiments [2]. Amberg studied the urban structure by the SAR high-resolution image and found that stage division method has more accuracy [3]. Borghys extracted the urban built-up land by L band in the high-resolution SAR image [4]. Xu hanqiu et al take advantage of the NDBI, MNDWI and SAVI and the urban land use has been classified by the maximum likelihood classification method, and precision achieved 91.2 percentages [5]. Considering that, according as the former research achievements of urban built-up land extraction, this paper we select SPOT5 in 2003 and Quick bird in 2007 as data sources which covers research area, the urban built-up land has been extracted by SAVI, PRWI and textural features indexes. Experiments prove the method has the characteristics of simplicity, convenience and efficiency.

SPOT5 has widespread usage, especially in land use, agriculture and forest resources monitoring and so on. It has three image forming apparatus, including HRG, VEGETATION and HRS. The HRS consists of 2.5m and 5m resolutions PAN band, 10m multi-spectral band and 20m SWIR band. Quick bird has 1m high-resolution of images and usages in urban planning, land use, port construction, and environment and military and so on. The GIS database updating is the most important application. It have a 0.61m resolution PAN band and R, B, G, NIR 2.44m multi-spectral resolution bands.

2   Extraction Method of Urban Built-Up Land

Urban built-up land mainly consists of constructions, roads, green land and space and so on, many of urban-built land are mixed pixel, and the phenomenon exists for the same deciduous with different spectral values. At present, the classification method based on statistics, threshold method of optical spectrum structure, textures analysis method and the classification method of geological experts are the most commonly used methods to extract the urban built-up land [6].

The classification based on statistical methods contain supervised classification and unsupervised classification methods. Unsupervised classification methods, as one of the most easiest and important method, is low precision and seldom used the urban built-up land extraction based on K-MEANS method, fuzzy comprehensive judgment and dynamic clustering analysis. Supervised classification methods mostly include minimum distance method, maximum likelihood method, fuzzy classification and artificial neural networks and so on. Maximum likelihood method and artificial neural networks method is most representative algorithm in the extraction of urban built-up land at present. ANN method is not based upon hypothetical probability distribution, and typically has high precision and robustly characteristics. Although the classification based on statistical methods become mature and could be used widespread, it has lower precision and no more than 80 percentage [7], [8].

The basic principle of threshold method of optical spectrum structure is that the absorptive capacity and reflectivity function from the same real word entity with different wave bands, the absorptive capacity and reflectivity function from different objects on earth in the same wave band. It uses a spectrometer sampling method to measure the mean value of spectrum from different objects on earth, drawing out the characteristics points from a spectral curve. Different brightness has got by distinctions between the urban built-up land wave band and other objects wave band, and choosing a suitable threshold value distinguishes the two objects. At present, it is one of the most frequently used ways to extract the urban built-up land by threshold method of optical spectrum structure.

The extraction of urban built-up land based on spectrum start from the concept of analysis of different spectrum curves and excavates the spectrum characteristics, and eventually achieved the extraction of urban built-up land. However, threshold method of optical spectrum structure cannot overcome the phenomenon of "different objects same image" and same objects different spectral values. Generally speaking, spectrometric value of road, dry riverbed and bare land is quite similar with urban built-up land's, and it is not easy to different between the two objects.

Because of the influence of terrain, river and many other factors, the spatial distribution of urban built-up land take distinct regular and obvious region difference, the classification method of geological experts' immediate reaction of the geographical feature. Commonly, urban built-up land mainly distribute in the areas with low height and gradient smaller low. In addition, urban built-up land has significant relationship with surface feature nearby, for example, some urban built-up land distribution along the river and it is easy to discriminate. It is necessary to study the characteristics of space distribution and spatial analysis technology with GIS. So the connection between RS and GIS play an important role in the extraction of urban built-up land. The classification method of geological experts' makes full advantage of the all kinds' geosciences knowledge and makes the classification result accord with fact; it is an excellent classification method.

3 Extraction of Urban Built-Up Land Information

3.1 Data Preprocessing

The SPOT5 and Quick bird image as the data sources and the cloud-free image were acquired in 2003 and 2007. Data preprocessing include radiometric calibration, registering, and geometric correction. Ancillary data included an urban vegetation inventory data layer, topographic map, which is in a scale of one-million, the land use map in 2003 and 2007, a digital elevation model (DEM). The data preprocessing has been implement in the Erdas imagine 9.1 software. The RMS is less than 0.5 pixels after registering.

3.2 Extraction of Urban Built-Up Land Information

Although the brightness value of urban built-up land is easy to confuse with the brightness of road, dry riverbed and bare land. There are very significant differences between the urban built-up land and roads, dry riverbed and bare land in the textural features. Textural features has the discriminate ability which is different from remote sensing image, and is used to the pattern recognition of urban built-up land and could solute effective the different objects same image and same objects different spectral values. At present the most commonly used textural features methods include statistical method, model method, based on mathematic method. With the resolution of images, the textural features are becoming clearer. The textural features have become powerful tools of extraction of urban built-up land now; its application will become wider and deeper.

In general, urban land use types mainly contain vegetation, water and urban built-up land. It is not practical to extract the urban built-up land according to a single model or algorithm. So this study discard the traditional method of NDBI which is used by the Landsat images, it finally decided to adopt the SAVI, PRWI and textural features as the three wave band of R,G, B. We got the color image combination (Fig.1). The urban built-up land can be used to extract effectively. The experiments show that the extraction process used the SAVI, PRWI and textural features are useful, simple and high resolution [9], [10], [11]. The study reduces the redundant data and the three wave bands are separate or negative correlation with each other. The researchers can clearly see the urban built-up land in the color combination images, which is a bright red shows.

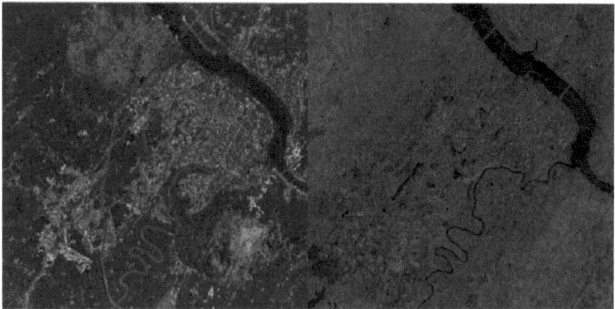

Fig. 1. The color combination image in2003 and 2007

It is found that in figure.1. SAVI is the B1 band, PRWI is the B2 band and the textural feature is the B3 band, the structure of urban built-up land is clearly presented by the color combination. The textural feature of band B3 larger than B1 band and B2 band, and it is the only characteristics of the three bands. Based on the previous studies and through several logical expressions simple, the urban built-up land is extracted. The logical expressions as follows:

$$\text{If B3>B1 and B3>B2 then 1 else null} \tag{1}$$

Where B1 is the SAVI wave band, B2 is the PRWI wave band and B3 is the textural feature. In this study, logical expressions are run in the modeler of the Erdas imagine 9.1. The urban built-up land information has been got by logical operation modeler (Fig.2).

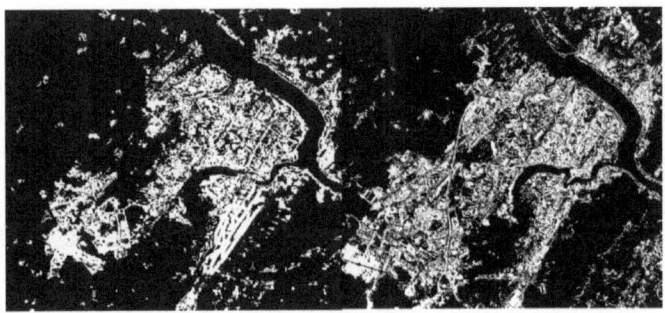

Fig. 2. The urban built-up land in 2003 and 2007

4 Analysis of Urban Built-Up Land Changes

It is necessary to evaluate the classification precision after the extraction information has been achieved. This study employs the same period land use map to evaluate the two extraction image by 256 random points (Table 1).

Table 1. Accuracy assessment

2003		2007	
Types	Urban Built Up Land	Types	Urban Built Up Land
Production accuracy（%）	87.33	Production accuracy（%）	85.37
User accuracy（%）	93.21	User accuracy（%）	90.24
Kappa	0.84	Kappa	0.86
Overall accuracy（%）	91.46	Overall accuracy（%）	92.70
Overall Kappa	0.8115	Overall Kappa	0.8068

With reference to Figure 2 we can found that the change of urban built-up land is located in the new city and areas surrounding the cities. The development direction of urban built-up land takes the trend of transferring from old cities to new cities with further speed and degree. The urban built-up land is crossing the Jialing river bridge with its direction trend following northeast, and joint with the Shuitu country and Jingguan country. The change of urban built-up land show up the urban spatial morphology and it is in compliance with the urban planning of research area in recent years.

Some thematic information of urban built-up land was transferred to Excel for statistics, and then we got the urban built-up land area in 2003 and 2007. The urban built-up land area is 1259.93 hm2 in 2003, covering rapidly increasing an area is 1964.53 hm2 in 2007. In the first several years, urban built-up land area growth an additional 704.6 hm2 and registers an average increase of 24.87 percentage from 2003 to 2007.

5   Conclusions

In this paper, SPOT5 in 2003 and Quick bird in 2007 are data source; combining with SAVI, PRWI and textural features, the urban built-up land has been extracted and analyzed at last with high precision of 91.46 percentages and 92.70 percentages. Results show that this method which employs SAVI, PRWI and textural features based on Multi-sensor Data Fusion Algorithms can automatic (semi-automatic) extract the urban built-up land quickly and accurately in high resolution remote sensing images. It is easier, more convenient, strong practicability and in high precision.

Acknowledgments. We thank the vital comments made by the reviewers and the editorial team. This work is supported by the key project of Shanghai leading academic disciplines of China under grant No. J50103, and partially by the key program of Shanghai science and technology committee under grant No. 08DZ2292200 and key project of the national technology support program of China under grant No. 2008BAC38B03.

References

1. Jun, L., Shixin, W., Xiaolei, Z.: Temporal-spatial characteristics of the urbanization of rural land in Xinjiang. Chinese journal of population, resources and environment 4, 37–44 (2006)
2. Hui, X., Shaogang, N.: Methodology of retrieving residential area from remotely sensed image. Research of soil and water conservation 13, 319–321 (2006)
3. Borghys, D., Perneel, C., Acheroy, M.: Automatic detection of built-up Parcas in high resolution polar metric SAR images. Pattern Recognition Letters 23, 1085–1093 (2002)
4. Ponana, V., Prudant, J., Kana'a, T.F.N., Dzana, J.G., Asse, N.: Multitemporal urban dynamics with multitemporal ENVISAT/ERS SAR images and multispectral HRV SPOT optical image using data fusion approach. In: Proc. Of the 2004 Envisat and ERS Symposium, Salzburg, Austria (2004)
5. Hhanqiu, X.: Remote sensing information extraction of urban built-up land based on a data-dimension compression technique. Journal of image and graphics 10, 223–229 (2005)
6. Deyi, L., Dapeng, W., Anding, Z., et al.: Research progress of residential area information automatic extraction methods based on remote sensing image. Yunnan geographic environment research 18, 48–51 (2006)
7. LO, C.P.: Land Use Mapping of Hong Kong Landsat Images: An evaluation. International Journal of Remote Sensing 2, 231–252 (1981)
8. Gao, J., Skillcorn, D.: Capability of SPOT XS data in producing detailed land cover maps at the urban- rural periphery. International Journal of Remote Sensing 19, 2877–2891 (1998)
9. Chengfan, L.: Changes of urban land-use by remote sensing monitoring. Southwest University master's degree paper (2009)
10. Rutian, B., Zhongke, B.: Land characteristic information and classification in opencast coal mine based on remote sensing images. Transactions of the CSAE 23, 77–81 (2007)
11. Huanjun, L., Bai, Z., Zongming, W., et al.: Soil saline-alkalization evaluation basing on spectral reflectance characteristics. J. Infrared Millim. Waves 27, 138–142 (2008)

Coordinated Control and Localizing Target System for Multi-UAVs Based on Adaptive UKF

Hengyu Li, Jun Luo, Lei Li, Jin Tong, and Shaorong Xie

School of Mechatronics Engineering and Automation, Shanghai University
No.149, Yanchang Rd., 200072 Shanghai, China
{lihengyu,luojun,lileinlp,jintong,srxie}@shu.edu.cn

Abstract. Unmanned Aerial Vehicle (UAV) has enormous application in military and civilian. Compared with a single platform, cooperative UAVs offer efficiency and robustness in performing complex tasks, and multi-UAVs' coordinative operations are recently becoming a focus of research. In this paper, a direction finding and location system for Multi-UAVs is proposed, which is based on the navigation strategy of the minimizing target location accuracy. In order to reduce the influence of the direction finding error, this article uses the data fusion method of adaptive UKF to achieve optimal position. This objective is to release the dependence of normal UKF on the priori knowledge of noise distribution, which is difficult to obtain in real systems. The experimental results validate that the presented method is valid. Compared with the conventional methods using UKF, this system based on adaptive UKF has high accuracy and robustness.

Keywords: multi-UAVs, coordinated control, localizing target system, adaptive UKF.

1 Introduction

Unmanned Aerial Vehicles (UAVs) has enormous application in military and civilian, which can work in dangerous, complex environment and unknown areas. Compared with a single platform, cooperative UAVs offer efficiency and robustness in performing complex tasks. As a result, multi-UAVs' coordinative operations are recently becoming a focus of research [1-4]. The task allocation of Multi-UAVs is to divide the mission to each UAV by degree of a whole benefits, least costly, and the optimal implementation of related tasks. In target orientation and crossing location, this work is focused on rational layout for several sensors to improve positioning accuracy [3]. Due to the system of target orientation and crossing location has comprehensive orientation and noise immunity, thus, the system of the target orientation and crossing location is chosen for target search and location in this paper.

The orientation and location is a process that system collects the noisy angle information through many UAVs platform first, gets the target position by data fusion and evaluates speed correctly. This issue is modeled as nonlinear system in the Cartesian coordinate, and the most popular one for the nonlinear system is the Extended

R. Chen (Ed.): ICICIS 2011, Part I, CCIS 134, pp. 249–258, 2011.
© Springer-Verlag Berlin Heidelberg 2011

Kalman Filter (EKF). Although widely used, EKF suffers from the deficiencies including the requirement of sufficient differentiability of the state dynamics, the susceptibility the requirement of sufficient differentiability of the state dynamics, the susceptibility to bias and divergence during the estimation. Unscented Kalman Filter (UKF) provides a derivative-free way to the state parameter estimation of nonlinear system with the same computational complexity as that of EKF. So UKF still into the framework of Kalman-type filters, which can only achieve good performance under a priori assumptions [5-6]. But in practice, the UAVs' system for working on dynamic environment, the system has the uncertainty factors by variability and outer complex environment, so the assumptions are usually not totally satisfied. The wrong prior information of noise may not only lead to a serious decline for KF's evaluation, but also even cause the divergence. Because the orientation error of UAV has a great effect on navigation and location for UAV, an adaptive filter is used to solve the problem in the paper. Then, test results are encouraging.

2 Adaptive UKF for Active Estimation

Fig.1 shows the structure of the adaptive UKF, which is proposed by J. D. Han [5-8]. The AUKF is composed of two parallel UKFs. At every time step, the master UKF estimates the states using the noise covariance obtained by the slave UKF, while the slave UKF estimates the noise covariance using the innovations generated by the master UKF. The two UKF are independent in the AUKF structure. By estimating the noise covariance, the AUKF is able to compensate the estimation errors resulting the noise covariance.

Consider the general discrete nonlinear system:

$$\begin{cases} x_{k+1} = f\left(x_k, u_k\right) + w_k \\ y_k = h\left(x_k\right) + v_k \end{cases} \tag{1}$$

Where x_k is the state vector, $x_k \in \mathfrak{R}^n$; y_k is the output vector at time k , $y_k \in \mathfrak{R}^m$; u_k is the known input vector, $u_k \in \mathfrak{R}^r$; w_k, v_k are respectively the disturbance and sensor noise vector, which are assumed Gaussian white noise with zero mean.

2.1 Master UKF

The main UKF estimation can be expressed as:

(1) Initialization

$$\begin{cases} \hat{x}_0 = E\left[x_0\right] \\ P_{x_0} = E\left[\left(x_0 - \hat{x}_0\right)\left(x_0 - \hat{x}_0\right)^T\right] \end{cases} \tag{2}$$

(2) Time update

$$
\begin{cases}
w_0^m = \dfrac{\lambda}{n+\lambda} \\[2mm]
w_0^c = \dfrac{\lambda}{n+\lambda} + \left(n - \alpha^2 + \beta\right) \\[2mm]
w_i^m = w_i^c = \dfrac{\lambda}{2(n+\lambda)} \qquad i = 1, \cdots, 2n \\[2mm]
\eta = \sqrt{n+\lambda} \\[2mm]
\lambda = n\left(\alpha^2 - 1\right)
\end{cases}
\tag{3}
$$

Where w_i^m , w_i^c are weights; α determines the spread of the sigma point; β is used to incorporate prior knowledge of the distribution of x , n is the dimension of augmented state.

$$
\begin{cases}
\mathcal{X}_{k-1} = \left[\hat{x}_{k-1}, \hat{x}_{k-1} + \sqrt{(n+\lambda)P_{X_{k-1}}}, \hat{x}_{k-1} - \sqrt{(n+\lambda)P_{X_{k-1}}}\right] \\[2mm]
\mathcal{X}_{k|k-1}^* = f\left(\mathcal{X}_{k-1}\right) \\[2mm]
\hat{x}_{k|k-1} = \displaystyle\sum_{i=0}^{2n} w_i^m \mathcal{X}_{i,k|k-1}^* \\[2mm]
P_{X_{k|k-1}} = \displaystyle\sum_{i=0}^{2n} w_i^c \left(\mathcal{X}_{i,k|k-1}^* - \hat{x}_{k|k-1}\right)\left(\mathcal{X}_{i,k|k-1}^* - \hat{x}_{k|k-1}\right)^T + Q^x \\[2mm]
\mathcal{X}_{k|k-1} = \left[\hat{x}_{k|k-1}, \hat{x}_{k|k-1} + \sqrt{(n+\lambda)P_{X_{k|k-1}}}, \hat{x}_{k|k-1} - \sqrt{(n+\lambda)P_{X_{k|k-1}}}\right] \\[2mm]
\gamma_{k|k-1} = h\left(\mathcal{X}_{k|k-1}\right) \\[2mm]
\hat{y}_{k|k-1} = \displaystyle\sum_{i=0}^{2n} w_i^m \gamma_{i,k|k-1}
\end{cases}
\tag{4}
$$

Where Q^x is noise covariance.

(1) Measurement update

$$
\left\{
\begin{aligned}
P_{y_k y_k} &= \sum_{i=0}^{2n} w_i^c \left(\gamma_{i,k|k-1} - \hat{y}_{k|k-1} \right) \left(\gamma_{i,k|k-1} - \hat{y}_{k|k-1} \right)^T \\
&\quad + R^x \\
P_{x_k y_k} &= \sum_{i=0}^{2n} w_i^c \left(\chi_{i,k|k-1} - \hat{x}_{k|k-1} \right) \left(\gamma_{i,k|k-1} - \hat{y}_{k|k-1} \right)^T \\
K_{x_k} &= P_{x_k y_k} P_{y_k y_k}^{-1} \\
P_{x_k} &= P_{x_{k|k-1}} - K_{x_k} P_{y_k y_k} K_{x_k}^T \\
\hat{x}_k &= \hat{x}_{k|k-1} + K_{x_k} \left(y_k - \hat{y}_{k|k-1} \right)
\end{aligned}
\right.
\tag{5}
$$

Where R is the measurement noise covariance; the slave filter estimates the diagonal elements of the noise covariance matrix of Q^x / R^x for the master UKF.

2.2 Slave UKF

Consider the diagonal elements of the noise covariance matrix of the master UKF is θ, $\theta \in \mathfrak{R}^l$. If the changing rule of θ is known in advance, define the state equations of the slave UKF as:

$$
\theta_k = f_\theta \left(\theta_{k-1} \right) + w_{\theta k}
\tag{6}
$$

Else if the changing rules of θ is unknown in advance, define θ_k as noise driven uncorrelated random drift vector, and the state equations of the slave UKF as:

$$
\theta_k = \theta_{k-1} + w_{\theta k}
\tag{7}
$$

Where $w_{\theta k}$ is Gaussian white noise with zero mean. Take the diagonal elements of the noise covariance matrix of the master UKF as the observation signal of the system, and based on (5) we can get the observation equation of the slave UKF as:

$$
\hat{S}_k = g(\theta_k) = diag \left[\sum_{i=0}^{2n} w_i^c \left(\gamma_{i,k|k-1} - \hat{y}_{k|k-1} \right) \left(\gamma_{i,k|k-1} - \hat{y}_{k|k-1} \right)^T + R^x \right]
\tag{8}
$$

Take the diagonal elements of the noise covariance matrix of the master UKF as the measured value of the Slave UKF. $S_k = diag \left(v_k v_k^T \right)$, where, $v_k = y_k - \hat{y}_{k|k-1}$. where v_k is the innovation, and also can be entitle as residual error, y_k is observation value of the master UKF at time k, and $\hat{y}_{k|k-1}$ is estimated value of corresponding UKF.

(1) Initialization

$$\begin{cases} \hat{\theta}_0 = E[\theta_0] \\ P_{\theta_0} = E\left[\left(\theta_0 - \hat{\theta}_0\right)\left(\theta_0 - \hat{\theta}_0\right)^T\right] \end{cases} \tag{9}$$

(2) Time update

$$\begin{cases} \vartheta_{k-1} = \left[\hat{\theta}_{k-1}, \hat{\theta}_{k-1} + \sqrt{(l+\lambda) P_{\theta_{k-1}}}, \hat{\theta}_{k-1} - \sqrt{(l+\lambda) P_{\theta_{k-1}}}\right] \\ \vartheta^*_{k|k-1} = f_\theta\left(\vartheta_{k-1}\right) \\ \hat{\theta}_{k|k-1} = \sum_{i=0}^{2n} w^m_{\theta i} \vartheta^*_{i,k|k-1} \\ P_{\theta_{k|k-1}} = \sum_{i=0}^{2n} w^c_{\theta i}\left(\vartheta^*_{i,k|k-1} - \hat{\theta}_{k|k-1}\right)\left(\vartheta^*_{i,k|k-1} - \hat{\theta}_{k|k-1}\right)^T + Q^\theta \\ \vartheta_{k|k-1} = \left[\hat{\theta}_{k|k-1}, \hat{\theta}_{k|k-1} + \sqrt{(l+\lambda) P_{\theta_{k|k-1}}}, \hat{\theta}_{k|k-1} - \sqrt{(l+\lambda) P_{\theta_{k|k-1}}}\right] \\ \varsigma_{k|k-1} = g\left(\vartheta_{k|k-1}\right) \\ \hat{S}_{k|k-1} = \sum_{i=0}^{2n} w^m_{\theta i} \varsigma_{i,k|k-1} \end{cases} \tag{10}$$

(3) Measurement update

$$\begin{cases} P_{S_k S_k} = \sum_{i=0}^{2n} w^c_{\theta i}\left(\varsigma_{i,k|k-1} - \hat{S}_{k|k-1}\right)\left(\varsigma_{i,k|k-1} - \hat{S}_{k|k-1}\right)^T \\ \qquad\quad + R^\theta \\ P_{\theta_k S_k} = \sum_{i=0}^{2n} w^c_{\theta i}\left(\vartheta_{i,k|k-1} - \hat{\theta}_{k|k-1}\right)\left(\varsigma_{i,k|k-1} - \hat{S}_{k|k-1}\right)^T \\ K_{\theta_k} = P_{\theta_k S_k} P^{-1}_{S_k S_k} \\ P_{\theta_k} = P_{\theta_{k|k-1}} - K_{\theta_k} P_{S_k S_k} K^T_{\theta_k} \\ \hat{\theta}_k = \hat{\theta}_{k|k-1} + K_{\theta_k}\left(S_k - \hat{S}_{k|k-1}\right) \end{cases} \tag{11}$$

Where R_θ is the measurement noise covariance; Q_θ is the process noise covariance; Weights $w^m_{\theta i}$, $w^c_{\theta i}$ are calculated as equation (4), the dimension of estimator is l.

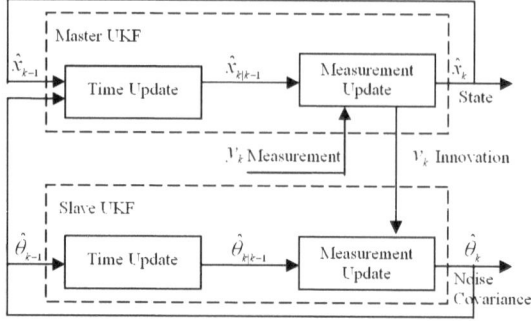

Fig. 1. The structure of adaptive UKF

3 Direction Finding and Location System for Multi-UAVs

Fig. 2 shows the structure of the direction finding and location system for multi-UAVs.

$$\begin{cases} S_{ABCD} = \dfrac{4R^2 \sin\alpha_1 \sin\alpha_2}{\sin^3(\alpha_1 + \alpha_2)} \times \Delta\theta_{max}^2 \\[2mm] R = \dfrac{L \sin\theta_1 \sin\theta_2}{\sin\beta} \\[2mm] CEP = r_{0.5} = 0.75L\sqrt{\left(\sin^2\theta_2 \sigma_{\theta_1}^2 + \sin^2\theta_1 \sigma_{\theta_2}^2\right)\Big/\sin^4\beta} \end{cases} \tag{12}$$

The system positioning accuracy depends on the size of the S_{ABCD}, and which associated with the dual-UAVs position relationship and the accuracy of finding direction instruments. CEP is the circular error probability, which depends on

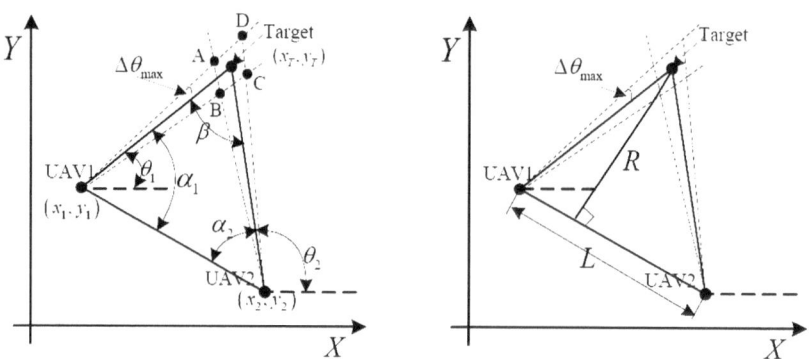

Fig. 2. The schematic diagram of the direction finding and location system

L, σ_{θ_1}, σ_{θ_2}, θ_1, θ_2 and β. Whare L is basedline length between two UAVs, σ_{θ_1} and σ_{θ_2} are variance of sensor measurement error of the UAV1 and UAV2, respectively. θ_1 and θ_2 are azimuth of the UAV1 and UAV2, respectively.

And we can get the system state equation as:

$$\begin{cases} x_T(k+1) = x_T(k) + \dot{x}_T(k) \times \Delta T + \omega_1 \\ y_T(k+1) = y_T(k) + \dot{y}_T(k) \times \Delta T + \omega_2 \\ \dot{x}_T(k+1) = \dot{x}_T(k) + \omega_3 \\ \dot{y}_T(k+1) = \dot{y}_T(k) + \omega_4 \end{cases}$$
(13)

Where $x_T(k+1)$ is the target location in x direction during $k+1$ moment, $y_T(k+1)$ is the target location in y direction during $k+1$ moment, $\dot{x}_T(k)$ and $\dot{y}_T(k)$ represent the change rate of the target direction, respectively. ΔT is the sampling period, $\omega = (\omega_1, \omega_2, \omega_3, \omega_4)$ is the process noise.

The system measurement equation is defined as:

$$\begin{cases} \theta_1(k) = \arctan\left(\dfrac{y_T - y_1}{x_T - x_1}\right) + v_1 \\ \theta_2(k) = \arctan\left(\dfrac{y_T - y_2}{x_T - x_2}\right) + v_2 \\ \theta(k) = \begin{bmatrix} z_1(k) \\ z_2(k) \end{bmatrix} = h(X_T(k), X_1(k), X_2(k)) + v(k) \end{cases}$$
(14)

Where $V(k) \sim N(0, diag(\sigma_1^2, \sigma_2^2))$ is observation noise.

The direction finding and location system formula can be expressed as:

$$dV = CdX + dX_s$$
(15)

Where $dV = [d\theta_1, d\theta_2]^T$ is the observation error vector; $dX = [dx, dy]$ is the position error vector; dX_s is the address error vector.

$$C = \begin{bmatrix} -\dfrac{\sin^2 \theta_1}{y - y_1} & \dfrac{\cos^2 \theta_1}{x - x_1} \\ -\dfrac{\sin^2 \theta_2}{y - y_2} & \dfrac{\cos^2 \theta_2}{x - x_2} \end{bmatrix}$$
(16)

Equation (15) can be converted into Equation (17):

$$dX = C^{-1}\left[dV - dX_s\right] \tag{17}$$

The positioning covariance matrix can be expressed as:

$$P = E\left[dX \cdot dX^T\right] = C^{-1}\left\{E\left[dX \cdot dX^T\right] + E\left[dX_s \cdot dX_s^T\right]\right\}C^{-T} \tag{18}$$

Where σ_s^2 is UAV coordinate positioning error variance, and $\sigma_{\theta_1}^2 = \sigma_{\theta_1}^2 = \sigma_\theta^2$, thus:

$$E\left[dV \cdot dV^T\right] = \begin{bmatrix} \sigma_\theta^2 & 0 \\ 0 & \sigma_\theta^2 \end{bmatrix} \tag{19}$$

$$E\left[dX_s \cdot dX_s^T\right] = \begin{bmatrix} \dfrac{1}{\left(x-x_1\right)^2 + \left(y-y_1\right)^2} & 0 \\ 0 & \dfrac{1}{\left(x-x_2\right)^2 + \left(y-y_2\right)^2} \end{bmatrix} \tag{20}$$

$$R = \begin{bmatrix} \sigma_\theta^2 & 0 \\ 0 & \sigma_\theta^2 \end{bmatrix} \tag{21}$$

The state vector and measurement vector of the UKF can be expressed as:

$$\begin{cases} x = \left[x_T, y_T, \dot{x}_T, \dot{y}_T\right] \\ y = \left[\theta_1(k), \theta_2(k)\right] \end{cases} \tag{21}$$

4 Simulation Results

Assume the Initial state vector: $\hat{x}_0 = 0$; $\hat{P}_{x_0} = diag\left\{10^{-7}, 10^{-7}, 10^{-7}, 10^{-7}\right\}$. In the study, the application of the adaptive UKF is mainly used for estimation performance measurement during measurement noise changes. Meanwhile, the estimated amount of the slave UKF is the diagonal elements of the measurement noise covariance matrix for the master UKF. The system measurement noise variance and the zero mean variance is expressed as R_T^x and Q_T^x, respectively. $R_T^x = diag\left\{10^{-8}, 10^{-8}\right\}$, $Q_T^x = diag\left\{10^{-16}, 10^{-16}, 10^{-12}, 10^{-12}\right\}$. Q^x and R_0^x are the noise variance of the master UKF parameters, where $Q^x = Q_T^x$, $R_0^x = diag\left\{10^{-10}, 10^{-10}\right\}$. The parameters of the slave UKF are assumed as: $\hat{\theta}_{R_0} = diag\left\{R_0^x\right\}$, $\hat{P}_{\theta_{R_0}} = diag\left\{10^{-20}, 10^{-20}\right\}$, $Q^{\theta_R} = diag\left\{10^{-22}, 10^{-22}\right\}$, $R^{\theta_R} = diag\left\{4\times10^{-20}, 4\times10^{-20}\right\}$.

In order to demonstrate the system's advantages, some simulation experiments are carried on. Fig.3 is the simulation results of the targeting system in x direction (left:AUKF; right:UKF). Fig.4 is the simulation results of the targeting system in x direction (left:AUKF; right:UKF). The results show the target location system with AUKF is better than the system with normal UKF. In other word, with incorrect a priori noise statistic information, the target location system with normal UKF cannot produce satisfying estimations due the violation of the optimality conditions. On the contrary, the target location system with AUKF has better performance. Assume the

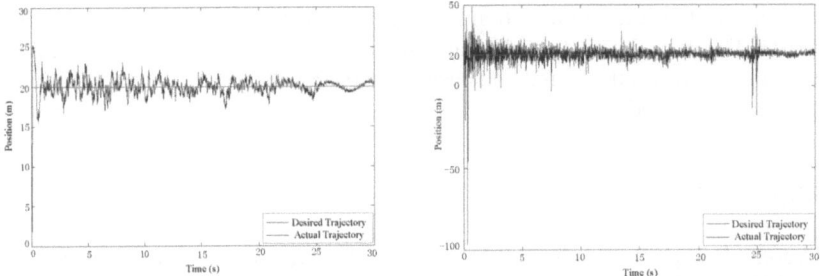

Fig. 3. The simulation results of the targeting system in x direction (left:AUKF; right:UKF)

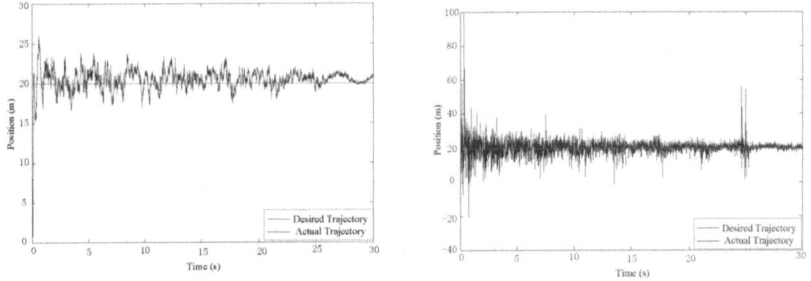

Fig. 4. The simulation results of the targeting system in y direction (left:AUKF; right:UKF)

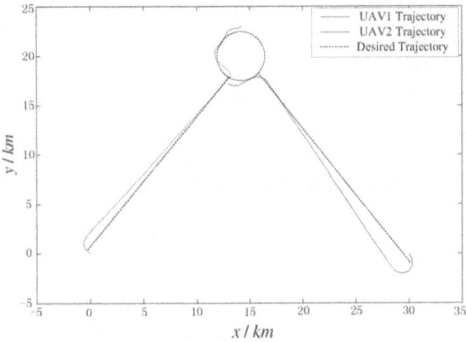

Fig. 5. The flight trajectory diagram of the dual-UAVs searching target based on adaptive UKF

two UAVs respectively start to search target from A (0,0) and B (25km, 0), and the target position is (20km, 20km). The test results is shown as Fig .5, and it can be seen that the coordinated control and localizing target system based on AUKF for Multi-UAVs gives quite satisfactory result and has robust stability.

5 Conclusion

This paper presents a direction finding and location system for Multi-UAVs. Within the control, an active estimation module executed by adaptive Unscented Kalman Filter is integrated into the direction finding and location system to improve its performance. The experimental results validate that the presented method is valid. Compared with the conventional methods using UKF, this system based on adaptive UKF has high accuracy and robustness.

Acknowledgments

This research is jointly sponsored by National Natural Science Foundation of China (No. 60975068, No. 50975168), National High Technology Research and Development Program of China (863, No. 2009AA04Z211), and "Shu-guang" project supported by Shanghai Municipal Education Commission and Shanghai Education Development Foundation (No. 09SG37)

References

1. Karl, S.: Passive Position Location Estimation Using the Extended Kalman Filter. IEEE Transactions on aerospace and electronic system AES-23(4), 558–567 (1987)
2. Daniel, J.P., Pedro, D.L., Gregory, J.T., George, Y.: Cooperative Control of UAVs for Localization of Intermittently Emitting Mobile Targets. IEEE Transactions on system, man, and Cybernetics-part B: Cybernetics 39(4), 959–970 (2009)
3. Gregory, J.T., Pedro, D.L.: Localizing RF Targets with Cooperative Unmanned Aerial Vehicles. In: Proceedings of the 2007 American Control Conference, pp. 5928–5933. IEEE Press, New York (2007)
4. Patrick, V., Izhak, R.: A Framework and Analysis for Cooperative Search Using UAV Swarms. In: Proceedings of the 2004 ACM Symposium on Applied computing, pp. 79–86. ACM, New York (2004)
5. Victor, M.M., Pigazo, A.: Kalman Filter: Recent Advances and Applications. Published by I-Tech Education and Publishing KG, Vienna (2009)
6. Song, Q., Han, J.D.: An Adaptive UKF Algorithm for the State and Parameter Estimations of a Mobile Robot. Acta Automatica Sinica 34(1), 72–79 (2008)
7. Peng, Y., Han, J.D., Huang, Q.J.: Adaptive UKF based tracking control for unmanned trimaran vehicles. International Journal of Innovative Computing, Information and Control 5 (10B), 3505–3516 (2009)
8. Jiang, Z., Song, Q., He, Y.Q., Han, J.D.: A Novel Adaptive Unscented Kalamn Filter for Nonlinear Estimation. In: 45th IEEE International Conference on Decision and Control, pp. 4293–4298. IEEE Press, New York (2007)

Applying Fuzzy Data Mining to Telecom Churn Management

Kuo-Hsiung Liao and Hao-En Chueh[*]

Department of Information Management, Yuanpei University,
No. 306, Yuanpei Street, Hsinchu 30015, Taiwan
liao@mail.ypu.edu.tw, hechueh@mail.ypu.edu.tw

Abstract. Customers tend to change telecommunications service providers in pursuit of more favorable telecommunication rates. Therefore, how to avoid customer churn is an extremely critical topic for the intensely competitive telecommunications industry. To assist telecommunications service providers in effectively reducing the rate of customer churn, this study used fuzzy data mining to determine effective marketing strategies by analyzing the responses of customers to various marketing activities. These techniques can help telecommunications service providers determine the most appropriate marketing opportunities and methods for different customer groups, to reduce effectively the rate of customer turnover.

Keywords: Telecommunications industry, Churn management, Fuzzy theory, Data mining, Marketing activity.

1 Introduction

According to statistics produced by the Institute for Information Industry of Taiwan, mobile phone users in Taiwan numbered 26 million as of the second quarter of 2009. This statistic indicates that the popularization rate of mobile phones in Taiwan has already reached 100 % and that mobile communications service is one of the most indispensable information and communication services in contemporary life.

Additionally, the portable line number service recently provided by the government permits users to change their telecommunications provider without changing their original mobile line number. This has made it easier for users to change their telecommunications service providers in consideration of their own best interests. To maintain market share and profitability, telecommunications service providers implement various policies and management mechanisms in an attempt to retain customers and avoid serious customer churn problems [1, 15, 16, 17, 20, 21].

A common churn management procedure is to analyze information about past churners, build a model for prediction of customer churn, use this prediction model to determine from current customer information those customers that are likely to churn, and then commence various marketing activities or events. However, whether

---

[*] Corresponding author.

R. Chen (Ed.): ICICIS 2011, Part I, CCIS 134, pp. 259–264, 2011.

churn management strategies have been successful must be examined according to whether or not customer churn rate has truly been reduced. Thus, to assist telecommunications service providers in successfully retaining potential churners, this study used fuzzy data mining techniques [3, 6, 10, 11, 12, 14, 24, 29] to analyze the responses of customers to various marketing activities and thus determine effective marketing strategies.

2 Literature Review

Numerous previous studies have proposed methods for assisting telecommunications service providers in solving problems of customer churn management. [2, 5, 6, 7, 8, 9, 13, 18, 19, 22, 25, 26, 27, 28]. Xia et al.[28] proposed the study of architecture using support vector machines to churn prediction model, and with a variety of data mining technology framework to compare the customer churn predictive model, including neural networks, decision-making trees, logistic regression, and Bayesian classifier, the experiments confirmed the structure using support vector machines churn out of the prediction model, the prediction accuracy than other data mining techniques to the prediction accuracy of better.

Tsai et al. [25] presented the research in the use of data mining techniques to find association rules that may affect the customers of the loss of an important factor, then these factors and the use of decision tree to construct the neural network technology a customer churn prediction model, and applied to telecommunications value-added services MOD (multimedia on demand) customer churn prediction. The study also experiments confirmed that pre-use association rules to carry out factor analysis of customer churn predictive model selection accuracy of the analysis of association rules is better than no prediction model. In addition, the study also confirmed that the experimental use of decision tree-based prediction model than the structure of neural network prediction model has better prediction results.

The main purpose of the past studies described above was to build an effective customer churn prediction model to forecast which customers are likely to churn. The provision of this information could then assist telecommunications service providers in organizing various marketing activities or events. However, from the perspective of telecommunications service providers, determining which customers are likely to churn does not guarantee that providers can successfully retain these potential churners and thus reduce their customer churn rate. Rather, effective marketing activities are essential for customer churn management.

3 Fuzzy Data Mining

Fuzzy set theory is proposed by L. A. Zadeh, professor of the University of California at Berkeley in 1965 [29]. Suppose we have a universe of discourse, X , and the elements of X is x_i , i.e. $X = \{x_i\}$. Then, some of unclearly attributes can be represented as fuzzy sets. Assume that A is a fuzzy set defined on X , then the degree of membership of an element belonging to the fuzzy set A can be expressed as a membership function μ_A, and its value is normalized to between 0 and 1. The membership function is shown as the follows [29]:

$$\mu_A : X \to [0,1], \ 0 \le \mu_A(x_i) \le 1, x_i \in X . \tag{1}$$

There are three basic operators of fuzzy sets: union, Intersection, and complement.

Two fuzzy sets A and B defined on X, then the symbol of the union operator is $\mu_{A \cup B}(x)$, and the definition of the union operator is as follows:

$$\mu_{A \cup B}(x) = max(\mu_A(x), \mu_B(x)), x \in X ; \tag{2}$$

Two fuzzy sets A and B defined on X, then the symbol of the intersection operator is $\mu_{A \cap B}(x)$, and the definition of the intersection operator is as follows:

$$\mu_{A \cap B}(x) = min(\mu_A(x), \mu_B(x)), x \in X ; \tag{3}$$

A fuzzy set A defined on X, then the symbol of the complement operator is $\mu_{\bar{A}}(x)$, and the definition of the complement operator is as follows:

$$\mu_{\bar{A}}(x) = 1 - \mu_A(x), x \in X . \tag{4}$$

In this study, the fuzzy sets can be used to assist in dealing linguistic means and avoiding the boundary shape problem.

Data mining is defined as use of automated or semi-automated method from a large number of data collections to extract the potential, unknown, meaningful and useful information or patterns [3, 6, 10, 11, 12, 14, 23, 24]. The main technologies of data mining include classification, prediction (trend) analysis, cluster analysis, association rules analysis, sequential patterns analysis and so on.

This study uses ID3 decision tree algorithm [23] for the last customer for the call center do in order to retain customers reflect the results of various marketing activities to identify successful and effective customer retention strategy to reduce customer churn. ID3 is a widely used algorithm of classification task. Classification is the process of mining a classifier from a set of pre-defined training data that can describe and distinguish data classes or concepts, such that the found classifier can assign a class or concept to a new un-defined data. In general, classification (mining a classifier) involves three major tasks: data representation, which represents data in machine-readable structures, classifier construction, which constructs a classifier from a set of training data, and classifier evaluation, which evaluates classifier accuracy with a set of testing data and in terms of various evaluation functions. Classification has been popularly applied on insurance risk analysis, credit approval, medical diagnosis, etc. Under the previous literature can also be found using the decision tree algorithm to solve the problem of churn management has a good effect [25].

4 Experiment and Results

The experimental dataset used in this study came from the randomly sampled customer retention activities and the responses of customers of a telecommunications company in Taiwan whose contracts were due to expire between June and July 2008.

From the customers whose contracts were due to expire in June and in July 2008 respectively, 400 customers were randomly selected from each of the following groups: customers with monthly bills of NT$ 0 ~ NT$300, customers with monthly bills of NT$301 ~ NT$800, and customers with monthly bills of NT$801 ~ NT$1000. Each group of 400 customers in the different bill amount ranges were then divided further into two subgroups of 200 customers each. Customer retention marketing programs were implemented by sending direct mail (DM) and through telemarketing. During this retention marketing process, customers could choose the marketing programs that they wanted. The finally marketing results of the activities recorded in Table 1. To category various customer groups to effective marketing, in this study, churn rate will be converted into a fuzzy set [29] called effective marketing, $\mu_{EM}(x)$,

$$\mu_{EM}(x) = \begin{cases} 1.0 & x < 10 \\ 0.8 & 10 \le x < 30 \\ 0.6 & 30 \le x < 50 \\ 0.4 & 50 \le x < 70 \\ 0.2 & 70 \le x < 90 \\ 0 & 90 \le x \end{cases}, \tag{5}$$

where x is the churn rate.

The established marketing model [23] is shown as in Figure 1. Through the marketing model that, for the customers whose monthly bills from NT$801 to NT$1000, regardless of their contractual maturity date in June or July, when the telephone marketing is used, effective marketing is the extent of up to 0.8; but If mailing DM is used, then the degree of effective marketing is 0.2 only. For the customers whose

Table 1. The result of customer marketing activities

Customer group	Contract expires	Bill payment	Marketing method	Churn rate	Effective marketing
1	June	NT$0 ~ NT$300	Telecom marketing	83%	0.2
2	June	NT$0 ~ NT$300	Sending DM	75%	0.2
3	June	NT$301 ~ NT$800	Telecom marketing	52%	0.4
4	June	NT$301 ~ NT$800	Sending DM	96%	0
5	June	NT$801 ~ NT$1000	Telecom marketing	13%	0.8
6	June	NT$801 ~ NT$1000	Sending DM	87%	0.2
7	July	NT$0 ~ NT$300	Telecom marketing	82%	0.2
8	July	NT$0 ~ NT$300	Sending DM	78%	0.2
9	July	NT$301 ~ NT$800	Telecom marketing	52%	0.4
10	July	NT$301 ~ NT$800	Sending DM	96%	0
11	July	NT$801 ~ NT$1000	Telecom marketing	26%	0.8
12	July	NT$801 ~ NT$1000	Sending DM	89%	0.2

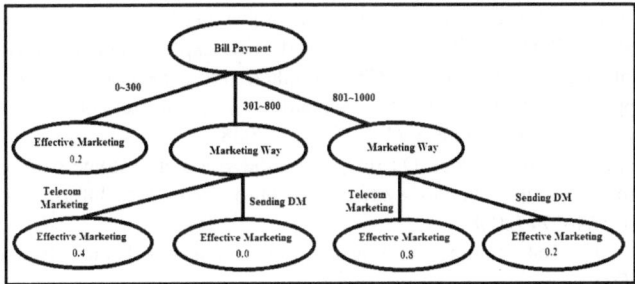

Fig. 1. Telecom marketing model

monthly billing amount from NT$ 0 to NT$300, you must use the same telephone marketing, the degree of effective marketing is 0.4; if mail DM is used, then it is completely not effective marketing. In addition, for the customers whose monthly bills from NT$ 0 to NT$301, no matter what kind of marketing, the degree of effective marketing is very low, only 0.2.

5 Conclusions

Most of previous researches, the emphasis being given to construct a customer churn predictive model to identify in advance the list of possible loss of customers. However, the ability to identify the possible loss of potential customers does not mean that you can retain the possible loss of those customers live, in order to reduce customer churn rate, must present an effective marketing strategy. To this end, this study uses fuzzy data mining techniques to analyze the past records of results of various marketing activities to establish a marketing model. In this study, the proposed marketing model can provide companies on determining the best marketing strategies for different customer groups.

References

1. Ahn, J.H., Han, S.P., Lee, Y.S.: Customer churn analysis: Churn determinants and mediation effects of partial defection in the Korean mobile telecommunications service industry. Telecommunications Policy 30(10-11), 552–568 (2006)
2. Au, W., Chen, K.C.C., Yao, X.: A novel evolutionary data mining algorithm with applications to churn prediction. IEEE Transactions on Evolutionary Computation 7(6), 532–545 (2003)
3. Berry, M.J.A., Linoff, G.: Data mining techniques: For marketing, sales, and customer support. John Wiley & Sons, Chichester (2004)
4. Berson, A., Simith, S., Thearling, K.: Building data mining applications for CRM. McGraw-Hill, New York (2000)
5. Chu, B.H., Tsai, M.S., Ho, C.S.: Toward a hybrid data mining model for customer retention. Knowledge-Based Systems 20(8), 703–718 (2007)
6. Chueh, H.-E., Lin, N.P., Jan, N.-Y.: Mining Target-oriented Fuzzy Correlation Rules in Telecom database. In: The 2009 International Conference on Advances in Social Networks Analysis and Mining, pp. 165–199 (2009)

7. Chueh, H.-E., Lin, S.-C., Jan, N.-Y.: Mining the Telecom Marketing Information to Optimizing the Customer Retention Strategies. Accepted: ICIC Express Letters, Part B: Applications
8. Coussement, K., Van den Poel, D.: Churn prediction in subscription services: An application of support vector machines while comparing two parameter-selection techniques. Expert Systems with Applications 34(1), 313–327 (2008)
9. Coussement, K., Van den Poel, D.: Integrating the voice of customers through call center emails into a decision support system for churn prediction. Information & Management 45(3), 164–174 (2008)
10. Dunham, M.H.: Data mining. Introductory and Advanced Topics. Pearson Education, London (2003)
11. Fayyad, U., Uthurusamy, R.: Data mining and knowledge discovery in databases. Communications of the ACM 39, 24–27 (1996)
12. Han, J., Kamber, M.: Data Mining: Concepts and Techniques. Morgan Kaufmann, San Francisco (2001)
13. Hung, S.Y., Yen, D.C., Wang, H.Y.: Applying data mining to telecom churn management. Expert Systems with Applications 31, 515–524 (2006)
14. Kantardzic, M.: Data mining-Concepts, models, methods, and algorithms. John Wiley & Sons, Chichester (2003)
15. Keaveney, S.M.: Customer switching behavior in service industries: An exploratory study. Journal of Marketing 59, 71–82 (1995)
16. Kim, H.S., Yoon, C.H.: Determinants of subscriber churn and customer loyalty in the Korean mobile telephony market. Telecommunications Policy 28(9), 751–765 (2004)
17. Kim, M.K., Park, M.C., Jeong, D.H.: The effects of customer satisfaction and switching barrier on customer loyalty in Korean mobile telecommunication services. Telecommunications Policy 28, 145–159 (2004)
18. Lejeune, M.: Measuring the impact of data mining on churn management. Internet Research: Electronic Network Applications and Policy 11(5), 375–387 (2001)
19. Luo, B., Shao, P., Liu, D.: Evaluation of three discrete methods on customer churn model based on neural network and decision tree in PHSS. In: The First International Symposium on Data, Privacy, and E-Commerce, pp. 95–97 (2007)
20. Mattersion, R.: Telecom churn management. APDG Publishing, Fuquay-Varina (2001)
21. Mozer, M.C., Wolniewicz, R., Grimes, D.B., Johnson, E., Kaushanky, H.: Predicting subscriber dissatisfaction and improving retention in the wireless telecommunications industry. IEEE Transactions on Neural Networks 11(3), 690–696 (2000)
22. Ngai, E.W.T., Xiu, L., Chau, D.C.K.: Application of data mining techniques in customer relationship management: A literature review and classification. Expert Systems with Applications 36(2), 2592–2602 (2009)
23. Quinlan, J.R.: Induction of Decision Trees. Machine Learning 1(1), 81–106 (1986)
24. Tan, P.N., Steinbach, M., Kumar, V.: Introduction to data mining. Pearson Addison Wesley, London (2006)
25. Tsai, C.F., Chen, M.Y.: Variable selection by association rules for customer churn prediction of multimedia on demand. Expert Systems with Applications 37, 2006–2015 (2010)
26. Tsai, C.F., Lu, Y.H.: Customer churn prediction by hybrid neural networks. Expert Systems with Applications 36(10), 12547–12553 (2009)
27. Wei, C.P., Chiu, I.T.: Turning telecommunications call details to churn prediction: a data mining approach. Expert Systems with Applications 23(2), 103–112 (2002)
28. Xia, G.E., Jin, W.D.: Model of Customer Churn Prediction on Support Vector Machine. Systems Engineering-Theory & Practice 28(1), 71–77 (2008)
29. Zadeh, L.A.: Fuzzy sets. Information and Control 8, 338–353 (1965)

Towards a Pre-computed Relation Matrix for Semantic Web Service

Luokai Hu[1,2], Shi Ying[2], and Kai Zhao[2]

[1] Hubei University of Education, Computer School, Wuhan China, 430205
[2] State Key Lab of Software Engineering, Wuhan University, Wuhan China, 430072
luokaihu@gmail.com

Abstract. Aiming at the complicated semantic matching problem of service's input and output data items in the service composition process, a pre-computed relation matrix for Semantic Web Services is presented. Based on the semantic relation reasoning method of concept in Domain Standard Ontology, the automatic matrix generation algorithm is given. Finally, the matrix based automatic service composition algorithm is proposed. Pre-computed service relation matrix can greatly improve the performance of automatic composition and provide a new approach for organizing the Semantic Web Services connections.

Keywords: Semantic Web Service, Domain Standard Ontology, Relation Matrix, Semantic Reasoning.

1 Introduction

With the increasing of Web service resources, the research on the description, publication, search and composition of Web service have become blossomed. Semantic Web service, which combines the Semantic Web and Web services technology, was proposed to provide a good foundation for the automatic discovery, composition and execution. By using of Semantic Web service technology, we can establish semantic model of Web services to achieve high accuracy, high degree of automation, machine-understandable semantic Web service description, discovery, composition, execution, dynamic configuration, and eventually reuse of the semantic Web services[1]. Currently, the ability and performance of semantic description and reasoning have become the main challenges of automatic semantic Web service composition. On the one hand, inadequate description capacity can not support effective reasoning. On the other hand, poor reasoning performance is unable to adapt to the large-scale application of semantic Web services.

The purpose of our work is to present, in one hand, a Domain Standard Ontology comprised of five sets of concept and in another hand, a pre-computed relation matrix before automatic service composition using semantic reasoning capability of OWL language. The relation matrix which describes the connections of a service's input data and another's output data provides the infrastructure for automatic service composition.

R. Chen (Ed.): ICICIS 2011, Part I, CCIS 134, pp. 265–270, 2011.

2 Domain Standard Ontology (DSO)

Domain Standard Ontology reflects the most common abstract concepts and relations in a particular application domain. The DSO of a particular domain is the default ontology for semantic annotation of WSDL.

2.1 The Abstract Concept of Domain Standard Ontology

The abstract concept set of DSO ψ is the union of five concept subsets.

$$\psi = \Lambda \cup \Delta \cup \Gamma \cup \Theta \cup \Xi$$

(1) **Simple Concept.** The set of simple concept is expressed with Λ.
A simple concept can be recursively defined as:

① Simple concept is the concept which does not appear in the left side of GCI;
② If a concept is a simple concept, its inverse concept is also a simple concept;
③ If a concept C_s appears in the left side of GCI and the concepts which appears in the concept expression of GCI right side are all simple concepts, C_s is simple concept. That is, $C_s \in \Lambda$ iff $\forall C(C \diamond w \wedge C_s \sqsubseteq w \rightarrow C \in \Lambda)$, where w is a concept expression,

$C \diamond w$ indicates all the concepts in the concept expression.

(2) **Compositive Concept.** The set of Compositive Concept is expressed with Δ.
The concept C_c is composed of two concepts C_1 and C_2, formally expressed as:

$$C_c = C_1 \triangle C_2, \text{ where } C_1, C_2 \in \psi, C_c \in \Delta$$

Both C1 and C2 can be called ComponentConcept, such as CustomerName, Flight-TicketNumber.

(3) **Inverted Concept.** The set of inverted concept is expressed with Γ.
A concept C_i is the inverted of the concept C, expressed as $C_i = \neg C$, $C \in \psi$.

(4) **Conjunctive Concept.** The set of conjunctive concept is expressed with Θ.
A concept C_{con} is conjuncted with two concepts C_1 and C_2, expressed as $C_{con} = C_1 \wedge C_2$,

$C_1, C_2 \in \psi$.

(5) **Disjunctive Concept.** The set of disjunctive concept is expressed with Ξ.
A concept C_{dis} is disjuncted with two concepts C1 and C2, expressed as $C_{dis} = C_1 \vee C_2$.

2.2 Modeling and Reasoning of DSO with OWL-DL

OWL-DL[2] is selected as the ontology modeling language of DSO. Because of space constraints, we use the description logic $\mathcal{SHOIN}$[3] for the formal description of the concept and relation of these concepts and only the modeling and reasoning of simple and compositive concepts are given as follows, similar to the other three kinds of concept.

(1) Modeling of the simple concept relation in DSO

① Synonym: If two concepts C and D have synonym relation between them, then $C \equiv D$ is modeled in DSO.

② Antonym: If two concepts C and D have antonym relation between them, then $C \equiv \neg D$ or $D \equiv \neg C$ is modeled in DSO.

③ Hypernym: If concept C is the generalization of D, then $D \sqsubseteq C$ is modeled in DSO.

④ Hyponym: If concept C is inherited from D, then $C \sqsubseteq D$ is modeled in DSO.

(2) Modeling and reasoning of compositive concept relation in DSO
Suppose a composition concept $C_{c1} \in \Delta$ is composed of C_1 and C_2 $C_{c1} = C_1 \triangle C_2$ and

$C_{c2} \in \Delta$ is composed of D_1 and D_2 $C_{c2} = D_1 \triangle D_2$.

① Synonym: C_{c1} and C_{c2} are synonym, **Iff** C_1 and D_1 are synonym **AND** C_2 and D_2 are synonym.

② Antonym: C_{c1} and C_{c2} are antonym, **Iff** C_1 and D_1 are antonym **AND** C_2 and D_2 are synonym **OR** C_1 and D_1 are synonym **AND** C_2 and D_2 are antonym.

③ Hypernym: C_{c1} is hypernym of C_{c2}, **Iff** C_1 is hypernym or synonym of D_1 AND C_2 is the hypernym or synonym of D_2 **BUT** $(C_1$ and $D_1)$ and $(C_2$ and $D_2)$ are not synonym at the same time.

④ Hyponym: We can reason about the hyponym relation of C_{c1} and C_{c2} similar with their hypernym relation.

3   Semantics Based Relation Matrix (SBRM)

On the basis of the DSO and its reasoning approach, the connection relation between input of a service and output of another can be generated into a matrix.

3.1   DSO Based Semantic Web Service Relation Matrix Building Algorithm

For a Semantic Web Service SWS_i, the algorithm for creating the relation between SWS_i and another SWS is as follows. The resulting matrix is shown in Fig. 1.

```
Procedure void filling(SWS sws_i, SWS sws_j)
var O_sws_i ;
capture the output of sws_i
var I_sws_j ;
capture the input of sws_j
Begin
/*cell(x, y) specifies the cell of the SBRM, where x
and y respects the row and column respectively */
cell(sws_i, sws_j) = null ;
  if(sws_i==sws_j)
    cell(sws_i, sws_j) = null ;
  else if(O_sws_i part I_sws_j || O_sws_i full I_sws_j)
    switch (semantic relation between O_sws_i and I_sws_j)
```

```
/*inter[] is the matched items between two Service's
input and output */
      case exact: cell(sws_i, sws_j)= (inter[], 3) ;
      case subsume: cell(sws_i, sws_j)= (inter[], 2) ;
      case generic: cell(sws_i, sws_j)= (inter[], 1) ;
  else
      cell(sws_i, sws_j)= (0, 0) ;
End
```

	SWS_0	SWS_1	SWS_2	SWS_3	SWS_4	SWS_5	SWS_6	......
SWS_0	null	(inter[],3)	...	...	...	...	...	
SWS_1	(inter[],2)	null	(inter[],1)	...	...	...	...	
SWS_2	(inter[],3)	(inter[],2)	null	...	...	...	...	
SWS_3	(inter[],3)	(inter[],2)	...	null	...	...	...	
SWS_4	...	...	...	...	null	...	...	
SWS_5	...	...	...	...	...	null	...	
SWS_6	...	...	...	...	...	...	null	
......								

Fig. 1. DSO based Relation Matrix for Semantic Web Service (SBRM)

When a service SWS_i from the SBRM is to be deleted, remove the row and column where the deleted service SWS_i is located in. When service SWS_i is to be added to the SBRM, procedure *filling* should be called.

3.2 SBRM Based Semantic Web Service Composition Algorithm

One of the aims of establishing SBRM is to find automatically and rapidly a composite service which will satisfy the request. The Composition algorithm explores the SBRM in depth-first and backward chaining strategy.

```
Procedure Map<SWS[][], int[]> Composition (SWS[] sws,
OutputOfRequest[] O_req, InputOfRequest[] I_req)
/* O_req and I_req is respectively the output and input
items of service composition request */
var SWS[n] temp = null ;
var int m = max ;
var SWS[m][m] goal = null ;
var Map<SWS[m][m] s, int[m] v> result = null ;
Begin
  foreach (sws[i] in sws){
    search a set of semantic web service "temp" in sws
/* compliantWith(x, y):
When the semantic relation between x and is exact, sub-
sume or generic, the compliantWith is true, otherwise
false */
    if(compliantWith(union(temp.output), O_req))
      copy temp to goal[i] ;
  }
  repeat
```

```
/*I_goal[i] is the union of input items of all services
in goal[i]*/
  if(I_goal[i]!=I_req)

    I_rest = I_req∪I_goal[i] - I_req∩I_goal[i] ;
  else{
    result.s[i] = goal[i] ;
    continue ;
  }
  for(int j=0; j<m; j++)
    for(int k=0; k<n; k++){
      if(cell(sws[k],goal[i][j])!=null&&cell(sws[k],
goal[i][j])!=(0,0)&&!sws[k] in goal[i]&&I_rest !=∅){
        I_rest=I_rest-cell(sws[k], goal[i][j]).right ;
        add sws[k] to goal[i] ;
        add cell(sws[k],goal[i][j]).left to result.v[i];
      }
      if(I_rest = = ∅)
        result.s[i] = goal[i] ;
    }
  until there is no goal[i] left in goal ;
  descending sort result.s, value by result.v ;
  return result ;
End
```

4 Related Works

In the semantic Web service description, the most representative work is three recommendation standards of W3C, namely by the order of time: OWL-S[4], WSMO[5]
and SAWSDL[6]. Both OWL-S and WSMO uses the ontology to describe Web services directly. On the contrary, SAWSDL, the new W3C recommendation, uses an
external ontology to express semantic information. Semantic annotation method
which is the most common in the semantic Web area is employed to annotate relevant
information in WSDL in order to achieve the semantic description of Web services. In
our previous work, a Semantic Web Service Description Language (WSDL4S[7]) has
been proposed to support the annotation and reasoning using DSO.

M. Paolucci earlier proposed a semantic Web service matching method which is
based on the semantic relation of input and output items in service description. They
divided the matching degree between the input of a service and the output of another
into four levels, Exact, Plug-in, Subsume and Fail.[8] On this basis, I. Horrocks further proposed Intersection level.[9] But such reasoning activities which are required
to carry out in each automatic services matching or composition seriously hampered
the performance of service matching and composition.

On the other hand, I. Constantinescu and D. Barreiro proposed matrix model of
Web services respectively [10,11], but their work did not involve any semantic infor-
mation. F. Lecue presented OWL-S or WSMO based causal links to realize service
composition.[12] H.N. Talantikite proposed an OWL-S based semantic network of
Web services.[13] Their work is built on a semantic Web service description method.
But they do not give a clear semantics reasoning algorithm.

5 Conclusion

As many problems involved in Semantic Web Service composition, automatic composition is very difficult. Firstly, based on the Domain Standard Ontology and its reasoning approach, we pre-established the relation matrix for semantic Web services before the service composition. On the actual operation of service composition, when a user submits a request of service composition, system can find all the composable sequences of semantic Web service according to the service connection relation matrix. In the case of no user involvement, the service sequence with the largest connection degree is selected automatically. Otherwise user-specified service sequence is selected. The SBRM greatly improves efficiency of service composition.

Supporting pre-condition and effect of Semantic Web Services in the relation matrix is the focus of future research work.

Acknowledgments. This work was supported by the National Natural Science Foundation of China under Grant (No. 60773006) and the youth project of Hubei University of Education Grant (No. 2009C015).

References

[1] McIlraith, A.S., Martin, L.D.: Bringing Semantics to Web Services. IEEE Intelligent Systems 18(1), 90–93 (2003)

[2] W3C, Web Ontology Language (OWL) (2004), http://www.w3.org/2004/OWL/

[3] Baader, F., Calvanesethe, D.: Description Logic Handbook: Theory, implementation, and applications. Cambridge University Press, Cambridge (2002)

[4] Martin, D., Burstein, M., Hobbs, J., et al.: OWL-S: Semantic Markup for Web Services (2004), http://www.w3.org/Submission/OWL-S

[5] Bruijn, J., Bussler, C., Domingue, J., et al.: Web Service Modeling Ontology (WSMO) (2005), http://www.w3.org/Submission/WSMO/

[6] Kopecky, J., Tomas, V., Carine, B., et al.: SAWSDL: Semantic annotations for WSDL and XML schema. IEEE Internet Computing 11(6), 60–67 (2007)

[7] Hu, L., Ying, S., Zhao, K., et al.: A Semantic Web Service Description Language. In: WASE International Conference on Information Engineering (ICIE 2009), Taiyuan, China, pp. 449–452 (2009)

[8] Paolucci, M., Kawamura, T., Payne, R.T., et al.: Semantic Matching of Web Services Capabilities. In: Horrocks, I., Hendler, J. (eds.) ISWC 2002. LNCS, vol. 2342, pp. 333–347. Springer, Heidelberg (2002)

[9] Li, L., Horrocks, I.: A Software Framework for Matchmaking Based on Semantic Web Technology. In: The 12th International Conf. on World Wide Web, pp. 331–339 (2003)

[10] Constantinescu, I., Faltings, B., Binder, W.: Type Based Service Composition. In: World Wild Web (WWW 2004), New York, USA, pp. 268–269 (2004)

[11] Claro, B.D., Albers, P., Hao, J.: Selecting web services for optimal composition. In: ICWS International Workshop on Semantic and Dynamic Web Processes, Orlando, USA (2005)

[12] Lecue, F., Leger, A.: A Formal Model for Semantic Web Service Composition. In: Cruz, I., Decker, S., Allemang, D., Preist, C., Schwabe, D., Mika, P., Uschold, M., Aroyo, L.M. (eds.) ISWC 2006. LNCS, vol. 4273, pp. 385–398. Springer, Heidelberg (2006)

[13] Talantikite, N.H., Aissani, D., Boudjlida, N.: Semantic Annotation for Web Services Discovery and Composition. Computer Standards & Interfaces 31(6), 1108–1117 (2009)

Precise Localization of Facial Features
Based on Cascade Fusion

Ying Chen[1], Chunlu Ai[1], and Chunjian Hua[2]

[1] School of IoT Engineering, Jiangnan University,
1800 Lihu Road, Wuxi, China
[2] School of Mechanical Engineering, Jiangnan University,
1800 Lihu Road, Wuxi, China
{chenying,cjhua}@jiangnan.edu.cn

Abstract. A simple and successful scheme for locating the facial features in images at the presence of complex condition context is presented. Multiple fusion steps are taken in cascade. Based on the estimation of the color distribution of the facial features, eye and mouth probability map is constructed using Gaussian Mixture Model (GMM), a fusion strategy on probability maps is then constructs eye, mouth, and skin binary maps. Then the binary fusion is implied to obtain candidate location of each component. Finally, the components are verified by taking facial geometry into consideration. Experiments show that more accurate detection results can be obtained as compared to other state-of-art methods.

Keywords: facial feature, feature localization, Gaussian Mixture Model, feature fusion[1].

1 Introduction

The problem of facial feature detection is an important research topic in many fields such as automatic face recognition, facial expression analysis and audio visual automatic speech recognition. A wide variety of approaches have been proposed in the area. Many detection methods [1, 2] adopt the idea of the cascaded AdaBoost classifier proposed by Viola and Jones [3]. SVM classifier is also used for detection [4, 5]. Other methods include regression and probability approaches [6-8]. Everingham compared the approaches in [6] and indicated that the simple probability model outperforms the others.

The method presented in this paper extends and improves the idea of localizing the facial features under probabilistic framework. A probability fusion following a binary fusion strategy is designed to obtain candidates of each facial component which are verified via statistical distribution of facial geometry. Finally, the experimental sets have been augmented to prove the robustness of the method against different acquisition conditions.

[1] This work has been supported by "the Fundamental Research Funds for the Central Universities" (JUSRP10926).

R. Chen (Ed.): ICICIS 2011, Part I, CCIS 134, pp. 271–277, 2011.

2 Precise Facial Feature Localization

Among the various facial features, eyes and mouth are the most prominent features for various applications such as face recognition and 3D face pose estimation. This section describes the strategy conceived to achieve precise eye and mouth localization.

The employed face candidate detector is a custom reimplementation of the Viola–Jones detector. The Chroma/luma features distribution of the facial components, which are robust to the variation of the context conditions such as lighting, viewpoints, camera type and setting, and the person's tan and ethnic group, are modeled to be mixture of Gaussian, and the distribution parameters are obtained during training process. Meanwhile, the facial geometry feature which is robust to rotation and scale variation is also designed, whose statistical distribution is also modeled with GMM. For each test image, probability fusion and binary fusion process is taken, which highlights candidates of each facial component separately. Facial geometry statistical learned above is used to verify the location of each component.

2.1 Features Selection

In the probability based methods, the feature vector representation is a main issue for the improvement of the performance.

YCbcr color space is widely used in facial issue. Instead of using simple feature vector [Cb Cr Y], the paper designs an adjusted pixel-wise feature for each facial component by exploiting special characteristics of each facial component.

Based on the observation that both dark and bright pixels are found around eyes in the luma component [9, 10], while usually little luma change is found around brow and skin areas, the pixel-wise feature to highlight eyes is then constructed as (1):

$$x_e = 1 - \frac{Y \ominus S_1}{Y \oplus S_1 + 1} \tag{1}$$

where Y is the luma component, S_1 is a disk structuring function, $\oplus$ and $\ominus$ respectively means grayscale dilation and erosion operations.

It is also observed that compared to skin, higher Cr values are found in the mouth areas, and the mouth has a relatively low response in Cr/Cb but has a high response in Cr^2 [9]. Therefore, the pixel feature to highlight mouth is constructed as (2):

$$x_m = \mathrm{H}\left[Cr^2 * (Cr^2 - \eta \cdot Cr/Cb)^2\right] \ominus S_2 \tag{2}$$

where S_2 is a line structuring function, $\eta = \lambda \cdot \dfrac{\sum Cr^2}{\sum Cr/Cb}$ is a factor to balance the importance of Cr^2 and Cr/Cb, where λ is a constant which could be set to 0.85~0.95, and $\mathrm{H}(\cdot)$ is a histogram equalization operator to strengthen the contrast.

We generate facial geometry features from training images that determine the geometry structure of facial components. An eye-mouth triangle is formed for all possible combinations of the two eye candidates and one mouth candidate. The triangle example on a labeled facial image is illustrated in blue in Fig. 1, where line L1 joins the mouth center (x_m, y_m) and the left eye center (x_{el}, y_{el}), line L2 joins the mouth center (x_m, y_m) and the right eye (x_{er}, y_{er}), and line L3 is drawn joining the eye centers, α_1 is the angle between line L3 and L1, and α_2 is the angle between line L3 and L2. Therefore, we take $x_t = [\alpha_1, \alpha_2]$ as the spatial feature.

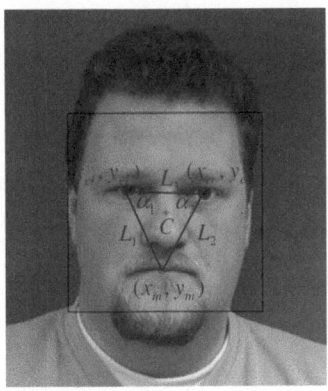

Fig. 1. Illustration of spatial feature

3 Probability Model and Fusion

3.1 Probability Model

To model the distribution of chroma&luma for each pixel over the full range of permissible variations, and spatial features for each facial component, Gausian Mixture Model (GMM) is employed to represent classes' distribution in both appearance and spatial feature spaces.

Given feature vector as $x = \{x_1, x_2, \cdots, x_n\}$ where n is the dimension of the feature vector, distribution of samples is modeled by the following formula:

$$p(x \mid \theta) = \sum_{i=1}^{M} w_i p_i(x \mid \theta_i) \tag{3}$$

where M is the number of mixture components, $p_i(x)$ is a normal PDF parameterized by a mean vector μ_i, and a covariance matrix Σ_i, $p_i(x) \sim N(\mu_i, \Sigma_i)$, w_i is the weight of the component $p_i(x)$, $0 < w_i < 1$ for all components, and $\sum_i w_i = 1$.

$\theta_i = (w_i, \mu_i, \Sigma_i)$ is the parameter vector of component i and will be estimated through given training data. The parameters of Gaussian probability density functions (pdfs) are estimated with the expectation maximization (EM) algorithm [11], and the mixture number M is computed via cross validation [12].

Training examples are taken from images of one individual (No. 145) in multi-PIE [13] with different pose, expression and illumination. Taking x_e from eye and brow training examples as feature vectors in GMMs, two mixture models $p(x_e \mid \theta_e)$ and $p(x_b \mid \theta_b)$ are established to describe eye and brow feature distribution. Similarly, taking x_m from mouth training examples, $p(x_m \mid \theta_m)$ are constructed to describe mouths distributions.

Different from extracting training data from sample images, skin distribution $p(x_s \mid \theta_s)$ is established by extracting skin training data $x_s = [Cb \quad Cr]$ from currently detected face area, which is expected to have more accurate description of the current sample. The extraction formula is as:

$$x_s = F(u + h/2 + (-\kappa \cdot h/2 : \kappa \cdot h/2), v + w/2 + (-\kappa \cdot w/2 : \kappa \cdot w/2)) \qquad (4)$$

where (u, v) is the coordinate of upper-left corner of the detected rectangle, w and h are the width and height of the rectangle, and κ is a constant which is usually set to 0.2.

For spatial description, $p(x_t \mid \theta_t)$ are constructed using x_t as the spatial feature vectors.

3.2 Cascade Fusion

In this subsection, three fusion strategies, namely probability fusion, logistical fusion and spatial fusion, are described. The strategies help to realize precise facial features localization.

According to the learned Gaussian model mentioned in subsection 4.1, the probability maps of facial components in a test ROI is constructed. The maps of one individual are illustrated in (a), (b), (d) and (e) in Fig. 2.

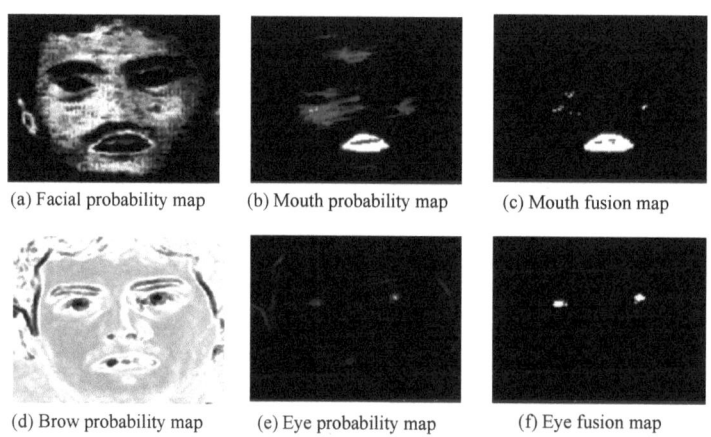

(a) Facial probability map   (b) Mouth probability map   (c) Mouth fusion map

(d) Brow probability map   (e) Eye probability map   (f) Eye fusion map

Fig. 2. Probability maps and the fusion results

As shown in Fig. 2(b) and (d), some facial areas have high mouth probability, and sometimes eye pixels have low probability, which is not strange because of the variation on illumination or poses. To eliminate this negative effect, probability fusion strategies are designed as (5) and (6), based on a simple but practical assumption that the probability of each component pixel to be the component should be larger than to be its neighboring components:

$$F_e = p(x_e \mid \theta_e) > p(x_b \mid \theta_b) \ AND \ p(x_e \mid \theta_e) > p(x_s \mid \theta_s), \tag{5}$$

$$F_m = p(x_m \mid \theta_m) > p(x_s \mid \theta_s) \tag{6}$$

According to (5) and (6), the binary eye & mouth maps are established, which are illustrated in Fig.2(c) and (f).

In most of the testing cases, the localization for each facial component can be realized based on F_e and F_m, after simple morphological and blob operations. However, as illustrated in Fig.3 (a), sometimes it becomes a little difficult due to the changes on facial context, such as glass-wearing, mouth-opening and beard-furnishing. To solve the problem, we combine our binary eye & mouth maps with the non-skin binary map B_s. Binary fusion strategy is illustrated as (7) and (8), and the results are shown in Fig. 3(b), following the results after morphological operation in Fig. 3 (c).

$$B_e = F_e \ AND \ B_s \tag{7}$$

$$B_m = (F_m \ AND \ BC \ ) \ OR \ B_s \tag{8}$$

where BC is the eroded skin convex binary image, which helps to reduce the size of ROI. Furthermore, to eliminate negative effective brought by beard, B_m is modified according to (8).

$$B_m' = (F_m \ AND \ BC \ ) \ OR \ (B_s \ AND \ (1 - B_d)) \tag{9}$$

where B_d is the binary beard map produced by thresholding beard map M_d which is constructed by:

$$M_d = Cb/Cr * Y \tag{10}$$

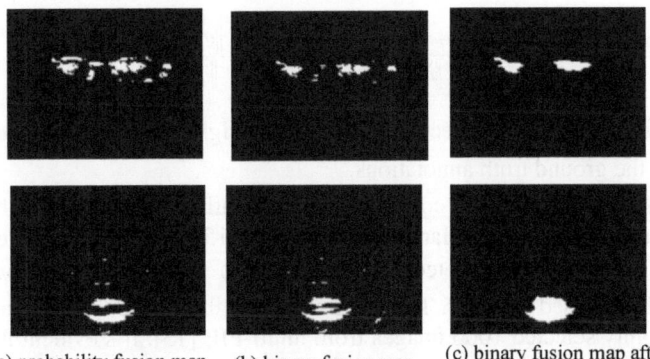

(a) probability fusion map   (b) binary fusion map   (c) binary fusion map after morphological operation

Fig. 3. Binary fusion and the fusion results

For possible more than one candidate, now we form an eye-mouth triangle for all possible combinations of the two eye candidates and one mouth candidate, which is supported by predefined rules about the spatial location of facial components. The rules are defined with $p(x_t \mid \theta_t)$ which are constructed in 3.1. The score for each combination is computed for each verified eye-mouth triangle based on their binary fusion maps. We remain the triangle with the highest spatial probability score that exceeds a threshold which is simply set to 0.5 in the experiments.

4   Experimental Results

We have evaluated our algorithm on several face image databases including multi-PIE [13] and AR [14]. These color images have been taken under varying conditions. None of these images has been used to train the statistical models. Examples of localization results are shown in Fig. 4.

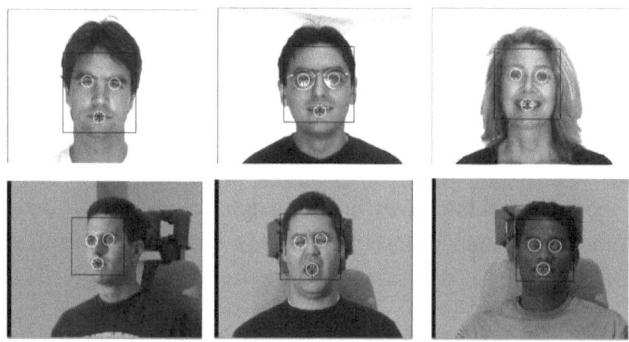

Fig. 4. Facial features localization results

In order to assess the precision of the facial component localization, we refer to the measure proposed by Campadelli *et al.* [4]. The localization criterion is defined in terms of the eye center positions according to:

$$d_e = \frac{\max\left(\|q_l - \hat{q}_l\|, \|q_r - \hat{q}_r\|\right)}{\|q_l - q_r\|}, d_m = \frac{\|q_m - \hat{q}_m\|}{\|q_l - q_r\|} \tag{11}$$

where $\hat{q}_{l/r}$, $\hat{q}_m$ stand for the detected eyes (left and right) and mouth positions, while $q_{l/r}$, q_m are the ground truth annotations.

In Table 1, our algorithm is compared with recently published SVM-based work [4] and the newly-developed Harr-based detector [15] in terms of aforementioned d_e and d_m. Note that only the detected position which is closest to the ground truth is remained in Harr-based detector. The test images are the whole images from AR [14] and the randomly selected 1000 images from multi-PIE [13]. It's evident from table 1 that the proposed method shows better performance in terms of precision as compared to the other two approaches.

Table 1. Localization results on AR face database for different algorithms

Methods	eye		mouth	
	$d_e \leq 0.1$	$d_e \leq 0.25$	$d_m \leq 0.1$	$d_m \leq 0.25$
Ref. [4]	60.2%	99.3%	92.3%	97.7%
Ref. [15]	26.0%	90.6%	89.2%	99.8%
Proposed method	79.2%	98.6%	95.2%	98.8%

5 Conclusion

We have demonstrated the probability fusion strategy in colour space can be pursued for precise facial feature localization. The approach is robust to illuminations, expressions and poses.

References

1. Wang, P., Ji, Q.: Multi-view face and eye detection using discriminate features. Comput. Vis. Imag. Underst. 105(2), 55–62 (2007)
2. Niu, Z., Shan, S., Yan, S., Chen, X., Gao, W.: 2D Cascaded AdaBoost for eye Localization. In: Proc. 18th Int. Conf. Patt. Recogn., vol. 2, pp. 1216–1219 (2006)
3. Viola, P., Jones, M.: Robust real time object detection. Int. J. Comput. Vis. 57(2), 137–154 (2004)
4. Campadell, P., Lanzarott, R., Lipor, G.: Precise eye and mouth localization. Int. J. Pattern Recognition and Artificial Intelligence 23(3), 359–377 (2009)
5. Tang, X., Ou, Z., Su, T., Sun, H., Zhao, P.: Robust precise eye location by AdaBoost and SVM techniques. In: Wang, J., Liao, X.-F., Yi, Z. (eds.) ISNN 2005. LNCS, vol. 3497, pp. 93–98. Springer, Heidelberg (2005)
6. Everingham, M., Zisserman, A.: Regression and Classification Approaches to Eye Localization in Face Images. In: Proc. Int. Conf. on Automatic Face and Gesture Recognition, Southampton, UK, pp. 441–448 (April 2006)
7. Fasel, I., Fortenberry, B., Movellan, J.: A generative framework for real time object detection and classification, Comput. Vis. Imag. Underst., pp. 182–210 (2005)
8. Ma, Y., Ding, X., Wang, Z., Wang, N.: Robust precise eye location under probabilistic framework. In: Proc. IEEE Int. Conf. Automatic Face and Gesture Recognition, pp. 339–344 (2004)
9. Hsu, R.L., Abdel-Mottaleb, M., Jain, A.K.: Face Detection in Color Images. IEEE Trans. on Pattern Analysis and Machine Intelligence (PAMI) 24(5), 696–706 (2002)
10. Zhou, Z., Geng, X.: Projection functions for eye detection. Pattern Recogn. 37(5), 1049–1056 (2004)
11. Dinov, I. D.: Expectation Maximization and Mixture Modeling Tutorial , California Digital Library, Statistics Online Computational Resource (December 9, 2008), http://repositories.cdlib.org/socr/EM_MM
12. Alpaydin, E.: Introduction to Machine Learning, 2nd edn. (Adaptive Computation and Machine Learning). The MIT Press, Cambridge (February 26, 2010)
13. Gross, R., Matthews, I., Cohn, J., Kanade, T., Baker, S.: Guide to the CMU multi-PIE database, Technical report, Carnegie Mellon University (2007)
14. Martinez, A.M., Benavente, R.: The AR face database, CVC Tech. Report #24 (1998)
15. Castrillón, M., Déniz, O., Hernández, D., Lorenzo, J.: A comparison of face and facial feature detectors based on the Viola–Jones general object detection framework, Machine Vision and Applications (2007), doi:10.1007/ s00138-010-0250-7

Multi Scale Toggle Contrast Operator Based Image Analysis

Xiangzhi Bai, Fugen Zhou, Zhaoying Liu, Bindang Xue, and Ting Jin

Image Processing Center
Beijing University of Aeronautics and Astronautics, Beijing 100191, China
jackybxz163@163.com

Abstract. Toggle contrast operator could extract image features and has been used in different applications. In this paper, the toggle contrast operator is used for image decomposition and reconstruction. By using multi scale structuring elements, toggle contrast operator decomposes the original image as different images which contain image features of different scale. Also, the original image could be reconstructed from the decomposed images without any loss. Therefore, this image decomposition and reconstruction method could be used for different applications. An example of image enhancement application has been also demonstrated.

Keywords: Image decomposition and reconstruction; Toggle contrast operator; Mathematical morphology; Image enhancement.

1 Introduction

Decomposing image as different images which contain different image features and then processing the decomposed images to obtain an efficient result following different application purposes is important transform for image processing. Some transforms have been proposed to achieve this purpose, such as wavelet transform [1], curvelet transform [2], morphological pyramid transform [3] and so on. Two very important steps in these transforms are image decomposition and reconstruction. The purpose of the image decomposition is transforming the original image as different images which contain different image features corresponding to different image scales. Then, the decomposed images could be used for different image application purpose. The purpose of image reconstruction is transforming the processed decomposed images into the final image which achieves the application purposes. Many transforms need image sampling when they are used for image decomposition and reconstruction, which may loss some useful image information. So, un-sampling transform may be an efficient alternating way.

In this paper, a new image decomposition and reconstruction method based on multi scale toggle contrast operator is proposed, which is an un-sampling transform. Toggle contrast operator [4] could efficiently extract image features. Multi scale toggle contrast operator is used to decompose the original images as different images which represent different image features of different image scales. Also, the final

R. Chen (Ed.): ICICIS 2011, Part I, CCIS 134, pp. 278–283, 2011.

image could be reconstructed from the processed decomposed images. Moreover, the whole procedure of decomposition and reconstruction do not need image sampling and will not loss any image information. Therefore, the proposed method would be very useful for image processing. An application of image enhancement is demonstrated to show the efficient performance of the method. Moreover, the proposed method could be widely used for different applications.

2 Toggle Contrast Operator

Mathematical morphology is an important theory for image processing and is based on geometry and set theory [4]. Let f and B represent gray scale image and structuring element, respectively. Morphological dilation ($\oplus$) and erosion ($\ominus$) operations of f (x, y) using B (i, j) are defined as follows.

$$f \oplus B(x, y) = \max_{u,v}(f(x-u, y-v) + B(u,v)),$$

$$f \ominus B(x, y) = \min_{u,v}(f(x+u, y+v) - B(u,v)).$$

By using morphological dilation and erosion, one type of toggle contrast operator is defined as follows.

$$TCO(x, y) = \begin{cases} f \oplus B(x,y), & if \ f \oplus B(x,y) - f(x,y) < f(x,y) - f\ominus B(x,y) \\ f\ominus B(x,y), & if \ f \oplus B(x,y) - f(x,y) > f(x,y) - f\ominus B(x,y) \\ f(x,y), & else \end{cases}.$$

This definition indicates that the gray value of each pixel in TCO is selectively replaced by the gray value of the same pixel in the result of dilation, erosion or the original image. The replaced pixels are with gray values close to the gray values of the same pixels in the original image.

3 Image Decomposition and Reconstruction

3.1 Multi Scale Toggle Contrast Operator

Structuring element in toggle contrast operator is a very important parameter. The extracted image features correspond to the used structuring element. However, there is only one structuring element used in toggle contrast operator. To extract all the features, multi scale structuring elements should be used. Suppose there are n scales of structuring elements $B_1, B_2, ..., B_n$. $B_i = \underbrace{B_1 \oplus B_1 ... \oplus B_1}_{dilation \quad i \quad times}$, $1 \leq i \leq n$. Then, the multi scale dilation and erosion of $f(x, y)$ using $B_i(u, v)$ are defined as follows.

$$f \oplus B_i(x, y) = \max_{u,v}(f(x-u, y-v) + \breve{B}_i(u,v)),$$

$$f \ominus B_i(x, y) = \min_{u,v}(f(x+u, y+v) - B_i(u,v)).$$

Based on multi scale dilation and erosion, multi scale toggle contrast operator could be calculated as follows.

$$TCO_i(x, y) = \begin{cases} f \oplus B_i(x, y), & if \ f \oplus B_i(x, y) - f(x, y) < f(x, y) - f \ominus B_i(x, y) \\ f \ominus B_i(x, y), & if \ f \oplus B_i(x, y) - f(x, y) > f(x, y) - f \ominus B_i(x, y) \\ f(x, y), & else \end{cases}$$

3.2 Image Feature Extraction

The results of dilation and erosion have the following relationships relate to the original image. $f \oplus B(x, y) \geq f(x, y)$, $f \ominus B(x, y) \leq f(x, y)$. So, the gray values of the pixels in the result of toggle contrast could be divided into three classes: (1) pixels with gray values larger than the gray values of the same pixels in the original image, which represent the image features produced by dilation operation and is denoted by D; (2) pixels with gray values smaller than the gray values of the same pixels in the original image, which represent the image features produced by erosion operation and is denoted by E; (3) pixels with gray values equal to the gray values of the same pixels in the original image. Therefore, toggle contrast could be used to extract image features. The images features D and E are calculated as follows.

$$D(f)(x, y) = \max(TCO(f)(x, y) - f(x, y), 0),$$

$$E(f)(x, y) = \max(f(x, y) - TCO(f)(x, y), 0).$$

Then, the original image could be obtained by using D and E as follows.

$$f = TCO(f) - D(f) + E(f). \tag{1}$$

3.3 Image Decomposition

Based on multi scale toggle contrast operator using multi scale structuring element, multi scale image features D_i and E_i could be calculated as follows.

$$D_i(f)(x, y) = \max(TCO_i(f)(x, y) - TCO_{i-1}(f)(x, y), 0),$$

$$E_i(f)(x, y) = \max(TCO_{i-1}(f)(x, y) - TCO_i(f)(x, y), 0).$$

$$TCO_0(f)(x, y) = f.$$

At each scale, the original image is decomposed into there images: $TCO_i(f)$, $D_i(f)$ and $E_i(f)$. $D_i(f)$ contains image details produced by dilation operation. $E_i(f)$ contains image details produced by erosion operation. $TCO_i(f)$ represents smoothed images which is the base image at scale i.

After this decomposition, the decomposed images could be processed following different application purposes.

3.4 Image Reconstruction

Based on expression (1), the original image could be reconstructed as follows.

$$f = TCO_0(f) = TCO_1(f) - D_1(f) + E_1(f)$$

$$= TCO_2(f) - D_2(f) + E_2(f) - D_1(f) + E_1(f)$$

$$= TCO_n(f) - D_n(f) + E_n(f) - ... - D_1(f) + E_1(f)$$

$$= TCO_n(f) - (D_n(f) + ... + D_1(f)) + (E_n(f) + ... + E_1(f)).$$

$$= TCO_n(f) - \sum_{i=1}^{n} D_i(f) + \sum_{i=1}^{n} E_i(f).$$

$$= TCO_n(f) - F(D_i(f)) + G(E_i(f)). \tag{2}$$

This expression indicates that, the original image could be easily reconstructed by using the decomposed three types images $TCO_i(f)$, $D_i(f)$ and $E_i(f)$.

3.5 Property

The procedure of image decomposition indicates that, this method does not need image sampling. So, the image could be decomposed without any information loss. And, the original image could be completely reconstructed from the decomposed image and does not need image sampling. So, the image could be reconstructed without any information loss. This will completely maintain the effect of image processing for different applications.

More importantly, different definition of the functions F and G in expression (2) may result in more efficient result.

4 Application of Image Enhancement

To show the efficiency the proposed method for image decomposition and reconstruction, an application of image enhancement is demonstrated.

4.1 Image Enhancement

A simple strategy of image enhancement is enhancing the image details of the original image. And, an efficient way is to obtain the largest gray values of pixels in image details at all scales. So, a simple image enhancement algorithm based on the multi scale toggle contrast operator is demonstrated below.

Step 1: Decompose the original image by using multi scale toggle contrast operator;

Step 2: Define F=G = $\max\limits_{i}$;

Step 3: *Reconstruct* the result image using expression (2).

4.2 Experimental Results

To show the efficiency of the image enhancement algorithm, the histogram equalization algorithm (HE) [5, 6] and contrast limited adaptive histogram equalization algorithm (CLAHE) [5] is used in this paper to compare with the proposed algorithm based on the proposed image decomposition and reconstruction method.

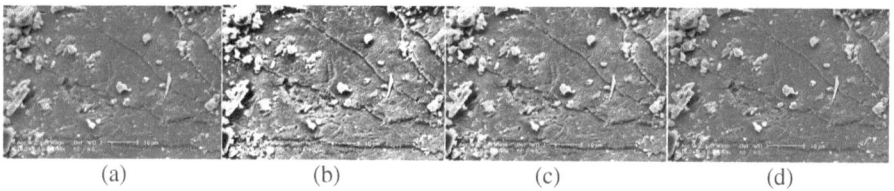

(a)   (b)   (c)   (d)

Fig. 1. Enhancement of mineral image. (a) Original image; (b) Enhanced result of HE; (c) Enhanced result of CLAHE; (d) Enhanced result of the proposed algorithm.

Figure 1 is an example of mineral image enhancement. Some details of the original image are not clear. Although HE makes some image details clear, many bright regions of the original image are over enhanced, which heavily affects the further application of the enhanced image. CLAHE obtains a better result than HE, but many regions are also over enhanced. The proposed algorithm based on image decomposition and reconstruction by using multi scale toggle contrast operator not only makes the original image clear, but also keeps the gray distribution of the original image, which achieves a better result than CLAHE and HE.

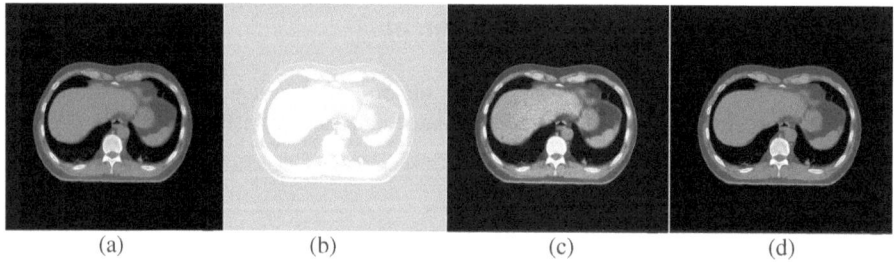

(a)   (b)   (c)   (d)

Fig. 2. Enhancement of medical image. (a) Original image; (b) Enhanced result of HE; (c) Enhanced result of CLAHE; (d) Enhanced result of the proposed algorithm.

Figure 2 is an example of medical image enhancement. HE could not enhance the original image because of large number of black pixels in the original image. CLAHE enhances the contrast of the original image, but some noises are also produced, especially in the bright regions. The proposed algorithm based on image decomposition and reconstruction by using multi scale toggle contrast operator enhances the original image and makes the edge regions clear, which performs better than CLAHE and HE.

The experimental results show that because the image decomposition and reconstruction by using multi scale toggle contrast operator could extract image details. The decomposed images could be used easily used for image enhancement. Moreover, the proposed image decomposition and reconstruction could be also used for other image applications.

5 Conclusions

A new image decomposition and reconstruction method based on multi scale toggle contrast operator is proposed in this paper. Toggle contrast operator using multi scale structuring elements could decompose the original image into different images which contain image features corresponding to different image scales. Also, the original image could be reconstructed from the decomposed images without any loss. Moreover, this image decomposition and reconstruction method does not need image sampling. An example of image enhancement application shows that the proposed image decomposition and reconstruction method is useful and efficient. More importantly, this method could be also used for other image application areas, such as image segmentation, image coding and so on.

Acknowledgments. This work is partly supported by the National Natural Science Foundation of China (60902056) and the Aeronautical Science Foundation of China (20090151007).

References

1. Yang, G.Z., Hansell, D.M.: CT Image Enhancement with Wavelet Analysis for the Detection of Small Airways Disease. IEEE Transactions on Medical Imaging 16, 953–961 (1997)
2. Candes, E.J., Donoho, D.L.: Curvelets – a Surprisingly Effective Nonadaptive Representation for Objects with Edges. In: Rabut, C., Cohen, A., Schumaker, L.L. (eds.) Curves and Surfaces, pp. 105–120
3. Morales, A., Acharya, T., Ko, S.: Morphological Pyramids with Alternating Sequential Filters. IEEE Transactions on Image Processing 4, 965–977 (1995)
4. Soille, P.: Morphological Image Analysis-Principle and Applications. Springer, Germany (2003)
5. Huang, K.Q., Wang, Q., Wu, Z.Y.: Natural Color Image Enhancement and Evaluation Algorithm Based on Human Visual System. Computer Vision and Image Understanding 103, 52–63 (2006)
6. Wan, Y., Shi, D.: Joint Exact Histogram Specification and Image Enhancement through the Wavelet Transform. IEEE Transactions on Image Processing 16, 2245–2250 (2007)

Prototype Design and Motion Analysis of a Spherical Robot

Shengju Sang[1,2], Ding Shen[2], Jichao Zhao[2], Wei Xia[2], and Qi An[1]

[1] School of Mechanical and Power Engineering, East China University of Science and Technology, Shanghai, P.R. China, 200237
[2] School of Information Science and Technology, Taishan College, Shandong Taian, P.R. China, 271021
{sang1108,sd-jack,zjc,xiwei0102}@163.com, anqi@ecust.edu.cn

Abstract. This paper describes a prototype analytical studies of a spherical robot with an internal mechanism for propulsion. The spherical robot is actuated and steered through a couter-weight pendulum connected to the main axle, a driving motor and a steer motor. On the basis of the structural characteristics of the spherical robot, its dynamic model is derived by applying the Lagrange-Routh equations briefly. The simulation model is established based on ADAMS software. The dynamic analysis and simulation are given to verify the validity of this design.

Keywords: spherical robot, prototype design, kinematics and dynamic model, analysis and simulation.

1 Introduction

The spherical robot as a member of the new type of mobile robots has made its debut in recent years. It consists of a ball-shaped outer shell to accommodate the whole mechanism inclusive of control devices and energy sources. They are believed to have several benefits, such as, locomotion with minimal friction, constrained spaces, omni-directions movement without ever overturning and so on. These advantages provide the spherical robots with stronger viability than the traditional mobile robots.

The spherical robots have been studied by using a variety of mechanisms. Halme et al. [1] developed the first spherical robot named Rollo from Helsinki University of Technology. It is a ball shape exploratory robot platform. The initial autonomous prototype operated on the sprung central member concept but this design was rejected in later prototypes. A spherical shape vehicle, called Spherical Mobile Robot (SMR) is proposed by Giulio Reina et al. in the Politecnico of Bari [2]. Bicchi et al. [3] developed a spherical vehicle consisting of a hollow sphere with a small car resting on the bottom. Spherobot was designed from Michigan State University, the open-loop control strategies which require less computation are implemented by Mukherjee et al. [4]. Bhattacharya et al. [5] proposed a driving mechanism that is a set of two mutually perpendicular rotors attached to the inside of the sphere. Ferriere et al. [6] developed a universal wheel to actuate a spherical ball to move the system, and in

R. Chen (Ed.): ICICIS 2011, Part I, CCIS 134, pp. 284–289, 2011.

their mechanism, the actuation system is out of the sphere. Spherical robots named August which can traverse omni-directionally were implemented in Azad University of Qazvin and the University of Tehran [7]. In the last decade, many other researchers have presented a lot of spherical robots [8,9]. They have made a great progress in a number of aspects, such as mechanism designing, dynamic modeling and control methods. Many spherical robots have been developed on the basis of the principles of gravity center offset and angular momentum conservation [11].

This paper presents a spherical robot that can achieve many kinds of unique motion, such as all-direction driving and motion on rough ground, without loss of stability. The prototype of the spherical robot is illustrated in Fig. 1. A semi-hard transparent plastic shell with the diameter of 400 mm was chosen for the tests to allow visual inspections of the behavior of the mechanisms during operation.

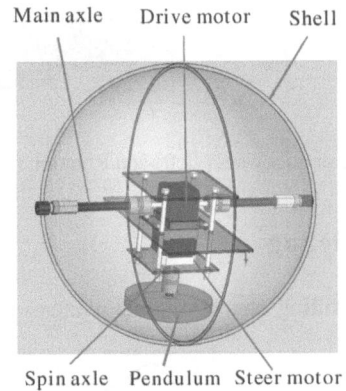

Fig. 1. Prototype of the spherical robot

2   Design

The spherical robot presented in this paper has an external spherical shape. It is composed of a spherical shell, a main axle, spin axis, a pedulum, a steer motor which mainly controls the steering motion and a drive motor for forward or backward. Fig.1 shows the structure of the spherical mobile robot.

The spherical shell is made up of acrylic material having 5 mm thickness. The inner radius of the robot is 195 mm. The transparent acrylic spherical shell enables researchers to monitor the state of internal mechanism while in motion. The spherical robots work on the principle of change in the center of gravity. A crucial aspect of the design is to place the internal components such that the center of mass of the robot is exactly at the geometric center of the sphere. This is very important so that the robot will not tip over on its own. The easiest way to achieve this is to place all the parts symmetrically. It is absolutely critical that there be no relative motion between the two hemispheres while in motion. This can be achieved by an arrangement for screwing a connecting rod along the axis of the sphere.

A counter-weight pendulum is connected to the main axle that runs through the whole sphere. The batteries used are placed at the end of the pendulum, thus lowering the center of mass for the robot. Two step motors are employed in the spherical robot. One motor raises the pendulum and, by moving the center of mass, creates momentum forward or backwards as shown in Fig. 2(left). The rotation of the steer motor causes the counter-weight pendulum to rotate about the spin axis (see the right part of Fig. 2). As a result, the robot will rotate in opposite direction accoding to the principle of angular momentum.

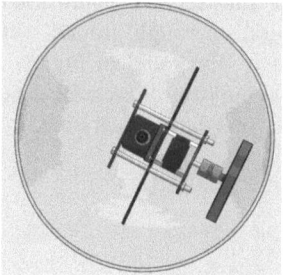 

Fig. 2. Movement forward or backwards (left) and Rotation in opposite direction (right)

3 Mathematical Modeling

Consider a spherical robot rolling on a horizontal plane as Fig.3.

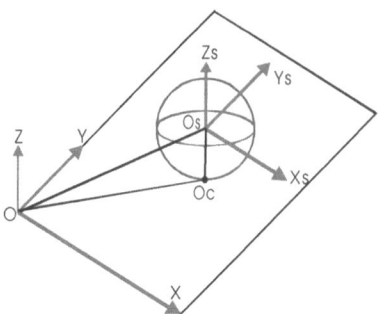

Fig. 3. Coordinates setup of the spherical mobile robot

The dynamic model in this paper is basically derived by using kinetic energy associated with generalized and quasi-velocities. These velocities are obtained from the non-slipping constraint condition of the robot. The simplified Boltzman-Hamel equation (1) is used to model the dynamic motion of the robot.

$$\frac{d}{d_t}\frac{\partial \overline{T}}{\partial \omega_l} + \sum_{j=1}^{n}\sum_{s=1}^{n}\beta_{sl}\gamma_{sj}\frac{\partial \overline{T}}{\partial \omega_j} - \sum_{j=1}^{n}\beta_{jl}\frac{\partial \overline{T}}{\partial q_j} = N_l \tag{1}$$

where, ω is the vector of quasi-velocities, $\overline{T}$ is the kinetic energy, N_I is the generalized force, β and γ are the coefficients, I denotes independent quasi coordinates and n is the number of the generalized coordinate q_j.

An inertial coordinate frame is attached to the surface and denoted as XYZ with its origin at the point O. The body coordinate axes $X_sY_sZ_s$, parallel to XYZ, are attached to the sphere and have their origin at O_s. The set of generalized coordinates describing the sphere consists of 1) coordinates of the contact point O_c on the plane, and 2) any set of variables describing the orientation of the sphere.

Because the spherical robot cannot move in Z direction, five variables $(x, y, \varphi, \beta, \psi)$ are enough to describe its configuration. Let (x, y) be the coordinates of O_s in the reference coordinates, and (φ, β, ψ) be the rotation angles around three coordinate axes, namely, X, Y, and Z, which denote the pose of the spherical robot. The chosen quasi-velocities of the robot can be expressed in matrix form as

$$\begin{bmatrix} \dot{x} \\ \dot{y} \\ \dot{\psi} \\ \dot{\varphi} \\ \dot{\beta} \end{bmatrix} = \begin{bmatrix} 0 & \gamma & 0 & 1 & 0 \\ -\gamma & 0 & 0 & 0 & 1 \\ \cos\psi\tan\beta & -\sin\psi\tan\beta & 1 & 0 & 0 \\ -\cos\psi\sin\beta & \sin\psi\sin\beta & 0 & 0 & 0 \\ \sin\psi & \cos\psi & 0 & 0 & 0 \end{bmatrix} \tag{2}$$

where, $\omega_1, \omega_2, \omega_3$ are the projections of the angular velocities of the robot on axes X_s, Y_s, Z_s of the moving coordinate frame $O_sX_sY_sZ_s$, which is parallel with fixed frame $OXYZ$ shown in Fig.3, x and y are geometric center of the robot, r is radius of the robot and φ, β, ψ are the pose of the robot in the XYZ Euler angles.

Hence, the dynamic equation can be expressed by quasi-velocities as

$$mr^2\dot{\omega}_1 7/5 = m_1^0 - rv_2$$
$$mr^2\dot{\omega}_2 7/5 = m_2^0 - rv_1 \tag{3}$$
$$mr^2\dot{\omega}_3 2/5 = m_3^0$$

where, m_i^0 i (i=1,2,3) are the projections of the main moment m0 on axes X_s, Y_s, Z_s of the moving coordinate frame $O_sX_sY_sZ_s$ on the robot, V1 and V2 are the projections of force vector V on axes x and y, and m is the mass of the robot.

4 Control Method

The spherical robot and its internal units are considered as multi-body dynamics in most models. Moreover, the rolling without slipping motion of spherical robots results in a nonholonomic constraint. Accordingly, various control laws are developed based on the model. The most common approach to reduce a complex dynamic model into a usable form for control is through linearization. However, an approximate linearization of nonholonomic systems causes loss of controllability. Hence, it is necessary to maintain controllability of the system during linear approximation.

Fuzzy logic control for wheeled mobile robots has been introduced in Ref. [10]. The control Algorithm including longitudinal motion, lateral motion, speed controller and roll angle controller will be discussed in another article in details.

5   Simulation and Discussion

ADAMS is the most widely used multi-body dynamics and motion analysis software nowaday. Unlike most CAD embedded tools, Adams incorporates real physics by simultaneously solving equations for kinematic, static, quasi-static, and dynamics.

The detail analysis and simulation of the spherical robot has been discussed in Ref. [11]. In this section, simulation results on the spherical robot by ADAMS using a time step 0.01s are presented to demonstrate the effectiveness of the design and verify the path following performance.

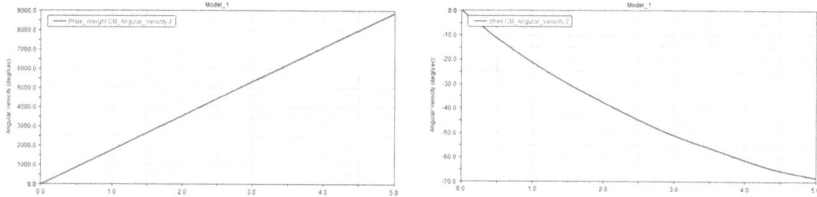

Fig. 4. Angular velocity of the pendulum (left) and angular velocity of the shell (right)

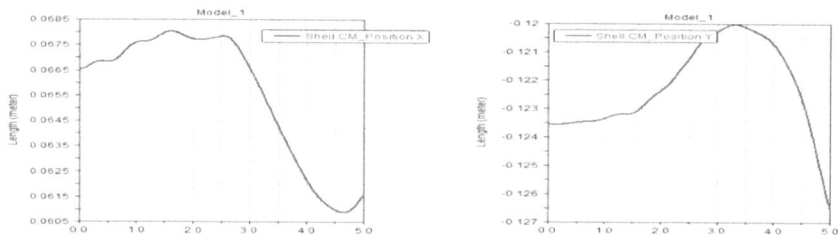

Fig. 5. Movement of the robot in x axis (left), Movement of the robot in y axis (right)

Fig. 4 shows angular velocity of the spherical robot as well as the pendulum. Fig. 5 shows Movement of the robot on the x-y plane.

For several missions, the experimental results agree well with those of the model. In each case, the experimental trajectory follows the predicted one within a reasonable accuracy. Some factors that contribute to these inaccuracies are: 1) the center of mass of the robot is not exactly at the geometric center of the robot; 2) imperfections on the surface of the sphere; and 3) open-loop nature of the robot control.

6   Conclusions

A mathematical model of the spherical robot motion has been developed in this paper. The model is validated through a set of simulations. Simulations and experimental trajectories of the robot on the plane are found to agree to a reasonable accuracy and the methods are effective. However, experiments also show that the spherical robot has a strong tendency to oscillate and the uneven ground could make the robot oscillate for a long time. So the approaches have good feasibility and it is expected to be improved in the future.

Acknowledgments. The work was partially supported by the Natural Science Foundation of Shandong, China (2009ZRA01105), the science and technology development fund of Tai'an (20083002 and 20092016).

References

1. Halme, A., Schonberg, T., Wang, Y.: Motion control of a spherical mobile robot. In: 4th IEEE International Workshop on Advanced Motion Control, pp. 100–106. IEEE Press, Mie University (1996)
2. Reina, G., Foglia, M., Milella, A., Gentile, A.: Rough-terrain traversability for a cylindrical shaped mobile robot. In: Int. Conf. on Mechatronics, pp. 148–155. IEEE Press, Los Alamitos (2004)
3. Bicchi, A., Balluch, A.: Introducing the 'SPHERICLE': an experimental testbed for research and teaching in nonholonomy. In: Proc. of the 1997 IEEE Int. Conf. Robotics and Automation, pp. 2620–2625. IEEE Press, Albuquerque (1995)
4. Mukherjee, R., Minor, M.A., Pukrushpan, J.T.: Simple Motion Planning Strategies for Spherobot: A Spherical Mobile Robot. In: Proc. IEEE Int. Conf. on Decision and Control, pp. 2132–2137. IEEE Press, Los Alamitos (1999)
5. Bhattacharya, S., Agrawal, S.K.: Spherical Rolling Robot: A Design and Motion Planning Studies. In: Proc. of Int. Conf. on Robotics and Automation. IEEE Press, Los Alamitos (2000)
6. Ferriere, L., Raucent, B., Campion, G.: Design of Omnimobile Robot Wheels. In: Proc. of Int. Conf. on Robotics and Automation, pp. 3664–3670. IEEE Press, Los Alamitos (1996)
7. Javadi, A., Mojabi, P.: Introducing august: a novel strategy for an omnidirectional spherical Rolling Robot. In: Proc. of Int. Conf. on Robotics and Automation. IEEE Press, Los Alamitos (2002)
8. Zhan, Q., Liu, Z., Cai, Y.: A Back-stepping Based Trajectory Tracking Controller for a Non-chained Nonholonomic Spherical Robot. Chinese Journal of Aeronautics 21, 472–480 (2008)
9. Oumer, N.W.: Development of Wireless Control System for a Spherical Robot. Master's thesis, Helsniki University of Technology (2009)
10. Sang, S., Zhao, J., Wu, H., An, Q.: Fuzzy Logic Control for Wheeled Mobile Robots. In: 6th Int. Conf. on Fuzzy Systems and Knowledge Discovery, pp. 237–241. IEEE Press, Los Alamitos (2009)
11. Sang, S., Zhao, J., Wu, H., Chen, S., An, Q.: Modeling and Simulation of a Spherical Mobile Robot. J. ComSIS (Special Issue) 7, 51–62 (2010)

An Algorithm of Fast Mining
Frequent Neighboring Class Set

Gang Fang, Hong Ying, and Jiang Xiong

College of Math. and Computer Science, Chongqing Three Gorges University
Chongqing 404000, P.R. China
cqwzjsjfg@163.com, dcs-yh@263.net, xjcq123@sohu.com

Abstract. For these prombles that present frequent neighboring class set mining algorithms have more repeated computing and redundancy neighboring class sets, this paper proposes an algorithm of fast mining frequent neighboring class set, which is suitable for mining frequent neighboring class set of objects in large spatial data. The algorithm uses the approach of going back to create database of neighboring class set, and uses the approach of generating proper subset of neighboring class set to compute support by descending search, it only need scan once database to extract frequent neighboring class set. The algorithm improves mining efficiency by two ways. One is that it needn't generate candidate frequent neighboring class set, the other is that it needn't repeated scan database when computing support. The result of experiment indicates that the algorithm is faster and more efficient than present algorithms when mining frequent neighboring class set in large spatial data.

Keywords: neighboring class set, proper subset, going back, descending search, spatial data mining.

1   Introduction

Mining spatial association rules from Geographic Information Databases are known as discovery spatial co-location pattern as in [1], which are some implicit rules expressing construct and association of spatial objects in Geographic Information Databases, and also expressing hierarchy and correlation of different subsets of spatial association or spatial data in Geographic Information Databases as in [2]. Nowadays, in spatial data mining, there are mainly three kinds of mining spatial association rules as in [3], such as, layer covered based on clustering as in [3], mining based on spatial transaction as in [2, 4, and5] and mining based on non-spatial transaction as in [3]. The first two methods may be also used to mine frequent neighboring class set, the spatial association as in [4, 5] is quite single, because they only express spatial association among these objects which are all close to objective. However, neighboring class set expresses another spatial association among these objects which are close to each other. MFNCS as in [2] uses the similar method of Apriori to search frequent neighboring class set, and so the algorithm has some repeated computing and superfluous neighboring class set, its efficiency is not efficient. Hence, this paper

R. Chen (Ed.): ICICIS 2011, Part I, CCIS 134, pp. 290–295, 2011.

proposes an algorithm of fast mining frequent neighboring class set, denoted by FMFNCS, which may avoid repeated computing and scanning database.

2 Definition and Problem Description

Every object in spatial domain constitutes spatial data set, which is expressed as data structure, denoted by <Object Identify, Class Identify and Spatial Location>. Here, identify of different class in spatial data set is denoted by Class Identify, identify of different object instance in the same class is denoted by Object Identify, location coordinate of object is denoted by Spatial Location. We regard an object as an instance of corresponding class, and so spatial data set is made up of these instances of spatial Class Identify. Sets of Class Identify are thought as a class set, denoted by C = $\{C_1, C_2 ... C_m\}$ means there are m different classes.

Definition 1. Neighboring Class Set, it is a subset of class set in spatial data set, which is expressed as $\{C_{t1}, C_{t2} ... C_{tk}\}$ ($t_k \leq m$) denoted by NCS. Let I = $\{i_{t1}, i_{t2} ... i_{tk}\}$ be an instance of neighboring class set denoted by NCS = $\{C_{t1}, C_{t2}, ..., C_{tk}\}$, here, i_{tj} is an instance of C_{tj} ($j \in 1, 2... k$).
Example, let $\{D, E, G\}$ be a NCS, and I = $\{D_3, E_1, G_2\}$ is an instance of NCS.

Definition 2. Neighboring Class Set Length, its value is equal to the number of class set contained in neighboring class set. If the length of NCS is equal to k, it is denoted by k-NCS.

Definition 3. Right Instance of Neighboring Class Set, let $I=\{i_{t1}, i_{t2}, ..., i_{tk}\}$ be an instance of NCS, if $\forall$ i_p and i_q ($i_p, i_q \in I$), and dist (i_p, i_q) $\leq$ d, and then we think **I** be an right instance of NCS. Here, **d** is the minimal distance used by deciding two spatial objects are close to each other, Euclidean distance is expressed as dist (i_p, i_q).

Definition 4. Neighboring Class Set Support, it is equal to the number of right instance of neighboring class set, which is denoted by support (NCS).

Definition 5. Frequent Neighboring Class Set, its support is not less than the minimal support given by user.

As above knowledge, mining frequent neighboring class set is expressed as follows:
    Input: (1) Class set is denoted by C = $\{C_1, C_2 ... C_m\}$, instance set is denoted by I = $\{i_1, i_2 ... i_n\}$, each i_k ($i_k \in$ I) is expressed as above mentioned data structure. (2) Minimal distance is denoted by **d**. (3) Minimal support is denoted by **s**.
    Output: Frequent neighboring class set.

3 The Algorithm of Fast Mining Frequent Neighboring Class Set

3.1 Using the Method of Going Back to Create NCS Database

To find corresponding NCS of right instance in spatial data set, the algorithm uses the method of going back to create NCS database used by a specifically data structure.

Structure neighboring class set {

   Int Count; //saving the number of right instance belong to NCS

   Int Length; // saving Neighboring Class Set Length

   Int [m] Location; // saving the location of class in spatial class set} NCS

Input: (1) Class set is denoted by C = {C_1, C_2... C_m}. (2) Right instance set is denoted by I = {i_1, i_2... i_n}.

Output: The array as NCS of saving neighboring class set.

Step 1: Scanning a right instance from right instance set to gain the class as C_j contained in each i_k ($i_k \in I$) by its i_k.Class Identify, and gain the location as No_j of the class as C_j in class set as C. And NCS of i_k is made of these classes frontal gained.

Step 2: Computing corresponding value of neighboring class set denoted by **Order** via the approach, that is **Order** = $\sum_{j=1}^{L} 2^{No_j - 1}$ (Length of NCS is denoted by L)

Step 3: If NCS [Order-1].Count=0, namely, there is not information of neighboring class set, and then saving this information which is expressed as follows:

Count=1, Length=L, Location [0] =No_1, Location [1] =No_2... Location [L-1] =No_L.

Otherwise, there is information of neighboring class sets, only let Count=Count+1.

Step 4: Repeated executing from step1 to step3 until finishing scanning all right instances, and finally inputting NCS.

Example, here class set is expressed as C = {D, E, F, G, H}, the first three right instances are express as I_1 = {D_3, F_5, G_6, H_5}, I_2 = {D_3, E_4, H_2}, I_3 = {D_2, F_4, G_5, H_3}.

Using the method of going back to create NCS database is expressed as follows:

NCS of I_1 is expressed as {D, F, G, H}, and the location sequence is expressed as {1, 3, 4, 5}, and then Order=$2^{(1-1)}$ + $2^{(3-1)}$ + $2^{(4-1)}$ + $2^{(5-1)}$ =29, because of this, namely, NCS [Order-1]. Count = 0, this information is saved in NCS [28] as follows:

Count=1, Length=4, Location[0]=1, Location[1]=3, Location[2]=4, Location[3]=5.

NCS of I_2 is expressed as {D, E, H}, and the location sequence is expressed as {1, 2, 5}, and then Order=$2^{(1-1)}$ + $2^{(2-1)}$ + $2^{(5-1)}$ =19, for NCS [Order-1].Count = 0, this information is saved in NCS [18] as follows:

Count=1, Length=3, Location[0]=1, Location[1]=2, Location[2]=5.

NCS of I_3 is expressed as {D, F, G, H}, and the location sequence is expressed as {1, 3, 4, 5}, and then Order=$2^{(1-1)}$ + $2^{(3-1)}$ + $2^{(4-1)}$ + $2^{(5-1)}$ =29, but NCS [Order-1]. Count = 1, i.e. NCS [28] has already saved information, and Count=Count+1=2....

3.2 The Method of Generating Proper Subset of Neighboring Class Set

Let NCS be a neighboring class set, its information is expressed as Count=1, Length=L, Location [0] =No_1, Location [1] =No_2... Location [L-1] =No_L. Aiming at this NCS, the process of generating its proper subset is expressed as follows:

Input: a neighboring class set as NCS.

Output: an integer array as PS which saves subsets of NCS.

Step 1: Gaining the sum of proper subset, which is denoted by Num=2^{Length}-2, here void is also one of proper subsets, but it is not considered.

Step 2: Via binary bit of a number from 1 to (2^{Length}-2), the location of class contained in proper subset would be gained, and after computing corresponding value of proper subset of NCS, it will be written to PS. The process is expressed as follows:

Firstly, gaining the value from $(2^{Length}-2)$ to 1 by descending, and then the value is turned into binary system, the location as No_j is gained from right to left according to binary bit. Finally, computing corresponding value of proper subset, which is denoted by Order, Order=$\sum 2^{Location[No_j-1]-1}$ is written to PS.

Step 3: Repeating step2 until variable is equal to 1, and inputting PS.

Example, here is a NCS as {D, E, H}, which is saved in NCS [18] as follows:

Count=1, Length=3, Location[0]=1, Location[1]=2, Location[2]=5.

The process of generating proper subset is expressed as follows:

Num=$2^{Length}-2=6$, variable is from $2^{Length}-2$ to 1, denoted by X.

X= 6 = $(110)_2$, $No_1=2$, $No_2=3$, Order = $2^{Location[No_1-1]-1}+2^{Location[No_2-1]-1}=18$, PS [0] =18.

Via chapter 3.1, corresponding neighboring class set of this value should save in NCS [Order-1], which is expressed as {E, H}. Obviously, it is one of proper subset.

X= 5 = $(101)_2$, $No_1=1$, $No_2=3$, Order = $2^{Location[No_1-1]-1}+2^{Location[No_2-1]-1}=17$, PS [1] =17.

In a similar way, corresponding neighboring class set of this value should save in NCS [16], which is expressed as {D, H}. Obviously, it is one of proper subset.

X= 4 = $(100)_2$, $No_1=3$, Order = $2^{Location[No_1-1]-1}=16$, PS [3] =16.

In a similar way, corresponding neighboring class set of this value should save in NCS [15], which is expressed as {H}. Obviously, it is one of proper subset.

X= 3 = $(011)_2$, $No_1=1$, $No_2=2$, Order = $2^{Location[No_1-1]-1}+2^{Location[No_2-1]-1}=3$, PS [4] =3.

In a similar way, corresponding neighboring class set of this value should save in NCS [2], which is expressed as {D, E}. Obviously, it is one of proper subset.

X= 2 = $(010)_2$, $No_1=2$, Order = $2^{Location[No_1-1]-1}=2$, PS [5] =2.

In a similar way, corresponding neighboring class set of this value should save in NCS [1], which is expressed as {E}. Obviously, it is one of proper subset.

X= 1 = $(001)_2$, $No_1=1$, Order = $2^{Location[No_1-1]-1}=1$, PS [6] =1.

In a similar way, corresponding neighboring class set of this value should save in NCS [0], which is expressed as {D}. Obviously, it is one of proper subset.

3.3 The Process of Mining Frequent Neighboring Class Set

Input: (1) Class set is denoted by $C = \{C_1, C_2...C_m\}$. (2) Instance set is denoted by $I = \{i_1, i_2...i_n\}$. (3) The minimal distance is denoted by **d**. (4) The minimal support is denoted by **s**.

Output: Frequent neighboring class set.

Step 1: Computing the entire right instance as **I'** from instance set as **I** by the minimal distance as **d**.

Step 2: Gaining neighboring class set as NCS after scanning once right instance set via the method of going back in chapter 3.1.

Step 3: Scanning once NCS by descending, aiming to each NCS[j], via the method of generating proper subset in chapter 3.2, and gaining an integer array as PS_j, $\forall$ $PS_j[t]$ ($PS_j[t] \in PS_j$), let NCS[$PS_j[t]$-1].Count= NCS[$PS_j[t]$-1].Count+ NCS[j].Count.

Step 4: Rescanning NCS to find all these NCS[j](NCS[j].Count $\geq$ s), and writing j to F after deleting corresponding label as j_k of subset of NCS[j] from F.

Step 5: Output NCS [F[i]] by the reverse method of going back.

4 The Analysis and Comparing of Capability

At present, there are very little documents of research frequent neighboring class set. MFNCS as [2] uses idea of Apriori to find frequent neighboring class set, which is made of three stages, firstly, computing all the frequent 1-NCS, secondly, generating all the 2-NCS by range query, and generating all the k-NCS (k > 2) by iteration. The algorithm has some repeated computing and superfluous neighboring class sets. In order to indicate superiority of proposed algorithm, denoted by FMFNCS, we compare the algorithm with MFNCS as follows:

4.1 The Analysis of Capability

Let $C = \{C_1, C_2...C_m\}$ be a class set, and let $I = \{i_1, i_2...i_n\}$ be an instance set, let n_k ($n=\sum n_k$) be the number of instance of C_k.

Time Complexity. Computing of FMFNCS mainly includes four parts which are expressed as computing right instance, creating NCS database, computing proper subset of NCS and search frequent NCS. Time complexity is expressed as follows:

$$(2^m - 1)[n^2 C_m^2 / m^2 + 3 + (2^m - 4)/2].$$

Computing of MFNCS mainly includes three parts which are expressed as computing all the frequent 1-NCS, generating all the 2-NCS by range query and generating all the k-NCS (k>2) by iteration. Time complexity is expressed as follows:

$$(2^m - 1)[n^2 C_m^2 / m^2 + n + (2^m - 1)].$$

FMFNCS need not generate candidate frequent NCS in mining process and it hasn't superfluous NCS. And it need scan once database to reduce repeated computing. Therefore, FMFNCS is more efficient than MFNCS.

Space Complexity. Space complexity of MFNCS is expressed as O ($\alpha \cdot 2^m$), α is parameter about support. Space complexity of FMFNCS is expressed as O ($\beta \cdot 2^m$), β is parameter about support and class set length. If right instances in spatial data set are hyper dispersion, space utilization ratio of FMFNCS is too low.

4.2 The Comparing of Experimental Result

Now we use result of experiment to testify above analyses. Two mining algorithms are used to generate frequent neighboring class set from 12267 right instances, whose class sets are expressed as value from 3 to 8191, neighboring class set length is not equal to 1, the number of spatial class set is denoted by m=13, the number of right instance included by these neighboring class set observe the discipline, namely, Order of NCS is denoted by 8191 has one right instance, Order of NCS is denoted by 8190 has two right instances, Order of NCS is denoted by 8189 has one right instance, Order of NCS is denoted by 8188 has two right instances, ….

Experimental circumstances: Intel(R) Celeron(R) M CPU 420 @ 1.60 GHz, 1.24G, language of the procedure is Visual C# 2005.NET, OS is Windows XP Professional. The experimental result is expressed as Fig. 1. The comparing of runtime is expressed as Fig. 2 as support and length of neighboring class set changes.

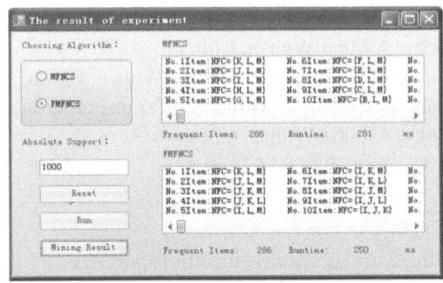

Fig. 1. The experimental result

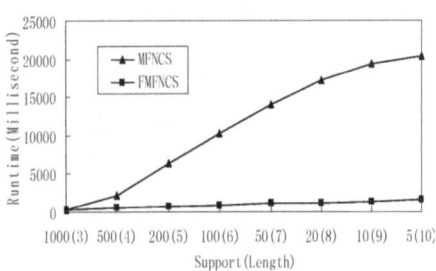

Fig. 2. The comparing of runtime

5   Conclusion

This paper proposes an algorithm of fast mining frequent neighboring class set, which may efficiently avoid repeated computing and scanning database. It is more efficient than presented algorithm when mining frequent neighboring class set.

Acknowledgments. This work was fully supported by science and technology research projects of Chongqing Education Commission (Project No. KJ091108), and it was also supported by science and technology research projects of Wanzhou District Science and Technology Committee (Project No. 2010-23-01) and Chongqing Three Gorges University (Project No. 10QN-22, 24 and 30).

References

1. Ma, R.H., Pu, Y.X., Ma, X.D.: GIS Spatial Association Pattern Ming. Science Press, Beijing (2007)
2. Ma, R.H., He, Z.Y.: Mining Complete and Correct Frequent Neighboring Class Sets from Spatial Databases. Journal of Geomatics and Information Science of Wuhan University 32(2), 112–114 (2007)
3. Zhang, X.W., Su, F.Z., Shi, Y.S., Zhang, D.D.: Research on Progress of Spatial Association Rule Mining. Journal of Progress in Geography 26(6), 119–128 (2007)
4. Liu, Y.L., Fang, G.: The research and application of a transaction complement mining algorithm. Journal of Computer Engineering and Applications 44(35), 168–170 (2008)
5. Fang, G., Liu, Y.L.: Application of Binary System Based Spatial Mining Algorithm in Mobile Intelligent Systems. Journal of Southwest University (Natural Science Edition) 31(1), 95–99 (2009)

Research and Development Trends of Car Networking

Wei He[1,2], Zhixiong Li[3], and Guotao Xie[3]

[1] ITS Institute, Engineering Research Center of Transportation Safety (Ministry of Education),
Wuhan University of Technology, 430063 Wuhan, China
[2] Transportation Research Center, Wuhan Institute of Technology, 430073 Wuhan, China
[3] Key Laboratory of Marine Power Engineering and Technology (Ministry of Transportation),
Wuhan University of Technology, 430063 Wuhan, China
hewei@mail.wit.edu.cn, lzx_520@163.com

Abstract. With the rapid development of the world economy, road transport has become increasingly busy. An unexpected incident would cause serious traffic disaster due to traffic accidents. To solve this problem, the intelligent transportation system (ITS), which is important for the health developments of the city transportation, has become a hot topic. The car networking provides a new way for intelligent transportation system. It can ensure intelligent control and monitoring of urban road with high performance. This paper described the concept of car networking and related technology both in oversea and domestic. The importance of car networking to achieve vehicle and details of the car networking related technologies were illustrated firstly. Then, attentions focus on the research nodus of the car networking. Lastly, the development trend of car networking research was discussed.

Keywords: Intelligent transportation system (ITS), urban road, car networking, research and development trend.

1 Introduction

With the rapid development of the digital, network, information and intelligent, improve the urban transport system is becoming increasingly. Car networking concept start walks into the people's vision. Vehicle networking is a identification technology that electronic tags which loaded on a vehicle via radio frequency identification technology to achieve extraction and effective use of the attribute information and static, dynamic information for all vehicles on the information network platform, and according to different functional requirements to regulate effectively and to provide integrated services for all vehicles, and achieve the ultimate goal of intelligent transportation and wisdom city [1-6].

2 Situation and Development of Car Networking

2.1 Overseas

In order to alleviate traffic jam, European cities has begun to deploy a collaborative communication system between road and car. Road can direct dialogue with car

R. Chen (Ed.): ICICIS 2011, Part I, CCIS 134, pp. 296–301, 2011.

through a simple lights, crossroads, or other infrastructure receptors, etc, can directly obtain new roads, understand the potential risks. The European Union government hopes to complete the system build and test run before 2013. Because of traffic jam, caused by time, fuel and other damage is considerable, the implementation of this technology will greatly improve the situation.

The United States has apply vehicle electronic information system to military equipment. Land combat vehicles fusion countless complex electronic components, Through these electronic components to command and control, communications, intelligence, surveillance and reconnaissance, manipulation of defensive or offensive weapon system and the vehicle itself. American's IVHS system and Japan's VICS system achieve intelligent traffic management and information service through the establishment of an effective information and communication.

CeBIT show in Germany in 2010 to display the "CeBIT intelligent transportation system" shows a complete industrial chain of intelligent traffic handling system. The system use the U.S. Global Positioning System (GPS) and Galileo positioning system signals, to ensure accurate data and get the optimal location of usability. According to the latest EU plans the Galileo positioning system will initially be used to provide search and rescue services before 2014.

2.2 Current Status of the Research in Domestic

"2030 Future Car" revealed a beautiful picture of the future automotive society to people in Shanghai World Expo. Intelligent Vehicle Networking enables the car connected with the traffic information net, intelligent Grid and community information network, which can help drivers get real-time information and do a wise travel-related decision. Besides, cars not only can rely on Vehicle Networking to achieve unmanned vehicles, but can prevent accidents and park intelligently.

In China, Intelligent Transportation continues to accelerate the pace of development, especially in Beijing, Shanghai and other big cities. Some features of vehicle information systems and related service can be an important addition to Intelligent Transportation. At the same time, integration with the Intelligent Transportation will accelerate car service market in China.

2.3 Developmental of Vehicle Networking

Today, most large and medium cities in China, the traffic congestion is people who feel tired and growing traffic accident pose a threat to the lives of the people, and the emergence of networked vehicles will greatly improve the situation, which has the following advantages :

(1) Vehicle Networking can enhance the efficiency of the road usage. Intelligent transportation technology can reduce traffic congestion by about 60%, short-distance transport efficiency by nearly 70% and increase the existing road network capacity by 2 ~ 3 times. Besides, the number of stops can be reduced by 30%, travel time decreased by 13% to 45% and the efficiency in the use of vehicles can be increased by 50% or more.

(2) Vehicle Networking can reduce vehicle energy consumption. China's oil consumption be after the United States, ranking second in the world dependence on

oil imports reached 56%. Transportation vehicle fuel oil consumption accounted for 40%. Under the control of intelligent traffic, the average speed increased. Because of that, the fuel consumption and emissions be reduced, fuel consumption can be reduced by 15% also.

(3) Vehicle Networking can reduce traffic accidents. Intelligent transportation technology will greatly enhance the management of roads and reduce traffic accidents efficiently. Vehicle safety accident rate can be reduced by 20%. Each year, the number of deaths caused by traffic accidents will be decreased by 30% to 70%.

3 Technology of Car Networking

3.1 Network Infrastructure of Car Networking

Vehicle networking must be based on the public network, which should connected with the car and cover all the places that the car go to. Besides, the net should be 7×24-hour online. That can achieve voice, images, data and other information transmission. Only public communication network to meet these conditions.

Nowadays, the based communication network that the three major operators buillt has many advantages, such as extensive coverage, excellent performance and high reliability. Especially 3G, the net construction will be completed this year, and in the next two years, it will be achieve the basic coverage. The rapid development of 3G mobile communication network can provide broadband wireless information transmission channel, to better achieve nationwide wireless roaming, and can handle images, video streaming and other forms of media, which provides a solid network network infrastructure for Vehicle networking.

In fact, Shanghai Telecom services as mobile communications and information services providers in the entire automotive industry chain, not only coordinate national CDMA communications network, but designed specifical national voice + data flow of the package for the OnStar (OnStar), transform the country move communications network billing model. Because of that, Shanghai GM's vehicles can pass the country and get the communication network services.

3.2 Car Networking Related Technologies

There are several levels of vehicle network: the bottom is the intelligent transportation system, providing the vehicle network infrastructure required; the second layer is the core of networked vehicles - Intelligent Internet car, and connected to the Internet; third layer is the vehicle Internet services, such as security services, emergency rescue services.

Intelligent Transportation is a transportation of a real-time, accurate, efficient Integrated transportation management and control systems established by using advanced sensor technology, communication technology, data processing, network technology, automatic control technology, and information dissemination technology in the organic management system[1].

Intelligent Transportation System (ITS) improve the transport operating environment by improving transport infrastructure and traffic information services. Many countries are actively developing intelligent transportation system-related technologies, such as the adjustment of public transport and the intelligent parking control system, never stop toll collection system and advanced traveler system, and so on. Now, the Volvo S80 can occur in the eye shadow of the obstacle to remind drivers; lane departure warning system to monitor whether the vehicle is in motion the gradual missed Drive; a dynamic maintaining system of Mercedes-Benz vehicles and radar assisted dynamic intelligent cruise control system of Lexus can make vehicles maintain a fixed distance from the vehicle in front.

3.3 Hot and Difficult Technology of Car Networking

a) RFID: RFID is a non-contact automatic identification technology, through the RF signal automatic target recognition and access to relevant data, to identify work without human intervention and can work in a variety of harsh environments. It can identify high-speed moving objects and operating multiple tags, With non-contact, reading distance, environmental adaptability, can carry more information storage, high-speed characteristics of batch reading. Applied it in the automatic identification and management of moving vehicles, vehicles can be collected through the RFID sensor devices and other information connected with the network to achieve the vehicle identification and management of intelligent network, build "a Car networking" management platform, provide urban traffic management and supervision of the relevant service functions. Have broad application prospects[2].

With the RFID chip technology and process development, improve the sensitivity, making the paste label on the windscreen of the car as a reliable source of information RFID electronic license become possible. And the corresponding adaptation of the RFID reader technology continues to upgrade the kernel, The RFID front-end information acquisition system performance will be increased. Currently, part cities of China has applications to achieve better in management of motor vehicle road and bridge fees and track down the intelligent management of city vehicles. But in the application of the promotion, there were some problems are focused on the following two aspects:

(1) The dates security and confidentiality of the RFID tag and system directly affect the reliability and authenticity of the whole system, as well as data protection operations.

(2) Reasonable definition of the application platform to build applications in many fields, making the " Car networkinged" to provide efficient management and service operations.

b) Wireless Technology: Real-time information exchange between and interaction between car and road, car and car is the core technology of the Car networking, undoubtedly, wireless technology play a major role in this process[3].

Technology used in vehicle location, communications and fees is DSRC (Dedicated Short Range Communication) and VPS(Vehicle Positioning System). DSRC is a microwave technology, a special technology on intelligent transportation systems used for motor vehicles payment without stopping. DSRC standards mainly involve two types of equipment: RSU(Road-Side Unit) and OBU(On-Board Unit). It is through communication between the RSU and the OBU, motor vehicles with OBU passed by arrangement with RSU antenna mast with the speed of (50 ~ 60Km / h), RSU vehicles and roadside equipment to achieve the data exchange. VPS use Global Positioning System(GPS) and Global System for Mobile Communication(GSM), motor vehicles payment without stopping by communication device with the car. Have a wider range of applications on Car navigation and voice communications for help field.

But wireless technology should meet the requirements of networking applications which interact real-time and make tradition compatible with future. Without compatibility and transition, there can be no real Car networking applications, today how to achieve compatibility and transition of old and new systems is a hot and difficult topic in the development of Car networking. "Compatibility" and "interaction" means as follows:

Firstly, it should be compatible with the current signal system of the road, making vehicles in the network interact with road information; Secondly, it should be compatible with the current cresset system of the road, making the state of networked car interact with each other at the same time; Thirdly, it should be compatible with the current indication system of the road, making vehicles in the network interact with digital navigation systems; Fourthly, it should be compatible with the current toll system of the road, making vehicles in the network interact with charging system; Fifthly, it should be compatible with the current control system of the road, making vehicles in the network interact with control systems.

4   Summary and Development Trends

Up to data EN-V has completely subverts the DNA of traditional car, and it will make future urban transport to achieve zero fuel consumption, zero emissions, zero congestion and zero accidents. EN-V will provide a more convenient, more intelligent and more environmental-friendly way to travel with electrification and Car networking technology.

However, at this stage, the development of Car networking technology remains gaps between our country and USA under smart economic system. At first we should focus on the development of Car networking technology, research in-depth and overcome related technical difficulties to promote the rapid development of information technology; At the same time, facing the development situation of Car networking that it seems automobile production enterprise as the key drivers and seems vehicle information service as the main point, the closed technical standards and services may be as a barrier when Car networking becomes popularized in the future. Therefore, it is an extremely important and urgent issue to set up a unified standard of Car networking technology.

With the coming of "vehicle networking Age", car companies should focus on the research of automotive information system, and make the full integration of automotive technology and mobile communication technology. Vehicle information is one of forward-looking technology over the practical application of Car networking; In addition, automotive intelligence is the development trends of future automotive. Research on automotive technology will also change, from the traditional internal combustion engine research with the energy of oil to the electric and intelligent research with the energy of hydrogen and electricity; meanwhile, the more complex electronics electric system of intelligent automotive will become, the bigger electric load will bear, and power-supply system will be faced with comprehensive upgrade.

Acknowledgments. This project is sponsored by National Basic Research Program of China (2006CB705505), Development Program of China (2006AA11Z214) and the Program of Introducing Talents of Discipline to Universities (No. B08031).

References

1. Mehta, M., Guinan, M.: The utilisation of multi-antenna enhanced mobile broadband communications in intelligent transportation systems. In: 7th International Conference on Intelligent Transport Systems Telecommunications, Sophia Antipolis, France, pp. 424–427 (2007)
2. Peng, J., Wu, P.: Study of drivers' EEGs and application in intelligent transportation systems. In: 9th International Conference of Chinese Transportation Professionals: Critical Issues in Transportation System Planning, Development, and Management, Harbin, China, pp. 1576–1583 (2009)
3. Toh, C.K.: Future application scenarios for MANET-based intelligent transportation systems. In: Proceedings of Future Generation Communication and Networking, Jeju Island, Korea, pp. 414–417 (2007)
4. Uradzinski, M., Kim, D., Langley, R.B.: The usefulness of internet-based (NTrip) RTK for navigation and intelligent transportation systems. In: 21st International Technical Meeting of the Satellite Division of the Institute of Navigation, Savannah, GA, United states, pp. 1967–1975 (2008)
5. Kumar, P., Jain, S.S., Singh, P.: Need of intelligent transport system for India. J. Inst. Eng. India: Civ. Eng. Div. 82, 6–69 (2001)
6. Elhillali, Y., Tatkeu, C., Deloof, P., Sakkila, L., Rivenq, A., Rouvaen, J.M.: Enhanced high data rate communication system using embedded cooperative radar for intelligent transports systems. Transp. Res. Part C Emerg. Technol. 18, 429–439 (2010)

A Research on MIMO Radar Based on Simulation

Zeng Jiankui and Dong Zhiming

Electronic Information School,
Chongqing University of Science and Technology, China
demesne@126.com

Abstract. MIMO radar (Multiple input multiple output radar) is a new radar developed recently. It outperforms the conventional phased radar in target detection. In this paper, the non-ideal factor of transmitting signal is considered. Firstly, the signal model of MIMO radar is investigated. And then the steps of the signal processing in MIMO radar are researched. At last, a simulation platform is established with the MATLAB to testify the advantage of MIMO radar over its conventional counterpart.

Keywords: signal processing, MIMO radar, target detection, simulation.

1 Introduction

It has been recently shown that multiple-input multiple-output (MIMO) system has the potential to dramatically improve the performance of the communication systems over single antenna system. Unlike the traditional beam-forming approach, which uses highly correlated signals of transmitting or receiving antenna arrays to steer a beam towards a certain direction in space, MIMIO makes use of the independence between signals from different transmitters and receivers to improve the more information received from the target and the robustness of the transmit-receive link.

MIMO radar is a novel radar technique developed recently [1] which is divided into two kinds. One kind of MIMO radar is refer to as collated antenna MIMO radar[2], the other kind of MIMO radar is widely separated antenna MIMO radar[3] which is also called multistatic MIMO radar. For the first kind of MIMO radar, Fishler[4] aimed at building the multistatic MIMO radar to counter targer's RCS-fluctuating and improve the detection performance; Berkerman[5] proposed MIMO radar can forming narrow beam; Fishler[6] verify that the CRB of MIMO radar is better than conventional phased radar.

The second kind of MIMO radar is widely research [7,8,9]. In this kind of MIMO radar, antennas transmit orthogonal signals. But the antennas are not separated widely as in first kind MIMO radar. Usually, the distance between antennas is half of the wavelength. As it has been researched, the kind of MIMO radar has many advantages such as high resolution, low intercept probability etc. In this paper, we investigate the signal model and signal processing of the collated antenna MIMO radar (in this paper, it is refer to as MIMO radar). Then a simulation platform is founded to testify the advantage of MIMO radar and some simulation result is presented.

R. Chen (Ed.): ICICIS 2011, Part I, CCIS 134, pp. 302–307, 2011.

In this paper, we investigate the advantage of the T-MIMO radar over phased array radar in the non-ideal factor on the transmitting signal. As it was well known, the transmitter is not stable; its signal may have much non-ideal component such as the phase instable which may significant impair the detector performance. From this paper, it can be seen that when the non-ideal factor is same in MIMO radar and phased array radar, the detector performance of MIMO radar is better than phased array radar. The reason is that MIMO radar false signal is not correlate as in phased array radar which will produce false target in the detector.

The remainder of this paper is organized as followed. First, signal model and signal processing of MIMO radar is introduced which includes the non-ideal factor in transmitting signals. Then the simulation system for MIMO radar is described. And then, simulation results are shown. Finally, some conclusions are drawn.

2 Signal Model

It is assume that the radar transmit array is composed of $L_1 \times L_2$ antennas. In MIMO radar model, the array is divide into L_2 sub-arrays. Each sub-array has L_1 antennas which transmits signal with p_t power. The array is shown in figure 1. Contrarily, in conventional phased radar, each antenna send the same signal.

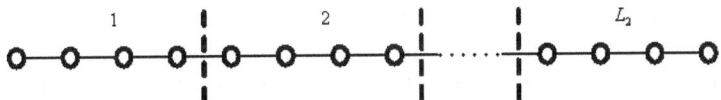

Fig. 1. The configuration of radar array

Because of the instability of the radar transmitter, the radar signal is not a pure ideal signal. It has many components which will affect the detector. Main source of these non-ideal factors includes signal source, the amplifier, the timer, etc. The important non-ideal factor which greatly impair the detector are the signal amplitude instability, the phase instability, the impulse duration instability and signal frequency instability and signal spur etc. Especially, the signal spur will significantly damage the detector performance because the signal spur will produce false target which will be detected by detector. Reducing beamformer gain (eg, through beamspoiling) can thus be of some help. Better still, when the source of the spur is waveform related, MIMO can offer a great benefit. Since the MIMO transmit waveforms are orthogonal, many spurs (e.g. those due to phase truncation and quantization in DDSs) will not be coherent across the array. As a result, these spurs will not be subject to array gain on transmitting, thereby reducing interference - both to the radar itself and to other RF systems.

Supposed the ideal transmitting LFM signal is

$$s(t) = E_0 e^{j(2\pi f_0 t + \frac{1}{2}\mu t^2)} \tag{1}$$

At receiver, the echo is processed by matched filter (MF), and judged by the detector. The output of the MF is

$$
\begin{aligned}
g(t) = E_0{}^2 e^{j\pi(kt(T-t)-\mu t^2)} \cdot \frac{\sin(\pi\mu t(T-|t|))}{\pi\mu t(T-|t|)}(T-|t|) \\
+E_0 \cdot b_m e^{j\pi((f_m-kt)(T-t)-\mu t^2)} \cdot \frac{\sin(\pi(f_m-\mu t)(T-|t|))}{\pi(f_m-\mu t)(T-|t|)}(T-|t|)
\end{aligned}
\tag{2}
$$

In (2), the first item is the real target echo. The second item is false target produced by the signal spur. It can be seen that the position of the false target is $\Delta t = f_m / \mu$, the amplitude of the false target is $b_m / 2E_0$. Where, the f_m and b_m is the frequency and the amplitude of the phase noise, respectively. In the conventional phased array radar, the false target is added up correaltely. Then the false target amplitude is so strong that it can be judge by the detector. But in the MIMO radar, because all the false target of different signal is un-correlate, they cannot be added up. It shall impair the detector performance.

3 MIMO Radar Signal Processing and Simulation System

At each receiver, the signal is firstly separated by a bank of band filter. The filter frequencies are different and are same with the frequency of each send signal. The target echo is sum of all transmitting signal. So, it include all the send signal components. Processed by the match filters, each signal component is separated. Each transmit signal is obtained now. Those separated signals are multiply by a coefficient and then sum up. This is equivalent to DBF at both transmitter and receiver.

And then, the moving target detection (MTD) is employed to find the velocity of the target. At last, the constant false alarm is used to detect the target.

To verify the advantage of MIMO radar, we established a simulation system using MATLAB. The system is divided into 3 models, the signal producing model, the wave propagation model and the signal processing modelIn signal producing model, the appropriate waveform is produced which include the LFM signal (linear frequency modulation), frequency coding signal and phase coding signal. The signal model also include phase noise which is describe in (2).

The echo signal which include the target echo, clutter and noise flow to the signal processed model which is show in figure 2.

The signal is firstly converted to digital signal by a A/D. And the it is processed by a Matched Filter(MF). The MF impulse response is the transmit signal. The output of the MF is exploited to beam formed to decided the direction of the arriving (DOA). The moving target indication (MTI) and moving target detection (MTD) technique is employed to cancel the clutter and find the velocity of target. And then, CFAR algorithm is used to calculate the detection threshold. At last, the founded target is shown in the monitor.

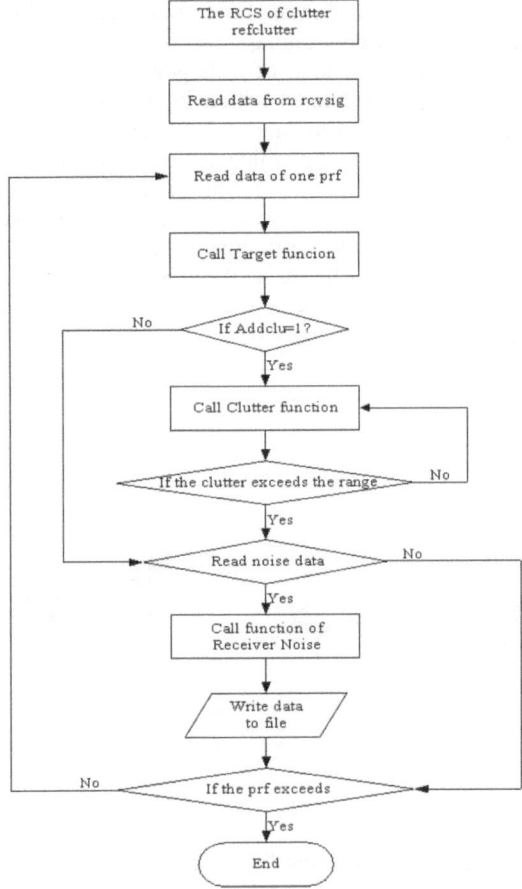

Fig. 2. The transmit signal model frame

The signal is firstly converted to digital signal by a A/D. And the it is processed by a Matched Filter(MF). The MF impulse response is the transmit signal. The output of the MF is exploited to beam formed to decided the direction of the arriving (DOA). The moving target indication (MTI) and moving target detection (MTD) technique is employed to cancel the clutter and find the velocity of target. And then, CFAR algorithm is used to calculate the detection threshold. At last, the founded target is shown in the monitor.

In our simulation platform, a interface for is provided for the input of parameter such as the number of antenna, the power of sending signal, the target range, velocity, direction, etc.

4   Simulation Result

In this section, the simulation system with MATLAB is employed to verify the MIMO radar advantage over its conventional counterpart. In this simulation system, we consider three kind of orthogonal signals, linear frequency modulate (OFDM LFM), phase code signal and frequency code signal.

In our simulation system, three kind of orthogonal signal is produced. And then, the radar transmit antenna is simulated which include carrier frequency modulate, power magnified etc. A target is simulated which return the wave. At the receiver, digital signal processing is simulated which includes DBF, MF, MTD and CFAR detector. Using this simulation system, under the situation of the same spur in MIMO radar and phased array radar. We compare the detector of these two kinds of radar.

When the phase noise is -30dB, we compare the MIMO radar and phased array radar. As showed in figure 3 and figure 4. As it is shown, in phase radar, the false target is stronger than weak target. So it will be judged by the detector. In MIMO radar, the false target will not be judged.

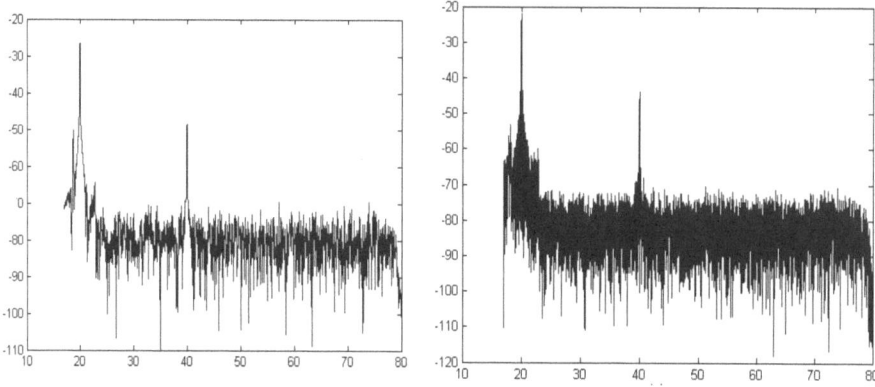

Fig. 3. The output of phased array radar   **Fig. 4.** The output of MIMO radar

From the simulation, we can see that in phase array radar, the false target will be detected. But in MIMO radar, there is no false target.

5   Summary

In this paper, we investigated the MIMO radar advantage over phased array radar on signal phase noise. As it well known, the transmitted signal is not an ideal signal, it may include many non-ideal factor such as phase noise. These may produce a false target which will be judge by the detector. We first analyze the source of signal. In MIMO radar, because the spur of different signal is not correlate, they will not add up. So, these spur will not impair the detector. This is demonstrated by a simulation system.

References

1. Zi-shu, H.: MIMO radar and its technical characteristic analysis. ACTA electronic sinica 33(12A), 2441 (2005)
2. Li, J., Stoica, P.: MIMO Radar with Colocated Antennas. IEEE Signal Processing Magazine 24, 106 (2007)

3. Haimovich, A.M., Blum, R.S., Cimini, L.J.: MIMO radar with widely separated antennas. IEEE Signal Processing Magazine 25, 116 (2008)
4. Fishler, E., et al.: Spatial Diversity in Radars Models and Detection Performance. IEEE Trans. On Signal processing 54, 823–838 (2006)
5. Bekkerman, I., Tabrikian, J.: Target detection and localization using MIMO radars and sonars. IEEE Trans. On signal processing 54, 3873–3883 (2006)
6. Fishler, E., et al.: MIMO radar: An idea whose time has come. In: Proceeding of the IEEE Radar Conference, Philadelphia, PA, p. 71 (2004)
7. Rabideau, D.J., Parker, P.: Ubiquitous MIMO multifunction digital array radar. In: The Thirty-Seventh Asilomar Conference on Signals, Systems and Computers, p. 1057 (2003)
8. Forsythe, K.W., Bliss, D.W., Fawcett, G.S.: Multiple-output Multiple-input (MIMO) radar. In: The Thirty-Seventh Asilomar Conference on Signals, Systems and Computers, p. 54 (2003)
9. Khan, H.A., et al.: Ultra wideband Multiple-output Multiple-input radar. In: 2005 IEEE International Radar Conference, Arlington, Virgrinia, p. 900 (2005)

Curriculum Reform Research of Computer Network Technology Based on School-Enterprise Cooperation

Peng Liu[*]

Department of Communication Engineering, Chongqing College of Electronic Engineering,
Chongqing, 401331, China
pengliu789@yahoo.com.cn

Abstract. There is growing concern about falling levels of student engagement with school science, as evidenced by studies of student attitudes, and decreasing participation at the post compulsory level. College-enterprise cooperation model is a new model of cultivating application-typed talents in college by cooperating with enterprises. In the paper, we analyze the teaching problems in the course of "Computer Network Technology", propose guidelines with teaching practice. Then we explored the reform ways to enhance students' self-learning ability. Finally, the conclusion is given.

Keywords: computer network technology; school-enterprise cooperation; practical training.

1 Introduction

Computer network technology is an exciting field that presents many opportunities for a student to be proficient in both computer systems and applications. The rapid spread of computers and advances in information technology has generated a need for highly trained workers to design and manage new information systems that use these technologies to meet the needs of the business organization [1]. The Computer networking technology program prepares graduates with skills needed to design and install secures network systems based on customer requirements, monitor network traffic and security, and maintain computer network hardware and software. As a practical subject, it requires not only the theoretical knowledge such as concepts, principles, processes and technical points, but also the practical application of these types of knowledge. However, as a long time, communication students in university have paid more attention to the professional knowledge, with less care about good practical teaching system for students in the training. The result showed the graduates while had a more complete professional knowledge, but failed to engineering ability and they cannot fully meet the needs of the community. In order to enhance the quality of students in university, we present a new model of cultivating application-typed talents in computer network technology by cooperating with enterprise. It always

---

[*] This author partially supported by the Science Foundation of Chongqing College of Electronic Engineering in China (Research on the congestion control for networked control systems).

R. Chen (Ed.): ICICIS 2011, Part I, CCIS 134, pp. 308–311, 2011.

stresses the improvement of hands-on ability and concerns about the ideas and methods of educating students [2].

School-enterprise cooperation model is a new model of cultivating application-typed talents in university by cooperating with enterprises [3]. Its basic connotation includes school-enterprise cooperation, two-way participation and mutual benefits. Based on the mutually beneficial and win-win cooperation of students, enterprise, society and school, school has introduced the industry's talent needs, good human resources, technical resources, innovative approaches and operating mode to the talent training process, and has created a new talent training model for school-enterprise cooperation. School has also developed and implemented a series of scientific quality assurance management system [4].

As a national communication college, the communication department in Chongqing College of Electronic Engineering has set a goal since its establishment: "To cultivate international communication engineer with an innovative sense". College actively adapts to the needs of economic and social development, promotes the school institutional reform and deepen school-enterprise cooperation [5-7].

The rest of the paper is organized as follows. Section 2 presents guidelines for computer network technology curriculum reform. Section 3 discusses designing a computer network technology curriculum based on school-enterprise cooperation. Section 4 presents evaluation systems for the curriculum. Conclusions are presented in Section 5.

2   Guidelines for Computer Network Technology Curriculum Reform

The ultimate goal of the course is to train network technology engineer. It always stresses the improvement of hands-on ability and concerns about the ideas and methods of educating students. To address these problems, we focused on engineered reforming professional practice of network technology engineering education system. The goal is to train students' skill in network technology engineering development and professionalism, to set objectives and assessment mechanisms, and then melt to form an overall training mechanism combines theoretical basis, experimental teaching, engineering practice to allow students own the basic knowledge, scientific literacy, expertise, innovation, engineering capability and professionalism, to get a comprehensive and balanced development. To achieve this goal, curriculum should use bilingual teaching and teach with the combination of E-learning and face to face instruction. We absorbed the advantages of similar courses abroad, combined with actual conditions to set the content of instruction.

3   Designing a Computer Network Technology Curriculum Based on School-Enterprise Cooperation

Based on the guidelines described above, we developed an innovation framework based initially on previous experience with innovation projects. There are three innovation instances in curriculum development.

• The contents of theory & practice update slowly

Most textbooks are difficult to catch up with the development of science and cause textbooks aging. As such textbook, it can only teach an idea of solving computer problems for students, but not face the social needs and applications. So, open teaching should be adopted, in addition, using the newer textbooks, we should supplement extracurricular readings, references, periodicals and the latest information on the internet.

• Theory teaching and experiment are disjointed, the experimental lessons are less

The experimental lessons of "computer network technology" are less because of various reasons in many colleges and universities, such as: shortage of funds, shortage of equipments, shortage of teachers and so on.

• The quality of qualified teachers can't keep up

It requires teachers to change their concept of education and teaching, have broader professional technical knowledge, and have a stronger sense of responsibility and confidence.

From the description above, it is evident that the proposed curriculum reform would strongly affect the teaching practice of the teachers. Hence, evaluation of teaching should also be reformed in step with this aim.

• Make full use of social resources to address the funding shortages and update teaching resources, practice bilingual teaching

Statistics show that business-to-school-enterprise cooperation in running schools and providing schools with practical training internship sites are highly enthusiastic, it is noteworthy. Therefore, teachers and students can obtain the latest, the most abundant and comprehensive information in relevant fields through the school-enterprise cooperation system. Teachers and students can be more in-depth learning for the knowledge points which are interested. In this way, students and teachers can share teaching resources easily.

• To learn while teaching, to stimulate teachers and students a common interest in learning.

In the school-enterprise cooperation model, schools and businesses should always exchange and communication. And in order to improve student self-learning ability, we should collect a large number of relevant information from the Internet, books, periodicals and so on. Teachers can take this opportunity to collect some of the textbook cannot get the information through the integration of information, classification, and the preparation of a really suitable for students in secondary vocational education and teaching materials, teaching continuously in a later study, modify, forming a complete set of detailed teaching materials to form the distinctive teaching.

• To organize teachers into the plant, to develop the social practice and practical ability and to enhance the quality of qualified teachers

It is only through the actual operation on the operational positions, teachers can put their energy to be released. The teachers are regularly arranged to attend some teaching trainings and researches. Out-going trainings opportunities will be provided to each teacher at least once a year to encourage them to participate actively in researches and technical developing, update their knowledge architectures and improve their operational skills.

4 Evaluation Systems for the Curriculum

The term curriculum program evaluation includes two aspects: the evaluation of students and the evaluation of the training mode.

With the help of the science foundation of Chongqing College of Electronic Engineering, the college has formed an all-round teaching quality assurance and monitoring system. College has established quality control and improvement mechanism with capacity-cultivating as its core and based on the four links of "preparation, implementation, summary, feedback". Student capability maturity assessment is combined with college assessment and enterprise assessment. College assessment is made by course examination, theory test, practical ability assessment, questionnaire survey, lectures attending, interviews and visits, etc. Enterprise assessment focuses on student ability to solve practical problems and the overall quality assessment.

5 Conclusions

Enhancing the cultivating of student's engineering capabilities is critical for the vocational engineering education. To achieve a further cooperation with enterprises, improve the quality of talent training, department of communication engineering has made a lot thorough study and practice, formed its own characteristics, and obtained good teaching results. Besides, students' hands-on ability and problem-solving ability are enhanced in the process of actual business cases.

References

1. Jones, A., Carr, M.: Teachers' Perceptions of Technology Education: Implications for Curriculum Innovation. Research in Science Education 22, 230–239 (1992)
2. Switzer, J.S.: Teaching Computer-Mediated Visual Communication to a Large Section: A Constructivist Approach. Innovative Higher Education 29, 89–101 (2004)
3. Kulm, G., Li, Y.: Curriculum research to improve teaching and learning: national and cross-national studies. Mathematics Education 41, 709–715 (2009)
4. Tatnall, A.D.: Using actor-network theory to understand the process of information systems curriculum innovation. Educ. Inf. Technol. 15, 239–254 (2010)
5. Liu, P.: An Approximate Discrete Controller for Networked Control Systems with Time Delay. Journal of Computational Information Systems 4, 1955–1959 (2008)
6. Liu, P.: A New Congestion Controller for Multilayer Networked Control Systems with persistent Disturbances. Key Engineering Materials 2, 805–810 (2010)
7. Liu, P.: A New Decision-Making for Nonlinear Input-Output Systems with Persistent Disturbances. In: 2010 International Conference on the Development of Educational Science and Computer Technology, pp. 422–425. IEEE Press, Wu Han (2010)

Industry Cluster's Adaptive Co-competition Behavior Modeling Inspired by Swarm Intelligence

Wei Xiang and Feifan Ye

Faculty of Mechanical Engineering and Mechanics, Ningbo University, Ningbo, P.R. China
xiangwei@nbu.edu.cn

Abstract. Adaptation helps the individual enterprise to adjust its behavior to uncertainties in environment and hence determines a healthy growth of both the individuals and the whole industry cluster as well. This paper is focused on the study on co-competition adaptation behavior of industry cluster, which is inspired by swarm intelligence mechanisms. By referencing to ant cooperative transportation and ant foraging behavior and their related swarm intelligence approaches, the cooperative adaptation and competitive adaptation behavior are studied and relevant models are proposed. Those adaptive co-competition behaviors model can be integrated to the multi-agent system of industry cluster to make the industry cluster model more realistic.

Keywords: Co-Competition; Swarm Intelligence; Adaptation; Industry Cluster.

1 Introduction

An industry cluster is a geographic concentration of interconnected businesses including suppliers and manufacturers in a particular field. Adaptation is regarded as one of the key characteristics to ensure the sustainable development of the cluster [1]. Individuals in a cluster are now operating as nodes in a network of suppliers, customers, and other specialized service functions. They need to be flexible and adaptive because their operations are always subject to a variety of uncertainties, like customer demand, supplier capacity, or supplier's capacity utilization. In other words, individuals' role can be partners or competitors, and such role may be shifted dynamically so as to adapt to the changing opportunities. In cluster, there exist several cases required for cooperative behavior, like when there exists a big order or complicated order which exceeds the individual's load or capability, or several individuals want to form alliance for earning a big cake, etc. Such cooperative behavior is not the always choice of individuals; it is often replaced by competitive behavior as enterprise always purchases individual maximum profit. Such adaptive co-competition behavior is quite common in industry cluster in reality. It is actually determined by accumulating information from environment and learning from historical decision.

The term 'Cluster' is originally from the phenomenon of social inserts. Following characters in social inserts, like highly flexibility in structure, self-autonomy, decentralization in terms of management etc, is quite similar to the characters of

R. Chen (Ed.): ICICIS 2011, Part I, CCIS 134, pp. 312–319, 2011.

industry cluster. Therefore, the study on self-adaptation of industrial clusters can be inspired by self-organization mechanism of the natural biological system - swarms. Swarm Intelligence (SI) is artificial intelligence based on the collective behavior of decentralized, self-organized systems. In this paper, the adaptive co-competition behavior of the individuals is represented using some swarm intelligence mechanism.

2   Review of the Literature

Industry cluster is a complex adaptive system (CAS). Agent based modeling and simulation is widely accepted to be a useful tool in studying the adaptation of CAS. However, the application of agent based modeling for industrial cluster is rarely found in the literature, only some related work on agent-based distributed supplier chain modeling were published [2]. The cooperation and competition mentioned in those agents' adaptive coordination mechanism in supply chain model are the great reference to this study. In most literature studies, game theory is recognized as effective approach modeling the individual cooperation among multiple agents. The individuals either adopt to be cooperative or to be non-cooperative, the different strategies were examined under various supply chain models [3]. As mentioned in these studies, one of the main questions here is whether the cooperation is stable. As in reality, seldom the individual enterprises always keep the cooperative behavior to others all the time.

Instead of using game theory, our study differs from those works in the individuals behavior modeled with swarm-inspired adaptive co-competition behavior. Inspired by the self-adaptation found in nature swarms like ants, both heterogeneous ants and whole colony can always show near optimal co-competition behavior. Therefore, swarm intelligence is integrated with agent coordination, thus the individual agent can adapt to be either cooperative or to be competitive with others in the cluster dynamically according to the current external environment, individual's local status information, as well as the historical decision.

There exists several SI algorithms and applications, like Ant Colony Optimization inspired by ant foraging, Ant Clustering algorithm inspired by ant sorting eggs and corpse behavior, division of labor inspired by wasp differentiation and task specialization behavior, Robots' co-operation and collaboration inspired by ants cooperative transport behavior[4]. The successful applications were reported in several areas, like robotics, manufacturing, telecommunications etc. However, the application in industry cluster or supply chain area is rare in the literature. In this study, the contribution is to propose co-competition behavior model which is referenced to ant colony's foraging behavior and cooperative transport behavior. The most successful application of ant colony's foraging behavior is the Ant colony optimization (ACO). ACO solves combinational optimization problems using foraging behavior patterns of ant colonies: indirect communication by pheromone and positive feedback mechanism. Some ACO works related to industry cluster can be found in virtual enterprises' or cluster's partner selection problem [5]. As to cooperative transport behavior: Cooperation occurs when individuals achieve together a task that could not be done by a single one, the individuals must combine their efforts in order to successfully solve a problem that goes beyond their individual abilities. Currently, such cooperative transport has been reported to be used in the robots cooperation [6], however, there is no work published in industry cluster or virtual enterprise areas.

3 Adaptive Co-competition Behavior Model

Individuals in the cluster adopt cooperative behavior or competitive behavior in dealing with orders according to current situation as well as its historical decisions. The decision to be cooperative or to be competitive itself is adaptive. When there exists a high customer demands, individuals may pay more on individual's maximum profit and adopt competitive behavior. On the contrast, when outside market is recessed, individuals are more likely to be cooperative and bid for big cake or attractive price by alliance. In this section, such two behaviors' modelings inspired by swarm are presented in detail respectively.

First, some terms are given as following to make a clearer explanation of the model:

$p_{ij}(t)$: denotes the probability of enterprise i to select task j at time t;

$\tau_{ij}(t)$: is the pheromone intensity of task j at time t, which can be any information that represents the demand of task j;

$\theta_{ij}(t)$: is the response threshold of enterprise i to task j at time t, which is determined by enterprise i's core capability for task j;

δ_j: is the incremental pheromone value for task j during a time period;

a_{ij}: is the amount of pheromone decreased due to enterprise i works for task j;

$f(x)$: is a threshold function of x due to enterprise's workload, which satisfies: $f(x) < 0$, if workload x <B; $f(x)> 0$, if x>B, B is a positive constant.

λ: denotes the learning (forgetting) factor for task;

$e_{ij}(t)$: represents the execution state of enterprise i for task j at time t, $e_{ij}(t)=1$ means enterprise i execute task j, otherwise $e_{ij}(t)=0$;

$\xi_i(t)$:denotes the workload of enterprise i at time t, $\xi_i(t) = \dfrac{\sum_{j=1}^{m} a_{ij} e_{ij}(t)}{C_i}$, where C_i is the total capability of enterprise i, m is the number of tasks;

3.1 Adaptive Co-operation Behavior Inspired by Cooperative Transport Behavior in Swarm

In nature, ants are capable of collectively retrieving large prey that is impossible for a single ant to retrieve. Usually, a single ant finds a prey item and tries to move it alone; when unsuccessful, it recruits nest mates and then a group of ants work together to move the item back. Although this scenario seems to be fairly well understood, the mechanisms underlying cooperative transport - that is, when and how a group of ants move a large prey item to the nest - remain unclear. However, it is known that the underlying coordination in collective transport seems to occur through the item being transported: a movement of one ant engaged in group transport is likely to modify the stimuli perceived by the other group members, possibly producing, in turn, orientation or positional changes in these ants. The basic model for group transport in robots was presented by Kube and Zhang [6] for coordinating a group of homogeneous robots without direct communication. Zhang et al.[7] solved the a cooperative collection task in robots by the model inspired by Ant System algorithm (AS) and employs the artificial pheromone as a clue for task difficulties. However, It is fair to say that the published research works are far to mature. Until now, no other application besides robots' cooperative transport has been reported.

Similar to cooperative transport in ants or robots, individual enterprises sometime need to work together to fulfill a big task due to individual's capability limitation. In such case, the cooperative behavior is required among several enterprises to satisfy the following two features: notify other enterprises to learn the task difficulties; map appropriate number of enterprises to the tasks; and partner selection for alliance.

By comparing the cooperative behavior in ant colony and industry cluster, we find that the task may increase its stimulus intensity as long as no enough enterprises joining in for cooperation. Moreover, the cooperation, no mater happened in ants, robots, or industry cluster, may lead to deadlock situation when all individuals are waiting for others to joining in. However, the differences are in twofold: (1) ants or robots have no sense of the task difficult, while individual enterprise can get the information of task quantity, so the task pheromone update will be different in two cases; (2) ants or robots are either idle or fully-loaded, while individual enterprise may have different workload, which will effect the probability of selecting task.

By referencing to cooperative transport behavior in ants, the novel cooperative behavior model is proposed to describe the cooperation among the individual enterprises in industry cluster in this study. The model is formulated as following:

$$\tau_{ij}(t+1) = \left(\tau_{ij}(t) + \delta_j - \sum_{i=1}^{n} a_{ij} e_{ij}(t) \right) w\!\left(T_{w_{ij}}\right) \tag{1}$$

$$\text{Where,} \quad w\!\left(T_{w_{ij}}\right) = \begin{cases} 1 & T_{w_{ij}} \le T_{tolerance} \\ \mu & T_{w_{ij}} > T_{tolerance} \end{cases} \tag{2}$$

$$\theta_{ij}(t+1) = \theta_{ij}(t) + f\!\left[\xi_i(t)\right] \tag{3}$$

$$p_{ij}(t) = \frac{\tau_{ij}^2(t)}{\tau_{ij}^2(t) + \theta_{ij}^2(t)} \tag{4}$$

Here, Equation (1) is the artificial pheromone about task j sensed by enterprise i. n is the number of the individuals. The pheromone intensity τ_{ij} is the driving force for individual enterprise i to select the task j. The more the pheromone intensity, the more attractive the task j is to the individual enterprises in cluster. Hence, once there is enterprise selecting the task j, τ_{ij} should be decreased with certain amount. In addition, as long as the task j is not selected, the pheromone intensity will be added with an additional constant, δ_j. The content in bracelet of Equation determines the task difficulty. Equation (2) is the task deadlock consideration [6]. μ is a constant that satisfies $0 < \mu < 1$; $T_{w_{ij}}$ is the waiting time since individual enterprise i finds that it can't perform task j; $T_{tolerance}$ is a positive constant; $w(x)$ is a segmentalized function of x, used to eliminate the "task deadlock" situation. When $T_{w_{ij}} > T_{tolerance}$, if enterprise i finds that it still can't perform task j individually or cooperatively with other members it recruits, it decreases the "sensing" pheromone about the task locally by multiple a value of μ ($0 < \mu < 1$). Thus the enterprise gets more chance to try other tasks of the same type through probability computing according to (4). In this way, task deadlock is eliminated.

Not like individual ants, which are either fully idle or fully loaded, individual enterprises in industry cluster should consider the workload. When workload is high, which means enterprise is busy with tasks already, then enterprise should increase its threshold θ_{ij} accordingly. $f[\xi_i(t)]$ in (3) is the factor considering workload. The enterprise workload ξ_i is used as a feedback for the response threshold θ_{ij} computing, allowing θ_{ij} increasing when the workload is high ($f[\xi_i(t)] > 0$, when $\xi_i(t) > B$), with the result that the probability to select task j decreases. This will ensure that when individual enterprise is busy, it will not accept task any more, otherwise, if it is too free, it can easily take task. Equation (4) formulates the probability of individual enterprise i to select task j at time t.

3.2 Adaptive Competition Behavior Inspired by Ant Foraging in Swarm

It is quite common that several individuals bid for a task. In Li et al. work [8] for task scheduling in a grid environment, the wasps are given a strength value which is regarded as the workload of the grid wasp. The bigger the strength value, the less the probability of wasp wining the bid. Compared with Li's wasp competition model, the competition in industry cluster should not only consider the workload of the individual enterprise, but also should consider some other factors like the bidding price, lead time, etc. Moreover, individual enterprises should take competitive action and learn from historical bidding policy.

In this paper, Ant System algorithm (AS) is used to model competition adaptation in industry cluster. The pheromone plays an important role in AS. Ants deposit pheromone, and make decision based on the detected pheromone, gradually, the whole ant colony achieves a good global performance. Here, individual enterprise is regarded as an ant, and the pheromone for enterprise needs to be defined properly as a clue for workload of individual enterprise. The AS-based model is proposed as following:

$$\tau_{ij}(t) = \frac{C_i}{\sum_{j=1}^{q} a_{ij} e_{ij}(t)} \tag{5}$$

$$\eta_{ij}(t+1) = \eta_{ij}(t) + \Delta\eta \cdot (1 - e_{ij}(t)) \tag{6}$$

$$p_{ij}(t) = \frac{\tau_{ij}^{\alpha}(t) \cdot \eta_{ij}^{\beta}(t)}{\sum_{l=1}^{m} \tau_{il}^{\alpha}(t) \cdot \eta_{il}^{\beta}(t)} \tag{7}$$

The pheromone τ_{ij} is formulated in (5) for representing workload. The more the workload of individual enterprise, the lower the pheromone value. Such pheromone should be updated whenever the individual has the workload update, such as receiving a new task or fulfilling a task.

η_{ij} is the heuristic desirability of selecting task j; $\Delta\eta$ is the learning incremental from history bidding; $e_{ij}(t)$ represents the execution state; Equation (6) shows that heuristic desirability η_{ij} is updated in a self-reinforcing way: If the individual successful bid type of task j before, the current heuristic desirability maintain the same as previous, otherwise, current heuristics increases a value of $\Delta\eta$ so as to increase the attraction for enterprise i. The probability of enterprise i winning task j is formulated in (7). α , β are two tunable parameters that control the relative weights of τ_{ij} and η_{ij} . Therefore, the individual with higher pheromone (i.e. low workload) and higher heuristics will have more chance for successful bidding. By such AS-based model, it is possible for each individual adaptively compete for bidding tasks in environments.

4 Multi-agent Industry Cluster Modeling Integrated with SI

Multi-agent system has advantages for automation, decentralization and flexibility. It can manifest self-organization and complex behaviors even when the individual strategies of all their agents are simple. By analyzing the characteristics of industry cluster's whole life development – from cluster forming, operation, to evolution, the individuals' behavior and the relationships among individuals can be abstracted, and then a multi-agent system (MAS) for industry cluster can be implemented for further simulation.

4.1 Agent Definition

The operation of an industry cluster involves individuals dealing with the tasks in the cluster, either cooperatively or competitively. Therefore, individual enterprises, the tasks and the cluster environment consists the whole cluster. Each individual is regarded as an enterprise agent, while the opportunities and tasks in cluster are built as task agents as well. The cluster environment is represented by an industry cluster manager agent. These three basic types of agents help to build a bottom-up model of the industry cluster.

The cluster manager agent behaviors like a manager or yellow page, all agents can register to it and get useful information by communication message. Task agent is created whenever there is an order appearing in the cluster. Once the task agent is created, it is registered to the cluster environment, then call for a proposal to all enterprise agents with relative capability, and accept bid based on its criteria. When the order is finished production by enterprise agent, it is deleted from the cluster environment.

Enterprise agent is to model an enterprise in the cluster. It is defined with several behaviors to make the agent with intelligent and auto behavior. For example, the register behavior helps the enterprise agent to register to the cluster for its core capabilities; the monitor behavior helps to keep recording its status and historical decisions. When its production load is less than a threshold or there exists several failing bidding because of competitive strategy, it will go for cooperative strategy for future opportunities or tasks; the contract-net responder behavior helps individual enterprise agent to adaptively bid for tasks according to both local status, external sensor of task demand, and the historical decisions. The section 3 mentioned co-competition behavior model inspired by swarm intelligence is integrated with the contract-net responder behavior of the enterprise agent.

4.2 MAS Implementation

The system is flexible and scalable as agents associated with real entities can be easily added or removed from the system, as in the real world, tasks continuously arrive at the cluster environment, and leave the cluster when they are finished processing. Figure 1 shows the framework of the multi-agent industry cluster model under JADE platform. All types of agents communicate each other based on the defined ontology and FIFA protocol. In order to manifest the collective or adaptive behavior of the industry cluster, the swarm intelligence is further integrated with the agents' behavior and coordination in Multi-agent system.

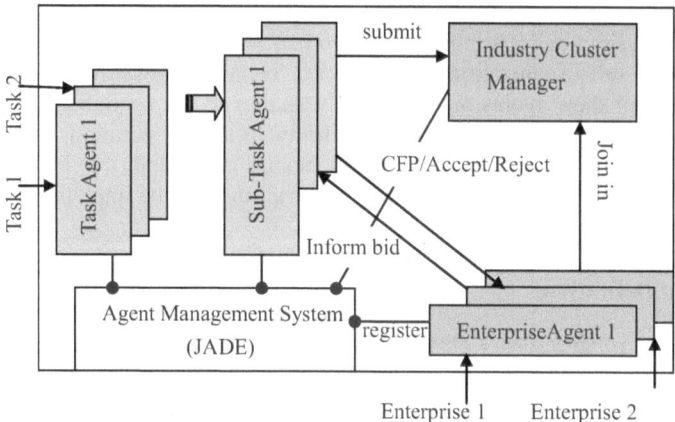

Fig. 1. Framework of multi-agent industry cluster system

With a multi-agent industry cluster model, a series of simulations can be studied to analyze the individual and cluster development in dynamic environment. Several internal and external dynamic factors need to be identified and considered as the simulation variables. The simulation on the multi-agent industry cluster will be our future work.

5   Conclusion and Future Work

Adaptation is important to the development of industry cluster. It helps the individual to adjust it behavior to dynamic changes in environment and collectively form cluster's adaptation as well. Adaptation analysis can be solved based on agent-based industry cluster model. Both individual enterprises and tasks appeared in cluster can be regarded as agents. In order to make the model more realistic, agents should be integrated with adaptive behavior. This paper is focused on the study on co-competition adaptation modeling of industry cluster, which is inspired by swarm intelligence mechanisms. The cooperative adaptation and competitive adaptation behavior are studied and relevant models are proposed inspired by ant cooperative transportation and ant foraging behavior and their related swarm intelligence approaches.

With the proposed swarm intelligence-based multi-agent industry cluster model, future work should be focused on the identification of dynamic factors in inner and outer cluster environment and the simulations on dynamic adaptation analysis.

Acknowledgments. The Project-sponsored by SRF for ROCS, SEM and NSF(70871062), and SRF for Zhejiang PEM (Y200804210).

References

1. Carbonara, N., Giannoccaro, I., Albino, V.: The competitive advantage of geographical clusters as complex adaptive systems: an exploratory study based on case studies and network analysis. In: ICCS 2006 (2006)
2. Lee, J.H., Kim, C.O.: Multi-agent systems applications in manufacturing systems and supply chain management: a review paper. International Journal of Production Research 46(1), 233–265 (2009)
3. Nagarajan, M., Sosic, G.: Game-theoretic analysis of cooperation among supply chain agents: review and extensions. European Journal of Operational Research 187(3), 719–745 (2008)
4. Garnier, S., Gautrais, J., Theraulaz, G.: The biological principles of swarm intelligence. Swarm Intelligence 1, 3–31 (2007)
5. Kang, K., Zhang, J., Xu, B.S.: Optimizing the selection of partners in collaborative operation networks. In: Huang, D.-S., Heutte, L., Loog, M. (eds.) ICIC 2007. LNCS (LNAI), vol. 4682, pp. 836–850. Springer, Heidelberg (2007)
6. Kube, C.R., Zhang, H.: Task Modelling in Collective Robotics. Auton. Robots 4, 53–72 (1997)
7. Zhang, D.D., Xie, G.M., Yu, J.Z., Wang, L.: Adaptive task assignment for multiple mobile robots via swarm intelligence approach. Robotics and Autonomous Systems 55, 572–588 (2007)
8. Li, H.X., Cheng, C.T., Pang, L.J.: High-efficiency Dynamic Task-Scheduling Algorithm for Grids. J. of South China Univ. of Tech (Natural Science Edition) 34(1), 82–86 (2006)

Empirical Study on Relationship Capital in Supply Chain-Based on Analysis of Enterprises in Hunan Province

Lu Shan and Ou-yang Qiang-bin

Management-Business School of Hunan University of Commerce, 410205 Changsha, China
lushan20031020@163.com

Abstract. Based on the existing theories and studies, this thesis aims to propose a theoretical model for describing the relationship between the relationship capital in the supply chain and its influencing factors, and meanwhile, the EFA (exploratory factor analysis) and CFA (confirmatory factor analysis) are carried out on 188 sample data. Through the evaluation of goodness of fit on the structure model as well as assumption testing, it turns out that there are four influencing factors for the relationship capital in the supply chain, namely, capability and reputation of the cooperation companies in the supply chain, input in specific assets and transfer cost, which are in a positive correlation with relationship capital separately. Then a decision-making basis is provided for the practice of relationship capital in the supply chain.

Keywords: supply chain, relationship capital, influencing factors, structural equation model.

1 Introduction

As the mechanism for reducing complexity, relationship capital plays an important role in the collaboration of the supply chain. At present, most of the existing studies are focusing on explicit contracts and there are less of them targeting on relationship capital-based supply chain coordination [1]. Because of the incompleteness of contracts and the uncertainty of environment, most of the activities need to be carried out through coordination among the enterprises. Therefore, it is necessary to research on the influencing factors and formation conditions of relationship capital to realize a better cooperation in the supply chain.

There are some literatures exploring on the role of relationship capital in JV enterprises. Inkpen & Beamish believe that "relationship" is the key for the success of cooperation in JV enterprises [2]. Luo also points out that relationship capital plays a positive role in the performance of a JV enterprise [3]. Lin Li & Zhou Pengfei propose that relationship capital formed by alliances can provide the members of the alliances with competitive advantages that cannot be copied or imitated [4]. Some scholars studied the measurement indices of relationship capital. Sarkar holds the opinion that relationship capital consists of several dimensions, such as mutual trust, commitment on mutual benefit and cooperation and communication [5]. Roy proposes that four

R. Chen (Ed.): ICICIS 2011, Part I, CCIS 134, pp. 320–325, 2011.
© Springer-Verlag Berlin Heidelberg 2011

indices, namely, strength, quality, tightness and quantity of relationship, can be used to measure the relationship capital between the enterprises [6]. Bao Gongmin and Wang Qingxi consider that relationship capital is mainly influenced by the partners' actions to shown their trust and specific investment [7].

The studies above are basically normative analysis, focusing on the relationship capital among companies of the alliances instead of relationship capital in the supply chain which lead to the indirect instruction to the management of relationship capital in the supply chain. In this paper, the author, based on the existing studies both at home and abroad, tries to establish a theoretical model for relationship capital in the supply chain and verify it through empirical studies, so that it can provide a reliable theoretical guidance for domestic companies to execute the strategy of relationship capital cooperation in the supply chain.

2 Research Model

According to the meaning of relationship capital, trust and commitment are the two key elements. Duysters believes that behavioral factors such as trust and commitment are found to be important drivers [8]. As a result, it is possible to use trust and commitment to measure the relationship capital in the supply chain. Mayer, Davis & Schoorman find that capability is the most frequent antecedent for trust. Reputation of a company spreads easily in the industry, which helps improve the reliability of the company. Investing in restricted assets is one of the effective ways to improve the level of trust, which directly affects the quality of the alliance relationship capital.

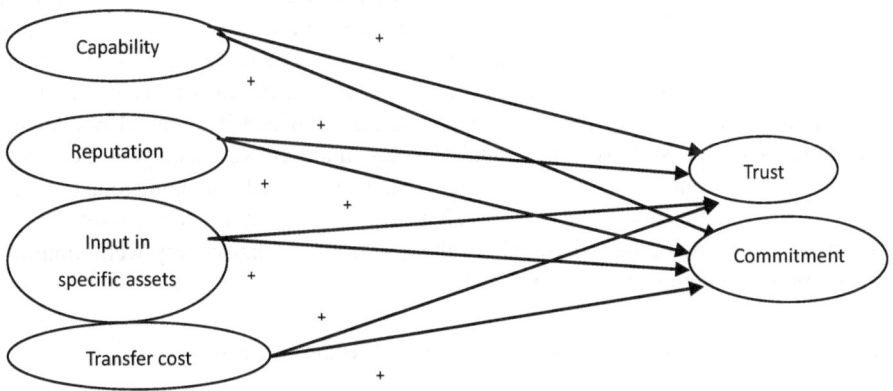

Fig. 1. Research model of relationship capital in supply chain

Based on the above analysis of the relationship between relationship capital on the supply chain and its influencing factors, i.e. capability of the cooperation company, its reputation, transfer cost and input in specific assets, it is verified that there is some theoretic link among these factors. This thesis proposes the research model for relationship capital in the supply chain, as shown in Figure 1, which describes the relationship between the two measurement indices of relationship capital and its four influencing factors. In Figure 1, the arrow linking the two variables shows the cause-and-effect relationship between the variables. The variable at the end of the arrow is exogenous variable and the variable at the point of the arrow head is endogenous variable. "+" means the two variables are in a positive correlation. There are eight positive correlations assumed in Figure 1, for example, "positive correlation between capability of a company and trust".

3 Data Collection and Analysis

3.1 Questionnaire Design and Sampling

First, the measurement indices for variables are designed based on the related existing studies in a draft questionnaire, and then twenty companies are selected from different industries with different scales in Hunan province, which are consulted several times for the modification of the draft. Second, the draft is discussed and modified within the workgroup. Finally, the final version of the questionnaire is determined. The final questionnaire, with the problem-oriented idea, focuses on the key elements of the research model for relationship capital in the supply chain, by adopting the internationally-used, simple and structuralized form.

In order to ensure the quality of the questionnaire, individuals surveyed must be CEO or other senior managements from the departments of the company, for they know very well about the cooperation companies in the supply chain. 325 copies of the questionnaire are sent out, 209 of them are returned and 21 copies are invalid because of noncooperation of companies and incomplete information. So there are 188 valid copies (with the returning rate of 58 %), which meet the requirement of a big sample in SEM method (at least 100). In addition, from the distribution of the positions of individuals surveyed, 97 of them are senior managers, which is about 51.6 % of the total number of the surveyed individuals; 34 are middle-level managers, i.e. about 18.1% of the total number; 39 are department managers, i.e. 20.7 % of the total number, and in general, senior managements take about 90.4 % of the surveyed. Therefore, it is regarded that the surveyed individuals of the questionnaire know very well about the cooperation companies in the supply chain.

3.2 Assumption Testing: Structural Equation Model Analysis

CFA is carried out in this part, in which the measurement items of each factor are analyzed in terms of reliability and validity and the effectiveness is also verified for each of the dimensions of potential variables. Meanwhile, the relationships among the potential variables are analyzed by Structural Equation Modeling (SEM) and the related assumptions are also analyzed and verified. Here the software of AMOS 5.0 is adopted for the analysis.

As shown in Figure 1, there are six variables, which have already been studied by lots of scholars. Based on these studies, the research in this thesis aims at the design of the measurement items for the variables, by taking into consideration the features of the

Table 1. Measurement items of variables

Variables	Measurement items	Load value	Cronbach'α
Capability ξ_1	The cooperation company is strong in its innovation capability.	0.73	0.8453
	Businesses are dealt in time.	0.69	
	The cooperation company is strong in its responsive ability.	0.76	
	The cooperation company often gives suggestions on our businesses.	0.82	
Reputation ξ_2	The cooperation company usually fulfills its commitments.	0.83	0.8121
	The cooperation company has great concern about the interests of its customers.	0.66	
	The cooperation company has a good reputation in the industry.	0.82	
	Services provided by the cooperation company are satisfying.	0.79	
Input in specific assets ξ_3	The cooperation company inputs a significant amount of specific material assets in the mutual cooperation.	0.75	0.7986
	We have to input a large amount of specific material assets if we cooperate with this company.	0.67	
	The cooperation company inputs a significant amount of specific labor assets in the mutual cooperation.	0.79	
	We have to input a large amount of specific labor assets if we cooperate with this company.	0.75	
Transfer cost ξ_4	It will cost a lot in adjusting the operation processes if the cooperation is terminated.	0.76	0.7894
	It will cost a lot in establishing new business procedures if the cooperation is terminated.	0.69	
	It will cost a lot in re-training employees if the cooperation is terminated.	0.75	
Trust η_1	We generally do not doubt about the information provided by the cooperation company.	0.76	0.8235
	We are convinced that the cooperation company will abide by the contracts.	0.85	
	The cooperation company discusses questions with us in a frank and sincere way.	0.84	
	The cooperation company does not disclose any of our secrets.	0.69	
Commitment η_2	The cooperation company will not gain any illegal interests from us.	0.78	0.8198
	The cooperation company fulfills its obligations and commitments in a serious way.	0.76	
	The cooperation company will try its best to help us whenever we need it.	0.82	
	We will try our best to help the cooperation company whenever it needs us.	0.71	

surveyed individuals. In the questionnaire, there are 23 measurement items in total for the six variables and the surveyed individuals are required to answer the questions by the commonly-used seven-grade scores. For the 23 measurement items, the inadequate items are deleted according to the results of EFA, and Table 1 shows the 23 measurement items for the formal data analysis. The minimum in the Cronbach values of the six variables is 0.7894>0.6, which means that there are strong correlations among the related measuring variables of the factors. 23 measurement items are loaded on the related factors (whose load values are all over 0.5) according to the expected modeling. In addition, the results of CFA illustrate that the measurement model has a high degree of goodness of fit, and since Chi-square=22.119, Chi-square/DF =1.209<3.0, GFI=0.978>0.90, CFI=0.973>0.90; RMSEA=0.006<0.05, this shows there is a favorable degree of goodness of fit between the data and the measurement model.

The aim of this study is to judge whether the four factors described in the model are the influencing factors for relationship capital in the supply chain, and Table 2 shows the results of the assumption testing. In Table 2, the assumption is verified that capability of the cooperation company is in a positive correlation with the item of trust (0.253, P<0.1), which means that favorable capabilities of a company help establish credibility among companies in the supply chain; the assumption is verified that reputation of the cooperation company is in a positive correlation with the item of trust (0.487, P<0.1), which means that keeping a good reputation plays a positive role in improving relationship capital under the quickly changing circumstances; the assumption is verified that input in specific assets is in a positive correlation with the item of trust (0.290, P<0.1), which means that the more the input in specific assets are, the higher the degree of credibility among companies in the supply chain; the assumption is verified that transfer cost is in a positive correlation with the item of trust (0.289, P<0.1). With the same method, it is verified that capability, reputation, input in specific assets and transfer cost of the cooperation company are in a positive correlation with the item of commitment separately. Therefore, it is obvious that capability, reputation, input in specific assets and transfer cost of the cooperation company are the influencing factors of relationship capital in the supply chain which can help facilitate supply chain cooperation in an effective way.

Table 2. Analyzing results of the total sample through structural equation model

Relations between variables	Standard path coefficient	Whether assumptions are supported
Capability ⟶ Trust	0.253	H1: support
Reputation ⟶ Trust	0.487	H2: support
Input in specific assets ⟶ Trust	0.290	H3: support
Transfer cost ⟶ Trust	0.289	H4: support
Capability ⟶ Commitment	0.279	H5: support
Reputation ⟶ Commitment	0.537	H6: support
Input in specific assets ⟶ Commitment	0.210	H7: support
Transfer cost ⟶ Commitment	0.212	H8: support

4   Conclusion

This thesis, based on the existing studies, proposes the research model of influencing factors for relationship capital in the supply chain, with eight assumptions which are used for describing the mechanism of the interrelations between each of the influencing factors and the relationship capital. SEM is adopted as the basic framework for empirical analysis, while software like SPSS 11.0 and AMOS 5.0 are applied for EFA and CFA of the sample data. The empirical study demonstrates that capability, reputation, input in specific assets and transfer cost of the cooperation company are the influencing factors of relationship capital in the supply chain and they are in a positive correlation with relationship capital separately.

Acknowledgement

The work in the paper is supported by Hunan Nature Sciences Fund item (10JJ6112), and Outstanding Youth of Scientific Research Project of Hunan Provincial Education Department (09B056).

References

1. Cachon, G.: Supply chain coordination with contracts, Working Paper, University of Pennsylvania (2002)
2. Inkpen, A.C., Beamish, P.W.: Knowledge bargaining power and the instability of international joint ventures. Academy of Marketing Review 1, 177–202 (2006)
3. Luo, X., Griffith, D.A., Liu, S.S., Shi, Y.: The effects of customer relationships and social capital on firm performance: A Chinese business illustration. Journal of International Marketing 4, 25–45 (2004)
4. Li, L., Pengfei, Z.: Knowledge Learning, Conflict Management and Relational Capital in Knowledge Alliances. Science of Science and Management of S&T 4, 107–110 (2004)
5. Sarkar, M.B., Echambadi, R., Cavusgil, S.T., Aulakh, P.S.: The influence of complementarity, compatibility, and relationship capital on alliance performance. Journal of the Academy of Marketing Science 4, 358–373 (2007)
6. Roy, J.P.: International joint venture partner selection and performance: The role of the host country legal environment, York University (2005)
7. Bao, G., Wang, Q.: On the Building and Maintenance of Strategic alliance Relational Capital. R & D Management 3, 9–14 (2004)
8. Duysters, G.M., Heimeriks, K.H.: Alliance capabilities -How can firm s improve their alliance performance? In: Sixth International Conference on Competence-Based Management, IMD, Lausanne (2002)

Hard-Failure Diagnosis Using Self-tuning Kalman Filter

Xiuling Xu and Xiaodong Wang

College of Mathematics, Physics and Information Engineering, Zhejiang Normal University
{jkxxl,wxd}@zjnu.cn

Abstract. Sensor is the necessary components of the engine control system. Therefore, more and more work must do for improving sensors reliability. Hard failures are out-of range or large bias errors that occur instantaneously in the sensed values. The objective of the hard-failure diagnosis algorithm is to improve the overall demonstrated reliability of engine control system by using analytical redundancy to detect sensor failures. A new self-tuning Kalman filter based on engine model has been designed to avoid the flaw of classical Kalman filter which needs to accurately know the model parameter and statistical characteristic of noise in system. The self-tuning Kalman filter has been used in hard-failure and simulations have been done in fault sensors in the paper. From the simulation results, the conclusion can be deduced that the fault diagnosis method designed using self-tuning Kalman filter can detect sensor failures successfully, isolate sensed signal, and accommodate signal timely.

Keywords: hard-failure; Kalman filter; self-tuning filter; fault detection and isolation; residual; engine.

1 Introduction

Over the past years hydromechanical implementations of engine control systems have matured into highly reliable units, however, there is a trend toward greater engine complexity to meet ever-increasing engine performance requirements. Consequently the engine control has become increasingly complex. Because of the trend in digital electronics the control has evolved from a hydromechanical to a full-authority digital electronic implementation. Nevertheless, great efforts have been done for improving the reliability of the Full-Authority Digital Electronic Control (FADEC) system [1, 2], especially engine control sensor. Engine sensor is the necessary components of the engine control system. Therefore, more and more work must do for improving sensors reliability. Hard failures are out-of range or large bias errors that occur instantaneously in the sensed values. Two methods are available for incorporating sensor redundancy to detect hard failure [3, 4]. The first method, hardware redundancy, involves adding multiple identical sensors to the control system [5]. A technique such as voting can then be used to detect and isolate sensor failures so that a faulty sensor can be eliminated from the system. Redundant multiple sensors, however, do have some drawbacks when incorporated into a control system. Adding redundant sensors to the controls hardware will increase the weight, cost, and complexity of the control system. The second method of incorporating sensor redundancy is software or analytic redundancy [6].

R. Chen (Ed.): ICICIS 2011, Part I, CCIS 134, pp. 326–334, 2011.

This method requires the controls computer, through software, to determine when a sensor failure has occurred without redundant hardware sensors in the control system. The controls computer can then provide an estimate of the correct value of the failed sensor's output to the control algorithm. This paper describes an advanced sensor failure detection, isolation, and accommodation algorithm based the second method. The implementation was achieved using parallel processing and a high level programming language. The algorithm is described and the hardware and software considerations necessary to achieve the real-time implementation are discussed along with some of the practical experience gained during the process.

2 Algorithm Description

The algorithm detects, isolates, and accommodates sensor hard-failure in engine control system. The algorithm incorporates advanced filtering and detection logic and is shown in Fig.1.

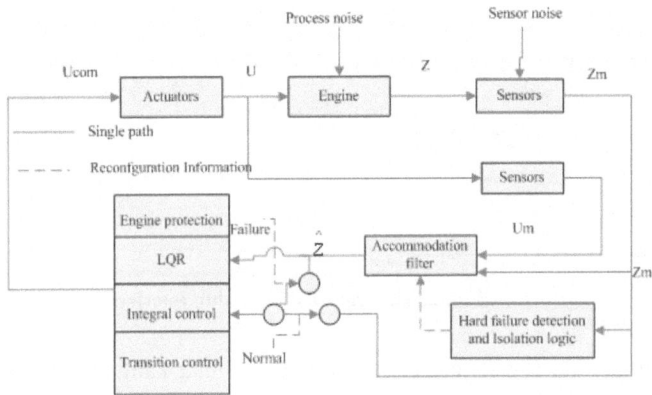

Fig. 1. Tested System with Hard-failure Diagnosis Algorithm

The algorithm consists of thee elements: (1) hard failure detection and isolation logic, (2) an accommodation filter, (3) the algorithm interface. These are shown as part of tested system in fig.1. The decision can be seen that kalman filter is the key from Fig.1. The algorithm inputs are the measured engine inputs U_m and the measured engine outputs Z_m. The algorithm outputs are optimal estimates $\hat{Z}$ of the engine outputs Z. The algorithm has two modes of operation, normal and failure. During normal mode operation, when no sensor failure is happened, the normal mode accommodation filter uses all the measured information to determine $\hat{Z}$. In failure mode operation, one of the five sensors has failed. A threshold process takes place once the failure has occurred. First the failure is detected. Once a failure is known to have occurred, the specific faulty sensor must be isolated. Finally, when isolation has occurred, the failure is accommodated by reconfiguring the normal mode accommodation filter which generates the estimates $\hat{Z}$. The algorithm interface is shown in detail in Fig.2. The tested system control includes four major logic sections: (1) transition control, (2) integral control, (3) LQR control, (4) engine protection logic.

In the normal, no failure mode the output of the accommodation filter, $\hat{Z}$ is fed to the LQR portion of the control while sensor outputs are fed to the integral portion of the control. When a failure of sensor i is accommodate, the output of the reconfigured accommodation filter, $\hat{Z}$ is fed to LQR. However, the i element of $\hat{Z}$ replaces the i sensor output, which is faulty, in the integral control.

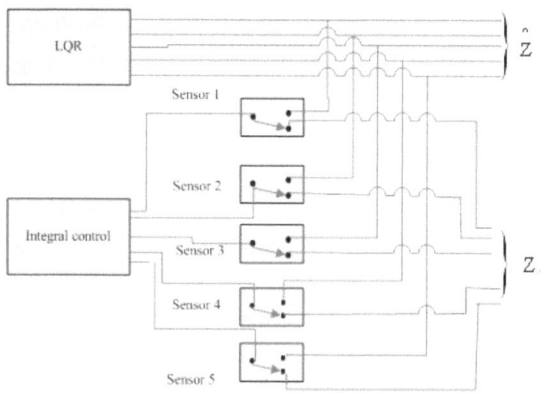

Fig. 2. The Dgnosis Algorithm Interface

From Fig.1 and Fig.2, results can be deduced that kalman filter is the key in the method. It applies on not only hard-failure detection, isolation, but also accommodation. Therefore, it need do great effort to design kalman filter. It also can be seen that U are engine inputs, Z_m are engine outputs, $\hat{Z}$ are optimal estimates of the engine outputs Z, and γ are residual generated by kalman filter. A set of residual vector γ can be received from sensed outputs of engine control system by kalman filter, that is $\gamma = Z - \hat{Z}_m$.

3 Accommadation Filter

From Fig.1, the conclusion can be seen that the sensor failure diagnosis algorithm is strongly dependent on accommodate filter, Kalman filter. Kalman filter is very powerful in estimations of past, present and even future states. It is greatly vital of the method designed in the paper. Kalman filter can generates residual vector γ, detect and isolate fault sensors using γ, finally can accommodate sensed outputs Z_m using the optimal estimates $\hat{Z}$ of fault sensors.

3.1 Self-tuning Kalman Filter

Performance of the accommodation filter and the detection and isolation logic is strongly dependent on a model of the engine. The model used has a linear dispersed-space structure as follows.

$$\begin{cases} X(t+1) = \Phi X(t) + BU(t) + \Gamma W(t) \\ \quad\quad Z(t) = HX(t) + V(t) \end{cases} \tag{1}$$

The self-tuning Kalman filter means that the model of noise can be obtained through statistical characteristic before filtering. A t the same time, the mean value and variance of noise matrix not only can be gotten, but also the gain matrix and error variance can be obtained . Self-tuning Kalman filter has been designed in the paper to overcome disadvantage of avoid the flaw of classical Kalman filter which needs to accurately know the model parameter and statistical characteristic of noise in system. The equation (1) is full considerable, and $X(t) \in R^4$, $Z(t) \in R^5$. In order to show problem simplicity for single input and single output system, the supposed can be put as equation (2)(3)(4).

$$E[W_k] = 0, Cov[W_k, W_j] = E[W_k W_j^T] = Q_k \delta_{kj} \tag{2}$$

$$E[V_k] = 0, Cov[V_k, V_j] = E[V_k V_j^T] = R_k \delta_{kj} \tag{3}$$

$$Cov[W_k, V_j] = E[W_k V_j^T] = 0 \tag{4}$$

Used Fadeeva expresions, the engine state-space model can transfer CARMA model [4,5]. The algorithm as follows:

$$F_0 = I_n, a_0 = 1$$

$$a_i = -(1/i)trace(\Phi F_{i-1}), i = 1, \cdots, n$$

$$F_i = \Phi F_{i-1} + a_i I_n, i = 1, \cdots, n-1$$

$$A(q^{-1}) = 1 + a_1 q^{-1} + a_2 q^{-2} + \cdots a_n q^{-n}$$

$$F(q^{-1}) = I_n + F_1 q^{-1} + F_2 q^{-2} + \cdots F_{n-1} q^{1-n}$$

$$B(q^{-1}) = HF(q^{-1})Bq^{-1}$$

$$C(q^{-1}) = HF(q^{-1})\Gamma q^{-1}$$

So CARMA model:

$$A(q^{-1})Z(t) = B(q^{-1})U(t) + D(q^{-1})\varepsilon(t) \tag{5}$$

$$D(q^{-1})\varepsilon(t) = C(q^{-1})W(t) + A(q^{-1})V(t) \tag{6}$$

The quotient of $D(q^{-1}), C(q^{-1}), A(q^{-1})$ and variance Q_ε of $\varepsilon(t)$ are known number. According to [7, 8], the self-tuning Kalman filter as follows:

$$\hat{x}(t/t) = \varphi \hat{x}(t-1/t-1) + \hat{K} z + [I_n - K_f H] * Bu(t-1)$$

among :

$$\hat{\varphi} = (I_n - \hat{K} H)\phi$$

$$\hat{K} = \begin{vmatrix} H \\ HF_1 \\ \\ HF_{\beta-1} \end{vmatrix}^{-1} \begin{vmatrix} I_m - Q_\varepsilon Q_\varepsilon^{-1} \\ d_1 - a_1 Q_v Q_\varepsilon^{-1} \\ \\ d_{\beta-1} - a_{\beta-1} Q_v Q_\varepsilon^{-1} \end{vmatrix} \tag{7}$$

The equations of general Kalman filter can be deduced as below [9].

$$\hat{X}_{k+1} = \hat{X}_{k+1/k} + K_k Z_{k+1/k} = \hat{X}_{k+1/k} + K_k (Z_k - H_k \hat{X}_{k+1/k})$$

$$\tilde{Z}_{k+1/k} = Z_{k+1} - \hat{Z}_{k+1/k} = H_{k+1} X_{k+1} + V_{k+1} - H_k \hat{X}_{k+1/k} = H_{k+1} \tilde{X}_{k+1/k} + V_{k+1}$$

$$\hat{X}_{k+1/k} = \Phi_{k+1,k} \hat{X}_k + G_{k+1,k} U_k$$

$$K_{k+1} = P_{k+1/k} H^T_{k+1} (H_{k+1} P_{k+1/k} H^T_{k+1} + R_{k+1})^{-1}$$

$$P_{k+1/k} = \Phi_{k+1,k} P_k \Phi^T_{k+1/k} + \Gamma_k Q_k \Gamma_k^T$$

In the kalman filter equations, the matrix Φ, G, H are typical state space system matrices where X is the 4×1 vector of estimates of the engine's state variables and γ is the 5×1 vector of residuals. The matrix K is the kalman gain matrix. All the system matrices as well as the kalman gain matrix are scheduled as a function of operating point to model variations in engine dynamics. Almost all of the matrices' elements are nonzero, thus, almost all the elements must be multiplied through the filter equations. In a word, the self-tuning Kalman filter can be designed.

$$K_k = \hat{K}, \ R_k = Q_v, \ Q_{k-1} = Q_w, \ P_k = P_{k-1}$$

Beginning term:

$$\hat{X}_0 = E(X_0) = X(0)$$

$$P_0 = E\{(X_0 - \hat{X}_0)(X_0 - \hat{X}_0)^T\} = E\{(X_0 - X(0))(X_0 - X(0))^T\} = P(0)$$

3.2 Hard-Failure Diagnosis

Hard-failure is defined as out-of-range or large bias errors that occur instantaneously in the sensed values. The hard-failure diagnosis algorithm compares the absolute value of each component of the residual with its own threshold. If the residual absolute value is greater than the threshold, a failure is detected and isolated for the sensor corresponding to the residual element. Threshold sizes are initially determined from the standard deviation magnitudes are then increased to account for modeling errors in the accommodation filter. In this paper, one kalman filter is used in hard-failure diagnosis. The hard failure detection and isolation logic is shown in Fig.3.

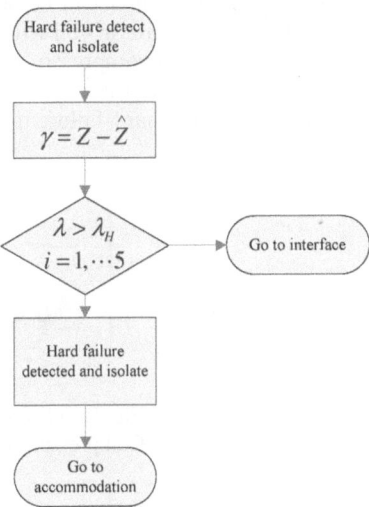

Fig. 3. Hard-failure Detection and Isolation Logic

The hard-failure detection threshold values λ_H (Table 1) are twice the magnitude of the standard deviation of the noise on the sensors. If the residual γ absolute value is greater than the threshold, the fault will be detected and isolated for the fault sensor.

Table 1. Hard-failure Detection Threshold

Sensor	i	Standard deviations	Detection threshold
XNLC	1	300rpm	600rpm
PT3	2	0.035Mpa	0.07Mpa
XNHC	3	300rpm	700rpm
T45C	4	20K	40K

4   Experiments

Engine simulation is used to predict the engine response to the induced failures on ground and the proposed flight conditions. Each sample time is 0.02 sec. Simulation for single hard-failure is first evaluated, and then, continual sensor failures of different sensors in the hard-failure are evaluated.

4.1   Single Sensor Happened Hard-Failure

Example: sensor of compressor speed has done hard-failure
When fault step has been given 820rpm for sensor of compressor speed on 100th sample, the residual of self-tuning Kalman filter can be seen to exceed threshold of sensor of compressor speed on 101st sample, alarm yell will be given, then the fault can be isolated. So the sensed signal for sensor of compressor speed will be replaced by the optional estimates of self-tuning kalman filter. Therefore accommodation of compressor speed has been accomplished in hard-failure diagnosis (Fig.4, Fig.5).

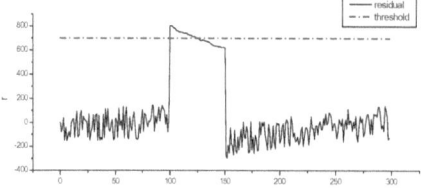

Fig. 4. Hard-failure on Compressor Speed Sensor Curve

Fig. 5. Self-tuning Filter Residual Curve of Compressor Speed

4.2   Continual Sensors Happened Hard-Failure

Example: fan speed and mixed chamber inlet temperature happened hard-failure
When fault step has been given for sensor of fan speed on 100th sample while 150th sample on the sensor of mixed chamber inlet temperature, the residuals of Kalman filter can be seen to exceed threshold of sensor of compressor speed and mixed chamber inlet temperature, alarm yell will be given, then the faults can be isolated respectively. From the simulation curves, the conclusion can be drawn that the algorithm designed in the paper can detect and isolate fault immediately, then accommodate sensed signal in time and in effect (Fig.6, Fig7, Fig.8, Fig.9).

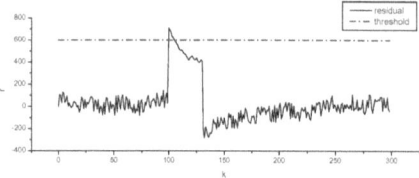
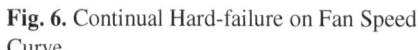
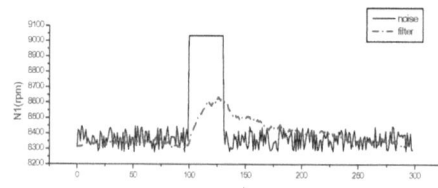

Fig. 6. Continual Hard-failure on Fan Speed Curve

Fig. 7. Self-tuning Filter Residual Curve of Fan Speed

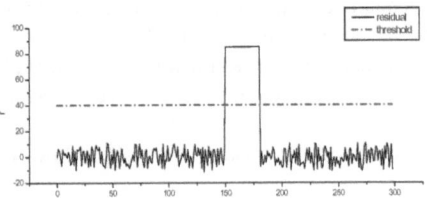 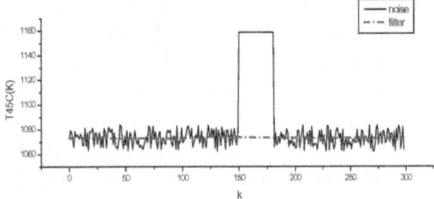

Fig. 8. Continual Hard-failure on Inlet Temperature Curve

Fig. 9. Self-tuning Filter Residual Curve of Inlet Temperature

5 Conclusion

In this paper, a new self-tuning Kalman filter for improving sensors reliability has been designed to avoid the flaw of classical Kalman filter which needs to accurately know the model parameter and statistical characteristic of noise in system. From the simulation curves, conclusion can be drawn that singularity fault of sensor not only can be detected and isolated timely, accommodated the sensed signal by the optional estimates reliably, also the continual fault of sensors can be done respectively and efficiently. The hard-failure diagnosis algorithm based on self-tuning can be used accurately and successfully.

Acknowledgement

The Project Supported by Zhejiang Provincial Natural Science Foundation of China (Y7100050).

References

1. Wang, S., Wang, Q., Cheng, J.: Using generalized likelihood ratio technique for detecting failures of engine control system sensors. In: Proceeding of the Second Asian /Pacific International Symposium on Instrumentation, Measurement and Automatic Control, pp. 191–194 (2003)
2. Fang, C.: Condition monitoring and fault diagnostic system of engine. International Aviation 6, 66–68 (2005)
3. Sanjay, G.: Controls and health management technologies for intelligent aerospace propulsion systems. In: AIAA-2004-0949, First Intelligent Systems Technical Conference (September 2004)
4. Takahisa, K., Donald, L.S.: Application of a bank of kalman filters for aircraft engine fault diagnosis. In: NASA/TM-2003-212526 the American Society of Mechanical Engineers and the International Gas Turbine Institute Atlanta, Georgia (June 2003)
5. Duan, Z., Cai, Z., Yu, J.: Unknown fault detection foe mobile robots based on particle filters. In: Proceedings of the 6th World Congress on Intelligent Control and Automation, pp. 5452–5457. IEEE, Los Alamitos (2005)

6. Takahisa, K.: Aircraft engine sensor/actuator/component fault diagnosis using a bank of kalman filters. In: NASA/CR-2003-212298, Aerospace Information (March 2003)
7. Kobayashi, T., Simon, D.L.: Evaluation of an enhanced bank of Kalman filters for in-flight aircraft engine sensor fault diagonosis. Journal of Engineering for Gas Turbines and Power 127, 497–504 (2005)
8. Yu, G., Zhang, S.: Switching ARIM A model based forecasting for traffic flow. In: ICASSP,Canana, vol. 2, pp. 429–432 (2004)
9. Zhang, P., Hung, J.: Gas path component fault diagonosis uding square root unscented Kalman filter for aeroengines. Journal of Aerospace Power 23(1), 169–173 (2008)

Research on the Structure Transformation of Landing Craft

Linfang Su, Xiao Liang[*], and Zhibin Li

College of Marine Engineering, Dalian Maritime University, Dalian, China
liangxiao19801012@126.com

Abstract. With the development of naval ship, many loading crafts with small displacement are replaced. However, it can be reused in coastline and multi-islands areas by improving carry capacity because the retired ships have excellent performance and unique construction. Therefore, how to transform a loading ship with small displacement into a civil carrier with large capacity was discussed. A three-dimensional ship model was established in MAXSURF, and the idealistic transformed model could be obtained by static stability calculation. Then, the model was verified by IMO regulation in stability at large angles of inclination. The total longitudinal flexural strength of the craft in sagging and hogging condition and the local strength were calculated and tested in detailed. The results show that to increase the principal dimensions of the landing craft can improve the carrying capacity successfully, which is an economic, convenient and feasible approach and can provide reference for the transformation and reutilization of the retired ships.

Keywords: Landing craft; strength analysis; finite element method; ship structure; MAXSURF; ANSYS.

1 Introduction

Nowadays many retired ships have been discarded, which is so wasteful. Because the aim of the landing craft building is for the war, the safety margin of strength and stability is more than the civil ship's, so it can be transformed into a larger capacity civil carrier. In the paper, the research is to increase the length of paralleled middle body of the landing craft can improve the carrying capacity successfully, which is economic, convenient and feasible approach.

In the paper, the hydrostatic stability was calculated, and the idealistic transformed model could be obtained. Then, the model was studied in stability and strength. According to the equal displacement approach, the stability was calculated by using MAXSURF. By means of ANSYS, the total longitudinal flexural strength and the local strength were calculated. Finally, the model was verified to meet the civil ship construction and inspection criterion.

---

[*] Corresponding author.

R. Chen (Ed.): ICICIS 2011, Part I, CCIS 134, pp. 335–340, 2011.
© Springer-Verlag Berlin Heidelberg 2011

2 Ship Stability Calculation

2.1 The Hydrostatic Stability Calculation

In this paper, taken a landing craft for example, the hydrostatic stability[1] is calculated in different length and different state which include the full load offshore, full load inshore, no-load offshore, and no-load inshore. Then the total trim was obtained. According to the principle of avoiding trim by the bow at full load, the idealistic lengthened value could be calculated. After a three-dimensional ship model was established, the stability at large angles of inclination was calculated and tested by IMO regulation.

Table 1. The principal dimensions of this landing craft

principal dimension	values
Overall length(L)	27.6 m
Length on waterline(L_{WL})	26.9 m
Molded breadth(B)	5.4 m
Molded depth(D)	2.7 m
Calculated draft(T)	1.29 m
Displacement(Δ)	153.4 t

Because the landing craft has unique construction, the original ship model is established according to the principal dimensions. The model is imported to HYDROMAX, and the no-load weigh and the center of gravity were calculated. Then the compartment of the ship model is plotted out. The compartment definition is given as follows:

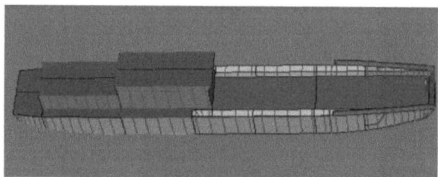

Fig. 1. Compartment definition

The stability is calculated at different length, and it is from 27.6m to 28.6m, 29.6m, 30.6m, 31.6m, 32.6m, and 33.6m, which refer to various hydrostatics parameters, such as weight, center of gravity, center of buoyancy, position of transverse metacenter and position of longitudinal metacenter. By means of the "Specified Condition" program, the other hydrostatics parameters can be gotten, which takes into account the longitudinal trim.

According to the results at different length, the ship longitudinal trim trend can be obtained. The trend of longitudinal trim at two conditions, full load offshore and full load inshore. From the calculation, it can be concluded as: with the paralleled middle body lengthening, the trend of the longitudinal trim values is decline. When the lengthened paralleled body is up to 6m, the values of longitudinal trim are 0.005m and 0.152m in full load offshore and full load inshore conditions. If the trim by the bow happens, there will be some troubles, such as decreasing in steerageway, taking wave on the deck easily and rudder racing, etc. For avoiding the trim by the bow, the lengthen value was chosen as 6m.

2.2 The Intact Stability Calculation

According to the equal displacement in curve of intact stability theory, the stability at large angles of inclination at different length is calculated in HYDROMAX. For checking the stability of ship in various load state, the arm of stability is needed to calculate in different displacement. The equal volume waterlines [2] method has two types. The first one is suitable to sea ships that have higher freeboard and the straight curve of broadsides. The second one is suitable to river boats that have lower freeboard and broadsides extraversion. In the paper, the first one is adopted. When ship float, center of buoyancy is B_0.

When an angle of athwartship inclination is φ, the ship float on the waterline $W_\varphi L_\varphi$, at which the center of buoyancy is B_φ, the coordinates are y_{B_φ} and Z_{B_φ}, the arm of stability is shown as follows:

$$l = \overline{GZ} = \overline{B_0 R} - \overline{B_0 E} = y_{B_\varphi}\cos\varphi + (Z_{B_\varphi} - \overline{KB_0})\sin\phi - \overline{B_0 G}\sin\varphi \tag{1}$$

Obviously, if the location of $B_\varphi(y_{B_\varphi}, z_{B_\varphi})$ can be gotten, the arm of stability that is l can be calculated.

Proceeding on incline an infinitely small angle d_φ, the inclining waterline is $W_{\varphi+d\varphi}L_{\varphi+d\varphi}$, which volume is equal to the one under $W_\varphi L_\varphi$.

$$d y_{d\varphi} = \overline{B_\varphi B_{\varphi+d\varphi}}\cos\varphi \tag{2}$$

$$d z_{d\varphi} = \overline{B_\varphi B_{\varphi+d\varphi}}\sin\varphi \tag{3}$$

$$\overline{B_\varphi B_{\varphi+d\varphi}} = \overline{B_\varphi B_{\varphi+d\varphi}} \tag{4}$$

Because the equation is shown as follows:

$$\overline{B_\varphi B_{\varphi+d\varphi}} = \overline{B_\varphi M_\varphi} d\varphi \tag{5}$$

So $\overline{B_\varphi M_\varphi}$ can be gotten, which is shown as follows:

$$\overline{B_\varphi M_\varphi} = I_\varphi / \nabla \tag{6}$$

I_φ is a moment inertia in vertical axis of the area under waterline($W_\varphi L_\varphi$) to the center of floatation (F_φ).

$$d y_{B_\varphi} = \overline{B_\varphi M_\varphi} d\varphi\cos\varphi \tag{7}$$

$$d z_{B_\varphi} = \overline{B_\varphi M_\varphi} d\varphi\sin\varphi \tag{8}$$

The state that an angle in athwartship inclination is Z_i similar to the overlap integral of countless infinitely small athwart ship inclination angles ($d\varphi$), which is shown as follows:

$$y_{B_\varphi} = \int_0^\phi \overline{B_\varphi M}_\varphi \cos\varphi d\varphi \tag{9}$$

$$z_{B_\varphi} = \overline{K B_0} + \int_0^\phi \overline{B_\varphi M}_\varphi \sin\varphi d\varphi \tag{10}$$

If the I_φ can be calculated and the $B_\varphi(y_{B_\varphi}, z_{B_\varphi})$ can be gotten by formula of (6) and (10), the arm of stability (l) can be calculated by formula (1). It is a key step to calculate the location of the equal volume under waterline. Actually, to solve the problem is adopted the repeated iteration method. Given $d\varphi$ and the initial waterline location on the midline, the program calculate the displacement that be compared with the given displacement, which process isn't stop until the difference between the calculated displacement and the given displacement less than the given error.

2.3 The Inspection of the Results

The HYDROMAX adopt the IMO A.749 (12) regulation. In the full load offshore condition, the freeboard is low and GZ is maximum. After the stability at large angles of inclination is calculated, the results at 33.6m length meet the IMO regulation. The calculation method in the other conditions, such as full load inshore, no-load offshore, no-load inshore, is similar to the above. All the results meet the IMO regulation.

3   Calculation of the Overall Strength and Local Strength

3.1 The Total Strength Calculation

In the paper, the total longitudinal flexural strength [3] of the craft at 33.6m in sagging and hogging condition is calculated by HYDROMAX. Considering safety, the wave height is set to be 4m. The calculation of the sagging bending moment and the hogging bending moment in the wave is shown as follows:

$$M_{hog} = M_{SW} + 0.19C_W L^2 (B_{wl2} + K_2 B_{tn})C_B = 1.53\times10^9 N \cdot MM \tag{11}$$

$$M_{sag} = M_{SW} + 0.14C_W L^2 (B_{wl2} + K_3 B_{tn})(C_B + 0.7) = -1.98\times10^9 N \cdot MM \tag{12}$$

M_{SW} — Still water bending moment; B_{tn} — The width of the cross-structure (the width of the tunnel). Coefficients K_2, K_3 can be gotten from the following formulas:

$$K_2 = 1 - \frac{z - 0.5T}{0.5T + 2C_W}, \quad K_3 = 1 - \frac{z - 0.5T}{0.5T + 2.5C_W} \tag{13}$$

Z — The height from the base line to the wet deck. The results are used in the calculation in local strength.

3.2 The Local Strength Calculation

In calculation of the local strength, the finite element ship model is built in ANSYS[4]. The total length of the model is 12m, which is divided into NO1, NO2, and NO3. The SHELL63 [5] are used to mesh deck, bulkhead, broadsides, ribs, brackets, etc. The BEAM4 [6] are used to mesh girder, stiffening beams, deck's transverse beams, longitudinal beams, etc. The ship model is divided into 516105 units [7].

The boundary conditions are two aspects. First, two sides are rigid fixing, in the left side restrict Ty,Tz,Rx,Rz and in the right side restrict Ty,Tz,Rx,Rz. Second, all the nodes in the central longitudinal section are restricted the Ty, Rx and Rz.

Putting the appropriate loads on the ship model is very important to the successful calculation. The external loads consist of the wave load, the gravity load and the inertial load. The wave load, which includes the hydrostatic pressure and the hydrodynamic pressure, is put on the shell element. The draft at full load offshore is 1.291m, in which the water pressure is equal to one in the baseline. The pressure in the other station can be calculated by interpolation method. The gravity load include the cargo load, such as 40t tank weight (the width of caterpillar is 623mm and the area interfaced with inner bottom is 4050mm). The inertial load has gotten, $M_{hog} = 1.53 \times 10^9 N \cdot M$ and $M_{sag} = -1.98 \times 10^9 N \cdot M$.

The analysis includes the following 4 load states:

Load state 1: Hogging, NO.2 full load, NO.1 and NO.3 no load; Load state 2: Sagging, NO.2 full load, NO.1 and NO.3 no load; Load state 3: Hogging, NO.2 no load, NO.1 and NO.3 full load; Load state 4: Sagging, NO.2 no load, NO.1 and NO.3 full load. The deformation map in the fourth state is as follow:

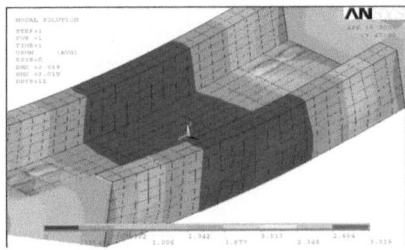

Fig. 2. The deformation map in the fourth state

4 Conclusions

Firstly, in this paper, it is discussed how to transform the landing craft, especially in increasing the principal dimensions. Secondly, after calculating the hydrostatic stability and intact stability, it can be obtained that increasing the principal dimension of the landing craft meet the stability criterion. Thirdly, after calculating the total longitudinal flexural strength and the local strength, it is verified that the transformed landing craft meet the corresponding regulations. Fourthly, the lengthened landing craft is tested to meet the civil ship construction and inspection criterion. Another conclusion, the retired naval ship can improve the carrying capacity to 28% through increasing the principle dimension.

References

1. Bai, S.Z., Hua, C.M.: A research of ship biomimetic fin stabilization at zero forward speed. In: Mechatronics and Automation, ICMA, pp. 114–118 (2008)
2. Sheng, Z.B., Liu, Y.Z.: Principles of Navel Architecture, pp. 87–99. Shang HaiJiao Tong University Press (2003)
3. Wang, F.H., Wang, W., et al.: Study on Hull Girder Strength Calculation Methods of Large Naval Ship. Journal of Ship Mechanics 9(3), 48–59 (2005)
4. R.Y.: The analysis of structure by means of ANSYS6.1. Peking University Press (2002)
5. Bathe, K.J., Dvorkin, E.N.: A Formulation of General Shell Elements -The Use of Mixed Interpolation of Tensorial Components. Int. Journal for Numrial Methods in Engineering 22(3), 697–722 (1986)
6. Guo, S.X.: Dynamic stochastic finite element methods for the damaged structure. Engineering Computation and Computer Simulation Theories and Application, pp. 35–41. Hunan University Press, Changsha (1995)
7. You, M.Y., Xie, L.Y.: Dividing the mesh and applications in engineering using ANSYS. Machinery (9), 37–39 (2007)

Dynamic Reasoning under Probabilistic Uncertainty in the Semantic Web

Limin Chen[1,2] and Zhongzhi Shi[1]

[1] Key Laboratory of Intelligent Information Processing, Institute of Computing Technology,
Chinese Academy of Sciences, Beijing, 100190, P.R. China
[2] Graduate University of Chinese Academy of Sciences, Beijing, 100049, P.R. China
{chenlm,shizz}@ics.ict.ac.cn

Abstract. Towards a full realization of the Semantic Web as a source of processable information and services, we extend description logic ALCO@ to admit dynamic reasoning under probabilistic uncertainty. In our formalism, the crisp knowledge is encoded in DL-knowledgebase, and the uncertain one is in conditional constraints; atomic actions are represented in terms of their preconditions (conditional constraints) and effects (possibly negated ALCO@-assertions involving only atomic concepts). We also summarize some reasoning tasks in the new formalism and provide algorithms for them. This work is strictly related to the practical need of DL-based reasoning in the Semantic Web and is much closer than the prior formalisms to a practical formalism in the Web setting full of uncertain information and dynamic processing.

Keywords: Semantic Web, Dynamic Reasoning under Uncertainty, Description Logic.

1 Introduction

Description logics (DL for short) [1] play an important role in the Semantic Web in that they are the logical foundations of the Web ontology language OWL (recommended by W3C). However, there exist at least two gaps between DLs and a practical formalism for agents with incomplete knowledge in the Web full of static information (provided by ontologies) and dynamic processing (provided by Web applications).

GAP One: *DLs are originally designed for representing static knowledge, while the dynamic information processing is a primary characteristic of the Web.*

Not only serves as a repository for information, the Web also provides services, with a long term aim to make the Web support shared processing as well as the shared information [2].

GAP Two: *DLs are logics with Boolean truth values, and hence cannot deal with uncertainty which is another intrinsic feature of the Web content.*

The need for handling uncertainty in the Semantic Web domain has been recognized for a long time and the efforts in this field have culminated in a W3C Group Report [3].

R. Chen (Ed.): ICICIS 2011, Part I, CCIS 134, pp. 341–347, 2011.
© Springer-Verlag Berlin Heidelberg 2011

Although there have been some investigations on extending DLs to bridge the two gaps, i.e., integrating DLs with action formalisms, or augmenting DLs to cope with uncertain information separately [4-11], there is little work towards the DL-based dynamic reasoning under probabilistic uncertainty for the Semantic Web. In the first regards, dynamic extensions of DLs mainly aim to bridge the expressiveness gap among the existing mainstream action formalisms in the background of the Sematic Web: their underlying languages are either first (or higher) order and do not admit decidable reasoning, or are decidable but only propositional. As for DL-based uncertainty representing and reasoning, to our knowledge, Giugno's and Lukasiewicz's works are the only approach to extend description logics with probabilistic uncertainty for the Semantic Web [6-7], although probabilistic description logics before the Semantic Web vision has been investigated, such as [8-11]. The main flaw in such formalisms is their lack of consideration for dynamic reasoning, which is of ever-increasing importance due to the abundance of computations provided by web services.

Obviously, a full realization of the Web as a source of processable information and services demands formalisms capable of representing and reasoning about actions under uncertainty, which cannot be satisfied by the current DL-based formalisms. Towards such a vision, we proposed a formalism for the Semantic Web. It is a probabilistic extension of the dynamic description logic D_ALCO@, which in turn extends DL ALCO@ by representing actions in a PDL[12]-like manner. Note that reasoning about actions in a probabilistic setting is not a new topic and there are many literatures in this aspect, yet they are not nearly related to our DL-based formalism.

Paper's Outline. We first gave a brief overview of dynamic description logic D_ALCO@ (Sec.2), then detailed PD_ALCO@ in Sec.3, including its syntax, semantics and some reasoning notions. Sec.4 summarizes some tasks of dynamic reasoning under uncertainty and also provides algorithms for them. Finally, we conclude the paper in Sec.5.

2 A Brief Revisit to Dynamic Description Logic D_ALCO@

(Syntax) Primary alphabets of D-ALCO@ include: i) N_R for role names; ii) N_C for concept names; iii) N_I for individual names; and iv) N_A for atomic action names. The concepts and roles in D-ALCO@ are the same as that in $ALCO$ with "$C, D \rightarrow C_i \mid \{o\}$ $\mid \neg C \mid (C \sqcap D) \mid @_o C \ (C \sqcap D) \mid \exists R. \ C$" & "$R \rightarrow P$", where $C_i \in N_C$, $o \in N_I$, $P \in N_R$. We use $\bot, \top, (C \sqcup D)$, and $\forall R. \ C$ to short $(C \sqcap \neg C)$, $\neg \bot$, $\neg(\neg C \sqcap \neg D)$, and $\neg \exists R. \ \neg C$, resp.

Formulas in D-ALCO@ are built with: $\varphi, \psi \rightarrow C(u) \mid R(u,v) \mid \neg \varphi \mid \varphi \vee \psi \mid <\pi>\varphi$, where $u, v \in N_I$, $R \in N_R$ and π is an action defined later. We define the logical connectives "$\rightarrow$" and "$\leftrightarrow$" in terms of "$\neg$", "$\vee$", as usual, and define "$[\pi]\varphi$" as "$\neg<\pi>\neg\varphi$". **ABox** and **TBox** in *D-ALCO* are the same as that in *ALCO*. Here we assume that readers have some familiarity with DL and omit some details of them.

An atomic action in D-ALCO@ is defined as $\alpha \equiv (Pre, Eff)$, where i) $\alpha \in N_A$ is the name of the atomic action; ii) *Pre* is a finite set of formulas; and iii) *Eff* is a finite set of formulas of the form $C(a)$ or $R(a,b)$, or their negations. D_ALCO@

actions are built with: $\pi, \pi' \rightarrow a \mid \varphi? \mid \pi \cup \pi' \mid \pi ; \pi' \mid \pi^*$, where a is an atomic action, and φ is a formula. An action box is a finite set of atomic actions.

(**Semantics**) A D-ALCO@ interpretation is a triple $M = (\Delta, W, I)$, where Δ is a set of individuals, W is a set of possible worlds and I associates each $w \in W$ a first-order interpretation $I(w)$. M interprets ALCO@-parts in possible world w as $I(w)$ does, and interprets actions as accessibility between possible worlds. Due to space limit, we refer the interesting readers to [13] for more details.

3   Extending D-ALCO@ with Probabilistic Uncertainty

In this section we present PD_ALCO@, a formalism admitting dynamic reasoning under probabilistic uncertain settings for the Semantic Web. It employs conditional constraints [7] to express interval restrictions for conditional probabilities over concepts, and lexicographic entailment for probabilistic reasoning.

(**Syntax**) Concepts and roles in PD_ALCO@ are built up with the same syntax rules as that for roles and concepts in ALCO@, resp. The definitions of axioms, TBox and ABox in PD_ALCO@ are also the same as those corresponding definitions in ALCO@. The set N_I of individuals in PD_ALCO@ is divided into two disjoint sets: the set I_C of classical individuals and the set I_P of probabilistic individuals which are those individuals in N_I related to which we store some probabilistic knowledge.

A *conditional constraint* is an expression of the form $(C|D)[l,u]$, where C, D are concepts free of probabilistic individuals, and l, u are reals in $[0,1]$. The conditional constraint $(C|D)[l,u]$ encodes an interval restriction for conditional probabilities over concepts C and D : for a randomly chosen individual o, if $D(o)$ holds, then the probability of $C(o)$ lies in $[l,u]$.

A PTBox $PT =(T,P)$ consists of a TBox T and a finite set of conditional constraints P. A PABox $PA=P_o$ for $o \in I_P$ is a finite set of conditional constraints that are specific probabilistic knowledge about o.

Atomic actions in PD_ALCO@ differ from that in D_ALCO@ in that they allow probabilistic knowledge in their preconditions.

Definition 1. An atomic action in D-ALCO@ is defined as $\alpha \equiv (Pre, Eff)$, where i) $\alpha \in N_A$ is the name of the atomic action; ii) *Pre* is a finite set conditional constraints (generally or specific to some individuals) specifying the action's preconditions; and iii) *Eff* is a finite set of possibly negated primitive ALCO@-assertions.

Actions are built with: $\pi, \pi' \rightarrow a \mid \varphi? \mid \pi \cup \pi' \mid \pi ; \pi' \mid \pi^*$, where a is an atomic action, and φ is a possibly negated ALCO@-assertion or a conditional constraint.

Dynamic conditional constraints (dynamic c-constraints for short) are more complex than conditional constraints and built up with $f \rightarrow cc \mid <\pi>f$, where π is an action and cc is a conditional constraint.

A dynamic probabilistic knowledge base in KB=$(T,P,\{P_o\}_{o \in Ip}, A_C)$ consists of a PTBox (T,P), a PABox P_o for each $o \in I_P$, and an A_C. Informally, a dynamic probabilistic knowledge base extends a probabilistic knowledge base in [7] by an ActionBox which encodes the dynamic aspects of the domain.

(Semantics) A PD_ALCO@ interpretation is a pair $Pr = (M, \mu)$ consisting of a D_ALCO@ interpretation $M = (\Delta, W, I)$ and a probability function over Δ, i.e., μ: $\Delta \rightarrow [0,1]$ subject to for each $o \in \Delta$, $\mu(o) \geqq 0$ and $\Sigma \mu(o)=1$.

Pr interprets concepts and roles at $w \in W$ as $I(w)$ does: 1) $A^{Pr,w}=A^{M,w}=A^{I(w)} \subseteq \Delta$; 2) $P^{Pr,w}= P^{I(w)} \subseteq \Delta \times \Delta$; 3) $(\neg C)^{Pr,w}=\Delta \setminus C^{Pr,w}$; 4) $(C \sqcap D)^{Pr,w} = C^{Pr,w} \cap D^{Pr,w}$; 5) $\{o\}^{Pr,w}=\{o\}$; 6) $(@_o C)^{Pr,w} =\Delta$ if $o \in C^{Pr,w}$ and $= \emptyset$ o.w.; 7) $(\forall R.C)^{Pr,w} = (\forall R.C)^{I(w)} = \{ x \mid \forall y \in \Delta$ subject to $(x, y) \in R^{I(w)}$ implies $y \in C^{I(w)}\}$.

The probability of concept C in $Pr = (\Delta, W, I, \mu)$ at $w \in W$, noted $Pr_w(C)$, is defined as

$$Pr_w(C)=\Sigma \mu(o), \text{ for each } o \in C^{Pr,w} \tag{1}$$

We abbreviate $Pr_w(C \sqcap D)/Pr_w(D)$ as $Pr_w(C|D)$ when $Pr_w(D) \neq 0$.

Pr satisfies $(C|D)[l,u]$ at possible world w, noted $Pr,w \models (C|D)[l,u]$ iff $Pr_w(D)=0$ or $Pr_w(C|D) \in [l,u]$. Pr satisfies a set P of conditional constraints at w, noted $Pr,w \models P$, iff $Pr,w \models p$ for each $p \in P$.

Actions are still interpreted as accessibility between possible worlds in Pr: 1) $\alpha^{Pr} = (Pre, Eff)^{Pr} = \{ (w,w') \mid w,w' \in W$ such that $Pr,w \models Pre$ and $I(w) \rightarrow_a I(w')\}$; 2) $(\varphi?)^{Pr} = \{ (w,w) \mid (w,w) \in W$ such that $I(w) \models \varphi\}$; 3) $(\pi \cup \pi')^{Pr} = (\pi)^{Pr} \cup (\pi')^{Pr}$; 4) $(\pi ; \pi')^{Pr} = \{ (w,w') \mid \exists w_t \in W$ such that $(w,w_t) \in (\pi)^{Pr}$ and $(w_t,w) \in (\pi')^{Pr} \}$; 5) $(\pi^*)^{Pr} = $ the reflexive and transitive closure of $(\pi)^{Pr}$.

The updated probability of concept C from w in $Pr=(\Delta, W, I, \mu)$ w.r.t. atomic action a, noted $Pr_{a,w}(C)$, is defined as $Pr_{a,w}(C)= Pr_v(C)$, where $(w,v) \in \alpha^{Pr}$.

Pr satisfies a dynamic c-constraint $<\pi>f$ at w, noted $Pr,w \models <\pi>f$, iff there exists $v \in$ such that $(w,v) \in (\pi)^{Pr}$ and $Pr,v \models f$. Pr satisfies a finite set F of dynamic c-constraints at w, noted $Pr,w \models P$, iff $Pr,w \models f$ for each $f \in F$. A dynamic c-constraint f is satisfiable iff there exists a Pr subject to $\exists w$ such that $Pr,w \models f$.

Pr verifies $(C|D)[l,u]$ at w iff $Pr_w(D)=1$ and $Pr,w \models (C|D)[l,u]$. Pr falsifies $(C|D)[l,u]$ at w iff $Pr_w(D)=1$ and $Pr,w \not\models (C|D)[l,u]$. A finite set F of conditional constraints tolerates a conditional constraint f w.r.t. TBox T iff there exists a $Pr=(\Delta, W, I, \mu)$ subject to $\exists w \in W$, such that $Pr,w \models F$ and Pr verifies f at w.

PTBox $PT=(T,P)$ is *consistent* iff i) T is satisfiable, and ii) there exists an ordered partition $(P_0,...,P_k)$ of P such that each P_i with $i \in \{0,...,k\}$ is the set of all conditional constraints that are tolerated w.r.t. T by $P \setminus (P_0 \cup ... \cup P_{i-1})$.

The results in [7] apply to our formalism too. The ordered partition is called the *z-partition* of P, and is unique if it exists.

A knowledge base KB=$(T,P,\{P_o\}_{o \in Ip}, A_C)$ is *consistent* iff i) (T,P) is consistent, ii) $T \cup P_o$ is satisfiable for each $o \in I_P$, and iii) $T \cup Eff$ is satisfiable for each atomic action $\alpha= (Pre, Eff)$ in A_C.

We next generalize the notions of *lexicographical preference* and *lexicographical entailment* to the dynamic setting as follows. First we use the *z-partition* $P_0,...,P_k$ of P to define a lexicographic preference relation on probabilistic dynamic interpretations. For PD_ALCO@ interpretations $Pr=(\Delta, W, I, \mu)$ and $Pr'=(\Delta', W', I', \mu')$, we say Pr at w is *lexicographically preferable* (or *lex-preferable*) to Pr' w' iff there exists $i \in \{0,...,k\}$

such that $|\{F \in P_i \mid Pr, w \models F\}| > |\{F \in P_i \mid Pr', w \models F\}|$ and $|\{F \in P_j \mid Pr, w \models F\}| = |\{F \in P_j \mid Pr', w \models F\}|$ for all $i < j \leqslant k$.

For a TBox I and a set F of conditional constraints, an interpretation Pr at w is a *lexicographically minimal* (or *lex-minimal*) model of $T \cup F$ iff no interpretation Pr' at $w' \models T \cup F$ and is lex-preferable to Pr at w.

$(C|D)[l,u]$ is a *lexicographic consequence* (or *lex-consequence*) of a set F of conditional constraints w.r.t. $PT = (T, P)$, $F \vdash^{lex} (C|D)[l,u]$ w.r.t. PT, iff $Pr_w(C) \in [l,u]$ for every lex-minimal model Pr at w of $T \cup F \cup \{(D|\top)[1,1]\}$. $(C|D)[l,u]$ is a *tight lexicographic consequence* (or *tight lex-consequence*) of F w.r.t. PT, denoted $F \vdash^{lex}_{tight}$ $(C|D)[l,u]$ w.r.t. PT, iff l (resp., u) is the infimum (resp., supremum) of $Pr_w(C)$ for all lex-minimal models Pr at w of $T \cup F \cup \{(D|\top)[1,1]\}$. Note that $[l,u]=[1,0]$ (where $[1,0]$ represents the empty interval when no such model exists.

Given a TBox T and a set F of conditional constraints, $T \cup F$ is satisfiable iff there exists an interpretation Pr that satisfies $T \cup F$ at some w. A conditional constraint $(C|D)[l,u]$ is a logical consequence of $T \cup F$, denoted $T \cup F \models (C|D)[l,u]$, iff each Pr at w that models $T \cup F$ also models $(C|D)[l,u]$; $(C|D)[l,u]$ is a tight logical consequence of $T \cup F$, denoted $T \cup F \vdash_{tight} (C|D)[l,u]$, iff l (resp., u) is the infimum (resp., supremum) of $Pr_w(C)$ subject to eachl Pr at w models $T \cup F$ with $Pr_w(D) > 0$.

A dynamic c-constraint $<\pi> (C|D)[l,u]$ w.r.t. PT is a *lexicographic consequence* (or *lex-consequence*) of F w.r.t. PT, denoted $F \vdash^{lex} <\pi> (C|D)[l,u]$ w.r.t. PT, iff $Pr_w(C) \in [l,u]$ for every lex-minimal model Pr at w of $T \cup F \cup \{(D|\top)[1,1]\}$, where $(w,w') \in \pi^{Pr}$. $<\pi> (C|D)[l,u]$ is a *tight lexicographic consequence* (or *tight lex-consequence*) of F w.r.t. PT, denoted $F \vdash^{lex}_{tight} <\pi> (C|D)[l,u]$ w.r.t. PT, iff l (resp., u) is the infimum (resp., supremum) of $Pr_w(C)$ for all lex-minimal models Pr at w of $T \cup F \cup \{(D|\top)[1,1]\}$ and $(w,w') \in \pi^{Pr}$. Note that $[l,u]=[1,0]$ (where $[1,0]$ represents the empty interval when no such model exists.

A (dynamic) conditional constraint f is a *lex-consequence* of PT, denoted $PT \vdash^{lex} f$, iff $\emptyset \vdash^{lex}_{tight} (C|D)[l,u]$ w.r.t. PT,; and f is a tight lex-consequence of PT, denoted $PT \vdash^{lex}_{tight} f$, iff $\emptyset \vdash^{lex}_{tight} f$, w.r.t. PT. A (dynamic) conditional constraint f about a probabilistic individual $o \in I_P$ is a *lex-consequence* of a $KB=(T,P,\{P_o\}_{o \in Ip}, A_C)$, denoted $KB \vdash^{lex} f$, iff $P_o \vdash^{lex} f$; and f is a tight lex-consequence of KB, denoted $K \vdash^{lex}_{tight} f$, iff $P_o \vdash^{lex}_{tight} f$.

4 Dynamic Reasoning under Uncertainty in PD_ALCO@

The main reasoning tasks in PD_ALCO@ include: i) PTBox Consistency (*PTCon*): Decide whether a given PTBox $PT = (T,P)$ is consistent; ii) Probabilistic Dynamic Knowledge Base Consistency (*PDKBCon*): Decide whether a probabilistic dynamic knowledge base $KB=(T,P,\{P_o\}_{o \in Ip}, A_C)$ is consistent; iii) Tight Lex-Entailment (*TLexEnt*): Given a $KB=(T,P,\{P_o\}_{o \in Ip}, A_C)$, a finite set F of conditional constraints, for concepts free of probabilistic individuals C and D, and action π from A_C, compute the rational numbers $l, u \in [0,1]$ such that $F \vdash^{lex}_{tight} (C|D)[l,u]$ w.r.t. PT.

The undying idea for *PTCon* is the same as that in [7], whose algorithm pt-consistency can be apply directly to PD_ALCO@. For *PDKBCon*, we can decide a dynamic probabilistic knowledge base's consistency according to the corresponding definition.

The *TLexEnt* can be reduced to the probabilistic reasoning in [6,7] by a concept regression process w.r.t. actions like that in [13] via the following theorem.

Theorem 2. $F \vdash^{lex} <\pi> (C|D)[l,u]$ w.r.t. PT, iff $F \vdash^{lex} (C^{Reg(\pi.\varepsilon)}|D^{Reg(\pi.\varepsilon)})[l,u]$ w.r.t. PT, where PT is a PTBox, F is a set of conditional constraints, $<\pi> (C|D)[l,u]$ is a dynamic c-constraint, and $\pi.\varepsilon$ is the accumulative effects computed by Equ.2.

For a possibly negated ALCO@-assertion φ, we define $\varphi^{\neg}$ to be ψ if φ is negated of the form $\neg\psi$, and $\neg\varphi$ o.w. The accumulative effects of action π can be computed by (2) inductively until σ is π.

$$\sigma.\varepsilon \rightarrow (\varnothing,\varnothing).\varnothing \mid \sigma;(Pre, Eff). (\varepsilon \setminus Eff^{\neg}) \cup Eff \tag{2}$$

For a concept C and $\pi.\varepsilon$, the computed $C^{Reg(\pi.\varepsilon)}$ holds the following property:

Lemma 3. For any $Pr = (\Delta, W, I, \mu)$, concept C and $\pi.\varepsilon$, $(w,v) \in \pi^{Pr}$ implies $(C)^{Pr,w} = (C^{Reg(\pi.\varepsilon)})^{Pr,v}$.

So, with Theorem 2, the tasks of dynamic reasoning under uncertainty in PD_ALCO@ can be reduced to the probabilistic reasoning in [6,7], which in turn can be reduced to the following two problems:

i)   Satisfiability (*SAT*): decide whether $T \cup F$ is satisfiable, where T is a TBox and F is a set of conditional constraints;

ii)   Tight Logical Entailment (*TLogEnt*): Given a TBox T, a finite set F of conditional constraints, concepts C,D free of probabilistic individuals, compute the rational numbers compute the rational numbers l, $u \in [0,1]$ such that $T \cup F \vdash_{tight} (C|D)[l,u]$.

The problems *SAT* and *TLogEnt* has been shown they can be reduced to deciding the satisfiability of classical DL-knowledgebase, deciding the solvability of linear constraints and computing the optimal value of linear programs in [7]. We refer the interested readers to \cite{lukas:08} for further technical details.

Due to the space limit, we omit the construction process of $C^{Reg(\pi.\varepsilon)}$ and the algorithms and the proofs concerned. We refer the interesting readers to the corresponding technical report [14] for more details.

5   Conclusions

We proposed PD_ALCO@ admitting dynamic reasoning under probability uncertainty. The main motivation behind this work is to develop a framework for the description logic based practical reasoning tasks in the Semantic Web where much information gathered from various resources is likely to be uncertain and many Web applications bring dynamics to the Web. It may be seemed as a PDL-like extension of description logics with probabilistic uncertainty. This work is strictly related to the practical need of DL-based reasoning in the Semantic Web and is much closer than the prior formalisms to a practical formalism in the Web setting full of uncertain information and dynamic processing. We think it will be of some interest to researchers in the field.

Acknowledgments. This work is supported by the National Natural Science Foundation of China under Grant No. 60775035, 60933004, 60903141, 60970088, 61035003, 61072085, the National Basic Research Program of China under Grant No. 2007CB311004, and the National Science and Technology Support Plan under Grant No. 2006BAC08B06.

References

1. Baader, F., Horrocks, I., Sattler, U.: Description Logics. In: van Harmelen, F., Lifschitz, V., Porter, B. (eds.) Handbook of Knowledge Representation, pp. 135–179 (2007)
2. Martin, D., Domingue, J.: Semantic Web Services, Part 1. IEEE Intelligent Systems 22(5), 12–17 (2007)
3. Laskey K. J., Laskey, K. B. Costa, C. G. , et al.: Uncertainty Reasoning for the World Wide Web (2008), http://www.w3.org/2005/Incubator/urw3/XGR-urw3-20080331/
4. Baader, F., Lutz, C., Milicic, M., Sattler, U., Wolter, F.: Integrating Description Logics and Action Formalisms: First Results. In: AAAI 2005, pp. 572–577 (2005)
5. Chang, L., Shi, Z., Qiu, L., Lin, F.: Dynamic Description Logic: Embracing Actions into Description Logic. In: DL 2007, pp. 243–250 (2007)
6. Giugno, R., Thomas, L.: P-SHOQ(D): A Probabilistic Extension of SHOQ(D) for Probabilistic Ontologies in the Semantic Web. In: Flesca, S., Greco, S., Leone, N., Ianni, G. (eds.) JELIA 2002. LNCS (LNAI), vol. 2424, pp. 86–97. Springer, Heidelberg (2002)
7. Lukasiewicz, T.: Expressive Probabilistic Description Logics. Artificial Intelligence 172(6-7), 852–883 (2008)
8. Heinsohn, J.: Probabilistic Description Logics. In: UAI 1994, pp. 311–318 (1994)
9. Jaeger, M.: Probabilistic Reasoning in Terminological Logics. In: KR 1994, pp. 305–316 (1994)
10. Koller, D., Levy, A., Pfeffer, A.: P-classic: A Tractable Probabilistic Description Logic. In: AAAI 1997, pp. 390–397 (1997)
11. Jaeger, M.: Probabilistic Role Models and the Guarded Fragment. Int. J. Uncertain. Fuzz. 14(1), 43–60 (2006)
12. Foo, N., Zhang, D.: Dealing with The Ramification Problem in the Extended Propositional Dynamic Logic. In: Advances in Modal Logic, pp. 173–191 (2002)
13. Chang, L., Lin, F., Shi, Z.: A Dynamic Description Logic for Representation and Reasoning About Actions. In: Zhang, Z., Siekmann, J.H. (eds.) KSEM 2007. LNCS (LNAI), vol. 4798, pp. 115–127. Springer, Heidelberg (2007)
14. Chen, L., Shi, Z.: Dynamic Reasoning under Probabilistic Uncertainty in the Semantic Web. Technical report, ICT(2010), http://www.intsci.ac.cn/users/chenlm/TR_DU.htm

PLS Regression on Wavelet Transformed Infrared Spectra for Prediction of Coal Contents

Yanming Wang, Deming Wang, Haihui Xin, Xiaoxing Zhong, and Gouqing Shi

School of Safety Engineering, China University of Mining and Technology,
Xuzhou 221116, China

Abstract. Study on multivariate calibration for infrared spectrum of coal was presented. The discrete wavelet transformation as pre-processing tool was carried out to decompose the infrared spectrum and compress the data set. The compressed data regression model was applied to simultaneous multi-component determination for coal contents. Compression performance with several wavelet functions at different resolution scales was studied, and prediction ability of the compressed regression model was investigated. Numerical experiment results show that the wavelet transform performs an effective compression preprocessing technique in multivariate calibration and enhances the ability in characteristic extraction of coal infrared spectrum. Using the compressed data regression model, the reconstructing results are almost identical compared to the original spectrum, and the original size of the data set has been reduced to about 5% while the computational time needed decreases significantly.

Keywords: multivariate calibration, wavelet transform, regression model, coal infrared spectrum.

1   Introduction

It is difficult to measure the contents of coal directly, and one potential method is using the infrared spectral properties and establishing the multivariate calibration models. But the huge data sets of the infrared spectrums greatly enhance the modeling complexity and reduce the analysis efficiency.

In order to enhance the predictive ability of multivariate calibration models, raw data are often pre-processed for the elimination of irrelevant information prior to calibration. Some approaches to the pre-process of raw data are first- and second-order derivation, standard normal variation (SNV), multiplicative scatter correction (MSC), Fourier transform (FT) and orthogonal signal correction (OSC) [1] , [2]. Applying the wavelet transform (WT) [3] as a preprocessing method shows the ability of compression and de-noising complicated signals and images. Wavelet transformation is becoming increasingly more popular in analytical chemistry, where it has been applied in the feature extraction, noise suppression, data compression and classification of NIR spectra [4], [5], [6], [7].

The main goal of this report is to present wavelet compression method applied to infrared spectrum analysis of coal. Discrete wavelet transformation is used to

R. Chen (Ed.): ICICIS 2011, Part I, CCIS 134, pp. 348–353, 2011.
© Springer-Verlag Berlin Heidelberg 2011

decompose the spectrum at different resolution levels. A large data set of spectrums is compressed and the non-significant coefficients are eliminated. Based on the wavelet pre-processing, compressed data regression model is performed.

2 Methods

2.1 Wavelet Transform and Data Compression

The discrete wavelet transform, which is easy to understand and also fast to calculate, was selected to be applied. In discrete wavelet analysis, a spectral signal $f(\lambda)$ is represented as the sum of orthogonal wavelet function $\psi_{j,k}(\lambda)$ at different scales:

$$f(\lambda) = \sum_{j=-\infty}^{+\infty} \sum_{k=-\infty}^{+\infty} C_{j,k} \psi_{j,k}(\lambda) \tag{1}$$

where $C_{j,k}$ are the wavelet coefficients.

A fast wavelet transform can be implemented by using simple procedures similar to Mallat's algorithm [9]. In fast wavelet transform, the signal $f(\lambda)$ is represented by a sum of the data obtained at different resolution levels of the original spectrum through the following formula:

$$f(\lambda) = \sum_{k} C^{J} \sqrt{2^{J}} \varphi_{J,k}(\lambda) + \sum_{j=1}^{J} \sum_{k} D^{j} \sqrt{2^{j}} \psi_{j,k}(\lambda) \tag{2}$$

where $\varphi_{J,k}(\lambda)$ and $\psi_{j,k}(\lambda)$ representing the scaling and wavelet function respectively, and J is the highest resolution level assigned in the WT calculation.

The wavelet basis functions are a family of functions that are obtained from a single wavelet called the 'mother' wavelet by translation and scaling. It is typically selected based on the signal processing problem domain. In this paper, we have used the orthogonal wavelet basis from the Daubechies family. DbN wavelets have properties appropriate for analyzing smooth signals with several vanishing moments, like plume spectrums.

The wavelet transform itself does not produce a compressed version of the original. Compression is achieved by eliminating the wavelet coefficients that do not hold valuable information. There are many possible threshold selection rules that can be applied to the estimation of a cut-off value in the wavelet domain. In the present study, recovered energy thresholding strategy was applied to select the wavelet coefficients. The percentage of recovered energy can be easily checked for an orthonormal wavelet analysis using the following expression:

$$RE = \frac{\sum_{j} |D_{e}^{j}|^{2}}{\sum_{j} |D^{j}|^{2}} \times 100\% \tag{3}$$

350   Y. Wang et al.

where $\sum_j \left|D^j\right|^2$ is the total energy of the spectrum signal, and $\sum_j \left|D_e^j\right|^2$ represents the total energy of the signal once the wavelet coefficients have been selected. This method removes all non-significant wavelet coefficients corresponding to all frequencies with exception of the lowest frequency band.

The compression ratio is given by the formula:

$$CR = \frac{\text{number of selected wavelet coefficients}}{\text{total number of wavelet coefficients}} \tag{4}$$

These two diagnostic parameters have been used in order to evaluate and compare the performance of the procedures applied on the studied signals.

2.2 Calibration Method

Partial least squares (PLS), is a projection method that models the relationship between the response $\mathbf{Y}$ and the predictors $\mathbf{X}$. The blocks are decomposed as follows

$$\mathbf{X} = \mathbf{TP'} + \mathbf{E} \tag{5}$$

$$\mathbf{Y} = \mathbf{UQ'} + \mathbf{F} \tag{6}$$

Here, $\mathbf{T}$ and $\mathbf{U}$ are the score matrices and $\mathbf{P}$ and $\mathbf{Q}$ are the loading matrices for $\mathbf{X}$ and $\mathbf{Y}$, respectively, $\mathbf{E}$ and $\mathbf{F}$ are the residual matrices. The x-scores t_a are linear combinations of the $\mathbf{X}$-residuals or $\mathbf{X}$ itself.

$$t_a = \left(\mathbf{X} - \mathbf{T} * \mathbf{P}\right) * \bar{\mathbf{w}} \tag{7}$$

where $\bar{\mathbf{w}}$ is the weight vector. This is done in a way to maximize the covariance between $\mathbf{T}$ and $\mathbf{U}$. $\mathbf{U}$ is related to $\mathbf{T}$ by the inner relation

$$\mathbf{U} = \mathbf{bT} + \mathbf{H} \tag{8}$$

where $\mathbf{b}$ is diagonal matrix, $\mathbf{H}$ is Residual matrix. The predictive formulation for $\mathbf{Y}$ is as follows

$$\mathbf{Y} = \mathbf{T'Q} + \mathbf{G} \tag{9}$$

where $\mathbf{G}$ is the residual matrix.

The quality of the results provided by the different pre-processing methods applied and PLS-regression models developed can be evaluated from a practical standpoint by testing and comparing the predictive power of the respective models. Thus, a useful index to test the quality of the results of a PLS-calibration model is the root-mean-square error ($RMSE$) of the residuals obtained, defined as

$$RMSE = \sqrt{\sum_{l=1}^{N} \left(\bar{q}_l - q_l\right)^2 \Big/ N} \tag{10}$$

where $\overline{q}$ the reference is value, and q is the calculated value and N is the total number of samples or spectra. On the other hand, the relative *RMSE* over the response range can also be employed:

$$RRMSE = \frac{RMSE}{Max\left(\overline{q}\right) - Min\left(\overline{q}\right)} \times 100\% \tag{11}$$

3 Results and Discussions

The wavelet analysis was carried out using the Wavelet Toolbox (for use with MATLAB). PLS calculation was implemented in MATLAB 7.0. The Daubechies wavelet functions, resolution levels have to be selected to give optimal performance. In this paper, the compression ratio *CR* measures the compression efficiency of the selected method while *RRSMES* measures the similarity between the original and reconstructed IR spectrum. Table 1 shows the results of compressing the IR spectrum with different Daubechies wavelet functions at resolution levels of 3 to 7 when *RE*=99%. Compression ratio has minimum value at resolution level 5 for different Daubechies wavelet functions. The Daubechies-2 wavelet function has the better compression efficiency than the others. For the same recovery energy threshold value, every case performs similar lower error.

Table 1. Compression results of IR spectrum using different wavelets and resolution levels

resolution level	Db2		Db4		Db6		Db8	
	CR	RRSME S(%)	CR	RRSME S(%)	CR	RRSME S(%)	CR	RRSME S(%)
3	0.1331	2.11	0.1336	2.09	0.1345	2.12	0.1364	1.96
4	0.0948	2.16	0.0908	2.14	0.0934	2.24	0.0956	2.09
5	0.0762	2.19	0.0772	2.20	0.0857	2.18	0.0861	2.11
6	0.0766	2.22	0.0780	2.15	0.0888	2.12	0.0914	1.87
7	0.0793	2.19	0.0788	2.16	0.0905	2.01	0.0925	1.82

The comparison between the original PLS model and the data compressed PLS model are presented in this section. All the spectrums of training and text sets are decomposed by Daubechies-2 wavelet function at resolution level 5. All PLS models have been variable centered, and all components included have been considered significant by cross-validation. Results from the original PLS model with 601 variables and the data compressed PLS models using different recovery energy is displayed in Table 2. The compressed regression models show similar results compared to the original PLS model down to *RE*=96%. In this case, the original data set was compressed to 5% of its original size. On the other hand, the data compressed PLS models cost less computing time than the original PLS model.

Table 2. Modeling results for the original PLS model, and for the data compressed PLS models

	RE(%)	CR	C		H		Cost Time(s)
			RRSME C(%)	RRSME P(%)	RRSME C(%)	RRSME P(%)	
Original PLS model	-	-	3.02	3.27	3.36	3.44	5.7
Data Compressed PLS models	98	0.0621	2.93	3.13	2.97	3.12	1.3
	96	0.0552	3.09	3.22	3.37	3.43	1.3
	94	0.0481	3.29	3.55	3.78	4.27	1.2
	92	0.0435	3.75	4.13	4.59	5.34	1.2

Fig.1 displays the original mean spectrum and the reconstructed spectrum using compressed regression model. As shown in the figure, it is possible to reconstruct the IR spectrum using compressed wavelet coefficients.

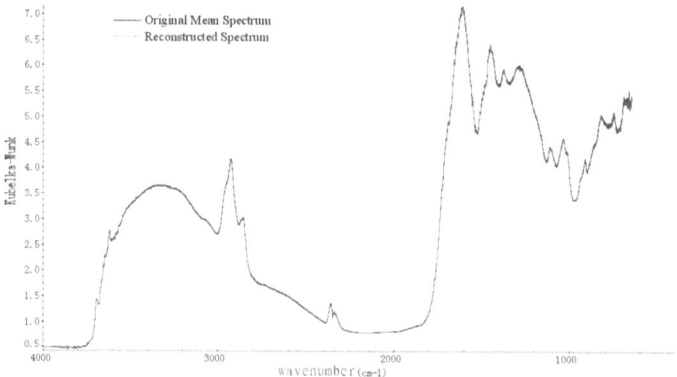

Fig. 1. The original mean spectrum and the reconstructed spectrum (RE=96%)

4 Conclusions

This work proposes a multivariate calibration method for simultaneous multi-component determination of coal, which is based on partial least squares regression combined with discrete wavelets transform as pre-processed compressing tools. The numerical experiments indicate that the wavelet transformation is a very powerful method for compressing data and Daubechies wavelet function works satisfactory for coal infrared spectrum compression. The regression example in this work shows that instead of using all spectral variables for original PLS model; the compressed data regression model reduces the original size of the data set to about 5% and the reconstructing results are almost identical compared to the original spectrum. In conclusion, the wavelet transform can be used as an effective compression preprocessing technique in multivariate calibration for coal infrared spectrum.

Acknowledgement

This work was supported by the State Key Laboratory Research Foundation of Coal Resources and Mine Safety (No. SKLCRSM08x06), the Fundamental Research Funds for the Central Universities (No. 2010QNA01), and the Scientific Research Foundation for the Introduction of Talent of China University of Mining & Technology.

References

1. Trygg, J., Wold, S.: Orthogonal projections to latent structures. Journal of Chemometrics 16, 119–128 (2002)
2. Bernard, J.W., Willis Jr., A.R.: An experimental study of fuel droplet ignition. AIAA Journal 7(1), 2288–2292 (1969)
3. Daubechies, I.: Ten Lectures on Wavelets. SIAM, Philadelphia (1992)
4. Trygg, J., Wold, S.: PLS regression on wavelet compressed NIR spectra. Chemometrics and Intelligent Laboratory Systems 42(1), 209–220 (1998)
5. Jetter, K., Depczynski, U., Molt, K.: Principles and Applications of Wavelet Transformation to Chemometrics. Analytica Chimica Acta 420(2), 169–180 (2000)
6. Esteban, I., González, J.M., Pizarro, C.: OWAVEC: a combination of wavelet analysis and an orthogonalization algorithm as a pre-processing step in multivariate calibration. Analytica Chimica Acta 515(1), 31–41 (2004)
7. Nicolaï, B.M., Theron, K.I., Lammertyn, J.: Kernel PLS regression on wavelet transformed NIR spectra for prediction of sugar content of apple. Chemometrics and Intelligent Laboratory Systems 85(2), 243–252 (2007)
8. Young, S.J.: Nonisothermal Band Model Theory. Journal of Quantitative Spectroscopy and Radiative Transfer 18, 1–28 (1976)
9. Mallat, S.G.: A theory for multiresolution signal decomposition: The wavelet representation. IEEE Trans. on Pattern Analysis and Machine Intelligence 11(7), 674–693 (1989)

The Case of Web-Based Course on Taxation: Current Status, Problems and Future Improvement

Zhigang Qin

Department of Public Economics, School of Economics, Xiamen University,
Xiamen, China, 361005
qzg@xmu.edu.cn

Abstract. This paper mainly introduces the case of the web-based course on taxation developed by Xiamen University. We analyze the current status, problems and future improvement of the web-based course. The web-based course has the basic contents and modules, but it has several problems including unclear object, lacking interaction, lacking examination module, lacking study management module, and the learning materials and the navigation are too simple. According to its problems, we put forward the measures to improve it.

Keywords: Web-based course, Web-based education, E-learning.

1 Introduction

The rapid development of information technologies continues to change the way people educate, work, shop, communicate, and play. In recent years, many Chinese universities have developed a lot of web-based courses in order to set up an e-learning environment for students and share the education resources. What are the current status and problems of the web-based courses? How to improve the web-based courses in the future? These are important questions. In the study, we take a web-based course on taxation as a case, to analyze the current status and problems of the web-base courses in Chinese university, and discuss the future improvements for the web-base courses.

2 Current Status of the Web-Based Course on Taxation

The web-based course on taxation was developed by the Department of Public Economics, School of Economics, Xiamen University. The web-based course on taxation can be found from "http://210.34.5.31/taxation/index.htm". Fig.1. shows the navigation page of the web-based course after enter the course.

There are four buttons on the top left in the navigation page. They are "explanation of the course", "relevant websites", "reference books", and "help". "Explanation of the course" shows the basic information of the course, such as the textbook, the study object, the abstract of the course, and the study requirements. "Relevant websites" gives a list of the relevant websites for learners. "Reference books" gives a list of

R. Chen (Ed.): ICICIS 2011, Part I, CCIS 134, pp. 354–359, 2011.
© Springer-Verlag Berlin Heidelberg 2011

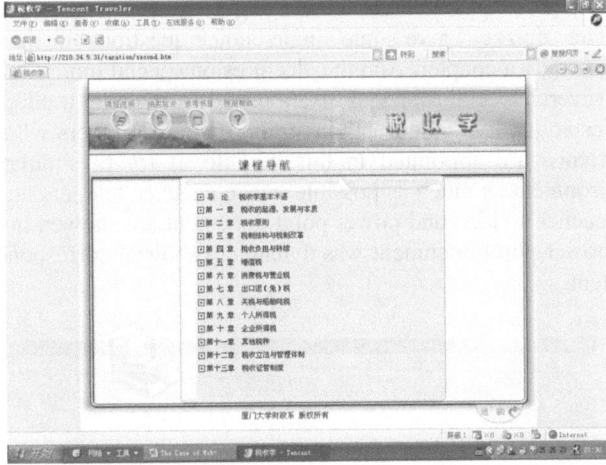

Fig. 1. The navigation page of the web-based course on taxation of Xiamen University

recommended books that can be read for reference. "Help" illustrates how to use the web-based course, such as buttons and navigations of the course, the meaning of the icons and symbols etc.

In the center of the navigation page, there is a content list of the course according to the chapters. Click on the list, it will link to the learning pages of the chapter as Fig.2.

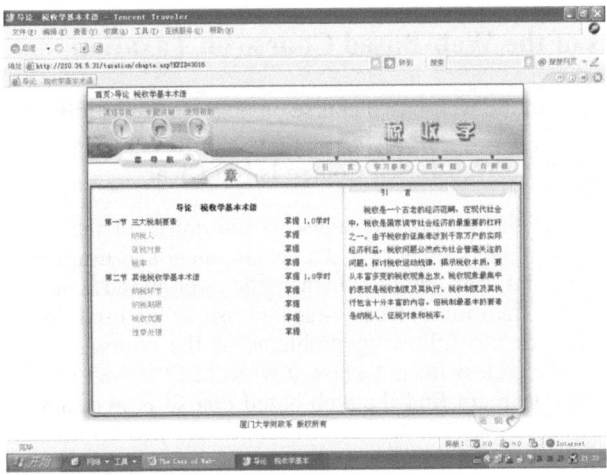

Fig. 2. The learning page of the web-based course on taxation of Xiamen University

The learning pages of the every chapter includes "main learning materials", "learning requirements", "questions for thinking", "quizzes", and "lectures on special topics". The "main learning materials" use text and flash to illustrate the main knowledges of the chapter. The "learning requirements" list the study objects of the relevant materials. The "questions for thinking" give some questions for the learner to think deeply. The "quizzes" give some single choice questions for the learner to text themselves after study a chapter. And the "lectures on special topics" give four videos of lectures on several special topics of taxation. In this module, it adopt video stream technology to establish live videocast classroom online. Teachers who have years of teaching experience are appointed in this module. It try to simulate face-to-face classroom environment as much as possible, make distance learners attain knowledge more direct. Teacher's video and power point document are showed in the same page as Fig.3. The power point document was dynamicly showed corresponds to teacher's prelection content.

Fig. 3. The "lectures on special topics"

3   Problems of the Web-Based Course on Taxation

The main problems of the web-based course on taxation are as follows:

3.1   The Object of the Web-Based Course Is Not Clear

The first problem of the web-based course is the object of the course is not clear. There is not a clear strategy object for the development and usage of the course. The course developers did not know whether the web-based course is used as a supplement for the traditional face-to-face class, or is used by the self-learned students. So it causes the following problems of the course. The teachers of the traditional face-to-face class do not know how to use the web-based course in their teaching, and the e-learners find the web-based course is not enough for their self-learning.

3.2   Lacking Interaction

The web-based course fouces on teaching only. It puts a lot of texts about the teaching contents on the web, but it lacks interaction. If the users of the web-based course have some problems, they can not find a way to ask and can not interact with the teachers and other learners. The problem make the course is not attactive to the distant learners.

3.3 Lacking Examination Module

The web-based course lacks an examination module. It has "questions for thinking" and "quizzes" after every section. But the "questions for thinking" have not reference answers, the users of the web-based course can not know whether their answers are correct or not, and what the problems of their answers are. The "quizzes" have single choice questions only. Although they have reference answers, the system can not give some explanation according to the users answers.

3.4 Lacking Study Management Module

The web-based course lacks a study management module. Users can not save their study progress in the computer. Every time, when someone enters the course, it will start from the same first page. The users have to memorize their own study progress by themselves. And if the teachers use the web-based course to teaching, them also can not get some ideas about the study progress of the students. It makes it difficult for the teachers to control the teaching progress.

3.5 The Learning Materials Are Too Simple

The learning materials of the web-based course on taxation are still too simple. Most of the learning materials are text, and some use flash to illustrate important knowledge points. These kinds of learning materials are not interesting enough for the self-learned students.

3.6 The Navigation Is Too Simple

Although the web-based course has a course navigation in the first page, and every chapter has a chapter navigation, the navigation function of the course is still too simple. Users can only choose the page from the menu in the navigation. They can not search by key words. And there are not links to the relevant topics in every learning materials. It is not convenient for the users.

4 Future Improvements of the Web-Based Course on Taxation

In order to solve the above problems of the web-based course on taxation, it can be improved as follows:

4.1 Set a Clear Object for the Web-Based Course

The first step to improve the course is to set a clear object for the course. As socialization of education trending evident, more and more people prefer lifelong education as their new learning choice. So the major object for the web-based course should be served the self-learned students. And for the students in the traditional class, the web-based course can be a teaching assistant of the teachers. Meanwhile, the students can use it as reference after the class.

4.2 Add an Interaction Module

The web-based course should be added an interaction module. The interaction of the web-based course includes the interaction between students and system, the interaction between students and teacher, and the interaction among the students. In order to improve the interaction between students and system, the course can be added a "Frequently Asked Questions, FAQ" module. The FAQ module collects the questions and answers that the students will encounter frequently. And it should has key words search fuction. When the users of the course come up against any problem, they can search the FAQ firstly. Email, BBS, Blog, and even WiKi can be used to improve the interaction between students and teacher, and the interaction among the students. Questions put by both learners and teachers during the instructional process will be processed and record in database of the FAQ, which reflect difficulties and key points in teaching. More times to use, more abundant will the database be.

4.3 Add an Examination Module

Examination function helps learners detect their learning effect. The web-based course should be added an examination module. In the examination module, teachers can upload examination questions and answers and other learning enchiridions via network. Distance learners can set item difficulty by themselves when they take online stochastic test. The examination should not only include objective questions such as single-choice tests, multiple-choice tests, and judgments, but also include subjective questions. After the students take the examination, the module can not only give the reference answers, but also give evaluation and reasons according to the students answers.

4.4 Add a Study Management Module

The web-based course should be added a study management module. The users can login the study management module by username and password. The study management module can save the study progress, quiz result etc. for the users. It can help the users to continue their study easily next time. And it will provide information to help the teachers to control the teaching progress.

4.5 Add Richer Learning Materials and Improve the Navigation

The course should use richer learning material to make it more interesting and more attractive to students. It can use more videos, games, cases analysis etc. to enrich the learning materials. The web-based course should provide key words search and the links to relevant topics in order to improve the navigation.

5 Conclusions and Further Work

This paper mainly introduces the case of the web-based course on taxation developed by Xiamen University. We analyze the current status, problems and future improvement of the web-based course. The web-based course has the basic contents and modules, but it has several problems including unclear object, lacking interaction, lacking examination module, lacking study management module, and the learning materials and the navigation are too simple. According to its problems, we put forward the measures to improve it.

And there are still many problems should be researched in the improvement of this web-based course. Such as, how to design the games for learning materials, how to design the collaborative learning tache, etc.

References

1. Du, J., Li, F., Li, B.: The Case of Interactive Web-Based Course Development. In: Leung, E.W.C., Wang, F.L., Miao, L., Zhao, J., Kleinberg, R.D. (eds.) WBL 2008. LNCS, vol. 5328, pp. 65–73. Springer, Heidelberg (2008)
2. Kuo, C.W., Yang, J.M., Lin, Q.P., Chang, M.: E-Learning: The Strategies of Learning Culture and Arts. In: Chang, M., Kuo, R., Kinshuk, Chen, G.-D., Hirose, M. (eds.) Edutainment 2009. LNCS, vol. 5670, pp. 101–107. Springer, Heidelberg (2009)
3. Gore, P.J.W.: Developing and Teaching Online Courses in Geology at the Two-year College Level in Georgia. Computers & Geosciences 26, 641–646 (2000)
4. Lin, C.B., Young, S.S.C., Chan, T.W., Chen, Y.H.: Teacher-oriented Adaptive Web-based Environment for Supporting Practical Teaching Models: a Case Study of "School for All". Computers & Geosciences 44, 155–172 (2005)
5. Duchastle, P.: Learning Environment Design. Journal of Educational Technology Systems 22(3), 225–233 (1993-1994)
6. Wilson, B.G.: Designing E-Learning Environments for Flexible Activity and Instruction. ETR&D 52(4), 77–84 (2004)

A Novel Block Encryption Based on Chaotic Map

Pengcheng Wei, Huaqian Yang, Qunjian Hang, and Xi Shi

Department of Computer Science, Chongqing Education of College, Chongqing 400067, China
wpc75@163.com,
{yhq_cq,eshixi,hmomu}@163.com,gmail.com,sina.com

Abstract. A chaotic block cryptographic scheme based on Chebyschev map is proposed. With random binary sequences generated from the couple Chebyschev map with different initial condition, the plaintext block is permuted by a key-dependent shift approach and then encrypted by the classical chaotic masking technique. Simulation results show that the proposed algorithm has excellent cryptographic properties such as diffusion and confusion properties and it can resist the know-plaintext attacks and chosen-plaintext attacks.

Keywords: Chaotic Maps; Block Cipher; Chebyschev map; binary sequences.

1 Introduction

The application research of information security using chaos theory has become an area of active research due to some good properties of chaotic signals and many research results are obtained [1-6]. Matthews [1] firstly proposed a kind of chaotic sequences cipher, and discussed the problem on using Logistic chaotic map to construct a key stream generator. Habutsu et al. [2] presented a chaotic encryption system based on a piecewise linear tent chaotic map. After that, Biham [3] pointed out this system can be easily decrypted by chosen-ciphertext attack, and complexity degree of known-plaintext attack is 2^{38}. In [4], Kocarev et al. proposed a block encryption algorithm based on chaotic Logistic map, and discussed the relationship between cryptography and chaos theory, and similarities of their crucial concepts such as mixing property and sensitivity to changes in initial conditions and parameters. Besides, Wong [5] proposed a fast chaotic cryptographic scheme based on the dynamic updating the look-up table, and no random number generator is required in this new scheme. Murali [6] studied a heterogeneous chaotic system and employed conventional synchronization method based on cryptography to realize secure information communication. There is no doubt that these research results can act an instruction role to latter research on chaos cryptography.

There are three drawbacks with the porposed cryptosystem: Firstly, the distribution of the ciphertext is not flat enough to ensure high security as the occurrence probability of cipher block decays exponentially as the number of iterations increases. Secondly, the encryption speed of these cryptographic schemes is very slow since the necessary numbers of iterations in the chaotic map for encrypting an 8-bit symbol is at least 250. The highest is even 65532. Thirdly, the length of ciphertext is at least twice that of plaintext, a byte of message may result in several tens of thousands of

R. Chen (Ed.): ICICIS 2011, Part I, CCIS 134, pp. 360–367, 2011.

iterations that need two bytes to carry. This will lead to huge ciphertext files for encrypting large multimedia files.

To overcome these drawbacks, a novel block cryptosystem based on a chaotic map is proposed in this paper. We will take advantage of the chaotic map properties and propose a novel chaotic block cryptographic scheme based on the Chebyschev map, With random binary sequences generated from the couple Chebyschev map with different initial condition, the plaintext block is permuted by a key-dependent shift approach and then encrypted by employing the classical chaotic masking technique. Simulation results illustrate that the distribution of the ciphertext is very flat that the entropy measured is almost equal to the ideal value. Moreover, the encryption time is very fast while the length of ciphertext is the same as that of the plaintext.

2 Random Binary Sequences Generation

2.1 Chebyschev Map

A particularly interesting candidate for chaotic sequences generators is the family of Chebyschev map, whose chaoticity can be verified easily with many other properties are accessible to rigorous mathematical analysis. The independent binary sequences generated by a chaotic Chebyshev map [7],[8] were shown to be not significantly different from random binary sequences. For this reason, a kth-order Chebyshev map [8] is employed for the design of the intended image encryption scheme. This map is defined by

$$f(x_{n+1}) = \cos(k \arccos(x_n)), -1 \le x_n \le 1, n = 1,2,3\cdots . \tag{1}$$

Here, the map is chaotic for $k \ge 2$ and we use $k = 4$ in this study. Fig.2. shows two time series of this map, with initial values differed only by 10^{-5}; indicating that the map can generate good chaotic (pseudorandom) sequences satisfying a basic requirement of a cryptosystem that demands such randomness. Fig. 1. further shows its statistical correlation curves.

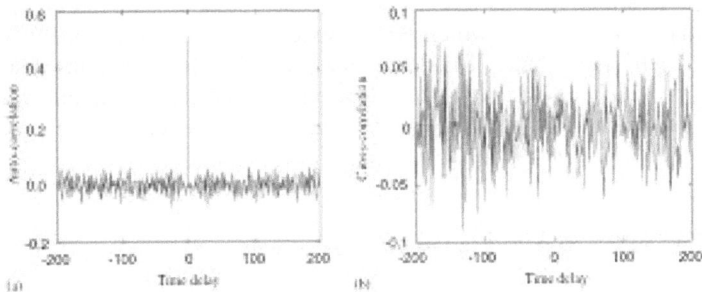

Fig. 1. The statistical correlation curves of a chaotic Chebyshev sequence: (a) Auto-correlation curve of the chaotic sequence when the initial value of 0.60000; (b) Cross-correlation curve of two chaotic sequence when their initial values are 0.60000 and 0.60001, respectively

2.2 Random Binary Sequences Generation

In order to improve the complexity and the period of the chaotic Sequence under the finite-precision circumstances, the chaotic sequence is generated from the couple Chebyschev map with different initial condition, Fig. 3. is the structure of chaotic sequence generator.

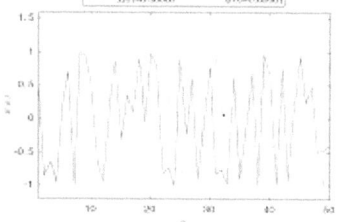

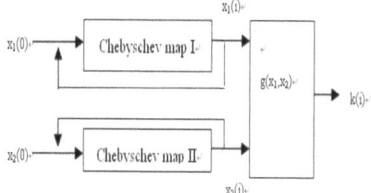

Fig. 2. Two time series of the Chebyshev with slightly different initial values

Fig. 3. Chaotic sequence generator

In Fig. 3., the chaotic sequence is defined as:

$$k(i) = g(x_1(i), x_2(i)) = \begin{cases} 1, & x_1(i) > x_2(i) \\ NULL, & x_1(i) = x_2(i) \\ 0, & x_1(i) < x_2(i) \end{cases} . \qquad (2)$$

We can obtain a binary sequence $\{B_t(k^n(x))\}_{n=0}^{\infty}$ from Eq.(2).

As a result, a binary sequence $B_i^n = \{b_i(\tau^n(x))\}_{n=0}^{\infty}$ (where n is the length of the sequence and $\tau^n(x)$ is the nth iteration of the Chebyschev map) can be obtained. It is composed of independent and identically distributed binary random variables [8].

The sequence B_i^n takes three significant roles in our algorithm: (a) permuting each plaintext block before it is encrypted. (b) encrypting the plaintext by employing chaotic masking technique, which is used extensively in conventional cryptosystems such as Khufu and Khafre, FEAL, IDEA, *etc* [9]. (c) determining the number of iterations in the chaotic map. Note that the binary sequence is random, which implies that the number of iterations of the chaotic map in our encryption process is also random.

3 The Proposed Algorithm

The block cipher studied in this paper operates on 64-bit plain-text blocks, and the length of key is 64 bits. Suppose plain-text is $M = M_1 M_2 \cdots M_k$, and its corresponding cipher-text is $C = C_1 C_2 \cdots Ck$, where k is number of blocks. Secret key $K = K_1 K_2 \cdots K_n$, where $n = 8$.

The proposed scheme is described in detail as follows:

Step 1: Input the plain-text, convert the plain-text into binary message M.

Step 2: Divided the binary message M into N-bits(N=64) plain-text blocks, let $M = M_1 M_2 \cdots M_k$, denoted $M_i = M_i^1 M_i^2 \cdots M_i^N$.

Step 3: Generate two values that are relative to chaotic system iteration.

$$\begin{cases} X_s = (K_1 \oplus K_2 \oplus \cdots K_n) / 256 \\ N_s = (K_1 + K_2 + \cdots K_n) \bmod 256 \end{cases}. \tag{3}$$

Step 4: Calculates the initial value and iteration times of the chaotic system (1)

$$\begin{cases} X = (X_s + R_{i-1} / 65535) \bmod 1 \\ N = floor(N_s + X * 256 \end{cases}. \tag{4}$$

R_{i-1} denotes the right half part of C_{i-1}, where C_{i-1} is the output block of former round.

Step 5: Based on the method described in Section 1, Iterates the chaotic map (1) N times with the initial value X, and obtain binary sequences $A_j = B_i^1 B_i^2 \cdots B_i^{64}$, and $A_j' = B_i^{65} B_i^{66} \cdots B_i^{70}$.

Step 6: Convert the binary sequences A_j' into integral value D_j, then permute the message block M_j with left cyclic shift D_j bits.

Step 7: Perform the following manipulation with sequences M_j and A_j:

$$C_j = M_j \oplus A_j. \tag{5}$$

where $\oplus$ is the XOR operation. As a result, the cipher-text block C_j for the message block M_j is obtained.

Step 8: If all the plain-texts have already been encrypted, the algorithm would terminate. Otherwise, let go to step 4.

The decryption process is almost the same as encryption one. We only need to replace Eq. (7) with:

$$M_j = C_j \oplus A_j. \tag{6}$$

4 Experiment Results and Analysis

Security is a major issue of a cryptosystem. In the proposed chaotic cryptographic scheme the sequences B_i^n, A_j' and A_j are random and unpredictable. These random properties are desirable for cryptographic security. In this section, we apply both theoretical and simulation results to elucidate some aspects of the security of the proposed scheme.

4.1 Diffusion Property

As we know, two main cryptographic properties of a good cipher are diffusion and confusion, which are commonly ensured by the balance and avalanche properties of the cipher-text in conventional cryptography [9]. Diffusion means spreading out the influence of a single plaintext symbol over many ciphertext symbols so as to hide the statistical structure of the plaintext. We examine the correlation between two vertically adjacent pixels, horizontally adjacent pixels, and two diagonally adjacent pixels, respectively. Relevant coefficient is defined as follow:

$$r_{xy} = \operatorname{cov}(x, y)\big/\sqrt{D(x)D(y)}\,. \tag{7}$$

Where is variance, is variance, x and y denote the gray value of image. In numerical computation, the discrete forms were used [10].

Firstly, randomly select 1000 pairs of pixels from an image, then calculate in term of formula (7),($N = 1000$). Signs r_{xy}^{h} , r_{xy}^{v} and r_{xy}^{d} denote relevant coefficient of between horizontal, vertical and diagonal adjacent pixels. In plain-image, r_{xy}^{h} is 0.9355, r_{xy}^{v} is 0.8663 and r_{xy}^{d} is 0.8545. In chipper-image, r_{xy}^{h} is 0.90187, r_{xy}^{v} is 0.0276 and r_{xy}^{d} is 0.0196. Because an plain-image has visual meaning, gray value of pixel varies slowly. Hence, relevant coefficient of between pixels is larger than cipher-image's in three adjacent cases. Whereas the cipher-image resembles noise, that is consistent with the law of statistics.

The distribution status of 1000 pair's adjacent pixels on (x,y)-(x+1,y) gray plane, which are chosen randomly, is shown in Fig.4, that is a help to understand the relevant coefficient in three adjacent cases. For example, (a) of Fig.4, random pairs in original image form a long and narrow strip on (x,y)-(x+1,y) gray plane, however,

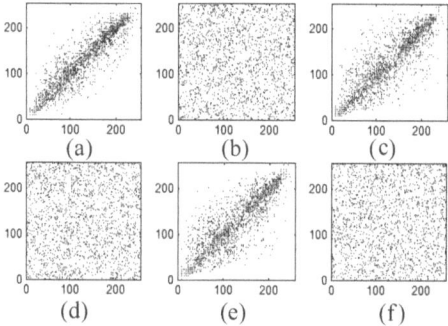

Fig. 4. Pixel gray value on location(x,y). (a), (c)and(e) indicate two vertically adjacent pixels gray value ,horizontally adjacent pixels gray value, and two diagonally adjacent pixels gray value on location(x,y) in plain-image respectively. (b), (d) and(f) indicate two vertically adjacent pixels gray value, horizontally adjacent pixels gray value, and two diagonally adjacent pixels gray value on location(x,y) in cipher-image respectively. Relevant coefficient of (a-f) are 0.9365, 0.0276, 0.8663, 0.0201, 0.8545, 0.0196.

these pixel pairs in the cipher-image behave a random distributive status, which almost fill the whole (x,y)-(x+1,y) gray plane. From the point of view of cryptography, this kind of random contribution, which is one of characters a good encryption algorithm should possess, fully shows that the proposed encryption system possesses a favorable diffusion performance of plain-text.

4.2 Confusion Property

Confusion means that the relation of between encryption key and cipher-text is masked, the statistic relation between secret encryption and cipher-text become complexity as possible, and attacker can not educe the encryption key from cipher-text. The image Camerman.bmp of size 256×256 and a full black image (namely, value of all pixels is 0) are encrypted using the same encryption key.The histogram of plain-images and cipher-images are drawn in Fig.5, respectively.

We find that, although the histogram of two plain-images has their distributive characters respectively, the histogram of two ciphered images are fairly uniform. It is very difficult to educe secret key from cipher-text when attacker try to attack by using the known-plaintext attacks or chosen-plaintext attacks [9].

4.3 Permutation Analysis

As stated in [8], the sequences $A_j^{'}$, A_j are independent and identically distributed binary random sequences. It is impossible to predict the next value from the previous ones unless one knows the initial value x_0 exactly. At the same time, only a part of the real-valued trajectory x_j of the chaotic map is used in the process of generating these sequences. Even if the cryptanalyst obtains the whole sequence A_j and $A_j^{'}$, there is insufficient knowledge to recover the real-valued sequence x_j. Therefore the estimation of x_0 and the subsequent reconstruction of the chaotic system are impossible.

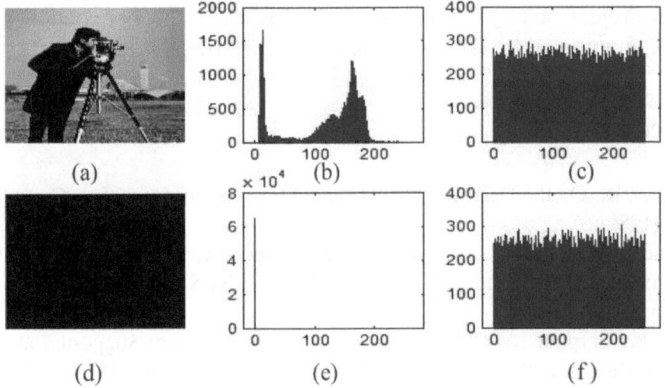

Fig. 5. (a)Is an image named Cameraman.bmp; (d)is a full black image; (b)and (e) are the histogram of two plain-image; (c)and(f) The corresponding histogram of cipher-image

Permutation is a basic operation for almost all conventional cryptographic systems (DES, IDEA, *etc*. [9]). In these systems, the permutation only rearranges the elements of the input block in a predefined way, once and for all, by the designer of the cipher system that is usually not influenced by the key. In practical situations, it is trivial and can be negligible in differential cryptanalysis. However, the key-dependent permutation makes it dependent on the key D_j. The permutation is then different for different message blocks. As the sequence D_j is generated from the chaotic map controlled by a secure key and with good random characteristics and sensitive dependence on initial conditions and system parameters, certain relationship between plaintext and entries of the look-up table found in [5] no longer exists. The difficulty of cryptanalysis is thus increased.

5 Conclusion

In this Letter, a new block cryptosystem scheme based on the Chebyschev map is presented. In this new scheme, the chaotic properties such as ergodicity and sensitive dependence on initial conditions and system parameters are appropriately utilized while the drawbacks and weaknesses of the existing algorithms are effectively overcome. Theoretical and experimental results indicate that the ciphertext distribution of our proposed scheme is very flat that the entropy measured is almost equal to the ideal value. The encryption speed is made faster while the length of ciphertext is the same as that of the plaintext. As a result, the proposed scheme is suitable for practical use in the secure transmission of confidential information over the Internet.

Acknowledgments

The work described in this paper was supported by a grant from CityU (No. 9041384), the Natural Science Foundation of China (No. 60703035), by Natural Science Foundation Project of CQ CSTC (NO. 2009BB2227), the Foundation of Chongqing Education Committee (No. KJ091501, KJ091502, KJ101501, KJ101502).

References

1. Matthews, R.: On the Derivation of a Chaotic Encryption Algorithm. Cryptologia XIII (1), 29–42 (1989)
2. Habutsu, T., Nishio, Y., Sasase, I., Mori, S.: A Secret Cryptosystem by Iterating a Chaotic map. In: Davies, D.W. (ed.) EUROCRYPT 1991. LNCS, vol. 547, pp. 127–140. Springer, Heidelberg (1991)
3. Biham, E.: Cryptanalysis of the Chaotic-Map Cryptosystem Suggested at EUROCRYPT 1991. In: Davies, D.W. (ed.) EUROCRYPT 1991. LNCS, vol. 547, pp. 532–534. Springer, Heidelberg (1991)
4. Kocarev, L., Jakimoski, G.: Logistic Map as a Block Encryption Algorithm. Phys. Lett. A 289(5), 199–206 (2001)

5. Wong, K.W.: A Fast Chaotic Cryptographic Scheme with Dynamic Look-up Table. Phys. Lett. A 298(4), 238–242 (2002)
6. Murali, K.: Heterogeneous Chaotic Systems Based Cryptography. Phys. Lett. A 10, 184–192 (2000)
7. He, Z.Y., Zhang, Y., Lu, H.T.: The Dynamic Character of Cellular Neural Network with Application to Secure Communication. Journal of China Institute of Communications 20, 59–67 (1999)
8. Kohda, T., Tsuneda, A.: Statistics of Chaotic Binary Sequences. IEEE Trans. Information Theory, 104–112 (1997)
9. Schneier, B.: Applied Cryptography, 2nd edn. Wiley, Chichester (1996)
10. Chen, G.R., Mao, Y.B., Chui, C.K.: A Symmetric Image Encryption Scheme Based on 3D Chaotic Cat Maps. Chaos, Solitons and Fractals 42, 749–761 (2000)

Fuzzy Evaluating Customer Satisfaction of Jet Fuel Companies

Haiying Cheng[1] and Guoyi Fang[2]

[1] Department of Computer and Electronic, Huazhong University of Science and Technology
Wuchang Branch, Wuhan, 430074, China
[2] Shenzhen Chengyuan Aviation Oil Ltd., Co., Shenzhen, China
whchy11@163.com

Abstract. Based on the market characters of jet fuel companies, the paper proposes an evaluation index system of jet fuel company customer satisfaction from five dimensions as time, business, security, fee and service. And a multi-level fuzzy evaluation model composing with the analytic hierarchy process approach and fuzzy evaluation approach is given. Finally a case of one jet fuel company customer satisfaction evaluation is studied and the evaluation results response the feelings of the jet fuel company customers, which shows the fuzzy evaluation model is effective and efficient.

Keywords: Jet fuel supply; Customer satisfaction; Fuzzy evaluation; Analytic hierarchy process.

1 Introduction

In the customer-oriented environment of jet fuel market competition, customer satisfaction gradually affects the survival and development of jet fuel companies. Thus increasing customer satisfaction has become the hot topic in the academic and business. In this situation, how to establish a scientific and reasonable customer satisfaction evaluation index system to evaluate customers' satisfaction must be an important issue in jet fuel business.

In recent years, business customer satisfaction in different fields, different applications, different ways and different types are studied and some researches are achieved. From the cost, facilities, business and service, Li Xiaobin evaluates the customer satisfaction and analysis on the basic theory. He proposes a freight service customer satisfaction evaluation system and a random sample of the freight customer satisfaction survey [1]. Lee Diansheng studies the port-logistics business customer satisfaction and theoretical models. He builds a customer satisfaction index system and analyzes the customer satisfaction survey results with the score and weight analysis approach [2]. Wu Rongzhen proposes the public transport services and a public transport services passenger satisfaction evaluation index system is given based on fuzzy comprehensive evaluation model [3]. Zhou Jianheng analyzes the customer satisfaction factors of third-party logistics based on the integrated performance indicator by a fuzzy evaluation method [4]. Wang Ying applies customer satisfaction

R. Chen (Ed.): ICICIS 2011, Part I, CCIS 134, pp. 368–373, 2011.

theory to combine the characteristics of the retail business and gives a customer satisfaction evaluation index system of a retail business model and conducts an empirical study of Wal-Mart supermarket [5].

However, those studies take less attention on the current literature of jet fuel companies to evaluate their customers' satisfaction. In this paper, the jet fuel company filling operations are studied and customer satisfies evaluation index system is established, which combines with the fuzzy analysis and evaluation methods. A case of jet fuel company customer satisfaction evaluation is given finally.

2 Evaluation Index System Analyses

2.1 The Principles of Evaluation Index System

Jet fuel company customer satisfaction evaluation index system can enhance the customer satisfaction of the jet fuel companies. To fully reflect the status of customer satisfies and operational characteristics of jet fuel filling factors, we must format a hierarchical and comprehensive evaluation index system. Several basic principles of establishing customer satisfaction index system that should be obeyed are shown as follows:

Guidance Quality. Because the view of customer satisfaction is used to design evaluation index system, selecting clients is the most critical step.

Measurability. For customer satisfaction need be quantized, it must be possible for statistical calculation, evaluation and analysis. To get the subjective indexes, a simple and effective quantitative method should be used.

Practicability. Since the correlation of indexes is small, the evaluation model should be simple and practical.

Dynamics. As customer expectations and needs always change in the market, customer expectations should keep adjusting dynamically in real time.

2.2 Index System

In accordance with the principles of the index system, we consider the filling operations characteristics of jet fuel companies, the analysis of relevant documents, interviews and questionnaires of the airline. A jet fuel company customer satisfaction evaluation index system based on the five dimensions as time, business, security, fee and service, is shown in Table 1.

The goal of customer satisfaction evaluation index system is marked as A. And the primary level indexes are listed as time (B_1), business (B_2), security (B_3), fee (B_4) and service (B_5). The second level indexes are marked with C_{ij} such as Wait time(C_{11}), Filling time(C_{12}), Appointment time(C_{13}), Time flexible(C_{14}), Filling quantity flexibility(C_{21}), Filling quantity accuracy(C_{22}), Filling process rationality(C_{23}), Filling facilities advancement(C_{24}), Safety awareness(C_{31}), Safeguard steps (C_{32}), Emergency treatment(C_{33}), Level of fees(C_{41}), Fee structure(C_{42}), Service awareness(C_{51}), Service attitude(C_{52}), Complaints handling(C_{53}).

3 Fuzzy Evaluation Model

3.1 Weights of Evaluated Indexes

During the evaluation process of jet fuel company customer satisfaction, the influence of each index is different. The scientific rationality installing of index weight will directly impact the final evaluation results. The paper uses AHP approach to decide the weight of indexes. The steps are as follow: (1) Build hierarchical level structure model; (2) Construct decided matrix; (3) get the max feature values and vectors of matrix; (4) consistency check the evaluation matrix, if the estimation consistency of each matrix element is so bad, the estimation should be done again until the elements are consistency. Then the feature vector can be used as the weight vector of indexes.

Assume the index level B has m primary level indexes. The next level C which composes index B_i has n_i second level indexes. The weight vector of index level B is marked as $W_A = (w_1, w_2, \ldots, w_m)$, the weight vector of the next level index which B_i belongs is marked as $W_{Bi} = (w_{i1}, w_{i2}, \ldots, w_{ini})$.

There are two kinds of weight vectors as standardized weight vectors (Eq.1) and normalized weight vectors (Eq.2).

$$\sum_i w_i = 1 \qquad (1)$$

$$\bigvee_i w_i = 1 \qquad (2)$$

3.2 Evaluation Remark Set and Results Analyses

According the feature of jet fuel company customer satisfaction evaluation, the evaluation index level can be divided into four levels as very satisfied, satisfied, general and not satisfied.

$V = \{V_1, V_2, V_3, V_4\}$, Where, V_1, V_2, V_3, V_4 means different evaluation level for each index, respectively.

Evaluation Matrix. The ith primary level evaluation matrix R_i is shown as Eq.3. Where r_{ijk} is the grade of membership for the kth remark of the index C_{ij}. There are four evaluation levels in this paper, so e is 4. The evaluation matrix is as Eq.4.

$$R_i = \begin{pmatrix} r_{i11} & r_{i12} & \cdots & r_{i1e} \\ r_{i21} & r_{i22} & \cdots & r_{i2e} \\ \cdots & \cdots & \cdots & \cdots \\ r_{in_i1} & r_{in_i2} & \cdots & r_{in_ie} \end{pmatrix} \quad i=1,2,\ldots, m \qquad (3)$$

$$R = (R_1, R_2, \ldots, R_m)^T \qquad (4)$$

There are two evaluation matrixes as standardized matrix (Eq. 5) and normalized matrix (Eq.6):

$$\sum_{k=1}^{e} r_{ijk} = 1 \tag{5}$$

$$\bigvee_{k=1}^{e} r_{ijk} = 1 \tag{6}$$

Evaluation Vector. For the two levels fuzzy evaluation, the main steps are as below:
The evaluation vector of the second level indexes is shown in Eq.7.

$$B_i = W_{Bi} \circ R_i = (b_{i1}, b_{i2}, ..., b_{ie}), \qquad i = 1, 2, ..., m \tag{7}$$

Where $\circ$ is the comprehensive evaluation composite operator. There are three types' composite operators as follow:

$M(\wedge, \vee)$, the single factor determine type is Eq.8.

$$b_{ik} = \bigvee_{j=1}^{n_i} (w_{ij} \wedge r_{ijk}) \tag{8}$$

$M(\cdot, \vee)$, the main factor determine type is Eq.9.

$$b_{ik} = \bigvee_{j=1}^{n_i} (w_{ij} r_{ijk}) \tag{9}$$

$M(\cdot, +)$, the weighted average type is Eq.10.

$$b_{ik} = \sum_{j=1}^{n_i} w_{ij} r_{ijk} \tag{10}$$

B_i compose the evaluation matrix B. After evaluating the primary level indexes, the total evaluated vector A is Eq.11.

$$A = W_A \circ B = (a_1, a_2, ..., a_e) \tag{11}$$

According with the principle of maximum membership, the evaluation level of jet fuel company customer satisfaction can also be decided from the evaluation vector's single value handling, which is to calculate the evaluation value V of the object and evaluate the customer satisfaction with V.

4   Case Study

One south jet fuel company designed customer satisfies questionnaires to survey the customer satisfaction for the company. The paper uses the return back questionnaires to fuzzy evaluate the customer satisfaction. The fuzzy evaluation steps are as below.

Get the indexes weights. With the AHP approach, each level indexes weights of jet fuel company customer satisfaction evaluation index system are decided and the results are shown in Table 1.

Table 1. Standardized Weights and Normalized Weights

Primary index	Standardized weight	Normalized weight	Second index	Standardized weight	Normalized weight
B_1	0.303	1.000	C_{11}	0.488	1.000
			C_{12}	0.141	0.289
			C_{13}	0.185	0.380
			C_{14}	0.185	0.380
B_2	0.112	0.370	C_{21}	0.427	1.000
			C_{22}	0.229	0.537
			C_{23}	0.207	0.485
			C_{24}	0.136	0.319
B_3	0.279	0.922	C_{31}	0.163	0.303
			C_{32}	0.540	1.000
			C_{33}	0.297	0.550
B_4	0.122	0.401	C_{41}	0.667	1.000
			C_{42}	0.333	0.500
B_5	0.184	0.608	C_{51}	0.169	0.382
			C_{52}	0.387	0.874
			C_{53}	0.443	1.000

Get the evaluating result. The jet fuel company evaluates its service satisfaction by customers' voting. The evaluating results are shown in Table 2. In Table 2, VS means very satisfied, NS means not satisfied.

Table 2. Evaluating results

Index	VS	Satisfied	General	NS	Index	VS	Satisfied	General	NS
C_{11}	7	9	4	0	C_{31}	8	6	5	1
C_{12}	8	7	3	2	C_{32}	6	7	6	1
C_{13}	6	10	2	2	C_{33}	7	9	4	0
C_{14}	8	9	3	0	C_{41}	5	8	5	2
C_{21}	6	9	3	2	C_{42}	7	8	3	2
C_{22}	5	9	5	1	C_{51}	6	8	5	1
C_{23}	9	6	4	1	C_{52}	6	8	5	1
C_{24}	5	10	4	1	C_{53}	7	9	2	2

Construct the second level evaluation matrix R_i and evaluate the second level. Use the three composite operators to evaluate respectively. When evaluating with composite operators $M(\wedge,\vee)$ and $M(\cdot,\vee)$, weight vector and evaluation matrix need normalized format. When evaluating with composite operator $M(\cdot,+)$, weight vector and evaluation matrix need standardized format.

Evaluate the primary level. The evaluating results are shown in Table 3 by evaluating with three composite operators.

Evaluating result analyses. According the principle of maximum membership, the results of three composite operators' evaluation are consistency. The evaluating level of the jet fuel company customer satisfaction is satisfied.

Table 3. Evaluating Results of Three Composed Operators

Composed operator	Very satisfied	Satisfied	General	Not satisfied
$M(\wedge,\vee)$	0.857	1.000	0.857	0.250
$M(\cdot,\vee)$	0.790	1.000	0.790	0.135
$M(\cdot,+)$	0.329	0.412	0.205	0.053

5 Conclusions

For the jet fuel supply market, achieving the customs greatest satisfaction is the most important condition for jet fuel companies to have success in market compete. The paper builds the jet fuel company customer satisfaction evaluation index system and gives the fuzzy evaluation model. One jet fuel company customer satisfaction is evaluated with the model and the satisfaction result has been found. The evaluating result of the case shows that this method has great function, which is simple and easy to operate and the evaluating result has higher reliable.

References

1. Li, X.B., Li, B.F.: Evaluation of Railway cargo transport customer satisfaction. J. Railway Transport and Economy. 32(5), 38–42 (2010)
2. Li, D.S., Wang, J.: Research on Customer Satisfaction Evaluation System of Port Logistics Enterprises. J. Logistics Technology 28(6), 88–90 (2009)
3. Wu, R.Z., Zhai, D.D., Xi, E.C., Li, L.: Evaluation model of satisfaction degree for urban public transit service. J. Journal of Traffic and Transportation Engineering 9(4), 65–70 (2009)
4. Zhou, J.H., Liu, Y.: Fuzzy Synthesis in Customer Satisfaction Degree of 3PL. J. Journal of Donghua University (Natural Science) 35(1), 94–97 (2009)
5. Wang, Y., Qiao, M., Zhang, Y.: An Empirical Study and Evaluation of Enterprise Customer Satisfaction. J. Information Science 26(12), 1182–1185 (2008)

The Research of the BDAR for ATS

Chengjin Gao[1], Sheng Sheng[2], and Lin Wang[3]

[1,2,3] Engineering College Air Force Engineering University Xi'an, China
ordin.gao@yahoo.com.cn

Abstract. The BDAR of weapons is an emphasis research in military domain. But the BDAR research for support equipment, which is the foundation of BDAR, is ignored. Thus, this paper studies of the BDAR of ATS that can test certain kind of missile. Firstly, this paper expatiates on the methods and steps that design the ATS with BDAR function. Then, this paper puts forward the idea that using Evolvable Hardware to design the ATS in order to satisfy its Combat Resilience which is based on the thought of reconfiguration. At last, this paper uses HLA to simulate the entire repair process when ATS is damaged in battlefield, validating the design of reconfigurable ATS is reasonable or not.

Keywords: BDAR, ATS, Combat Resilience, EHW, HLA.

1 Introduction

Battlefield Damage Assessment and Repair (BDAR) is a series of expedient actions to return the disabled weapons to a mission-capable or limited mission-capable condition by using emergency diagnosis and repair techniques on the battlefield. BDAR is appeared at the Fourth Middle East War in 1973 for the first time. Later, BDAR has been researched comprehensively by several countries and used in many local battles [1]. Nowadays, the emphasis of BDAR research is to study how to diagnose and repair the disabled weapons using uninjured support equipments. However, it is unrealistic to only study the weapons, because the support equipments are also easily damaged in the real war. That is out of question to rush to repair the weapons if having no uninjured support equipments. It is highly necessary to study the BDAR of support equipments, which is the foundation of repairing the damaged weapons. As a result, the emphasis of this paper is to study the BDAR of an auto-test system (ATS), which is used to test some kinds of missiles in an emergency.

2 Steps of the BDAR for ATS

At the wartime, it is not allowed to put up the missiles on the fighter-plane before the missiles are tested. The performance is bad or good of ATS will influence the battle effectiveness of missiles directly, which will affect the results of the war finally. Thus, when the ATS is damaged on the battlefield, it must be rushed to repair. The flow of the BDAR toward ATS is shown as Fig. 1:

R. Chen (Ed.): ICICIS 2011, Part I, CCIS 134, pp. 374–379, 2011.
© Springer-Verlag Berlin Heidelberg 2011

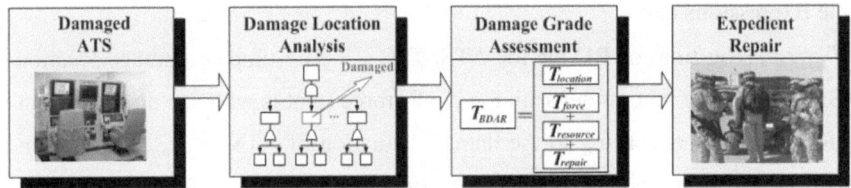

Fig. 1. Flow Chart of the BDAR toward ATS

2.1 ATS Damage Location Analysis (ATSDL)

It must has two preconditions before doing ATS Damage Location Analysis, that is: ① to establish the ATS Basic Function Items (ATSBFI); ② to found the ATS Damage Tree (ATSDT).

ATS Basic Function Items (ATSBFI) is the indispensable item when ATS is testing the missiles. If the ATSBFI is damaged, it will result in the test mission failure. All kinds of spare items and redundant systems do not belong to BFI.

ATS Damage Tree (ATSDT) is to make a certain system-level damage event (e.g. ATS cannot boot-strap) as a start (that is top event), and then find out all the BFI (the every reasons why ATS cannot boot-strap) which result in this event according to the damage phenomena. After that, doing analysis step by step until make sure the final cause (they are bottom events) that conduce to system-level damage and can be rushed to repair. ATSDT of certain damage is shown as Fig. 2:

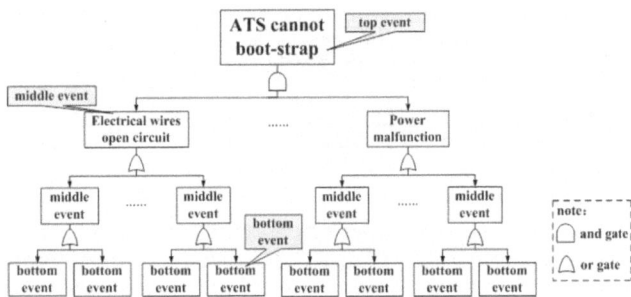

Fig. 2. ATSDT of certain damage

2.2 ATS Damage Grade Assessment (ATSDGA) [2]

Compared with the standard maintenance procedures, the most prominent factor of BDAR procedures is the time limits. So the grade of ATS damage must be defined by the emergency time of BDAR (T_{BDAR}).

$$T_{BDAR} = T_{location} + T_{repair} + T_{force} + T_{resource} \qquad (1)$$

In the Expressions (1):

T_{BDAR} : The time of BDAR for ATS. $T_{location}$: The time of damage location for ATS. T_{force} : The time of determining repair force (that is who can do the repair) and the force arriving according to the damage situation of ATS. $T_{resource}$: The time of determining repair resource and the resource arriving according to the damage situation of ATS. T_{repair} : The estimated time of repair the damage.

The relationship between ATSDGA and T_{BDAR} is shown as Table 1:

Table 1. The Relationship between ATSDGA and T_{BDAR}

ATS Damage Grade	The Range of T_{BDAR}
Slight Damage	0~2h
Secondary Damage	2~24h
Serious Damage	24~96h
Obsolescence	>96h

T_{force} , $T_{resource}$ and T_{repair} are separately determined by repair force, repair resource and estimated time of repair.

① The Setup of Repair Force in Wartime

The setup of repair force under combat situations is the determinant of Damage Grade Assessment (DGA) and the foundation of BDAR is shown as Fig. 3:

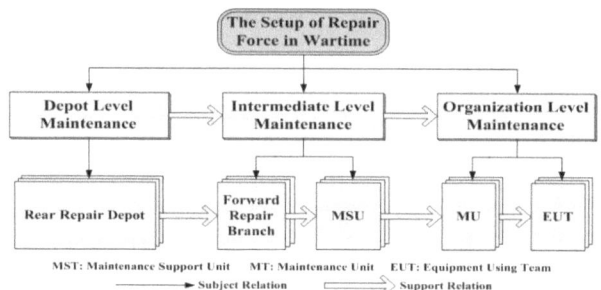

MST: Maintenance Support Unit   MT: Maintenance Unit   EUT: Equipment Using Team
———► Subject Relation   ⇒ Support Relation

Fig. 3. The Setup of Repair Force in Wartime

Equipment Using Team (EUT, which is composed of crew who operate the ATS) will rush to repair the ATS when it is damaged. If damage exceeds EUT repair capacity, Maintenance Unit (MU, which consists of organizational mechanics who may be trained in assessing battle damage and field repair procedures) is called. Maintenance Support Unit (MSU, which consists of direct support/general support mechanics and technical specialists who are trained in assessing battle damage in addition to their specialty) is called when ATS damage exceeds MU repair capacity.

If MSU still could not repair it, ATS will be sent to the Forward Repair Branch, and the Rear Repair Depot provides the top-level maintenance.

② The Configuration of Repair Resource in Wartime

The repair resource of ATS consists of Battlefield damage repair kits (including essential test tools, equipments, spare parts, components and materials available) and BDAR manual. The configuration of repair resource is the source of resource that repairs disabled ATS.

③ The estimate of repair time

The estimated time of ATS repair is determined by the repair time (the time of renewing the ATSBFI) of every damaged component.

3 Design for the Combat Resilience of ATS——Reconfiguration

BDAR is an important factor to keep and renew battle effectiveness, and conquer the enemy finally. But it is impossible for unit, maintenance and operation crew to determine the ability of equipment, which can or cannot be repaired, easy or difficult to emergency repair. This ability, which is called Combat Resilience (CR), is a kind of design characteristic [3].

This paper adopts the concept of configuration to design the CR of ATS, that is to say, to design the configurable ATS. The realization base of configuration is to determine the Configurable Units (CU), which is the smallest unit and element for the CR of ATS. CU should make one card realize different types of equipments' functions through configuration just as the Ai7 series of Teradyne and also should combine different modules into different equipment just as the SI of Agilent. So we can use the Evolvable Hardware (EHW) to design the configurable ATS.

The hardware framework of configurable ATS is shown as Fig. 4. It has two parts: Reconfigurable Auto-Test Equipment (RATE) and Reconfigurable Test Unit Adapter (RTUA).

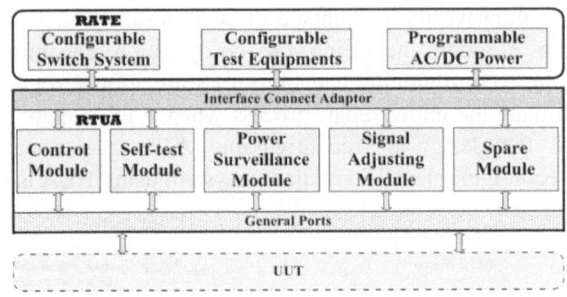

Fig. 4. The Hardware Framework of Configurable ATS

RTAE consists of configurable switch system, configurable test equipments and programmable AC/DC power. RTUA consists of control module, self-test module, power surveillance module, signal adjusting module and spare module. All of these modules are designed for EHW. Evolvable hardware block diagram based CU is shown as Fig. 5.

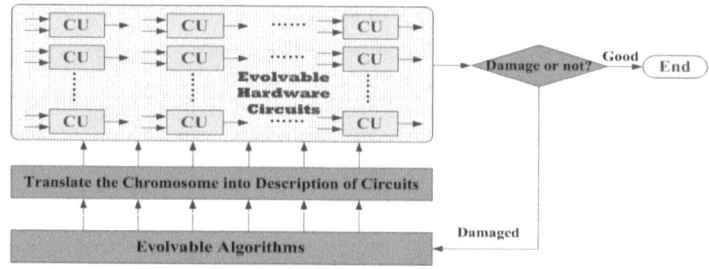

Fig. 5. Evolvable Hardware Block Diagram Based CU

Configurable Unit, which is the smallest unit and element for the CR of ATS, consists of FPGA and FPTA. FPGA realizes the evolvable design of digital circuits in ATS. This paper adopts the Visual Configurable Circuits to realize the inner configuration of evolvement aim circuit in order to achieving the chromosome coding of FPGA effectively, predigesting complexity of evolvement aim circuit and reducing the compute cost. [4][5]. FPTA realizes the evolvable design of analog circuits in ATS. It is a programmable transistor array and can realize the configuration in transistor-level, so it can produce many kinds of analog circuits (such as gate circuit, amplifier circuit, AD conversion circuit and filter circuit, etc.) [6][7].

4   Do Simulation for Reconfigurable ATS Using HLA

The reconfigurable ATS with BDAR function has complex structure, so its design and production is very difficulty. This paper adopts simulation technology to validate the design feasibility of reconfigurable ATS in order to reduce cost and improve production efficiency. HLA (High Level Architecture), which is advanced firstly by DOD at 1995, is a universal framework of creating computer simulation system. The aim of HLA is to improve the percentage of cost and efficiency when building the simulation system through increasing the co-operation capability of simulation application and the reconfiguration capability of simulation resource [8]. This paper uses HLA to simulate the entire repair process when ATS is damaged in battlefield, thus to validate the design of reconfigurable ATS is reasonable or not. The construction of reconfigurable ATS simulation system using HLA is shown as Fig. 6:

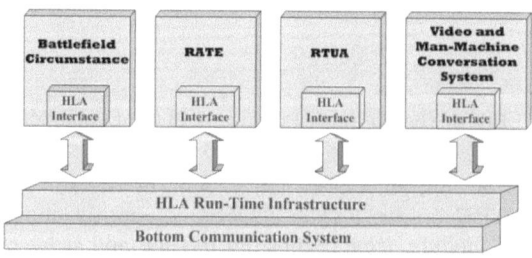

Fig. 6. Reconfigurable ATS Simulation System

5 Conclusion

This paper studies the BDAR of support equipment for the first time and expatiates on the contents and methods that research the ATS with BDAR function including: ① Steps that design the ATS with BDAR function. ② Based on the concept of reconfiguration, this paper puts forward the idea that using Evolvable Hardware to design the ATS in order to satisfy its Combat Resilience. ③ Use HLA to simulate the entire repair process when ATS is damaged in battlefield, thus validate the design of reconfigurable ATS is reasonable or not.

References

1. Jiezhong, H., Jianjun, Y., Ruopeng, Y.: Operational Research of Equipment Assurance Technology. National Defense Industry Press, Beijing (2006)
2. Quan, S., Shuangshan, M., Guangyan, W., Qiwei, H.: Theory and Technology of Equipment Battlefield Damage. National Defense Industry Press, Beijing (2007)
3. Jianping, L., Quan, S., Maosheng, G.: Theory and Application of BDAR. Publishing House of Enginery Industry, Beijing (2000)
4. Guoliang, D., Liang, Y., Qiang, Z., Jie, Z.: Evolvable Hardware Based on Virtual Reconfigurable Circuits. Computer Engineering 34(7), 243–244 (2008)
5. Ping, Z., Yedan, Z.: Design and Realization of an Evolvable IP Core. Microcontrollers & Embedded Systems (10), 8–10 (2004)
6. Kaiyang, Z., Youren, W.: Evolving Analog Circuits Based on Cell Arrays. Computer Measurement & Control 13(10), 1102–1104 (2005)
7. Zebulum, R.S., Keymeulen, D., Duong, V., Guo, X., Ferguson, M.I., Stoica, A.: High Temperature Experiments Using Programmable Transistor Array. In: Genetic and Evolutionary Computation Conference (GECCO), Seattle, WA (June 2004)
8. Yan, Z., Jianwei, D.: Design of HLA Emulation Program. Publishing House of Electronics Industry, Beijing (2002)

Secure Biometric E-Voting Scheme

Taha Kh. Ahmed and Mohamed Aborizka

Arab Academy for Science and Technology and Maritime Transport
2033 Cairo, Egypt
Tk_alyasien@hotmail.com, m_rizka@cairo.aast.edu

Abstract. The implementation of the e-voting becomes more substantial with the rapid increase of e-government development. The recent growth in communications and cryptographic techniques facilitate the implementation of e-voting. Many countries introduced e-voting systems; unfortunately most of these systems are not fully functional. In this paper we will present an e-voting scheme that covers most of the e-voting requirements, smart card and biometric recognition technology were implemented to guarantee voter's privacy and authentication.

Keywords: E-Voting, E-Democracy, E-Token, Biometric Recognition.

1 Introduction

Election is the process that gives the citizens the rights to select candidates to represent them in a democratic pattern. Election deals with the democracy and freewill of citizens, for this reason voting process considered to be very critical and sensitive process, therefore election implementation must serve many requirements in order to deliver a trustworthy election. These requirements can be defined as user conventions requirements and delivery of secure voting process requirements [1-2].

Due to the fast development of network technology the world is going toward the use and implementation of the e-technology in every aspect in our life including e-governments. E-voting becomes one of these technologies. E-voting refers to the use of hardware and software to establish an electronic system, useful in voting process, by generating an electronic ballot that replaces the paper ballot [9]. E-voting was introduced by e-governments especially in Europe in order to serve voting convention by providing remote system so the voter can cast his/her vote whenever and wherever he/she can. These systems will increase voter's participation and will fast up the votes counting.

Introducing remote voting technique over the internet (e-voting) will serve voter's convention. The main idea of this technology is to speed up the ballot counting and increase voters' participation by providing remote voting process.

In this paper we introduce a secure e-voting system. Our system will try to meet both voter's convention requirements and voting security requirements. It will also try to add privacy to authentication by implementing biometric recognition techniques [3].

The structure of the paper is as follows, the next section discuss briefly e-voting schemes to show strength and weakness. Section 3 provides a general description of

R. Chen (Ed.): ICICIS 2011, Part I, CCIS 134, pp. 380–388, 2011.
© Springer-Verlag Berlin Heidelberg 2011

our scheme. Section 4 discusses the scenario of internal and external interactions between the components of our scheme. Section 5 discusses the implementation issues of the scheme. Finally conclusion and future work are included in section 6.

2 Motivation

Motivation behind building new e-voting system is to establish a system that fulfills all or most of the main ideal e-voting properties by looking through all these properties and try to satisfy them during the development of e voting system. e-voting systems deals with the freewill of people, something that many nations fought for it, this make building e-voting system a critical job. Some researchers suggested more complicated requirements but we will focus here on the main requirements. These requirements are:

- *Privacy*: It is the inability to link a voter to a vote. Voter privacy must be preserved during the election as well as after the election for a long time.
- *Eligibility*: Only eligible voters participate in the election. They should register before the Election Day and only registered eligible voters can cast votes.
- *Uniqueness*: Only one vote for a voter should be counted. It is important to notice that uniqueness does not mean un-reusability, where voters should not vote more than once.
- *Uncoercibility*: Any coercer, even authorities, should not be able to extract the value of the vote and should not be able to coerce a voter to cast his vote in a particular way. Voter must be able to vote freely.
- *Receipt-freeness*: It is the inability to know what the vote is. Voters must neither be able to obtain nor construct a receipt which can prove the content of their vote to a third party both during the election and after the election ends. This is to prevent vote buying or selling.
- *Fairness*: No partial tally is revealed before the end of the voting period to ensure that all candidates are given a fair decision. Even the counter authority should not be able to have any idea about the results.
- *Transparency*: The whole voting process must be transparent. Bulletin boards may be used to publicize the election process. The security and reliability of the system must not rely on the secrecy of the network which cannot be guaranteed.
- *Accuracy*: All cast votes should be counted. Any vote cannot be altered, deleted, invalidated or copied. Any attack on the votes should be detected. Uniqueness should also be satisfied for accuracy.
- *Robustness*: Any number of parties or authorities cannot disrupt or influence the election and final tally. To have confidence in the election results, robustness should be assured. However, there are numerous ways for corruption. For example; registration authorities may cheat by allowing ineligible voters to register; ineligible voters may register under the name of someone else; ballot boxes, ballots and vote counting machines may be compromised.
- *Mobility:* a system is mobile if there are no restrictions (other than logical ones) on the location from which the voter can cast.

Our prototype will try to focus on solving security requirement such as integrity, authentication, confidentiality and verifiability by implementing some protocols that guarantee a more secure and stable e-voting system.

3 Existing and Potential Solutions

In Europe the interest in implementing and developing an internet voting system increased in the last few years with the growing interest on e-governments and it's rule in e-democracy. Most of the European countries still in the studying stage of implementing e-voting, few countries implemented the remote voting system, for example in the Netherlands in 2004 in the European Parliamentary elections. In Spain the *Generalitat de Catalunya* (the government of the autonomous region of Catalonia located in the north-east of Spain) organized its own remote electronic voting pilot that was run in parallel to the 2003 Elections to the Parliament of Catalonia [GC03]. In Great Britain, remote electronic voting systems were used in the local elections of 30 municipalities. The target group consisted of the citizens who have the right to vote and are resident abroad and electors resident in there countries but are temporarily abroad on the Election Day. In 2003 the United States of America, had many attempts to use e-voting systems. The Voting over the Internet (VOI) project was used in the general elections of 2000 in four states. The Internet votes were legally accepted, but their amount was small (84 votes) [11]. Another e-voting project named Secure Electronic Registration and Voting Experiment (SERVE) was developed for primary and general elections in 2004 in the United States of America. The eligible voters of SERVE were mainly overseas voters and military personnel. In Estonia e-voting system was applied first time in the municipal elections in 2005. The second implementation was in 2007 in Parliamentary elections. There were 5.4 per cent of e-votes among all votes.

This paper will focus on (SERVE) e-voting system implemented by United States and the Estonian e-voting system. We will try to analysis these two systems and compare it to our suggested system.

In the last few years a numerous numbers of researches proposed different e-voting systems and many countries implanted these systems. However, this number of e-voting systems can be categorized into three main categories [4].the first category is based on blind signature technique [5] [6]. The second category is based on mixed nets [7]. The last category is based on homomorphic signature properties [8]. In general all of the above mentioned systems were designed in a way that the voter can't be linked to his/her vote. Our system is categorized under the "blind signature" based systems, that the system will be designed to serve anonymity of the voter and it will add the biometric recognition to add privacy to authentication.

4 E-Voting System Component

Our prototype contains several components that interact together in the e-voting three stages (registration phase, voting phase and tallying phase) to deliver a robust e-voting system. In this section we will define the components and the security tools used to build our e-voting system architecture.

4.1 E-Voting Servers

Our prototype will require implementing few application servers that will run in committee's location. According to the design each stage will require a set of servers to run.

- *Registration server (RS):* It is responsible for monitoring and controlling the first stage of the election process. Registration server has many duties to perform; it register only eligible voters to participate in the elections by applying a set of rules provided by the election authority. The voting server implements its duties by issuing a voting certificate to the voters, which allow its holder to cast his/her vote.
- *Privacy server (PS):* Is responsible to provide anonymity identify to the voter, this process is consider the most important process so that the voter can't be linked to its vote. The privacy server implements its duty by first confirming the voter's certificate, then verifying the generated anonymous identity generated by the voter.
- *Voting server (VS):* It is responsible for receiving and recording voter's votes. It implements it by accepting voter's anonymous identity and authenticates it, after authentication it records the votes and sends it to the votes counting server.
- *Tallying server (TS):* It is responsible of counting the votes to be tallied then to the public.
- *Certificate authority (CA):* It is responsible to confirm the person's identification data received by the registration server in the registration and identification stage and to provide personal information about the voter where the registration server can use this information to take a decision about the state of the voter is he/she is eligible or not.

4.2 Security Mechanism of E-Voting

Different Security components are applied to the system. The following components are used in our system implementation.

- *Digital certificate:* Are used to maintain authentication.
- *Public key infrastructure technique:* PKI will be used to support the usage of digital certificate where each voter will be required to generate private and public key to use in voting process. Also PKI will be used to maintain part of the voter's privacy when generating the unique identity used in voting. The unique identity is used to make linking the voter to the vote impossible.
- *Hashing technique:* Is used with existing PKI to maintain accuracy and non duplication. Accuracy is maintained in the voting phase. The hash of the voter's UID and choice of candidate is added to its encryption using the committee's public key. When the committee's receives the total message, it decrypts the original message and compares its hash to the hash received to make sure that no alteration has been made to the vote. Non duplication is achieved through the existence of a unique identity for every voter that can be linked to the voter. The unique identity is the hash of the encryption of the committee's digital signature

using the voter's public key. The generated unique identity is stored with the voter's choice of candidates to prevent duplication of votes.

- *Blind signature technique:* The privacy requirement in this scheme is based on using PKI with blind signature to insure complete prevention to link a vote to the voter. Blind signature is used to sign the unique identity of the voter without revealing it. Since blind signature can be implemented using public key signing algorithm.

- *Biometric smart token:* Biometric Smart Token in EVSE system and we will use the finger print as a template, to verify the voter in the elections with the Match-On-Card technology the fingerprint is verified inside the secure environment of the Smart token. In this case the fingerprint template stored on the Smart token cannot be extracted. It can only be used internally by the Smart Card itself. Signing contracts or documents is only one application where the biometric verification in Smart token can be used.

5 E-Voting System Architecture

Different components are interacting together to provide a secure modern e-voting system that satisfy the needs of public and democracy. Figure 1 gives an abstract view of interaction between different components. The following discuss the scenario of the three voting stages the system runs into.

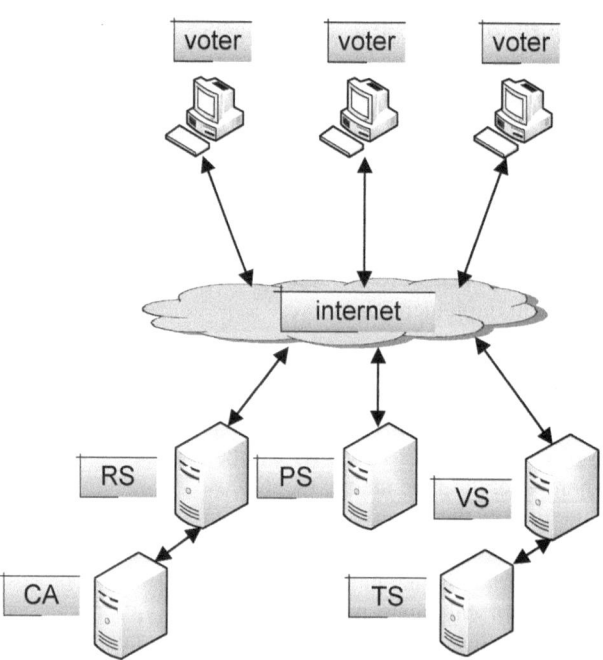

Fig. 1. Abstract View of Scheme Interactions

5.1 Registration Phase

Each citizen has to provide his/her personal e-token which contain the national digital certificate (NDC) and his/her fresh sample of biometric identity to the election committee to gain his/her voting rights. The citizen inserts his/her e-token and enters his/her username and password and his/her live biometric sample to activate the e-token. The biometric scanner will convert the biometric sample into biometric template (biometric in a binary form).

1. The biometric template is bound with a voter public key (public key of voter's digital certificate stored in e-token) and the result will be send to the registration server.

2. The registration server will unbind the received message then it will authenticate the voter who wants to register by using challenge response message (if the voter fails to pass the message or his/her keys was not found in the ineligible list the registration session will be terminated. Otherwise, the session will continue).

3. The registration server checks the received public key and biometric hash key in the ineligible list, and already registered list. If he/she is already registered the registration server will send him/her the election certificate and end the registration. If not found, then request the voters credentials from certificate authority (CA) to be sure the citizen is eligible.

4. The certificate authority will reply with voter's credentials.

5. The registration server checks the uniqueness of the received public key and biometric template. The registration server creates a voting digital certificate containing all required information and the digital signature. The registration server updates the registered voters database.

6. The registration server then sends the voter's certificate (certificate serial number, unique pair of public/private keys, digital stamp of current election, and the public key of election committee.

7. The new voter's certificates are uploaded to the citizen e-token. The e-token validates the received voting digital certificate and digital stamp and then securely stores it.

5.2 Voting Phase

After registration phase ends, the citizens who become registered voters are ready to cast their votes. Currently, each voter has a valid voting digital certificate (VDC) that grants him/her the right to cast his/her vote in the current election. The advantage of the proposed scheme is that, in addition to casting votes, the system gives the voter the ability of using anonymous identity while voting, so that no one can trace the citizen's real identity based on the vote he/she cast. On the other hand, while the system supports anonymous voting, the system also will be always sure that the anonymous voter is eligible to cast his/her vote, and he/she can cast it according to the rules and settings of the current election. The scenario for obtaining anonymous identity and casting votes is as follows:

1. The voter generate a unique identification number using some data stored in the voter's e-token, the process of generating the unique identification number is by encrypting the digital stamp of election committee with the voter's biometric template and hash the result using one way hash function.

2. The voter blinds the UID with his/her blind signature and signs the output with the stored private key of VDC.

3. The voter encrypts the result of previous step by public key of election committee and then sends the result to the anonymous identity server (AIS) (election certificate is used to authenticate the voter to AIS server).

4. The AIS decrypt the message using private key of election committee and blindly signs the blinded UID using the committee's private key.

5. The AIS then encrypts the signed UID by VDC public key.

6. The AIS sends the signed UID to the e-token and recorded voter as authenticated so that the voter can't request another blind signature.

7. The e-token decrypts the message using voter's private key, unbinds the signed UID, verify it, and store it.

8. The voter now can connect to voting server and authenticate him/her self using his/her anonymous ID and voting certificate.

9. The voting server verify that the user is eligible, if the voter is eligible then The voter make his/her voting choice, and sends the signed unique anonymous identity and the choice of candidate to the voting server.

10. The committees voting server insures that the signed unique anonymous identity is not found in the voting database, then records the received signed unique anonymous identity and choice of candidates in the voting database.

11. The committees voting server sends an acknowledgment to the voter that his/her vote was successfully recorded.

5.3 Tallying Phase

At the end of the voting phase; the next and final phase begins, which is the tallying phase. In the counting phase, the votes stored in the centralized database in the committee's voting server are counted, and the results are to be announced to the public.

6 Scheme Implementation Issues

The current Implementation of our proposed secure e-voting scheme is implemented using the following algorithms for symmetric key encryption, Advanced Encryption Standard (AES) with 128 bit key size and a modified version of AES for smart card [10], the RSA [11] for digital signature purpose, MD5 as a hash function, and D. Chaum blind signature algorithm [12]. The time performance of the system was out of the scope of our research. Finally the proposed e-voting system does not cover bribe and coercion problems [13].

7 Conclusion

E-voting technology is important to e-government to form the electronic democracy. E-democracy become a concern for the developed countries especially in Europe and America to establish firm bonding with the people, this will increase the trust in the governments. Building a trustworthy e-voting system requires to satisfy at least four main requirements for a successful e-voting system, which are; security, privacy, accuracy, and mobility. Also consider to build a well structured system that functions in high performance that can serve any number of voters. In this paper we proposed an e-voting remote system that we believe it serve the e-voting successful requirements. Providing secure, anonymous, mobile system that also implements the biometric recognition technique that provides the best way to serve authentication and privacy. Our system requires further work to be done in the future. It can be summarized in three phases. The first phase will be completing the security suite of our e-voting to include different algorithms and protocols that should make the system more flexible. The second phase will be a modification to our system to provide an accepted solution to bribe and coercion problems. The last phase will be a real time and practical testing outside the lab for the release version of our secure e-voting system to report the performance and the reliability of the system.

References

1. Lambrinoudakis, C., Gritzalis, D.: Building a reliable e-voting system: functional requirements and legal constraints. In: Hameurlain, A., Cicchetti, R., Traunmüller, R. (eds.) DEXA 2002. LNCS, vol. 2453, p. 435. Springer, Heidelberg (2002)
2. Krimmer, R., Triessnig, S.: The development of remote e-voting around the world: A review of roads and directions. In: Baldoni, M., Son, T.C., van Riemsdijk, M.B., Winikoff, M. (eds.) DALT 2007. LNCS (LNAI), vol. 4897, pp. 1–15. Springer, Heidelberg (2008)
3. Jain, A.K., Nandakumar, K., Nagar, A.: Biometric Template Security. EURASIP J. Adv. Signal Process. Article Id 579416, 1–17 (2008)
4. Hirt, M., Sako, K.: Efficent Reciept-Free Voting Based on Hommomorphic Encryption. In: Encrypt 2000 (2000)
5. Ibrahim, S., Kamat, M., Salleh, M., Aziz, S.R.A.: Secure E-Voting With Blind Signature. In: Proceedings of IEEE 4th National Conference on Telecommunication Technology, Shah Alam, Malaysia (2003)
6. Carroll, T.E., Grosu, D.: A Secure and Efficient Voter-Controlled Anonymous Election Scheme. In: Proceedings of International Conference on Information Technology: Coding and Computing, ITCC 2005 (2005)
7. Jakobsson, M.: Flash mixing. In: Proc. of the 18th ACM Symposium on Principles of Distrbuted Computing (PODC 1999), pp. 83–89. ACM Press, New York (1999)
8. Benaloh, J., Tuinstra, D.: Receipt-Free Secret Ballot Elections (extended abstract). In: Proceedings 26th ACM Symposium on the Theory of Computing (STOC). ACM, New York (1994)
9. E-voting deadlock. Elsevier computer fraud and security 2008(2), 1 (2008)
10. Lu, C.-F., Kao, Y.-S., Chiang, H.-L., Yang, C.-H.: Fast implementation of AES cryptographic algorithms in smart cards. In: International Carnahan Conference on Proceedings IEEE 37th Annual (2003)

11. Rivest, R., Shamir, A., Adleman, L. : A method for Obtaining Digital Signatures and Public Key Cryptosystems. Communications of the ACM (February 1978)
12. Chaum, D.: Blind signatures for untraceable payments. In: CRYPTO 1982, pp. 199–203. Plenum Press, New York (1982)
13. Ku, W.-C., Ho, C.-M.: An e-Voting Scheme against Bribe and Coercion. In: Proceedings of the 2004 IEEE International Conference on e-Technology, e-Commerce and e-Service (EEE 2004) (2004)

Glowworm Swarm Optimization Algorithm for Solving Numerical Integral

Yan Yang and Yongquan Zhou

College of Mathematics and Computer Science, Guangxi University for Nationalities
Nanning, Guangxi 530006, China
yongquanzhou@126.com

Abstract. A new method for solving numerical integration based on artificial glowworm swarm optimization algorithm is presented. The method can not only compute usual definite integral for any functions, but also compute singular integral and oscillatory integral. The simulation results show that the proposed algorithm for solving numerical integration has higher precision.

Keywords: glowworm swarm; optimization algorithm; fitness; numerical integration.

1 Introduction

Solving numerical integration is one of the common problems in scientific calculations and engineering technology field, such as the PID involving integral calculation. So far, people have made a lot of researches to solve numerical integration using theoretical and computational methods. There are some traditional methods such as Newton method, Gauss method, Romberg method, and Simpson's method, etc [1]. At present, some scholars calculate the numerical integration with evolutionary strategy, particle swarm algorithm and neural network algorithm [3-5], [9]. However, if the antiderivative is not easy to obtain or the integrand can not find antiderivative, we would not gain integral value with the traditional methods.

A new method for solving numerical integration based on artificial glowworm swarm optimization (GSO) algorithm is presented, and the basic idea of the algorithm is that generate some point randomly in the integral interval, regard each point as an artificial glowworm, optimize the points according to the moving principle of artificial glowworms and get more precise integration values. The method can not only compute usual definite integral for any functions, but also compute singular integral and oscillatory integral.

2 Glowworm Swarm Optimization (GSO) Algorithm

Glowworm swarm optimization (GSO) algorithm is proposed in 2005[4]. The GSO algorithm was applied to multimodal optimization, noise issues, theoretical foundations, signal source locatisation, addressing the problem of sensing hazards and pursuiting of multiple mobile signal sources problems. And the basic principle of the

R. Chen (Ed.): ICICIS 2011, Part I, CCIS 134, pp. 389–394, 2011.

GSO algorithm is as follows: Luciferin induces glowworm to glow to attract mates or prey. The brighter the glow more is the attraction, meanwhile the higher of the luciferin, then glowworm moves towards the position having hight luciferin. The luciferin value is corresponding to the fitness function value, so glowworm looks for the position having highest luciferin value to determine the optimal value of the fitness function in dynamic decision domains.

A set of N glowworms are randomly deployed in a m-dimensional workspace. According to the similarity of luciferin value, divide the swarm into nei neighbors and each glowworn i selects a neighbour j with a probability P_{ij} and moves toward it within its decision domains range R_d ($0 < R_d^i < R_s$), where R_s is a circular sensor range of glowworm i. The position of glowworm i is x_i ($x_i \in R^m, i = 1, 2, \cdots, N$), which is a potential solution. Put x_i into the objective function and gain the fitness function value $J(x_i)$ and luciferin value l_i. Estimate the solution with luciferin value. The algorithm can gain the optimal value of functions. The equations that modeled the luciferin-update, probability distribution used to select a neighbour, movement update and local-decision range update are given below:

$$l_i(t) = \max\{(0, (1 - \rho) * l_i(t - 1) + \gamma * J(x_i(t)))\} \tag{1}$$

$$P_j(t) = \frac{l_j(t)}{\sum_{k \in N_i(t)} l_k(t)} \tag{2}$$

$$x_i(t + 1) = x_i(t) + s\left(\frac{x_j(t) - x_i(t)}{\|x_j(t) - x_i(t)\|}\right) \tag{3}$$

$$r_d^i(t + 1) = \frac{r_s}{1 + \beta * D_i(t)} \tag{4}$$

Where, $N_i(t) = \{ j : \|x_j(t) - x_i(t)\| < r_d^i(t); l_i(t) < l_j(t)\}$ is a neighbour of glowworm i consisting of those glowworms that have a relatively higher luciferin value and that are located within a dynamic decision domain. If the luciferin value of glowworm i is greater than j's and the distance between the glowworm i and j is less than the dynamic decision domain, divide glowworm j into the neighbours of glowworm i.

$$D_i(t) = \frac{N_i(t)}{\pi * r_s^2}$$

is the neighbour-density of glowworm i at iteration t and β is a constant parameter. The constant parameter β affects the rate of change of the neighbourhood range. The constant parameter ρ decides whether algorithm has memory. A value $\rho = 0$ renders the algorithm memory less where the luciferin value of each glowworm depends only on the fitness value of its current position. However, $\rho \in (0, 1)$ leads to the reflection of the cumulative goodness of the path followed by the glowworms in their current luciferin values. The constant parameter γ can scale the function fitness values. The value of step-size S influences the range of objective function.

3 GSO Algorithms for Solving Numerical Integral

Set objective function $f(i)$ as fitness function in the GSO algorithm, the processes of artificial GSO algorithm for solving numerical integral are as follows:

Step 1. Determine the individual expression. The individual in expressions is consisted of position X and luciferin value L of glowworm, each part has D components as follows: $X_i = (x_{i1}, x_{i2}, \cdots, x_{id})$, $L_i = (l_{i1}, l_{i2}, \cdots, l_{id})$. Where D is the node number of the integral interval. $(x_{i1}, x_{i2}, \cdots, x_{id})$ is the node of the integral interval. $(l_{i1}, l_{i2}, \cdots, l_{id})$ is the luciferin value related to the node and it is used to adjust the change of each node.

Step 2. Initialize a population. Randomly generate a group containing N glowworm individuals in the search space. Each glowworm individual (X_i, L_i) contains D components.

Step 3. Determine the fitness function. Place the each glowworm individual between the left and right endpoints of integral interval. Each glowworm divides the integral interval into $D+1$ sections and $D+2$ nodes. Separately calculate the distance d_j ($j = 1, 2, \cdots, D+1$) between two adjacent nodes of the $D+2$ nodes. Then calculate the corresponding function values of the $D+2$ nodes and the function value of intermediate nodes of the $D+1$ sections. Finally, find the corresponding function values of left endpoint, middle node and right endpoint of each section. The minimum of function is w_j and the maximum is W_j, where $j = 1, 2, \cdots, D+1$. So the fitness of each glowworm individual i is defined as follows:

$$f(i) = \frac{1}{2} \sum_{j=1}^{d+1} d_j \left| W_j - w_j \right|,$$

The more approximate zero the individual fitness value is, the more excellent the individual is.

Step 4. Judge termination condition. If the condition meets the termination condition, the algorithm ends and outputs optimal solutions. Otherwise, turns to step5.

Step 5. According to the artificial GSO algorithm, update the population and calculate the fitness value of new individual. For glowworm i, the update formulas of luciferin value and position are below:

$$l_{id}(t) = \max\{(0,(1-\rho)*l_{id}(t-1)+\gamma*J(x_{id}(t)))\}$$

$$x_{id}(t+1) = x_{id}(t) + s\left(\frac{x_{jd}(t) - x_{id}(t)}{\left\|x_{jd}(t) - x_{id}(t)\right\|}\right)$$

where, $d = 1, 2, \cdots, D+1$, s and γ are nonnegative, $\rho \in (0.2, 0.7)$.

Step 6. Repeat Step5 until it reaches the termination condition and choose the best individual as the result.

Step 7. End the algorithm. Obtain the integration value by expression $\sum_{j=1}^{D+1} m_j d_j$, and $(m_1, m_2, \cdots, m_{D+1})$ is the function values related to midpoints of $D+1$ sections which are divided by left endpoints, optimal individuals and right endpoints of integral intervals.

4 Numerical Experiment Results

In order to verify the feasibility and validity of the algorithm, code the algorithm in Matlab7.0 and calculate examples in references [5], [6]. The swarm size N is fixed to 15. Set the initial luciferin $l_0 = 5$, moving step-length $step = 0.01$, initial decision domains range $R_0 = 3$, circular sensor range $R_s = 3$ and neighbour number is $nei=5$, $\rho \in (0.2, 0.7)$, $\beta \in (0.05, 0.09)$ and maximum iterations $iter\_\max = 100$. The breakpoint $D = 100$.

Example 1. The reference [8] has calculated the integral values of functions $(1+x^2)^{\frac{1}{2}}$, x^2, x^4, $1/(1+x)$, $\sin x$ and e^x with trapezoid method and Simpson method in the integral interval from 0 to 2. The results of this paper and reference [8] are shown in Table 1.

Table 1. Integral values of corresponding numerical functions

$f(x)$	$(1+x^2)^{\frac{1}{2}}$	x^2	x^4	$1/(1+x)$	$\sin x$	e^x
Accurate value	2.958	2.667	6.400	1.099	1.416	6.389
Trapezoid method	3.326	4.000	16.000	1.333	0.909	8.389
Simpon method	2.964	2.667	6.667	1.111	1.425	6.421
GSO	2.8217860 18863031	2.3372386 39056741	5.0798205 10899253	0.991418 31579456	1.41534 921610 7424	5.405118 93671873 1

Example 2. Calculate the integral $\int_0^{48} \sqrt{1 + \cos^2 x} \, dx$.

There was some difficulties to calculate the above integral function with Romberg method [7], and obtained the result 58.47082 with Composite Simpson's rule. The result is 58.5205 calculated with neural network in reference [5]. The accurate value is 58.4704691. Due to the integrand is a periodic function and the cycle is π , also $48 = 15\pi + 0.8761$, we can calculate the above integral as follows:

$$\int_0^{48} \sqrt{1 + \cos^2 x} \, dx = 15 \int_0^{\pi} \sqrt{1 + \cos^2 x} \, dx + \int_0^{0.8761} \sqrt{1 + \cos^2 x} \, dx$$

Table 2 shows the results of this paper and references [8], [9].

Table 2. Integral values of corresponding numerical functions

$f(x)$	Simpson's	Neural network	ES	GSO	Accurate value
$\sqrt{1 + \cos^2 x}$	58. 47082	58. 5205	58. 47065	58.460228 087204669	58.4704691

Example 3. Calculate the singular integral

$$f(x) = \begin{cases} e^{-x}, 0 \le x < 1 \\ e^{-x/2}, 1 \le x < 2 \\ e^{-x/3}, 2 \le x \le 3 \end{cases}$$

The best results are 1.5459805 and 1.5467 calculated respectively with ES [9] and neural network [3-5]. The accurate value is 1.546036 and the result calculated with artificial GSO is 1.532449804351269. Table 3 shows the results of this paper and references [8], [9].

Table 3. Integral values of corresponding numerical functions

$f(x)$	Neural network	ES	GSO	Accurate value
$e^{-x/i}, i = 1,2,3$	1.5467	1.5459805	1.540285006836290	1.546036

Example 4. Calculate the integral $I = \int_0^1 e^{-x^2} \, dx$.

The antiderivative of the integrand is not elementary function, so we can not calculate the integral value with Newton-Leibniz formula. References [7-9] calculated the integral values respectively with Rectangle method, Trapezoid method and the Simpson method. Table 4 shows the results of this paper and references [8], [9].

Table 4. Integral values of corresponding numerical functions

$f(x)$	Rectangle method	Trapezoid method	Simpson method	ES	GSO	Accurate value
e^{-x^2}	0.77782	0.74621	0.74683	0.74683	0.7478901 03019663	0.746824

5 Conclusions

In this paper, we put forward a new method for solving numerical integration based on artificial glowworm swarm optimization algorithm. The simulation examples of numerical integration validated the algorithm was effective and enforceable. Meanwhile, the algorithm need low requirements for integrand and it can not only compute usual definite integral for any functions, but also compute singular integral and oscillatory integral.

Acknowledgements

This work is supported by Grants 0991086 from Guangxi Science Foundation.

References

1. Chen, Y.J.: WZ-method and asymptotic estimates for a kind of definite Integrals with parameter (in Chinese). Journal of South China Normal University 4, 1–6 (2009)
2. Krishnanand, K.N., Ghose, D.: Glowworm swarm optimisation: a new method for optimising multi-modal functions. Int. J. Computational Intelligence Studies 1(1), 93–119 (2009)
3. Xu, L., Li, L.: Neural Network Algorithm for Solving Numerical Integration (in Chinese). Journal of System Simulation 20(7), 1922–1924 (2008)
4. Wei, X., Zhou, Y., Lan, X.: Numerical integration method study based on function network (in Chinese). Computer Science 36(4), 224–226 (2009)
5. Wang, X., He, Y., Zeng, Z.: Numerical integration study based on triangle basis neural network algorithm (in Chinese). Journal of Electronics & Information Technology 26(3), 394–399 (2004)
6. Rouillier, F., Zimmermann, P.: Efficient isolation of polynomial's real roots. Journal of Computational and Applied Mathematics 162, 33–50 (2004)
7. Burden, R.L., Faires, J.D.: Numerical analysis, pp. 190–206. Thomson Learning, Inc., Brooks/ Cole (2001)
8. Wang, X.H., He, Y.G., Zing, Z.Z.: Numerical integration study based on triangle basis neural network algorithm. Journal of Electronics & Information Technology 26(3), 394–399 (2004)
9. Zhou, Y., Zhang, M., Zhao, B.: Solving numerical inregration based on evolution strategy method (in Chinese). Chinese Journal of Computers 31(2), 196–206 (2008)

An Energy Aware Ant Colony Algorithm for the Routing of Wireless Sensor Networks

Deqiang Cheng, Yangyang Xun, Ting Zhou, and Wenjie Li

School of Information and Electrical Engineering, China University of Mining and Technology,
Xuzhou, Jiangsu, 221008, P.R.C
{Deqiangcheng,Xyy871004,Tingting04041616,Lwjljd}@163.com

Abstract. Based on the characteristics of routing protocol for wireless sensor networks, an energy aware ant colony algorithm (EAACA) for the routing of wireless sensor networks is proposed in this paper. When EAACA routing protocol chooses the next neighbor node, not only the distance of sink node, but also the residual energy of the next node and the path of the average energy are taken into account. Theoretical analysis and simulation results show that compared with the traditional ACA algorithm for the routing of wireless sensor network, EAACA routing protocol balances the energy consumption of nodes in the network and extends the network lifetime.

Keywords: Ant colony algorithm, Energy aware, WSN.

1 Introduction

The wireless sensor network (WSN) sends information through the sensor nodes by the self-organizing network. In order to establish the reliable links between the sensor nodes in the wireless network, the routing protocol is vital. Extensive research results have shown that the routing protocol has a direct influence on the performance of wireless sensor networks [1][2][3].

According to the network architecture of WSN, the routing protocol is divided into planar routing protocol and hierarchical routing protocol [2][4]. Hierarchical routing protocol has better scalability for large networks. However, the sensor nodes can not been deployed rapidly because of the complexity of network topology. In addition, the cluster head node undertakes communicating with external nodes, cluster scheduling and other important work. So, the quick energy consumption of cluster head nods can make the network failure. Compared with the hierarchical routing protocol, sensor nodes in planar routing protocol have the characteristics of same status, high redundancy, high reliability and network robustness. But, due to lack of management schemes nodes with planar routing protocol can not optimize routing paths and communication resources.

Based on the above considerations, this paper makes use of ant colony optimization to select the shortest path from the source node to sink node for the effective and fast transmission of data in the network. For the nodes of WSN, the energy is limited. So taking the energy restriction of wireless sensor node into account, an ant colony algorithm based on energy aware EAACA (Energy Aware Ant Colony Algorithm)

R. Chen (Ed.): ICICIS 2011, Part I, CCIS 134, pp. 395–401, 2011.

routing protocol is proposed for wireless sensor networks. When EAACA routing protocol chooses the next hop neighbor nodes, the distance to the sink node is considered, meanwhile the residual energy of the next hop node and the average energy of the path are taken into account. Simulation results show that, EAACA routing protocol balances the energy consumption of nodes in the network and extends the network lifetime.

2 Wireless Sensor Network Model for Routing Algorithm

Compared with the wireless sensor networks model with fixed transmitting power, the WSN with adaptive transmitting power is more energy-saving, and can further extend the network lifetime[2][4].

In the wireless sensor networks with adaptive transmitting power, the wireless transmission power of node is exponential decay with increasing distance to the other node. Two wireless channel transmission models were proposed in reference [5]. When the distance d between the sending node and receiving node is less than a value of d_0, the free-space model is use, so the transmission power attenuation factor of sending node is d^2. Otherwise the multi-path fading model is used, and the transmission power attenuation factor is d^4.

$$E_{TX}(k,d) = \begin{cases} kE_{elec} + k\varepsilon_{fs}d^2, & d < d_0 \\ kE_{elec} + k\varepsilon_{mp}d^4, & d > d_0 \end{cases} \quad (1)$$

$$E_{RX}(k) = kE_{elec} \quad (2)$$

Communication characteristics and energy consumption models affect the advantages and performance of protocol. The wireless transmission and energy consumption model defined in the reference [7] is used in this paper. The total energy consumption of each communications is defined as equation (3).

$$E_T = E_{TX} + E_{RX} = 2E_{elec} \times k + \varepsilon_{fs} \times k \times d^2 = k(2E_{elec} + \varepsilon_{fs} \times d^2) \quad (3)$$

The transmitting power and receiving power are defined as equation (4) and equation (5) respectively.

$$P_t = E_{elec} + \varepsilon_{fs} \times d^2 \quad (4)$$

$$P_r = \frac{P_t \lambda^2}{(4\pi)^2 d^2} \quad (5)$$

Where λ is the wavelength. When a node receives signal with transmission power P_t and received power P_r, the distance between transmit and receive node is

$$d = \frac{\lambda}{4\pi}\sqrt{\frac{P_t}{P_r}} \quad (6)$$

In EAACA routing protocol, the information of each node includes matrix vector of the distance to each neighbor node. So, according to these distance, the node can use dynamic transmission power to send the ant packets to the next hop neighbor node with the purpose of using less energy to ensure the entire network connectivity.

3 Design of EAACA Routing Protocol

The proposed EAACA protocol includes the route discovery and route maintenance process. In the route discovery process, the sensor nodes establish all valid paths to the destination node by sending a query packet (forward ant), if the ants find the destination node, then the destination node generates a response packet (backward ant). The backward ant goes back to the sending node along the reverse path, and releases pheromone while it returns. The concentration of pheromone is in inverse proportion to the distance to the destination node. Therefore, the stronger concentration of the pheromone represents the shorter distance to destination node. Once all the paths are set up, the source node begins to release the data packets and the packets transmit along the path with the highest pheromone concentration. In route maintenance process, the sensor nodes send a certain number of probe packets to the destination node periodically to monitor the quality of the existed, meanwhile probe new route to the destination node. To reduce the control packet overhead, the number of probe packets is restricted by the current concentration of pheromone [6][8][9][11].

3.1 Pheromone Rule

At a certain time interval, the source nodes release a certain number of ants periodically in the network, all forward ants find all valid paths from the source to the destination node, and all the visited node are stored in the ant packet field carried by ants. Each node maintains a simple pheromone table in the networks. The pheromone table is built the path during searching process.

Pheromone Enhancement. When the query packet or probe packet gets to the destination node, the destination node generates a response packet, and sends it back along the reverse path. The response packet in each visited node release a certain amount of pheromone $\triangle\tau$. In traditional ACA algorithms, pheromone increment as equation (7) [9][10].

$$\Delta\tau = c \times (HOP_{max} - hop_{count}) \tag{7}$$

Where c is the variable parameter, HOP_{max} represents the maximum allowed number of hops for query data packets and probe data packets in the network; hop_{count} represents hops of the packet to the destination node. Therefore, when node receives the response packet from the destination node by the nth neighbor node, the node will update the pheromone concentration $\tau_{n,d}$ as equation (8).

$$\tau_{n,d} = (1-\rho) \times \tau_{n,d} + \Delta\tau \tag{8}$$

Where ρ is the pheromone evaporation coefficient; $1-\rho$ is the pheromone residue factor; the range of ρ is [0, 1]. EAACA not only considers the distance of path, but also considers the energy level of path; so, the pheromone concentration is improved as follows:

$$\Delta \tau = c \times (HOP_{max} - hop_{count}) \times Eavg_n \qquad (9)$$

Each node updates pheromone table as equation (10):

$$\tau_{n,d} = (1-\rho) \times \tau_{n,d} + \frac{\Delta \tau}{\omega \cdot hop_{count}} \qquad (10)$$

Where ω is the control factor; hop_{count} is hops of the current node packet to the destination node (the number of nodes visited by backward ants).

Pheromone Evaporation. In EAACA algorithm, the pheromone evaporation scheme is defined as equation (11), and the range of evaporation rate ρ_1 is [0, 1]. ρ_1 is used to set the speed of pheromone evaporation, the greater value represents the faster evaporation of pheromone concentration.

$$\tau_{n,d} = \begin{cases} \tau_{n,d} \times \rho_1 & \text{if } \tau_{n,d} \times \rho_1 >= \tau_{n,d} \_ default \\ \tau_{n,d} \_ default & \text{if } \tau_{n,d} \times \rho_1 <= \tau_{n,d} \_ default \end{cases} \qquad (11)$$

The concentration of pheromone can not be reduced to 0 or negative value, so equation (11) guarantees pheromone concentration no lower than the $\tau_{n,d}$_default, and the value of $\tau_{n,d}$_default represents the lower limit of the pheromone concentration. During the process of searching path to destination node, $\tau_{n,\ d}$_default ensures that every neighbor could be the next-hop node.

Routing Selection. In a certain intermediate node, forward ants choose the next-hop neighbor based on the probability. Selecting probability in the traditional ACA routing algorithm is defined as formula (12).

$$P_{n,d} = \begin{cases} \dfrac{\tau_{n,d}^{\alpha}}{\sum\limits_{n \in nodes\_visit_p} \tau_{i,d}^{\alpha}} & i \in N_m - nodes\_visit_p \\ 0 & otherwise \end{cases} \qquad (12)$$

Where $P_{n,\ d}$ is the transfer packets probability of one node to the nth neighbor nodes; $\tau_{n,d}$ is the value in the pheromone table; $\tau_{n,\ d}$ represents the pheromone concentration of the neighbor node n to the destination node d.

In EAACA routing algorithm, for calculating the packet transfer probability to the next hop neighbor, the residual energy of node is considered. So, the improved transfer probability is defined as formula (13):

$$P_{n,d} = \begin{cases} \dfrac{\tau_{n,d}^{\alpha} E^{\beta}(n)}{\sum\limits_{n \in nodes\_visit_p} \tau_{i,d}^{\alpha} E^{\beta}(i)} & i \in N_m - v\_node_p \\ 0 & otherwise \end{cases} \qquad (13)$$

Where $E=1/$ $(E_{initial}-E_s)$, and $E_{initial}$ is the initial energy of nodes; E_s is the actual energy of the nodes; β is the expectation heuristic factor; α and β are importance parameters to control pheromone concentration, which represent weights of nodes with more residual energy and the shorter path.

4 Simulation Results and Performance Analysis

4.1 Simulation Parameters

WSN nodes are arranged in the area of 200 x 200m^2, and wireless transmission distance is 40m between nodes. The simulation parameters are shown in Table 1.

Table 1. Experiment simulation parameters

Parameters	Value
Node initial energy	2[J]
Sink number	1
ε_{fs}	10[pJ/bit/m^2]
E_{elec}	50[nJ/bit/m]
E_{DA}	5[nJ]
MAC layer protocol	802.11

According to the proposed routing protocol based on ant colony algorithm, the algorithm parameters are defined as follows: $\alpha=1.5$; $\beta=1.5$; $\rho=0.5$; $\rho_1=0.8$.

4.2 Analysis of Simulation Results

The simulation mainly compares EAACA routing algorithm with the traditional ACA routing algorithm in the average residual energy and energy loss ratio of the network nodes.

Average residual energy is the basic standards to measure the merits of routing protocol. For 10 sets of different network nodes, the average residual energy of nodes after running 200s is shown in Figure 1. It can be seen that the average residual energy of nodes in the proposed EAACA is higher than that of the traditional ACA. It is due to EAACA routing protocols considered the energy factors when the data packets select the next hop node, and they transfer packets according to the probability of distance and the weight of energy. Thus, a single node is avoided to death early because of excessive energy consumption. The energy consumption of the network is saved to extend the network lifetime.

Energy loss ratio is that the total energy consumption of the network divided by all the number of successfully received packets. Energy loss ratio not only reflects the energy consumption situation of nodes in the network, but also shows the efficiency of receiving data packets successfully by the sink node. when there are 200 nodes in WSN, the situation of energy loss ratio with the time changing is shown as Figure 2. It can be seen from Figure 2, the EAACA protocol saves more energy than traditional ACA protocol, makes the network live longer and has higher reliability.

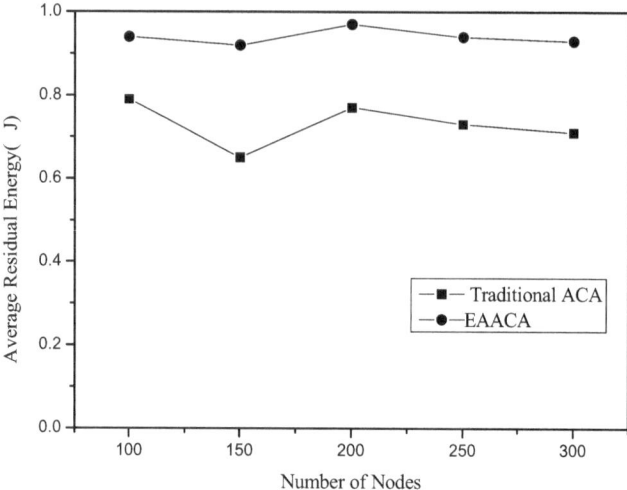

Fig. 1. Comparison of average residual energy

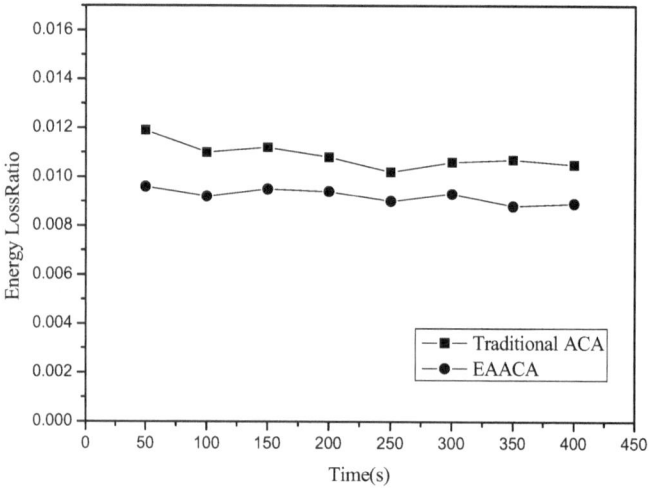

Fig. 2. Comparison of energy loss ratio

5   Conclusions

The ant colony algorithm for wireless sensor networks has the advantage of selforganization, stronger local searching ability and so on. However, the wireless sensor network is energy-limited, so EAACA routing algorithm based on energy level is proposed in this paper. Simulation results show that the proposed EAACA algorithm has improved significantly in the part of average remaining energy, the energy loss ratio, and greatly extends the network life cycle.

Acknowledgments. The work in this paper is part of a project sponsored by The Postdoctoral Science Foundation of Jiangsu, China (0901056C).

References

1. Jennifer, Y., Biswanath, M., Dipak, G.: Wireless Sensor Network Survey. Computer Networks 52, 2292–2330 (2008)
2. Akyildiz, I.F., Su, W., Sankarasubramaniam, Y., Cayirci, E.: A survey on sensor networks. IEEE Communications Magazine 116, 102–116 (2002)
3. Akkaya, K., Younis, M.: A Survey on Routing Protocols for Wireless Sensor Networks. Ad Hoc Networks 3, 325–349 (2005)
4. Toumpis, S., Tassiulas, L.: Optimal Deployment of Large Wireless Sensor Networks. IEEE Transactions on Information Theory 52, 2935–2953 (2006)
5. Rappaport, T.: Wireless Communication: Principles and Practice. Prentice-Hall Inc., New Jersey (1996)
6. Selcuk, O., Karaboga, D.: Routing in Wireless Sensor Networks Using Ant Colony Optimization. In: First NASA/ESA Conference on Adaptive Hardware and Systems, pp. 401–404. IEEE Press, New York (2006)
7. Heinzelman, W., Chandrakasan, A., Balakrishnan, H.: Energy-efficient Communication Protocol for Wireless Microsensor Networks. In: The Hawaii International Conference on System Sciences, pp. 1–10. IEEE Press, C. A (2000)
8. Wang, J., Xu, J., Xu, J.: Wireless Sensor Networks Routing Protocol Based on Ant Colony Optimized Algorithm. Journal of System Simulation 20, 4898–4901 (2008) (in Chinese)
9. Sim, K.M., Sun, W.H.: Multiple Ant Colony Optimizations for Network Routing. In: The First International Symposium on Cyber Worlds, pp. 277–281. IEEE Press, New York (2002)
10. Kamali, S., Opatrny, J.: A Position Based Ant Colony Routing Algorithm for Mobile Ad-hoc Networks. Journal of Networks 3, 31–41 (2008)
11. Tseng, Y., Chang, Y., Tzeng, B.: Energy Efficient Topology Control for Wireless Ad Hoc Sensor Networks. Journal of Information Science and Engineering 20, 27–37 (2004)

A Kind of Decay-Curve Inertia Weight Particle Swarm Optimization Algorithm

Yan Sun[1,2], Shishun Zhu[1], Qiang Li[3], Daowei Zhu[1], and Shujun Luo[4]

[1] Military Transportation University, Department of Automobile Engineering, Tianjin, China
[2] 66417 troops, xuanhua, China
[3] North China University of Technology, College of Mechanical Electronical and Engineering, Beijin, China
[4] Military Transportation University, Department of Military logistics, Tianjin, China

Abstract. Based on the research results published in existing relevant references, the basic principles of the standard particle swarm optimization (PSO) algorithm are elaborated and analyzed. To the shortcomings of the standard particle swarm optimization algorithm such as the success rate, number of iterations, running time and the local optimum in the optimization process, a new kind of decay-curve inertia weight Particle Swarm Optimization Algorithm (CPSO) is presented and the astringency analysis is finished. The comparison between the CPSO algorithm and the standard PSO algorithm through the experiment a analysis show that, the CPSO algorithm is apparently better than the standard PSO algorithm both in the convergence speed an convergence precision.

Keywords: decay-curve inertia weigh; PSO; convergence performance.

1 Introduction

The PSO idea was originally introduced by J. Kennedy et al. in 1995 as an optimization technique inspired by swarm intelligence and theory in general such as bird flocking, fish schooling and even human social behavior [4], [7], [8]. Furthermore, the whole idea and structure of the algorithm is inspired by evolutionary computation. Later PSO has turned out to be a worthy alternative to the standard Genetic Algorithm (GA) and other iterative optimization techniques.

Since the introduction of PSO in 1995 several research articles have been published on the subject. Shi and Eberhart investigated the problem of finding good parameter setting with the PSO model [11]. Further, the interaction between particles has been researched in 1999 regarding the "swarm neighborhood topology" [10]. Even though much work has been done in this area during the last eight years, only a small part of it has been concerned with testing and comparison with traditional optimization techniques like GA and other evolutionary approaches. There has been an empirical study concerning the performance of the PSO and an analytical comparison between the PSO model and the GA approach [5], [13]. P. J. Angeline compared the performance between a standard Evolutionary Algorithm (EA) and a basic PSO and concluded that the performance of the two different methods is competitive [1].

R. Chen (Ed.): ICICIS 2011, Part I, CCIS 134, pp. 402–409, 2011.
© Springer-Verlag Berlin Heidelberg 2011

Angeline's main point was that the PSO often converges significantly faster to the global optimum than the EA but has difficulties in fine tuning solutions. Hence, the performance of the PSO flattens out with a loss of diversity in the search space as the overall result.

In the paper, a new kind of decay-curve inertia weight Particle Swarm Optimization Algorithm is presented and the astringency analysis is finished. The results of application example proved that practical optimization parameters can be obtained in limited time by the method, and it is a kind of effective way to solve the problem of dynamic optimization method on electromechanical coupling system.

2 Elementary Particle Swarm Optimization Algorithm

Kennedy and Eberhart proposed the PSO algorithm conceptually based on social behavior of organisms such as herbs of animals, schools of fish and flocks of birds. PSO is a pseudo- optimization method (heuristic) inspired by the collective intelligence of swarms of biological populations. PSO is a zero- order, non- calculus-based method (no gradients are needed), can solve discontinuous, multimodal, non-convex problems [10]. It includes some probabilistic features in the motion of particles. The system initially has a population of random solutions. Each potential solution, called particle, is given a random velocity and is flown through the problem space. The particles have memory and each particle keeps track of previous best position and corresponding fitness. The previous best value is called as *pbest*. Thus, *pbest* is related to a particular particle. It also has another value called *gbest*, which is the best value of all the particles *pbest* in the swarm. The basic concept of PSO technique lies in accelerating the particle towards its *pbest* and the *gbest* locations at each time step. Acceleration has random weights for both pbest and gbest locations. The step-by-step algorithm of PSO is given below [10].

Step 1: Initialize a population (array - N) of particles with random positions and velocities of d dimensions in theproblem space.

Step 2: For each particle, evaluate the desired optimization fitness function in d variables.

Step 3: Compare particle's fitness evaluation with particles *pbest*. If current value is better than *pbest*, then set *pbest* value equal to the current value and the *pbest* location equal to the current location in d dimensional space.

Step 4: Compare fitness evaluation with the population's overall previous best. If the current value is better than *gbest*, then reset *gbest* to the to the current particles array index and value.

Step 5: Change the velocity and position of the particle according to (5) and (6) respectively. Vid and Xid represent the velocity and position of ith particle with d dimensions respectively and ran1 and ran2 are two uniform random functions.

$$v_{id}(k+1) = wv_{id}(k) + c_1 r_1 \left[p_d(k) - x_{id}(k) \right] + c_2 r_2 \left[p_g(k) - x_{id}(k) \right]$$

$$x_{id}(k+1) = x_{id}(k) + v_{id}(k+1)$$

Step 6: Repeat Step 2 until a criterion is met, usually a sufficiently good fitness or a maximum number of iterations/function evaluations.

Where, ω is called the inertia weight controls the exploration and exploitation of the search space because it dynamically adjusts velocity. *Vmax* is the maximum allowable velocity for the particles. c1 and c2 termed as cognition and social components respectively are the acceleration constants. r1 and r2 are two random between 0 and 1 number. pid and pgd are particle best ever position and particle best position in swarm respectively. The computation time taken by the PSO algorithm is comparatively less than the GA. Hence, PSO algorithm is used as an optimization tool to calculate the optimized future control sequence in MPC system.

3 Adaptive Leap Particle Swarm Optimization

For the CPSO which the population scale is M, $X_i = (x_i^1, x_i^2, ..., x_i^D)$ $(i = 1, 2, ..., M)$, is defined as the feasible solution of the particle in D dimension optimization problem, $V_i = (v_i^1, v_i^2, ..., v_i^D)$ is the flying velocity the optimum position that the particle has passed is marked as $P_i = (p_i^1, p_i^2, ..., p_i^D)$, the optimum solution in feasible field is p_g. For the objective function $G(X)$, the evolution of the CPSO in $k+1$ times can be decided by following equation:

$$p_i^d(k+1) = \begin{cases} p_i^d(k) & \text{if } G(x_i(k+1)) \leq G(p_i^d(k)) \\ x_i^d(k+1) & \text{if } G(x_i(k+1)) > G(p_i^d(k)) \end{cases} \quad (d = 1, 2, ..., D)$$

The renewal evolution expression is:

$$v_i^d(k+1) = (k\alpha + \beta)^{-(2n-1)} v_i^d(k) + c_1 r_{1i}^d(k) \left[p^d(k) - x_i^d(k) \right] + c_2 r_{2i}^d(k) \left[p_g(k) - x_i^d(k) \right] \quad (1)$$

$$x_i^d(k+1) = x_i^d(k) + v_i^d(k+1) \quad (2)$$

here: α, c_1, c_2 are the selected positive real number, $r_{1i}^d(k), r_{2i}^d(k)$ is random number in the field of [0, 1]. To induce Eq.(2) to Eq. (1), we can deduce the following equation:

$$x_i^d(k+1) = x_i^d(k) + (k\alpha + \beta)^{-(2n-1)} v_i^d(k) + c_1 r_{1i}^d(k) \left[p^d(k) - x_i^d(k) \right] + c_2 r_{2i}^d(k) \left[p_g(k) - x_i^d(k) \right] \quad (3)$$

From Eq.(2), we get:

$$v_i^d(k) = x_i^d(k) - x_i^d(k-1) \quad (4)$$

To combine Eq.(4) and (3), we get:

$$x_i^d(k+1) = x_i^d(k) + c_1 r_{1i}^d(k) \left[p^d(k) - x_i^d(k) \right] + c_2 r_{2i}^d(k) \left[p_g(k) - x_i^d(k) \right] \quad (5)$$

With the increase of generation number k, $e^{-\alpha k}$ is gradually tend to become zero, Eq.(5) will become the following form:

$$x_i^d(k+1) = x_i^d(k) + c_1 r_{1i}^d(k) \left[p_i^d(k) - x_i^d(k) \right] + c_2 r_{2i}^d(k) \left[p_g(k) - x_i^d(k) \right] \qquad (6)$$

According to Eq.(6), it is obvious to know that the random vector $\{x_i^d(k)\}$ is operated in iterative way by the vector $p_i^d(k)$ and $p_g(k)$, which is acted by random disturbance $r_{1i}^d(k)$ and $r_{2i}^d(k)$.

4 Analysis of CPSO Algorithm Convergence

To seek design variable vector $X \in F$, F is the feasible field, in order that the objective function $G(\mathbf{X})$ can be optimized.

Presupposition 1. Feasible region Ω of problem(P) is bounded closed region. Target function $f(x)$ is continuous on region Ω.

Definition 1. Suppose that $\{X(k)\}$ is population series produced by algorithm CPSO where $x(k) \in X(k)$ is optimization individual of k generation population. Suppose that $f(x(k)) \le f(x(k-1))$ exist, and certain point $x(N)$ self or one limit of series is infinitesimal point of problem P, then algorithm M is called as local convergence.

Lemma 1. If problem P has local minimal point x^*, then $\lim_{t \to \infty} p_g(t) = x^*$

Proof. Considering that $P_g(t)$ is particle swarm optimization individual during iterative process t times, thus formulation $f(p_g(t)) \le f(p_g(t-1))$ is obtained. Substitute formulation (1) into formulation (2), the following formulation is obtained

$$x_{id}(t+1) = x_{id}(t) + (k\alpha + \beta)^{-(2n-1)} \times v_{id}(t) + c_1 \times r_1 \times (p_{id}(t) - x_{id}(t)) + c_2 \times r_2 \times (p_{gd}(t) - x_{id}(t)) \quad (7)$$

Because that $v_{iD}(t) = x_{iD}(t) - x_{iD}(t-1)$, then

$$x_{id}(t+1) = x_{id}(t) + (k\alpha + \beta)^{-(2n-1)} \times (x_{id}(t) - x_{id}(t-1)) + c_1 \times r_1 \times (p_{id}(t) - x_{id}(t)) + c_2 \times r_2 \times (p_{gd}(t) - x_{id}(t))$$

For particle swarm optimization individual, $p_{gD}(t) = p_{iD}(t)$, the above equation (7) is updated as follows:

$$x_{id}(t+1) = x_{id}(t) + (k\alpha + \beta)^{-(2n-1)} \times (x_{id}(t) - x_{id}(t-1)) + (c_1 \times r_1 + c_2 \times r_2) \times (p_{gd}(t) - x_{id}(t)) \qquad (8)$$

Where $x(t)$ will be gradually approach particle swarm optimization value $p_g(t)$, and $|v_{iD}| > 0$.

Suppose that $p_g(t)$ is not local minimal point, then $r > 0$ is in existence. This makes the following equation $f(x) < f(p_g(t))$ establish, where $\|x - p_g(t)\| \leq r$. Because of $f(x)$ being continuous, the equation $f(x(t')) < f(p_g(t))$ required from the equation (8), during $x(t)$ approach to $p_g(t)$, $t' < t$, $\|x(t') - p_g(t)\| \leq r$. Obviously, the above result is contradiction to the existed condition, thus the above supposition can not come into existence. The conclusion is as follows, $P_g(t)$ is local minimal point.

Theorem 1. CPSO algorithm is local convergence

Proof For particle swarm optimization individual, $p_g(t) = p_i(t)$, because of $\lim\limits_{x \to \infty} x(t) = p_g(t)$, $\lim\limits_{x \to \infty} x(t) = x^*$, where x^* is local minimal point, and having the following sequence $f(p_g(t)) \leq f(p_g(t-1)) \leq \cdots \leq f(p_g(0))$, CPSO algorithm is local convergence from the definition 1.

Lemma 2. Suppose that $\Delta x_{iD} = v_{iD}$, $r_1, r_2 \sim N(0,1)$, Then, $\Delta x_{iD} \sim N(\mu_D, \sigma_D)$
Proof Obtained from equation (1),

$$\Delta x_{id} = (k\alpha + \beta)^{-(2n-1)} \times v_{id} + c_1 \times (p_{id} - x_{id}) \times r_1 + c_2 \times (p_{gd} - x_{id}) \times r_2,$$

Suppose that

$$\phi_1 = (k\alpha + \beta)^{-(2n-1)} \times v_{id}, \phi_2 = c_1 \times (p_{id} - x_{id}), \phi_3 = c_2 \times (p_{gd} - x_{id})$$

then $\Delta x_{iD} = \phi_1 \phi_2 r_1 + \phi_3 r_2$

For CPSO, during the running process of particle swarm, the formulation (7) give particle a stronger velocity impulse, this makes ϕ_1, ϕ_2, ϕ_3 become nonzero variable during the searching process. Because of $r_1, r_2 \sim N(0,1)$, obviously $\Delta x_{iD} \sim N(\mu_D, \sigma_D)$ is proper.

Theorem 2. Suppose that particle swarm sequence $\{x(k)\}$ is produced by CPSO algorithm, where $x^*(k) \in X(K)$ is optimization individual of k generation particle swarm, i.e. $x^*(k) = \arg\min\limits_{1 \leq i \leq \mu} f(x_i(k))$. If target function and feasible area of problem (P) is satisfied with supposition 1, then $p\{\lim\limits_{k \to \infty} f(x^*(k)) = f^*\} = 1$, i.e. particle swarm sequence is convergence to global optimum solution at probability being 1.

5   Performance Test of Arithmetic

To test the effect of optimization algorithms, CPSO and PSO are applied to solve the optimal value function of the four classical test functions.

Sphere: $f_1(\mathbf{x}) = \sum_{i=1}^{n} x_i^2, -100 \le x_i \le 100, n = 30$,

Schaffer's f6: $f_2(\mathbf{x}) = 0.5 + \dfrac{\sin^2(\sqrt{x_1^2 + x_2^2}) - 0.5}{[1 + 0.001(x_1^2 + x_2^2)]^2}, -100 \le x_i \le 100, n = 2$

Rastrigrin: $f_3(\mathbf{x}) = \sum_{i=1}^{n} (x_i^2 - 10\cos(2\pi x_i) + 10), -5.12 \le x_i \le 5.12, n = 30$

Griewank: $f_4(\mathbf{x}) = \dfrac{1}{400} \sum_{i=1}^{n} (x_i - 100)^2 - \prod_{i=1}^{n} \cos(\dfrac{x_i - 100}{\sqrt{i}}) + 1, -600 \le x_i \le 600, n = 30$

Algorithm parameters are set as follows:

PSO and the CPSO's population size were taken $m = 10$ and $m = 30$, $c_1 = c_2 = 2$ were, PSO weight $w = 0.5$, CPSO adjustment factor $\alpha = 0.03, \beta = 1, n = 1$.

Trial function's target value selects the target value in many literature to use, as shown in Table 1.

Table 1. Goal for test functions

函数	Sphere	Rosenbrock	Schaffer's f6	Rastrigrin	Griewank
目标值	0.01	100	10^{-5}	100	0.1

Table 2. Performance comparison of the two algorithma (m=10)

function	Algorithm	Success rate	Iterations	Run time (t)
Sphere	PSO	1	1368.75.	0.206
	CPSO	1	826.74	0.135
Schaffer's f6	PSO	0.75	1808.33	0.053
	CPSO	1	1568.44	0.038
Rastrigrin	PSO	0.97	600.76	0.154
	CPSO	1	647.29	0.143
Griewank	PSO	0.96	1149.60	0.257
	CPSO	1	993.78	0.188

Three algorithms run 100 time and receive the average of optimal rate, the average number of iterations and the average running time, As shown in Table 2 and Table 3.

Table 3. Performance comparison of the two algorithma (m=30)

function	Algorithm	Success rate	Iterations	Run time (t)
Sphere	PSO	1	316.76	0.148
	CPSO	1	306.65	0.121
Schaffer's f6	PSO	1	959.46	0.056
	CPSO	1	434.25	0.028
Rastrigrin	PSO	1	226.89	0.144
	CPSO	1	223.87	0.134
Griewank	PSO	0.98	433.08	0.286
	CPSO	1	318.66	0.185

From Table 2 and Table 3 shows, CPSO algorithm in success rate, number of iterations and running time is better than PSO algorithm.

6 Conclusions

Particle swarm optimization (PSO) algorithm is a new optimization technique originating from artificial life and evolutionary computation. PSO is easily understood, realized. PSO has few parameters need to be tuned, and has been applied widely. To overcome the problem of premature convergence on PSO, proposes an improved particle swarm optimization (CPSO), which is guaranteed to keep the diversity of the particle swarm and to improve performance of basic PSO algorithm. Four benchmark functions are selected as the test functions. The experimental results show that the CPSO can not only significantly speed up the convergence, effectively solve the premature convergence problem, but also have good stability.

References

1. Kennedy, J., Eberhart, R.C.: Particle swarm optimization. In: Proc. of the IEEE Int'l Conf. on Neural Networks, pp. 1942–1948. IEEE Press, Perth Australia (1995), http://www.engr.iupui.edu/~shi/Coference/psopap4.html (1999-6-8)
2. Parsopoulos, K.E., Vrahatis, M.N.: On the computation of all global minimizers through particle swarm optimization. IEEE Trans. on Evolutionary Computation 8(3), 211–224 (2004)

3. Krink, T., Vesterstrom, J.S., Riget, J.: Particle swarm optimization with spatial particle extension. In: Proc. of the IEEE Int'l Conf. on Evolutionary Computation, pp. 1474–1497. The Institute of Electrical and Electronics Engineers(IEEE) Inc., Honolulu (2002)
4. Kazemi, B.A.L., Mohan, C.K.: Multi-phase generalization of the particle swarm optimization algorithm. In: Proc. of the IEEE Int'l Conf. on Evolutionary Computation, pp. 489–494. The Institute of Electrical and Electronics Engineers(IEEE) Inc., Honolulu (2002)
5. Hu, X.H., Eberhart, R.C.: Adaptive particle swarm optimization: Detection and response to dynamic system. In: Proc. of the IEEE Int'l Conf. on Evolutionary Computation, pp. 1666–1670. The Institute of Electrical and Electronics Engineers (IEEE) Inc., Honolulu (2002)
6. Xie, X.F., Zhang, W.J., Yang, Z.L.: A dissipative particle swarm optimization. In: Proc. of the IEEE Int'l Conf. on Evolutionary Computation, pp. 1456–1461. The Institute of Electrical and Electronics Engineers (IEEE) Inc., Honolulu (2002)
7. Ratnaweera, A., Halgamuge, S.K., Watson, H.C.: Self-organizing hierarchical particle swarm optimizer with time-varying acceleration coefficients. IEEE Trans. on Evolutionary Computation 8(3), 240–255 (2004)
8. Clerc, M., Kennedy, J.: The particle swarm——Explosion, stability, and convergence in a multidimensional complex space. IEEE Trans. on Evolutionary Computation 6(1), 58–73 (2002)
9. Cristian, T.I.: The particle swarm optimization algorithm: convergence analysis and parameter selection. Information Processing Letters 85(6), 317–325 (2003)
10. Li, H., Tang, H.W., Guo, C.H.: The convergence analysis of a class of evolution strategies. Operations Research (OR) Trans. 3(4), 79–83 (1999) (in English with Chinese abstract)
11. Guo, C.H., Tang, H.W.: Global convergence properties of evolution strategies. Mathematica Numerica Sinica 23(1), 105–110 (2001) (in English with Chinese abstract)

Performance Analysis of Cooperative Virtual Laboratory Based on Web[*]

Zheng Gengzhong[1] and Liu Qiumei[2]

[1] Department of Mathematics and Information Technology,
Hanshan Normal University, Chaozhou 521041, Guangdong, China
[2] Library, Hanshan Normal University, Chaozhou 521041, Guangdong, China

Abstract. Indexes such as autonomy, interaction, promptness, cooperation and distributed are very important to evaluate the performance of cooperative virtual laboratory based on web(CVLW).The characteristics of CVLW are analyzed in this paper, and virtual laboratory is regarded as a special network, network analysis method is used to analyze the important index of response time. The analysis is advantageous to improve the utilization efficiency of virtual laboratory and provide useful references for better study the interoperability of CVLW.

Keywords: Virtual laboratory, Cooperation, Responding time, Performance analysis.

1 Introduction

Collaborative virtual laboratory based on web(CVLW) is a distributed system, which integrate the computer supported cooperative work(CSCW) and virtual laboratory [1,2]. CVLW can provide users with a virtual network platform and have a more flexible form and interaction compared with the traditional virtual laboratory [3]. Response time as a time metric of virtual experimental system, emphasizing the validity, accuracy, and cooperation of multiple tasks, which is a key problem to be solved in CVLW. In CVLW, network delay will lead packet to be lost and experimental data inaccurate, thus experimenters will have no interest in the virtual laboratory, and lead the working of CVLW become low efficiency. For these reasons, in the paper, based on analysis the characteristics of virtual laboratory, we regard virtual laboratory as a special network and analysis the important index of response time by creating a logical network model. Through the analysis of response time, we can improve the efficiency of CVLW and make experimenters in different geographic locations complete experiment project more easily, thus improve the interoperability of virtual laboratory.

The remaining sections are organized as follows: In section 2, we study the performance analysis model of CVLW. In section 3, we make an empirical analysis of CVLW. Section 4 concludes the paper.

---

[*] This work is proudly supported by the National Natural Science Foundation of China (No. 60974082, No.60703118). Team project of Hanshan Normal University (No. LT201001).

R. Chen (Ed.): ICICIS 2011, Part I, CCIS 134, pp. 410–415, 2011.
© Springer-Verlag Berlin Heidelberg 2011

2 Performance Analysis Model of CVLW

2.1 Study Objective

In the communication network of CVLW, the objective of the performance analysis is: for a given time t_0, if a node proposes a requirement, how to use the appropriate algorithm to calculate other nodes' probability of response time $t \leq t_0$.

The research objectives can be convert to how to create the structure function corresponding to the task which to be resolved. Let function $\delta(x)$ is the response time of CVLW, and $\delta(x) \leq t_0$, so the probability of response time can be expressed as: $R(G, time) = \{P_r \delta(x)\}$. Assume the structure function of CVLW is $\delta(f)$, $\delta(f)$ denote the data transmit time between node s and node t under the state of f. Since the communication of CVLW is duplex, so we have:

$$R(G, time) = P\{\delta(f) \leq \frac{t_0}{2}\} = P\{traffic_{(s,t)} \geq \frac{2}{t_0}\}$$

Since the reciprocal of unit data transmission time is traffic, so the probability of response time is to calculate the probability of traffic. Let $M = \left\lceil \frac{t_0}{2} \right\rceil$, assume there have $N+1$ levels of traffic between node s and node t, the probability in several response time can be shown in Table 1:

Table 1. Relationship between data delay and probability

Data delay	Probability
∞	P_0
1	P_1
1/2	P_2
...	
1/N	P_n

Through the above analysis, we can get $R(G, time) = P_n$, and calculate the probability of responsed time by using related algorithm to find the smallest path of all nodes in network. The solution step is list as follows:

(1) Convert physical map into logic diagram;
(2) Find the minimum path sets of the network;
(3) Use "d" grade minimum path algorithm to obtain all of the smallest d-level path;
(4) Solve the probability of the given response time.

2.2 Network Model

As a distributed system, CVLW can be regard as a communication subnet, the method of network analysis can be used to study the performance of the communication subnet.

Assume the network model of CVLW is $N(V,E,W)$, where $V = \{v_1,v_2,...,v_p\}$ is the set of p nodes, $E = \{e_1,e_2,...,e_q\}$ is the set of q edges[4], v_i is the element of V which is called vertice, e_k is the element of E which is called edge, the weight of (v_i,v_j) is w_{ij}, $w_{ij} \in W$. Let v_s and v_j is the any vertice in network, then the best result is to find a way which is the smallest way in all of the roads from v_s to v_j, the

mathematical model is: $W(P^*) = \min \sum W_{ij}, (v_i,v_j) \in P$.

2.3 Solving Traffic Probability with Minimal Path Set Algorithm

From the above analysis, we can know that the analysis of response time can be transformed into the problem of solve traffic probability among nodes. So minimal path set algorithm can be used to solve the problems.

Assume $N_f = \{a_i \in E \mid f_i > 0\}, Z_i = \{a_i \in E \mid f_i = 0\}, l_{ij} = (\delta_{i1},\delta_{i2},...,\delta_{in})$, where

$\delta_{ij} = \begin{cases} 1 & i = j \\ 0 & i \neq j \end{cases}$, let $S_f = \{a_i \in N_f \mid \delta(f - l_i) < \delta(f)\}$, define the structure function of $N(V,E,W)$ is δ, f is the state vector of δ, when $\delta(f) = d$, i.e., the data flow between node s and node t is d, and $N_f = S_f$, then f is the smallest d-level path in $N(V,E,W)$.

Assume data flow expected value between node s and node t is d, then the communication ability is d, and its probability is $p_r\{f \mid \delta(f) \geq d\}$, which means the probability that at least d unit data can be transmit between node s and node t. If $p^1, p^2,..., p^k$ is the smallest path among all paths between node s and node t, for each p^i, the maximum data stream flowing through it is $L_j = \min\{c_i \mid e_i \in p^j\}$ and data flow f is the d-level minimum path, t is the traffic through the k minimum path, assume $t = (t_1,t_2,...,t_k)$, then $\sum_{i=0}^{k} t_i = d$ $t_i \leq l_i$ $i = 1,2,...,k$ and $\sum_j \{t_j \mid e_j \in p^j\} \leq c_j$ $j = 1,2,...,m$.

Based on the above analysis, we can calculate the minimum path of CVLW through "d" grade minimum path algorithm, the algorithm is list as follows:

(1) Calculate the maxium capacity of p^j, and $L_j = \min\{c_i \mid e_i \in P^j\}$ $j = 1,2,...,k$;

(2) Find all of the feasible solutions by the following equations $(f_1,f_2,...,f_k)$;

$$\begin{cases} \sum_{i=1}^{k} f_i = d \\ f_j \leq L_j \quad j = 1,2,...,m \\ \sum_j \{f_j \mid a_j \in P^j\} \leq c^i \quad i = 1,2,...,m \quad j = 1,2,...,k \end{cases}$$

(3)   Convert   feasible   solution   to   the   candidate   minimum   path $X = (x_1, x_2, ..., x_m)$ $x_i = \sum_j \{ f_j \mid a_j \in P^j \}$.

3 Empirical Analysis

Figure 1 shows a physical structure of CVLW among Fudan University, Xidian University, Northwestern University and Tsinghua University. Assume Northwestern University send a request to Fudan University, now we need to calculate the probability of response time $\leq 2/3$ which Tsinghua University response to Northwestern University.

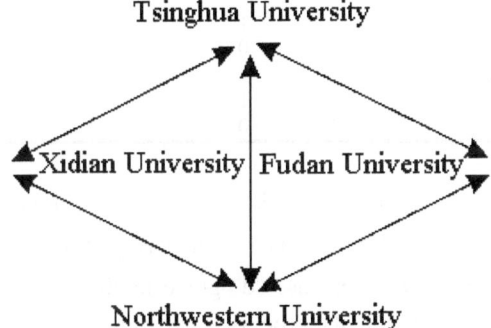

Tsinghua University

Xidian University | Fudan University

Northwestern University

Fig. 1. Physical structure of CVLW

According to the previous analysis, function $\delta(x)$ is the response time of CVLW, and $\delta(x) \leq 2/3$. Ignore the time of process information, and assume communication is full duplex.

Since $t_0 = 2/3$,   and $R(G, time) = P^r \{ \delta(f) \leq 2/3 \} = P^r \{ traffic_{(s,t)} \geq \dfrac{2}{2/3} \}$ thus $d = 2$.

Convert figure 1 into the network topology as figure 2 shows, table 2 shows the possible states and probability of each path.

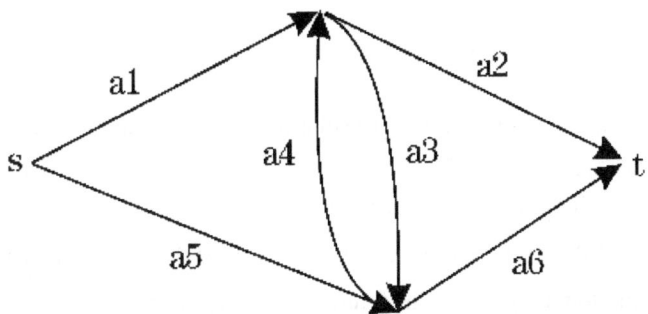

Fig. 2. Network topology of CVLW

Table 2. Relationship of network topology between edge state and probability

Path	Possible state	Probability
a_1	3	0.15
	2	0.15
	1	0.10
	0	0.15
a_2	2	0.60
	1	0.20
	0	0.20
a_3	1	0.80
	0	0.20
a_4	1	0.90
	0	0.10
a_5	1	0.90
	0	0.10
a_6	2	0.60
	1	0.30
	0	0.10

Given $C = \{C_1, C_2, C_3, C_4, C_5, C_6\} = \{3, 2, 1, 1, 1, 2\}$, with join matrix method [5], we can get four minimum path, namely $P^1 = \{a_1, a_2\}, P^2 = \{a_1, a_3, a_6\}$, $P^3 = \{a_2, a_4, a_5\}, P^4 = \{a_5, a_6\}$, and use "d" grade minimum path algorithm to solve the probability of response time, the processes are list as follows:

(1) $L_1 = \min\{3, 2\} = 2, L_2 = \min\{3, 1, 2\} = 1, L_3 = \min\{2, 1, 1\} = 1, L_4 = \min\{1, 2\} = 1$;

(2) Find a feasible solution of $f_1 + f_2 + f_3 + f_4 = 3$ $(f_1, f_2, f_3, f_4) \le (2, 1, 1, 1)$;

$$\sum_j \{f_i \mid a_1 \in p^j\} = f_1 + f_2 \le 3$$

$$\sum_j \{f_i \mid a_2 \in p^j\} = f_1 + f_3 \le 2$$

$$\sum_j \{f_i \mid a_3 \in p^j\} = f_2 \le 1$$

$$\sum_j \{f_i \mid a_4 \in p^j\} = f_3 \le 1$$

$$\sum_j \{f_i \mid a_5 \in p^j\} = f_3 + f_4 \le 1$$

$$\sum_j \{f_i \mid a_6 \in p^j\} = f_2 + f_4 \le 2$$

f_1, f_2, f_3, f_4 is the non-negative integer solutions of the equations, and there are four feasible solutions: $F^1 = (2, 1, 0, 0), F^2 = (1, 1, 1, 0), F^3 = (2, 0, 0, 1), F^4 = (1, 1, 0, 1)$;

(3) Convert feasible solution to the candidates minimum path;

$X^1 = (3, 2, 1, 0, 0, 1), X^2 = (2, 2, 1, 1, 1, 1), X^3 = (2, 2, 0, 0, 1, 1), X^4 = (2, 1, 1, 0, 1, 2)$

(4) Because the topology shown in figure 2 has a cycle. So one by one check each candidate two level minimum path;

$X^2 = (2,2,1,1,1,1)$ is not a three level minimum path, the remaining three are minimum path. The reliability of response time can be calculated after all three level minimum path have been found.

Since $P^1, P^2, ..., P^K$ is the minimum path of d level, thus $R_d = P_X\{X : \delta(X) \geq d\} = P_X\{\cup_I^K\{X : X \geq P^I\}\}$.

Using the method of state decomposition to solve the above equation, we can get the probability of communication ability between node s and node t as follows:

$$R_0 = P_X\{X : \delta(X) \geq 0\} = P_X\{\cup_{I=1}^K\{X : X \geq P^I\}\} = 1$$

$$R_1 = P_X\{X : \delta(X) \geq 1\} = P_X\{\cup_{I=1}^K\{X : X \geq P^I\}\} = 0.99$$

$$R_2 = P_X\{X : \delta(X) \geq 2\} = P_X\{\cup_{I=1}^K\{X : X \geq P^I\}\} = 0.88$$

$$R_3 = P_X\{X : \delta(X) \geq 3\} = P_X\{\cup_{I=1}^K\{X : X \geq P^I\}\} = 0.61$$

$$R_4 = P_X\{X : \delta(X) \geq 4\} = P_X\{\cup_{I=1}^K\{X : X \geq P^I\}\} = 0.20$$

The above datas show that complete probability calculate of the system function under given work conditions and specified time in CVLW can measure system reliability, and provide a valuable reference for the selection of a reasonable, economical and reliable scheme of CVLW.

4 Conclusion

CVLW is a virtual laboratory based on virtual prototype and CSCW, which is consisted of virtual device and virtual experimental platform. Autonomous, interactive, timely, collaborative and distributed are the key indexes to measure the performance of CVLW. In the paper, we make a qualitative analysis of the response time, the analysis can help experimenters to achieve better transparency and improve interactive operational in the operation of virtual experiments. What is more, the study can further improve efficiency in the use of virtual laboratory and provide useful references for better study the interoperability of virtual laboratory.

References

1. Luo, W., He, P.: Research on Key Technologies in Cooperating Virtual Lab. Computer simulation 12, 252–254 (2004)
2. Wang, R., Shi, C.: Research Net Cooperate Virtual Lab Based on VP. Computer Engineering and Applications 18, 143–144 (2003)
3. Shi, C., Cai, P.: Research and Development on a Virtual Laboratory Supporting Computer Cooperative Work. Computer Engineering and Applications 30, 150–152 (2003)
4. Ni, X., Yi, H.: VM-based design of B/S collaborative system. Computer Integrated Manufacturing Systems 2, 157–159 (2005)
5. Xin, K.: Minimum path acquired by the liaison matrix. Water Conservancy & Electric Power Machinery 3, 56–58 (2004)

Numerical Simulation of Gas Leaking Diffusion from Storage Tank

Hongjun Zhu and Jiaqiang Jing

Department of Petroleum Engineering, Southwest Petroleum University, Xindu Road 8#,
Xindu district, 610500 Chengdu, China
ticky863@126.com, jjq@swpu.edu.cn

Abstract. Over 80 percents of storage tank accidents are caused by gas leaking. Since traditional empirical calculation has great errors, present work aims to study the gas leaking diffusion under different wind conditions by numerical simulation method based on computational fluid dynamics theory. Then gas concentration distribution was obtained to determine the scope of the security zone. The results showed that gas diffused freely along the axis of leaking point without wind, giving rise to large range of hazardous area. However, wind plays the role of migrating and diluting the leaking gas. The larger is the wind speed, the smaller is the damage and the bigger is the security zone. Calculation method and results can provide some reference to establish and implement rescue program for accidents.

Keywords: numerical simulation; computational fluid dynamics; leaking diffusion; security zone.

1 Introduction

In recent years, explosion is usually presented in oil-gas field surface installations and chemical refineries. Most of these incidents are caused by gas leaking. In August 12, 1989, heaviest explosion accidents occurred in Huangdao oil store, giving rise to 5 oil tanks and 36,000 tons of crude oil burned, 19 people killed and 35.4 million RMB lost. In October 21, 1993, gas leaked from gasoline tank in Jinling petrochemical company refinery, leading to combustion explosion and burning area reached to 23437.5 m^2, 2 people killed and 389,600 RMB lost. And economic losses of 3.25 million RMB are result from disastrous fire of tank in Banpo oil store in April 24, 2004. Thus, it is urgently needed to know the diffusion rule of leaking gas, in order to establish rescue program and reduce losses.

Ehsan Nourollahi [1] had studied the characteristics of gas leaking from pipelines. Tian G.S. [2] proposed a method to calculate the leakage rate of gas. And diffusion rule of smoke in small size was obtained by Jin Y. [3]. With the rapid development of computer technology, numerical methods have been used to simulate the leaking gas. Peide Sun [4] simulated the deformation of rock and gas leaking flow in parallel. Hu X.Q. [5] simulated gas containing hydrogen sulfide leaking from high-pressure

R. Chen (Ed.): ICICIS 2011, Part I, CCIS 134, pp. 416–421, 2011.
© Springer-Verlag Berlin Heidelberg 2011

pipeline. And Qin Z.X. [6] analyzed the diffusion and explosion of gas from natural gas pipelines.

However, most of the above studies are about gas leaking from pipelines, which can not describe the diffusion rule of gas leaking from tank. Therefore, in this paper, gas leaking diffusion under different wind conditions was simulated based on computational fluid dynamics theory.

2 Governing Equations and Numerical Method

2.1 Governing Equations

The Navier-Stokes equations were solved to obtain the flow field of gas leaking from tank, which include continuity equation and momentum equation expressed as follows:

$$\frac{\partial \rho}{\partial t} + \nabla(\rho v) = 0 \tag{1}$$

$$\frac{\partial(\rho v)}{\partial t} + \nabla(\rho v v) = -\nabla p + \nabla \tau + \rho g + F \tag{2}$$

where ρ is the density of fluid, v is the velocity, τ is the viscous stress, p is the pressure, F is the other volume force and g is gravitational acceleration.

The equations of mass and momentum were solved using version 12.0.16 of the general purpose CFD code FLUENT. The discretization of the equations is implemented using a power-law differencing scheme in a staggered grid system. Velocities are stored at cell surfaces and scalars, such as pressure and volume fraction, are stored at the center of the cell. Second-order upwind difference scheme is employed in the discretization of momentum equations. PRESTO format is used to discretize the pressure terms, and SIMPLE algorithm is applied in the coupling of the pressure and velocity.

2.2 Geometry and Mesh

For the present study, geometry and mesh have been generated in GAMBIT which is a commercial CAD software package. The geometry and mesh distribution used for computational model has been shown in Fig.1. The diameter of leaking aperture is 0.1m and computational domain is a 100m×100m square with two tanks and two buildings in it.

Gas is leaking from the aperture in vertical direction with uniform velocity. Wind blows from the left in horizontal direction. If there is no wind, the left boundary is also an outlet for leaking gas.

The nature gas used in the simulation is a mixing gas containing 93.5% CH_4 and 6.5% H_2S. The density of CH_4 is 0.6679 kg/m^3, dynamic viscosity and thermal conductivity of which is 1.087×10^{-5} Pa·s and 0.0332 W/(m·℃), respectively. While the density, dynamic viscosity, and thermal conductivity of H_2S are 1.46 kg/m^3,

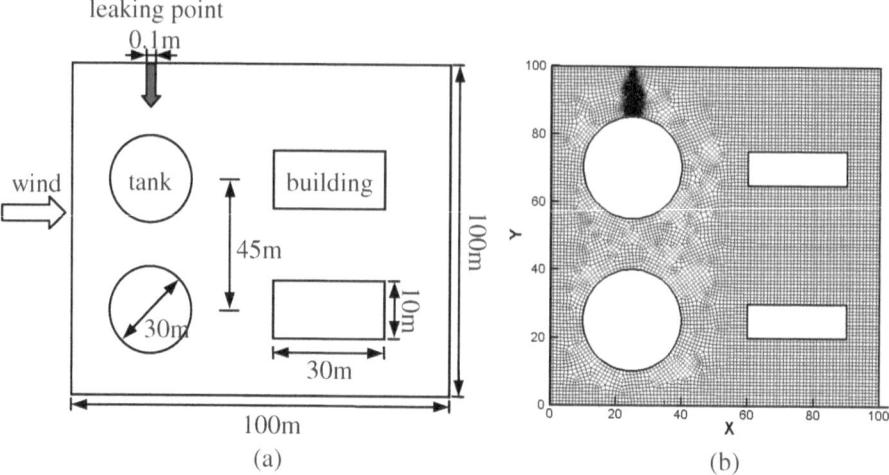

Fig. 1. Geometry and mesh of computational domain. (a) shows the geometry model. (b) shows the mesh for simulating.

1.2×10^{-5} Pa·s and 0.0134 W/(m·°C), respectively. The specific-heat-capacity of CH_4 and H_2S are all got according to piecewise-polynomial.

2.3 Boundary Conditions

Uniform velocity profile was assumed at the inlet boundary for leaking point (u_1=200m/s) and wind inlet (u_2=0, 3, 5 or 8m/s). And pressure outlet (relative p=0) was used for the exit of computational zone.

3 Results and Discussion

Wind has an important impact on the diffusion of leaking gas. It is different for diffusion in environment with different wind speed. Shown from Fig.2, we can see that gas diffused freely along the axis of leaking point without wind. The concentration in leaking point is large, which reduced gradually with the diffusion in surrounding. When there is wind coming from the left of computational domain, the trace of leaking gas would deviate from the vertical direction. And the larger is the wind speed, the greater is the deviation.

Due to the large velocity of gas in leaking point, wind had no significant effect on the initial segment, whose influence presented obviously in the region far away the point. Wind increased the heat and mass transfer between leaking gas and air, promoting the diffusion of gas. And natural gas has a trend of diffusing leeward. The larger is the wind speed, the more significant is the trend. So Fig.2 shows that concentration contours distributed densely on the windward side. While the concentration contours distributed sparsely in the Leeward side.

Concentration distribution: CH$_4$ H$_2$S

No wind

Wind speed
u=3m/s

Wind speed
u=5m/s

Wind speed
u=8m/s

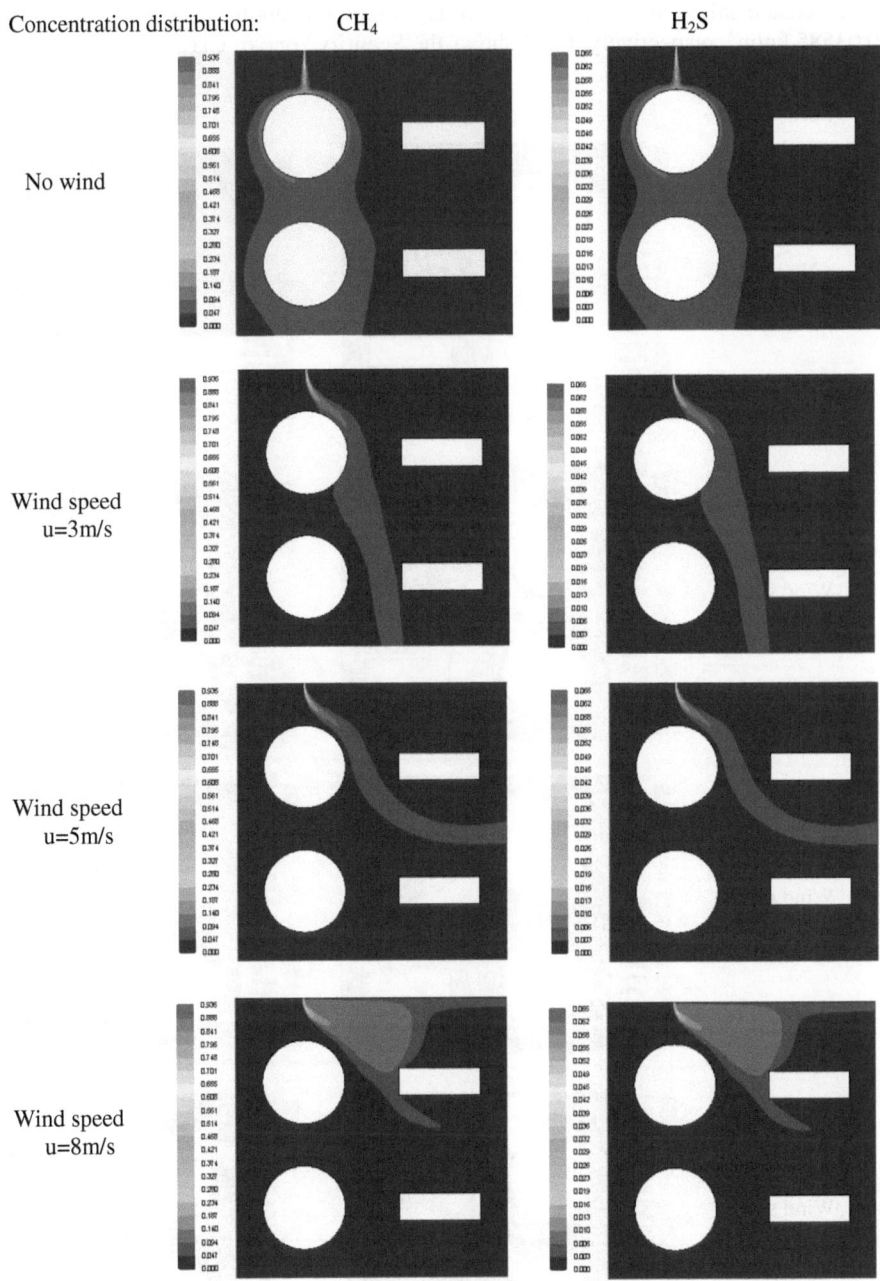

Fig. 2. Concentration distribution of CH$_4$ and H$_2$S in computational domain with different wind speed

To ensure safety, the concentration of H_2S and CH_4 should be below 20mg/m^3 and 0.03585 kg/m^3, respectively. Fig.3 shows the Security zone of CH_4 and H_2S.

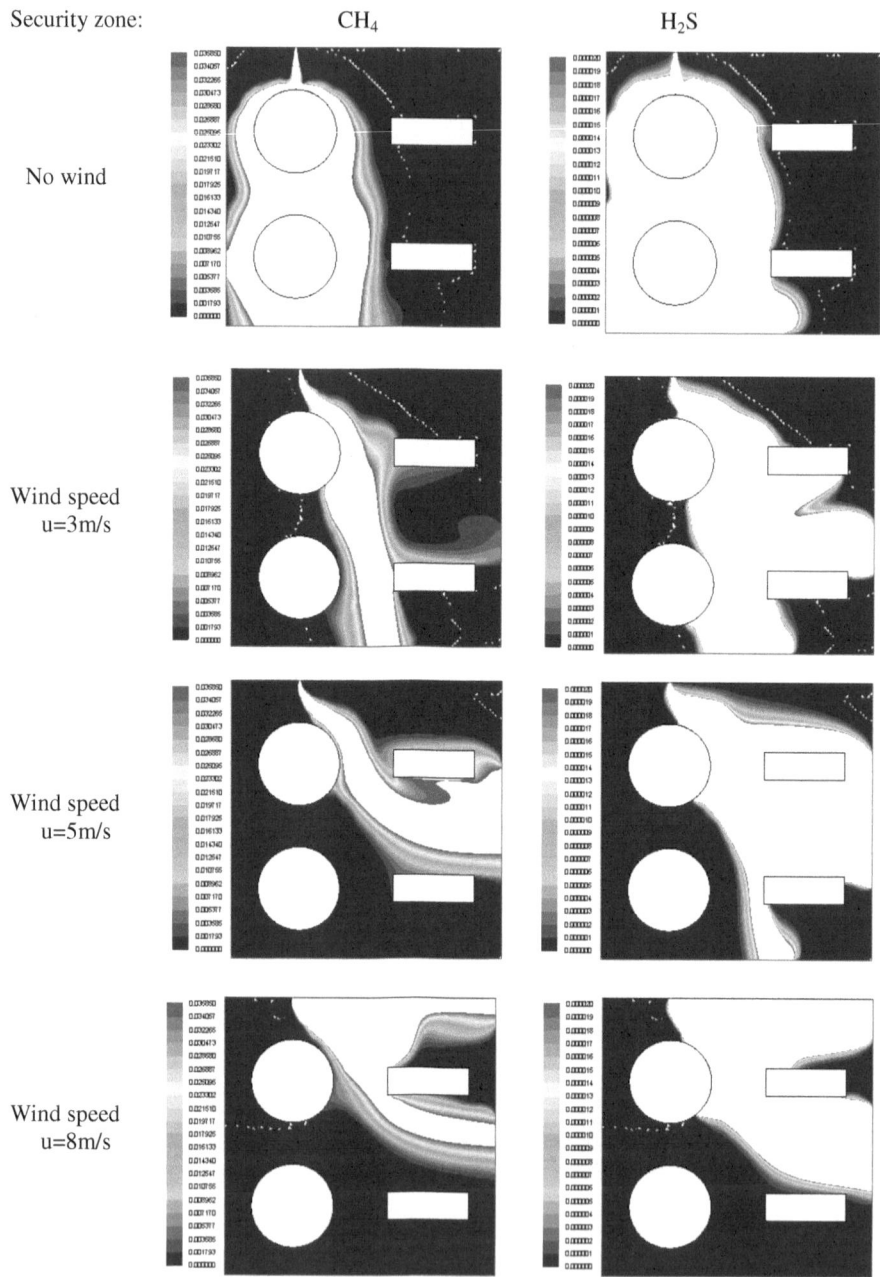

Fig. 3. Security zone of CH_4 and H_2S in computational domain with different wind speed

Large range of hazardous area was formed in the computational domain when there is no wind, due to leaking gas diffused freely in the space. The wind is helpful to natural gas diffusion. However, the consequence is different for different wind speed. The damage is decreasing with the increase of wind speed, leading to the raise of the security zone.

4 Conclusions

In this work, a numerical study is presented to understand the gas leaking diffusion from storage tank. Visual numerical simulation results are obtained as follows:

♦ Wind plays an important role on the diffusion of leaking gas. Gas diffused freely along the axis of leaking point without wind. However, the trace of leaking gas would deviate from the vertical direction due to the influence of wind. Natural gas has a trend of diffusing leeward. The larger is the wind speed, the more significant is the trend.

♦ Leaking gas diffused freely in the space without wind, giving rise to large range of hazardous area. While security zone in the computational domain is increasing with the increase of wind speed.

Acknowledgments. Research work was co-financed by the China National Natural Science foundation and Shanghai Baosteel Group Corporation (No.: 51074136), and supported by the Grand National Science & Technology Specific Project (No.: 2008ZX05026-04-004). Without their support, this work would not have been possible.

References

1. Nourollahi, E.: Simulation of Gas Pipelines Leakage Using Characteristics Method. In: Simulation of Electrochemical Processes III, pp. 1–12. WIT Press, Southampton (2006)
2. Tian, G.: Study on simulating leak of gas from pipe. Journal of Shandong Jianzhu University 14, 56–60 (1999)
3. Jin, Y., Zhou, W., Ruan, Y.: CFD Numerical Simulation of Gas Diffusion. Journal of Safety and Environment 2, 21–23 (2002)
4. Sun, P.: Numerical Simulations for Coupled Rock Deformation and Gas Leak Flow in Parallel Coal Seams. Geotechnical and Geological Engineering 22, 1–17 (2004)
5. Hu, X.: Numerical Simulation of the Multicomponent Nature Gas Diffusion on the High Pressure Leaking Pipeline. China university of petroleum, Dongying (2007)
6. Qin, Z.: Natural gas pipeline leakage diffusion explosion numerical simulation. Southwest petroleum university, Chengdu (2007)

An Orthogonal Wavelet Transform Blind Equalization Algorithm Based on the Optimization of Immune Clone Particle Swarm

Guo Yecai and Hu Lingling

School of Electrical and Information Engineering,
Anhui University of Science and Technology, Huainan 232001, China
guo-yecai@163.com

Abstract. On the basis of the analyzing the futures of particle swarm aglorithm, orthogonal wavelet transform constant modulus blind equalization algorithm (WTCMA), and immune clone algorithm, an orthogonal wavelet transform constant modulus blind equalization algorithm based on the immune clone particle swarm optimization is proposed. In this proposed algorithm, the diversity of population in particle swarm algorithm is effectively regulated via the immune clone operation after introducing the immune clone algorithm into particle swarm optimization. Therefore, the local extreme points and the premature convergence caused by the diversity variation of population in the evolution late of the particle swarm algorithm are avoided and the global search capability of particle swarm optimization algorithm is improved. So, the proposed algorithm has fastest convergence rate and smallest mean square error. The performance of the proposed algorithm is proved by computer simulation in underwater acoustic channels.

Keywords: particle swarm optimization algorithm; immune clone algorithm; wavelet transformation; diversity of populations; blind equalization.

1 Introduction

Inter-symbol interference (ISI) must be eliminated by blind equalization techniques without training sequence to improve the efficiency of communication system and save the bandwidth-limited underwater acoustic channel. As shown in [1], wavelet transform(WT) may be used to transform the input signals of blind equalization system to reduce the autocorrelation of the input signal and improve the convergence rate but its best weight vector is searched via the stochastic gradient descent algorithm and they easily fall into local convergence in the searching process. Particle Swarm Optimization(PSO) algorithm is a random global search optimization algorithm[2, 3], the population of particle swarm is on behalf of a group of the potential solutions of the problem and the speed and position of the population are constantly optimized via the current population. The basic idea of the PSO algorithm is to find the global optimum via making full use of the mutual cooperation of individuals in population and information sharing. It is suitable for solving the

R. Chen (Ed.): ICICIS 2011, Part I, CCIS 134, pp. 422–427, 2011.

complex problem with nonlinear multi-objectives, but easily appears premature convergence duo to reductions of species diversities of population with the evolution process[4] and it is greatly dependence on the initial population. Immune clone algorithm [5 ~7] is a heuristic algorithm with global and local search ability in the immune biology system, can adovid getting into local extreme in the search process and maintain the species diversity. In particle swarm optimization based on immune clone algorithm, when the species diversity becomes poor, the species diversity still can be improved via updating the particle groups using the immune clone algorithm.

In this paper, the immune clone algorithm and particle swarm algorithm are applied to wavelet constant modulus blind equalization algorithm, an orthogonal wavelet transform constant modulus blind equalization algorithm based on the optimization of immune clone particle swarm(IC-PSWTCMA) is proposed and outperforms orthogonal wavelet transform constant modulus blind equalization algorithm based on the particle swarm optimization(PSO-WTCMA) and orthogonal wavelet transform constant modulus blind equalization algorithm(WT-CMA) in improving convergence rate and reducing mean square error.

2   Orthogonal Wavelet Transform Blind Equalization Algorithm

In orthogonal wavelet transform constant modulus blind equalization algorithm (WTCMA), $a(n)$ is the transmitted signal sequence, $y(n)$ is the equalizer input sequence, $R(n)$ is orthogonal wavelet transform of $y(n)$, $w(n)$ is the weight vector; $\psi(\cdot)$ is a memoryless nonlinear function and used to generate error function; $e(n)$ is the error of the equalizer; $z(n)$ is the output sequence of the equalizer.

Let $L = M_w = 2^J$, L denotes the length of equalizer, V is the orthogonal wavelet transform matrix, $R(n)$, which is   orthogonal wavelet transform maxtrix of $y(n)$, is given by

$$R(n) = y(n)V .$$
(1)

$$z(n) = W^T(n)R(n) .$$
(2)

The equalizer error function is written as

$$e(n) = R^2_{CM} - |z(n)|^2 .$$
(3)

where, $R^2_{CM} = E\{|a(n)|^4\}/E\{|a(n)|^2\}$, According to least mean square criterion, the weight vector $W(n)$ of the equalizer is written as

$$W(n+1) = W(n) - \mu \hat{R}^{-1}(n)e(n)R^*(n) .$$
(4)

where, μ is defined as the iterative step-size, $\hat{R}^{-1}(n) = \mathrm{diag}[\sigma^2_{1,0}(n), \sigma^2_{1,1}(n), \cdots, \sigma^2_{J,k_J-1}(n),$ $\sigma^2_{J+1,0}(n), \cdots, \sigma^2_{J+1,k_J-1}(n)]$, $\sigma^2_{j,k}(n)$ and $\sigma^2_{J+1,k}(n)$ are the average power estimation of the wavelet transform coefficient and the scale transform coefficient, respectively. We call Eq.(1)~Eq.(4) as the orthogonal wavelet transform constant modulus blind equalization algorithm (WT-CMA).

3 Orthogonal Wavelet Transform Blind Equalization Algorithm Based on Immune Clone Particle Swarm Optimization

The PSO algorithm based on immune clone algorithm can make up for the defect of falling into local extreme in particle swarm algorithm.

A. Algorithm theory

The specific ideas of the IC-PSO are as follows: In D dimension search space, let M denote the number of particles. The particle position vector is regarded as the weight vector of blind equalizer. Firstly, the particles are randomly initialized, i.e., the speed and location of the antibody are initialized. The number of the randomly initialization particles are equal to the number of weight vectors. Assume that the number of the initial population is N and given by $N = [N_1, N_2, \cdots, N_M]$. N_i denotes the i th individual and corresponds to a weight vector of the equalizer. The optimal solution of weight vector will be used as antigen and particle as antibody, the affinity expresses the proximity degree between antibody and antigen, and the PS's fitness function is used as the antibody affinity(i.e., the objective function will be optimized). After one iteration of algorithm, the antibody (particle) with higher affinity (fitness) will be selected to carry out immune clone operation in order to produce a new generation of antibody groups(particle swarm). In fact, the immune clone operation includes selection, cloning, high-frequency variation and then selection. Then, the optimal solution obtained by the immune clone is further optimized by particle swarm algorithm. The optimal solution in each iteration will continues to immunization cloning, after the iteration ends, the optimal position vector is selected and regarded as the initialization vector of the equalizer weight vector.

B. Determination of Fitness Function

It is necessary to construct an appropriate cost function to apply the optimization algorithm to blind equalization algorithms. The weight vector of equalizer is updated via minimizing the cost function. However, in PSO algorithm, the best fitness is obtained by iteration process, whereas in the immune clone algorithm, the evolution process is carried out by selecting the highest affinity antibody, so the fitness function of the PSO is defined as the affinity function of antibody to carry out optimization. Therefore, the fitness function of the IC-PSO algorithm is defined as

$$f(W_i) = 1 / J(W_i) .\tag{5}$$

where, $J(W_i)$ is the cost function of equalizer, W_i is the position vector of the i th particle and corresponds to the weight vector individual of the equalizer.

C. Algorithm Design

On the basis of making full use of the advantages of IC-PSO algorithm, orthogonal wavelet transform blind equalization algorithm based on IC-PSO algorithm can optimize the wavelet equalizer weight vector, greatly improve the convergence accuracy and reduce the steady state error. Theoretical analyses show that IC-PSO algorithm has the following characteristics:

(1) The IC-PSO algorithm maintains the fast convergence rate of particle swarm optimization algorithm and the information-sharing.

(2) In immune clone operation, cloning operation expands the search space, the immune gene operation including the crossover and mutation operation improves the diversity of population via the high-frequency variation. The best individual genes can be inherited via selection operation to improve the optimization ability of the algorithm and to avoid algorithm degradation.

The steps of the IC-PSO algorithm are as follows:

Step 1: In D dimensional space, M particles are randomly generated and regarded as antibodies. The position vector and velocity vector of the particle are randomly initialized and the various initial parameters of the system are given.

Step 2: Calculate the fitness value or the affinity of the current each particle or antibody. The fitness function of the particle is used as the antibody affinity.

Step 3: Cloning operation carries out the cloning of each individual of the population separately according to the size of individual affinity(fitness) and the cloning copy proportion. Let Y denote the number of particles with larger fitness value and X be the sizes of the cloned population in Y.

Step 4: For population X, after the immunization genetic operation including the crossover and high frequency mutation are done, a new population X' of particles is generated, and the fitness of population X' is recalculated.

Step 5: According to the fitness value, a new population Y' of particles is selected from the population X' and assume that $Y'=Y$. If the number of the selected particles with maximum fitness via updating the particle population from the current population is less than the number of the selected particles with maximum fitness via the immune cloning algorithm, the immune clone particles are used to replace the particles of the initial population. Accordingly, the good genes are inherited to maintain the population diversity and the extreme individuals. The individual extreme *pbest* in the current population and the global extreme *gbest* are calculated.

Step 6: According to the iterations of the population groups, the particle velocity and position are further updated and the fitness of particles recalculated to carry out the immune clone operation. The individual extreme *pbest* and global extreme *gbest* are compared and updated. The particle velocity and position are updated by as follows[4]:

$$v_{id}(k+1) = wv_{id}(k) + c_1 * r_1 * (p_{id}(k) - x_{id}(k)) + c_2 * r_2 * (p_{gd}(k) - x_{id}(k)) . \qquad (6)$$

$$x_{id}(k) = x_{id}(k) + v_{id}(k+1) \qquad (7)$$

$$x_{id}(k) = x_{id}(k) + v_{id}(k+1) \qquad (8)$$

where, $i = 1, \cdots, M$, $d = 1, \cdots, D$, c_1 and c_2 are the learning factor, r_1 and r_2 are random number within [0,1]. N is the maximum iterations of the particle swarm optimization algorithm. w is the inertia weight, w_{max} and w_{min} are the largest and smallest of the inertia weight. x_i represents the location of the i th particle and $x_i = (x_{i1}, x_{i2}, \cdots, x_{iD})$, v_i represents the velocity of the i th particle and $v_i = (v_{i1}, v_{i2}, \cdots, v_{iD})$. The individual

extreme   value $p_i = (p_{i1}, p_{i2}, \cdots, p_{iD})$ and   the   global   extreme   value
$p_g = (p_{g1}, p_{g2}, \cdots, p_{gD})$.

Step 7: Termination operations. If the number of iterations has reached to the maximum, the global optimal location vector p_{gbest} is selected and $p_{gbest} =$ $(p_{g1}, p_{g2}, \cdots, p_{gD})$. In this case, the weight vector of the equalizer is completely initialized; otherwise, return to Step 2.

D. The choice of the optimal weight vector

In selecting the best individual, we take into account of the algorithm's real-time, randomness, and the zero-forcing condition of the blind equalization algorithm, the optimal location vector of the finally output particle is regarded as the initial weight vector of blind equalizer.

4 Simulation Results

To present the effectiveness of the proposed algorithm, the simulation tests with underwater acoustic channel were carried out and compared with the WTCMA and the PSO-WTCMA. 16QAM signals were transmitted to the underwater acoustic channel, whose impulse response is given by $h = [0.9656\ -0.0906\ \ 0.0578\ 0.2368]$ [13], the weight length of equalizer was set to 16, the SNR was set to 20dB, the population size was 100, the clone copy factor was 0.8, the optimal crossover probability was 0.2, the mutation probability was 0.1, the maximum evolution generation was 500, the 8th tap of the weight vector for the WTCMA was initialized to one; other parameters were shown in Table 1. Simulation results were shown in Fig.1.

Table 1. Simulation parameters

Algorithms	Simulation Step-size	Wavelet	Decomposition level	Power initialization	β value
WTCMA	0.0006	DB4	2	6	0.999
PSO-WTCMA	0.000015	DB4	2	6	0.999
IC-PS-WTCMA	0.000028	DB4	2	10	0.99

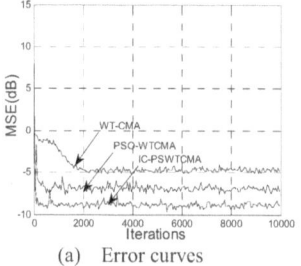

(a)   Error curves

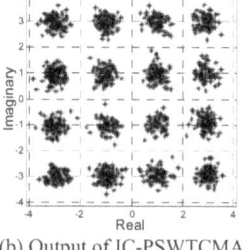

(b) Output of IC-PSWTCMA

Fig. 1. Simulation Results

From the Fig.1(a), we can know that the convergence rate of IC-PSCMA has an improvement of about 200 steps and 1400 steps comparison with that of the PSO-WTCMA and WTCMA, respectively. The IC-PSWTCMA has a drop of about 1.5dB and 3.5dB for MSE(mean square error) comparison with the PSO-WTCMA and WTCMA.

5 Conclusions

On the basis of analyzing wavelet transform and the IC-PSO algorithm, an orthogonal wavelet transform constant modulus blind equalization algorithm based on the optimization of Immune Clone Particle Swarm(IC-PS-WTCMA) is proposed. This proposed algorithm not only maintains the simplicity and the easy realization of the particle swarm optimization process, but also improves the performance of the global optimization of PSO algorithm. Theoretical analyses and simulation results with underwater acoustic channels show that the proposed algorithm has faster convergence speed and smaller residual mean square error comparison with WTCMA and PSO-WTCMA. Thus, the proposed algorithm has practical value in engineering.

Acknowledgment

This paper is supported by Specialized Fund for the Author of National Excellent Doctoral Dissertation of China (200753), Natural Science Foundation of Higher Education Institution of Jiangsu Province (08KJB510010) and "the peak of six major talent" cultivate projects of Jiangsu Province (2008026), Natural Science Foundation of Higher Education Institution of Anhui Province (KJ2010A096), Natural Science Foundation of Jiangsu Province(BK2009410).

References

1. Han, Y., Guo, Y., Li, B., Zhou, Q.: Momentum Term and Orthogonal Wavelet-based Blind Equalization Algorithm. Journal of System Simulation 20(6), 1559–1562 (2008)
2. Huang, S.: Survey of Particle Swarm Optimization Algorithm. Computer Engineering and Design 30(8), 1977–1980 (2009)
3. Kennedy, J., Eberhart, R.C.: Particle Swarm Optimization. In: Proceedings of the 1995 IEEE International Conference on Neural Networks, pp. 1942–1948. IEEE, New York (1995)
4. Huang, H., Chen, Z.: Novel Arithmetic Based on Particle Swarm Optimization. Journal of System Simulation 19(21), 4922–4925 (2007)
5. Gao, Y., Xie, S.: Particle Swarm Optimization Algorithms with Immunity. Computer Engineering and Applications 40(6), 4–6 (2004)
6. Hu, C., Zeng, J.: Immune Particle Swarm Optimization Based on Sharing Mechanism. Journal of System Simulation 16(20), 4278–4285 (2008)
7. Ma, W., Jiao, L., Shang, R.: Immune Clone SAR Image Segmentation Algorithm. Journal of Electronics & Information Technology 31(7), 1749–1752 (2009)

A Support Vector Machine Blind Equalization Algorithm Based on Immune Clone Algorithm

Guo Yecai and Ding Rui

School of Electrical and Information Engineering,
Anhui University of Science and Technology, Huainan 232001, China
guo-yecai@163.com

Abstract. Aiming at affecting of the parameter selection method of support vector machine(SVM) on its application in blind equalization algorithm, a SVM constant modulus blind equalization algorithm based on immune clone selection algorithm(CSA-SVM-CMA) is proposed. In this proposed algorithm, the immune clone algorithm is used to optimize the parameters of the SVM on the basis advantages of its preventing evolutionary precocious, avoiding local optimum, and fast convergence. The proposed algorithm can improve the parameter selection efficiency of SVM constant modulus blind equalization algorithm(SVM-CMA) and overcome the defect of the artificial setting parameters. Accordingly, the CSA-SVM-CMA has faster convergence rate and smaller mean square error than the SVM-CMA. Computer simulations in underwater acoustic channels have proved the validity of the algorithm.

Keywords: immune clone algorithm, support vector machine, blind equalization algorithm, parameter selection.

1 Introduction

In underwater acoustic communication, constant modulus blind equalizer can greatly eliminate inter-symbol interference(ISI) at the receiver and improve the bandwidth utilization and may be described as a classifier, but its convergence rate is slow and its steady-state mean square error(MSE) is large[1]. SVM based on the principle of structural risk minimization may be regarded as a classifier and a machine learning method in a small sample of circumstances[2]. SVM constant modulus equalization algorithm(SVM-CMA) can overcome the lose efficacy of the traditional CMA in a small sample of learning situations and its local convergence and has fast convergence rate and small mean square error, but in the construction process of the support vector machine, the parameter settings has a greater influence on the final classification accuracy[3~5]. The appropriate parameters can improve the precision and the generalization ability of SVM, whereas parameter selection methods, such as the repeated experiments, the artificial selection, etc., are based on the subjective experience of the researchers and it is necessary to spend more time to select these parameters.

In this paper, on the basis of making full use of the global search capability of the immune clone selection algorithm, support vector machine constant modulus blind

R. Chen (Ed.): ICICIS 2011, Part I, CCIS 134, pp. 428–433, 2011.
© Springer-Verlag Berlin Heidelberg 2011

equalization algorithm based on immune clone algorithm is proposed. The parameters in the proposed algorithm are automatically determined instead of the artificial selection method, so the proposed algorithm has faster convergence speed and smaller mean square error, and its learning time can be greatly reduced at the same time.

2 SVM Blind Equalization Algorithm

In basic structure of SVM constant modulus blind equalization algorithm, $a(n)$ is the transmitted signal, $h(n)$ is the impulse response vector of the channel, $v(n)$ denotes white Gaussian noise vector, $y(n)$ is called as the input signal of equalizer, $w(n)$ is weight vector of equalizer, $z(n)$ is the output signal of equalizer. According to ISI space geometrical theory, the blind equalization problem may be regarded as the function regression problems constructed by SVM and the parameters of the function is used to determine the equalizer weight vector. The partial structure of SVM blind equalization structure is shown in Fig.1.In Fig.1, the input signal vector of the equalizer is $x_i(n)$, $i = 1, 2, \cdots, N$, and $x_k(n) =$

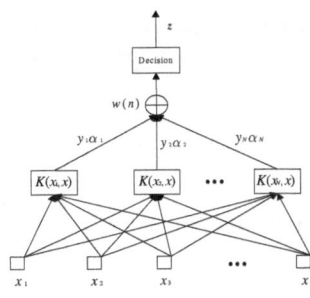

Fig. 1. SVM blind equalizer

$\{x(n), \cdots, x(n-M+1)\}$. M is the length of equalizer. The output of channel is given by

$$x(n) = \sum_{k=1}^{M-1} a(k)h(n-k) + v(n) \cdot \qquad (1)$$

The output of SVM blind equalizer is given by

$$Z(k) = \sum_{k=0}^{M-1} w(n)x(n-k) = w^T(n)x(n) \cdot \qquad (2)$$

where T is transpose operation of matrix. According to the principle of structural risk minimization and the constant modulus feature of the transmitted signals, the weight vector of the equalizer can be estimated in precision ε. The minimum cost function is defined as

$$J(w(n)) = \frac{1}{2}\|w(n)\|^2 + C\sum_{k=1}^{N}(\xi(k) + \tilde{\xi}(k)) \cdot \qquad (3)$$

Where C is a Penalty coefficient, $\xi(i)$ and $\tilde{\xi}(i)$ denote the positive slack variables.

In order to minimizing equation (3), the constraint conditions are given as follows

$$\begin{cases} R_2 - (w^T(n)x_k)^2 \le \varepsilon + \xi(k) \\ (w^T(n)x_k)^2 - R_2 \le \varepsilon + \tilde{\xi}(k) \cdot \\ \quad \xi(k), \tilde{\xi}(k) \ge 0 \end{cases} \qquad (4)$$

where. $R_2 = E[|a(n)|^4]/E[|a(n)|^2]$ In this constraint conditions, the weight vector $w(n)$ of the equalizer is quadratic, accordingly, it is impossible to find the optimization weight vector in equation (3) via SVM's linear programming method. According to the Iterative Reweighted Quadratic Programming algorithm for the right (IRWQP) [6], the quadratic constraint conditions in equation (4) may be rewritten into the linear constraint conditions,i.e.,

$$\begin{cases} (w^T(n)x_k)Z(k) - R_2 \leq \varepsilon + \tilde{\xi}(k) \\ R_2 - (w^T(n)x_k)Z(k) \leq \varepsilon + \xi(k) \end{cases} . \tag{5}$$

In order that the original minimization problem can be turn into convex quadratic programming problem or dual problem, i.e., the maximization problem of the following function.

$$J'(w) = -\frac{1}{2}\sum_{k,j=1}^{N}(\tilde{\alpha}(j) - \alpha(j))(\tilde{\alpha}(k) - \alpha(k))(Z(j)Z(k))K < x_{j}.x_k >$$

$$-\varepsilon\sum_{j=1}^{N}(\tilde{\alpha}(j) + \alpha(j)) + \sum_{j=1}^{N}(\tilde{\alpha}(j) - \alpha(j)) . \tag{6}$$

Subject to

$$\begin{cases} \sum_{j=1}^{N}(\tilde{\alpha}(j) - \alpha(j)) = 0 \\ 0 \leq \tilde{\alpha}(j) \leq C, j = 1, \cdots, N \end{cases} . \tag{7}$$

Where, $K < x_{j}.x_k >$ denotes the Inner product function of support vector machine.

After comparing the original problem with the dual problem, the weight vector of the equalizer can be expressed as

$$w(n) = \sum_{k=1}^{N}(\tilde{\alpha}(k) - \alpha(k))Z(k)x_k . \tag{8}$$

In equation (8), Lagrange multipliers $\tilde{\alpha}(k)$ and $\alpha(k)$ can be solved through equatipn (6) and equation (7).

The recursively formula of weight vector $w(n)$ is written as

$$w(n) = \lambda w(n-1) + (1-\lambda)w(n) . \tag{9}$$

where n is the number of iterations, λ is step-size.

3   Immune Clone Algorithm Blind Equalization Algorithm Based on SVM

In support vector machine blind equalization algorithm, some parameters such as the kernel function, the C Penalty coefficient, ε-insensitive loss function, etc. , have to be determined. Suddenly, the different parameter settings can seriously affect the learning performance of SVM. In this paper, we will introduce the immune clone selection algorithm into support vector machines blind equalization algorithm to determine parameters C and ε .When the immune clone selection algorithm is applied to the parameter optimization of the SVM-CMA, the specific steps of the implementation are as follows:

Step 1: Initialization of population
The initial population is generated by stochastic method and each antibody corresponds to a set of parameters C and ε .

Step 2: Determination of affinity
The affinity between the antibody and antigen is computed.

Step 3: Clone selection
The antibodies of the initial population are ranked from small to large order according to the size of affinity. After the clone expansion operation to the best antibody is carried out according to the following equation to get the expansion antibody group.

$$N = \sum_{i=1}^{n} \left\lfloor \frac{\beta n}{i} \right\rfloor .$$

(10)

Where, N denotes the size of clones, β is a clone controlling factor, and $\lfloor \ \rfloor$ represents round numbers. The number of clone antibodies is proportional with the affinity.

Step 4: Elite crossover strategies [7,8]
Elite Crossover Principle are as follows: In the implementation of the immune algorithm, for the given elite crossover probability P_{kc} , each individual $a(t)$ in the antibodies produces a random number R within [0,1]. If the random number R is less than the elite crossover probability P_{kc} , $a(t)$ is selected and intersected with the current elite individual $b(t)$. In crossover process, $a(t)$ and $b(t)$ are put into a small mating pool and intersected according to the selected strategies, such as single point crossover, two points crossover, multi-point crossover and consistent crossover, etc., to get a pair of progeny individuals $a'(t)$ and $b'(t)$. Then, $a(t)$ in the population is replaced with $a'(t)$, whereas $b'(t)$ is abandoned. By elite crossover operation, antibodies inherit the fine mode of the elite individuals, and will not disrupt the fine mode. This operation outperforms the traditional crossover operation in the advantages[7,8].

Step 5: High frequency mutation
Each cloning antibody of the antibody population carries out high frequency mutation to produce the mutation population A^* . High frequency mutation, as the clone selection operator of a major operation, can prevent the evolutionary precocious and increase the diversity of antibodies.

Step 6: Computation of affinity values
Recalculating the antibody affinity after mutating at high frequency.

Step 7: Selection

The n high affinity antibodies is selected from the mutation population A^* to replace n low affinity antibodies in the initial antibody population, n is inversely proportional to the average affinity value of the antibodies.

Step 8: Termination operations

According to the number of the evolution generation, whether the evolutionary process ends. When the number of the evolution generation doesn't exceed the maximum evolution generation, the operation returns to the step 2 to sequentially execute the step 2 to step 7. When the number of the evolution generation exceeds the maximum evolution generation, the operation ends and the optimal solution of the global parameters is obtained.

Based on the above process, the parameters of SVM can be optimized to improve the performance of SVM blind equalization algorithm.

4   Simulation Results

To present the effectiveness of the proposed algorithm, the simulation tests were carried out and its performance is compared with CMA and SVM algorithm. In tests, The size of antibody was set to 100, the clonal controlling factor was set to 0.6, the elite crossover probability was equal to 0.2, the mutation probability was 0.1, the maximum number of iterations was set to 200. The ranges of the parameters C and ε are within $[1,30]$ and $[0.00001, 0.1]$, respectively. The weight length of equalizer was set to 32; the SNR was set to 20dB. The impulse response of channel was given by $h=[0.9656\ -0.0906\ \ 0.0578\ 0.2368]$, 16QAM signals were transmitted. For the CMA, the sixth tap coefficient of the equalizer was set to one, the step-size μ_{CMA} was set to 0.00003. For the SVM blind equalization algorithm, the step size λ_{SVM} was set to 0.9, and $N_{SVM} = 1000$, $C_{SVM} = 28$, $\varepsilon_{SVM} = 0.4$. For the CSA-SVM, the step-size λ_{WT-SVM} was set to 0.9, $C_{CSA-SVM} = 2.7813$, $\varepsilon_{CSA-SVM} = 0.0737$, and $N_{CSA-SVM} = 1000$. The simulation results were shown in Fig.2.

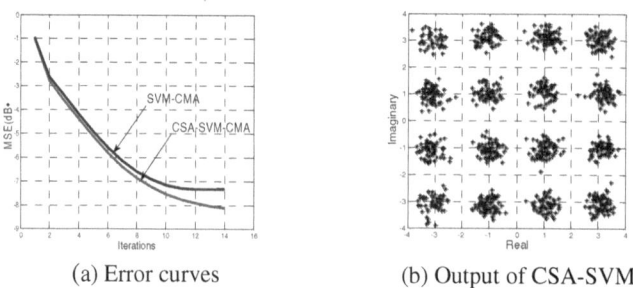

(a) Error curves   (b) Output of CSA-SVM

Fig. 2. Simulation Results

From the Fig.2 it is seen that the mean square error(MSE) of CSA-SVM-CMA has drop of about 1dB comparison with the SVM-CMA and that the output constellations of the CSA-SVM-CMA are the clearest in all algorithms.

5 Conclusions

A support vector machine constant modulus blind equalization algorithm based on immune clone algorithm is proposed. In this proposed algorithm, the optimal parameters of the support vector machine can be determined via making full use of the global search ability of the immune clone algorithm and its avoiding local optimum. Accordingly, the proposed algorithm has fast convergence rate and small mean square error. Simulation results in underwater acoustic channels have proved the advantages of the proposed algorithm.

Acknowledgment

This paper is supported by Specialized Fund for the Author of National Excellent Doctoral Dissertation of China (200753), Natural Science Foundation of Higher Education Institution of Jiangsu Province (08KJB510010) and "the peak of six major talent" cultivate projects of Jiangsu Province(2008026), Natural Science Foundation of Higher Education Institution of Anhui Province (KJ2010A096), Natural Science Foundation of Jiangsu Province(BK2009410).

References

1. Guo, Y.: Blind Equalization Technology. Press of Hefei University of Technology (2007)
2. Santamria, I., Ibanez, J., Vielva, L., et al.: Bind Equalization of Constant Modulus Signals Via Support Vector Regression. In: Proceedings of IEEE International Conference on Acoustics, Speech, and Signal Processing, vol. 4, pp. 737–740. IEEE publication, Hong Kong (2003)
3. Song, H., Wang, C.: Decision feedback equalizer based on non-singleton fuzzy support vector machine. 30(1), 117–120 (2008)
4. Liu, F., An, H., Li, J., Ge, L.: Build Equalization Using Support Vector Regressor for Constant Modulus Signals. In: 2008 International Joint Conference on Neural Networks (IJCNN 2008), pp. 161–164. IEEE, Los Alamitos (2008)
5. Li, J., Zhao, J., Lu, J.: Underwater Acoustic Channel Blind Equalization Algorithm Based on Support Vector Machines. Elementary Electroacoustics, 4–6 (2006)
6. Kisialiou, M., Luo, Z.: Performance Analysis of Quasi-Maximum Likelihood Detector Based on Semi-Definite Programming
7. Cooklev, T.: An Efficient Architecture for Orthogonal Wavelet Transforms. IEEE Signal Processing Letters 13(2), 77–79 (2006)
8. Yao, Q., Tian, Y.: Model Selection Algorithm of SVM Based on Artificial Immune. Computer Engineering 15(34), 223–225 (2008)

A Service Access Security Control Model in Cyberspace

Li Qianmu[1,*], Yin Jie[2], Hou Jun[1], Xu Jian[1], Zhang Hong[1], and Qi Yong[1]

[1] School of Computer Science & Technology, Nanjing University of Science & Technology, 210094 Nanjing, China
[2] School of Computer Science & Technology, Jiangsu Police Institute, 210094 Nanjing, China
{liqianmu,yinjie,houxiaozhu,dolphine.xu,njust,njqiyong}@126.com

Abstract. A service access control model in cyberspace is proposed, which provides a generalized and effective mechanism of security management with some items constraint specifications. These constraint specifications are organized to form a construction, and an enact process is proposed to make it scalable and flexible to meet the need of diversified service application systems in cyberspace. The model of this paper erases the downward information flow by extended rules of read/write, which is the breakthrough of the limitations when applying the standard role-based access control in cyberspace.

Keywords: Cyberspace; Service Access; Security Control Model.

1 Introduction

Large-scale information management and a large number of service requests exist in cyberspace. There is an urgent need to use an easy-to-manage, service-oriented access control mechanism to reduce management complexity.

This paper designs a Service-Orient Access Control Model (SOACM) of cyberspace, including the user, the service space and operation these three orthogonal concepts. User, service and operation are limited sets. User is the caller of service computing, subject of access control, service space is all original and dynamic increasing services, operation is the basic unit of user behavior. The coordinate system of the user, the service space and operation these three concepts show in fig.1, Denote mapping as $F : U \times WS \times OP \rightarrow \{0\,1\}$ which nodes in space (U, WS, OP) maps $\{0,1\}$ sets. If node (u_i, ws_i, op_i) maps 1, indicate that user u_i has authorization to execute operation op_i on service space node ws_i. If node (u_i, ws_i, op_i) map 0, indicate that user u_i do not have authorization to execute operation op_i on service space node ws_i. So service-oriented application access control can be expressed as space node sets which mapping "1" in the space (U, WS, OP), namely subset D generate from space (U, WS, OP):

$$D = \{(u_i, ws_i, op_i) \mid u_i \in U, ws_i \in WS, op_i \in OP, and F(u_i, ws_i, op_i) = 1\}$$

---

[*] Corresponding author.

R. Chen (Ed.): ICICIS 2011, Part I, CCIS 134, pp. 434–439, 2011.
© Springer-Verlag Berlin Heidelberg 2011

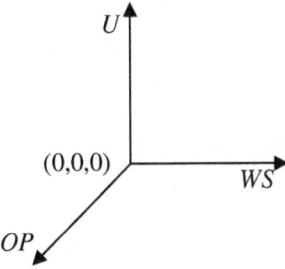

Fig. 1. Space (U,WS,OP) , which U axis, WS axis, OP axis are respectively express elements of the user, the service space and the operation sets, this coordinate origin is not in the three sets, denoted as $(0,0,0)$. (u_i, ws_i, op_i) in space (U,WS,OP) represent user u_i execute operation op_i on ws_i in service space.

2 Access Control Model SOACM

Definitions (predefined sets standards) USERS, ROLES, OPS, OBS and SESSIONS are respectively user set, role set, operation set, object set and session set of the system. Their meanings are defined by RBAC standard.

Definitions (classified grades set, CLASSES). classified grades index is the sensitivity of the data. if we use integer to indicate classified grades index, LOW indicates that the minimum classified grades, the highest classified grades is HIGH and LOW $\leq$ HIGH, then $\forall l \in CLASSES \Rightarrow l \in [LOW..HIGH]$. CLASSES is all classified grades sets.

Definitions (scope, CATEGORIES). the $I=\{CAT_1, CAT_2, ..., CAT_n\}$ is the system divides category sets, according to a characteristic. CAT_i ($1 \leq i \leq n$) is a category name. Scope $CATEGORIES=\{C_1, C_2, ..., C_k\}(k\geq1)$ is a subset of I .That is $CATEGORIES \subseteq I$.

Definitions (user roles distribution, UA). $U A \subseteq USERS \times ROLES$, It is the distribution relations of many-to-many mapping the user to the role. $Assigned\_users(r)=\{u \in USERS | (u,r) \in UA\}$ will map the role r (excluding succession role) to the user set, $assigned\_users(r:ROLES) \rightarrow 2^{USERS}$.

Definitions (user authority set, PRMS). $PRMS=2^{(OPS \times OBS)}$, is a user's authority set.

Definitions (the role of authority arrangement, PA). $PA \subseteq PRMS \times ROLES$ is arrangements relations of many-to-many mapping the authority to the role. $Assigned\_permissions(r)=\{p \in PRMS \mid (p,r) \in PA\}$ will map the role r (excluding succession role) to the authority set, $assigned\_permissions(r:ROLES) \rightarrow 2^{PRMS}$.

Definitions (authority mapping, Op and Ob). $Op(p:PRMS) \rightarrow \{op \subseteq OPS\}$ maps the operation set of authority p. $Ob(p:PRMS) \rightarrow \{ob \subseteq OBS\}$ maps the object set of p.

Definitions (role inheritance relationship, RH). $RH \subseteq ROLES \times ROLES$ is ROLES the partially ordered set structure, which is known as the inheritance relationship and is expressed as $\rightarrow$. $r_1 \rightarrow r_2 \Rightarrow authorized\_permissions(r_2) \subseteq authorized\_ permissions$ (r_1). $Authorized\_users(r)=\{u \in USERS | r' \rightarrow r, (u, r) \in UA\}$ maps the role r and all roles' users of inheriting the role r, *authorized_users(r:ROLES)*→2^{USERS}. *Authorized_permissions(r)*={$p \in PRMS$| r' →r, $(p, r')\in PA$} maps the role r and all roles' authorities of inheriting the role r, *authorized_permissions(r:ROLES)* →2^{PRMS}.

Definitions (session mapping). *Session_users(s: SESSIONS)*→*USERS* maps the session s to the corresponding user. *Session_roles(s)* ⊆ {$r \in ROLES$|($\exists r'$ →r) (*session_user(s)*, r') ∈ *UA* } maps the session to the corresponding role sets, *session_roles(s:SESSIONS)*→2^{ROLES}.

Session_roles (s) maps all roles than can be used in session s (including the role of inheritance).

Definitions (security level, *LABELS*). Security level *LABELS* ⊆ *CLASSES*×$2^{CATEGORIES}$ is classified grades and the range combination. *Class(l:LABELS)*→ {*class*⊆*CLASSES*} maps the classified grades of security level l. *Category(l:LABEL)*→ {*category*⊆ *CATEGORIES*} maps the range of security level.

Such as the security level *l* = {confidential, (Ministry of Personnel, Ministry of Finance)}, *Class (l)* = secret, *Category (l)* = (Ministry of Personnel, Ministry of Finance). It should be noted that the security level can be across multiple ranges.

Users can arrange multiplicate security level in SOACM model.

Definitions (role security level arrangements, RSA). Role security level arrangements *RSA* ⊆ *ROLES*×*LABELS* is the many to one mapping relation between roles and the security level. *Role_label (r:ROLES)*={$l \in LABELS$|(r, l)∈*RSA*} maps the security level of r, *role_label(r:ROLES)*→{l ∈ *LABELS*}. *Role_label_RH(r:ROLES)* ={$l \in LABELS$|$\exists r'$, r→r' ∧ (r', l)∈*RSA*} maps r and the security level of the role that r inherits, *role_label_RH(r:ROLES)*→2^{LABELS}.

Although the role and security level is the many to one mapping relation (a role only is arranged a security level), *role_label_RH* can be mapped multiple security levels by inheritance.

SOACM establish access control strategy according to a service hierarchical structure, thus the access control strategy is more direct-viewing.

Definition Class Privilege_Authorize(PA) is a connection class between role and service, an instance is a two tuples (r, s), represent the authorization relationship that role r to service s. denote as pa(r, s). each two tuple (r, s) in class is not redundant.

Definition Class Satus_Authorize(SA) is a connection class between actor and role, an instance is a two tuples (a,r), denote that actor a is authorized some role r. each two tuple (a,r) in class is not redundant.

The definition of responsibility separation class is a self association class in role class, an instance is a two tuples (role1, role2), represent conflicts of interest relations between the two roles. responsibility separation has two type : static responsibility separation(SSD) and dynamic responsibility separation(DSD). The former stipulate that an actor cannot simultaneously be authorized two kind of roles, the latter stipulate that an actor can authorize this two roles. But SSD and DSD are mutual, namely a SD relation can not be static and dynamic at the same time, obviously, SD relation non-reflexive, symmetry, not transitivity.

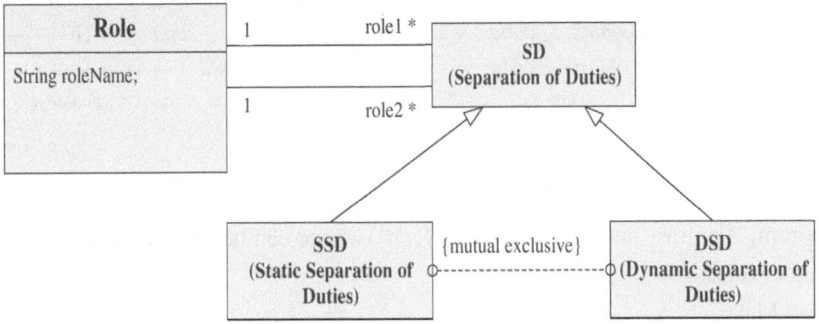

Fig. 2. separation relation of duties between two roles can be divided into static and dynamic. Inheritance role for the organization and management of large role in regulating the service authority (PA to the Service) and the authorized user specification (from SA to the Actor). For the two roles, the role of inheritance and separation of duties are mutually exclusive; and separation of duties can be derived from the role of super-role. To simplify the calculation of service as the role of authority and the management authority, in accordance with the succession of semantic roles may determine a set of rules so that the role can automatically inherit the role of the super-powers norms, but also allows users to automatically grant super role, and automatically activated. Each PA SA or an object that contains all the powers of constraint conditions. We first definition of similar size and power of the same concept. Similar is the meaning of power, the two power p1 and p2, if the PA category, for the same services; If the SA category for the same role.

C1. PA a target that exists in the context of a specific role have access to a service:

$$\forall r \in Role, s \in Service\ (\exists pa\,(r,s) \in PA \leftrightarrow (CC\,(pa\,(r,s).context\ \_\ cond\,) \rightarrow r \xrightarrow{cc} s))$$

C2. Role if a right to access a certain operation, the necessary conditions for the right to visit the operation of the interface:

$$\forall r \in Role,\ \forall s \in Operation\ ,\forall i \in Interface\ \ (\exists pa\,(r,s) \in PA \wedge s \triangleleft i$$
$$\rightarrow \exists pa\,'(r,i) \in PA,\ pa\,'(r,i).context\ \_\ cond\ = pa\,(r,s).context\ \_\ cond\,)$$

C3. Role if a right to access a certain interface, its role is the necessary condition for the right to visit the ultra-Interface Interface:

$$\forall r \in Role,\ \forall s, s' \in Interface\ \ (\exists pa\,(r,s) \in PA \wedge \exists g\,(s',s) \in Generaliza\quad tion$$
$$\rightarrow \exists pa\,'(r,s') \in PA,\ pa\,'(r,s').context\ \_\ cond\ = pa\,(r,s).context\ \_\ cond\,)$$

C4. Role if a right to access a certain operation, and the implied operation of another operation, then the role in the conversion of Context conditions also have the right to visit the implied operation:

$$\forall r \in Role, \forall s_1, s_2 \in Operation\ ((s_1 \xrightarrow{cf} s_2) \wedge \exists pa_1(r,s_1) \in PA$$
$$\rightarrow \exists pa_2(r,s_2) \in PA,\ pa_2(r,s_2).context\ \_\ cond = cf\,(pa_1(r,s_1).context\ \_\ cond\,))$$

Theorem: Role as a service and r s, if the C2, C3, C4 from a number of objects pa (r, s), then the final target only one PA, on condition that these pa Context (r, s) Context object and set conditions:

$$\forall r \in Role,\ \forall s \in Service\ (\exists pa_1(r,s),\ pa_2(r,s) \in PA \rightarrow \exists pa\,(r,s) \in PA,$$
$$pa\,(r,s).context\ \_\ cond\ = pa_1(r,s).context\ \_\ cond\ \vee pa_2(r,s).context\ \_\ cond\,)$$

Prove. $\exists pa_1(r,s),\ pa_2(r,s) \in PA$

$\Rightarrow (CC(pa_1(r,s).context\_cond) \rightarrow (r \xrightarrow{cc} s)) \wedge (CC(pa_2(r,s).context\_cond) \rightarrow (r \xrightarrow{cc} s))$

$\Rightarrow (CC(pa_1(r,s).context\_cond) \vee CC(pa_2(r,s).context\_cond)) \rightarrow (r \xrightarrow{cc} s)$

$\Rightarrow CC(pa_1(r,s).context\_cond \vee pa_2(r,s).context\_cond) \rightarrow (r \xrightarrow{cc} s)$

$\Rightarrow \exists pa(r,s) \in PA, pa(r,s).context\_cond = pa_1(r,s).context\_cond \vee pa_2(r,s).context\_cond$

3 The Model Analysis

Theorem: Arbitrary subset in the (U,WS,OP) space can be expressed by a union of a group of roles.

Prove: Make

$D = \{(u_i,ws_i,op_i) \mid u_i \in U, ws_i \in WS, op_i \in OP, andF(u_i,ws_i,op_i)=1\}$ arbitrary subset in the (U,WS,OP) space, B is a collection of D' values from U .Arbitrarily admitted $u_i \in B$, $i = 1,2,\dots$ n, make

$$D_i = \{(u_i,ws_j,op_j) \mid ws_j \in WS, op_j \in OP, andF(u_i,ws_j,op_j)=1\} =$$
$$\{(u_k,ws_k,op_k) \mid u_k \in U, ws_k \in WS, op_k \in OP, andH_i(ws_k,op_k)=1,G_i(u_k)=1\}$$

Of which:

$$H_i(ws,op) = F(u_i,ws,op), ws \in WS, op \in OP; G_i(u) = \begin{cases} 1, & ifu = u_i, \ u \in U \\ 0, & ifu \neq u_i \end{cases}$$

Obviously, $D = D_1 \cup D_2 \cup \cdots \cup D_n$, namely D can use a collection of a group of roles to indicate, therefore, a group of roles can express an arbitrary subset in the (U,WS,OP) space, that is to say using role-based access control model can implement arbitrary Access Control Strategy, which proves SOACM model is universal.

4 Conclusions

The SOACM model has the following characteristic: (1) generality. May realize many kinds of access control strategy which define by user based on different service demand, namely the model may realize authorization rule identified by access control strategy. (2) Autonomous control. Domain access control strategy of each management domain can be developed independently by the user, namely the establishment of access control strategy in a management domain do not interfere by other access control strategy and distribution structure of service computing. At the same time, when some entity joins or the withdrawal visit, At the same time, when some entity joins or the withdrawal visit, there is no impact on access control strategy of other organizations, and its own access control strategy never change due to join or withdraw from the service. (3) Mutual operation of access control between multiple management domain. Provide a single system image of the cross-organizational authorization mechanism, realize mutual operation of access control in each management domain, namely cross-domain management authority.

Acknowledgments. This work is supported by Jiangsu Six Categories Peak Funding, NUST Research Funding (No.2010XQTR04), Jiangsu Public Security Department Scientific Project and the National Natural Science Foundation of China under Grant No. 60903027 and No. 90718021.

References

1. Role Based Access Control, American National Standard for information Technology, BSR INCITS 359[S], Draft 4/4 (2003)
2. Park, J.S., Sandhu, R., Ahn, G.: Role-Based Access Control on the Web. ACM Transactions on Information and System Security 14(1), 37–71 (2010)
3. Nyanchama, M., Osborn, S.: Modeling Mandatory Access Control in Role-Based Security Systems. In: IFIP Workshop on Database Security. Proceedings of the Ninth Annual IFIP TC11 WG11.3 working conference on Database security IX: status and prospects: status and prospects, Rennselaerville, New York, United States, pp. 129–144 (2009)
4. Osborn, S., Sandhu, R., Nunawer, Q.: Configuring Role-Based Access Control To Enforce Mandatory And Discretionary Access Control Policies. ACM Transaction on Information and System Security 13(2), 85–106 (2010)
5. Osborn, S.: Mandatory access control and role-based access control revisited. In: Proc. of the Second ACM Workshop on Role-based Access Control. Fairfax, VA, pp. 31–40 (2007)

A Motor Speed Measurement System Based on Hall Sensor

Wen-cheng Wang

School of Information and Control Engineering, Weifang University,
Weifang 261061 China
wwchpaper@126.com

Abstract. The working principles of Hall sensor has been introduced in this paper. To the defects of traditional methods, it proposed the designing strategy of motor speed measurement system based on single chip microcontroller with integrated chip. The hardware circuits including power module, data processing module and data display module have been described and it focuses on the analysis speed measurement module. The speed data can be obtained through counting impulse signals and displayed on LED. Experience shows that the system have high stability, it can meet the needs of DC motor speed measurement.

Keywords: Hall sensor; DC motor; speed measurement; control system.

1 Introduction

DC motor has been widely used in machinery manufacturing, electric power, metallurgy and other fields because of its good start, braking and speed performance. In the industrial measurement and control system, in order to control the motor rotation better, it is often needed to continuously measure its speed. Higher the motor speed resolution, the better control of the motor. Now, the commonly used speed measurement methods include centrifugal tachometer method, tachogenerator method, gleaming method, photoelectric encoder method and Hall element method, et al.. Since the Hall element has the performances of small size, simple external circuit, dynamic, long life, debugging and convenient, it can be made with a variety of sensors and widely used in displacement measurement, angle measurement, speed measurement and counting, and so on [1-3].

So, after analyzing the characteristics of Hall element, a design method of speed measurement system is proposed. The hardware circuits and software are introduced. It adopt Hall sensor to gather pulse signals from motor, and the pulses are send to single chip machine after procession. In order to accurately measure speed, the system was designed to obtain instantaneous speed and ensure the measurement in real time.

The rest of this paper is organized as follows. Section 2 introduces the principle of Hall sensor. Section 3 described the framework of hardware and unit circuits in details. After that, the flow chart of software is presented in section4. In section 5, some experimental results are analyzed with some real examples. Finally, the last section gives some concluding remarks.

R. Chen (Ed.): ICICIS 2011, Part I, CCIS 134, pp. 440–445, 2011.

2 Principle of Hall Element

As a speed sensor of measurement system, the Hall element has many advantages such as small size, light weight and easy installation, et al.. Its working principle is Hall-effect: A metal or semiconductor chips are placed in a magnetic field, when the sheet is connected to current I , on both sides of the sheet surface will produce a trace of the Hall voltage U_H , if it changes the strength of magnetic field, the size of the Hall voltage will changes accordingly. With the formula expressed as:

$$U_H = K_H \times I \times B .\tag{1}$$

Where K_H is the sensitivity coefficient of Hall device, I is the electric current and B is the magnetic induction intensity.

If a Hall element is installed nearly to the turntable, when turntable rotates with the shaft, the Hall element is affected by magnetic field generated by the magnet, so it outputs pulse signal whose frequency is proportional to speed, then speed can be calculated by measuring the pulse period or frequency[4,5]. The connection circuit of device and electronic properties are shown in Fig.1.

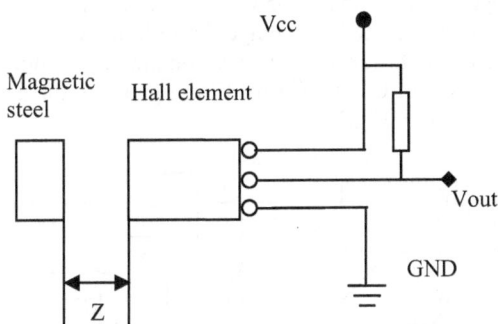

Fig. 1. The connection circuit of device

The relationship of pulse period and motor speed is

$$n = 60/(P \times T)\tag{2}$$

Where n is the motor speed, P is the pulse number of a round for the motor, and T is the period of square wave signal.

3 Hardware Design

According to the requirements of actual control, this paper has designed the hardware connection diagram of DC motor speed measurement based on microcontroller AT89S51. The system mainly includes four parts: keyboard circuit, power circuit, speed measurement circuit and displaying circuit [6]. The overall structure of the system is shown in figure 2.

The working process is as follows. Firstly, the control commands are inputted to single chip microcontroller by the keyboard, the pulse signals corresponding to motor

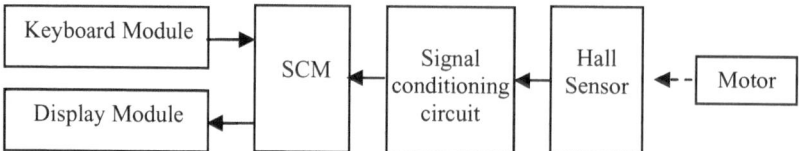

Fig. 2. The overall structure of system

speeds are collected through the Hall sensor. Then, the operational status is displayed on the LED.

3.1 Microcontroller

This system uses AT89S51 as CPU, it is an 8-bit CMOS microcontroller with the characters of 4KB Flash, low-power and high performance. It is compatible with standard 80C51 instruction set and 80C51 guidelines foot structure, which can be applied to many embedded control system to provide high cost-effective solutions.

3.2 Power Circuit

The operating voltage of AT89S51 is +5V while the lighting voltage is 220V, 50Hz AC. So, it is needed to convert to DC voltage through the rectifier bridge. Because the obtained DC voltage through transformer may contain AC component, so it is needed the filter circuit composed of C1 and C3 for filtering. Then, the 5V voltage can get by 7805. The circuit is shown in Fig.3.

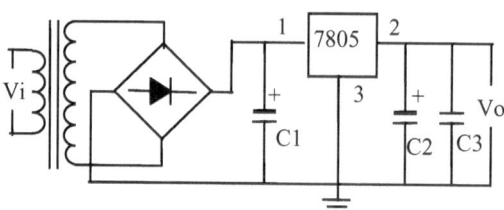

Fig. 3. Circuit of system power

3.3 Keyboard

Two switches SW1, SW2 of the system connect to P2.0, P2.1, respectively. Where SW1 is used for system restarting, SW2 is used for system setting. The method to judge whether the key is pressed down is as follows. Setting port P2 for high level firstly, then testing pin level start from P2.0 to P2.1 one by one. If a pin is low-level, it means the key is pressed down, then corresponding treatment is needed to be done to achieve key function. If the pin is high level, then it is not treated.

3.4 Display Circuit

The System uses LEDs to display the data. It is composed with four LEDs with a total positive, and the bit-choice side is driven with a transistor S8550. The display mode of system is dynamic scanning.

3.5 Speed Measurement Circuit

Motor speed circuit is designed mainly based on Hall sensor UGN-3501T, which is an integrated sensitive device produced by the United States SPRAGUE Company. Hall sensor measures speed signal from permanent magnet DC motor. When the shaft has a turn, a certain amount of pulses are produced, they are outputted by the Hall device circuit and become the counting pulses of rotation counter. By controlling counting time, it can achieve that counting values of counter is corresponding to shaft speed. The speed measurement circuit is showed in Fig.4.

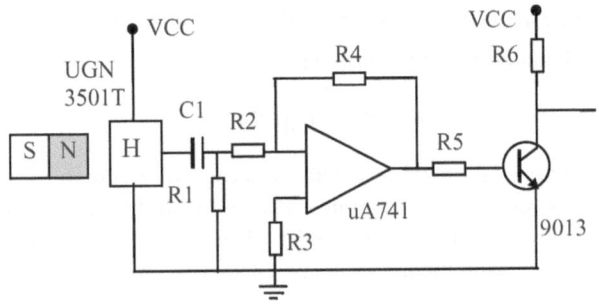

Fig. 4. The speed measurement circuit

4 Software Design

In this paper, the program is compiled with Keil C51. This system uses INT0 interrupt of microcontroller to count on speed pulses. When single chip microcontroller is powered on, the system enters a state of readiness. The first step is initialization, the timer T1 works on the external event count mode to count the speed pulse, T0 works on mode 1. The pulse number is read one time per seconds, this value is the pulse signal

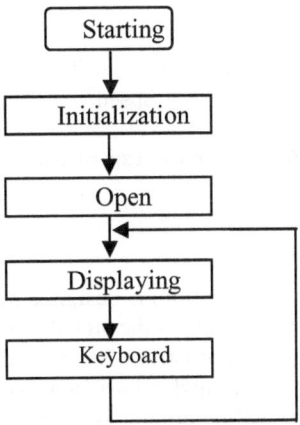

Fig. 5. The flowchart of main program

frequency; according to equation (1) the speed of the motor is calculated. The software of Speed detection device mainly includes: speed measurement subroutine, data processing subroutine and display routines, et al.. The main flowchart is shown in Fig.5.

5 Experiment

In order to verify the accuracy of measurements, the comparison test has been conducted. The true value n_0 is measured with high precision instrument and the measurement value n_x is the value from the display of system. The measurement error ε can be calculated with this formula:

$$\varepsilon = |n_x - n_0| / n_0. \tag{3}$$

The graphical representation of test data is shown in figure 6. The measurement results show that the errors are all within ± 4%, and with the increase of the speed, the relative errors become smaller and smaller. Thus, the experiment shows that the system has high measurement accuracy, and can meet the needs of speed measurement of DC motor.

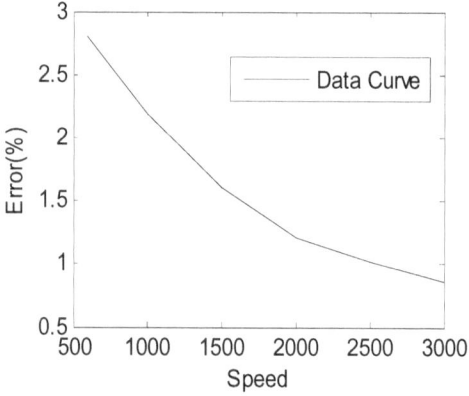

Fig. 6. Data curve of experimental results

6 Conclusion

In this paper, a speed measurement system is designed based on SCM technology and Hall sensor. The microcontroller obtained the signals from Hall sensor to achieve the continuous speed monitoring and control. Experiments show that the hardware interface circuit is simple, reliable, and robust, with some theoretical and practical values and can meet the functional requirements of speed regulation. Especially when the measurement space is limited, or sensors installed under the conditions of the inconvenience, this method has obvious advantages.

References

1. Yao, R.B., Sun, H.B.: The Design of Rotation Rate Measurement System Based on STC89C51RC. Journal of Lianyungang Teachers College (4), 84–87 (2007)
2. Yang, J.S., Liu, F.: Application study of hall sensor A44E in cartwheel s resurver. Electric Measurement Technology 32(10), 100–102 (2009)
3. Xu, C.J., Wu, Y.H., Wu, J.F., et al.: High Degree Accuracy Speed Measurement Method Using Hall Sensor Based on FPGA. Instrument Technique and Sensor (10), 99–101 (2009)
4. Li, J.B., Liu, M.L.: Hall Sensor Based on the Speed Measurement System. Journal of Henan Institute of Science and Technology 37(3), 54–56 (2009)
5. Ding, Z.Q.: Design of Motor Speed Measurement Device Based on Hall Effect Sensor. Journal of Agricultural Mechanization Research (5), 81–83 (2010)
6. Shao, X.T., Chen, M., Li, J.: Monolithic microcomputer measuring of a motor rotation speed signal Based on linear Hall sensor. Electric Test (12), 46–48 (2008)

Fault Reporting Based on Geographic Information of Distribution Network Fault Locating System

Sun Quande[1], Li Kaiyang[2], and Wang Chunsheng[1]

[1] Henan Jiaozuo Power Supply Company, No.169 Minzhu Road,
Jiefang District, 454000 Jiaozuo, Henan, China
[2] Huazhong University of Science and Technology, No 1037 Luoyu Road,
Hongshan District, 430074 Wuhan, Hubei, China

Abstract. For the Fault identification on Non-Control Area of Distribution network, a new method of distribution network fault is locating. Distribution network model based on GIS is introduced, mixed by Model of power system distribution network and Model of Geographic Information System (GIS) data. Distribution network fault locating algorithm based on rough set theory is constructed, as well as implementation process of fault locating.

Keywords: Geographic Information System (GIS); Distribution Network; Fault locating System.

1 Introduction

Nowadays, the fault location of distribution network framework's large area of the branch line is mainly depended on the fault reporting information from users, and then users called to complaint power fault address and time and so on. Then the electric workers answered the messages, including the regions planning to power cut or when the maintenance workers would arrive. However, several problems are not correctly settled. These problems would be decided by the fault reporting based on geographic information of distribution network fault locating system, which avoided the huge investment on communication equipment, shortened the power cut time.

2 Distribution Network Analysis Based on GIS Application

GIS is applied here and there on the device and operation management of distribution network, because of its formidable features such as display, inquiry, count. What's more, other professional analysis of power based on the spatial analysis, the network analysis is only on the initial stage [1]. Network analysis functions of GIS could achieve these points, as network upstream analysis, network downstream analysis, tracking of common ancestor, and network connectivity analysis, etc. They all would be the basis of fault location.

R. Chen (Ed.): ICICIS 2011, Part I, CCIS 134, pp. 446–452, 2011.
© Springer-Verlag Berlin Heidelberg 2011

2.1 Distribution Network Model

Distribution network included distribution substations, distribution lines, breakers, isolating switch, and distribution transformers [2]. The breakers, RMU, isolating switch, and switching stations are always used as switches, so they could be replaced by switches [3]. Figure 1 shows distribution network structure of Gong One Line.

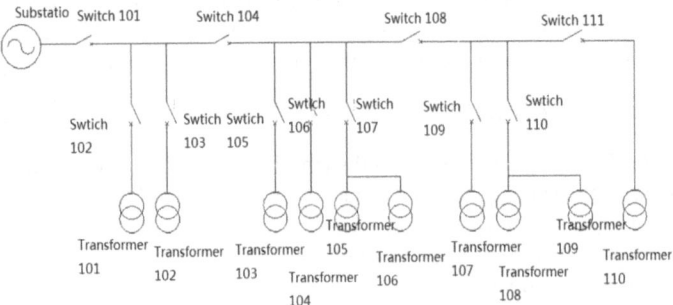

Fig. 1. Gong One Line Distribution network structure

This Tree-lined distribution network is expressed as:

$$A = \{S, L_i, K_j, T_k | i = 1,2, \dots n_1; j = 1,2, \dots n_2; k = 1,2, \dots n_3\} \tag{1}$$

On the formula, n_1 n_2 n_3 means the numbers of line or equipment; S means power source (distribution substations); L means Power Supplying line; K means switch; T means transformers.

To describe the distribution network deeply, let all the equipment showed as Device Names, including coding; category; graphic properties; related properties; management properties. Distribution network model involves three information data: spatial information; attribute information; relationships.

2.2 Distribution Network Model Based on GIS

GIS treats the breaker, isolating switch, fuse as point features; distribution lines as line features; rivers and buildings as surface elements. For the every element, GIS describe and store three corresponding information data: spatial information; attribute information; relationships. All the distribution network GIS data are stored in the Geospatial Database ('Geodatabase' for short). For the power users, Geodatabase could reflect several benefits: first, users could have a choice to create the custom elements, which may be used to describe transformers, lines, cables, instead of point elements or line elements; second, data entry and editing could be more precise; third, data model is more intuitive handling; fourth, elements have rich related environmental; fifth, the idea multi-user concurrency editing Geography data comes true.

To establish distribution network model based on GIS, power source(S), switch (K_j), transformer (T_k) are treated as the vertex of distribution network topology, distribution network line (L_i) as the line of distribution network topology. What's more, distribution network should not be on closed-loop operation. So distribution network means open-loop dissipative network with variable structure. In the GIS data model, one or more layers could be chosen from simple feature class. For example, conductor layers and equipment layers on certain routes could be assembled as a new geometric network; or make all layers as a new geometric network. On the new geometric network, Lines mean the line elements on the original layers, Points mean power source, switch, transformer and other point elements on the original layers, as well as new contact as T contact and caused by the different line's model. Then distribution network based on GIS data model is completed:

$$A = \{P_i, L_j | i = 1,2,\dots n; j = 1,2,\dots m\} \tag{2}$$

On the formula, P_i means all contacts of distribution network; L_j means lines connected by all contacts. At the same time, for the purpose to describe all the network elements in distribution network (at the distribution network, except the new contact as T contact and caused by the different line's model, other network elements means specific equipment). They are always shown as network element attributes, including ID; Feature Class; Feature Category; Feature Run Number; Feature State; Others. The distribution network model based on GIS is constructed. Then the point elements and line elements in distribution equipment acting as a connectivity role are stored in a data set. Create a new Geometric Network by the GIS tools, and connect all the distribution equipment, ready for the network analysis. Figure 1 corresponds to the distribution network shown in Figure 2 geometric network. On the Figure 2, 1, 2, 3...9 means T-junction generated by geometric network.

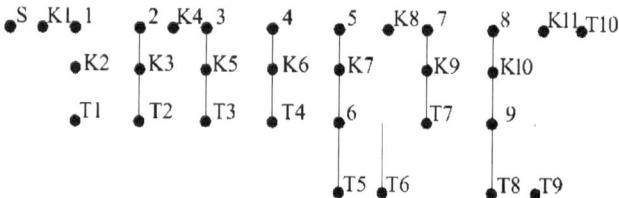

Fig. 2. Gong One Line Based on GIS

2.3 Analysis of Distribution Network Model Based on GIS

Because Geometric network of distribution network topology analysis algorithm is based on the topology analysis of GIS, the topological analysis functions based on the GIS development platform achieve faster network topology analysis. Using the topology analysis functions provided by ArcGIS, a connected analysis would be finished to the entire distribution network, as well as several connected analysis to a single-circuit. For example, set power source as source, each power equipment as sink, then simulate the current of distribution network by flow. It would be obtained through the network analysis that the network topology of the line in real time and a wiring diagram circuit. This set the stage for the distribution network fault analysis. The advantage of this stage is reveal clear and intuitive, reporting equipment and address failure with the shown on map, which give the operator great decision support.

3 Algorithm of Distribution Network GIS Fault Location Based on Rough Set Theory

Rough set theory is dealing with uncertainty and new tools for the mathematical imprecision [4]. Most important feature is not required to provide data processing required to solve the problem other than any prior information collection, analysis and can effectively deal with imprecise, inconsistent, incomplete, and other incomplete data and find hidden knowledge reveal the potential law.

3.1 Automatically Form a Decision Table

Dynamic encoding on distribution network is to form a decision table. Distribution flow chart dynamic coding is shown on Figure 3. The first input is the ID of outlet switch. For instance Figure 1, search from outlet switch down to the transformer at the end of the line. The transformer properties contain ID and run number, which are marked as T_1, $T2...T_{10}$. Then the corresponding power user areas are marked as the same number T_1, $T2...T_{10}$. Search the near power user area containing the equipment along the line. If the user could be found, mark 1; else mark 0. Automatically turn the formation of fault-based fault location CALLS decision table (Table 1). In this table, '1' means that users have called the customer service center to report faults; '0' means have not. Assuming K_1 switch fails, the connect power users theoretically will call. When K_2 or T_1 fails, the user T_1 will call, as well as other users will not. In accordance with a failure only occurs at the same time in the power system, form 16 decision rules.

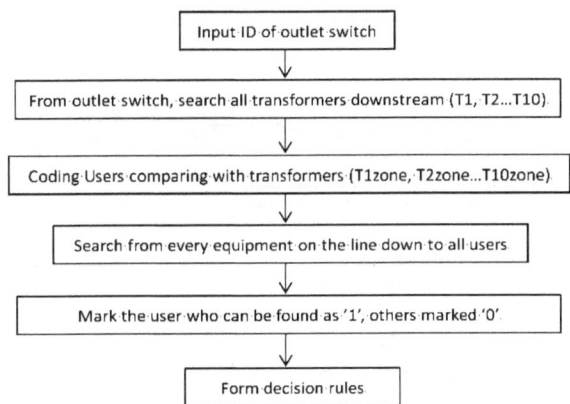

Fig. 3. Distribution network flow chart dynamic coding

Table 1. Fault Location Decision Table

Sample number	A	B	C	D	E	F	G	H	I	J	Fault element
1	1	1	1	1	1	1	1	1	1	1	K1
2	1	0	0	0	0	0	0	0	0	0	K1 or T1
3	0	1	0	0	0	0	0	0	0	0	K3 or T2
4	0	0	1	1	1	1	1	1	1	1	K4
5	0	0	1	0	0	0	0	0	0	0	K5 or T3
6	0	0	0	1	0	0	0	0	0	0	K6 or T4
7	0	0	0	0	1	1	0	0	0	0	K7
8	0	0	0	0	1	0	0	0	0	0	T5
9	0	0	0	0	0	1	0	0	0	0	T6
10	0	0	0	0	0	0	1	1	1	1	K8
11	0	0	0	0	0	0	1	0	0	0	K9 or T7
12	0	0	0	0	0	0	0	1	1	0	K10
13	0	0	0	0	0	0	0	1	0	0	T8
14	0	0	0	0	0	0	0	0	1	0	T9
15	0	0	0	0	0	0	0	0	0	1	K10 or T11
16	0	0	0	0	0	0	0	0	0	0	No fault

3.2 Reduce Decision Table

Using recursive call, simplify all the N condition attributes. When K condition attribute is deleted, record decision attribute as DS_k If DS_k and DS_0 different, the condition attribute is not omitted; else, the condition attribute could be omitted. Simplify the Table 1 by decision table reduction process in Figure 4, and then decision table reduction could be got (Figure 4).

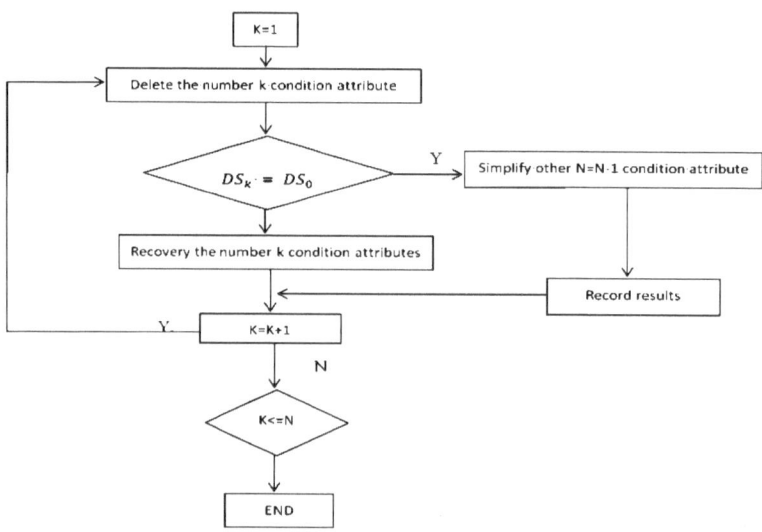

Fig. 4. Decision Table Reduction Chart

Table 2. Decision Table Reduction

Sample number	A	B	C	D	E	F	G	H	I	J	Fault element
1	*	1	*	*	*	1	*	*	1	1	K1
2	1	0	0	0	0	0	0	0	0	0	K1 or T1
3	*	1	0	0	0	0	0	0	0	0	K3 or T2
4	*	0	*	*	*	1	*	*	1	1	K4
5	0	0	1	0	0	0	0	0	0	0	K5 or T3
6	*	*	*	1	0	0	0	0	0	0	K6 or T4
7	*	*	*	*	1	1	0	0	0	0	K7
8	*	*	*	*	1	0	0	0	0	0	T5
9	*	*	*	*	0	1	0	0	0	0	T6
10	*	*	*	*	*	0	*	*	1	1	K8
11	*	*	*	*	*	*	1	0	0	0	K9 or T7
12	*	*	*	*	*	*	*	1	1	0	K10
13	*	*	*	*	*	*	*	1	0	0	T8
14	*	*	*	*	*	*	*	0	1	0	T9
15	*	*	*	*	*	*	*	*	0	1	K10 or T11
16	0	0	0	0	0	0	0	0	0	0	No fault

In Table 2, '*' means whether the user called for failure, no effect on the correct failure positioning of the distribution network. As well as every important characteristics of the region fault information, this has the same positioning capability with original decision table. This rough set theory-based fault location method uses the regional information set redundancy complaints, avoiding errors and uncertainty information caused by human factors, to achieve the aim of correct positioning.

4   Implementation Process of Fault Location

Fault location of the implementation process includes the following three steps:

1) Generate a power supply circuit wiring diagram. There are all communications (house numbers, phone numbers, and addresses) about power users in system database. When customer service hotlines (95598) are called, user's house number and address are recorded. So the transformer supplies for him could be found. It would do benefit to reduce complaints in the actual failure occurred during the user because of the distribution network systems are not familiar with the possibility of false positives. Then Search investment reported the transformer power supply failure point S with the fault location system in the network analysis tools Arc Engine. According to this point, power supply circuit diagram could be drawn. User who votes fault is not always the one in the new failure zone, because some users do not know where the area is planned power outage or equipment maintenance. So this information must be filtered out first. If the transformer could find the source supplying power, the line it in fails. Then ID of outlet switches and transformers should be output to an array file, because scheduling departments cannot monitor this failure.

2) Based on power supply circuit logic diagram (Figure 2), dynamic coding all the geometric network device nodes on the failure of power supply circuit, such as breakers, isolating switches, fuses, transformers. The decision table is based on codes, simplify decision table, and output fault sections in the decision table.

3) Mark fault sections on the GIS map with highlight, and show the cause of the malfunction and details about fault equipment [5].

5 Conclusion

In low voltage distribution network, there are many non-control areas, with much fault, ineffective positioning, and not intuitively. To avoid these abuses, this system use GIS and the rough set theory, according to the information on user's fault complaints, finding the location of the point of failure quickly. In the practical application, more methods could be used to efficiently shut the time of repairing distribution network fault, like GIS fault recovery vehicle system, to improve the level of power customer service.

References

1. Chang, K.-s.: Introduction To Geographic Information System. Science Press, Beijing (1999)
2. Cassel, W.R.: Distribution Management System: Functions and Payback. IEEE Trans. on Power Systems, 796–801 (1993)
3. Trussell, L.V.: GIS based Distribution Simulation and Analysis. Electricity Distribution (2001)
4. Resconi, G., Kovalerchuk, B.: Agents' model of uncertainty. Knowledge and Information Systems 18(2), 213 (2009)
5. Normak, Per-ludivg: Trimble introduces New Family of Trimble trident analyst software providing advanced GIS and CAD information extraction for mobile mapping. Computer Weekly News, p. 107, Atlanta (2010)

Key Curriculum Reform Research on Numerical Analysis

Zhong Li and Chensong Peng

Department of Mathematics and Science, Zhejiang Sci-Tech University, Hangzhou, 310018, Zhejiang, China
lizhong@zstu.edu.cn

Abstract. Based on the current undergraduate teaching characteristics and the actual teaching situation of numerical analysis curriculum, this paper gives a useful discussion and appropriate adjustments for this course's teaching content and style, and it also proposes some new curriculum reform plans to improve the teaching effectiveness which can develop student's abilities of mathematical thinking and computational practice.

Keywords: Numerical analysis; College teaching; Curriculum reform.

1 Introduction

Numerical Analysis is a course which studies various numerical computation methods and the theory for solving different mathematical and applied problems. Its research content is broad, rich and practical. It not only has high abstraction and rigorousness characteristics of pure mathematics, but also has highly technical and practical features for extensive applications. That means numerical analysis is a combination field of mathematics and computer science. Therefore it becomes a core course of mathematics and information science major in colleges and universities [1,2].

In the current domestic and overseas teaching and research on numerical analysis course, they normally focus on its theoretical content and ignore its practice and application guidance, which makes it as a relatively abstract mathematics course. For many undergraduates, because it's difficult to understand and master its main content, they are easy to be boring for learning this course, which is hard to achieve the expected teaching effectiveness [3,4]. In view of this reason, many domestic and foreign universities have done the teaching reform on numerical analysis curriculum. During the teaching process, they arrange some numerical computation method tests and large-scale integrated experiments and so on. However, we find these reforms are not enough to achieve the expected effectiveness, one reason is that even the students are able to make some experiments, they do not know why these methods should be done like this and where these methods can be applied for, i.e., they do not fully grasp the main content of computational methods. On the other hand, with the rapid development of computers and other related technologies, the content of numerical analysis and corresponding central issue has also changed, which is inconsistent with

R. Chen (Ed.): ICICIS 2011, Part I, CCIS 134, pp. 453–458, 2011.
© Springer-Verlag Berlin Heidelberg 2011

the traditional teaching content. We need to combine some new contents of numerical analysis in time to take some proper teaching adjustment on numerical analysis course [5,6].

This paper does the research based on the existing problems in teaching numerical analysis course. Through the reform and construction of its teaching content, method and other aspects, we mobilize the student's enthusiasm for learning this course; broaden student's learning knowledge; let them know the practical application when understanding the relevant theory.

2 Numerical Analysis Key Course Teaching Reform

2.1 Current Numerical Analysis Teaching Situation

Numerical Analysis is a fundamental course in mathematics and information science major of Zhejiang Sci-Tech University. By learning the course, students can understand the characteristics of various numerical computational methods, and use these numerical methods to solve some mathematical problems, build a solid foundation for solving practical application problems combining with the computer technology. The main content of this course includes polynomial interpolation, function approximation and computation, numerical integration and numerical differentiation, numerical solution of ordinary differential equations, numerical solution for nonlinear equation and linear equations, etc. When teaching this course, students can proficiently use the numerical computation software and do some numerical computations experiments by the programming language, which achieve the harmonious teaching effect of its theory and practice. Based on the teaching syllabus and the student's actual condition, the course is mainly on the way of the classroom teaching and is supplemented by the computer experiment. There is 48 hours of the classroom teaching, which is to introduce the basic principles and concepts of main numerical computation methods. The teaching content hour is compact, we need to arrange the reasonable content for the classroom teaching so that students can understand and master the modern scientific computing and numerical methods in principle, and they are also able to apply relating knowledge to solve real application problems. The specific teaching content hour arrangement is shown in table 1.

The main problem of current course teaching is that when introducing the specific numerical computation method and related mathematical knowledge, some students, especially in information sciences major, feel boring and difficult to understand relevant content. This course also requires better hands-on computer programming capabilities, but some students in mathematics major have not the appropriate preparation and training, which cause the weak practical programming ability. What's more, the development of research on numerical analysis is rapid and the related hot research field is also changed, we should adjust and update the teaching content [7,8]. Therefore, in order to effectively serve for its teaching process, we urgently need to do the teaching reform on numerical analysis course to explore new teaching ideas and teaching methods for students.

Table 1. Schedule of teaching content hour arrangement of Numerical Analysis

Teaching Mode / Teaching hours / Course content (Knowledge unit)	Theory teaching	Exercise class	Discussion class	Total
unit 1: Introduction	2			2 class hours
unit 2: Interpolation method	7	1		8 class hours
unit3: Function approximation and computation	7	1		8 class hours
unit4: Numerical integration and numerical differentiation	6	1	1	8 class hours
unit 5: Numerical solution of differential equations	6	1	1	8 class hours
unit 6: Numerical method for solving nonlinear equation	6			6 class hours
unit7: Direct numerical method for solving linear equations	4			4 class hours
unit8: Iteration method for solving nonlinear equations	3	1		4 class hours
Total	41	5	2	48 class hours

2.2 Numerical Analysis Teaching Reform Implementation

The basic teaching reform of numerical analysis course in mathematics department is mainly to adjust the course content according to the actual situation; perform appropriate reforms based on the existing teaching problems; try some new teaching methods and train the professional teaching faculty; improve undergraduate's interest in learning this course, so that they can truly understand the main content of the course. Detailed implementation plans are

(1). Reform of teaching content and curriculum system
While teaching numerical analysis course, we regularly communicate with students, know the student's learning state of math or information science major in time, adjust and modify the traditional numerical analysis syllabus, reduce or remove some relatively difficult sections appropriately, such as function approximation, numerical eigenvalue calculation, etc. We also increase some new contents related to numerical analysis, such as parallel computing, genetic algorithms and neural network computing, etc. In the course system, we appropriately change the simple mode teaching by the lecturer, increase answering time for solving student's question and stimulate the learning interest of students.

(2). Teaching reform of theoretical knowledge

For the students in information science major, they are relatively lack of mathematical theory knowledge. For mathematics students, their computer hands-on programming ability is relatively weak. The teacher should let the students prepare to learn corresponding weak knowledge first, so that when introducing the basic theory of computation methods and do the large-scale experiment, the difficulty of teaching numerical algorithms can be reduced. In addition, when introducing the specific numerical method, the teacher can use the heuristic teaching, for example, give questions before the class teaching, guide the students to preview and self-learn the relating content which can also reduce the classroom teaching burden and simplify the task of classroom teaching. When explaining various computational methods, the lecturer can teach them by comparing different algorithms and find their relationship between them, emphasis on the comparability and relevance of algorithms so that students are no longer isolated to learn these numerical methods, which help them deepen the understanding of various algorithms. In addition, the teacher can introduce some new research progress in the relating numerical computation field so that the students will not feel boring to learn this course. The teacher can also recommend some important journals and conferences of numerical analysis, help student download the relevant papers from the website, so that students obtain the newest research knowledge in the related field.

(3). Experiment (practice) reform and development

We modify previous large-scale experiment content, increase some numerical method description for solving meaningful application problems, and combine the experiment content with other courses such as mathematical modeling course, and so on. Through the experimental training, we hope to improve the student's learning interest and the ability to solve practical problems. In addition, students need to develop the hands-on ability, pay attention to the relationships between the programming for realizing the computational algorithm and the existing computational application software. If some students are not familiar with the programming language and the related software before doing the experiment, the teacher should increase some class hours to introduce the programming language and application software such as VC, Matlab, etc. After the experimental time, the teacher can ask students to learn these relating contents by themselves to strengthen the practice ability.

(4). Combination of traditional teaching and multimedia teaching

In our course reform, we take the reform on the past teaching method which is mainly based on the blackboard teaching. We add the multimedia teaching methods, such as using PPT to explain some parts of the course content. We make use of the network, audio, video and other information resource, give the full influence of graphics, image, animation and other tools to enhance the teaching effect. These measures are not only consistent with the characteristics of the course, but also increase the diversity of teaching content which makes the classroom teaching lively and interesting. In addition, we can recommend the original foreign materials and use the bilingual teaching mode for teaching some parts of them.

(5). Exercise assignment and examination arrangement

Certain arrangement of after-school exercises can help students review and understand the content of the class. According to the student's actual state, the teacher should arrange a number of exercises with moderate difficulty and give some different kinds of exercises associated with theoretical knowledge and practical application problems, so that the students can be trained to develop the independent thinking capacity. For the experiment section, the teacher should provide the large-scale experimental homework, the students choose relevant programming language to realize the algorithm and solve the problem. The experimental score can be referred as a proportion recorded in the final performance of this course. Finally, we need to establish a certain number of the exercise base for each chapter of numerical analysis course. Final exam can be randomly selected from the exercise base. The final score can be determined by the final written test, the experimental score and the usual performance, which increases the objectivity and impartiality of learning this course.

2.3 Specific Reform Schedule Plan

The course reform schedule can mainly be divided into two phases:

(1). We do the appropriate modification on the teaching syllabus of numerical analysis. Through the questionnaires, the communication between teachers and students, attending the teaching conference or other styles, we know what theoretical knowledge students don't understand clearly, which section students are more interested in, and what experiments students are difficult to do, etc. We improve the corresponding teaching contents in time. We also analyze and summarize relevant information to complete the mid-term research report.

(2). According to the mid-term report, we adjust and update the contents of numerical analysis in the next year's teaching. We complete the teaching reform of this course's content and system, improve the teaching method and the experimental teaching, reorganize the teaching note and construct the exercise library; complete the reform research summary report, publish one related reform research paper.

2.4 Goal of Course Reform

Through the teaching reform research of numerical analysis course, we will develop the teaching note in the past few years, summary the relevant teaching material, improve the existing curricula syllabus, the teaching calendar, modify the after-school exercise set and the examination paper, arrange the multimedia teaching material and tool. The students learning this course can benefit from them. The goal of this course reform is to form our teaching characteristics of numerical analysis in mathematics and information science major of Zhejiang Sci-Tech University. In addition, through this teaching reform, we will practice the teaching ability of our young teachers, establish the reasonable team for teaching numerical analysis course.

3 Summary

We compare the teaching effect for recent students learning numerical analysis course. After the teaching reform, we find that the student's fear of difficulty related to this course has been reduced, while the student's interest, confidence and enthusiasm in learning this course is increased, and the computer programming ability has also been promoted. Furthermore, the final exam score of this course has greatly been improved. Current numerical analysis educational reform has gotten some progress.

Acknowledgment

This research was supported by Numerical Analysis Key Course Construction Project of Zhejiang Sci-Tech University (Grant No. ZDKC0901); National Natural Science Foundation of China (Grant No.60903143, 51075421).

References

1. Kincaid, D., Cheney, W.: Numerical Analysis: Mathematics of Scientific Computing, 3rd edn. American Mathematical Society, Providence (2003)
2. Li, Q.Y., Wang, N.C., Yi, D.Y.: Numerical Analysis. Huazhong University of Science and Technology Press (2004) (in Chinese)
3. Sun, Z.Z., Yuan, W.P., Wen, Z.C.: Numerical Analysis, 2nd edn. Southeast University Press (2002) (in Chinese)
4. Yuan, W.P., Sun, Z.Z., Wu, H.W., et al.: Computing Methods and Laboratory, 3rd edn. Southeast University Press (2003) (in Chinese)
5. Wan, Z., Han, X.L.: New Viewpoints and Practices for Reforming the Teaching of the Course: Numerical Analysis. Journal of Mathematics Education 17(2), 65–66 (2008)
6. Chen, Z., Li, W.X.: Key Course Construction and Practice Discussion of Numerical Analysis. Journal of Yangtze University (Natural Science Edition): Sci & Eng. 6(1), 345–346 (2009) (in Chinese)
7. Song, S.H., Zhu, J.M., Tang, L.Y., et al.: Research on Teaching Reform of Advanced Numerical Analysis. Journal of Higher Education Research 31(4), 66–67 (2008) (in Chinese)
8. Zhong, B.J., Huang, T.Z.: Investigating Teaching of Numerical Analysis course. China University Teaching 9, 31–32 (2008) (in Chinese)

The Topic Analysis of Hospice Care Research Using Co-word Analysis and GHSOM

Yu-Hsiang Yang[1], Huimin Bhikshu[2], and Rua-Huan Tsaih[1]

[1] Dept. of Management Information Systems, National Chengchi University, Taipei (Taiwan)
[2] Dharma Drum Buddhist College (DDBC), Taipei (Taiwan)
yuxiang1001@gmail.com, huimin2525@gmail.com,
tsaih@mis.nccu.edu.tw

Abstract. The purpose of this study was to propose a multi-layer topic map analysis of palliative care research using co-word analysis of informetrics with Growing Hierarchical Self-Organizing Map (GHSOM). The topic map illustrated the delicate intertwining of subject areas and provided a more explicit illustration of the concepts within each subject area. We applied GHSOM, a text-mining Neural Networks tool, to obtain a hierarchical topic map. The result of the topic map may indicate that the subject area of *health care science and service* played an importance role in multidiscipline within the research related to palliative care.

Keywords: topic-map, co-word, GHSOM, hospice care, palliative care, terminal care.

1 Introduction

Since the first scholarly paper in terminal care appeared in 1952 [1] according to SCIE (Science Citation Index Expanded) and SSCI (Social Science Citation Index) databases, explorations of the possibilities of hospice care or palliative care have seen a vigorous development, especially in the last fifteen years. Recently, bibliometric or informetric method was used to analyze a good deal of research relevant to palliative care. Payne and Turner offered a conceptual mapping of fields of research concerned with death and dying, which they suggested that there is a greater acknowledgement of the differing epistemological and theoretical frameworks used by researchers [2]. However, their results were based on their professional judgments, not by systemic methods. In this study, we proposed a hierarchical mapping model using co-word analysis and Growing Hierarchical Self-Organizing Map (GHSOM) [3-4] in order provide a hierarchical topic map of palliative care research.

The objectives of this study were to reveal the major topics or conceptual interrelations of research related to hospice care as an example, in order to gain a better understanding of the quantitative aspects of recorded data and discover features of research relevant to hospice care embedded in the SCIE and SSCI databases. Thus, we adopted GHSOM in co-word analysis to cluster the conceptual topics into a representation of dynamic 2-dimentional interrelated structures within the data.

R. Chen (Ed.): ICICIS 2011, Part I, CCIS 134, pp. 459–465, 2011.
© Springer-Verlag Berlin Heidelberg 2011

2 Dataset and Method

The dataset used in this study was derived from the SCIE and SSCI Databases of the Web of Science, created by the Institute for Scientific Information. It comprehensively indexes over 1,950 journals across 50 social sciences disciplines. It also indexes individually selected, relevant items from over 3,300 of the world's leading scientific and technical journals.

An empirical search command was used by "Topic= ("palliative care*") OR Topic= ("hospice care*") OR Topic= ("terminal care*") refined by Document Type= (Article or Review) "to retrieve data related to hospice care. The documents specifically included articles or reviews in the study. Book reviews, papers of proceeding, letters, notes, meeting abstracts were not taken into consideration. A total of 6,828 papers published between 1952 and 2009 were found.

The study applied co-word analysis with GHSOM to cluster the major topics of a large collection of documents based on research related to hospice care, and provide a topical landscape of the field. Self-Organizing Map (SOM) was designed according to the concept of unsupervised artificial neural networks to process high-dimensional data and provided visual results [5-8]. However, SOM requires a predefined number of nodes (neural processing units) and implements a static architecture. These nodes result in a representation of hierarchical relations with limited capability. GHSOM approach was developed to overcome these limitations, and is often applied in field the information extraction [3, 9-11]. GHSOM is based on the characteristic of SOM, but it can automatically grow its own multi-layer hierarchical structure, in which each layer encompasses a number of SOMs, as shown in Figure 1.

The process of applying GHSOM to topic analysis is illustrated in Figure 2. The three phases are: the data preprocessing phase; the clustering phase; and the interpreting phase.

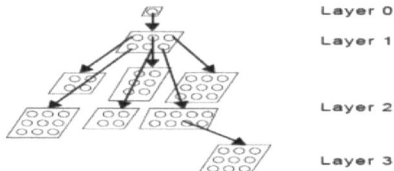

Fig. 1. Structures of GHSOM [9]

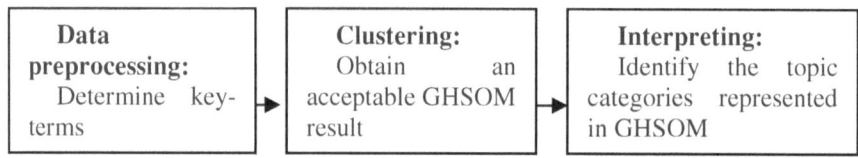

| **Data preprocessing:** Determine key-terms | **Clustering:** Obtain an acceptable GHSOM result | **Interpreting:** Identify the topic categories represented in GHSOM |

Fig. 2. The three phases of the topic analysis process

In the data preprocessing phase, key-terms such as titles, keywords, and subject categories are used to represent the contents of the documents. Meaningful key-terms describing the articles are extracted directly from the documents without any manual intervention. These key-terms are weighted according to a *tf* x *idf* the state-of-the-art weighting scheme shown in equation (1) [9-10, 12-13].

$$w_i(d) = tf_i (d) \times \log (N / df_i)$$
    (1)

In equation (1), $w_i(d)$ represents the weight of the ith term in document (d), $tf_i(d)$ represents the number of times the ith term appears in document (d), N represents the total number of documents, and df_i represents how many documents contain the ith term. The resulting key-term vectors were used for GHSOM training.

In the clustering phase, the GHSOM experiment[1] was conducted through the trial and error method, using various values for breadth and depth and different normalizations to gain an acceptable GHSOM model for the analysis. The results of GHSOM are shown as Figure 2.

In the interpreting phase, for each node of GHSOM of the first-layer and some nodes of the second-layer which will be re-grouped into the layer 3, we counted the df_i value of each key-term in all articles cluster them into a particular node and assigned a key-term with the highest df_i value (or several key-terms if their df_i values were very close) as the topic category. If there were more than five topics, we would denote it as multidisciplinary. For the remaining nodes, the utmost five important key-terms would be automatically assigned by the GHSOM using the $tf \times idf$ weighting scheme.

3 Results

Through the process of applying GHSOM to topic analysis as showed in Figure 2, we obtained the result as showed in Figure 3 in the clustering phase. The model comprised four layers and 58 nodes. All 6,828 articles were clustered into a SOM of 2 x 3 nodes in layer 1, where all articles that had been clustered into the six nodes were further re-grouped into a SOM of 2 x 2 (i.e. node 1, 2, 3, 5, 5, and 6) respectively. The articles clustered into nodes 1.4, 3.3, 3.4, 4.1, 5.2 and 6.3 were further re-grouped into a SOM of 2 x 2 nodes in layer 3. The articles clustered into node 3.4.2 were further re-grouped into a SOM of 2 x 2 nodes in layer 4.

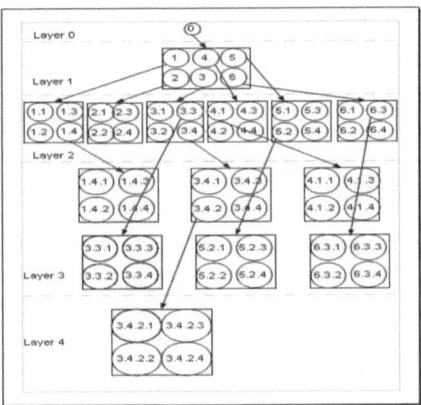

Fig. 3. The GHSOM result

---

[1] We used GHSOM toolbox in the Matlab R2007a® package to conduct the GHSOM experiment.

In the interpreting phase, for each node of GHSOM, we count the df_i value of each key-term in all articles cluster them into a particular node and assigned a key-term with the highest df_i value (or several key-terms if their df_i values were very close), as the topic category. If there were more than five topics, we would denote it as multidisciplinary. The results are presented in Figures 4, 5, 6 and 7, in which the number in the parenthesis refers to the number of clustered articles. For instance, there were 1002 articles clustered into node 1, and based upon the interpretation, it was named the "end, death and life", articles in node 2 as "health care science and service" category, and so on.

1	3	5
end death life	MED,GEN&INTL nursing	PEOH health care SCI & SRV
(1002)	(2183)	(1174)
2	4	6
health care SCI & SRV	oncology	clinical neurology MED,GEN&INTL health care SCI & SRV
(502)	(1068)	(897)

Fig. 4. First-layer interpretation results of GHSOM. MED, GEN&INTL is the abbreviation for medicine, general & internal; SRV is services; SCI is science; PEOH is public, environmental, and occupational health.

1.1	1.3	3.1	3.3	5.1	5.3
death end quality ethics communication (142)	life death end euthanasia SOC.SCI.biomedical (160)	SOC.SCI.biomedical ethics medical.ethics GERI&GERO SOC.issues (225)	nursing (507)	PEOH health.care.SCI&SRV MED,GEN&INTL home needs (196)	PEOH health.policy&services health.care.SCI&SRV PEOH (411)
1.2	1.4	3.2	3.4	5.2	5.4
life end death cancer-patients patient (229)	end health.care.SCI&SRV life (471)	pediatrics parents pediatric.palliative.care child children (108)	health.care.SCI&SRV MED,GEN&INTL (1343)	PEOH health.care.SCI&SRV MED.GEN&INTL (492)	neoplasms PEOH health.care.SCI&SRV MED,GEN&INTL palliative.treatment (75)
2.1	2.3	4.1	4.3	6.1	6.3
health.care.SCI&SRV MED,GEN&INTL cancer PEOH life (105)	cancer oncology life patients quality-of-life (140)	oncology (409)	surgery carcinoma GAST&hepatology stents (171)	clinical.neurology pain cancer.pain palliative.MED anesthesiology (84)	clinical.neurology health.care.SCI&SRV MED,GEN&INTL (540)
2.2	2.4	4.2	4.4	6.2	6.4
health.care.SCI&SRV MED,GEN&INTL cancer oncology clinical.neurology (99)	cancer oncology pain quality-of-life symptoms (158)	rehabilitation health.care.SCI&SRV oncology cancer (282)	cancer oncology survival therapy palliation (206)	clinical.neurology management attitudes patient quality-of-life (39)	MED,GEN&INTL clinical.neurology pain management breakthrough.pain (234)

Fig. 5. Second-layer interpretation result of GHSOM. GAST is gastroenterology; GERI&GERO is geriatrics & gerontology; SOC is social; SCI is science; PSY is psychology; MULTID is multidisciplinary; INTERD is interdisciplinary.

1.4.1	1.4.3
end death life decision-making of-life (79)	end care life death (221)
1.4.2	**1.4.4**
of-life.care end death quality GERI&GERO (113)	cancer death end life children (58)

4.1.1	4.1.3
quality-of-life advanced.cancer RNAD.CTRL-trial fatigue FUNC.assessment (24)	oncology patients quality-of-life therapy respiratory.system (86)
4.1.2	**4.1.4**
oncology cancer quality-of-life cell.lung-cancer supportive (86)	cancer oncology management quality-of-life (213)

3.3.1	3.3.3
nursing care advance.directives services dementia (31)	nursing nurses experiences (99)
3.3.2	**3.3.4**
PSY,MULTID care SOC.SCI,biomedical oncology stress (62)	nursing (315)

5.2.1	5.2.3
PEOH health.care.SCI&SRV MED,GEN&INTL cancer health (84)	PEOH health.care.SCI&SRV MED,GEN&INTL death cancer-patients (68)
5.2.2	**5.2.4**
PEOH health.care.SCI&SRV MED,GEN&INTL research SOC.SCI,INTERD (51)	PEOH health.care.SCI&SRV MED,GEN&INTL (289)

3.4.1	3.4.3
care death (301)	care EDU terminally ill medical (140)
3.4.2	**3.4.4**
MED,GEN&INTL (827)	health.care.SCI&SRV pharmacology&pharmacy EDU,scientific.disciplines (75)

6.3.1	6.3.3
clinical.neurology health.care.SCI&SRV MED,GEN&INTL (331)	clinical.neurology health.care.SCI&SRV MED,GEN&INTL end-of-life.care ill.cancer-patients (77)
6.3.2	**6.3.4**
MED,GEN&INTL health.care.SCI&SRV clinical.neurology cancer pain (510)	health.care.SCI&SRV MED,GEN&INTL clinical.neurology cancer management (81)

Fig. 6. Third-layer interpretation result of GHSOM. MED, GEN&INTL is the abbreviation for medicine, general & internal; GERI&GERO is geriatrics & gerontology; RNAD refers to random; CTRL is control; FUNC is functional; SRV is services; EDU is education; PEOH is public, environmental, and occupational health; SOC is social; SCI is science; PSY is psychology; MULTID is multidisciplinary; INTERD is interdisciplinary.

3.4.2.1	3.4.2.3
MED,GEN&INTL care urology&nephrology (199)	MULTID (250)
3.4.2.2	**3.4.2.4**
decision-making of-life.care united-states aids advance.directives (63)	MED,GEN&INTL (315)

Fig. 7. Fourth-layer interpretation result of GHSOM. MED, GEN&INTL is the abbreviation for medicine, general & internal.

Based on these dominant topical clusters in the collection of articles, further specific topics were obtained in layer 2, (Figure 5). For instance, articles in the "end, death and life" category were further re-grouped into sub-category topics including "death", "end", "quality", "ethics" and "communication" in node 1.1. Articles in a number of nodes of layer 2 (that is, nodes 1.4, 3.3, 3.4, 4.1, 5.2, and 6.3) were further re-grouped into more specific subcategories in layer 3, as shown in Figure 6. And articles in node 3.4.2 of layer 3 was further re-grouped into more specific subcategories in layer 4, as shown in Figure 7.

4   Conclusions

To sum up, the study shows that the variety of research appeared to be scattered across a wide range of subject areas. However, the GHSOM tool had all of the benefit of SOM, in providing a map from a higher dimensional input space to a lower dimensional map space, as well as providing a global orientation of independently growing maps in the individual layers of the hierarchy, which facilitated navigation across branches. The topic map using GHSOM in co-word analysis illustrated the delicate intertwining of subject areas and provided a more explicit illustration of the concepts within each subject area. The result of the topic map may indicate that the subject area of *health care science and service* played an importance role in multidiscipline within the research related to palliative care.

References

1. Cameron, C.S.: Professional Attitudes and Terminal Care. Public Health Rep. 67, 955–959 (1952)
2. Payne, S.A., Turner, J.M.: Research methodologies in palliative care: a bibliometric analysis. Palliat 22, 336–342 (2008)
3. Dittenbach, M., Rauber, A., Merkl, D.: Uncovering hierarchical structure in data using the growing hierarchical self-organizing map. Neurocomputing 48, 199–216 (2002)
4. Rauber, A., Merkl, D., Dittenbach, M.: The growing hierarchical self-organizing map: exploratory analysis of high-dimensional data. IEEE Transactions on Neural Networks 13, 1331–1341 (2002)
5. Campanario, J.: Using neural networks to study networks of scientific journals. Scientometrics 33, 23–40 (1995)
6. Kohonen, T.: Self-organized formation of topologically correct feature maps. Biological cybernetics 43, 59–69 (1982)
7. Kohonen, T., Kaski, S., Lagus, K., Salojarvi, J., Honkela, J., Paatero, V., Saarela, A.: Self organization of a massive document collection. IEEE Transactions on Neural Networks 11, 574–585 (2000)
8. Noyons, E., van Raan, A.: Monitoring scientific developments from a dynamic perspective: self-organized structuring to map neural network research. Journal of the American Society for Information Science 49, 68–81 (1998)
9. Rauber, A., Merkl, D., Dittenbach, M.: The growing hierarchical self-organizing map: exploratory analysis of high-dimensional data. IEEE Transactions on Neural Networks 13, 1331 (2002)

10. Shih, J., Chang, Y., Chen, W.: Using GHSOM to construct legal maps for Taiwan's securities and futures markets. Expert Systems with Applications 34, 850–858 (2008)
11. Li, S.T., Chang, W.C.: Design And Evaluation Of A Layered Thematic Knowledge Map System. Journal of Computer Information Systems 49 (2009)
12. Wolfram, D.: Applied informetrics for information retrieval research. Greenwood Publishing Group, Westport (2003)
13. Salton, G.: Automatic text processing: the transformation, analysis, and retrieval of information by computer. Addison-Wesley, Reading (1989)

An Approach to Feature Selection Based on Ant Colony Optimization and Rough Set

Junyun Wu, Taorong Qiu, Lu Wang, and Haiquan Huang

Department of Computer, Nanchang University, Nanchang, Jiangxi 330031, China
taorongqiu@163.com

Abstract. Feature selection plays an important role in many fields. This paper proposes a method for feature selection which combined the rough set method and ant colony optimization algorithm. The algorithm used the attribute dependence and the attribute importance as the inspiration factor which applied to the transfer rules. For further, the quality of classification based on rough set method and the length of the feature subset were used to build the pheromone update strategy. Through the test of data set, results show that the proposed method is feasible.

Keywords: Feature selection; Ant colony optimization algorithm; Rough set.

1 Introduction

Feature selection is extensive and it spreads throughout many fields, including data mining, pattern recognition, machine learning and signal processing .As a result of the data sets with a high dimensional space, feature selection is particularly necessary[1,2]. Currently, many researchers have studied a number of feature selection methods. These feature selection methods can be divided into global search strategy, random search strategy and heuristic search strategies[3-6]. The "branch and bound" [7] approach used global search strategy can be get the relatively optimal feature subset. However, with the data set increases, the algorithm efficiency will decrease. The random search strategy combined feature selection with simulated annealing algorithm, tabu search algorithm and genetic algorithm[8] while basis with probabilistic reasoning and sampling. In the random search strategy, the evaluation of the characteristics importance can be statistical scores of the characteristics or the contribution to the classifier[9]. Heuristic search strategy of feature selection methods commonly include forward selection and backward selection. Forward selection method can be called greedy method[10].

Ant colony algorithm is a heuristic optimization algorithm[11]. It has advantages such as strong robustness, good distributed compute system, easy to combine with other methods. This paper proposed a method for feature selection which combined the rough set method and ant colony optimization algorithm. The algorithm used the attribute dependence and the attribute importance as the inspiration factor which applied to the transfer rules. For further, the quality of classification based on rough set method and the length of the feature subset are used to build the pheromone update strategy.

R. Chen (Ed.): ICICIS 2011, Part I, CCIS 134, pp. 466–471, 2011.

2 Feature Selection Algorithm Based on Ant Colony Optimization Method and Rough Set

2.1 Algorithm Description

The main steps of proposed feature selection algorithm are as follows:

Input: dataset $T = (U, A, V, f)$ and the parameters of the algorithm.

Output: feature subset CS(Characters-Set).

(1) Initialization

• Determine the maximum of allowed iterations $Wmax$; let candidate feature subset H=C;
• Calculate the relative core (condition attribute to the decision attribute) and add the core attributes into the current feature subset;
• The concentration of pheromone on each feature node at the initial moment is denoted by $\tau_i(0) = \tau_0$. In the feature selection problem, the concentration of pheromone on node i is attribute significance $\sigma_{CD}(i)$.

(2) Solution generation and evaluation

• Assign any ant randomly to one feature and visiting features, each ant builds solutions completely. For the nuclear property, ants put them into the feature subset automatically.
• Sort selected subsets according to the evaluation function. Then, select the best subset.

(3) Check the stop criterion

Exit, if the number of iterations is more than the maximum allowed iteration and the feature subset have been found out, otherwise continue.

(4) Pheromone updating

Update the pheromone concentration on each node. Here the attribute dependency based on rough set method and the length of the feature subset are used to construct the pheromone update strategy.

(5) Generation of new ants

In this step previous ants are removed and new ants are generated. Go to (2).

(6) Output feature subset CS(Characters-Set).

2.2 State Transition Rule

Here the algorithm uses rough set dependency and attributes significance to construct the transition rule. That is, the probability that ant k will move from feature i to feature j in its solution at time step t:

$$P_{ij}^k(t) = \begin{cases} \dfrac{\alpha * \tau_j(t) + (1-\alpha) * \gamma_{ij}(t)}{\displaystyle\sum_{m \in H}(\alpha * \tau_m(t) + (1-\alpha) * \gamma_m(t))} & if \quad j \in H \\ \\ 0 & otherwise \end{cases} \tag{1}$$

Where H is the current feature subset; $\tau_j(t)$ and $\gamma_{ij}(t)$ are respectively the pheromone value on node j and the dependency between i and j; α is a parameter that determine the relative importance of the pheromone value and the dependency.

2.3 Pheromone Update Rule

After all ants have completed their solutions, the addition of new pheromone by ants and pheromone evaporation are implemented by the following rule applied to all the nodes:

$$\tau_i(t+1) = (1-\xi)\ \tau_i(t) + \xi * \sum_{k=1}^{n}\Delta\tau_i(t) \tag{2}$$

where $\xi \in (0,1)$ is the pheromone trail decay coefficient. The main role of pheromone evaporation is to avoid stagnation. Therefore, the presence of ξ, not only can improve the iterative process of searching the optimal solution, but also effectively expand the search space.

When the colony complete one iteration, each ant k deposits a quantity of pheromone, on each node that it has used according to Eq.(3):

$$\Delta\tau_i^k(t) = 1/(\theta * L(S)_t^k + \eta * (\gamma(S)_t^k)^{-1}) \tag{3}$$

Where $L(S)_t^k$ represent the length of feature subset searched by ant k at t moment; $\gamma(S)_t^k$ represent the dependency between the feature subset and decision attribute set. θ and η are two parameters that control the relative weight of length and dependency of feature subset.

From Eq.(3) we can see that in the case of θ and η value determined, $L(S)_t^k$ smaller and $\gamma(S)_t^k$ greater, the increment of pheromone is also greater. The probability of choice for these nodes is greater. This formula can not only get a shorter feature subset, but also a greater dependence. On the other hand, this formula means that the dependence and feature subset length have different significance for feature selection task.

2.4 Evaluation Criteria Based on the Dependency and the Length of the Feature Subset

The evaluation criteria plays an important role in the algorithm based on ACO and RS. It is denoted as follows:

$$\varepsilon\ (\ S) = n\ /(\ \theta * L(S) + \eta * (\gamma(S))^{-1})\qquad(4)$$

where n is the number of condition attributes in the data set; $L(S)$ is the length of the feature subset and $\gamma(\ S\ )$ is the dependency between the feature subset and decision attribute set. θ and η are two parameters that control the relative weight of length and dependency of feature subset, can be called weight parameters. From the definition of the function, when θ and η value determined, with $L(S)$ smaller and $\gamma(\ S\ )$ greater, the function value is greater. Therefore, the shorter and greater dependency subset can be searched by ants.

3 Experimental Design and Results Analysis

3.1 Dataset

7 data sets form UCI and Internet have been selected to validate the effectiveness of the algorithm. Table 1 shows the description of data sets.

Table 1. Description of data sets

NO.	Name	Dimensional number	Sample number	Source
1	Weather	4	14	Internet
2	Car1	7	20	Internet
3	Car2	9	21	Internet
4	Vote	16	83	UCI
5	Zoo	16	72	UCI
6	Soybean	35	114	UCI
7	Splice	60	83	UCI

3.2 Experimental Methods

Experimental conditions for hardware is Intel(R) Core(TM)2 Duo CPU 1.80GHz, 160G hard disk, 1G memory. The experiment has been executed on WindowsXP, VC6.0 experimental platform. The three feature selection algorithm including feature selection algorithm based on ACO[14-17], feature selection algorithm based on RS[10,18] and the proposed algorithm in this paper have been applied to test and compare on the 7 data sets. The experimental results or comparison includes two indexes: one is the length of feature subset and the other is the precision of feature subset which is according to the evaluation function.

In the feature selection algorithm based on ACO, the optimal combination parameter has been applied, they were set as $\rho = 0.5$, $\alpha = 3$, $\beta = 1$ and the ant population is 1.5 times of the number of attributes. In this paper, the parameters were set as $\theta = 0.2$, $\eta = 0.8$, $\rho = 0.5$ and the ant population is 1.5 times of the number of attributes.

3.3 Experimental Results

In order to express clearly, the feature selection algorithm based on ACO, the feature selection algorithm based on RS and the proposed algorithm in this paper were respectively called algorithm1,algorithm2 and algorithm3.The experimental results are the average of algorithm iteration for ten times. Test results shown in table 2:

Table 2. Test results for three methods in different data sets

NO.	Algorithm1		Algorithm2		Algorithm3	
	L(S)	ε(S)	L(S)	ε(S)	L(S)	ε(S)
1	4	2.5	3	2.85714	3	2.85714
2	6	3.18182	3	2.16867	2	5.0
3	4	4.39024	7	3.75	4	4.6875
4	8	6.3755	6	8.0	3	9.16996
5	6	8.0	9	6.15385	1	8.4472
6	7	17.3759	10	12.4365	6	16.16745
7	6	30.0	6	30.0	5	35.428

According to the results of the experiment can be further analyzed. For dataset1, algorithm1 and algorithm3 get a same feature subset on length and accuracy. The reason is the core computing in the two kinds of methods. That is feature subset must include the core attribute set. For dataset2, algorithm2 and algorithm3 get a subsets which have the same length, but the accuracy of the subsets different. This is because algorithm3 considered the influence of attribute dependence on feature subsets quality. Besides, in pheromone updating strategy, the ants were guided by the quality of feature subsets. In a word, through the experiment test, we can conclude that whether the ants can obtain the optimal and shorter subset depends on the characteristics of the data sets. For example, since dataSet5, dataSet6, dataSet7 are core-less, so the difference of feature subset length and accuracy between algorithm1 and algorithm3 is not obvious. In view of this, the core computing is very important in the task of feature selection.

4 Conclusion

A new feature selection algorithm based on ACO and RS have been proposed in this paper. The method combined attribute significance and dependency effectively to construct state transition rules, which improved the efficiency of ant colony searching. In addition, in order to get the optimal feature subset, attribute dependency based on rough set method and the length of the feature subset are used to construct the pheromone update strategy. The results based on the test show that the proposed method is feasible. However the algorithm will decrease the efficiency with the data set size increases. Therefore, searching the optimal minimum feature set in large data sets and incomplete data sets is the main contents of the future work.

References

1. Liu, H., Motoda, H.: Feature Selection for Knowledge Discovery and Data Mining. Kluwer Academic Publishers, Dordrecht (1998)
2. Guyon, I., Elisseeff, A.: An Introduction to Variable and Feature Selection. Journal of Machine Learning Research 3, 1157–1182 (2003)
3. Kudo, M., Sklansky, J.: Comparison of Algorithms that Select Features for Pattern Classifiers. Pattern Recognition 33(1), 25–41 (2000)
4. Sun, Z.H., Bebis, G., Miller, R.: Obieet Deteetion Using Feature Subset Selection. Pattern Recognition 37(11), 2165–2176 (2004)
5. Jain, A.K., Duin, R.D.W., Mao, J.C.: Statistical Pattern Recognition: A Review. IEEE Transaction Pattern Analysis and Machine Intelligence 22(1), 4–37 (2000)
6. Kudo, M., Sklansky, J.: Comparison of Algorithms That Select Features for Pattern Classifiers. Pattern Reeognition 33(l), 25–41 (2000)
7. Chen, X.W.: An Improved Branch and Bound Algorithm for Feature Selection. Pattern Recognition Letters 24(12), 1925–1933 (2003)
8. Wang, L.: Intelligent optimization algorithms and applications. Tsinghua university press, Beijing (2004)
9. Wu, B.L., Abbott, T., Fishman, D., et al.: Comparison of Statistical Methods for Classification of ovarian Cancer Using Mass Spectrometry Data. Bioin for Maties 19(13), 1636–1643 (2003)
10. Swiniarski, R.W., Skowron, A.: Rough Set Methods in Feature Selection and Recognition. Pattern Recognition Letters 24(6), 833–849 (2003)
11. Dorigo, M., Maniezzo, V., Coloni, A.: Ant System: Optimization by a Colony of Cooperating Agents. IEEE transactions on SMC 26(1), 8–41 (1996)
12. Zhang, W.X., Wu, W.Z., Liang, J.Y.: Rough Set Theory and Methods. Science Press, Beijing (2001)
13. Liu, Q.: Rough sets and Rough Reasoning. Science Press, Beijing (2005)
14. Wang, Y., Xie, J.Y.: An Adaptive Ant Colony Algorithm and the Simulation. Journal of system simulation 14(1), 31–33 (2002)
15. Uncu, O., Turksen, I.B.: A Novel Feature Selection Approach: Combining Feature Wrappers and Filters. Information Sciences 177(2), 449–466 (2007)
16. Vafaie, H., Imam, I.F.: Feature Selection Methods: Genetic Algorithms vs. Greedy-like Search. In: Proceedings of International Conference on Fuzzy and Intelligent Control Systems (2004)
17. Wei, J.X., Liu, H.: Document Clustering Algorithm Design and Simulation Based on the Genetic Algorithm. Nanjing university journal (Natural sciences) (03), 432–438 (2009)
18. Wang, G.Y., Zhao, J.: Theoretical Study on Attribute Reduction of Rough Set Theory: Comparison of Algebra and Information Views. In: Proceedings of the Third IEEE International Conference on Cognitive Informatics, ICCI 2004 (2004)
19. Qiu, T.R., Liu, O., Huang, H.K.: A Granular Approach to Knowledge Discovery in Relational Databases. Acta Automatica Sinica 35(8), 1071–1079 (2009)

A New Adaptive Deformable Model Using Gradient Vector Flow

Bin Zhao*, Siyuan Cheng, and Xiangwei Zhang

Guangdong University of Technology, Guangzhou, China

Abstract. In this paper we proposed and demonstrated a new approach to adaptive estimate of gradient vector flow (GVF) deformable contour based on B-spline representation. An extension of the GVF deformable model is presented, and the method is based on the improved dynamic GVF force field which can increase the external force's capture range and convergence speed. Then, a specific strategy of adaptive deformable contour knots insertion process, based on fitting accuracy, are proposed, and this approach can automatically add knots in the contour curve according to the reconstruction error analysis. The improved iterative algorithm can reduce the iterative number, and increase fitting accuracy and efficiency. Finally, using computer simulation, the experiments reported in this paper demonstrate an efficient procedure and fine performance of the approach.

Keywords: Deformable model; Gradient Vector Flow; B-spline; finite element.

1 Introduction

This Deformable model, known as snakes, which have been researched and applied extensively in the areas of edge detection, image segmentation, shape modeling, and visual tracking. Snakes were first introduced by Kass [1] in 1987. Deformable model is curve or surface that deform under the influence of internal smoothness and external image forces to delineate object boundary. Compared to local edge based methods, deformable models have the advantage of estimating boundary with smooth curves that bridge over boundary map. The reconstruction object boundary is represented as a parameter curve or surface, and an energy function is associated with the curve. The curve deforms by the internal and external forces, so the problem of reconstruct transform as the energy minimization process. When initialized far away from the object boundary, however, the models may be trapped by spurious edges or high noise. A number of methods have been proposed to improve the snake's performance. The balloon model was introduced by Cohen [2] to enlarge the capture range of the model. Among a variety of deformable model method, the gradient vector flow technique by Xu [3] recently gains a wide attention due to its ability to

---

* This work is supported by the National Natural Science Foundation, China (No. 50775044, 50805025), Provincial Natural Science Foundation of Guangdong (No. 8151009001000040), and the Production, Teaching and Research Integration Project of Guangdong Province (No. 2009B090300044).

R. Chen (Ed.): ICICIS 2011, Part I, CCIS 134, pp. 472–482, 2011.
© Springer-Verlag Berlin Heidelberg 2011

deal with concave regions. GVF deformable model presented a new external force field, which computed as a diffusion of the gradient of an edge map derived from the image as the external force, instead of image gradients.

From the original philosophy of snake, an alternative approach is using a parametric B-spline representation of the deformable contour. Such a formulation of the deformable model allows for the local control and a compact representation. Moreover, this formulation has less number of control parameters and the smoothness requirement has implicitly built into the model. Razdan [4] presented an adaptive interpolation to choose the knot to the B-spline curve fitting, in order to obtain reasonable knot he considered the original data points that reflect the shape information, including arc length and curvature distribution of the known parameterization curve. The data set with noise is more insensitive to the method, but it did not consider the curve approximation error. Li [5] and others proposed the arrangement guideline of knots, and can gain more knots than expected with curvature filtering. Park [6] presented a B-spline approximation method of regular points, which need pre-estimate the number of control points to calculate the curvature of the rough approximation curve of original data points. Finite element solvers are a basic component of simulation applications, they are common in computer graphics and simulations.

In this paper, we proposed a new adaptive approach to enhance the GVF model performance, which consists of the improved dynamic GVF force field and a strategy of automatic deformable contour knots insertion. The structure of this paper is arranged as follows. In section 2, a review of the snake and GVF deformable model are presented, and section 3 introduces the B-snake model. In section 4, an improved adaptive GVF model is proposed. The experimental results are shown in section 5, and this paper concludes in section 6.

2   GVF Deformable Model

In this section, we review the mathematic formulation of classical snakes and GVF deformable model, and the advantages and weakness of each method is described, too.

2.1 Snakes

The deformable models also called snakes, first proposed by Kass [1]. The snakes are elastic curves or surfaces defined within an image that can move through the image domain to minimize a specified energy function. A classical 2D snake is a curve $v(s) = (x(s), y(s))$, where $s \in (0,1)$ is the independent variable of Fourier transform formal which describe the model boundary, and $x(s)$ and $y(s)$ are coordinates of control points. The energy function is usually formed by internal and external forces as:

$$E_{energy} = E_{\text{int}\,er}(v(s)) + E_{ext}(v(s)) \tag{1}$$

The internal energy function $E_{int\,er}$ deals with intrinsic properties of the deformable model, and tends to elastically hold the curve together and to keep it from bending too much. Kass gave a parametric representation of the internal energy function that defined as:

$$E_{int} = \frac{1}{2} \int_0^1 \left(\alpha(s)|v'(s)|^2 + \beta(s)|v''(s)|^2 \right) ds \tag{2}$$

where $\alpha(s)$ and $\beta(s)$ are weighting parameters that control the tension and rigidity of the contour, respectively. The first order derivative $v'(s)$ discourages stretching and makes the model behave like an elastic string. While the second order derivative $v''(s)$ discourages bending and makes the model behave like a rigid rod. We can control the deformable contour's tension and rigidity by the coefficients $\alpha(s)$ and $\beta(s)$.

The external energy function E_{ext} intends to guide the contour towards the image edge. Typically, the external forces is derived from the image so that it takes on smaller values at the feature of interest such as boundaries. The external energy is defined by:

$$E_{ext} = -\left| \nabla[G_\sigma(x, y) * I(x, y)] \right|^2 \tag{3}$$

where $G_\sigma(x, y)$ is a two-dimensional Gaussian function which standard deviation σ, $I(x, y)$ represents the image.

Using variation calculus and Euler-Lagrange differential equation, (1) can be solved and the solution defined as the force balance (4).

$$\alpha X^{''} - \beta X^{'''} - \nabla E_{ext}(X) = 0 \tag{4}$$

where $F_{int} = \alpha X^{''} - \beta X^{'''}$ and $F_{ext} = -\nabla E_{ext}(X)$ comprise the component of a force balance equation such that

$$F_{int} + F_{ext} = 0 \tag{5}$$

The internal force F_{int} discourages stretching bending while the external potential force F_{ext} drives the deformable contour towards the desired image boundary. (4) is solved by making the deformable contour dynamic by treating X as a function of time t as follows:

$$X_t(s,t) = \alpha X^{''}(s,t) - \beta X^{'''}(s,t) - \nabla E_{ext} \tag{6}$$

By discretizing the equation and solving the discrete system iteratively, the solution to (6) can be obtained [7]. When $X(s,t)$ stabilizes, the solution of (4) is achieved.

Classical snakes suffer from three intrinsic drawbacks. The original contour is very sensitive to parameters and the algorithm is mostly dependent of the initial position; capture range is also limited. Finally, boundary concavities always leave the contour split across the boundary.

2.2 GVF Deformable Model

Xu and Prince [3] and [8] present a new theory of external forces for deformable contour models that called gradient vector flow (GVF). The gradient vector flow is an external force field, which obtained by solving a vector diffusion equation that diffuses the gradient vector of a gray-level edge map computed from the image without blurring the edges. The idea of the diffusion equation is taken from physics. This model produces a field with strong forces near the edges, but also extending the gradient map farther into homogeneous regions using a computational diffusion process, which is also responsible for creating vectors that point into boundary concavities.

The gradient vector flow field is defined as the vector field $V(x, y) = [u(x, y), v(x, y)]$ that minimizes the energy function

$$\varepsilon = \iint (\mu(u_x^2 + u_y^2 + v_x^2 + v_y^2) + |\nabla f|^2 |\mathbf{V} - \nabla f|^2) dx dy \tag{7}$$

where $f = |\nabla G_\sigma(x, y) * I(x, y)|$ is the edge map function which is derived by using an edge detector on the original image convoluted with a Gaussian kernel, u and v are two functions corresponding to s, μ is a regularization parameter governing the trade-off between the first term and the second term in the integrand. Adjusting the parameter μ can make V approximately equal to the greater gradient of the edge map by minimizing energy functional, and the greater the noise, the greater μ.

Using the calculus of variations, the GVF field can be obtained by solving the corresponding Euler-Lagrange equations. Since the GVF is not a deterministic expression, it cannot be solved from the energy function. But the deformable contour can be optimized by the condition of balance of the force instead. Similar to (4), the force balance equation of GVF model can be expressed as

$$\alpha X'' - \beta X''' + \chi V = 0 \tag{8}$$

where χ is a proportional coefficient. This variational formulation follows a standard principle, in particular, when the gradient of edge map is large, the second term dominates the integral and it keeps the external force field nearly equal to the gradient. However, it keeps the field to be slowly varying in homogeneous regions where the gradient of the edge map is very small. In addition, when the gradient of the edge map $|\nabla f|$ is small, the energy is dominated by the sum of the squares of the partial derivatives of the vector field, resulting a large coverage field. The effect of this variational formulation is that the result is made smooth when there is no data, and the total energy is minimized when $V = \nabla f$.

The larger capture range and concavity tracking ability of GVF model are attributed to the diffusion equation which can diffuse the region of influence of edge gradient. The GVF deformable contour is appropriated for the complex convex-concave boundary approximation, and the force field is more regular than the conservative force. Furthermore, the GVF deformable contour is insensitive to the initialization of the contour, and has better robustness of the absolute value of gradient, even the noise.

3   The Finite Element Equation of GVF Model

Cohen firstly implemented the finite element method for deformable model [9]. Finite element analysis is a numerical method for solving partial differential equations, with better numerical stability and less computational complexity, there-fore, FEM is widely used in science and engineering. In this paper, we restrict our attention to the common case of cubic uniform B-spine curves, and propose a finite element method to solve the energy function problems of GVF deformable contour presented by B-spline curves.

3.1   Cubic B-Spline Contour

Spline curve is a widely used function approximation tool, and the spline representations of deformable contour were addressed in [10] and [11]. The B-spline deformable contour is described as the linear combination of the B-spline basis functions and control points, and each segment of B-spline curve is one unit of finite element mesh, which is called line unit. For the cubic uniform B-spline curve, every unit can be approximated by four control points in sequence as shown in Fig. 1.

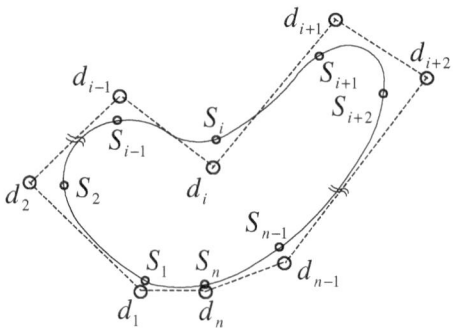

Fig. 1. Close cubic B-spline curve

Each curve segment is a linear combination of four polynomials. The cubic B-spline curve segment $e_i(s)$ is defined as follows:

$$e_i(s) = N_s \cdot d_s \tag{9}$$

where the parameter s is normalized between 0 and 1 , and $d_s = [d_i \quad d_{i+1} \quad d_{i+2} \quad d_{i+3}]^T$ $(i = 0, \cdots n)$ are control points of contour, $N_s = [B_{0,3}(s) \quad B_{1,3}(s) \quad B_{2,3}(s) \quad B_{3,3}(s)]$ are function matrixes of the B-spline deformable contour sequence. Then the B-spline deformable contour (B-snake) can be presented by

$$X(s) = \sum_i e_i(s) \tag{10}$$

where $B_{i,3}(s)$ are 3th degree B-spline basis functions as follow:

$$
\begin{cases}
B_{0,3}(s) = \dfrac{1}{6}(1-s)^3 , \\[2mm]
B_{1,3}(s) = \dfrac{1}{6}(3s^3 - 6s^2 + 4) , \\[2mm]
B_{2,3}(s) = \dfrac{1}{6}(-3s^3 + 3s^2 + 3s + 1) , \\[2mm]
B_{3,3}(s) = \dfrac{1}{6}s^3 ,
\end{cases} \tag{11}
$$

Gradient vector flow force is selected as the external force of B-spline deformable model, and GVF force field V is defines as:

$$
V = (u(x_0, y_0), v(x_0, y_0)), \cdots, (u(x_{n-1}, y_{n-1}), v(x_{n-1}, y_{n-1})) \tag{12}
$$

where $(x_0, y_0), \cdots, (x_{n-1}, y_{n-1})$ are the knot points in the deformable contour.

3.2 Finite Element Equation

In order to obtain the finite element equation of the deformable curve we calculate the energy deformation of each element, the element stiffness matrix K_s is given as follows:

$$
K_s = \int_0^1 (\alpha \frac{\partial N_s^T}{\partial s} \frac{\partial N}{\partial s} + \beta \frac{\partial^2 N_s^T}{\partial s^2} \frac{\partial^2 N_s}{\partial s^2}) ds \tag{13}
$$

And the element load vector F_s is given by:

$$
F_s = \int_0^1 N_s^T E_{ext}(e_i) \, ds \tag{14}
$$

The finite element equation of the deformable curve can be formulated by assembling the sequences of B-spline curve that defined as:

$$
KP = V \tag{15}
$$

where K is global stiffness matrix, P is global node vector, V is the external force vector. The iterative function can be obtained by the method of [9] and [12], using finite difference to discretize the equation with time t as follows:

$$
x^{t+1} = x^t + \Delta t F_{x^t} \tag{16}
$$

where Δt is the time step. For solving the equation don't need matrix inversion as well as the linear system becomes an iterative step for vector, therefore the convergence speed can be improved greatly. When the difference between two successive iterations is sufficiently small the iterative process terminates.

4   Adaptive Deformable Model

Processing the gradient mapping using the diffusion equation as the external energy is to use the diffusion effect of GVF field in homogeneous region. But the smoothness of the boundary is not the feature what we expected. In the image boundary, we hoped that make full use of gradient itself characteristic. To deal with these problems we developed an adaptive GVF deformable model. This improved method is presented in detail as follows.

4.1   Improved GVF

Classical edge map has three basic properties: The gradient of an edge map ∇f has vectors point toward the image contour which extend perpendicular to the edges; the gradient vectors have magnitudes only in the immediate vicinity of edges and in homogeneous regions ∇f is nearly equal to zero. By calculating the diffusion equation, the gradient mapping can be extend to the region far away from the boundary and homogeneous region, and obtain the vectors which point toward the concavity bottom inside the boundary, too. However, the smoothness of the boundary is not what we expected features. Near the edge contour, we hope to have full use of the characteristic of gradient itself. Based on the above analysis, a dynamic GVF force is introduced to provide an evolution mechanism as well as all the characteristics owned by the original GVF force field. The improved GVF force is inspired by the property of the GVF field, combining the model force field with the feature of the image region, and the proposed of external force can be expressed as:

$$F_{ext} = \varphi(V + kn(s)) + \gamma \nabla f \qquad (17)$$

where $\varphi = | e - \gamma |$, and $\gamma = e^{\frac{\nabla f}{\|\nabla f\|}}$. The control coefficients of external force is defined as dynamically change according to the characteristic of target image, γ can enhance the effort of edge map gradient near the image boundary; and φ ensures that the diffusion gradient vector flow V could be more effective in the region far away from the edge. In addition, the pressure force $kn(s)$ is added to the external force of model to reduce the fitting time in homogeneous region. The Fig.2 shows the corresponding gradient vector flow field.

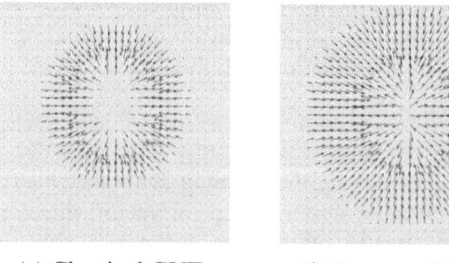

(a) Classical GVF   (b) Improved GVF

Fig. 2. A ellipse corresponding GVF field

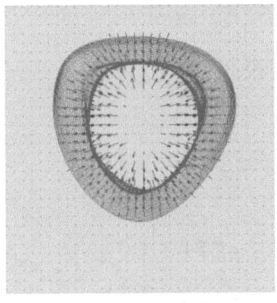 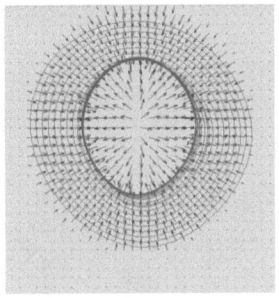

(a) Iteration 150 (GVF)   (b) Iteration 25(improved GVF)

Fig. 3. Comparison of the GVF and the improved GVF

To some extent the improved GVF is similar to the classical GVF. When the initial contour is far away from the image boundary, the GVF diffusion force field dominates the external force of model, with the performance of smooth diffusion. While the deformable contour moves to image boundary nearby, the external force switches to be dominated by the edge gradient. Fig. 3 demonstrates the performance of the improved GVF scheme compared to the classical GVF method. Fig. 3 (a) illustrates the iteration 150 with GVF, and Fig. 3 (b) is iteration 25 with improved GVF. It can be easily observed that the capture range of external force is increased, as well as the convergence speed.

4.2 Adaptive B-Spline Approach

Using the B-spline deformable model method to reconstruct the image contours or discrete scan data, one of the key factors to obtain accurate reconstruction contour is to control the B-spline curve fitting error. Based on the improved GVF deformable model, this paper presents a B-spline deformable contour fitting method with adaptive error control.

Firstly, the control points of deformable contour are deter-mined appropriately around the target boundary manually in the image, and the number and location of control points are in accordance with the external GVF force field and the general trend of image boundary. Supposes $d_i (i = 1, \cdots n)$ are control points determined, and the initial deformable contour is the cubic B-spline curve constituted by these n control points. Then compute the deformation process of the model which approximating with the effort of internal energy and external energy, and the deformable contour moves to the target boundary gradually. After the iterative calculation of GVF deformable has ended, carries on the fitting accuracy analysis. If the fitting error can not satisfy the permitted range, the deformable model will automatically insert a new knot in the curve segment to refine the knots vector, and calculate the new control point strategy.

Suppose that the knot S_j is expected to insert between S_i and S_{i+1}. The new control points sequence are $d = (d_0, \cdots, d_i, d_j, d_{i+1}, \cdots, d_n)$, and the control point d_j is determined by:

$$d_j = (1-\alpha_j)d_i + \alpha_j d_{i+1} \qquad (18)$$

where

$$\alpha_j = \begin{cases} 1 & j \leq i-1 \\ \dfrac{S_t + 2 + (j-i)}{3} & i \leq j \leq i+2 \\ 0 & j \geq i+3 \end{cases} \qquad (19)$$

Then continue the deformable contour curve fitting again, and the iterative calculation is repeated until the whole contour curve can satisfy the required precision.

5 Experiments and Results

In validating the performance of the proposed method, we applied it on the reconstruction of aircraft model image. In the experiment, the model parameters were chosen as: $\alpha = 0.5$, $\beta = 0.4$, $\chi = 0.6$, $k = 0.2$ and iteration number is 150. Fig. 4(a) shows the initial location and the primary deformation result, and (b) is the local contour with the larger fitting error. Fig. 5(a) demonstrates how to insert knots in local contour curves with larger fitting error, and to continue the fitting iteration again with new knots strategy. Repeating the iteration progress until the whole deformable contour satisfies the fitting accuracy. Fig. 5(b) shows the final result.

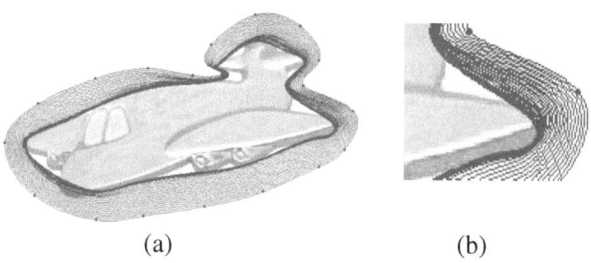

(a)   (b)

Fig. 4. The initial contour fitting result

From the figures it can be seen that the new algorithm enhance the GVF model performance. The model defines some control points to obtain the primary deformable contour, then according to the error analysis, the new knots are automatically inserted only in the larger error section of contour curve. The adaptive solver reduces the often high computational cost of simulations, and the fitting precision is also improved by the adaptive knots insertion.

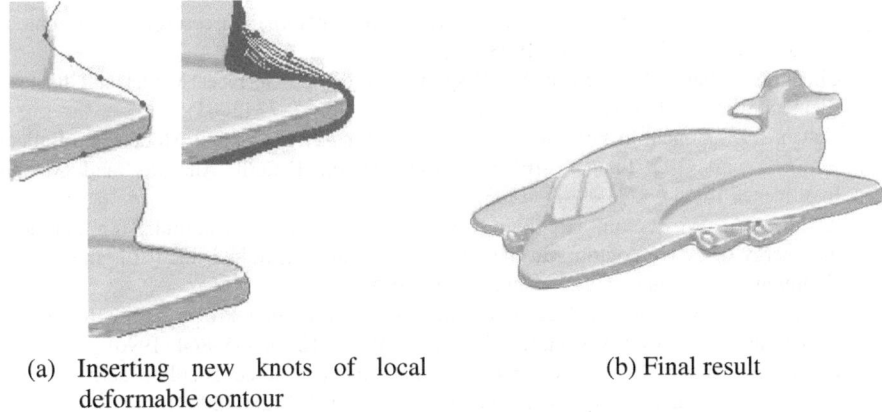

(a) Inserting new knots of local
    deformable contour

(b) Final result

Fig. 5. Adaptive refinement of deformable contour

6 Conclusions

In this paper, we have presented a new method using gradient vector flow for image approximation. An improved dynamic GVF force field and a strategy of adaptive deformable contour knots insertion have been introduced. Solving the extremum of energy functional of the B-spline GVF model with finite element method by iteration, and calculating the functional equation by iterative method until the approximation of initial contour satisfies the given precision. The experiment has shown that the proposed method can achieve accurate and efficient approximation, and also be of great value in reducing the often high computational cost of simulations.

In future work we intend to test this method comprehensively, the use of Non-uniform rational B-spline could be an interesting area, and we hope that the proposed strategy will be more powerful and robust in real applications.

References

1. Kass, M., Witkin, A.T., Terzopoulos, D.: Snakes, Active contour models. International Journal of computer vision 1(4), 321–331 (1988)
2. Cohen, L.D.: On Active Contour Models and Balloons. CVGIP: Image Understanding, vol 53(2), 211–218 (1991)
3. Xu, C., Prince, J.L.: Snakes, shapes, and gradient vector flow. IEEE Trans. On Image Processing 7, 359–369 (1998)
4. Razdan, A., Mongkolnam, P., Farin, G.: Reverse Engineering Using a Subdivision Surface Scheme, http://3dk.asu.edu/archives/publiction/
5. Li, H., Ching, Y.S., Tien, D.B., Ping, Z.: Realization of handwritten numerical recognition based on constant curvature character. Tuxiangshibie Yu Zidonghua 2(3), 152–154 (2005)
6. Jeong, J., Kim, K., Park, H., et al.: B-Spline surface approximation to cross-sections using distance maps. International Journal, Advanced Manufacturing Technology 15, 876–885 (1999)

7. Xu, C., Jerry, L.: Generalized gradient vector flow external forces for active contours. Signal Processing 77, 131–139 (1998)
8. Cheng, S., Zhang, X.: Deformable B-spline Curves and Surfaces Model and Its Finite Element Solution. Journal of Chongqing University 26, 75–77 (2003)
9. Cohen, L.D., Cohen, I.: Finite-Element Methods for Active Contour Models and Balloons for 2-D and 3-D Images. IEEE Transaction on Pattern Analysis and Machine Intelligence 15(11), 1131–1147 (1993)
10. Amini, A.A., Weymouth, T.E., Jain, R.C.: Using dynamic programming for minimizing the energy of active contours in the presence of hard constraints. In: IEEE International Conference on Computer Vision, pp. 95–99 (1988)
11. Amini, A.A., Weymouth, T.E., Jain, R.C.: Using Dynamic Programming for Solving Variational Problems in Vision. IEEE Trans. on PAMI 12(9), 855–864 (1990)
12. Cheng, S., Zhang, X., Jin, C.: Finite element method based B-spline active contour. Journal of information and computational science 1(2), 275–280 (2004)
13. Luo, S.: Automated Medical Image Segmentation Using a New Deformable Surface Model. International Journal of Computer Science and Network Security 6(5), 109–115 (2006)

A Comparative Study of Different Distances for Similarity Estimation

Zhong Li, Qiaolin Ding, and Weihua Zhang

School of Electrical and Electronic Engineering, North China Electric Power University
071003 Baoding, Hebei, China
ncepulz@126.com

Abstract. Distance metric is widely used in similarity estimation. The smaller the distance is, the greater the similarity is. The Minkowski distance metric are usually chosen as the similarity measure in the conventional similarity metrics. In this paper, the most popular Euclidean and Manhattan distance, and the morphology similarity distance we have proposed are compared as similarity estimation measure distance. We cluster thirty random datasets using the fuzzy c-mean algorithm, recognize the Iris data from the UCI repository, and the experiment results are compared and analyzed.

Keywords: Similarity Estimation, Distance, Shape Similarity.

1 Introduction

Similarity has been a research topic in the field of psychology for decades. Tversky describes the similarity concept as "an organizing principle by which individuals classify objects, form concepts, and make generalizations"[1]. Similarity is fundamental to the definition of many science areas, and a measure of the similarity between two vectors drawn from the same feature space is essential to most research works.

Usually, the word "similarity" means that the value of s(x, x') is large when x and x' are two similar vectors (or samples, or patterns, or instances), the value of s(x, x') is small when x and x' are not similar. Very often a certain measure of dissimilarity is used instead of a similarity measure. A dissimilarity measure is denoted by d(x, x'), $\forall$ x, x'$\in$X. Dissimilarity is frequently called a distance, and the smaller the distance is, the greater the similarity is. The popular similarity measures maybe the Manhattan and Euclidean distances.

Traditionally, a multidimensional vector is treated as a point of the feature space, we calculate the distance between the points to measure the similarity. In our previous works[2], vectors were treated as polygons, and based on the characteristic of the difference between vectors, the morphology similarity distance(MSD) was proposed for similarity estimation. In this paper, we shall first illustrate the most used distance measures for similarity estimation and the MSD, then test and analyze these distance

R. Chen (Ed.): ICICIS 2011, Part I, CCIS 134, pp. 483–488, 2011.

measures on thirty random datasets, and the Iris data from the UCI(University of California Irvine) Machine Learning Repository.

2 Distance Measure for Similarity Estimation

For different applications, a number of pertinent distance measures have been proposed and discussed. The most common similarity index is the Minkowski metric[3]. Given N patterns, $x_i = \left(x_{i1}, ..., x_{in} \right)^T$, i=1,2,...,N, the Minkowski metric for measuring the dissimilarity between the jth and the kth patterns is defined by

$$d (j, k) = \left(\sum_{i=1}^{n} \left| x_{ji} - x_{ki} \right|^r \right)^{1/r} .$$ (1)

Where $r \geq 1$. The well known widely used Manhattan distance($r=1$) and the Euclidean distance($r=2$) can be seen as special cases of Minkowski distance. The Manhattan and Euclidean distances have been suggested that it is not appropriate for many problems[4], and finding a suitable distance measure becomes a challenging problem when the underlying distribution is unknown and could be neither Gaussian nor Exponential[5].

The Manhattan and Euclidean distances are computed by the absolute difference of vectors, the characteristic of the differences between the vectors is ignored. We had used polygons but not points to respect the vector[2], explained the relationship of polygons shape similarity and characteristic of the differences between vectors, and proposed the MSD for similarity estimation, and it was defined as

$$d_{MSD} (j,k) = L_2 \times \left(2 - d_{ASD} / L_1 \right) .$$ (2)

Where L_2 is the Euclidean distance, L_1 is the Manhattan distance, and d_{ASD} is the absolute sum of the difference, it is defined by

$$d_{ASD} (j,k) = \left| \sum_{i=1}^{n} \left(x_{ji} - x_{ki} \right) \right| .$$ (3)

3 Random Data FCM Clustering

Fuzzy c-mean algorithm(FCM) is a data clustering technique wherein each data point belongs to a cluster to some degree that is specified by a membership grade. It was originally introduced by Jim Bezdek in 1981[6]. In order to compare and analyze the similarity estimation character of the classical Manhattan distance, the Euclidean distance and the MSD, we do cluster analysis on thirty random datasets using the FCM clustering algorithm with these three different distances separately.

3.1 Test Data

We have thirty random test datasets totally, each dataset has 200 samples and it is produced by a rand function, this rand function generates arrays of random numbers whose elements are uniformly distributed in the interval (0,1). We get each test dataset from the rand function as follows: Dataset = rand (200, 2).

3.2 Test Method

The test parameters of the FCM were set as follows: the stop criterion for the iteration was $\varepsilon = 0.0001$, $m=2$, $c=2$ and 4 separately, and all began with a randomly initialized μ_{ij}, the norm d_{ij}^2 were the Euclidean distance, the Manhattan distance and the MSD separately. So we cluster each test dataset three times and get 180 test results totally. The clustering result pictures of one test dataset are shown in figure 1($c=2$) and figure 2($c=4$).

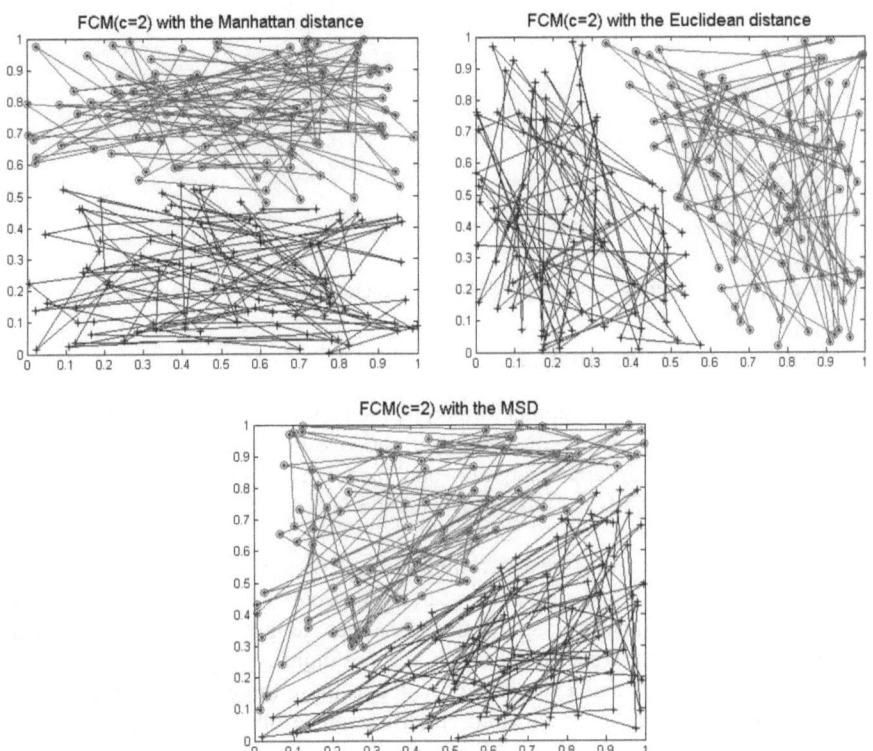

Fig. 1. The clustering results by FCM ($c=2$) of a test dataset with different distance

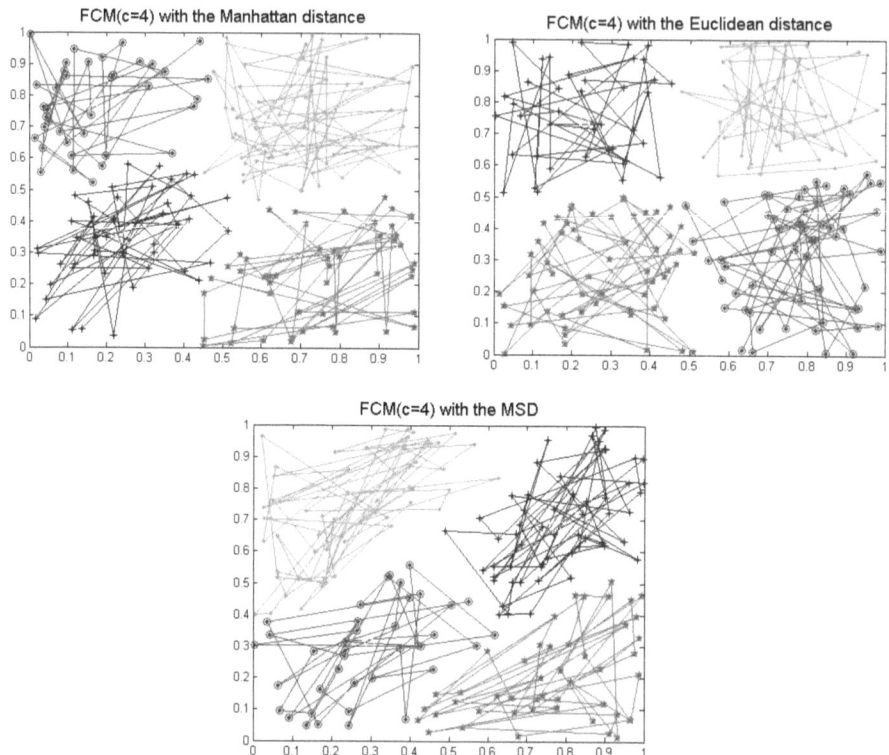

Fig. 2. The clustering results by FCM (*c=4*) of a test dataset with different distance

3.3 Experiment Results Analysis

According to the shape of the points formed by the two or four clusters, we can classify all the experiment results by the shape of the points formed. All graphs can be classified to eight types appreciatively, and named as Type A, Type B, Type C and Type D for the FCM($c=2$), Type E to Type H for the FCM($c=4$), shown as in figure 3.

Look at these graphs, and treat two-dimensional vectors as polygons, it is easy to understand that each point in these graphs respects a rectangle. By the shape similarity, we can classify rectangle into three types: length-bigger rectangle, width-bigger rectangle and square. A closer look at these eight type graphs, it is found that all rectangles in Type D and Type H are divided as these three types appreciatively. It seems that we may get the conclusion: classification result Type D and Type H, the rectangle shape similarity is taken into account.

According the classification method above, we classify all the 180 test results, and list the results in table 1. From table 1, we find that results of the FCM with the Manhattan or Euclidean distance are separated into almost all these types, but for the FCM with the MSD, all the results are only belong to Type D and Type H. Therefore,

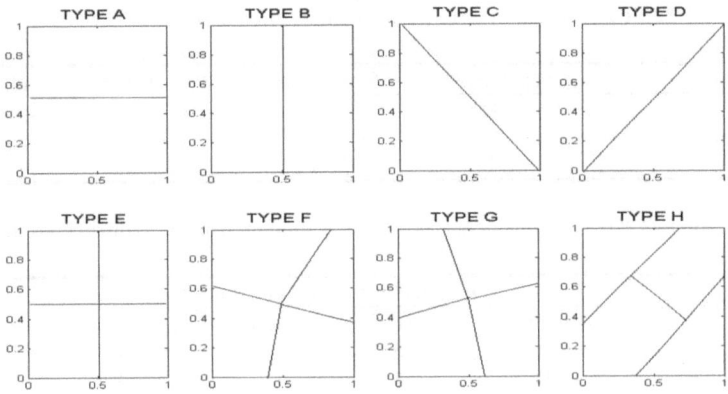

Fig. 3. Eight types of clustering results of FCM ($c=2,4$)

Table 1. The distribution of the FCM ($c=2,4$) results

Distance	Type A	Type B	Type C	Type D	Type E	Type F	Type G	Type H
Manhattan	13	10	4	3	11	9	10	0
Euclidean	5	6	9	10	12	7	11	0
MSD	0	0	0	30	0	0	0	30

these statistical clustering results show that: using the MSD as similarity estimation measurement, the shape similarity is taken into counted.

4 Recognition Test

The recognition experiments on the Iris data set include two steps. First, we calculate the arithmetic mean as the centroid of each type data, then compute the Manhattan distance, the Euclidean distance and the MCD from each sample to these centroids separately, and classify all the Iris data.

The well known Iris dataset contains 3 classes (Setosa, Versicolor and Virginica) of 50 samples each, where each class refers to a type of iris plant. The data have four attributes information: sepal length, sepal width, and petal length, petal width[7]. Clearly, the Iris data respect the size and shape message of three type of iris plant. It has been confirmed that Setosa is linearly separable from the other two, and due to the close similarities between Versicolor and Virginica, they are not linearly separable from each other[8]. We calculate the centroids of the three kinds of iris plants and list it in table 2.

The result of recognition by the different distance to their centroids is recorded in table 3, it illustrates the Setosa can be classified correctly by all the three distances, but the other two kinds iris plant can not classified correctly. For all the Iris data, using the Manhattan distance, the Euclidean and the MCD, the incorrectly recognition number are 11, 11 and 7, error rates are 7.333%, 7.333%, and 4.667% separately.

Table 2. The centroids of the three kinds of plant of the Iris database

Plant type	Sepal length	Sepal width	Petal length	Petal width
Setosa	5.006	3.248	1.462	0.246
Versicolor	5.936	2.77	4.26	1.326
Virginica	6.588	2.974	5.552	2.026

Table 3. The result of recognition by the different distance to their centroids

Distance type	Incorrectly recognition number				Error rate
	Setosa	Versicolor	Virginica	Total	
Manhattan	0	3	8	11	7.333%
Euclidean	0	4	7	11	7.333%
MSD	0	2	5	7	4.667%

5   Conclusions

Homogeneity has same or similar shape is so common in the abstract and in nature, and shape similarity is a very important factor for classification and object recognition. This paper compares the classical Manhattan distance, the Euclidean distance, and the morphology similarity distance by FCM clustering on random datasets and recognition test on the wellknown Iris data. Experiment results indicate that the morphology similarity distance maybe a better shape similarity measurement.

References

1. Tversky, A.: Features of similarity. Psychological Review 84(4), 327–352 (1977)
2. Li, Z., Yuan, J., Zhang, W.: Fuzzy C-Mean Algorithm with Morphology Similarity Distance. In: 6th International Conference on Fuzzy Systems and Knowledge Discovery. IEEE Press, Tianjin (2009)
3. Jain, A.K., Dubes, R.C.: Algorithms for Clustering. Prentice-Hall, Englewood Cliffs (1988)
4. Zakai, M.: General distance criteria. Information Theory, 94–95 (January 1964)
5. Sebe, N., Lew, M.S., Huijsmans, D.P.: Toward improved ranking metrics. Pattern Analysis and Machine Intelligence 22, 1132–1143 (2000)
6. Bezdek, J.C.: Pattern Recognition, C: with Fuzzy Objective Function Algorithms. Plenum, New York (1981)
7. Fisher, R.A.: The use of multiple measurements in taxonomic problems. Annual Eugenics 7, 179–188 (1936)
8. Gates, G.W.: The Reduced Nearest Neighbor Rule. Information Theory, 431–433 (May 1972)

Reliability Analysis for CNC Machine Tool Based on Failure Interaction

Yingzhi Zhang, Rui Zheng, Guixiang Shen, and Bingkun Chen

College of Mechanical Science and Engineering, Jilin University, Changchun, China

Abstract. CNC machine tool is a kind of typical complex system with complicated structure and failure styles. The failure rate of one component in such a complex system is not only influenced by its natural failure, but also by interactive failure of the other components. However, the assumption that all of the components are failure independent was essential of a traditional reliability analysis, which may lead to unacceptable analysis errors. In this paper, a non-fatal shocked reliability model is proposed based on failure interaction. Weibull distribution is commonly used in reliability analysis, so a special case of the reliability model for this is given subsequently, and then applied to analyze the failure data of a certain type of CNC machine tool. The analysis result can illustrate the natural failure rates of mechanical and electrical subsystems, and even show the failure interactions between them.

Keywords: Failure interaction, CNC machine tools, Non-fatal shock, Reliability analysis.

1 Introduction

CNC machine tool is a kind of typical complex system. The complication of its structure and functions make it difficult to find out the failure laws of components. The traditional reliability analysis for the CNC machine tool is mainly based on the assumption that all of its components are failure independent. However, numerous industrial experiences have shown that the assumption of independent failures has been unrealistic and has led to unacceptable analysis errors [1]. Therefore, the dependent failure should be considered when analyzing the reliability of the CNC machine tool.

Cho and Parlar [2] classified the dependencies between components into economic, structural and stochastic ones:

Economic dependence between components implies that performing maintenance on several components jointly costs less money and/or time than the sum of all components separately.

Structural dependence refers to some systems where several components form an integral part. Then maintenance of a failed component implies to maintain the other components in this integral part.

Stochastic dependence implies that the states of some component (e.g., the age, the failure rate or the state of failure) can affect the states of the others.

R. Chen (Ed.): ICICIS 2011, Part I, CCIS 134, pp. 489–496, 2011.

In these three categories of independencies, stochastic dependence is the chief one that applied in reliability analysis. Meanwhile, among different cases of stochastic dependence, the failure interaction is the most high-frequency one. The failure interaction means that the failure of one component can affect or modify one or more of the remaining components of the system [3]. The failure interaction can be divided into three kinds:

[1] Type I failure interaction: the failure of a component can induce a failure of other component with probability p, and has no effect on the other component with probability $1-p$. Then, one component has two types of failure. One is natural, and the other is induced. Murthy and Nguyen [4] first proposed such a type of failure interaction for a two-component system. Murthy and Nguyen [5] extends Type I failure interaction to multi-component system. Murthy and Wilson [6] discussed the estimation for Type I failure interaction model under different data structures. Jhang and Sheu [7] extended the fixed probability in Murthy and Nguyen [5] to be a probability function of time.

[2] Failure rate interaction: The failure of one component in multi-component will act an interior shock to affect or modify the failure rates of the other components. Murthy and Nguyen [4] proposed a special type of failure rate interaction which is named as Type II failure interaction. Yong Sun and Lin Ma [8] developed an analytical model based on failure rate interaction.

[3] Shock damage interaction: When component 1 fails, it causes a random amount of damage to component 2. Component 2 will fail when its accumulated damage exceeds a special level.

Here, we propose a non-fatal shocked reliability model for a two-component system subject to Type I failure interaction. The rest of this paper is organized as follows. We will give the non-fatal shocked reliability model in section 2, and non-fatal shocked Weibull model will be given subsequently as a special case. In Section 3, non-fatal shocked Weibull model will be applied to analyze the failure data of a certain type of CNC machine tools, and the analysis result can illustrate us the internal failure law of mechanical and electrical subsystems. Finally, section 5 concludes this paper.

2   Non-fatal Shocked Reliability Model

According to Type I failure interaction, the failure causes of one component, which are named shocks in this paper, can be divided into two types. One is from interior (e.g., abrasion, aging and corrosion) of the component and causes its natural failure, while the other brings the induced failure and comes from the effect of the other components. Non-fatal shock is defined as that the occurrence of this shock only causes the component to fail with some certain probability.

We firstly state assumptions before giving the model:

The research objects of the model are two components (denoted as component 1 and component 2) in the same system. The term 'component' usually includes subsystem unless specified.

[1] Shock $Z_1(t)$ ($Z_2(t)$), whose intensity function is $\lambda_1(t)$ ($\lambda_2(t)$), is derived from component 1 (component 2). It can cause component 1 (component 2) to fail immediately with probability p_1 (p_2), and keep component 1 (component 2) not failed with probability $1 - p_1$ ($1 - p_2$). Shock $Z_1(t)$ ($Z_2(t)$) has no effect on the failure state of component 2 (component 1).

[2] Shock $Z_3(t)$ comes from the dependence between component 1 and component 2 with the intensity function $\lambda_3(t)$. The occurrence of shock $Z_3(t)$ can induce both the components to fail with probability p_{00}, make only component 1 (component 2) fail with probability p_{01} (p_{10}), and has no effect on the states of both component 1 and component 2 with probability p_{11}.

[3] All the three shocks occur independently and accord to non-homogeneous Poisson process.

Let $N_i(t)$ denote the number of shock $Z_i(t)$ over the interval $(0,1)$, and the cumulate intensity function is given by

$$\Lambda_i(t) = \int_0^t \lambda_i(t)dt, i = 1,2,3$$

[4] Let $M_j(t), j = 1,2$ be the failure numbers of component j over the interval $(0,t)$.

Then the probability that component 1 suffers from k-times shock $Z_1(t)$ but never fails over the interval $(0,t)$ is given by

$$P\{N_1(t) = k, M_1(t) = 0\} = \frac{[\Lambda_1(t)^k]}{k!} exp(-\Lambda_1(t))(1 - p_1)^k$$

The reliability function of component 1 suffering merely shock is given by

$$R_{11}(t) = \sum_{k=0}^{\infty} \frac{[\Lambda_1(t)]^k}{k!} exp(-\Lambda_1(t))(1 - p_1)^k \tag{1}$$

The occurrence of shock $Z_2(t)$ has no effect on component 1, so the reliability function of component 1 after merely shock $Z_2(t)$ equals to 1. That is $R_{12}(t) = 1$. The probability that component 1 suffers from k-times shock $Z_3(t)$ but never fails over the interval $(0,t)$ is given by

$$P\{N_3(t)=k, M_3(t)=0\} = \frac{[\Lambda_3(t)^k]}{k!} exp(-\Lambda_3(t))(P_{10}+p_{11})^k$$

and the reliability function $R_{13}(t)$ is given by

$$R_{13}(t) = \sum_{k=0}^{\infty} \frac{[\Lambda_3(t)]^k}{k!} exp\left(-\Lambda_3(t)\right)\left(P_{10}+p_{11}\right)^k \qquad (2)$$

Therefore, the reliability function of component 1 can be expressed as

$$R_1(t) = R_{11}(t) \cdot R_{12}(t) \cdot R_{13}(t) = (\sum_{k=0}^{\infty} \frac{[\Lambda_1(t)]^k}{k!} exp(-\Lambda_1(t))(1-p_1)^k) \cdot (\sum_{k=0}^{\infty} \frac{[\Lambda_3(t)]^k}{k!} exp(-\Lambda_3(t))(p_1 0+p_1 1)^k)$$
(3)

Eq. 3 can be rewritten as

$$R_1(t) = R_{11} \cdot (t) \cdot R_{13}(t) = exp(-p_1\Lambda_1(t)) \cdot exp(-(p_{01}+p_{00})\Lambda_3(t)) \qquad (4)$$

After the similar process, we can achieve the reliability function of component 2, then

$$R_2(t) = R_{22} \cdot (t) \cdot R_{23}(t) = exp(-p_2\Lambda_2(t)) \cdot exp(-(p_{10}+p_{00})\Lambda_3(t)) \qquad (5)$$

In Eq. 4 and Eq. 5, $R_{11}(t)$ and $R_{22}(t)$ are the natural reliability functions of component 1 and component 2 respectively. Meanwhile, $R_{13}(t)$ and $R_{23}(t)$ denote the reliability of component 1 and component 2 respectively when they are effected by failure interaction.

Particularly, when the intensity functions of the three shocks are all according to exponential distribution, i.e., $\lambda_i(t) = \gamma_i \beta_i t^{\beta i-1}$, the reliability functions of component 1 and component 2 can be expressed by

$$R_1(t) = exp(-p_1\lambda_1 t^{\beta_1} - (p_{01}+p_{00})\gamma_3 t^{\beta_3}) \qquad (6)$$

$$R_2(t) = exp(-p_2\lambda_2 t^{\beta_2} - (p_{10}+p_{00})\gamma_3 t^{\beta_3}) \qquad (7)$$

Let $(1/\eta_i)^{\beta_i} = p_i\gamma_i, i=1,2$, $(1/\eta_3 1)^{\beta_3} = (P_{01}+p_{00})\gamma_3$ and $(1/\eta_3 2)^{\beta_3} = (P_{11}+p_{00})\gamma_3$, Eq. 6 and Eq. 7 can be rewritten as

$$R_1(t) = R_{11}(t)R_{13}(t) = exp(-(t/\eta_1)^{\beta_1})exp(-(t/\eta_{31})^{\beta_3}) \qquad (8)$$

and

$$R_2(t) = R_{22}(t)R_{23}(t) = exp(-(t/\eta_2)^{\beta_2})exp(-(t/\eta_{32})^{\beta_3}) \qquad (9)$$

Eq. 8 and Eq. 9 have the form of Weibull distribution, so they can be named as non-fatal shocked Weibull model. Non-fatal shocked Weibull model is more adaptable in reliability analysis, and it is applied in the following section to analyze the failure data of a certain type of CNC machine tool.

3 Reliability Analysis of CNC Machine Tools

3.1 Preliminary Analysis to Failure Data

Mechanical subsystem and electrical subsystem are two main subsystems in CNC machine tools. It is commonly considered that the times to failure of the both subsystems are according to Weibull function. The data relates to the testing of 20 CNC machine tools of the same type during one year's time. We use the WPP plot (for more information, please refer to Nelson W[8]) to select an appropriate model formulation to model the failure times. The WPP plot of the failure data is shown in Fig. 1.

As can be seen from Fig. 1, the plotted points of both the subsystems are not scattered along a straight line, implying that the two-parameter Weibull is not appropriate to model the failure time. Considering that there are failure interactions between mechanical and electrical subsystems, Eq. 8 and Eq. 9 are used to model the time to failure of mechanical subsystem and electrical subsystem.

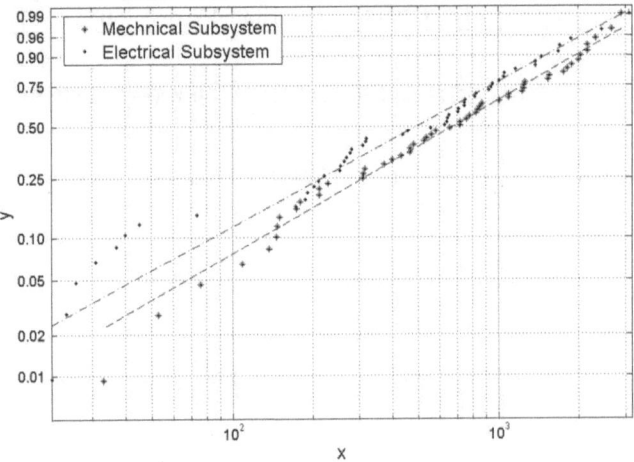

Fig. 1. WPP Plots for Mechanical Subsystem and Electrical Subsystems

3.2 Reliability Functions of CNC Machine Tools

There are 7 parameters in Eq. 8 and Eq. 9, which brings many difficulties to estimate their value. Maximum Likelihood Estimate (MLE) can be used to estimate the parameters. Furthermore, we can also use ReliaSoft Weibull++ for a simple and quick estimation. Noticing that there is the same parameter in Eq. 8 and Eq. 9, it is necessary to combine the two formulas to estimate the parameters. We should adjust the parameter β_3 in the two formulas to make them equal. The values of parameters after estimation are given in Table 3, where D_n and $D_{n,\alpha}$ are two parameters of Kolmogorov-Smirnov test. When $D_n < D_{n,\alpha}$, the parameter estimates then can be accepted. As can be seen in Table 1, the parameters have a good match to model the failure times of mechanical and electrical subsystems. Then we can achieve the reliability functions of mechanical and electrical subsystems which are shown in Eq. 10 and Eq. 11 respectively.

$R_{M1}(t)$ and $R_{E2}(t)$ are the respective natural reliability of the mechanical and electrical subsystems. $R_{M3}(t)$ and $R_{E3}(t)$ denote the interactive failures of the two subsystems.

Then the failure rate charts of the two subsystems, which are shown in Fig. 2 and Fig. 3, can be achieved.

Table 1. Model Parameter Estimates

β_1	η_1	β_3	η_{01}	D_n	$D_{n,\alpha}$
1.6162	1671.5	0.6500	2546.9	0.1261	0.1660
β_2	η_2	β_3	η_{02}	D_n	$D_{n,\alpha}$
1.4511	1294.0	0.6500	1838.4	0.0821	0.1692

$$R_M(t) = R_{M1}(t)R_{M3}(t) = exp(-(t/1671.5)^{1.6162})exp(-(t/2546.9)^{0.6500}) \qquad (10)$$

$$R_E(t) = R_{E2}(t)R_{E3}(t) = exp(-(t/1294.0)^{1.4511})exp(-(t/1838.4)^{0.6500}) \qquad (11)$$

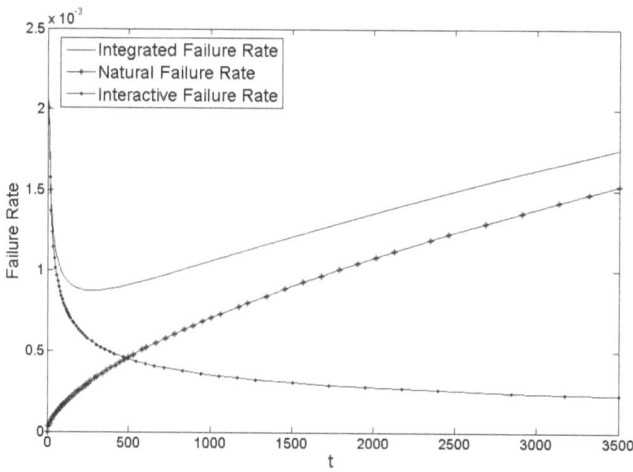

Fig. 2. Failure Rate Chart of Mechanical Subsystem

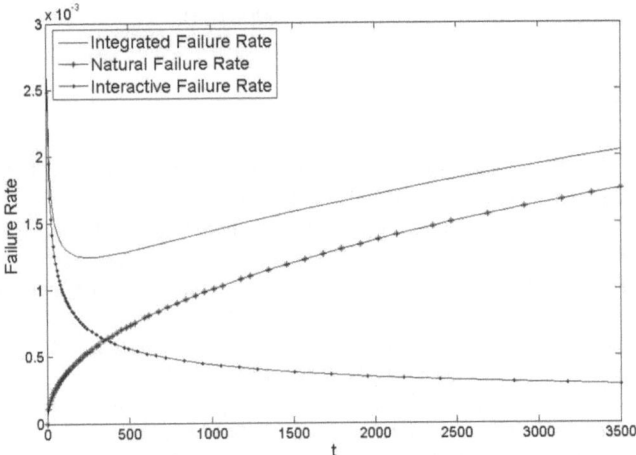

Fig. 3. Failure Rate Chart of Electrical Subsystem

3.3 Conclusions of Reliability Analysis

From the two charts, several conclusions then can be drawn as below:

[1] The integrated failure rates of mechanical and electrical subsystems are both descended sharply in the beginning, which are dominated by their failure interactions. When their integrated failure rates drop to some certain degree, they ascend slowly with the effect of their natural failure rate.

[2] The natural failure rates of mechanical and electrical subsystems are both ascended with time, with the reason that the fatigue and aging of subsystems are aggravated along the time.

[3] In the before 500 hours, the failure interactions of the two subsystems effect more than their natural failure. After then, the natural failure dominates the subsystem's failure.

4 Conclusion

In this paper, we had presented a non-fatal reliability model for a two-component system subject to failure interaction between components. The model was then applied to analysis the interactive failure of CNC machine tools to illustrate the internal law of failure. The extension of this work to considering multi-component system is also a possibility.

Acknowledgments. This paper was supported by National Natural Science Foundation of China (No. 50875110), Project "High-end CNC machine tools and basic manufacturing equipment" supported by scientific and technological major special project (No. 2009ZX04001-031-05), and cutting-edge science and interdisciplinary innovation projects of Jilin University (No. 200903165).

References

[1] Sun, Y., Ma, L., Mathew, J.: An analytical model for interactive failures. Reliability Engineering and System Safety 91, 495–504 (2006)
[2] Cho, D., Paralar, M.: A survey of maintenance models for multi-unit systems. European Journal of Operational Research 51, 1–23 (1991)
[3] Lai, M.-T.: A discrete replacement model for a two-unit parallel system subject to failure rate interaction. Quality and Quantity 43, 471–479 (2009)
[4] Murthy, D.N.P., Nguyen, D.: Study of two-component system with failure interaction. Naval Research Logistics Quarterly 32, 239–247 (1985)
[5] Murthy, D.N.P., Nguyen, D.: Study of multi-component system with failure interaction. European Journal of Operational Research 21, 330–338 (1985)
[6] Murthy, D.N.P., Wilson, R.: Parameter estimation in multi-component systems with failure interaction. Applied Stochastic Models and Data Analysis 10, 47–60 (1994)
[7] Jhang, J.P., Sheu, S.H.: Optimal age and block replacement policies for a multi-component system with failure interaction. International Journal of Systems Science 31, 593–603 (2000)
[8] Nelson, W.: Applied Life Data Analysis. Wiley and Sons, New York (1982)

Distribution Network Information System of Jiaozuo Based on ArcObject

Wang Chunsheng[1], Sun Quande[1], and Li Kaiyang[2]

[1] Henan Jiaozuo Power Supply Company, No.169 Minzhu Road,
Jiefang District, 454000 Jiaozuo, Henan, China
[2] Huazhong University of Science and Technology, No 1037 Luoyu Road,
Hongshan District, 430074 Wuhan, Hubei, China

Abstract. Describe the distribution network information system of Jiaozuo, which comes from analysis, design, to development by the true examples. And introduce how to achieve some of the typical functions by components of Arcobject.

Keywords: Geographic Information System (GIS); Distribution Network; Arcobject.

1 Introduction

Power GIS is an integrated information system of power information in the production and management, which is connected by electrical equipment, substations, transmission and distribution networks, power users and power load, and other core business[1]. This system provides such information, like electrical equipment and facilities, status of power network, production and management, the power market, as well as other natural environment information as mountains, rivers, topography, towns, roads streets, buildings, meteorology, hydrology, geology and resources. Power GIS platform based on a common GIS, which could be used to seek data, pictures, images, maps, technical information and management knowledge. Besides the basic characteristics of GIS, power GIS also has the following characteristics:

1) Because the parameters of power system are real-time and dynamic changes, the real-time information should be timely collected, processed, and analyzed. Power GIS has high requirements of data processing, storage capacity and transmission speed.

2) Multi-attribute data of distribution network requires GIS sufficiently stable and reliable. According to power technical standards and power industry business needs, the system has good maintainability. Power GIS should achieve the data one input and multiple outputs, in order to ensure consistency of data operations the unified data management and multi-layer protection, high reliability and accuracy of building business systems.

3) Power system is a large and complex system, distribution network and wide area dispersion of power facilities and equipment, the diversity of large real-time

R. Chen (Ed.): ICICIS 2011, Part I, CCIS 134, pp. 497–501, 2011.

information, system interface complex, covering a wide range of information, the various voltage levels and network multi-user connection. So GIS should has the capabilities with topology analysis and conversion.

4) Stand-alone GIS-way power station has lagged behind, and does not fit the practical needs of electric power enterprise information systems. Power industry is the application of GIS platforms installed in the LAN environment, the network application and development on the integration of information, sharing of resources.

5) GIS in the electric power network connectivity based on geometric analysis, advanced applications is the key to power GIS technology and a variety of advanced applications can be combined.

2   System Analysis and Development

2.1   System Requirements

The Jiaozuo distribution network information system is divided into three large pieces of information: basic GIS capabilities, distribution network analysis and management capabilities and WebGIS. Some of the basic GIS functionality including map display, query, statistics, this part roughly has the same functions as any common GIS platform, which could be applied independently from the distribution system. Distribution Network Analysis and Management section includes switch analog operation, listing operation of power supply, power supply range analysis, power optimization program analysis, outage management, load density analysis, the best path, fault repair, the user equipment reports, which functional modules based on the basic GIS functions, with strong professional and targeted. WebGIS functions including map display, query, customer feedback, is a simple Web platform.

2.2   Development Platform

This project uses ESRI's ArcObject as a secondary development platform, which belongs to ESRI's ArcGIS software family. Using ArcObject secondary development, there are two common mode:

1) VBA customization:

In the ArcCatalog and ArcMap applications to bind a VBA (Visual Basic for Application) compiler, it is easy to use VBA, simple to customize the program interface personalization, personalized toolbar and extend part of the geographic features. Use VBA development is simple, but the independence of poor, biased towards a single function.

2) COM component development:

Another development model of ArcObject is the application of COM technology. COM is Microsoft's Component Object Model (Component Object Model) of the acronym, ArcObject to provide a framework for component development using the popular programming language, developers can implement all the features of commercial GIS software.

With the appearance of COM, software development and organization reached a new height. It is a powerful integration technology, so you can run the program in the various decentralized organization of software modules together to make the application at a higher degree of be customized to make the software more flexible, more dynamic.

This system is used in the VB COM component in the development of technologies used to achieve all the features of the system. In ArcObject, there are two important high-level COM components: MapControl and PageLayoutControl. They package many low-end, scattered components together, to form a powerful high-level application components. Using MapControl and PageLayout-Control, such functions can be achieved: Show map layers; zoom in, zoom, roam; generate graphical elements (such as points, lines, circles, polygons); that NOTE; identify the elements of the map is selected, the space or attribute query; marked map elements; management control settings; management control of the display properties; management page attributes; increase in the control and find elements; load the map document to the control; available directly from Explorer and drag and drop ArcCatalog data to the control; print page design and other functions. Most functions of ArcGIS are realized by these two controls.

2.3 Development Plan

The Jiaozuo distribution network information system using client / server model, data is divided into two parts: spatial data and attribute data. Spatial data is the basic geographic data, such as: roads, rivers, housing and so on, which is stored as GeoDataBase structure; attribute data includes distribution network parameters, such as: equipment, accounting information, history, graphic data distribution network, customer information, but also the data from the customer service system and distribution automation system, which stored in ordinary relational database. In the management of these data, the use of a database engine --- ArcSDE provided by ArcGIS --- can unify the two kinds of data into together.

The client is installed in the Electric Power Bureau of certain computer terminals within the LAN, suitable for middle and upper management personnel to use, such as scheduling classes and repair classes. Such managers can simply use existing data for analysis, decision-making in the management of basic data without editing a large number of updates. Windows2000 and the main module based on ArcObject should be installed in the GIS client, which should connect to the server by ArcSDE, to call the data. The working end can configure the printers.

WebGIS servers communicate with remote client, to receive and respond to requests for Web browsers and interact with the services provided by Web application server. Web application server, in this system, provides a key to view the network information, instead of all of the network management operations. Some functions, Such as security access control, simple query statistics, could be achieved by direct accessing to the database. Some features of the development use B / S model, which applies to online information dissemination, to meet the user's large number of query and browse. By the way, Web server install software, like Windows2000, ARCIMS etc.

Most of the development of the system are focused on the client, briefly described as below:

1) ArcObject classes used by the library are included in the esriCore.olb. There are three kinds: Abstract Class, Component Class and General Class. Abstract Class cannot be created, and it can only be used for the parent of other classes. General Class cannot be created, but such objects can be created other classes, as an attribute, or instantiated by object of other classes. Component Class can be created, or be created explicitly. For all of the class of ArcObject supported by VB, Esri Object Library must be added as a reference to the VB compiler.

2) The realization of the basic GIS functionality is relatively easy, because they do not involve professional models. It can be achieved directly by ArcObject. To display the map in the form file, the MapControl form must be added into the control to the program. MapControl support such map files, as mxd, shp, lyr format, even can display the data in GeoDataBase as the map. There are two ways adding a map file to the MapControl. One is pre-specified map files, that map is loaded up when first run the program. This approach is relatively simple, but poorly inflexible and cannot be changed after loading the map. The other way is by a loader to add the map when the program is running. Here is the map file loading subroutines:

3) Distribution network analysis and management functions expand from the basic GIS functions, which is upgraded from common GIS platform to a professional power GIS.

Take the connectivity analysis as an example. In the distribution network, connectivity analysis is mainly used to determine whether there is electricity at some point, same as whether the point connect with a known power supply source (substation or transformer). To achieve connectivity analysis in ArcObject, first create the geometric network. Geometric network is the network model, containing only two elements points and lines, abstracted from a variety of networks in reality, such as electric power network, computer network, road network, rail network and other. It is the basis of network analysis in the ArcObject. Generally, pre-generated geometric network should be done by ArcMap before the analysis.

The connectivity analysis to go through the following steps:

1) Connect the GeoDataBase, read the geometric network data, then achieve the piont by calling the method of OpenFeatureDatasetNetwork.

2) Set the source node by clicking the left mouse button on the map to set. The program should be added into the mouse response function of MapControl-OnMouseDown. Then use the m-ipPoints. AddPoint function method, to record the every point you click by the left mouse button.

3) Set the sink nodes. When double-click the left mouse button on the map, the program could add the response function of Map-ControlOnDoubleClick. Once the sink nodes set, the program will perform connectivity analysis algorithm, to judge whether the similarities between two points.

4) When the operation is finished, if the two points linked, the module generates a fold line between two points, and displayed on the map:

The result of connectivity analysis is shown in Figure, a line between two points:

3   Conclusion

ArcObject, as a GIS development platform, is a product leader in its class. It provides functionality far beyond similar products. Not only that, it support large development environment through the COM component technology, and a large free help system, so that developers can put more energy into the software architecture analysis, and database design. So it can be predicted that ArcObject will certainly become the mainstream of secondary development platform for GIS.

References

1. Chang, K.-S.: Introduction To Geographic Information System. Science Press, Beijing (1999)
2. Cassel, W.R.: Distribution Management System: Functions and Payback. IEEE Trans. on Power Systems, 796–801 (1993)
3. Trussell, L.V.: GIS based Distribution Simulation and Analysis. Electricity Distribution (2001)
4. Resconi, G., Kovalerchuk, B.: Agents' model of uncertainty. Knowledge and Information Systems 18(2), 213 (2009)
5. Normak, Per-ludivg: Trimble introduces New Family of Trimble trident analyst software providing advanced GIS and CAD information extraction for mobile mapping. Computer Weekly News, p. 107, Atlanta (2010)

Design and Implementation for Low Network Loaded and Automatically Photographic Surveillance System

Linying Jiang and Heming Pang

Software College, Northeastern University, Shenyang,
110819 Liaoning, China

Abstract. For the weakness of traditional video surveillance system which over-reliance on human, this paper proposed a design and implementation scheme for a infrared sensor-based and automatically photographic video surveillance system, which better solved the problem of inefficient and taking up too much system space for traditional video monitor system; Besides, this paper worked out two data transmission optimization schemes: infrared trigger and non-infrared trigger, which greatly reduces the network traffic load.

Keywords: video surveillance, infrared sensor, S3C2410, ARM Linux.

1 Introduction

With the development of Internet and broadband network technology, networked digital video based on embedded video server occupies market gradually. Compared with traditional simulation video surveillance and multimedia computer platform (embedded system) digital video surveillance, the advantages of networked digital video system are mainly reflected in: system strong expansion capability, low maintenance costs, monitoring easily and so on[1][2].

However, most network video surveillance systems can't work effectively when ensuring the security of surveillance sites under the condition of no person on duty[3], such as midnight. Some network surveillance systems provide a full video recording capability, which just videoing mechanically. Its shortcomings mainly include: the saved video files take up too much system space; most video files do not have any values and have to clean up regularly. Therefore, this paper presents a new surveillance scheme, which reads infrared sensor signal continuously to determine whether there are illegal objects in surveillance sites. Once detected invasion, it will take pictures of surveillance sites continuously and save all these photos.

2 System Architecture

Fig. 1 shows the architecture of surveillance system, the CPU of front-end machine uses ARM9 S3C2410, on which running Linux operating system. The mainly principles of Fig. 1 are: front-end computer connects a series of digital cameras based on ZC301 chip via USB interface and collects video data by video capture module.

R. Chen (Ed.): ICICIS 2011, Part I, CCIS 134, pp. 502–508, 2011.

Through serial port, front-end machine connects a sensor expansion board, on which connects an infrared sensor and collects infrared sensor signal by infrared sensor signal acquisition module. After finishing the collection of video data and infrared sensor signal, front-end machine will have data communications with control center via socket. Then, control center displays the video data on Java Applet GUI. Users can use terminals to access control center and obtain image data via Internet.

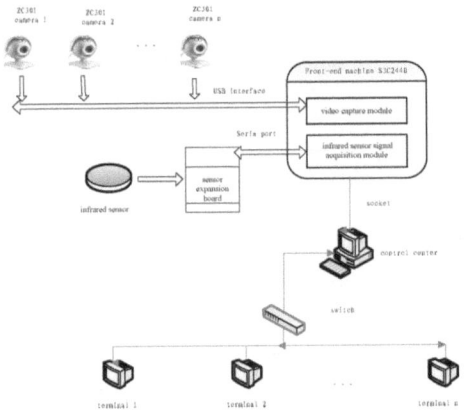

Fig. 1. System architecture

3 Video Surveillance Module Design

3.1 Video Data Capture Module

The embedded linux operation system used in this system has already contained video4linux video device driver, which provides video devices with a range of application programming interface function. Since the SMIC micro-ZC301 series cameras have an approximately 71% coverage in camera market, so most of the current linux versions have loaded video4linux driver by default. This paper is mainly about the aspects of program design to capture video images for USB camera device files /dev/video0 after loading the video4linux driver successfully. Fig. 2 shows the process of capturing video data.

There are two ways for video capturing: one is mmap() memory mapping method; the other is read() reading device directly method. The read() method reads data through kernel buffer, while the mmap() method maps the device file into memory, bypassing the kernel buffer. The fastest disk access is usually slower than the slowest memory access, so mmap() method accelerates I / O access. In addition, mmap() system call allows processes to share memory by mapping the same file. The process can access to files just as the way as accessing memory. While accessing, it only needs to use pointers rather than call the file manipulation functions. Because of the above advantages of mmap(), the program implementation uses memory mapping method, that is mmap() mode.

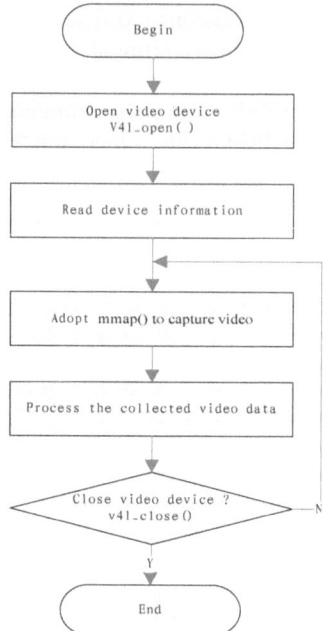

Fig. 2. Flow diagram of capturing video data

3.2 Image Processing Module

This system uses a SMIC micro-ZC301 camera and its image compression and coding is implemented by DSP hardware of itself. The ZC301 is JPEG-encoded bit-stream, so, in order to display images in a terminal, it only needs to have a JPEG decoding for the collected image data.

Libjpeg is a widely used JPEG compression / decompression library. It can read and write JPEG image files in JFIF format. Through libjpeg library, each application can read from JPEG compressed image for one or more scan lines (the so-called scan line is an image line consisted by a line of pixel spots), and other jobs, such as color space conversion, down-sampling/up sampling, color quantization are completed by libjpeg. The specific decoding process is shown in Fig.3.

3.3 Video Data Receiver Module

Control center collects decoded image data from front-end machine through Java socket programming and then displays the collected image data on Java Applet GUI. In order to achieve B / S architecture video surveillance mode, it needs to pack Java Applet image display program into jar package and embedded it into web page in the form of GUI through <applet> tags of HTML. As long as the web page is published to web server (e.g. Apache, etc.) of control center, terminals can monitor the target surveillance sites through Internet.

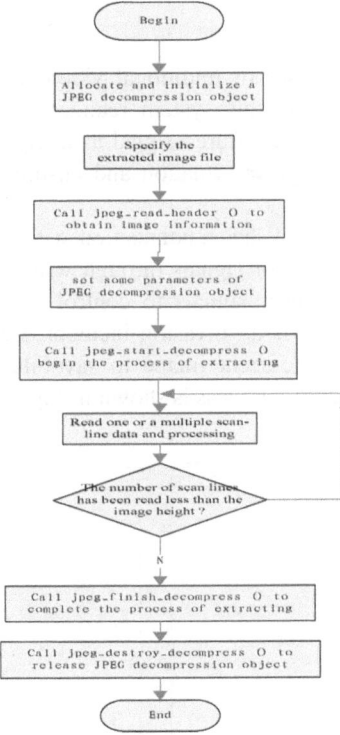

Fig. 3. Flow diagram of libjpeg decoding

This system receives the image data through Java Applet and it is completed by the following core steps:

(1) Create a socket. Socket connection = new Socket (m_strServer, port);

(2) Obtain input stream object: InputStream in = connection.getInputStream ( );

The reason for obtaining input stream object in is that it can obtain image data by calling the read function of the object in.

(3) Obtain image data: n = in.read(buffer, 0, HDRLEN);

What read function return is the current byte number read into buffer. The return value will be -1 if there is an exception occurs during read operation. The initial value of HDRLEN is 50, which means at most 50 bytes data is allowed to read into the buffer at one time.

(4) Image Display: BufferedImage image = ImageIO.read(new ByteArrayInput Stream(buffer2)); ImageIcon icon = new ImageIcon(image); m_label.setIcon(icon);

Through the above mention steps, the image data is encapsulated into java applet panel m_label in the form of picture.

3.4 Image Auto-Save Module

In order to overcome weaknesses of traditional video surveillance system, such as over-reliance on human control, this system realizes infrared sensor-based image auto-save feature. By treating the infrared signal as a trigger to save video image, it can avoid sending useless image information and ensure no missing any suspicion information at the same time.

After front-end machine establishes a connection with control center, open sensor module and capture infrared sensor signals through write() and read() function, then send the collected infrared sensor signals to control center through socket. If the signal value is 1, that is, there is an invasion incident occurring in the surveillance site, the system will save the current image to saveFile directory through write() function of ImageIo. The specific process is shown in Fig. 4.

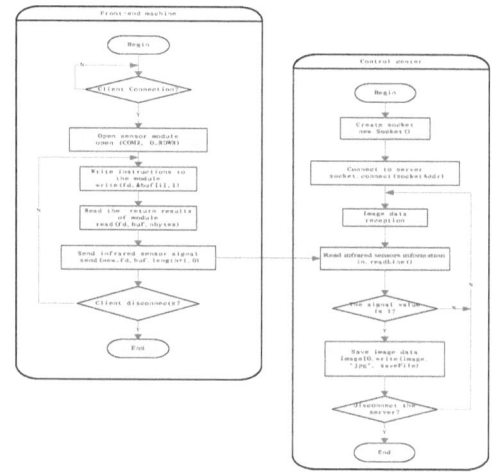

Fig. 4. Flow diagram of image auto-saved

4　Optimization of Sending Data

With the number of external cameras increasing, the amount of data sent concurrently per second increases continually, which makes the network load heavier and heavier and increases the packet loss rate. Shown as Fig. 5, red line represents the network traffic of sending infrared sensor signal at a certain time, while blue line represents the network traffic of sending image data concurrently in multi-camera mode. In such a high network load conditions, infrared sensor signal is likely to lose. However, under no person on duty circumstance, the stable transmission of infrared sensor signal is extremely important and the security risk brought by losing such signal should not be overlooked.

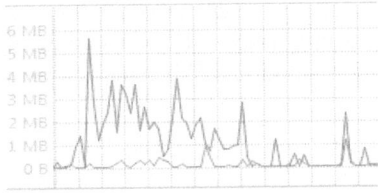

Fig. 5. Network traffic of sending data concurrently in multi-camera mode

To solve this problem, this system designs two modes of sending data: infrared trigger mode and non-infrared trigger mode. In non-infrared trigger mode (suitable for having person on duty condition), system only transmits image data. While in infrared trigger mode (suitable for no person on duty), system will send infrared sensor signal first, if there is no invasion, control center will return a refusal signal (default value is true) to front-end machine to refuse image data transmission; if there is an invasion, control center will set the refusal signal to false and ask for sending image data.

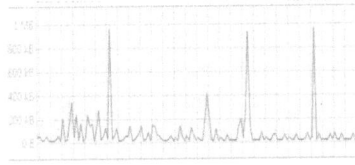

Fig. 6. Network traffic of non-infrared trigger mode

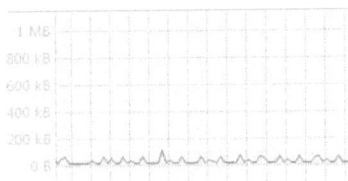

Fig. 7. Network traffic of infrared trigger, no invasion mode

By contrasting Fig.6 with Fig.7, it is clearly that, in non-infrared trigger mode, if front-end machine connects only one camera, the network traffic of sending image data per second is about 150KB; in infrared trigger mode, if there is no invasion incident, control center only sends infrared sensor signal and its network traffic is only a few dozen KB. By taking infrared sensor signal as a trigger to determine whether to send image data or not, it reduces the infrared sensor signal loss rate and saves the network traffic greatly.

5   Conclusion

As people's awareness of security increasing, intelligent network video surveillance system will become more and more popular. It can also develop into a series of more intelligent monitoring systems, such as automatic alarm, automatic recording, etc based on this system. Security issue will always be the focus of people's attention and this system presents a new solution to this issue and has broad market space[4].

References

1. He, S.-Q., Yang, M.-H.: Research on Real-time Performance of Embedded Video Surveillance System. Computer Engineering 35(4), 235–237 (2009)
2. Zhang, W.-W.: Design and Implementation of Embedded Video Surveillance System Based on ARM. Nanjing University of Science and Technology, Nan Jing (2007)
3. Network. Overview and Design for Remote Network Video Monitoring System [EB/OL] (January 14, 2009) (2010-2-4),
   http://info.secu.hc360.com/2009/01/140857149093-4.shtml
4. FREEDOM_ASIC. Image acquisition of USB Camera Based on XScale in Linux [EB/OL] (January 19, 2009) (2010-2-4),
   http://hi.baidu.com/freedom_asic/blog/item/5824251372dda524dc 540143.html

The Research on Incentive Mechanism of Knowledge Creation in IT Enterprise

Si-hua Chen

Institute of Information Resource Management School of Information Management,
Jiangxi University of Finance and Economics, Nanchang, China, 330013
doriancsh@yahoo.com.cn

Abstract. In the era of knowledge economy, in order to maintain sustainable development, the key is by management to find the best way to continuously discover new knowledge and make it form core competency. IT industry especially which favors new technology and new products, knowledge creation competition is a strategic issue concerning the survival of enterprises. Therefore, on the basis of analyzing the characteristics of knowledge workers of IT enterprises, this paper proposes contract incentive mechanism. we found through designing a reasonable incentive mechanism the Pareto dominance risk-sharing and Pareto dominance effort level can be achieved simultaneously.

Keywords: Knowledge creation, IT enterprise, Incentive, Pareto dominance.

1 Introduction

This instruction file for Word users (there is a separate instruction file for LaTeX users) may be used as a template. Kindly send the final and checked Word and PDF files of your paper to the Contact Volume Editor. This is usually one of the organizers of the conference. You should make sure that the Word and the PDF files are identical and correct and that only one version of your paper is sent. It is not possible to update files at a later stage. Please note that we do not need the printed paper.

In the era of knowledge economy, knowledge is the first resource of organization and becomes the key strategic factor of economic growth. German scholars Mertins Kai, Peter Heisig etc consider that knowledge has the same features with currency, that is its value appears only when it is used — knowledge can be useful only when it is shared.[1]. In other words, knowledge develops in exchange and appreciate in use. Knowledge creation is the activity which applies new elements and concepts to production, management and other economic or social activities so as to bring value to business or society. Through knowledge management, on the basis of knowledge acquisition, diffusion, and sharing we constantly pursue new developments and apply knowledge to new areas to therefore stimulate the continuously enhancement of the core competency of enterprises. TAO(2006) proposes knowledge and the ability to create and apply knowledge is the most important source of an organization to keep sustainable competitive advantage[2]. The importance of knowledge creation arouses great research interest of academia. The focus of research of knowledge creation has

R. Chen (Ed.): ICICIS 2011, Part I, CCIS 134, pp. 509–514, 2011.

transferred from early definition of concepts and significance to the process of knowledge creation. At present there are many scholars who have propose the theory of knowledge creation.

Many Chinese scholars also have made studies on knowledge creation. HE Chuanqi(2005) thinks that knowledge creation is the process of discovering and creating new knowledge for economic and social interests. Knowledge creation appears in the whole process of knowledge production, dissemination and application. He considers that broadly knowledge creation has three forms, that is implementing knowledge creation through R&D activities, implementing knowledge creation in the process of knowledge production, dissemination and application, the proliferation and application of new knowledge for economic and social interests. He Chuanqi's "knowledge creation" view to large degree is influenced by the "Technology Innovation Statistical Manual" of OECD. In fact he accepted the basic meaning of enterprise innovation and divided enterprise innovation into technology innovation, process innovation, product innovation, management innovation and institutional innovation[3].

IT Enterprises as typical representative of high-tech enterprises have distinctive features, possessing the characteristics of knowledge-intensiveness and talent-clustering. Knowledge competition is the largest features of competition of IT companies. It can be said that knowledge is the core of uniting capital and talents of IT enterprises while knowledge creation is the driving force to support the growth of IT enterprises and is the major source of long-term competitive advantages of IT enterprises. Therefore, how to effectively motivate employees to implement knowledge creation has significant theoretical and practical meaning. The focus of studies is mainly on the incentive mechanism of knowledge employees[4-15]. The literature of motivating knowledge worker is still few.

This paper will follow the below steps: the second part we propose the hypotheses; the third part puts forward the model; On the basis of analyzing the model, the forth part summarizes incentive mechanism; the fifth part is acknowledge.

2   Hypothesis

Human is the carrier of knowledge and is also the subject of knowledge creation. Therefore, the essence of motivating knowledge creation is the motivation of the knowledge employees who participate in knowledge creation. In the following parts, we name enterprises as principal, employees participating in knowledge creation as agent. Before putting forward the model, we propose the following hypotheses.

Hypothesis 1: there exists non-symmetric information between principal and agent. Principal does not have private information while agent has the private information which principal can hardly observe. Because the information principal has is different from the one agent has and principal can not directly observe the true information of agent, it is necessary for principal to design a incentive mechanism.

Hypothesis 2: principal's action goal is different from agent's. If their action goals are the same, agent will consciously choose the action beneficial to principal and there is no need for principal to design a incentive mechanism.

Hypothesis 3: Both principal and agent meet the hypothesis of bounded rationality. Principal hopes to get the maximum expected utility from the incentive mechanism he designs and therefore the objective function of which principal designs incentive mechanism is the maximization of expectation. Similarly agent hopes to be able to choose the behaviors which can maximize his expected utility, meet participation constraint and incentive compatibility constraint.

Hypothesis 4: principal has the initiative in the design of mechanism and has the capability to realize promise. That is as long as the mechanism does not discontinue and does not change he can perform it. The hypothesis means the incentive mechanism principal designs is comparatively stable. It runs through the whole time of agent's activities until the completion of payment.

Hypothesis 5: agent has the right to choose different levels of efforts.

3 Model

Parameter description :

A: action space of agent; a : action of agent , $a \in$ A; Θ:nature space.

θ : nature, the exogenous random variable. When agent chooses action a, the exogenous variable θ is determined, $\theta \in \Theta$.

$x(a,\theta)$: an observable outcome determined by both a and θ.

$\pi(a,\theta)$: the utility determined by both a and θ . The direct ownership of π belongs to principal. $\partial \pi / \partial a > 0$, π is strictly increasing concave function of a. π is strictly increasing function of θ.

$s(x)$: incentive contract. According to the q observed, based on contract $f(q)$, principal provide payment for agent. Due to the interest conflict between principal and agent, $s(x)$ contract is very important. Only when principal provide enough incentives, agent will behavior according to principal's wish.

$c(a)$: cost of agent, $c' > 0$, $c'' > 0$. $c' > 0$ means agent hopes himself to pay less efforts.

$v(\pi - s(x))$: expected utility function of principal. $v' > 0$, $v'' < 0$. Principal is risk-neutral and risk-averse. The marginal disutility of effort is increasing.

$u(s(\pi)) - c(a)$: expected utility function of agent. $u' > 0$, $u'' < 0$. Agent is risk-neutral and risk-averse. The marginal disutility of effort is increasing. This means except that principal can provide enough incentives for agent, agent won't work hard as principal wishes.

$g(\theta)$: density function of θ.

$f(x,\pi,a)$: joint density function of x, π, a.

We suppose utility is an observable variable and only π is observable. Therefore, $x = \pi$. Whether it is awards or punishments of principal on agent can only be decided by π. According to hypothesis 3, principal hopes to get the maximum expected utility from the incentive mechanism he designs. Therefore, the expected utility function of principal can be expressed in the following way:

$$\max \int v(\pi(a,\theta) - s(x(a,\theta))) g(\theta) d\theta \qquad (1)$$

Principal's problem is to choose a and $s(x)$ to maximize the above utility function. However, according to hypothesis 2, the action goal of agent is different from the one of principal. According to hypothesis 3, agent is also pursuing his own maximum utility. According to hypothesis 5, agent has the right to choose different actions. Therefore, principal faces two constraints from agent. The first constraint is participation constraint. That is the expected utility agent gets from accepting contract should not be less than the one he gets from not accepting contract. The maximum expected utility agent gets from not accepting contract is determined by other market opportunities he faced and we use $\bar{u}$ on behave of it.

The second constraint is incentive compatibility constraint. Because principal can not observe agent's action and agent always chooses the action which maximizes his own expected utility, principal's a can only be realized by the utility maximization action of agent. In other words, if a is action principal wants and $a' \in A$ is any action agent can choose, then only when the expected utility agent gets from choosing a is larger than the one agent gets from choosing a', agent will choose a.

The mathematical descriptions of participation constraint and incentive compatibility are as follows:

$$\int u(s(x(a,\theta))) g(\theta) d\theta - c(a) \geq \bar{u} \qquad (2)$$

$$\int u(s(x(a,\theta))) g(\theta) d\theta - c(a) \geq \int u(s(x(a',\theta))) f(\pi,a') d\theta - c(a') \qquad (3)$$

The above is model description of contract incentive. However, the incentive of knowledge creation in IT enterprises is a little bit different. Generally speaking the knowledge creation groups in IT enterprises and enterprises can constrain and observe the effort level of knowledge employees by designing all kinds of working disciplines, rules and regulations. That is to say actions of knowledge employees in IT enterprises are observable. What they can choose is whether they participate. If they don't participate, they can choose to leave enterprises. Therefore, in the situation that agent's effort levels can be observed, incentive compatibility constraint is superfluous and we only need to unite equation (1) and (2).

Constructing Lagrangian function:

$$L(a, s(\pi)) = \int v(\pi(a,\theta) - s(x(a,\theta))) g(\theta) d\theta + \lambda [\int u(s(x(a,\theta))) g(\theta) d\theta - c(a) - \bar{u}] \qquad (4)$$

We seek first derivatives of a and $s(\pi)$ and make them equal to 0. They are simplified as:

$$Ev'[\frac{\partial \pi}{\partial a} - \frac{1}{u'} \frac{\partial c}{\partial a}] = 0 \qquad (5)$$

E is expectation operator. $v'\dfrac{\partial \pi}{\partial a}$ can be explained as the marginal utility of effort

level of a which is measured by utility of principal. $\dfrac{v'}{u'}\dfrac{\partial c}{\partial a}$ can be explained as the

marginal cost which is measured by utility of principal. Therefore, (5) is a typical condition of pareto dominance: the expected marginal utility of efforts is equal to the expected marginal cost. That is to say, when a can be observed by principal, we can reach pareto dominance. Specifically if principal is risk-neutral($v''=0, v'=1$), then

$$E[\frac{\partial \pi}{\partial a}-\frac{1}{u'}\frac{\partial c}{\partial a}]=0 \qquad (6)$$

Optimal risk-sharing means u' is a constant. Therefore,

$$E\frac{\partial \pi}{\partial a}=\frac{1}{u'}\frac{\partial c}{\partial a} \qquad (7)$$

$E\dfrac{\partial \pi}{\partial a}=\dfrac{\partial}{\partial a}\int \pi(a,\theta)g(\theta)d\theta$ is marginal expected output, $\dfrac{1}{u'}\dfrac{\partial c}{\partial a}$ is the marginal

rate of substitution of monetary income and effort of agent.

4 Conclusion

From above analysis we get a conclusion: when principal can observe agent's effort level (that is IT enterprises can constrain and observe the effort level of knowledge employees in knowledge creation by all kinds of working disciplines, rules and regulations), there exists a optimal contract which can realize pareto dominance risk sharing and pareto dominance effort level at the same time. The optimal contract can be described as followings:

$$s=\begin{cases} s^*(\pi)=s^*(\pi(a^*,\theta)), a \geq a^* \\ \underline{s}, a < a^* \end{cases} \qquad (8)$$

Enterprise ask knowledge employees to choose effort level of a^*. If knowledge employees are observed to choose $a \geq a^*$, principal will pay employees according to $s^*(\pi(a^*,\theta))$. Otherwise, employees can only get $\underline{s}$. As long as $\underline{s}$ is small enough, employees will not choose $a < a^*$.

Acknowledgments. It is a project supported by the This work is supported by the NSFC(70663002, 710730073).

References

1. Mertina, K., Heisig, P., Vorbeck, J.: Knowledge management concepts and best practices. Tsinghua University Press, Beijing (2004)
2. Tao, H., Dai, C.-j.: Game Analyses of Organization's Tacit Knowledge. Journal of Information 7, 74–78 (2006)
3. Zhang, F., He, C.-q.: The principle and the path of knowledge innovation. Bulletin of the Chinese Academy of Sciences 20, 389–394 (2005)
4. Kohn, A.S.: Why incentive plans cannot work. Harvard Business Review 71, 54–63 (1993)
5. Gibbons, R.: Incentives in Organizations. Journal of Economic Perspective 12, 115–132 (1998)
6. Prendergast, C.: The Provision of Incentives in Firms. Journal of Economic Literature 37, 377–463 (1999)
7. Dixit, A.: Incentives and Organizations in the Public Sector. The Journal of Human Resource 37, 696–727 (2002)
8. Gibbons, R.: Incentives Between Firms (and Within). Management Science 51, 2–17 (2005)
9. Fehr, E., Falk, A.: Psychological foundations of incentives. European Economic Review 46, 687–724 (2002)
10. Rob, P.: Social capital, corporate culture and incentive intensity. Journal of Economics 33, 243–257 (2002)
11. Fehr, E., Schmidt, K.M.: Fairness and incentives in a multitask principal-agent model. Scandinavian Journal of Economics 106, 453–474 (2004)
12. Bandiera, O., Barankay, L., Rasul, I.: Social preferences and the response to incentives evidence from personnel data. Quarterly Journal of Economics 120, 917–962 (2005)
13. Lin, Y.: Supervision, peer pressure and incentives in a labor-managed firm. China Economic Review 2, 215–229 (1991)
14. Itoh, H.: Incentives to help in multi-agent situations. Eoonommica 59, 611–636 (1991)
15. Drago, R., Garvey, G.T.: Incentives for helping on the job: theory and experiment. Journal of Labor Economics 16, 1–25 (1998)
16. Itoh, H.: Cooperation in hierarchical organizations:an incentive perspective. Journal of Law, Economics and Organization 8, 321–345 (1992)

Computational Simulation of Submarine Oil Spill with Current

Wei Li[*], Yongjie Pang, and Hongwei Li

Science and Technology on Underwater Vehicle Laboratory, Harbin Engineering University,
Harbin, China
weiwei99231@126.com

Abstract. Nowadays, the oil spill models are usually based on the sea surface and few of them are for submarine oil spill. Therefore, the simulation for submarine pipeline oil spill is discussed by FLUENT in this paper to forecast the trajectory of oil. The coupling of pressure and velocity under unsteady-state condition is solved by pressure implicit with splitting of operators algorithm, and the boundary condition of nonlinear free surface is solved by volume of fluid. The simulation of oil particles motion is carried out. Furthermore, the quantity and trajectory of spilled oil under different operating pressure and current velocity are compared and analyzed. The results show that the submarine diffusion scope of spilled oil is smaller with larger operating pressure or lower current velocity.

Keywords: submarine, simulation, oil spill, current.

1 Introduction

The increasing oil spill accidents have led to much oil leaking into the sea and badly destroyed the balance of ecological environment. At present, the modeling for forecasting oil spill behavior and incidence is usually based on sea surface [1, 2] or offshore zones [3, 4]. However, the numerical modeling for submarine oil spill is relatively lacking. Abascal has forecasted the trajectory of submarine oil spill using radar galvanic current [5], but the approach can only supply partial real-time information, and may not support emergency behavior for the influence of weather and night. Li [6], Johansen [7] and Dasanayaka [8] have also carried out the research on submarine oil ejecting, but they all aim at oil gas mixture and can not contribute to forecasting oil spill greatly. Reed [9] has established an oil spill estimation computer system, which also does not refer to forecasting the trajectory of submarine oil spill.

In order to forecast the trajectory of submarine oil spill exactly, we discuss the oil spill of submarine pipeline orifice using FLUENT [10] in this paper. The coupling of pressure and velocity under unsteady-state conditions is solved by pressure implicit with splitting of operators (PISO) algorithm, and the boundary conditions of nonlinear free surface are solved by volume of fluid (VOF). The initial and boundary conditions are defined by UDF of FLUENT. The mathematical model simulates the whole

---

[*] Corresponding author.

R. Chen (Ed.): ICICIS 2011, Part I, CCIS 134, pp. 515–520, 2011.
© Springer-Verlag Berlin Heidelberg 2011

course that oil particles generate from submarine pipelines and rise up to sea surface by buoyancy action. We also discuss the interactivity between oil and water particles, and analyze the oil particles motion with different conditions.

2 Mathematics Model and Methods

The control equations include the continuity equation, the momentum equation and the turbulent current mode of unsteady- incompressible-viscous fluid. The calculation adopts finite volume method and discrete scheme adopts the first order upwind difference scheme.

Sea surface condition belongs to two-phase flow and submarine pipeline oil spill belongs to three-phase flow, which is suitable to use VOF method. The volume fraction a_q is introduced as the volume of substance q in the cell. $a_q=0$ means null, while $a_q=1$ means full. $q=1,2,3$ represents the gas, water and oil, respectively. At nonlinear free surface, a_q should satisfy following conditions:

$$\frac{\partial a_q}{\partial t} + \mathbf{v} \cdot \nabla a_q = 0 \; ; \; q = 1,2,3 \tag{1}$$

$$\sum_{q=1}^{n} a_q = 1 \tag{2}$$

Where, equation (2) is the control condition of calculation. The symbol v is the average velocity of cell. As the density of each port is different through the whole flow field, we adopt following method to calculate the density in the cell where two substances mixes together.

$$\rho = \sum_{q=1}^{n} a_q \rho_q \tag{3}$$

VOF model can simulate two types of immiscible fluids by solving the separate momentum equation and processing the volume ratio of each fluid which cross the domain, expressed as equation (4)

$$\frac{\partial}{\partial t}(\rho \mathbf{v}) + \nabla \cdot (\rho \mathbf{v} \mathbf{v}) = -\nabla P + \nabla \cdot \left[\mu \left(\nabla \mathbf{v} + \nabla \mathbf{v}^T \right) \right] + \rho g + \mathbf{F} \tag{4}$$

3 Simulation and Analysis

3.1 Wave Flume Model

Based on FLUENT, we use GAMBIT to establish numerical model and generate meshes. The flow field is initialized by the pressure-based solver and macro of DEFINE_INIT (my_init_phase, mixture_domain). The model of k-ε and PISO are adopted to solve turbulent flow problems under unsteady conditions. For the boundary conditions, we choose the pressure inlet, symmetry boundary and wall.The parameters are chosen according to the submarine pipelines, oil properties and Bohai conditions. The designing parameters of pipelines are referenced [11, 12].

The pressure in oil pipeline is different according to different positions of oil spill, so we define several operating pressure as oil particles spilling pressure, such as 100600pa, 100800 pa, 101000pa and 102000pa. And current velocity is defined as 0.1 m/s. Moreover, the current velocity of each sea area is different, so we define current velocity as 0.3m/s, 0.5 m/s and 0.8 m/s, while operating pressure is 101000pa.

3.2 Oil Spill Analysis

The oil is spilled and quickly forms the jet current or plume current with low operating pressure. When spilled oil reaches a certain horizon plane and the dynamical character of jet current or plume current is not important enough, the spilled oil current is dispersed by coming water current to form oil particles. This process is shown in Fig. 1.

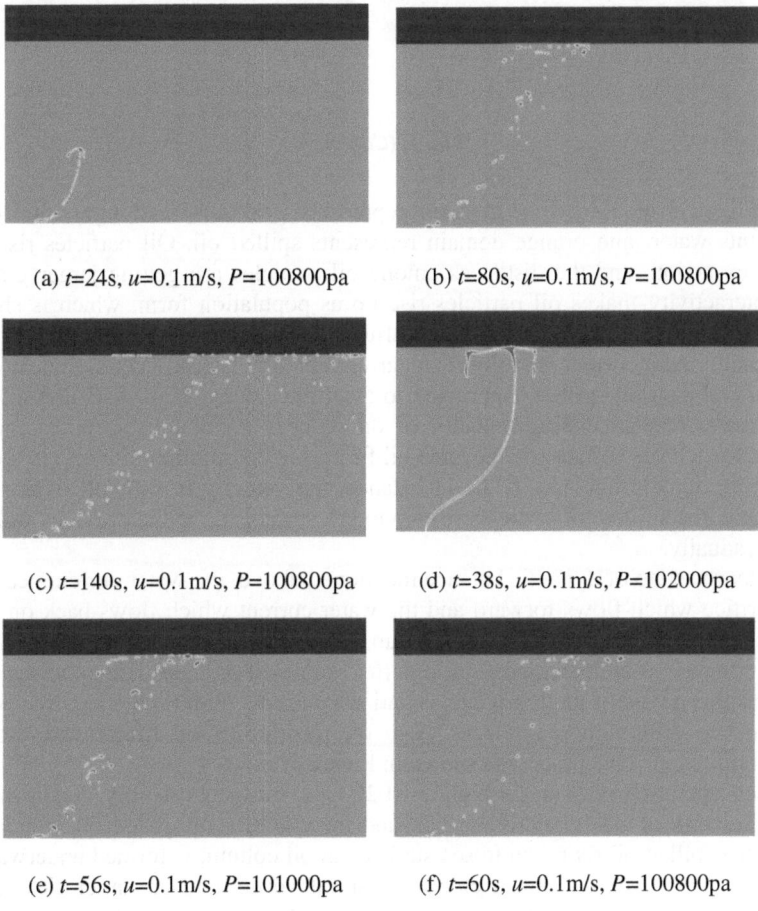

(a) t=24s, u=0.1m/s, P=100800pa   (b) t=80s, u=0.1m/s, P=100800pa

(c) t=140s, u=0.1m/s, P=100800pa   (d) t=38s, u=0.1m/s, P=102000pa

(e) t=56s, u=0.1m/s, P=101000pa   (f) t=60s, u=0.1m/s, P=100800pa

Fig. 1. Distribution of oil-water-gas

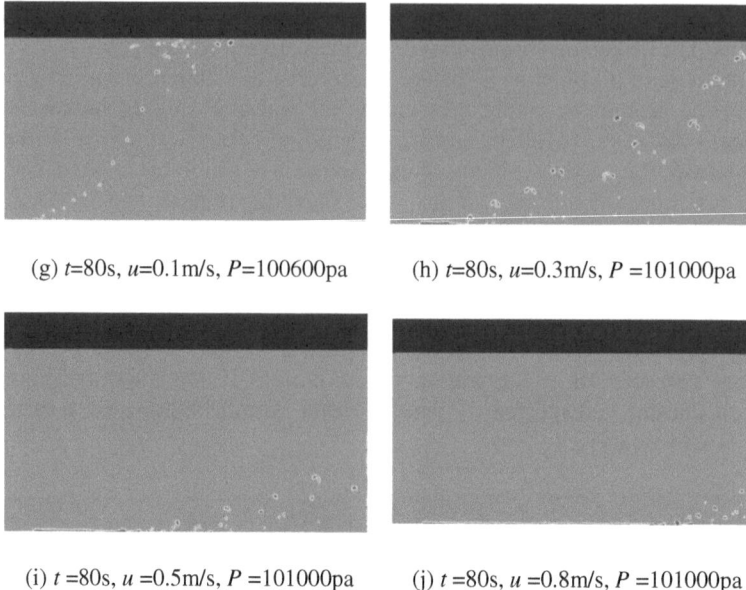

(g) t=80s, u=0.1m/s, P=100600pa   (h) t=80s, u=0.3m/s, P =101000pa

(i) t =80s, u =0.5m/s, P =101000pa   (j) t =80s, u =0.8m/s, P =101000pa

Fig. 1. (*Continued*)

In Figure 1(a), dark blue domain represents gas (air), and light blue domain represents water, and orange domain represents spilled oil. Oil particles rise up by buoyancy action, and the distances among oil particles are getting larger gradually. The interactivity makes oil particles rise up as population form, which is shown in Figure 1(b). The spilled oil particles influence the seawater current and cause the variation of local current velocity. The current velocity is relatively high near oil spill orifice, and then oil spill is suppressed to a certain extent. With sustained spilling of oil particles, the ascending velocity of oil reduces continuously. When initial oil particles reach sea surface and become oil films, the distribution of current velocity in the whole domain becomes to be in balance, the velocity of oil spill is also stable. Therefore, the spilled oil particles rise up to sea surface along the previous wake flow trace gradually.

Under the state of dynamic balance mentioned above, the water current near the oil spill orifice which flows forward and the water current which flows back on surface generate a clockwise spiral vortex and an anticlockwise spiral vortex, respectively. With influence of anticlockwise spiral vortex, some oil particles rise up to sea surface and generate a type of motion which is anti sea current. With time going by, the rising oil particles drift with sea current. Also the position of oil films move along the current direction. This process is shown in Figure 1(c).

When operating pressure is high as 102000pa, oil ejects rapidly. Meanwhile, the rising velocity of oil is relatively high and the quantity of spilled oil is increasing. While the spilled oil rising up to sea surface, an oil column is formed underwater. By the influence of sea current, a clockwise spiral vortex and an anticlockwise spiral vortex appear around the oil spill orifice and at the end of oil column, as shown in Figure 1(d).

The simulation results under different operating pressure as 101000pa, 100800 pa and 100600 are shown in Figure 1(e) to Figure 1(g).

We can see from Figure 4 to Figure 7, if operating pressure is greater than 102000pa, the spilled oil rise up to sea surface as a continuous oil column; if operating pressure is less than 101000pa, the spilled oil rise up to sea surface as oil particles. With operating pressure increasing, the spilled oil quantity is getting greater, and the ascending velocity is getting higher, and the stretched distance of spilled oil is shorter. Moreover, the distribution of current velocity in one vertical plane is more non-uniform, and spiral vortex is stronger. The anti direction drift of oil particles near sea surface is more obvious.

According to the analysis above, the conclusion can be drawn that different operating pressure can cause different oil spill trajectory, when the other conditions are fixed. When operating pressure is high enough, the sea current has little influence on oil spill, and we can control and reclaim oil spill more easily. However, when the operating pressure is low, the stretched extent underwater and oil films area on surface increase, which is difficult for the spilled oil to be controlled.

As the density of oil and seawater is almost the same, when current velocity rises continuously with the same operating pressure, the influence of sea current is strengthened. Meanwhile, the influence of buoyancy is relatively weakened. When the current velocity is low ($u=0.1$m/s), as shown in Fig. 5, the influence of buoyancy becomes dominant to the rising spilled oil. When the current velocity is $u=0.3$m/s, $u=0.5$m/s and $u=0.8$m/s, as shown in Figure 1(h) to Figure 1(j), the influence of sea current dominates obviously, and oil particles move with sea current after spilled immediately. Therefore, the higher current velocity is, the longer submarine drift distance is.

When the operating pressure is fixed, the influence of sea current is little on the spilled oil quantity at unit intervals. So the operating pressure becomes a key influencing factor. By the analog analysis, we can obtain that the oil drift extent varies with current velocity. If current velocity is high enough, the spilled oil maybe attaches to sea floor and increases the problems for oil control and recovery. As the species and quantity distribution of benthos is simple and the oil degradation capability of benthos is poor, the pollution of the oil may exit for a long time.

4 Conclusions

We have discussed the two-dimension and three-phase flow numerical modeling for submarine pipeline oil spill by FLUENT and analyzed the motion of oil particles with different operating pressure and current velocity. We have not only obtained the spilled oil quantity at each time, but also simulated the drifting trajectory meantime, which can supply effective information for emergency decision. The simulation results indicate that the operating pressure and current velocity are key factors which influence oil spill behavior and incidence, and they determine the position and area of surface oil films, which are very important for forecasting the oil spill behavior and incidence. In this paper, we only discuss two factors above, and other oceanic conditions will be discussed in further research.

References

1. Zhu, S., Dmitry, S.: A numerical model for the confinement of oil spill with floating booms. Spill Science & Technology Bulletin 7(5), 249–255 (2002)
2. Xie, H., Yapa, P.D., Nakata, K.: Modeling emulsification after an oil spill in the sea. Modeling emulsification after an oil spill in the sea 68, 489–506 (2007)
3. Guo, W.J., Wang, Y.X.: A numerical oil spill model based on a hybrid method. Marine Pollution Bulletin 58, 726–734 (2009)
4. Guo, W.J., Wang, Y.X., Xie, M.X., Cui, Y.J.: Modeling oil spill trajectory in coastal waters based on fractional Brownian motion. Marine Pollution Bulletin 58, 1339–1346 (2009)
5. Abascal, A.J., Castanedo, S., Medina, R.: Application of HF radar currents to oil spill modeling. Marine Pollution Bulletin 58, 238–248 (2009)
6. Li, Z., Yapa, P.D.: Modeling gas dissolution in deepwater oil/gas spills. Journal of Marine Systems 31, 299–309 (2002)
7. Øistein, J., Rye, H., Cooper, C.: Deepspill-field study of a simulated oil and gas blowout in deep water. Spill Science & Technology Bulletin 8(5), 433–443 (2003)
8. Dasanayaka, L.K., Yapa, P.D.: Role of plume dynamics phase in a deepwater oil and gas release model. Journal of Hydro-environment Research 2, 243–253 (2009)
9. Reed, M., Emilsen, M.H., Hetland, B.: Numerical model for estimation of pipeline oil spill volumes. Environmental Modelling & Software 21, 178–189 (2006)
10. Wang, R., Zhang, K., Wang, G.: Fluent technology basis and application instance. Tsinghua University Press, Beijing (2007)
11. Liu, J., Hu, H.: The design of submarine pipeline in chengdao oil field. China Offshore Platform 11(5), 214–217 (1996)
12. Zhao, S., Liu, J.: Submarine Pipeline Design of Chengdao Oilfield. Oil & Gas Storage and Transportation 16(5), 32–36 (1997)

Study on Engineering Consciousness and Ability Fostering of Applied Talents in Engineering Education

Wang dong ping

Department of Modern Science & Technology
Agricultural University of Hebei
Baoding, Hebei, China
qceftgh@126.com

Abstract. Fostering problem of innovative applied talent in engineering education is important problem of modern industry development and innovative national construction. The paper analyze detailedly Engineering ability connotation and engineers quality feature, and point out Status and problems of higher engineering education in China, and put forward effective way of constructing engineering consciousness and ability fostering environment of innovative engineering science and technology talent in order to improve student's innovation consciousness and engineering ability.

Keywords: innovation consciousness, engineering consciousness, engineering ability, applied talents.

1 Introduction

Engineering is an important part of modern civilization, economic operation and social development, and impact on all aspects of human life. With the rapid development of world science and technology updates, engineering and technology play a more important role on economic and social development. And training quality of engineering qualified scientists and technicians will determine the quality of engineering technology's level and development speed and the country's industrial competitiveness. And innovative engineering talent cultivation has become the key issue of industrial development and innovative national construction of the 21st century. But for a long time, undergraduate talents cultivation are affected by the traditional idea with value theory and neglect practice, and trained engineering professionals is not high quality of innovation, and engineering practice is not strong. Especially under the context of higher education popular but education resource-constrained, the phenomenon with lacking of innovative spirit, weak practical ability and disjointing between talent foster and economic and social development are becoming more prominent. Therefore, training student's engineering spirit and consciousness and developing student's innovative potential which is converted to innovative indeed are the first problem of engineering education.

R. Chen (Ed.): ICICIS 2011, Part I, CCIS 134, pp. 521–528, 2011.
© Springer-Verlag Berlin Heidelberg 2011

2 Engineering Ability Concept and Engineers Quality

2.1 Engineering Ability Concept

Engineering itself is a kind of innovation design work. In economic activities, the engineering is defined as intermediate link which the market demand are converted to manufacture process, including production design and quality definition, also including project management, operation management and related activities. Therefore, essence of engineering is innovation, and engineering education is to cultivate innovative engineering technology talents. Ability refers to have the stable psychological characteristics of personality which fulfill any activities and is get according repeat training during the use of intelligence, knowledge and skills, and it shows mind-body energy when knowing and changing the world depending on self-intelligence, knowledge and skills. It includes general ability and special ability: general ability is referred to put up thinking ability, learning ability, observation ability, memory, etc in general activities. Special ability refers to possess analytical ability, innovational ability, organizational ability coordinal ability, etc in specific activities. The students' engineering ability in the high engineering education refers to the practical ability and energy about students' comprehensive quality that performed in engineering practical activities, and the goal of international engineering is to train the future engineers who have comprehensive quality that suit the development of international engineering and the creation of state and social need.

2.2 Engineers Features

The American National Engineering Academy has put forward the corn quality of the future engineers in 《the 2010 Engineer Plans》 : there are strong analysis ability, flexible practice ability, high creativity and good communication ability, business and management skills, a high level of professional ethics, intense professional consciousness and ability of lifelong learning. The American engineering and technology of engineering educational training authentication committee have made 11 items of professional talents article evaluation standards: (1) ability with applied mathematics, science and engineering knowledge;(2) ability with designing experiment analysis and date management;(3)ability with designing a component, a system or a process according to the needing;(4)a variety of ability with training comprehensive;(5)ability with checking, guidance and solving the engineer problems;(6)understanding the professional ethics and social responsibility;(7)ability with effective expression and communication;(8)knowing the global environment and social influence because of the engineering problems;(9) ability with lifelong learning;(10)having the knowledge of the present time relevant problems;(11) ability with applying a various skills and modern engineering tools to solve practical problems.

According to the association of Australia's engineers and quality engineer's "double model of quality", engineer will be divided into two kinds of basic knowledge and basic skills. Basic knowledge include: engineering discipline knowledge, formal and informal informational sources knowledge, the latest technology and skill, engineering tools. Basic skills include: professional technical ability, communication skills, study ability, analysis ability, information's choices and decisions, interpersonal skills, risk and dangerous analysis, synthetic ability, comprehensive ability from multiple side. From this we can see, these standards are basic same with American standard, also focus on engineering technology knowledge, mastery of the latest project tools and interpersonal skills, problem analysis ability, etc.

National Academy of Engineering in the UK describe a changeful industrial view in the context of globalization and complication for the research of future engineering graduates. If every company need to successful operation in such a complex and capricious environment, it must find professional technical engineering graduates with scientific and practice ability, and these graduates must have strong interpersonal skills, including the ability to present situation of business as shown Fig 1. As can be seen from the figure 1, the engineer has three types: engineer as specialist, engineer as integrator, engineer as change agent. Among them, that engineer as specialist shows that the market have sustained needing for specialist with international level, and engineer as integrator reflect engineering is in a complex environment and needs the engineer with diversification skills, and in order to promote new industrial development in the uncertain future, engineer as change agent must have creativeness, innovation and leadership. Intersection part denote , technical skill, social skills and quality forming core competence of engineering graduates, at one time skills of engineering graduates possessing should be the set of various subjects ability. Obviously, engineering graduates need to undertake engineer roles of above three kinds.

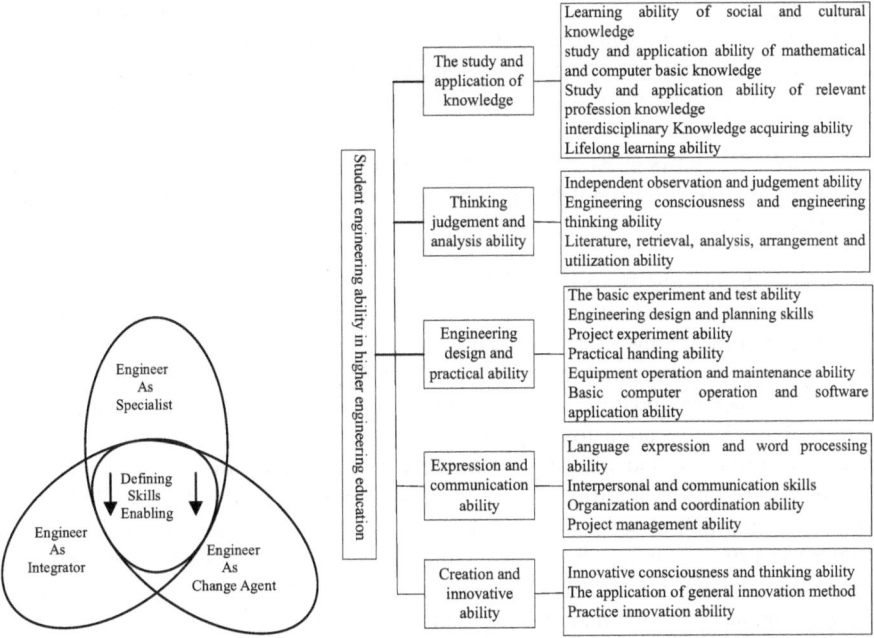

Fig. 1. Future engineering graduate prospect **Fig. 2.** Students work ability structural system in higher engineering education

At present, with the rapid development of new subject, more and more engineering problems need to be solved in creative thoughts, so it requires that university foster engineering science and technology talent that not only grasp broad and deep professional knowledge, but also possess outstanding professional experience of the field, the ability to construct products and system, good teamwork spirit and the ability of human communication, the ability to exchange culture, and economical mind. Accordingly, the education department have established a "quality" project requiring higher education focus on efforts to improve the quality, especially on the spirit of innovation and practical ability of the students. For the students, they should have the ability of learning and application the knowledge, thinking and analysis ability of judgment, engineering design and practice, communication skills and abilities to create innovations[1]. The structure of engineering abilities is showed in figure 2.

3 Necessity of Engineering Consciousness and Ability Fostering of Applied Talent in Engineering Education

Since Beiyang University was found in 1895, the higher engineering education has been developing more than a hundred years. Particular in the recent 20 years, The higher educational scope and level have great development. The engineering students are more than 7,000,000 in 2008(Chinese education net). There are 36 countries and religions acknowledge mutually educational background with China. We are not only creasing the experience and accumulating the fund, but also strength our national power and raising political economy in the internationality, and it is a miracle in the history of the people's economic and society. But facing with current new situation of economy and society development, there are still disparity and shortage to train the engineering science talent in our country higher engineering education.

3.1 Applied Talents of Engineering Education Fostering Are Difficult to Adapt Economy Development Requirement because of Producing and Learning Disjunction

At present, the process factories which mainly use cheap labor are towards to southeast Asia and other areas where the labor is cheaper, and China has huge press facing with industrial reforming and updating. However, Overall condition of our country's engineering science and technology talent development can't adapt to the requirement of industrial structure updating and new industrialization development in which prominent problem is education foster pattern can't adapt to development requirement because of producing and learning disjunction. For example, in Tsinghua University, perhaps only 25% scientific research can sign contract with the establishment to transform in which about 30% can achieve success, namely only 7.5% scientific research can bring economic benefit[2]. China need a great deal high quality talent for quick development in industrial chain. Because of educational concept, school-running mechanism, teachers, the management and the teaching link etc questions, the quality of the engineering education can't meet the requirement of industry on talent and of youth on job. China engineering academy ever has given a research to the 5,000 engineering science and technology talent, and 21.8% people think that student of universities fostering far from or basically not fit country technology development demands; and 52.4% of respondents recognize that quality of engineering major student of our country is very common[3].

3.2 Because Innovation Consciousness Culture Environment Is Lacked, Practice and Innovation Ability of Applied Talent of Engineering Education Fostering Are Weak

Long-term planning system make our country higher education management system form very strong commonness restriction, and single culture mode, inculcation type teaching way and rote learning examination manner not only cause no innovative knowledge base, but also make student form intense seeking same thought and form difficult seeking different thought which is very important for innovation. However, at present engineering training in teaching process which still mainly locate classroom and laboratory is lacked combination and harmonious development with society , especial corporation engineering practice. Even though factory practice with a period is arranged, students seldom can indeed direct contact actual production process because of restriction of practice field and manage condition, or practice training is very different with practical production because practice content is planed to enclose firmly teaching project. Investigation show that 60.4% of respondents think current engineering education can not provide abundant engineering training for student, and engineering students commonly are lacked importance understand for engineering design and applying integration knowledge to settle problem[4]. Moreover, Quite a lot of students in engineering graduate have poor operating ability, low settling practice problem ability, narrow specialty knowledge, bad communication ability and low engineering interest degree etc problems. According to a investigation of employing units involving in IT industry, manufacturing industry, transportation industry, construction industry, posts and telecommunications industry, education and development industry etc many industries, in which 44.0% of employing units think that employed engineering graduate are lacked of science attitude and spirit(such as attitude of preciseness and painstaking, spirit of daring to doubt, criticism and being bold in making innovations etc), 40.2% think their engineering consciousness(such as economy manage consciousness, ethic consciousness and moral consciousness etc) and innovation consciousness are deficiency, 38% think they cannot well recognize and form and settle engineering problem. moreover, some employing units still think engineering graduate don't flexible use technology and modern tool which are necessary for engineering practice, and they don't skillfully operate experiment and analyze and explain the data, and their work ability of independence, communication ability of language and letter and lifelong learning literacy are low[5].

4   The Construction of Engineering Consciousness and Ability Fostering Environment of Applied Talent in Engineering Education

Under the new situation of global economic integration and industrial upgrading, quantity and quality of engineer is inevitably set a higher request. Although engineering graduates must go through the project practices trainings for many years before they become a real engineer, but the school of engineering education play a vital role in whether they can become qualified engineers in the future. Engineering consciousness and ability fostering of innovative engineering science and technology talent is a complicated systematic project, so we should adjust the personal training plan, establish virtual study experiment situation, develop the assistant professor project, establish enterprise project training center and conduct technical innovation and so on to found an environment which stimulates student's engineering consciousness and ability cultivation, and explore method and strategy of the innovative engineering science and technology fostering.

4.1 Establishing the "Big Engineering" Concept, and Optimizing Talent Training Plan in Engineering Education

At present, China has entered the great industrial age that the information technology stimulate industrialization and the industrialization promote information, whose core is to take the road to industrialization which make a full use of high technology content, good economic benefit, low resource consumption, litter environmental pollution, human resource advantages being fully exerting. So, engineering science and technology talent of university fostering not only has the foundation of natural science and engineering science, but also must have the quality of humanities social science which surpasses engineering specialized technology category, such as economy, society, law, management, environment and so on. Accordingly, when we make talents training program of engineering education, we must establish the "big engineering" concept , and put engineering into a large system which include economy, society, science, humanity, environment and so on, and set the curriculum whose main features is cross-professional integration and application of many multi-disciplinary courses, and emphasis on coordination of engineering and natural, engineering and social, and try to achieve the cross and integration and mutual penetration between the various disciplines and technical fields, meanwhile strengthen the humanities, economics, law in the curriculum, in order to facilitate the forming of engineering major student's engineering ethics, engineering spirit and consciousness.

Setting up virtual experimental environment to establish learning platform for engineering ability education.

In order to further understand and learn engineering courses and stimulate innovation consciousness and ability in engineering specialized courses teaching and experiment, we set "big engineering" concept, and adopt VRML language combining with JavaScript language, and merge 3-D stereo environment, scene roaming, dynamic explosion, virtual demonstration operation and experiment assistant etc module, and construct distance education system based on virtual reality, and create distance virtual studying and experiment situation. SQL SERVER and ACCESS are adopted to set up network and stand-alone edition data-base, and each teaching and experiment course is integrated as direct management material as shown in figure 3. Function module of hanging type structure are designed in order to realize increasing continuously new module and making new function along with expansion of subject and major, and knowledge network system of many subject cross are constructed to make students master relaxedly reorganization and debugging in virtual training, then realize distance allopatry multi-person collaborative work and communication.

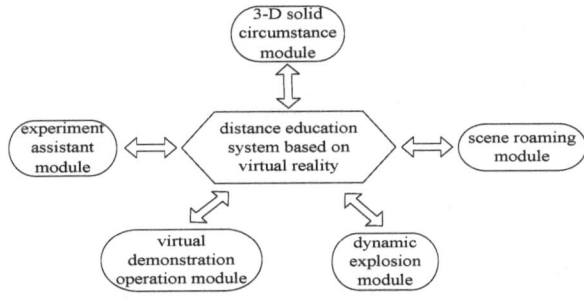

Fig. 3. Distance education system based on virtual reality

Meanwhile, project develop study of virtual reality and hardware-in-the-loop simulation method, and train student's communication and collaboration ability in created "autonomous learning" circumstance, and make students be enlightened by invention-creation in imitation.

4.2 Expanding the Practice Space to Increase the Engineering Ability of Applied Talent of Engineering Education

Innovation environment is important condition of the knowledge innovation. Cultivating student's innovation consciousness and innovation ability, the most important way is to build a strong learning atmosphere and a practice platform. In order to improve these abilities and reduce the blindness of student autonomous learning, practice link is strengthened in engineering students fostering, and innovation and practice platform are constructed.

1) Developing professor assistant engineering: Subject research project is throughout textbook compiling, classroom teaching and practice activities. Under the lead and guidance of professors with innovation experience, research platform is put up for fostering innovative engineering science and technology talent, student's engineering consciousness and engineering ability is trained in scientific research.

2) Setting up enterprise engineering training centre: Engineering practice education need the support of the internal and external environment. If engineering practice environment of universities want to keep up to step of social economy and construction development, only depending on national investment can not be achieved temporarily. University cooperates with many enterprises to run a school, and utilize enterprise source and get united with the required direction of corporation talent, and set up enterprise engineering training centre in order to achieve the win-win of the university engineering talent cultivation and manpower resource needed by enterprise.

3) Holding science and technology innovation activity: Through holding various forms skill competition convey "theory with practice" and "combining education with productive labor" educational idea to students and society, and construct an innovative atmosphere in order to train student's innovative spirit and ability.

Acknowledgment

The author thanks funding support of agricultural university of Hebei teaching and research project (08-B20), (10-A15), (08-A5).

References

1. Fu, Y.: Engineering ability structure and training ways of Higher Engineering Education. Journal of Technology College Education 25(3), 79–80 (2006)
2. Cha, J.Z., He, Y.C.: Three great strategy of Engineering Education in China. Press of Beijing Institute of Technology (2009)
3. Pan, Y.H.: Why is the last in world of China engineering education ability. Wen hui daily (5) (September 28, 2007)
4. Hen, B.Q., Yang, H.G.: How to foster future engineer, China education newspaper (2) (September 10, 2007)
5. Li, Q.F., Zhao, Y.F.: Survey of practical ability for university students from the perspectives. Higher education development and evaluation 24(1), 106–115, 124

Application Research of Improved Grey Forecasting Model in Load Forecasting

Yuansheng Huang, Wei Fang, and Zhou Fan

School of Business Administration, North China Electric Power University,
Baoding 071003, China
fangwei_ncepu@yahoo.cn

Abstract. As the most common grey model, GM (1,1) is useful for power load forecasting. Based on the slide average method, the paper improves the original data and the traditional GM (1,1) model effectively, and compares the forecast results between traditional GM (1,1) model and improved GM (1,1) model. Finally, it improves the effectiveness of power load forecasting.

Keywords: gray model, load forecasting, moving average method, GM(1,1).

1 Introduction

On Load Forecasting Method for Power System is a typical kind of grey system, and it uses some parts of the data to predict future data. The GM (1,1) model is a more common grey model, its first order differential equation is gray, through the GM (1,1) model requires only the load of the original data. The main characteristics of this method is the algorithm is simple, fast, less in the case of historical data, showed growth or decline of a class of data, its predictions were able to achieve good accuracy. However, the gray model itself has some limitations, the data dispersion, the greater, the larger the gray scale, the prediction accuracy is worse, the forecast for too long not ideal. Consider the above limitations, this paper moving average method using the original series; Grey has been improved, so that the data only increases the weight of the year, while avoiding excessive volatility in the value.

2 Traditional GM (1, 1) Model

Grey system theory is put forward in the international arena by Professor Deng Julong first, Grey characteristics of the data in the analysis of small, little understanding of the behavior of the data to explore the potential mechanism of less data, less comprehensive data based on the phenomenon, reveals little data, little background information on the variation of things. GM (1,1) model is the most commonly used as a gray model, which is a variable that contains only a single first-order differential equations to construct the model as an effective load forecasting model is GM (1,n) model is a special case. Establishment of GM (1,1) model requires only a few columns.

R. Chen (Ed.): ICICIS 2011, Part I, CCIS 134, pp. 529–534, 2011.

Set the known historical load raw data sequence is:

$$X^{(0)} = \{x^{(0)}(1), x^{(0)}(2),\ldots\ldots x^{(0)}(n)\} \quad (1)$$

Using an accumulated generating series:

$$X^{(1)} = \{x^{(1)}(1), x^{(1)}(2),\ldots\ldots x^{(1)}(n)\} \quad (2)$$

Where, $x^{(1)}(k) = \sum_{i=1}^{k} x^{(0)}(i)$

Establishment of the following first order differential equation $x^{(1)}(k)$:

$$\frac{dX^{(1)}}{dt} + aX^{(1)} = u \quad (3)$$

Where, a, u is the unknown factor.

Determine the data matrix B, Y_n:

$$(4)$$

$$B = \begin{bmatrix} -\frac{1}{2}(x^{(1)}(1) + x^{(1)}(2)) & 1 \\ -\frac{1}{2}(x^{(1)}(2) + x^{(1)}(3)) & 1 \\ \cdots & \cdots \\ -\frac{1}{2}(x^{(1)}(N-1) + x^{(1)}(N)) & 1 \end{bmatrix}$$

$$Y_n = \begin{pmatrix} x^{(0)}(2) \\ x^{(0)}(3) \\ \vdots \\ x^{(0)}(n) \end{pmatrix} \quad (5)$$

With the least square method:

$$A = (a,u)^T = (B^T B)^{-1} B^T Y_n \quad (6)$$

The coefficients a, u into the formula (3) and then solve the differential equation. Let $x^{(0)}(0) = x^{(1)}(0)$, the gray prediction model available:

$$\hat{x}^{(1)}(k+1) = \left[x^{(0)}(1) - \frac{u}{a} \right] e^{-ak} + \frac{u}{a} \quad k = 1,2,\cdots,n \quad (7)$$

Type the first order of the cumulative reduction (1-IAGO) to restore opera-
tions $\hat{x}^{(0)}(k+1) = \hat{x}^{(1)}(k+1) - \hat{x}^{(1)}(k)$, that is to get the original $x^{(0)}$ series prediction model is:

$$\hat{x}^{(0)}(k+1) = (1 - e^{a})\left[x^{(0)}(1) - \frac{u}{a}\right]e^{-ak} \quad k = 0,1,2,\cdots,n \tag{8}$$

Grey system has obvious advantages: the principle is simple, requires less sample
data, easy operation, and short-term forecasting accuracy. It applies only to the
amount to be predicted with a constant exponential growth rate of the short or me-
dium-term load forecasting, for the E-type, S-shaped curve, and no significant
changes of the curve and long-term load forecast, the forecast errors. Therefore, the
need for ordinary gray GM (1, 1) model is improved.

3   Improved Gray GM (1, 1) Model Based on Moving Average Method

Gray model method is suitable for a strong exponential load forecasting, and this
method should make choice to the data. Meanwhile, if you make the choice, you
should choose the date uniformly-spaced, and make the latest data as a reference
point, make the earliest data to go to stay, but the latest data must be added. The purpose of making the model advanced is weakening the impact of outliers, strengthen-
ing the general trend of the original series, in order to make the transformation of raw
data as far as possible changes in the sequence of exponential increase. When the
original series growing too fast, we should be modified so that the rate of change
changes. In order to achieve the purpose, this paper chooses the moving average
method.

Through the application of the original average method, the impact of outliers can
be weaned, as far as possible the original data transformed into a sequence of incremental changes.

Set the known historical load raw data sequence is:

$$\{x^{(0)}(t)\} \quad t = 1,2,\cdots,n \tag{9}$$

Moving average value is calculated as follows:

$$x^{'(0)}(t) = \frac{x^{(0)}(t-1) + 2x^{(0)}(t) + x^{(0)}(t+1)}{4} \tag{10}$$

The computation not only increases the weight of the year data, but also avoids excessive volatility of the data. This improved method can be used for the calculation of the
two end points to calculate the following formula:

$$x^{'(0)}(1) = \frac{3x^{(0)}(1) + x^{(0)}(2)}{4} \tag{11}$$

$$x^{'(0)}(n) = \frac{x^{(0)}(n-1) + 3x^{(0)}(n)}{4} \tag{12}$$

Through the above steps to improve the original data, the remaining steps with the original GM (1, 1) model calculation steps.

4 Application Sample

Through the improved grey model, this paper adopted moving average method based on the improved GM (1,1) model for load forecasting, and used Mat lab software to achieve specific load forecasting process. This paper selected a place 1995-2003 annual electricity consumption by 9 sets of data modeling, load forecasting and the next three years, and then compared with the actual values to test the practical application of this model. Nine consecutive years in an area of electricity consumption in the following Table 1 (unit: billion kwh):

Table 1. Nine consecutive years in an area of electricity consumption

year	1995	1996	1997	1998	1999	2000	2001	2002	2003
serial number	1	2	3	4	5	6	7	8	9
use value	602.01	645.83	691.62	793.56	813.02	886.46	931.94	1014.16	1088.02

Combine raw data, calculate using MATLAB software and the GM (1,1) model, and reach the results showed in Table 2:

Table 2. The calculation result of traditional gray model

year	1995	1996	1997	1998	1999	2000
serial number	1	2	3	4	5	6
use values	602.01	645.83	691.62	793.56	813.02	886.46
calculated values	602.01	657.5	706.6	759.5	816.2	877.2
absolute uncertainty	0	11.6700	14.9800	-34.0600	3.1800	-9.2600
Relative error	0.00%	1.77%	2.12%	4.48%	0.39%	1.06%
year	2001	2002	2003	2004	2005	2006
serial number	7	8	9	10	11	12
use values	931.94	1014.16	1088.02	1152.34	1245.62	1340.66
calculated values	942.8	1013.3	1089.0	1170.4	1257.9	1351.9
absolute uncertainty	10.8600	-0.8600	0.9800	18.06	12.28	11.24
Relative error	1.15%	0.08%	0.09%	1.57%	0.99%	0.84%

Combine raw data, calculate using MATLAB software and the improved GM (1,1) model, and reach the results showed in Table 3:

Table 3. The calculation result of improved gray model

year	1995	1996	1997	1998	1999	2000
serial number	1	2	3	4	5	6
use values	602.01	645.83	691.62	793.56	813.02	886.46
calculated values	602.01	661.9	704.9	761.3	816.5	875.7
absolute uncertainty	0	16.0700	13.2800	-32.2600	3.4800	-10.7600
Relative error	0.00%	2.48%	1.88%	4.06%	0.43%	1.20%
year	2001	2002	2003	2004	2005	2006
serial number	7	8	9	10	11	12
use values	931.94	1014.16	1088.02	1152.34	1245.62	1340.66
calculated values	939.2	1007.2	1080.2	1158.5	1242.5	1332.6
absolute uncertainty	7.2600	-6.9600	-7.8200	6.1600	-3.1200	-8.0600
Relative error	0.77%	0.69%	0.71%	0.53%	0.25%	0.60%

The traditional model of the above results and improved GM (1,1) comparison of the results can be seen that the results of the next three years to improve the prediction accuracy of the results higher, the improved GM (1,1) model to accurately predict electricity use, and the actual value of the absolute error even smaller, so you can confirm the improved GM (1,1) model, the effectiveness of load forecasting.

5 Conclusions

This paper establishes the mathematical model through nine years of historical data, and predicts the load values of the next three years, and then test effect to prove reliability of the improved GM(1,1)method. This paper uses the forecasting process the original GM (1,1) prediction model and the improved GM (1,1) prediction model. By comparing the two model calculations of data, improved GM (1,1) prediction model improves the accuracy of the load to prove that moving average method using gray prediction for the original series, improved the prediction accuracy has been further improved.

References

[1] Yan-li, N.: Application of optimal combined forecasting method in electricity prices fore-casting. Electric Power Science and Engineering 4, 30–32 (2005)
[2] Wang, Y.-L.: Adaptive forecasting method for time-series data streams. Zidonghua Xuebao/Acta Automatica Sinica 33(2), 197–201 (2007)

[3] Jiang, C.-w.: Research of forecasting method on chaotic load series with high embedded dimension. Power System Technology 28(3), 25–28 (2004)

[4] Deng, J.: A novel grey model GM (1, 1 | τ, r): generalizing GM (1, 1). Journal of Grey System 13(1), 1–8 (2001)

[5] Yu, M.-s.: Application of combined optimum grey model to mid and long term load forecasting. Journal of Shenyang University of Technology 29(2), 153–156 (2007)

[6] Lei, M.: A novel grey model to short-term electricity price forecasting for NordPool power market. In: Proceedings of the 2009 IEEE International Conference on Systems, Man and Cybernetics. SMC (2009)

An Adaptive Multi-agent System for Project Schedule Management*

Yongyi Shou and Changtao Lai

School of Management, Zhejiang University,
310058 Hangzhou, China
{yshou,changtao86}@zju.edu.cn

Abstract. A multi-agent system is established for project schedule management, considering the need for adaptive and dynamic scheduling under uncertainty. The system is realized using Java. In the proposed system, three types of
agents, namely activity agents, resource agents, and a monitoring agent, are
designed. Duration and resource requirement self-learning operators are
developed for activity agents in order to model the self-learning and adaptive
capacities of an agent in its local environment; moreover, a monitoring operator
is also presented for the monitoring agent. The system allows the user to set up
simulation parameters or scheduling rules according to their own preferences.
Simulation results from an example showed that the system is effective in supporting users' decision-making process.

Keywords: multi-agent system; project scheduling; decision support system.

1 Introduction

With the development of project management, a variety of techniques for scheduling
have been proposed. However, commercial software tools, such as Primavera Project
Planner and Microsoft Project, have not included the advanced optimization algorithms appeared in literatures [1]. Traditional methods play important roles in the
implementation of a project, but with constant challenges too. This is because the real
project is usually uncertain (with uncertain duration and resource requirements, etc.)
and progressive (which requires dynamic scheduling) and is distributed for resource
allocations (team members may be geographically decentralized), thus brings high
complexity especially to the scheduling of large-scale projects (it requires adaptive
control), which results in insurmountable difficulties for traditional management
techniques from theory to application.

Agent technology which originates from the mid-1980s provides new methodology
for solving the dynamic scheduling and collaboration problem in a distributed environment. In this paper, combining the characteristics of an agent such as autonomy,
social ability, reactivity, etc. [2], we developed a self-learning and self-adaptive
scheduling procedure to achieve the self-learning behaviors of project activities, as

---

* The paper is supported by Zhejiang Provincial Natural Science Foundation of China
(R7100297).

R. Chen (Ed.): ICICIS 2011, Part I, CCIS 134, pp. 535–540, 2011.
© Springer-Verlag Berlin Heidelberg 2011

well as the adaptive control of the entire project; hence a multi-agent system for project schedule management was established.

2 Resource-Constrained Project Scheduling

To describe the profile of resource-constrained project scheduling problem, the following symbols and corresponding definitions will be used in this paper.

Two types of makespans are presented. One is the planned makespan, denoted by D^p, which is calculated through the critical path method (CPM) without considering the resource constraints; the other is the real makespan, denoted by D^r.

A project consists of a set of J activities $j = 1, 2, \ldots, J$, where activities 1 and J are dummy start and end activities respectively. π_j denotes the attribute of activity j, whose value is either CPA when activity j appears in critical path or $NCPA$ otherwise.

Activity j may be in one of four states, denoted by ξ_j, where $\xi_j = 0, 1, 2,$ or 3, representing available, eligible, executing, or finished state respectively. We adopt the assumption that activities are non-preemptable while processing. The types of duration of activity j include planned duration d_j^p, optimistic duration d_j^{om}, pessimistic duration d_j^{pm} and real duration d_j^r. All are assumed to be non-negative integers, and d_j^p, d_j^{om}, and d_j^{pm} are determined in the planning stage, while d_j^r is uncertain.

A set of K resources index by k are available for the project, including renewable and nonrenewable ones. τ_k is introduced to represent resource attribute, whose value is either 0 when resource k is renewable or 1 otherwise. TR_k denotes the total amount of resource k, and CR_k represents the available amount in the current period.

The planned requirement of resource k for activity j is denoted rq_{jk}^p, and the real one is denoted by rq_{jk}^r. The former is determined in the planning stage, while the latter is uncertain and is determined by adjusting rq_{jk}^p in the dynamic scheduling stage.

In addition, we will use the following symbols and their definitions. Let t denotes the simulation clock, where $t = 1, 2, \ldots, D^r$. Φ denotes the activity agent group, and $AA_j \in \Phi$ is an agent for activity j. Similarly, Γ denotes the resource agent group, and $RA_k \in \Gamma$ is an agent for resource k. The only monitoring agent is represented by MA. The set of immediate predecessors of i activity j is denoted by IP_j. $S_{t_0}^{cpa}$ is a set of critical activities at time t_0, where $S_{t_0}^{cpa} = \{j \mid \pi_j = CPA \wedge t = t_0, j = 1, 2, \ldots, J\}$. Moreover, four kinds of agent groups are defined, i.e., AG_{t_0}, EG_{t_0}, SG_{t_0}, and FG_{t_0}, where, $AG_{t_0} = \{AA_j \mid AA_j \in \Phi, \xi_j = 0 \wedge t = t_0\}$, $EG_{t_0} = \{AA_j \mid AA_j \in \Phi, \xi_j = 1 \wedge t = t_0\}$, $SG_{t_0} = \{AA_j \mid AA_j \in \Phi, \xi_j = 2 \wedge t = t_0\}$, and $FG_{t_0} = \{AA_j \mid AA_j \in \Phi, \xi_j = 3 \wedge t = t_0\}$, indicating that activity agents are available, eligible, executing, and finished, respectively.

3 The Multi-agent System

The multi-agent system for project schedule management designed here contains an agent network shown in Figure 1, where a number of resource agents, activity agents and a monitoring agent are involved.

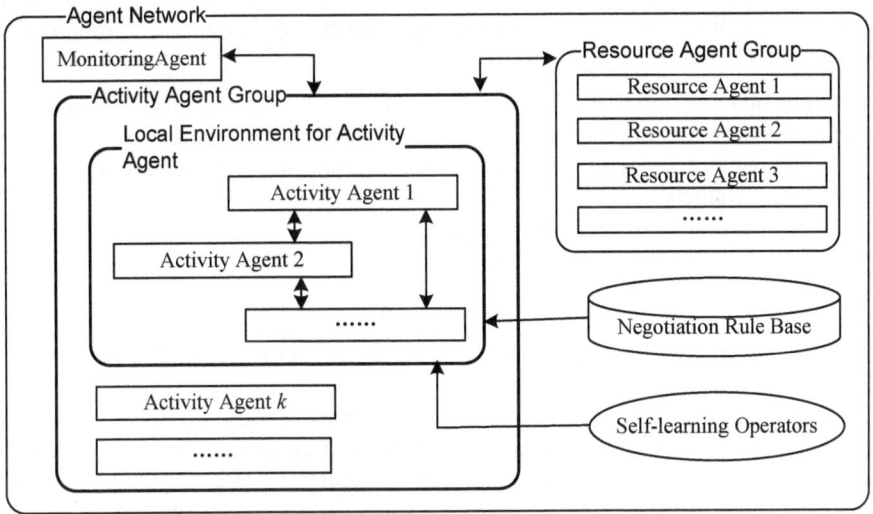

Fig. 1. The Agent Network Model

An agent may play either of the following two roles: (1) to encapsulate the project components, such as departments, activities, and resources; (2) to package the project functions, such as communication, collaboration, and service.

Typically, the attributes of an activity or a resource and the corresponding scheduling/allocation procedure can be encapsulated as an agent. For example, Yan *et al.* defined a service agent to exercise the functions such as duration calculation and resource allocation [1]. Homberger designed schedule agents and a mediator agent, the former is used for scheduling project activities, while the latter is used to generate alternative allocations to be evaluated by schedule agents [3]. In this paper, we design three types of agents: activity agent – AA_j for activity j, resource agent – RA_k for activity k, and a monitoring agent – MA.

The index, schedule status, attribute, and functions of activity j are encapsulated in AA_j. Its primary function is to determine the real duration and resource requirements through its duration self-learning operator *durationSelfLearningOperator( )* and resource requirements for self-learning operator *resourceSelfLearningOperator( )*.

RA_k is responsible for allocating resource k to AA_j who submits the request for resource k. Its decision-making is purely reactive. The model of RA_k contains only attributes.

MA is responsible for the coordination of negotiations among activity agents, by monitoring operator *controlAgents( )*, and to re-determine the critical path when one critical path activity finishes.

Operators for Activity Agents. AA_j and AA_k ($k \in IP_j$) form a local environment. The self-learning operators of AA_j include duration self-learning operator and resource requirement self-learning operator, which reflect the capacity of self-learning and adaptive in local environment. The basic ideology for designing self-learning operators is: the completion situation of predecessors of one activity may affect the activity's real duration and real resource requirements. Therefore, the duration of the activity will be handled as follows:

(1) The planned duration d_j^p, optimistic duration d_j^{om}, and pessimistic duration d_j^{pm} of an activity are part of project planning, thus are determining factors.

(2) The random factor of duration is modeled using was estimated using beta distribution [4]. Namely:

$$\mu_j = (d_j^{om} + 4d_j^p + d_j^{pm}) / 6 , \qquad (1)$$

$$\sigma_j^2 = [(d_j^{pm} - d_j^{om}) / 6]^2 , \qquad (2)$$

where μ_j and σ_j^2 are the mean and the variance of the real duration of activity j, respectively.

(3) As an important piece of information, the biases of real duration and planned duration of predecessors will be considered by activity agents. The fuzzy factor of activity duration, dev_j, can be determined by the geometric mean of these deviations. In real situation there may be exceptional events. If this occurs (here an occurrence probability of exceptional events is pre-set), then change the sign of dev_j.

(4) Finally, the real duration is calculated as:

$$d_j^r = N(\mu, \sigma^2) \cdot (1 + dev_j) . \qquad (3)$$

The resource requirement self-learning operator is similar to the duration operator, in which the random factor of resource requirements adopts a uniform distribution:

$$U((5 / 9) \cdot rq^p_{jk}, (13 / 9) \cdot rq^p_{jk}) . \qquad (4)$$

Operator for Monitoring Agent. One task for MA is that, to re-identify critical path activities (CPA) of the project when any critical path activity finishes. If an activity's latest finish time is equal to its earliest finish time, then the activity will be marked as a critical path activity, otherwise non-critical path activity (NCPA); when a resource conflict occurs, the CPA has the highest execution priority.

The eligible agent group EG_{t_o} at time t_0 also forms a local environment. In this local environment, if at current time there are several activities in an eligible state (their predecessors are all completed) and the current amount of resources are available to meet the needs of the each activity (but not necessarily meet the total demand), then the activity agent will determine their scheduling sequence through negotiations, so as to resolve resource conflicts.

We simplified the negotiations among activity agents, where some priority rules are employed to determine the scheduling sequence. The basic rule is: if an eligible activity is exactly a CPA, then it can immediately be scheduled; otherwise, the scheduling sequence is determined using the priority rule selected by the user. We consider eight priority rules: SPT (shorter processing time), LPT (longer processing time), FIS (fewer immediate successors), MIS (more immediate successors), SRR (smaller resource requirements), GRR (greater resource requirements), EST (earlier start times), and EDD (earlier due dates) [5].

The procedure of the MA agent also involves the termination of activity agents. If the sum of start time and real duration of an activity agent equals to the current simulation clock, then the activity agent stops.

We developed a simulation system for project schedule management using JAVA. The system includes four modules that are data access, initialization, simulation, and results output, as well as a graphical user interface (GUI) which implements the user's interaction with the system. In addition, the system includes two types of files that are project data and simulation results.

4 Example and Simulation

An example which evolves from the instance J3011_10 in J30 of PSPLIB [6] is used with some modifications to test the multi-agent system. The project is composed of 32 activities with two dummy ones. Original durations are used as optimistic durations, and the planned durations are 1 unit more than optimistic ones, while the pessimistic ones are 2 units more than optimistic ones. There are four kind of resources, of which resources R_1 and R_2 are renewable, and resources R_3 and R_4 are nonrenewable, where $TR_1 = 15$, $TR_2 = 14$, $TR_3 = 100$, $TR_4 = 140$.

In the multi-agent system, users can perform a single simulation, or a stepping simulation based on simulation clock; users can also perform a multiple simulation and get statistical results, thus supporting the real project decision-making.

Priority rules such as SPT from [5] are used, and a number of 500 simulations are carried out for each priority rule; statistics for the real makespans of the project are worked out, and the distributions of real makespans are also calculated. It can be observed from Figure 2, that the real makespans are close to a beta distribution.

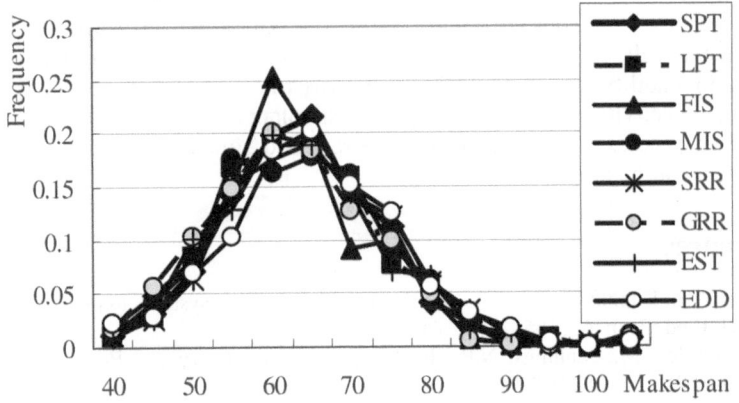

Fig. 2. Statistics for the Frequency of Makespans

Table 1 shows some statistical results for the real durations in which column 6 gives the number of project failures during simulations. Through the analysis of Table 1, we can draw the following conclusions:

(1) The effect of priority rules on the simulation results is not significant. This shows that the self-learning mechanism reacts to the different results of the consultation to make adaptive adjustments. The average duration under GRR is smallest, while the one under EDD is largest, but the difference is trivial.

(2) The real makespan in simulation results is stable. This shows that through multiple simulations, the average of the results can be used for decision-making.

(3) The difference between the maximum and minimum durations is relatively large, which shows that in extreme cases, the difference among implementations of the project may be very large, one implementation of the project may either be much more efficient than the scheme, or only result in failure. This indicates that the uncertainty has significant effects on the implementation of the project planning.

Table 1. The simulation results

Priority rules	Average durations	Std.	Minimum duration	Maximum duration	Failure times
SPT	61.51	9.35	37	94	4
LPT	61.55	10.05	36	94	0
FIS	60.09	9.48	37	92	1
MIS	61.25	10.02	31	91	5
SRR	62.73	10.37	35	106	2
GRR	59.82	9.82	31	88	4
EST	61.15	10.22	35	93	6
EDD	62.83	10.58	34	93	2

5 Conclusions

We designed and realized a multi-agent system for resource constrained project scheduling problem under uncertain environment. Duration self-learning and resource requirements self-learning operators are designed for activities to reflect the agent's self-learning ability; and meanwhile the priority rules are used to handle the negotiations among activity agents. The system can simulate the user's adaptive and dynamic scheduling process for a project, and the repeated simulation results can assist the user's decision-making.

References

1. Yan, Y.H., Kuphal, T., Bode, J.: Application of multiagent systems in project management. Int. J. Prod. Econ. 68, 185–197 (2000)
2. Wooldridge, M., Jennings, N.R.: Intelligent Agents: Theory and Practice. Knowl. Eng. Rev. 10(2), 115–152 (1995)
3. Homberger, J.: A multi-agent system for the decentralized resource-constrained multi-project scheduling problem. Int. T. Oper. Res. 14, 565–589 (2007)
4. Clark, C.E.: The PERT model for the distribution of an activity time. Oper. Res. 10, 405–406 (1962)
5. Knotts, G., Dror, M., Hartman, B.C.: Agent-based project scheduling. IIE. Trans. 32, 387–401 (2000)
6. Kolisch, R., Sprecher, A.: PSPLIB - A project scheduling problem library. Eur. J. Oper. Res. 96, 205–216 (1996)

Using F-Metric to Construct a New Niederreiter Public Key Cryptosystem

Mu Han[1,*], Hong Zhang[1], and Chun-gen Xu[2]

[1] School of Computer Science and Technology, Nanjing University of Science and Technology,
NanJing 210094, China
[2] School of Sciences, Nanjing University of Science and Technology, China

Abstract. In this paper we show how to construct a new public key cryptosystem against known attacks, together with the reduction of the public-key. In terms of F-Metric, the maximum F-distance code is constructed, a new modification of the Niederreiter public key cryptosystem based on maximum F-distance codes is proposed. We chooses a random matrix as an extra secret key to hide the structure of the public key, it makes such cryptosystem is security.

Keywords: F-Metric, the maximum F-distance code, Niederreiter public key cryptosystem, random matrix, security.

1 Introduction

The first code-based public-key cryptosystem is introduced and investigated in [1]. The system is based on Goppa codes in the Hamming metric. Its dual version, Niederreiter public-key cryptosystem[2] is based on the difficulty of finding a coset leader of a coset of the code. The main drawback of public-key cryptosystem based on Hamming metric is large public key sizes.

In 1991 Gabidulin, Paramonov and Tretjakov proposed a variant of the McEliece scheme (GPT) [3] using rank distance codes instead of hamming distance codes. Smaller public-key sizes have been proposed for GPT than for the original McEliece cryptosystem, as general decoding algorithms are much slower for the rank metric than for the hamming metric. However, recently Overbeck showed that rank distance codes do not seem to be a good choice for cryptographic applications [4].

Other metrics, for instance, the F-metrics suggested in [5]. Moreover, these metrics can provide new possibilities for both correcting special types of errors and applications in other fields, for example, in cryptography.

In this paper, we use F-metric to construct a maximum F-distance code, and a new modification of the Niederreiter public key cryptosystem based on maximum F-distance codes is proposed.

The paper is structured as follows: Firstly, we give a short introduction to McEliece and Niederreiter Cryptosystems and General properties of F-metrics. Secondly, we show how to construct the maximum F-distance code. Then, we present

---

* Corresponding author.

R. Chen (Ed.): ICICIS 2011, Part I, CCIS 134, pp. 541–546, 2011.

a new modification of Niederreiter public key cryptosystem. Finally, we analyze the security of the new Niederreiter Cryptosystem.

2 Preliminaries

2.1 McEliece and Niederreiter Cryptosystems

McEliece public-key cryptosystem[1] is based on the difficulty of decoding linear codes in Hamming metric. Its dual version, Niederreiter public-key cryptosystem [2] is based on the difficulty of finding the smallest with a given syndrome.

For a given code, McEliece public-key cryptosystem and Niederreiter public-key cryptosystem are equivalent [6].

One of the great advantages of McEliece and Niederreiter cryptosystem is the work-function of encryption-decryption.

The main drawback of McEliece and Niederreiter cryptosystems remains the size of the public-key.

Table 1 sums up the characteristics of these systems when they both use [1024, 524, 101] –binary codes. It then shows that it is preferable to use the version proposed by Niederreiter.

Table 1. Performance of McEliece, Niederreiter and RSA public-key cipher

	McEliece [1024,524,101] binary code	Niederreiter [1024,524,101] binary code	RSA 1024-bit modulus Public exponent=17
public-key size	67072 bytes	32750 bytes	256 bytes
Number of information Bits transmitted per encryption	512	276	1024
Number of binary operations performed by the encryption per information bit	514	50	2402
Number of binary operations performed by the decryption per information bit	5140	7863	738112

2.2 F-Metric [5]

Let Ω be a n-dimensional vector space F_q^n, where F_q is a finite field with q elements. The **span**<X> of a subset $X \subset \Omega$ is the smallest subspace $F_X \subseteq \Omega$ containing X. Any subset $C \subset \Omega$ is called a code.

Let $F := \{F_1, F_2, \ldots, F_N\}$ be any family of subsets $F_i \subset \Omega$ such that $< \bigcup_{i=1}^{N} F_i >= \Omega$.

Definition 1. The F-norm(F-weight), N_F, of a vector $x \in \Omega$ is the cardinality of the smallest subset I of the set $\{1, 2, \ldots, N\}$ such that x belongs to $< \bigcup_{i=1}^{} F_i >$.

Definition 2. The F-distance between vector x and y is the norm of their difference, i.e., $d_F(x,y) = N_F(x-y)$.

Definition 3. The F-distance of a code $C \subset \Omega$ is the integer $d_F(C) := \min \{ d_F(x,y) \mid x,y \in C, x \neq y\}$.

Definition 4. If all elements of a family $F := \{F_1, F_2, \ldots, F_N\}$ are vectors, then the metric generated by the family is called a projective F-metric. In this case, we will denote elements of the family by f_i, i.e., $F := \{f_1, f_2, \ldots f_N\}$.

Proposition 1. (Generalised Singleton Bound): For any linear code $C \subseteq F_q^n$ of dimension k the following equality holds: $d_F(C) \leq n-k+1$.

We refer to a code meting this bound as a code with the maximum F-distance.

Define the mapping $\varphi : F_q^N \to \Omega$ as $\varphi(e_i) = f_i$ $(i=1, \ldots, N)$, where $\{e_1, e_2, \cdots e_N\}$ is a standard basis in F_q^N and $\{f_1, f_2, \ldots f_N\}$ are vectors that define the F-metric.

Definition 5. The parent code is the kernel $P := \ker(\varphi) \subset F_q^N$.

3 The Maximal F-Distance Code

$$\text{Let } F = \begin{pmatrix} u_1 & u_2 & \cdots & u_N \\ u_1 x_1 & u_2 x_2 & \cdots & u_N x_N \\ \cdots & \cdots & \cdots & \cdots \\ u_1 x_1^{n-1} & u_2 x_2^{n-1} & \cdots & u_N^{n-1} x_N^{n-1} \end{pmatrix} \quad (n \leq N) , \tag{1}$$

$x_i \in F_q$ are pairwise distinct, and $u_i \in F_q$ are nonzero, $i=1, \ldots, N$.

As vector $f_1, f_2, \cdots, f_N$ that define the F-metric, take columns of a generalised Vandermonde matrix F. This F-metric is Vandermonde F-metric. The parent code for this F-metric is a generalised Reed-Solomon code.

$$\text{Let } G^T = \begin{pmatrix} v_1 & v_2 & \cdots & v_k \\ v_1 y_1 & v_2 y_2 & \cdots & v_k y_k \\ \vdots & \vdots & \cdots & \vdots \\ v_1 y_1^{n-1} & v_2 y_2^{n-1} & \cdots & v_k y_k^{n-1} \end{pmatrix} , \quad \text{where } v_i \in F_q \text{ are nonzero}$$

and $y_i \in F_q$ are pairwise distinct. Let $x_i \neq y_i$, so the matrix $(F \mid G^T)$ is also a generalized Vandermonde matrix.

$$(F|G^T) = \begin{pmatrix} u_1 & u_2 & \cdots & u_N & v_1 & v_2 & \cdots & v_k \\ u_1x_1 & u_2x_2 & \cdots & u_Nx_N & v_1y_1 & v_2y_2 & \cdots & v_ky_k \\ \cdots & \cdots & \cdots & \cdots & \cdots & \cdots & \cdots & \cdots \\ u_1x_1^{n-1} & u_2x_2^{n-1} & \cdots & u_N^{n-1}x_N^{n-1} & v_1y_1^{n-1} & v_2y_2^{n-1} & \cdots & v_ky_k^{n-1} \end{pmatrix}. \tag{2}$$

Proposition 2. The code C defined by the matrix G^T is a code with the maximum F-distance: $d_F(C)=n-k+1$. Consequently, the code corrects up to $t_k = [\dfrac{n-k}{2}]$ F-errors.

By $G H^T = 0$, we obtained the transposed parity-check matrix of the maximum F-distance C is

$$H^T = \begin{pmatrix} z_1 & z_2 & \cdots & z_{n-k} \\ z_1y_1 & z_2y_2 & \cdots & z_{n-k}y_{n-k} \\ \vdots & \vdots & \cdots & \vdots \\ z_1y_1^{n-1} & z_2y_2^{n-1} & \cdots & z_{n-k}y_{n-k}^{n-1} \end{pmatrix}, \text{ where } z_i \in F_q \text{ are nonzero and } y_i \in F_q \text{ are}$$

pairwise distinct.

Let $c=g+e$, where g is the code vector, and e the error vector. Denote t as $t = N_F(e)$, if $t \le t_k$, then fast decoding of the maximum F-distance codes may be carried out just as for generalized Reed-Solomon codes.

4   Construction of the System

A public-key cryptosystem that uses an error vector as a plaintext was first introduced by Niederreiter[2]. Niederreiter use generalized Reed-Solomon codes in his system. A parity-check matrix H of a GRS code premultiplied by a nonsingular matrix S, which hides the structure of H, is chosen as a public key: $H_{pub}=SH$. Sidel'nikov and Shestakov[7] gave a polynomial algorithm to recover the structure of generalized Reed-Solomon codes, thus breaking completely the system. We proposed to choose matrices of rank 1 to hide the structure of the public key.

The cryptosystem is constructed in the following way.

First, a legitimate user chooses a transposed parity-check matrix $H^T = (z_i y_i^j)$ of a linear maximum F-distance code C over $GF(q)$ with a fast decoding algorithm in the F-mertic.

Next, One choose a nonsingular square matrix S of order $(n-k)$ over $GF(q)$ and a permutation matrix P of order n over $GF(q)$.

● A secret key: X, S, H^T, P.

● A public key: $H_{pub}^T = P(H^T + X)S$, where X is a matrix of rank 1. The hiding matrix X may be chosen as follows:

(1) Choose any vector $\bar{b} = (b_1, b_2, \cdots, b_n)$, $b_i \in GF(q)$, from any coset of F-weight $d_F - 1 = n-k = 2t_k = r$ of the given the maximum F-distance code;

(2) Calculate a syndrome $\bar{x} = \bar{b}H^T = (x_1, x_2, \cdots, x_{d_F - 1})$;

(3) Calculate $X = \overline{a}^{-T} \overline{x}$, where $\overline{a} = (a_1, a_2, \cdots, a_n)$ and not all zero laments $a_i \in GF(q)$ are chosen randomly;

● A plaintext: A plaintext is an n-dimension vector $\boldsymbol{m} = (m_1, m_2, \cdots, m_n)$, where $m_i \in GF(q)$ and $N_F(\boldsymbol{m}) \le t_k - 1$, where t_k is the error-correcting capability of the code defined by H^T in the space with the $\boldsymbol{F}$-metric.

● Encryption: $c = \boldsymbol{m} H_{pub}^T$.

● Decryption: $c = \boldsymbol{m} P(H^T + X)S = \boldsymbol{m} PH^T S + \boldsymbol{m} PxS = \overline{m} H^T S + \overline{m} xS$. The legal user knows that $\overline{m}X$ is either 0 or a vector λx, where λ depends on the value of $\boldsymbol{m}$ and x is fixed. Thus, the decoding complexity is increased not more then n times.

5 Cryptanalysis

Two kinds of attacks on public-key cryptosystems based on error-correcting codes can be considered. The first kind of attacks is based on getting a plaintext from an intercepted ciphertext. The second attack is based on getting private keys from known public keys. Here possible attacks against each system will be investigated.

Attack 1. (Getting the secret key from the public key): Given a public key $H_{pub}^T = P(H^T + X)S$ it is necessary to find X, S, H^T, P. First of all note that without the matrix X structure, the public key becomes $H_{pub}^T = P(H^T)S$ which equivalent to the standard Niederreiter case. This standard case has been broken by Sidelnikov and Shestakov. So a legal user chooses some random X as an extra secret key and adds it to the original public key to produce a new modified public key , it makes such cryptosystem is effective for resisting the attack based on getting private keys from known public keys.

Attack 2. (Getting a plaintext from a ciphertext): Pick a $k \times k$ submatrix G_{t^k} of G_{pub} consisting of the $i_1th, i_2th, \ldots, i_{t^k} th$ columns of G_{pub}, where $G_{pub} H_{pub}^T = 0$. Even in that case to decrypt a message the attacker needs to locate positions $i_1, i_2, \ldots, i_{t^k}$ of nonzero elements of the message $\overline{m}$. After that the attacker can calculate components $m_{i_1}, m_{i_2}, \ldots m_{i_{t^k}}$ of the message $\overline{m}$ and verify the derived message $\overline{m}$. The attack would still require $C_N^{t_k}(t_k^3 + t_k n)$ calculations. If $q=2^8$, $n = 60$, $k=20$, $t_k = \left[\dfrac{n-k}{2}\right] = 20$, then the size of public-key is 9600 bytes, and need 2^{81} calculations.

6 Conclusion

We construct a new Niederreiter Public Key Cryptosystem based on $\boldsymbol{F}$-metric. Using these $\boldsymbol{F}$-metrics to increase complexity of the system making it harder to attack allowing for smaller key-sizes. However, If some new and more efficient decoding methods about error-correcting codes base on F-metric are proposed, we should make further researches on the security of the public-key cryptosystem presented.

References

1. McEliece, R.J.: A Public-key Cryptosystem Based on Algebraic Coding Theory. Technical report, Jet Propulsion Lab. DSN Progress Reprot (1978)
2. Niederreiter, H.: Knapsack-Type Cryptosystem and Algebraic Coding Theory. Probl. Control Inform. Theory 15(2), 159–166 (1986)
3. Gabidulin, E.M., Paramonov, A.V., Tretjakov, O.V.: Ideals over a Non-Commutative Ring and their Application in Cryptology. In: Davies, D.W. (ed.) EUROCRYPT 1991. LNCS, vol. 547, pp. 482–489. Springer, Heidelberg (1991)
4. Overbeck, R.: Structural Attack for Public key Cryptosystems based on Gabidulin Codes. Journal of Cryptology 21, 280–301 (2008)
5. Gabidulin, E.M., Simonis, J.: Metrics Generated by Families of Subspace. IEEE Trans. Inf. Theory 44(5), 1336–1341 (1998)
6. Li, Y.X., Wang, X.M.: On the Equivalence of McEliece's and Niederreiter's Public-Key Cryptosystems. IEEE Trans. Inf. Theory 40(1), 271–273 (1994)
7. Sidelnikov, V.M., Shetakov, S.O.: On the insecurity of Cryptosystem Based on Generalized Reed-Solomon Codes. Discrete Math. 2(4), 439–444 (1992)

Flax Fibers as Reinforcement in Poly (Lactic Acid) Biodegradable Composites

Yuan Yuan[1], Minghui Guo[1], and Yong Wang[2]

[1] Key Lab of Bio-based Material Science and Technology of Ministry of Education,
Northeast Forestry University, Harbin, China
[2] Department of Graduate Education, Northeast Agricultural University, Harbin, China
gmh1964@126.com

Abstract. In our research, poly (lactic acid) (PLA) film was used in combination with flax fibers as reinforcement to generate biodegradable composites by a film stacking technique and hot-press. The research of the relationship between the main process parameters and the performance of the board are done by the orthogonal experiments, then the various factors to influence the performance were analyzed and the optimal parameters were determined. The results showed that with the increasing of flax addition (30%~50%) and silane addition (1%~5%), the tensile strength and modulus increased, but the flexural strength and modulus increased then decreased with the increasing of flax addition (30%~50%). During the hot-press temperature (190℃~210℃) increasing, the tensile strength, flexural strength and modulus all increased. And the optimal parameters are determined by the flax addition 40%, silane addition 5%, hot-pressing temperature 190℃, and hot-pressing time 3 min.

Keywords: Flax fibers; Poly (lactic acid); Biodegradable composites; Silane treated.

1 Introduction

In recent years, as the people's awareness of environmental protection is approaching danger, and seeking the renewable resources to produce high polymer materials is a general development orientation for Polymer Science and technology. The composites prepared by nature plant fibers and oil based plastic had a wider application of automotive interior parts, structural parts, Interior and exterior decoration materials [1].

Plackett et al. [2] used the polylactide film and jute fiber mats to generate composites by a film stacking technique. Shanks et al. [3] prepared the composite materials from PLA with flax fibers, where the flax fibers had been subjected to interstitial polymerization to replace the water in the cellulose fibers. Oksman et al. [4] manufactured the composite materials of flax fibers and PLA with a twin-screw extruder and then compression moulded to test samples. The stiffness of test samples was 8.4 GPa.

Chunhong Wang et al. [5] prepared flax fibers reinforced polylactide composites by means of moulding pressing technology. Wenna Zhang et al. [6] studied the effect of changing the angle of layer on the mechanical property of the composites.

R. Chen (Ed.): ICICIS 2011, Part I, CCIS 134, pp. 547–553, 2011.
© Springer-Verlag Berlin Heidelberg 2011

In this study, PLA film was used in combination with flax fibers as reinforcement to generate biodegradable composites by a film stacking technique and hot-press. The research of the relationship between the main process parameters and the performance of the board are done by the orthogonal experiments, then the various factors to influence the performance were analyzed and the optimal parameters were determined.

2 Experimental Materials and Methods

2.1 Materials

PLA was converted into a film approximately 0.2 mm in thickness and was purchased from Jiangyin Gaoxin Chemical Fiber Company. In vacuum drying oven, the PLA film was dried for 8 hours at 80℃, then stored in the dryer prior to use. Flax fiber was supplied by Harbin Changlong Flax Company. Vinyltriethoxysilane (HD-20 silane) was used as the fiber surface modifying coupling agent and was purchased from Guangzhou Haoji Trade Company. Ethanol for analysis was purification reagents and was purchased from Tianjing Guangfu Technological Company.

2.2 Processing

For the surface treatment of the flax fiber, HD-20 silane was dissolved for hydrolysis in a mixture of water-ethanol (50:50 w/w). Next, the fibers were sprayed by the solution at specific volume. Then the fibers were kept in air for 2 days. Lastly, the fibers were oven dried at 100℃ for 2 h.

To ensure that all absorbed moisture was removed and to prevent void formation, the flax fibers and the PLA film were dried at 80℃ under vacuum for 10 h before processing. The biodegradable composites containing different weight percentages of fibers were produced by hot-press using the film-stacking procedure. Lay-ups (150mm×150mm) were prepared in which sections of flax fiber were stacked up with several PLA film layers on either side. After pre-compression, the whole assembly was carefully placed on the laboratory press with a temperature and pressure control. The biodegradable composite samples (180 mm long ×180 mm wide×3 mm thick) were cut to desired shapes for test.

Flax addition, silane addition, the hot-press temperature and the hot-press time were selected as variable factors as showed in Table 1. According to a preliminary test, determining that flax addition (30%, 40% and 50%), silane addition (1%, 3% and 5%), the hot-press temperature (190℃, 200℃ and 210℃) the hot-press time (3min, 5min and 7 min), and hot press was 3MPa.

Table 1. Factors and levels of the orthogonal test

Levels	Factors			
	A Flax Addition (%)	B Siane Addition (%)	C Hot-press Temperature (℃)	D Hot-press Time (min)
1	30	1	190	3
2	40	3	200	5
3	50	5	210	7

2.3 Testing and Characterization

The tensile tests were conducted according to GB/T 1040.2-2006, with tensile speed 50mm/min. And the flexural tests were conducted according to GB/T9341-2000, with flexural speed 5 mm/min. Each value reported is the average of six sample tests and error bars correspond to plus or minus one standard deviation.

3 Results and Discussion

3.1 Variance Analysis of the Orthogonal Test

Table 2 showed that the tensile and flexural properties were also strongly attracted by the process parameters which were all linked together. The tensile and flexural strength were taken as the index of the test together, and the factors on the performance indexes were measured by range (R). The level on the indexes were reflected by average score (Ki). The bigger was the value, the better was the performance. The approximate analysis as showed in Table 2.

Table 2. Variance analysis of the orthogonal test

Properties		A	B	C	D
Tensile Strength	K_1	266.2	286.0	289.0	282.2
	K_2	304.3	275.3	280.9	283.6
	K_3	282.3	291.5	282.9	287.0
	$R_{(j)}$	6.35	2.70	1.35	0.80
	F Value	97.12^{**}	18.02^{**}	4.73^{*}	1.62
Flexural Strength	K_1	211.2	215.1	251.2	232.8
	K_2	247.5	236.7	209.3	233.9
	K_3	232.6	239.5	230.8	224.6
	$R_{(j)}$	6.05	4.07	6.98	1.55
	F Value	45.50^{**}	24.37^{**}	60.00^{**}	3.53

F0.05 (2,9)=4.26; F0.01(2,9)=8.02; * the factor effect is significant, F>F0.05; ** the factor effect is highly significant, F>F0.01.

For the tensile strength, $R_A>R_B>R_C>R_D$, so the factor on the tensile strength for ordering was A>B>C>D. As $K_{2A}>K_{3A}>K_{1A}$ showed, the factor A on the level 2 was better than the other two levels. At the same time, as $K_{3B}>K_{1B}>K_{2B}$, $K_{1C}>K_{3C}>K_{2C}$, and $K_{3D}>K_{2D}>K_{1D}$ showed, the optimum technological condition was $A_2B_3C_1D_3$ for the tensile property. In the same way, the factor on the flexural strength for ordering was C>A>B>D, and the the optimum technological condition was $A_2B_3C_1D_2$. But the hot-press time had no remarkable effect on the mechanical properties, so it was suitable to shorten the hot-press time for improving the test efficiency and reducing energy consumption, so the optimum technological condition was $A_2B_3C_1D_1$.

3.2 Effect of Flax Addition on the Mechanical Properties

According to range analysis of orthogonal test, the influence factors were silane addition 5%, the hot-press temperature 190℃, the hot-press time 3 min, and the preinstall density 1.0g/cm³. Fig. 1-A showed the tensile property the samples with increase of flax addition from 30% to 50%. Comparing with flax addition 30%, the tensile strength of flax addition 70% increased from 32.61MPa to 50.64MPa, up 55.29 percent, and the tensile modulus increased from 4.49GPa to 6.42GPa, up 42.98 percent.

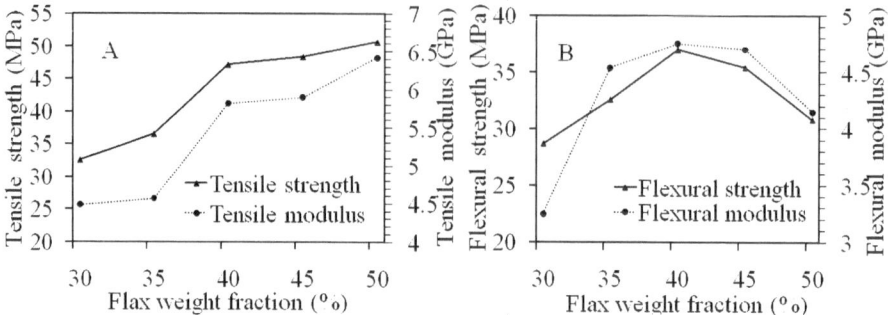

Fig. 1. Relationship between mechanical properties and flax weight fraction

But the flexural property increased with increase of flax addition from 30% to 40%, the flexural strength increased from 28.68MPa to 36.97MPa, up 28.91 percent, and the flexural modulus increased from 3.25GPa to 4.75GPa, up 46.15 percent. During the flax addition from 40% to 50%, the flexural strength decreased from 36.97MPa to 30.81MPa, down 16.66 percent, and the flexural modulus decreased from 4.75GPa to 4.15GPa, down 12.63 percent, as showed in Fig. 1-B.

In experiment range, due to the flax fiber with the higher specific strength and modular ratio, the mechanical properties of the biodegradable composites increased with increase of flax addition. While the PLA content of the biodegradable composites reduced, it was hypothesized that this may be due to a shortage of PLA to fully wet out between the flax fibers [7]. So the mechanical properties of the biodegradable composites were better at the flax addition 40%.

3.3 Effect of Silane Addition on the Mechanical Properties

Under the condition of preinstall density 1.0g/cm³, flax addition 40%, the hot-press temperature 190℃, and the hot-press time 3 min as showed in Fig.2-A and Fig.2-B. During increase of silane addition from 1% to 5%, the tensile and flexural properties increased, and the tensile strength increased from 39.83MPa to 52.64MPa, up 32.16 percent, and the tensile modulus increased from 4.86GPa to 6.35GPa, up 30.66 percent, and the flexural strength increased from 28.79MPa to 36.42MPa, up 26.50 percent, and the flexural modulus increased from 3.19GPa to 4.54GPa, up 42.32 percent.

The results indicated that, in acidic conditions, owing to one part of the group in silane coupling agent could provide more effective chemical cross linking reaction with hydroxyl groups in flax fiber surfaces to weaken flax fiber surface polarity [8], while another part of the group can be used with the PLA chemical reaction or physical wound. Thus for flax fiber and PLA based substrate, two kinds materials

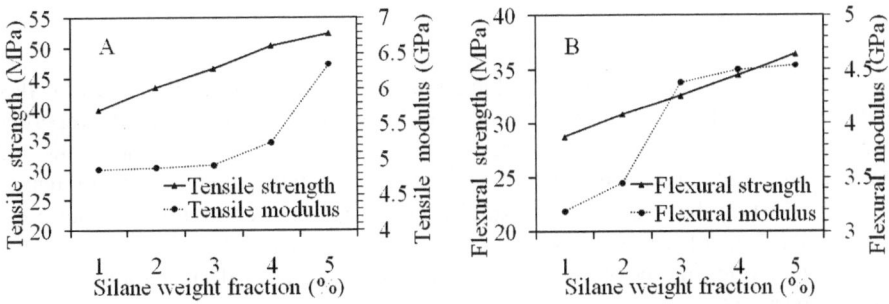

Fig. 2. Relationship between mechanical properties and silane weight fraction

with very different polar bonded together [9], with increasing the affinity between flax fiber and PLA, forming the good boundary layer of cohesion strength, and improving performance of the biodegradable composites. So silane addition 5% was suitable.

3.4 Effect of Hot-Press Temperature on the Mechanical Properties

Under the condition of preinstall density $1.0g/cm^3$, flax addition 40%, silane addition 3%, and the hot-press time 3 min, during the hot-press temperature increasing in a range of 190℃ to 210℃. Fig. 3-A and Fig.3-B showed that the tensile and flexural properties decreased, and the tensile strength increased from 50.61MPa to 36.64MPa, down 27.60 percent, and the tensile modulus increased from 6.79GPa to 5.44GPa, down 19.88 percent, and the flexural strength increased from 43.68MPa to 32.81MPa, down 24.88 percent, and the flexural modulus increased from 5.67GPa to 4.08GPa, down 28.04 percent.

It indicated PLA melted then overflowed from the flax surface at over high temperature, and when the flax fiber given a force without PLA surrounded, the brittleness of the biodegradable composites increased, easy to break. It might cause the fiber degradation, so the mechanical properties decreased [10]. So the hot-press temperature between 190℃ and 200℃ was better, less than 210℃.

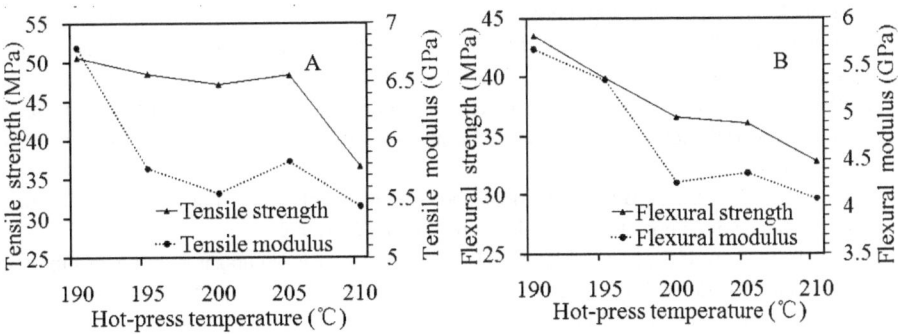

Fig. 3. Relationship between mechanical properties and hot-press temperature

4 Conclusion

For the mechanical properties of the biodegradable composites, with increase of flax addition (30%~50%), the flexural properties increased, but the flexural properties increased then decreased. During increase of silane addition (1%~5%), the tensile and flexural properties increased. When the hot-press temperature increased in a range of 190℃ to 210℃, the tensile and flexural properties decreased. While, the hot-press time (3min~7min) had no remarkable effect on the mechanical properties, so it was suitable to shorten the hot-press time for improving the test efficiency and reducing energy consumption.

In view of the economic cost and the properties of the biodegradable composites, the optimal parameters are determined by flax addition 40%, silane addition 5%, the hot-press temperature 190℃, the hot-press time 3min.

Acknowledgment

It is a project supported by Northeast Forestry University graduate science and technology innovation project (project name, "Processing Technics of Flax Fibers as Reinforcement in Poly (Lactic Acid) Biodegradable Composites"), Heilongjiang Province key science and technology research project (GA09B201-07), Harbin key science and technology research project (GJ2007GG002235), and Basic research in universities of the central business fees earmarked funds projects (DL09EB01-1).

The corresponding author is Guo Minghui, and the email address is gmh1964@ 126.com.

References

1. Clemons, C.: Wood-plastic Composites in the United States: the Interfacing of Two Industry. Forest Products 52, 10–18 (2002)
2. Plackett, D., Andersen, T.L., Pedersen, W.B., Nielsen, L.: Biodegradable Composites Based on L-polylactide and Jute Fibres. Compos Sci. Technol. 63, 1287–1296 (2003)
3. Shanks, R.A., Hodzic, A., Ridderhof, D.: Composites of Poly (Lactic Acid) with Flax Fibers Modified by Interstitial Polymerization. Appl. Polym. Sci. 99, 2305–2313 (2006)
4. Oksman, K., Skrifvars, M., Selin, J.F.: Natural Fibres as Reinforcement in Polylactic Acid (PLA) Composites. Compos Sci. Technol. 63, 1317–1324 (2003)
5. Wang, C.H., Wang, R., Shen, L., Jiang, Z.H.: Forming Technology of Flax Noil Fibers Reinforced Polylactide Biodegradable Composites. Acta Materiae Compositae Sinica 25, 63–67 (2008)
6. Zhang, W.N., Li, Y.B.: Fabrication and Characterization of Flax Fiber Reinforced Polylactic acid Composite. Textile Research 30, 49–53 (2009)
7. Lee, B.H., Kim, H.S., Lee, S., Kim, H.J., Dorgan, J.R.: Bio-composites of Kenaf Fibers in Polylactide: Role of Improved Interfacial Ahesion in the Carding Process. Compos Sci. Technol. 69, 2573–2579 (2009)

8. Wu, J.S., Yu, D.M., Chan, C.M., Kim, J., Mai, Y.W.: Effect of Fiber Pretreatment Condition on the Interfacial Strength and Mechanical Properties of Wood Fiber/PP Composites. Appl. Polym. Sci. 76, 1000–1010 (2000)
9. Duan, L.F., Liu, W.P., Li, B.H.: Effects of Silane Coupling Agent on Properties of HDPE/Wood Flour Composites. Plastic Sci. Technol. 34, 36–39 (2006)
10. Shibata, S., Cao, Y., Fukumoto, I.: Lightweight Laminate Composites Made From Kenaf and Polypropylene Fibres. Polym. Testing 25, 142–148 (2006)

A Novel Framework to Maximum Lifetime for Wireless Sensor Network

Feng Sheng[1], Qi Xiao-gang[2], and Xue Ji-long[2]

[1] College of Science, Xidian University, Xi'an, 710126
[2] Department of Applied Mathematics, Xidian University, Xi'an 710071, China
{shengfeng2008,qixiaogang,xuejilong}@gmail.com

Abstract. In this paper, a novel framework is presented to prolong the lifetime of wireless sensor networks to the maximum. This framework consists of two parts. One is a novel topology management mechanism called electric fan topology mechanism (EFTM) and the other is an efficient routing protocol called maximum lifetime routing (MLR). EFTM provides a scheduler strategy to save much energy by turning off some transceivers periodically. MLR is based on the work of EFTM, which selects nodes with high-energy reserves as router. Though we turn off some transceivers periodically, we have developed receiver-based packet routing policy and last-mile algorithm to accommodate rapid change of topology and to guarantee the robust of networks. Simulation results show that MLR based on the work of EFTM extends the lifetime of networks to the maximum. MLR is suitable for large scale non-real time wireless sensor applications. When all trajectories are unavailable, nodes can still send packets to sink efficiently. The network using MLR can adapt to the rapid change of network topology very well.

Keywords: Maximum lifetime, TEDD, energy map, electric fan topology.

1 Introduction

The advance of micro sensor technology makes it easy to develop sensor devices of low cost and small size. These devices are organized as wireless sensor networks (WSNs) to monitor specified phenomenon or environment. WSNs may have a large scale depending on the acceptable accuracy and/or fault-tolerant. Since WSNs has an unattended nature, sensor node is energy-constrained and needs to use energy efficiently in order to live longer [1-3].

One of the most important challenges of designing wireless sensor networks is to extend lifetime of the network. Much of the work has been done to extend the network lifetime by making the energy of WSNs more efficient [4-8]. Most of them can be classified as cluster-based hierarchical protocol. For example, LEACH [4] is a typical adaptive clustering protocol. In LEACH, nodes organize themselves into local clusters with one node acting as cluster-head. The idle ordinary nodes can turn into sleep status. Cluster heads form a backbone network connected to sink node. But if the distance between cluster head and the sink increases, the energy consumption is proportional to the square of the distance at least.

R. Chen (Ed.): ICICIS 2011, Part I, CCIS 134, pp. 554–564, 2011.
© Springer-Verlag Berlin Heidelberg 2011

In this paper, a novel framework is presented to prolong the lifetime of wireless sensor networks to the maximum. This framework consists of a novel electric fan topology management mechanism (EFTM) and an efficient routing protocol named maximum lifetime routing (MLR). EFTM provides a scheduler strategy to save much energy by turning off some transceivers periodically. MLR is based on the work of EFTM, which chooses the node with high-energy reserves as router.

Electric fan topology mechanism is the basement of the framework. The new topology management mechanism works as follows. At one interval, only some nodes are working, and other nodes go to sleep. For example, in Figure 1, sink is located in the center of the networks. At one interval, nodes near trajectories of sector 1, 3, 5, 7 are working, and nodes near trajectories of sector 2, 4, 6, 8 are sleeping. At another interval, nodes near trajectories of sector 1, 3, 5, 7 are sleeping, and nodes near trajectories of sector 2, 4, 6, 8 are working (Just the node near trajectory and the node with low energy reserves can turn off its transceiver). Sleeping node can save much energy.

MLR is comprised of three main parts. The first part is the architecture for generating trajectories that pass through region with higher energy reserves and avoid low-energy areas. The main idea is to select a set of nodes that are most suitable for disseminating information and to find the best curve or the best set of curves passing through or near these selected points. The second part is an algorithm, called Last-mile (LM) algorithm. Users of LM algorithm are those which are not located in or near any trajectory. They use the LM algorithm to route packets to trajectories or sink. The third part of MLR is a packet forwarding mechanism learned from TEDD.

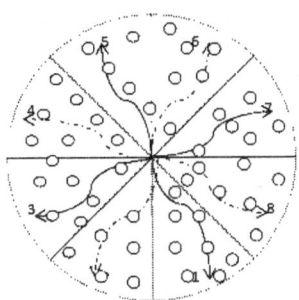

Fig. 1. Electric fan topology

The rest of this paper is organized as follows. Section 2 discusses the related work. Electric fan topology mechanism is described in Section 3. Section 4 discusses the detail of route strategy MLR. In Section 5, simulation results are analyzed. Finally, the conclusion is presented.

2 The Related Work

The number of routing algorithm may be not less than the number of existing wireless sensor networks. Among all algorithms proposed in the literature, the closest to the one presented in this work is TEDD [9]. The key idea is to embed a curve in the packet to be disseminated from a sink node to sensor nodes, and then intermediate nodes forward it in a unicast manner to those nodes that lie close to the curve. TEDD extends the principles of TBF by incorporating the usage of the energy map. It defines a receiver-based data dissemination policy, i.e., each node upon receiving a packet decides itself whether to relay it or not. In TEDD, the decision to forward a packet or not is based on the node geographical location and the packet information. The forwarding decision process uses a temporization policy: before relaying a packet, the current node waits a small time interval. After this, if no neighbor relays the packet, the node transmits it. TEDD eliminates the need of route table maintenance and presents a robust behavior in dynamic topology.

Algorithm 1 presents the basic operation of TEDD. When a node receives a packet, it verifies whether it is inside the received network sector. If it is not, it drops the packet. If it is inside the network sector, the node verifies if its distance to the reference point is higher than the communication range. If the calculated distance is higher than the communication range, the node drops the packet. If it is not, the node waits for a delay time that is calculated according to its distance to the reference point. The smaller the distance is, the less the delay is. After the delay time, if any of its neighbors had retransmitted the packet, the node drops the packet. Otherwise, the node selects the reference point, and forwards the packet.

Algorithm 1. TEDD—receiving packet
Input: the received packet
If the node is inside the received network sector then
   Calculate its distance to the reference point
   If this distance value is less or equal to the communication range then
      Calculate the delay time
      Wait the delay time
      If any of its neighbors retransmitted this packet then
         Drop the packet
      Else
         Calculate the reference point
         Forward the packet
      End if
   Else
      Drop the packet
   End if
Else
   Drop the packet
End if

However, TEDD has two main drawbacks. First, TEDD focus routing activity on nodes with high-energy reserves, but it does not have a plan to save energy at all. Actually, it uses much energy, because almost all nodes (except the low-energy node) stay on-line to be ready as a router all the time. The on-line status indicates the transceiver is working. Second, in TEDD, sink node has to calculate route for every sensor node, and to embed a curve in the packet to be disseminated from a sink node to sensor nodes. The result is that sink node is so busy, and the amount of packets used for delivering route information increases a lot. Therefore, we need to improve all above, especially the first one.

3 Electric Fan Topology Mechanism

In this section, we present the detail of electric fan topology mechanism for wireless sensor networks. First, some background should be given. Then, we give an overview of the process when framework works. At the end of this section, EF algorithm will be presented.

3.1 Background

In [10], Hill et al. states that WSNs should embrace the philosophy of getting the work done as quickly as possible and going to sleep. The best way to save energy is to turn off parts of transceivers of nodes that are not needed, as modeled by a state-based energy dissipation model (SEDM) presented in [11].

How can we turn off some transceivers of nodes without affecting the normal operation of network? LEACH [4] is a typical adaptive clustering protocol. In LEACH, nodes organize themselves into local clusters, with one node acting as the local base station or cluster-head. The idle ordinary node can turn into sleep status. Cluster-heads form a backbone network connected to sink node. It looks like a perfect solution, but it's not so perfect actually.

$$p(r) \sim \frac{p(s)}{d^f} \tag{1}$$

In Eq. (1), f is a number between 1.5 and 2.5 [12], p(r) is the received power, p(s) is the transmit power, and d is the distance between receiver and sender. In general, the distance between two clusters heads is 4~7 times greater than the distance between two ordinary nodes in an adaptive LEACH protocol. It's too expensive. We define hops from sink node to node x as hop(x). Another possible solution is showed as following. Nodes within hops between hop(x) and hop(x+2) work, but nodes within hop between hop(x+2) and hop(x+4) sleep and so on. Obviously, it's not a good idea, because sleeping node will prevent its neighbors from sending data to sink node and others. So a new topology management mechanism which looks like an electric fan when the algorithm works (see Figure 1) is presented in this paper.

The new topology management mechanism prolongs lifetime of wireless sensor networks by employing energy-saving technique which consists of placing transceivers of some nodes in sleep mode and reducing device capabilities. Clearly, a trade-off exists between the strategy of energy-saving and network performance in terms throughput and the delay of data delivery.

3.2 Framework of EF Algorithm

Electric fan topology mechanism (EFMT) has two main functions. First, it should provide basic condition to choose the node with high-energy reserves as router for route protocol. Second, it can turn off some transceivers periodically without producing shake to the networks. The second function is the core of EFMT.

To complete the first function, we should have one method to inspect some interesting states of node, including whether its transceiver is sleeping or not and how much energy it reserves. Energy information of nodes can be provided by energy map

[13] [14]. As EF algorithm controls all nodes in a centralized way, it can provide the status of nodes.

Now we introduce the core function of EFMT. Sector is the schedule unit of EFMT, and trajectory [15] is base element of sector. But in our work, trajectory not only can be used to route packets, but also can be used to manage nodes.

Before EFMT working, we need to build trajectories. We find nodes with high-energy reserves between sink node and sensor node from energy map, and generate a route maintenance packet (RMP), which contains necessary coordinates of high-energy reserves nodes for building a trajectory. Obviously, the resulting trajectory should link sink node with sensor node.

There is no need to distribute a trajectory to every pair of sink node and sensor node. Because if like that, sink node has to calculate route for every sensor node, the result is that sink node is so busy, and the amount of packets for delivering route information increases a lot. In an area, we just select one or a few nodes as target node(s), and construct trajectory between sink node and target node(s). As the broadcast nature of radio signals, when RMP is disseminated, nodes near the trajectory can detect that and store it in local memory. Of course, there are still some nodes that are not located in or near the trajectory, and we have developed LM algorithm for those. We will discuss LM algorithm in next section.

After building the trajectories, we should have an effective mechanism to manage those trajectories. Electric fan topology mechanism defines the whole wireless network as an irregular disk, and sink node is located in the center of the irregular disk. The irregular disk is divided into N equal divisions based on the scale of WSNs and the communication range of the node. Sector is the schedule unit of EFMT. We build one or a few trajectories depending on the peak level of packets business in every sector and manage those trajectories using sector as unit. Each sector has a corresponding number among 0~N-1. At one dispatch interval, we allow that only either even number or odd number of sector can be scheduled to run. In such way, EFMT turns off some transceivers efficiently and skillfully.

In short, every sector is a container in EFMT, which can manage several trajectories at one time. We should rebuild the trajectory of section periodically to avoid the consumption of energy unfairly.

Now we summarize the working process of EFMT.

What sink node does for maintaining networks route is described as follows.

1) Sink initializes itself. 2) Broadcast one required command to collect information of nodes, such as node's coordinate, node's residual energy and so on; 3) Sink uses the fresh information to update local energy map. 4) Sink selects target node. Then sink selects high-energy reserves nodes between sink node and target node. 5) Sink generates a route maintenance packet (RMP), which contains necessary coordinates of high-energy reserves nodes for building a trajectory and command to turn off some nodes' transceivers; 6) A packet routing mechanism is used to transmit RMP along the trajectory to target node. 7) Sink repeats above periodically.

What ordinary node does for maintaining network route is described as follows.

1) When it received command required sending local information to sink, node does it. 2) Nodes near the trajectory will receive the RMP; 3) After receiving RMP, node builds the trajectory and stores the trajectory result in local memory. If node receives one sleep command from the RMP, it will sleep for some interval indicated

by the RMP. 4) When next RMP comes, node updates its local trajectory information, retransmits the RMP to other nodes and so on. 5) If node is not located in the point near the trajectory, the unique way for it to route packet is to use the Last-mile algorithm.

3.3 EF Algorithm

It is noted that the state of sector running or sleeping has no effect on the nodes that are not located in or near any trajectory. Last-mile algorithm can deal with those special nodes.

Algorithm 2. Electric fan algorithm
If sectors of even kind had been dispatched last time
   Dispatches sectors of odd kind to run;
   Dispatches sectors of even kind to sleep;
Else
   Dispatches sectors of even kind to run;
   Dispatches sectors of odd kind to sleep;
End if

---

4 Route Strategy

4.1 Generating Trajectory

We hope that packets can be transmitted to target nodes through region with higher energy reserves, and nodes of low-energy areas avoid working as a router between sink node and target node. So we should make node with high-energy reserves work as router when packets need to be transmitted from sink to target node or from target node to sink. Maybe we can use virtual circuit solution of ATM communication system, but routers need to maintain the next router of the way to the target node. Obviously, it's expensive for nodes. As wireless sensor network use air as communication medium unlike wire network using wired medium, so wireless sensor network is a delicate network and the routing entity of node often can't reflect the real network status. More serious one is that transceiver needs to be turned off periodically for saving energy. All of above affect routing entities and topology of the network. We find an original solution for above problem at [9] [13]. For TEDD, trajectory represents the most suitable routing path and will be attached to every sending packet. This method can eliminate the need of maintaining routing entity. Moreover, if a receiver-based packet routing policy is used, routing protocol can achieve more robust.

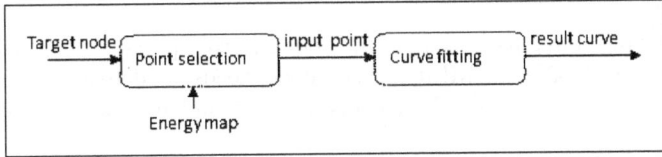

Fig. 2. Trajectory generation

The architecture of generating trajectory is showed in Figure 2. It is a simple solution, but for MLR, it is enough. We use cubic spline interpolation [16] as our curve fitting solution. The other detail of how to fitting trajectory can be found at [9, 15].

4.2 Last-Mile Algorithm

In the simplest cast of MLR, every sector has just one trajectory, like the sector 5 of figure 3. It's obvious there are some nodes which are not local in or near any trajectory. Last-mile algorithm is prepared for those nodes to send packet to the sink or nodes keeping one or more trajectories in hands.

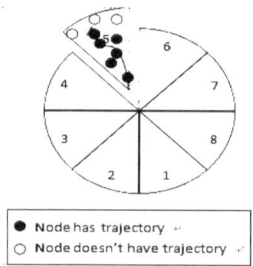

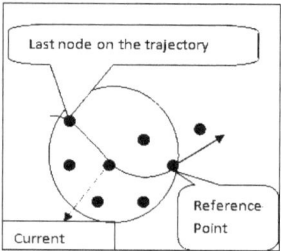

Fig. 3. Nodes near trajectory   **Fig. 4.** Packet routing

The node running LM algorithm should have one neighbor node at least, and also should know some information of its neighbor, such as residual energy, whether sleep or not, hops to sink node and so on.

Algorithm 3. Last-mile algorithm
   //assume: hop(x) is hops from node x to sink node.
   Input: current node's on-line neighbors
   Select two nodes Q and P. Among all input nodes, Node Q has most reserves
        energy
   and node P has second most reserves energy. Hops of Q or P should be equal or
        lesser
   than hop(current node).
      If (hop(Q) > hop(P))
      Send the packet to Q with probability 0.7;
      Else
      Send the packet to P with probability 0.7;
      End if

4.3 Packet Route Mechanism

In the process of routing packets, after the node received packet, it does not conserve the trajectory in TEDD. In MLR, sensor node needs to deliver packets back to sink node, so when received RMP, every node should update its local trajectory information.

Our solution of updating trajectory is as follows. First, after sink node has selected one target node, it selects high-energy reserves nodes between sink node and the target node. Then sink generates a route maintenance packet (RMP), which contains necessary coordinates of high-energy reserves nodes to build a trajectory. If RMP is ready, a packet routing mechanism is used to transmit RMP along the trajectory to target node. The node near the trajectory will receive the RMP. Once node had received RMP, it builds the trajectory and stores the result in local memory. When next RMP came, node updates its local trajectory information. Repeat above periodically.

MLR just defines one data flow mode rather than two modes of TEDD. Because we use a new topology management mechanism, named Electric fan algorithm, so every sector of sensor field has limited nodes. If broadcast function is needed, broadcasting to the whole sector will be more efficient. Famous key elements of TEDD may include such one: high latency. So in MLR, we have a formula.

$$delayTime = \frac{d}{flag} \qquad (2)$$

In Eq. (2), d is the distance from the current node to the reference point and the default flag is 1, 000. If transceiver has good sensitivity, flag can be set larger than 1000. After delay time, if not any packet had been retransmitted, the current node retransmits.

The proposed temporization policy of TEDD is based on the distance from the current node to a point ahead on the curve, called reference point. In particular, the reference point is the point (not necessarily a node) closest to the curve localized at the circumference with center at the current node and radius equals to the node communication radius (Figure 4). In each relay, the selection of the reference point is determined by the previous hop of the trajectory. Each node that receives a packet adjusts its delay time using its distance to the reference point sent in the packet, and the delay time is proportional to the distance.

Except the adaption above, the basic operation of packet routing mechanism of MLR is the same as algorithm 1, which is developed in the reference [9].

5   Simulation Result

5.1   Define Scenario

Simulation parameters are presented in Table 1. In our simulation, 500 nodes are deployed in a sensor field 40×40m² randomly. It's assumed that every node knows its own location and sink knows the coordinates of all nodes. Sink is a special node: no restriction in energy and memory. Sink is placed at the center of sensor field.

Table 1. Simulation parameters

Parameters	Values	Parameters	Values
Number of Nodes	500	Sensor field size	40×40m²
Initial energy	40J	Number of Events	10^{12}
Frequencies of event	1 per second	Power consumption	Mica2 OEM
Communication range	Ordinary node: 5m; Sink: 7m		

Our team had developed a new simulator for WSNs, named Micro simulator for WSNs, which is based on the work of NS2. Micro simulator uses scheduler and event mechanism of NS2. The objective of Micro simulator is to develop a micro simulator just for WSNs. In order to analyze the performance of MLR, we use Micro simulator as our simulation platform.

In this simulation, we use three routing protocols MLR, Tw-TEDD, RG. Tw-TEDD is a degraded version of MLR. Tw-TEDD doesn't use electric fan algorithm, but it needs to track how many times the trajectory had been used. Before distributing the new trajectory to nodes, sink sets a restriction to times of trajectory used. If using times of trajectory is close to restriction, the trajectory should be abandoned, and a new trajectory to the same target node should be rebuilt by sink. Before the new trajectory installed, no packet transmission is permitted. RG is a random gossip routing protocol. A sensor node randomly selects one of its neighbors to send the data. Once the neighbor node receives the data, it selects another sensor node randomly.

5.2   Simulation Result

In Figure 5, percentage of dead nodes is showed. The X-axis shows the simulation time while the left Y-axis shows percentage of dead nodes. From the curve, it shows that in MLR, the curve is almost straight before 900×10^9 seconds, then the curve suddenly bending. It indicates nodes almost die at the same time. Tw-TEDD does well too. But for random gossip' blindness of selecting route, it needs to pay a lot, and it does not have a good result.

In Figure 6, the relationship between simulation time and average residual energy of networks is described. There are some differences among three curves. Obviously, MLR performs best. The MLR curve represents the relationship between simulation time and average residual energy of networks of MLR, as MLR turns off some transceivers periodically to save energy, so it has outstanding performance. The title of maximum lifetime routing protocol for WSNs is deserved for MLR.

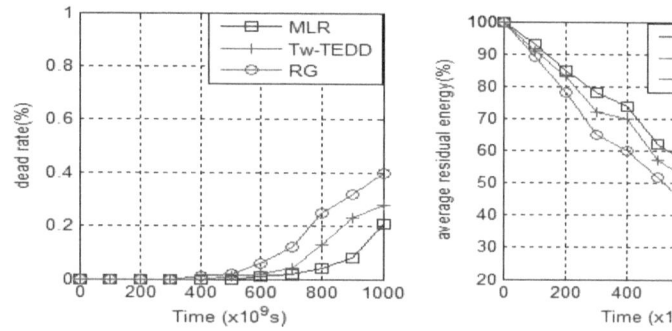

Fig. 5. Percentage of dead nodes   **Fig. 6.** Average residual energy

In Figure 7, the relationship between average delay time and the number of transmitted packets is described. The delay time is the interval from the moment called send function by top level application to the moment packet received by receiver. If the sending process is blocked because the transmitter had been closed, the delay of this process also need to be calculated into delay time in our simulation. It explains the average delay time of sending the number of packets, for example, the average delay time of transmitting 60x10^8 packets is 19×10^{-3} seconds. MLR has high delay time because it turns off some transceivers periodically. So MLR is not a good solution for real time environment!

In Figure 8, we can see that under the condition that the number of events is same, routing protocol needs to send how many packets to the networks for reporting those events to sink from the start point of running networks to a moment. Random gossip routing protocol loses the game because the node of random gossip is just like the man who is running in desert without compass or GPS. As nodes of MLR and Tw-TEDD have learnt the "secret" perfect way to sink, they run well.

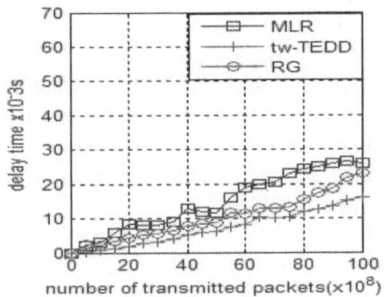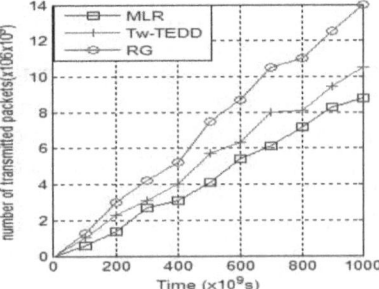

Fig. 7. Delay time   **Fig. 8.** Packets number

6 Conclusion

In this paper, a novel framework is presented to prolong the lifetime of wireless sensor networks to the maximum. This framework consists of a novel electric fan topology management mechanism and an efficient routing protocol named maximum lifetime routing (MLR). The novel electric fan topology management mechanism (as we know we are the first one to do this) provides a scheduler strategy to save much energy by turning off some transceivers periodically. MLR can be used to choose the node with high-energy reserves as router. When last-mile algorithm integrated with TEDD routing method, an efficient general routing protocol is proposed. Except those, we can add more useful characteristics to the framework easily, such as data aggregation, flow control and so on.

Simulation results show that MLR extends the lifetime of networks to the maximum. MLR is suitable for large scale non-real time wireless sensor applications. Another interesting thing is that even though all trajectories are unavailable, nodes can still send packets to sink efficiently, because MLR has Last-mile algorithm in reserve. Moreover, as MLR uses a receiver-based packet routing policy, it can adapt to the rapid changing of network topology very well.

References

1. Ephremides, A.: Energy Concerns in Wireless Networks. IEEE Wireless Communication 9, 48–59 (2002)
2. Goldsmith, A.J., Wicker, S.B.: Design Challenges for Energy-Constrained Ad hoc Wireless Networks. IEEE Wireless Communication 9, 8–27 (2002)
3. Kim, B., Kim, I.: Energy Aware Routing Protocol in Wireless Sensor. International Journal of Computer Science and Network Security 6(1), 201–207 (2006)
4. Heinzelman, W.R., Chandrakasan, A., Balakrishnan, H.: Energy-Efficient Communication Protocol for Wireless Micro sensor Networks. In: Proceedings of the Hawaii International Conference on System Sciences, Maui, Hawaii, January 4-7 (2000)
5. Lindsey, S., Raghavendra, C.S.: PEGASIS: Power Efficient Gathering in Sensor Information Systems. In: IEEE Aerospace Conf. Proc., vol. 3(9-16), pp. 1125–1130 (2002)
6. Manjeshwar, A., Agrawal, D.P.: TEEN: a Routing Protocol for Enhanced Efficiency in Wireless Sensor Networks. In: International Parallel and Distributed Processing Symposium, vol. 3, 30189a (2001)
7. Manjeshwar, A., Agarwal, D.P.: APTEEN: A Hybrid Protocol for Efficient Routing and Comprehensive Information Retrieval in Wireless Sensor Networks. Parallel and Distributed Computing Issues in Wireless Networks and Mobile Computing, 195–202
8. Rodoplu, V., Meng, T.H.: Minimum Energy Mobile Wireless Networks. IEEE JSAC 17(8), 1333–1344 (1999)
9. do Val Machado, M., Goussevskaia, O., et al.: Data Dissemination in Autonomic Wireless Sensor Networks. IEEE Journal on Selected Areas in Communications 23(12), 2305–2319 (2005)
10. Hill, J., Szewczyk, R., Woo, A., Hollar, S., Culler, D., Pister, K.: System architecture directions for networked sensors. In: Proc. 9th Int. Conf. Arch. Support Programming Languages and Operating Systems, pp. 93–104 (November 2000)
11. Mini, R.A.F., Loureiro, A.F., Nath, B.: A state-based energy dissipation model for wireless sensor networks. In: Proc. 10th IEEE Int. Conf. Emerging Technol., Factory Autom. (2005)
12. Santi, P.: Topology Control in Wireless Ad Hoc and Sensor Networks. John Wiley & Sons Ltd, Chichester
13. Mini, R.A.F., Loureiro, A.A.F., Nath, B.: The Best Energy Map of a Wireless Sensor Network. source, `http://www.cs.rutgers.edu/dataman/papers/2004-5/04sbrc-budget.pdf` contributors: CiteSeerX
14. Mini, R.A.F., Nath, B., Loureiro, A.A.F.: Prediction-based Approaches to Construct the Energy Map for Wireless Sensor Networks. source, `http://www.cs.rutgers.edu/~mini/sbrc.ps.gz` contributors: CiteSeerX
15. Niculescu, D., Nath, B.: Trajectory Based Forwarding and Its Applications. In: Proceedings of the 9th Annual International Conference on Mobile Computing and Networking, Routing and Forwarding, pp. 260–272 (2003)
16. Press, W.H., Teukolsky, S.A., Vetterling, W.T., Flannery, B.P.: Numerical recipes, 3rd edn. Cambridge University press, Cambridge (2007)

Enhancing Security by System-Level Virtualization in Cloud Computing Environments

Dawei Sun[1], Guiran Chang[2], Chunguang Tan[1], and Xingwei Wang[1]

[1] School of Information Science and Engineering, Northeastern University,
Shenyang, P.R. China, 110004
sundaweicn@163.com, tcg1978@gmail.com, wangxw@mail.neu.edu.cn
[2] Computing Center, Northeastern University, Shenyang, P.R. China, 110004
chang@neu.edu.cn

Abstract. Many trends are opening up the era of cloud computing, which will reshape the IT industry. Virtualization techniques have become an indispensable ingredient for almost all cloud computing system. By the virtual environments, cloud provider is able to run varieties of operating systems as needed by each cloud user. Virtualization can improve reliability, security, and availability of applications by using consolidation, isolation, and fault tolerance. In addition, it is possible to balance the workloads by using live migration techniques. In this paper, the definition of cloud computing is given; and then the service and deployment models are introduced. An analysis of security issues and challenges in implementation of cloud computing is identified. Moreover, a system-level virtualization case is established to enhance the security of cloud computing environments.

Keywords: Cloud Computing; Security; Virtualization Techniques; Issues; Challenges.

1 Introduction

Many trends are opening up the era of cloud computing [1] [2] [3], a large-scale distributed computing paradigm driven by economies of scale, in which a pool of abstracted, virtualized, dynamically-scalable, highly available, and configurable and reconfigurable computing resources (e.g., networks, servers, storage, applications, data, and so on) can be rapidly provisioned and released with minimal management effort in the data centers. And services are delivered on demand to external customers over high-speed Internet, together with the "X as a service (XaaS)" computing architecture, which is broken down into three segments: "applications", "platforms", and "infrastructure". Its arms are to provide users with more flexible services in a transparent manner and with ever cheaper and more powerful processors.

Virtualization techniques have become an indispensable ingredient for almost every cloud computing environment. By the virtual environments, cloud provider is able to run varieties of operating systems as needed by cloud users. Virtualization can improve reliability, security, and availability of applications by using consolidation,

R. Chen (Ed.): ICICIS 2011, Part I, CCIS 134, pp. 565–570, 2011.
© Springer-Verlag Berlin Heidelberg 2011

isolation, and fault tolerance. In addition, it is possible to balance the workloads by using live migration techniques to relocate applications from failing datacenters, and isolate fault systems for repair.

In this paper, the definition of cloud computing is given; and then the service and deployment models are introduced. An analysis of security issues and challenges in implementation of cloud computing is identified. Moreover, a system-level virtualization case is established to enhance the security of cloud computing environments.

The remainder of this paper is organized as follows. In section 2, we give the definition of cloud computing and the service and then deployment models are introduced. Section 3 analyzes the security issues and challenges in implementation of cloud computing. Section 4 establishes a system-level virtualization case to enhance security of cloud computing environments. Finally, conclusions are given in section 5.

2 Cloud Computing Overview

2.1 Definition of Cloud Computing

Many formal definitions about cloud computing have been proposed in both academia and industry. By IBM definition [4], it is a pool of virtualized computer resources. By Forster et al definitions [1], it is a large-scale distributed computing paradigm that is driven by economies of scale, in which a pool of abstracted, virtualized, dynamically-scalable, managed computing power, storage, platforms, and services are delivered on demand to external customers over the Internet.

While one provided by NIST (National Institute of Standards and Technology) [3] appears to include key elements of cloud computing: it is a model for enabling convenient, on-demand network access to a shared pool of configurable computing resources (e.g., networks, servers, storage, applications, and services) that can be rapidly provisioned and released with minimal management effort or service provider interaction. The essential characteristics about cloud computing can be described: on-demand self-service, broad network access, resource pooling, rapid elasticity, and measured service. The common characteristics are massive scale, homogeneity, virtualization, resilient computing, low cost software, geographic distribution, service orientation, and advanced security technologies.

2.2 Service Models of Cloud Computing

An analysis of the products and services released by Google [5], Amazon [6], IBM [4] [7], Microsoft [8], Salesforce, [9], and so on, the best known cloud service providers. The service model of cloud computing can be categorized as follow (as shown in Figure 1) [1] [3]: (1) Software as a Service (SaaS). The capability provided to the cloud user is to use the cloud servicer applications running on a cloud infrastructure. The applications are accessible from various client devices through a thin client interface such as a web browser. The consumer does not manage or control the underlying cloud infrastructure. Salesforce CRM [9] is a SasS cloud case; (2) Platform as a Service (PaaS). The capability provided to the consumer is to deploy onto the cloud infrastructure consumer-created or acquired applications created using programming languages and tools supported by the provider. The consumer does not manage or control the underlying cloud infrastructure including network, servers, operating systems, or storage, but has control over the deployed applications and possibly application hosting environment configurations. Google App Engine [5] is a PasS cloud case. Microsoft Azure [8] is another PasS cloud case; (3) Infrastructure as a Service (IaaS). The capability provided to the consumer is to provision processing, storage, networks, and other fundamental computing resources where the consumer is able to deploy and run arbitrary software. The consumer does not manage or control the underlying cloud infrastructure but has control over operating systems, storage, deployed applications, and possibly limited control of select networking components. Amazon Elastic Compute Cloud (EC2) [6] is an IaaS cloud case.

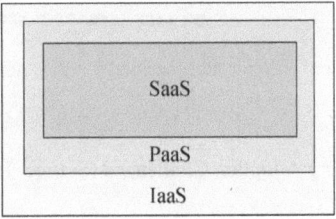

Fig. 1. Cloud Computing Service Model

2.3 Deployment Models of Cloud Computing

The service model of cloud computing can be categorized as follow [3] [10]: (1) Private cloud. The cloud infrastructure is operated solely for an organization. It may be managed by the organization or a third party and may exist on premise or off premise; (2) Community cloud. The cloud infrastructure is shared by several organizations and supports a specific community that has shared concerns (e.g., mission, security requirements, policy, and compliance considerations). It may be managed by the organizations or a third party and may exist on premise or off premise; (3) Public cloud. The cloud infrastructure is made available to the general public or a large industry group and is owned by an organization selling cloud services; (4) Hybrid cloud. The cloud infrastructure is a composition of two or more clouds (private, community, or public) that remain unique entities but are bound together by standardized or proprietary technology that enables data and application portability (e.g., cloud bursting for load-balancing between clouds).

3 Cloud Computing Security Challenges

Based on a survey conducted by IDC in 2009, the major challenges that prevent cloud computing from being adopted are recognized by organizations as shown in Figure 2.

It is clear that security issue is the most important challenge in cloud computing application. Without a doubt, putting your data in someone else's hard disk, running your software using someone else's CPU appears daunting to many. Well known

Q: Rate the challenges/issues of the 'cloud' /on-demand model

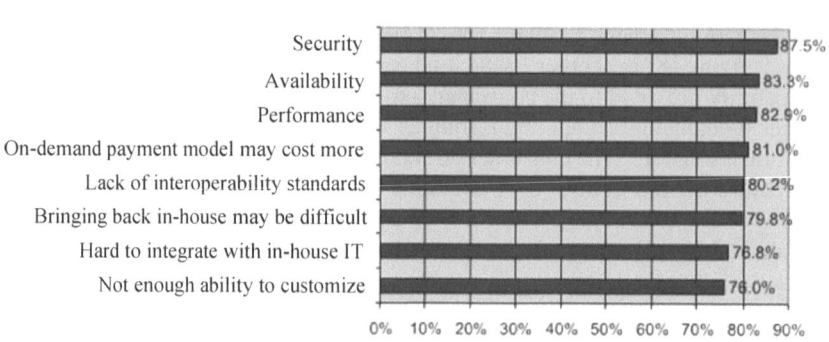

(Scale: 1 = Not at all concerned 5 = Very concemde)

Source: IDC Enterprise Panel, 3Q09, n=263, September 2009

Fig. 2. Cloud Computing Adoption Challenges (Source: IDC Survey, Sep. 2009)

security issues can be summary as follows [3] [10] : (1) data dispersal and international privacy laws; (2) need for isolation management; (3) multi-tenancy, One application instance may be serving hundreds of companies (3) logging challenges; (4) data ownership issues; (5) quality of service guarantees; (6) dependence on secure hypervisors; (7) attraction to hackers (high value target); (8) security of virtual OSs in the cloud; (9) possibility for massive outages; (10) encryption needs for cloud computing; (11) lack of public SaaS version control.

4   System-Level Virtualization Techniques to Enhance Security

Virtualization is a technique for hiding the physical characteristics of computing resources from the way in which other systems, applications, or end users interact with those resources. It includes making a single physical (e.g., a server, an OS, or application) resource appearing to function as multiple logical resources, or it can include making multiple physical resources appearing as a single logical resource [11] [12].

System-level virtualization is the faithful reproduction of an entire architecture in software which provides the illusion of a real machine to all software running above it. It is classified into two categories (see Figure 3): Bare-metal virtualization and Hosted virtualization. Bare-metal virtualization is used for the reason that it has direct access to hardware resource and its performance is comparable to that of native execution. In contrast, hosted virtualization incurs additional overhead due to the layering of the VMM on top of the host OS when service resource requests from the VMs [13].

System-level virtualization can improve dependability and enhance security of cloud systems for a number of reasons and the three major justifications are: (1) system consolidation. It is the major market for virtualization solutions. It enables the

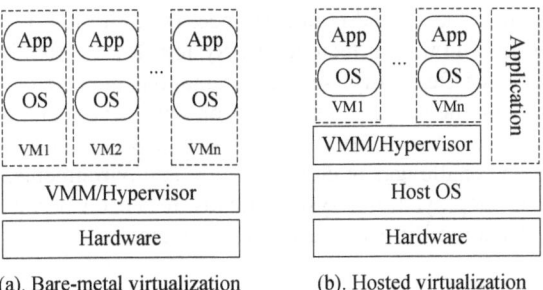

Fig. 3. Classification of system-level virtualization

sharing of expensive servers among different applications with guarantees that each application will have its own view of the system and is isolated from each other. This allows service providers to consolidate works to fewer servers and also to support incompatible or legacy operating environments without the need to separate the hardware and achieve integrity of the cloud system. In addition, server consolidation can increase function unit reuse degree, reduce hardware cost, improve resource utilization, save power and achieve system load balance; (2) isolation. It aims at improving the security and reliability of a system by isolating the execution environment for applications in VMs which cannot corrupt the bare hardware. Isolation forbids a misbehaving virtual machine to consume other machine resources, provides fairness according to the shares of virtual machines, and improves the reliability and availability of the cloud system. The applications running on the VMs are well defined entities, and are isolated from all other applications and even from the core host operating system; and (3) live migration. The capability of live migrating the entire VMs, makes it possible to improve the quality of service by balancing the global loads among several servers without interruption the application execution and by moving the VMs when a failure is predicted for a specific server. It also enables a transparent programmable downtime of the servers by using live migration the VMs to other servers before a server is shut down for maintenance.

In addition, some other capabilities of system-level virtualization can also enhance the maintainability, enhance the security of cloud systems, such as VM pause/ unpause, VM checkpoint/ restart. These mechanisms enable the implementation of three fault tolerance policies: (1) reactive fault tolerance; (2) proactive fault tolerance; and (3) hybrid policies mixing both reactive and proactive fault tolerance.

5   Conclusions and Future Works

As a novel pas-as-you-go business model, Security is one of the challenges to be addressed before cloud computing is widely applied, and Virtualization technique is one of the most important means to improve the security of current heterogeneous cloud platforms. System-level Virtualization techniques have become an indispensable ingredient for almost cloud computing system. By the virtual environments, cloud provider is able to run variety of operating systems as needed by each cloud user. Virtualization can improve reliability, security, and availability of applications by using consolidation, isolation, and fault tolerance. In addition, it is possible to balance the workloads by live migration techniques. System-level virtualization offers enormous opportunities for flexibility, security management, and deployment of cloud systems. It is clear that the scope of virtualization will expand in the future.

Future works include more rigorous cloud virtualization case and further analysis of security issues and challenges in cloud computing environments. The cloud virtualization case will be deployed and systematically tested on private cloud computing platform of State Taxation Bureau of Liaoning Province.

Acknowledgments. This work is supported by the National Natural Science Foundation of China under Grant No. 61070162, No. 71071028, No. 60802023 and No. 70931001; the Specialized Research Fund for the Doctoral Program of Higher Education under Grant 20070145017; the Fundamental Research Funds for the Central Universities under Grant No. N100604012, No. N090504003 and No. N090504006. The authors gratefully thank Junling Hu for her help and comments.

References

1. Foster, I., Zhao, Y., Raicu, I., Lu, S.Y.: Cloud Computing and Grid Computing 360-degree compared. In: The Grid Computing Environments Workshop, GCE 2008, pp. 1–10. IEEE Press, Texas (2008)
2. Andrzej, G., Michael, B.: Toward dynamic and attribute based publication, discovery and selection for cloud computing. Future Generation Computer Systems 26, 947–970 (2010)
3. Mell, P., Grance, T.: Presentation on effective and secure use of cloud computing paradigm. National Institute of Standards and Technology, Information Technology Laboratory, http://csrc.nist.gov/groups/SNS/cloudcomputing/index.html
4. IBM Cloud computing (white paper version 1.0), http://www.ibm.com/developerworks/websphere/zones/hipods/
5. Google App Engine (2010), http://code.google.com/intl/zh-CN/appengine/
6. Amazon Elastic Compute Cloud (Amazon EC2) (2010), http://aws.amazon.com/ec2/
7. IBM Cloud computing (2010), http://www.ibm.com/ibm/cloud/
8. Microsoft, Azure (2010), http://www.microsoft.com/windowsazure/
9. Salesforce, CRM (2010), http://www.salesforce.com/cn/crm/
10. Dillon, T., Chen, W., Chang, E.: Cloud Computing: Issues and Challenges. In: 24th IEEE International Conference on Advanced Information Networking and Applications, AINA 2010, pp. 27–33. IEEE Press, Los Alamitos (2010)
11. Alain, R.: Using virtualization to improve durability and portability of industrial applications. In: 6th IEEE International Conference on Industrial Informatics, Korea, pp. 1545–1550. IEEE Press, Daejeon (2008)
12. Chowdhury, N.M.K., Raouf, B.: A survey of network virtualization. Computer Networks 54, 862–876 (2010)
13. Scott, S.L., Vallée, G., Naughton, T., Tikotekar, A., Engelmann, C., Ong, H.: System-level virtualization research at Oak Ridge National Laboratory. Future Generation Computer Systems 26, 304–307 (2010)

Enabling Two Levels of Adaptation: A Framework for Traffic-Aware and Context Management Deployment

Chin-Ling Chen[*] and Jia-Ching Wang

Department of Information Management
National Pingtung Institute of Commerce
Pingtung, Taiwan 900

Abstract. This paper presents a novel approach in that it provides both inter-service adaptation by reconfiguring current available services in reaction to environment changes and intra-service adaptation by selecting the appropriate parameters to best adaptation. A highly scalable JXTA middleware is used in context-aware framework, which provides the unified interfaces for service operating on JXTA so that the services can access directly to the context environment. We experiment some simulations to demonstrate its ability to adaptation.

Keywords: adaptation, context-aware, JXTA.

1 Introduction

The rapid change of internet environment and the high availability of multimedia services have nominated the requirements for context-aware services (CAS) and service provisioning as the key to support various multimedia services for users. The early concept of context was introduced by [1]. Usually the context is associated with the resulting information provided by various sensors. Any information that is used to characterize the situation of an entity as well as the interaction between entities is considered to be context. We may divide CAS techniques into two categories: service platform designing [1-11] and communication adaption [12-17].

Recently much effort has been concentrated on the designing of flexible CAS framework in which a service platform is used for context collection, delivering and distribution [1-6]. However, this kind of framework lacks in scalability and modularity. A new autonomous approach [7-9] in which agents discover and communicate other agents has been proposed to solve the above mentioned problems. This framework deals both with the context information provided in many network locations by brokers through an open simple API, and the way the context information distributes. Nevertheless, this framework limits in deciding reliable context information. In [10-11], the concept of rule-based functions (enablers) has been addressed to manage personal

---

[*] Corresponding author.

R. Chen (Ed.): ICICIS 2011, Part I, CCIS 134, pp. 571–580, 2011.
© Springer-Verlag Berlin Heidelberg 2011

reachability, manage implicit context, and adapt modality to the context. This framework uses a generic approach that enables processing and exchange of the context information distributed in context domain, over administrative domains, and in protocol layers. However, the issues regarding user preference, configuration and management of sensors and user status still cannot be solved in this research. Communication adaption [12-17] make decision to deliver the possible services that match in the best way end-user's requirements according to current environment resources like available networks and user devices. The dissemination of messages according to users' location and other attributes opens up new possibilities in context-aware systems.

The basic functions P2P technology requires includes files sharing, distributed computing, and instant messager services. Currently most P2P applications are specific to a single platform and are unable to communicate and share data with other applications. JXTA [18] enables peers providing various P2P services to locate each other and communicate each other. In addition, JXTA technology is designed to be independent of programming languages, transport protocols and deployment platforms. This has led us to the choice of JXTA.

In this paper, we design an adaptive context awareness mechanism that supports a scale of flexibility by adding or deleting context entity in adapting to changes in resources and use JXTA middleware to support a degree of scalability by allowing direct participation of users. Two levels of adaptation can be achieved in the framework: inter-service and intra-service. In inter-service adaptation, the unit of service is implemented as a context object that provides kinds of value-added service, allowing context awareness mechanism to benefit from the aggregated functionality of service combination. Intra-service adaptation reacts in selecting the appropriate parameter in case of more than one choices on the list.

2   Adaptive Context-Aware Framework

The set of services includes four categories: video, audio, text and instant message. Video service is assumed to be of two types (Table 1) and audio service is grouped into five classes (Table 2). In this case, we have $W_{v2}>W_{v1}$ and $W_{a5}>W_{a4}>W_{a3}>W_{a2}>W_{a1}$. User can specify one or more services for the person on the contacts list. There are three types of states in user status. They are idle, busy and meeting, corresponding to the capability to receiving all services, text and instant message, and instant message only, individually. Users may switch to the other states as his behavior changes. In order to detect internet environment, network status is characterized by three parameters: available bandwidth *(ABW)*, packet loss rate *(Loss)* and transmission delay *(Delay)*. What kinds of services provided to the user depends mostly on network status.

The proposed mechanism consists of three modules- *context analysis, context decision* and *context adaptation*. The *context analysis* is interested in the current status of environmental contexts, including hardware environment, specified user preferences, user status and network status. *Context analysis* supports the acquisition of context data to establish corresponding object. It may happen that not all the environmental parameters can be detected and collected completely. The more context information it gathers, the more accurate decision it ensures. *Context analysis* reports every change in the context that it monitors to context decision. In *context decision*, one filter rule is created for each context object with confining the scope associated with the status of an environment context. Let P_i represent the weighted value of context entity i for each service, where $i = 1, 2, 3$ and 4 indicate hardware environment, specified user preferences, user status, and network status, individually. When $P_i = 1$, the service for context entity i is allowed to open. Otherwise ($P_i = 0$), close. A series of services can be combined together to form a service combination (SC), which is defined by a vector (T, I, V, VT, A, AT), where T is text service, I is instant message service, V is video service, VT is video format type, A is audio service and AT is audio format type. All the lists of service combination for four context entities are shown from Table 3 to Table 6. Context decision is responsible for checking the context object against the filter rule and then generates an appropriate service combination. All the rule filters for four context entities are represented from Fig.1 to Fig.4. The service can be dynamically added or removed to adapt to the vigorous changes in the characteristics of internet environment. Context adaptation can be achieved at two levels. At the coarse grained level (inter-service), two or more service combinations are monitored simultaneously and adaptation is required in case of choice confliction. Let A_i be the set of service combination for context entity i and F be the set of adaptation result. I is an index set, where $I = \{1, 2, 3, 4\}$. We have

$$F = \bigcap_{i \in I} A_i$$

Table 1. List of video format types

RTP payload type	Video format type	Weight
26	JPEG	W_{v1}
34	H.263	W_{v2}

Table 2. List of audio format types

RTP payload type	Audio format type	Weight
0	G.711/U-law	W_{a2}
3	GSM	W_{a4}
4	G.723	W_{a5}
5	DVI	W_{a3}
14	MPEG-audio	W_{a1}

Table 3. List of SCs *hardware environment* (P_1)

	T	I	V	VT	A	AT
SC #1	1	1	0	N/A	0	N/A
SC #2	1	1	0	N/A	1	All
SC #3	1	1	1	All	0	N/A
SC #4	1	1	1	All	1	All

Table 4. List of SCs *specified user preferences* (P_2)

	T	I	V	VT	A	AT
SC #1	1	1	N/A	N/A	N/A	N/A
SC #2	1	1	0	N/A	N/A	N/A
SC #3	1	1	1	Optional	N/A	N/A
SC #4	1	1	1	Optional	0	N/A
SC #5	1	1	1	Optional	1	Optional

Table 5. List of SCs *user status* (P_3)

	T	I	V	VT	A	AT
SC #1	1	1	1	All	1	All
SC #2	1	1	0	N/A	0	N/A
SC #3	0	1	0	N/A	0	N/A

Table 6. List of SCs *network status* (P_4)

	T	I	V	VT	A	AT
SC #1	1	1	1	All	1	All
SC #2	1	1	0	N/A	0	N/A
SC #3	1	1	0	N/A	1	{3, 4}
SC #4	1	1	0	N/A	1	{3, 4, 5}
SC #5	1	1	1	{34}	1	All
SC #6	1	1	0	N/A	1	All

There are situations after the coarse adaptation decision is made. For example, $F = \{1, 1, 1, \{26, 34\}, 1, \{0, 3, 4, 5, 14\}\}$. This service combination provides user for text, instant message, all types of video and audio services. In this case, finer grained adaptation (intra-service) must be made to optimize its performance. In this case, $W_{v2} > W_{v1}$ and $W_{a5} > W_{a4} > W_{a3} > W_{a2} > W_{a1}$, H.263 and G.723 are, therefore, chosen.

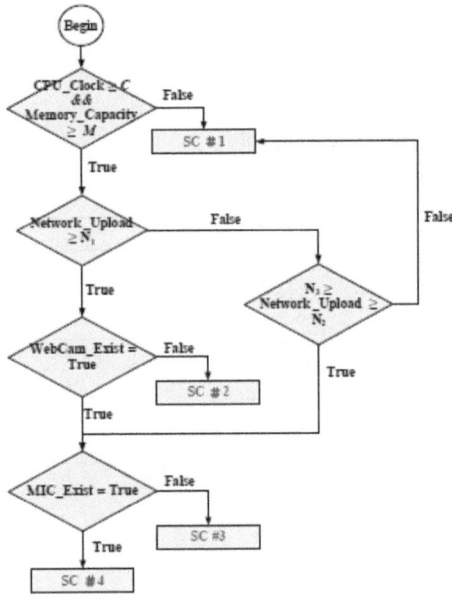

Fig. 1. Rule filter of *hardware environment* (P_1)

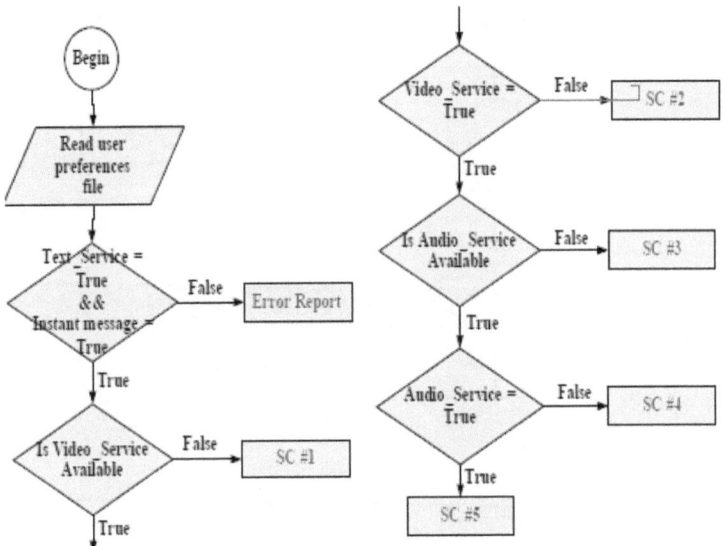

Fig. 2. Rule filter of *specified user perferences* (P_2)

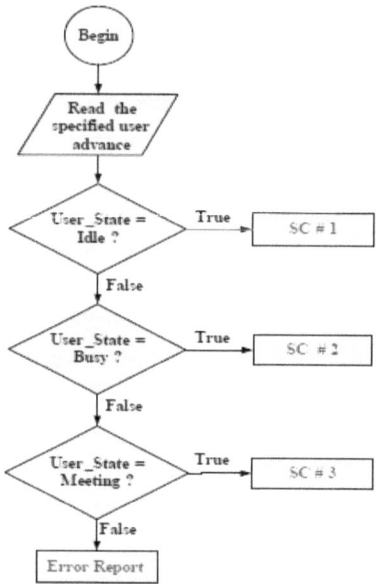

Fig. 3. Rule filter of *user status* (P_3)

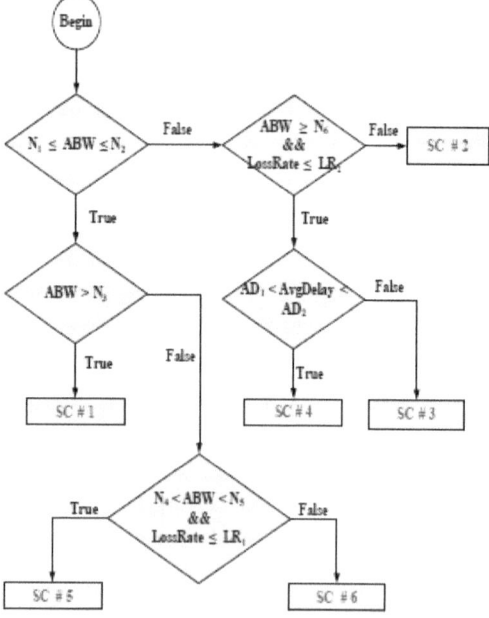

Fig. 4. Rule filter of *network status* (P_4)

3 Experiments and Evaluation

In this section, two scenarios are experimented to study the performance of the system. In the first scenario, we use discrete time based simulation for studying the effects of continuous video and audio stream by measuring the following parameters: transmission rate, loss rate and average delay. Table 7 indicates the experimental result. MPEG-audio and JPEG, has larger transmission rates (38.9 and 2,093 kbps, individually) in the audio and video stream types. We assign the weighted value based on the inverse of average transmission rate in the first scenario (Table 8). The second scenario is carried out to find the threshold of loss rate that leads to discontinuous stream playback. Figure 5 represents various volumes of jamming traffic for running 300 seconds to generate packet loss. For jamming traffic, one packet length is about 1,060 byte long. Table 9 represents the threshold value of playback discontinuity for various stream types. The threshold value indicates the level of performance uncertainty (loss rate) the user can tolerate. DVI and H.263 has the larger threshold value of loss rate in audio (31.3%) and video (38.5%) stream types, respectively. The second scenario assigns the weighted value accordingly based on the threshold value of each stream type (Table 10).

Table 7. Performance results of various stream types

Type	Avg trans rate (kbps)	Delay (ms)
G.711(U-law)	70	59.99
G.723	12	59.96
DVI	39	59.98
GSM	19	59.99
MPEG-Audio	72	156.82
JPEG (video)	2,093	3.80
H.263 (video)	170	24.25

Table 8. List of weighted value- scenario 1

Type	Weight
G.711/U-law	W_{a2}
GSM	W_{a4}
G.723	W_{a5}
DVI	W_{a3}
MPEG-audio	W_{a1}
JPEG	W_{v1}
H.263	W_{v2}

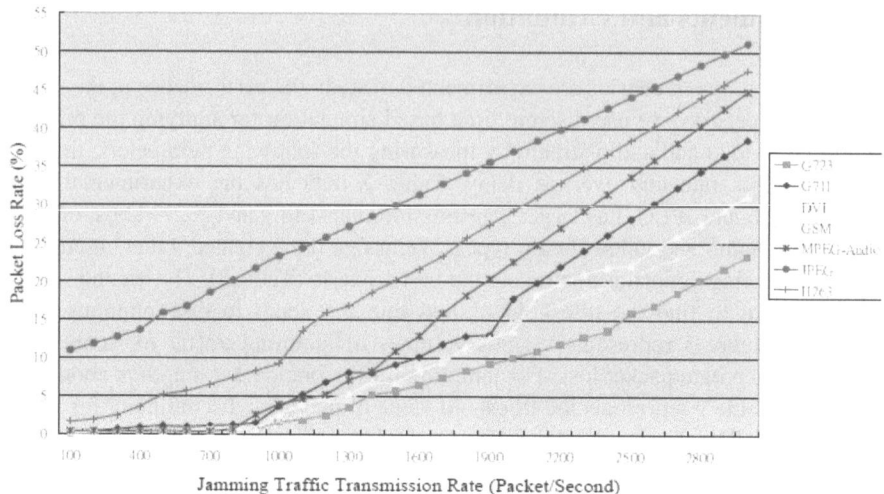

Jamming Traffic Transmission Rate (Packet/Second)

Fig. 5. Packet loss rate as a function of trassmission rate

Table 9. Discontinuity threshold of various stream types

Type	Avg trans rate (kbps)	Delay (ms)
G.711(U-law)	1,000	3.61
G.723	2,500	15.91
DVI	3,000	31.31
GSM	19	59.99
MPEG-Audio	1,500	10.97
JPEG (video)	100	10.98
H.263 (video)	2,500	38.54

Table 10. List of weighted value- scenario 2

Type	Weight
G.711/U-law	W_{a1}
GSM	W_{a3}
G.723	W_{a4}
DVI	W_{a5}
MPEG-audio	W_{a2}
JPEG	W_{v1}
H.263	W_{v2}

4 Conclusions

We have designed an adaptive context aware framework to efficiently manage the overall resource allocation within internet. Services combination can be achieved by reconfiguring itself dynamically in reaction to contextual changes. The JXTA middleware enables applications to use the framework to provide effective detection of changing environment of internet so that adaptation can be carried out efficiently. To validate the functionality of the proposed system, we experiment two scenarios under light and heavy loading conditions. The performance result indicates the ability of the system to adapt dynamically to the changing characteristics of internet environment. A new adaptive context-aware framework applied to mobile environment will be the topic of our future works. The framework is also required to provide some advanced mechanisms such as monitoring composite events, reusing the object, and minimizing the unnecessary objects. The ways to compromise multiple context providers across various administrative domains must be also further investigated.

References

1. Godbole, A., Smari, W.W.: Human perspective based context acquisition, learning and awareness in the design of context aware systems. In: IEEE Military Communications Conference, MILCOM 2006, vol. 1, pp. 102–109 (2006)
2. Bernardos, A.M., Tarrio, P., Iglesias, J., Casar, J.R.: Deploying context-aware services: A case study of rapid prototyping. In: 6th IEEE Consumer Communications and Networking Conference, CCNC 2009, vol. 6(1), pp. 1342–1346 (2009)
3. Chiti, F., Fantacci, R., Archetti, F., Messina, E., Toscani, D.: An integrated communications framework for context aware continuous monitoring with body sensor networks. IEEE Journal on Selected Areas in Communications 27(4), 379–386 (2009)
4. Cadenas, A., Gonzalez, J.M., Sola, O.M.: Context-aware processing of mobile device sensor information: Car accident detection hosted service. In: 6th IEEE Consumer Communications and Networking Conference, CCNC 2009, vol. 6(1), pp. 1362–1366 (2009)
5. Cho, K., Hwang, I., Kang, S., Kim, B., Lee, J., Lee, S., Park, S., Song, J., Rhee, Y.: HiCon: A hierarchical context monitoring and composition framework for next-generation context-aware services. IEEE Network 22(4), 34–42 (2008)
6. Wood, A.D., Stankovic, J.A., Virone, G., Selavo, L., He, Z., Cao, Q., Doan, T., Wu, Y., Fang, L., Stoleru, R.: Context-aware wireless sensor networks for assisted living and residential monitoring. IEEE Network 22(4), 26–33 (2008)
7. Serrano, J.M., Serrat, J., Strassner, J.: Ontology-based reasoning for supporting context-aware services on autonomic networks. In: IEEE International Conference on Communications, ICC 2007, vol. 1, pp. 2097–2102 (2007)
8. Wong, W.S., Aghvami, H., Wolak, S.J.: Context-aware personal assistant agent multi-agent system. In: 19th IEEE International Symposium on Personal, Indoor and Mobile Radio Communications, PIMRC 2008, vol. 19(1), pp. 311–314 (2008)
9. Saghir, B.E., Crespi, N.: A generic layer model for context-aware communication adaptation. In: IEEE Wireless Communications and Networking Conference, WCNC 2008, vol. 9(1), pp. 3027–3032 (2008)

10. Bossche, B.V.D., Strobbe, M., Jans, G.D., Hollez, J., Turck, F.D., Dhoedt, B., Demeester, P., Maas, G., Vlerken, B.V., Moreels, J., Janssens, N., Pollet, T.: Design of the pCASE platform for enabling context aware services. In: IFIP/IEEE International Symposium on Integrated Network Management, IM 2007, vol. (1), pp. 872–875 (2007)
11. Costa, P.D., Almeida, J.P.A., Pires, L.F., Sinderen, M.: Evaluation of a rule-based approach for context-aware services. In: IEEE Global Telecommunications Conference, GLOBECOM 2008, vol. 27(1), pp. 1657–1661 (2008)
12. Park, J.-T., Nah, J.-W., Wang, S., Chun, S.-M.: Context-aware mobility management with energy efficiency for multimedia streaming service in wireless LAN. In: 6th IEEE Consumer Communications and Networking Conference, CCNC 2009, vol. 6(1), pp. 1267–1272 (2009)
13. Garcia-Luna-Aceves, J.J., Mosko, M., Solis, I., Braynard, R., Ghosh, R.: Context-aware packet switching in ad hoc networks. In: 19th IEEE International Symposium on Personal, Indoor and Mobile Radio Communications, PIMRC 2008, vol. 19(1), pp. 1426–1431 (2008)
14. Saghir, B.E., Crespi, N.: An intelligent assistant for context-aware adaptation of personal communications. In: IEEE Wireless Communications and Networking Conference, WCNC 2007, vol. (1), pp. 2378–2383 (2007)
15. You, J., Lieckfeldt, D., Reichenbach, F., Timmermann, D.: Context-aware geographic routing for sensor networks with routing holes. In: IEEE Wireless Communications and Networking Conference, WCNC 2009, vol. 10(1), pp. 2589–2594 (2009)
16. Geiger, L., Durr, F., Rothermel, K.: On contextcast: A context-aware communication mechanism. In: IEEE International Conference on Communications, ICC 2009, vol. 32(1), pp. 1589–1593 (2009)
17. Giaffreda, R., Barria, J.: Service delivery in collaborative context-aware environments using fuzzy logic. In: IEEE International Conference on Communications, ICC 2007, vol. 1, pp. 2045–2049 (2007)
18. Gong, L.: JXTA: a network programming environment. IEEE Internet Computing 5(3), 88–95 (2001)

Bacteria Foraging Based Agent Feature Selection Algorithm

Dongying Liang[1], Weikun Zheng[1], and Yueping Li[2]

[1] Shenzhen Institute of Information Technology
liangdy@sziit.com.cn, zhengwk@sziit.com.cn
[2] Shenzhen Polytechnic
leeyueping@gmail.com

Abstract. This paper provides an agent genetic algorithm based on bacteria foraging strategy (BFOA-L) as the feature selection method, and presents the combined method of link-like agent structure and neural network based on bacteria foraging algorithm (BFOA). It introduces the bacteria foraging (BF) action into the feature selection and utilizes the neural network structure achieve fuzzy logic inference, so that the weights with no definite physical meaning in traditional neural network are endowed with the physical meaning of fuzzy logic inference parameters. Furthermore, to overcome the defects of traditional optimization methods, it applies the agent link-like competition strategy into the global optimization process to raise the convergence accuracy. The curve tracing test results show that this algorithm has good stability and high accuracy.

Keywords: bacteria foraging, agent, feature selection, fuzzy neural network.

1 Introduction

Optimization problems widely exist in scientific research and engineering practice. Due to the complexity of objective function and constraint conditions, to solve global optimization problems become more and more difficult, especially the optimization of high-dimension complex functions, which is still an open problem. In recent years, with the development of optimization methods such as Genetic Algorithm (GA), Particle Swarm Optimization (PSO) and Evolutionary Algorithm (EA), how to apply these algorithms into global optimization problems has gradually become the research focus.

GA, PSO and differential EA have been successfully applied in many optimization problems. However, they have defects such as slow convergence speed and weak global optimization capability, and are easy to fall into local optimal solution. In 2002, K.M.Passino brought forward the bacterial foraging algorithm (BFOA). In the BFOA model, the solution to optimization problems corresponds to the status of bacterial in the search space, namely, the majorized function adaptive value. BFOA algorithm includes three steps: chemotaxis, replication and dispelling. This algorithm is featured by swarm intelligence algorithm parallel search and easy jump out of local

R. Chen (Ed.): ICICIS 2011, Part I, CCIS 134, pp. 581–588, 2011.
© Springer-Verlag Berlin Heidelberg 2011

minimum. Ref [2] puts forward a multi-agent genetic algorithm (MAGA). This method can fix the agents on grids, which enables each agent to compete or cooperate with its neighborhood (a natural evolution phenomenon) and avoids the occurrence of premature convergence. However, if there are few agents in the swarm, the above problems also occur in the algorithm. In the past, some researchers put the stress on the optimal utilization of Hybrid Genetic Algorithm (HGA). Ding[9] brought forward a hybrid search algorithm integrating GA and Ant Colony Optimization (ACO), and probed into the advantages of search space and the best solution of utilization.

In view of the above, aiming at the dynamic neighborhood competition, this paper puts forward the intelligent agent genetic evolutionary algorithm based on BFOA chained competition strategy (BFOA-LA). The bacterial foraging chemotaxis process can assure the local search capability of bacteria. The replication process can fasten the search speed of bacteria. However, for complicated optimization problems, the chemotaxis and replication cannot prevent the bacteria from getting into local infinitesimal. By utilizing the mutual competition and intercross of link-like intelligent agents, this method is beneficial for enhancing the global search capability. Besides introducing the variation mode of intelligent agents, BFOA-LA method adopts the dispelling process to strengthen the global optimization ability of the algorithm. This algorithm not only preserves the diversity of swarm individuals in evolution to gain higher convergence speed, but also controls the number of optional characteristics flexibly.

2   Description

2.1   Fuzzy Neural Network Structure Based on Bacterial Foraging and Adaptive Link-Like Agent Genetic Algorithm

The traditional fuzzy neural network is defective in aspects such as slow convergence rate of learning, easy fall into local minimum, poor real-time learning ability, and generalization ability. Here it integrates the adaptive link-like agent and bacterial foraging algorithm (BFOA), and adds the replication and dispelling of BFOA as a learning strategy into the neural network training process to build the hybrid adaptive link-like agent network, which can effectively make up the deficiency of traditional BP network. This algorithm has combined the coevolution idea and adopts the multi-sub-population parallel searching mode. This idea is that partition the whole population into multiple sub-populations first, and each subpopulation then adopts the link-like agent genetic algorithm for evolution. The subpopulations share and transfer genetic information by sharing agents, to reach the aim of finding satisfactory solution by multi-subpopulations collectively. It thus effectively raises the optimization rate.

According to the methods in [2], it constructs the circular link-like agent structure as shown in Fig. 1. The agent and agents in its neighborhood compete and co-operate each other. The sharing agent transmits the genetic information of the previous subpopulation to the current subpopulation, which is beneficial for diffusing the genetic information among the swams.

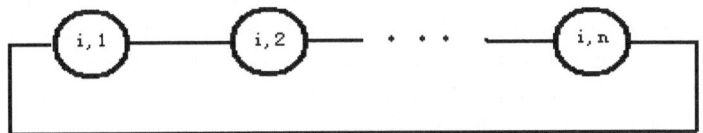

Fig. 1. Link-like Agent Structure

Conduct network weights training on the basis of the constructed circular link-like agent structure (as shown in Fig. 1).

BFOA-BP network model contains multiple comparatively independent four-layer structure agent fuzzy neural network BP network. Each agent occupies one grid. Being restrained by the local sensing ability, the agent can only make interaction with the surrounding agents. Based on this networked agent, make the network weights training.

The training of fuzzy neuron network is to find the optimal structure and connection weights, so that the difference between the output of neuron network and the target function is very small. Adopt the genetic algorithm to train the network weights. This scheme adopts the two-step approach to learn. The first step is the initial stage of neural network, in which the adaptive link-like agent genetic algorithm is used to solve the network initial parameter setting in the blind equalization algorithm. It introduces the bacteria foraging algorithm and utilizes two basic actions of the bacteria: surging (pushing the bacteria to move forward) and dispelling (randomly determining the surging direction of bacteria). It puts forward the improved agent network initial parameter algorithm based on BFOA, and applies it to the optimal structure for optimizing the solving system. The second step is the parameter identification phase; that is, to solve the iteration problem with the traditional BP algorithm.

The construction methods of the algorithm are as below:

First Step: Initialize the population and encode. Design the population size adaptive adjustment algorithm. Here adopt the average hamming distance between current generation population individuals to improve the search efficiency of best-of-run solution.

Second Step: Calculate the fitness. Calculate the fitness value of each individual according to the training results. The fitness value decides the propagation and extinction of an individual. The formula of the fitness function is as below:

$$f(n) = \cfrac{1}{2\left[|x(n)|^2 - \cfrac{M\left(|x(n)|^4\right)}{M\left(|x(n)|^2\right)} \right]^2} \tag{1}$$

Third Step: Select the adaptive selection operator. In Fig. 1, the cycle of chain structure of agent selection method using neighborhood competition, each bacteria flowing through the roll to determine the direction of chemotaxis by surging determining step. In the evolutionary process, the bacteria can adaptively select the adaptive step size selection operator confirmed to accelerate the convergence, as the selection process is conducted in the local environment, and therefore difficult to create "local top edge" and lead to premature fall into the local extreme, and difficult to miss the fine individuals in the population.

Fourth Step: The bacteria produce the next iteration group. Firstly, tournament selection method and the replication of bacteria foraging algorithm mixing ratio of action where the combination of the replication operator. Reproduction of bacteria follow the "survival of the fittest" principle, to trend the process of accumulation and fitness of the bacteria as a standard, the better half of the bacteria to replicate group split, copy, sub-network has the same structure with the parent network and network weight, to accelerate the optimization speed; bad half of the bacterial group of death, removing half of poor fitness network. Tournament selection method select the number of each individual one of the highest fitness among genetic individuals. Then combine these two methods are adaptive proportional replication operator, the bacteria produce a new NP to ensure high fitness individuals to large probability to go to the next generation of genetic and into the next iteration. In this process, to maintain population diversity and maintain the network diversity, the probability of a certain part of the network to re-select the initial weights assigned, that a certain number of bacteria in the completion of replication, based on the adaptive fitness of the bacteria crossover probability and mutation probability, to complete the dispersed operations.

Fifth Step: The design adaptive termination rule. Calibration method using two generations. In the completion of each generation of genetic operation, when the genetic algebra is greater than a threshold, or compare the current generation of the best individual in population in the population with previous generations of the best in the Hamming distance between individuals, weak in a particular threshold, then the genetic operations to stop, otherwise continue to the next generation of genetic manipulation. Iterative algorithm after the termination of the best chromosome. Then converted into the right connection coefficient, membership parameters.

Sixth Step: When the genetic algorithm iteration stops, it provides a global optimal initial value to the fuzzy neural network. Then it implements optimal search locally with the traditional BP algorithm, until the precision requirements are satisfied. The iterative formula of network weight value can be obtained according to the gradient descent method.

2.2 Algorithm Implementation

Based on the above analysis, it puts forward the adaptive link-like agent genetic algorithm combining the neighborhood dynamic competition and bacteria foraging strategy for feature selection. The process is as below:

```
Begin
  i = 0;
  Initialize population G(i)
  while the quit condition false do
```

```
      Make G(i) to form a multi-subpopulation
      collaborative network agent structure in the
      sequence of subpopulation 1(i), subpopulation
      2(i), … subpopulation N(i).
   for n = 1:N
      Use the BP algorithm to train the Nth network;
      Dispel, network weights re-initialization;
      Select N subpopulation networks with optimal
      fitness for replication,
      Update the optimum individual information of this
      subpopulation;
   end for
Combine subpopulation 1(i), subpopulation 2(i), … sub-
population N(i) in sequence into population G(i + 1)
   Select the feasible solution of the i generation from
   the optimum individuals of N subpopulations;
Update the evolution counter times;
      i := i + 1;
   end //while
end.
```

By adopting adaptive link-like agent genetic algorithm, it can avoid the defect of previous BP algorithm (easy fall into local optimum) and obtain the globally best-of-run solution. The link-like neighborhood competition strategy can arouse fierce competition between agents in process of agent evolution, which is in accordance with the character of the nature in survival of the fittest. This agent only competes with agents in the neighborhood. The computing cost is low, and the convergence rate is high.

3 Experimental Results and Analysis

To validate the performance of the algorithm in this paper, validate the feature selection algorithm with the tests as below. To evaluate the above algorithm, compare with the PSO and EA algorithms. Select five common Benchmark functions for numerical experiments. Among them, the former three functions are single-mode functions with single minimum point; and the latter two functions are multimode functions with multiple local minimum points. For function description, value range and theoretical extreme value, please refer to Table 1.

Table 1. Test Functions

Function	Value Range	Theoretical Extreme value
$f_1(\bar{x}) = \sum_{i=1}^{D-1}[100(x_{i+1} - x_i^2)^2 + (x_i - 1)^2]$	$(-100,100)^n$	$f_1(\bar{1}) = 0$
$f_2(\bar{x}) = \sum_{i=1}^{D}[x_i^2 - 10\cos(2\pi x_i) + 10]$	$(-10,10)^n$	$f_2(\bar{0}) = 0$
$f_3(\bar{x}) = \frac{1}{4000}\sum_{i=1}^{D}x_i^2 - \prod_{i=1}^{D}\cos(\frac{x_i}{\sqrt{i}}) + 1$	$(-600,600)^n$	$f_3(\bar{0}) = 0$
$f_4(\bar{x}) = -20\exp(-0.2\sqrt{(\frac{1}{D}\sum_{i=1}^{D}x_i^2)}) - \exp(\frac{1}{D}\sum_{i=1}^{D}\cos 2\pi x_i) + 20 + e$	$(-32,32)^n$	$f_4(\bar{0}) = 0$
$f_5(\bar{x}) = [\frac{1}{500} + \sum_{j=1}^{25}\frac{1}{j + \sum_{i=1}^{2}(x_i - a_{ij})^6}]^{-1}$	$(-65.536, 65.536)^2$	$f_5(-31.95, -31.95) = 0.998$

Table 2. Mean Value and Variance of Best-of-run Solution of Each Algorithm after 30 Times' Independent Tests under the Max. Evolutionary Generations

Function	D	BFOA-LA		PSO		EA	
		Mean value	Variance	Mean value	Variance	Mean value	Variance
f1	100	53.725	9.2636	131.438	39.7556	89.263	28.7231
f2	100	18.3748	5.2336	15.1032	5.9621	23.0013	10.4136
f3	100	0.2523	0.0274	0.8332	0.5871	0.2367	0.1218
f4	100	1.7563	0.5028	1.8951	1.5023	1.9858	1.6563
f5	100	0.9998	0.0000	0.9998	0.0017	0.9998	0.0042

Table 3. Mean Value and Variance of Best-of-run Solution of the Three Algorithms (dimension n = 19, 20)

n	Mean best-of-run solution(Std Dev)		
	BFOA-LA	PSO	EA
19	0.7627(0.0335)	0.7963(0.0049)	0.9491(0.0731)
20	0.8754(0.0295)	0.8953(0.0047)	0.9634(0.0849)

For fair comparison, initialize the same random seeds for all algorithms. Fig. 2 gives out the hybrid bacteria and link-like agent genetic algorithm iteration operation results for the feature selection of benchmark test with this algorithm. Table 2 presents the mean value and variance of best-of-run solution of each algorithm after 30 times' independent tests under the max evolutionary generations. The data in Fig. 2

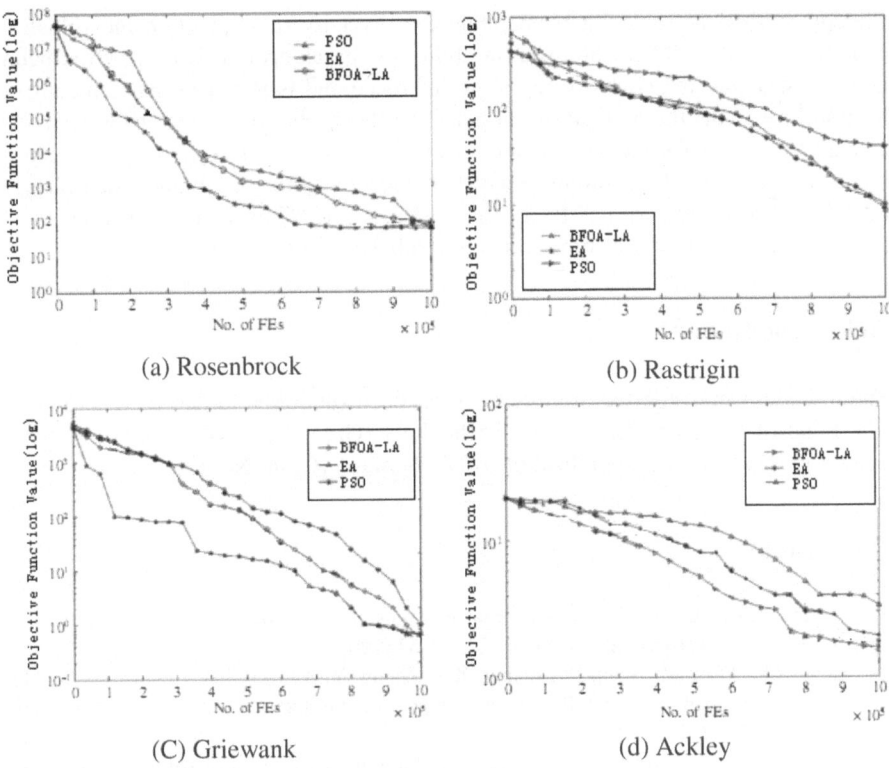

Fig. 2. Optimization Sketch Map of Benchmark Functions

shows that the result of the algorithm of this paper is obviously superior to that of PSO and EA. Moreover, the mean value and variance of it obtained on the five test functions are not higher than those of PSO and EA. The hybrid bacteria and link-like agent genetic algorithm can get satisfactory optimization result within the stipulated evolutionary generations and even get satisfactory solution. Fig. 2 shows that the sample set has relatively sound linear separability in the corresponding characteristic subspace. The genetic algebra and execution time of the link-like agent genetic algorithm are both lower than those of the corresponding algorithm. It indicates that the convergence of the link-like agent genetic algorithm is quick and the evolution efficiency is high.

4   Conclusions

As for the defect of traditional genetic algorithm in easily fall into local optimum, this paper puts forward a new agent genetic algorithm based on the link-like competition strategy combing BFOA and fuzzy neural network. This algorithm introduces the circle link-like agent structure, and adopts the BFOA combining link-like competition strategy method in selection to maintain the diversity of population individuals in evolution and the global optimization ability of the algorithm. It utilizes the neural network structure to achieve fuzzy logic inference and high-performance feature selection. It restrains the prematurity of genetic, effectively raises the convergence rate, and greatly enhances the global optimization ability. The feature selection experiments for benchmark functions prove that the algorithm has higher identification accuracy and lower complexity. It has greatly reduced the computing time of the software and raised the real-time ability and robustness of the detection system.

Acknowledgment

The research work reported in this article has been supported in part by Youth Scientific Fund of Shenzhen Institute of Technology (Grant No. QN-08008), and Nature Scientific Funds of Shenzhen Institute of Technology (Grant No. LG-08004).

References

1. Passino, K.M.: Biomimicry of Bacterial Foraging for Distributed Optimization and Control. IEEE Control Systems Magazine 22, 52–67 (2002)
2. Zeng, X.P., Li, Y.M., Wang, J., Zhang, X.J., Zheng, Y.M.: Link-like Agent Genetic Algorithm for Feature Selection Based on Competition Strategy. Journal of System Simulation 20(8), 1973–1979 (2008)
3. Liu, Y., Passino, K.M.: Biomimicry of social foraging bacteria for distributed optimization: Models, principles, and emergent behaviors. J. Optimization Theory Applicat. 115(3), 603–628 (2002)
4. Kim, D.H., Abraham, A., Cho, J.H.: A hybrid genetic algorithm and bacterial foraging approach for global optimization. Inform. Sci. 177(18), 3918–3937 (2007)
5. Tripathy, M., Mishra, S.: Bacteria foraging-based to optimize both real power loss and voltage stability limit. IEEE Trans. Power Syst. 22(1), 240–248 (2007)
6. Biswas, A., Dasgupta, S., Das, S., Abraham, A.: Synergy of PSO and bacterial foraging optimization: A comparative study on numerical benchmarks. In: Proc. 2nd Int Symp. Hybrid Artificial Intell., pp. 255–263. Springer, Heidelberg (2007)
7. Ratnaweera, A., Halgamuge, K.S.: Self organizing hierarchical particle swarm optimizer with time-varying acceleration coefficients. IEEE Transactions on Evolutionary Computation 8(3), 240–254 (2004)
8. Tang, W.J., Wu, Q.H., Saunders, J.R.: A novel model for bacteria foraging in varying environments. In: Gavrilova, M.L., Gervasi, O., Kumar, V., Tan, C.J.K., Taniar, D., Laganá, A., Mun, Y., Choo, H. (eds.) ICCSA 2006. LNCS, vol. 3980, pp. 556–565. Springer, Heidelberg (2006)
9. Ding, J.L., Chen, Z.Q., Yuan, Z.Z.: On the Combination of Genetic Algorithm and Ant Algorithm. Journal of computer research and development 40(9), 1351–1356 (2003)

Research on the Interrupt Functions Based on the CAN Controller of LPC2300 Series ARM Chips

Tu Li[1], Song Juanjuan[2], and Liu Jun'an[3]

[1] Department of Computer Science, Hunan City University Yiyang, Hunan, 413000, China
tulip1907@163.com
[2] Department of Chemical and Environmental Engineering, Hunan City University Hunan,
Yiyang, 413000, China
s-jj-18@163.com
[3] Department of Machinery Engineering, Hunan Institute of Engineering Xiangtan, Hunan,
411101, China
Liu_jun_an@163.com

Abstract. In this paper, LPC2300 CAN controller driver were completed With the standard C programming language, which including the hardware abstraction layer program description and user interface. In order not to affect the normal operation of the CAN controller, the acceptance filter is set to bypass mode, We closed the acceptance function of the filter.

Keywords: ARM, CAN, Interface functions, filter.

1 Introduction

LPC2300 Series, a 32-bit ARM microprocessor produced by PHILIPS / NXP Company, is designed for the device's connection performance with powerful function and good cost efficiency. It supports 10/100 Ethernet, full speed（12Mbps）USB 2.0 and CAN 2.0B, and it has 512KB - ISP/IAP Flash, 58KB – RAM, 10-bit A/D and D/A transformer and a IRC oscillator. Some devices are embedded with SD memory interface. Controller Area Network (CAN) is a high performance and real time serial communication network. LPC2300 series ARM CAN controller integrates a complete CAN protocol (follow CAN specification V2.0B) program. It can greatly streamline the cable (wiring harness), and has a powerful diagnostic monitoring. And it can play a major role in the application of automotive, industrial, high-speed network and lowcost devices.

2 Features of CAN Controller

LPC2300 CAN controller is a serial interface with send and receive buffers, but it does not contain acceptance filter. The acceptance filter is a separate module, It can filter on all CAN channels identifier. The structure shown in Figure 1.

R. Chen (Ed.): ICICIS 2011, Part I, CCIS 134, pp. 589–595, 2011.
© Springer-Verlag Berlin Heidelberg 2011

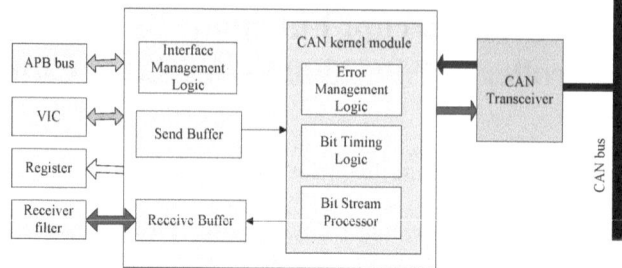

Fig. 1. The structure of LPC2300 CAN controller

CAN controller is a peripheral of ARM LPC2300 series ARM chips, which including complete receiving and sending CAN modules, and it has the capabilities of error detection.

CAN controller is fully controlled by the processor, CPU written the internal data to the transmit buffer through the bus, and then start the CAN controller to send it, The sending data through the bit stream manager, error management logic, bit sequential logic test components and the CAN transceivers in turn, and ultimately completed a CAN data transmission, Figure 2 shows the data transmission process. Of which:

- Bit stream manager: Converte the data into binary code which sent on the bus
- Error management logic: Detect the state of the bus and error status and whether there was an error sending
- Bit timing logic: manage the send timing on the bus;
- CAN transceiver: Convert the bit stream data into the differential level which was transported on the CAN bus transmission.

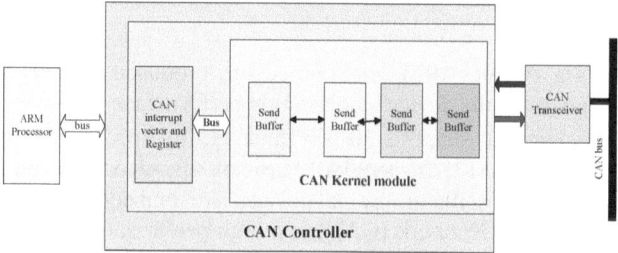

Fig. 2. CAN data transmission

The CAN data reception and the data transmission is a reverse process. when the CAN transceiver Detected that there is data on CAN bus, It Convertes the differential level signals on bus into bit stream data, after the error manager and the bit timing logic unit checked on the bit stream data and the timing, and then after the bit stream manager convert the bit stream datas into byte datas, and stored it to the receive buffer. When a frame has been received, the data receive interrupt generate in the receive buffer (notice the CPU has received a frame of new data), and change the value in the status register.

2.1 The Structure of Library Functions

Figure 3 shows the LPC2300 CAN controller driver file structure, the user's applications need to include LPC2300CAN_Driver.h files, then add LPC2300 CAN_Driver.c file to the current project , and copy the LPC2300 CAN controller driver library to the current project, then you can call driver functions from the library.

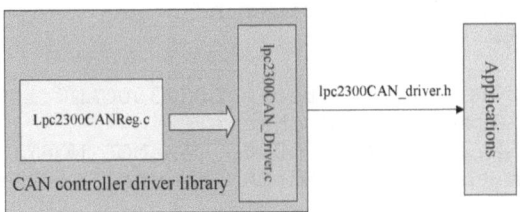

Fig. 3. The structure of library functions

2.2 Application of the Driven Functions

The function library contains most of operations associated with the CAN controller, these operations are invisible for the user, the user can complete the operation of the CAN only need to call the appropriate interface functions. In order to make the library package better, users can not know the type of the return value, so the user can only use a non-pointer variable to receive the data, Untyped pointer variables were cast in the driver library, which will be completely invisible to users. So users only need to know how to use the interface functions.

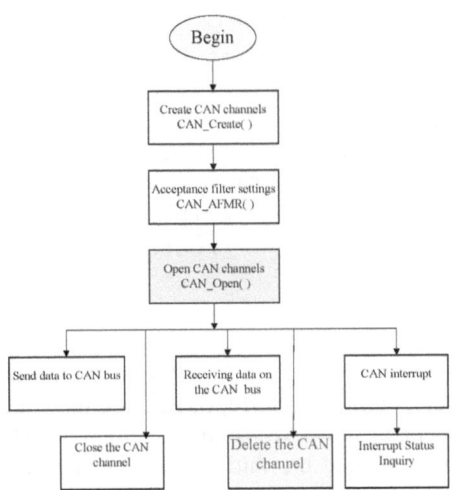

Fig. 4. The structure of CAN driver library

Create and Open a CAN Channel(CAN_Create( ), CAN_Open( ))
When the LPC2300's CAN controlleris in use, the users first need to create a channel and get the structure variable pointer of the CAN channel information, and then operate the CAN controller according to the structure variable pointer of the CAN channels . Code 1 shows CAN_Create ( ), CAN_Open ( ) in the program examples.

```
   Code 1:   Create a CAN channel
#include "config.h"
#include "..\LPC2300CAN_Driver.h"
int main(void)
 {
  void*pLPC2300CAN0=CAN_Create(LPC2300CAN0,100,24000000);
          // Create a CAN channel
  CAN_Open(pLPC2300CAN0,1000000,CAN_MOD_NOR);
       // Open the specified CAN-channel
  ...
  While(1);
}
```

Send and Receive the Data (SendDatToCAN( ), RecDatFromCAN( ))

The function of sending data and receiving data is the most frequent function of the application in the CAN driver library. SendDatToCAN () and RecDatFromCAN () are sending data to the CAN bus and receiving the data from the CAN bus. Note that the CAN data transmission is sent in units of frames, so Users need to fill in the information of the outgoing data frame when sending data, The data frame structure is defined in LPC2300CAN_Driver.h, which is defined as shown in code 2.

```
   Code 2   The structure of the Frame data
#define FILFRAME(dlc,rtr,ff)(dlc|(rtr << 4)|(ff<<5))
   // Fill in the information of RFS frame
typedef struct _caninfo
{
    unsigned char canrfs;      //Information   of        the
frame[0~3]bit--DLC,[4]bit--RTR,[5]bit--FF
    unsigned int  canid;       //ID of the frame
    unsigned int  candat[2];   //Data
}CANINFO;
```

Interruption (__irq xxx( ))
Only three interruption is enabled in the LPC2300 driver functions library (receive interrupt, transmit interrupt, bus error interrupt), Because there are differences among the processors, we only conducted CAN common settings (such as CAN controller interrupt enable, IER register), and the initialization of interruption associated with the processor requires users to program.

In the specific steps of LPC2300 CAN interrupt initialization, CAN refers to the CAN channel 0 and CAN channel 1, the specific steps described below.

(1) Set the interrupt select register (VICIntSelect), set the CAN controller interrupt with IRQ interrupt. (The CAN interrupt channel number is 23);

(2) Assign the address of the interrupt function to VICVectAddr23, the No. 23 Interrupt Vector Address Register (CAN interrupt);

(3) Set the CAN interrupt in the highest priority, Priority register is equal to 0: VICVectPri23 = 0;

(4) Enable the CAN interrupt vector, the register VICIntEnable | = (1 <<23).

Code 3:   CAN Interrupt initialization

```
void CANIrqInit(void)
{
    // Enable the interrupt vector of CAN1/CAN2
    VICIntSelect &= (~(1<<23));
        // Set the channel to IRQ interrupts
    VICVectAddr23 = (unsigned int)CANIntPrg;
        // Set the interrupt entry address
    VICVectPri23 = 0;
        // Set the interrupt of NO.23 channel    as the
highest priority
    VICIntEnable |= (1<<23);
        // open the CAN interruption
}
```

Note that when exit the interrupt:

(5) Clear the interrupt address ,VICVectAddr = 0;

(6) The flag of the receiver interruption will not reset with the reading of the data, so before exiting the interrupt, users must reset it with method of software (Clearing the flag of the receiving interrupt has been completed in the RecDatFromCAN ( ) function);

(7) When the receive buffer receives a frame of data, the system will generate a receive interruption. when reading the data, be sure to clear receive buffer (Clearing the receive buffer has been completed in the RecDatFromCAN () function), or it will cause continuous interruption;

Code 3 shows the steps of the user initializate the CAN controller.Code 4 shows the example of interrupt in the application.

Code 4   The Application of CAN Interruption in the Program

```
void __irq CANIntPrg(void)
{
  unsigned char status = IcrStatus();
  if((status & 0x01) == 0x01) //receive the interrupt
    { // Receive the code
       buffer = RecDatFromCAN((status & 0xc0)>>6);
       if((status & 0xc0)>>6 == 0x00)
           // Data sent from the No.1 channel
         { dat2 = *buffer;      }
       else  // Data sent from other channels
```

```
            {dat1 = *buffer;}
            flag = 1;
        }
    if((status & 0x3f) == 0x02)
        {//Send the code    }
    if((status & 0x3f) == 0x04)
        {// add code if there is bus error interruption }
        VICVectAddr = 0;
}
int main (void)
{void*pLPC2300CAN0=CAN_Create(LPC2300CAN0,100,24000000);
        //create a CAN channel
 void*pLPC2300CAN1=CAN_Create(LPC2300CAN1,100,24000000);
 CAN_Open(pLPC2300CAN0,1000000,CAN_MOD_NOR);
        // Open the CAN channel that created
 CAN_Open(pLPC2300CAN1,1000000, CAN_MOD_NOR);
 CANIrqInit(); // CAN Interrupt initialization
        while(1)
        {
        if(flag == 1)
            {
                SendDatToCAN(pLPC2300CAN1,&dat2);
                SendDatToCAN(pLPC2300CAN0,&dat1);
                flag = 0;
            }
        }
    return 0;
}
```

3   Conclusion

The CAN receiving data process has an additional CAN Acceptance Filter than sending data process, the main function of the acceptance filter is whether the data from the receive buffer meets the needs of the users (If the current data is not within the scope of the filter, it will be lost), in order to improve the efficiency of CAN controller. CAN Acceptance Filter and the CAN controller is not in the same module, so this is not described in this paper.

References

1. Hall, M., Maillet, S.: Windows CE: Inside the Build System. Embedded Operating System Development, USA (2004)
2. ISO11898 Road Vehicle sinterchange of digital information controller area networks for high speed communication, pp. 21–27. ISOS Publications and E2products, Geneva (1993)

3. PHILIPS Semiconducter. SJA 1000 stand2alone CAN controuer [EB/OL] (December 15, 1997),
   `http://www.nxp.com/acrobatdownload/applicationnotes/AN97076.Pdf`
4. Hank, P.: A new CAN controller stportingdiagncsis and system optmizottion. In: Determination of Bit Timirg Parameters for the CAN Controller SJA1000, Application Note AN96116, 1996 4th International CAN Conference, Berlin, Germany, pp. 123–127 (1997)
5. Andrews, G.R.: Foundations of multithreaded, par2allel and distributed programming, pp. 36–40. Addison Wesley, Pearson (2002)

Data Recognition and Filtering Based on Efficient RFID Data Processing Control Schemes

Hsu-Yang Kung, Chiung-Wen Kuo, and Ching-Ping Tsai

Department of Management Information Systems,
National Pingtung University of Science and Technology, Taiwan, R.O.C.
{kung,m9756005,tcp}@mail.npust.edu.tw

Abstract. Radio Frequency Identification (RFID) applications have changed gradually from a single vendor and single application to being integrated into applications for supply chains. The primary function of RFID middleware is to process large amounts of data within a short period. High performance and efficiency are difficult to achieve in a RFID data processing control scheme when the volume of RFID data is large. This work is designed the core functions of RFID middleware and developed data processing control scheme that includes data recognition, data filtering and data searching processes. The control scheme for RFID data recognition is used to identify data with false positives and then to obtain corrected data objects. The data filtering control scheme is used to solve problems associated with RFID expansion under a large amount of work and data. The proposed data searching method is based on the EPC (Electronic Product Code) and uses the Hash to accelerate information filtering efficiency.

Keywords: RFID Middleware, RFID Data Filtering, Data Recognition, Hash-based Data Searching.

1 Introduction

Radio Frequency Identification (RFID) technology [3] has matured rapidly and its tag is small. It has a large capacity, good durability and declines prices. The primary focus is now on RFID middleware development. Achilleas[1] et al. also identified the main challenges is associated with data filtering and transfer of RFID data. The RFID system will be in the near future. Therefore, RFID middleware must provide scalable and reliable data management.

This work is designed the core functions for RFID middleware and developed a novel data processing control scheme, which includes data recognition, data filtering, and data searching functionalities. The control scheme for RFID data recognition is utilized to determine situations with false positives and then obtain corrected data objects. The control scheme for data filtering is applied to solve problems associated with RFID expansion in a scenario with large amounts of work and data. The proposed data searching method is based on the encoding characteristics of EPCGlobal, and uses the Hash to accelerate information filtering efficiency.

R. Chen (Ed.): ICICIS 2011, Part I, CCIS 134, pp. 596–601, 2011.

The remainder of this work is organized as follows. In section 2, we introduce the related research on RFID middleware. Section 3 shows the architecture of RFID middleware. In section 4, we present the Hash function to filter RFID data. Finally, section 5 concludes this work.

2   Related Work

In this work, our middleware is divided into five sorting methods proposed by scholars' reference. The sequences are device adaption and management, data processing, process design, standardization, and efficiency.

1.   Device adaption and management
(1) Zehao et al. [7] proposed RFID middleware device management based on agent. These agents were the Control Agent and Device Agent. The core is the Control Agent, which manages all device agents and their lifecycles.
(2) Libe et al. [6] designed a Reader Agent, Logical Reader Agent, and Device Monitor Agent to manage and monitor all readers.

2.   Data processing
(1) Achilleas et al. [1] designed a Filter that receives input from readers or other filters. Filter input is includes distributed parameters of reference services (e.g., database queries and web services). The filtering process can be defined as a set of (XML) documents.
(2) Zehao et al. [7] designed a data management module responsible for data processing (e.g., tag data aggregation, filtering tags, and stability of tag events).

3.   Process design
(1) Achilleas et al. [1] proposed a filtering process from data input to output defined by a XML file. Additionally, a filter has more than one output for a user with the situation on the application.
(2) Libe et al. [6] designed a graphical user interface through which many agents handle work. Such as the reader monitors, collects and filters data, and outputs data.

4.   Standard
(1) Achilleas et al. [1] designed a middleware framework base on EPCglobal.
(2) Hwang et al. [2] proposed an Aspect-Oriented Programming (AOP)-based framework for middleware. According to the EPCglobal standard for development of API, this provides customized middleware.

5.   Efficiency
(1) Notably, EPCglobal proposed distributed middleware architecture, Application Level Events (ALE). Device control, data filtering, and storage to companies as a group, alone the burden of the workload. For example, John et al. [5] present project of RFID application.
(2) Jian Feng[4] developed the method of Middleware Load Balancing. This method constructs multi-host middleware, and shares and sends information to other middleware. When the workload exceeds a middleware threshold, some readers will be transferred to another middleware.

3 Research Architecture

The Middleware comprises a RFID device, middleware, and application. The structure of these components is described as follows.

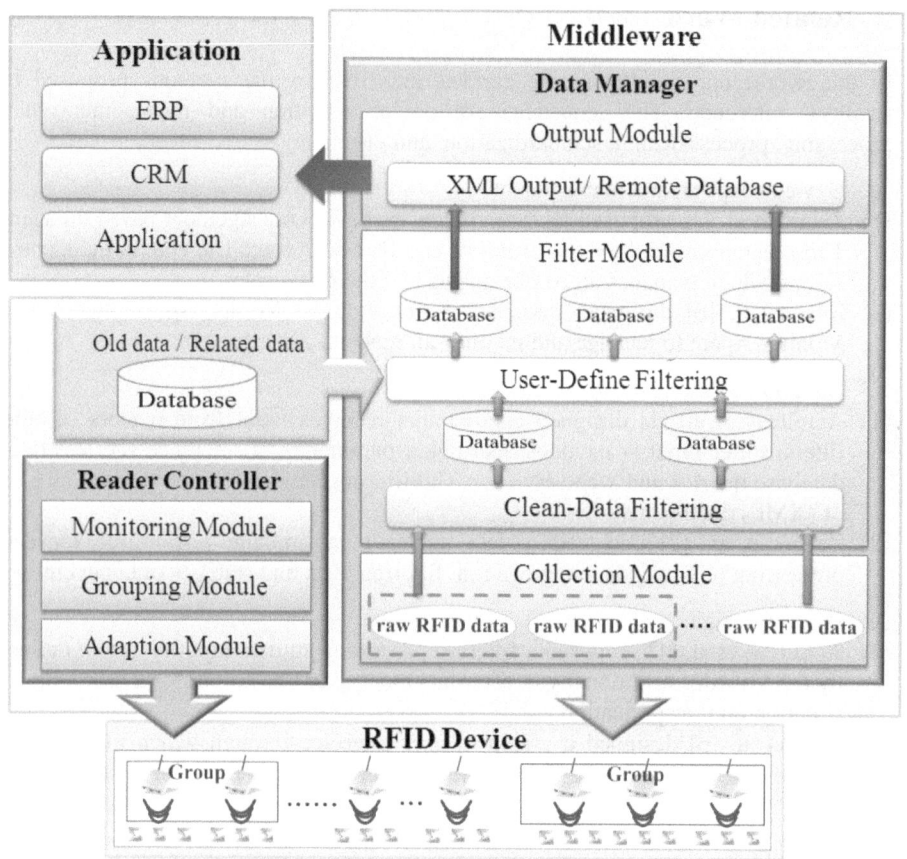

Fig. 1. RFID Middleware Architecture

1. RFID Device
This part describes the RFID Reader and Tag, which have different equipment specifications. Middleware must connect various readers to achieve the aim of a single user interface.

2. Middleware
Middleware has two core components—the Data Manager and the Reader Controller. The Data Manager is responsible for data filtering, collection, and storage. The Reader Controller is responsible for connecting readers, grouping and monitoring readers.

(1) Data Manager:
a. Collection Module: The reader effectively collects and reads data, and transmits data to the corresponding filtration module for processing.
b. Filter Module: This module has multiple filter functions. This module uses the Hash function to filter duplicate data, and lets users filter specific data. That function is also called data classification.
c. Output Module: A user can set a data flow as output from the Filter Module. Additionally, data can be saved to a database specified by a user or as output data in the XML format.

(2) Reader Controller:
a. Monitoring Module: This module helps users manage readers. A user can monitor the working condition of readers for real-time monitoring and troubleshooting.
b. Grouping Module: This module manages many readers, each reader has different application scenarios. Thus, this work designed a grouping function, such that a group has the same application scenarios. A user can then control multiple readers in a group simultaneously.
c. Adaption Module: This module controls readers from different manufacturers. Then users did not develop each different Reader.

3. Application
The data was transform to information by middleware. Then this module delivers information to other application system or database. Therefore, a user can refer to the designation database or obtain data in the XML format.

4 Research Methods

1. Clean-data Filtering
Clean-data Filtering filters duplicate data to reduce the amount of data. This work sets a particular unit of reading the range. It is not a reader of reading the range. Therefore, it is the same between the same readers reads tags and the time difference in repeated and overlapping multi-readers. Traditional methods repeat data filtering, such that when a reader reads a new tag, the reader has to read into the previously all tag data which will be compared to determine whether data are repeated. This approach requires a considerable amount of resources, resulting in slow system operation. To increase the filtration rate, this work uses a hash function for repeat information filtering.
    In this work, the characteristics of EPC codes can be divided. The EPC code is split into EPCFront and Hash (Item and Serial) (Fig. 2). The filtering algorithm is described as follows. The Hash Filter algorithm reads each new entry of EPC code in the last two columns of serial and item calculates the hash function. The hash value is then calculated and compared with hash values already in the hash table. If the hash table does not have the same hash value, then this hash value is added to the hash table. If the hash table has this hash value, then the remaining fields in the EPC code are added to the EPCFront of the same hash value in the hash table (Table 1).

```
Public void hash(String new EPC){
      For(int  i=0 ;  i< Hash  Table  has  stored  of  the
number; i++){
            If( Hash(new EPC) = Hash1(i)){
                  DupKey=2;
                  If(epcFront(new EPC) = any one epcFront
in the Hash(i)){
                        DupKey=1;
                        Break;
                  }
            }
      If(DupKey = 0){
            Add new EPC to Hash table.
      }Else if(DupKey=2){
            Add new EPC's epcFront to HashTable.
      }Else{
            EPC is duplicates.
      }
  }
```

Table 1. Hash Table

Hash(Item, Serial)	epcFront
Hash1	epcFront1, epcFront2
Hash2	epcFront3
Hash3	epcFront4, epcFront5

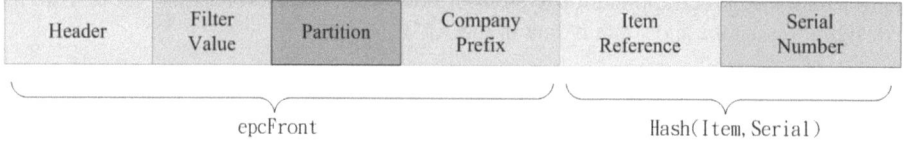

Fig. 2. EPC code(SGTIN96)

This work used Minimal Perfect Hash Function within the Minimal Perfect Hashing (MPH) algorithm. This work improved the MPH Function, such that it meets the EPC code. The MPH Function, $H(x, y)$, has the condition that variables x and y cannot be the same, and x must be greater than y. However, the EPC code cannot meet these conditions in this work. Thus, this work designs a new Hash function. The Hash function can generate a perfect hash table. This hash function is tested and verified by reduction ad absurdum. This work then proves that EPC codes result in a perfect hash table.

The hash function (Eq. 1) was under the two conditions—both of x and y must be positive integers or zero, and N is must be a positive integer. Further, $0 \leq x$ and $y \leq N$, Then hash value in equation 1 will not be same.

$$H(x, y) = 2N(x-1) + y-x(x-1)/2 \ (1) \tag{1}$$

2. User-Defined Filtering

The RFID data are used in different application situations and used repeatedly. Thus, different application situations require different filtering data. User-Defined Filtering is designed by users, it means that the users can control the data of duplicate filter and also transform data to information according to the application situation.

Based on the following information and inquiry types, users can customize information filtering and search functions.

(1)   Classified information
a.   Information can be classified according to EPC fields (e.g., Header, Filter Value, Company, and Item Reference).
b.   Filtering is according to user needs and information not required, or only retains the information needed (e.g., Header, Filter Value, Company, and Item Reference).
(2)   Inquiries by the respective need
a.   Queries are according to the EPC field (e.g., Header, Filter Value, Company, and Item Reference).

5   Conclusions

This work proposes a novel RFID middleware architecture and process. This process increases the efficiency of data processing in various application scenarios. It used a Hash function and the concept of layered filtering for rapid data filtering and error data filtering, the user-defined filtering that provided cross-platform XML format output and designated storage database. It can easily combine information with the application. This work also uses the mathematical verification method to confirm that proposed hash function can generate a perfect hash table without duplicated data.

Acknowledgments. This work is partially supported by the National Science Council, Taiwan, R.O.C., under the grant No. NSC 99-2220-E-020-001.

References

1.   Anagnostopoulos, A.P., Soldatos, J.K., Michalakos, S.G.: REFiLL:A lightweight programmable middleware plafform for cost effective RFID application development. Pervasive and Mobile Computing 5(1), 49–63 (2009)
2.   Hwang, H.J., Choi, J.T.: Design of an Aspect-Based Framework to Improve the Dynamic Management of RFID middleware. Computer and Information Technology (2007)
3.   Jaroodi, J.A., Aziz, J., Mohamed, N.: Middleware for RFID systems: An overview. In: 33rd Annual IEEE International Computer Software and Application Conference, pp. 154–159 (2009)
4.   Cui, J.F.: Mobile Agent based Load Balancing for RFID Middleware. In: The 9th International Conference, vol. 2, pp. 973–978 (2009)
5.   Mo, J.P.T., Sheng, Q.Z., Li, X., Zeadally, S.: RFID Infrastructure Design; A Case Study of Two Australian RFID Projects. IEEE Internet Computing 13(1), 14–24 (2009)
6.   Massawe, L.V., Aghdasi, F., Kinyua, J.: The Development of a Multi-Agent Based Middleware for RFID Asset Management System Using the PASSI Methodology. In: Sixth International Conference on Information Technology: New Generations, pp. 1024–1048 (2009)
7.   Liu, Z., Liu, F., Lin, K.: Agent-based Device Management in RFID Middleware. Wireless Communications Networking and Mobile Computing (2008)

Research on Operating Performance Evaluation of Electric Power Enterprises Based on F-AHP

Yuansheng Huang, Wei Fang, and Mingxi Shi

School of Business Administration, North China Electric Power University,
Baoding 071003, China
fangwei_ncepu@yahoo.cn

Abstract. The paper evaluated the operating performance of electric power enterprises by using Analytic hierarchy process (AHP) and the Fuzzy comprehensive evaluation. Using AHP to determine the weight of index can avoid fuzzy logic caused by complicated decision-making, and Fuzzy comprehensive evaluation can deal with the equivocal message effectively. Combine these two methods can make decision-making more scientific, and the paper take an example to prove the validity of this method.

Keywords: electric power enterprises, operating performance, AHP, Fuzzy comprehensive evaluation.

1 Introduction

With the further development of reform in power market, the research on regulatory theory of electric power enterprises has become an important study subject. The regulatory method based on performance is a kind of incentive regulation models, and this model has advantages, such as incentive of cost minimization, improve investment efficiency and stimulate the information disclosure. In the domestic, searching for more effective method of performance evaluation and supervision which suit for electric power enterprises is particularly important.

Due to many factors that influence the operation of electric power enterprise, we can not get all accurate data in the process of evaluation, and it must have partial incomplete information and ambiguous condition. Therefore, this paper used the analytic hierarchy process (AHP) to index the values of subjective, and then, combined all qualitative judgment to determine the weight of each decision factors, so to avoid the error caused by logic reasoning in complex decision-making.

In addition, in the model selection, the fuzzy comprehensive evaluation is a new evaluation method in recent years, it can give every membership result from object belongs to different classes, and the decision maker can make decision according to the maximum subjection principle. Because the weights and matrix of member are obtained by people's subjective judgment, so fuzzy comprehensive evaluation is a kind of comprehensive evaluation methods based on subjective information. When expert panel can not obtain the fixed opinion, the fuzzy comprehensive evaluation method is a good evaluation method.

R. Chen (Ed.): ICICIS 2011, Part I, CCIS 134, pp. 602–608, 2011.

Therefore, according to the actual conditions of electric power enterprises, the paper propose a flexible and comprehensive evaluation method for evaluating the operating performance of electric power enterprise based on AHP and the fuzzy comprehensive evaluation.

2   Constructing Evaluation Index System of Operating Performance for Electric Power Enterprise

2.1   Construction of Evaluation Index System

The principle of establishing the comprehensive evaluation index system in electric power enterprise are, the objective principle, the overall principle, the feasibility principle, the general principle and it must be combined with development. The paper established relative evaluation index system on operating performance for electric power enterprise, it is below:

Table 1. The evaluation index system of operating performance for electric power enterprise

	One class indexes	Secondary indexes
Index system	Economic operation (U_1)	Average price of electricity purchasing(u_{11})
		Net assets(u_{12})
		Income of sold electricity(u_{13})
		Line loss rate(u_{14})
		Average rate of load(u_{15})
		Maximum load(u_{16})
	The quality of power supply (U_2)	Length of power distribution line(u_{21})
		Variable capacity(u_{22})
		Qualification rate of voltage(u_{23})
		Supply reliability of power(u_{24})
		Qualify rate of frequency(u_{25})
	Service (U_3)	Supply area(u_{31})
		The number of users in supply area(u_{32})
		Capacity of limit electricity(u_{33})
		Solution of providing power(u_{34})
		Satisfaction rate of complaints and return(u_{35})
		Turnover rate of total asset(u_{36})
		Turnover rate of inventory(u_{37})

2.2   Using AHP to Determine Indexes Weights

Analytic hierarchy process (AHP) make various factors in complex problems into interconnected orderly, it use mathematical method to determine weights in each level. This method will make judge and thinking qualitative and calculating convenient. Its specific steps are as follows:

(1) Determine the evaluation target, the evaluation sample set and the weights for samples.

(2) Construct judgment matrix.

(3) Get the weight vector in every layer through normalized processing, biggest eigenvalue and correspondence eigenvector of judgment matrix, the method is as follows:

Firstly, calculate continuous product of elements W_k in each line;

Secondly, calculate $\overline{W_k}$ in each line;

Third, get the normalized processing $\overline{W_k} = [\overline{W_1}, \overline{W_2}, \cdots, \overline{W_k}]$ and weight vectors: $W = (W_1, W_2, \cdots, W_m)$

$$W_k = \overline{W_k} \bigg/ \sum_{k=1}^{m} \overline{W_k} \tag{1}$$

Fourth, calculate CI=(λ_{max} - n)/(n-1), and make consistency test according to CI/CR<0.1

Fifth, the index weight of the first layer is W_i, the index weight of the second layer is W_{ij}, and the combination weights is:

$$W^1 = W_i \times W_{ij} \tag{2}$$

3 Constructing Fuzzy Comprehensive Evaluation Model

Fuzzy comprehensive evaluation evaluate the object and factors based on fuzzy mathematics principle, it analyze the comprehensive practical problem. The paper construct a fuzzy evaluation model with two layers, the modeling process is as follows:

(1) Determine factors set as U
One class indexes set is

$$U = (U_1, U_2, \cdots, U_i) \tag{3}$$

Secondary indexes set is

$$U_i = (U_{i1}, U_{i2}, \cdots, U_{ij}) \tag{4}$$

(2) Determine evaluation set as V
The evaluation set is

$$V = \{v_1, v_2, \cdots, v_5\} \tag{5}$$

They represent "Outstanding, good, medium, poor, very poor ". Each evaluation set is available to membership degree, and the size of the degree is limited in [0, 1].

(3) Fuzzy comprehensive evaluation for secondary indexes

The weight set of secondary index is

$$W_k = (W_{k1}, W_{k2}, W_{k3} \cdots W_{kn})$$ (6)

Using the mathematical model as:

$$(w_{i1}, w_{i2}, \cdots, w_{ik}) \begin{bmatrix} r_{i11} & r_{i12} & \cdots & r_{i1m} \\ r_{i21} & r_{i22} & \cdots & r_{i2m} \\ \vdots & \vdots & \vdots & \vdots \\ r_{ik1} & r_{ik2} & \cdots & r_{ikm} \end{bmatrix} = (b_{i1}, b_{i2}, \cdots, b_{ik})$$ (7)

The evaluation vector $B_i = (b_{i1} \quad \cdots \quad b_{in})$ is result matrix of the secondary indexes.

(4) Fuzzy comprehensive evaluation for one class indexes
The weight set of one class indexes is

$$W = (w_1, w_2, w_3)$$ (8)

Using the mathematical model as:

$$(w_1, w_2, \cdots, w_i) \begin{bmatrix} b_{11} & b_{12} & \cdots & b_{1j} \\ b_{21} & b_{22} & \cdots & b_{2j} \\ \vdots & \vdots & \vdots & \vdots \\ b_{i1} & b_{i2} & \cdots & b_{ij} \end{bmatrix} = (b_1, b_2, \cdots, b_j)$$ (9)

The final evaluation result is

$$B = (b_1, b_2, \cdots, b_j)$$ (10)

(5) The quantification of comprehensive evaluation result which converts 100 points
Given a transformation matrix, evaluation result will be transformed into specific value according to comprehensive evaluation value result A of evaluation objects, and the expression of A is:

$$A = B \bullet C^T$$ (11)

4 Empirical Analyze

Take power supply enterprise for example, we can evaluate the relative operation performance. The index in index system can be represented by membership (0-1) in fuzzy math, it says good evaluation means good membership and bad evaluation means bad membership, the membership set is (0.8, 0.7, 0.6, 0.5, 0.4, 0.3, 0.2). According to the opinion from expert group (A and B, C, D) for index of each level, we can get matrix below.

$$R_1 = \begin{bmatrix} 1 & 0.4 & 0.6 & 0.7 \\ 0.7 & 0.5 & 0.6 & 0.5 \\ 0.8 & 1 & 0.5 & 1 \\ 0.8 & 0.5 & 0.4 & 0.4 \\ 0.4 & 0.7 & 0.8 & 0.6 \\ 0.6 & 0.8 & 1 & 0.7 \end{bmatrix}, \quad R_2 = \begin{bmatrix} 0.8 & 1 & 0.6 & 0.7 \\ 0.6 & 0.5 & 1 & 0.5 \\ 1 & 0.6 & 0.4 & 0.5 \\ 0.7 & 0.5 & 0.6 & 1 \\ 0.4 & 0.6 & 0.5 & 1 \end{bmatrix},$$

$$R_3 = \begin{bmatrix} 0.6 & 1 & 1 & 0.5 \\ 1 & 0.6 & 0.6 & 0.4 \\ 0.5 & 0.4 & 0.5 & 0.6 \\ 0.4 & 0.5 & 0.5 & 1 \\ 0.7 & 0.6 & 1 & 0.5 \\ 1 & 0.6 & 0.6 & 0.4 \\ 0.6 & 1 & 0.5 & 0.7 \end{bmatrix}$$

4.1 Using AHP to Determine Each Index Weight

(1) Determine the weight of secondary index

According to the principle for determine weight in AHP, we can construct every judge matrix of secondary index and calculate the weight of secondary index.

$$C_{V1} = \begin{bmatrix} 1 & 1/2 & 3 & 1/4 & 1/2 & 1/3 \\ 2 & 1 & 1/2 & 1/3 & 1/2 & 1/2 \\ 1/3 & 2 & 1 & 1/4 & 1/3 & 1/2 \\ 4 & 3 & 4 & 1 & 3 & 2 \\ 2 & 2 & 3 & 1/3 & 1 & 1/3 \\ 3 & 2 & 2 & 1/2 & 3 & 1 \end{bmatrix}$$

The weight vector is obtained by value method

$$W_1 = (0.0890, 0.0934, 0.0777, 0.3630, 0.1482, 0.2287)$$

After inspection, the consistency meets the requirements.

Similarly, the calculation results are as follows:

$$C_{V2} = \begin{bmatrix} 1 & 2 & 2 & 2 & 4 \\ 1/2 & 1 & 1/2 & 1/2 & 2 \\ 1/2 & 2 & 1 & 1/2 & 3 \\ 1/2 & 2 & 2 & 1 & 3 \\ 4 & 1/2 & 1/3 & 1/3 & 1 \end{bmatrix}$$

$$W_2 = (0.3510, 0.1330, 0.1903, 0.2511, 0.0746)$$

$$C_{V3} = \begin{bmatrix} 1 & 2 & 1/3 & 1/2 & 1/3 & 1/4 & 1/3 \\ 1/2 & 1 & 1/2 & 1/4 & 1/2 & 1/3 & 1/4 \\ 3 & 2 & 1 & 1/2 & 2 & 3 & 1/2 \\ 2 & 4 & 2 & 1 & 3 & 2 & 2 \\ 3 & 2 & 1/2 & 1/3 & 1 & 1/2 & 1/3 \\ 4 & 3 & 1/3 & 1/2 & 2 & 1 & 2 \\ 3 & 4 & 2 & 1/2 & 3 & 1/2 & 1 \end{bmatrix}$$

$$W_3 = (0.0636, 0.0530, 0.1698, 0.2630, 0.0961, 0.1670, 0.1875)$$

(2) Determine the weight of the first class index
The judge matrix of the first class index is as follows:

$$C_V = \begin{bmatrix} 1 & 1/2 & 3 \\ 2 & 1 & 3 \\ 1/3 & 1/3 & 1 \end{bmatrix}$$

The weight of the first class index is

$$W = (0.3325, 0.5278, 0.1396)$$

After inspection, the consistency meets the requirements.
    (3) Calculate the combined weight
    The combined weight of single factor is

$$W_1' = (0.0296, 0.0311, 0.0258, 0.1207, 0.0493, 0.0760)$$

$$W_2' = (0.1853, 0.0702, 0.1004, 0.1325, 0.0394)$$

$$W_3' = (0.0089, 0.0074, 0.0237, 0.0367, 0.0134, 0.0233, 0.0262)$$

4.2 Fuzzy Comprehensive Evaluation

(1) Comprehensive evaluation of secondary indexes
    Take a comprehensive evaluation for secondary indexes according to the principle of fuzzy comprehensive evaluation and weight calculated above, the result is

$$B_1 = W_1 \bullet R_1 = (0.2339, 0.2089, 0.2130, 0.1931)$$

$$B_2 = W_2 \bullet R_2 = (0.3993, 0.3705, 0.3207, 0.3869)$$

$$B_3 = W_3 \bullet R_3 = (0.0877, 0.0894, 0.0840, 0.0927)$$

(2) Comprehensive evaluation of the first class indexes

According to formula above, the evaluation of the first class

$$B = W \bullet R = (0.3325, 0.5278, 0.1396) \bullet \begin{bmatrix} 0.2339 & 0.2089 & 0.2130 & 0.1931 \\ 0.3993 & 0.3705 & 0.3207 & 0.3869 \\ 0.0877 & 0.0894 & 0.0840 & 0.0927 \end{bmatrix}$$

$$= (0.3008, 0.7275, 0.2518, 0.2814)$$

(3) Quantification of comprehensive evaluation result

Use the transformation matrix C= (95, 85, 70, 50, the result can be transformed into 100 points:

$$A = B \bullet C^T = (0.3008, 0.2775, 0.2518, 0.2814) \bullet [95,85,70,50]^T = 83.8595$$

The calculation results shows that the comprehensive evaluation result of power supply enterprise is outstanding, it means the relative operating performance of the enterprise in the fierce competition environment is superior.

5 Conclusion

The paper constructs a reasonable set of evaluation index system through combing analytic hierarchy process and fuzzy comprehensive evaluation, this combination can take various factors for comprehensive consideration, it also get a variety of different opinions on the evaluation, reduce the random errors of power enterprise, and make evaluation for partial operating performance more rationality.

References

1. Tseng, F.M., Yu, H.C., Tzeng, G.H.: Applied hybrid Grey Model to forecast seasonal time series. Technological Forecasting and Social change 67, 291–302 (2001)
2. Yao, A.W.L., Chi, S.C., Chen, C.K.: Development of an integrated grey fuzzy-based electricity management system for enterprises. Energy 30, 2759–2771 (2005)
3. Dong, C.: The theory and application of neural network by matlab. National Defence Industry Press, Beijing (2005) (in Chinese)
4. Hsu, C.C., Chen, C.Y.: Applications of improved grey prediction model power demand forecasting. Energy Convers Manage 44, 2241–2249 (2003)
5. Gerard Adams, F., Shachmurove, Y.: Modeling and forecasting energy consumption in China: Implications for Chinese energy demand and imports in 2020. Energy Economics (30), 1263–1278 (2008)
6. Yan-chang, L., Shuai, X.: Application of neural network-based corrected intelligent residual error gray models to load forecast. East China Electric Power 35(11), 30–33 (2007) (in chinese)

Efficient Reference Picture Management Schemes for H.264/AVC Decoding System

Chunshu Li, Kai Huang, Min Yu, and Xiaolang Yan

Institute of VLSI Design
Zhejiang University
Hangzhou, China
{lics,huangk,yumin,yan}@vlsi.zju.edu.cn

Abstract. Inter-frame prediction with multiple reference pictures is one of the several advanced techniques in H.264/AVC standard. However, it also brings high implementation complexity. In this paper, we present two effective schemes and DPB storage arrangement for efficient reference picture management. One scheme is for direct mapping between reference picture index and DPB picture index and another scheme is to replace refidx of co-located block with its dpbidx in temporal direct prediction mode. These two schemes are utilized to optimize motion vector generation and reference block access, two kernel functions of inter-frame prediction. Experimental results show that the proposed schemes are able to reduce CPU workload by 80% and improve system throughput performance by 22.1%. Both schemes help our implemented decoder achieve real-time decoding of 1080p main profile H.264 video stream with 110 MHz clock frequency at the hardware cost of 53k and 37k gates for MC and MVPG modules respectively.

Keywords: H.264, Reference Picture Management, Direct Prediction Mode, Motion Compensation.

1 Introduction

The predominance of H.264/AVC over those previous video standards is accredited to a series of aggressive coding methods of which new inter prediction algorithm contributes most. Motion algorithm of H.264/AVC decoder is mainly composed of Motion Vector Predictor (MVP) generation and Motion Compensation (MC).

The MVP generation (MVPG) derives the motion data which points to a reference block in one of at most 16 reference frames. As specified in H.264/AVC main profile, there are two prediction modes adopted during MVPG: 1) the traditional spatial correlation prediction mode which utilizes motion data of the spatially neighboring blocks. It obtains MV and reference index of neighboring blocks according to the reference picture list (RefPicList) of current picture; 2) the direct prediction mode which relies on a co-located block in the co-located picture. However co-located picture has its own reference picture list. Therefore more challenges are brought into MVPG owing to two different reference picture lists used in current picture and co-located picture.

R. Chen (Ed.): ICICIS 2011, Part I, CCIS 134, pp. 609–620, 2011.
© Springer-Verlag Berlin Heidelberg 2011

During MC process, the required reference block is located and fetched to generate current block with the help of the motion vector (MV) and reference index (refidx) derived from MVPG. All decoded pictures are stored to global picture buffer (DPB, decoding picture buffer). Moreover, all necessary reference blocks are also read from DPB. These DPB access are also the bottleneck to H.264/Video decoder system because of limited DRAM bandwidth. Therefore efficient managing reference pictures in DPB is able to great improve MC performance.

Many researches have been conducted to improve MVPG [2][3] and MC [5-8] while few of them pay attention to the reference picture management scheme. In [2], only the traditional spatial correlation prediction mode is given without the solution to the much more complicated direct prediction mode. In [3], it described a method to bridge two reference picture lists used in current picture and co-located picture for direct prediction mode. However all calculations for the position of co-located block are accomplished by software CPU. It is not efficient for real-time video decoding with high resolution. Han Bin proposed a loop buffer in [5] to solve the problem about picture storage. It demands on two-move mapping process to get reference block address in DPB according to its reference index. Other works [6-8] wrote less about reference picture management. However, it still requires further research on reference picture management owing to its great effect on inter prediction of video decoder, especially for main profile with Macroblock-Adaptive Frame-Field Coding (MBAFF).

In this paper, we proposed two efficient schemes for reference picture management in H.264/AVC main profile decoding system. The first scheme is for direct mapping between reference picture index (refidx) and DPB picture index (dpbidx). A systematical hardware and software architecture for inter prediction was also given based on this reference picture management scheme. The second scheme is to replace refidx of collated block with its dpbidx in temporal direct prediction mode so as to avoid the problem of two different reference picture lists. Furthermore, the storage arrangement of DPB based on these two schemes was specified to satisfy different requirements of picture structure. The experiment results shows these two schemes can decrease the work load of software CPU by 80% and improve the performance of hardware inter prediction accelerator by xx% with xx% DRAM access reduction.

The rest of the paper is organized as follows. Section 2 analyzes the traditional algorithm of mapping refidx to DPB index (dpbidx) in MC, and the MVPG algorithm which focuses on idrect prediction mode. Section 3 presents the details of two proposed reference picture management schemes and DPB storage arrangement. The experimental results are given in Section 4. Finally, section 5 concludes the paper.

2   Relevant Algorithm Analysis

2.1   Mapping refidx to dpbidx Algorithm in MC Process

In MC process, the reference picture is determined according to the refidx value of current decoded block One decoded picture should be transferred into DPB as the reference for its following picture. Fig.2(b) illustrates the traditional method for determining the position of reference block in DPB. After the decoded picture is transferred into DPB, a look up table (DPB_LUT) which contains 16 entries is used for registering the usage status of DPB. After the Reference Picture Initialization and Reordering process, the RefPicList is generated for inter-frame prediction of current. The refidx is first mapped to lutidx which indicates the reference picture registered in DPB_ LUT. Then lutidx is mapped to dpbidx and the entry number of reference picture in DPB is determined. The exact storage position of reference block is further determined by MVs of the current block.

In usual video decoding system, the MC operation works as the bottleneck, this two-move mapping scheme significantly drop the system performance.

2.2 Motion Vector Predictor Algorithm

In H.264/AVC motion estimation, there are two prediction modes, spatial prediction mode and direct prediction mode, according to tree-structure macroblock (MB) partitions from 16x16 to 4x4.

Spatial Prediction Mode
For the traditional spatial prediction mode, the MVP of the current block is chosen from the candidate motion vector of neighboring partitions on the left, top and top-right (or top-left if the top-right one is not available). MVP is adopted based on either non-median operation or median operation. Non-median operation works when the current block size is 16x8 or 8x16. A quick selection is used for this operation according to the reference pictures of neighboring partitions. For median operation, a median selection between the motion vectors of neighboring blocks is adopted for MVP the estimation of current block.

Direct Prediction Mode
Direct prediction mode is composed of spatial direct mode and temporal direct mode. There is not any motion information for one MB in B slice bitstream. Both forward and backward motion data are derived according to the temporal correlation between the current decoded block and the co-located block in the backward reference picture.

The detailed prediction progress for temporal direct prediction modes is illustrated as follows:

Step 1: Get the Motion Data of Co-located Block

The co-located picture is assigned to 0-indexed entry in reference picture list 1 (RefPicList1). For the simple case that there are only frame or field group of pictures (GOP) in the bitstream, the position of the co-located block in co-located picture is exactly same as the current block in the decoded picture. However, for the case of MBAFF or PAFF, the position mapping scheme (col_mapping) becomes more complex with three different kinds of conditions, One_To_One, Frame_To_Field and Field_To_Frame, according to the coding structure of current MB and co-located MB. Then the motion data (mvCol and refCol) can be derived.

Step 2: Derivation of Reference Index

The backward refidx (refidxL1) points to the entry indexed 0 in RefPicList1.

The forward refidx is generated through a mapping procedure which transfers the refidx of co-located block (refidxCol) to refidxL0 of current block. The picture index of co-located block is different from that in current RefPicList0. Therefore mapping procedure is necessary to bridge these two different reference picture lists.

Three different mapping schemes are shown in Fig.1. In condition of One_To_One, both co-located block and current block share the same decoding structure. As shown in

Fig.1(a), it is direct mapping scheme through the lookup table of DPB. In condition of the Frame_To_Field, co-located block and current block are decoded as frame block and field block respectively. As shown in Fig.1(b), its mapping scheme is more complex owing to the translation from frame index to field index. In condition of Filed_To_Frame, its mapping scheme also needs to handle the translation from field index to frame index as shown in Fig.1(c).

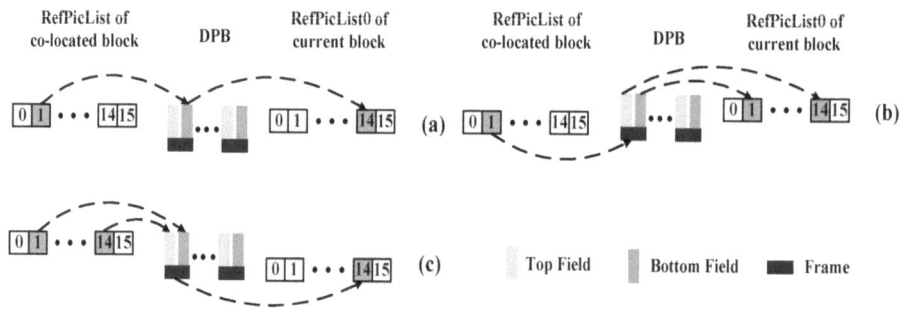

Fig. 1. Three different mapping strategies between different reference picture lists

Typically, each mapping strategy is required to translate from refidxCol to dpbidx, and then from dpbidx to refidxL0. As mentioned in Mapping refidx to dpbidx algorithm, each mapping process from refidx to dpbidx or from dpbidx to refidx needs to two moves. Therefore there are totally four moves to bridge the refidxCol and refidxL0 in the typical way. It brings more complexity to design the decoder and obviously reduces its efficiency. Furthermore, four index lookup tables, from refidx to lutidx, from lutidx to refidx, from lutidx to dpbidx and from dpbidx to lutidx, are necessary to be stored during decoding a picture. It brings extra hardware cost.

Step 3: Derivation of MV
The bi-directional MV of current block are derived by scaling the mvCol with the factor DistScaleFactor calculated according to the picture order counts(POCs) of two reference pictures and current picture.

3   Proposed Reference Picture Management Schemes

3.1   Direct Mapping Scheme between refidx and dpbidx

To reduce the time consumption caused by two-move mapping operation, a direct mapping scheme between refidx and dpbidx is established as shown in Fig.2(a).

Compared with the traditional method illustrated in Fig.2(b), the total number of DPB entry is increased to 17 from 16. Different from the process of Decoding-Marking-Transferring during storing one picture, it is simplified to the process of Storing-Marking shown in Fig.3. At the beginning of video decoding, the 0-indexed entry in DPB is allocated to the first decoded picture. Then the entries indexed from 1 to 16 are sequentially allocated to the following 16 decoded pictures. During the 17th picture decoding, one of the 16 entries used previously should be retired for the 18th picture storage. The retired entry is chosen according to the reference picture requirement of the 18th picture decoding. During the remaining time of the decoding process, any decoded picture is stored into the entry retired in last picture decoding process. In this process, the time-consuming operations for transferring are avoided which benefits greatly to the decoding system's performance and power cost.

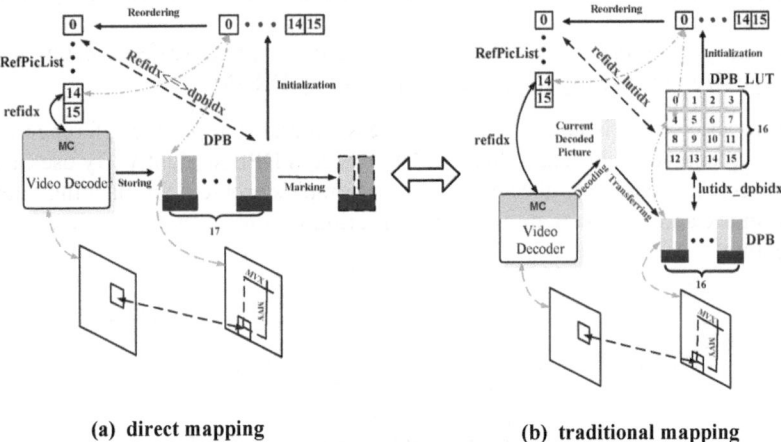

(a) direct mapping   (b) traditional mapping

Fig. 2. Mapping between refidx and dpbidx

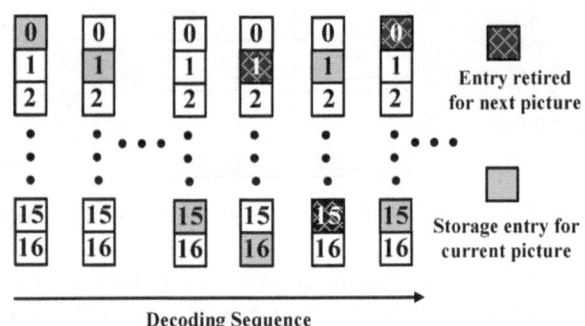

Decoding Sequence

Fig. 3. Storing-Marking process for storing pictures into DPB

In the proposed scheme, a direct linking between refidx and dpbidx is established by software and the DPB_LUT structure is concealed by hardware as shown in Fig.4. A usual NALU sequence is composed of SPS, PPS and coded slices. The decoding works for PPS, SPS and the header of coded NALU slice are partitioned to be processed by software.

CPU is expected to deal with both initialization and reordering operations on reference pictures in DPB. Furthermore it is necessary to generate two tables to map from refidx to dpbidx and from dpbidx to refidx respectively. All slice data decoding works are partitioned to be processed by hardware accelerator for higher performance. Before each slice data decoding, CPU runs reference picture management driver software to generate necessary information for hardware motion compensation accelerator. These information are stored in memory as the interface between CPU software node and MC hardware accelerator. They can be separated to three different parts:

1) Necessary parameters for video sequence, picture and slice. They are usually implemented as register file for target hardware accelerator.
2) Two refidx/dpbidx tables corresponding to current slice. They are usually implemented as register file or on-chip memory for easy accessing by hardware accelerator.
3) 17-entry DPB for decoded picture storage and next picture reference. Owing to its large size, it is usually implemented as off-chip DRAM.

Hardware accelerator is able to use its address generator to get the reference picture address through two tables and drive DMA to access DPB straightly. By use of direct mapping scheme, hardware accelerator avoids complex problem for mapping reference picture index and improves motion compensation efficiency with simple addressing architecture.

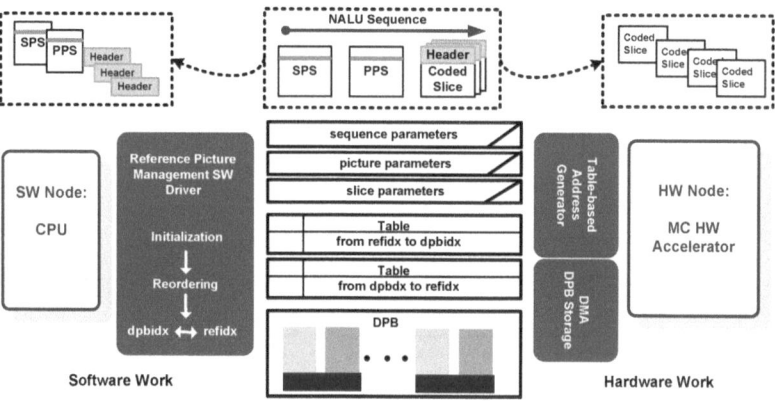

Fig. 4. Direct mapping between dpbidx and refidx on software/hardware decoding system

With proposed scheme, CPU software decoding works with hardware accelerator in parallel. Hardware accelerator is working for N slice, while CPU is working for N+1 slice. Therefore, CPU has enough time to manage reference picture and prepare all necessary information for its slice data decoding in hardware accelerator.

3.2 Replacing refidxCol with dpbidxCol in Temporal Direct Prediction Mode

The mapping process from refidxCol to refidxL0 comprises four moves in traditional process method. To locate the reference block in MC process, current refidxL0 (refidxL0Curr) should be transferred back to current dpbidx (dpbidxCurr). Thus it totally takes 6 mapping moves to generate the address of reference picture in DPB for current block as illustrated in Fig.6(a). According to the temporal direct prediction algorithm, both dpbCol and dpbCurr point to the same entry in DPB. Traditional method is too complex and leads to low efficiency. Compared with the traditional method, the proposed scheme uses dpbidx to replace refidx and stores it into memory when decoding the co-located picture.

Table 1 lists the bit width needed to mark refidx, dpbidx and MV respectively in the case of level 4.2. For MBAFF, it is necessary to use two bits to indicate top field, bottom field or frame in a DPB entry pointed by refidxCurr. Besides it also needs to indicate whether the current block is intra-prediction or inter-prediction. Therefore, 2 more bits are required to be combined into dpbidx so as to indicate these information. As shown in Table 1, for each block, there is 33(26+7)-bit data stored into memory during decoding process. It is obviously inefficient because bus width is usually 32 bit or 64 bit. To address this problem, the proposed scheme keeps 32-bit data width by reducing dpbidx width to 6 bits.

Table 1. Bit width needed to mark refidx, dpbidx and MV

Info		Range	Bit width	
refidx		[0,31]	5	
dpbidx		[0,16]	5+2	
MV	Horizontal	[-2048,2047.5]	14	26
	Vertical	[-512,511.5]	12	

Table 2. Rules for reducing dpbidx bit width to 6 bits

Cond	Description			
	dpbidx[5:4]		dpbidx[3:0]	
			Intra	Inter
1	00:frame indicated 10:bottom field indicated 01:top field indicated 11:intra-prediction indicated		4'd0 fixed	dpbidxCurr[3:0]
2	2'b11 fixed		4'd15 fixed	
3	00:frame indicated 10:bottom field indicated 11:intra-prediction indicated 01:top field indicated		4'd0 fixed	dpbidxCurr[4:0] -5'b1

Three rules are used to compress dpbidx into 6 bit as specified in Table 2. Three conditions are described as follows:

Condition 1: The value of dpbidxCurr is smaller than the entry index of current picture storage (dpbidx_Currpic) which is derived by CPU software before hardware accelerator starts to work.

Condition 2: The value of dpbidxCurr equals to the dpbidx_Currpic in the case that top or bottom filed refers to the opposite field of the same frame.

Condition 3: The value of dpbidxCurr is larger than dpbidx_Currpic.

With this scheme, the corresponding dpbidxCol value can be accessed from memory straightly when dealing with the current block. After some adjustment on dpbidxCol according to the mapping scheme of co-located block position, the dpbidx of current block is able to derive as the flow shown in Fig.5.

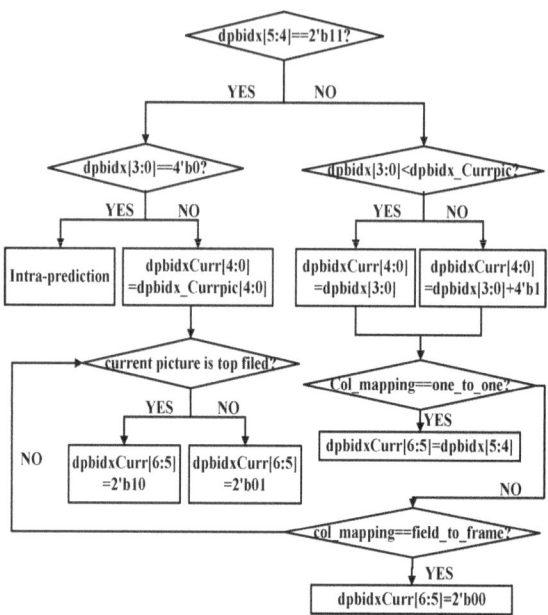

Fig. 5. The flow to derive current block dpbidx

This prediction addressing logic in hardware accelerator takes only one move to generate dpbidxCurr, while the traditional way has to use 6 moves, as shown in Fig.6(b).

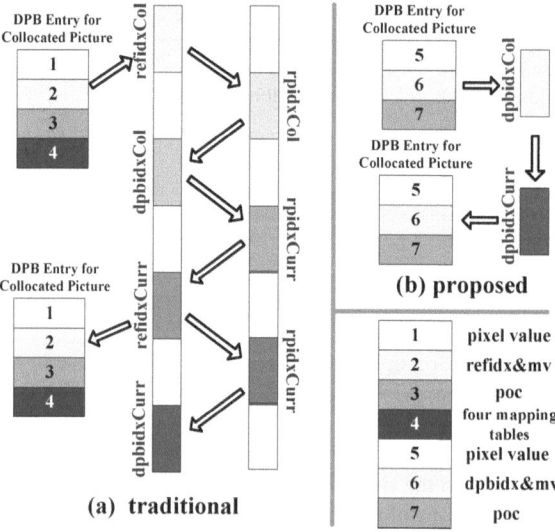

Fig. 6. Comparison between traditional and proposed methods in temporal direct prediction

3.3 Self-adaptive DPB Storage Arrangement Scheme

DPB stores all the information required by inter prediction process including the pixel value, MV, dpbidx and POC value. As shown in Fig.7, the proposed design makes an adaptive arrangement for these information according to decoding structure (field or frame) of the decoded picture and block. Pixel values are stored exactly in their geometric positions considering that each reference pixel will be located according to the geometric span of MV. Both MVs and dpbidx of one block are packaged into one word with the highest 6 bits for dpbidx and the rest 26 bits for MVs. Motion information of the blocks within one MB are stored together. The storage sequence of those blocks within one MB follows their decoding sequence defined in H.264 standard.

Motion information storage for inter-MB level varies according to the structure of decoded picture. For the simplest frame format shown in Fig.7(a), storage is in units of MB and in a way of geometric position mapping. For the field decoded picture, top and bottom fields are stored separately as shown in Fig.7(b). Fig.7(c) illustrates that when it comes to the MB-pair format, motion information storage is in units of MB pair.

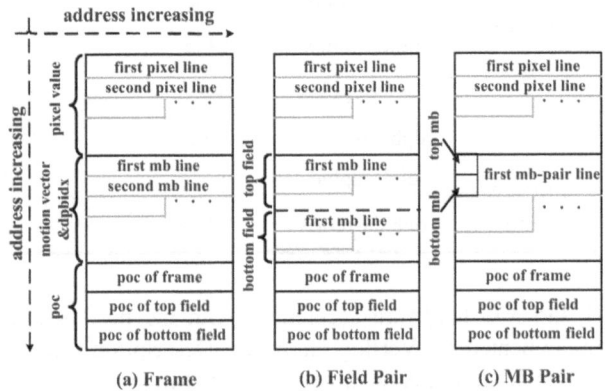

Fig. 7. DPB storage arrangement

4   Implementation Results

The initialization, reordering and marking operations on reference pictures in DPB are implemented into C code as a driver program running on CPU. To verify the effectiveness of our work, we built a platform with CK510E processor[9] for running software driver codes of reference picture management and MVPG/MC hardware accelerator[10] using proposed dpbidx mapping scheme for inter predictor generation. The two mapping tables between refidx and dpbidx are implemented in on-chip SRAM, and DPB is implemented in off-chip SDRAM.

Compared to the traditional way using four mapping tables, the work load of proposed method is reduced by 80% which is shown in Table 3.

Table 3. Comparison between traditional method and proposed method in RISC work load

		Traditional	Proposed	Reduce
ASM Code	text	17745	12366	30.3%
	bss	8	4	50.0%
	data	16	12	25.0%
CPU load		2 MIPS	0.4MIPS	80%

As for the on-chip memory cost, the traditional method stores four tables into memory which costs 1728 bits, while the proposed design reduces the memory cost by 50% the details of which are shown in Table 4.

Table 4. Comparison between traditional method and proposed method in memory cost

Schemes	Table name	Size(bit)	Total(bit)
Traditional Method	refidx-lutidx	32x6	1728
	lutidx-refidx	64x5	
	lutidx-dpbidx	64x7	
	dpbidx-lutidx	128x6	
Proposed Design	refidx-dpbidx	32x7	864
	dpbidx-refidx	128x5	

Both MVPG and MC hardware accelerator with the proposed dpbidx mapping scheme were implemented by Verilog Hardware Description Language (HDL) and synthesized by Design Compiler with SMIC 65nm Silicon Process. For the system throughput performance measurement, the dedicated testing sequences generated by JM 8.6 encoder were used to verify the target design which covers almost all the attributes of the main profile H.264/AVC decoder with level 4.2.

Table 5 illustrates the proposed reference picture management scheme's contribution to improvement of the whole decoding system's throughput performance. Both values in Table 5 are generated based on our own hardware platform. As can be seen that the proposed scheme improves the system throughput performance by 22.1%

Table 5. Comparison between traditional method and proposed method in throughput performance based our own hardware platform

Schemes	Cycles/MB
Traditional Method	avg 585
Proposed Method	avg 456

From the results of our experiment, the proposed design can achieve real-time decoding of HD 1080p (1920x1088 @30fps) video stream when operating at 110 MHz. The hardware implementation results and some comparisons are shown in Table 6 which illustrates that our design outperforms other designs in the same field in both hardware costs and system performance.

This advancement is ascribed greatly to the proposed two optimization techniques according to four aspects:

Firstly, the whole picture transferring operation is avoided by altering the marking and storage sequence based on 17 entries of DPB. The storage position of each decoded picture is determined during the marking operation of last picture. Therefore it can be straightly stored into DPB.

Secondly, for the complex mapping process from refidx to the actual storage position of reference picture in DPB, the proposed design reduces the traditional two-move process to one move which establishes a direct relationship between refidx and dpbidx.

Thirdly, by storing dpbidx in place of refidx into DPB, the most complex prediction mode in MVPG process, namely direct prediction mode, is simplified greatly with the reduction from six moves to one moves only. New data package is able to efficiently improve bus bandwidth.

Lastly, all decoded data are well organized with a self-adaptive DPB storage management scheme.

Table 6. Comparison of proposed design with other works

Module		Gate Count	Cycles/MB	Performance
MVPG	[2]	52k	max 260 avg 160	1080p,basiline,108M
	[3]	41k	28~260	1080p, high,60fps,266M
	[4]	62k	max 310	1080p, AVS Jizhun,6.2,148.5M
	Proposed	37k	avg 90	1080p, main,30fps,80M
MC	[6]	60.6k	avg 500	QCIF@30fps 1.5M
	[7]	93k	avg 851	CIF@30fps 20M
	Proposed	53k	avg 456	1080p@30fps 110M

5 Conclusion

To address the challenges brought by multiple reference pictures in H.264/AVC, this paper proposed two effective reference picture management schemes and the corresponding DPB storage arrangement so as to improve the performance of both software CPU and hardware accelerator. The proposed reference picture management schemes are able to make use of DPB structure and its picture index to avoid unnecessary operations in MVPG and MC. Experimental results show the feasibility and efficiency of target software and hardware platform with the proposed schemes.

References

1. Joint Video Team (ITU-T Rec.H.264 and ISO/IEC 14496-10 AVC): Draft ITU-T Recommendation and final Draft International Standard of Joint Video specification (2003)
2. Yin, H., Zhang, D., Wang, X., Xia, Z.: An efficient MV prediction VLSI architecture for H.264 Video Decoder. In: IEEE International Conference on Audio, Language and Image Processing, pp. 423–428 (2008)
3. Yoo, K., Lee, J., Sohn, K.: VLSI architecture design of motion vector processor for H.264/AVC. In: IEEE International Conference on Image Processing, pp. 1412–1415 (2008)
4. Zheng, J., Deng, L., Zhang, P., Xie, D.: An Efficient VLSI Architecture for Motion Compensation of AVS HDTV Decoder. Journal of Computation Science & Technology 12(3), 370–377 (2006)
5. Han, B., Wang, J., Liu, M.: The management of reference frame list in H. 264 decoder. Journal of Microcomputer Information 23(9-2), 290–292 (2007)
6. Xu, K., Choy, C.: A Power-Efficient and Self-Adaptive Prediction Engine for H.264/AVC Decoding. IEEE Trans. Very Large Scale Integrated Circuits 16(3), 302–313 (2008)
7. Yang, K., Zhang, C., Du, G., Xie, J., Wang, Z.: A Hardware-Software Co-design for H.264/AVC Decoder. In: Proc. IEEE Asia Solid-State Circuit Conference, pp. 119–122 (2006)
8. Lei, Y., Li, H., Zheng, Z., et al.: A H.264 Video Decoder with Scheme of Efficient Bandwidth Optimization for Motion compensation. In: IEEE International Symposium on Communications and Information Technologies, Sydney, pp. 531–534 (2007)
9. Li, C., Huang, K., Feng, J., De, M., Ge, H., De, M., Ge, H., Yan, X.: A High Efficient Memory Architecture for H.264 Motion Compensation. In: IEEE International Conference on Application-specific Systems, Architectures and Processors, Rennes, France (2010)
10. Hangzhou C-Sky Microsystems Corporation. CKCORE User Manual, China (2006)

Research on the Algorithm for 3L-CVRP with Considering the Utilization Rate of Vehicles

Han-wu Ma[1,2], Wei Zhu[1], and Sen Xu[1]

[1] School of Business Administration, Jiangsu University, Zhenjiang 212013, China
[2] Institute of Systems Engineering, Southeast University, Nanjing 210096, China
mahanwu@126.com

Abstract. Integrated optimization of vehicle routing problem and container loading problem has become a research hotspot in current logistics distribution. Firstly, a mathematical model of the three-dimensional loading capacitated vehicle routing problem (3L-CVRP) is made out under the assumption of which the delivered items are rectangular, considering the rotation of items, last in first out (LIFO) rule and the loading of fragile items which are all in accordance with the realistic conditions, and the objective is to minimize the total driving distance and maximize the utilization rate of vehicle. Then, in order to solve this problem, this paper divides the process of routing and loading into two levels, and a new algorithm which combined Tabu Search (TS) with Local Search (LS) is presented. At last, the feasibility and effectiveness of the method and algorithm is proved by the adoption example.

Keywords: Vehicle Routing Problem, Container Loading Problem, Tabu Search, Local Search.

1 Introduction

The vehicle routing problem (VRP) is to find the minimum cost routes to be traveled by a fleet of vehicles. The container loading problem (CLP) is mainly used to design the loading solution with high quality, in order to increase the utilization rate of vehicles, which can reduce the number of employed vehicles and the transportation costs. These two problems have been widely studied, but the research on the combination of them is very limited. Taking the tobacco distribution in china for example, the distribution method used by many tobacco distribution centers is fixing-time and fixing-route method which will make the tobacco distribution centers cannot determine the specific tobacco distribution route according to the daily actual dynamic demand of retail customer points. And when in the low season or the peak season, the tobacco distribution centers employ the same amount of vehicles, which will increase the no-load ratio and the transportation costs. How to solve the distribution problem of home delivery in the shortest distance, and improve the utilization rate of vehicles, and reduce the number of employed vehicles, all these problems should be addressed immediately for distribution centers which are similar with tobacco distribution centers in china.

R. Chen (Ed.): ICICIS 2011, Part I, CCIS 134, pp. 621–629, 2011.

The VRP has been very extensively studied since it was formally first introduced by Dantzig and Ramser [1] in 1959, and a lot of research branches are derived from this problem. The CVRP is one of the most common and the most important research branches. The character of CVRP is that each vehicle must meet the loading capacity constraints which usually include the restriction of total weight or total volume, while in real life, the loading capacity constraints are often more complex. For example, during the logistics and distribution, if you cannot find a suitable loading program to put all the required items of customers into a same vehicle, then you cannot use one vehicle to distribute all the required items of these customers, and you must use more vehicles or you must put these items into different vehicles in order to distribute all the items. This will surely increase the transportation costs, and then we attached multi-dimensional loading constraints to the CVRP.

Gendreau et al [2] was the first to consider the vehicle routing problem with three-dimensional loading constraints, in this paper, a tabu search approach was proposed to address the 3L-CVRP, where the three-dimensional loading sub-problem was also solved by a tabu search metaheuristic. Fuellerer et al [3] employed a local search to solve the loading sub-problem along with an ant colony optimization routine to find an overall solution to the 3L-CVRP problem. Tarantilis et al [4] employed the Tabu search was for routing aspects of the problem and used a collection of packing heuristics for checking the feasibility of loading in paper. From literature review of 3L-CVRP research, we can see that all the authors build the 3L-CVRP model through increasing constraints on the basis research of 2L-CVRP which they had studied, and strive to innovate in the algorithm. However, the scholars did not consider the utilization rate (weight or volume) of vehicles, and the final result may appear that one vehicle only distribute one or a few customers, although it still meets the shortest total distribution distance, the company must employ a larger number of vehicles to distribute the items. From the view of operating costs for distribution centers, this is not the ideal state.

The purpose of the paper is to optimize the whole on the basis of combining the VRP with the CLP. A Tabu search which combines the Tabu search with guided local search was presented to solve the 3L-CVRP. The paper divides the process of routing and loading into two levels. In order to get the high utilization rate of vehicles, the number of employed vehicles was judged finally. If the number of employed vehicles was not at the least, split the route with the lowest utilization rate into other routes in order to find a better route program. At last, the feasibility and effectiveness of the method and algorithm is proved by the adoption example.

The rest of this paper is organized as follows:After the introduction, a clear detailed description of the problem is provided. In Section 3, the proposed algorithm is presented. Computational results are described in Section 4. Finally, conclusions are summarized.

2   Problem Description

The 2L-CVRP is defined as follows. A completely undirected graph G is given. Let $G=(V,E)$, in which $V = \{v_0, v_1, v_2, \ldots, v_n\}$ is a set of n+1 vertices corresponding to the depot (v_0) and the customers ($v_1, v_2, \ldots, v_n$). Let $E=\{(i,j)|(i,j{\in}V), i{\geq}0, j{\geq}0, i{\neq}j\}$ and E is the set of edges. For each edge, the associated traveling cost C_{ij} is defined, which corresponds to the cost of transition from v_i to v_j, and $c_{ij}=c_{ji}$ .In the central depot (v_0), a set of t identical vehicles is available. Each vehicle has a weight capacity D and a three-dimensional rectangular loading space length L, height H and width W. The rectangular loading surface is denoted as $S=W{\times}H{\times}L$ .Each customer v_i (i= 1,2,..., n) requires the delivery of a set of mi three-dimensional items I_{ik} ($1{\leq}k{\leq}m$) having width w_{ik} , height h_{ik} and length l_{ik} with total weight d_i . Let $s_i=\sum_{j=1}^{m_i} w_{Iij}h_{Iij}l_{Iij}$ denote the total amount of space needed by customer v_i .

In 3L-CVRP, we assume that all items are rectangular boxes. The items can only be placed orthogonally inside a vehicle; however, items can be rotated by 90^0 on the width-length plane. Some items are also marked fragile. The objective of 3L-CVRP is to find a set of at most t routes (one per vehicle), each one including the depot, so that the following conditions are satisfied:

(1) Every vehicle starts from the depot, visits a sequence of clients and returns to the depot;(2) All customers are served by exactly one vehicle;(3) No vehicle carries a total weight that exceeds its capacity;(4) The utilization rate of vehicle on average is a maximum;(5) The overall length of the edges included in the routes is a minimum;(6) All items for a particular vehicle can be orthogonally packed while satisfying the following loading constraints:(6.a) (Fragility Constraint) no non-fragile items are placed on top of fragile items;(6.b) (Supporting Area Constraint) all items have a supporting area ($\underset{\sim}{A}$) of at least percent of their base area (A). That is $\underset{\sim}{A} \geq aA$ ($0 < a \leq 1$) ;(6.c) (LIFO constraint) the loading of each vehicle must obey the following LIFO rule. When customer i is visited, all of its corresponding items I_{ik} must not be stacked beneath nor be blocked by items of later customers. An item is considered blocked if it will overlap any item of a later customer when it is moved along the Z axis towards the door.

The loading space of a vehicle is represented in the positive orthant of a Cartesian coordinate system, with the W edge, the H edge, and the L edge respectively parallel to the X axis, the Y axis, and the Z axis. The origin is at the deepest, bottommost, leftmost corner. The container's loading/unloading door lies at the $W{\times}H$ rectangle originating from point (0, 0, L).

3 The Proposed Algorithm

We design an algorithm which combines Tabu Search with Local Search to solve 3L-CVRP. The whole algorithm can be divided into two levels: the overall framework uses Tabu Search to arrange the route of each vehicle; an efficient inner Local Search is invoked for the loading solution. In order to obtain good quality initial solution, a heuristic algorithm was used, this algorithm is the improvement of Clarke-Wright savings algorithm: every time when it merges the paths, the new generate path will be called to use the loading algorithm, only when the new path can successfully solved the problem then it can merge the paths. Although the Local Search algorithm is not complete, it cannot find the loading program for some complex situations. Its efficiency is high, and it makes the Tabu Search algorithm in outer layer can search in larger space during a short time, which can enhance the overall optimized ability of the algorithm.

3.1 Local Search for Loading

Algorithm 1. Local Search Algorithm for Loading

Local Search Algorithm for Loading
1 Calculate the total weight of all items S_{weight} and total volume S_{volume}; if $S_{\text{weight}}>D$, or $S_{\text{volume}}>S$, return false;
2 Generate the initial solution X^0; let the current solution $X= X^0$;

3 Iterate σtimes:
    3.1 Let $len1$ = return value which use Deepest-Bottom-Left-Fill algorithm;
    3.2 If $len1$ = nitems, then save the loading program, return true;
    3.3 Let $len2$ = return value which Maximum Touching Area algorithm;
    3.4 If $len2$ = nitems, then save the loading program, return true;
    3.5 Let len = max ($len1$, $len2$), i=one of random integers in [1, len + 1], j= one of random integers in [1, n_{items}]; exchange the value of $X[i]$ and $X[j]$;

4 Return false

The solution of this algorithm is expressed as an ordered sequence which is a composition of all the items to be loaded. Put these items into the carriages based on this sequence by using heuristic algorithm, getting the coordinates of these items. The length of this sequence is $n_{\text{items}} = \Sigma_{i=1}^{h} m_{c_i}$, in which each item was represented by two-tuples (type number of items, the location of customer in the path). So it provided so much information such as the type of each items, the customers that require for items and the location of customers in the route.

Let X be the current solution sequence, len be the maximum return value which use Deepest-Bottom-Left-Fill [5] and Maximum Touching Area [6] algorithm that put X as input parameters. That is, two heuristic loading algorithms were used for processing X in this paper. Loading up to len items, and in the load (len + 1) pieces of the items is bound to fail. The Local Search algorithm for Loading is shown in Algorithm 1.

3.2 Tabu Search Algorithm for the 3L-CVRP

All vehicles traveling routes were directly used to represent solutions in this algorithm, and the ordered sequence of customers were directly used to represent each route, and each solution included all the n vertices. In the specific implementation of the algorithm, each route is a type of structure *route_s*, in which including an integer variable which was used to represent the number of points in the route of customers, a one-dimensional array which was used to represent numbers that the customers were delivered by order, and a real variable which was used to represent the length of this route; each solution is a type of structure *routes_s*, in which including an integer variable represents the number of routes, one-dimensional array which is a type of structure *routes_s* was used to store each route information, a real variable which was used to represent the total length of all routes, in addition, there are members saving the loading programs which save the position of each item in the vehicle(the coordinates of back of the lower left corner and the front of lower right corner).

Algorithm 2. Tabu Search Algorithm for the 3L-CVRP

Tabu Search Algorithm for the 3L-CVRP
1 Setting the parameters of TS algorithm;
2 Using an improvement of Clarke-Wright savings algorithm to generate the initial solution *initial_sol*, if the return value is false , output "Fail", end;
3 Let the current optimal solution *best_sol* = *initial_sol*, the current solution *current_sol= initial_sol*;
4 Initialize the tabu list *tabu_table*, let *tabu_table[u][v]*=-∞, 0≤u, v≤n;
5 Let the number of current iterations *current_iter* = 0;
6 If meet the criterion of termination, turn 13;
7 Let the best candidate solution be *next_sol*; let *found_next = false*, means that it has not yet found the optimal candidate solution; use (*u, v*) to identify the neighborhood transformation that transform the current solution into optimal candidate solutions.
8 Cycle φ times:
8.1 Let φ be the numbers that transform; If the current solution has only one route, let *k*= 1; Otherwise, randomly selected *k* value according to some probability of 3 transformation
8.2 Use no.*k* transformation to transform *current_sol*, if the transformation fails, continue to cycle. Otherwise, Let the candidate solution be *candidate_sol*, the identify of this transformation is (*u',v'*);
8.3 Calculate the value of adaptation of *candidate_sol*;
8.4 If *found_next=true*, and the value of adaptation of *candidate_sol is* not less than the value of adaptation of *next_sol*, continue to cycle;
8.5 If the value of adaptation of *candidate_sol is* not less than the value of adaptation of *best_sol*, and *current_iter-tabu_table* [*u'*][*v'*]< φ , that is to say the *candidate_sol* has been tabu and it do not meet the criteria of contempt, continue to cycle;
8.6 The newly generated routes in *candidate_sol was* called loading algorithm. If any route loading failed, continue to cycle;
8.7 Copy the loading program from *current_sol* that have not change the route in *candidate_sol*;
8.8 Let *found_next = true*, u= *u'*, v= *v'*, *next_sol = candidate_so*;
9 If *found_next =false*, let *current_sol = best_sol*, turn 12;
10 Let *current_sol = next_sol, tabu_table[u][v]* =*tabu_table[v][u]=current_ite*;
11 If *current_sol* is better than *best_so*l, let *best_sol = current_sol, best_iter = current_iter*;

12 Let *current_iter* =*current_iter* + 1, turn 6;
13 If the number of *best_sol* routes has been the minimal, then output the route programs and loading plans of *best_sol*. Otherwise, get into the following cycle:

   13.1 Put this *best_sol* routes in descending order according to loading rate, merger the points in lowest loading rate route into the route that including the nearest point.

   13.2 Calculate the total weight of all items S_{weight} and Total volume S_{volume}; if $S_{weight}>D$, or $S_{volume}>S$, delete this point, merger this point into the route that including the second nearest point, continue;

   13.3 Use the loading algorithm to check the loading;

   13.4 If the number of *best_sol* routes has not been the minimal, continue;

14 If best_sol≤t, output "Fail", Otherwise, output the the route programs and loading plans of *best_sol*.

4 Computational Results

In order to verify the performance of the proposed algorithm, the proposed algorithm was tested on a test set obtained by modifying instances from the literature. The instances from the literature can be downloaded at www.or.deis.unibo.it/research.html, 5 instances were derived from these 27 instances. For details of the datasets, the reader can refer to [2].The loading space was defined as $W = 25$, $H = 30$, and $L = 60$.We have implemented the algorithm in C and run it on a 2.0 GHz Core Duo notebook with 1024MB RAM under Windows XP. The parameters of the algorithm in this experiment are set as follows:

The threshold of supporting area: $\alpha=0.75$; The maximum number of LS iterations: $\sigma=200$;The number of candidate solutions that was generated at TS each iteration: $\varphi=500$;Tabu length: $\phi=30$;The termination criterion parameter of TS algorithm: $\theta_1 = 4000$, $\psi =1000$, $\theta_2 = 6000$.

In order to better illustrate the validity of the model and algorithm, experiments considered the constraint of the fragile, LIFO rules and supporting area constraint. Standard constraint: 3L-CVRP in standard case, that is the constraint of the fragile, LIFO rule and supporting area constraints; No fragile constraint: cannot have to meet the constraint of fragile, the other two conditions must be met; No LIFO rule: cannot meet the LIFO rule, the other two conditions must be met; Without supporting area constraint: cannot meet the supporting area constraint, the other two conditions must be met; Without all the constraints: the three conditions cannot be met.

Table 1 shows operating results of the selected instances in the Standard constraint.

As can be seen in Table 1, during all the instances with the different number of customers, the vehicle's average load factor of weight is very high, and the highest reached 96.74%, the lowest also reached 84.6%. From a single route in this test, the loading factor of weight of many vehicles are 100%; Compared to the vehicle's average loading factor of weight, the loading factor of volume is not very high, it is due to that items which customers required have high density, if the vehicle is not fully loaded, the vehicle's weight has been fully loaded. In response to this condition, the distribution center can replace those vehicles with the vehicles of greater loading capacity in order to load more items.

Table 1. Operating results under the standard constraint

N.O	N.O of C	N.O of I	Maximum N.O of V	Initial NO of V	N.O of R	Total Distance	AR of W	AR of V	TIME
2	15	26	5	5	5	332.927	92.73%	33.22%	17.42
4	20	36	6	7	6	447.983	95.40%	36.86%	46.53
9	25	50	8	9	8	630.182	95.57%	44.85%	164.06
16	35	63	11	11	11	694.004	96.74%	33.53%	34.14
24	75	143	16	16	15	1122.775	84.6%	53.97%	588.76

Table 2. The comparison of operating results under the different constraints

N.O	2		4		9		16		24	
Indicators.	Result	%gap	Result	%gap	Result	%gap	Result	%gap	Result	%gap
No fragile constraint										
N.O of R	5		6		8		11		15	
Total Distance	332.927	0	447.983	0	630.128	-0.01%	692.423	0.23%	1116.42	-0.56%
TIME	8.95	-48.62%	36.03	-22.6%	133.08	-18.9%	12.91	-62.2%	468.00	-20.5%
No LIFO rule										
N.O of R	5		6		8		11		15	
Total Distance	332.927	0	447.983	0	628.238	-0.31%	692.423	-0.23%	1060.051	-5.6%
TIME	3.44	-80.25%	11.2	-76.0%	41.22	-74.9%	4.5	-86.82	269.58	-54.2%
Without support area constraint										
N.O of R	5		6		8		11		15	
Total Distance	332.927	0	447.983	0	628.238	-3.1%	692.423	-0.23%	1103.825	-1.68%
TIME	7.25	-58.38%	24.80	-46.7%	111.03	-32.3%	7.13	-79.115	367.59	-37.6%
Without all the constraints										
N.O of R	5		6		8		11		15	
Total Distance	332.927	0	447.983	0	625.096	-0.8%	692.423	-0.2%	1051.51	-6.35%
TIME	2.75	-84.2%	6.26	-86.6%	24.67	-85.0%	2.44	-92.9%	152.19	-74.2%

N.O of C is the number of customers; N.O of I is the total number of items; Maximum N.O of V is the maximum number of vehicles; Initial NO of V is the number of vehicles in initial solution. N.O of R is the number of routes; Total Distance is the total driving distance; AR of W is the vehicle's average load factor of weight; AR of V is the vehicle's average load factor of volume; TIME is the running time.

Table 2 shows the comparison of operating results under the different constraints. The %gap is the percent improvement over the corresponding algorithm solution value.

From the total driving distance of comparison in Table 2, the results after removing the fragility constraint have averagely been improved by 0.56%; a stronger effect is obtained by removing the supporting area constraint and the LIFO constraint: The improvements are 1.68% and 5.59%, respectively. The removal of all the three constraints yields an overall average solution value's improvement of 6.35%.The table also shows the comparison of running time, the results after removing the relevant constraints were improved greatly. Remove the LIFO rules, the running time was improved most obviously, and the maximum improvement reached 80.25%. Therefore, both from the total driving distance traveled or from the running time, the greatest impact on the calculation results is from the LIFO rules. This article assumes that the distribution center employed the same types of vehicles, although the loading factor of a single vehicle has only a little change, the vehicle's average loading factor of weight and the volume does not change because the number of employed vehicles does not change in these 4 conditions.

In addition, from the view of running time, algorithm of TS + LS can get the results within 600 seconds, this algorithm has a very clear advantage in time-consuming. The experiment demonstrates that the result of our proposed algorithm is superior to those results reported so far (The comparison of operating results with other results of literature was omitted in this paper). It also shows obvious advantages in terms of efficiency when applying this algorithm on large-scaled instances.

5 Conclusions

This paper addresses the 3L-CVRP with considering utilization rate of vehicle. To the best of our knowledge, it is the first time for considering utilization rate of vehicle in 3L-CVRP. From the computational results, it is shown that the algorithm which combined Tabu Search with Local Search achieves good results. For constructing the initial solution, an improvement of Clarke-Wright savings algorithm is employed. The feasibility and effectiveness of the method and algorithm is proved by the adoption example. The results can further optimize the allocation of resources and reduce transportation cost. And the results are particularly suitable for distribution centers which are similar with tobacco distribution centers in china that have its own delivery vehicles and its vehicles are used repeatedly.

The importance of the 3L-CVRP with considering utilization rate of vehicle is mainly reflected in two aspects. Theoretically, being composed of two NP-hard optimization problems, it is also a highly complex NP-hard problem. For practical applications, this problem may exist at many companies. So the future work is to further improve the performance of this algorithm, and extend it to solve the problems that are close to the logistics and transportation needs in real life.

References

1. Dantzig, G.B., Ramser, J.H.: The Truck Dispatching Problem. Management Science 6, 80–91 (1959)
2. Gendreau, M., Iori, M., Laporte, G., Martello, S.: A Tabu Search Algorithm for a Routing and Container Loading Problem. Transportation Science 40(3), 342–350 (2006)
3. Fuellerer, G., Doerner, K.F., Hartl, R.F., Iori, M.: Metaheuristics for vehicle routing problems with three dimensional loading constraints. European Journal of Operational Research 201, 751–759 (2010)
4. Tarantilis, C.D., Zachariadis, E.E., Kiranoudis, C.T.: A hybrid metaheuristic algorithm for the integrated vehicle routing and three-dimensional container-loading problem. IEEE Transactions on Intelligent Transportion Systems 10(2), 255–271 (2009)
5. Baker, B.S., Coffman Jr., E.G., Rivest, R.L.: Orthogonal Packings in Two Dimensions. SIAM Journal on Computing 9(4), 846–855 (1980)
6. Lodi, A., Martello, S., Vigo, D.: Heuristic and Metaheuristic Approaches for a Class of Two-Dimensional Bin Packing Problems. Informs Journal On Computing 11(4), 345–357 (1999)
7. Ma, H.W., Yang, X.: The Research on the Model of ILRIP for Distribtion Network Based on JITD. Chinese Journal of Management Science 17, 394–398 (2009)

Simulation of a Signalized Intersection Delay Model

Minghui Wu[1,2], Lian Xue[1,*], Hui Yan[1], and Chunyan Yu[3]

[1] School of Computer and Computing Science, Zhejiang University City College
Hangzhou, Zhejiang, 310015, P.R. China
[2] Department of Computer Science and Engineering, Zhejiang University
Hangzhou, Zhejiang, 310027, P.R. China
[3] College of Mathematics and Computer Science, Fuzhou University
Fuzhou, Fujian, 350108, P.R. China
xuel@zucc.edu.cn

Abstract. Signalized intersection delay is an important evaluation index of the signalized intersection capacity and level of service. This paper presents a signalized intersection delay model for signalized intersection. The model uses time series and queuing theory. It discusses the operation characteristics of the process of arrival and leaving and optimizes the intersection signal timing and gets the best signal cycle time. A scientific model and a more complete analysis are founded in the paper. These methods have a good reference value to the relevant departments.

Keywords: Signalized intersection, delay, queuing theory, forecast, timing optimization.

1 Introduction

With the development of China's economic and raise living standards, all service industries are also increasingly to fierce competition. As the standards of enterprise management, service concept and corporate image, service quality in recent years receives a double concern by service and customers.

Traffic flow theory [1] [2] began in the 30's; literature [3] and [4] provided a Poisson solve the problem of traffic flow in the numerical calculation examples. However, with the development of new transport, it is found the original method of probability theory to some extent already does not apply to the current rapid development of the traffic situation. And the new theories which have become more sophisticated, such as Queuing Theory[5] and fluid Mechanics Theory[6], are more applicable to the present traffic conditions. After Adams used the queuing theory on the pedestrian delays without the traffic lights in 1936, queuing theory are more widely used in traffic engineering.

Queuing theory can simulate the queuing process. It can reflect the concept of personalized service by improving the key and details during queuing process, relieve the customer impatience and leave people a relatively free space during queuing process. It truly reflects a "people-oriented" service concept.

---

* Corresponding author.

R. Chen (Ed.): ICICIS 2011, Part I, CCIS 134, pp. 630–635, 2011.

In this paper, vehicles operating characteristics of a signalized intersection is analyzed. It uses MINITAB and MATLAB7.0 to calculate the delay time when the vehicle is in the signalized intersection and other vehicles running Eigen value.

2 The Short-Term Traffic Flow Prediction of Basing on Time Series

Intersection of external vehicles to arrive on the forecast of operating characteristics of the vehicle plays an important role in prediction, so the establishment of an appropriate prediction model to forecast is an important part. Intersection of a section now known in 18 cycles (60 seconds per cycle) and external traffic flow data, such as shown in Table 1:

Table 1. Intersection external traffic flow data table

Cycle	External traffic flow (Cars)	Cycle	External traffic flow (Cars)	Cycle	External traffic flow (Cars)
1	25	9	21	17	25
2	33	10	35	18	39
3	36	11	36	19	42
4	20	12	29	20	23
5	23	13	20	21	28
6	30	14	32	22	36
7	35	15	33	23	33
8	22	16	32	24	31

The signalized intersection of 18 cycles to reach the number of vehicles outside for trend analysis and seasonality analysis. If the long term trend, a time series, it was a long-term trend, you can use the trend of the sequence to be legitimate, if less Trend describes the parameters of time series prediction is the trend of change over time, can be transformed into a " smooth "time-series [8].

Observed no significant growth trend found in Figure 1, and then to the seasonal analysis of the sequence. Again observe the timing diagram, found that the sequence may exist, "seasonal" features actual quotes here because of the seasonal timing is not presented in the real season, but a cyclical change. Seasonal changes in sub-up of two types: regular seasonal changes and seasonal variations changes.

For the regular seasonal changes, the best model to describe the use of additive decomposition. Additive model [9]:

$$Y_t = Trend + Seasonal + Error \tag{1}$$

For the variable seasonal variations, should be used to describe the multiplicative decomposition model. Multiplicative model [9]:

$$Y_t = Trend \times Seasonal \times Error \tag{2}$$

Additive model used here to predict the timing, forecasting the next 18 cycles of external traffic flow, the results shown in table 2.

Table 2. Prediction Results Table additive

Cycle	Forecast(Cars)	Cycle	Forecast(Cars)
25	32	34	30
26	30	35	27
27	25	36	31
28	32	37	35
29	36	38	32
30	30	39	27
31	28	40	35
32	34	41	37
33	35	42	31

3 Traffic Signal Model

Forecast the arrival rate of vehicles in the traffic signal intersection and queue length and the corresponding delays is very important for the implementation of traffic signal control and management. In this paper, stochastic service system theory is used to forecast the vehicle's arrival rate in the signalized intersection, queue length and delay time.

See the signalized intersection i as a service, the arrival of all vehicles at signalized intersection i as the arrival of customers (Vehicles which reach the stop line of each signalized intersection are subject to Poisson distribution, there are four directions of the stop line in a signalized intersection, and Poisson stream confluence is still Poisson stream. So vehicles which reach the stop line of signalized intersection i are subject to Poisson distribution). There are signals to control in Signalized intersection i, different phase followed by the flow of traffic through intersections, vehicles which reach the stop line of signalized intersection i are subject to Poisson distribution. But from a complete cycle, there will always be a green light in a certain phase at any time, that is to say the intersection is a continuous service for the customer (vehicle). The time of service from the help dest for the vehicles can be seen as a negative exponential distribution with independent, thus signalized intersection i can be seen as a $M / M / 1$ system.

So the system mentioned above is called $M / M / 1$ queuing system and in this system, customers receive services.

Average waiting time

$$\bar{W} = \frac{\rho}{u(1-\rho)} \tag{3}$$

The average length of stay

$$\overline{T} = \frac{\rho}{\mu(1-\rho)} + \frac{1}{\mu} \qquad (4)$$

Average length of the ranks

$$\overline{N}_1 = \frac{\rho}{1-\rho} \qquad (5)$$

And $\rho = \dfrac{\lambda}{U}$ is the service's intensity.

4 The Forecast of $\overline{N}, \overline{W}, \overline{T}$

Under the observation, the average service rate of the signal intersection is $\mu = 43$, that is, the intersection per cycle (a period of 60 seconds per week) that can pass through 43 cars.

In accordance with the time series obtained outside the next 18 cycles the number of vehicles predicted to reach the average captain intersection $\overline{N}$, the average waiting time $\overline{W}$, the average length of stay $\overline{T}$. The results are as follows Table 3:

Table 3. Forecast Results table of $\overline{N}, \overline{W}, \overline{T}$ (time series analysis)

Cycle	$\overline{N}$ (Cars)	$\overline{W}$ (Second)	$\overline{T}$ (Second)	Cycle	$\overline{N}$ (Cars)	$\overline{W}$ (Second)	$\overline{T}$ (Second)
25	5	3.488	4.287	34	3	2.031	2.727
26	3	1.703	2.29	35	2	1.42	2.13
27	2	1.301	2.01	36	4	3.051	3.6
28	4	2.657	3.32	37	6	4.22	5.01
29	6	4.302	5.11	38	3	2.11	2.71
30	3	1.81	2.39	39	2	1.446	2.13
31	2	1.43	2.02	40	5	3.48	4.27
32	4	3.00	3.5	41	8	5.301	5
33	6	4.302	5.11	42	3	2.21	3

5 Signal Timing Optimization

The intersection of heavy urban transportation, generally setting the lights to regulate traffic. Capacities of a signalized intersection design and signal control are closely linked. Select optimal solution to maximize the traffic capacity of intersections, reduce delays, to solve bottleneck problems. Signalized intersection is the best cycle times for each light interval between the best. Is calculated as follows [11]:

$$C_0 = \frac{(1.4 + k)L + 6}{Y - 1} \qquad (6)$$

Where: L is the total lost time per cycle(s); Y is the maximum sum of phase flow ratio; K is the parking compensation parameters, according to different optimized requirements, required the most hours of fuel, taken $K = 0.4$; when it is the minimum consumption, taken $K = 0.2$, when it is the minimum delay, taken $K = 0$.

6 Conclusion

This paper studies the arrival of vehicles through the intersection operation and the characteristics of them in signalized Intersections. Then on the basis of that, make use of time series and queuing theory to establish delay model and forecast of vehicles in signalized Intersections. This research gives a solid theoretical foundation of enhancing the efficiency of road, reducing vehicle delay, and be adapt to the rapid development of transport, etc, and also provide an effective method to enhance the capacity of public services.

Acknowledgment

This work was supported in part by a grant from the National Natural Science Foundation of China (No.60805042) and a grant form Program for New Century Excellent Talents in Fujian Province University (No.XSJRC2007-04).

References

1. Yu, J., Yang, C.: Traffic flow theory. Hefei University of Technology 28(1) (2004)
2. China Road and Traffic Engineering Handbook Editorial Association. Traffic Engineering Manual. People's Traffic Press, Beijing (2001)
3. Kinzer, J.P.: Application of the probability to problem of highway traffic. Proc. Inst. Traffic Eng. 3(5) (1934)
4. Adams, W.F.: Road traffic considered as random series. JIns Civil Eng. 3(4) (1936)
5. Zhang, Y.N., Dong, D.-C.: Skew Intersection set in the waiting area of vehicles. East China Jiaotong University 25(6) (2008)
6. Wu C., Chang Y.: Expressway toll plaza toll lane configuration. Highway Engineering 33(5) (2008)
7. Daniel Neil, L., Love, D., Huber, M.: Traffic Flow Theory. People's Traffic Press, Beijing (1983)
8. Tang Ying-hui, TANG Xiao-wo. Queuing Theory - Fundamentals and Applications [M]. Beijing: Cambridge University Press, 2000.

9. Peng, Z., Shaodi, W.: A class of time-varying time series model parameters estimation. Nanjing University of Posts and Telecommunications 18(5-6) (1998)
10. Quanru, P.: Stochastic service system in the transport network application. Jiangsu University, Zhenjiang (2007)
11. Zhengyan, C., Zhixuan, J., Hong, Z.: Signalized Intersection Delay Analysis, p. 26. Taiyuan University of Technology, Taiyuan (2005)

Matlab for Forecasting of Electric Power Load Based on BP Neural Network

Xi-ping Wang[1] and Ming-xi Shi[2]

[1] Department of Economy and Management, North China Electric Power University,
Baoding 071003, China
wxpmm@126.com
[2] Department of Economy and Management, North China Electric Power University,
Baoding 071003, China

Abstract. Modeling and predicting electricity consumption play a vital role both in developed and developing countries for policy makers and related organizations. Improve load forecasting technology level is not only beneficial to plan power management and make reasonable construction plan, but also good for saving energy and reducing power cost, and then, it can improve the economic benefits and social benefit for power system. BP neural network is one of the most widely used neural networks and it has many advantages in the power load forecasting. Matlab has become the best technology application software which has been internationally recognized, the software has many characteristics, such as data visualization function and neural network toolbox, for these, it is the essential software when we do some research on neural network.

Keywords: Electric power load, Matlab, BP neural network, forecast.

1 Introduction

Along with the rapid development of modern science and technology, various load forecasting methods has been put out. It is a well-known fact that Artificial Neural Networks (ANN) can model any nonlinear relationship to an arbitrary degree of accuracy by adjusting the network parameters. It is also better to use models that can handle nonlinearities among variables as the expected nature of the consumption data of electric power. Using BP neural network technology for power load forecasting is a new research method, it can imitate human intelligence, adapt itself for large non-structure and the law, besides, it can get the information by autonomous learning, memory, reasoning and optimization calculation, and Matlab can realize the BP neural network for forecasting.

2 Research Methodology

The BP neural network is Back Propagation neural network, the signal is forward but the error is spread propagation, it is the most sophisticated neural network and is the

R. Chen (Ed.): ICICIS 2011, Part I, CCIS 134, pp. 636–642, 2011.

most widely used. BP network is a multilayer feed forward neural network, when the transfer function of neurons is 'S' function, the output of entire network is limited in a small range, but if the transfer function of neurons is 'purelin' function, the output can take any value[1]. Fig. 1 gives a basic BP neurons model, the number of input is R, all inputs are connected by proper weights called w, and the output of network can be expressed as:

$$a = f(w \times p + b) \tag{1}$$

'f' is the transfer function which connect input and output, the BP neurons model is as follows:

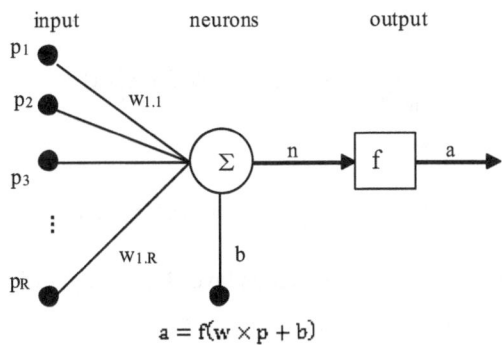

$$a = f(w \times p + b)$$

Fig. 1. BP neurons model

2.1 Number of Network Layer

In fact, increase the number of hidden layers can improve the nonlinear mapping capacity of BP network, but if the number of hidden layers above a certain value, it will increase training time of network. Therefore, in applying the BP neural network for predicting, select a network which has one hidden layer is enough.

2.2 Number of Neurons in Each Network Layer

The node number of input and output is closely related with the sample, according to the historical data, the number of neurons in the input is 4 and the number of neurons in the output is 1. In reality, we can get the number of neurons in hidden layer according to the empirical formula, the common empirical formula is:

$$i = \sqrt{(n + m)} + a \tag{2}$$

'i' is the number of neurons in hidden layer, 'n' is neurons number of input layer, 'm' is neurons number of output layer, 'a' is constant and $1 < a < 10$. Thus, we can set the number of neurons of hidden layer in this neural network for 11.

3 BP Algorithm

The learning of BP neural network is to be supervised, it need to provide input vector 'p' and expectations 't', the weights and deviation in training process are adjusted according to corresponding network performance, and finally we can achieve the expected function. The default performance function of network is average variance in forward neural network, and the goal of learning process is how to make average error minimize[2,3,4].

3.1 The Weights Adjust between Hidden Layer J and Output Layer P

In BP algorithm, the adjustment and output of weights are relative to the partial differential, the partial differential is[5]:

$$\frac{\partial E(n)}{\partial w_{jp}(n)} = -e_{kp}(n) \cdot f\left(u_p^p(n)\right) \cdot v_j^J(n) \tag{3}$$

Define the local gradient as:

$$\delta_p^p(n) = -\frac{\partial E(n)}{\partial u_p^p(n)} = e_{kp}(n) \cdot f\left(\dot{u}_p^p(n)\right) \tag{4}$$

The iteration value of $w_{jp}(n)$ between hidden layer J and output layer P is:

$$w_{jp}(n+1) = w_{jp}(n) + \Delta w_{jp}(n) \tag{5}$$

3.2 The Weights Adjust between Hidden Layer I and Hidden Layer J

It is similar with above, the weights adjust between hidden layer I and hidden layer J is also along with the descent direction of gradient, and the adjust value is:

$$\Delta w_{ij}(n) = -\eta \frac{\partial E(n)}{\partial w_{ij}(n)} = \eta \delta_j^J(n) \cdot v_i^I(n) \tag{6}$$

The local gradient is:

$$\delta_j^J(n) = -\frac{\partial E(n)}{\partial u_j^J(n)} = -\frac{\partial E(n)}{\partial v_j^J(n)} \cdot \frac{\partial v_j^J(n)}{\partial u_j^J(n)} = -\frac{\partial E(n)}{\partial v_j^J(n)} \cdot f\left(\dot{u}_j^I(n)\right) \tag{7}$$

The iteration value between hidden layer I and hidden layer J is:

$$w_{ij}(n+1) = w_{ij}(n) + \Delta w_{ij}(n) \tag{8}$$

3.3 The Weights Adjust between Input Layer M and Hidden Layer I

It is similar with above, the adjust value between any two nodes from two different layers is:

$$\Delta w_{mi}(n) = \eta \delta_i^I(n) \cdot x_{km}(n) \tag{9}$$

The local gradient is:

$$\delta_i^l(n) = f\big(u_i^l(n)\big) \cdot \sum_{j=1}^{J} \delta_j^l(n) w_{in}(n) \tag{10}$$

4   The Usage of Matlab Based on BP Neural Network

4.1   Sample Data Processing

The number of node in input layer, output layer and hidden layer depend on the complexity of the object. The sample data is the quantity of electric power load in ZhongWei city between 2009 and 2010, they are shown below:

Table 1. The electric power used by industrial enterprises between 2009 and 2010

Month	Quantity (TWH)	Month	Quantity (TWH)
2009.01	2.60	2009.10	4.77
2009.02	2.71	2009.11	5.18
2009.03	2.90	2009.12	4.54
2009.04	2.77	2010.01	5.33
2009.05	3.00	2010.02	5.22
2009.06	3.44	2010.03	4.55
2009.07	4.12	2010.04	5.76
2009.08	4.33	2010.05	5.79
2009.09	4.62		

We input the quantity of four months, with these four data, we can get the quantity of fifth month, we also take the quantity of 2010.04 and 2010.05 as the test samples, it is as follows:

Table 2. Sample data

training sample	Input	Output
1	2009.01–2009.04	2009.05
2	2009.02–2009.05	2009.06
3	2009.03–2009.06	2009.07
4	2009.04–2009.07	2009.08
5	2009.05–2009.08	2009.09
6	2009.06–2009.09	2009.10
7	2009.07–2009.10	2009.11
8	2009.08–2009.11	2009.12
9	2009.09–2009.12	2010.01
10	2009.10–2010.01	2010.02
11	2009.11–2010.02	2010.03
test sample		
1	2009.12–2010.03	2010.04
2	2010.01–2010.04	2010.05

4.2 Model Building

Input the command in command window of Matlab:

```
p0=[2.60 2.71 2.90 2.77 3.00 3.44 4.12 4.33 4.62
    4.77 5.18 4.54 5.33 5.22 4.55 5.76 5.79]
for i=1:11
    p(:,i)=[p0(i) p0(i+1) p0(i+2) p0(i+3)]';
    t(i)=p0(i+4);
end
net=newff(minmax(p),[11,1],{'logsig','purelin'},
'trainlm'),
net.trainparam.show=100,
net.trainparam.epoch=2000,
net.trainparam.goal=1e-4,
[net,tr]=train(net,p,t);
```

We can get the training diagram of neural network as follows:

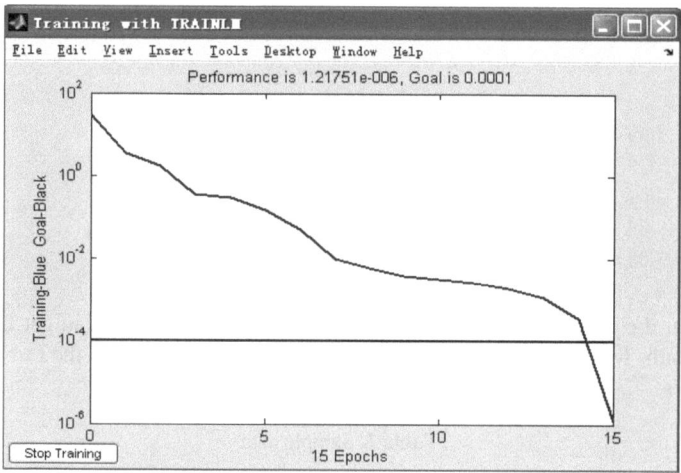

Fig. 2. Training diagram of neural network

4.3 Simulate the Network

Input the command:

```
ptest(:,1)=[p0(12) p0(13) p0(14) p0(15)]';
ptest(:,2)=[p0(13) p0(14) p0(15) p0(16)]';
ttest(1)=p0(16);
ttest(2)=p0(17);
result_test=sim(net,p)
result_test1=sim(net,ptest)
result=[result_test result_test1];
ttest2=[t ttest];
result2=[ttest2' result' (result-ttest2)']
```

The expected output, forecasting results and forecasting error are as follows:

```
result2 =

     3.0000     2.9998     -0.0002
     3.4400     3.4396     -0.0004
     4.1200     4.1180     -0.0020
     4.3300     4.3289     -0.0011
     4.6200     4.6190     -0.0010
     4.7700     4.7705      0.0005
     5.1800     5.1785     -0.0015
     4.5400     4.5412      0.0012
     5.3300     5.3289     -0.0011
     5.2200     5.2193     -0.0007
     4.5500     4.5511      0.0011
     5.7600     5.2295     -0.5305
     5.7900     5.0647     -0.7253
```

Among them, the first column is expected output, the second column is actual output, the third column is absolute errors, use these data, we can calculate the relative error, they are: -0.0067%, -0.0116%, -0.0486%, -0.0254%, -0.0216%, 0.0105%, -0.0290%, 0.0264%, -0.0206%, -0.0134%, 0.0242%, -10.1444%, -14.3207%. It can be seen that the error of training sample is very small, but the error of test sample is 10% above, obviously if we want to use this network extrapolation to get more accurate prediction, we must get a large number of samples.

4.4 Drawing Shows

The expected output and actual output are shown below:

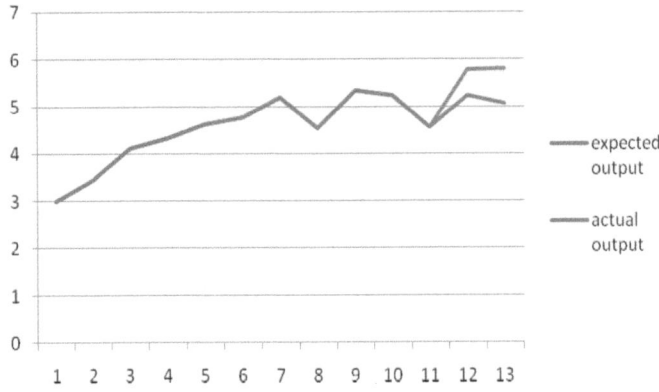

Fig. 3. Contrast diagram between expected output and the actual output

5 Summary

In the practical application of artificial neural network, BP neural network is the most popular. The neural network toolbox of Matlab can set learners free from the complex programming work.

Acknowledgements

This research was supported by the Social Science Foundation of Hebei province under Grant HB10XGL121 and the project supported by "the Fundamental Research Funds for the Central Universities (09MR44)".

References

1. Deng, J.L.: Control problems of grey systems. Syst. Control Lett. 1, 288–294 (1982)
2. Yao, A.W.L., Chi, S.C., Chen, C.: Development of an integrated grey fuzzy-based electricity management system for enterprises. Energy 30, 2759–2771 (2005)
3. Ranjan, M., Jain, V.K.: Modeling of electrical energy consumption in Delhi. Energy 24, 351–361
4. Hsu, C.C., Chen, C.: Applications of improved grey prediction model power demand forecasting. Energy Convers Manage 44, 2241–2249 (2003)
5. Chang, N.B., Tseng, C.: Optimal evaluation of expansion alternatives for existing air quality monitoring network by grey compromise programming. Environ Manage 56, 61–67 (1999)

Application of Bayesian Networks in Situation Assessment

Xi Su[1], Peng Bai[1], Feifei Du[2], and Yanping Feng[1]

[1] Science Institute of Air Force Engineering University Xi'an China
[2] Military Transportation University Tianjin China

Abstract. The present development of situation assessment and the advantages of Bayesian Networks' application in it are introduced in this paper. Particularly, network-construction methods and the temporal inference technology in Bayesian Networks for situation assessment are deeply analyzed, and accordingly it is concluded that the development current of Bayesian Network' application in situation assessment is to promote its coding capability of military-realm knowledge, temporary semantics as well as module inference ability. Finally, existing major problems in all aspects of Bayesian Networks' application in situation assessment are analyzed and a beneficial research idea is therefore put forward in this paper.

Keywords: Bayesian Networks; situation assessment; temporal inference; network-construction.

1 Introduction

According to acquired massive incomplete and inaccurate information with interferences as well as deceptions, modern wars require commanders to make decisions quickly under high uncertainty and time pressures. Situation Assessment (SA) therefore becomes a necessity of modern wars. There are different definitions from different angles mainly include the definition in the JDL model and the cognition definition based on artificial intelligence promoted by Endsley[1]. The widely adopted one in military domain is the definition in JDL models: situation assessment is to establish a view including battle operations, events, time, positions and the organization form of military strength factors, and help commanders to make fast and correct decisions with the battle field synthetic situation chart formed by relating the observed battle strength distribution, circumstances of the battle field, adversary's intentions and mobility to ascertain reasons of events and assess enemy's military strength structure and using characteristics. Practically, the third class model of Endsley situation assessment is adopted a function model to assist researchers to comprehend SA theoretically and lay a foundation for the application of artificial intelligence in SA.

2 Present Application of Bayesian Networks in Situation Assessment

Since 1988 when J.Pear[4] promoted its clear definition, Bayesian Networks has became a hot research field of expression and inference of inaccurate knowledge in

R. Chen (Ed.): ICICIS 2011, Part I, CCIS 134, pp. 643–648, 2011.
© Springer-Verlag Berlin Heidelberg 2011

artificial intelligence for more than two decades. It is a directed acycline graph with nodes to denote variants and the arcs among these nodes to denote direct causality or relevance of variants. As a combination of artificial intelligence, probability, graph theory and decision theory, Bayesian Networks can be deemed as a standard cognition model to infer under uncertain conditions, and it is widely applied to inferences with inner uncertainty and decision issues.

Compared with expert system and neural networks, another two processing methods of artificial intelligence, advantages of Bayesian Networks applied to situation assessment are demonstrated below. Firstly, Bayesian Networks is the combination of graph theory and Bayesian inference. Like neural networks, Bayesian Networks also uses nodes and directed arcs to express realm knowledge. New information can be propagated by directed arcs among nodes and information reserved in networks can also be specified by experts or studied from samples. Links among nodes not only have obvious practical meanings but also accord with comprehensions of military-realm knowledge. Secondly, knowledge in Bayesian Networks can be updated while knowledge in expert systems can not be updated. Once the expert system is constructed, its knowledge is changeless and difficult to be stored. Thirdly, in its construction, Bayesian Networks has already encoded expert knowledge, while neural networks begin with no knowledge at all and must acquire knowledge through learning. And lastly, time propagation algorithm embodies situation assessment's continuity through computing accumulation effects of situations according to both new evidence and the evidence arrived with time sequences. The temporal continuity doesn't exist in memoryless expert systems and neural networks.

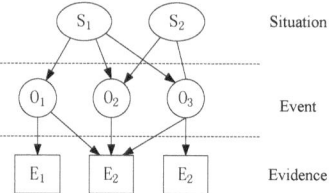

Fig. 1. An example of standard Bayesian Network for situation assessment

Due to Bayesian Networks' merits enumerated upon, the situation assessment research based on Bayesian Networks develops quickly abroad[2] and gets the progress that some situation assessment systems based on statistics-level single platforms including pilotless aircraft platforms, airborne avionics systems[6], vessel anti-missile strategy[7], pilot assisted situation assessment systems and so on are putted into practice. Nodes in Bayesian Networks for situation assessment denote military event and among nodes directed arcs and conditional probability represent causality or relevant relations among events and intensity of relations respectively. In assessment, military events and intelligence detected in situation awareness process are adopted as evidences and evidence propagation and inference algorithm of Bayesian Networks are used to update reliability of other events. When uncertain evidences are known, through this evidence inference the probability of other events can be inferred to judge enemy purposes and to predict targets of enemy actions. A standard Bayesian Networks for situation assessment is showed in Fig1.

3 Bayesian Network Construction for Situation Assessment

To apply Bayesian Networks to battlefield situation assessment, the corresponding Bayesian Network must be constructed firstly. Present Bayesian Networks construction mainly includes learning construction, artificial construction and two-phase modeling [5] combining advantages of the two before. In battlefield situation assessment, massive training data can not be acquired for Bayesian Networks to learn. Therefore, firstly, abundant knowledge expressed by rules is provided by military experts according to experiences and intelligence, and then manual modeling and networks construction modification through model training are accomplished by BN experts. The construction steps are demonstrated as follows:

The first step is to ascertain node contents. Bayesian Networks is constituted by nodes corresponding different events. Consequently, events and their complete state-spaces in situation assessment realm must be ascertained first. The second step is to ascertain node relations. Since situation assessment includes a great deal of factors and intricate relations, BN construction staff and military experts must ascertain these relations together to establish the topology structure of Bayesian Networks. Finally, the conditional probability table should be formed. Since military knowledge is necessary in probability allocation, it is usually assigned by military experts according to experiences.

Being aimed at specific setting, traditional situation assessment Bayesian Networks (SABN), though expert knowledge is coded, still has very limited coding knowledge due to setting restriction. Its construction is hard, time consuming and difficult to be transplanted, while its program modification and maintenance are inconvenient too. Accordingly, SABN can not fulfill requirements of large complicated system networks' construction. Laskey[2] advanced using Bayesian Networks to establish knowledge base, which is also called BN segment, and link networks segments in line with certain rules to construct SABN dynamically in situation assessment. Based on this theory, domestic similar research, using Bayesian Networks modules for dynamic construction, presents dynamic construction of hierarchy SABN [8] according to characteristics of situation assessment. Introduced into Bayesian Networks' construction by Koller[3], object oriented method makes probability characteristics embodies objects' relations and establish the model of probability relations to enhance its expression ability of knowledge. Domestic researchers who applied OOBN theory to situation assessment presented examples of expressing battlefield situation information with object oriented method and realized object oriented situation information's storage in the relation database.

Adopting either Bayesian Networks segment method or object oriented method can both be seemed as means of fully encoding expert knowledge with Bayesian Networks, in other words, combining Bayesian Networks with expert systems. This combination, on one hand, conquers static restrictions of expert systems and achieves better storage, acquirement and update of knowledge. On the other hand, it can also make Bayesian Networks more pragmatic. Only inference technology which can adequately congregate expert knowledge and has friendly human-computer interaction interfaces will thrive in the future.

4 Inferences of Bayesian Networks in Situation Assessment

4.1 Temporal Inference of Bayesian Networks in Situation Assessment

There are mainly two methods to denote time in BN. One is to change a system into a series of snapshots from the starting time to the ending time by Dynamic Bayesian Networks (DBN). Embodying a complete network structure, each snapshot denotes the present system state, temporal causality among relevant nodes of successive two networks and the variant of nodes along with time. Sine practical problems to be resolved in situation assessment, however, are always the changes of networks structures and variants to be decided or inferred, it is not a stationary Markov process and difficult to be simulated by DBN. Aimed this problem, flexible structure varied DBN, which actually presents not only the directed acycline gragh of networks and the conditional table of static Bayesian Networks in each time slice but also the transition matrix between every two time slices, is introduced in reference[9]. Its corresponding inference algorithm is also researched on the basis of discrete Bayesian Networks inference algorithms. Apparently, this method needs modeling staff have deep comprehension of the whole change process of the system as well as large computation quantity. It is therefore hard to be realized in situation assessment.

The second method is to apply temporal expansion to BN. Improved by Kanazawa, discrete time networks model time into a series of points and consider events happen instantaneously and facts happen on a series of time points. Both events and facts are denoted by random variants. Berzuni advanced that some nodes should be added into networks to denote temporal spaces, however, it could evidently increase the magnitude and complexity of networks. Tawfid and Neufeld proposed to deem conditional probabilities among nodes as functions of time, which needs to acquire extrapolation knowledge of probability changes along with time as well as to specify values of each node in different times. According to space algebra theory, Temporal Abduction Problem (TAP) introduced by Santos, considers each event has a relevant temporal space in which event happens. Relations among events are denoted as a directed arcs sum or directed acycline gragh with weights from causes to results in which directed arcs fulfill all possible relations of temporal sets. Though it is very flexible in denoting relations among events, this method would enormously promote the complexity of system construction and inference due to the introduction of abduction random variants. In the research work of reference[8], the definition of time polymer put forward by Young is introduced to denote a military event changing along with time, and each time polymer contain a group of time spaces which means that events may happen in these time spaces and the possible states set of events. In other words, the time space is a group of sets containing temporal random variants and each of them corresponds a time space. The relation between time polymer is called time causality. The Bayesian Networks with temporal inference meaning is constructed through temporal rebuilding of nodes and arcs in Bayesian Networks.

4.2   Probability Inference of Bayesian Networks in Situation Assessment

According to present references, various comprehensions of situation assessment correspond various inference algorithms in SABN, however, there is almost no inference algorithms particularly aimed at SABN. A widely adopted method is to standardize SABN and apply conventional BN inference algorithms to it, Belief Propagation (BP) presented by Pearl, leveled assumption evidence inference algorithms, variant elimination, for instance. Otherwise, basic algorithms are improved to attain better situation comprehension and inference results such as Loopy Belief Propagation algorithm based on loopy networks, inference algorithms used in structure varied DBN and object oriented inference algorithms in OOBN. A distinct characteristic of BN is probability inference with specific meanings. However, probability theory cannot express the uncertainty of all knowledge in military realm and in low level processes of information fusion processing multi-sources heterogeneous data through adopting different uncertainty inference methods according to characteristics of various data can merely acquire uncertain information rendered to the situation assessment system later. This process is usually overlooked by present process methods and probability meanings of all levels' events or clues are directly assumed to infer. How to eliminate this uncertainty within the framework of probability inference is a pretty valuable research direction. In addition, including strategy, battle and statistics levels situation assessment should take advantage of characteristics of both these levels and structure modules of subsystems in levels to make local inferences which can fulfill time as well as accuracy requirements of each level with the purpose of simplifying system inference and reducing communication pressure.

4.3   Analysis of Bayesian Networks' Inference Algorithms

Research results of algorithms' complexity indicate that learning, accurate inference and approximate inference are all NP difficult. If temporal inference semantics is added into NP difficult probability inference of Bayesian Networks, the complexity of networks learning and inference algorithms will evidently soaring. At the same time of developing normal inference algorithms, characteristics of factors, relations, levels of practical situation assessment systems must be well combined and therefore make nodes and segments of Bayesian Networks in situation assessment fully reflect these characteristics to use them as internal information in inference. A present trend of complicate system modeling is modulated and leveled Bayesian Networks based on statistic, battle and strategy levels, geography field as well as function field. Developing reliable networks link algorithms and inference algorithms with more specific aims will promote the inference efficiency of Bayesian Networks in situation assessment.

5   Conclusions

Since the birth of Bayesian Networks, it has been effectively applied to situation assessment realm and some laboratory prototype systems combining Bayesian Networks with other methods to assess situations have also appeared and developed into practice gradually. It can better express knowledge in military realm; on the other hand, it also has solid teaching foundations. Nevertheless, there are still many problems resting in Bayesian Networks' application in situation assessment. First of all, there are no generally acknowledged BN models for situation assessment including the SA function model, the situation assumption model and the mathematic model. Secondly, present expert knowledge coding of Bayesian Networks is still mainly aimed at settings. Because the knowledge that a certain Bayesian Network can express is limited, the Bayesian Networks' application is obviously restricted. The last problem is that there is no effective algorithms combining temporal and space inference in the Bayesian probability inference. Present research on BN in situation assessment introduces some beneficial thoughts to resolve these problems but the concepts, models and methods still need to be improved. Evaluating concepts of situation assessment, realization methods and assessment standards in practice and fully integrating knowledge of military experts, recognition ability of commanders and functions of the military command and control system will construct a situation assessment system which is an excellent combination of knowledge denotation, dynamic storage and update, recognition models and inference technologies.

References

1. Endsley, M.: Theoretical Underpinnings of Situation Awareness: A Critical Review. Situation Awareness Analysis and Measurement (2000)
2. Laskey, K.B.: Hypothesis Management in Situation -Specific Network Construct. In: 17th Conference On UAI, Morgan Kanfmann, San Mateo (2001)
3. Koller, D., Pfeffer, A.: Object-Oriented Bayesian Networks. In: Proceedings of the Thirteenth Annual Conference on Uncertainty in Artificial Intelligence, UAI 1997 (1997)
4. Pearl, J.: Probabilistic Reasoning in Intelligent Systems: Networks of Plausible Inference. Morgan Kaufmann, San Mateo (1988)
5. Zhang, M., Wang, B.: The realization of target grouping technology in situation detection. Electrooptics and control 11(1) (2004)
6. Waltz, E., Linas, J.: Muslti-sensor Data Fusion. Artech House, Boston (1990)
7. Steinberg, A.N., Bowman, C.L., White, F.E.: Revisions to the JDL Data Fusion Model. In: Proceedings of 3rd NATO/IRIS Conference, Quebee, Canada (1998)
8. Bullen, B.: A Bayesian Methodology for Effects Based Planning. Information Fusion for Command Support, pp. 5-1 – 5-8 (2005)
9. Mahoney, S.M., Laskey, K.B.: Constructing Situation Specific Belief Networks. In: Proceedings of the 14th Conference on Uncertainty in Artificial Intelligence, pp. 370–378 (1998)

Preliminary Analysis on the Relative Solution Space Sizes for MTSP with Genetic Algorithm

Junling Hao

School of Information Technology and Management Engineering,
University of International Business and Economics, 100029 Beijing, China
getuo@tom.com

Abstract. It is well known that the chromosome design is pivotal to solve the multiple traveling salesman problems with genetic algorithm. A well-designed chromosome coding can eliminate or reduce the redundant solutions. One chromosome and two chromosome design methods and a recently proposed two-part chromosome design are firstly introduced in this paper. Then the preliminary quantitative comparison analysis of the solution spaces of three different chromosome design methods is presented when the number of cities is linear with the travelers. The concept of relative solution space is proposed in order to compare the relative size of the solution spaces. The solution space of two-part chromosome design is much smaller than those of the traditional chromosome design. The result given in this paper provides a good guideline for the possible algorithmic design and engineering applications.

Keywords: Multiple traveling salesperson problem, genetic algorithm, chromosome design, solution space.

1 Introduction

The multiple traveling salesperson problem (MTSP) [1] involves scheduling m>1 salespersons to visit a set of n>m locations so that each location is visited exactly once while minimizing the total distance traveled by the salespersons. The MTSP is similar to traveling salesperson problem (TSP) to seek an optimal tour without sub-tours. In the MTSP, the n cities must be partitioned into m tours, with each tour resulting in a TSP for one salesperson. The MTSP is more difficult than the TSP because it requires determining which cites to assign to each salesperson, as well as the optimal ordering of the cities within each salesperson's tour.

The most common application of the MTSP is in the area of scheduling [2]. The scheduling job on a production line is often modeled as a TSP. If the production operation is expanded to have multiple parallel lines to which the jobs can be assigned, the problem can be modeled as a MTSP [3]. Vehicle scheduling problem (VSP) [4] is another problem as a model of MTSP. The VSP consists of scheduling a set of vehicles, all leaving from and returning to a common position, to visit a number of locations such that each location is visited exactly once [5]. A variation on TSP that can also be modeled as a MTSP involves using one salesperson to visit n cities in a series of m smaller sub-tours.

R. Chen (Ed.): ICICIS 2011, Part I, CCIS 134, pp. 649–655, 2011.

Due to the computational complexity of the MTSP, it is necessary to employ heuristics [6] to solve problems of realistic size. Genetic algorithms (GAs) [7] are heuristics that researchers have applied to TSP. More recently, researchers studying VSP have expanded the use of GAs for TSP to consider MTSP. Most of the researches on using GAs for the VSP have focused on using two different chromosome designs for MTSP. Both of these chromosome designs can be manipulated using classic GA operators developed for TSP; however, they are also prone to produce redundant solutions to the problem. The research [1] introduced a new chromosome for MTSP that works with classic GA TSP operators while dramatically reducing the number of redundant solutions in the solution space, thereby improving the efficiency of the search.

Different chromosome designs decide different magnitudes in terms of search spaces because they have distinct abilities to elude the redundant solutions to the problem. Furthermore, different solution spaces in magnitudes have important effects on the performance of search algorithms. The solution spaces of three different chromosome design methods are quantitatively compared and analyzed under the linear relation between cities n and salespersons m in this paper. The concept of relative solution space is introduced in order to compare the relative size of the solution spaces. The solution space of two-part chromosome design is much smaller than those of the traditional chromosome design.

The remainder of this paper is organized as follows. Three chromosome design methods used for MTSP are presented and contrasted in Section 2. The quantitative comparison analysis of the solution spaces corresponding to three different chromosome design methods is presented in Section 3. Finally, conclusions are reached in Section 4.

2 Three Chromosome Representations for MTSP

Three different chromosome designs are introduced in this section, which are commonly employed when solving MTSP using GAs. We also discussed their properties, weaknesses and advantages for solving MTSP.

2.1 One Chromosome Technique

The one chromosome technique [8] is illustrated as Fig.1 (where n = 15 and m = 4). In Fig. 1, the first salesperson would visit cities 2, 5, 14 and 6 (in that order). The second salesperson would visit cities 1, 11, 8 and 13 (in that order), and so on for the rest salespersons.

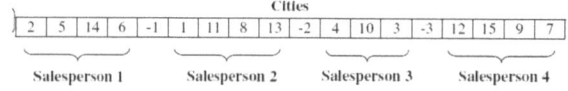

Fig. 1. One chromosome technique for MTSP with 4 salespersons and 15 cities

The n cities are represented by a permutation of the integers from 1 to n for this technique. This permutation is partitioned into m sub-tours by insertion of $m-1$

negative integers that represent the change from one salesperson to the next. Any permutation of these $(n+m-1)$ integers represents a possible solution to the problem. There are $(n+m-1)!$ possible solutions with this chromosome coding method to the problem. However, many of the possible chromosomes are redundant. For example, simply exchanging the values of the first five genes with those of the next five genes would produce an equivalent (redundant) solution.

2.2 Two Chromosome Technique

The two chromosome technique is illustrated as Fig.2 (where n = 15 and m = 4). The first chromosome is a permutation of the n cities and the second specifies one salesman to the city at the same place of the first chromosome [5]. Salesperson 2 visits cities 2, 8, 12 and 9 (in that order). Salesperson 1 visits cities 5, 14, 10 and 15 (in that order) and so on for the rest salespersons.

Cities

2	5	14	6	1	11	8	13	4	10	3	12	15	9	7

Salespersons

2	1	1	3	4	3	2	4	4	1	3	2	1	2	3

Fig. 2. Two chromosome technique for MTSP with 4 salespersons and 15 cities

There are $n!m^n$ possible solutions to the problem, where n is the number of cities and m is the number of salespersons for this technique. However, many of the possible solutions are redundant. For example, the first two genes in each of the above chromosomes can be interchanged to create different chromosomes that result in an identical (or redundant) solution.

2.3 Two-Part Chromosome Technique

The two-part chromosome technique is illustrated as Fig.3. Salesperson 1 visits cities 2, 5, 14 and 6 (in that order), salesperson 2 visits cities 1, 11, 8 and 13 (in that order), and so on for the rest salespersons. The first part of the chromosome is a permutation of integers from 1 to n, representing the n cities. The second part of the chromosome is of length m and represents the number of cities assigned to each of the m salespersons. The values assigned to the second part of the chromosome are constrained to be m positive integers that sum to the number of cities to be visited.

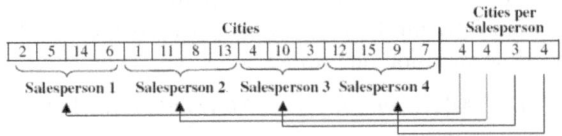

Fig. 3. Two-part chromosome technique for MTSP with 4 salespersons and 15 cities

The two-part chromosome method reduces the size of the search space ($n!C_{n-1}^{m-1}$) due to the elimination of some (but not all) redundant solutions. For example, cities assigned to salesperson 1 always appear first in the two-part chromosome followed by the cities assigned to the second salesperson. This was not the case in either of the previous two chromosomes, where cities for a given salesperson could appear in any relative position in the chromosome.

2.4 The Relative Solution Space Size for Different Chromosome Techniques

Carter and Ragsdale [1] gave the sizes of the solution spaces for each of the above chromosomes which are summarized below and also gave the proof that the solution space for the two-part chromosome is smaller than those of the other two techniques when $n > m \geq 1$. Three different solution space sizes are denoted as $C_{one} = (n+m-1)!$, $C_{two} = n!m^n$ and $C_{t-parrt} = n!C_{n-1}^{m-1}$. We have known that $C_{t-parrt} \leq C_{one} \leq C_{two}$ whenever $n > m \geq 1$ [1].

3 Quantitative Comparison Analysis on the Solution Spaces Corresponding to Three Different Chromosome Techniques

It is not enough if we know nothing more than their relative relation in sizes, which is a motive for the further quantitative research of this paper.

3.1 Relative Solution Space

The relative solution spaces (RSS) are defined according to the relative relation in their sizes, which are denoted as C_{31} and C_{32}. It is obvious that $0 < C_{31}, C_{32} < 1$.

$$C_{31} = \frac{C_{t-part}}{C_{one}} = \frac{n!C_{n-1}^{m-1}}{(m+n-1)!} \tag{1}$$

$$C_{32} = \frac{C_{t-part}}{C_{two}} = \frac{n!C_{n-1}^{m-1}}{n!m^n} \tag{2}$$

It is easy to see that RSS is a dualistic function with variables of n and m. The changing rules or some deterministic trends of RSS will be analyzed.

3.2 Preliminary Illustrating Analysis of RSS

The quotient operation of the factorial and combinatorial terms in Equations.(1,2) make the analysis very difficult. Firstly, *Mathematica* computing platform [9] is used to illustrate the possible variation rules of RSS through 3D graphics.

$Plot3D[C_{31}, \{m,1,100\}, \{n,m,100\}]$: $Plot3D[C_{32}, \{m,1,100\}, \{n,m,100\}]$

Observed from Fig.4 we can see that RSS decreases very fast and approaches to zero. C_{32} is much fast approaching to zero than C_{31}. When n and m are about 30, C_{32} is probably 10^{-37} and C_{31} is about 4×10^{-5}.

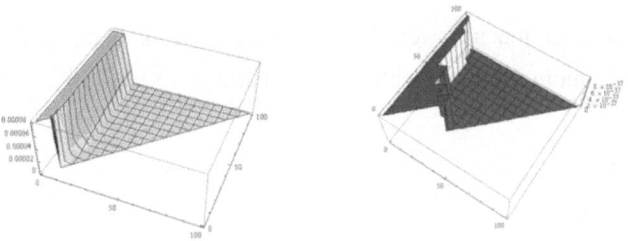

Fig. 4. 3D graphics of C_{31} (left) and C_{32} (right) with n and m

3.3 Preliminary Analysis When m Is Constant

When RSS is looked on as a dualistic function of n and m, it is very difficult to make an explicit analysis about RSS. Furthermore, n is varying from situations and m is constant in realistic problem. For example, the number of salespersons of an express corporation is usually steady during a period of time. Supposing m and n are large integers and m is constant, RSS is analyzed as follows.

$$C_{31} = \frac{C_{t-part}}{C_{one}} = \frac{n! C_{n-1}^{m-1}}{(m+n-1)!} \rightarrow \frac{1}{(m-1)!} \ (n \rightarrow +\infty) \tag{3}$$

$$C_{32} = \frac{C_{t-part}}{C_{two}} = \frac{n! C_{n-1}^{m-1}}{n! m^n} \text{ has no limit when } n \rightarrow \infty \tag{4}$$

$C_{31} \rightarrow \frac{1}{(m-1)!} \ (n \rightarrow +\infty)$ indicates that the relative solution space C_{31} is approaching to $\frac{1}{(m-1)!}$ with cities n is increasing if salesman m is constant. It can be seen that the solution space of two-part chromosome is $\frac{100}{(m-1)!}\%$ of that of one chromosome. C_{32} has no limit means that it depends on the number of salesman m rigorously. If we let m, besides n, approaches to infinity, it is easy to see that $C_{32} \rightarrow 0$, which is consistent to the qualitative analysis of [1].

3.4 Quantitative Comparison on the Solution Spaces with n=km

The above relative solution space analysis are simply given under the unitary condition of m<n. The possible relation of n and m are not considered which should have some inherent relevance in real world problem. For example, m will be mostly decided by n, if n stands for the possible delivery sites of a dairy industry and m is the number of hired mailing persons. Generally speaking, n is a linear function of m (n=km and k is constant) because every hired man is responsible for a somewhat equal number of delivery sites in this situation.

3.4.1 Illustrating RSS When n=km

RSS C_{31} and C_{32} are illustrated with n=2m and n=10m as Figs. 5-6.

Observed from Figs.6-9 we have two conclusions. The first is that both C_{31} and C_{32} approach to zero very fast if m is larger than 2. This indicates that solution space of two-part chromosome is much smaller than those of other two. The other is that C_{32}

approaches to zero much faster than C_{31} which shows that solution space C_{two} dominates C_{one} more and more with n (or m) increase.

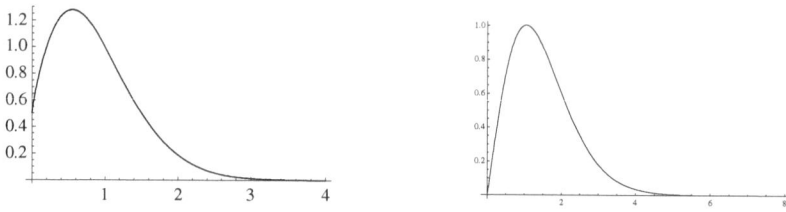

Fig. 5. Illustrating RSS C_{31} (left) and RSS C_{32} (right) when n=2m

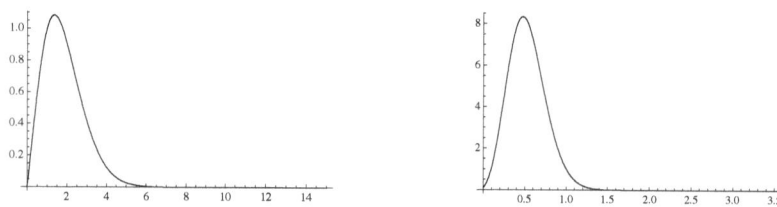

Fig. 6. Illustrating RSS C_{31} (left) and RSS C_{32} (right) when n=10m

3.4.2 Quantitative Comparison of the Solution Spaces When n=2m

Due to the analyzing difficulty of C_{31} and C_{32} for general case, the linear relation n=2m is considered for quantitative comparison of the solution spaces with *Stirling* formula and approximate analysis [10].

$$
C_{31} = \frac{C_{t-part}}{C_{one}} = \frac{n!\,C_{n-1}^{m-1}}{(m+n-1)!}
$$

$$
\sim \frac{\sqrt{2\pi n}\,(\frac{n}{e})^{n}\,\sqrt{2\pi(n-1)}\,(\frac{n-1}{e})^{n-1}}{\sqrt{2\pi(n+m-1)}\,(\frac{n+m-1}{e})^{n+m-1}} \cdot \frac{1}{\sqrt{2\pi(m-1)}\,(\frac{m-1}{e})^{m-1}\,\sqrt{2\pi(n-m)}\,(\frac{n-m}{e})^{n-m}}
$$

$$
= \sqrt{\frac{m(m-1)}{\pi(3m-1)(m-1)m}} \cdot \frac{m^{2m}\,(m-\frac{1}{2})^{2m-1}}{(m-\frac{1}{3})^{3m-1}\,(m-1)^{m-1}\,m^{m}} \cdot \frac{2^{4m-1}\,e^{5m-2}}{3^{3m-1}} \tag{5}
$$

When m is adequately large, the first, second and third part of (5) can be approximated to $\sqrt{\frac{2}{3\pi m}}$, $(\frac{1}{m})^{m-1}$ and $\frac{3}{2e^{2}}(\frac{16e^{5}}{27})^{m}$ respectively. Furthermore, the approaching speed to zero of C_{31} mainly lies on the second part. We hold on to dominating term and ignore the secondary parts, then we obtain that $C_{31} \sim (\frac{1}{m})^{m}$. The other form of the conclusion is rewritten as

$$
C_{one} \sim C_{t-parrt} \cdot O(m^{m}) \tag{6}
$$

Similarly, we have
$$
C_{two} \sim C_{t-parrt} \cdot O(m^{2m}) \tag{7}
$$

It is easy to conclude that the above quantitative analysis comparison of the solution spaces is consistent with the qualitative analysis of [1] and even more accurate than that of reference [1].

4 Conclusion

As we know that different chromosome coding techniques for MTSP result in different solution space sizes. Of course, different space sizes have definitive impacts on the search algorithms. [1] only gave the order in magnitudes for three solution spaces. The quantitative analysis and comparison on the solution spaces are illustrated and analyzed in this paper based on *Stirling* formula and approximate analysis.

Acknowledgments. This research is supported by the "Keynote Fostering Project of Management Science and Engineering of the University of International Business and Economics, Beijing, China".

References

[1] Carter, A.E., Ragsdale, C.T.: A new approach to solving the multiple traveling salesperson problem using genetic algorithms. European Journal of Operational Research 175, 246–257 (2006)

[2] Pinedo, M.L.: Scheduling: theory, algorithms, and systems, 3rd edn. Springer, Heidelberg (2008)

[3] Carter, A.E., Ragsdale, C.T.: Scheduling pre-printed newspaper advertising inserts using genetic algorithms. Omega 30(6), 415–421 (2002)

[4] Bunte, S., Kliewer, N.: An overview on vehicle scheduling models. Public Transport 1(4), 299–317 (2010)

[5] Park, Y.B.: A hybrid genetic algorithm for the vehicle scheduling problem with due times and time deadlines. International Journal of Productions Economics 73(2), 175–188 (2001)

[6] Michalewicz, Z., Fogel, D.B.: How to solve it: Modern heuristics. Springer, Heidelberg (2000)

[7] De Jong, K.A.: Evolutionary Computation-A unified approach. The MIT Press, Cambridge (2006)

[8] Tang, L., Liu, J., Rong, A., Yang, Z.: A multiple traveling salesman problem model for hot rolling schedule in Shanghai Baoshan Iron and Steel Complex. European Journal of Operational Research 124(2), 267–282 (2002)

[9] Xu, A.: Mathematica and mathematical experiments, Publishing House of Electronics Industry, Beijing (2004)

[10] Zhang, Z.S.: Mathematical analysis. Peking University Press (1990)

Hybrid Artificial Fish Swarm Algorithm for Solving Ill-Conditioned Linear Systems of Equations

Yongquan Zhou, Huajuan Huang, and Junli Zhang

College of Mathematics and Computer Science Guangxi University for Nationalities
Nanning, Guangxi 530006, China
yongquanzhou@126.com

Abstract. Based on particle swarm optimization (PSO) and artificial fish swarm algorithm (AFSA), this paper proposes a hybrid artificial fish swarm algorithm (HAFSA). The method makes full use of the fast local convergence performance of PSO and the global convergence performance of AFSA, and then is used for solving ill-conditioned linear systems of equations. Finally, the numerical experiment results show that hybrid artificial fish swarm algorithm owns a better global convergence performance with a faster convergence rate. It is a new way to solve ill-conditioned linear systems of equations.

Keywords: Particle swarm optimization, hybrid artificial fish swarm Algorithm, ill-conditioned linear systems of equations.

1 Introduction

In survey data processing, model parameter estimation, engineering design fields and many other areas, numerical calculations often involve the problems of solving linear systems of equations. However, as a result of the existence of model error, measurement error, calculation error and other errors, the true theoretical solution of linear systems of equations is usually difficult to obtain [1]. If a smaller disturbance of the original data or the presence of errors can lead to greatly changing the solution of linear systems of equations, such systems of equations are called ill-conditioned linear systems of equations [2]. For such systems of equations, the direct method and the iterative approach that are commonly used often fail to solve them. At present, the commonly used methods to solve ill-conditioned linear systems of equations are singular value decomposition (SVD) and conjugate gradient method in the iterative approach. But both methods have a few limitations: conjugate gradient method has difficulty in determining the best number of iterations, whereas SVD method is sensitive to the truncated position of singular value. Therefore, it is very necessary to find other effective algorithms for solving ill-conditioned linear systems of equations.

In 2002, artificial fish swarm algorithm (AFSA) is by Li Xiao-lei proposed [3]. So far AFSA has been applied to many fields such as artificial neural network, pattern recognition, parameter estimation, distinguish method and so on. The study found that AFSA owns a good global search capability, but it owns slower velocity of convergence. This paper takes particle swarm optimization (PSO)[4] as a local search operator and embeds it into AFSA, and proposes a hybrid artificial fish swarm

R. Chen (Ed.): ICICIS 2011, Part I, CCIS 134, pp. 656–661, 2011.

algorithm (HAFSA) based on PSO, which use the proposed HAFSA to solve ill-conditioned linear systems of equations. Numerical experiments show that the proposed algorithm can obtain more accurate solution.

2   Definition of Ill-Conditioned System of Equations

Definition 2.1[5]: Let A be nonsingular square matrix, $\| A \| \bullet \| A^{-1} \|$ is called the condition number of A and is written as $cond(A)$, that is, $cond(A) = \| A \| \bullet \| A^{-1} \|$.

Definition 2.2[5]: Let A be nonsingular square matrix, if $cond(A) > 1$, $Ax = b$ is said to be ill-conditioned system of equations; If $cond(A)$ is more close to 1, $Ax = b$ is said to be well-conditioned system of equations.

3   Hybrid Artificial Fish Swarm Algorithm (HAFSA)

3.1   The Basic AFSA

Artificial fish swarm algorithm (AFSA) is a stochastic optimization algorithm based on swarm intelligence, which has a good global search capability and is not sensitive to the initial value and parameter selection. It is simple, easy to implement and owns good robustness. The mathematical model is described as follows:

Assume that N artificial fishes are initially randomly deployed in the objective function space R^m, $X = (x_1, x_2, \cdots x_n)$ represents the state of each artificial fish (AF), where x_i ($i = 1, \ldots, n$) is the optimal variable. $Y = f(X)$ expresses food concentration of the current location of the AF, where Y represents the objective function. $d_{i,j} = \| X_i - X_j \|$ denotes the distance between the AF i and j, *visual* and δ represent the visual distance and crowd factor of the AF respectively, *step* and *trynumber* express the step of the AF moving and the maximum number of the AF attempts respectively.

3.1.1   Behavior Description

In each iteration, the artificial fishes update themselves mainly though AF-Prey, AF-Swarm and AF-Follow. The specific behaviors of the AF are expressed as follows:

(1) **Random Behavior:** Random behavior is that the AF moves at random within the *visual*. When the AF finds food, it will move quickly toward the direction with the food increasing gradually.

(2) **AF-Prey:** AF-Prey is a kind of behavior that the fishes move toward the direction with more food. That is to say, the AF X_i selects randomly a state X_j

within the *visual* , and then their objective function values are calculated respectively. If Y_j is better than Y_i, X_i moves a step toward X_j, or else X_i will continue to move randomly and select a state X_j within the *visual* . If the advance condition is not satisfied after *trynumber* attempts, X_i will move randomly and get a new state.

(3) **AF-Swarm:** AF-Swarm is a kind of optimization behavior that each AF moves toward the center of the nearby partners as much as possible and avoids overcrowding in the moving process. The AF X_i searches the number of its fellows and the central position of its fellows within the *visual* , if the central position is better and the fishes around it are not too crowded, the AF X_i will move a step toward the central position, or else AF-Prey is carried out.

(4) **AF-Follow:** AF-Follow is a kind of behavior that the fishes move toward the optimal direction within the *visual* . That is to say, the AF X_i searches the partner with the best function value within it's *visual* , if the fishes around the best partner are not too crowded, the AF X_i will move a step towards the best partner, or else AF-Prey is executed.

(5) **Bulletin Board:** Bulletin board is used to record the state of the optimal AF. At the end of each iteration, the current state of the AF will be compared with the state on the bulletin board, if the current state of the AF is better, the state on the bulletin board will be updated by the current state of the AF, or else the state on the bulletin board will not be updated. After the end of the iterations of the entire algorithm, the state on the bulletin board is outputted, that is to say the optimal value is found.

3.1.2 Behavior Choices

According to the character of the problem to be solved, each AF evaluates the current environment, and then selects an appropriate behavior to perform. For example, if the problem is solving $\max f(x)$, AF-Swarm is firstly simulated, and secondly AF-Follow is simulated, then the states after the movement are evaluated, the better behavior of improving its state will be executed, the default behavior is AF-Prey. Finally, a lot of the artificial fishes gather around a few local extreme values, which is helpful to obtain the global extreme value. What's more, a lot of the artificial fishes gather around the better local extreme value, which is useful to get the global optimal value, so as to achieve the purpose of our optimization.

3.2 PSO

Particle swarm optimization (PSO) is an evolutionary computation technique that simulates migration and gather of a flock of birds searching for food. It describes the interaction behaviors among the particles that fly with a certain speed in the n -dimensional search space. In PSO, the velocity and the position of each particle are dynamically adjusted according to its own flying experience as well as the experience of neighboring particles. The motion states of particles are expressed as follows:

$$v_i(k+1) = wv_i(k) + c_1 rand()(pbest - x_i(k)) + c_2 rand()(gbest - x_i(k))$$
$$x_i(k+1) = x_i(k+1) + v_i(k+1)$$

Where $x_i(k) = (x_{i1}, x_{i2}, \cdots, x_{iD})$ represents the current position of the i-th particle, $v_i(k) = (v_{i1}, v_{i2}, \cdots, v_{iD})$ expresses the current velocity of the i-th particle, w is called the inertia factor, $rand()$ is a random number uniformly distributed in the interval $[0,1]$, c_1 and c_2 are two positive constants called acceleration coefficients, $pbest$ denotes the best historical position that the i-th particle has passed, $gbest$ denotes the best historical position that the entire swarm has passed.

3.3 The HAFSA

The procedure of the AFSA algorithm can be described as follows:

Step 1. Initialization. Initialize population size N, the visual distance $visual$, crowd factor δ, the step $step$ of the AF moving, the maximum number $trynumber$ of the AF attempts, acceleration coefficients c_1 and c_2, the inertia factor w, the probability p of local search, the maximum number K_t of iterations of PSO. Randomly initialize the positions of N artificial fishes in the search space.

Step 2. Bulletin board initialization. Calculate the fitness value of each AF, initialize bulletin board using the position and the fitness value of the AF with the best fitness value.

Step 3. Behavior choices. For each AF, AF-Follow and AF-Swarm are simulated respectively, the better behavior of improving its state will be executed, and the default behavior is AF-Prey.

Step 4. Update bulletin board. After each AF completes an iteration, its current fitness value will be compared with the fitness value on the bulletin board, if it is better than the fitness value on the bulletin board, the position and the fitness value on the bulletin board will be updated by the current position and fitness value of the AF, otherwise the position and fitness value on the bulletin board will not be updated.

Step 5. Implement PSO. If the random number $r \in (0,1)$ is less than p, where $p \in (0,1)$ is a given probability of local search, $N/2$ better artificial fishes will be selected as initial population of PSO, and then PSO is executed for them, that is, AFSA is thinned locally.

Step 6. Update bulletin board. After implementing PSO for $N/2$ better artificial fishes, these artificial fishes are evaluated respectively. If the current fitness value of the AF is better than the fitness value on the bulletin board, the position and the fitness value on the bulletin board will be updated by the current position and fitness value of the AF, otherwise the position and fitness value on the bulletin board will not be updated.

Step 7. Judge terminal condition. Repeat Step 3 ~ Step5 until the fitness value on the bulletin board satisfies error bound.

Step 8. The algorithm terminates. Output the optimal solution and the optimal value, that is the position and the fitness value of the AF on the bulletin board.

4 Numerical Simulations Results

In order to investigate the performances of the proposed HAFSA, the following three typical problems are used. For each test problem, the parameters of HAFSA are set as follows: population size N =50, the visual distance $visual$ =0.8, the step of the AF moving $step$ =0.3, crowd factor δ =1.5, the maximum number of the AF attempts $trynumber$ =6, the probability of local search p =0.25, the maximum number of iterations of PSO K_t =20, acceleration coefficients c_1 =2.0, c_2 =2.0, the inertia factor w =0.1. The proposed HAFSA is coded in MATLAB 7.0 and implemented on 1.8GHz PIV PC with 256MB RAM. Each experiment is independently executed 20 times. The mean function value and the average number of iterations out of 20 runs are regarded as measures and compared with the results obtained by the other methods. Comparative results are as follows:

Example 1[6]: Solve ill-conditioned linear system of equations

$$A \cdot x = b \text{, where } A = \begin{bmatrix} 1 & 0.99 \\ 0.99 & 0.98 \end{bmatrix}, b = \begin{bmatrix} 1 \\ 1 \end{bmatrix}$$

The exact solution of systems of equations is x_1 =100, x_2 =-100, simulation results and comparisons are listed in Table 1.

Table 1. Statistical results of different methods for Example 1

Methods	x_1	x_2	Iterations	Time (s)
HAFSA	100	-100	45	2.979
AFSA	100	-100	220	14.265
Zhang[6]	100.0348	-99.9788	—	—

From Table 1, it can be obviously found that the best solutions obtained by HAFSA and AFSA are both the exact solution, they are superior to the result reported in [6].

Example 2[7]. Solve seriously ill-conditioned linear system of equations $H \cdot x = b$ that consists of the Hilbert coefficient matrix, where

$$h_{i,j} = \frac{1}{i+j-1} \text{ , } (i, j = 1, 2, 3, 4, 5) \text{ , } b_i = \sum_{j=1}^{5} h_{i,j} \cdot j$$

This is a typically seriously ill-conditioned linear systems of equations, its exact solution is x_1 =1, x_2 =2, x_3 =3, x_4 =4, x_5 =5, simulation results and comparisons are shown in Table 2.

Table 2. Statistical results of different methods for Example 2

Methods	x_1	x_2	x_3	x_4	x_5	Iterations	Time(s)
HAFSA	1.0005	1.9993	2.9775	4.0597	4.9615	145	12.7
AFSA	1.0011	1.9854	3.0454	3.9499	5.0176	295	21.91
CSM[7]	0.9994	2.0108	2.9511	4.0758	4.9621	15852	—

From Table 2, it is observed that the best solution obtained by HAFSA is better than the results obtained by the other methods. Besides, iterations and time of HAFSA are also less than those of the other methods.

5 Conclusions

AFSA is a novel swarm intelligence algorithm and has the better global search capability, but its local convergence speed is slower. PSO is easy to implement and its local convergence speed is faster, but it is easily premature. In view of their advantages and disadvantages, this paper attempts to combine these two algorithms and proposes a hybrid artificial fish swarm algorithm. The proposed HAFSA is applied to solving ill-conditioned linear systems of equations. Numerical simulations show compared with the basic AFSA, the proposed algorithm not only owns faster convergence efficiency but also can obtain more precise solutions.

Acknowledgements

This work is supported by Grants 0991086 from Guangxi Science Foundation.

References

1. Chen, N.: A neural-network algorithm for solving the singular linear systems. Journal of Natural Science of Hunan Normal University 30(3), 38–41 (2007)
2. Zhang, W.: Memory gradient algorithm for solving ill-conditioned linear systems. Journal of Shanghai Maritime University 25(3), 94–96 (2004)
3. Li, X.-l., Shao, Z.-j., Qian, J.-x.: An optimizing method based on autonomous animats: Fish-swarm algorithm. Systems Engineering and Theory and Practice 22(11), 32–38 (2002)
4. Kennedy, J., Eberhart, R.C.: Particle swarm optimization. In: Proceedings of the IEEE International Conference on Neural Networks Perth, pp. 1942–1948. IEEE Press, Australia (1995)
5. Zhu, F., Li, D., Li, S.: Computational Methods, pp. 80–83. Wuhan University Press, Wuhan (2003)
6. Zhang, Y., Zhang, P., Zhang, C.: An exact method for solving the ill-conditioned simultaneous equations. Journal of Harbin Institute of Technology 27(6), 26–28 (1995)
7. Zou, J., Qian, J.: Composite structure method for ill-conditioned linear equations. Journal of Tsinghua University (Science and Technology) 41(4), 231–234 (2001)

A Survey on Social Image Mining

Zheng Liu[1,2]

[1] School of Computer Science and Technology, Shandong Economic University,
Ji'nan 250014, China
[2] Shandong Provincial Key Laboratory of Digital Media Technology, Ji'nan 250014, China
Lzh_48@126.com

Abstract. With the rapid development of Web2.0 technology, we have witnessed great interest and promise in social image mining as a hot research field. Discovering and summarizing knowledge from these multimedia data enables us to mine useful information from the real world. In this paper, the approaches of three kinds of information mined from social images are reviewed: geographic information, hot events of the society and information about personal photo collections. Several key theoretical and empirical contributions in the current decade related to social image mining are discussed. Based on the analysis of what has been achieved in recent years, we believe that social image mining will be paid more and more attentions in the near future.

Keywords: Social Image, Web 2.0, Landmark, Hot Events, Personal Photo Collections.

1 Introduction

Recent years have witnessed the prosperity of social media and the success of many social websites, such as Flickr, Youtube etc. These websites allow users not only to create and share media data but also to comment and annotate them. On the one hand, the rapid increase of social media websites makes many related applications useful, such as categorization, recommendation and searching. The rich metadata in these websites also offer us opportunities to tackle the problems encountered in multimedia analysis and understanding. In this paper, the methods of three kinds of information mining are discussed: geographic information, hot events of the society and information about personal photo collections.

The rest of the paper is organized as follows. Section 2 introduces some related works about geographic information mining. Section 3 presents some pioneering works in hot events mining in recent years. In section 4, we survey the works in personal photo collections mining. In Section 5, we conclude the whole paper.

2 Geographic Information Mining

Geographical information is often represented in the form of a longitude-latitude pair in order to represent the locations where the photos are taken. In recent years, the use

R. Chen (Ed.): ICICIS 2011, Part I, CCIS 134, pp. 662–667, 2011.

of geographical information has become more and more popular. With developments in low-cost GPS chips, many cell phones and digital cameras have been equipped with GPS receivers, and then are able to record the locations when taking photos. The recent works about geographic information mining are as follows.

Gao et al.[1] present a travel guidance system named W2Go, which can automatically recognize and rank the landmarks for travelers. In this paper, a novel Automatic Landmark Ranking (ALR) method is proposed by utilizing the tag and geo-tag information of photos in Flickr and travelling information from Yahoo Travel Guide. W2Go adopts geo-tags to locate the positions where the photo was taken, and computes the probability of a tag to be a landmark. Then, the candidate landmarks are ranked by combining the frequency of tags, user numbers in Flickr, and user knowledge in Yahoo Travel Guide. R. Abbasi et al. [2] proposed a method to identify landmark photos using tags and social Flickr groups without depending on GPS coordinates for these photos. The information they used only are Flickr tags and user groups information. They apply a SVM classifier for which the training data is extracted from Flickr groups to find relevant landmark-related tags.

In paper [3], the authors concentrated on the way to organize a large-scale geo-tagged photos, working with 35 million photos downloaded from Flickr. The proposed approach combines content analysis based on text tags and image data with structural analysis based on geospatial data, and use the spatial distribution of where people take photos to define a relational structure between the photos taken at popular places. The authors also developed classification methods for predicting locations from visual, textual and temporal features. These methods illustrate that both visual and temporal features improve the ability to estimate the location of a photo compared to using only textual tags.

L. S. Kennedy et al. [4] used both context- and content-based methods to generate representative sets of images for location-driven features and landmarks. They use location and other metadata, such as tags associated with images, and the images' visual features to solve this problem. They present an approach to extract tags which could represent landmarks.

In paper [5], K. Yanai et al. described two approaches to analyze the relationship between words and geographical locations by a large scale geo-tagged images on Flickr. They use image region entropy and geo-location entropy to describe relations between location and image visual features. From experimental results, the authors showed that low image entropy concepts may have high geo-location entropy. Afterwards, they propose a novel method to choose representative photos for specific regions around the world, by which the users could automatic find cultural differences for a given concepts.

In a recent research work [6], Zheng et al. worked on the landmark recognition. They built a web-scale landmark recognition engine exploiting 20 million GPS-tagged photos of landmarks together with online tour guide systems. Experimental results show that the engine can achieve high recognition performance efficiently. The authors believe that recognizing non-landmark locations accurately is still a hard problem for us to tackle.

Adrian Popescu et al. [7] developed a system named MonuAnno which automatic annotate geo-referenced landmarks images. The proposed system exploits both image localization information and image visual content analysis. The annotation is obtained by a two steps k-NN algorithm. Firstly, only neighboring landmarks of a new unannotated geo-tagged image will be recognized as candidate annotations. Second, the authors introduce a verification step to prune false ones in candidate annotations.

In paper [8], the authors presented a prototype system which can automatically generate landmarks using pedestrian navigation directions from geo-tagged photos. Both navigation images selecting and images with directional instructions enhancing are executed automatically. This work also shows a clear direction for further research fields for landmark-based navigation systems.

W. Chen et al. [9] present a novel data-driven approach which depends on online photos sharing websites, e.g. Flickr, for automatically generating tourist maps. The proposed algorithm uses the geographical areas as input and then finds geo-tagged photos from online photo collections. The algorithm generates a set of points of interest (POIs) for the area by clustering the photos based on their locations and identifying the popular tags for each cluster. After retrieving additional photos based on these discovered POI tags, the authors use image matching to find the most representative landmark images.

3   Hot Events Mining

Detecting events from Web has attracted increasing research interests in recent years. It is a great opportunity for us to mining hot events from social images. The related works have been done are listed as follows.

In [10], the authors exploited satellite images corresponding to photo location data and investigate their novel applications to recognize the photo-taking environment. The satellite information are then combined with classical visually event detection approaches. They employed both color and structure-based visual vocabularies to characterize ground and satellite images respectively. Combining both photo and satellite could obtain great performance enhance compared to the ground view methods.

M. Cooper et al. [11] present several variants of an automatic unsupervised algorithm to partition a photo collection by temporal similarity alone, or temporal and content-based similarity together. The main steps of this paper are as follows. First, inter-photo similarity is quantified at multiple temporal scales to identify likely event clusters. Second, the final clusters are obtained according to one of three clustering goodness criteria and the clustering criteria trade off time complexity and system performance.

T. Rattenbury et al. [12] applied each tag's usage patterns to extract semantics of tags, unstructured text-labels assigned to resources on the Web. They mainly concentrate on the problem of extracting place and event information from tags which are provided by Flickr users.

Chen et al. [13] exploited the rich metadata of Flickr photos to automatically detect events. Specifically, they use the user-defined tags to obtain the content of photos and rely on the metadata of time and location to analyze the distribution of photos through tags. The authors try to tackle this problem by using different methods, such as simultaneously considering time and location dimensions and performing wavelet transform. Then, a timeline array is used to efficiently map tags to either periodic or aperiodic events.

4   Personal Photo Collections Mining

In the recent years, the increasing popularity of digital cameras, cell phones and other digital devices has resulted in prosperity of personal photo collection which is usually located on storage devices or on the Web. Millions of new personal photos are uploaded to Flickr every month. With such large amount of personal photo collection, It is hard for users to browse photo collection or search for photos. Therefore, it is of great importance to discover useful information from photo collections. Unlike isolated photos, the photos in a collection have rich metadata, such as user-defined tags, user comments, GPS coordinate and the time when the photo is taken. There are several works about personal photo collections mining in the recent years.

Recent work by Wu et al. [14] applied human face clustering technology to find social relationships from personal photo collections. Co-occurrence of identified faces as well as inter-face distances which are inferred from in-image distance and typical human face size are used to compute link strength between any two identified persons. Therefore, social clusters as well as social importance of individuals can be calculated.

Tang et al. [15] proposed a novel approach combining time, color, and local structural information in a cascade framework so that computation complexity could be reduced. Time clustering is often used with image visual similarity. In this work, time information can be used to reduce the computation load if the photos are limited in a certain time interval.

M. Naaman et al. [16] described the contextual metadata which is related to a photo, given time and location, as well as a browser interface that utilizes that metadata. Then, they present the results of a user study and a survey that together expose which categories of contextual metadata are most useful for recalling and finding photos.

Cao et al [17] used conditional random fields to describe relationships of different photos in a sub-collection to annotate photos by scene category and also annotate sub-collections by event category. This work made full use of the inherent event based organization and strong inter-photo correlations that are characteristic of personal collections to improve image collection annotation. Furthermore, Cao et al. [18] proposed another approach to model the photo correlations using both visual similarity and the temporal coherence, and construct a framework for label propagation. In this work, high-confidence annotation labels are first obtained for certain photos and then propagated to the remaining photos in the same collection, according to time, location, and visual similarity.

Quack et al. [19] developed a system for linking photos to relevant Wikipedia articles. Their approach mainly relies on retrieving geo-tagged photos from those websites using a grid of geospatial tiles. The downloaded photos are clustered into potentially interesting entities through a processing pipeline of several modalities, including visual, textual and spatial proximity. The resulting clusters are analyzed and are automatically classified into objects and events. Using mining techniques, they then find text labels for these clusters, which are used to arrange each cluster to a corresponding Wikipedia article in a fully unsupervised manner. A final verification step uses the contents from the selected Wikipedia article to verify the cluster-article assignment.

5 Discussion and Conclusions

Due to the rapid advancement of digital technology in the last few years, there has been an increasingly large amount of images available on the Web. With the recent spreading of Web 2.0 sites, more and more individual users began to upload photos taken by themselves to image community websites. Therefore, it is of great importance to mine useful information from social images. In this survey, we have summarized the existing approaches to mining three kinds of information from social images. From above, we strongly believe that, in the near future, this research field will be paid more and more attentions by the researchers and will promote the fundamental theories research in the related fields.

Acknowledgements

This work is supported by the National Natural Science Foundation of China (Grant No.60970048), Research Foundation of Shandong Economic University ("Research on Key Problems of Automatic Image Annotation", 2008), and Project of Shandong Province Higher Educational Science and Technology Program (Grant No.J10LG69).

References

1. Gao, Y., Tang, J., Hong, R., Dai, Q., Chua, T.-S., Jain, R.: W2Go: A Travel Guidance System by Automatic Landmark Ranking. In: Proceedings of the seventeen ACM international conference on Multimedia, MM (2010)
2. Abbasi, R., Chernov, S., Nejd, W., Paiu, R., Staab, S.: Exploiting flickr tags and groups for finding landmark photos. In: Boughanem, M., Berrut, C., Mothe, J., Soule-Dupuy, C. (eds.) ECIR 2009. LNCS, vol. 5478, pp. 654–661. Springer, Heidelberg (2009)
3. Crandall, D.J., Backstrom, L., Huttenlocher, D., Kleinberg, J.: Mapping the world's photos. In: WWW 2009 (2009)
4. Kennedy, L., Naaman, M.: Generating diverse and representative image search results for landmarks. In: WWW 2008 (2008)
5. Yanai, K., Kawakubo, H., Qiu, B.: A visual analysis of the relationship between word concepts and geographical locations. In: CIVR 2009 (2009)
6. Zheng, Y., Zhao, M., Song, Y., Adam, H., Buddemeier, U., Bissacco, A., Brucher, F., Chua, T., Neven, H.: Tour the world: building a web-scale landmark recogntion engine. In: CVPR 2009 (2009)
7. Popescu, A., Moëllic, P.-A.: MonuAnno: Automatic Annotation of Georeferenced Landmarks Images. In: CIVR 2009, Santorini, Greece, July 8-10 (2009)
8. Hile, H., Vedantham, R., Liu, A., Gelfand, N., Cuellar, G., Grzeszczuk, R., Borriello, G.: Landmark-Based Pedestrian Navigation from Collections of Geotagged Photos. In: Proceedings of ACM International Conferenceerence on Mobile and Ubiquitous Multimedia, MUM 2008. ACM Press, New York (2008)
9. Chen, W., Battestini, A., Gelfand, N., Setlur, V.: Visual summaries of popular landmarks from community photo collections. In: ACM International Conference on Multimedia, pp. 789–792 (2009)

10. Luo, J., Yu, J., Joshi, D., Hao, W.: Event recognition: viewing the world with a third eye. In: ACM International Conference on Multimedia, pp. 1071–1080 (2008)
11. Cooper, M., Foote, J., Girgensohn, A., Wilcox, L.: Temporal event clustering for digital photo collections. ACM Transactions on Multimedia Computing, Communications, and Applications 1(3), 269–288 (2005)
12. Rattenbury, T., Good, N., Naaman, M.: Towards automatic extraction of event and place semantics from flickr tags. In: SIGIR (2007)
13. Chen, L., Roy, A.: Event Detection from Flickr Data through Wavelet-based Spatial Analysis. In: CIKM 2009, Hong Kong, China, November 2-6, pp. 523–532 (2009)
14. Wu, P., Tretter, D.: Close & Closer: Social Cluster and Closeness from Photo Collections. In: Proceedings of the 17th ACM international conference on Multimedia. ACM Press, New York (2009)
15. Tang, F., Gao, Y.: Fast Near Duplicate Detection for Personal Image Collections. In: Proceedings of the 17th ACM international conference on Multimedia. ACM Press, New York (2009)
16. Naaman, M., Harada, S., Wang, Q.: Context Data in Geo-Referenced Digital Photo Collections. In: Proceedings of the 12th ACM International Conference on Multimedia, pp. 196–203. ACM Press, New York (2004)
17. Cao, L., Luo, J., Kautz, H., Huang, T.S.: Annotating Collections of Photos Using Hierarchical Event and Scene Models. In: IEEE Proceedings Computer Vision and Pattern Recognition (2008)
18. Cao, L., Luo, J., Huang, T.: Annotating photo collections by label propagation according to multiple similarity cues. In: ACM Conference on Multimedia (2008)
19. Quack, T., Leibe, B., Gool, L.V.: World-scale mining of objects and events from community photo collections. In: Proc. of Conf. on Content-based Image and Video Retrieval, New York, NY, USA, pp. 47–56 (2008)

Binocular Vision-Based Position and Pose of Hand Detection and Tracking in Space

Chen Jun, Hou Wenjun, and Sheng Qing

Beijing University of Posts and Telecommunications, Automation School
100876 Beijing PRC
Rockychen09@gmail.com

Abstract. After the study of image segmentation, CamShift target tracking algorithm and stereo vision model of space, an improved algorithm based of Frames Difference and a new space point positioning model were proposed, a binocular visual motion tracking system was constructed to verify the improved algorithm and the new model. The problem of the spatial location and pose of the hand detection and tracking have been solved.

Keywords: Frames Difference, Camshift algorithm, Space Point Positioning Model.

1 Introduction

Computer Vision is one of the most popular research topics in Artificial Intelligence, and target tracking and stereo vision is the core content of Computer Vision. Stereo vision is the use of two cameras simulate human visual features from images or image sequences extract information, to recognize three-dimensional features of the objective world and the objects shape and motion[1] .

Currently, the study of stereo vision tracking system is very popular, but most are limited to the space object position detection and motion tracking, lack of object pose detection, especially soft objects. In order to solve this problem, an improved Frames Difference algorithm and Space Point Positioning Model were proposed in this paper, a real-time spatial location and pose detection and tracking system was constructed.

2 Moving Target Detection and Tracking

2.1 Image Segmentation

Frames Difference is a commonly used method of image segmentation, low sensitivity to light changes, simple to meet the real-time requirements, but also has its drawbacks: some of the adjacent frames overlap there will be empty (see in Figure 1), the image will be divided into several separate parts, cannot extract the object of continuous information. Frames Difference was improved in this paper, first of all, obtain the

R. Chen (Ed.): ICICIS 2011, Part I, CCIS 134, pp. 668–675, 2011.

information of the contours in frame difference[2], second, calculate the centers of these small comtours, then calculate the center of these centers, at last, use a rectangular block to fill the empty positions (shown in Fig 2.).The improved frames difference method can effectively solve the hollow portion adjacent frames overlap problem.

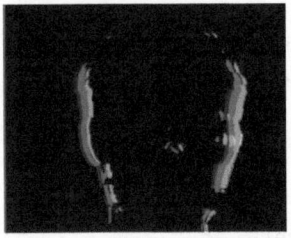

Fig. 1.   **Fig. 2.**

2.2 CamShift Moving Target Tracking

CamShift motion tracking method is the improvement of MeanShift algorithm, the basic principle is to track the color information of the target as the characteristics, these calculated information projected onto to the next frame, with the site image as a new source of maps of the next frame, you can repeat this process to achieve continuous tracking of targets [3] [4], because the color matched CamShift algorithm is found by moving objects in motion the process of target motion, little change in the color information, so Camshift algorithm has good robustness.

In this paper pre-extraction of color information of the hand in building manpower color histogram, the whole window as the initial search window, the CamShift has changed from a semi-automatic algorithm for tracking algorithm to an automatic algorithm.

MinShift algorithm is the core of CamShift, the process is as follows:

1)   Select the window size and initial position

2)   Calculate the centroid coordinate of the region

Zero-Order moment of the region : $M_{00} = \sum_{x=1}^{m} \sum_{y=1}^{n} I(x, y)$

First moment of the region :

$$M_{10} = \sum_{x=1}^{m} \sum_{y=1}^{n} xI(x, y) \quad M_{01} = \sum_{x=1}^{m} \sum_{y=1}^{n} yI(x, y)$$

Centroid coordinates of the region : $\left(x_c, y_c\right) = \left[\dfrac{M_{10}}{M_{00}}, \dfrac{M_{01}}{M_{00}}\right]$

3)   To adjust the center of the window to this centroid

4)   Repeat steps 2 and 3 until convergence center of the window

the calculation of the direction of regional principal axes:

the second moment for the region of hand :

$$M_{20} = \sum_{x=1}^{m} \sum_{y=1}^{n} x^2 I(x, y) \quad M_{02} = \sum_{x=1}^{m} \sum_{y=1}^{n} y^2 I(x, y)$$

Axis direction of the region : $\theta = \dfrac{\arctan\left[\dfrac{2\left[\dfrac{M_{11}}{M_{00}} - x_c y_c\right]}{\left[\dfrac{M_{20}}{M_{00}} - x_c^2\right] - \left[\dfrac{M_{02}}{M_{00}} - y_c^2\right]}\right]}{2}$

2.3 Staff Position and Pose Detection in Space

2.3.1 Triangulation

To test the staff's position in space, the usual method is to use two main axis parallel to the camera, using the triangle rule to strike [5]. Figure (3) is a non-dimensional distortion correction of the camera coordinate system, the image pixel coordinate system is based on the upper left corner of the origin, the two plane alignment, the camera coordinate system to the left of the camera projection center as the origin.

In figure (3), the main axis intersection with the image plane is (c_x, c_y), point P in the image plane coordinates are $(p_{x1}, p_{y1})(p_{x2}, p_{y2})$, the distance between the camera main axis is T, focal length is f.

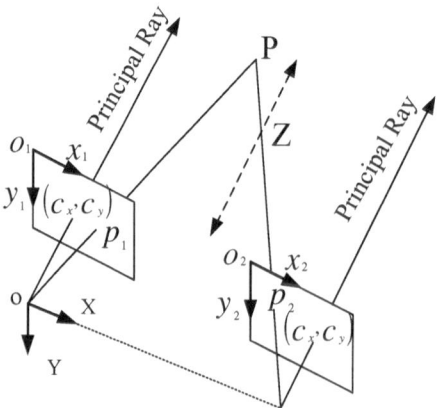

Fig. 3.

The position of point $P(X, Y, Z)$ in the camera coordinate system coordinate can be calculated using similar triangles as follows:

$$\frac{T-(p_{x1}-p_{x2})}{Z-f} = \frac{T}{Z} \Rightarrow Z = \frac{fT}{(p_{x1}-p_{x2})} \tag{2-1}$$

$$\frac{(p_{x1}-c_x)}{X} = \frac{f}{Z} \Rightarrow X = \frac{T(p_{x1}-c_x)}{(p_{x1}-p_{x2})} \tag{2-2}$$

$$\frac{(p_{y1}-c_y)}{Y} = \frac{f}{Z} \Rightarrow Y = \frac{T(p_{y1}-c_y)}{(p_{x1}-p_{x2})} \tag{2-3}$$

2.3.2 Improved Spatial Point Location Mode

In the space for the movement of hand, the pose should also be known, this problem can not be solved only through the triangle model, so the triangle model was changed in this paper, At first, two cameras will be placed into a 90 ° angle, assuming the main axis of two cameras in the same plane, the two main optical axis, respectively Y, Z axis, with its intersection of the camera coordinate system to establish the origin, MN for the hand of the central axis, P as it's center, M_1N_1 and M_2N_2 in the two pixels are the projection plane, p_1p_2, respectively, at its center, $(c_{x1}c_{y1})$ and $(c_{x2}c_{y2})$ were the two main optical axis and plane of pixels corresponding to the intersection, ,the length of O_1O is T_1, the length of O_2O is T_2, O_1 and O_2 to the corresponding pixel distance from the plane (two camera focal length) were f_1, f_1 shown in Figure (4).

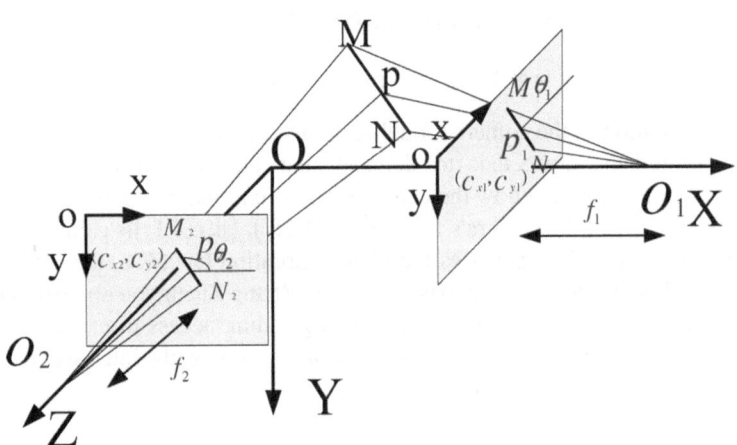

Fig. 4.

Using similar triangles can know point (X, Y, Z) in the camera coordinate system and hand pose, respectively, we can see from the camera 1 and 2:

$$\frac{f_1}{T_1} = \frac{p_{y1}-c_{y1}}{Y_1} = \frac{c_{x1}-p_{x1}}{Z} \Rightarrow \begin{cases} Y_1 = \frac{T_1(p_{y1}-c_{y1})}{f_1} \\ Z = \frac{T_1(c_{x1}-p_{x1})}{f_1} \end{cases} \tag{2-4}$$

$$\frac{f_2}{T_2} = \frac{p_{y2}-c_{y2}}{Y_2} = \frac{p_{x2}-c_{x2}}{X} \Rightarrow \begin{cases} Y_2 = \frac{T_2(p_{y2}-c_{y2})}{f_2} \\ X = \frac{T_2(p_{x2}-c_{x2})}{f_2} \end{cases} \tag{2-5}$$

$$Y = \frac{Y_1+Y_2}{2} = \frac{\frac{T_1(p_{y1}-c_{y1})}{f_1}+\frac{T_2(p_{y2}-c_{y2})}{f_2}}{2} \tag{2-6}$$

2.3.3   Camera Calibration

In practice, There will be a significant distortion on the edge of the imager, which called radial distortion, the following formula is created to adjust the radial position (fish eye Lens need k_3):

$$x = x(1 + k_1 r^2 + k_2 r^4 + k_3 r^6) \tag{2-7}$$

$$y = y(1 + k_1 r^2 + k_2 r^4 + k_3 r^6) \tag{2-8}$$

In additional, tangential distortion is due to manufacturing defects resulting from the lens not being exactly parallel to the imaging, two additional parameters p_1 and p_2 were introduced to adjust this distortion:

$$x = x + [2p_1 y + p_2(r^2 + 2x^2)] \tag{2-9}$$

$$y = y + [2p_2 x + p_1(r^2 + 2y^2)] \tag{2-10}$$

Spatial point location in the camera model is in the case of no distortion, so these two aberration should be corrected, to demand that the five distortion parameters $\{k_1 k_2 k_3 p_1 p_2\}$, also need to know the camera optical axis and the imaging device main intersection $(c_x c_y)$ and the camera's focal length $(f_x f_y)$, $(c_x c_y f_x f_x)$ is called the camera intrinsic parameters. This paper uses the plate calibration OpenCV, the set Z to 0, to solve the focal length and the main axis offset with Zhang Zhengyou algorithm [6], and the distortion parameters is based on Brown's algorithm, access to camera distortion parameters, the use of distortion map correction of the camera, the intrinsics matrix and the distortion matrix as follows:

$$\text{intrinsic matrix: } M = \begin{bmatrix} f_x & 0 & c_x \\ 0 & f_y & c_y \\ 0 & 0 & 1 \end{bmatrix} \tag{2-11}$$

$$\text{distortion matrix: } N = \{k_1 k_2 p_1 p_2\} \tag{2-12}$$

3 Experimental Results and Analysis

3.1 Experimental Conditions

Two Logitech UVC USB camera were used to build real-time staff position and pose tracking system in this paper, the camera resolution is 130 million pixels, support the 640X480 video collection, belonging to the low-end cameras, and a 7X8 chess board was made, the box size length of 20mm, so the parameters in the matrix M units is mm/20, the main axis from the intersection of the two camera distances T_1, T_2 are 400mm.

3.2 Camera Calibration

Use of the aforesaid methods to calibrate the camera 1 and 2, the rotation of the chess box was set at 10 times to get the intrinsic matrix and distortion matrix as follows:

$$M_1 = \begin{bmatrix} 804.7 & 0 & 333.8 \\ 0 & 804.7 & 242.4 \\ 0 & 0 & 1 \end{bmatrix} \quad N_1 = \{0.35 \quad -1.20 \quad 0.02 \quad 0.02\}$$

$$M_2 = \begin{bmatrix} 874.3 & 0 & 377.5 \\ 0 & 872.7 & 221.4 \\ 0 & 0 & 1 \end{bmatrix} \quad N_2 = \{0.91 \quad -6.18 \quad -0.02 \quad 0.03\}$$

3.3 Experimental Data and Analysis

The experiment was based on the experimental platform built above, from the interception of the nine images, seeing in the following table, Angle 1 and Angle 2 means the angle between the central axis and the negative X-axis in the two coordinate system, (x_1, y_1) and (x_2, y_2) are the position of the hand in the two coordinates.

Frames	Angle 1	Angle 2	X_1	Y_1	X_2	Y_2
1(185)	87	91	303	237.5	173.5	277
2(249)	80	84	434	311	405.5	306
3(504)	136	99	525.5	259	335.5	284
4(346)	127	70	344.5	271.5	288	267.5
5(359)	75	89	318.5	297.5	291.5	286.5
6(459)	46	92	392.5	313	446	270.5

With the formula (3-4) - (3-6), the center of the hand in coordinates of the location the space can be Calculated, and the angle around the Z axis and X axis rotation, a model of hand was built with 3DMAX, the virtual scene [7]was built with OpenGL , the virtual hand position and pose were contrast with the image above, as shown below:

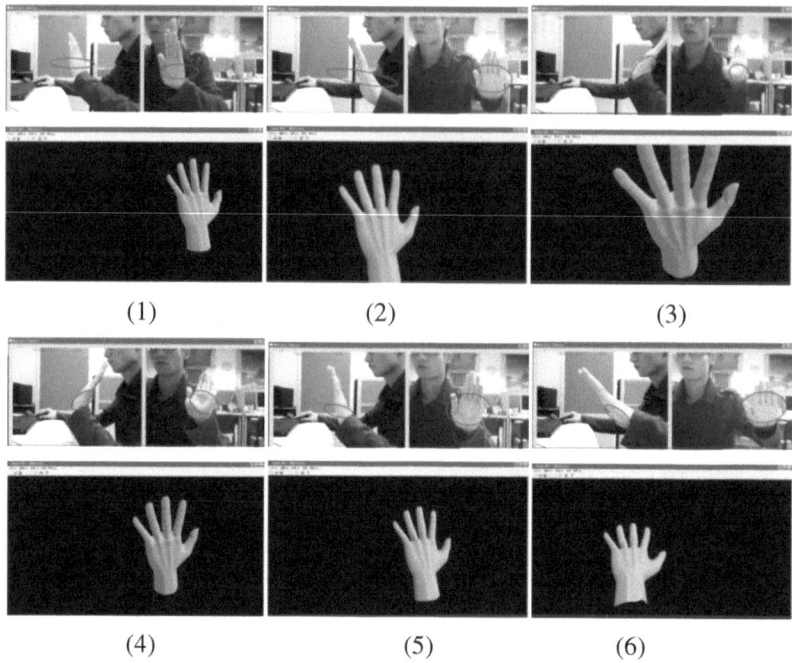

(1)   (2)   (3)

(4)   (5)   (6)

The following conclusions can be drawn from the experimental data and image comparison above:

1. The position of the virtual hand not only corresponding to the spatial location of the real hand in pictures, but also could well reflect the changes of the hand in spatial location.
2. When the hand around the X axis and Z axis, although there are some errors, but the virtual hand can be broadly reflect the pose of actual hand and angle changes.

4   Conclusion

In summary, using two ordinary camera to capture the spatial position and pose of hand to create a virtual interactive manual system is feasible, this user-friendly system can be widely used in virtual games, virtual assembly systems.

The system still needs further improvement, the question that the hand around the Y axis should be solved, the other is to increase the precision of the angle captured.

References

1. Wang, T.: The Review and Prospect of Computer Vision. Journal of Wuhan Automotive Polytechnic University 20(1) (February 1998)
2. Carr, H., Snoeyink, J., van de Panne, M.: Progresssive topological simplification using contour trees and lacal spatial measures. In: 15th Western Computer Graphics Symposium, Big White, British Columbia (March 2004)

3. Bradski, G., Kaebler, A.: Learning OpenCV, vol. 10. O'Reilly Media, Inc., Sebastopol (2009), Learning OpenCV
4. Fu, S.-h., Zhang, X.-h.: Moving targets real-time detecting methods based on the image sequences. Optical Technique 30(2), 215–217 (2004)
5. Ma, S., Zhang, Z.: Computer Vision. Science Press, Beijing (1998)
6. Zhang, Z.: A flexible new technique for camera calibration. IEEE Transaction on pattern Analysis and Machine intelligence 22, 1330–1334 (2000)
7. Peace Dove Studios. OpenGL Advanced Programming and Visualization System, 1 (2003)

Linear Feedback Anti-control of Chaos in Permanent Magnet Synchronous Motor

Jingyue Wang[1], Haotian Wang[2], and Lixin Guo[3]

[1] School of Automobile and Transportation, ShenYang Ligong University,
Shenyang 110159, China
Abswell@126.com
[2] School of Automation, Shenyang Aerospace University, Shenyang 110136, China
Whatian@163.com
[3] School of Mechanical Engineering, Northeastern University, Shenyang 110004, China
Guolx@mail.neu.edu.cn

Abstract. In order to take advantage of chaos in permanent magnet synchronous motor system, the permanent magnet synchronous motor systems with smooth and non-smooth air-gap models are studied. The chaos anti-control methods by the addition of linear feedback are dissertated and analyzed by numerical solution. The chaos in systems is anti-controlled. The allowable range controlling variables and the chaos orbits of the systems under anti-control are obtained. The systems obtain the new chaotic attractors with the completely different topology.

Keywords: Permanent magnet synchronous motor (PMSM), Chaos, Anti-control of chaos, Linear feedback, Topology.

1 Introduction

In 1989, Kuroe and Hayashi [1] introduced the chaos phenomena in motor sport when the motor parameters are in certain areas in the 20th IEEE Power Electronics Specialists Conference. the motor will have a chaotic motion, suddenly showing a large torque or small. The situation in some of the practical application is not allowed. Therefore, how to control and eliminate this chaos becomes a subject of concern [2-8]. However, it soon discovered that in some cases chaos in the motor can provide great convenience for us. Chaos brings the irregular movement can improve the efficiency of the grinding machines, can make the quality of mixing cement mixer greatly and can be used in medical equipment pacemakers, etc. In these applications, people want stable system to appear chaos phenomena or to strengthen the original chaotic phenomena, i.e. anti-control of chaos [9-10]. Zhang and Li [11] constructed a linear controller, which allow the original or even a stable non-chaotic system of permanent magnet synchronous motor to get a new chaotic attractor. Zhang et al. [12] also constructed a linear controller, which make the original system present chaos behavior. Using delay state feedback controller, chaos is anti-controlled by Meng et al. [13]. Meng et al. [14] proposed a control strategy of chaos and chaotic anti-control with the

R. Chen (Ed.): ICICIS 2011, Part I, CCIS 134, pp. 676–685, 2011.

minimum of the energy method. Kong et al. [13] made permanent magnet synchronous motor exact linearization by differential geometry theory, and achieved chaotic anti-control. In general, the study of anti-control of Chaos in Permanent Magnet Synchronous Motor is less.

Based on the above analysis, in this paper, the permanent magnet synchronous motor systems with smooth and non-smooth air-gap are controlled to a chaotic orbit by a linear feedback controller. Numerical simulation shows that the control method is effective and feasible. It can provide the theoretical basis of chaotic motion.

2 The Mathematical Model of PMSM

The axis current i_d, i_q of the stator d, q and the rotor angular velocity ω as state variables, using $d - q$ coordinates axis, the mathematical model of PMSM can be written as [14]

$$\begin{cases} \dfrac{di_d}{dt} = (u_d - R_1 i_d + \omega L_d i_q)/L_q \\ \dfrac{di_q}{dt} = (u_q - R_1 i_q - \omega L_d i_d - \omega \psi_r)/L_q \\ \dfrac{d\omega}{dt} = [n_p \psi_r i_q + n_p (L_d - L_q) i_d i_q - T_L - \beta \omega]/J \end{cases} \quad (1)$$

After the affine transformation and the time scale transformation, the dimensionless mathematical model of PMSM is

$$\begin{cases} \dfrac{dx}{dt} = -\dfrac{L_q}{L_d} x + yz + \tilde{u}_d \\ \dfrac{dy}{dt} = -y - xz + \alpha z + \tilde{u}_q \\ \dfrac{dz}{dt} = \sigma(y - z) + \varepsilon xy - \tilde{T}_L \end{cases} \quad (2)$$

$$\alpha = \frac{n_p \psi_r^2}{R_1 \beta} , \ \sigma = \frac{L_q \beta}{R_1 J} , \ \tilde{u}_q = \frac{n_p L_q \psi_r u_q}{R_1^2 \beta} , \ \tilde{u}_d = \frac{n_p L_q \psi_r u_d}{R_1^2 \beta} , \ \varepsilon = \frac{L_q \beta^2 (L_d - L_q)}{L_d J n_p \psi_r^2} ,$$

$\tilde{T}_L = \dfrac{L_q^2 T_L}{R_1^2 J}$, $n_p = 1$, Where The non-dimensional quantities have been introduced,

Where x, y, z represent respectively d, q - axis stator current and rotor angular velocity ω, and u_d, u_q, T_L represent d, q -axis voltage and external torque, respectively, ψ_r represents permanent magnetic flux, R_1 represents Stator windings, β represents viscous damping coefficient, J represents rotational inertia, n_p represents pole pairs. R_1, β, J, L_d, L_q and T_L are all positive. When $L_d = L_q$, the system is smooth air-gap PMSM. Otherwise, the system is non-smooth air-gap PMSM. In the system parameters, ψ_r is affected the greatest impact by the working environment and conditions. The system shows a very complicated nonlinear dynamics with ψ_r value changes.

3 The Linear Controller Design

The definition of a n-dimensional non-linear chaotic system as follows

$$\begin{cases} \dot{x} = F(X(t), t) \\ \dot{y} = DX \end{cases}.$$ (3)

Where, F is a nonlinear smooth vector function. X is the system state variable, $X = [x_1, x_2, \cdots, x_n]^T$. y is the output of system. The constant matrix D is $1 \times n$. The linear feedback controller of the system is $U = Ky$. Where, K is a feedback gain matrix. The linear feedback controller is added to the system. Then the controlled system is

$$\dot{x} = F(X(x), t) + U.$$ (4)

4 Anti-control of Chaos in Smooth Air-Gap PMSM

From (1), we get the smooth air gap permanent magnet synchronous motor system model

$$\begin{cases} \dfrac{dx}{dt} = -x + yz + \tilde{u}_d \\ \dfrac{dy}{dt} = -y - xz + \alpha z + \tilde{u}_q \\ \dfrac{dz}{dt} = \sigma(y - z) - \tilde{T}_L \end{cases}.$$ (5)

The system, with system parameters $\tilde{u}_d = -0.27$, $\tilde{u}_q = -0.42$, $\tilde{T}_L = 1.2$, $\alpha = 20$, $\sigma = 20$, was chosen for analysis. Suppose the initial point of the system is (0.01, 0.01, 0.01). Take time step of 0.005s, with fourth order fixed step Runge-Kutta method for numerical integration of Equation (5), we can obtain the time history of motion, the phase trajectory and Poincaré map in Figure 1, Figure 2 and Figure 3. From these figures, we can conclude the system is stable.

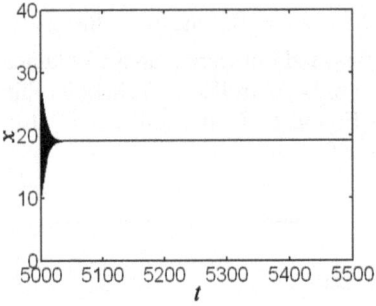

Fig. 1. Time course diagram of the stable system

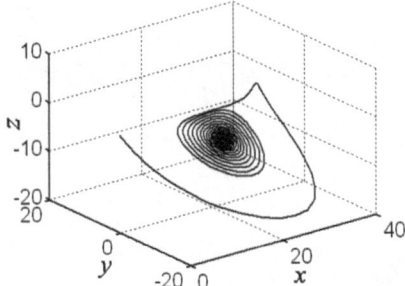

Fig. 2. Phase portrait of the stable system

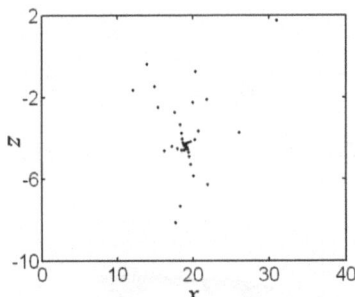

Fig. 3. Poincaré map of the stable system

If $K = [k_1, k_2, k_3]^T$, x is the system output, the equation of the controlled system is

$$\begin{cases} \dfrac{dx}{dt} = -x + yz + \tilde{u}_d + k_1 x \\[2mm] \dfrac{dy}{dt} = -y - xz + \alpha z + \tilde{u}_q + k_2 y \,. \\[2mm] \dfrac{dz}{dt} = \sigma(y - z) - \tilde{T}_L + k_3 z \end{cases} \tag{6}$$

When $k_1 = 0.6$, $k_2 = -1.2$, $k_3 = 10.2$ the time history of motion of the controlled system, the phase trajectory and Poincaré map are obtained, as shown in Figure 4 to 6. It is obvious that the system is controlled to a chaotic orbit. The corresponding strange attractors are shown in Figure 6. In this time, it is also only one half the original chaotic attractors in Figure 9.

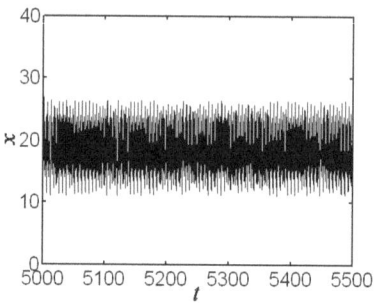

Fig. 4. Time course diagram of the controlled system

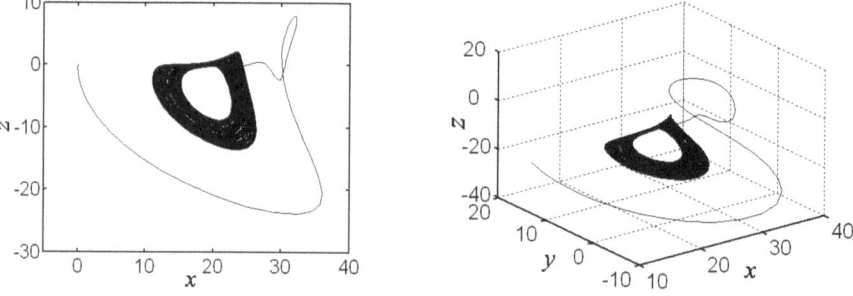

Fig. 5. Phase portrait of the controlled system

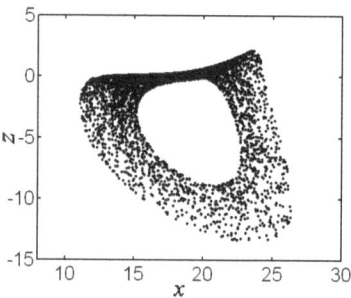

Fig. 6. Poincaré map of the controlled system

When $k_1 = 0.6$, $k_2 = -1.2$, $k_3 = 10.34$, we can obtain the time history of motion of the controlled system in Figure 7, the phase trajectory in Figure 8 and Poincaré map in Figure 9. The corresponding strange attractor are shown in Figure 9. It is obvious that the new chaotic attractors are different from that in Figure 6.

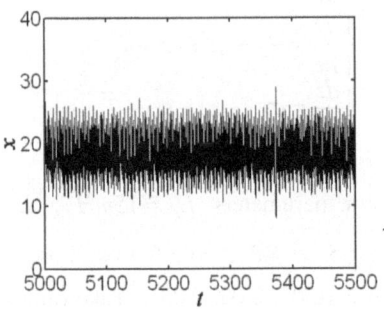

Fig. 7. Time course diagram of the controlled system

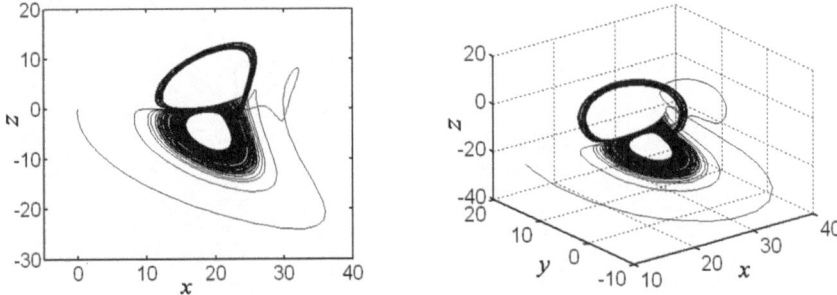

Fig. 8. Phase portrait of the controlled system

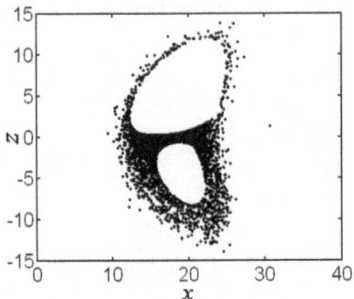

Fig. 9. Poincaré map of the controlled system

5 Anti-control of Chaos in Non-smooth Air-Gap PMSM

The non-smooth air gap permanent magnet synchronous motor system model is

$$\begin{cases} \dfrac{dx}{dt} = -\dfrac{L_q}{L_d}x + yz + \tilde{u}_d \\[2mm] \dfrac{dy}{dt} = -y - xz + \alpha z + \tilde{u}_q \\[2mm] \dfrac{dz}{dt} = \sigma(y - z) + \varepsilon xy - \tilde{T}_L \end{cases} \quad . \tag{7}$$

The system, with system parameters $L_d = 15mH$, $L_q = 10mH$, $\tilde{u}_d = -0.27$, $\tilde{u}_q = -0.42$, $\tilde{T}_L = 1.2$, $\alpha = 5$, $\sigma = 8$, $\varepsilon = 0.98$, was chosen for analysis. Suppose the initial point of the system is (0.05, 0.02, 0.05). Take time step of 0.005s, with fourth order fixed step Runge-Kutta method for numerical integration of Equation (7), we can obtain the time history of motion, the phase trajectory and Poincaré map in Figure 10, Figure 11 and Figure 12. From these figures, we can conclude the system is stable.

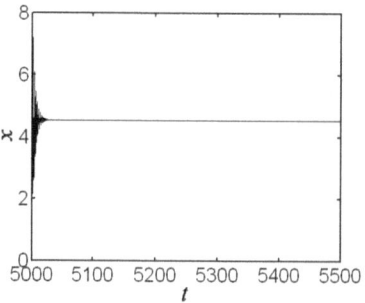

Fig. 10. Time course diagram of the stable system

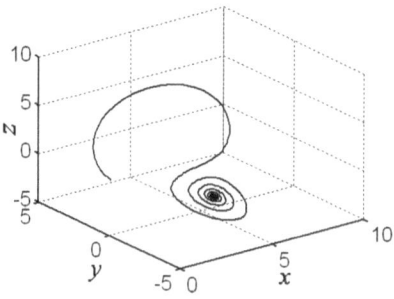

Fig. 11. Phase portrait of the stable system

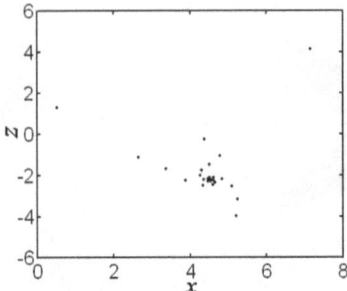

Fig. 12. Poincaré map of the stable system

If $K = [k_1, k_2, k_3]^T$, x is the system output, the equation of the controlled system is

$$\begin{cases} \dfrac{dx}{dt} = -\dfrac{L_q}{L_d}x + yz + \tilde{u}_d + k_1 x \\ \dfrac{dy}{dt} = -y - xz + \alpha z + \tilde{u}_q + k_2 y \\ \dfrac{dz}{dt} = \sigma(y - z) + \varepsilon xy - \tilde{T}_L + k_3 z \end{cases} \tag{8}$$

When $k_1 = 0.06$, $k_2 = -0.02$, $k_3 = 7.5$, Figure 13 shows the time history of motion of the controlled system, Figure 14 shows the phase trajectory and Figure 15 shows the Poincaré map. From these figures, we can conclude the system is chaotic. The system obtains a new chaotic attractor, which is similar to Lorenz attractor.

When we wanted to make use of the chaotic motion, the system can be controlled by using the above method, and rapidly emerge chaos. The system is controlled by using sensors to collect the d, q - axis stator current and the rotor angular velocity ω, adjusting the feedback coefficient k_1, k_2, k_3. This control method is easy to implement in the system and costs less.

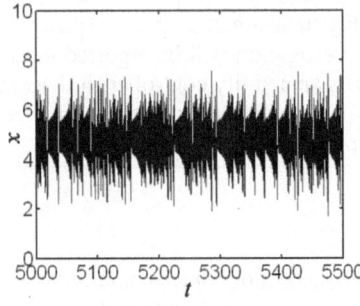

Fig. 13. Time course diagram of the controlled system

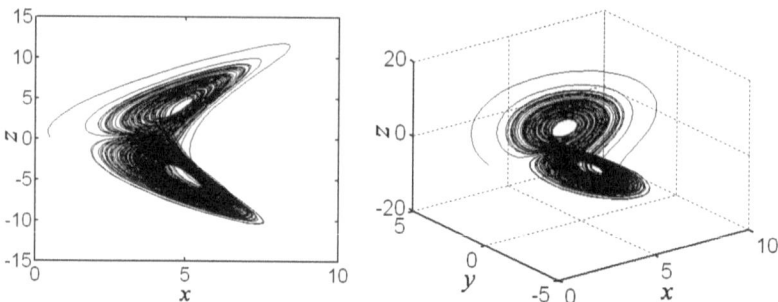

Fig. 14. Phase portrait of the controlled system

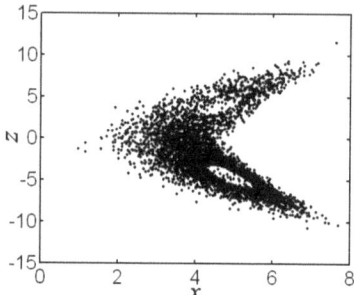

Fig. 15. Poincaré map of the controlled system

6 Conclusion

In this paper, we have studied an anti-control method of chaos in the permanent magnet synchronous motor systems with smooth and non-smooth air-gap models. To take advantage of the chaotic characteristics of permanent magnet synchronous motor, by applying the linear feedback controller, the original permanent magnet synchronous motor systems with smooth and non-smooth air-gap show chaotic motion, which allows us to use good chaos properties. In these new chaotic systems, there are abundant and complex dynamical behaviors. The new attractors and their forming mechanism need further to study and explore. Their topological structure should be completely and thoroughly investigated. It is expecting that more detailed theory analysis and simulation investigation will be reported in the near future elsewhere. The linear feedback controller is an activity controller. It does not affect the original system parameters, only need to change the control parameters. This method has better prospect in engineering application.

References

1. Kuroe, Y., Hayashi, S.: Analysis of bifurcation in power electronic induction motor drive system. In: IEEE Power Electronics Specialists Conference Rec. Milwaukee, WI, USA, pp. 923–930 (1989)

2. Nakashima, S., Inagak, I.Y., Mik, I.I.: Sensorless initial rotor position estimation of surface permanent magnet synchronous motor. IEEE Transactions on Industry Applications, 1598–1603 (2000)
3. Corleym, J., Lorenz, R.D.: Rotor position and velocity estimation for a salientpole permanent magnet synchronous motor at stand still and high speeds. IEEE Transactions on Industry Applications, 784–789 (1998)
4. Wai, R.: Total sliding-mode controller for PM synchronous servo moter drive using recurrent fuzzy neural network. IEEE Transactions on Industrials, 926–944 (2001)
5. Calvo, M., Malik, O.P.: Synchronousmach in esteady state permanent estimation using neural network. IEEE Trans. on Energy Conversion, 237–144 (2004)
6. Harb, A.M.: Nonlinear chaos control in a permanentmagnet reluctance machine. Chaos, Solitons & Fractals 19, 1217–1224 (2004)
7. Ataei, M., Kiyoumarsi, A., Ghorbani, B.: Control of chaos in permanent magnet synchronous motor by using optimal Lyapunov exponents placement. Physics Letters A 17, 4226–4230 (2007)
8. Li, D., Wang, S.L., Zhang, X.H., et al.: Impulsive Control of Permanent Magnet Synchronous Motors with Parameters Uncertainties. Chin. Phy. B 17, 1678–1682 (2008)
9. Chen, G., Ueta, T.: Yet another chaotic attractor. International. Journal of Bifurcation and Chaos 29, 1465–1466 (1999)
10. Chen, G.: On feedback control of chaotic dynamic system. International Journal of Bifurcation and Chaos 2, 407–411 (1992)
11. Zhang, Z., Li, Z.: Anti-control of chaos in the permanent-magnet synchronous motors. Journal of Jinan University (Natural Science) 22, 44–46 (2001)
12. Zhang, B., Li, Z., Mao, Z.: Anti-control of its chaos in the permanent-magnet synchronous motors. Control Theroy And Applications 19, 544–548 (2002)
13. Meng, Z., Sun, C., An, Y.: Chaos anti-control of PMSM based on exact linearization via delay-time state variable feedback. Electric Machines and Control 11, 282–286 (2007)
14. Meng, Z., Sun, C., An, Y., Hongmin, Y.: Chaos analysis and energy minimization control method of permanent magnet synchronous motors. Electric Drive Automation 29, 11–14 (2007) (in Chinese)
15. Kong, Q., An, Y., Sun, C., Cao, J.: Variable Structure Chaos Anti-Control of an Exact linearized PMSM. Techniques of Automation & Applications 27, 8–9 (2007) (in Chinese)
16. Li, Z., Zhang, B., Mao, Z.Y.: Strange attractors in permanent magnet synchronous motors. In: IEEE 1999 International Conference on Power Electronics and Drive Systems, pp. 150–155. The Hong Kong Polytechnic University, Hong Kong (1999)

An Infrastructure for Personalized Service System Based on Web2.0 and Data Mining

Yu Liu[1], Weijia Li[1], Yuan Yao[2], Jing Fang[1], Ruixin Ma[1], and Zhaofa Yan[1]

[1] School of Software, Dalian University of Technology, Dalian 116620, P.R. China
[2] Link Scholar Technology Co. Ltd., Dalian 116025, P.R. China

Abstract. With the development of information technology, personalized web portals are becoming more and more popular. Personalization offers great opportunities to obtain information more effective and efficient, and personalized services can provide significant user benefits since they adapt their behaviors to better support the users. The paper designs an infrastructure of personalized service system through a case study. It provides a platform where users can share resources and exchange information about research papers, which is implemented at www.linkscholar.net.

Keywords: web2.0; data mining; recommendation system; personalization.

1 Introduction

With the continuous development of information technology, Internet users show a growing demand for a wide range of features. Information browsing is no longer the sole purpose of surfing the Internet, and people have the hope of getting valuable information at any time, as well as a request that the Internet is able to provide screening, integration and optimization of personalized information services [1].

Individual information service is this kind of service which is user-centric, and based on the user's information. Individual customization means that according to different information needs of users, to provide targeted information services and systems. By means of collection and analysis of users' information, individual recommendation learns users' interests and behaviors, finds the potential demands for information of users to take the initiative to recommend the information, and supplies the users with a better network experience, to save searching time and enhance efficiency.

In March 1995, at the meeting of the American Association for Artificial Intelligence, Carnegie Mellon University's Robert Armstrong and others proposed individual navigation system "WebWatcher", Stanford University's Marko Balabanovic and others proposed individual recommendation system "LIRA" [2]. The three systems mark the beginning of individual services. In 1996, Yahoo! launched the individual portal "My Yahoo!" [3].

R. Chen (Ed.): ICICIS 2011, Part I, CCIS 134, pp. 686–691, 2011.
© Springer-Verlag Berlin Heidelberg 2011

Although the research institutes have carried out related studies for individual information services theory, technology and products. Many results of the low level of automation and poor quality are far from meeting the people's individual needs. Data mining is an important tool to solve this difficulty, which can supply the right service actions with strong support and reliable guarantee. With the help of the data mining technology to deal with user's behaviors, comments and paper information, we can get the user interest models and other relevant models which are the key of setting up initial individual page and individual recommendation services' quality.

This project can meet the needs of scientists and technicians, which is based on Science and Technology web sites, focuses on individual customization, data mining, individual recommendation, and researches individual information services system and data mining. The general users can personalize the interfaces and manage the research papers by their own, and at the same time, the background system using the data mining technology can recommend corresponding papers to users by the configuration and the browsing records from the users. The project is not only the basic research of individual services and data mining, but also will greatly promote the organization of network technology papers platforms and the individuation development. Its research results have not only an important academic value but as well produce large social economic benefits.

2   An Infrastructure for Personalized Service System

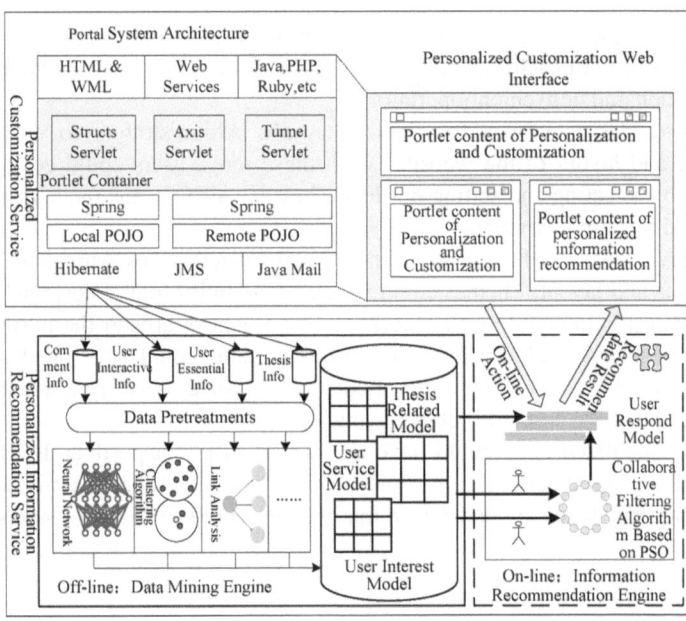

Fig. 1. System structure of user-centered science and technology paper service platform

2.1 Customization Service Platform

In a personalized interface, users could configure the website according to his or her requirements with the modules that he or she is interested in. At the same time, customization platform is also used to show the results of personalized recommendation.

2.2 Service Platform for Personalizing Information Recommendation

(1) Data mining engine: off-line operation. Data mining, based on content structure and using aspects, discovers users' interest with various algorithms and establishes models that users are interested in.
(2) Information recommendation engine: on-line operation. Modeling based on users' browsing action and data mining engine, returns users the recommended results.

3 Customization Service

This science and technology paper service platform should not only be used as a user-centered service platform that provides personalized information but also an information collection platform that collects users' information and obtains related information for target users by the use of data mining and recommendation system.

3.1 Web Interface Customization

Users could choose the different overall system interface modules, page components, layout and the way of each sub-module views according to their own styles to achieve personalization and convenient operations.

Portal provides interfaces for final users and administrators to customize the appearance and layout of the website. With these tools, users could customize their own pages by selecting and setting portlets. They can also change the layout and color (if permitted by administrator).

Users are allowed to have one or more personalized pages with their own color themes, skins and layout. Themes could be used to identify font, color, pitch and other visual elements; skin could be the accessories and control around the portlet, such as sidebar, border, and shadow and so on. Different skins could be applied to different portlets so that the websites' appearance could be adjusted to satisfy any requirements, and users could move portlet to set the layout.

Every personalized page could have a group of different portlets. Portlets on the web page could be determined by final users or administrators. Administrators can designate portlets which are needed, so that they will not be deleted by users.

3.2 Service Content Customization

Portal provides content customization and integration to achieve centralized access. Behavior analysis and content recommendation could be achieved by portal. Framework that supports the portal and web services uses SOAP to integrate Web services or other functions provided by distant portal into independent local atomic portlet components. These components could be deployed by being collaborated into more advanced portlets so that portal could obtain information from local and distant Web service as well as other distant portal. By integrating contents and applications from different sources using the block way, websites could provide more new services to users.

In addition, customization service platform could provide more functions. On the one hand, users could point out the contents he or she concerns about. On the other hand, users could edit models established by data mining technology in the system, which are convenient for engine to provide more accurate recommendations.

Portal integrates data mining technology and data analysis system to provide models that users are interested in by collaborating and analyzing corresponding business data.

3.3 Services Customization

Services customization means users could set ways of receiving services such as e-mail, telephone reforming and expert advice so that users could get information services based on his or her own time and geographic location.

The portal platform allows users control how they receive alerts: via portal-based web alert, e-mail or any additional delivery mechanisms configured by the portal administrator. Similar technology could be applied to services customization. By implementing Portal services recommendation component, users could set their own ways of obtaining information.

4 Personalized Information Recommendation Services

Web Data Mining is a kind of comprehensive analysis tools and pivotal technology for assisting Personalized Information Service, which tracks users' behavior data and relevant comments submitted by users on the Web site of scientific research. It collects users' information, then analyses users' data and establishes models users interested in using Data Mining technology to realize personalized recommendation.

4.1 User Data Collection

Data collection is a process acquiring information related with user's features, preferences or activities, and it provides necessary data sources for the establishment of user's model. User's information includes user's registration information, interactive information with system, browsing information and comments. Comments are the information submitted by the user voluntarily, which can better reflect the user's interest.

4.2 User Preference Model and Transference model

Regarding to different information, we take different measures. For comments submitted to Papers Web Site by users, we use Web content Data Mining Techniques; for interacting information between the user and system, we take the Techniques of

Web Mining; for the link relationship among users and articles browsed on Web site and the structure of personalized homepages collocating, we make use of the Techniques of Web Structure Mining. Then the final job is to establish the user preference model synthetically by integrating all kinds of information, especially users' current comment data, which is prepared for Personalized Information Recommendation later.

In addition, the user's interest is not set in stone, and always changes as time passes by. As a result, the updating strategy of User Preference Model is one of the key problems, which relates to whether Information Recommendation can be realized accurately. The updating of User Preference Model means improving the model's precision and the quality of recommendation. According to user's direct and connotative viewpoints to the recommendation system, the updating strategy improves the primary model and ensures that the model can match the up-to-date user's preferences.

4.3   Resource Expression and Related Model Analysis

According to the paper's title, authors, keywords, and basic information of the thesis papers, papers are classified by information. Creating the corresponding eigenvector model for each type of paper guides the user preferences excavation to enhance the accuracy of the recommendation.

At the same time, the importance of a paper is based on the paper's eigenvector; the popularity of a paper is based on the case the paper viewed by users; the relevance model of papers is based on the users' browsing situation. As time goes on, the relevance model of papers are incrementally updated.

4.4   Service Model and Information Recommendation Techniques

Customer service model includes: user fractionizing model, user recommendation model, user response model and user washed-away model. The user fractionizing model classifies user's type based on user's action model; the user recommendation model means recommending resources that users may be interested in according to the user preference point; the user response model means searching for users interested in particular types of information resources, and then realizing one-on-one service to these users and analyzing the users' response to recommendation; the user washed-away model refers to search features of washed-away users to find facts impacting users' churning to improve the Web site's service and service quality, and as far as possible to reduce the risk of loss of customers.

4.5   Online Services Recommendation

Online services recommendation is the last process to use mining techniques. It attains the current user' access operations and services request module to implement recommendation algorithm, generate recommendation interface by calculating, and then send recommendation interface to client browser. So it provides personalization services for users.

5 Summary

Personalization is a significant use of Internet with the emergence of huge volume of information on the Internet. In this paper, we present a new infrastructure for personalized service system based on web2.0 and data mining, which can meet the needs of the user recommendation, interface friendly, operation simply and recommendation accurately.

We first show the structure of the user-centered science and technology paper service platform, and then give a comprehensive introduction of its two important components: the Customization Service, which works as an information collection platform for the data mining and recommendation system, and also the Personalized Information Recommendation Service, which is essential for the process of collecting, analyzing the users' data and generating the recommendation interface.

With the development of information technology and Web 2.0, the combination of data mining and personalized services is bound to be increasingly closer, so this system will become more and more mature.

Acknowledgments. This work was under Grand by the Natural Science Foundation of China (No.60803074) and the Fundamental Research Funds for the Central Universities (No. DUT10JR06).

References

1. Zeng, C., Xing, C., Zhou, L.: The Overview of Personalized Service Technologies. Journal of Software 13, 1952–1961 (2002)
2. Balabanovic, M., Shoham, Y.: Learning Information Retrieval Agent: Experiments and Automated Web Browsing. In: Proceedings of the AAAI Spring Symposium Series on Information Gathering from Heterogeneous. Distributed Environments, pp. 13–18 (1995)
3. Li, Z., Wang, J.: Research and realization of personalization service system based on Web mining. Information Technology 10, 142–145 (2007)

Research of Optimized Agricultural Information Collaborative Filtering Recommendation Systems

Fang Kui[1,*], Wang Juan[2], and Bu Weiqiong[3]

College of Information Science and Technology, Hunan Agricultural
University, Changsha 410128, China
fk@hunau.net

Abstract. The problems of information overload and resource disorientation which is caused by information explosion become more serious, especially for lots of farmers, who know little computer technologies. In order to provide information and knowledge conveniently, timely and efficiently to farmers, researchers do studies on recommendations system. In this paper, key technologies in recommender system are introduced. we provide a solution that construct a non-missing data user evaluation matrix through the clustering of the items. Addressing the differences in farmers' rating behavior, before making predictions, we normalize the user evaluation matrix.

Keywords: Collaborative filtering; recommendations system; rating matrix; user similarity.

1 Overview

In the course of agricultural informational service, one of the important tasks is how to help farmers to get useful information through internet. As farmers have limited knowledge about computer technology, especially the filtering and judgment abilities are weak when there is numerous information on the net. Thus in order to provide a individuation agricultural information service, we provide a agricultural information recommendations system based on collaborative filtering, which generates the set of nearest neighbors firstly, then predicts the interests about other information and provides the usable information to users.

1.1 Recommendation System

In 1997, Resnick&Varian defined the recommender system[1], in electronic commerce systems, the recommender systems that simulate the process about salesmen Recommend products to users can provide product information and suggestion to customers, to find favourite products. In brief, the purpose of the recommender system is to recommend suitable products to users, according to their requirements.

---

* Corresponding author.

R. Chen (Ed.): ICICIS 2011, Part I, CCIS 134, pp. 692–697, 2011.

Recommender systems were classified into several kinds, as Item-based recommender system, recommendations system based on collaborative filtering, recommendations system based on data mining by different techniques.

(1) Item-based recommender system[2]

Item-based recommender system computes the similarity between items and users' interests. It's under the basic ideas that users' preferences can be described by a user profile, and for each item, we extract the feature to form the feature vector. When a user is commended, we calculate the similarities between the user profile and the item feature matrix, then commend items using these similarities.

(2) Collaborative Filtering Recommended System [3]

Collaborative filtering recommended system is the most success recommendation technology. it analyzed users' interests to determine the nearest neighbor set. The evaluation prediction was formed by integrating the evaluation from the similar users[4]. The process of Collaborative filtering recommended system was divided into three parts, describe the user profile, generate the nearest neighbor set depending on similarities, and produce the recommendation result.

(3) Recommended system of Data Mining[5]

With increasing of the number of users and items, there are large number of user transaction data, registration data, evaluation data, and so on. Meanwhile, servers maintain lots of log data, cart Information and so on. Facing with these massive data, in order to improve the quality and efficiency of the recommendation system, we introduce variety of data mining technology (association rules, sequential pattern mining, clustering, classification, etc.) into recommendation system. Recommendation systems based on data mining mainly involve with the three key technologies, such as processing the raw data, Pattern expression, and application of data mining algorithms.

(4) Hybrid Recommendation System[6]

Because of advantages and disadvantages in both content-based filtering and collaborative filtering, researchers proposed a hybrid recommendation model, which can remain the advantages of both mode, and has higher quality than the formers.

2 An Optimized Agricultural Information Recommendations System Based on Collaborative Filtering

This system is a subsystem of Hunan agricultural information service platform, which analyzes evaluation information, then calculates similarities between the current user and other users, and generates nearest neighbor set of the current user, finally recommends services to users.

2.1 Evaluation Matrix with No-Missing

In general Collaborative filtering modules, First, build a user evaluation matrix based on historical information second, calculate the similarity between users. Then Generate the nearest neighbor set. Finally, according to the nearest neighbor set, recommend information which users may be interested in to. The specific process is shown in Fig.1.

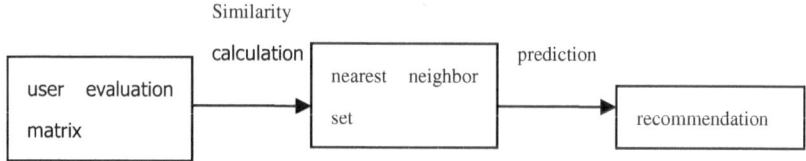

Fig. 1. The Flow Chart of Collaborative Filtering

For the problem of sparsity of collaborative filtering system, usually there are two solutions: 1) interpolation method, Reducing dimensions 2) instead the missing with a default value, such as average. However, the shortage of both methods is evident. Thus if couldn't fully reflect users' individual interests or hobbies, we can not fundamentally solve the sparsity.

In order to effectively deal with this problem, before calculating the similarity between users, we determine the similarity between the items. Then generate items clusters and find the nearest neighbors of each cluster, Finally, according to the user evaluation of the nearest neighbors predict the rating of target information. Then the rating matrix is built. The process shown in Fig.2.

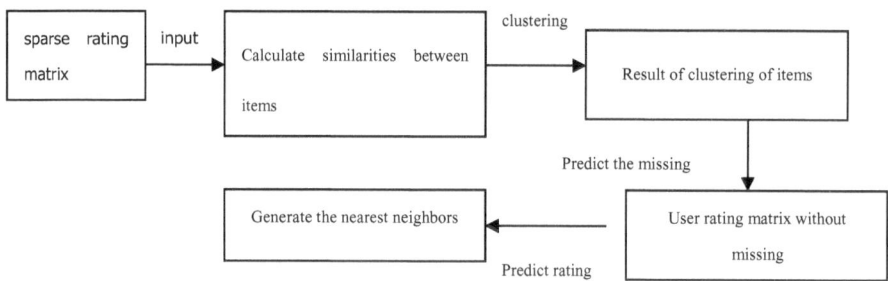

Fig. 2. The Improved Flow Chart of Collaborative Filtering

Let Ui is the item set rated by user i and user j, and the item rated by User I is credited to Ki ,

$$Ui,j=Ki+Kj \tag{1}$$

The items user i didn't rate is Ni,

$$Nf=Ui,j-Ki \tag{2}$$

According to the evaluation that User i and user j rated to the similar items, we can predict the evaluation of the Ni. To the active item r∈Ni, Pi represents the evaluation that user I predicted the item r.

(1) Calculate the similarities between items

To caculate the similarity between item n and item r, first, depending on user ratings on item r and item n calculate the similarity between item n and item r, using the similarity measure, which noted as Sim (r, n).

(2) Items Clustering

There are many Clustering method, such as k-means algorithm, Clara algorithm, can be used. This paper introduces the method of Between-groups Linkage, which can calculate the sum of squares of Euclidean distance. After clustering, find the nearest neighbors of items r, which is expressed as Hr={K1,K2,... , Kn}, r∉ Hr, where highest similarity is k1, and so on.

(3) using the prediction method which proposed by Sarwar [7].

$$P_{i,r} = \frac{\sum\limits_{n \in H_r} Sim_{r,n} \times R_{i,n}}{\sum\limits_{n \in H_r} \left(\left|Sim_{r,n}\right|\right)}$$ (3)

Where simr, n represents the similarity between item r and Kn; Ri, n represents the evaluation of the item n rated by user i.

2.2 Finding the Nearest Neighbor Set

After getting the no missing user evaluation matrix, the main task is calculation of similarities between target user and other users. Then select the top-N similar users as the target user's nearest neighbors set. At present: Person correlation coefficient, Cosine correlation, Relevance of the modified cosine are used widely in similarity measure. This paper adopts the Person correlation coefficient to calculate the similarity of user interest.

2.3 Standardization of User Evaluation[8]

As user's ratings are related to their personalities, for example, the conservative user's ratings may be lower than real scores, and the optimistic ones may give higher ratings. Therefore, user rating must be standardized. The standard formula shown as follows:

$$P_{k,m}(X_{a,b}) = X_{a,b} - (\overline{X}_a - \overline{X}_k) - (\overline{X}_b + \overline{X}_m)$$ (4)

Where Pk,m(Xa,b) is a standardized function.Xa, b is the evaluation of itemb rated by user a. $\overline{X}_a$, $\overline{X}_k$ is the average rating of Usera and Userk. $\overline{X}_b$, $\overline{X}_m$ is the average rating of Itemb and Itemm.

2.4 Recommended Results

With the nearest neighbor set, the target user's interest can be predicted, and generate recommendation result. Usually, according to the different purpose of the

696 F. Kui, W. Juan, and B. Weiqiong

recommendation, there are can various recommendation forms. TOP-N used in this paper to recommend possible item set to users.

3 Conclusion

To test the recommendation method proposed in this paper, first, collect the initial evaluation information. After pretreatment, it's a relatively sparse matrix.

Table 1. Initialized Matrix of User Evaluation

	Item1	Item2	Imem3	Item4	Item5
User1	-	4	-	4	2
User2	3	-	4	5	-
User3	-	5	-	-	3
User4	1	1	-	-	5
User5	3	-	2	-	1
User6	-	-	-	-	3
User7	4	-	-	-	-
User8	-	4	2	-	-
User9	5	-	-	-	-
User10	-	-	4	-	2

Then calculate the similarities between items using person related coefficient, and obtain the result of clustering of items.

Then we get the user evaluation matrix without deletion items.

Then calculate the similarities between users , and receive the nearest neighbors of user n ,U. U1={U6, U3, U4}; U2={ U4, U6, U7}; U3={ U6, U1, U4}; U4={ U2, U6, U1}; U5={ U9, U8, U1}; U6={ U4, U2, U1}; U7={ U9, U2, U4}; U8={ U5, U2, U4}; U9={ U7, U2, U4}; U10={ U1, U6, U4}.

After standardization, the standard evaluation matrix was formed, then we can predict the evaluation about the items which is not evaluated by the active user and get the commendation result by TOP_N principle.

Acknowledgment

In this paper, we Optimized the algorithm of Recommendations System Based on Collaborative Filtering. firstly, form the items clusters based on the similarities between items, secondly, predict the missing value of the evaluation matrix, which can solve the sparsity problem. Befor predicting, the evaluation matrix should be standardized, which overcomed the evaluation's discrepancy coming from differences in users characters, which make the user evaluation is more referable.

This paper is supported by the HuNan Municipal Science and Technology Projects (2010J05) and of Hunan Science and Technology Programs (2008FJ3046).

References

1. Resnick, P., Varian, H.R.: Recommender systems. Communications of the ACM 40(3), 56–58 (1997)
2. Ge, M.: The research about Collaborative Filtering Recommendations System based on content clustering Shandong Normal University (2008)
3. Wei, T., Peng, Y.: Overview of improvement of Collaborative Filtering Recommendations System based on e-commerce applications. Computer Engineering and Science 30(10), 61263 (2008)
4. Wu, Y., Zhen, H.: The Hybrid Algorithm in Automated recommendation about education resource. Computer Application and Software 25(12), 202–203 (2008)
5. Li, D., Yu, G.: The Research and implement of Recommendations System based on Hybrid Algorithm. Tongji University (2008)
6. Zhou, L., Xu, M., Zhang, Y., Zhang, Z., Zhang, Z.: Collaborative Filtering courses Recommendations System model. Computer Engineering and Applications 27(4), 1315–1318 (2010)
7. Deb, K.: Multi2objective genetic algorithms: problem difficulties and construction of test problems. Evolutionary Computation 7(3), 2052230 (1999)
8. Wang, J., de Vries1, A.P., Reinders, M.J.T.: Unifying Userbased and Itembased Collaborative Filtering Approaches by Similarity Fusion. In: Proc. 29th ACM SIGIR Conference on Information Retrieval, pp. 501–508 (2006)
9. Song, Z., Wang, H., Yang, J.: Applications about Collaborative Filtering in personalized recommendation. Journal of Hefei University of Technology: natural science edition 31(7), 1059–1064 (2008)
10. Zhao, L., Hu, N., Zhang, S.: Design of personalized recommendation algorithm. Journal of Computer Research and Development 39(8), 9862991 (2002)
11. Deng, A., Zuo, Z., Zhu, Y.: The algorithm about Collaborative Filtering Recommendations System based on content clustering. Mini-Micro Systems 25(9), 166521670 (2004)

An IPv6 Multihomed Host for Outbound Traffic

Chin-Ling Chen* and Sheng-Lung Cao

Department of Information Management,
National Pingtung Institute of Commerce,
Pingtung, Taiwan 900

Abstract. Though the technology of IPv6 network has become mature in recent years, it still takes long to dispose IPv6 in an all-round way in the internet. In this research, we have designed an IPv6 multihomed host architecture to connect both IPv6 network and 6to4 network. This paper describes a load balance mechanism that allows applications on multihomed devices to utilize the individual networks efficiently to transmit streams that could be part of a session. We experiment the relevant parameters in the IPv6 testbed environment to demonstrate its effectiveness.

Keywords: IPv6, multihomed host, load balance, redundancy.

1 Introduction

Two types of multihoming techniques have been proposed in recent years: multihomed host [1] and multihomed site [2-9]. Multihomed host means that a host connects to two or more internet service providers instead of one. With multihomed hosts a key decision is not simply which network/interface to use but which interface to use for which stream and under what circumstances. Many studies have addressed issues on multihomed site. There are two possible approaches to link assignment of multihomed site. The first approach is static, and usually it announces non-overlapping or over lapping [2] prefixes to different links. For non-overlapping prefix, the traffic destined to these two prefixes to two different links will reach the network via the two respective links. Overlapping prefix splits a prefix into longer prefixes and the original prefix is also announced. Another static scheme applies hashing [3] for distributing traffic over multiple links to obtain better load balancing performance. Table-based hashing can also distribute traffic load according to unequal weights. However, this approach does not consider dynamic traffic load characteristics. The load distributed among access links cannot be balanced evenly because the hashing function is biased for a given traffic load. The second approach is dynamic, which usually requires a table to record the route selection so that all the subsequent packets of a connection will follow the

---

* Corresponding author.

R. Chen (Ed.): ICICIS 2011, Part I, CCIS 134, pp. 698–703, 2011.
© Springer-Verlag Berlin Heidelberg 2011

same route. Network Address Translation (NAT)-based approach [4] translates the source address in an outgoing packet to the external address of a multihomed NAT gateway, so that the returned traffic can be affixed to the corresponding link. BGP peering scheme [5-7] provides fault tolerance without the changes of normal operation of Internet. When connectivity between enterprise and ISP goes down, the failed IP prefixes will be advertised to the other available ISPs.

In this research, we have designed and implemented an IPv6 multihomed host based on Linux platform. The proposed architecture provides redundancy of connectivity to internet by utilizing IPv6 and 6to4 [10] links. We design a load balance algorithm based on the evaluation of both throughput and latency. The load balance mechanism uses active probing to collect related information on user network and makes a decision regarding the selection of an appropriate access link based on the load of the link bottleneck direction. The algorithm achieves a significant reduction of packet loss rate with a moderate number of link shifts.

2   Multihomed Host

We assume a static route selection scheme in the networks. The choice was made to simplify the analysis. Assume W is the set of source destination pairs and the source is defined as the outgoing interface of multihoming host. According to the static priority routing model, the route set R_w consists of N_w routes. For each set R_w, with $N_w > 1$ there exists a routing policy $\mathcal{R}_w$, which specified the schedule for finding available routes. An outgoing flow might try the first route in the set and, if no capacity is available, the second route and so on. Each route consists of an arbitrary combination of links between source and destination.

We have designed and implemented the load balance mechanism by using rtt based throughput threshold scheme. In order to select an appropriate access link, the collection of information regarding both throughput and rtt is required. We first measure the round trip time via each access link for their destination gateway. Let T_i indicate the throughput processed by route i at one probing period, where $i= 1, 2$. T_{max} and T_{min} are defined to be maximum and minimum throughput for route i in the route set R_w. For a flow-granularity load based link selection algorithm, we calculate the load difference between two access links. If the load difference exceeds the load threshold T_{th}, we may conclude that significant load imbalance occurs and the outbound flow will be redirected to the least loaded link during next probing period. The load threshold is used to avoid severe oscillation of route switching.

However, an access link may be available but it cannot be used to reach certain remote subnets in case of upstream congestion. To provide accurate estimation of subnet traffic, we introduce round trip time (rtt) into the model. The rtt is calculated based on the average of these rtt measurements for n runs during one probing period. The link assignment algorithm measures rtt_i for route i. rtt_{max} and rtt_{min} are defined as maximum and minimum rtt for roue i in the route set R_w. If rtt_{max} exceeds the rtt threshold rtt_{th}, the load   offered   to   the   subnet   is   more   than   it   can   handle.   Congestion might build up in the subnet. We use the latency ratio α, which is defined as rtt_{max}/rtt_{min}, to find out the other possible available access link. There is plenty of room of optimization if the rtt ratio is more than an order of magnitude. If the latency ratio(α) exceeds the rtt threshold (rtt_{th}), the load threshold (T_{th}) is reduced by the value rtt_{min}/rtt_{max} ($1/\alpha$). The smaller T_{th} is incentive to redirect the traffic flow to the least loaded link. The load threshold T_{th} is scaled back when the network is perceived to be in the steady state. If the switching behavior is silent for some certain period D, the load threshold T_{th} is scale up with incremented by β, where $0 < \beta < 1$ The algorithm is given below:

For each probing period
{
    IF $rtt_{max} > rtt_{th}$
        { **IF** (rtt_{max} / rtt_{min}) > M_{th}
            { $T_{th} = T_{th}/(rtt_{min}/rtt_{max})$; }
        }
    ELSE
        { *count++*;
        IF *count* > D;
            { $T_{th} = T_{th} + \beta$;
            count = 0;}
        }
    IF ($T_{max} - T_{min}$) > T_{th}
        {Redirect traffic flow to T_{min} link; }
}

3   Experiments and Evaluation

We have executed experiments on the mutihomed host over the current IPv6 internet to evaluate the performance of the proposed scheme. The IPv6 host has connected a local network to the two network backbone (Fig. 1). The host can forward packets from a local network to one of the two backbones in two ways. There two probing sites use different ISPs and thus together represent a typical multihoming site. Two internet backbones offer IPv6 network address prefixes for the network environment. They are 3ffe:3600:1000::/48 and 3ffe:3600:2000::/48.

The host measures the *rtt* for the destination gateway at regular intervals and selects the optimum link based on load balance algorithm. We start the latency probing tasks on both sites at the same time. Each probe transaction uses ICMP6 ECHO REQUEST and ECHO RESPONSE to measure the rtt and thus the network latency to the probed subnet. Every five minutes, the host carries out four measurements in the interval of one second. The latency-based link selection algorithm chooses the faster of these two links, and its latency is the smaller of the two.

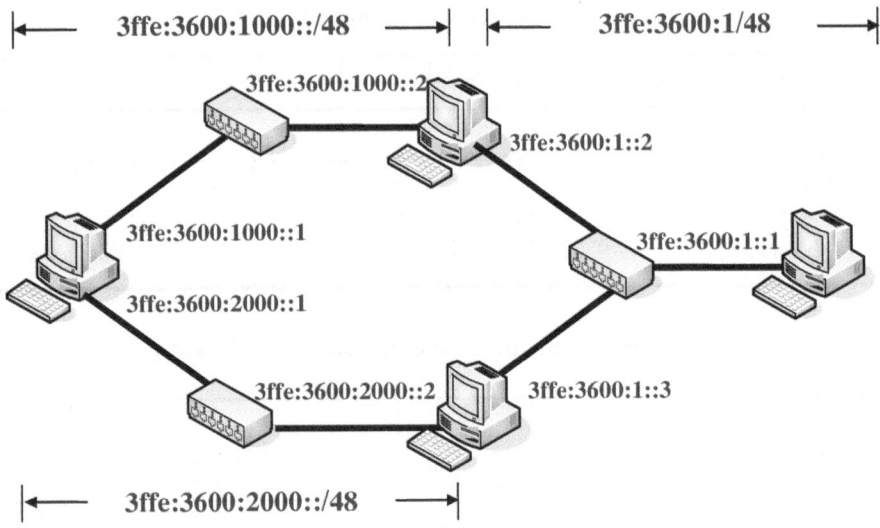

Fig. 1. Experimental environment

We evaluated and compared two performance metrics— packet loss rate, holding time and Average Link Switching (ALS). The packet loss typically represents the sum of the packet lost during the time switching to the other link. Holding time denotes the total access time obtained by one link before switching to the alternative. ALS is defined as the total number of link switching to the total number of active flows. In order to analyze these two metrics, we conduct two sets of experiments. In the first set, we focus on the effect of different parameters on load threshold in the proposed scheme. The second set examines the ability of the proposed scheme in minimizing the loss rate under various loading conditions. We compare the proposed approach with two other schemes: static [2] and dynamic [4]. In static scheme, the path for a flow is set up beforehand and does not undergo any shift at any later time. In dynamic scheme, the outgoing link for each flow is selected based on their rrt measurement.

Table 1 represents the simulation results of ALS, holding time and loss rate for different T_{th} values. We found that the ALS is reduced dramatically in case of T_{th} over 25. The holding time before switching increases as threshold T_{th} increases. The table also shows that small value of threshold T_{th} suffers excessive packet loss. The proposed mechanism experiences trivial packet loss rate in case of T_{th} exceeding 25. There is an optimal value of threshold T_{th} (25) for achieving reduction of link flapping, packet loss as well as holding time before switching.

Table 2 represents the values of latency ratio(α) under different load conditions. We found that the impact of load imbalance between two access links ($\Delta\rho$) is greatly on latency ratio(α). When the difference between two links' load is significant, the value of α is high. Fig. 2 shows that the load difference has not significantly effect the loss rate for all three schemes in both light and medium loading conditions ($\Delta\rho$ <0.6). The proposed scheme becomes smooth with slow increased trend as the offered load is over

Table 1. Simulation results for different T_{th} values

Load threshold (MB)	5	25	50	75	100	125	150
ALS	50	10	5	3	2	2	2
Holding time (s)	100	480	900	1200	1500	1800	2200
Loss rate (%)	0.02	0.0037	0.0014	0.0014	0.0008	0.0006	0.0006

Table 2. Latency ratio(α) for different loading conditions ($\Delta\rho$)

eth0 \ eth1	$rtt_{0\%}$	$rtt_{10\%}$	$rtt_{20\%}$	$rtt_{30\%}$	$rtt_{40\%}$	$rtt_{50\%}$	$rtt_{60\%}$	$rtt_{70\%}$	$rtt_{80\%}$	$rtt_{90\%}$	$rtt_{100\%}$
$rtt_{60\%}$	4.72	3.86	3.08	2.44	1.94	1.34	1	—	—	—	—
$rtt_{70\%}$	9.56	7.81	6.23	4.94	3.93	2.70	2.02	1	—	—	—
$rtt_{80\%}$	13.18	10.77	8.59	6.81	5.42	3.73	2.79	1.37	1	—	—
$rtt_{90\%}$	15.92	13.01	10.38	8.22	6.55	4.50	3.37	1.66	1.20	1	—
$rtt_{100\%}$	21.35	17.44	13.92	11.03	8.78	6.04	4.52	2.23	1.61	1.34	1

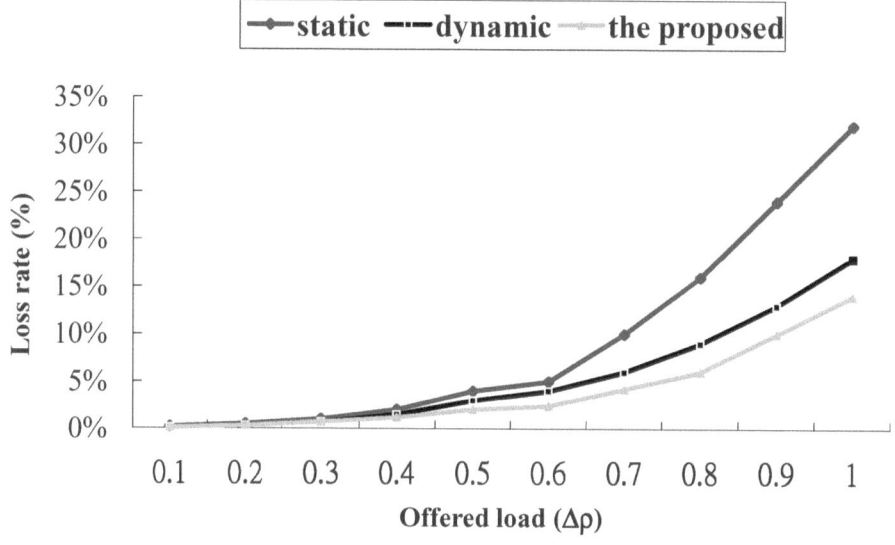

Fig. 2. Loss rate as a function of offered load

0.6. However, both static and dynamic schemes experience significant loss rate in heavy loading condition. The significant imbalanced load between two access links usually leads to frequent switching, thus resulting in high loss rate.

4 Conclusions

In this study, we propose a simple means of supporting multihomed host in an IPv6 network, by designing one link selection algorithm based on the evaluation of both throughput and rtt. The traffic may be distributed piecemeal and routed via the most optimal combination of the currently active network interfaces. We experiment a multihomed host in both IPv6 and 6to4 networks, and examine its performance in supporting efficient load balance. The simulation shows that the proposed adaptive mechanism can achieve a lower loss rate under any loading condition as compared with the other two schemes. In future, we will address the issues in maximizing the utilization of available bandwidth by making use of the resource available on all its interfaces.

References

1. Habib, A., Christin, N., Chuang, J.: Taking advantage of multihoming with session layer striping. In: IEEE INFOCOM 2007-IEEE International Conference on Computer Communications, vol. (1), pp. 2696–2701 (2007)
2. Zhu, Y., Dovrolis, C., Ammar, M.: Combining multihoming with overlay routing (or, how to be a better ISP without owning a network). In: IEEE INFOCOM 2007-IEEE International Conference on Computer Communications, vol. (1), pp. 839–847 (2007)
3. Cao, Z., Wang, Z., Zegura, E.: Performance of hashing-based schemes for internet load balancing. In: IEEE INFOCOM 2000-The Conference on Computer Communications, vol. (1), pp. 332–341 (2000)
4. Tüxen, M., Rüngeler, I., Stewart, R., Rathgeb, E.P.: Network address translation for the stream control transmission protocol. IEEE Network 22(5), 26–32 (2008)
5. Teruhi, S., Uematsu, Y.: End-node-based congestion-aware network load balancing. In: IEEE International Conference on Communications, ICC 2004, vol. 27(1), pp. 2174–2178 (2004)
6. He, J., Rexford, J.: Toward internet-wide multipath routing. IEEE Network 22(2), 16–21 (2008)
7. Amaral, P., Bernardo, L., Pinto, P.: DTIA: An architecture for inter-domain routing. In: IEEE International Conference on Communications, ICC 2009, vol. 32(1), pp. 2191–2196 (2009)
8. Akella, A., Maggs, B., Seshan, S., Shaikh, A.: On the performance benefits of multihoming route control. IEEE/ACM Transactions on Networking 16(1), 91–104 (2008)
9. Huang, C.-M., Lin, M.-S.: Partially reliable-concurrent multipath transfer (PR-CMT) for multihomed networks. In: IEEE Global Telecommunications Conference, GLOBECOM 2008, vol. 27(1), pp. 2494–2498 (2008)
10. Shirasaki, Y., Miyakawa, S., Yamasaki, T., Takenouchi, A.: A Model of IPv6/IPv4 Dual Stack Internet Access Service. RFC 4241 (December 2005)

A New Practical Electric Vehicle Battery Management System

Yanpeng Shi[1,*] and Guoxin Wu[2]

[1] Department of Information Engineering
Liaoning Provincial College of Communications,
Shenyang, 110122 China
shiypeng@163.com
[2] Key Laboratory of Modern Measurement & Control Technology (Ministry of Education),
Beijing Information Science & Technology University,
Beijing, 100192, China
wgx1977@msn.com

Abstract. The lithium battery gradually becomes the mainstream of traction battery owing to its small volume, light weight, high voltage, high power, less self discharge, long service life and other advantages. However certain management is required during the application of Li-ion battery for its obvious nonlinearity, inconsistency and time-variant characteristics. If lithium batteries are used in power equipment in serial, they may have different charge and discharge due to different internal characteristics, when one battery deteriorates, the behavior characteristics of the entire battery pack will be limited so as to lead to deteriorated battery pack performances. The lithium power battery pack management system designed here is installed inside lithium battery pack, takes MCU as the control core and equalizes energy of each lithium battery while achieving over charge, over discharge, overcurrent and short circuit protection.

Keywords: The lithium battery; electric automobile; management system; data processing.

1 Introduction

The lithium battery gradually becomes the mainstream of traction battery owing to its small volume, light weight, high voltage, high power, less self discharge, long service life and other advantages. However certain management is required during the application of Li-ion battery for its obvious nonlinearity, inconsistency and time-variant characteristics. Besides, lithium battery has high charge and discharge requirements; over charge, over discharge, over discharge current or short circuit causes temperature rise and severely damages the performances of lithium battery so as to shorten its service life[1], [2].

---

* The work is supported by National Natural Science Foundation of China (NSFC, No: 50975020) and Funding Project For academic Human Resources Development in Institutions of Higher Learning Under the Jurisdiction of Beijing Municipality(IHLB) (PHR201008443).

R. Chen (Ed.): ICICIS 2011, Part I, CCIS 134, pp. 704–710, 2011.

If lithium batteries are used in power equipment in serial, they may have different charge and discharge due to different internal characteristics, when one battery deteriorates, the behavior characteristics of the entire battery pack will be limited so as to lead to deteriorated battery pack performances. It's necessary to carry out real-time monitoring against lithium battery during charge and discharge, provide over voltage, current and temperature protection and balance battery-to-battery energy in order to maximize its excellent performances and prolong service life.

2   General Schematic Design of System

The lithium power battery pack management system designed here is installed inside lithium battery pack, takes MCU as the control core and equalizes energy of each lithium battery while achieving over charge, over discharge, overcurrent and short circuit protection. States of battery pack are displayed via LCD and historical performance status of each lithium battery is read via communication port reserved in advance[3], [4].

Intelligent management system of power lithium battery is mainly comprised of charge module, data acquisition module (including voltage, current, and temperature data acquisition), balance module, electric calculation module, data display module and storage and communication module. The system chart is as shown in figure 1.

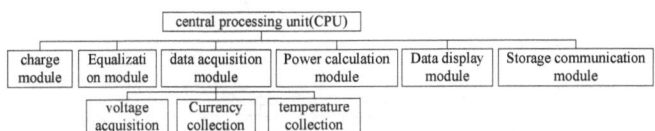

Fig. 1. Management System Structure Diagram takes MCU as main controller, judges the battery pack is in charge, discharge or idle state and whether there is overcurrent via acquisition of current information and takes handling measures in response to relevant states

After acquisition and analysis of voltage of each battery, the system decides whether balance module is started to equalize energy of the entire battery pack and judges whether there is over charge or discharge. Temperature acquisition is mainly for over temperature protection. Working status, current, voltage of each battery, remaining electric quantity and temperature information is shown through LCD module. Realization methods of each module will be described in following sections.

2.1   MCU: Atmega 8

MCU applied to this system is the high performance 8-digit MCU ATmega8 launched by ATMEL. This MCU has all performances and characteristics of high grade AVR MCU, supports In System Programming (ISP), and requires only one self-made download cord for MCU system development. ATmega8 MCU has 6 A/D conversion channels, including 4 channels having 10-digit accuracy and may be directly applied to battery voltage measurement during design. Performances of ATmega8 make it an embedded efficient MCU with high adaptability, flexibility and low cost and particularly suitable for use at development stage.

2.2   Principle and Realization of Charge Control Module

Conventional charge method of lithium battery is carried out in pre-charge, constant current and constant voltage stages in a time sequence as shown in figure 2.

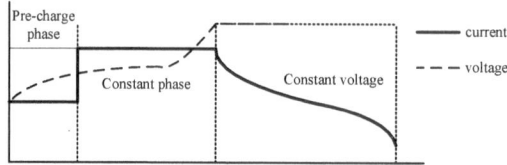

Fig. 2. Constant current and constant voltage stages in a time sequence

As management system is placed in battery box with battery pack and external charger is applied, versatility of the management system will be reduced when communication channels are added to form a loop control with external charger. To improve versatility and enable management system and external charger to work separately, this battery management system adopts intermittent charge method as shown in figure 3.

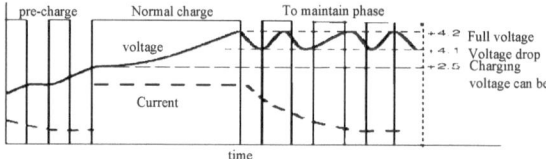

Fig. 3. Intermittent charge method is to ON and OFF charging circuit in an intermittent manner at pre-charge and maintaining stages to change charge current equivalently so as to meet the performance requirement for low current at pre-charge and maintaining stages and high current during normal charge

If battery pack with management system is charged, matching external constant power supply charger shall be connected; the constant voltage shall be: $U = 4.2v * N + \text{voltage loss}$, where N refers to battery quantity. The current limit shall be 0.3C (C refers to battery capacity) of conventional current of the power lithium battery. System initialization must be carried out prior to charging and then battery pack shall be charged with intermittent charge method.

2.3   Principle and Realization of Voltage Sampling Module

During charge of lithium battery, the terminal voltage shall be controlled below 4.2V to prevent battery damage caused by over discharge; it is required that voltage of each lithium battery must be inspected in real-time manner during charging. The management system applies voltage sampling inspection scheme as shown in figure 4[5].

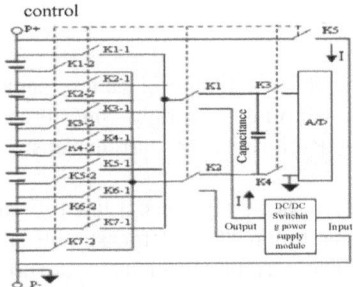

Fig. 4. The working principle is as follows: push SPDT switch K1 and K2 upward to voltage measurement position, and connect capacitances to multi-way switch controlled by MCU kn-1, kn-2 (n=1, 2, 3, 4, 5, 6 and 7) ends of each battery in a synchronous manner to charge capacitors until the capacitor voltage equals to single battery to be measured, then disconnect multi-way switch controlled by MCU kn-1 and kn-2, and close switch K3 and k4 to connect A/D converter for measurement. This scheme uses 10-bit A/D converter directly and requires no additional A/D chip so as to save the design costs. Analog switch in actual circuit is realized by relay.

Power battery pack is a battery module consisting of multiple individual batteries, due to difference between individual batteries in terms of internal characteristics, the battery pack is imbalanced after certain times of charge and discharge so as to affect the efficiency and security of power battery pack seriously. Over charge, discharge, current and temperature and other phenomena occurring during charge and discharge of battery pack sharpen the difference of battery characteristics to cause imbalance between individual lithium batteries in terms of capacity, voltage and other performances and finally lead to abrupt degradation of characteristics of entire battery pack and accelerated damage to partial battery. Therefore, balance between individual batteries in the pack must be solved during the combined use of battery pack.

Resistance, capacitor and transformer balance or other schemes might be applied to balance the capacity between individual batteries. As the management system is in response to large capacity power lithium battery pack, if resistance balance is adopted, there would be high balance speed but too much energy waste; if capacitor balance is used there would be low balance current so that it is unlikely to achieve balance between power lithium batteries. Hence, transformer balance scheme which balances efficiency and speed is applied to this balance module. DC/DC switch power supply module is used directly in specific design. Depending on small power consumption, high efficiency, small volume, light weight and other advantages, switch power supply module is ideal for using as balance module directly. During specific use, it is judged that whether energy balance is needed for battery pack according to voltage of individual batteries detected. If necessary master balance switch K5, and switch K1 and K2 are pushed downward to balance position, and carry out additional charge for the battery with the lowest voltage with energy of the entire battery pack until difference between individual batteries is within the range required by the system.

2.4 Realization of Sampling

Current is the key parameter for estimate of battery capacity so that it imposes high requirement for current sampling accuracy, interference resistance capacity and linearity error. LTSR25-NP closed loop current sensor from LEM is used in this design[6].

This element has excellent accuracy, decent linearity and best response time. With 25A current rating and maximum 80A of measurable current, it meets the requirements of system design. The current sensor may convert charge current into 0V~5V voltage signal which is sent to 10-bit A/D converter in MCU and discharge current with 0.2A of accuracy may be detected after conversion. The working curve is as shown in figure 5.

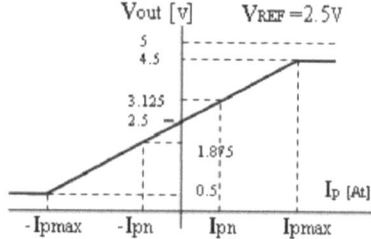

Fig. 5. Working Curve of LTSR25-NP Current Sensor. In the figure, VREF means voltage at reference point and is 2.5V by default, and IP means current to be detected.

Digital temperature sensor DS18B20 from DALLAS Semiconductor Company is used in battery management system for temperature detection. The sensor has single chip structure and outputs 9~12-bit characters without additional A/D converter. One-wire bus protocol is adopted for communication, i.e. operations against DS18B20 might be completed via one data cord. As each DS18B20 contains unique sequence code, each bus may be connected with multiple DS18B20 units therefore DS18B20 is characterized by easy connection and flexible system setting, and is suitable for multiple point temperature detection system, in particular of temperature detection and control system combined with MCU.

LCD selects DM12864M character and graphical dot matrix crystal display module which displays Chinese characters and graphic and with 8,192 Chinese characters (16x16 dot matrix), 128 characters (8x16 dot matrix) and 65x256 dot matrix display RAM. Main technical parameters and display characteristics are as follows:

Power supply VDD: 3.3V~5V (built-in booster circuit and requiring no negative voltage);
Display size: 128 row x 64 line;
LCD type: STN;

Interface with MCU: 8 or 4-bit in parallel/3-bit in serial;

Multiple software functions: cursor display, picture shift, self-defined character, and sleep mode, etc.

This system uses serial interface to display total voltage of battery pack, voltage of individual batteries, charge and discharge current, charge and discharge time, working temperature and remaining power quantity and others via liquid crystal module.

The lithium battery management system writes charge and discharge information, including voltage of individual battery, charge and discharge time, working temperature, and battery power quantity into Flash storage chip SST25VF020 for storage trough real-time sampling during the charge or discharge process of lithium battery. Historical data stored in Flash may be read via serial port and upper level PC communication if necessary.

As SST25VF series of Flash storage chip, SST25VF020 has following characteristics: 2M of total capacity; single supply read and write operations with 2.7V~3.3V of working voltage; low power consumption, with 7mA of working current and 3μA of standby current; up to 33MHz of clock frequency; 100 years storage of data; SOIC and small sized WSON sealing.

3 Software Design

Software design of the system is completed with MCU C language. The main flow chart is shown below.

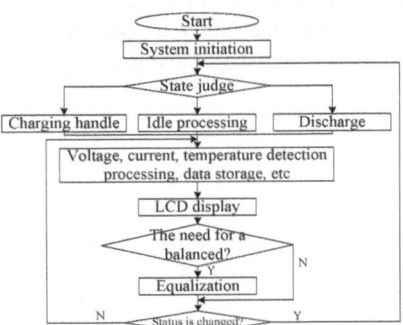

Fig. 6. The system mainly covers individual voltage measurement program, current detection program, temperature detection program, energy balance program, charge management program, LCD display program, data storage and communication program and other program modules

3.1 Voltage Measurement Program

Voltage of individual batteries is measured with 10-bit A/D converter of MCU. The software uses "mean screening value" filtration method in order to improve measurement accuracy. For measuring analog quantity of each battery, several measurements shall be conducted continuously, the highest and lowest values are screened out, and the remaining measurement values are averaged to acquire the best measurement result, and then battery voltage is obtained based on voltage calculation method. Upon the completion of voltage measurement, "bubble sort" program is run to sort all battery voltages, mark batteries with minimum and maximum voltage and serve the balance module.

3.2 Charge Management Program

The charge stage of battery is judged through voltage of individual battery detected, and MCU pulse width modulation (PWM) is used to control MOSFET to achieve charge at low current at pre-charge stage and maintaining impulse charge at charge stage. Charge circuit is opened automatically when completion of charge is detected. The charge management module judges whether the battery is in normal status via voltage, current and temperature detected, opens charge and discharge circuits immediately via MOSFET and illuminates failure prompt lamp in case of over voltage, current or temperature or other phenomena.

4 Conclusion

This design provides intelligent management system to power lithium battery; the system provides the battery pack with various protection and energy balance controls to maximize the entire performance of lithium battery pack. The prototype developed has been tested on Thunder Sky lithium battery pack consisting of 10x100AH batteries in serial, has acquired 6A of maximum balance current and approximately 80% of balance efficiency, with performances fully meeting requirements of power lithium battery pack for energy balance, and shall have good application prospect and promotional value.

References

1. Zhang, A.L., ChaI, Q.H., Shen, W.: Assessment of the potential use of electric and hydrogen powered vehicles in China. Journal of Tsinghua University(Science and Technology 49(9), 107–109 (2009)
2. Ran, Z.Y., Wang, J.P., Chen, Y.H., Wang, Y., Si, X.Y.: BatteryManagemen t System Used for HEV. Journal of Chongqing University of Technology 24(2), 1–5 (2010)
3. Metz, B., Davidson, O., De Coninck, H., et al.: IPCC special report carbon dioxide capture and storage. IPCC [EB/OL] (2005),
   http://www.ipcc.ch/ipccreports/srccs.htm
4. Edwards, R., LarivéJ, F., Mahieu, V., et al.: Well-to-Wheels analysis of future automotive fuels and powertrains. EUCAR, CONCAWE, JRC// IES, London (2006)
5. Niels, J.S., Mutasim, A.S., Naim, A.K.: Energy management strategies for parallel hybrid vehicles using fuzzy logic. Control Engineering Practice 11, 171–177 (2003)
6. Liu, B.J., Wang, Y., Yin, T.M.: EV Battery Management System. Electrical Automation 32(1), 60-62(81) (2010)

Dynamic Methods of Component Composite Service Selection Based on Trust-Aware

Yuan Bo[1], Wang BinQiang[1], Zhao Bo[1], and Song Shasha[2]

[1] National Digital Switching System Engineering & Technology Center,
Zhengzhou, China
yuanbonet@163.com
[2] Institute of Information Engineering, Information Engineering University
Zhengzhou, China
songss@ndsc.com.cn

Abstract. Trust concept and Trust Degree are introduced into ForCES system and trustaware service selection problem in component service composition is discussed. The mathematic models based on exclusive components and shared components are established. The dynamic selection problem of service composition is researched deeply. An dynamic selection methods CCSSGA is designed based on GA. The method is under the environment of service providing perfect service without exceeding threshold and rejecting service with exceeding threshold, or it is under the environment of service's QoS descending when the invoke number increase. The CCSSGA has good effect through experiments and results analysis.

Keywords: Trust degree; service composition; QoS; ForCES; dynamic selection method.

1 Introduction

IETF ForCES (Forwarding and Control Elements Separation) architecture has become one of the international design goals that can work as open network architecture. The basic idea of the ForCES[1-5] is that dividing a router into control and forwarding components, that it may be constituted by several components and communication protocols. Users can select the appropriate set of service-oriented component which can constitutes reconfigurable routing switching system from the set of component for specific business needs.

In practice, ForCES routing system provides flexible user-oriented routing service. Data exchanging aggregates a number of components (such as packet classification, lookup, priority scheduling, etc.). Service composition selection problem is a hot research issue in recent years, there has been much study for this research [6-12]. Literature [6,7] use a non-linear programming method executing services composition from a global perspective. Literature [8] established parameter system of QoS, abstracted grid service composition model of scheduling problem, and gived an algorithm based genetic algorithm. But these work regard the service selection problem

R. Chen (Ed.): ICICIS 2011, Part I, CCIS 134, pp. 711–716, 2011.

as a pure optimization problem, they did not consider service parameters might change during the execution of services composition.

The remainder of the paper is organized as follows. Section 2 of the article discussed the trust-aware service portfolio selection problem and established a mathematical model; In section 3, the dynamic service composition component selection was discussed deeply, a dynamic selection method CCSSGA was designed; in Section 4, simulation results show CCSSGA having good impression; Finally, the paper is concluded in section 5.

2 Component Mathematical Model of Service Composition

We classify component by the same service attributes as a component class in ForCES system, a component class contains multiple component members. In the process of component services there are two cases that are exclusive components and shared components. Exclusive components: components provide service realization only for one combination of service, scheduling engine finished combination of service components by service order, and computed a separate operating cost and QoS. Shared components: a component provided services for multiple service combination implementation, the capacity of component service is fixed. Components running costs and service quality of service affected by a number of combinations.

A.   Mathematical models of exclusive component

There are m kinds of components and each class has n elements, the trust matrix of

component is $\begin{bmatrix} tr_{11} & tr_{12} & \cdots & tr_{1n} \\ tr_{21} & tr_{22} & \cdots & tr_{2n} \\ \vdots & \vdots & \ddots & \vdots \\ tr_{m1} & tr_{m2} & \cdots & tr_{mn} \end{bmatrix}$, the cost matrix of service is $\begin{bmatrix} c_{11} & c_{12} & \cdots & c_{1n} \\ c_{21} & c_{22} & \cdots & c_{2n} \\ \vdots & \vdots & \ddots & \vdots \\ c_{m1} & c_{m2} & \cdots & c_{mn} \end{bmatrix}$,

response time matrix is $\begin{bmatrix} t_{11} & t_{12} & \cdots & t_{1n} \\ t_{21} & t_{22} & \cdots & t_{2n} \\ \vdots & \vdots & \ddots & \vdots \\ t_{m1} & t_{m2} & \cdots & t_{mn} \end{bmatrix}$. We use the component selection

matrix $\begin{bmatrix} x_{11} & x_{12} & \cdots & x_{1n} \\ x_{21} & x_{22} & \cdots & x_{2n} \\ \vdots & \vdots & \ddots & \vdots \\ x_{m1} & x_{m2} & \cdots & x_{mn} \end{bmatrix}$ to represent which component is selected by the

combination of service, $x_{ij} = \begin{cases} 1, & x_{i.j} \text{ is choosed} \\ 0, & \text{others} \end{cases}$, the function of Combination of trust

services, service costs, response time and the elements of trust, service costs, response times are that:

$$f(tr_{11}, tr_{12}, \cdots, tr_{1n}, \cdots, tr_{ij}, tr_{m1}, \cdots, tr_{mn}) = \sum_{i=1}^{m} \sum_{j=1}^{n} x_{ij} tr_{ij} \qquad (1)$$

$$g(c_{11}, c_{12}, \cdots c_{1n}, \cdots, c_{ij}, c_{m1}, \cdots, c_{mn}) = \sum_{i=1}^{m} \sum_{j=1}^{n} x_{ij} c_{ij} \tag{2}$$

$$m(t_{11}, t_{12}, \cdots, t_{1n}, \cdots, t_{ij}, t_{m1}, \cdots, t_n) = \sum_{i=1}^{m} \sum_{j=1}^{n} x_{ij} t_{ij} \tag{3}$$

Trust degree is the positive effect of parameters, service costs and response time is the negative effect of parameters. We can get optimization objectives of service portfolio selection problem, such as (4), (5) shows. T_r is trust the service, C is service costs and T is response time constant. Such optimization problem is multi-choice knapsack problem which is NP-hard problem.

Object:

$$\begin{cases} \max(f(tr_1, tr_2, \cdots, tr_i, \cdots, tr_n)) \\ \min(g(c_1, c_2, \cdots, c_i, \cdots, c_n)) \\ \min(m(t_1, t_2, \cdots, t_i, \cdots, t_n)) \end{cases} \tag{4}$$

Constraints:

$$\begin{cases} f(tr_1, tr_2, \cdots, tr_i, \cdots, tr_n) > Tr \\ g(c_1, c_2, \cdots, c_i, \cdots, c_n) < C \\ m(t_1, t_2, \cdots, t_i, \cdots, t_n) < T \end{cases} \tag{5}$$

B. Mathematical models of shared components

A component can support multiple services simultaneously, With service object increasing, service delivery and QoS of components will decline, so we can't select the components accordance with the original selection criteria.

Utility function that equation(6) shows the number of service components can support at T time, $Ulist(N_{ij}, T)$ represents the set of services that component N_{ij} could Supported. $|Ulist(N_{ij}, T)|$ represents the number of services which are executing. α is standardized coefficient constant.

$$U_{ij}(N_{ji}, T) = \alpha |Ulist(N_{ij}, T)| \tag{6}$$

Utility function equation(7) shows the price of component service at T time, $Cost(N_{ij}, T)$ represents the service costs of component N_{ij} at the moment T, β is standardized coefficient constant., $C_{ij}(N_{ij}, T)$ is a service costs of portfolio service.

$$C_{ij}(N_{ij}, T) = \beta \frac{\sum_{\forall N_{ij} \in U_{ij}(N_{ij}, T)} Cost(N_{ij}, T)}{|Ulist(N_{ij}, T)|} \tag{7}$$

Formula(1) shows function of trust degree that between portfolio service and components. Formula(3) shows function of response time that between portfolio service and components. Formula(8) shows function of service cost that between portfolio service and components.

$$g(c_{11}(N_{ij}, T), c_{12}(N_{ij}, T), \cdots c_{1n}(N_{ij}, T), \cdots, c_{ij}(N_{ij}, T),$$

$$c_{m1}(N_{ij}, T), \cdots, c_{mn}(N_{ij}, T)) = \sum_{i=1}^{m} \sum_{j=1}^{n} x_{ij} c_{ij}(N_{ij}, T) \tag{8}$$

Such problem is NP-hard problem too.

3   Dynamic Selection Based on Genetic Algorithm Approach

Because the multi-objective scheduling is a NP-hard problem. The genetic algorithm based on evolutionary theory[13,14] is suitable for solving such complex optimization problems. Crossover operator is a GA searching operator. The step for Component Composite Service Selection Genetic Algorithm(CCSSGA):

(1) (Initial population). Determining the probability of hybridization p_c, mutation probability p_m, population size N. Using Direct integer encoding and random algorithm to generate initial population which is $X(0)$. Evolution algebra $t = 0$.

(2) (Hybrid). We selected hybrid parents (X^i, X^j) from $X(t)$ in proper order, doing hybrid mode operation using Hybrid Probability p_c. Hybrids Collection is Out_1.

(3) (Variation). we make uniform mutation Against Out_1 using p_m. The result is Out_2.

(4) (select). We randomly select individual which number is $N-1$ from the set $X(t) \cup Out_1 \cup Out_2$, total selecting number is N, $X(t+1)$ is composition of the next generation, $t = t+1$.

(5) When the termination condition is met, the algorithm stopped; Otherwise, transferring step (2).

4   Simulation and Result Analysis

Experiment computer is IBM X3200M2 CPU 3.0GHz, RAM 2GB, Hard disk250GB. GA is implemented by Java. Algorithm parameters are that: Crossover probability is 0.8, Mutation probability is 0.2, $\alpha=\beta=0.001$, the largest number of shared supporting services of component is 10, maximum number of algorithm iterations is 300. Figure 1 shows the test object.

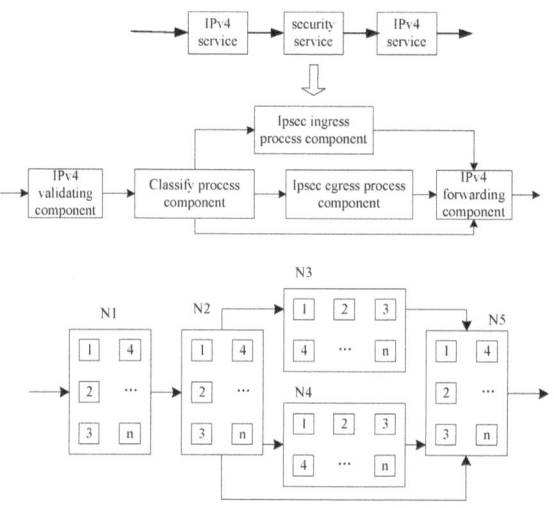

Fig. 1. Routing switching system component security services portfolio example

We used 5 kinds of component, Each type of component has 100 members, N1~N4 are services exclusive style component, N5 is service shared component, $N_{1,8}$ means the 8th component in Component Class 1. Selecting $\{N_{1,9} \; ; \; N_{2,36} \; ; \; N_{3,55} \; ; \; N_{4,87}\}$ from services exclusive style component set and setting parameters is optimal value. Selecting $\{N_{5,47} \; ; \; N_{5,88}\}$ from service shared component set and setting parameters is optimal value. So in the figure 2 there are two optimal path $N_{1,9}{\rightarrow}N_{2,36}{\rightarrow}N_{3,55}{\rightarrow}$ $N_{4,87}{\rightarrow}N_{5,47}$; $N_{1,9}{\rightarrow}N_{2,36}{\rightarrow}N_{3,55}{\rightarrow}N_{4,87}{\rightarrow}N_{5,88}$. There are two test purpose, one is examining the hit rate of the optimal path. The other is examining when components $N_{5,47}$ beyond its limits, using the following algorithm can select the appropriate components again. So we validated the effectiveness of algorithm in trust of components, service costs, response time, etc.

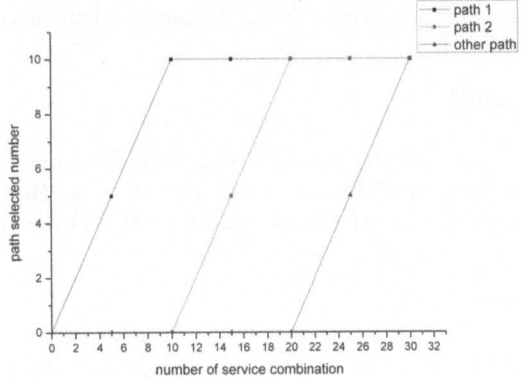

Fig. 2. Times of omposite services and path selected

From figure 3, when M<10, It has not reached the threshold of component $N_{5,47}$ in path 1, all composite services using the path 1; when 10<M<20, component $N_{5,47}$ have reached the saturation number 10, But the rest of composite services do not meet the threshold of path 2, Therefore, all the composite services using the path 1 and path 2. When 20<M, the number of services is beyond the capability of path 1 and path 2. Portfolio service began to use other paths, The path 1 and path 2 maintain the same amount of saturated. Composite service execution path selection according with the service upper threshold value that proved the validity of the algorithm.

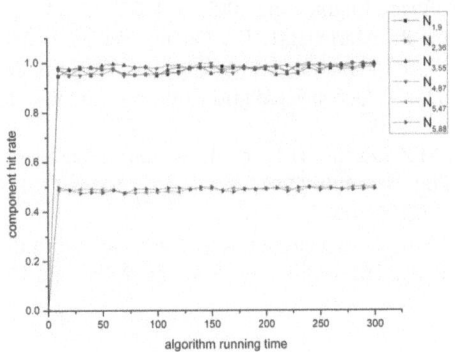

Fig. 3. Algorithm running time and component hit rate

From figure 4, With the increasing of the number of service composition, components {N1,9 ; N2,36 ; N3,55 ; N4,87} remained relatively high hit rate. The hit rate of $N_{5,47}$, and $N_{5,88}$ unchanged.

5 Conclusion

This paper analysisd component service composition problem of ForCES System, according to the characteristics of grid environment and the different needs of component composition, we discussed selection of service composition component based on trust-aware. A new evolution operator was designed and a genetic algorithm CCSSGA was designed to solve this problem. In the future, we will research dynamic task selection algorithm which considering dependent combinations of components.

Acknowledgment

This work is supported by the National High-Tech Research and Development Plan of China under Grant No.2008AA01A323 and National High-Tech Research and Development Plan of China under Grant No. 2009AA01A334 and No.2009AA01A346.

References

1. Wang, W.-M., Dong, L.-G., Zhuge, B.: Analysis and implementation of an open programmable router based on forwarding and control element separation. Journal of Computer science and Technology 23(5), 769–779 (2008)
2. Khosravi, H., Anderson, T.A.: IETF RFC 3654, Requirements for Separation of IP control and Forwarding (2003)
3. Yang, L., Dantu, R., Anderson, T.A., et al.: IETF RFC 3746, Forwarding and Control Element Separation (ForCES) Framework (2004)
4. Wu, H.-b., Xu, M.-w.: Intra-router routing mechanism for ForCES architecture. Journal of Tsinghua University (Science and Technology) 48(1), 124–127 (2008)
5. Halpern, J., Deleganes, E.: ForCES Forwarding Element Model [DB/OL] (2007-10-07), http://www.ietf.org/internet-draft/draft-ietfforces-model-08.txt
6. Zeng, L., Bloualem, B.: Qos-aware middleware for Web services composition. IEEE Transactions on Software Engineering 30(5), 311–327 (2004)
7. Zeng, L., Boualem, B., Marlonetal, D.: Quality driven Web services composition. In: Proceedings of the 12th International Conference on World Wide Web, pp. 411–421 (2003)
8. Wang, Y., Hu, C., Du, Z.: QoS-awared grid workflow schedule. Journal of Software 17(11), 2341–2351 (2006)
9. Zhang, W.Z., Hu, M.Z., Zhang, H.L., et al.: A multi-objective evolutionary algorithm for grid Job scheduling of Multi-QoS constraints. Journal of Computer Research and Development 43(11), 1855–1862 (2006)
10. Li, B., Wang, L.: A hybrid quantum-inspired genetic algorithm for multi-objective flow shop scheduling. IEEE Transactions on Systems, Man, and Cybernetics 37(3), 576–591 (2007)

An Optimization Multi-path Inter-Session Network Coding in Wireless Sensor Networks

Zhuo-qun Xia[1], Chao Liu, Xue-han Zhu, Pin-chao Liu, and Li-tong Xie

School of Computer and Telecommunication Engineering,
Changsha University of Science and Technology, Hunan Changsha 410114 China

Abstract. Wireless sensor networks (wsns) typically provide several paths from a source to a destination, and by using such paths efficiently. This has the potential not only to increase multiplicatively the achieved end-to-end rate, but also to provide robustness against performance fluctuations of any single link in the system. Network coding is a new technique which improves the network performance. This paper we analyze how to using network coding according to the characteristic of multi-path routing in the wsns. As a result, an optimization multi-path inter-session network coding is designed to improve the wsns performance.

Keywords: Wireless sensor networks, inter-session network coding, multi-path routing.

1 Introduction

A wireless sensor network consists of light-weight, low power, small size sensor nodes. There are many areas of applications of sensor networks vary from military, civil, healthcare, and environmental to commercial [1,2]. Data communication in wireless sensor networks (wsns) exhibits distinctive characteristics. Routing in wsns still relies on simple variations of traditional distance vector or link state based protocols, thus suffering low throughput and less robustness. Routing in WSNs exhibits distinctive characteristics significantly affecting routing protocol design. There are some reasons. For instance, wsns is of some highly loss links large and dynamic network size; and data packet size is small (mostly less than 50 bytes); in addition, wsns includes many time-sensitive data.

Network coding has emerged as an important potential approach to the operation of communication networks, especially wireless networks [3]. In general; network coding is performed by encoding multiple packets either from the same user or from different users. The former is called intra-session network coding P[3,4], while the latter is called *inter-session* network coding P[5], [6].

---

[1] Foundation item: Project (091053604) supported by National Student innovative pilot project of China.

R. Chen (Ed.): ICICIS 2011, Part I, CCIS 134, pp. 717–721, 2011.

In wireless sensor networks, sensor nodes may have multiple sensors (light, temperature, seismic) with different transmission characteristics. Packets from a sensor for an application constitute its data flow. For several classes of applications a sensor node may initiate multiple flows that have diverse requirements in terms of transmission rate, reliability, delay and throughput towards the sink. In wsns, usually tens or thousands of sensor nodes are deployed scattered way in an area with one or more sinks. Myriad and divergent types of traffic from simple periodic events to unpredictable bursts of messages are generated by sensor nodes. Moreover, for achieving reliability and load balancing, several multi-path routing protocols have been proposed. But the limitation of these protocols is traffic overhead. Thus the occurrence of congestion in this situation is more likely. The situation becomes worse when congestion occurs in multiple paths. In this paper, we design an optimized multi-path inter-session network coding to improve the wsns performance.

This paper is organized as follow: in section 2 we discuss the related works and our contributions, we give model of multi-path inter-session network coding and how to operate network coding in section 3, and section 4 introduces the conclusion.

2   Related Work and Contributions

There are some papers on applying network coding in wireless sensor network. Haiyang LiuP[7]P etc introduced Chaotic Routing (CR), a set based broadcasting routing framework for WSNs. CR leverages the emerging mesh networking concepts of opportunistic routing and practical wireless network coding. In paper [8], ZHENG GUO design a network coding scheme for underwater sensor networks and explore its performance through simulation. TAO CUI proposed a jointly opportunistic source coding and opportunistic routing (OSCOR) protocol for correlated data gathering in wireless sensor networksP[9]. OSCOR improves data gathering efficiency by exploiting opportunistic data compression and cooperative diversity associated with wireless broadcast. The paper [10] represented the first attempt to address passive link loss inference under network coding traffic in wireless sensor networks. In paper, it shows that network coding changes the fundamental connection between path and link successful transmission probabilities. However, these papers do not consider combine the multi-path and network coding. We will design an optimization multi-path inter-session network coding to improve the wsns performance.

The contribution of this work is twofold: On one hand, our work is one of the original works designing a multi-path inter-session network coding in wireless sensor networks. On the other hand, we optimize the multi-path network coding according to the each path costs in wsns.

3   Multi-path Inter-Session Network Coding

In this section, we propose a multi-path network coding in wireless sensor networks.

3.1 Model of Multi-path Inter-Session Network Coding

Using multi-path inter-session network coding, we firstly introduce the assignment of the data flows in multi-path; then propose an optimization framework for addressing questions of multi-path routing in wireless sensor networks.

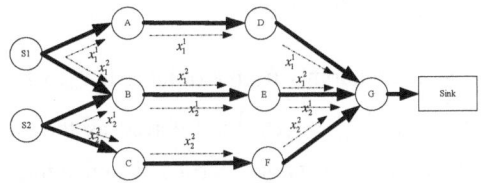

Fig. 1. Multi-path transmission in wireless sensor networks

Consider the scenario depicted in Figure 1. We have two sources of traffic, each of which is aware of two paths leading to its sink node. For example, Source 1 (positioned at s1) can send packets to sink node at rates x_1^1 on path (s1, A, D, G) and x_1^2 on path (s1, B, E, G). In the same way, Source 2 (positioned at s2) can send packets to sink node at rates x_2^1 on path (s2, C, F, G) and x_2^2 on path (s2, B, E, G). Under the current channel conditions, the path (B, E, G) is a link using network coding.

We consider the cost metric of the system to be the number of transmissions required to support a given traffic matrix. We suppose that it is cheaper for Source 1 to send all its traffic on path (s1, A, D, G). However, notice that there is an opportunity for utilizing network coding on a path (B, E, G). So s1 and s2 will send their data packets to node B; then node B send coded packets to node E.

The paper [11] proposes optimality and derives a primal-dual algorithm that lays the basis for multi-path network coding. We refer to the optimization method to optimize the multi-path inter-session network coding. The optimization scheme includes three main models. First the system set a feasible rate set; then a utility maximization is given; and the flows are scheduled according to the utility maximization which should be optimized. The detail of scheme is given in paper [11].

3.2 The Inter-Session Network Coding Implement

(1) Network coding construction

In this paper, we assume that coding for multiple source destination pairs. The routes from the source to the destination are determined by a routing protocol. We use routing protocols that provide multiple paths/routes from the source to the destination. The intermediate nodes on the routes are referred to as *relays*. Node encoder is operated using linear network coding. It receives packets from the synchronizer and encodes these packets. This operation is illustrated in formula (1).The coded data packets are mixed data packets on a single linear mixture. In particular, we assume that the listened packet p_j in the middle nodes is a single data packet. There are k groups of packet with length is n. The forwarding nodes will encode the listened new data packets. In addition to as the encoded payload an additional header is added to the output packet that contains information about the packets and fragments used for encoding.

$$A_i = \sum_{j=1}^{n} a_{ij} p_j, \qquad i = 1, 2, \cdots, k \tag{1}$$

The coefficient a_{ij} is picked randomly from a finite field F_q, where q is the size of the field. The set of coefficients $\left(a_{i1}, \cdots, a_{in} \right)$ is referred as the *encoding vector*. Each packet to be transmitted in the network carries its encoding vector. The source determines the amount of redundancy that it injects into the network by determining n_θ. When the source simply forwards the n packets, we have $n' = n$ and $a_{ij} = 1$, $j = i$, $a_{ij} = 0$, $j \neq i$.

For inter-session network coding, multiple nodes which receive data from environments will further encode packets. If the relay nodes receiving data store incoming packets in a local buffer for a certain period of time and then linearly combines the packets in the buffer. Suppose a relay node r, receives m incoming packets, $p_1^r, \cdots, p_m^r$ Let $f_{i1}, \cdots, f_{ik}$ denote the encoding vector carried by p_i^r, $i = 1, \cdots, m$, Relay r computes m' outgoing packets, $y_1^r, \cdots y_{m'}^r$ by linearly combining the incoming packets. That is $y_i^r = \sum_{j=1}^{m} h_{ij}^r p_j^r$, $i = 1, \cdots, m'$. The coefficient h_{ij} is picked randomly from the finite field F_q.

(2) Decoding implement

Decoding at the sink node is straightforward. The sink node will decode the received mixed data packets. To deliver data packets with the original form, both the uncoded and coded packets will to be buffered. Each arriving packet is inspected by the decoder to determine whether this packet is required for the decoding process or not. If not, it is not encoded; and it is forwarded to the upper layer. When the sink node receives n packets with linearly independent encoding vectors, it recovers the original n packets by matrix inversion. When there are multiple source-destination pairs, a unique node ID is assigned to each node. Packets from a source carry the node ID of that source.

4 Conclusions

A rich body of work has been reported on how network coding can improve performance in both wired and wireless networks. In this paper, we propose an optimization multi-path inter-session network coding in wireless sensor networks. The future work is to demonstrate the performance of the scheme in the test bed.

References

1. Wireless sensor networks (WSN),
   http://www.ececs.uc.edu/~njain/research.html
2. Estrin, D., Govindan, R., Heidemann, J., Kumar, S.: Next century challenges: Scalable coordinate in sensor network. In: Proceedings of the 5th ACM/IEEE International Conference on Mobile Computing and Networking, pp. 263–270. IEEE Computer Society, Seattle (1999)
3. Ahlswede, R., Cai, N., Li, S.-Y.R., Yeung, R.W.: Network information flow. IEEE Trans. Inf. Theory 46(4), 1204–1216 (2000)
4. Chen, L., Ho, T., Low, S., Chiang, M., Doyle, J.: Optimization based rate control for multicast with network coding. In: Proc. of IEEE INFOCOM, Anchorage, AK (May 2007)
5. Traskov, D., Ratnakar, N., Lun, D.S., Koetter, R., Medard, M.: Network coding for multiple unicasts: An approach based on linear optimization. In: Proc. of IEEE ISIT, Seattle, WA (July 2006)
6. Wang, C.C., Shroff, N.B.: Beyond the butterfly: Graph-theoretic characterization of the feasibility of network coding with two simple unicast sessions. In: Proc. of IEEE ISIT, Nice, France (June 2007)
7. Liu, H., Kolavennu, S.: Chaotic Routing: A Set-based Broadcasting Routing Framework for Wireless Sensor Networks. In: The 2008 International Conference on Embedded Software and Systems (July 2008)
8. Guo, Z., Xie, P., Cui, J., Wang, B.: On Applying Network Coding to Underwater Sensor Networks. Ad Hoc Networks 7(4), 791–802 (2009)
9. Cui, T., Chen Ho, L., Low, T., Andrew, S.H.: Opportunistic Source Coding for Data Gathering in Wireless Sensor Networks., 1–11, 8-11 (October 2007)
10. Lin, Y., Liang, B., Li, B.: Passive Loss Inference in Wireless Sensor Networks Based on Network Coding. In: HINFOCOM 2009, IEEEH, April 19-25, pp. 1809–1817. Rio de Janeiro, Location (2009)
11. Radunović, B., Gkantsidis, C., Key, P.: An Optimization Framework for Opportunistic Multipath Routing in Wireless Mesh Networks. In: IEEE INFOCOM 2008 proceedings (2008)

Exploring the Intrinsic Motivation of Hedonic Information Systems Acceptance: Integrating Hedonic Theory and Flow with TAM

Zhihuan Wang

Shanghai Maritime University
zhwang@shmtu.edu.cn

Abstract. Research on Information Systems (IS) acceptance is substantially focused on extrinsic motivation in workplaces, little is known about the underlying intrinsic motivations of Hedonic IS (HIS) acceptance. This paper proposes a hybrid HIS acceptance model which takes the unique characteristics of HIS and multiple identities of a HIS user into consideration by interacting Hedonic theory, Flow theory with Technology Acceptance Model (TAM). The model was empirically tested by a field survey. The result indicates that emotional responses, imaginal responses, and flow experience are three main contributions of HIS acceptance.

Keywords: Hedonic information systems, intrinsic motivation, IT acceptance, TAM, Hedonic theory, Flow.

1 Introduction

Recently, Hedonic information systems (HIS) [1] has drawn significant attentions in IT research. With the fundamental difference between utilitarian IS (UIS) and HIS, previous extrinsic motivation driven models including Technology Acceptance Model (TAM) [2-3] and the Unified Theory of Acceptance and Use of Technology (UTAUT) [4] are found to be problematic or ineffective in predicting individual acceptance of HIS [5-6]. Therefore, additional intrinsic motivators are introduced to investigate the acceptance of entertainment oriented IS. For instance, [7] examined user intentions to explore a technology over time from both hedonic and instrumental perspectives. [8] proposed an Interactivity-Stimulus-Attention Model (ISAM) to explain how intrinsic motivation influences user acceptance of purely hedonic gaming systems. Many other research attempt to use a single positive feeling like fun [9], enjoyment [1, 10-11], playfulness [12-13] and attractiveness [10] to capture the influence of the underlying intrinsic motivation of HIS on user acceptance.

However, given the rich emotional responses of interacting with HIS like online games, a single dimension emotion appears to be insufficient and difficult to model or represent all of these emotional responses. [14], indeed, noted that conceptualizing intrinsic motivation as a single emotion like enjoyment may be limited our understanding of user motivation. In addition, according to [15], an IS user may have multiple identities. For instance, an ebay user is an IT user and a shopper. Both

R. Chen (Ed.): ICICIS 2011, Part I, CCIS 134, pp. 722–730, 2011.

identities can influence whether the user accepts ebay.com [15]. However, most of the previous research are failed to recognize the multiple identities of an IS user and their influence on IS acceptance [15]. This may limit our understanding of the underlying motivations of user acceptance of HIS, and may even mislead our understanding of IS acceptance [16].

The purpose of this study therefore is to explore the underlying intrinsic drivers of users' behavior intention to interacting with a HIS by proposing a HIS acceptance model which takes the unique characteristics of HIS and multiple identity nature of a HIS user into consideration. The structure of this paper is as follow. The next section addresses the theoretical background and hypotheses of this study. Then, we introduce the data collection and analysis approach, which is followed by a discussion of the results. Finally, a conclusion is offered.

2 Theoretical Background and Hypotheses

The theoretical background of this research covers several well established theories including hedonic theory [17], Flow theory [18], and Technology Acceptance Model (TAM) [2]. All of these theories are integrated in the context of HIS acceptance based on the overlapped identities of a HIS user.

2.1 Multiple Identities of a HIS User and Research Model

Identities of a HIS user and their influence on acceptance are rarely investigated [15]. According to [15], an IS user is not simply a computer user, he or she may have other identities. For instance, a user of ebay.com is not only a computer user but also plays the role of a shopper. [19] examined user acceptance of the web-based virtual world from the perspective of hedonic product consumption considering a virtual world user as a hedonic consumer. Moreover, the initial classification of IS into UIS and HIS [1] is also derived from customer behavior research which distinguishes utilitarian and hedonic products [17, 20]. It suggests that an HIS could probably be viewed as a particular hedonic product, while a HIS user could also be considered a hedonic consumer.

In addition to a hedonic consumer, a HIS user may also be considered as a player. The main reason lies in the similar experiences between interacting with an HIS and play-related activities. According to [1], "hedonic information systems aim to provide self-fulfilling value to end users" and "in their purest form, interacting with a hedonic information system is designed to be an end in itself". while play activities can produce experiences enjoyed for players' own sake, without any external rewards [21]. Such experiences of play are referred to variously as "autotelic" [22], "inherently pleasurable" [23], and "nonutilitarian" [24].

This common experience between interacting with a HIS and play experience implies that a user's interaction with a HIS could be viewed as a type of play [12-13]. Therefore, a HIS user could probably also be viewed as a player. This study therefore considers that a HIS user has three identities: a computer user, a hedonic consumer and a player.

In order to reflect the triple identities of a HIS user, a hybrid HIS acceptance research model is proposed which extends the TAM with intrinsic motivations from hedonic theory and flow theory as shown in Fig. 1. This model is developed based on TAM aiming to reflect that a HIS user is primarily a computer user, Integrating imaginal responses and emotional responses, two main contribution of hedonic consumption, reflects that a HIS user also acts as a hedonic consumer; Integrating flow experience with TAM indicate that a HIS user is also a player as flow experience represents an optimal experience of play where skills and challenges are matched [25].

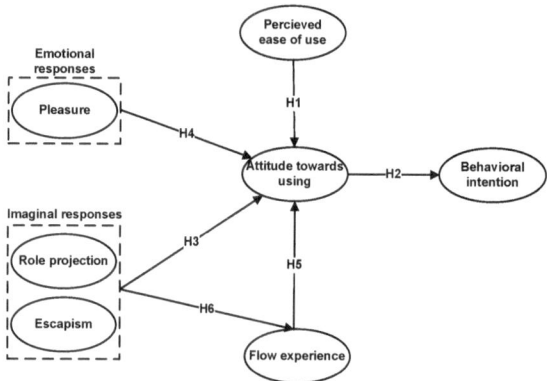

Fig. 1. Research model for HIS acceptance

2.2 Technology Acceptance Model and HIS Acceptance

Perceived ease of use is an assessment of the mental effort involved in the use of IS. According to [1], in the context of HIS, the achievement of external goals is subordinate to using the system itself. As a result, perceived ease of use may play a more central role in predicting user acceptance of HIS. Studies on HIS [26-27] also note that perceived ease of use is a strong and direct predictor of users' intention to use MMS. Therefore, in the context of HIS, we expect that perceived ease of use has a positive influence on HIS acceptance. Thus, we propose the following hypothesis:

H1: Perceived ease of use has a positive influence on users' attitude towards using a HIS.

Perceived usefulness is defined as "the degree to which a person believes that using a particular system would enhance his or her job performance" [2, p. 320]. It is found to be problematic for HIS [1, 28-29] we will not include perceived usefulness in our research model.

In the context of HIS acceptance, intrinsic motivations are the main drivers of the acceptance of a HIS [1]. People's feelings (e.g., enjoyment and fun) of the systems a play more important role [1]. Thus, attitude should have a direct influence on users' intention to use a HIS. We hypothesize:

H2: Attitude towards using a HIS has a positive influence on behavioral intention to use the HIS.

2.3 Hedonic Theory and HIS Acceptance

Hedonic theory is developed to explain and describe the intrinsic motivations underlying the hedonic consumption of aesthetic products such as ballet, music, and movies [17]. It posits that the unique consumption experience is the main contribution of hedonic consumption. This unique experience refers to imaginal and emotional responses [19, 30]. Imaginal Responses mainly refer to role projection and escapism [19, 31]. While emotional responses mainly refer to pleasure [7].

Since a HIS user is also acts as a hedonic consumer, theories which work well for hedonic consumption may be equally applicable for HIS acceptance. Therefore, we hypothesize:

H3: Imaginal responses have a positive influence on attitude towards using a HIS
    H3a: Role Projection has a positive influence on attitude towards using a HIS.
    H3b: Escapism has a positive influence on attitude towards using a HIS.
H4: Pleasure has a positive influence on attitude towards using a HIS.

2.4 Flow Experience and HIS Acceptance

The concept of flow was introduced [22 p. 36], and defined as "the holistic sensation that people feel when they act with total involvement". To supplement the concept of flow, [32] suggest two attributes as the principal components of optimal flow: concentration and enjoyment. [33] suggests that distortion in time perception is an important construct of flow state.

Flow is also introduced to explain the adoption and usage of some HIS. Hsu and Lu's [28] finds that flow is strongly related to individual's intention to play online games. This is consistent with a recent study on mobile gaming which suggests that people's attitude towards mobile gaming is significantly influenced by a flow experience [10]. Thus we hypothesize:

H5: Flow experience has a positive influence on attitude towards using a HIS
Since imaginal responses (role projection and escapism)is a type of deep mental involvement [31], we also hypothesize :

H6: Imaginal responses have a positive influence on flow.
    H6a: Role Projection has a positive influence on flow.
    H6b: Escapism has a positive influence on flow.

3 Research Methodology

3.1 Data Collection

Empirical data was collected by an online survey which was hosted on surveymonky.com. An advertisement which includes a link to this online survey was developed and distributed through the advertising platform of Facebook.com, targeting people who are particularly interested in video games. Therefore, the advertising of the survey will be automatically displayed on potential participants' screen. If they are interested in the survey, they may click the advertisement and be directed to the online survey to take part in the survey. Totally, we received 294 responses and 226 of them are completed. The majority of the participants are experienced young online game players. Most of them are play games in a weekly and daily basis. 65.5% of the participants are male. About 85% of the participants are not older than 25.

3.2 Measurement

All of the measures and their items are adapted from previous research and rephrased particularly to fit the context of online gaming. Perceived ease of use (EOU), Attitude (ATT) and Behavioral Intention (BI) are adapted from TAM. Hedonic theory related measures, Escapism (ESC) and Role Projection (RP), are from [19]. The three measures (Enjoyment, Time Distortion, and Concentration) used to measure the flow experience are from two studies: Enjoyment (ENJ) and Time Distortion (TD) are adapted from [13] and Concentration (Con) is from [34]. Pleasure used to represent emotional responses is from [38].

4   Data Analysis and Results

The overall data analysis strategy used in this study follows the two-step analysis procedures [35] which first examines the measurement model, namely, the psychometric properties of all scales are first assessed through Confirmatory Factor Analysis (CFA). Then, it examines the structural model.

4.1 The Measurement Model

Measurement model analysis mainly involves convergent validity and discriminant validity. Convergent validity refers to the extent to which the indicators of a construct that are theoretically related should highly correlate [36]. Our analysis indicated that the factor loadings for all items are greater than acceptable level (0.6) and at a significant level of 0.001. Each construct satisfies the recommended levels of composite reliability (0.7) and Average Variation Extracted (0.5) [37]. Therefore, convergent validity is shown. Discriminant validity is the extent to which the measure is not a reflection of other variables, and there is a variation in the sample on the key variables[36]. CFA analysis showed that all indicators load more strongly on their corresponding constructs than on other constructs. Moreover, our analysis also found that inter-construct correlations are much greater than square root of AVE (Average Variance Extracted). This indicates that all constructs share more variance with their own indicators than with other constructs. Thus, according to [37] discriminant validity is shown.

4.2 Structural Model

Fig.2 presents the result of our study with overall explanatory power, including the variance explained, path coefficients and their significant level. In addition, the solid lines represent the significant paths while dotted lines are for non-significant paths. According to Fig. 2, emotional responses (Pleasure) and flow experience have significantly influence users' attitude. Imaginal responses (escapism and role projection do not have a direct influence on attitude but are mediated by flow experience. The path between Attitude and Behavioral intention is the most strong and significant relationship in this model. Generally, the combination of emotional responses and flow experience explained 41.3% of the variance of Attitude, while attitude, in turn, explained 33.2% of the variance of Behavioral intention.

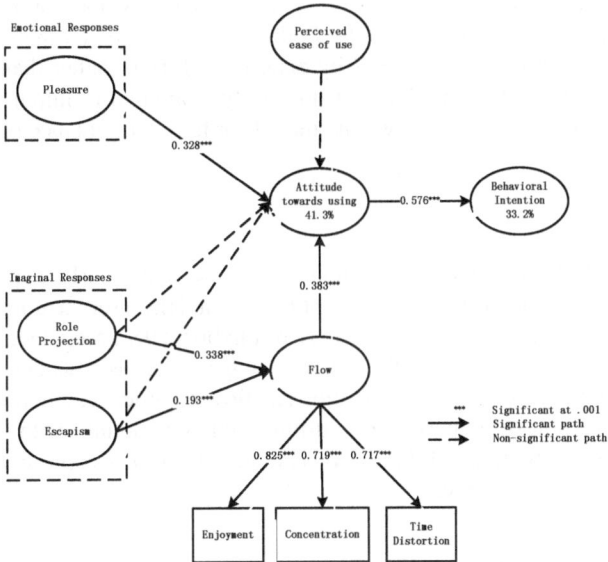

Fig. 2. Results of path analysis

5   Discussion and Limitations

For TAM, perceived ease of use does not have a significant influence on attitude towards using a HIS. Possible reason is that most of the participants are exerienced game players [4].

The influence of imaginal responses on atttitude towards using a HIS and flow experience, to our knowledge, has not been tested by other researhers before. This is the first attemp to understand the effect of role projection and escapism on flow and HIS acceptance. It is suprising that both role projection and escapism do not have a significant influence on attitude towards using a HIS but mediated by flow experience. As a result, both emotional responses and imaginal responses influence the acceptance of HIS. Since emotional responses and imaginal responses are adapted from hedonic theory, the viewpoint of a HIS user as a hedonic consumer is well supported.

The result of data analysis indicates that flow experience has a strong influence on attitude, which is consistant with the finding of recent research on mobile game acceptance [10], another typical HIS. This result also support the insight that a HIS user is not only an IT user but also a player who does not use the system but plays with the system.

However, our study is not without limitations. When generalizing the findings of this study, some limitations need to be taken into consideration. One important limitation of this study is its sample. Most of the participants in this study have rich experience in playing online games, and people have no or little online gaming experience are not included. Thus the survey bias may have crept into the research design as those non-users are not included in the sampling frame. It is conceivable that an experienced user's motivation to play an online game follows a different pattern from that of an initial-user. The findings of this research therefore are more likely to reflect the acceptance of HIS by experienced users rather than initial-users. Caution is advised when the findings of this study is applied to initial acceptance of HIS. We urge other researchers to test the model for initial acceptance of HIS.

6 Conclusion

In conclusion, HIS acceptance is a relatively new and poorly explored area of research. This study identifies three identities of a HIS user: a computer user, a hedonic consumer and a player, and proposed a hybrid HIS acceptance model which integrates hedonic theory, flow with TAM. It suggests that user acceptance of HIS is highly related with such intrinsic motivations as flow experience, emotional responses and imaginal responses experienced during their interacting with HIS. Further research can use the findings of this study as a basis to further explore the underlying motivations of HIS acceptance.

Acknowledgment

This work was supported in part by Shanghai Science Commission Project (No. 09DZ2250400, 10692103500, 09530708200, 08170511300) and Shanghai Education Commission Project (No. J50604, 11YZ137).

References

1. Van der Heijden, H.: User Acceptance of hedonic information systems. MIS Quarterly 28(4), 695–704 (2004)
2. Davis, F.D.: Perceived Usefulness, Perceived Ease of Use, and User Acceptance of Information Technology. MIS Quarterly 13(3), 319–340 (1989)
3. Davis, F.D., Bagozzi, R.P., Warshaw, P.R.: User Acceptance of Computer Technology: A Comparison of Two Theoretical Models. Management Science 35(8), 982–1003 (1989)
4. Venkatesh, V., et al.: User Acceptance of Information Technology: Toward a Unified View. MIS Quarterly 27(3), 425–478 (2003)
5. Scheepers, R., Scheepers, H., Ngwenyama, O.K.: Contextual influences on user satisfaction with mobile computing: findings from two healthcare organizations. European Journal of Information Systems 15(3), 261–268 (2006)
6. Taylor, S., Todd, P.A.: Understanding information technology usage: a test of competing models. Information Systems Research 6(2), 144–176 (1995)

7. Magni, M., Susan Taylor, M., Venkatesh, V.: [']To play or not to play': A cross-temporal investigation using hedonic and instrumental perspectives to explain user intentions to explore a technology. International Journal of Human-Computer Studies 68(9), 572–588 (2010)
8. Lowry, P.B., et al.: Proposing the Interactivity-Stimulus-Attention Model (ISAM) to Explain and Predict the Enjoyment, Immersion, and Adoption of Purely Hedonic Systems. In: Special Interest Group on Human-Computer Interaction 2007 Pre-ICIS Workshop, Montreal (2007)
9. Okazaki, S., Skapa, R., Grande, I.: Global youth and mobile games: applying the extended technology acceptance model in the U. S.A, Japan, Spain, and the Czech Republic. Advances in International Marketing 18, 253–270 (2007)
10. Ha, I., Yoon, Y., Choi, M.: Determinants of adoption of mobile games under mobile broadband wireless access environment. Information & Management 44(3), 276–286 (2007)
11. Davis, F.D., Bagozzi, R.P., Warshaw, P.R.: Extrinsic and Intrinsic Motivation to Use Computers in the Workplace. Journal of Applied Social Psychology 22(14), 1111–1132 (1992)
12. Webster, J., Martocchio, J.J.: Microcomputer Playfulness: Development of a Measure With Workplace Implications. MIS Quarterly 16(2), 201–226 (1992)
13. Agarwal, R., Karahanna, E.: Time flies when you're having fun: Cognitive absorption and beliefs about information technology usage. MIS Quarterly 24(4), 665–694 (2000)
14. Malhotra, Y., Galletta, D.F., Kirsch, L.J.: How Engogenous Motivations Influence User Intentions: Beyond the Dichotomy of Extrinisic and Instrinsic User Motivation. Management Information System 25(1), 267–299 (2008)
15. Koufaris, M.: Applying the Technology Acceptance Model and Flow Theory to Online Consumer Behavior. Information Systems Research 13(2), 205–223 (2002)
16. Ayyagari, R.: Examination of hedonism in TAM research. In: Proceedings of the 2006 Southern Association for Information Systems Conference (2006)
17. Hirschman, E., Holbrook, M.B.: Hedonic Consumption: Emerging Concepts, Methods and Propositions. Journal of Marketing 46(3), 92–101 (1982)
18. Csikszentmihalyi, M.: Flow: the Psychology of Optimal Experience. Harper & Row, New York (1990)
19. Clyde, W.H., Jiming, W.: User Acceptance of Virtual Worlds: The Hedonic Framework. Database for Advances in Information Systems 38(4), 86–89 (2007)
20. Holbrook, M.B., Hirschman, E.: The experiential aspects of consumption: Consumers fantasies, feelings, and fun. Journal of Consumer Research 9(2), 132–140 (1982)
21. Day, H.I.: Play: A ludic Behavior. In: Day, H.I. (ed.) Advances in Intrinsic Motivation and Aesthetics, pp. 225–250. Plenum, New York (1981)
22. Csikszentmihalyi, M.: Beyond boredom and anxiety: the experience of play in work and games. Jossey-Bass, San Francisco (1975)
23. Calder, B.J., Staw, B.M.: Self-perception of intrinsic and extrinsic motivation. Journal of Personality & Social Psychology 31(4), 599–605 (1975)
24. Hutt, C.: Toward a taxonomy and conceptual model of play. In: Day, H.I. (ed.) Advances in Intrinsic Motivation and Aesthetics, pp. 251–298. Plenum, New York (1981)
25. Csikszentmihalyi, M.: Play and Intrinsic Rewards. Journal of Humanistic Psychology 15(3), 41–63 (1975)
26. Hsu, C.-L., Lu, H.-P., Hsu, H.-H.: Adoption of the mobile Internet: An empirical study of multimedia message service (MMS). Omega 35(6), 715–726 (2007)

27. Lee, M.K.O., Cheung, C.M.K., Chen, Z.: Understanding user acceptance of multimedia messaging services: An empirical study. Journal of the American Society for Information Science & Technology 58(13), 2066–(2077)
28. Hsu, C.-L., Lu, H.-P.: Why do people play on-line games? An extended TAM with social influences and flow experience. Information & Management 41(7), 853–868 (2004)
29. Pagani, M.: Determinants of adoption of third generation mobile multimedia services. Journal of Interactive Marketing 18(3), 46–59 (2004)
30. Lacher, K.T., Mizerski, R.: An Exploratory Study of the Responses and Relationships Involved in the Evaluation of, and in the Intention to Purchase New Rock Music. Journal of Consumer Research 21(2), 366–380 (1994)
31. Hirschman, E.: Predictors of self-projection, fantasy fulfillment, and escapism. Journal of Social Psychology 120(1), 63–76 (1983)
32. Ghani, J.A., Deshpande, S.P.: Task characteristics and the experience of optimal flow in human-computer interaction. The Journal of Psychology 128(44), 381–391 (1994)
33. Novak, T., Hoffman, D., Yung, Y.: Measuring the customer experience in online environments: A structural modelling approach. Marketing Science 19(1), 22–44 (2000)
34. Ghani, J.A., Supnick, R., Rooney, P.: The experience of flow in computer-mediated and in face-to-face groups. In: DeGross, J.I., et al. (eds.) Twelfth International Conference an Information Systems B2 - Twelfth International Conference an Information Systems. GVU, New York (1991)
35. James, L.R., Muliak, S.A., Brett, J.M.: Casual analysis: assumptions, models, and data. Sage, Los Angeles (1982)
36. Chin, W.: The Partial Least Squares Approach to Structural Equation Modeling. In: Marcouiides, G.A. (ed.) Modern Methods for Business Research. Lawrence Eribaum Associates, Mahwah (1998)
37. Fornell, C., Larcker, D.F.: A second generation of multivariate analysis: Classification of methods and implications for marketing research. In: Houston, M.J. (ed.) Review of marketing, pp. 407–450. American Marketing Association, Chicago (1987)

Vision-Guided Robot Tracking Algorithm Based on Characteristic Description of Maneuvering Target

Yuan Zhang, Peng Wang, Xin Li, Shaochen Kang, Jinglei Xin, and Wenhao Jiang

School of Mechanical & Power Engineering, Harbin University of Science and Technology,
Xuefu road. 52, 150080 Harbin, People's Republic of China
Wp_hust@yahoo.com.cn

Abstract. The change of appearance characteristic is caused by changing viewpoint in the maneuvering target tracking. The traditional Camshift tracking algorithm based on a single color histogram model is not robust to this variation. In this paper, image moment invariant is proposed to describe maneuvering target to enhance model description, through its recursive algorithm to optimize the target model and refresh the weight value. The experiment result demonstrates that, comparing with the single fixed model and the self-adaption single model, the new algorithm can adapt for the appearance variation of the target rapidly and with small calculated amount.

Keywords: Target tracking, invariant moment, Camshift, Vision-guided robot.

1 Introduction

Target tracking is widely used in the military and the civil, the mainly application fields including vehicle monitoring [1], highway traffic control, air defense, ballistic missile defense, air attack, ocean surveillance, battlefield surveillance, air traffic control and so on [2]. As the research focus of maneuvering target tracking, the accuracy and the real-time should be ensured at the same time, but it's hard to realize in the actual situation.

Meanshift, as a typical representative of the matching searching algorithms [3], is emphasized and widely researched owing to its small calculated amount and strong adaptability for target transformation and rotation variation [4]. There are two basic versions: Camshift and Standard Meanshift, they both show the target model with color-based histogram [5], get the weighted image centroid through iterating to track target. Camshift gives the pixels equal weights during the calculation and computes the weighted image with back-projection produced from object histogram, and the weighted image called probability graph. Standard Meanshift weights the pixels with kernel functions satisfying some condition and gets the iterative formula [6], which can obtain the centroid position of the target, with the Bhattacharyya coefficient between the maximum target model and the candidate target model [7]. Essentially, the purpose of the iteration is to get the weighted image centroid, while the weighted image here is more complicated than the probability graph.

R. Chen (Ed.): ICICIS 2011, Part I, CCIS 134, pp. 731–736, 2011.

The variation of the observed angle changes the target appearance characteristic when the vision-guided robot tracks maneuvering target. The traditional Camshift based on single color histogram can't meet this change, so the image moment invariant characteristic is introduced to describe maneuvering target to enhance the description in this paper.

2 The Research for Maneuvering Target Moment Invariant

From the content above, we find that the different order geometry moments and central moments can show the different characterizations. In this paper, the solely invariant set which can describe the variations of the maneuvering target, such as size, translation, rotation and etc, is needed. The invariant represents a special character because it is sole for an image, while there is no business with the distance and the movement of the camera. It is hard to distinguish the target with the standard model considering deformation, central position and zoom of the maneuvering target at some time.

The moment invariant character is the moment characteristic keeping invariable after translation, rotation and zoom, the 7 moment invariants is shown as below:

$$\left(\begin{array}{l} M_1 = \eta_{20} + \eta_{02}, M_2 = (\eta_{20} - \eta_{02})^2 + 4\eta_{11}^2 \\ M_3 = (\eta_{30} - 3\eta_{12})^2 + (3\eta_{21} - \eta_{03})^2 \end{array}\right. \tag{1}$$

Where η_{20}, η_{02}, η_{11}, η_{30}, η_{03} and η_{21} are respectively second order central moments and third order central moments which are zero order central moments processed by normalization.

If these characteristic values are calculated by the formula of normalization central moment, the computation amount is large, so it can't meet the real-time. In the applications, the three moment groups are modified as below.

$$t_1 = M_1, t_2 = M_2, t_3 = \sqrt[5]{M_3^2} \tag{2}$$

Moment technology supplies a way that maneuvering target is decomposed into a series of finite eigen values; this way is simplicity and very diversification. In the applications, especially real-time pattern recognition, the operation speed is crucial, so the research for rapid moment algorithm is necessary.

The recursive algorithm can speed up the calculation, it decomposes 2D image into two cascaded one-dimensional moments:

$$m_{KL} = \sum_{i=1}^{N} i^K \sum_{i=1}^{M} j^L x_{ij} = \sum_{i=1}^{N} i^K S_{iL} \tag{3}$$

Where $S_{iL} = \sum_{i=1}^{M} j^L x_{ij}$.

The advantage of the way is that multiplication is omitted in low order moment calculation, for example, calculate line i zeroth order moment S_{i0}:

$$S_{i0} = \sum_{j=1}^{M} x_{ij} \qquad (4)$$

Recursive summation: $S_{i0}(j) = S_{i0}(j-1) + x_{ij}(j)$, Where the initial value of S_{i0} is 0. The first moment is shown as:

$$S_{i1} = \sum_{j=1}^{M} j x_{ij} \qquad (5)$$

Under the recursive summation calculation, with $j \equiv (j-1)+1$, the first moment S_{i1} is shown as:

$$\sum_{j=1}^{M} j x_{ij} = \sum_{j=2}^{M} (j-1) x_{ij} + \sum_{j=1}^{M} x_{ij} \qquad (6)$$

Expand the recursive formula, we can get:

$$\sum_{i=1}^{M} j x_{ij} = \sum_{i=3}^{M} (j-2) x_{ij} + \sum_{i=2}^{M} x_{ij} + \sum_{i=1}^{M} x_{ij}$$

$$= x_{iM} + \left(x_{iM} + x_{i(M-1)} \right) + ... + \sum_{j=3}^{M} x_{ij} + \sum_{j=2}^{M} x_{ij} + \sum_{j=1}^{M} x_{ij} = \sum_{i=1}^{M} \sum_{n=M+i-j}^{M} x_m \qquad (7)$$

The multiplication is omitted based on this method; superficially, there are more addition operations but actually not, that is because of the recursive formula below:

$$S_{i1}(j) = S_{i1}(j-1) + S_{i0}(j) \qquad (8)$$

There are only 2M addition operations in this algorithm. Similarly, the second moment S_{i2} can be calculated with $j^2 \equiv (j-1)^2 + (j-1) + j$:

$$S_{i2} = \sum_{j=1}^{M} j^2 x_{ij} \qquad (9)$$

The recursive formula of S_{i2} is:

$$S_{i2}(j) = S_{i2}(j-1) + S_{i1}(j) + S_{i1}(j-1) \qquad (10)$$

Similarly, the third moment can be calculated with $j^3 \equiv (j-1)^3 + j^3 + j^2 + (j-1)^2 - j$. The horizontal calculation can be done based on the vertical moment; firstly, take the output of vertical moment S_{iL} as the import of the horizontal calculation, and then calculate the horizontal moment same as the vertical.

3   The Maneuvering Target Dynamic Model

The movement of the target is autonomously maneuvering, what's more, the system signals and the noise interferences are random, so under the controlled condition, this system can be taken as widely stationary random process. The dynamical tracking model can be described with mathematics as:

$$Z(t) = \varphi(\Delta t)Z(t - \Delta t) + \delta(t) + E(t - \Delta t) \tag{11}$$

Where $Z(t)$ is the state of the system at time t; $\varphi(\Delta t)$ is state transfer matrix of the invariant moment within Δt; $\delta(t)$ is initial state; $E(t)$ is the estimation error.

In this paper, the target moves in the horizontal plane perpendicular to the camera and its variation size is small within the whole visual field, so the search window can be ensured with the position and the area of the target, what's more, the target is in the maneuvering movement state most of the time, so the speed factor can't be omitted, the effect of the target characteristic combined with the movement speed should be taken into consideration.

Assume that the moment invariant information has been obtained based on characteristic matching at time t-1, complete the steps below at time t:

1) Refresh the tracking model state;
2) Camshift;
3) Weight refreshing: refresh the current sample weight with the moment invariant factor;
4) State estimation;
5) Target identification: matching identification with estimating state and target characteristic.

4   The Experiment and Analysis

Firstly, mobile robot is taken as maneuvering target. Set the order to make it move within the visual field and track it with Meanshift algorithm and the new algorithm researched in this paper respectively. The new algorithm defines the sampling scope around the target neighborhood with the invariant information characteristic, and then make the every particle moves towards the neighboring local extreme point combined with Meanshift, it enhances the accuracy and the real-time of tracking with the effective sampling. The contrasting experiment results are shown as Fig.1 and Fig.2.

From the contrast we can get that it is easy to cause unsuccessful tracking when the maneuvering target moves out of the search window, while the new algorithm combined the moment invariant characteristic description can solve the problem, thus ensuring the stability of the tracking.

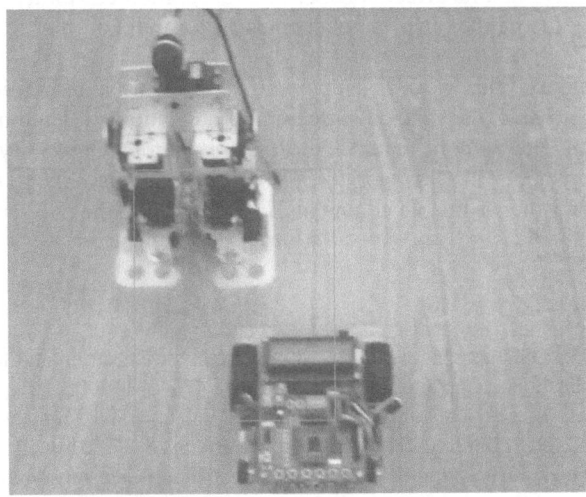

Fig. 1. The traditional Camshift tracking result

Fig. 2. The algorithm proposed here tracking result

5 Conclusions

The method of the moment invariant is brought in Camshift algorithm in this paper, so a new Camshift tracking algorithm is produced, and then through designing and optimizing the target characteristic description model to self adaptively switch or combine according to the current tracking environment successfully so that the robustness of tracking on the variation appearance target is better. This scheme mechanism is clear and its effect is good. The recognition capability of the model will be enhanced by fusing the other target characteristics in the further research.

Acknowledgments. This work is supported by National Natural Science Foundation of China (No. 61071205) and post-doctoral Foundation of Heilongjiang Province (LBH-Z09212). The authors would like to thank Harbin University of Science and Technology for supporting this work. The authors would also like to thank the editors and reviewers for their valuable comments and for making the paper more readable.

References

1. Xu, K., Li, W.: Feature Extraction Based on Amplitude Spectrum and Moment Invariants and Its Application. Acta Automatica Sinica 32(3), 470–474 (2006)
2. Yan, B.: Fast Target-Detecting Algorithm Based on Invariant Moment. In: Nagel, W.E., Walter, W.V. (eds.) Infrared Technology, vol. 23(6), pp. 8–12 (2001)
3. Peng, J.: The Hand Tracking for Humanoid Robot Using Camshift Algorithm and Kalman Filter. Journal of Shanghai Jiaotong University 40(7), 1161–1165 (2006)
4. Zhang, H.: Object tracking algorithm based on CamShift. Computer Engineering and Design 27(11), 2012–2014 (2006)
5. Xu, K.: Object tracking algorithm with adaptive color space based on CamShift. Journal of Computer Applications 29(3), 757–760 (2009)
6. Ding, Z.: Motive object Detection Based on Camshift Algorithm. Computer Knowledge and Technology 5(36), 10532–10533 (2009)
7. Wang, P., Ye, X.: The Research of Bionic Robot DynamicTarget Tracking System. Applied Mechanics and Materials 33, 332–336 (2010)

Fuzzy Comprehensive Evaluation of Peak Load Unit Based on Entropy Weight

Zhengyuan Jia, Zhou Fan, and Shaohui Chen

School of Business Administration, North China Electric Power University,
Baoding 071003, China
jzy111111@126.com, fanzhou2836@163.com

Abstract. The paper summarized and analyzed the index system which influence peak load unit based on the design scheme of peak load units, and selected the peak load units In this paper, the scheme of peak load units are selected through fuzzy comprehensive evaluation method based on entropy weight, using the entropy weight method to determine the weights, by this method the problem of weight allocation can be avoided. The fuzzy comprehensive evaluation method overall evaluating the peak load unit and selecting optimal peak load units. Use the case analysis to prove the method is scientific and reasonable.

Keywords: Peak Load Unit, Entropy Weight, Fuzzy Comprehensive Evaluation.

1 Introduction

The function of peak load unit is to adjust the peak value, frequency and modulation of power system, it is important to maintain the security and stability of power system. Select the appropriate peaking units can not only reduce environment pollution, but also produce considerable economic benefit and social benefit, so, the appropriate select of peak load unit is essential to entire society.

The paper select the appropriate peak load unit based on entropy of fuzzy comprehensive evaluation method, determine the index weight by the use of entropy method. The traditional methods to determine the index weight are subjective assignment method, but use entropy weight to determine the weight is a better way to avoid the subjective factors which can make bias. The paper use Fuzzy comprehensive evaluation method to conduct an overall evaluation of the cycling unit.

2 Program Targets System Peak Load Units

Peak load unit is auxiliary system for a particular power project, the function is adjust the peak value, frequency and modulation of power system, it also can keep the power system operated safety and stability. It must take economic factors, economic feasibility and design benefits into account so as to avoid the cost when construct the peak load units. The cost which can avoid purchase expense for power grid refers to

R. Chen (Ed.): ICICIS 2011, Part I, CCIS 134, pp. 737–743, 2011.
© Springer-Verlag Berlin Heidelberg 2011

the volume and capacity for power station design, and the cost is necessary to avoid total cost. In addition, peak load unit construction must take both environmental factors and social factors into account.

The select plans of peak load units are as follows:

(1) Coal-fired scheme
(2) The cycle unit combined gas and steam
(3) 70% coal-fired and 30% the cycle unit(scheme of 70% coal-fired)
(4) 50% coal-fired and 50% the cycle unit(scheme of 50% coal-fired)
(5) 30% coal-fired and 70% the cycle unit(scheme of 30% coal-fired)

Due to the differences among design scheme, it must bring the different influence for economy, society and environment, so, the paper obtain the index system according to a scientific and reasonable comprehensive analysis and the index system are as follows:

Table 1. Index system peak load units

The optimal program of peak load unit	Economic feasibility	Finance net present value(Million Yuan)
		Financial internal rate of return %
		Investment (Million Yuan)
		Payback period (Years)
		ROI %
	Environmental feasibility	Farmland (mu)
		Air pollution (harmful gas emissions)
		Water Pollution
		Ash and ash field
		Ecological impact
	Social feasibility	Resource conditions
		Technical conditions
		Financial condition
		Solve the employment
		Demolition

3   Entropy Weight Coefficient Determined

The entropy is a concept in thermodynamics, which was first introduced by the information theory of Shannon. The basic idea of entropy method is that the bigger the difference degree index, the weight is more important. How to calculate the index among entropy is the key link of the conversion, which directly affects the correctness of the objective weight of each index, it also impact the safety and rationality of the evaluation. In the information theory, entropy reflects the degree of its value disorder, the smaller the value system, the smaller the disorder. We can get index weight and utility according to the evaluation of information entropy, use judge matrix we can determine the index weight. The calculation procedure is as follows:

(1) Construct the evaluation matrix with dimension of m×n

$$R = (r_{ij})_{mn} = \begin{pmatrix} x_{11} & x_{12} & \cdots & x_{1n} \\ x_{21} & 22 & \cdots & x_{2n} \\ \vdots & \vdots & \vdots & \vdots \\ x_{m1} & x_{m2} & \cdots & x_{mn} \end{pmatrix} \tag{1}$$

x_{ij} is the j index value of i object, $(i = 1,2,3. \cdots m; j = 1,2,3, \cdots .n)$.

(2) Normalized processing for judging matrix B:
Normalized processing for positive indicator

$$b_{ij} = \frac{x_{ij} - \min(x_{ij})}{\max(x_{ij}) - \min(x_{ij})} \tag{2}$$

Normalized processing for reverse indicator

$$b_{ij} = \frac{\max(x_{ij}) - x_{ij}}{\max(x_{ij}) - \min(x_{ij})} \tag{3}$$

$\max(x_{ij})$ is the most satisfying and $\min(x_{ij})$ represents the most unsatisfying.

(3) According to the definition of entropy, the entropy of evaluation indexes are

$$H_i = -\frac{1}{\ln m}(\sum_{j=1}^{m} f_{ij} \ln f_{ij}) \tag{4}$$

$$f_{ij} = \frac{b_{ij}}{\sum_{j=1}^{m} b_{ij}} \tag{5}$$

While $\ln f_{ij} = 0$, and there $f_{ij} \ln f_{ij} = 0$.

(4) Calculate the entropy of evaluation index.

$$W = (w_i)_{1 \times n} \tag{6}$$

$$w_i = \frac{1 - H_i}{n - \sum_{i=1}^{n} H_i} \tag{7}$$

$$\sum_{i=1}^{n} w_i = 1. \tag{8}$$

Different weight can reflect the different influence of different index in decision-making. The smaller value and larger weight for entropy, it means the index provides more useful information.

4   Fuzzy Comprehensive Evaluation

4.1   The Fuzzy Comprehensive Evaluation Can Generally Be Summarized in the Following Steps:

(1) Establish the factor set $U = (u_1, u_2, u_3 \cdots u_n)$,

(2) Give the evaluation level $V = (v_1, v_2, v_3, v_4) = ($Very good; good; general; poor$) = (90, 80, 70, 60)$

(3) Establish the membership function. Using expert scoring method, the number of expert is p, the number of index is n, and the judge matrix is c_{np}.

$$c_{np} = \begin{pmatrix} c_{11} & c_{12} & \cdots & c_{1m} \\ c_{21} & c_{22} & \cdots & c_{2m} \\ \vdots & \vdots & \vdots & \vdots \\ c_{n1} & c_{n2} & \cdots & c_{nm} \end{pmatrix} \quad (i = 1,2,3,\cdots,n; \ j = 1,2,3,\cdots,m) \tag{9}$$

Where c_{ij} said the number of notes on the index i and evaluation level j by p experts.

Membership is:

$$r_{ij} = \frac{c_{ij}}{p} \tag{10}$$

(4) Create index membership matrix R

$$R = \begin{pmatrix} r_{11} & r_{12} & \cdots & r_{1m} \\ r_{21} & r_{22} & \cdots & r_{2m} \\ \vdots & \vdots & \vdots & \vdots \\ r_{n1} & r_{n2} & \cdots & r_{nm} \end{pmatrix} \tag{11}$$

4.2   The Fuzzy Comprehensive Evaluation Model

Obtain the matrix of the fuzzy comprehensive evaluation factors according to the fuzzy mathematics

$$Q = WR = (w_1, w_2, \cdots, w_n). \begin{pmatrix} r_{11} & r_{12} & \cdots & r_{1m} \\ r_{21} & r_{22} & \cdots & r_{2m} \\ \vdots & \vdots & \vdots & \vdots \\ r_{n1} & r_{n2} & \cdots & r_{nm} \end{pmatrix} \tag{12}$$

Where Q is the fuzzy set of V,

$$Q = (q_1, q_2, q_3, \cdots, q_m)$$

Evaluation results:

$$P = V.Q^T \tag{13}$$

5 Empirical Analysis

The paper design five plans for selecting appropriate peak load unit according to the power structure and energy resource of power system. We can process the original data by soft according to feasibility study of economy and the result is as follows:

Table 2. Evaluation of the program's economic value

plan	Financial NPV (Million Yuan)	Financial internal rate of return %	Investment (Million Yuan)	Payback period (Years)	ROI %
1	204705.1	23.43	298311	13.2	20.5
2	184523.2	25.21	264598	12.6	16.5
3	223480.6	22.01	314562	15.8	18.6
4	268962.2	18.23	394562	16.4	25.6
5	146523.2	26.32	221563	11.2	24.2

Entropy method is used to determine index weight and we can construct the normalized comparison matrix according to the above formula.

$$B = \begin{pmatrix} 0.4752 & 0.6428 & 0.5563 & 0.6154 & 0.5604 \\ 0.3103 & 0.8628 & 0.7512 & 0.7307 & 1.0000 \\ 0.6285 & 0.4672 & 0.4624 & 0.1154 & 0.7692 \\ 1.0000 & 0.0000 & 0.0000 & 0.0000 & 0.0000 \\ 0.0000 & 1.0000 & 1.0000 & 1.0000 & 0.1538 \end{pmatrix}$$

According to the formula, we also obtained:

$$H_i = \begin{pmatrix} 1.2314 & 1.1356 & 1.2561 & 1.1523 & 1.0845 \end{pmatrix}$$

$$W_i = \begin{pmatrix} 0.2691 & 0.1577 & 0.2978 & 0.1771 & 0.0983 \end{pmatrix}$$

A Judge is the first to create a single matrix. Assumed rate of 10 experts, the financial net present value of this factor, 6 people think that the feasibility of this program very good, 2 people think it is better, two people think in general. On to do a similar evaluation of other factors, then the expert evaluation matrix C.

$$C_{ij} = \begin{pmatrix} 6 & 2 & 2 & 0 \\ 5 & 4 & 0 & 1 \\ 4 & 4 & 1 & 1 \\ 5 & 1 & 3 & 1 \\ 7 & 2 & 1 & 0 \end{pmatrix}$$

According to the index membership function, the membership matrix of indicators
R

$$R = \begin{pmatrix} 0.6 & 0.2 & 0.2 & 0 \\ 0.5 & 0.4 & 0 & 0.1 \\ 0.4 & 0.4 & 0.1 & 0.1 \\ 0.5 & 0.1 & 0.3 & 0.1 \\ 0.7 & 0.2 & 0.1 & 0 \end{pmatrix}$$

Fuzzy comprehensive evaluation of economic viability is

$$Q_1 = W_1.R_1 = (0.2691 \ 0.1577 \ 0.2978 \ 0.1771 \ 0.0983) \begin{pmatrix} 0.6 & 0.2 & 0.2 & 0 \\ 0.5 & 0.4 & 0 & 0.1 \\ 0.4 & 0.4 & 0.1 & 0.1 \\ 0.5 & 0.1 & 0.3 & 0.1 \\ 0.7 & 0.2 & 0.1 & 0 \end{pmatrix}$$

$$= (0.5168 \ 0.2734 \ 0.1466 \ 0.0633)$$

Similarly, the fuzzy comprehensive evaluation of environmental feasibility and social feasibility are

$$Q_2 = (0.2356 \ 0.4586 \ 0.1214 \ 0.1844)$$
$$Q_3 = (0.3187 \ 0.2514 \ 0.1623 \ 0.2676)$$

According to the formula, the final result of fuzzy comprehensive evaluation is

$$P = V.(W.Q)^T = V.(W. \begin{pmatrix} Q_1 \\ Q_2 \\ Q_3 \end{pmatrix})^T$$

$$= (90 \ 80 \ 70 \ 60) \times ((0.3 \ 0.3 \ 0.4) \times \begin{pmatrix} 0.5168 & 0.2734 & 0.1466 & 0.0633 \\ 0.2356 & 0.4586 & 0.1214 & 0.1844 \\ 0.3187 & 0.2514 & 0.1623 & 0.2676 \end{pmatrix})^T$$

$$= 78.46$$

Using the same method we can get other solutions of fuzzy comprehensive evaluation score for each scheme, and then, obtain the optimal plan for adjusting the peak load.

6 Summary

The paper evaluated the plan of adjusting peak load comprehensively based on entropy fuzzy comprehensive evaluation method. From examples we can see that this method is not only scientific and practical, but also can avoid a lot of errors which indexes cannot be objective and reasonable evaluation.

References

1. Jia, Z., Fan, Z., Jiang, M.: Distribution Network Planning Based on Entropy Fuzzy Comprehensive Method. In: 2010 International Conference on AMM, vol. 780, pp. 26–28 (2010)
2. Yang, K., Liu, Y., Wang, L.: Entropy-based fuzzy evaluation model for optimal selection in the construction. Sichuan Building Science (2009)
3. Jiang, H., Wang, Z., Liu, C.: The quality of highway projects Fuzzy comprehensive evaluation. Shanxi Architecture (2010)
4. Czajkowski, L.D.: Entropy-based fuzzy comprehensive evaluation method in the application of thermal power plant site. Coal (2010)
5. Li, J., Liu, J., Niu, D.: Based on Standards for Power Grid Corporation confidence crisis management capacity entropy weight and fuzzy synthetic evaluation. North China Electric Power University (2009)
6. Xieji, J., Liu, C.: Fuzzy Mathematics and Its Applications. Huazhong University Press, Wuhan (2000)

Molecular Variation of *Potato Virus Y* in China

Hongyi Yang[1,2], Nana Zhang[2], Debin Li[2], and Lili Li[3,*]

[1] College of Horticulture, Northeast Agricultural University, Harbin, China
[2] College of Life Sciences, Northeast Forestry University, Harbin, China
[3] College of Horticulture, Shenyang Agricultural University, Shenyang, China
lilili0622@yahoo.com.cn

Abstract. *Potato virus Y* (PVY) is an important viral pathogen infecting *Solanaceous* crops. The study was conducted to analyze the characterization of molecular variation of PVY isolates in China. Sequence analysis of coat protein (CP) gene for 48 Chinese isolates of PVY showed nucleotide identities ranged from 76.8 to 100.0%. Phylogenetic analysis showed that all PVY isolates formed five groups, and there was not a tendency for isolates to group according to their geographical origin or hosts. Recombination analysis showed that no typical recombination event was found. A high level of sequence variability was found among PVY isolates, and it was likely to have several complicated strains of PVY in China.

Keywords: *Potato virus Y*; Variation; Phylogenetic analysis.

1 Introduction

Potato virus Y (PVY) is an important viral pathogen infecting *Solanaceous* crops, and the significant yield losses could be caused by PVY [1]. Two main strains of PVY are differentiated on the basis of their reaction in *Nicotiana tabacum*: PVY^O inducing a systemic mottle and PVY^N with a veinal necrosis [2]. In addition, two strains including PVY^C and PVY^{NTN}, which caused severve chlorotic mosaic or mottle in the virus indicator plants, were also reported. PVY occurs naturally in commercial cultivars of potato. The virus particles of PVY are filamentous, approximately 680-900 nm in length. Recently, the complete nucleotide sequence of PVY was elucidated, and the genome of PVY consisted of a ssRNA of about 9700 nt [3]. Biological indexing is the earliest method for PVY detection, but the symptoms are complicated for different strains. Mild strains usually cause slight mottle, but severe strains cause extreme loss, and the leaves are small and distorted [2].

Studies on the molecular variation of virus based on the nucleotide and amino acid sequences are becoming an important topic. The virus isolates of different geographical origin are the basic materials for studying molecular variation, fortunately, nucleotide sequences of a great deal of isolates in China has been reported. The study was conducted to analyze the characterization of molecular variation of PVY.

---

[*] Corresponding author.

R. Chen (Ed.): ICICIS 2011, Part I, CCIS 134, pp. 744–748, 2011.

2 Materials and Methods

2.1 Nucleotide and Amino Acid Sequences of Chinese PVY Isolates

The nucleotide sequences of coat protein (CP) gene for 4 PVY isolates, corresponding to 4 strains (PVY^C, PVY^O, PVY^N, and PVY^{NTN}), were obtained form GenBank with the accession numbers: PVU09509, EF026074, EF026075, and NC_001616, respectively. The position of nucleotide and deduced amino acid in CP for Canadian isolate (GenBank accession numbers: PVU09509) was defined as the referenced criterion for other isolates in the study. The different hosts and geographical origins of PVY isolates were showed in Table 1 in the study.

Table 1. The different hosts and geographical origins of PVY isolates

GenBank Acc. No.	Host	Geographical origin	Isolate
PVU25672		Beijing	
GU550507	tobacco	Shandong	SD
AY742716		Shandong	Qingzhou
AY742732		Heilongjiang	Mudanjiang-13-5
AY742728		Heilongjiang	Mudanjiang-11-1
AY742731		Heilongjiang	Mudanjiang-8-3
AY742727		Heilongjiang	Mudanjiang-8-2
AY742733		Beijing	HXCH-2
GU073999	tobacco	Heilongjiang	
FJ766533	potato	Guizhou	guiyang
AY742721		Anhui	Fengyang-12-3
AY742720		Anhui	Fengyang-10
AY742729		Anhui	Fengyang-8-2
AY742719		Anhui	Fengyang-8-1
AY742718		Anhui	Fengyang-6
AY742717		Anhui	Fengyang-4-1
AY742730		Anhui	Fenggang-5
AY742725		Anhui	Fenggang-1
GU074000		Dalian, Liaoning	Dalian
AY742714		Beijing	
AY742722		Beijing	Beijing-2-1
AY742724		Beijing	Beijing-0-3
AY742723		Beijing	Beijing-0-1
AY841257	tobacco		AFY1
AY601681		Yunnan	2
AY601680		Yunnan	1
AY841269	tobacco		XCH46
AY841268	tobacco		XCH44
AY841266	tobacco		XCH43
AY841265	tobacco		XCH39
NC_001616			
EF026074	potato	USA	PVY-Oz

Table 1. (*Continued*)

GenBank Acc. No.	Host	Geographical origin	Isolate
AY841263	tobacco		XCH38
AY841264	tobacco		XCH36
AY841262	tobacco		XCH35
AY792597		Shandong	SD-TA
AY841261	tobacco		XCH31
AY841260	tobacco		XCH30
AY841259	tobacco		XCH25
AY841258	tobacco		XCH25
HM036205	potato	Xinjiang	Ur2-PVYCP7
HM036204	potato	Xinjiang	Ur2-PVYCP6
HM036203	potato	Xinjiang	Ur2-PVYCP5
HM036202	potato	Xinjiang	Ur2-PVYCP3
HM036201	potato	Xinjiang	Ur2-PVYCP2
HM036200	potato	Xinjiang	Ur2-PVYCP1
EF063710	potato	Guizhou	SL053
AY841267	tobacco		XCH47
AY742715		Shenyang	Shenyang
PVU09509	potato	Canada	
EF026075	potato	USA	PB312

2.2 Analysis of Sequences

Multiple sequence alignment of the nucleotide and deduced amino acid sequences was carried out by CLUSTAL X (1.83), and the blank region was artificially modified. Identities of nucleotide and amino acid sequences were calculated using the LaserGene software (DNASTAR, Madison, WI). Phylogenetic analysis was carried out by MEGA 4.0 [4].

The aligned sequences were checked for incongruent relationships that might have resulted from recombination, using RDP, GENECONV, BOOTSCAN, MAXCHI, CHIMAERA and SISCAN programs in RDP2 [5]. These analyses were done using default settings for the different detection programs.

3 Results and Discussion

In 52 isolates of China, the hosts of 26 isolates were reported in GenBank. The isolates were isolated from tobaccos or potatoes, other hosts were not found. Multiple sequence alignment of nucleotide sequences of CP (801 nt) was conducted between all 52 isolates of PVY, and the blank region of CP was artificially modified. The alignment of deduced amino acid sequences of CP gene was also carried out, and percent of nucleotide and amino acid sequence identifies were calculated by LaserGene software. Sequence analysis of CP gene of various PVY isolates showed nucleotide identities ranged from 76.8 (between isolate Beijing and Mudanjiang-13-5) to 100.0% (between Heilongjiang's isolate Mudanjiang-8-3, Mudanjiang-8-2, and Anhui's isolates Fengyang-10, Fengyang-6, Fengyang-8-2). The variation of deduced amino acid sequences of CP gene was slight, and amino acid sequences of some isolates were the same, but the variation of amino acid sequences of isolates of Heilongjiang was high.

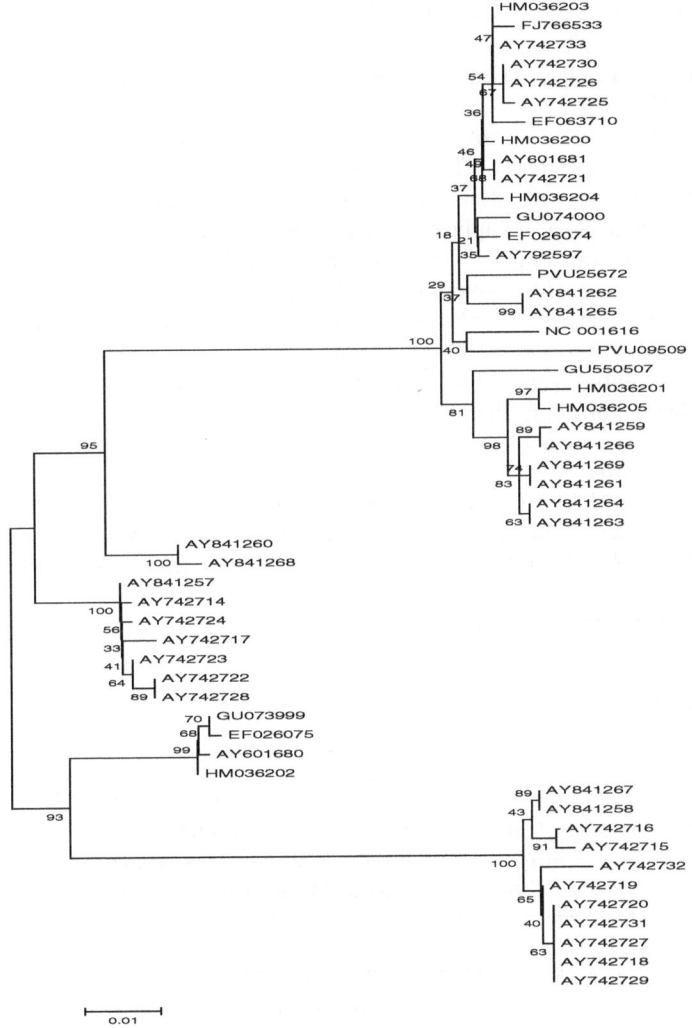

Fig. 1. Phylogenetic tree based on the nucleotide sequences of CP of PVY. Bootstrap value was signed in branchs.

Phylogenetic tree was obtained by MEGA 4.0 based on the nucleotide sequences of CP gene of PVY (Fig. 1). There was not a tendency for isolates to group according to their geographical origin or hosts, and it was similar to the tree based on the deduced amino acid sequences of CP gene. Phylogenetic analysis showed that all PVY isolates formed five groups. Group 1, the biggest one, consisted of 26 Chinese isolates and 2 American isolates, and it was likely to be a mixed group concluding strains PVY^O, PVY^N, and PVY^C. Group 2 had only 2 isolates from tobacco. Group 3 was composed by 7 isolates from Beijing, Anhui, and Heilongjiang, and the isolates had high identities of nucleotide. Group 4 consisted 3 Chinese isolates and 1 American isolate, the group was possible the representative for strain PVY^{NTN}. Group 5 was mainly made up of isolates from Anhui and Heilongjiang. On the whole, the variation of CP gene of Chinese PVY isolates was very complicated, and the isolates came mainly from tobacco and potato, in addition, presumably, 4 strains of PVY were possible in existence in China.

In the study, there was not a tendency for isolates to group according to their geographical origin or hosts. The *Solanaceous* crops were very abundant in China. Molecular variation and strain differentiation were more advantageous in the condition of huge area, complicated terrain and various entironments. There were probable several strains of PVY in China, which could be obtained through analysis of nucleotide sequence and symptoms in indicator plants.

Recombination analysis showed that typical recombination events were not found using RDP, GENECONV, BOOTSCAN, MAXCHI, and CHIMAERA programs in RDP2. Few potential recombination events could be found by analysis with SISCAN programs, but it was not further testified and had a low P-value.

Acknowledgments. The study was supported by China Postdoctoral Science Foundation (20080430877, 200902369), Postdoctoral Science Foundation of Heilongjiang (LBH-Z08252), Science and Technology Innovation Foundation for Talented Scholars of Harbin (RC2008QN002060), Specialized Research Fund for the Doctoral Program of Higher Education (20090062120009), and the Fundamental Research Funds for the Central Universities (DL09CA13).

References

1. Valérie, B., Michel, T., Flora, C., Pierre, L., Camille, K., Emmanuel, J.: Improvement of Potato virus Y (PVY) Detection and Quantitation Using PVY^N- and PVY^O- Specific Real-time RT-PCR Assays. J. of Virol. Methods 134, 261–266 (2006)
2. Hull, R.: Matthews' Plant Virology, 4th edn. Academic Press, San Diego (2002)
3. Robaglia, C., Durand-Tardif, M., Tronchet, M., Boudazin, G., Suzanne, A.M., Francine, C.D.: Nucleotide Sequence of Potato Virus Y (N Strain) Genomic RNA. J. Gen. Virol. 70, 935–947 (1989)
4. Kumar, S., Tamura, K., Nei, M.: MEGA3: Integrated Software for Molecular Evolutionary Analysis and Sequence Alignment. Brief. in Bioinformatics 5, 150–163 (2004)
5. Martin, D., Rybicki, E.: RDP: Detection of Recombination amongst Aligned Sequences. Bioinformatics 16, 562–563 (2000)

The Overview of Entity Relation Extraction Methods

Xian-Yi Cheng, Xiao-hong Chen, and Jin Hua

School of Computer Science and Technology Nantong University, Nantong 226019, China
xycheng@ntu.edu.cn

Abstract. The Information extraction can be defined as the task of extracting information of specified events or facts, and then stored in a database for the users' querying. Only with the correct relationship between the various entities, the database can be correctly store in. Entity relation extraction becomes a key technology of information Extraction system. In this paper, we analyze the status of entity relation extraction method; propose several problems for this field to be solved.

Keywords: Text mining, entity relation, information extraction.

1 Introduction

In the field of information extraction, entity is the basic information elements of the text, and it is the basis of proper understanding of the text[1]. Narrowly defining, the entity is the concrete or abstract entities in the real world, such as person, organization, company, location, etc. Generally, it's expressed by Unique identifier (proper name), such as person's name, organization's name, company's name, location's name and so on. Broad defining, the entity can also contain the time, the expressions of quantifier. The exact meaning of the entity can only be determined by specific application, for example, in specific application, the address, e-mail, telephone number, ship number, conference name, etc. can be use as named entity.

Relation is seen as the link of two entities within a period of time or space[2]. In the Research of information extraction, relation detection plays a key role in the identification and description of events. Thus, the extraction of semantic relation between entities is an important information extraction in the field of basic research. It's used in many research domains, such as, Information retrieval, question answering, ontology construction, information filtering, machine translation, etc.

If we assume, the main function of information extraction is automatically converted form text into data form, the entity extraction determines various elements of the form, and then the entity relation extraction determines the relative position of these elements in the form.

Before discussing the entity relation extraction, firstly we define what are relations and the classification of relations.

From a mathematical perspective, relation is equal to a subset of the Cartesian product; from a computer perspective, relation is a two- dimensional table; from a logical perspective, relation is more than binary predicate. It is noted that the relation

R. Chen (Ed.): ICICIS 2011, Part I, CCIS 134, pp. 749–754, 2011.
© Springer-Verlag Berlin Heidelberg 2011

what we discussing does not include function, functional relations, unary predicted, numerical relations, event relations, logical relations, etc.

It is more complex in the classification of relations, form the formal of the relations, it has: binary relations and multi-relations; grammatical relations, semantic relations and pragmatic relations; explicit relations and implicit relations. Form the environment of the relations, it has: web entity relations and plain text entity relations. From the pattern of the relations, it has: pre- defined relations and non-pre-defined relations. In recently research, it always pays attention to binary relations, grammatical relations, explicit relations, web relations and pre-defined relations.

The seven pre-defined entity relations we frequently used giving by

ACE (automatic content extraction, ACE) are: part-whole relations (PART-WHOLE), physical relations(PHYS), generic-affiliation relations (GEN-AFF), Metonymy relations (METONYMY), agent- artifact(ART), organizational affiliation relations (ORG-AFF), personal-social relations (PER-SOC), each category also includes a number of sub-types[3]. HowNet also predefines a number of relationships[4].

2 Knowledge-Based Entity Relation Extractions

This method of extraction uses linguistic knowledge, before the implementation of extraction, it constructs a pattern set based on words, speech or semantic, and then stored in database. During the relation extraction, the Pretreatment sentence fragment will try to match with the pattern in the pattern set. IF the match is successful; we can conclude that this sentence fragment has a corresponding relationship property of the pattern.

During using the knowledge-based entity relation extraction method, the most difficult step is the construction of relations pattern. Initially, the construction of relations pattern depended on linguists, they analyzed the corpus related to the extraction task in depth, used the existing linguistic achievements, enumerated every possible expression of relationship, constructed the relation pattern by hand. On the one hand, this method make the period of construct the pattern too long, and make the application cost too high; on the other hand, if the extraction system is used for relation extraction in new fields, the Linguists need to extract features of the new field to re-construct relations pattern. This is very difficult to realize in reality. To solve this problem, several scholars have raised different solutions. Douglas E.[5] proposed FASTUS extraction system in MUC-6, express a variety of domain- dependent rules in a extensible, common mode through the introduction of the "macro" concept. Roman Yangarber et al.[6] proposed Proteus extraction system in MUC-7, the pattern constructing method of relation extraction in this system based on sample generalization.

3 Feature-Based Entity Relation Extractions

This method is not need to write knowledge rules by special experts, only need many samples used as training data, construct a classifier by a variety of learning method, express as multi- dimensional feature vector by training samples.

During the processing of entity relation extraction using machine learning method based on the feature vector, the most important aspect is the construction method of the sample feature vector. Only select the appropriate features, it can represent the entities correctly, and then improve the learning effect. The appropriate features of the so-called are the classification-related features; these features have a strong degree of differentiation.

The feature vector is a numerical representation of the instance, that is, the instance is converted into feature vector, among them, x_i is ith element of the n-dimensional feature vector. The purpose of the feature-based machine learning method is for a given set of training data (x1,y1)', (x2,y2)', ..., (xn,yn)', Which for the binary classification problem yi∈ {1,+1}, learning a classification function f, so that for a given new feature vector xi, f can classify it correctly.

The general method that the entities pair (E1,E2) construct the feature vector in a sentence given in fig.1.

E1.TYPE, E2.TYPE, E1.SUBTYPE, E2.SUBTYPE, Order

$$W_{i-w}, W_{i-w-1}, ..., W_{i-1}, W_{i+1}, ..., W_{i+w-1}, W_{i+w}$$

$$t_{i-w}, t_{i-w-1}, ..., t_{i-1}, t_{i+1}, ..., t_{i+w-1}, t_{i+w}$$

$$W_{j-w}, W_{j-w-1}, ..., W_{j-1}, W_{j+1}, ..., W_{j+w-1}, W_{j+w}$$

$$t_{j-w}, t_{j-w-1}, ..., t_{j-1}, t_{j+1}, ..., t_{j+w-1}, t_{j+w}$$

Fig. 1. The feature vector construction

Among them, E.TYPE is the class for the entity belongs, E.SUBTYPE is the subclass for the entity belongs. Order is the position relationship between the two entities, that is, 0 (E1 at the left side of E2), 1 (E1 at the right side of E2), 2 (E1 contains E2), 3(E2 contains E1). I and j respectively are the location of the two entities appearing one after another, Wk and tk respectively are the Chinese words and the speech in location k.

The vector that constructed by all the properties of the entities pair in a sentence is seen as xi, the classification mark is seen as yi, that constitutes a multi-classification sample (xi, yi). The multiple categories can be classified by the binary classifier, it has "one to many" and "two to two" classification methods, we use the "one to many" method.

4 Kernel-Based Entity Relation Extractions

Kernel-based methods can make use of many different forms of data organization to express entity relationship. While calculating the distance between the entities, it can use kernel function other than the inner product of eigenvectors. Any kernel function is implicitly calculating the dot product of the object feature vector in high- dimensional feature space, that is , in many cases, it can calculate their dot product not need to enumerate all the features. In natural language processing, the typical instances are the subsequence kernels and the parse tree kernels.

Compared with the feature vector based method, the advantage of Kernel-based method is that it can express entity relation more flexible, and it can colligate multi-disciplinary knowledge and information through the kernel function mapping. The kernel function has complex excellent properties, thus the final entity relationship distance can be completed by the kernel methods from many different information sources, improving the accuracy. Zelenko proposed a machine learning method based on kernel function for the relation extraction[7]. He firstly defined the kernel function based on shallow parse expression in the text, and designed an efficient dynamic programming algorithm to calculate the value of kernel function. Secondly, used the support vector machine (SVM) and voting perceptions algorithm respectively to achieve information extraction, the experiments showed that the kernel method has very good performance.

5   Hybrid Model-Based Entity Relation Extractions

Though the machine learning system become the mainstream recently, Particularly for simple marking problems, knowledge engineering system (rule-based) in general compared to the standard information extraction systems such as: MUC, ACE, and KDD, their performance is the best.

The advantage of the knowledge engineering system is to use the manual mode to extract entities and entity relationships, model can be understood, and can be improved, but improving the effect of pure machine learning system requires additional training data. The impact of adding additional data quickly becomes very small, while the cost of manual annotation of data increases linearly.

TEG is a hybrid entity relation extraction system[2], it is based on knowledge engineering and machine learning systems together. System is based on SCFG. The grammar rules for extraction are artificial regulations, and the probability is trained by a set of annotations. The disambiguation capability of PCFG makes the knowledge engineering system write simple rules, thus eliminating the artificial workload required.

In addition, the training set scale required is lesser than pure machine learning system required (under the same accuracy). Moreover, the rule- establishing and corpus-annotating can balance with each other.

TEG grammar description is composed by the statement and rules, Rules are mainly follow the classic rules of grammar, can be simply written by symbols [ ] and | , the conterminal in the rule must be declared before using. Some extracted entities required, events and instances can be declared as the output concept. In addition, it also needs to declare two types of terminator: glossary and n-gram.

Glossary is a series of terms that is clear or extracted by a single semantic category introduced from external resources. The instances in glossary are: village, city, state, gene, protein, human surname, job name, etc. Some linguistic concepts such as propositions can be considered as the glossary. Actually, for each term, glossary and the conterminal in the rule are equivalent.

N-gram is more complex. When using in rules, it can be extended to any term. However, the probability of generating a given term is not defined in the rule, but it can be obtained from the training set, and based on the previous or the first few terms. Therefore, the one of possibilities of using the n-gram is that TEG rule is context-sensitive.

6 Social Network-Based Entity Relation Extractions

That social networks research shows that social networks are an important feature which is the network shown in the community structure. Numerous studies found that many networks are heterogeneous, which is the nature of social networks. It is not a large number of identical nodes connected randomly, but rather a combination of many types of nodes. There are more connections between nodes in the same type, and different types of connections between nodes are relatively small. So the researchers to meet the same type of nodes and edges between these nodes posed by the sub-graphs are networks group or community (Community), shown in Fig.2.

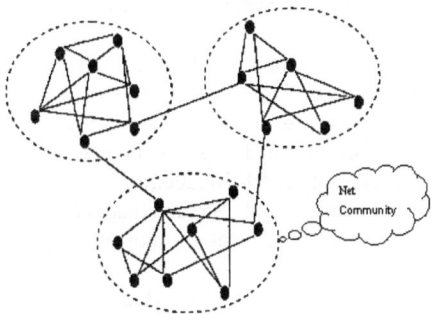

Fig. 2. Network of community structure

According to the above characteristics of the community, it can determine the semantic relations in the named entity feature vector and its similarity in structure of the network, the same community named entities with similar characteristics; as expressed by each node represents a semantic feature vector for each of the named semantic entity relationship attribute, so the network of a community has the same semantic relation to a class of named entity pairs. So, just over the network from different communities can be found to achieve the semantic relationship of the named entity clustering[8].

7 Other Methods

Skounakis extracted three types of dualistic entity relations from the scientific literature with the model of HHMM[9]. Dan Roth proposed to identify the entity and the entity relation in the sentence with the means of probabilistic framework[10], and fully considered of interdependence between the entity and the entity relationship. In Literature[11], it introduced a method of the whole information methodology which is used to complete the multi-entity relation extraction, while the clear entity relations and the implied entity relations in the text are extracted at the same time.

8   Conclusions

Entity relation extraction has two main ways: knowledge engineering methods and machine learning methods. It needs to summarize manually from the large corpus of knowledge engineering approach and the template system is easy to be in trouble when transplanting, and machine learning methods in the system transplantation have shown very strong advantages, therefore, machine learning methods become a primary way on the research of entity relation. The mixed method reduces the difference from relation extraction system based on the learning and based on knowledge.

References

1. Zhao, J.-z.: A Research for Semantic Relation Automatic Extraction Among Named Entities in Chinese Professional Domain. Huazhong Normal University (master(s thesis), Shanhai (2007)
2. Feldman, R.: Text Mining Handbook. Cambridge University Press, Cambridge (2007), http://www.cambridge.org/9780512836579
3. http://www.nist.gov/speech/tests/ace/index.htm
4. Liu, Q., Li, S.: Word Similarity Compu-ting Based on Hownet. Computational Linguistics and Chinese Language Processing 7, 59–76 (2002)
5. Appelt, D.E., Hobbs, J.R., Bear, J., et al.: SRI International FASTUS System: MUC-6 Test Results and Analysis. In: Proceedings of the 6th Message Understanding Conference (MUC-6), pp. 237–248 (1995)
6. Yangarber, R., Grishman, R., Tapanainen, P., Huttunen, S.: Unsupervised discovery of scenario-level Patterns for information extraction. In: Proeeedings of the Applied Natural Language Processing Conference (ANLP 2000), Seattle,WA (2000)
7. Grishman, S.Z.R.: Extracting Relations with Integrated Inofrmation Using Kernel Methods. In: ACL (2005)
8. Skounakis, M., Cren, M., Ray, S.: Hierarchieal Hidden Markov Models for Information Extraction. In: Proceedings of the 18th International Joint Conference on Artificial Intelligence, pp. 1010–1018. Morgan Kaufmann, Acapuleo (2003)
9. Dan, R., Wen-tau, Y.: Probabilistic Reasoning for Entity & Relation Recognition. In: 19th international Conference on Computational Linguistics (2002)
10. Zhang, S.: Research on Key Technologies of the Informstion ExtraCtion, vol. 5. Doctoral Dissertation of Beijing University of Posts and Telecommunications, Peiking (2007)

Detailed Design and Analysis on Error Handing and Controlling Protocol in Mobile Payment*

Xu Yong and Yan Tingting

School of Economics and Commerce, South China University of Technology,
Guangzhou University City, Guangzhou 510006, China
xuyong@scut.edu.cn, ytt0114@126.com

Abstract. This paper puts forward a detailed design of Error Handing and Controlling Protocol (EHCP) on the basis of Micro Payment Transaction Protocol (MPTP) used by China Mobile and the frame design of EHCP. Messages sending and receiving among three parties in the payment system is described. Finally, the analysis illustrates that our protocol achieves the goals of high security, fairness and efficiency.

Keywords: mobile payment; protocol; security.

1 Introduction to the Frame Design of EHCP

Aimed to perfect mobile payment communication mechanism and solve mobile payment security issues, improving the completion rate of the payment when error occurred, literature [1] has proposed the framework design of protocol EHCP.

EHCP is based on the MPTP used by China Mobile, used to solve some accidental problems in special conditions, such as the forced interruption caused by client terminal's low battery, or resource-exhausted caused by vendor's overloaded server. Customer C has two choices offered by EHCP after error occurred, to execute the termination protocol or the recovery protocol. The operating environment of EHCP contains three entities, including Customer C, vendor V, and Broker B. In EHCP, when discuss the error occurred in the transaction of C and B, there is an assumption that broker B is completely creditable without any errors. To distinguish types of errors, this article proposed a four-phase model based on his original transaction processing of MPTP.

In Phase One, customer C sends payment commitment M, vendor V checks and handles it. In Phase Two, customer C sends the first half part of Paywords, vendor V checks and handles it. And in Phase Three, vendor V sends goods, customer C checks and handles them. At last in Phase Four, customer C sends the latter half part of Paywords, V checks and handles it.

---

* The National Soft Science Research Program, 2010B070300016.

R. Chen (Ed.): ICICIS 2011, Part I, CCIS 134, pp. 755–760, 2011.
© Springer-Verlag Berlin Heidelberg 2011

2 The Detailed Design of EHCP

2.1 Notations

IDC, IDV, IDB: the identities of party C, V and B. They contain the contact information of customer, vendor and broker;

K_{CV}, K_{CB}, K_{VB}: secret keys shared by C and V, V and B, C and B. They are used in symmetric encryption algorithm;

PK_C, PK_V, PK_B: public keys in public-key algorithm;
SK_C, SK_V, SK_B: private keys in public-key algorithm;
A_C, A_V: certificates issued to customer and vendor by broker;
TID: the identity of transaction;
W_0: the root of the payword chain;
(W_i, i): the payment pair;
$H^Y(X)$: a cryptography hash function;
T: timestamp;
$(M)_K$: the message M symmetrically encrypted with the key K;
$Sign_X()=\{H()\}SK_X$: the signature of X;
A→B: A send message to B;
$M=\{ID_V,A_C,W_0,n,L_i,T,G,P,\{\{ID_V,A_C,W_0,n,L_i,T,G,P\}SK_C,K_{CV}\}PK_V\}$:payment commitment sent to V by C;
$I=\{W_0,n,L_i,T,G,P\}$: the plaintext of the payment information sent to V by C;

2.2 The Detailed Design of Termination Protocol

1) Error occurred in Phase One
Owing to the error occurred in Phase One, implementing termination protocol will not bring about any loss to both sides of the transaction, it is no need to investigate the causes. Customer C can ask for the termination right from broker B. The details of the protocol are given below:

Message 1 C→B: $\{F_{Abort}, TID, ID_B, ID_V, I, \{F_{Abort}, TID, ID_V\}SK_C\}$

In the message 1, F_{Abort} is the representation of C's request for termination, furthermore, $\{F_{Abort}, TID, ID_V\}SK_C$ is the evidence to show C has sent the request. At the exact time receives message 1, broker B will first check the boolean variables $B_{Recovered}$ and $B_{Aborted}$. (Termination protocol and recovery protocol can not be run concurrently when EHCP is executing. The boolean variables $B_{Recovered}$ and $B_{Aborted}$ are needed, and initialized False) B accepts the request when the value of boolean variables are both Fasle, and then confirms C's registration by sending message 2 and message 3:

Message 2 B→C: $\{F_{confirmAbort}, ID_C, ID_V, TID, \{F_{confirmAbort}, ID_C, ID_V, TID\}SK_B\}$

Message 3 B→V: $\{F_{confirmAbort}, ID_C, ID_V, TID, \{F_{confirmAbort}, ID_C, ID_V, TID\}SK_B\}$

$F_{confirmAbort}$ is the representation that B has accepted the termination request. Termination protocol ends when C and V receive message 2 and 3.

2) Error occurred in Phase Two

Comparing with the former situation, protocol needs to consider how to ensure the customer's benefit without loss when implementing termination protocol in this phase. Message 1, 2 and 3 are sent in turn to confirm the termination of transaction. Then customer C asks broker B to invalid the paywords sent by C to prevent these paywords from being used to liquidate with broker by illegal vendors.

$$\text{Message 4 C} \rightarrow \text{B: } \{ID_B, ID_C, ID_V, TID, A_C, W_0, T\} \, K_{CB}$$

Broker B decrypts C's certificate A_C and extracts payment information including several combination of commitment M, W_0 and (Wi, i), such as $(M, W_0, (Wi, i))$, $(M', W_0', (Wi, i)')$, etc. Compare these information with I got in message 1, then make sure that which information is belong to the exact transaction to terminate. Compute $W_0' = H^i(Wi)$ for i=n, n-1,…,1. If $W_0' = W_0$, the conclusion is that A_C record the correct payment information. According to this information, B will invalid the paywords in its database.

2.3 The Detailed Design of Recovery Protocol

1) Error occurred in Phase One

When error occurred in Phase one, C sends the recovery request. Payment commitment M can only continued sending as far as the request has confirmed by B, and then it is similar to start a new payment.

$$\text{Message 5 C} \rightarrow \text{B: } \{F_{Recovery}, ID_B, ID_V, TID, \{F_{Recovery}, ID_V, TID\}SK_C, \{K_{CV}\} \, PK_B\}$$

In the message 5, $F_{Recover}$ is the representation of C's request for recovery, furthermore, $\{F_{Recovery}, ID_V, TID\}SK_C$ is the evidence to show C has sent the request. Session key K_{CV} used between C and V is sent to B to ask for a new one. At the exact time receives message 5, broker B will first check the boolean variables $B_{Aborted}$. If the value of $B_{Aborted}$ is False, set the value of $B_{Recovered}$ to True, and then send message 6 and 7.

$$\text{Message 6 B} \rightarrow \text{C: } \{F_{confirmRec}, ID_C, ID_V, TID, \{F_{confirmRec}, ID_C, ID_V, TID\}SK_B, (K'_{CV})PK_C\}$$

$$\text{Message 7 B} \rightarrow \text{V: } \{F_{confirmRec}, ID_C, ID_V, TID, \{F_{confirmRec}, ID_C, ID_V, TID\}SK_B, (K'_{CV})PK_V\}$$

$F_{confirmAbort}$ is the representation that B has accepted the recovery request. Since C and V has respectively received the evidence of recovery permission $\{F_{confirmRec}, ID_C, ID_V, TID\}$ SK_B and the new session key K'_{CV} included in message 6 and 7, a new MPTP executes between C and V.

2) Error occurred in Phase Two

Referring to the error handling process in Phase One, C asks broker B to implement recovery protocol, and obtaining the session keys between customer C and vendor V from B.

$$\text{Message 5 C} \rightarrow \text{B: } \{F_{Recovery}, ID_B, ID_V, TID, \{F_{Recovery}, ID_V, TID\}SK_C, \{K_{CV}\} \, PK_B\}$$

Message 6 B→C: {$F_{confirmRec}$, ID_C, ID_V, TID, {$F_{confirmRec}$,ID_C,ID_V,TID}SK_B, $(K'_{CV})PK_C$}

Message 7 B→V: {$F_{confirmRec}$, ID_C, ID_V, TID, {$F_{confirmRec}$,ID_C,ID_V,TID}SK_B, $(K'_{CV})PK_V$}

According to the handling and controlling process descript in the literature [1], the protocol can be descript as:

IF amount_type=1 THEN

Message 4 C→B: {ID_B, ID_C, ID_V, TID, A_C, W_0, T} K_{CB}

Message 8 B→C: {ID_C, ID_V, TID, W_0, (Wi, i), $Sign_B(W_0,(W_1,1),...,$ (Wi, i)),T} K_{CB}

Message 9 C→V: {ID_C,ID_V, TID, W_0, $(W_1,1)$,...(Wi, i), {ID_C,ID_V, TID, W_0, $(W_1,1)$,...(Wi, i)} SK_C, $Sign_B(W_0,(W_1,1),...,$(Wi, i)) } K'_{CV}

ELSE

Message 10 C→V: {ID_C,ID_V, TID, W_0,T, $(W_1,1)$,...(Wi, i), T_1,...Ti} K'_{CV}

In large payment situations, broker B signs on the Paywords when he confirms that Paywords have been sent, then C sends these Paywords with signature to V by message 9. Vendor V verifies the validity of C' identity and B' signature, and uses these Paywords to update the original database. It will bring about no loss even the vendor does not get the last Paywords when error occurred.

In both cases above, V checks and handles the information in message 9 and 10 sent by customer. After that, V sends message 11 to C as a response.

Message 11 V→C: {ID_C,ID_V,I,T, (Wi, i),{ID_C,ID_V,I,T, (Wi, i) } SK_V } K'_{CV}

C continues the transaction implementing before error occurred after getting message 11, and sends the rest Paywords to V.

3) Error occurred in Phase Three

Message 5, 6 and 7 are sent the same as above. Considering the contents of communication of digital goods and the contents of communication of physical goods is different, so the protocol can be shown as below:

IF transaction_type =1 THEN

Message 12 C→V: {ID_C, ID_V, TID, W_0, T, j', $(W_1,1)$,..., i), T_1,...Ti} K'_{CV}

IF $B_{Recovered}$=False OR j'> j V continues to transfer digital goods from the (j' + 1) units

ELSE exit protocol

ELSE

Message 13 C→V: {ID_C, ID_V, TID, W_0, T, $(W_1, 1)$, ...(Wi, i), T_1,...Ti} K'_{CV}

Message 14 V→C: {TID, G, P, $Sign_V$ (TID, G, P)} K'_C

When the trading goods is digital goods, C sends message 12 to V. Vendor distinguishes whether the information is reasonable. If so, continues to transfer goods from the (j' + 1) units. When the trading goods is physical goods, as the transaction

ID is unique, as long as customer C provides the document to prove that C has paid for the Paywords, vendor sends the receipt to C.

4) Error occurred in Phase Four

Through the discussion in lecture [1], it is concluded that the execution process of recovery protocol in this phase is as same as the process of Phase Two.

3 Analysis

3.1 Security Issues

The design of EHCP is in full consideration of securities about transaction and money and goods, especially the security of digital goods.

Transaction security

In EHCP, transmission of communication content and party authentication are ensured by cryptological technique and the secret keys. Simply by the keys to authenticate the communication parties is not enough. However, certificates are issued to customers and vendors by broker to ensure that the identity is legal and available.

Customer firstly conducts a conversation with vendor after he chooses to execute the recovery protocol. In this way, we ensure that original error has been solved in EHCP. That is to say customer and his terminal, vendor and its server, wireless network are all available, which greatly increase the possibility of implementing recovery protocol Money security.

At the improving of MPTP, we adding a field to customer's certificate named send_paychain which is sent by broker B. The adding field is used to record the payment message (mostly are commitment M, W_0 and Paywords) that C has sent to V, ensuring C can ask to invalid the specific Payword in the record by returning the certificate to broker B when the protocol terminated or interrupted, so as to prevent losing funds form not receiving goods.

3.2 Fairness Analysis

The termination protocol must be started by customer. It is fair for both parties in trading: (1) customer initiates the mobile payment, so customer has the right to choose termination; (2) only if the error occurred in Phase One or Two, can execute the termination protocol. So whether customer starts termination protocol or not, vendor will not loss anything since it does not send any digital goods or dispatch commitment; (3) customer can ask broker to invalid the Paywords sent by himself. It is fair to customer because he will not loss money while he can not get the goods; (4) broker notices both C and V to end the transaction when the request of termination is accept.

In the executing of recovery protocol, fairness is reflected reference to (1), (4) items above. In addition, although customer has the right to initiate EHCP, he can start the protocol only when some error occurred during mobile payment. It ensures the fairness of transaction process from another side because customer can not end a normal trading.

3.3 Efficiency Analysis

It costs large mount of resources of software, hardware, wireless networks and time to dealing with the error in mobile payment. Together with the weak computing of mobile device and limited bandwidth of wireless networks, it is very important to solve efficiency issues.

In EHCP, treatments are carried out at terminals as possible to reduce online operations and reduce burden of wireless networks. EHCP is divided into termination protocol and recovery protocol. Both of these two protocols are divided into several phases. In order to reduce the communication traffic between C and V, customer chooses the way to deal with the error payment on his terminal, and then the corresponding protocol block is executed directly.

In short, EHCP is adaptable for personal mobile devices from the perspective of computation, storage and processing speed, especially for upcoming 3G mobile terminal.

4 Conclusion

Combining with the feasibility and conciseness of actual operation, this paper gives the detailed design of EHCP based on the frame design of EHCP, and analyzes the characteristics of EHCP from security, fairness and efficiency. As a new electronic payment instruments, mobile payment is carrying people's longing for digital life. From the date of birth, mobile payment is in good graces of all the parties in the industry. It is sure that EHCP will play a role in standard formulation and mobile payment will also have greater development in the near future.

References

1. Xu, Y., Tingting, Y.: Frame Design on Error Handing and Controlling Protocol in Mobile Payment. South China University of Technology, Guangzhou (2009)
2. Kungpisdan, S., Srinivasan, B.: A Secure Account-Based Mobile Payment Protocol. In: Proceeding of the International Conference on Information Technology. Coding and Computing (2004)
3. Peng, B., Fu, C., Han, L.: ECC Based Mobile Electronic payment. Journal of Huazhong University of Science and Technology (Natural Science Edition), 82–85 (October 2008)
4. Xu, Y., Yan, T.: A Design of Electronic Payment Standard Based on CNAPS(N). In: The International Conference on Information Science and Engineering, ICISE 2009 (2009)
5. Fun, T.S., Beng, L.Y., Likoh, J., Roslan, R.: A Lightweight and Private mobile Payment Protocol by Using Mobile Network Operator. In: Proceeding of the International Conference on Computer and Communication Engineering, vol. 03, pp. 162–166 (2008)

Author Index